Ernest Hemingway

A to Z

ERNEST HEMINGWAY

A TO Z

The Essential Reference to the Life and Work

CHARLES M. OLIVER

Facts On File, Inc.

Ernest Hemingway A to Z

Copyright © 1999 by Charles M. Oliver

Checkmark Books
An imprint of Facts On File, Inc.
11 Penn Plaza
New York NY 10001

Library of Congress Cataloging-in-Publication Data

Oliver, Charles M.
Ernest Hemingway A to Z : the essential reference to the life and work / Charles M. Oliver.
p.   cm.
Includes bibliographical references (p.   ) and index.
ISBN 0-8160-3467-2 (hardcover). — ISBN 0-8160-3934-8 (pbk.) (acid-free paper)
1. Hemingway, Ernest, 1899–1961—Encyclopedias. 2. Novelists, American—20th century—Biography—Encyclopedias. I. Title.
PS3515.E37Z7484 1999
813'.52—dc21   98-30042

Checkmark Books are available at special discounts when purchased in bulk quantities for businesses, associations, institutions or sales promotions. Please call our Special Sales Department in New York at (212) 967-8800 or (800) 322-8755.

You can find Facts On File on the World Wide Web at http://www.factsonfile.com

Cover design by Nora Wertz
Map by Jeremy Eagle and Patricia Meschino

Printed in the United States of America

VB Hermitage 10 9 8 7 6 5 4 3 2
(pbk) 10 9 8 7 6 5 4 3 2

This book is printed on acid-free paper.

*F*or Helen, who,

even after nearly thirty years

of Hemingway saturation,

still thinks I picked the right author.

CONTENTS

ACKNOWLEDGMENTS

Hemingway scholars have a reputation for helping one another with research ideas, so I owe a debt to several friends in Hemingway studies who have contributed to my education during the past several years, even if they haven't participated directly in the preparation of *Ernest Hemingway A to Z*.

I am especially grateful to those who read portions of the text in typescript and sent back extremely helpful suggestions and corrections. They are: Susan Beegel, Gerry Brenner, Albert J. DeFazio III, Robert E. Gajdusek, Peter L. Hays, Allen Josephs, Robert W. Lewis, Kenneth Marek, Ann Putnam, Ann Reynolds, Michael S. Reynolds, H. R. Stoneback, Bickford Sylvester, and William B. Watson.

I would like also to acknowledge the generous assistance of Stephen Plotkin, curator of the Hemingway Collection at the John F. Kennedy Library in Boston, Allan Goodrich, audiovisual archivist at the Kennedy Library, and his staff, especially Kristen Kidder and Rachel Murray, who helped with the photographs. Others to whom I owe thanks include Jennifer Wheeler, executive director of The Ernest Hemingway Foundation of Oak Park; Michael F. Plunkett and his staff in the Rare Book room at the Alderman Library, University of Virginia; the reference librarians at the Alderman; Jane Penner, librarian in the Department of Music, University of Virginia; the librarians at *The Kansas City Star* and *The Toronto Star* (for assuring me that the article *the* was included in the names of their newspapers when Hemingway worked for them); Al DeFazio and Frank M. Laurence for help with information about recent films; Robert Oliver at the University of Paris for chasing down some geographical details; Kenneth Marek, who provided maps of the Walloon Lake area in northern Michigan; R. Kent Rasmussen, author of *Mark Twain A to Z*, who offered early advice; and Anne Baxter at Facts On File for her patience and kindness; and Ohio Northern University for its loyal support of my work in Hemingway studies.

I owe special thanks to Peter Hays for recommending me to literary agent Julie Castiglia, who offered me this project and provided continued encouragement.

INTRODUCTION

1.

Ernest Hemingway, arguably the most popular American writer of the 20th century and certainly one of the best, killed himself at age 61 after a life of adventure and productivity like few others of his time.

He went to five wars, was wounded badly as an 18-year-old volunteer ambulance driver for the Italian army in World War I, and was among the first Americans to enter Paris after the Allied invasion of Normandy in World War II. Between those wars he covered the Greek army's retreat from Constantinople in 1922 for *The Toronto Daily Star,* the Spanish civil war in 1937 and 1938 for the North American Newspaper Alliance (NANA), and the Sino-Japanese War in 1941 for the newspaper *PM,* seeing frontline action in each of these conflicts.

He survived four automobile accidents and two airplane crashes, the latter occurring on consecutive days in East Africa in 1954, prompting premature obituaries in newspapers all over the world.

During the approximately 43 years of his maturity Hemingway wrote nine novels, four books of nonfiction, more than 100 short stories, nearly 400 articles, a play, and some poetry. He won the 1954 Nobel Prize for literature and a Pulitzer Prize. He was married four times and had three sons. For a period of about 20 years during the 1930s and 1940s he was in the news media almost daily, his experiences covered by reporters and photographers as if he were a Hollywood movie star. He was handsome, active, and intelligent.

No wonder, then, that nearly 40 years after his death, Hemingway is still more written about than all but a half-dozen other writers. Some of this writing is meant to diminish the stature of his work, on various ideological or theoretical grounds. At least one major university has removed all of Hemingway's works from its reading lists.

But the last 20 years have also produced a Hemingway Society, begun in 1980, with a scholarly journal and a newsletter with worldwide circulations, and societies in Oak Park, Illinois (his birthplace), northern Michigan (where his family spent their summers), and Japan (a place he never visited). Also since 1980 there have been more than 60 conferences devoted entirely or in part to Hemingway, more than 100 books, and more than 1,500 articles about Hemingway or his works. There are festivals each year in Oak Park and in Key West, Florida (where he had a home during the 1930s), a $7,500 Hemingway Foundation/PEN Award given each year for the best first book of fiction, and an industry of products named after Hemingway—clothes, hunting gear, fishing tackle, a house design, even a Hemingway wallpaper. And teachers of Hemingway's fiction still find his novels and stories to be among the best ways to interest their students in good literature.

All of this academic and commercial activity, however, has contributed to a mythology that grows by the year, created to a large extent by biographers repeating untrue stories about Hemingway or explaining events in his life by quoting his fiction. A character in John Ford's 1962 film *The Man Who Shot Liberty Valance* says, "When the legend becomes fact, print the legend." To a large extent, that is what has happened to Hemingway.

2.

This reference is meant to be a guide to the life and work of Ernest Hemingway, for those familiar with them, and, especially, for those readers who are discovering Hemingway for the first time, for whom it may serve as a comprehensive introduction and guide to study. The focus is on facts, the *who, what, where,* and *when,* and not on the *why.* I have attempted to avoid critical interpretation as far as possible, but readers may notice it creeping in now and then. Evaluation is sometimes unavoidable, if only for the sake of coherence.

A degree of subjective judgment is called for, for example, in determining the number of short stories Hemingway wrote. Some short story checklists include the "interchapters" of *In Our Time* (1925); several scholars have published as short stories fragments Hemingway cut from other stories or novels. There are two "fables" and an "allegory" that are sometimes called short stories, and two newspaper articles Hemingway later published as short stories. I include all such items in *Hemingway A to Z*, identified as short stories, "vignettes," "fragments," or "fables." And I have included juvenilia, the three stories Hemingway published in his high school literary magazine. Altogether, there are 104 "short stories" with entries in this book.

Ernest Hemingway A to Z includes plot summaries for each novel and short story, as well as Hemingway's one play. Nearly all the characters who appear before the reader and most of those who are merely offstage are identified, and summaries are included for each of Hemingway's four nonfiction books and 371 pieces of journalism, and it lists publication data for each of his 90 poems.

There are biographical entries for Hemingway, his family and friends, and for members of his circle of writers. There are entries for the important people, places, and events Hemingway refers to in his works and which shaped his life and his fiction. Entries are listed by easily recognized headings. People both fictional and real are listed last name first; for example, "Barnes, Jake" and "DiMaggio, Joe." The articles "a," "an," and "the" are placed last in a heading; for example, "*Old Man and the Sea, The.*" "Saint" and "San" are placed first; for example, "San Sabastián." Paris streets are usually listed under "rue"; for example "rue de l'Odéon." Other examples include "Capri bianca" (a wine), "Abruzzi" (a region of Italy), "Rube Goldberg" (a metaphor), and "Michelin map." Quotations from Hemingway's work preserve his original spelling and punctuation. Small caps indicate a cross-reference, but readers may assume that all Hemingway titles and

major characters have separate entries. Entries are filed alphabetically, letter by letter.

I have not named real-life prototypes for fictional characters, nor have I attempted to connect fictional events to Hemingway's own life. As with all good writers of fiction, Hemingway wrote from his experience, and for readers to attempt to (mostly) guess at parallels with "reality" is to diminish a work's value as art. The novels and short stories are works of fiction, and that is how they are treated in *Hemingway A to Z*.

The Sources for the Titles

Whereas the titles of novels, nonfiction books, story collections, short stories, and poetry are, for the most part, Hemingway's, the titles of newspaper and magazine articles are not. Those titles were usually written by copy editors. For the articles Hemingway wrote for *The Toronto Daily Star* and *The Toronto Star Weekly* I have used the titles William White chose for *By-Line Ernest Hemingway* and *Ernest Hemingway: Dateline Toronto*, because these two books are more accessible than are the original publications. In each entry, however, I have included the original newspaper headline published with the article. For the dispatches Hemingway wrote for the North American Newspaper Alliance (NANA), I have used the titles William Braasch Watson chose for each of the 30 dispatches collected for publicaton in *The Hemingway Review*. The dispatches are listed here, however, as "NANA Dispatch number 1," etc. For articles published in other magazines (*Esquire*, for example) I have used the title published with the article. For the short interchapters ("vignettes") used in *in our time* (1924) I have used the chapter numbering system from *In Our Time* (1925) and repeated in *The Short Stories of Ernest Hemingway* (1954 and later editions), because the latter volumes are more accessible. The interchapters are listed here as "Chapter 1," etc.

A comprehensive list of Hemingway's published writings is provided in the bibliography, Appendix V.

—Charles M. (Tod) Oliver
Charlottesville, Virginia

A

Aachen German city near the Belgian and Dutch borders and the first important German city to fall to the Allies in WORLD WAR II; mentioned in *Across the River and Into the Trees*. See General Walter Bedell SMITH.

A.B.C. Leading newspaper in Madrid during the 1930s, reflecting monarchist views; read by Philip RAWLINGS in *The Fifth Column* and referred to in both *For Whom the Bell Tolls* and *Death in the Afternoon*.

Abdel Krim (c. 1882–1963) Moroccan military officer, important in the administration of the Spanish zone, about whom Richard CANTWELL in *Across the River and Into the Trees* thinks when discussing the Moors with Renata. They "are excellent soldiers," against whom "we" Americans fought in WORLD WAR I.

Abdullah In *Green Hills of Africa* he is the "educated" tracker on safari with Hemingway in Tanzania.

Abraham Lincoln Brigade American volunteer soldiers, fighting for the Republic during the Spanish civil war (1936–39). See INTERNATIONAL BRIGADES.

Abruzzi Region in east-central Italy, extending from the watershed of the central Apennines to the Adriatic Sea, taking in the provinces of L'Aquila, Pescara, Chieti, and Teramo. The PRIEST in *A Farewell to Arms* urges Frederic HENRY to go to the Abruzzi on leave and visit his family at CAPRACOTTA. Frederic feels bad later when he returns to his unit in GORIZIA and realizes how disappointed the priest is that he had not gone to the Abruzzi.

absinthe A green, aromatic liqueur, 68 percent alcohol, made from wormwood and other herbs, most often anise; it has a bitter, licorice flavor. Its consumption was abolished in France in 1916 and it was banned in most Western nations but was legal in Spain during the 1920s and 1930s when Hemingway was there. In *The Garden of Eden* it is Catherine BOURNE's luncheon drink in HENDAYE, France, on the Spanish border on the Bay of Biscay. Later, in Madrid, it is referred to by David BOURNE's friend Colonel John BOYLE as "that wormwood-tasting truth serum." Besides Catherine and David Bourne, Robert JORDAN in *For Whom the Bell Tolls*

drinks absinthe, as do Jake BARNES, Brett ASHLEY, and Bill GORTON in *The Sun Also Rises*. See also PERNOD and PASTIS.

absolute constructions Grammatical concept, used by Hemingway as a stylistic device to enhance emotional impact. An absolute phrase consists of a noun or noun equivalent usually followed by a participle or participial phrase and used to modify a noun clause. Hemingway used these mostly at the end of sentences. In *A Farewell to Arms*, at the end of the paragraph in which Frederic HENRY describes his own wounding, he describes his friend Passini's wounding as well, stating in the last sentence: "Then he was quiet, biting his arm, *the stump of his leg twitching*." The italicized words form an absolute construction. In "Big Two-Hearted River" NICK says that the trout's back "was mottled the clear, water-over-gravel color, *his side flashing in the sun*."

"Absolute Lie, Says Dr. Banting, of Serum Report, An" Article, unsigned, published in *The Toronto Daily Star* (October 11, 1923), reprinted in William Burrill's *Hemingway: The Toronto Years* (1994). It was identified as a Hemingway story by *Star* librarian William McGeary. In it, Hemingway says that Dr. Frederick G. Banting, a Toronto doctor who discovered insulin, denies a report that he has been working on a serum that would combat pernicious anemia.

abstractions Several of Hemingway's characters are disturbed by abstract words concerning war. Frederic HENRY, for example, in *A Farewell to Arms* says that he "was always embarrassed by the words sacred, glorious, and sacrifice and the expression in vain. . . . [He] had seen nothing sacred, and the things that were glorious had no glory and the sacrifices were like the stockyards at Chicago if nothing was done with the meat except to bury it. There were many words that you could not stand to hear and finally only the names of places had dignity."

Robert JORDAN in *For Whom the Bell Tolls* asks himself if "big words make [war] more defensible? Did they make killing any more palatable?"

Abyssinia Unofficial name before World War II for the East African nation of Ethiopia. It is where Count

MIPPIPOPOLOUS, in *The Sun Also Rises,* says he received two arrow wounds in a war when he was 21 years old. And young Tom HUDSON, in *Islands in the Stream,* connects Abyssinia to an incident at his school in Paris. While Tom's father was on a trip to Abyssinia, the headmaster at young Tom's school tried to expel him for reading Joyce's *Ulysses* to his schoolmates.

Accademia Venice's main art gallery, the Galleria dell'Accademia is one of the two places (with SCUOLA SAN ROCCO, also in Venice) Richard CANTWELL in *Across the River and Into the Trees* would like to go every day to see the Tintoretto paintings.

"Across from the Post Office" Article, first published in William Burrill's *Hemingway: The Toronto Years* (1994). One of a series of articles Hemingway wrote for *The Toronto Daily Star* about the attempt by Germany to jumpstart the economy of the Ruhr Valley following World War I. The reason it was not published by the *Star* is unknown. It was "discovered" by Burrill in the Hemingway Collection at the John F. Kennedy Library in Boston.

"Across the Board" Poem written in 1949 and first published in *88 Poems* (1979).

Across the River and Into the Trees Hemingway's sixth novel (1950) and, with *To Have and Have Not,* generally considered to be one of his least successful. Early reviewers seemed to think Hemingway had lost his touch, although the late 20th-century response seems more favorable.

The protagonist, Colonel Richard CANTWELL, is a 50-year-old U.S. regular army officer stationed in Trieste in 1948. Cantwell has had four heart attacks when the novel opens "two hours before daylight" on a Sunday morning. He is with his young Italian friend Barone ALVARITO at the beginning of a duck hunting trip near the mouth of the TAGLIAMENTO RIVER, about 42 miles (70 km) east of Venice. Cantwell recalls the fourth heart attack, which had occurred the day before, in a flashback two-thirds of the way through the novel. He has the attacks that finally kill him that Sunday evening on the road back to Trieste.

Chapter 1 and the last six chapters are in time present. The first chapter takes place on Sunday morning; the last six, that same evening. Chapters 2 through 39 describe Cantwell's memories and thoughts as he contemplates the events leading to this weekend in Venice, including his final good-bye on Saturday afternoon to his 18-year-old friend and probable lover, RENATA, a contessa. Neither Venice nor Renata appears to the reader except as recalled by Cantwell.

The narrative is set in a duck blind in the marshes at the mouth of the river on Sunday morning and on the road back to Trieste on Sunday evening. The real set-

Ernest with Mary in Venice, 1949 (Copyright holder unknown; photo courtesy of the John F. Kennedy Library)

ting, however, is the mind of Cantwell as he tries to transcend the catastrophe taking place within his body. The novel is the story of a man struggling to control the terms of his own impending death. The duck-hunting trip is the frame through which he is seen considering his life as he awaits his death.

The transitional device Hemingway uses to move into and out of Cantwell's memory is simple and effective. At the end of chapter 1, Cantwell is trying to hold back his anger at a boatman and he thinks to himself, "Keep your temper, boy. . . ." Chapter 2 begins, "But he was not a boy," and near the beginning of chapter 40 Cantwell is brought back to the present by the sight of ducks coming in: "Boy, hell, he thought." Everything else in the novel—the bitter experience of his WORLD WAR II demotion from brigadier general to colonel, his previous heart attacks, and the romantic weekend in Venice with Renata—meals at the GRITTI PALACE HOTEL, drinks at HARRY'S BAR, a trip on the Venetian canals, and their final good-bye—take place only in his memory.

Cantwell selects carefully both the things he does on his last weekend in Venice and the things he remembers about those events on Sunday. Acts and memory are carefully controlled to allow him to feel that he is facing death with dignity. He focuses on his more pleasant memories, his military career, and particularly his love for Renata and the time they had had together the day before.

The idea that he must keep his temper reminds him of his Thursday visit to the doctor's office where he had been given a "clean" bill of health by a skeptical army surgeon. Cantwell had taken MANNITOL HEXANITRATE to speed up his blood flow so he could pass the doctor's test, but the doctor wasn't fooled: "[D]on't you ever run into anything, or let any sparks strike you, when you're really souped up on nitroglycerin," the doctor had told Cantwell. "They ought to make you drag a chain like a high-octane truck. . . . Your cardiograph was wonderful, Colonel. It could have been that of a man of twenty-five. It might have been that of a boy of nineteen." The doctor knows that Cantwell had forced the cardiograph to look good so he would be passed for the trip to Venice. Cantwell knows he does not have long to live, and he wants the trip as a kind of final farewell to the things he has most enjoyed in life. Cantwell's love for Renata provides the source of most of his memories while he's in the duck blind. There is some evidence that the 50-year-old colonel and the 18-year-old Renata have had a sexual relationship, although, as with such evidence in other Hemingway novels, it is ambiguous. Early in the novel, Cantwell sees two stakes in the water of a canal, "chained together but not touching," and he compares them to his relationship with Renata, implying a non-sexual love affair. However, with Cantwell in his room at the Gritti Palace Hotel, Renata says, "I can be your daughter as well as everything else." He says, "That would be incest." There is also a scene in a gondola under an army blanket that provides fairly convincing evidence of sexual activity. Some readers have inferred that Renata may be pregnant.

One of the complications in *Across the River* is the relationship of Alvarito to Renata and Cantwell. There is the suggestion—again, only from Cantwell's remembrance—that the friendship between Alvarito and Renata might one day lead them to marry, a prospect that does not displease Cantwell. It may be Alvarito whom Renata has in mind when she tells Cantwell that if she were going to have a baby she would have to marry someone; he is a baron, and she is a countess.

There is an unstated understanding between the two men. Each is aware of the other's love for Renata, and there is mutual respect. Finally, as Cantwell rides back toward Trieste and just before his final heart attacks, feeling they are imminent, he reiterates for himself this understanding. "You have said goodbye to your girl and she has said goodbye to you. That is certainly simple. You shot well and Alvarito understands. That is that." Cantwell has seemingly maintained control of the terms according to which he lives, including those of his impending death.

Maintaining control over one's life, even in the face of terrible odds, is one of the central themes in Hemingway's work. Nearly all of his main characters, men and women, fight for this control (see, especially, Jake BARNES, Frederic HENRY, and Catherine BARKLEY). *Across the River and Into the Trees* is the story of a professional soldier on the last day of his life, fighting to die with the dignity which he believes he has maintained throughout his military career.

The novel was published by Charles Scribner's Sons on September 7, 1950, in a first edition of 75,000 copies. It had been serialized previously in *Cosmopolitan* in its February–June issues, 1950.

"Active French Anti-Alcohol League" Article published in *The Toronto Daily Star* (April 8, 1922), reprinted in *Ernest Hemingway: Dateline Toronto* (1985). The headline in the *Daily Star* was "Anti-Alcohol League Is Active in France." Datelined "Paris," the story says that just as the "golden age of European culture" is beginning—"the present blissful time when the French bartender has at last learned to mix a good martini"—along comes the educational campaign of the "Ligue Nationale Contre Alcoolisme" to reduce drinking in France. "Thirst-driven Americans see the exhibit and shudder."

Adamo Hemingway's Italian chauffeur for part of his travels around the Spanish bullfight circuit in 1959 as he was preparing to write *The Dangerous Summer*. Adamo was an undertaker in Udine, Italy.

Adams, Dorothy Nick ADAMS's sister in "Fathers and Sons." When the Ojibway Indians Billy and Trudy tell Nick that Eddie Gilby, their half-brother, has said he wants to "sleep in bed with you sister Dorothy," Nick tells them he will kill Eddie before he lets that happen. This is the only Nick Adams story in which Dorothy is mentioned.

Adams, Helen Nick ADAMS's pregnant wife in "Cross-Country Snow." She does not appear in the story but is referred to by Nick and his friend George.

Adams, Nick The named protagonist in 12 short stories and one of the interchapters of *In Our Time* ("[Nick Sat Against the Wall. . .]"); most often referred to only as Nick, sometimes as Nicholas. Nick is generally considered to be the protagonist in three other stories in which he is not named: "The Light of the World," "In Another Country," and "An Alpine Idyll." Philip Young, one of the earliest academics to write about Hemingway works, includes eight more stories with Nick Adams as the main character (*Ernest Hemingway: The Nick Adams Stories* [1972]). Those eight, however, are fragments of short stories or novels.

In each of the Nick Adams stories, Nick witnesses a singular conflict, usually traumatic, sometimes merely dramatic, that leaves a psychological scar: an ex-prize-fighter, now brain-damaged, has to be knocked out occasionally by his caretaker to keep him from becoming violent ("The Battler"); a Swede, tired of running after committing an unidentified crime, merely turns his face to the wall when informed that two gunmen are looking for him ("The Killers"); the end of a love affair ("The End of Something" and "The Three-Day Blow"); the unhappy relationship between Nick's Christian Scientist mother and his doctor father ("The Doctor and the Doctor's Wife"); the CAESARIAN SECTION his father performs on an Indian woman, while her husband slits his own throat, apparently no longer able to stand her screaming ("Indian Camp"); or Nick's own experience of shell shock in a battle in northern Italy during WORLD WAR I ("A Way You'll Never Be").

Each of these stories connects to a key Hemingway theme: an experience itself is less important than how one deals with it. The Nick of "The Three-Day Blow," for example, gets drunk with a friend trying to forget the end of his love affair with Marjorie. The Nick of "The Killers" leaves town rather than stay while Ole ANDRESON passively awaits his own murder. The Nick of "The Battler," stunned by his experience with Ad FRANCIS and BUGS, can think of nothing else.

The other stories in which Nick is named as the main character are "Ten Indians," "Now I Lay Me," "Big Two-Hearted River" (parts 1 and 2), "Cross-Country Snow," and "Fathers and Sons" (the latter two stories the only ones in which Nick is married).

Young included in his book, as a "completed" Nick Adams story, "Summer People." According to Paul Smith, however, in *A Reader's Guide to the Short Stories of Ernest Hemingway* (1989), Hemingway had considered it "not much good" and had "never completed the typescript version of the original manuscript." The other seven fragments of works that Young includes in his book are "Three Shots" (cut from "Indian Camp"), "On Writing" (cut from "Big Two-Hearted River"), "The Last Good Country" (probably intended as the opening of a novel), "Night Before Landing" (probably cut from the opening of an unpublished novel), "The Indians Moved Away," "Crossing the Mississippi," and "Wedding Day," the last three unfinished short stories.

Adams, Willie Character in *To Have and Have Not.* See CAPTAIN WILLIE.

"a.d. in Africa: A Tanganyika Letter" Article, published in *Esquire* (April 1934), reprinted in *By-Line: Ernest Hemingway* (1967). The "a.d." stands for amoebic dysentery, and Hemingway, hunting on East Africa's Serengeti Plain in December 1933, describes trying to write without a typewriter and trying to hunt while recovering from a.d.

adjutant A military staff officer, usually an administrative assistant to a unit's commanding officer.

In the "Chapter 1" vignette of *In Our Time,* the adjutant in a unit of drunken soldiers wants the kitchen corporal, the incident's narrator, to put out his fires, even though the unit is 30 miles from the front.

In "A Way You'll Never Be," the adjutant informs Nick ADAMS that he fought in the Iritrea campaign in northern Italy in WORLD WAR I.

Admiral's compass Owned by Richard CANTWELL, in *Across the River and Into the Trees,* when he had a "small boat" on the Chesapeake Bay. It was a compass he remembers using during his march across France in WORLD WAR II.

Adrianople Modern Edirne, a city situated in eastern THRACE at the confluence of the MARITSA and Tundzha Rivers. It is the setting for the "Chapter 2" vignette of *In Our Time.* At the time of the sketch (1922), the town belonged to Greece by terms of the TREATY OF SÈVRES (1920); but it reverted to Turkey by provisions of the Treaty of Lausanne, following the LAUSANNE CONFERENCE in 1923. Hemingway reported on the fighting between the Turks and Greeks and the Lausanne peace talks for *The Toronto Daily Star.*

"a.d. Southern Style: A Key West Letter" Article, published in *Esquire* (May 1935), about amoebic dysentery.

"Advice to a Son" Poem written in Berlin in 1931 and first published in a German magazine annual, *Omnibus: Almanach auf das Jahr 1932.*

"Afghans: Trouble for Britain" Article, datelined "Constantinople," published in *The Toronto Daily Star* (October 31, 1922). Reprinted in *The Wild Years* (1962) and in *Ernest Hemingway: Dateline Toronto* (1985). The headline in the *Daily Star* was "Kemal Has Afghans Ready to Make Trouble for Britain." Hemingway provides background for Afghanistan's hatred of the British, most of it gathered from a friend of his, the Afghan minister for war, Shere Mohamet Khan. The British had long used Afghanistan as a buffer zone between India and Russia and had bombed the badly trained and defenseless Afghans in 1919. This explains why, Hemingway predicts, when Kemal, the Turkish leader, attacks Mesopotamia and the British forces there, a Kemal-trained Afghan army will come down the Khyber Pass to help the Turks.

aficionado   In Spanish, *afición* means "passion." In *The Sun Also Rises* an aficionado is one who is "passionate about the bullfights." The novel's main character, Jake BARNES, is an aficionado, as is Juanito MONTOYA, the owner of the Hotel Montoya in Pamplona, where all the best bullfighters stay.

Africa   In *The Old Man and the Sea* SANTIAGO dreams at night of the lions on the beaches of Africa, which he remembers as a boy sailing on a square-rigged ship along the African coast.

In *The Garden of Eden* Catherine BOURNE talks to her husband, David, about going to Africa, and later uses it metaphorically to explain how dark she wants to become on the beaches of the French Riviera. "I'll be your African girl too," she tells him. The story David is writing is about an experience he had as a boy hunting elephants in Africa with his father. See AFRICAN STORY.

"An African Betrayal"   This "short story" was lifted piecemeal from *The Garden of Eden,* where it is a work-in-progress by the novel's main character, David BOURNE. It was published as "An African Betrayal" in *Sports Illustrated* (May 5, 1986) and reprinted as "An African Story" in *The Complete Short Stories of Ernest Hemingway* (1987). See AFRICAN STORY.

"African Journal"   A three-part series of excerpts from Hemingway's journal, published in *Sports Illustrated* (December 20, 1971 and January 3 and 10, 1972), of

Ernest at safari camp in East Africa (Courtesy of the John F. Kennedy Library)

the East African safari he and his wife Mary took in at the end of 1953 and the beginning of 1954, including details of the two plane crashes that they survived. See also *True at First Light.*

African story   In *The Garden of Eden,* the untitled story that David BOURNE writes at LA NAPOULE, France, while living in a MÉNAGE À TROIS with his wife, Catherine BOURNE, and MARITA. While he is writing the story, his childhood experiences with his father in East Africa are "completely real" to him, while the present with Catherine and Marita seems "unreal and false," more like a dream or, sometimes, a nightmare.

Later, at the height of Catherine's "madness," the novel's omniscient narrator states that David "must go back into his own country, the one that Catherine was jealous of and that Marita loved and respected," the Africa where he was happiest.

The story comes out of his guilty childhood memory of an East African hunt with his father, when he inadvertently led his father and the African tracker, JUMA, to an old, beautiful elephant, which they then kill. The elephant is believed by Juma to be about 200 tons with tusks weighing 200 pounds. David writes about crying over the death of the elephant and the hatred he felt for his father; as an adult, he feels guilty for having caused the animal's death.

The narrative within *The Garden of Eden* about the writing of the African story is confusing, because two

Ernest and Mary on African safari, 1954 (Courtesy of the John F. Kennedy Library)

African stories are described, the first which David says he finished in "four days," and the second which he later describes but which includes the same characters as the first and which is evidently the same story. Chapter 18 begins, "He finished the story in four days," and he tells Marita that it is in the notebooks in the top of his suitcase. But later he tells Catherine that the story is "about half through." Chapter 21 begins, "The next day in the story was very bad. . . ." And chapter 22 begins, "He did not think that he could go on with the story that morning. . . ."

David tells Catherine that the story is about East Africa during the time of the MAJI-MAJI REBELLION, the uprising in Tanganyika (now Tanzania) in 1905–1907. It happened when David was "about eight years old." David is about 24 years old as he writes the story. See "An African Betrayal."

"After the Storm" The unnamed narrator of this short story—the first in the collection *Winner Take Nothing* (1933)—is the first person to find, after a hurricane, an ocean liner lying on its side just under the surface of the water west of the Florida keys. He is a sponge fisherman by trade, but it is clear that he has dived for ship treasures before. Although he can "stand on the letters of her name on her bow" with his head just out of water, it is 12 feet down to the porthole closest to the surface. He dives several times in a futile attempt to break the porthole glass but can see inside the ship a woman "with her hair floating all out" and the "rings on one of her hands."

He had been in a fight at the beginning of the story, just after the storm had ended, and the authorities finally find him and hold him under a $500 bond. By the time he gets free of the police and back to the sunken ship, the "Greeks had blown her open and cleaned her out."

The last paragraph explains that the liner had tried to enter Havana harbor when the hurricane hit, but the Cubans wouldn't let her in because of the danger to the harbor docks. The captain then tried to shelter her west of the Florida keys. She went down between the REBECCA LIGHT and the TORTUGAS ISLANDS, probably along the Rebecca shoals, where the water is as shallow as two fathoms in some places.

"After the Storm" was first published in *Cosmopolitan* (May 1932) and reprinted in *Winner Take Nothing* (1933).

"Age Demanded, The" Poem written in 1922 and first published in the German publication *Der Querschnitt* (February 1925).

aguacate Avocado trees at Thomas HUDSON's farm in the "Cuba" section of *Islands in the Stream*.

aguardiente Spanish word for *aqua vitae*, the "water of life," unmatured brandy or other spirits, distilled from grapes or from sugarcane in cane-growing countries. In *The Sun Also Rises*, Jake BARNES and Bill GORTON buy aguardiente for 40 centimes a glass on their bus trip from PAMPLONA to BURGUETE.

Agustín One of the guerrilla fighters helping Robert JORDAN in *For Whom the Bell Tolls*. When Jordan arrives at the guerrilla camp, Agustín befriends him and warns him that the band's leader, PABLO, is untrustworthy. After the bridge whose destruction is the guerrillas' objective is blown up and Pablo is back with the rest of his band, Agustín is quick to realize that, in order to have extra horses, Pablo had killed the five men who had helped him. At the end of the novel Agustín helps carry the wounded Jordan to temporary safety and promises to look after Maria, Jordan's lover.

aide In *The Fifth Column*, an aide to the officers in charge of the artillery observation post on the Extremadura Road near Madrid. He is tied up by Philip RAWLINGS and MAX (2) when they attack the post.

Aigle Town in Switzerland at the east end of Lake Geneva. In *Green Hills of Africa* Hemingway remembers drinking a glass of "brown beer sitting at the wood tables under the wisteria vine" in Aigle after he, his wife, and Chink DORMAN-SMITH had crossed the Rhone Valley after fishing the Stockalper River, the "horse chestnut trees in bloom." And he remembers that he and Chink talked about writing.

In *A Moveable Feast* Hemingway recalls a conversation with Hadley about being in Aigle; she remembers that while he and their friend Chink Dorman-Smith sat in the garden of an inn reading, she fished in the Rhône; and Ernest remembers how clear the Stockalper River was the day they were there and how murky the Rhône.

Aigues Mortes Small French village at the north end of a three-and-one-half-mile canal that runs southwest to GRAU DU ROI on the Mediterranean Sea coast. At the beginning of *The Garden of Eden* David and Catherine BOURNE live in a hotel in Grau du Roi looking out onto the canal, and they can see the towers of Aigues Mortes.

"'Air Line' Contribution" Article for Oak Park and River Forest High School newspaper, *The Trapeze* (November 10, 1916), reprinted in *Hemingway at Oak Park High: The High School Writings of Ernest Hemingway, 1916–1917* (1993).

"'Air Line' Contributions" Article for Oak Park and River Forest High School newspaper, *The Trapeze*

(November 24, 1916), reprinted in *Hemingway at Oak Park High: The High School Writings of Ernest Hemingway, 1916–1917* (1993).

Al   One of the two hitmen in "The Killers." He wears a derby hat and carries a sawed-off shotgun and tries to get MAX (1), the second killer, to "shut up" each time he tells GEORGE (5) too much about their plans to kill Ole ANDRESON. When Al comes out of the kitchen after guarding the tied-up Nick ADAMS and the Negro cook, the "cut-off barrels of the shotgun made a slight bulge under the waist of his too tight-fitting overcoat." And when the two killers leave the lunchroom, they are described as looking "like a vaudeville team" in "their tight overcoats and derby hats."

albacore   Member of the mackerel family of open-sea fishes that includes tuna and BONITO. The sixty species of mackerel are recognized by their deeply forked tails and streamlined bodies with smooth, almost scaleless skins with no iridescent sheen. Their firm, oily texture makes them commercially valuable. Both the albacore and bonito are used as bait by Santiago in *The Old Man and the Sea* in order to catch marlin.

Albert   Character in *To Have and Have Not*. See Albert TRACY.

Alcalde Peor   In Spanish, literally, "worst mayor," a name Thomas HUDSON gives to a Havana politician, a "new friend," whom Hudson meets in the process of getting drunk with HONEST LIL at Havana's FLORIDITA bar in *Islands in the Stream*.

Alerta   Havana newspaper, a copy of which is bought by Thomas HUDSON in *Islands in the Stream*. He reads the news about the Allied troop movements in Italy during February 1944.

Alfred's Sin House   Havana whorehouse in *Islands in the Stream*.

Algabeño (1) (1902–1936)   José García, Spanish bullfighter, known as Algabeño, one of the three bullfighters Hemingway saw at his first bullfights in Pamplona in July 1923. The other bullfighters on the Pamplona card that day were MAERA (Manuel García) and Rosario OLMOS. For a description of these fights, see "Pamplona in July" (*By-Line Ernest Hemingway*).

Algabeño (2)   A bullfighter referred to by Jake BARNES as one who is without "afición," without passion, in *The Sun Also Rises*. During the Fiesta SAN FERMÍN in Pamplona Jake and his friends hear that Algabeño is hurt during the bullfights in Madrid.

Algeciras   Town near Gibraltar at the southernmost tip of Spain, where the Hemingways landed in the spring of 1959, on their way to visit Bill and Annie DAVIS at their villa above Málaga, the first stop on Ernest's trip to cover the summer bullfights in preparation for writing *The Dangerous Summer*.

Alger, Horatio (c. 1832–1899)   American writer of more than 100 books for children, most of them meant to inspire readers to succeed through hard work and good moral values. In *The Sun Also Rises* Jake BARNES thinks that Robert COHN has taken the English writer W. H. HUDSON's books too seriously, as if, he says, they were as realistic as the novels of Horatio Alger.

Alice   Biggest of the five whores in "The Light of the World." She wore "one of those silk dresses that change colors," and the narrator thinks she must weigh 350 pounds.

alkali   Hydroxide, such as soda or potash, that is soluble in water. In his AFRICAN STORY in *The Garden of Eden* David BOURNE writes about "crossing the gray, dried, bitter lakes [in East Africa] his boots now white with crusted alkalis."

"[All armies are the same . . .]"   First line of a poem written about 1922 and first published in *88 Poems* (1979).

Allen, Gracie (1905–1964)   American comedienne and partner with George Burns from 1923 until her death. Harry and Marie MORGAN listen to the "George Burns and Gracie Allen" radio show after Morgan gets back from Cuba in part 1 of *To Have and Have Not*.

Alma   The First Comrade's girlfriend in *The Fifth Column*.

"Along With Youth"   Poem written in 1922 and first published in Hemingway's first book, *Three Stories & Ten Poems* (1923).

Alpine Club   Organization in western Austria during the 1920s of people who built and provisioned huts in the mountains for the use of summer hikers and winter skiers; mentioned in *A Moveable Feast*.

"Alpine Idyll, An"   This short story's "idyll" is told to the story's unnamed narrator and his skiing friend, JOHN (1), at an inn in GALTÜR (1), Austria, in May, just after a month of spring skiing in the Silvretta range of mountains on the southwest Austrian border with Switzerland. It is told by a sexton, who is "amused," and the old innkeeper, who is "disgusted."

The narrator and John had seen a graveyard burial on their way into town and so are curious when the sexton, whom they recognize as having been at the gravesite, comes into the inn with a peasant. As the sexton tells the story, the peasant OLZ (who has now left the inn) had just buried his wife that day, though she had been dead since December. He wasn't able to bring her down to their parish church from his home on the other side of the mountains until the snow melted. But the priest didn't want to bury her. It seems that Olz had laid his wife out in a shed on a woodpile. When she became stiff he stood her against the wall so he could get at the wood. Then he hung his lantern from her mouth every evening when he went for wood, and her face became distorted. Olz assured the priest that, yes, he loved his wife very much, but the priest insisted that what he had done to her "was very wrong." When the story's narrator asks the innkeeper if he thinks it's a true story, the innkeeper says, "Sure it's true. . . . These peasants are beasts." And the story ends with the narrator and his friend going back to their meal.

"An Alpine Idyll" was first published in the anthology *American Caravan* (September 1927) and reprinted in *Men Without Women* (1927).

Alpini Italian Alpine troops during WORLD WAR I. In *A Farewell to Arms,* one of the ambulance drivers in Frederic HENRY's unit, Manera, tells another, PASSINI, that Alpini are so loyal to the Italian cause that they would go to war even without threats by the CARABINIERI (Italian military police).

al sangue "Very rare," bloody, the way RENATA, in *Across the River and Into the Trees,* wants her steak cooked for dinner with Richard CANTWELL at the GRITTI PALACE HOTEL restaurant.

Alvarito, Barone Young Italian friend of Richard CANTWELL and RENATA, in *Across the River and Into the Trees,* who has known Renata since childhood. The barone is about 21 years old and is described as "almost tall, beautifully built in his town clothes, and . . . the shyest man the Colonel had ever known." At the end of the novel, Cantwell tells Alvarito, "I love Venice." Alvarito looks away, suggesting his understanding that Cantwell is talking about Renata. He says, in reply, "Yes . . . We all love Venice. Perhaps you do the best of all." Cantwell then repeats, "I love Venice as you know. Yes, I know," Alvarito says and "looked at nothing." That Alvarito also loves Renata suggests that there is an understanding, although never stated, that he and she might eventually marry. His sensibilities are such, however, that he would never mention the subject directly in a conversation with Cantwell.

Alvarito's mother's house In *Across the River and Into the Trees* Richard CANTWELL sees the house along the GRAND CANAL in Venice as he is taken by boat toward the GRITTI PALACE HOTEL. Cantwell remembers that the house was once lent to Lord Byron, "who was well loved" in Venice.

Alzira III Fishing boat owned by "father," one of the "haves" in *To Have and Have Not.* The boat's "master" is Jon JACOBSON, and there is a crew of 14. The boat is lost through carelessness, along with 600 dollars' worth of Harry MORGAN's fishing gear.

Amelie One of the two salesgirls in a Paris store from whom the AMERICAN LADY, in "A Canary for One," buys all of her dresses.

American, the The only identification used for one of the two main characters in "Hills Like White Elephants." He and his girlfriend, JIG, who is pregnant, are waiting in a train station near Zaragosa, Spain, for a train to take them to Madrid. He tries to convince her that an abortion is "really an awfully simple operation. . . . It's just to let the air in." The word "abortion" is never used in the story, but the conversation between the two young people shows their hesitancy to use the key word in their present relationship. The tension is so great between them that he cannot stop talking, trying to convince her that the operation is a simple one and that he will continue to love her whether she has the operation or not. He insists that he doesn't want her to have the operation unless she wants to, but he keeps coming back to the simplicity of it. Even after she begs him to stop talking, he can't, nervous as he is about her decision. At the end of the story, he carries their bags to the platform where the train is due momentarily, and, on his way back through the station's bar, he notices how "reasonably" all the other passengers are waiting for the train. When he asks Jig if she feels better, she answers, "I feel fine. . . . There's nothing wrong with me. I feel fine." But the American, in his insensitivity, misses her sarcasm.

American ambassador In *The Sun Also Rises* (probably 1925), an embarrassment to the American Jake BARNES because he's not an "aficionado"; that is, he has no passion for the bullfights. The ambassador commits the social mistake of wanting to talk to bullfighters just before they fight.

"American Bohemians in Paris" Article, published in *The Toronto Star Weekly* (March 25, 1922), reprinted in *The Wild Years* (1962), and in *By-Line: Ernest Hemingway* (1967). Datelined "Paris, France," the article describes how the "scum of Greenwich Village . . . has been skimmed off and deposited . . . on that section of Paris adjacent to the Cafe Rotonde." The Americans are searching for "atmosphere." The *TSW* headline read "American Bohemians in Paris a Weird Lot."

American church   The church in Paris on Avenue Hoche, where David and Catherine BOURNE were married, three weeks before the beginning of *The Garden of Eden*.

American Civil War   In *For Whom the Bell Tolls* Robert JORDAN, during the times when he's trying not to think about the civil war he's helping to fight in Spain in 1937, thinks about his GRANDFATHER (4), who had fought in the American Civil War with Quantrill, John Mosby, Grant, Sherman, Stonewall Jackson, Jeb Stuart, Phil Sheridan, McClellan, and "Killy-the-Horse Kilpatrick."

American Hospital (1)   Where Frederic HENRY recovers after his wounding in book 1 of *A Farewell to Arms*. The hospital has just been "installed," so the nurses are not prepared to treat patients and are surprised to see him when he is carried into the ward. Catherine BARKLEY is later assigned to the hospital, and it is probably during their lovemaking in Frederic's room that Catherine gets pregnant. Frederic refers to it as the "little hospital" in comparison with the OSPEDALE MAGGIORE, also in Milan.

American Hospital (2)   In Neuilly, France, a western suburb of Paris. In *A Moveable Feast* Hemingway describes trying to convince F. Scott Fitzgerald that "congestion of the lungs" is the same thing as pneumonia, and he tells Fitzgerald about an article he had read in the American Hospital at Neuilly while waiting to have his own throat "cauterized." Although Hemingway knew about various ailments and had been through a series of sore throats himself, he probably makes the story up in order to pacify Fitzgerald who has become paranoid about his condition.

American Lady   Character in "A Canary for One" who, on a train to Paris, is taking a caged canary to her daughter. Two years ago the American Lady had broken off a love relationship between her daughter and a man from Vevey, Switzerland, because a friend of hers had told her that "[n]o foreigner can make an American girl a good husband." The American Lady tells the story's narrator, "I couldn't have her marrying a foreigner."

This is only one of several ways in which the American Lady is trapped (caged like the canary) by her own life. She is slightly deaf and so afraid to leave the train at stops for fear of not hearing the boarding whistle. And she doesn't sleep in the *lit salon* compartment because she's afraid the very fast, *rapide*, train will wreck in the night. And she has for 20 years bought dresses from the same saleslady in Paris, because the woman has all the proper measurements; and now the daughter gets her dresses from the same store.

The American Lady, who is as trapped by life as her daughter or the canary, is referred to as "American Lady" 23 times in a fairly short story, indicating Hemingway's sarcastic attitude toward such caged women.

ametralladora   Spanish for THOMPSON SUBMACHINE GUN, mentioned in *To Have and Have Not*.

Amiens   Town in northern France where, in "My Old Man," the "old man" rides in a "couple" of horse races.

anarcho-syndicalist meeting   Gathering where the tall waiter in "The Capital of the World" goes to hear talks and give one himself about the coming "revolution" in Spain.

Anatolia   The name in ancient geography for all land east of the Aegean Sea; it's the modern name for Asia Minor. When HARRY in "The Snows of Kilimanjaro" uses the word he means Asiatic Turkey.

Anderson, Sherwood (1876–1941)   American novelist and short story writer, best known for *Windy McPherson's Son* (1916; rev. 1921), *Winesburg, Ohio* (1919), *Many Marriages* (1923), and *DARK LAUGHTER* (1925). Anderson's short stories influenced Hemingway, who had read and been impressed by Anderson's work while still in high school. When he went to Paris, Hemingway carried letters of introduction from Anderson to Gertrude STEIN, Sylvia BEACH, Lewis GALANTIER, and Ezra POUND. Anderson's letters were all highly complimentary of Hemingway's writing talents and stated that he and his wife Hadley were "delightful people to know."

Anderson, who was 22 years older than Hemingway, said that Ernest was a "young fellow of extraordinary talent . . . who was instinctively in touch with everything worth-while going on." Hemingway liked the stories in *Winesburg, Ohio* and used the "tough guy" style of writing—short and sometimes clipped sentences—in his own early stories, particularly the Nick ADAMS stories. Several critics noticed the similarity between Hemingway's "My Old Man" and Anderson's "I Want to Know Why." Both stories are about boys and their fathers and horse racing. And they both tend to romanticize a young boy's attitude toward his father.

Hemingway denied that Anderson influenced his writing. He argued that Anderson's recent work had "gone to hell, perhaps from people in New York telling him . . . how good he was." In spite of Hemingway's criticism, Anderson was one of several writers to write blurbs for *In Our Time* when it was published in 1925.

Hemingway's first novel, *The Torrents of Spring* (1925), makes fun of affectation in contemporary fiction, especially in Anderson's novel *Dark Laughter*. *Torrents* also was taken as a criticism of Anderson's style, but Hemingway said it was all a joke. He wrote Anderson a letter (May 21, 1926), explaining that John Dos Passos, Hadley, and he had lunched together the previous fall and had talked about *Dark Laughter*. Hemingway says that after lunch he went back to his apartment, started *Torrents of Spring*, and finished it in a week. He tells Anderson that *Torrents* is not what the critics say it is but simply a joke, not meant to be mean, but, nevertheless, "sincere." Writers who are struggling to write great stories, Hemingway told Anderson, ought to be able to tell their friends when their stories are "rotten."

Anderson thought the letter was "possibly the most self-conscious and patronizing" ever written from one writer to another. *Torrents* might have been an amusing parody, Anderson thought, if Max Beerbohm, a notable exponent of the genre, had written it in a dozen pages. Hemingway took Sherwood out for a drink when the latter arrived in Paris, and Ernest later told Maxwell PERKINS that Sherwood was not still angry about the parody. Anderson's report of the meeting in his own memoirs states that Hemingway asked him out for a drink, but that as soon as they were served, Hemingway drank his beer straight down, turned, and left the bar.

"[And everything the author knows . . .]" First line of a poem written in 1926 and first published in *88 Poems* (1979).

"And Out of America" Article, published in *transatlantic review* (August 1924), about Jean COCTEAU'S translations of English literature.

André Waiter at the café in GRAU DU ROI where David and Catherine BOURNE eat breakfast in *The Garden of Eden*.

Andrea A "Count," in *Across the River and Into the Trees*, and customer at HARRY'S BAR, "rather drunk," according to the bartender Ettore when Arnaldo calls on behalf of Richard CANTWELL to find out who is there.

Andrés Character in *For Whom the Bell Tolls*. See Andrés LOPEZ.

Andreson, Ole Swedish prizefighter in "The Killers," who refuses to leave his boardinghouse room when Nick ADAMS comes to warn him about the two men in HENRY'S LUNCH-ROOM who say they are going to kill him. The story's narrator does not say why Andreson is being hunted down, but Ole tells Nick that he "got in wrong," suggesting that he may have failed to throw a fight. He thanks Nick for "coming around," but he can't make up his mind to leave his room. The landlady tells Nick, "He's an awfully nice man." At the end of the story Nick believes that Ole will be killed.

androgyny In botany the word means a combination of male and female, a plant that has both staminate and pistillate flowers in the same cluster. In human beings an androgyne is a person who has both masculine and feminine characteristics or who is sexually attracted to both men and women—that is, bisexual. Androgyny—or perhaps more accurately "bisexuality"—is the key to Catherine BOURNE's character in *The Garden of Eden*. Three weeks or so after her marriage to David, she cuts her hair in order to change into a "boy," and she talks David into cutting his hair like hers so that he can be the "girl." (The *Random House Compact Unabridged Dictionary*, 1996, uses unisex hairstyles in its definition of "ambisexuality," a word synonymous with bisexuality.) Catherine's insistence on a sexual role reversal is the beginning of the friction that will, seven months later, destroy the marriage. The narrator in *Eden* often refers to "the dark magic" of the change that Catherine goes through, which, at times, becomes a kind of madness.

In *Islands in the Stream* during one of Thomas HUDSON's sexual dreams about his first wife, she says to him, "Should I be you or you be me?" He says, "You have first choice." She says, "I'll be you."

Andros Island Largest of the Bahama Islands, about 140 miles east-southeast of Miami, referred to in *Islands in the Stream*.

Anglo-American Club In Milan, where, in *A Farewell to Arms*, Frederic HENRY goes sometimes after his treatments at the OSPEDALE MAGGIORE in order to sit in the "deep leather-cushioned" chairs and read the magazines.

Angostura bitters Liquor made with the bitter aromatic bark of either of two South American trees of the rue family. Used as cocktail flavoring or a medicinal tonic; it has a rose-colored tint. Thomas HUDSON adds Angostura to his gin and tonic in *Islands in the Stream*. The bitters that Hudson uses has a "gull's quill in the cork." Angostura is referred to once as "Old Angus."

anis An "acrid" smelling drink, usually mixed with water, which turns it to a "milky yellow" color and which Robert JORDAN carries in a flask in *For Whom the Bell Tolls*. According to Jordan, "one cup of it took the place of the evening papers." It was one of the things "he had enjoyed and forgotten and that [had come] back to him when he tasted that opaque, bitter, tongue-numbing, brain-warming, stomach-warming, idea-changing liquid alchemy."

Anis del Mono   French and Spanish liqueur, made from oil of the anise plant, a member of the carrot family. Drunk by characters in *The Sun Also Rises.* Del Mono is a brand name.

Anis del Toro   Liqueur ordered by the two main characters in "Hills Like White Elephants." A young woman, JIG, tells her lover that the anis tastes like licorice and then agrees with him when he says, "That's the way with everything" in their lives together. He means, especially, the friction between them, created by her pregnancy and their attempt to agree on whether she should have an abortion. Anis del Toro is also drunk by characters in *The Sun Also Rises.* Del Toro is a brand name for this liqueur.

Anita   Character in *The Fifth Column.* See MOORISH TART.

Anllos, Juan (1897–1925)   Spanish bullfighter, "Nacional II," mentioned in *Death in the Afternoon.* According to Barnaby Conrad in *Gates of Fear* (1957), his name is spelled Anllo, and in 1925 he was killed in a bullring in Soria by a bottle thrown by a spectator. His older brother, Ricardo, known as "Nacional I" is also mentioned in *Death.*

Anna   Nurse mentioned in *Islands in the Stream,* who took care of Andrew HUDSON when he stayed with his mother in Rochester, New York.

Anselmo   "The old man," 67 years old, from BARCO DE AVILA, one of PABLO's band of guerrilla fighters in *For Whom the Bell Tolls,* killed by a fragment of the BRIDGE when it is blown up. When Robert JORDAN first meets him, the reader is told that Anselmo is speaking old Castilian and that it went something like this: "Art thou a brute? Yes. Art thou a beast? Yes, many times. Hast thou a brain? Nay. None. Now we come for something of consummate importance and thee, with thy dwelling place to be undisturbed, puts thy fox-hole before the interests of humanity. Before the interests of thy people. I this and that in the this and that of thy father. I this and that and that in thy this."

"Anthraxolite, and Not Coal, Declares Geologist Again"   Article, unsigned, published in *The Toronto Daily Star* (September 25, 1923).

Antonio (1)   Colonel at SEGURIDAD HEADQUARTERS in Madrid in *The Fifth Column.* After Philip RAWLINGS questions the First Comrade, who had allowed a prisoner to escape, he suggests to Antonio that the comrade be allowed to live. But after Rawlings leaves the office,

Antonio asks his assault guards to bring the First Comrade back for further questioning. He is also in charge of questioning and torturing a civilian who is captured by Rawlings and his German counterespionage colleague, MAX (2). The reports in the newspapers the next day state that 300 members of the FIFTH COLUMN had been rounded up, suggesting that the civilian had talked.

Antonio (2)   First mate on Thomas HUDSON's fishing boat, searching for the crew of a German submarine in the "At Sea" section of *Islands in the Stream.* Early in the search among the islands off the northeast coast of Cuba he and ARA, one of the Basques on board, find nine bodies, all burned by the Germans.

ants metaphor   Frederic HENRY, facing the death of Catherine BARKLEY near the end of *A Farewell to Arms,* remembers a time when he put a log, full of ants onto a campfire. The ants swarmed over the log, trying to escape. Frederic remembers thinking that he could be a "messiah" and rescue the ants, but, instead, he throws a cup of water on the log so he can make a fresh drink of whisky and water. He remembers thinking that the water probably only "steamed the ants." He remembers this experience when he realizes that Catherine is going to die, and he begins thinking about fate, that "they" will always "kill you in the end." He compares the "they" of Catherine's fate to his own "messiah" role with the ants.

Aosta   Italian town, north of Milan, in the foothills of the Italian Alps, about 18 miles by road south of the Great St. Bernard Pass. From Aosta the main character in "The Revolutionist" walks across the pass into Switzerland. The distance would include a rise of almost 1,800 yards.

In *A Moveable Feast* Hemingway writes that Hadley reminded him of the time when the two of them and their friend Chink DORMAN-SMITH walked through the snow of the St. Bernard Pass into Italy and "walked down all day in the spring to Aosta."

Aparicio, Julio (1932–)   One of the bullfighters whom Hemingway saw fight during the summer of 1959 as he traveled the Spanish bullfight circuit in preparation for writing *The Dangerous Summer.*

"Appointment with Disaster, An"   Title of part 3 of the three-part magazine version of *The Dangerous Summer,* published by *Life* in its September 19, 1960, issue. Part 1, "The Dangerous Summer," was published on September 5; part 2, "The Pride of the Devil," was published on September 12. See *The Dangerous Summer.* (1).

Apponyi, Count Albert (1846–1933)   Hungarian statesman, leader of his country's delegation to the Paris Peace Conference (1920); subject of Hemingway's article "Count Apponyi and the Loan" (*The Toronto Daily Star*, October 15, 1923).

Ara   Member of Thomas HUDSON's boat crew, one of two Basques on board, searching for the crew of a German submarine in the "At Sea" section of *Islands in the Stream.* He is the "wide-shouldered Basque," and he and ANTONIO (2), Hudson's first mate, find nine bodies, all burned by the Germans.

Aranjuez   One of the Spanish towns where bullfights were covered by Hemingway in the summer of 1959 in preparation for writing *The Dangerous Summer* for *Life* magazine. Antonio Ordóñez was on the bullfight program. Hemingway saw his first bullfight, outside of Madrid, in Aranjuez on May 30, 1923. It is described in *Green Hills of Africa.*

Archer, Fred   Lieutenant commander at the U.S. embassy in Havana, an old friend of Thomas HUDSON's in *Islands in the Stream.*

Archibald, Tommy   The jockey riding Kircubbin in the fixed horserace at St. Cloud, outside of Paris, in "My Old Man."

Ardennes (1)   Large, wooded plateau from northern France to southeastern Belgium and northern Luxembourg, the scene of several battles in both world wars, most notably the Battle of the Bulge (December 1944–January 1945). It is one of the areas where Richard CANTWELL fought during World War II, on his division's march to the Siegfried line on Germany's western frontier.

Ardennes (2)   Formerly a province, Ardennes is now a department in the region of Champagne. It is referred to by Jake BARNES in *The Sun Also Rises,* because it is from the adjoining Champagne region that Jake, and other Hemingway fictional characters, get their favorite wines.

Arévalo   The place in Spain where PABLO and his guerrilla fighters blew up a train a few weeks before they are joined by Robert JORDAN, in *For Whom the Bell Tolls.* The town is about 96 miles northwest of Madrid.

Argonne Forest   The Argonne Forest is in northeast France along the border with Belgium, Luxembourg, and Germany, the site of major battles in 1918 during WORLD WAR I. It is one of the places mentioned in "Soldier's Home," where Harold KREBS fought in that war with the U.S. Marines.

Arlen, Michael (1895–1956)   Writer, born in Bulgaria but brought up in England, where he took the name Michael Arlen in 1922 when he began to publish his

work. His original name was Dikran Kouyoumdjian. In *A Moveable Feast* Hemingway writes that F. Scott FITZGERALD described all the plots of Arlen's novels as they drove back to Paris from Lyon and that Scott thought that Arlen was the writer to watch. Arlen's best-known novel, *The Green Hat* (1924), had just been published and was a popular success.

In *The Fifth Column* Philip RAWLINGS tells Dorothy BRIDGES that she is "vulgar" to want to go to Saint Moritz. "Kitzbühel you mean," he says to her. "You meet people like Michael Arlen at Saint Moritz."

Arlington   U.S. National Cemetery where military personnel can be buried; Colonel Richard CANTWELL thinks about the cemetery in *Across the River and Into the Trees,* but without indicating he would like to be buried there.

Armagnac   Brandy distilled from wine from the district of Armagnac in Gascony, France. In *The Garden of Eden,* David and Catherine BOURNE usually drink it with Perrier water.

armorer's shop   In Milan, where, in *A Farewell to Arms,* Frederic HENRY buys a pistol the evening he catches the midnight train back to GORIZIA and the battlefront.

Arnaldo   At the GRITTI PALACE HOTEL in Venice, the "glass-eyed" waiter assigned to Richard CANTWELL's room in *Across the River and Into the Trees.* He tells Cantwell that his wife "still speaks" of the ducks that Cantwell gave him on his last trip into Venice.

"Arrival of Lloyd George, The"   Article, published in *The Toronto Daily Star* (October 5, 1923), reprinted in *Ernest Hemingway: Dateline Toronto* (1985). The headline in the *Daily Star* was "Lloyd George up Early as Big Liner Arrives." Datelined "New York," it is an interview with the former British prime minister as he arrives in New York on the *Mauretania.* Hemingway writes that in spite of the failure of the British delegation led by Lloyd George to the Genoa Peace Conference the year before (1922), he is a "survivor" and not thinking about the past.

arrow-heads   Indian relics belonging to the father of the unnamed main character/narrator in "Now I Lay Me." They are burned, along with other relics the father had collected, by the boy's mother, who does not understand their value.

"[Arsiero, Asiago . . .]"   First line of a poem about World War I towns of northern Italy, written in 1922 and first published in *88 Poems* (1979).

artichoke hearts   Part of a picnic David BOURNE and MARITA have, along with mustard sauce, TAVEL wine, and radishes, at LA NAPOULE beach, near the end of *The Garden of Eden*.

"Art of Fiction XXI: Ernest Hemingway, The" Interview with Hemingway by George Plimpton, editor of *The Paris Review*. Plimpton's key question: "What is the true function of art?" Hemingway's answer: "From things that have happened and from things as they exist and from all things that you know and all those you cannot know, you make something through your invention that is not a representation but a whole new thing truer than anything true and alive, and you make it alive, and if you make it well enough, you give it immortality."

The interview was No. 21 in Plimpton's "Art of Fiction" series for *The Paris Review*. It appeared in the spring 1958 issue.

"Art of the Short Story, The" Article, published in *The Paris Review* No. 79 (1981) and reprinted in *New Critical Approaches to the Short Stories of Ernest Hemingway*, edited by Jackson J. Benson (1990). It was written in 1959 for a proposed Scribner's student edition of Hemingway's short stories, but the idea for the book was abandoned. Hemingway generalizes in the essay about the "background" for several of his best-known stories, discussing in some cases the importance of what is left out as a way of describing, ostensibly for would-be writers, how to write fiction.

Arturo Bank clerk in "Out of Season," who stares at PEDUZZI from the "door of the Fascist café" when Peduzzi tips his hat to him.

Arusha The capitol of the Arusha Province in northeast Tanzania, about 50 miles southwest of Mt. Kilimanjaro. In *Green Hills of Africa* Hemingway remembers seeing a "wonderful pair of [sable] horns" in the game warden's office there.

At the end of "The Snows of Kilimanjaro," HARRY, dying of gangrene, dreams that Compton, a pilot, plans to refuel his plane in Arusha on its way to a Nairobi, Kenya, hospital. But instead of going to Arusha the plane turns "left" and flies to the top of Kilimanjaro.

"Ash Heel's Tendon, The" An unfinished early story fragment, written between 1919 and 1921, rejected for publication but published, with four other previously unpublished fragments, as a completed "short story" by Peter Griffin in the first volume of his biography, *Along With Youth: Hemingway, The Early Years* (1985). The sketch is about a killer who may be seen as an early version of the tough guys in Hemingway's later, successful short story "The Killers."

Ashley, Brett Leading female character, a 34-year-old Englishwoman, in *The Sun Also Rises*. A former V.A.D. (assistant nurse) during WORLD WAR I, Brett married Lord Ashley after her "true love . . . kicked off with the dysentery." She has been married to him since the war, but he does not treat her well. She is currently in Paris awaiting a divorce and preparing to marry another man, Mike CAMPBELL, with whom she hopes to find stability.

Brett had just begun to get her life back together when, at the beginning of the novel, she meets and falls in love with Jake BARNES. Although she is in love with Jake, the novel's narrator and the main character, he is sexually impotent from a wound received in the war. While she is able to satisfy him sexually in some way only hinted at, he cannot satisfy her. When Jake asks her if he and she couldn't just "live together," she tells him she would "just *tromper* [betray him] with everybody." She loves him, but she knows her own sexual appetites and that "living" with Jake would not be fair to him.

In nearly every scene in which Brett appears, Jake's narration makes clear the conflicting emotions she feels—her love for him, her sexual appetite, and her desire for a safer existence. This frustration is what motivates her throughout the novel and makes her one of Hemingway's most interesting characters.

The reader first meets her when she arrives with several homosexuals at the BAL MUSETTE, a dancing club in Paris. Jake is there with the prostitute GEORGETTE, whom he has picked up, and some friends, one of whom is Robert COHN. Jake says of the entrance of the homosexuals: "With them was Brett. She looked very lovely and she was very much with them." She feels safe with them, but she immediately sits with Jake and then dances with him, and the reader is quickly aware of their attraction. Cohn is infatuated with Brett on his first look, publicly enough to embarrass her. Jake explains to the reader that Cohn "looked a great deal as his compatriot must have looked when he saw the promised land." She leaves the club with Jake, but the taxi ride only presents further frustration for them both as they are jostled together in the cab's backseat.

Later Brett goes off to SAN SEBASTIÁN with Cohn, because, as she confesses to Jake, she thought it "would be good for him." Jake's sarcastic response is that she might, then, "take up social service." She realizes what a mistake she's made when, in Pamplona, Cohn cannot let go of her and so makes enemies of everyone, including his best friend Jake.

In the chaos that surrounds Brett and her friends at the festival—including constant drinking—she runs off with the bullfighter Pedro ROMERO. She leaves him in Madrid and sends telegrams to several places to persuade Jake to rescue her. The wire asks, "Could you come Hotel Montana Madrid am rather in trouble Brett." Jake accepts the call for help.

On the novel's last page, Brett and Jake are in a Madrid taxi on the GRAN VIA, Brett saying to him "Oh, Jake . . . . we could have had such a damned good time together," and Jake says, in the last line, "Yes . . . . Isn't it pretty to think so?"

Ashley, Lord Brett ASHLEY's second husband in *The Sun Also Rises*. She is in the process of divorcing him. He was in the British navy during WORLD WAR I and traumatized enough by the war that he sleeps, according to Brett, with a loaded revolver at his side.

askari East African word meaning a native soldier or policeman. In *The Garden of Eden* David BOURNE, in the AFRICAN STORY he is writing, uses the word to refer to an old, dead elephant, which was the "companion" or, perhaps, "friend" of the elephant David's father is hunting.

Asti Small town in the Italian Piedmont, known for its Asti Spumante, a sweet sparkling wine, which Frederic HENRY drinks with "a friend" in the whorehouse at GORIZIA at the beginning of *A Farewell to Arms*.

Astor, John Jacob IV (1864–1912) American multimillionaire and an inventor of, among other things, a bicycle brake. He built the Astoria section of what later became the Waldorf-Astoria Hotel in New York City. He is mentioned in *Islands in the Stream* in connection with an "old song" about his death on the *Titanic*.

Astra 7.65 A pistol, worn by Frederic HENRY at the beginning of *A Farewell to Arms*. He is skeptical of its value, because it "jump[s]" when he fires it.

Asturias, the In *The Fifth Column* the hotel manager in Madrid informs Philip RAWLINGS of the "bad news" that the fighting is almost finished at "the Asturias," a region of northwest Spain, facing the Bay of Biscay. In the Spanish civil war the region fell to the Nationalists in October 1937 after fierce fighting.

Atares A castle in Cuba, where, according to Thomas HUDSON in *Islands in the Stream,* revolutionaries had shot Colonel Crittenden and his men "when that expedition failed down at Bahía Honda forty years before" Hudson was born. See Colonel William L. CRITTENDEN.

"Athletic Association to Organize Next Week" Article for Oak Park and River Forest High School newspaper, *The Trapeze* (November 3, 1916), reprinted in *Hemingway at Oak Park High: The High School Writings of Ernest Hemingway, 1916–1917* (1993).

"Athletic Notes" (1) Article for Oak Park and River Forest High School newspaper, *The Trapeze* (November 24, 1916), reprinted in *Hemingway at Oak Park High: The High School Writings of Ernest Hemingway, 1916–1917* (1993).

"Athletic Notes" (2) Article for Oak Park and River Forest High School newspaper, *The Trapeze* (December

22, 1916), reprinted in *Hemingway at Oak Park High: The High School Writings of Ernest Hemingway, 1916–1917* (1993).

"Athletic Notes" (3) Article for Oak Park and River Forest High School newspaper, *The Trapeze* (February 2, 1917), reprinted in *Hemingway at Oak Park High: The High School Writings of Ernest Hemingway, 1916–1917* (1993).

"Athletic Notes" (4) Article for Oak Park and River Forest High School newspaper, *The Trapeze* (February 9, 1917), reprinted in *Hemingway at Oak Park High: The High School Writings of Ernest Hemingway, 1916–1917* (1993).

"Athletic Verse" Title covering three poems about football ("The Tackle," "The Punt," and "The Safety Man"), first published in the Oak Park and River Forest High School literary magazine, *Tabula* (March 1917). All three were reprinted in *88 Poems* (1979) and counted as separate poems. According to Nicholas Gerogiannis, editor of *88 Poems,* there is a question about the authorship, but the only surviving manuscript is in Hemingway's handwriting.

Atkinson, Dick One of JOE's teenage friends in "My Old Man."

Atlantic Monthly American magazine of the literary arts, founded in Boston in 1857, edited first by James Russell Lowell. Hemingway published three short stories and two poems in the magazine.

In *The Garden of Eden* Catherine BOURNE, realizing how upset her husband, David, is because she burned his short story manuscripts, tells him she will reimburse him for the loss by having someone at *Atlantic Monthly* estimate the value of the stories, which she will then double. In *A Moveable Feast* Hemingway writes that Gertrude Stein wanted to be published in this magazine.

"[At night I lay with you . . .]" First line of a three-line poem written about 1920–21 and first published in *88 Poems* (1979).

"At the End of the Ambulance Run" Article, unsigned, published in *The Kansas City Star* (January 20, 1918), reprinted in *Ernest Hemingway, Cub Reporter* (1970).

"At the Theater with Lloyd George" Article, published in *The Toronto Star Weekly* (October 6, 1923), reprinted in *Ernest Hemingway: Dateline Toronto* (1985). The headline in the *TSW* was "Lloyd George Attends Theatre in New York." Datelined "New York," the article covers the former British prime minister's attendance at the *Music Box Revue* on Broadway, the crowds that welcomed him and his family at the theater, and what his wife, Dame Margaret, and their daughter, Megan, wore.

Aurol, Madame   In *The Garden of Eden* the wife of the proprietor at the hotel in LA NAPOULE, France. She doesn't approve of the MÉNAGE À TROIS in her hotel, but she likes David BOURNE and gives him food and drink when he visits her kitchen.

Aurol, Monsieur   Proprietor at the hotel in LA NAPOULE where David and Catherine BOURNE stay while David writes his AFRICAN STORY.

Austrian offensive   In "A Natural History of the Dead," the Austrian offensive against the Italians in June 1918 was one of the events during which the narrator observed death.

Auteuil   One of the leading steeplechase racecourses in Paris, built about 1850 in the southeast corner of the BOIS de Boulogne. In *A Moveable Feast* Hemingway writes about going to the track "after work" during his early years in Paris with his wife Hadley. One day she bet on a horse named Chèvre d'or who started at 120 to 1 and led by 20 lengths before falling at the last jump, "with enough savings on him to keep us six months."

In "My Old Man," JOE's "old man" bought a horse at Auteuil for "30,000 francs," making Joe feel "proud" that his old man was an owner.

The track is also mentioned in *Islands in the Stream*, *The Garden of Eden*, and *Death in the Afternoon*.

"Author's Note"   A stylistic device Hemingway uses in *The Torrents of Spring* to enhance his PARODY of various contemporary writers of the post–World War I years. The author uses the "Author's Notes" to explain parts of the story, and some notes are nearly as long as the chapters. In one note he suggests that if the reader is confused or bored, he, Hemingway, would be glad to read anything the reader has written, "for criticism or advice," and that the reader can always find him "any afternoon" at the CAFÉ DU DÔME, in Paris, where he will be "talking about art" with Harold Stearns and Sinclair Lewis.

In another "Note" he says that he wrote the previous chapter (12, the last chapter in part 3) in two hours and then went to lunch with John DOS PASSOS, who told Hemingway that he had "wrought a masterpiece."

In yet another "note" he states that "It was at this point in the story, reader, that Mr. F. Scott FITZGERALD came to our home one afternoon, and after remaining for quite a while suddenly sat down in the fireplace and would not (or was it could not, reader?) get up and let the fire burn something else so as to keep the room warm."

l'Auto   One of the publications left behind by the bicycle racers in San Sebastián, which Jake BARNES reads while relaxing after the Fiesta SAN FERMÍN.

Avanti!   Official Italian Socialist newspaper, founded in 1912 by Benito Mussolini and edited by him during its early history. He was an antimilitarist, antinationalist, and anti-imperialist editor and vigorously opposed Italy's entry into World War I. *Avanti!*, which means "Forward!" is referred to in "The Revolutionist."

avenue de l'Opéra   On the Right Bank in Paris, running from the Opéra southeast to the rue de Rivoli. In *The Sun Also Rises,* Jake BARNES and GEORGETTE ride in a HORSE-CAB up this avenue to rue des Pyramides, "through the traffic of the rue de Rivoli, and through a dark gate into the Tuileries . . . then [turning] up the rue des Saints Pères."

l'Avenue's   Restaurant in Paris where Jake BARNES, Robert COHN, and Cohn's "fianceé," Francis, go for dinner at the end of chapter 1 in *The Sun Also Rises*.

Avignon   Town in southern France about 50 miles north of Marseilles on the main rail line between Marseilles and Paris. It is where, in "A Canary for One," the story's narrator sees "negro soldiers," led by a white sergeant, waiting on the station platform.

And it is where David and Catherine BOURNE get off the train on their honeymoon trip to GRAU DU ROI. They then ride their bicycles down to Nîmes and stay at the Imperator Hotel before riding farther south to AIGUES MORTES and on to Grau du Roi.

Avila   Spanish town in the western foothills of the Guadarrama Mountains, about 78 miles west of Madrid. In *For Whom the Bell Tolls* it is the town from which PILAR and PABLO start the Loyalist movement and where Pablo and other LOYALISTS kill the town's priest and other local FASCISTS. See PILAR'S STORY.

Ayers   In *Islands in the Stream* Thomas HUDSON remembers that his friend Roger DAVIS was in love with a girl in Paris named Ayers. Davis broke off the affair because he finally realized she was a "phony."

Aymo, Bartolomeo   One of the ambulance drivers with Frederic HENRY during the Italian army's retreat from Caporetto in *A Farewell to Arms*. He is killed by an Italian soldier at the beginning of the chaotic rush to get away from the attacking Austrian army. Frederic says of Aymo, "I liked him as well as any one I ever knew. I had his papers in my pocket and would write to his family."

Ayuntamiento   Office building in PAMPLONA, where Jake BARNES buys his bullfight tickets in *The Sun Also Rises*.

B

Babati Town in Tanzania, about 120 miles southwest of Mt. Kilimanjaro. The Hemingways left from Babati on their southward safari, the subject of *Green Hills of Africa.*

baboons Large, terrestrial monkeys of Africa and Arabia, mentioned in *Green Hills of Africa,* mainly because they "stink." Again, in *The Garden of Eden* baboons are eating wild figs in David BOURNE's AFRICAN STORY, and their droppings make a "foul" smell.

baby (1) In "Indian Camp," a baby boy is born to a young Indian woman by CAESARIAN SECTION. NICK's doctor father performs the operation.

baby (2) At the end of *A Farewell to Arms* Catherine BARKLEY's baby "looked like a freshly skinned rabbit" to Frederic HENRY, but he discovers a few minutes later that it was born dead.

backgammon A board game for two people, the board having two parts, each marked with 12 elongated triangles, and with each player having 15 pieces, which are moved in accordance with throws of the dice. In *The Garden of Eden* Catherine BOURNE sometimes plays backgammon with MARITA after dinner. According to the narrator of the story, "[t]hey always played it seriously and for money."

backpack NICK carries one with him on his fishing trip in "Big Two-Hearted River." He thinks it is too heavy with canned goods, but he is happy to eat the contents nevertheless.

Bacon, Grandpa NICK's grandfather in "The Indians Moved Away."

Bacuranao A town on the Bacuranao River about 15 miles east of Havana, Cuba. In *To Have and Have Not* there is a cove near the mouth of the river, where there used to be a "big dock for loading sand." Harry MORGAN and Mr. SING agree to meet there so that Morgan can pick up 12 Chinamen and take them, illegally, from Cuba to Florida.

In *Islands in the Stream* Thomas HUDSON thinks the German submarine crew he is searching for might be smart to land at Bacuranao.

Baedeker Handbooks for travel in countries and cities of western Europe, used almost universally by travelers during the first 20 years or so of the 20th century. In *Across the River and Into the Trees* Richard CANTWELL refers to the guide sarcastically, because it is used by a "pockmarked" American tourist whom he clearly dislikes.

Bains de l'Alliaz In Switzerland, the place to which Frederic HENRY and Catherine BARKLEY walk, on "the other side of the mountain" from their rented house above MONTREUX in *A Farewell to Arms.*

Bainsizza plateau In northeast Italy, just north of Gorizia, the site of heavy fighting during WORLD WAR I. According to Frederic HENRY in *A Farewell to Arms,* the "fighting . . . was over" by mid-September (1917). A "British major" reports to Frederic that 150,000 Italians had been lost in the fighting there and another 40,000 on the CARSO. See CAPORETTO, BATTLE OF.

baits Exactness in depth of baits is essential to SANTIAGO, in *The Old Man and the Sea.* Even though he has been 84 days without a fish, he is an expert fisherman, which the narrator makes clear by constant references to his knowledge of nature in general and of fishing in particular. "One bait was down forty fathoms. The second was at seventy-five and the third and fourth were down in the blue water at one hundred and one hundred and twenty-five fathoms. Each bait hung head down," and the hook was "covered with fresh sardines." Later the old man baits two additional lines but keeps them in the boat. Before he hooks the MARLIN (2) he catches a 10-pound albacore, which he says will make another "beautiful bait."

Baker, Carlos Heard (1909–1987) Author of the first major biography of Hemingway, *Ernest Hemingway: A Life Story* (1969), still the standard on which other biographers rely. Baker also authored the first major critical study of Hemingway's writings, *Hemingway: The Writer As Artist* (1952). He wrote a biography of Percy Bysshe Shelley and a volume of criticism, *Shelley's Major Poetry: The Fabric of a Vision* (1948), in addition to two novels, and a book of poetry. Baker taught at Princeton University from 1951 until his death in 1987.

Baker, Sir Samuel (1821–1893) Samuel White Baker, British traveler and sportsman, mentioned by Hemingway in *A Moveable Feast* as the author of *The Nile Tributaries of Abyssinia* (1872).

Bal Bullier Paris dance hall at 33, avenue de l'Observatoire during the 1920s, mentioned in *A Moveable Feast*. The Bal Bullier was a bit unusual for dance halls in the 1920s because it charged men 4–6 francs to enter but women only 2 $^1/_2$–4 francs. Most Paris dance halls charged the same for women and men.

"Balkans: A Picture of Peace, Not War" Article, published in *The Toronto Daily Star* (October 16, 1922), reprinted in *Ernest Hemingway: Dateline Toronto* (1985). The headline in the *Daily Star* was "Balkans Look Like Ontario, A Picture of Peace, Not War." Datelined "Sofia, Bulgaria," it's about a drunken Paris taxi driver causing Hemingway's typewriter to be bent so that this report is being written in pencil on the train while he crosses eastern Europe, where, he says that Croatia looks like eastern Ontario. The land is beautiful and "there can never be peace in the Balkans as long as one people holds the lands of another people—no matter what the political excuse may be."

"Ballot Bullets" Article, published in *The Toronto Star Weekly* (May 28, 1921), reprinted in *The Wild Years* (1962), reprinted in *Ernest Hemingway: Dateline Toronto* (1985). The headline in the *Star Weekly* was "Gun-Men's Wild Political War on in Chicago." Datelined "Chicago," the article is about Chicago politics, particularly about Anthony D'Andrea, a "defeated candidate for alderman in the 19th Ward," who was "shot down on his own doorstep." When Alderman John Powers won the election the previous November by 400 votes, D'Andrea protested the vote count, and a "series of killings commenced."

bal musette French term for any popular dancing hall. The Hemingways' first apartment at 74, rue Cardinal Lemoine in Paris was above a *bal musette*. In *A Moveable Feast* Hemingway writes that Ford Madox Ford invited him to one of the "evenings" he and some friends were having at the "amusing" *bal musette*. When Ford began to give him directions, Hemingway had a difficult time convincing him that he already knew its location.

In *The Sun Also Rises* Jake BARNES takes GEORGETTE to a *bal musette* on the rue de la Montagne Sainte-Geneviève, where they meet some of his friends.

bambini theory A theory about Italian art rendered by Richard CANTWELL's driver, JACKSON, in *Across the River and Into the Trees*. Jackson's theory is that Italians love babies, which is why so many Italian paintings depict women holding babies.

"Banal Story" Unnamed character in this two-page story is sarcastic about a "booklet" he is reading (in 1925) advertising *The Forum,* a magazine of arts and letters. The brochure describes stories and articles which, to the narrator, are "banal"—dull or stale. The ad states that "Patrons of the arts and letters have discovered *The Forum.*" It describes articles on a boxing match in Paris, a "twenty-one" foot snowfall in Mesopotamia, and a future cricket match in Australia. The narrator says, it is a "splendid booklet."

At the end of the page and a half of descriptions of other articles and stories, the "He" of the story lays down the booklet, and the narrator states that "meanwhile," Manuel Garcia MAERA, a famous bullfighter, is dying in Triana, Spain. And the "He" of the story is not mentioned again. It is difficult to tell whether the death of the bullfighter is meant as an example of or a contrast with the banality of the articles and stories described in the booklet advertising *The Forum*.

The narrator states that people at Maera's funeral bought "colored pictures of him to remember him by, and [so] lost the picture they had of him in their memories." At the end of the story, the narrator says that after Maera's funeral, "every one sat in the cafés out of the rain, and many colored pictures of Maera were sold to men who rolled them up and put them away in their pockets."

"Banal Story" was first published in *Little Review* (Spring-Summer 1926) and reprinted in *Men Without Women* (1927).

"Bandera Rosa" Spanish civil war song, sung in *The Fifth Column* by 25 comrades waiting downstairs in the Hotel Florida in act 2, scene 3.

banderillas According to Hemingway in the glossary of *Death in the Afternoon,* a banderilla is a "rounded dowel, seventy centimetres long, wrapped in colored paper, with a harpoon shaped steel point, placed in pairs in the withers of the bull in the second act of the bullfight."

banderilleros Bullfighters under the orders of the matador during a bullfight. They help with the capes and in placing the banderillas; mentioned and defined in *Death in the Afternoon.*

Bank of Odessa In showing prejudice against Russian tourists in Venice, Richard CANTWELL tells Ettore, a waiter at HARRY'S BAR, that he hopes CIPRIANI, the owner, doesn't take any checks from the Bank of Odessa in *Across the River and Into the Trees.*

"Bank Vaults vs. Cracksmen" Article, published in *The Toronto Star Weekly* (December 1, 1923), reprinted in *The Wild Years* (1962), reprinted in *Ernest Hemingway:*

Dateline Toronto (1985). The headline in the *Star Weekly* was "Fifty-ton Doors Laugh at Robbers' Tools,/ Bank Vaults Defy Scientific Cracksmen." It is about attempted bank robberies in Canada and particularly one on June 26, 1916, when five robbers blew a vault through the back wall of a Ville Marie bank but still did not get the vault open.

bar (1)   In "A Clean, Well-Lighted Place," the older waiter closes up his own café and goes to a bar for a cup of coffee. But he doesn't like bars and knows that a "clean, well-lighted café is a very different thing" from a bar.

bar (2)   In *The Garden of Eden*, a bar at the PALACE HOTEL (2) in Madrid, where David BOURNE reads the English-language newspapers and drinks a Spanish wine, MARISMEÑO, while waiting for his wife, Catherine.

barber, the   Italian barber at the AMERICAN HOSPITAL (1) in Milan in *A Farewell to Arms*. Frederic HENRY is shaved by the barber, who doesn't understand that Frederic is an American who has been wounded fighting on the side of the Italians; the barber thinks he is an Austrian officer. The PORTER (3) who brought the barber to the hospital laughs about it and tells Frederic that the barber had threatened to cut his throat.

Barbera   A grape originating in the Italian Piedmont and the principal grape in such wines as Botticino and Buttafuoco. Frederic HENRY has a bottle of Barbera in the backseat of his ambulance car during the retreat from CAPORETTO in *A Farewell to Arms*.

Barbusse, Henri (1873–1935)   French novelist, mentioned in *A Farewell to Arms*. Count GREFFI recommends the writer as one Frederic HENRY should read, especially *Le Feu* (1916), a firsthand account of the life of French soldiers during the early part of WORLD WAR I.

Barcelona   One of the towns on the Spanish bullfight circuit covered by Hemingway in *The Dangerous Summer*. It is where Antonio ORDÓÑEZ and Luis Miguel DOMINGUÍN fought their second fight on the same card.

Barco de Avila   The Spanish hometown of ANSELMO, "the old man" in *For Whom the Bell Tolls*.

Barkley, Catherine   Leading female character in *A Farewell to Arms*. She is an English assistant nurse with the British Army in WORLD WAR I, stationed in northern Italy. Her fiancé, a British soldier, has been "blown up" in the battle of the Somme in northern France, and she is "nearly crazy" over the loss. What Frederic HENRY, the novel's narrator and main character, doesn't tell the reader—perhaps because he doesn't know at the

time—is that the fiancé has been killed just before Frederic meets Catherine in the fall of 1916 (see SOMME, BATTLE OF THE) and that the trauma of her fiancé's loss is recent. In the garden of the villa that houses the British hospital, Catherine slaps Frederic when he tries to kiss her on what amounts to a first date. She apologizes almost immediately, however, and offers him a second chance at a kiss.

Frederic's first impression of Catherine is that she is "quite tall." She is blonde with "tawny skin and gray eyes," and she wears what "seems" to Frederic to be a nurse's uniform. He thinks she is "beautiful." She carries a rattan stick that belonged to her fiancé, to whom she was engaged for eight years. Catherine tells Frederic that she was a "fool" not to have married him; "I could have given him that anyway," she tells him. This experience of loss makes her an important foil to Frederic's initial immaturity. Even though the war has just begun, she is already aware of the horrors that war brings; Frederic is not.

The two become lovers. Then Frederic, recovered from his wounds, returns to the front leaving a pregnant Catherine behind.

Catherine Barkley is certainly more mature than Frederic during most of their love affair. Her strength is apparent when, in spite of the recent death of her fiancé in the war, she continues her duties as a nurse with the Italian army. But when Frederic escapes from the chaos of the retreat from Caporetto and returns to find Catherine in Stresa, he, too, has survived an ordeal, and matured.

Much of the early scholarly criticism of the women in Hemingway's fiction, including the character of Catherine Barkley, saw the women as sex objects, without much personality, whose main role was to please the male protagonists. Late-20th-century criticism, however, suggests that many, even most, of the leading female characters in Hemingway's fiction are not only multidimensional but also strong in their own right.

Bar Milano   In *The Sun Also Rises*, a "small, tough bar," where Jake BARNES and some of his friends, including EDNA, Bill's friend from BIARRITZ, go for food and drink during the Fiesta SAN FERMÍN in Pamplona.

Barnes, Djuna (1892–1982)   American novelist, poet, playwright, and illustrator, well known in the Paris literary circle of writers during the 1920s and 1930s. She is best known for her novel *Nightwood* (1936), about the homosexual and heterosexual loves of five grotesque characters. Barnes also wrote and illustrated *The Book of Repulsive Women: 8 Rhythms and 5 Drawings* (1915), and three plays produced by the Provincetown Players in 1919. In Paris she interviewed expatriate writers for articles to be published in various magazines. In 1923 BONI & LIVERIGHT published her *A Book* (expanded as *A*

Night Among the Horses in 1929 and revised as *Spillway* in 1962). Barnes also wrote *Ryder* (1928), a satire of a man's relationships to the women in his life.

Hemingway wrote about Barnes in a 1924 editorial for Ford Madox Ford's TRANSATLANTIC REVIEW. "Djuna Barnes, who according to her publishers is that legendary personality that has dominated the intellectual night-life of Europe for a century, is in town. I have never met her, nor read her books, but she looks very nice." The gossipy comment may have been as much a slam at Ford as at Barnes. Hemingway disliked Ford in part because of his constant puffing up of his own writing in *transatlantic* and in a regular newspaper editorial.

Barnes is generally considered a minor writer of her time, yet Janet FLANNER says in her "Introduction" to *Paris Was Yesterday: 1925–1939* (1972) that "Djuna Barnes was the most important woman writer we had in Paris. She was famous among us for her great short story, 'A Night among the Horses.' Within a short time after the publication of her novel *Nightwood* . . . it became available in a paperback edition and attained enormous popularity among young European intellectuals all the way from Rome to Berlin . . ." Flanner describes Barnes as "tall, quite handsome, bold-voiced, and a remarkable talker."

Barnes, Jake Main character and narrator of *The Sun Also Rises*. He is from Kansas City, but he lives in Paris at the time of the novel (1925). His flat is on the Left Bank across the street from the CLOSERIE DES LILAS, and "a little way down the Boulevard St. Michel." He works for an unidentified newspaper with offices on the Right Bank, probably the Paris edition of the *New York Herald Tribune*.

He and his Paris friends are members of what Gertrude STEIN called the "LOST GENERATION." Part of the first epigraph to the novel includes a quotation from her, "in conversation," in which she tells the author: "You are all a lost generation." Hemingway transfers this idea to Jake and his friends Robert COHN and Bill GORTON. They are "lost" in the sense that, although they are Americans, they feel their political and social beliefs are not compatible with what has happened in the United States after World War I. Jake was wounded in the genitals during the war and is IMPOTENT, though he denies it in a drunken conversation with Bill Gorton late in the novel. When Gorton tells Jake that some people "claim" that he is "impotent," Jake says, "No . . . I just had an accident." It is probable that he receives some form of sexual gratification in a scene in his Paris flat, after Brett ASHLEY sends Count MIPPIPOPOLOUS for champagne.

The exact nature of Jake's wound and of his "impotence" is never made clear. He is narrating his own story, however, and so is not likely to spell out the details. The "accident," whatever it was, is important to

the reader's understanding of Jake's character, because the resulting wound prohibits him from having a normal sexual relationship. Jake tries to keep a sense of humor: He says, "Well, it was a rotten way to be wounded. . . . In the Italian hospital we were going to form a society." He says that the Catholic Church recommends that he not think about it, but he cannot forget it, has trouble sleeping, and even though he suffered the wound at least seven years earlier, it still dominates his life.

He loves Brett, but because they cannot consummate their relationship, their friendship is a constant cause of frustration for both. In the PAMPLONA section of the novel, she runs off with the bullfighter Pedro ROMERO but soon after sends a telegram to Jake asking for his help, and he goes immediately to Madrid to rescue her from the "trouble" she says she's in—she's out of money. He sends a telegram, telling her he will be in Madrid the next day, and he then thinks to himself, "That seemed to handle it. That was it. Send a girl off with one man. Introduce her to another to go off with him. Now go and bring her back. And sign the wire with love."

Jake works hard at coping with his life, telling Cohn at one point, "Nobody ever lives their life all the way up except bullfighters." This attitude may account for Jake's enthusiasm for Paris, for the Pamplona fiesta, for wine and good food, and for the bullfights. He knows what "living well" is, and he tries to come to terms with the things he can do nothing about. Hemingway calls this attempt to play the cards one is dealt GRACE UNDER PRESSURE (he used the term in public for the first time in March 1926, while he was finishing *The Sun Also Rises*).

And in spite of Jake's comment about the Catholic Church telling him that the answer to his problem is to not think about it, Catholicism is still at the center of Jake's religious belief. He tells Brett that he is a "rotten Catholic" but that it is a "grand religion." He tells her that he has gotten things he has prayed for even if she hasn't, and when she confesses to him near the end of the novel that "deciding not to be a bitch" is what she has "instead of God," he reminds her that "[s]ome people have God . . . [q]uite a lot."

Jake's sexual impotence, caused by the war wound, is important to the reader's understanding of the novel as a whole. His physical impotence represents the general impotence of other expatriate Americans after the war, who went to Europe to escape a homeland they perceived to be culturally barren and indifferent to the war's devastating effects. On a larger scale, Jake's impotence signifies the frustration, the powerless, helpless feeling of anyone attempting to deal with a world that seems to have been stripped of meaning. Jake says, "I did not care what [the world] was all about. All I wanted to know was how to live in it."

Barney, Natalie (1876–1972) American literary figure who inherited a fortune, moved to Paris, and in 1909 established a home at 20, rue Jacob. She spent the next 60 years holding Friday salons there that included most of the best writers and painters from the United States, Great Britain, and France. She was also known for her frank, public expression of her lesbianism. Djuna BARNES wrote a "guidebook" about Barney's lesbian circle, titled *Ladies Almanack* (1928).

Hemingway, who was especially at ease with lesbian women, passed on to Gertrude STEIN and Alice B. TOKLAS the gossip that Barney had lost her sexual attractiveness (she was 48 when Hemingway met her) and made up for it by using props, such as polar bear rugs and polar bear pajamas, as "beauty aids." Hemingway told Stein and Toklas that Natalie's mind had "all the charming quality of a dog's in heat."

Barney is mentioned by Hemingway in *A Moveable Feast*, mostly in connection with BEL ESPRIT, Ezra POUND's plan to collect money from other writers and artists to give to T. S. ELIOT so that he could quit his banking job in London and devote his time to writing poetry. Barney was one of the early financial backers for Pound's plan. See also LESBIANISM.

Baron, the "An old friend" of Thomas HUDSON's, remembered in the "Cuba" section of *Islands in the Stream*. See PRINCESS.

barreras First row of seats at bullfights. Jake BARNES buys three tickets in the barreras for the first day of bullfights in PAMPLONA in *The Sun Also Rises*. He also buys three tickets for the SOBREPUERTOS, which are higher up and farther away from the blood.

bartender In "The Light of the World." When the story's narrator and his friend Tom enter the bar, the bartender immediately covers the two free-lunch bowls. And he won't serve either of them beer until he sees their money. After Tom insults him by spitting out a bite of the free-lunch pig's feet, the bartender kicks them out.

Barthou, Louis Head of the French delegation to the Genoa Economic Conference during April 1922, mentioned in several articles from the meeting, particularly "Barthou Refuses Conference."

"Barthou Crosses Hissing Tchitcherin" Article, published in *The Toronto Daily Star* (April 24, 1922), reprinted in *The Wild Years* (1962), reprinted in *Ernest Hemingway: Dateline Toronto* (1985). The headline in the *Daily Star* was "Barthou, Like a Smith Brother, Crosses Hissing Tchitcherin." Datelined "Genoa," the article reports on the exchanges between the leaders of the French and Russian delegations at the Genoa

Economic Conference (1922) and the effort by the leader of the British delegation, Lloyd George, at reconciliation. Tchitcherin "hisses" when he talks because of missing teeth.

"Barthou Refuses Conference" Article, unsigned, published in *The Toronto Daily Star* (April 18, 1922), reprinted in *Ernest Hemingway: Dateline Toronto* (1985). The headline in the *Daily Star* was "Barthou Refuses to Confer with Russians and Germans." Datelined "Genoa," the article reports that the leader of the French delegation to the Genoa Economic Conference, Louis Barthou, will take no further part in the conference unless the treaty just signed by Russia and Germany "is not immediately abrogated."

Bartlett, Soldier Sparring partner for boxer Jack BRENNAN, the main character in "Fifty Grand."

baseball In *The Old Man and the Sea*, baseball, the national sport of Cuba, is a constant, even thematic, factor. SANTIAGO reads about the American big league teams (the *Gran Ligas*) in the Havana papers before he leaves his village to go "out far" in search of great fish. During his three-day ordeal on the Gulf Stream he often wonders about how the teams are doing, particularly the Yankees and Joe DIMAGGIO. He thinks of DiMaggio especially, because of his ability to play in spite of a "bone spur," which the old man thinks about in comparison to his own "cramped" left hand. Other teams mentioned in the novel are "the Indians of Cleveland," "the Tigers of Detroit," "the Reds of Cincinnati," and "the White Sox of Chicago."

"Basketball Seasons Opens; Poor Lightweight Prospects" Article for Oak Park and River Forest High School newspaper, *The Trapeze* (December 8, 1916), reprinted in *Hemingway at Oak Park High: The High School Writings of Ernest Hemingway, 1916–1917* (1993).

Bas Meudon Short street on the Ile de Billancourt in southwest Paris, the location of La Pêche Miraculeuse restaurant; mentioned by Hemingway in *A Moveable Feast* as a place where he and Hadley could get *goujon*, a fish they liked.

Basque bar (1) In Havana, where, in the "Cuba" section of *Islands in the Stream*, Thomas HUDSON eats an occasional lunch and gets drunk during discussions with two acquaintances about young Tom Hudson's death in the war.

Basque bar (2) In SAINT-JEAN-DE-LUZ, France, where David BOURNE gets a drink, in *The Garden of Eden*.

Bassi, Fillipo Vincenza   Italian soldier who gets drunk with Frederic HENRY and other army buddies in book 1 of *A Farewell to Arms*.

Batista y Zaldívar, Fulgencio (1901–1973)   Cuban military leader, dictator (1934–40), and president (1940–44, 1952–59). He is president of Cuba during the time of *Islands in the Stream*. Thomas HUDSON and HONEST LIL drink to him, and then, getting drunker, to Roosevelt, to CHURCHILL, to STALIN, to Adolfo (Dolf) LUQUE, to Adolf HITLER, etc., etc.

In 1953 Batista honored Hemingway with the Order of Carlos Manuel de Céspedes—an ironic gesture because Céspedes was the Cuban leader whom Batista had toppled from government in 1933. By 1958 it was clear that Hemingway was worried about the possibility of civil war in Cuba. He was relieved when Batista fled to Ciudad Trujillo on December 31, 1958, and Fidel Castro took over the island the next day. Hemingway believed Batista had ruined the country, stealing an estimated $600 to $800 million from the Cuban people, and Hemingway wished Castro well in repairing the damage.

battle cruiser   In *The Garden of Eden*, on one of her trips to Nice, Catherine BOURNE sees a cruiser on the Mediterranean performing maneuvers. David, who had seen the ships earlier, thinks they may be on an anti-submarine assignment.

"Battle for Paris"   Article, published in *Collier's* (September 30, 1944), reprinted in *By-Line: Ernest Hemingway* (1967). This article is the third of six dispatches from the European sector of World War II, all published in *Collier's*. It is about the American forces slowly moving toward Paris along the road from Maintenon to Epernon to Rambouillet (about 21 miles southwest of Paris).

Hemingway translates from French civilians and resistance fighters to American army officers. He reports that "It was quite a strange life in the Hotel du Grand Veneur [the temporary army headquarters in Rambouillet] in those days," referring to the counter-intelligence work being done in order to locate the German forces and find the land mines the Germans had laid in their retreat. Hemingway ends the article by stating that "There was a report that General Le Clerc's Second French Armored Division was approaching Rambouillet on the road to Paris, and we wanted to have ready all the information on the German dispositions."

"Battle of Copenhagen, The"   Poem written by Hemingway and two wartime friends, Bill Horne and Y. K. Smith, about 1920, and first published in *88 Poems* (1979).

"'Battle' of Offenburg, The"   Article, published in *The Toronto Daily Star* (April 25, 1923), reprinted in *The Wild Years* (1962), reprinted in *Ernest Hemingway: Dateline Toronto* (1985). The headline in the *Daily Star* was "Ruhr Commercial War Question of Bankruptcy." This was the fourth of 10 articles Hemingway wrote for the *Daily Star* on the French-German situation in 1923, five years after the end of World War I. The town of Offenburg was at the southern limit of French-occupied Germany. The French wanted to protect it because it was a commercially important railway link for transporting coal from the Ruhr Valley south to Italy, but the effort was bankrupting France.

"Battle of Raid Squads"   Article, unsigned, published in *The Kansas City Star* (January 6, 1918), reprinted in *Esquire* (December 1968), and reprinted in *Ernest Hemingway, Cub Reporter* (1970).

battle police   Italian CARABINIERI officers at the wooden bridge over the TAGLIAMENTO RIVER, in *A Farewell to Arms*. They are pulling out of the line of retreating Italians the officers, all of whom they accuse of abandoning their troops. After a summary trial the accused officers are shot. It is from this threat of execution that Frederic HENRY escapes by diving into the river and making his way back to Milan.

"Battler, The"   One of several Nick ADAMS short stories in which Nick is traumatized by his experiences. Nick, on his way north from Chicago to northern Michigan, hops a freight train but is thrown off by a brakeman who lures him into approaching by saying, "I got something for you." Nick is not seriously injured, but he realizes that it was "a lousy kid thing to have done," getting suckered.

Nick sees a fire in a beechwood forest nearby and drops down off the tracks to investigate. He meets Ad FRANCIS, an ex-prizefighter with one ear and a misshapen face, but otherwise a very pleasant man as far as Nick can tell.

BUGS, a friend of Ad's, then comes into camp and is introduced by Ad as being "crazy" too. Bugs, a Negro and, as Nick finds out, the caretaker of Ad Francis, puts ham slices and eggs into a skillet for some sandwiches. Ad asks Nick for his knife, but Bugs tells him not to give it to him, adding to the tension that already exists between the two friends and Nick. Bugs continues to make sandwiches, but Ad picks a fight with Nick, saying, "Who the hell do you think you are?"

Nick tries to avoid a fight, and just before Ad hits him, Bugs "taps" Ad on the back of the head with a "cloth-wrapped blackjack," knocking him out. Bugs explains that every now and then Ad gets this way, and when he does, "I have to [hit him like that] to change him. . . ." Bugs explains further how Ad got the way he is, not just from the boxing but also because of newspaper stories about his sister being his fight manager, and how when they got married it "made a lot of unpleasantness."

Bugs tells Nick to leave before Ad wakes and suggests that he walk toward Mancelona, about two miles up the tracks. At the end of the story Nick is up the railway embankment and walking the tracks again before he notices the ham sandwich in his hand, showing Nick's focus on the ordeal. "The Battler" was first published in *In Our Time* (1925).

Battler, The (film)   An adaptation of the short story, excerpted from the film *Hemingway's Adventures of a Young Man,* produced by Martin Ritt in 1962; screenplay by A. E. HOTCHNER.

Battler, The (television play)   An adaptation of the short story, coauthored by A. E. Hotchner and Sidney Carroll and performed as a CBS "Playwrights '56" production (October 1955), starring Paul Newman.

Bavarian Alpenkorps   Famous German corps of soldiers who fought at the Battle of CAPORETTO during WORLD WAR I. Their commander, General von Berrer is mentioned in "A Natural History of the Dead," although his name is misspelled as "Behr." See General von BEHR.

Bayonne   Town in the southwest corner of France, about 15 miles from the Spanish border and five miles from the Bay of Biscay. It is where Jake BARNES and Bill GORTON arrange to meet Robert COHN on their way to PAMPLONA for the Fiesta SAN FERMÍN and where Jake drops off Gorton to catch the train back to Paris near the end of the novel.

It is also one of the places where Antonio ORDÓÑEZ and Luis Miguel DOMINGUÍN fought "mano a mano" on the 1959 bullfight circuit covered by Hemingway in preparation for writing *The Dangerous Summer.*

BBC   British Broadcasting Company. Mr. BOBBY in the "Bimini" section of *Islands in the Stream* says he listens to Big Ben chime, but everything else he hears broadcast from the BBC makes him "restless." The "Bimini" section takes place in the summer of 1934 or 1935, and Bobby is probably referring to reports of Hitler's increasing military activity on the continent.

Beach, Sylvia (1887–1962)   Proprietor of the SHAKE-SPEARE AND COMPANY (1) bookshop at 12, rue de l'Odéon in Paris from 1919 until 1941 when the Germans forced her to close down. She was important to the American and British expatriate writers who found their way to Paris after World War I and bought or borrowed English-language books from her store. But her most important contribution was the publication at Shakespeare and Company of James Joyce's

Ulysses in 1922 after several publishers had turned it down because of its sexual content.

In 1941 when the German army threatened to confiscate the books in her shop, she removed them to a third-floor apartment, one floor above her own apartment, which was just above the bookshop. The Germans never found the books. When she closed her shop she was taken by the Germans to an internment camp where she spent seven months before being released, and she spent the rest of the war hiding in Paris, most of that time in an American student hostel at 93, boulevard Saint-Michel. But her bookshop never opened again.

She wrote about her shop and literary experiences in *Shakespeare and Company* (1959). At the end of the book she describes Hemingway's finding her in rue de l'Odéon during the liberation of Paris and his willingness to go, at her request, with some of his soldier friends onto the roofs of houses along her street to kill German snipers. She says those were the last shots she heard fired on the rue de l'Odéon.

In *A Moveable Feast* Hemingway writes that Miss Beach "had pretty legs and she was kind, cheerful and interested, and loved to make jokes and gossip. No one that I ever knew was nicer to me." He and Hadley borrowed a number of books from the shop during their first years in Paris.

Bear Lake   Original name for WALLOON LAKE in northern Michigan, where Hemingway's parents bought land in 1898.

Bear River   Yogi JOHNSON in *The Torrents of Spring* walks across the bridge over the Bear River that flows through PETOSKEY into Lake Michigan.

Beaune   French wine from near the town of Beaune in the center of the Burgundy wine district. In *A Moveable Feast* Hemingway writes that he and his wife Hadley would have "a lovely meal and drink Beaune. . . . And afterwards [we would] read and then go to bed and make love."

Beauty   Nickname that David BOURNE uses in *The Garden of Eden* for both his wife, Catherine, and for Marita.

Bee-lips   Harry MORGAN's name for the lawyer, Mr. SIMMONS, in *To Have and Have Not.* Simmons encourages Harry to take four Cubans from Key West to Havana, and, in spite of mistrusting Bee-lips, Harry allows himself to be talked into the illegal crossing. Bee-lips is killed during the robbery of the FIRST STATE TRUST AND SAVINGS BANK by the Cubans.

Beerbohm, Sir Max (1872–1956)   Prominent English essayist, critic, and caricaturist, referred to in "Out of

Season." The YOUNG GENTLEMAN apparently doesn't like Beerbohm and so wonders why "the hell" PEDUZZI (1) would order Marsala wine since that's "what Max Beerbohm drinks."

"Before You Go on a Canoe Trip, Learn Canoeing" Article, unsigned, published in *The Toronto Star* (June 3, 1922), reprinted in William Burrill's *Hemingway: The Toronto Years* (1994). It was identified as a Hemingway story by *Star* librarian William McGeary, and an associate, Greg Clark. Hemingway offers advice about canoeing in an apparent response to a letter by two couples planning a trip to Algonquin Park. Campers are "made," he says at the end of the article, "not born."

Behr, General von   General von Berrer, commander of the Bavarian Alpenkorps at the Battle of CAPORETTO during World War I. In "A Natural History of the Dead," the narrator refers to him as "a damned fine general." Hemingway misspells his name as "von Behr."

Bel Esprit   Ezra POUND's name for a plan to collect money for T. S. ELIOT so that he could quit his job in a London bank and devote his time to writing poetry. Pound and Natalie BARNEY, a rich woman and patroness of the arts, developed the idea of collecting a part of the earnings of American and British writers and other artists in Paris and giving the money to Eliot. The idea of Bel Esprit died of natural causes when Eliot began to make money from *The Waste Land*, published in 1922.

Belgian boy   Teenager in *For Whom the Bell Tolls*, fighting with the 11th Brigade on the side of the Republic in the Spanish civil war. He is so traumatized by seeing death that he cries whenever spoken to by others.

"Belgian Lady and the German Hater, The"   Article, published in *The Toronto Daily Star* (April 28, 1923), reprinted in *The Wild Years* (1962), reprinted in *Ernest Hemingway: Dateline Toronto* (1985). The headline in the *Daily Star* was "A Brave Belgian Lady Shuts Up German Hater." This was the fifth of 10 articles Hemingway wrote for the *Daily Star* on the French-German situation in 1923, five years after the end of World War I. Datelined "Frankfurt-on-Main," the article describes a train trip Hemingway took from Baden to Württemberg, Germany, and of the Belgian lady who helped him through several narrow scrapes with various German authorities and especially with a German passenger who, thinking Hemingway was French, took all of his passionate hatred for the French out on him.

Bell, Mrs.   Woman who looks after Mrs. Hirsch's rooming house in "The Killers." She takes Nick ADAMS up to Ole ANDRESON's room when he asks to see him.

She later tells Nick that Andreson is "an awfully nice man. He was in the ring, you know."

Belleau Wood   Forest in northern France, northwest of Château-Thierry, where the U.S. Marines won an important battle in 1918 during WORLD WAR I. It is mentioned in "Soldier's Home" as one of the places where Harold KREBS fought with the marines.

Belloc, Joseph-Pierre Hilaire (1870–1953)   French poet and essayist, known for writing works in English during the first quarter of the 20th century. He wrote books of children's verse as well as history, particularly biographies of *Danton* (1899) and *Robespierre* (1901) and a four-volume *History of England* (1925–31).

In *A Moveable Feast* Hemingway writes about a conversation with Ford Madox FORD in which Ford talks about how neatly he had "cut" Belloc. Hemingway discovered later that it was not Belloc whom Ford had "cut"—a comment on Ford's usual drunken state.

"Bells Are Ringing for Me and My Gal, The"   "For Me and My Gal" was a popular song, published in 1917 with music by George W. Meyer and lyrics by Edgar Leslie and E. Ray Goetz. It was made famous after Judy Garland sang it in the movie *For Me and My Gal*. In *The Sun Also Rises* Bill GORTON sings about "IRONY AND PITY" to the tune of "For Me and My Gal." He's referring to Jake BARNES's "impotence."

Belmonte   Juan Belmonte was one of Spain's great bullfighters, and Hemingway used him as a character in *The Sun Also Rises*. In the novel he comes out of retirement (he's 33 years old) but is not expecting the competition that he gets from Pedro ROMERO. According to Jake BARNES, Belmonte's return "[has] been spoiled by Romero. Romero did always, smoothly, calmly, and beautifully, what he, Belmonte, could only bring himself to do now sometimes."

Belmonte is also mentioned in "The Undefeated" and in *Green Hills of Africa* during a discussion of "handsome" men.

Beloit College   Small college in Beloit, Wisconsin used as a reference, in *Across the River and Into the Trees*, to an unfair military advantage, as in a football game between, for example, a big university like "Minnesota" and a small college like "Beloit."

Benítez, General   In *Islands in the Stream* Thomas HUDSON asks his Cuban chauffeur about Benítez, a Cuban officer during World War II, and is told that the general is practicing riding a motorcycle along the Malecon, Cuba's central highway, in preparation for serving with a motorized division in Europe. The otherwise unidentified general is probably Manuel Benítez, who was a police chief in Havana during the early 1940s.

Benny Character in the "Bimini" section of *Islands in the Stream*. He helps the Constable get EDDY (3) home after a fight over the size of the broadbill SWORDFISH that David HUDSON catches. It looked as if it might weigh 1,000 pounds, but nobody believed Eddy when he said that, so they beat him up.

Bergman, Ingrid (1915–1982) Academy Award–winning movie actress born in Sweden who, after being cast by American movie mogul David O. Selznick in the 1939 English-language remake of *Intermezzo*, rose to Hollywood stardom and subsequently had a long and brilliant film career. She is referred to by Colonel CANTWELL in *Across the River and Into the Trees* as "Miss Bergman." She played Maria opposite Gary Cooper's Robert Jordan in the film and radio adaptations of *For Whom the Bell Tolls*. See MARIA (1).

Berrendo, Paco CARLIST lieutenant, who at the end of *For Whom the Bell Tolls* is climbing the hill on which Robert JORDAN lies wounded. The reader infers that Berrendo will be killed by Jordan before Jordan himself dies. Lieutenant Berrendo had earlier led the attack against EL SORDO and his men, calling in airplanes to bomb the hill where the PARTIZANS are making a last-ditch stand.

bersaglieri Crack infantry of the Italian army, referred to in *A Farewell to Arms*. According to Frederic HENRY, they are wearing red fezzes as he and the other ambulance drivers pass them in a long column of loaded mules on the road to the warfront. Later, AYMO, one of Frederic's ambulance car drivers during the retreat from CAPORETTO, wishes they could find some *bersaglieri*, because they have the "widest backs" and could help push the cars out of the mud.

"Best Rainbow Trout Fishing, The" Article, published in *The Toronto Star Weekly* (August 28, 1920), reprinted in *The Wild Years* (1962), and in *By-Line: Ernest Hemingway* (1967). The article is about the recent introduction of rainbow trout into Canadian waters and the difference between fishing for rainbow trout and fishing for brook or speckled trout. There's as much difference, Hemingway says, as there is between prizefighting and boxing. Contrary to the writing and pictures in magazines, for example, brook trout do not "jump" when hooked, whereas the rainbow always leaps whether the line is slack or tight. The *TSW* headline read "The Best Rainbow Trout Fishing in the World Is at the Canadian Soo."

Best Short Stories of 1923, The Anthology, edited by Edward O'Brien, which includes Hemingway's "My Old Man." The book was dedicated to Hemingway. In *A Moveable Feast* Hemingway describes his reaction to this first U.S. hardback publication. He writes that he laughed about the publication because O'Brien had misspelled his name (Hemenway) throughout the book and because the editor had broken his own rule about not publishing works that had not already been published in magazines. "My Old Man" was reprinted from *Three Stories and Ten Poems* but not from a magazine.

Best Short Stories of 1926, The Anthology, edited by Edward O'Brien, which includes Hemingway's "The Undefeated," reprinted from *This Quarter* (Autumn-Winter 1925–26).

Best Short Stories of 1937, The Anthology, edited by Edward O'Brien, which includes Hemingway's "The Snows of Kilimanjaro," reprinted from *Esquire* (August 1936).

Best Short Stories of 1940, The Anthology, edited by Edward O'Brien, which includes Hemingway's "Under the Ridge," reprinted from *Cosmopolitan* (October 1939).

"Betting in Toronto" Article, published in *The Toronto Star Weekly* (December 29, 1923), reprinted in *The Wild Years* (1962), reprinted in *Ernest Hemingway: Dateline Toronto* (1985). The headline in the *Star Weekly* was "Toronto Is the Biggest Betting Place in North America: 10,000 People Bet $100,000 on Horses Every Day." It's about betting on the "nod" in Toronto; that is, making bets through bookmakers without benefit of formal negotiations. The bookmakers fix the limit on how much a player can make, no matter how large the bet: Even if a horse's odds are 200 to 1, the maximum win in Toronto on a two-dollar bet is 30 dollars.

"Betty Co-ed" Popular fox-trot published in 1931, words and music by J. Paul Fogarty and Rudy Vallee. The full title is "Betty Co-ed: Collegiate Sweetheart Song."

It is one of the tunes that Mr. FRAZER hears on his radio in "The Gambler, the Nun, and the Radio." He thought the "best tunes . . . that winter" were "Sing Something Simple," "Singsong Girl," and "Little White Lies." Mr. Frazer thought that the more he listened to "Betty Co-ed," the more the "parody of the words . . . grew . . . obscene." So he "finally abandoned it and let the song go back to football." The parody was in his own, otherwise unstated thinking as he lay in his hospital bed. The words that might have influenced his thinking are "Flirtation is an art with Betty Co-ed, the college girl who's full of happy charm. She gets the men in rushes by well cultivated blushes. . . ." And from the chorus: "Betty Co-ed has lips as red as rose-buds, Betty Co-ed has eyes of navy blue, . . . Her voice is like a song-bird calling you. . . . Her heart's a perfect treasure so 'tis said, Betty Co-ed is lov'd by every college boy, But I'm the one who's lov'd by Betty Co-ed."

B.G. Brigadier General, the abbreviation used by Colonel Richard CANTWELL's driver, JACKSON, in refer-ring to Cantwell, even though Jackson, who is being sar-castic, knows Cantwell has been demoted to colonel.

Biarritz Fashionable French resort town on the Bay of Biscay, about 12 miles from the Spanish border. In *The Sun Also Rises* Count MIPPIPOPOLOUS offers Brett ASHLEY $10,000 to go with him to Biarritz. He also suggests Cannes and Monte Carlo, but she says no to all his offers. Biarritz is also where Jake BARNES and Bill GORTON drop off Mike CAMPBELL to catch the train for the short ride to SAINT-JEAN-DE-LUZ near the end of the novel.

In *Islands in the Stream* Thomas HUDSON thinks about the automobile accident in France that killed his sec-ond wife and their two sons: "What the hell do you sup-pose she was doing at Biarritz? . . . At least she could have gone to St.-Jean-de-Luz."

Biarritz is also referred to by David BOURNE in *The Garden of Eden*. He calls it a "horror." His wife, Catherine, drives to Biarritz alone on one of her trips to get her hair cropped short like a boy's.

bibis Swahili term of respect toward women, used in some East African nations, however, to refer to European concubines. As David BOURNE recalls with regret his boyhood experience with his father and JUMA on an elephant hunt in East Africa in *The Garden of Eden*, he thinks that he should have kept the elephant he found "secret" and let his father and Juma "stay drunk with their *bibis* at the beer shamba."

bicycles In describing the death that HARRY feels com-ing, in "The Snows of Kilimanjaro," the narrator uses the image of bicycles as one way of representing death. Harry "lay still and death was not there. It must have gone around another street. It went in pairs, on bicy-cles, and moved absolutely silently on the pavements."

Bienvenida, Antonio Mejías (1922–   ) One of the bullfighters whom Hemingway saw fight during his 1959 travels on the Spanish bullfight circuit in prepara-tion for writing *The Dangerous Summer*. He fought on the Barcelona card with the two bullfighters Hemingway was most interested in that summer, Antonio ORDÓÑEZ and Luis Miguel DOMINGUÍN.

Biffi's Restaurant in the GALLERIA in Milan where, in *A Farewell to Arms*, Frederic HENRY and Catherine BARKLEY go occasionally while he is recovering from his war wounds.

"Big Dance on the Hill, The" Article, really a vignette, maybe a poem, published in *The Toronto Star Weekly* (November 24, 1923), reprinted in *Ernest Hemingway: Dateline Toronto* (1985). It's about an awkward moment at a party and contains 31 lines, each beginning with "The." For example: "The arrival./ The vast crowd on the Floor./ The encounter with the boss." It was also reprinted in *88 Poems* (1979).

"Big Day for Navy Drive" Article, unsigned, pub-lished in *The Kansas City Star* (April 17, 1918), reprinted in *Ernest Hemingway, Cub Reporter* (1970).

"Big Hanna Club Meeting Hears Rousing Talk" Article for Oak Park and River Forest High School newspaper, *The Trapeze* (March 23, 1916), reprinted in *Hemingway at Oak Park High: The High School Writings of Ernest Hemingway, 1916–1917* (1993).

Big Harry Character in a story told by Mr. BOBBY, the bartender in the "Bimini" section of *Islands in the Stream*. See SUICIDES.

bight A bend in a river or coastline. In *To Have and Have Not* Harry MORGAN worries that a government boat may be hiding behind Garrison Bight, near Key West.

Big Lucie's daughter A girl who enters FREDDIE's PLACE "with that girl from their place," in *To Have and Have Not*. Both girls are prostitutes.

Big Red One U.S. Army division of soldiers who, according to Richard CANTWELL in *Across the River and Into the Trees*, "believed their own publicity" and who fought at HÜRTGEN FOREST in WORLD WAR II. See General Walter Bedell SMITH.

"Big Two-Hearted River: Part I" Short story in two parts. NICK, the story's only character, gets off a train in SENEY, in Michigan's Upper Peninsula, for an overnight trout fishing and camping trip. On the story's surface nothing much happens, but, as with nearly all of Hemingway's best fiction, what is not stated is more important than what is (see THEORY OF OMISSION).

In "Big Two-Hearted River" the reader "feels" gradu-ally the tension Nick is under from the detailed descrip-tions presented by the narrator in the story, the reader becoming aware that Nick is on the camping trip in order not to think about whatever it is that has traumatized him. The concentration on the details of camping and fishing is presented through Nick's thinking but in the third person.

Whatever caused the trauma is not stated, but it is the psychic wound that matters, not the reason for it, and the fact that Nick is working hard to forget it so he can get his life back together. The "swamp," across and down river, is a constant symbol of Nick's dread, but he is beginning to conquer it. See also "On Writing," the original ending to the story.

Both parts of "Big Two-Hearted River" were first published in *This Quarter* (May 1925) and reprinted in *In Our Time* (1925).

"Big Two-Hearted River: Part II" The second part of this short story begins on the morning of the second day, NICK concentrating on the details of fixing a breakfast of coffee and buckwheat pancakes and two onion sandwiches for lunch. He catches two big trout, and, while taking a break and wishing he had a book to read, he looks across and down the river to the swamp. Nick does "not want to go in there now. . . . In the swamp fishing was a tragic adventure. Nick did not want it." The swamp represents whatever it is that Nick is trying not to think about, whatever it is that has brought Nick to the river in the first place and that causes him to focus on the details of fishing and camping so he can keep his mind from "starting to work," to "choke" off thinking as he was able to do at the end of part 1. The reader feels at the end of the story that Nick will overcome his psychological wounding, because, although he has avoided the "tragic adventure," the narrator states in the last sentence: "There were plenty of days coming when he could fish the swamp."

Bill (1) NICK's friend in both "The End of Something" and "The Three-Day Blow." He appears at the end of the first story, after Nick has broken up with his girlfriend, MARJORIE. Clearly in on Nick's intentions, Bill asks, "Did she go all right?" Nick, still upset at the breakup, tells Bill to go away. In "The Three-Day Blow" Bill tries to convince Nick that breaking up with Marjorie was the right thing to do. He argues that she is not good enough for Nick. "Now she can marry somebody of her own sort. . . . You can't mix oil and water."

Bill (2) In "Big Two-Hearted River," NICK remembers that when HOPKINS left their camp on the Black River "a long time ago," having received a telegram stating that his first Texas oil well had come in, he gave his pistol to Nick and his camera to "Bill," gifts "to remember him [Hopkins] always by."

Bill's father A painter, mentioned in "The Three-Day Blow," the father of BILL (1). Bill and NICK decide that Bill's father has "had a tough time," but there is no

explanation, though it is clear that both boys understand what is meant.

Billy Brother of Nick ADAMS's Indian girlfriend, TRUDY, in "Fathers and Sons." He hunts with Nick's shotgun while Nick and Trudy make love in the Hemlock woods behind the Indian camp.

Bimini The North Bimini Islands are located about 60 miles due east of Miami and are made up of North and South Bimini, the North Island four miles long and about 300 yards wide for most of its length. The two main Bimini Islands are part of the Bahama "out islands." In *Islands in the Stream*, Thomas HUDSON's house is located at the southern end of North Bimini "on the highest part of the narrow tongue of land between the harbor and the open sea." The porch of Hudson's house is on the east side, facing "the sea," the ocean and sandy beaches. The west side is on the Gulf Stream side.

"Bimini" Title and setting for the opening section of *Islands in the Stream*. It is 1934 or 1935, and Thomas HUDSON has for visitors his three sons, "Young Tom," David, and Andrew, all vacationing from school and excited about the fishing and swimming at the island.

Bird, Bill Hemingway's fishing friend, who, when they first met, was director of the Continental branch of the Consolidated Press in the rue d'Antin in Paris. They went to the Genoa Conference together in 1922 and traveled together on a number of trips for their respective newspapers. Hemingway mentions Bird in the article "Fishing in Baden Perfect."

"Bird of Night" Poem written in 1921 and first published in *88 Poems* (1979).

Birmingham, George A. (1865–1950) Pen name of James Owen Hannay, Irish clergyman and writer, best known for writing farcical novels about Irish life, especially *Spanish Gold* (1908), which Hemingway mentions in *Green Hills of Africa*.

"Black Ass at the Cross Roads" Unfinished story based on one of Hemingway's WORLD WAR II experiences about a unit of Allied soldiers stationed at a crossroads that had become an escape route for Germans trying to get through enemy lines and back to Aachen, Germany. The story was first published in *The Complete Short Stories of Ernest Hemingway* (1987). "Black ass" is a Hemingway term for depression or melancholia.

"Black-Ass Poem After Talking to Pamela Churchill" Poem about melancholia ("black-ass"), written in 1949 and first published in *88 Poems* (1979). Pamela Churchill was, when the poem was written, the wife of Randolph Churchill, son of Winston.

Ernest with tuna at Bimini dock (Courtesy of the John F. Kennedy Library)

Black Christ, The   In *A Moveable Feast* Hemingway writes that he grew a beard and let his hair grow while he and Hadley were in Schruns, Austria, in the winter 1925–26 and that the people who saw him ski down the logging trails around Schruns called him "the Black Christ." When they saw him at the local Weinstube they called him "the Black Kirsch-drinking Christ."

blackjack, cloth-wrapped   The instrument BUGS uses, in "The Battler," to knock out his friend, Ad FRANCIS, to "change" him and keep him from fighting with Nick ADAMS. A blackjack is a short club, usually leather-covered, having a heavy head and a strap handle. Bugs's blackjack has a whalebone handle and a handkerchief wrapped around the heavy end to protect Ad's head from serious harm.

Blackman, Charlie   Friend of EDNA's from Chicago in *The Sun Also Rises*.

"Black Novel a Storm Center"   Article, published in *The Toronto Star Weekly* (March 25, 1922), reprinted in *Ernest Hemingway: Dateline Toronto* (1985). The headline in the *Star Weekly* was "Prize-Winning Book Is Centre of Storm." Under a Paris dateline, Hemingway reviews the controversy about the novel *Batouala*, by René Maran, "a Negro, winner of the Goncourt Academy Prize of 5,000 francs for the best novel of the year by a young writer," the awarding of the prize getting "condemnation, indignation and praise." The novel is critical of French imperialism in Africa. Hemingway ends the article by suggesting that the novel should be translated into English by "another Negro who has lived a life in the country two days' march from Lake Tchad and who knows English as René Maran knows French."

"Black Pig, The"   An otherwise unidentified novel mentioned in *A Farewell to Arms*. The PRIEST (2) calls it a "filthy and vile book."

Black River   Unidentified river where, in "Big Two-Hearted River," NICK remembers arguing with HOPKINS about how to make coffee and where "Hop" had received a telegram telling him that his first Texas oil well had come in.

Blaine, James G. (1830–1893)   Controversial member of the Republican Party but secretary of state under President James Garfield (1881) and the party's nominee for president against both Grover Cleveland and Benjamin Harrison. In "Up in Michigan" Jim GILMORE talks about the Republicans and Blaine with his friend D. J. Smith.

"[Blank Verse]"   Poem using punctuation alone to demonstrate blank verse. It was first published in the Oak Park and River Forest High School newspaper, *Trapeze* (November 10, 1916), reprinted in *88 Poems* (1979).

Blanquet (1881–1925)   The "greatest *peon de brega* who ever lived," according to PILAR in *For Whom the Bell Tolls*. "*Peon de brega*" is an archaic Spanish term for BANDERILLERO, a matador's assistant who holds the cape. His professional name was Enrique Belenguer Soler, and Pilar thinks he had a gypsy's ability to smell death on a person about to die.

Blazzard, Captain Howard   U.S. Army officer whose story of the infantry's breaking through the Siegfried Line is described in Hemingway's article "War in the Siegfried Line."

"Blind Man's Christmas Eve, The"   Article, published in *The Toronto Star Weekly* (December 22, 1923), reprinted in *Ernest Hemingway: Dateline Toronto* (1985). To a blind man on the streets of Toronto it was just "the twenty-fourth of December." The by-line is "John Hadley," in honor of Hemingway's son, John Hadley Nicanor Hemingway, born October 10, 1923.

Blindy   Main character in "A Man of the World." He was blinded in a fight with Willie Sawyer, who gouged his eyes out of their sockets and then bit them off. Blindy wanders between "The Flats" and a small, western U.S. town called Jessup and its two saloons, the PILOT and the INDEX. He fingers the slot machines for loose change, and he smells badly enough so that customers often leave the saloon early.

Sawyer had driven Blindy part way to town the night of the short story but had dropped him off suddenly when Blindy had reached over to touch his face. In the fight Blindy had lost his eyes, but he had managed to gouge out a portion of Sawyer's face in the process. When he reached over to touch the face, Sawyer had kicked him out of the car. "That's why he put me out of the car," Blindy says. "He ain't got no sense of humor at all. . . . You know that Willie Sawyer he'll never be a man of the world."

Blixen-Finecke, Baron Bror von   One of two white hunters Hemingway admires and writes about in his article "Notes on Dangerous Game: The Third Tanganyika Letter." The other white hunter is Philip PERCIVAL. Von Blixen was married for seven years to his cousin, Isak DINESEN, who went with him to Africa in 1914 and helped him run a coffee plantation in Kenya. Both were also big game hunters and guides. She is the author of *Seven Gothic Tales* (1934) and *Out of Africa* (1937).

Blonde Venus   In "Big Two-Hearted River," NICK remembers that HOPKINS's girlfriend was named the Blonde Venus.

"['Blood is thicker than water . . .']"   First line of a poem written in 1922 and first published in Carlos Baker's biography, *Ernest Hemingway: A Life Story* (1969).

blue-backed notebooks   The *cahiers* (stitched paper booklets used in France, about the size of U.S. college exam booklets) into which Hemingway wrote many of his earliest stories. In *A Moveable Feast* he states that all he needed in order to write were the blue-backed notebooks, two pencils (with a sharpener, but not a pocket knife because it wasted too much pencil), a café table on which to write, and "luck."

"Blue Hotel, The"   Short story by Stephen CRANE, published serially in *Collier's* (November 26–December 3, 1898). In *Green Hills of Africa* Hemingway tells Kandisky that Crane wrote "two fine stories" and names "The Open Boat" and "The Blue Hotel," the latter one the better of the two.

boat   Owned by the narrator of "After the Storm" and from which he tries to dive down to an ocean liner that sank during the storm and which is only 12 feet below the surface.

boatman   He takes Richard CANTWELL along the Grand Canal toward the GRITTI PALACE HOTEL in *Across the River and Into the Trees*. The boatman had lost five brothers during World War II, and Cantwell promises to try to get him a jeep engine for his boat.

boats, six   Richard CANTWELL is in the sixth boat on the duck hunting expedition in *Across the River and Into the Trees.* Four of the boats hunt in the "main canal toward the big lagoon to the north." The fifth boat hunts in a "side canal," and Cantwell's boat "turned south into a shallow lagoon."

Bobby   Dog (retriever) that picks up Richard CANTWELL's ducks on the Sunday morning duck-hunting trip in *Across the River and Into the Trees.*

Bobby, Mr.   Bobby Saunders is the owner of Thomas HUDSON's favorite bar, the PONCE DE LEÓN, on BIMINI in *Islands in the Stream,* most often referred to as Mr. Bobby's.

boca   Spanish word meaning a "mouth" or "entrance" to a low island (that is, a key or, in Spanish, *cayo*).

Boca Chica   Florida key just northeast of KEY WEST and the location of a camp being built by WPA workers in *To Have and Have Not,* set in the 1930s.

Boca Grande   Small key about 15 miles west of KEY WEST, Florida. In *To Have and Have Not,* it is where CAPTAIN WILLIE is headed after giving Harry MORGAN a chance to escape from U.S. agents. See also Frederick HARRISON.

Bocanegra   In *The Sun Also Rises* the name of the bull that kills Vincente GIRONES during the running of the bulls in Pamplona and which is later killed by Pedro ROMERO in the afternoon bullfights.

bock beer   In *Islands in the Stream* the beer that Thomas HUDSON remembers most from when he lived in Paris with his first wife.

boina   Spanish word used by the narrator in *The Garden of Eden* for the "beret" that David BOURNE wears occasionally.

Bois, le   Short for Bois de Boulogne ("bois" means woods or forest), a beautiful and celebrated 2,137-acre woods on the west side of Paris, that includes within its borders several restaurants and the LONGCHAMPS (1) and AUTEUIL horse racecourses, both built about 1850. In *The Sun Also Rises* Jake BARNES, Brett ASHLEY, and Count MIPPIPOPOLOUS eat dinner at a "restaurant in the Bois" the night the count brings a case of champagne to Jake's flat. At the restaurant, the count orders an 1811 bottle of brandy, explaining his seeming "ostentatious" order by saying, "I get more value for my money in old brandy than in any other antiquities."

The Bois is also one of the places to which Richard CANTWELL jokingly tells RENATA to tell the Venice gondolier to take them in *Across the River and Into the Trees.*

Boise   One of Thomas HUDSON's 11 cats, mentioned in the "Cuba" section of *Islands in the Stream.* He's called "Boy" for short.

Bolitho, William   See Bill RYALL.

Böllinger Brut 1915   In *The Garden of Eden* MARITA gives David BOURNE a case of this special champagne as a gift. There are a dozen or more brut champagnes produced by Böllinger each year, the word "brut" meaning not sweetened, extra dry.

Bologna   City in northern Italy, about 54 miles north of Florence, the setting for most of "The Revolutionist." It is also a town in "Che Ti Dice La Patria?" to which the two main characters travel.

Bone, John (?–1928)   Managing editor at *The Toronto Daily Star* during the years Hemingway worked for it (December, 1921–January, 1924). Bone was responsible for hiring Hemingway as a roving European reporter, writing feature stories on the economic conference in Genoa (April 1922), the Greco-Turkish fighting in the Near East (October 1922), the peace talks in Lausanne, Switzerland (December 1922), and the friction between Germany and France in the Ruhr Valley (April–May 1923).

Hemingway was paid $75 a week plus expenses for the work, a lot of money for a *Star* reporter, but Bone got some of his money back by selling the stories to U.S. newspaper under his own byline, a kind of plagiarism legal in Canada at that time.

Bonello, Aldo   One of the ambulance drivers with Frederic HENRY during the retreat from Caporetto in *A Farewell to Arms,* who "finishes off" the sergeant that Frederic shoots during the retreat. Bonello disappears later, perhaps a deserter, but Luigi PIANI seems suspect when he reports Bonello's disappearance to Frederic, suggesting that he may have shot him.

bongo   Reddish-brown antelope of tropical Africa, with white stripes and large, spirally twisted horns. In *Across the River and Into the Trees* Richard CANTWELL compares his friend ALVARITO to the bongo, because he thinks both of them are shy creatures.

Boni & Liveright   New York publishers of Hemingway's third book, *In Our Time* (1925). Hemingway was committed to a second book at Boni & Liveright but was able to break the agreement when Horace Liveright rejected *The Torrents of Spring* because it parodied one of the publisher's major writers, Sherwood ANDERSON. The rejection allowed Hemingway to publish both *Torrents* and *The Sun Also Rises* in 1926 with Charles Scribner's Sons, which then became Hemingway's permanent book publisher.

The official name of the company used an ampersand (&) rather than "and," as it appears in the first editions of *In Our Time* and *Dark Laughter*. But there are exceptions, as in Anderson's *Tar: A Midwest Childhood* (1926), which has an "and" on both the publication page and the cover.

Albert Boni and Horace Liveright were New York businessmen who started the publishing firm as a reprint house in 1917. Their first 12 Modern Library titles proved successful, but they split up in their second year over philosophical differences. Liveright retained ownership on a flip of a coin. He kept the Boni & Liveright name and began publishing the original works of such American writers as Ezra POUND, T. S. ELIOT, Djuna BARNES, and Upton SINCLAIR. In 1925, besides Hemingway's *In Our Time*, Liveright published Anderson's *Dark Laughter*, Theodore Dreiser's *An American Tragedy*, and Eugene O'Neill's *Desire Under the Elms*. Other authors published by Boni & Liveright include William FAULKNER, Hart Crane, Elizabeth Bowen, e.e. cummings, Ben Hecht, Robinson Jeffers, Edgar Lee Masters, Anita Loos, and Thornton Wilder.

Liveright incorporated in 1928 and changed the firm's name to Horace Liveright. Liveright died in 1933. The company, in bankruptcy, was purchased for $18,000, and the name was changed to Liveright Publishing Corporation. Gilbert Harrison, publisher of *The New Republic*, bought the company in 1969, and it became a subsidiary of W.W. Norton Publishers in 1974.

bonito   Sometimes called "skipjack," the bonito is a warm-water fish that can weigh as much as 20 pounds. In *The Old Man and the Sea* SANTIAGO fishes out where the bonito and ALBACORE are swimming, hoping to find a MARLIN among them. He catches a bonito while hooked to the marlin and, cutting the bonito into six strips, dries it for eating later. Both bonito and albacore are members of the mackerel family of open-sea fishes which includes tuna, the largest mackerel.

Bookman, The   Monthly U.S. literary magazine published from 1895 to 1933. David BOURNE in *The Garden of Eden* is angered by his publisher's notion that his second novel "validates" his first, and so David wonders to whom the publisher promised validation—certainly not, he thinks, to the journals that had reviewed his book, including *The Bookman*.

Book of Pirates   Book by Howard PYLE, published in 1921, which the narrator/father in "A Day's Wait" reads to his nine-year-old son, SCHATZ, who has the flu.

bookstalls   A fixture along the Left Bank quais (embankments) in Paris, where, Hemingway writes in *A Moveable Feast*, you could sometimes find English-language books. The bookstalls are still an attraction for Left Bank strollers.

bootblacks   In *The Sun Also Rises* Bill GORTON hires them to shine Mike CAMPBELL's shoes during one of their drunken sprees in PAMPLONA at the Fiesta SAN FERMÍN.

Booth's gin   In *The Fifth Column* Philip RAWLINGS and Anita drink Booth's gin at CHICOTE'S RESTAURANT while he waits for Max to report in from behind the Fascist lines.

Borrow, Henry   Maker of the Peerless Pounder at the PUMP-FACTORY in PETOSKEY, according to Yogi JOHNSON in *The Torrents of Spring*. "I carved it direct from the steel with this knife," Borrow tells Yogi and Scripps O'NEIL, holding up a "short-bladed, razorlike-looking knife." He says it took "eighteen months to get it right." The peerless pounder is part of the novel's PARODY, not clearly defined except that it's a handcarved steel pump that won a pump race in Italy.

Bosch, Hieronymus (c. 1450–1516)   Flemish painter, known for his satirical and grotesque paintings, his use of brilliant colors, bizarre animals and plants, and monstrous figures, often representing northern European folk tales. His best-known paintings include *The Garden of Earthly Delights*, *Temptations of St. Anthony*, and *Adoration of the Magi*.

He is mentioned by Richard CANTWELL, in *Across the River and Into the Trees*, who has decided that his own impending death has an "ugly face that old Hieronymus Bosch really painted."

Boss over and unders   A name for a shotgun with barrels over and under instead of side by side. In *Across the River and Into the Trees* Richard CANTWELL thinks about buying a Boss "over and under" shotgun for RENATA so she can go duck hunting.

Botin's   Restaurant in Madrid at 17 Calle de los Cuchilleros, near the Plaza Mayor. Jake BARNES and Brett ASHLEY have lunch "upstairs," the day he meets her at her Madrid hotel near the end of *The Sun Also Rises*. They order the restaurant's speciality, roast young suckling pig and *rioja alta* wine. A favorite Hemingway restaurant, it still exists.

boulevard Arago   In Paris, on which were located the tennis courts where Ernest and Hadley Hemingway, Ezra Pound, Harold Loeb, and others, played tennis in the 1920s; mentioned in *A Moveable Feast*.

boulevard du Montparnasse   Street in Paris known for its many Left Bank restaurants and cafés; mentioned in various works but especially in *The Sun Also Rises*.

boulevard Raspail   Avenue in Paris that forms, with the BOULEVARD DU MONTPARNASSE, the corner location of the CLOSERIE DES LILAS, a bar-restaurant frequented by Jake BARNES and his friends in *The Sun Also Rises*.

boulevard Saint-Germain   Wide Paris thoroughfare on the Left Bank, curving from the quai d'Orsay (across the river from the Place de la Concorde) to the quai Saint-Bernard (across the river from the Ile Saint-Louis). In *A Moveable Feast* Hemingway uses the street often as a point of reference. See SAINT-ETIENNE-DU-MONT.

boulevard Saint-Michel   In Paris, mentioned often by Hemingway but especially in *The Sun Also Rises* and *A Moveable Feast*.

Boulton, Dick   Half-breed Indian from the camp in "The Doctor and the Doctor's Wife," hired to cut logs for NICK's father, whose name is Henry in this story. Boulton accuses Henry of stealing the logs, but Henry considers them driftwood and is angry at having his integrity questioned. Boulton finds the name of the owner on one of the logs, and Nick's father says that, in that case, he had better not cut them up. Boulton challenges Henry further by continuing to call him "Doc" after Henry has asked him not to. The doctor walks away from the challenge, back to his cottage with Nick.

bouncer   At FREDDIE'S PLACE in *To Have and Have Not*. When Richard GORDON gets involved in a drunken brawl near the end of the novel, the bouncer knocks him out. Gordon and the SHERIFF are on their way to see Harry MORGAN's boat being towed in to KEY WEST.

Bourne, Catherine   Twenty-one-year-old androgynous wife of the main character, David BOURNE, in *The Garden of Eden*. Although the novel is told from David's point of view, Catherine is the more interesting character. Not only is she bisexual (see ANDROGYNY), she also has what, at the end of the 20th century, might be called a multiple personality condition.

After three weeks of marriage she wants to change into a boy, which creates the friction that determines the plot of the novel. At one point she identifies herself as "Peter" and calls David "Catherine." "You're my beautiful lovely Catherine. You were so good to change. . . . Please know and understand. I'm going to make love to you forever." Sometimes she refers to the two of them as "brothers." David, a writer, identifies himself to her as "the inventive type," and she identifies herself to him as "the destructive type," foreshadowing the outcome of their marriage. He calls her "devil."

She gets her hair cut, first at le GRAU DU ROI and later in BIARRITZ, as a boy's when he would "first go to public school," and again in CANNES when she insists that David get the same haircut, colored the same light silver. She tells David that in Biarritz the coiffeur asked her which public boys school she wanted to imitate, and she suggested the only English schools she could remember, Eton and Winchester. She declared for Eton "all the way" but then had the coiffeur shorten it some more until it was "either wonderful or terrible." Both the haircut and the color become an obsession for Catherine, evidence of her "craziness," a mental state that she recognizes but can't seem to do anything about.

David, unhappy and frustrated over his inability to prevent Catherine's deterioration, wraps himself more and more in his writing and later in his growing love for MARITA, the third member of their MÉNAGE À TROIS, a term not used by the narrator. Catherine becomes Marita's lover. Catherine had attended a girls school, and she tells David that she had chances there with other girls and had wanted to, but did not. "But now I have to." When she meets Marita, she falls in love with her immediately and can't wait to introduce her to David. Marita is lesbian when Catherine and David first meet her with her friend NINA, but once the threesome begins, and Marita realizes the madness in which she has become involved, she falls in love with David and, eventually prefers his company to that of Catherine.

Catherine tries to fight her jealousy over this change in the marriage, insisting to David and Marita that she loves them both and wants happiness for them and for herself. She is also jealous of the two novels David has written and of the short stories he is writing, especially the AFRICAN STORY, because it is not about her or about their marriage. At the end, she refers to this story as the "dreary dismal little [story] about your adolescence with your bogus drunken father." The only story she likes is the one she calls the "NARRATIVE," about their marriage and their triangular relationship with Marita. At the climax of the novel, which comes during the worst of her madness, she burns all the stories except for the "narrative." David, at the end, must accept his own inability to help her and allows her to leave.

The cause of Catherine's mental deterioration is never made clear. Colonel John BOYLE, a friend of David's in Paris and also a friend of Catherine's parents, tells David that her father, a "very odd type . . . killed himself in a car. His wife too." Boyle says, he's "no loss to you as a father-in-law." He also tells him that the mother was "very lonely they say." He calls the automobile accident a "[s]tupid way for grown up people to be killed." All of this suggests the possibility of a double suicide, which might foreshadow Catherine's "craziness."

Catherine, realizing that she needs help, tells David that they might drive to Switzerland after Marita leaves. David suggests that she could see a doctor there, and he tells her that they could "get some good advice and make a fun trip out of it." But in the end she refuses to go. Instead, she takes a train to Biarritz, leaving David and Marita to carry on a less troubled, more normal relationship and David to attempt to rewrite the stories she had burned.

Bourne, David   The main character in *The Garden of Eden,* through whose point of view the story is told. He is about 24 years old and his wife, Catherine, is 21. They have been married three weeks at the beginning of the novel, and the story takes place between March and September, probably in 1923 (see the novel's main entry).

Most of the honeymoon is financed by Catherine, who insists on it even to the extent that she belittles the income David has from his books. David is a writer with two novels already published. The first is titled *The RIFT* and is about his boyhood experiences in East Africa; the second is about flying planes in World War I. According to Catherine, the second novel is "the only good thing anyone ever wrote about flying," a compliment which David denies.

During the approximately four-month time span of *The Garden of Eden,* David writes short stories, one about his marriage with Catherine and eventually about the MÉNAGE À TROIS that develops with MARITA, and another about an experience when he was "about eight years old" with his father, hunting elephants in East Africa. Catherine explains to Marita, with sarcasm, that David is from Oklahoma but some "of his ancestors escaped from Oklahoma" and took him to Africa when he was a boy.

David had written the stories in *cahiers,* lined notebooks that French children use in school, and Catherine refers to them as "those ridiculous child's notebooks," showing the full extent of her jealousy to Marita, who has also read the African story and likes it.

David tries to be sensitive toward Catherine, especially for her need, even obsession, to change from female to male and back again. But it is also clear that he likes the change in their sexual relationship, even to the point of allowing his hair to be cut short and colored to match hers. And it is clear that, although it sometimes makes him uncomfortable, he likes the triangular romance that develops once they meet Marita. As it turns out, David's acquiescence to Catherine's sexual preferences—he can never say no—is precisely what brings the marriage to an end.

Boutet de Monvel, Louis Maurice (1851–1913) French painter and illustrator, mostly of children's books. In *A Moveable Feast* Hemingway refers to him in a description of Alice B. TOKLAS. He says that Gertrude Stein's companion (Alice) "had a very pleasant voice, was small, very dark, with her hair cut like Joan of Arc in the Boutet de Monvel illustrations and had a very hooked nose."

boy (1)   Sixteen-year-old character in "God Rest You Merry, Gentlemen." He appeals to the doctors WILCOX and FISCHER in a Kansas City hospital to castrate him because he can't stop sinning "against purity. . . . I can't stop it happening. . . . I pray all night and I pray in the daytime. It is a sin, a constant sin against purity." Doc Fischer tries to convince him that it's a normal thing in a boy, but he's not convinced. They send him away, but at one o'clock the next morning, Christmas day, he is back at the hospital, having attempted self-mutilation. But, as Doc Fischer explains to the story's narrator, the boy "didn't know what castrate meant," implying that he had cut off his penis, and that he might die from loss of blood.

Boy (2)   Short for BOISE, one of Thomas HUDSON's cats in *Islands in the Stream.*

Boyle, Colonel John   Friend of David BOURNE's in *The Garden of Eden.* Boyle has "deep blue eyes, sandy hair and a tanned face that looked as though it had been carved out of flint by a tired sculptor who had broken his chisel on it." They run into one another at the bar of the PALACE HOTEL (2) in Madrid when David and his wife, Catherine, are there during their honeymoon. The reader of *The Garden of Eden* learns about Catherine BOURNE's family from Boyle's conversation with David. The cause of her mental deterioration is never made clear, but Colonel Boyle, also a friend of Catherine's parents, says that her father killed himself and his wife in an automobile accident. Boyle tells David that he's "no loss to you as a father-in-law" and that her mother was "very lonely." He says that the accident was a "[s]tupid way for grown up people to be killed," suggesting the possibility of a double suicide.

Boyle, Jimmy   Police officer in the "Chapter 8" vignette who shoots two Hungarian robbers of a cigar store because he thinks they're Italians ("wops").

Boyne Falls grade   A train heading south on the G.R.&I. Railroad (Grand Rapids and Indiana) climbs this grade just north of Boyne Falls, Michigan, and, in *The Torrents of Spring,* it passes Scripps O'NEIL as he walks north along the tracks toward PETOSKEY from MANCELONA. The Boyne Falls grade is 20 miles north of Mancelona.

boys, the   In "The Snows of Kilimanjaro," HARRY dreams that "the boys," the gun-bearers and trackers, light the kerosene fires in order to guide a plane in to the campsite.

boys, three   Narrator of "In Another Country" has established a kind of camaraderie with three "boys," all about the narrator's age and all wounded and using rehabilitating machines provided by a doctor at the Milan hospital where they are all being treated. After the daily treatments, they walk together from the hospital to the Café Cova through the communist quarter, where some of the "toughs" of Milan lived and cat-called to them as they passed.

All of the soldiers had medals of various sorts for their wounds and their valor, but they were also wounded psychologically. The narrator says that they "were all a little detached, and there was nothing that held us together except that we met every afternoon at the hospital." A fourth "boy" joined them sometimes, a boy who had lost his nose in the war and who now has a black silk handkerchief over his face to hide the wound.

Bradbury, Ray (1920–)   One of the memorials to Hemingway following his death was written by the American science-fiction novelist and short story writer Ray Bradbury in a short story titled "The Kilimanjaro Machine" (*Life* magazine) and later titled "The Kilimanjaro Device" (in *I Sing the Body Electric!,* 1969). In the story, Hemingway, who has died, is walking along an Idaho dirt road. A pickup truck stops, and the driver gives him a ride. After a few miles, the truck takes off and flies Hemingway to the top of Mt. Kilimanjaro. Some of Bradbury's best-known works include *The Martian Chronicles, Fahrenheit 451,* and *Dandelion Wine.*

Braddocks, Henry   In *The Sun Also Rises* he is Robert COHN's "literary friend"; Jake BARNES is Cohn's "tennis friend." Braddocks, his wife, and some of their friends meet Jake and the prostitute GEORGETTE at a Paris restaurant.

Braddocks, Mrs.   Henry Braddocks's wife, a Canadian. Her first name is "Jo." She fails to get the joke when, in *The Sun Also Rises,* Jake BARNES introduces the prostitute GEORGETTE as Georgette Leblanc, the name of a famous French singer.

Bradley, Helène   Woman in *To Have and Have Not* with whom Richard GORDON has an unsuccessful sexual fling during the afternoon before the evening that his wife, Helen GORDON, tells him their marriage is over. Gordon becomes suddenly impotent when Tommy BRADLEY, Helène's husband, appears at the door of her bedroom to watch Gordon and Helène making love.

Bradley, Tommy   In *To Have and Have Not,* he appears at Helène BRADLEY's bedroom door just as Helène and Richard GORDON are beginning sexual intercourse.

brakeman   In "The Battler" he throws Nick ADAMS off a freight train he has hopped.

Braque, Georges (1882–1963)   French painter and illustrator, one of the founders of Cubism. Thomas HUDSON, in *Islands in the Stream,* reminds "young Tom" that he met Braque in Paris. He is also mentioned in *A Moveable Feast* (see TANK WAGONS).

Breaking Point, The (film)   Warner Brothers picture, released in October 1950 (97 minutes), based on Hemingway's novel *To Have and Have Not.*

Breda works   The ugly part of Venice, according to Hemingway, heavily industrialized. It reminds Richard CANTWELL, in *Across the River and Into the Trees,* of Hammond, Indiana.

Brennan, Jack   Main character in "Fifty Grand." He is a boxer, a "natural welterweight," preparing for a big fight in New York's Madison Square Garden, but he can't get his heart into it because he misses his wife and two daughters, who are across the river in New York from his training camp in New Jersey.

He's thinking about giving up the fight game in order to have more time with his family. So when his manager, John COLLINS, brings in a couple of "friends" to talk to him about throwing the fight, Brennan accepts the offer. The story's narrator, Jerry DOYLE, who is also Brennan's trainer, is not in the room when the "fix" is discussed, but the reader gets enough information from him to know both that the fix is on and that, although Doyle is not technically in on it, neither does he plan to do anything to stop it. Brennan tells Doyle that he's betting $50,000 on his opponent, Jimmy WALCOTT.

Brennan fights well for 10 rounds but tells Collins in between rounds that he "can't stay" because his "legs are going bad." And, according to the narrator, "He was sick as hell." He knew he was losing, but it was all right because the money he had bet on his opponent was safe. All he wanted to do now was "finish it off right to please himself. He didn't want to be knocked out." But in the 11th round, Walcott hits Brennan below the belt, so hard that the narrator/trainer says, "I thought the eyes would come out of Jack's head." Brennan knows, however, that if the referee calls the foul against Walcott, the $50,000 he bet on Walcott would be lost. So when the referee grabs Walcott, Brennan tells him the blow "wasn't low. . . . It was a accident." The referee looks at Brennan's manager, thinking he might throw in the towel that he's already holding, but Collins, in on the fix, doesn't stop the fight.

Doyle says Brennan's "face was the worst thing I ever saw—the look on it! He was holding himself and all his body together and it all showed on his face. All the time he was thinking and holding his body in where it was busted." But then Brennan starts to box again, and he lands both gloves solidly at Walcott's groin, sending him to the floor where Walcott grabs himself in pain.

The referee stops the fight and declares Walcott the winner "on a foul," a "popular win" for Walcott, because most of the crowd's money was on him, so there's no complaining about the decision. Back in the dressing room, Collins says, "They certainly tried a nice double-cross," suggesting that Collins and his two friends, and probably others, had bet on Brennan to win the fight, after increasing the bets, and the odds, against him. At the end of the story, Brennan says, "It's funny how fast you can think when it means that much money."

Brenta River   Forming in the Italian Alps northwest of Venice and flowing into the Venice lagoon just above the town of Mira, about seven miles due west. In *Across the River and Into the Trees,* Colonel Richard CANTWELL thinks about the "long stretch of the Brenta where the great villas were, with their lawns and their gardens and the plane trees and the cypresses."

Brescia   City across the lagoon from Venice and, in *A Farewell to Arms,* a major stop on the railway line between the northern Italian warfront and Milan. The train Frederic HENRY hops, during his escape from the war, stops at Brescia.

Brett Ashley   See Brett ASHLEY.

bridge   In *For Whom the Bell Tolls* Robert JORDAN is assigned to blow up a bridge across an unnamed river in the Guadarrama Mountains near SEGOVIA. He and the Spanish guerrilla fighters helping him manage to blow up the bridge, but Jordan is wounded in trying to get away, and, at the end of the novel, he lies on the floor of a forest, waiting to die.

bridge, pontoon   Bridge over the Ebro River near the eastern coast of Spain, at which the narrator of "Old Man at the Bridge" finds an old man more concerned about two goats, a cat, and four pairs of pigeons he is responsible for than he is for his own safety.

bridge, railway   A "long plain iron bridge" in *A Farewell to Arms,* spanning an unnamed river that Frederic HENRY and his ambulance drivers cross after abandoning their cars, stuck in the mud about eight miles southeast of UDINE. From this bridge, Frederic looks north to another bridge on the same river and sees German soldiers crossing, also toward Udine.

bridges   In *Across the River and Into the Trees* Richard CANTWELL mentions or thinks about several bridges in Venice, particularly along the GRAND CANAL: "under the white bridge and under the unfinished wood bridge . . . the red bridge on the right and [we] passed under the first high-flying white bridge . . . the black iron fretwork bridge on the canal leading into the Rio Nuovo."

Bridges, Dorothy   Main female character in *The Fifth Column*. She is American, "a tall handsome blonde girl," educated at Vassar, although she tells her lover Robert PRESTON that she "didn't understand *anything*" they taught her there.

She is a reporter for unnamed publications, writing about the Spanish civil war, apparently, but without leaving her room in the Hotel Florida, except to shop. She tells Preston, who accuses her of never working, that she's going to "finish that *Cosmopolitan* article just as soon as I understand things the *least* bit better."

Her second lover, Philip RAWLINGS, the play's main character, describes her to his friend MAX as having the same background that "all American girls have that come to Europe with a certain amount of money. . . . Camps, college, money in family . . . men, affairs, abortions, ambitions, and finally marry and settle down or don't marry and settle down."

She is important in the play primarily as someone for Rawlings to return to after his work in counterespionage for the Loyalist side in the war. She makes plans with him for traveling to exotic places after the war, but he is merely playing a game with her, knowing that they are plans that will never be carried out.

Brigata Ancona   World War I Italian military unit mentioned by RINALDI (2) in *A Farewell to Arms*. He suggests that Frederic HENRY and their friend the PRIEST (2) have a relationship like the "number of the first regiment of the Brigata Ancona." It's a vulgar allusion, because the regiment was the 69th.

Brigata Basilicata   One of the brigades of Italian soldiers seen by Frederic HENRY in book 1 of *A Farewell to Arms*. He identifies them by their "red and white striped collar mark."

brisa, light   A light *brisa*, or breeze, a Caribbean name for a northeast trade wind, typical on the GULF STREAM in September, the time of *The Old Man and the Sea*. At the end of the novel, SANTIAGO uses the breeze out of the northeast to sail back to his Cuban village. It is also referred to in the "Cuba" section of *Islands in the Stream*. "Blowing at gale force out of the northeast against the Gulf Stream it [the brisa] made a very heavy sea."

Brissago Swiss village on the west side of LAKE MAGGIORE just north of the border with Italy. In *A Farewell to Arms* Frederic HENRY and Catherine BARKLEY land there after rowing up the lake from STRESA. It's "a nice-looking little town."

"British Can Save Constantinople" Article, published in *The Toronto Daily Star* (September 30, 1922), reprinted in *The Wild Years* (1962), reprinted in *Ernest Hemingway: Dateline Toronto* (1985). The headline in the *Daily Star* was "British Strong Enough To Save Constantinople." Datelined "Constantinople," this four-paragraph story is about British troops arriving to protect the city, while the Turkish government decides if it will abide by the Allied peace terms arrived at earlier in the year.

"[British Colonial Coal Mines Swindle]" Article, "discovered" by William Burrill at the John F. Kennedy Library in Boston and published in part in *Hemingway: The Toronto Years* (1994). It is Hemingway's first "investigative reporting" story for *The Toronto Daily Star,* about the possible swindle of the public by a British Colonial Coal Mine official, Alfred F. A. Coyne. Hemingway's editor at the *Star,* Harry C. Hindmarsh, rejected the story for fear of a libel suit.

British doctor At the field station where Frederic HENRY is taken after his wounding in *A Farewell to Arms.* He looks at Frederic's leg wounds and sends him off to a hospital in Milan.

Britisher, the At the post hospital in book 1 of *A Farewell to Arms,* the Englishman, attached to a British ambulance unit, helps get special treatment for the wounded Frederic HENRY. He explains to one of the Italian doctors that Frederic is the "legitimate son of President Wilson," and later he says that he is the "only son of the American Ambassador." Frederic later leaves for the field hospital in one of the British ambulances.

British Hospital Hospital in GORIZIA, Italy, where, in *A Farewell to Arms,* Catherine BARKLEY is stationed as a nurse and where she and Frederic HENRY meet in the garden for their first romantic evening together.

"British Order Kemal to Quit Chanak" Article, unsigned, published in *The Toronto Daily Star* (September 30, 1922), reprinted in *Ernest Hemingway: Dateline Toronto* (1985). Datelined "Constantinople," it covers a dispatch from General Harington, the British commanding officer in Constantinople, to Mustafa Kemal of Turkey demanding that he "evacuate the Chanak area." The headline in *TDS* read "British Again Order Kemal to Quit Chanak."

"British Planes" Article, unsigned, published in *The Toronto Daily Star* (September 30, 1922), reprinted in *Ernest Hemingway: Dateline Toronto* (1985). Datelined "Constantinople," about additional British troops brought to Constantinople to protect Greeks and Armenians from an attack by Turks. Headline in *TDS* read "British Airplanes Over Turk Capital."

"broads," two Sitting at a table next to Jerry DOYLE, Jack BRENNAN, and Soldier BARTLETT in Hanley's restaurant at the beginning of "Fifty Grand." They overhear Brennan refer to another boxer, Kid Lewis, as a "kike," and one of the women calls Brennan an "Irish bum," whose "wife sews [his] pockets up every morning."

Brodie, Steve Spurious daredevil who pretended to have survived a jump off the Brooklyn Bridge in 1886. In thinking about taking a chance on buying dinner for the two INDIANS (1) at BROWN'S BEANERY, Yogi JOHNSON, one of the two main characters in *The Torrents of Spring,* remembers Brodie's faked act, the publicity from which allowed him to open a tavern in the Bowery that became famous. Yogi's "chance" works, too, because the two Indians become his friends.

Brooklyn Dodgers Major League baseball team from the beginning of the National League in 1891 until its move from Brooklyn, New York, to Los Angeles in 1958. In the "Cuba" section of *Islands in the Stream* Thomas HUDSON tells HONEST LIL, a Havana madam, that Hong Kong millionaires had scouts throughout China looking for girls to become prostitutes just as the Brooklyn Dodgers sent out scouts to look for ballplayers.

brothers SANTIAGO, in *The Old Man and the Sea,* who has knowledge and appreciation of all things natural, thinks of the fish, the birds, and even the stars as man's brothers. He speaks to the 1,500-pound marlin he has caught as "brother."

Brothers, The *The Brothers Karamazov,* a novel by DOSTOYEVSKY, published in 1879–80. Referred to by Hemingway in *A Moveable Feast* only as "The Brothers."

Browning, Elizabeth Barrett (1806–1861) English poet, best known for her love poems in *Sonnets from the Portuguese* (1850). See Robert BROWNING.

Browning, Robert (1812–1889) English poet, perhaps best known for his dramatic monologues "My Last Duchess" and "The Pied Piper of Hamelin" (1842). In *Across the River and Into the Trees,* Colonel Richard CANTWELL remembers that the married poets "Robert and Mrs. Browning" were not particularly well liked by the Venetians.

Brown's Beanery   The only eatery mentioned in *The Torrents of Spring* and an important setting in the novel because it's where Scripps O'NEIL meets the "elderly waitress," Diana, whom he later "marries." The Brown's Beanery sign in front reads "The Best by Test," and when the waitress sends an order to the kitchen, she yells, "A pig and the noisy ones."

Brown's Nautical Almanac   One of the navigational guides published annually by the British admiralty, beginning in 1767, and which provided information, charts, and tables for ships, particularly the position of the sun, moon, and planets at a given latitude and longitude on any day at any hour of the year. The U.S. began publishing similar almanacs in 1855. The almanac is mentioned in *A Moveable Feast* (see PILOT FISH).

Bruce (1)   Negro bartender, nicknamed "Red Dog" at the INDIAN CLUB in *The Torrents of Spring*.

Bruce (2)   One of Danny Hogan's assistants at his New Jersey training camp for prizefighters in "Fifty Grand." A "Negro," he rubs down the fighters after they've worked out.

Bruce, Audrey   One of the SEVEN TOURISTS in the "BIMINI" section of *Islands in the Stream*. Thomas HUDSON thought he had never seen a "lovelier face nor a finer body. Except one, he thought"—a reference to his first wife. Audrey Bruce is on the island to see Hudson's friend Roger DAVIS, whom she had met before at Cap d'Antibes and at the AUTEUIL racetrack in Paris, although Davis barely remembers the occasions. Her name then was Audrey Raeburn, and she had been there with her mother and Dick Raeburn, her mother's husband, whose name Audrey had taken. Her mother, "still" a drug addict, is now married to Geoffrey Townsend and lives in London. Both Dick Raeburn and Bill Bruce, Audrey's stepfather, are dead now, and Audrey would like to renew her friendship with Davis.

Bruce, Toby (1911–1984)   Friend of Hemingway' and sometimes chauffeur and handyman, from Piggott, Arkansas. They met through Pauline Pfeiffer HEMINGWAY's family in Piggott.

Brueghel, Pieter (c. 1525–1569)   Flemish painter, Pieter Brueghel the elder, known for his violent, apocalyptical paintings, a "very old-timer," according to Thomas HUDSON in *Islands in the Stream*. There was a Brueghel family of three famous Flemish painters: Pieter, the elder, and his sons, Pieter (1564–1637) and Jan (1568–1625).

In *Across the River and Into the Trees* it is probably the elder Brueghel whom Richard CANTWELL refers to in a conversation about painting with his driver, Jackson. Just the last name is used.

Brumback, Ted (1895–1955)   Friend of Hemingway's who worked with him for both *The Kansas City Star* and the American Red Cross during WORLD WAR I, when both men served with the ambulance corps attached to the Italian army in northern Italy. A week after Hemingway was wounded (July 8, 1918) Brumback wrote a letter to Hemingway's father, providing details of his son's serious condition and his "heroism" in carrying a wounded Italian soldier out of danger.

Brundi   Italian soldier, one of the "priest-baiters" in Frederic HENRY's Italian military unit in book 1 of *A Farewell to Arms*.

Bryan, William Jennings (1861–1925)   U.S. politician, lawyer, and newspaper editor. He was the prosecuting attorney in the 1925 Tennessee trial against John T. Scopes for teaching the Darwinian concept of evolution, rather than creationism, in his high school biology classes. His death on July 26, 1925, helps set the date of *The Sun Also Rises*.

Jake BARNES informs Bill GORTON that he read about Bryan's death "in the paper yesterday." Since the Fiesta SAN FERMÍN in PAMPLONA always begins on July 6 and Jake's statement to Gorton comes the week before the fiesta begins, it is clear that Hemingway fictionalized Bryan's death date. It is safe to assume, however, that the fiesta they attend is in July 1925. In addition, Brett ASHLEY tells Jake that Pedro ROMERO was born in 1905, and readers know he is 19 years old.

Buckley   An army patrol leader, the only named character in the "Chapter 3" vignette of *In Our Time*.

Budapest   Capital city of Hungary, mentioned in "The Revolutionist." It is where the "He" of the short story is tortured by the White Russian counterrevolutionaries before he escapes to Italy.

buffalo, three   Francis MACOMBER, in "The Short Happy Life of Francis Macomber," and the hunting guide, Robert WILSON, chase three bull buffalo, as Macomber regains his courage the day after he runs from a lion. They kill two buffalo and wound one, which then rushes from the bush and is killed by Macomber, who courageously stands his ground against the attack. The buffalo described is probably the Cape buffalo, known in East Africa for its fierceness. The story's narrator describes the "huge, black animals" as "big black tank cars," with "upswept wide black horns."

Bugatti   A small, fast, expensive racing car, produced by the Italian manufacturer Ettore Arco Isidore Bugatti

(1881–1947). In *The Garden of Eden,* a small blue car owned by David and Catherine BOURNE, which they call the "Bug," was purchased by Catherine.

"bugger"   In "Fathers and Sons," Nick ADAMS remembers that his father once defined "bugger" as a "man who has intercourse with animals." He called it a "heinous crime."

Bugs   In "The Battler," the "Negro" caretaker of Ad FRANCIS, an ex-prizefighter, both characters a little "crazy." Bugs tells Nick ADAMS, the story's main character, that he met Ad in jail. Bugs has to "change" Ad to keep him from fighting by "tapping" him on the back of the head with a "cloth-wrapped blackjack." Like Ad Francis, Bugs seems gentle when he talks with Nick but is in his own way dangerous, one of the shocks to the psyche Nick carries with him back toward the railroad tracks at the end of the story.

Buick   The "big Buick" with "one hundred and fifty ponies" is the car in which Colonel Richard CANTWELL is taken to Venice at the beginning of *Across the River and Into the Trees* and in which he has his fatal heart attacks at the end of the novel. He calls the car a *motoscafo,* which in Italian means "motorboat."

Buitrago   Spanish town about 39 miles north of Madrid and "on the other side of the [enemy] lines" in *For Whom the Bell Tolls.* It is across the Guadarrama Mountains from SEGOVIA.

bull, the (1)   In the "Chapter 11" vignette of *In Our Time* the bull is so tired from so much bad sticking by the bullfighter that he finally "folded his knees and lay down and one of the CUADRILLA leaned out over his neck and killed him with the PUNTILLO."

bull, the (2)   For a moment in the "Chapter 12" vignette of *In Our Time,* the reader gets the bull's point of view. In a sentence fragment: "The bull looking at him straight in front, hating."

bullfight   The term used in Spanish is *corrida* or *corrida de Toros.* "There is," according to Jake BARNES in *The Sun Also Rises,* "no Spanish word for bullfight." Hemingway says in *Death in the Afternoon,* that "[t]he bullfight is not a sport in the Anglo-Saxon sense of the word, that is, it is not an equal contest or an attempt at an equal contest between a bull and a man. Rather it is a tragedy. . . ." He says that from a "modern moral point of view, that is, a Christian point of view, the . . . bullfight is indefensible; there is certainly much cruelty, there is always danger, either sought or unlooked for, and there is always death, and I should not try to

defend it now, only to tell honestly the things I have found true about it."

Hemingway explains that in trying to learn to write, he realized that he needed to begin with the "simplest things, and one of the simplest things of all and the most fundamental is violent death." And since the "only place where you could see life and death, *i.e.,* violent death now that the wars were over, was in the bull ring and I wanted very much to go to Spain where I could study it." He says: "but the bullfight was so far from simple and I liked it so much that it was much too complicated for my then equipment for writing to deal with and, aside from four very short sketches, I was not able to write anything about it for five years—and I wish I would have waited ten."

As for morals, he says, "I know only that what is moral is what you feel good after and what is immoral is what you feel bad after and judged by these moral standards, which I do not defend, the bullfight is very moral to me because I feel very fine while it is going on and have a feeling of life and death and mortality and immortality, and after it is over I feel very sad but very fine."

Hemingway often spells "bullfight" and "bullfighting" with a hyphen.

bullfight critic, substitute   During the early stages of the bullfight in "The Undefeated," the substitute reporter for Madrid's *El Heraldo* newspaper makes notes about the fight in bullfight jargon, perhaps appropriate for "nocturnals" (night bullfights), since the crowd is not particularly knowledgeable. However, he decides that he doesn't need to stay for the entire fight (he has a date at Maxim's at midnight), and so he leaves just before the most important stage of the fight and the goring of Manuel GARCIA.

"Bullfighting, Sport and Industry"   Article, published in *Fortune* (March 1930), about the economics of the bullfight industry in Spain.

"Bull Fighting a Tragedy"   Article, published in *The Toronto Star Weekly* (October 20, 1923), reprinted in *The Wild Years* (1962), and in *By-Line: Ernest Hemingway* (1967). The article is a report of Hemingway's first bullfights, "on the outskirts" of Madrid, probably in late May 1923. The article is as detailed as the later writing Hemingway did on bullfighting, especially in *The Sun Also Rises* and *Death in the Afternoon.* And it has the same thematic idea, which *The Toronto Star Weekly* used in its headline over the story: "Bull Fighting Is Not a Sport— It Is a Tragedy."

He writes about his impressions of this first bullfight, which he says was "not the best. The best was in the little town of Pamplona high up in the hills of Navarre [which he saw in July] . . . where they have held six days of bullfighting each year since 1126 A.D., and where the bulls race through the streets of the town each morning at six o'clock with half the town running ahead of them." He adds, "I'm not going to apologize for bull fighting. It is a survival of the days of the Roman Coliseum. But it needs some explanation. Bull fighting is not a sport. It was never supposed to be. It is a tragedy. A very great tragedy. The tragedy is the death of the bull. It is played in three definite acts. . . ."

bull ranches Hemingway states in *Death in the Afternoon* that fighting bulls are raised at bull ranches in the Spanish provinces of Navarra, Burgos, Palencia, Logroño, Zaragoza, Valladolid, Zamora, Segovia, Salamanca, Madrid, Toledo, Albacete, and the regions of Extremadura, and Andalucía. "The biggest bulls and the best bred come from Andalucía and Castilla."

bulls For the best exposition on bulls in Hemingway, read chapters 11 through 14 of *Death in the Afternoon.*

bull's head, stuffed Over the desk of Madrid bullfight promoter Don Miguel RETANA, in "The Undefeated," hangs the head of "Mariposa," the bull that killed Manuel GARCIA's brother nine years before on April 27, 1909, setting the time of the story in 1918.

Bumby Nickname the Hemingways gave their son, John (Jack) Hadley Nicanor Hemingway, born October 10, 1923, in Toronto. In *A Moveable Feast* Hemingway writes about him during the early years when the family was in Paris.

Burberry Trademark for a British-made raincoat. "You can't get water through a Burberry," Richard CANTWELL, in *Across the River and Into the Trees,* remembers thinking to himself during an early Saturday morning walk in the rain of Venice.

Burguete Town in the Pyrenees Mountains of northern Spain, about 24 miles north of Pamplona. In *The Sun Also Rises* Jake BARNES and Bill GORTON stay "five days" there while on a fishing trip to the IRATI RIVER.

burlesque show A series of theatrical acts, usually involving slapstick humor, comedy skits, bawdy songs, and scantily clad women. In Hemingway's "A Pursuit Race" the only two characters work for a burlesque show, William CAMPBELL as the "advance man" and Mr. TURNER as the show's manager. The story's narrator makes clear in the opening paragraph that "pursuit race" is used metaphorically for life itself, so it is not difficult to read "burlesque show" as a metaphor, too.

Burnham The name Colonel Richard CANTWELL calls his driver, JACKSON, by mistake in *Across the River and Into the Trees.* Jackson corrects him and reminds him that

Burnham is "at the rest center at Cortina." It isn't clear whether Burnham is Cantwell's regular driver or the colonel is being deliberately abusive toward Jackson, who later wonders to himself why Cantwell is such "a mean son of a bitch . . . and he can be so God-damn nice."

Burns, George   See ALLEN, GRACIE.

Butler Name of the "old man" in "My Old Man," the father of the story's narrator, JOE. Butler is a Kentucky-born jockey, riding in European steeplechases in the 1920s. He seems to have thrown some races, not from anything Joe knows about his father but from the reader's inferences about what the son says he has overheard.

Butler may have thrown a race at the SAN SIRO course in Milan, or was paid to throw a race and didn't. He leaves Italy for Paris, where he has difficulty getting his jockey's license transferred. He wins some bets, however, enough to buy his own racehorse. Butler's horse, GILFORD, shows promise by taking third in a hurdle race, but in the PRIX DU MARAT, a "4500 meter steeplechase" at AUTEUIL, he is in a "crash" with several horses at a water-jump. Butler is killed, and Gilford breaks a leg and has to be shot. Joe says at the end that he is left with "nothing," but that's not quite true, because he has good memories of his father. His father's friend George GARDNER is right when he tells Joe that his "old man was one swell guy." He was at least to Joe.

"Butterfly and the Tank, The"   This short story is set in CHICOTE'S RESTAURANT in Madrid during the "second winter of shelling in the siege of Madrid" (1937) during the Spanish civil war. A civilian, called the "flit gun man," shoots his FLIT GUN at an older waiter who doesn't like it, but since many people in the overcrowded bar laugh at the waiter's anger, the "flit gun man" continues to shoot at him.

Finally the shooting becomes tiresome, and three men grab the civilian and throw him out of the bar. He comes stumbling back into the bar, bloody but unbowed, and shoots his flit gun at the crowd in general. He is pushed into a corner of the bar and shot dead, several other men draw guns and chaos ensues. The police discover that the civilian had loaded his flit gun with eau de cologne and was simply trying to add some gaiety to a wartime afternoon in a crowded bar.

The bar's manager suggests to the story's narrator that the man's "gaiety comes in contact with the seriousness of the war like a butterfly . . . and a tank." Knowing that the narrator is a writer, the manager suggests that he write a story about the incident and title it "The Butterfly and the Tank." The "flit-gun man" is also mentioned in Hemingway's play, *The Fifth Column.*

"The Butterfly and the Tank" appeared first in *Esquire* (December 1938) and then as the second of the "stories" in *The Fifth Column and Four Stories of the Spanish Civil War* (1969).

"Buying Commission Would Cut Out Waste"   Article, unsigned, published in *The Toronto Daily Star* (April 26, 1920), reprinted in *Ernest Hemingway: Dateline Toronto* (1985). An interview with Ralph Connable, head of Woolworth Company in Canada, about waste in the company's system of buying supplies.

Buzoni   One of the owners of steeplechase horses at the SAN SIRO track in Italy in "My Old Man."

B'wana Kabor   Swahili name for KARL in *Green Hills of Africa.*

By-Line: Ernest Hemingway   Anthology of 76 articles, edited by William White and published by Charles Scribner's Sons in 1967; subtitled "Selected Articles and Dispatches of Four Decades." The book is divided into five parts: "Reporting, 1920–1924" (30 articles); "*Esquire*, 1933–1936" (17 articles); "Spanish Civil War, 1937–1939" (12 articles); "World War II" (13 articles); and "After the Wars, 1949–1956" (four articles). See Appendix V for article titles.

Byron, Lord George Gordon (1788–1824)   English Romantic poet, mentioned by Richard CANTWELL, in *Across the River and Into the Trees,* in connection with his having once stayed in a house in Venice owned by ALVARITO's ancestors on his mother's side.

C

Cabañas A town "[d]own the coast from MARIEL," the place in Cuba where, in *To Have and Have Not,* Harry MORGAN is to take the four Cubans (see CUBANS, FOUR). Cabañas is about 40 miles west of Havana. *Cabañas* are also the tents used by fishermen on the beaches outside of Havana.

cabinet ministers, six Otherwise unidentified, they go before a military firing squad in the "Chapter 5" vignette of *In Our Time.*

cablese The "shorthand" style Hemingway sometimes used in sending his Spanish civil war stories to NANA (North America Newspaper Alliance) offices in London or New York for publication by their 60-plus newspaper subscribers. It was meant to save money on telegrams.

Hemingway omitted all apostrophes and hyphens, all words like "stop," "comma," "para," "quote," etc. He contracted words: "safternoon" for "this afternoon," "unbelieve" for "do not believe," etc. He also dropped articles, infinitives, auxilliary verbs, and short prepositions. He combined verbs and prepositions: "uplink" for "link up," "outfigured" for "figured out," "upthrusting," "inrushing," "upget," etc. Here is an example: "youd hear the double boom of the guns and then the whirling cloth ripping incoming rush and dirt would fountain brownly up among the grapevines." It is little wonder that few of Hemingway's Spanish civil war dispatches sent by telegram and syndicated by NANA ever appeared the same in any two newspapers. Editors had to create their stories from the author's cablese. The *Ernest Hemingway A to Z* author is indebted to Margaret Calien Lewis for the above description, taken from her unpublished master's thesis, *Ernest Hemingway's The Spanish War: Dispatches from Spain 1937–1938* (University of Louisville, 1968).

According to William B. Watson in his article, "A Variorum Edition of Dispatch 19" (*The Hemingway Review,* Spring 1988), Hemingway wrote two drafts of his dispatches, one in normal English, the other in "cablese." Here is the cablese version of the lead paragraph of NANA DISPATCH #6: "Since six o'clock smorning eyve been watching government attack on large scale designed eventually uplink forces heights coruna road with others advancing excarabanchel and casa del campo cutting

neck salient rebel forces thrust university citywards lifting rebel pressure exmadrid stop" (40 words).

The story edited in New York and sent to member newspapers reads: "Since six o'clock this morning I have been watching a Government attack on a large scale that is designed eventually to link up forces on the heights of the Coruña road with others advancing from Carabanchel and the Casa de Campo, cutting the neck of a salient [forwardmost enemy battle position] the rebel forces have thrust toward University City and lifting rebel pressure from Madrid" (61 words).

Cabo Blanco Off the coast of Peru, where Hemingway fished for marlin during the filming of *The Old Man and the Sea;* mentioned in *The Dangerous Summer.*

Cabot, John Moors (1901–) U.S. diplomat and author. He was ambassador to Sweden in 1954 when Hemingway won the Nobel Prize for literature and, when Hemingway chose not to go to Sweden for the ceremony, delivered his acceptance speech to the Swedish Academy on December 10, 1954.

Cadillac Town in Michigan where the cook in "The Light of the World" wants to go because his sister lives there. One of the customers at the station restaurant in the story remembers that it is also the hometown of Steve KETCHEL and Ad Wolgast, two prizefighters.

Cádiz Capital of Cádiz province in southwest Spain in Andalucia on the Bay of Cádiz. Hemingway's friends Carmen and Antonio ORDÓÑEZ have a home there, which the author used as a stopover several times during the summer of 1959 when he followed the bullfight circuit in preparation for writing *The Dangerous Summer.*

Cadorna, Il Generale Italian field marshal, head of the army general staff who reorganized the Italian army before World War I. Frederic HENRY, in *A Farewell to Arms,* calls him "fat and prosperous."

Caesarean section The surgical removal of the baby from the mother's uterus through an abdominal incision. Legend has it that Julius Caesar was born this way, thus the name.

In "Indian Camp," a Caesarian section is performed on a young Indian woman by NICK's father, a doctor. The operation is done with a jackknife and without any anesthetic, and then the incision is sewn up with nine feet of gut leader from some of the doctor's fishing line.

And, in *A Farewell to Arms,* it's the operation performed on Catherine BARKLEY in the hospital in LAUSANNE, from which she bleeds to death.

café (1) Near the hospital in LAUSANNE where Frederic HENRY goes, while Catherine BARKLEY is in labor, and waits for her baby to be born, in *A Farewell to Arms.*

café (2) In "The Undefeated," the bullfighter Manuel GARCIA goes to a café near the Puerto del Sol in Madrid looking for ZURITO (1) whom he hopes to talk into picing for him at the "nocturnals" the next night.

café (3) In Paris in "The Sea Change," the setting for the conversation between the unnamed girl and her lover, Phil, about the girl leaving him for a woman.

café (4) Otherwise unidentified setting for most of "A Clean, Well-Lighted Place." The older waiter tells the younger waiter, "This is a clean and pleasant café. It is well lighted." After he closes up, he goes to a bar for a cup of coffee, but he knows that a "clean, well-lighted café is a very different thing" from a bar or bodega. See WAITER, OLDER; WAITER, YOUNGER.

café (5) In *A Moveable Feast* Hemingway mentions "a good café" on place St.-Michel in Paris where he had a *café au lait* and a rum St. James and wrote a short story. A pretty girl came into the café, sat by herself near the window, and he kept looking up at her from his writing. See GIRL (6).

café (6) In CANNES where, in *The Garden of Eden,* David and Catherine BOURNE meet MARITA. It is interesting to note that the word *café* includes the accent mark only once in the novel, for a café crème that David orders. The accent mark, which is important in the French pronunciation of the word and which Hemingway knew about and used in all of his other works, was probably left out of *The Garden of Eden* by the editors at Scribner's.

café, station (1) In Montreux, Switzerland, the setting for part 1 of "Homage to Switzerland."

café, station (2) In Vevey, Switzerland, the setting for part 2 of "Homage to Switzerland."

café, station (3) In Territet, Switzerland, the setting for part 3 of "Homage to Switzerland."

Café Alvarez In Madrid, where the middle-aged waiter in "The Capital of the World" is drinking a "small beer" at the time the story's main character, PACO (2), is being killed back at the PENSION LUARCA while playing at being a matador.

Café Cambrinus In "The Mercenaries" it is on Wabash Avenue in Chicago, the setting for the story.

Café Cova Restaurant in the GALLERIA in Milan, Italy, near the Piazza del Duomo and Teatro alla Scala (opera house). In *A Farewell to Arms* Frederic HENRY eats there and often fantasizes about meals there during some of the worst moments of fighting in the war.

The Cova is also where the narrator of "In Another Country" and his wounded Italian army friends go after their hospital treatments for various mangled body parts.

Café Crillon In Paris at the deluxe Hotel Crillon, 10, place de la Concorde, one of the expensive cafés on the Right Bank, mentioned in *The Sun Also Rises.* It's where Jake BARNES was to meet Brett ASHLEY "at five o'clock," but she forgets the appointment.

Café de la Paix In Paris at 12, boulevard des Capucines, near the Opera, where Jake BARNES and Robert COHN have coffee at the end of chapter 5 in *The Sun Also Rises.*

It is also where the "old man" in "My Old Man" goes once or twice a week and sits "on the opera side."

Café de Paris In MAISONS-LAFITTE, France, where, in "My Old Man," JOE and his "old man" often sit at tables between work sessions at the racetrack.

Café des Amateurs Paris café, crowded when Hemingway describes arriving there at the beginning of *A Moveable Feast.* He describes it as "evilly run" and "crowded with drunkards," and he says he stayed away because of the "smell or dirty bodies" and the "sour smell of drunkenness." He refers to the café as the "cesspool of the rue Mouffetard."

Café de Versailles In Paris at 171, rue de Rennes, where Jake BARNES and his friends go for coffee at the end of chapter 1 in *The Sun Also Rises.*

Café du Dôme At 108, boulevard du Montparnasse in Paris. In *A Moveable Feast* Hemingway writes that the cafés Dôme and Rotonde, across from each other at the corner of boulevard du Montparnasse and boulevard Raspail, were popular because people wanted to be seen at such places and "in a way such places anticipated the [newspaper] columnists as the daily substitutes for immortality." It is also where Hemingway says he had a conversation with the 25-year-old artist Jules PASCIN, who was drunk, and two models he had with him. "He looked more like a Broadway character of the Nineties than the lovely painter that he was, and afterwards, when he had hanged himself, I liked to remember him as he was that night at the Dôme."

Jake BARNES mentions the café in *The Sun Also Rises.*

And it is where, in "Mr. and Mrs. Elliot," Hubert and Cornelia Elliot and their friends go, instead of the Rotonde across the street, because the Rotonde is "always so full of foreigners."

Café Fornos In the Madrid of "The Capital of the World," where some of the matadors and picadors, who stay at PACO (2)'s pension, are playing billiards during the time that Paco is being accidentally killed while playing at bullfighting.

Café Iruña First choice of the many eating and drinking places in PAMPLONA for Jake BARNES and his friends, in *The Sun Also Rises,* during their week at the Fiesta SAN FERMÍN.

Café Marinas In Bayonne, France, where Jake BARNES goes for dinner, in *The Sun Also Rises,* while relaxing after the Fiesta SAN FERMÍN. See CHÂTEAU MARGAUX.

Café Napolitain Paris sidewalk café, at No. 1, boulevard des Capucines, where Robert COHN and Jake BARNES have aperitifs at the end of chapter 2 in *The Sun Also Rises.* Georgette has a pernod with Jake, and then the two leave together. The name in the early 1920s was Café-Glacier Napolitain. "Glacier" means icemaker.

café on the corner In GRAU DU ROI, France, "facing the sea," where David and Catherine BOURNE, in *The Garden of Eden,* drink aperitifs and watch "the sails of the mackerel fishing boats out in the Gulf of Lions."

Café Rotonde At 103, boulevard du Montparnasse in Paris. Jake BARNES says, in *The Sun Also Rises,* that "No matter what café in Montparnasse you ask a taxi-driver to bring you to from the right bank of the river, they always take you to the Rotonde. Ten years from now it will probably be the Dome."

In his article titled "American Bohemians in Paris" Hemingway writes that "[y]ou can find anything you are looking for at the Rotonde—except serious artists."

The Elliots in "Mr. and Mrs. Eliot" dislike the Rotonde, because it is "always so full of foreigners."

Café Select At 99, boulevard du Montparnasse in Paris, often the choice of Jake BARNES, in *The Sun Also Rises,* for dinner or for meeting friends; he refers to it as "this new dive."

In *Islands in the Stream* Thomas HUDSON remembers that when he was living in Paris as a young man he painted a picture of the proprietor of the Select. And Hemingway refers to the café in *A Moveable Feast.*

Café Suizo In PAMPLONA in *The Sun Also Rises,* a secondary choice for Jake BARNES and his friends after the CAFÉ IRUÑA.

Cage, Miss The "young and pretty" nurse at the AMERICAN HOSPITAL (1) in Milan, where Frederic HENRY is taken after his wounding, in *A Farewell to Arms.* She is the first nurse to take care of him at the hospital. In the bright sunlight of the second day, he thinks she looks "a little older . . . and not so pretty."

cahiers The "cheap, lined, school" notebooks in which David BOURNE writes his stories that his wife, Catherine, burns at the climax of *The Garden of Eden.* He keeps them in a locked SUITCASE, along with a cardboard box of five pencils and a "cone-shaped sharpener." Catherine refers to them as "those ridiculous child's notebooks."

They are the "blue-backed notebooks" in which Hemingway wrote many of his stories while in Paris during the 1920s. They are similar to the examination booklets used by many U.S. colleges.

Cahors wine Red wine from the town of Cahors in southwest France. In *A Moveable Feast* Hemingway writes that he and Hadley drank "the good Cahors wine" at the restaurant Nègre de Toulouse in half or full carafes, "usually diluting it about one-third with water."

Caibarién Town on the northeast coast of Cuba where Thomas HUDSON's crew is taking him after his wounding near the end of *Islands in the Stream.*

Callaghan, Morley (1903–1990) Canadian novelist and short story writer. His novels include *Strange Fugitive* (1928), *Such Is My Beloved* (1934), and *A Passion in Rome* (1961). He also published a memoir of his years in Paris during the late 1920s. *That Summer in Paris* (1963), which discusses his friendship with Hemingway and F. Scott FITZGERALD.

Callaghan met Hemingway in Toronto in 1923, and the young reporter for *The Toronto Star* befriended Callaghan and his wife, Lowrey, who was herself a reporter for the newspaper. Hemingway went to them for moral support at times when he was particularly unhappy with the treatment he was getting from city editor Harry Hindmarsh, who seemed to thrive on making his newest reporters hate him.

Callaghan once said of Hemingway there is "[s]omething within him [that] drove him to want to be expert at every occupation he touched." In Paris the two boxed for exercise, and a story ran in *The New York Herald Tribune* reporting that Callaghan had knocked out Hemingway in one of their "matches." Hemingway was furious; Callaghan wrote to the newspaper, saying he had never knocked Hemingway out, and that they had boxed only a few times to work up a sweat.

Callejón Restaurant on the Calle Becerra in Madrid, where Hemingway stopped for meals at least twice during his travels on the bullfight circuit in 1959 in preparation for writing *The Dangerous Summer*.

"Call for Greatness" Article, published in *Ken* (July 14, 1938). Hemingway asks President Roosevelt to intervene on behalf on the Loyalists in Spain.

Calutina The name, in "Mr. and Mrs. Elliot," preferred instead of Cornelia by Mrs. Elliot's Southern family and friends. She teaches her husband, Hubert, to call her Calutina. See Cornelia ELLIOT.

Camagüey (1) Airfield in Cuba about 350 miles east-southeast of Havana, where Thomas HUDSON's first wife, now with the Army USO (in May 1944), flies in for a one-day visit in *Islands in the Stream*.

Camagüey (2) Name of the archipelago along the northern Cuban coast, islands that form the hunt zone for Thomas HUDSON as he and his fishing boat crew search for members of a German submarine crew in the "At Sea" section of *Islands in the Stream*. CAYO GUILLERMO and CAYO COCO, near where they finally find the Germans, are part of the chain.

Camargue Large island in the Rhône delta in the south of France, once a marshland but now reclaimed in part and used for extensive cattle raising. At the beginning of *The Garden of Eden*, which takes place in the mid-1920s, David and Catherine BOURNE can see from their hotel room in the Grau du Roi across the "low plain of the Camargue" to the towers of AIGUES MORTES.

Cambrinus Owner of the Café Cambrinus on Chicago's Wabash Avenue in the short story "The Mercenaries."

camion Low-slung truck. In *Across the River and Into the Trees* Richard CANTWELL remembers riding in a camion on the road between Monfalcone and Latisana in Italy during WORLD WAR I.

campaniles Bell towers, "pointed steeples," that Richard CANTWELL points out to his driver, JACKSON, particularly at Ceggia as they drive toward VENICE at the beginning of *Across the River and Into the Trees*.

Campari A bitter Italian aperitif, red in color, it derives its bitter flavor from quinine. Campari is often mixed with soda and ice, and is also used as a cocktail ingredient.

In "Get a Seeing-Eyed Dog," a short story set in Italy, Campari is mixed with gin: "Campari and Gordon's with ice."

Campbell, Mike Brett ASHLEY's Scottish fiancé in *The Sun Also Rises*. She introduces him to Jake BARNES and his friend Bill GORTON at the CAFÉ SELECT in Paris: "This drunkard is Mike Campbell," she tells Jake. "Mr. Campbell is an undischarged bankrupt." He is from a rich family but is careless with money. He goes with Brett and her friends to PAMPLONA for the bullfights and is more conspicuously drunk than any of the others because he is jealous of Brett's various lovers.

Jake says that "Mike was a bad drunk," Brett and Bill are good drunks, and "Cohn was never drunk." Bill asks Mike how he went bankrupt. "Two ways," Mike says. "Gradually and then suddenly." Mike wants to marry Brett after her divorce from Lord Ashley, and, at the end of the novel, Brett tells Jake that she's going back to Mike.

Campbell, William One of the two characters in "A Pursuit Race." He's an advance man for a burlesque show, and he has managed to stay ahead of the show from Pittsburgh to Kansas City. But he succumbs to alcohol and drugs and so gets caught by Mr. TURNER, one of the show's managers, in a Kansas City hotel room. The "pursuit race" of the story's title is a metaphor, which makes it is clear that Campbell has been caught by his pursuers. Mr. Turner is sympathetic but must get on with his work and so passes Campbell by, thereby putting him out of the race; and the larger pursuer, life itself, is in the process also of passing Campbell by, putting him out of the more important race.

"Camping Out" Article, published in *The Toronto Star Weekly* (June 26, 1920), reprinted in *The Wild Years* (1962), reprinted in *Ernest Hemingway: Dateline Toronto* (1985). The headline in the *Star Weekly* was "When You Camp Out, Do It Right." Most people going camping this summer, Hemingway suggests, will return having had a good time, but if someone "goes into the woods with a frying pan, an ignorance of black flies and mosquitoes, and a great and abiding lack of knowledge about cookery, the chances are that his return will be very different." Hemingway offers detailed directions for cooking over an open fire and tells readers at the end of the article that it is all right to talk about roughing it, but only the "real woodsman" can be comfortable on a camping trip to the woods.

"Canada's Recognition of Russia" Article, unsigned, published in *The Toronto Daily Star* (April 10, 1922), reprinted in *Ernest Hemingway: Dateline Toronto* (1985). Datelined "Genoa," this two-paragraph story reports that Canada's "chief interest in the Genoa Conference [which opened April 10, 1922] is the recognition of Russia." The headline in the *TDS* was "Canada's Chief Interest, Recognition of Russia."

"Canadians: Wild/Tame" Article, published in *The Toronto Star Weekly* (October 9, 1920), reprinted in *Ernest Hemingway: Dateline Toronto* (1985). The headline in the *Star Weekly* was "The Average Yank Divides Canadians into Two Classes—Wild and Tame." A then recent article in *Collier's Weekly* by William Stevens McNutt on what Canadians think of Americans inspired Hemingway to write this article on what Americans think of Canadians. Canada is, for Americans, Hemingway writes, the "North-West Mounted Police, winter sports, open snowy places replete with huskie dogs, Canadian whiskey, race reports from Windsor, the Woodbine and Blue Bonnets, and a firm and dominant passion that no one will slip him any Canadian silver."

"Canary for One, A" Two Americans, the unnamed narrator of this short story and his wife, are traveling by train along the Mediterranean coast of France to Marseilles and then north through Avignon to Paris. They are in a compartment with an "AMERICAN LADY" who is taking a caged canary to her daughter.

Two years earlier the American Lady had broken off a love relationship between her daughter and a man from Vevey, Switzerland, because a friend of hers had told her that "No foreigner can make an American girl a good husband." The American Lady tells the narrator, "I couldn't have her marrying a foreigner." The three traveling companions arrive in Paris and say good-bye. In the story's last line, the reader learns that the narrator and his wife are splitting up their marriage.

Each character is trapped like the canary in its cage. The narrator is in an apparently loveless marriage, although he only informs the reader of it in the story's last line and provides no details. The American Lady is trapped by, among other things, her attitude toward foreign men, an idea she had heard once from a friend. The daughter, though she does not appear in the story, is perhaps trapped most of all, by a domineering mother. She will receive the caged canary.

"A Canary for One" was first published in *Scribner's Magazine* (April 1927) and reprinted in *Men Without Women* (1927).

Canary Islands Off the coast of the western Sahara in West Africa, belonging to Spain. In *The Old Man and the Sea*, the night before SANTIAGO's three-day fishing adventure on the Gulf Stream, he dreams of the islands and of seeing lions playing on the beaches.

C. and M. In "The Light of the World," ALICE says to PEROXIDE, "you haven't got any real memories except having your tubes out and when you started C. and M." Although not further identified, the "C" is probably for "curettage," a medical term for cleaning the walls of body cavities and which would mean, in Hemingway's story, scraping the uterus after an abortion. The "M" may be for "mercury," a chemical element which at the time of the story (1930s) was used by doctors to cure syphilis.

Cannes French town on the Mediterranean seacoast, 21 miles southwest of Nice. It is mentioned in "A Canary for One" as a stop where the American Lady had gotten back on the train just before it left. Being a little deaf, she heard no departure signal.

And in *The Garden of Eden* it is one of the places where Catherine BOURNE gets her hair cut like a "boy's."

Cantwell, Gordon The brother of Colonel Richard Cantwell in *Across the River and Into the Trees*, who had died, apparently, in the war in the Pacific during WORLD WAR II.

Cantwell, Richard The 50-year-old protagonist of *Across the River and Into the Trees*. He is a "Colonel of Infantry in the Army of the United States, reduced from being a general officer," because he lost his regiment during a battle in WORLD WAR II. In trying to rationalize the loss, he remembers that it "was all the regiment I ever could have hoped for in this life until I lost it. . . . Under orders, of course. . . . So you leave one company dead along a draw. You lose one company complete and you destroy three others." He was an assistant divisional commander at the time of the defeat of his regiment.

During the time of the novel (1948), Cantwell is stationed in Trieste and waiting for his retirement. He has had three heart attacks and has two more during the weekend of the novel, all but the last of which take place in his recollections while he duck hunts at the mouth of the TAGLIAMENTO RIVER on Sunday morning.

He had been a lieutenant during WORLD WAR I, and many of his memories, especially at the beginning of the novel on his way from TRIESTE to VENICE with his driver, JACKSON, are of that time when he was 18 years old. He had been a hero in that war, receiving medals from three governments for bravery under fire: the *MEDAGLIA D'ARGENTO* from the Italian government; the VICTORIA CROSS (V.C.) from the British government; and the DISTINGUISHED SERVICE CROSS (D.S.C.) and the SILVER STAR from his own government.

The 50-year-old soldier ready for retirement is in love with RENATA, the 18-year-old Italian contessa who also loves him. She "compromises" her reputation by going to his hotel room in Venice, even if only for conversation. The sexual relationship is ambiguous, although some sort of sexual activity occurs beneath a blanket in a gondola.

In World War I Cantwell had been wounded near FOSSALTA, an Italian town along the PIAVE RIVER northeast of VENICE, and he remembers returning to the place of his wounding and leaving a "memorial." It was easy to find because the place was at a bend in the river, "where the heavy machine gun post had been," and where "the crater was smoothly grassed." He "relieved himself in the exact place where he had determined, by triangulation, that he had been badly wounded thirty years before." It was the "big fifteenth of June offensive in eighteen" (which sets the date of the novel at 1948). He sees that the grass there now grows green with the "iron" he had deposited, plus "Gino's leg, both of Randolfo's legs, and my right kneecap."

He is moody throughout the novel with nearly everyone except Renata. Early in the story, for example, as he and Jackson drive toward Venice, the driver thinks to himself, "He sure is a mean son of a bitch, . . . and he can be so God-damn nice." At Cantwell's death at the end of the novel, Jackson opens Cantwell's note requesting that in the event of his death the painting of Renata and his two shotguns should be returned to the GRITTI PALACE HOTEL in Venice. But Jackson thinks to himself, "They'll return them all right, through channels." It is the driver's moment of revenge on the colonel for the times when he has demanded that things be done "by the numbers."

Cantwell spends Sunday, the day of the novel and the last day of his life, thinking about the most important things that had occurred during his life, especially the events of the past two days. He particularly focuses on his love for Renata and what may happen to her after his death. Cantwell, a military officer accustomed to having everything in order, of doing everything by regulations, and knowing that the fatal heart attack may come at any moment, spends the last hours of his life doing something he loves, duck hunting at the mouth of a beautiful river, while reviewing his attempts to leave things in order with the people he cares most about, especially with Renata.

The "order" that the army has demanded of him throughout his career aids Cantwell as he attempts to maintain his dignity in the face of impending death.

Capa, Robert (1913–1954) Born Endre Friedman in Budapest, he did not change his name to Robert Capa until 1936, when his first photographs from the Spanish civil war were published in U.S. newspapers. His long and fruitful association with *Life* magazine began in January 1938 with his photographs of the fighting at Teruel. Capa and Hemingway became good friends during the Spanish civil war and World War II, and remained so until Capa's death during the French-Indochina War.

Cap d'Antibes The cap (cape) juts out into the Mediterranean Sea south of Antibes, on the French Riviera. In *To Have and Have Not* it is one of the "good" places, along with Switzerland, about which Helen GORDON reminds her husband, Richard, places they have visited in happier times. She reminds him of this while telling him that their marriage is over.

In *A Moveable Feast* Hemingway writes that in the summer of 1925, while he and Hadley were in Spain, where he started writing *The Sun Also Rises,* the F. Scott Fitzgeralds, whom they had met the spring before, were in Cap d'Antibes and that when the Hemingways saw Scott again in September back in Paris, he was considerably "changed."

capeas Informal bullfight, usually held in a village square with amateurs and aspirant bullfighters taking part. See *Death in the Afternoon.*

"Capital of the World, The" In this short story, a young boy named PACO (2) works as an apprentice waiter in the PENSION LUARCA in Madrid. His two older sisters, who work as chambermaids in the same hotel, had earned enough money to pay his way from their village in the poorest region of Extremadura to Madrid.

He is the youngest of three waiters working in the pension's restaurant, but he loves his work, because it is "done under bright lights, with clean linen, the wearing of evening clothes, and abundant food in the kitchen," and it all "seemed romantically beautiful." He also has a romantic notion about bullfighting, which will, during the evening the story takes place, lead him to his own death.

Of the eight or so people staying at the Luarca, for Paco "the only ones who really existed were the bullfighters." There are three matadors staying there, two picadors, and one "excellent" banderillero. Of the three matadors, one is ill, one has just passed his novice tests, and one is a "coward." The cowardly matador is upstairs trying to seduce Paco's older sister, who is making up the matador's room. In the restaurant, one of the waiters, Ignacio (2), is in a hurry to get to a meeting of the anarcho-syndicalists, a revolutionist group. Paco likes the way IGNACIO talks about the revolution, especially his idea about the "necessity for killing the priests and the Guardia Civil." All of his talk was very romantic-sounding to Paco, who tells him to go on to the meeting, that he will cover for him. ENRIQUE (1), the dishwasher, agrees with Paco that the two of them can finish up.

After the last customers leave, Paco takes a used napkin and pretends to be a matador, swinging his arms in imitation of "a slow sweeping VERONICA. He turned and, advancing his right foot slightly, made the second pass, gained a little terrain on the imaginary bull and made a third pass, slow, perfectly timed and suave." Enrique, who tries to talk Paco out of this dangerous game, finally agrees to use two other napkins to tie meat knives to two legs of a chair in order to play the bull to Paco's matador.

Paco's two sisters, meanwhile, are on their way to see Greta GARBO in *Anna Christie*. The bullfighters and their associates are at the Café Fornos; the first waiter is at his anarcho-syndicalist meeting; and the owner of the Pension Luarca is already asleep, all of this detail meant to set up the scene in the hotel's "deserted dining room."

Paco and Enrique are practicing their bullfighting techniques. In the role of the bull, Enrique moves toward Paco, who "swung the apron just ahead of the knife blade as it passed close in front of his belly and as it went by it was, to him, the real horn. . . . Then the bull turned and came again and, as he watched the onrushing point, he stepped his left foot two inches too far forward and the knife did not pass, but had slipped in as easily as into a wineskin. . . . and Paco slipped forward on the chair, the apron cape still held, Enrique pulling on the chair as the knife turned in him, in him, Paco."

Enrique runs for the all-night first-aid station down the street, but Paco falls to the floor, feeling the "life go out of him as dirty water empties from a bathtub when the plug is drawn." While his sisters are on their way back to the pension, having disliked the movie, Paco dies on the floor of the dining room, "as the Spanish phrase has it, full of illusions."

"The Capital of the World" was first published in *Esquire* (June 1936) as "The Horns of the Bull" and reprinted under its present title in *The Fifth Column and the First Forty-Nine Stories* (1938).

"Capital of the World" (ballet)   Adaptation of the short story for ballet, written by A. E. HOTCHNER and performed in December 1953 at the Metropolitan Opera House in New York.

Caporetto, Battle of   Beginning on October 24, 1917, the 14th Austrian Army—seven divisions and most of the artillery of which were German—attacked the Italian Second Army in the 12th battle for the ISONZO River area of northeastern Italy. The Italians retreated to the west, across the TAGLIAMENTO and Livenza Rivers. By the time the Austrian-German forces were slowed down on the plains north of Venice by outrunning their supply lines, the Italians had lost 40,000 killed or wounded and 275,000 captured; the Austrian army lost 20,000 killed or wounded. Caporetto is now called

Kobarid. Formerly in Austria, it was turned over to Italy in 1919 and then to Yugoslavia in 1947.

In *A Farewell to Arms*, Frederic HENRY and the ambulance drivers under his command are in the retreat from Caporetto, and it is at the bridge crossing the Tagliamento River that Frederic makes his "separate peace" from the war, diving into the river to avoid being shot by the CARABINIERI as an officer who they say has "betrayed" his men. Frederic remembers Caporetto as a "little white town with a campanile in a valley." There was a "fine fountain in the square."

The "Retreat from Caporetto" section of *A Farewell to Arms* was reprinted in the Hemingway-edited book of war stories, *Men at War* (1942).

The battle is mentioned in "A Natural History of the Dead" (in *Death in the Afternoon*) in connection with General von Behr of the Bavarian Alpenkorps, a "damned fine general."

Capracotta   In *A Farewell to Arms* it is the PRIEST (2)'s hometown in the ABRUZZI region of east-central Italy. The priest tells Frederic HENRY that it is forbidden to play the flute at night in Capracotta, because "it was bad for the girls to hear the flute at night."

Capri bianca   Italian white wine, remembered by Frederic HENRY as he fantasizes about Catherine BARKLEY in book 1 of *A Farewell to Arms*. During his convalescence in Milan, he and Catherine had ordered Capri bianca at the GRAN ITALIA restaurant, and they also drank it the evening they spent together in a run-down hotel waiting for his midnight train back to the war front.

It is the wine chosen by RENATA for dinner at the GRITTI PALACE HOTEL restaurant in Venice in *Across the River and Into the Trees*.

In *A Moveable Feast* Hemingway writes of Hadley's memory of a time at Cafe Biffi's in the Galleria in Milan when they had fruit cups of fresh peaches and wild strawberries with cold Capri wine.

Captain of artillery   In *A Farewell to Arms* he prevents Frederic HENRY from getting help in saving a seat on the crowded train in Milan, headed back to the war front.

Captain Ralph   Captain of a RUN-BOAT in the "BIMINI" section of *Islands in the Stream*. The boat carries supplies from Miami to Bimini once a week.

Captain Willie   Charter boat captain in *To Have and Have Not*. He helps Harry MORGAN by taking farther out to sea two government men who have chartered his fishing boat and, when they spot Harry dumping sacks of liquor overboard, want to arrest him for bootlegging. Captain Willie's last name is Adams.

"Captives" Poem about prisoners of war, written about 1920 and first published in Hemingway's first book, *Three Stories & Ten Poems* (1923).

Carabanchel Suburb of Madrid and the site of considerable fighting in the fall and winter of 1936 during the Spanish civil war. A line of Republican defense was established in Carabanchel that held against the Nationalists and insured that the war would last a long time. In *The Fifth Column* Max hides in one of the houses in Carabanchel while waiting to escape back to Madrid.

carabinieri Italian armed policemen, who, in *A Farewell to Arms,* are sent to where thousands of Italian soldiers, retreating from the Battle of CAPORETTO, have converged on a wooden bridge over the TAGLIAMENTO RIVER on the road between UDINE and Pordenone. Frederic HENRY refers to them as "battle police," because they have taken it upon themselves to pull out of the long lines of soldiers the officers, whom they first accuse of desertion and then shoot as betrayers of the Italian cause.

carbolic solution In "The Snows of Kilimanjaro," HARRY, the main character, dies from a scratch on his leg which he fails to protect properly. He forgets to put iodine on it, because he "never" infects, and then, when it gets worse, he uses a "weak carbolic solution when the other antiseptics ran out," and the solution "paralyzed the minute blood vessels and started the gangrene."

Carcassonne Medieval walled city in southern France, about 54 miles southeast of Toulouse. Carcassonne is divided by the Aude River and known as one of the architectural marvels of Europe. It is referred to near the end of *The Garden of Eden*. Catherine BOURNE, in telling her husband, David, that she is leaving the next morning from LA NAPOULE, says that she will "go by Arles and Montpellier" on her way to Carcassonne.

"Cardinal Picks a Winner, The" Article, published in *Ken* (May 5, 1938). It is about an accompanying photograph of dead children in the Spanish civil war, whom, Hemingway reports, the Cardinal did not believe Franco would bomb.

Cardinella, Sam The only named character in the "Chapter 15" vignette of *In Our Time*, one of five men hung "at six o'clock in the morning in the corridor of the county jail." He is so afraid that the guards have to carry him to the gallows. And while they are placing the hood over his head, he loses "control of his sphincter muscle," causing the guards to drop him, "disgusted." Cardinella is "strapped tight" to a chair when the drop falls.

Carlists Militant supporters of the rival claims of the successors of Don Carlos to the Spanish throne. During the SPANISH CIVIL WAR (1936–39) the Carlists joined with the monarchists, the military, and the new Fascist party, the FALANGE, against the Republican government.

Carmel, California Mentioned in *The Sun Also Rises*. It's where Robert COHN backed financially a review of the arts, which he later edited.

Carpenter, Henry One of the YACHTSMEN "haves" in *To Have and Have Not*. He and Wallace Johnston drink scotch and sodas on board *NEW EXUMA II* near where Harry MORGAN's boat is being towed at the end of the novel, but they are unconcerned for anyone but themselves. Carpenter is 38 and "M.A. Harvard"; Johnston is 36, also "M.A. Harvard."

Carpentier, Georges (1894–1975) French boxer, who won the light heavyweight championship of the world in 1920, knocking out Battling Levinsky in four rounds. He lost to Jack Dempsey the next year in a fight for the heavyweight championship. See Hemingway's article "Carpentier vs. Dempsey."

"Carpentier vs. Dempsey" Article, published in *The Toronto Star Weekly* (October 30, 1920), reprinted in *Ernest Hemingway: Dateline Toronto* (1985). The headline in the *Star Weekly* was "Carpentier Sure to Give Dempsey Fight Worth While." Hemingway believes that Carpentier "has a most excellent chance to defeat Dempsey" in their heavyweight championship fight the next year. U.S. newspaper editorial writers, however, believe that "Dempsey will hit him once and it will all be over." Dempsey did, in fact, beat Carpentier in Jersey City, New Jersey, notable as the first fight to gross more than $1 million in gate receipts.

"Car Prestige" Article, published in *The Toronto Star Weekly* (May 1, 1920), reprinted in *Ernest Hemingway: Dateline Toronto* (1985). The headline in the *Star Weekly* was "Keeping Up with the Joneses, the Tragedy of the Other Half." The Toronto social system seems to be "divided into those with [motorcars] and those without. To those with, those without are the Other Half."

Carso, the Northern Italian plateau between Trieste and Monfalcone along the Adriatic Sea. There was a battlefront on the Carso during WORLD WAR I, where, according to Frederic HENRY in *A Farewell to Arms,* the Italians lost 40,000 men.

Nick ADAMS, in "A Way You'll Never Be," asks the adjutant if he had been, "by any chance, on the Carso?"

"Cars Slaying Toronto's Splendid Oak Trees"   Article, published under the byline "Peter Jackson," published by *The Toronto Star Weekly* in the fall of 1923, reprinted in William Burrill's *Hemingway: The Toronto Years* (1994). It was "discovered" by Burrill in the Hemingway Collection at the John F. Kennedy Library in Boston. It is about automobile pollution killing the great old oak trees in Toronto's High Park. Hemingway used the Peter Jackson pen name on one other story for the *Star Weekly,* "Wild Gastronomic Adventures of a Gourmet."

carta del oro   According to the narrator of *To Have and Have Not* it is the "best" Bacardi rum at FREDDIE'S PLACE.

carts   The narrator of the "Chapter 2" vignette of *In Our Time* observes that during the Greek army evacuation of ADRIANOPLE the "carts were jammed for 30 miles along the KARAGATCH ROAD" between Adrianople and Karagatch.

Caruso, Enrico (1873–1921)   Italian tenor, famous for singing more than 50 operatic roles, mostly in Italian and French operas; he sang in many operas at the New York City Metropolitan Opera between 1903 and 1920. In *A Farewell to Arms,* Frederic HENRY's officer friends ask him to bring back from his military leave some phonograph records of Caruso.

In "Fathers and Sons," Nick ADAMS reads that Caruso had been arrested for MASHING.

Casablanca   Name given to the dock area and the heights above it, just across the harbor from Havana, Cuba. At the point of his worst pain in holding onto the marlin, SANTIAGO, in *The Old Man and the Sea,* remembers a hand-wrestling match he had with a "great negro from Cienfuegos" in the tavern of Casablanca. The fight lasted "one day and one night" and was finally won by Santiago, "who was not an old man then but was Santiago *El Campeón*" (the champion).

Casals, Pablo (1876–1973)   Spanish cellist, composer, and conductor, mentioned in *Across the River and Into the Trees.* RENATA's speaking voice reminds Richard CANTWELL of Casals playing the cello.

Castile   Region of north-central Spain, mentioned in *The Sun Also Rises* because of its bull-breeding ranch that supplies some of the bulls for the Fiesta SAN FERMÍN in PAMPLONA. The region is traditionally divided into "Old Castile," comprising the provinces of Avila, Burgos, Logroño, Santander, Segovia, and Soria, and "New Castile," the provinces of Ciudad Real, Cuenca, Guadalajara, Madrid, and Toledo.

cat (1)   In "Old Man at the Bridge," the old man takes care of two goats, a cat, and four pairs of pigeons.

cat (2)   The cat of "Cat in the Rain." The American wife sees it under a table, trying to stay dry, but when she goes outside her hotel to find it, it is gone.

cat (3)   At the end of "Cat in the Rain," it is a big tortoise-shell cat that the American wife gets, rather than the one she had seen out her hotel window in the rain.

cat (4)   Near the end of *The Old Man and the Sea* a cat passes SANTIAGO "on the far side" of the road as the old man walks to his shack after leaving the skeleton of his marlin at the town dock.

Catalan *cardel*   Heavyweight fishing line, used by SANTIAGO in *The Old Man and the Sea.* In order to avoid tangled lines after hooking the marlin, Santiago cuts away "two hundred fathoms of good Catalan *cardel* and the hooks and leaders."

cathedral (1)   In Bayonne, France, probably the Cathédrale Sainte-Marie, known in the 1920s, because of its Gothic beauty, as the Notre-Dame-de-Bayonne. Jake BARNES and Robert COHN take a "look" at the cathedral on a morning walk in *The Sun Also Rises.*

cathedral (2)   In Pamplona, referred to by Jake BARNES in *The Sun Also Rises* as the "great brown cathedral."

Cather, Willa (1873–1947)   American novelist of the early 20th century and subject of some Hemingway parody in *The Torrents of Spring.* The narrator criticizes Cather for writing about war in her Pulitzer Prize–winning novel *One of Ours* (1922), "where all the last part of it was taken from the [movie] action in the *Birth of a Nation,* and ex-servicemen wrote to her from all over America to tell her how much they liked it."

Catherine Barkley   See Catherine BARKLEY.

Catherine Bourne   See Catherine BOURNE.

Catholicism   Although Hemingway once wrote that he was a man of "no religion" and that a writer could not afford to show politics or religion in his writings, Hemingway converted to Catholicism and went to mass, especially during his years with Pauline Pfeiffer, a devoted Catholic, in KEY WEST.

"Cat in the Rain"   Short story about the loneliness of a young American woman, staying with her husband at a hotel in an unnamed Italian town on the Mediterranean Sea, the two of them the only Americans at the hotel.

She is bored, especially because her husband, GEORGE (2), is not paying much attention to her. It is raining, and, when she sees a cat under a table outside the hotel, trying to avoid getting wet, she tells her hus-

EH with Christopher Columbus at the Finca Vigía. (Courtesy of the John F. Kennedy Library.)

smooth"; she wants a "kitty to sit on [her] lap"; she wants to "eat at a table with [her] own silver . . . [and] candles"; she wants "it to be spring"; she repeats that she wants a "kitty"; and she wants "some new clothes."

At the end of the story, the maid brings a "big tortoise-shell cat" to the room and offers it to the wife. The maid tells her that the hotel owner had asked her to bring the cat to the "Signora." The story is an example of Hemingway's use of his THEORY OF OMISSION. The word "lonely" is not used, for example, perhaps because the wife herself doesn't realize that it is because she is lonely that she wants the cat (or any of the other things she "wants"). Nor is there any overt suggestion that the wife is dissatisfied with the marriage, although her desire for the cat and her husband's inattention suggest that.

"Cat in the Rain" was first published in *In Our Time* (1925).

cats, eleven Belonging to Thomas HUDSON in the "Cuba" section of *Islands in the Stream*. They are important companions to Hudson, especially after the death of his three sons. The names of the 11 cats are "Boise," "Goats," "Princessa," "Uncle Woolfie," "Willy," "Friendless," "Friendless's Brother," "Littless," "Furhouse," "Fats" ("El Gordo"), and "Taskforce." See under individual name.

Cavalcanti One of the "priest-baiters" in Frederic HENRY's Italian military unit in book 1 of *A Farewell to Arms*.

cavaliere ufficiale Richard CANTWELL's title, in *Across the River and Into the Trees*, for the manager of the GRITTI PALACE HOTEL in VENICE, in this case probably meaning "official gentleman."

cave In the Guadarrama Mountains near SEGOVIA in *For Whom the Bell Tolls*. It is where PABLO's guerrilla fighters are camped in preparation for their partizan work for the Spanish Loyalists. The novel's main character, Robert JORDAN, stays with them there while he prepares to blow up a nearby bridge.

caviar There are various kinds of fish eggs called caviar, but it is sturgeon eggs that David BOURNE gets in the kitchen of the hotel in LA NAPOULE where he and Catherine stay during the late summer, in *The Garden of Eden*.

Cayo Antón Island (at 22°26′ N; 78°05′ W) between Cayo Mégano Grande and Cayo Paredon Grande along Cuba's northeast coast, where Thomas HUDSON and his crew anchor offshore to search the island for members of a German submarine crew. They discover that the Germans had been there and had picked up a Cuban

band that she wants to go down and get it. He offers to go down but easily accepts her rejection of the idea, and goes on reading.

The wife likes the owner of the hotel, "an old man and very tall," who sends the maid with an umbrella to go outside with the wife. But when they get to the table the cat is gone. The wife "was suddenly disappointed." She realizes, now, how much she wanted the cat: "Oh, I wanted it so much. I wanted a kitty." George puts down his book when she returns to the room and, when she tells him the cat was gone and how much she wanted it, he wonders where the cat went but then picks up his book again.

She sits in front of the mirror and wonders aloud if it would be a good idea to let her hair grow out. George likes her hair the way it is. But she tells him that she's tired of looking like a boy, indicating to him how short her hair is. Then she begins to state all the other things she wants. She wants to "pull [her] hair back tight and fisherman as a guide. Note: For this island and the 12 following island-entries, see the map in Appendix I.

Cayo Coco   Large island in the Cuban Archipiélago de Camagüey off the northeast Cuban coast, searched by Thomas HUDSON and his crew during their attempt to find a German submarine crew. They search at Puerto Coco, a bay on the island (at 22°33′ N; 78°28′ W).

Cayo Confites   Island off the northeast coast of Cuba (at 22°11′ N; 77°49′ W), one of several islands Thomas HUDSON and his crew search in May 1944, looking for a German submarine crew. There's a radio station on the island, and Hudson hopes to send a radio message to Guantánamo to report on his progress. Hudson "saw the high lookout post on the sandy key and the tall signalling mast."

Cayo Contrabando   Cuban island between CAYO GUILLERMO and the west end of CAYO COCO, where, in *Islands in the Stream,* Thomas HUDSON and his crew close in on a German submarine crew they're searching for in May 1944.

After running his boat aground and waiting for the high tide to free it, Hudson motors around the point of Contrabando in the boat's dingy, and passes through the channel that separates it from "No Name Key" and other small keys. They see the turtle boat the Germans had stolen from Cuban fishermen, lying with her bow close to the shore and covered with new-cut mangrove branches.

Cayo Cruz   Long, narrow island off the northeast coast of Cuba (at 22°15′ N; 77°49′ W), just a few miles east of CAYO ROMANO, near the Old Bahama Channel. It's one of the islands where Thomas HUDSON and his crew think a German submarine crew they're looking for may have landed. Hudson anchors "in the lee" of the island.

Cayo Francés   Island off the northeast coast of Cuba, at the northwest end of the Archipiélago de Camagüey. It's from Cayo Francés that search planes "should" be flying, according to Thomas HUDSON, looking for German submarines in the "At Sea" section of *Islands in the Stream.*

Cayo Guillermo   Island off the northeast coast of Cuba (at 22°36′ N; 78°40′ W), one of several islands Thomas HUDSON and his crew search in May 1944, looking for a German submarine crew. It is south and west of Puerto Coco in the Romano island chain.

Cayo Guinchos   Tiny island (at 22°45′ N; 78°07′ W), about 50 miles north of the west end of Cayo Romano off the Cuban northeast coast just onto the Great

Bahama Bank. In the "At Sea" section of *Islands in the Stream,* Thomas HUDSON receives reports that airplanes sank a German submarine off Guinchos two weeks ago, and Hudson and his crew are searching for the German crew members through the islands along the Archipiélago de Camagüey.

Cayo Lobos   On the Great Bahama Bank, Cayo Lobos is an island about 40 miles off the Cuban coast, northeast of CAYO ROMANO. It is one of the islands where, in the "At Sea" section of *Islands in the Stream,* Thomas HUDSON thinks a German submarine crew may have gone.

Cayo Mégano   Small island off the north coast of Cuba (at 22°20′ N; 77°55′ W), officially named Cayo Mégano Grande. It is searched by Thomas HUDSON and his boat crew, looking for the crew of a German submarine.

Cayo Paredón Grande   Small Cuban island just off the north end of CAYO ROMANO. In the "At Sea" section of *Islands in the Stream* the island is "approximately twenty degrees off the port bow" of Thomas HUDSON's boat as it heads north from CAYO CRUZ, searching for a German submarine crew. There is a lighthouse on the north end of the island (at 22°29′ N; 78°10′ W), and Hudson thinks the keeper may have seen the turtle boat the Germans have stolen in their escape.

Cayo Romano   The main, long island in the Archipiélago de Camagüey off the northeast coast of Cuba. In the "At Sea" section of *Islands in the Stream* Thomas HUDSON and his crew search through the islands along the northeast side of Romano for a German submarine crew. There's an old house on the island and a "tall old-fashioned light," but it is almost uninhabitable now because of the insects.

It reminded Hudson of earlier times when he had known the island well, but now it was "there at its barest and most barren, jutting out like a scrubby desert . . . It was a wonderful key when the east wind blew day and night and you could walk two days with a gun and be in good country. It was country as unspoiled as when Columbus came to this coast. Then, when the wind dropped, the mosquitoes came in clouds from the marshes . . . and they could bleed a man to death."

Cayo Sal   Island/cape off the southeast coast of Cuba (at 20°00′ N; 75°52′ W), where a blimp was shot down, according to reports Thomas HUDSON has received in his search for a German submarine crew in *Islands in the Stream.* Hudson and his fishing-boat crew are searching north of the Cuban coast for the Germans.

Cecilia, Sister   The nun in "The Gambler, the Nun, and the Radio." She provides Mr. FRAZER with news of Cayetano RUIZ, the Mexican beet worker who has been shot and brought to the hospital where Sister Cecilia works and where Mr. Frazer is a patient with a broken leg. She tells him that she wants to be a saint. "Ever since I was a little girl I've wanted to be a saint. When I was a girl I thought if I renounced the world and went into the convent I would be a saint." When Mr. Frazer, trying to encourage her, says, "Of course you'll be a saint," she says, "No, probably I won't be. But, oh, if I could only be a saint! I'd be perfectly happy."

Ceggia Town in northern Italy, which Richard CANTWELL tells his driver about in *Across the River and Into the Trees,* particularly for its campaniles.

ceiba tree Outside the bedroom window at the FARM near Havana where Thomas HUDSON lives alone, particularly mentioned in the "Cuba" section of *Islands in the Stream.* He sees the shadow of its branches on the walls of his room when he can't sleep.

celery *rémoulade* Side dish at lunch for David and Catherine BOURNE at GRAU DU ROI, in *The Garden of Eden.* Rémoulade is a cold sauce made with mayonnaise and various condiments and herbs, in this case mixed with celery root. It goes with the sea bass David has caught, and they have it with radishes and pickled mushrooms.

Cendrars, Blaise (1887–1961) French poet associated with cubism, dadaism, and surrealism. In *A Moveable Feast* Hemingway writes that although a number of poets met regularly at the Closerie des Lilas, Cendrars was the only one he ever saw there. He had a "broken boxer's face" and a "pinned-up empty sleeve."

cendre French for "ash-colored," which, in *The Garden of Eden,* is the color of Catherine BOURNE's hair when she returns to LA NAPOULE from spending the morning with the coiffeur in CANNES.

Central Highway In Cuba, mentioned in the "Cuba" section of *Islands in the Stream.* It runs the length of Cuba, from Guane, near the southwest end, to Guantánamo at the eastern end.

Cervantes, Miguel de (1547–1616) Spanish novelist and poet, best known for *Don Quixote de la Mancha* (part 1 published in 1605; part 2 in 1615). In *Death in the Afternoon* Hemingway compares the art of bullfighting to the art of painting or writing, and the two Spanish writers he mentions are Cervantes and Lope de VEGA (Hemingway spelled it "da Vega").

Cesare One of the "priest-baiters" in Frederic HENRY's Italian military unit in book 1 of *A Farewell to Arms.*

Cézanne, Paul (1839–1906) French painter. His painting of "The Bathers" is remembered by Thomas HUDSON as he watches his crew bathe on the stern of his boat off of CAYO ANTÓN in the "At Sea" section of *Islands in the Stream.* But then he thought he would rather have Thomas EAKINS paint it, instead of Cézanne.

In *A Moveable Feast* Hemingway says that it's better to see paintings when you are hungry and that he "learned to understand Cézanne much better and to see truly how he made landscapes when he [Hemingway] was hungry."

Cézanne country Area around Aix-en-Provence in southern France is called "Cézanne country" by Catherine BOURNE in *The Garden of Eden,* because it looks like some of Cézanne's paintings.

Châlon-sur-Saône Town in France, south of Dijon, where Hemingway and Fitzgerald stayed on their way back to Paris from Lyon. They stopped there because it was raining, and Fitzgerald's car had no top.

Chambertin Wine, mentioned in *Across the River and Into the Trees,* that the unnamed wine offered to Richard CANTWELL and RENATA at the GRITTI PALACE HOTEL in Venice "is not." Chambertin is one of the most celebrated vineyards in the world, situated in the commune of Gevrey-Chambertin, in Burgundy's Côte d'Or region of France. In other words, the wine given to Cantwell and Renata at one of Venice's most expensive hotels is a disappointment. They wish for the Chambertin.

The vineyard is also mentioned in *Death in the Afternoon* in a comparison Hemingway makes between acquiring a taste for good wine and acquiring a taste for bullfights.

Chambery cassis Cassis is a black-currant liqueur. When David and Catherine BOURNE first meet MARITA and her friend NINA during a lunch in Cannes, in *The Garden of Eden,* David notices that Nina orders the cassis, while Marita, the "handsome one," orders a *fine à l'eau* (brandy and water).

Champagne Region in northeast France, known best because of its production of champagne, but it was also the setting for the second battle of the Marne (July 15–17, 1918) in WORLD WAR I. It is one of the places mentioned in "Soldier's Home" where Harold KREBS fought with the U.S. Marines. "Champagne" is an obsolete word meaning "battlefield."

Champagne is also where the drunken soldiers are headed in the "Chapter 1" vignette of *In Our Time.*

"Champs d'Honneur" Poem about the death of soldiers, written about 1920. It was first published in *Poetry* magazine (January issue, 1923) and then again in Hemingway's first book, *Three Stories & Ten Poems* (1923).

"Changed Beliefs"   Article, published in *The Toronto Star Weekly* (November 24, 1923), reprinted in *Ernest Hemingway: Dateline Toronto* (1985). It is about Hemingway's changed attitude toward Canada with a list of 10 beliefs he has changed. It is signed "A Foreigner."

Chantilly   Racetrack in Chantilly, France, about 24 miles north of Paris. Mentioned in "My Old Man."

Chaplin, Dunc (1894–1988)   Duncan Dunbar Chaplin, Jr., a baseball pitcher at Princeton (class of 1917) and a friend of F. Scott Fitzgerald's. According to Hemingway in *A Moveable Feast,* Chaplin was with Fitzgerald when he and Hemingway first met at the Dingo bar in Paris in April 1925. There is some dispute about this story, however, since Chaplin denied that he was in Paris in 1925 both to Fitzgerald biographer Matthew Bruoccoli and in a story in the *Princeton Alumni Weekly* (June 6, 1964).

"Chapter 1"   First of 16 vignettes of *In Our Time* (1925); it was first published in *Little Review* (Spring 1923), and then as "chapter 1" of *in our time* (1924). All of the vignettes were experiments in writing short, declarative sentences, something Hemingway had learned while a reporter on *The Kansas City Star.* Most of the vignettes are single paragraphs and appear as interchapters in *In Our Time.* The first 15 interchapters are listed below with the chapter numbers used in the more accessible book, *In Our Time.* The 16th is titled "L'ENVOI."

"Chapter 1" is between the short stories "On the Quai at Smyrna" and "Indian Camp" and is 112 words long. It is about a World War I incident of drunken soldiers walking along a road in the dark toward the Champagne region east of Paris and an adjutant trying to get the narrator, a "kitchen corporal," to put out his fires, even though the unit is 30 miles from the front.

"Chapter 2"   Vignette (131 words), which appeared first in *Little Review* (Spring 1923) and then in *in our time* (1924) as "chapter 3"; it was published as an interchapter between the short stories "Indian Camp" and "The Doctor and the Doctor's Wife" of *In Our Time* (1925). The short sentences (barely 10 words each on average) are meant to enhance the tension described by the evacuation of refugees from ADRIANOPLE during the Greek-Turkish War in 1922. The Greek cavalry is directing traffic west along the KARAGATCH ROAD, and the narrator describes the chaos of that retreat, including a woman having a baby in one of the carts.

"Chapter 3"   Vignette (75 words), which pictures a moment in a World War I battle at Mons, Belgium. The I-narrator describes how "we," the soldiers he is with, shot—"potted," he calls it—a German soldier climbing over a wall in a garden they are in. The piece was first published in *Little Review* (Spring 1923), and then in *in our time* (1924) as "chapter 4."

"Chapter 4"   Vignette (106 words), which appears between the short stories "The End of Something" and "The Three-Day Blow" in *In Our Time* (1925). The scene takes place on an unidentified battlefield/bridge between unidentified armies, though it is probably a World War I battle, and the "we"-narrator is probably British. The soldiers on the narrator's side have set up "an absolutely perfect barricade across the bridge. . . . It was absolutely topping." They "potted" (shot) the enemy soldiers who tried to get over the "old wrought-iron grating" barricade, and then their officers "worked on it" to try to get it out of the way. The narrator says that he and his comrades were "frightfully put out" when the enemy retreated. The short piece was first published in *Little Review* (Spring 1923), and then in *in our time* (1924) as "chapter 5."

"Chapter 5"   Vignette (129 words), placed between "The Three-Day Blow" and "The Battler" in *In Our Time* (1925). It is about the execution by firing squad of six cabinet ministers. The setting is vague. The ministers are shot against a hospital wall, and no names or nationalities are mentioned.

Historically, the scene is probably taken by Hemingway from the actual shooting of six Greek cabinet ministers, ordered by Colonel Nicholas PLASTIRAS, one of the Greek military leaders who had forced King Constantine to abdicate on September 27, 1922. Hemingway's fictional description of the scene is vivid. Five of the ministers stand "very quietly against the wall." But the sixth is sick, and when "they" fire the "first volley" he is "sitting down in the water with his head on his knees." The vignette was first published in *Little Review* (Spring 1923), and then in *in our time* (1924) as "chapter 6."

"Chapter 6"   Vignette (172 words). NICK and his friend RINALDI (1) are badly wounded during World War I. Rinaldi may be dead, and Nick is sitting against the wall of a church "where they had dragged him to be clear of machine-gun fire in the street." Rinaldi is face down against the wall. The bombed house across the street has a bedstead hanging out the front side. Two Austrian dead are in the shadow of the house, lying in the rubble.

Nick expects the stretcher bearers to show up momentarily. Meanwhile, he declares a "separate peace" and talks to Rinaldi about it. "Not patriots," he says. But Rinaldi is a "disappointing audience." This is the only one of the 16 vignettes with Nick as a character.

This sketch appears between "The Battler" and "A Very Short Story" in *In Our Time* (1925). It was first published in *in our time* (1924) as "chapter 7."

"Chapter 7" Vignette (135 words) about a soldier in northern Italy, scared badly from the battle he's in and praying to Jesus to save him from being killed. He promises Jesus that if He keeps him safe, he will "do anything [Jesus] asks." But when the shelling moves "further up the line," and the sun comes up the next morning and he's back in Mestre (near Venice) that night, he doesn't tell the prostitute he goes with about Jesus, and "he never told anybody."

This sketch appears between "A Very Short Story" and "Soldier's Home" in *In Our Time* (1925). It was first published in *in our time* (1924) as "chapter 8."

"Chapter 8" Vignette (139 words) concerns two Hungarians who rob a cigar store in an unnamed city, but it is mainly about two bigoted police officers, one of whom shoots the robbers in cold blood because he thinks they are Italians ("wops"). Officer DREVITTS is "frightened" by the killings, but Jimmy BOYLE says, "They're crooks, ain't they? . . . They're wops, ain't they?" And when Drevitts asks him how he knew they were "wops," Boyle says, "I can tell wops a mile off." But it turns out that they're not Italian; they're Hungarian.

The vignette appears between "Soldier's Home" and "The Revolutionist" in *In Our Time* (1925). It was first published in *in our time* (1924) as "chapter 9."

"Chapter 9" Vignette (139 words) about a bullfight afternoon in which the first two matadors are badly hurt, and the third matador, named the "Kid," has to kill five of the six bulls, "because you can't have more than three matadors." (The reader must infer that one of the first two matadors kills his first bull.) "The Kid" is so tired by the fifth bull that he can't "get the sword in." He finally makes it after at least five tries, and he sits down in the sand and throws up. His handlers hold a cape over him while the crowd "hollered and threw things down into the bull ring."

This vignette is placed between "The Revolutionist" and "Mr. and Mrs. Elliot" in *In Our Time* (1925). It was first published in *Little Review* (Spring 1923), and then in *in our time* (1924) as "chapter 2."

"Chapter 10" Vignette (119 words) that focuses on a horse that has been gored by a bull, its "entrails [hanging] down in a blue bunch." The picador riding the horse tries to get the horse's attention again, kicking in his spurs while the monos (bull ring servants) whack him on the back of the legs, blood pumping "from between the horse's front legs." At the end, the bull "could not make up his mind to charge" again.

Chapter 10 was first published in *in our time* (1924) as "chapter 12" and was reprinted in *In Our Time* (1925) as an interchapter between "Mr. and Mrs. Elliot" and "Cat in the Rain."

"Chapter 11" Vignette (136 words). A bullfighter performs so badly that the crowd comes over the barrera after him, and two men hold him while a third cuts off his pigtail, signifying that he is no longer a bullfighter. He gets drunk that night and admits that "I am not really a good bullfighter."

This vignette was published in *in our time* (1924) as "chapter 13" and reprinted as "Chapter 11" in *In Our Time*, placed between "Cat in the Rain" and "Out of Season."

"Chapter 12" Vignette (189 words). It presents a vivid description of the final moments in a bullfight, this one with the matador VILLALTA performing in the classical manner and killing cleanly. This is a particularly interesting vignette, because the style of this 1923 writing experiment may be recognized in later Hemingway fiction. There are 18 verbs, for example, in the 189-word piece, only one of which is a to-be verb; and there are seven ABSOLUTE CONSTRUCTIONS, a stylistic mannerism that Hemingway used often in later fiction.

Here is an example of a series of absolutes from the end of the first paragraph: "Then he cursed the bull, flopped the muleta at him, and swung back from the charge *his feet firm, the muleta curving* and at each swing *the crowd roaring*." The italics identify the absolutes.

The vignette was first published as "chapter 14" in *in our time* (1924) and as an interchapter in *In Our Time* (1925), placed between "Out of Season" and "Cross-Country Snow."

"Chapter 13" Vignette (282 words). Two bullfighters, the narrator and MAERA (1), try to get a third bullfighter, LUIS (1), to stop drinking and dancing with the riau-riau dancers, return to the hotel, and prepare for the afternoon's bullfighting. They are unsuccessful, and Maera complains because he knows that he and the narrator will have to kill Luis's bulls for him, "after he gets a [COGIDA]" (after he is gored by one of the bulls).

This is one of the longest of the vignettes, and it is placed between "Cross-Country Snow" and "My Old Man" in *In Our Time* (1925). It was first published as "chapter 15" in *in our time* (1924).

"Chapter 14" Vignette (206 words). This is a bullfight story describing the death of a matador who feels the bull's horn go all the way through him into the sand. "Some one" finally gets the bull by the tail, they pick up the bullfighter, MAERA (2), and run with him to the infirmary. A doctor finally arrives from the corral where he has been "sewing up picador horses." Maera feels death coming, and then "he was dead."

The piece was first published as "chapter 16" in *in our time* (1924) and then reprinted as an interchapter in *In Our Time* (1925), placed between "My Old Man" and "Big Two-Hearted River, Part I."

"Chapter 15" Vignette (275 words) describing the hanging of five men "at six o'clock in the morning in the corridor of the county jail." One of the men, Sam CARDINELLA, is so weakened from thinking about being hanged that the guards have to carry him to the gallows where they place him in a chair on the scaffold, and he is left sitting there "strapped tight" when the drop falls.

It was first published as "chapter 17" in *in our time* (1924) and then reprinted in *In Our Time* (1925), placed between parts 1 and 2 of "Big Two-Hearted River."

"Chapter Heading" Poem about "longer thoughts," written in 1921 and first published in *Poetry* magazine (January issue, 1923) and again in Hemingway's first book, *Three Stories & Ten Poems* (1923). It was also selected for publication in *Best Poems of 1923* (1924).

Charlevoix Town in northern Michigan between Lake Charlevoix and Lake Michigan, referred to as "Voix" by NICK and BILL (1) in "The Three-Day Blow." It is where Nick had planned to stay "all winter" in order to be near his girlfriend Marge—that is, until they break up (in "The End of Something").

Charlevoix, Lake Large lake in northern Michigan, best known in Hemingway studies for Horton Bay, a small town on the north side, three miles west of Walloon Lake, where the Hemingways built Windemere Cottage in 1899 and where Grace Hemingway built a studio cottage in 1919. Horton Bay is also where Ernest and Hadley Richardson were married on September 3, 1921. Lake Charlevoix is about 12 miles long and from one-and-a-half to two miles wide, with an eight-mile "South Arm." Near the end of the 19th century, lumber companies sent logs to the Lake Michigan ships by way of steamers on Lake Charlevoix.

Charlevoix road Parallel to the shoreline of Little Traverse Bay in northern Michigan, leading south from PETOSKEY, the setting for *The Torrents of Spring*.

Charlie Chaplins The word in Spanish is *"charlotadas,"* meaning comic bullfights. Rafael Dutrus, "Llapisera," organized the fights during the late 1920s and dressed like Charlie Chaplin, the silent film comedian. In Spain Chaplin was known as "El Charlot." According to Barnaby Conrad in *Gates of Fear* (1957) the *charlots,* the slang form of *charlotadas,* are "the worst

form of humor in the world," because they are absurd replicas of the real bullfight. The "charlots" are referred to in "The Undefeated."

Charo One of KARL's trackers and gun bearers in *Green Hills of Africa*. "All RAMADAN he never swallowed his saliva until sunset." He is, according to Hemingway, a "very serious and highly religious" Muslim. He is Karl's "very devout Mohammedan gun bearer."

Charters, James Barman at the Dingo Bar in Paris at 10, rue Delambre (now the Auberge du Centre). Charters wrote a memoir about Montparnasse, titled *This Must Be the Place* (1934), for which Hemingway wrote an "Introduction."

Chartreuse de Parme Novel (*Charterhouse of Parma*) by the French writer STENDHAL, published in 1839; mentioned by Hemingway in *A Moveable Feast*.

Château Margaux In the Médoc district of Bordeaux, one of the finest and most famous vineyards in the world. It produces *premier cru* (first growth) wines, one of only eight French red wines so classified.

Near the end of *The Sun Also Rises* Jake BARNES, trying to relax by himself in Bayonne, France, after a week of eating and drinking in Pamplona, goes to the Café Marinas for dinner and has a bottle of Château Margaux "for company." According to *Wine Spectator* (1996), a bottle of 1924 Château Margaux sold in 1987 for $230. That's not what Jake paid for it in 1925, but his choice of wines reflects his attempt to live his life well.

A Margaux wine is also the wine of choice for Frederic HENRY and Catherine BARKLEY in *A Farewell to Arms,* at the GRAN ITALIA restaurant in Milan.

Châteauneuf du Pape Red wine from the Châteauneuf du Pape village about 11 miles north of Avignon in the Rhône Valley of southern France. Mentioned in several of Hemingway's works, particularly in *A Moveable Feast*.

Chaves Name of a bullfighter for whom Manuel GARCIA, in "The Undefeated," is substituting. The real Chaves, a Spanish bullfighter, is mentioned in *Death in the Afternoon*.

Chekov, Anton Pavlovich (1860–1904) Russian playwright and short-story writer, known for a number of plays, including *The Seagull* (1897 and 1904), *Three Sisters* (1901), and *The Cherry Orchard* (1904).

In *A Moveable Feast* Hemingway states that he borrowed a number of books by Russian writers from Sylvia BEACH's American bookshop, SHAKESPEARE AND COMPANY (1), particularly books by Turgenev, Gogol,

Tolstoi, and Chekov. His name is more commonly spelled Chekhov.

Cherbourg   French town on the English Channel, one of the towns taken by Richard CANTWELL and his men, in *Across the River and Into the Trees*, on their march toward Paris in WORLD WAR II.

Chernex and Fontanivent   Two of the three villages in *A Farewell to Arms* that Frederic HENRY and Catherine BARKLEY walk past on the path from Mr. and Mrs. GUT-TINGEN's house, where they are staying, down the mountain into MONTREUX, Switzerland. Frederic can't remember the name of the third village.

Chesterton, G. K. (1874–1936)   British critic, novelist, and poet, admired by NICK in "The Three-Day Blow"; Nick quotes to BILL (1) a verse of one of Chesterton's poems, "The Flying Inn," which begins: "If an angel out of heaven/Gives you something else to drink, . . ."

"Che Ti Dice La Patria?"   The title of this short story translates as "What do you hear from home?" Although it was first published as nonfiction, Hemingway consid-ered it a short story, including it in *Men Without Women* (1927).

Two men, the story's narrator and his friend, GUY, take a 10-day trip around northern Italy in April 1927 (note dating below) to see if they can "see how things [are] with the country or the people." They drive in an old Ford coupé "from Ventimiglia to Pisa and Florence, across the Romagna to Rimini, back through Forli, Imola, Bologna, Parma, Piacenza and Genoa, to Ventimiglia again." They spend the night in Mentone across the border in France, glad to be out of Fascist Italy.

There are only two places in the story in which the trip's main purpose is mentioned. At one point, Guy says to the narrator, "Do you remember what we came to this country for?" And at the end of the story, that purpose is identified when the narrator says, "Naturally, in such a short trip, we had no opportunity to see how things were with the country or the people." It is Fascist Italy in 1927, and this last line is ironic, because the two characters learn a great deal during their 10-day trip about the influence of Fascism in northern Italy.

The story is divided into three sections, each describ-ing an incident showing the decadence in Italy follow-ing World War I and the rise of Fascism under Mussolini. In the first section, a young man asks them to take him the 12 miles to Spezia (La Spezia), and he is so insistent—offering to ride on the runningboard of the two-seat coupé—that they cannot refuse. He explains that he is a Fascist and so is used to "discom-fort" and to traveling. He is arrogant in his political beliefs and so says only "thanks" when they let him off—for an Italian the "lowest" form of gratitude.

In the second section, titled "A Meal in Spezia," they look for "somewhere simple" for lunch and pick a restaurant where the waitresses double as prostitutes. The narrator tells Guy that "Mussolini has abolished the brothels" and that this is a "restaurant," implying that, because of the ban, the prostitutes had to find a front for their main business. The waitress who waits on the travelers tries to force herself on Guy, who has to beg the narrator to get him out of there.

In the third section, titled "After the Rain," a "big car" splashes a "sheet of muddy water" onto the coupé, another act of arrogant Fascism. There is no heat in the restaurant in Sestri where they stop for lunch, and they eat in their hats and coats, as do the other customers. The narrator reads in a local newspaper about the "SHANGHAI FIGHTING" (which helps to date the story; the "Shanghai massacre," led by Chiang Kai-shek took place in April 1927). And, finally, while they wait for a train to pass, a Fascist on a bicycle tells them he can't read the numbers on their car's license plate. When the narrator cleans the plate, the Fascist asks for 25 lire, raising the "fine" to 50 lire when the narrator com-ments on the "dirty" Italian roads.

All of these incidents are meant to present a picture of "how things were with the country or the people" of northern Italy under Fascism in 1927. This idea is emphasized a bit at the end of the story when, after their 10 days of travel, they spend the night in Mentone, France, which "seemed very cheerful and clean and sane and lovely." The story's title suggests, also sarcasti-cally, that what one might "hear from home" during those days—if one's home is northern Italy—is that things are just fine, thank you; everything is fine.

"Che Ti Dice la Patria?" was first published as an arti-cle titled "Italy—1927" in *The New Republic* (May 18, 1927) and reprinted as a short story.

Chèvre d'Or   Horse at AUTEUIL that Hemingway's wife Hadley bet on at 120 to 1 odds, according to *A Moveable Feast*. The horse fell at the last jump, "with enough savings on him to keep us six months."

Cheyenne   American Indian tribe, mentioned in *The Garden of Eden*. See SIOUX.

Chicago Art Institute   Museum and art school in Grant Park, facing Michigan Avenue, incorporated in 1879. Hemingway visited the museum several times while growing up in Oak Park, a western Chicago sub-urb, and he writes in *A Moveable Feast* about getting his first look at the French impressionists at the Chicago Art Institute.

"Chicago Never Wetter Than Today"   Article, pub-lished in *The Toronto Star Weekly* (July 2, 1921), reprinted in *The Wild Years* (1962), reprinted in *Ernest*

Hemingway: Dateline Toronto (1985). The headline in the *Star Weekly* was "Chicago Never Wetter Than It Is Today." Datelined "Chicago," it is about how little was accomplished in Chicago by passage of the Prohibition amendment. The "explanation is very simple. In Chicago the city police take no part in enforcing the Eighteenth Amendment."

Chicago Tribune, The   Paris edition of the U.S. newspaper, a copy of which is purchased by David BOURNE in *The Garden of Eden.*

Chicago White Sox   Major League baseball team, mentioned in *A Farewell to Arms* as winning the American League pennant. The team was 100-54 in 1917 and defeated the New York Giants in the World Series, four games to two. This reference helps set the time of the novel, because it is the only season between 1913 and 1921 in which the Giants won the National League pennant.

Chicote, Pedro   Proprietor of CHICOTE'S RESTAURANT in Madrid during the 1920s. According to the narrator of "The Denunciation," he was a great bartender and "ran a fine bar."

Chicote's restaurant   In Madrid on the Gran Vía, one of Hemingway's favorite restaurant/bars. In "The Denunciation," it is described: "Chicote's in the old days in Madrid was a place sort of like The Stork [Club, in New York City], without the music and the debutantes, or the Waldorf's men's bar if they let the girls in."

Chicote's is mentioned several times in *The Fifth Column.* Today it's a combination bar and museum.

Chicuelo II (1934–1960)   One of the bullfighters whom Hemingway saw fight during his 1959 travels on the bullfight circuit in Spain in preparation for writing *The Dangerous Summer.* Chicuelo was killed in a plane crash the next year.

Chief Running Skunk-Backwards   A friend of the Negro bartender in the INDIAN CLUB in *The Torrents of Spring.*

chile peppers   Available at BOBBY's cafe and bar on BIMINI in *Islands in the Stream.* According to the novel's narrator, they come stuffed with a choice of salmon, bacalao, Chilean bonito, Mexican turtledoves' breasts, turkey meat, or mole.

"China's Air Needs"   Article, published in *PM* (June 17, 1941), reprinted in *By-Line: Ernest Hemingway* (1967). Datelined "Rangoon," the article argues that China doesn't have enough good pilots to compete

with the Japanese in an air war and that any aid that America gives to the Chinese air force would have to include pilots. This was the sixth of seven dispatches Hemingway wrote for *PM.* The headline read "Ernest Hemingway Says China Needs Pilots as Well as Planes to Beat Japanese in the Air."

"Chinese Build Air Field"   Article, published in *PM* (June 18, 1941), reprinted in *By-Line: Ernest Hemingway* (1967). Datelined "Manila," the article describes Hemingway's initial surprise, even irritation, that the U.S. ambassador to Chungking, Nelson Johnson, would say to him that the Chinese could build a proper airfield for American-built Boeing B17s, the "Flying Fortress," by a specified date—in this case March 30, 1941.

Two days after his interview with Johnson, Hemingway flew to Chengtu in north Szechwan Province to watch the airfield being built. The field was to be "a mile and an eighth long by a little over one hundred fifty yards wide, with a stone-filling and top dressing macadam runway five feet deep." Sixty thousand workers hauled away 286,000 cubic yards of gravel; another 35,000 workers crushed stone "with hand hammers." Szechwan Province by itself provided 100,000 workers, all working 12-hour shifts; there were 5,000 wheelbarrows and 200,000 baskets in use at one time. The chief engineer on the project, Chen Loh-Kwan (a University of Illinois graduate, Hemingway notes), made the deadline.

This was the seventh of seven dispatches Hemingway wrote for *PM.* The headline read "Ernest Hemingway Tells How 100,000 Chinese Labored Night and Day to Build Huge Landing Field for Bombers."

Chink   Friend of Hemingway's; see Eric Edward "Chink" DORMAN-SMITH.

Chink place   Café "uptown in Havana," where Harry MORGAN, in *To Have and Have Not,* can get "a good meal . . . for forty cents." "Chink" is a derogatory term for Chinese.

chinook wind   Warm, dry wind that blows occasionally down the eastern slopes of the Rocky Mountains. It is mentioned several times in *The Torrents of Spring* as affecting the lives of the people of northern Michigan, especially of the novel's main characters.

Chocko's Bar   In PAMPLONA, Spain, where Hemingway and Antonio ORDÓÑEZ spent some time during the fiesta in the summer of 1959 as Hemingway followed the bullfight circuit in preparation for writing *The Dangerous Summer.* The bar is described as "under the arcade outside the hotel Juanito Quintana used to own," a reference to the author's old friend from the

1920s and the hotel that was the prototype for the one where Jake BARNES and his friends stayed (*The Sun Also Rises*).

"Cholly Knickerbocker" Title of a syndicated gossip column in various newspapers during the 1920s and 1930s. In *Islands in the Stream* Audrey BRUCE has read in one of the columns that her friend Roger DAVIS is writing a "great novel." She travels to Bimini in order to see him again.

Chopin Ballade In *The Fifth Column,* Dorothy BRIDGES owns a phonograph record of the "Chopin Ballade in La Bemol Menor, Op. 47" and plays it on the phonograph she has in her hotel room. She also plays a recording of the "Chopin Mazurka in C Minor, Op. 33, No. 4."

Christian imagery Prevailing image in *The Old Man and the Sea.* The novel's main character is named SANTIAGO, which in Spanish means St. James, who, according to the New Testament, was a fisher of men.

During Santiago's two-day struggle to land the 1,500-pound marlin, he places a "sack" over his shoulder where the line is cutting him, and he "suffer[s]" from the pain of holding onto the huge fish, which turns out to be two feet longer than his 16-foot skiff. The old man's "left" hand, which cramps, "had always been a traitor and would not do what he called on it to do and he did not trust it." He thinks it may be a "sin" to kill the marlin, but he reminds himself that he was "born to be a fisherman as the fish was born to be a fish" and that "San Pedro [St. Peter] was a fisherman as was the father of the great DiMaggio."

In pain, he says aloud, "*Ay,*" which is, as the narrator says, "just a noise such as a man might make, involuntarily, feeling the nail go through his hands and into the wood." In fighting the sharks that are eating at the marlin, Santiago's mouth tastes "coppery and sweet." After he brings his skiff back to his home dock, leaving the remains of the marlin tied to it, he climbs the hill to his shack, "and at the top he fell and lay for some time with the mast across his shoulder." And, back in the shack, he "slept face down on the newspapers with his arms out straight and the palms of his hands up."

Santiago's wife, now dead, had decorated their cottage with religious pictures, including one of the "Virgin of Cobre," Cuba's patron saint, whom the old man prays to while undergoing his fight for the great fish.

Christian Science System of religious teachings, based on the Bible, the most important application of which is spiritual, as opposed to medical, healing. Nick's MOTHER (1) in "The Doctor and the Doctor's Wife" reads Christian Science literature.

"Christians Leave Thrace to Turks" Article, unsigned, published in *The Toronto Daily Star* (October 16, 1922), reprinted in *Ernest Hemingway: Dateline Toronto* (1985). The headline in the *Daily Star* was "Tired Christians, and Hungry, Leave Thrace to Turks." Datelined "Constantinople," this is a six-paragraph story about the thousands of Christians leaving Thrace with the Greek army as the Turks move into the city.

Christmas day In "God Rest You Merry, Gentlemen," a 16-year-old boy is brought into the emergency room of a Kansas City hospital, having attempted "self-mutilation." The two doctors in charge, Doc FISCHER and Doctor WILCOX, argue about the significance of the incident occurring on Christmas day.

"Christmas Gift! Christmas Gift!" Scripps O'NEIL in *The Torrents of Spring* remembers hearing children in the South crying this to one another.

"Christmas Gift, The" Article, published in *Look* magazine (April 20 and May 4, 1954), reprinted in *By-Line: Ernest Hemingway* (1967). This two-part article describes two airplane crashes Ernest and Mary were in during a two-day period (January 23 and 24, 1954) in East Africa. The article title refers to Hemingway's failure to find proper Christmas gifts before the near-fatal accidents.

After a three-day sight-seeing flight over the Belgian Congo and the lake region of Central Africa to Murchison Falls, the Cessna 180, in preparing to land, strikes a telegraph wire and is brought down by the pilot, Roy Marsh, into the bush. Mary suffers two broken ribs and shock, but the pilot and Ernest seem to be okay. The next day, taking off from Butiaba where they had gone downriver on the *Murchison*, a boat that had been used in the movie *The African Queen*, the de Havilland *Rapide* caught fire.

Hemingway writes of breaking one of the plane's windows with his head to escape but that he thought he was okay. It turned out that his injuries included a ruptured liver, spleen, and kidney, temporary loss of vision in his left eye, some loss of hearing in his left ear, a crushed vertebra, a sprained right arm and shoulder, a sprained left leg, paralysis of the sphincter, and first-degree burns on his face, arms, and head.

Part 2 of the article describes the painful car ride back to Entebbe and a plane ride then to Nairobi and a hospital. He describes a vice that he "commenced" there, that of "reading of one's own obituaries." He reports that several undeserved good things were said about him but also some inaccuracies, for example a German newspaper that reported that he had attempted to land the plane himself on the summit of Mt. KILIMANJARO.

"Christmas in Paris" Article, published in *The Toronto Star Weekly* with two other Christmas "tales," under the general heading "Christmas on the Roof of the World" (December 22, 1923), and reprinted as a short story in *Two Christmas Tales* (1959).

"Christmas on the Roof of the World" Article, published in *The Toronto Star Weekly* (December 22, 1923), reprinted in *By-Line: Ernest Hemingway* (1967). The article is in three parts: "Christmas on the Roof of the World," "A North of Italy Christmas," and "Christmas in Paris." The latter two parts were reprinted in a booklet titled *Two Christmas Tales* (The Hart Press, Christmas 1959).

Christmas on the Roof of the World Booklet, subtitled "A Celebration in the Swiss Alps," reprinting two articles from *The Toronto Star Weekly*, "Christmas on the Roof of the World" and "A North of Italy Christmas." Published by Redpath Press (1987), illustrated by Etienne Delessert.

Churchill, Sir Winston (1874–1965) British prime minister (1940–45 and 1951–55) best known for his stewardship of Britain during WORLD WAR II. He was also the author of several books, including *The Second World War* (six volumes, 1948–54) and *A History of the English-Speaking Peoples* (four volumes, 1956–58).

Hemingway blamed Churchill for ruining the military career of his good friend Chink DORMAN-SMITH, a British lieutenant general and chief of staff to General Claude Auchinleck during the 1942 African campaign in World War II. General Auchinleck had just won the first battle of Alamein—which turned the tide against the German Afrika Korps—when Churchill arrived in Cairo and demanded that the British troops attack again immediately. Auchinleck and Dorman-Smith talked him out of a second attack, because they were now depending on new, untrained troops. Churchill accepted their advice but relieved them of their command. General Bernard Montgomery replaced Auchinleck and immediately adopted Dorman-Smith's battle plan. Ironically, Montgomery delayed his attack to a later date than Dorman-Smith had recommended.

This episode probably served as the model for Hemingway's *Across the River and Into the Trees* (1950). In it Hemingway's main character, Colonel Richard CANTWELL, had been demoted because he was forced to make an "impossible" attack during a World War II engagement and so lost his regiment "under other people's orders." And Cantwell invents a drink called "MONTGOMERYS," which are "fifteen to one" Martinis, meaning fifteen parts gin or vodka to one part dry vermouth. Cantwell explains that the British Field Marshall wanted fifteen to one odds in his favor before he would attack, and then he would attack "tardily."

Churchill, Winston (1871–1947) U.S. historical novelist, a St. Louis–born graduate of the U.S. Naval Academy, best known for his novels *RICHARD CARVELL* (1899), *The Crisis* (1901), and *The Crossing* (1904), all popular during the first decade of the 20th century.

Church of Frari Santa Maria Gloriosa dei Frari in the Campo San Rocco in VENICE. Behind the corner of the apse Richard CANTWELL hides from "two young men . . . [m]aybe Fascists" whom he suspects are threatening him on his early Saturday morning walk, in *Across the River and Into the Trees*.

C.I.D. Criminal Investigation Department of Britain's Scotland Yard, referred to for their work by U.S. Army Colonel Richard CANTWELL in *Across the River and Into the Trees*.

cigar store In the "Chapter 7" vignette, it is where two Hungarian robbers are shot by one of the two police officers called to the scene because he thinks they're Italian ("wops").

Cinzano Brand name for a common Italian vermouth. In *The Sun Also Rises* Jake BARNES sees a man who is pushing a roller that prints the name on the sidewalk near Jake's office in Paris.

Frederic HENRY sends the porter at the AMERICAN HOSPITAL (1) in Milan for a bottle of Cinzano at a nearby wine shop in *A Farewell to Arms*.

Cipriani, Giuseppe Owner of HARRY'S BAR at 1323 San Marco, Calle Vallaresso in Venice, Italy, which opened in 1931. His son, Arrigo (Harry), became manager upon Giuseppe's retirement. The Cipriani family also owns Harry's Dolci in Venice, Bellini by Cipriani at 777 Seventh Avenue in New York, and Harry Cipriani at 783 Fifth Avenue in New York. Giuseppe Cipriani's first novel was published in 1991, titled *Heloise and Bellinis*. Harry's Bar is mentioned several times in *Across the River and Into the Trees*. Richard CANTWELL was there the day before the novel begins.

Circe Enchantress in Greek mythology who turns men into swine. In *The Sun Also Rises* Robert COHN compares Brett ASHLEY to Circe.

"Circulating Pictures" Article, unsigned, published in *The Toronto Star Weekly* (February 14, 1920), reprinted in *The Wild Years* (1962), and in *By-Line: Ernest Hemingway* (1967). The article is about an agreement between Toronto artists and a group of "young matrons" to rent paintings for six-month periods for 10 percent of each painting's assessed value. At the end of the rental period the painting goes back to the artist, "ready for sale." The *TSW* headline read "Circulating Pictures a New High-Art in Toronto."

This was thought to be Hemingway's first article for the *Star* until William Burrill "discovered" previously unidentified articles in the Hemingway Collection at the John F. Kennedy Library in Boston and published 25 of them in *Hemingway: The Toronto Years* (1994). See "New Ether to Credit of Toronto Surgeon."

"Circus, The" Article, published in *Ringling Bros. and Barnum & Bailey Circus Magazine and Program* (1953). It was the "introduction" to the 1953 circus program.

Cirque de Paris In Paris, at 18-20, avenue de la Motte-Picquet, when Hemingway was there in the 1920s. It was just to the west of the Hôtel des Invalides. The huge, dome-covered circus building straddled what is now the rue Ernest Psichari, with a passage leading to rue Duvivier. Hemingway also saw boxing matches there in the 1920s. The Mascart-Ledoux and Routis-Ledoux fights in particular are mentioned in *Green Hills of Africa*. The Cirque de Paris opened in May 1908; it had been the Cirque Métropole from January 1906 to February 1908. The last circus performance there was on June 15, 1930.

Ciudad Real Spanish town about 200 kilometers south of Madrid. It is one of the places where Antonio ORDÓÑEZ and Luis Miguel DOMINGUÍN fought "mano a mano" on the 1959 bullfight circuit covered by Hemingway in preparation for writing *The Dangerous Summer*.

Cividale Small town in northern Italy, about eight miles north of GORIZIA and about four miles east of UDINE, from which the Germans forced the Italians to retreat west of the TAGLIAMENTO RIVER after the Battle of CAPORETTO. Remembered by Frederic HENRY in *A Farewell to Arms*.

civilian Character in *The Fifth Column*, a member of the FIFTH COLUMN and one of two men captured by Philip RAWLINGS and MAX (2) at the artillery observation post on the Extremadura Road near Madrid. ANTONIO, the Comisario de Vigilancia (commissioner) at the Seguridad headquarters, questions him. As the curtain falls on this third scene of act 3, it is clear that Antonio will torture the civilian in order to get information. The next day's papers report that 300 members of the Fifth Column have been arrested.

Claridge Hotel In Paris at 74, avenue des Champs-Élysées, where, according to Hemingway in *A Moveable Feast*, Ernest WALSH had rented a "long, shiny" car with its uniformed chauffeur, in order for Walsh to visit Ezra Pound and impress two "girls" who were with him.

"Clark's Fork Valley, Wyoming, The" Article, published in *Vogue* (February 1939), reprinted in two *Vogue* books, *Vogue's First Reader* (1942) and *The World in Vogue* (1963), reprinted in *By-Line: Ernest Hemingway* (1967). It's about fly-fishing in September, and hunting mountain sheep or elk later in the fall in Wyoming's Clark's Fork, a branch of the Yellowstone. "It's a good country."

"Class Prophecy" Article for Oak Park and River Forest High School literary magazine, *Senior Tabula* (1917), reprinted in *Hemingway at Oak Park High: The High School Writings of Ernest Hemingway, 1916–1917* (1993). Written in the form of a short story.

Clausewitz, Karl von (1780–1831) Prussian general who wrote books on military science, particularly *On War*, which had a large impact on the military strategy and tactics of later officers of the German army. See "Program for U.S. Realism, A."

"Clean, Well-Lighted Place, A" In this short story an OLD MAN (5) is drinking brandy in the early morning hours at a café, probably in Spain, perhaps in Madrid. He is deaf, and the two waiters decide he may be 80 years old. The younger of the two waiters is in a hurry to get home to his wife and so has very little sympathy for the old man, who had tried to commit suicide the week before. The younger waiter says to him, knowing he can't hear, "You should have killed yourself last week."

The waiters don't know why he tried to kill himself or why he drinks to get drunk, but the older waiter, who lives alone, empathizes with him, preferring as the old man does a well-lighted place late at night. And he doesn't mind staying late at the café where he works, because he knows he won't get to sleep until dawn anyway. When the younger waiter refuses to give the old man "another" brandy, the older waiter asks him what difference another hour makes. The younger waiter says, "More to me than to him," and suggests that the old man can "buy a bottle and drink at home." But, the older waiter says, "It's not the same." The older waiter thinks to himself, "[I]t is the light of course but it is necessary that the place be clean and pleasant." A clean, well-lighted place is always better than home for a man alone.

The older waiter finishes closing up the café and goes to a bar, where he orders a small cup of coffee. But he doesn't like bars and so turns down a second cup and leaves. "A clean, well-lighted café," he believes, "was a very different thing." He starts for home where he knows he will not sleep until daylight. "After all, he said to himself, it is probably only insomnia. Many must have it."

"A Clean, Well-Lighted Place" was first published in *Scribner's Magazine* (March 1933) and reprinted in *Winner Take Nothing* (1933).

Clemenceau, Georges (1841–1929)   French statesman and twice premier (1906–09 and 1917–20). Called "the Tiger." He lived in the United States as a journalist and teacher, 1865–1869, returning to France to help overthrow the empire in 1870.

Hemingway interviewed him in September 1922 for *The Toronto Star,* but the article was rejected by *Star* editors because of Clemenceau's criticism of Canada's support of France during World War I. In another rejected article, written in October 1923, "Lloyd George the Great Survivor," Hemingway writes that following the Paris Peace Conference in 1919 when the "Big Four" statesmen failed to save the world for democracy, only British prime minister David Lloyd George "survives" and that Clemenceau is "a bitter and disillusioned old man."

Both of these articles were "discovered" by William Burrill in the Hemingway Collection at the John F. Kennedy Library in Boston and published in his book, *Hemingway: The Toronto Years* (1994).

"Clemenceau Politically Dead"   Article, published in *The Toronto Daily Star* (February 18, 1922), reprinted in *Ernest Hemingway: Dateline Toronto* (1985). The headline in the *Daily Star* was "Builder, Not Fighter, Is What France Wants." Datelined "Paris," Hemingway is surprised at how soon the French have forgotten what Clemenceau did for them during World War I. But now no one pays any attention to the former "Tiger of France." "The things Clemenceau says have turned sour in the mouths of the people. They do not taste like truth."

clerk (1)   At New York's Shelby Hotel in "Fifty Grand," where Jack Brennan stays the night of his fight with Jimmy Walcott at Madison Square Garden.

clerk (2)   At the U.S. embassy in Havana, in *Islands in the Stream,* ignored by Thomas HUDSON on his way to make his report to the ONI (Office of Naval Intelligence) on his German submarine findings. He ignores the clerk because his mustache is too thin and he has plucked his eyebrows.

clock   In "The Killers" there's a clock "on the wall behind the counter" in HENRY'S LUNCHROOM, where most of the story takes place. There is something of a mystery concerning the clock's significance, because the time of day is mentioned four times during the killers' wait in the lunchroom for Ole Andreson to show up. But the lunchroom owner, George, informs the killers that the clock is 20 minutes fast. So when the narrator tells us, for example, that "George looked up at the clock" and it "was a quarter past six," is it really quarter past six or five minutes before six? The signifi-

cance of this time confusion in "The Killers" has not been explained.

Closerie des Lilas   Café-restaurant at 171, boulevard du Montparnasse in Paris at the corner of boulevard Saint-Michel and boulevard du Montparnasse, frequented often by Hemingway and other writers in the 1920s. In *A Moveable Feast* Hemingway writes of having a beer there, thinking about what Gertrude STEIN had just said to him about his generation being "lost," and thinking also of Marshal Ney, whose statue is at the corner. He says of Closerie des Lilas that it was "one of the best cafés in Paris."

The restaurant is near where Jake BARNES's flat is located over a BAL MUSETTE in *The Sun Also Rises.*

And it is remembered by Thomas HUDSON in *Islands in the Stream* as he thinks about his Paris years in the 1920s.

clouds, cumulus and cirrus   Cumulus clouds are thick, but fluffy-looking, usually isolated, with a dark, horizontal base; cirrus clouds are wispy or feathery-looking and at heights above 20,000 feet. In *The Old Man and the Sea* they are the predominant clouds over the Gulf Stream in September, the time of the story.

club   Carried by Gulf Stream fishermen to subdue the bigger fish pulled alongside a boat, used by SANTIAGO in *The Old Man and the Sea* in his attempt to fight off the sharks as they attack his marlin.

Cluny   Art museum in Paris at the southeast corner of boulevard Saint-Germain and boulevard Saint-Michel, mentioned in *A Moveable Feast* and in *Islands in the Stream.* See EGLISE SAINT-ETIENNE DU MONT.

Clyne, Frances   Robert COHN's "mistress" for three years in *The Sun Also Rises,* before they split up in Paris and she returns to England. She has just received a divorce from her husband after a three-year wait, when Cohn breaks up with her. She tells Jake BARNES about Cohn's "little secretary" on the magazine Cohn backed in Carmel, California. She thinks the secret of the breakup is that Cohn "always wanted to have a mistress, and if he doesn't marry me, why, then he's had one." She is described as "a very tall girl who walked with a great deal of movement." She leaves for England at the end of part 1.

C.N.T.   *Confederacion Nacional de Trabajo,* an anarcho-syndicalist organization that took a leading part in the resistance against the military uprising that led to the Spanish civil war; referred to in *For Whom the Bell Tolls.*

coast, Cuban   In *The Old Man and the Sea,* the north coast of Cuba plays an important role, because it is the only landmark for SANTIAGO, whose skiff is pulled by a marlin first to the northwest and then to the northeast and out of the sight of land. Before he hooks the marlin, "the coast was only a long green line with the gray blue hills behind it." The next time he looks up, it is gone.

Coast Guard   At the KEY WEST Coast Guard base in *To Have and Have Not*. The base was established on Key West in 1846, named after the then U.S. president Zachary Taylor. There had been a U.S. naval station on the island since 1823.

Coast Guard officials confiscate Harry MORGAN's boat when they accuse him of transporting illegal liquor from Cuba to Florida. And as he heads for Cuba with four Cubans who have just robbed a bank, he spots a Coast Guard plane, this time hoping for their help. At the end of the novel, two Coast Guard men dive into the water to rescue Mrs. TRACY, Albert's wife, who has fallen off the dock where Harry's boat is tied.

From Cuba, pilots of Coast Guard planes search for SANTIAGO during the three days of his ordeal with the marlin in *The Old Man and the Sea*.

Coates, Liz   Main character in "Up in Michigan." She is a teenager, perhaps 16 or 17 years old and lives in HORTON BAY. She works at D. J. Smith's restaurant. Mrs. Smith thinks Liz is the "neatest" looking girl she has ever seen. Jim GILMORE works at the blacksmith shop, and Liz likes his way of walking, his mustache, his white teeth, and the fact that he doesn't look like a blacksmith. And she feels "funny" when she sees how white his arms are above his tan line as he washes outside the house.

Liz thinks about him a lot while he's on a deer hunting trip, and she's sure something will happen when he gets back. But when he returns, he gets drunk with his deer hunting friends and, drunk, sexually abuses Liz in an act that would be called at the end of the 20th century "date rape."

She's frightened by his drunken advances, but because she doesn't know what else to do, she lets him take her out to the dock, where she tries to stop him from sexual intercourse but cannot. Afterward, she is "cold and miserable and everything felt gone." It's her first sexual experience, and it isn't what she thought it would be. He falls asleep on top of her, and, after working out from under him, she covers him up with her coat and walks back to the house, while a "cold mist" comes "up through the woods from the bay."

Cobb, Ty (1886–1961)   Major League baseball player, who spent all but the last two years of his 24-year career with the Detroit Tigers and who had a lifetime batting average of .367. When, in *Islands in the Stream*, David asks his brother Andrew if he knows Ty Cobb's lifetime batting average, Andy gets it right.

Cocteau, Jean (1889–1963)   French writer, artist, and filmmaker, known for the surrealism that permeates his films, novels, and plays. He is perhaps best known in the United States for his play *Orphée* (1926) and for his films *Blood of a Poet* (1933) and *Orphée* (1949). In *Death in the Afternoon* Hemingway mentions him as the "literary protector" of the French novelist and poet, Raymond RADIGUET.

Cocteau is referred to as "Mr. Cocteau" in *Islands in the Stream*. Roger DAVIS tells "young Tom" that he had not gotten into the drug trade in Paris because de Quincey and Cocteau had "done so well in it."

cogida   Bullfight term meaning the tossing of a man by the bull. According to Hemingway in his glossary to *Death in the Afternoon*, "*cogida*" means "literally the catching; if the bull catches he tosses." The bullfighter is usually gored by the bull's horn(s).

cognac   French brandy, distilled from wine from the Cognac region and drunk by, among other Hemingway characters, Frederic HENRY in *A Farewell to Arms*.

Cohn, Louis Henry   Hemingway's first bibliographer. Cohn, owner of the bookstore "House of Books" in New York City, compiled *A Bibliography of the Works of Ernest Hemingway* (1931). It includes a description of all the novels, short stories, articles, and poems written by Hemingway and published before the summer of 1930. And it includes a list of the reviews written of Hemingway's major works. Cohn also published, through his "House of Books," a limited edition of *God Rest You Merry, Gentlemen* (1933).

Cohn, Robert   Jake BARNES's 34-year old "Jewish friend" in *The Sun Also Rises*. He was "once middleweight boxing champion of Princeton" and "was a member, through his father, of one of the richest Jewish families in New York, and through his mother of one of the oldest." He was, according to Jake, the novel's narrator, "married by the first girl who was nice to him." He was married for five years, had three children who are not mentioned in the novel again, and lost most of the $50,000 left to him by his father. And, just as he "had made up his mind to leave his wife, she left him and went off with a miniature-painter." Cohn's mother was sending him an allowance of about $300 a month.

He falls in love with Brett ASHLEY at first sight. When he meets her at the BAL MUSETTE, Jake describes him as looking at her "a great deal as his compatriot must have looked when he saw the promised land." Cohn goes to San Sebastian for a week with Brett, much to Brett's later regret, because he can't let her go, even after she makes it clear to him that the fling is over.

Cohn's role in the novel is as a foil for Jake and, later, as a foil for and the butt of much drunken anger by Jake's friends. Jake tells the reader at one point, "Somehow I feel I have not shown Robert Cohn clearly. . . . He had a funny sort of undergraduate quality about him; nothing he ever says stands out. . . . Externally he had been formed at Princeton. Internally he had been moulded by the two women who had trained him."

Because of this role as "foil," Cohn is one of the key characters in the novel. Jake is sarcastic about Cohn in the novel's opening sentence: "Robert Cohn was once middleweight boxing champion of Princeton. Do not think that I am very much impressed by that as a boxing title, but it meant a lot to Cohn." Although they continue to be friends, with regular tennis dates in Paris and mutual social friendships, Jake continues to make sarcastic remarks about him. And at the novel's climax, Cohn finally has taken all he can of Mike CAMPBELL's continual drunken baiting in Pamplona about Cohn's broken-off relationship with Brett and of Jake's sarcasm. He knocks out Jake and knocks down Mike. Then, because of his jealousy of the bullfighter Pedro ROMERO, who has become Brett's new lover, Cohn fights with Romero in his hotel room, leaving him bloody and scarred.

Cohn leaves Pamplona after these fights and, although the reader assumes he goes back to Paris, Jake does not know where he goes and does not bother to guess.

coiffeur (1)   At AIGUES MORTES, France, he cuts Catherine BOURNE's hair. "No decent girls had ever had their hair cut short like that in this part of the country and even in Paris it was rare and strange." It is the beginning of the "change" in Catherine.

The various coiffeurs that Catherine Bourne goes to, and later her husband, David, are key elements in the novel's conflict, because the "change" that takes place in their sexual roles begins with their short haircuts and light hair coloring.

coiffeur (2)   At CANNES, "Monsieur Jean," who cuts Catherine BOURNE's hair in *The Garden of Eden*. The narrator states that Jean is "about David's age," in other words in his mid-20s.

coiffeur (3)   At BIARRITZ, where Catherine BOURNE goes to get her hair cut on her way to Spain with her husband, David, in *The Garden of Eden*.

coiffeur's place   In MONTREUX, Switzerland, where Catherine BARKLEY gets her hair done while waiting to go to a Lausanne hospital for the birth of her baby in *A Farewell to Arms*.

Cojímar   Town about seven miles east of Havana, Cuba, mentioned in *To Have and Have Not*. And although it is not named in *The Old Man and the Sea*, it is probably SANTIAGO's home village.

Cojímar bar   Built "out of the rocks overlooking the harbor" at Cojímar, Cuba, about seven miles east of Havana, one of the places where Thomas HUDSON goes to drink in the "Cuba" section of *Islands in the Stream*.

coleta   Pigtail worn by a bullfighter, which signifies his status as a matador. In "The Undefeated," ZURITO (2) threatens to cut off the coleta of Manuel GARCIA, unless he performs well in the nocturnal for which he has signed a contract. At the end of the story, after Garcia is at first better than expected but then has bad luck and is severely gored, Zurito acts as if he is going to cut off Garcia's pigtail, but then he says he is only "joking," an act of kindness to the badly hurt Garcia.

Collected Poems of Ernest Hemingway, The   Pirated edition, published in Paris but without a publisher's name, date of publication, or copyright information. It has a section titled "Miscellaneous Poems," which includes: "Ultimately," "The Lady Poet with Footnotes," "The Age Demanded," "The Ernest Liberal's Lament," "The Soul of Spain," and "Neo-Thomist Poem." And in a section titled "Ten Poems," it has the 10 poems published originally in *Three Stories and Ten Poems* (1923): "Mitraigliatrice," "Oklahoma," "Oily Weather," "Roosevelt," "Captives," "Champs D'Honneur," "Riparto D'Assalto," "Montparnasse," "Along With Youth," and "Chapter Heading." There are three editions of this pamphlet, the third published in San Francisco by City Lights Press in 1960 that includes as an 11th poem in the "Ten Poems" section, "Valentine."

Six other unauthorized, "pirated," editions were also published, most of them copies of the earlier editions.

Collier's   U.S. magazine begun in 1887 by Peter F. Collier, a book publisher. In the decade before World War I it was a force in public affairs, especially with a series of articles by Samuel Adams that resulted in the federal Food and Drug Act of 1906.

Hemingway wrote six articles for the magazine in 1944, all concerned with the Allied Armies' progress across France into Germany during WORLD WAR II.

Collins, John   Jack Brennan's fight manager in "Fifty Grand." He and two other "friends," Happy Steinfelt and Lew Morgan, talk Brennan into throwing his fight with Jimmy Walcott, a fight scheduled for Madison Square Garden in New York. When Brennan gets hit hard in the groin by Walcott, Collins can't throw in the towel because he has bet heavily on Walcott to win the fight and so would lose all of his money.

Colonel, the   Otherwise unnamed U.S. officer and a friend of Thomas HUDSON, in *Islands in the Stream*. He oversees Hudson's search for German submarines in Cuban waters, and when he sends instructions to Hudson for the search that takes place in the "At Sea" section of the novel, he tells him to bring back a prisoner.

Colt automatic pistol, .22 caliber   In "Big Two-Hearted River," NICK remembers that when HOPKINS left for Texas to get rich in oil, he gave Nick his pistol.

"Comintern"   Spanish civil war song, sung in *The Fifth Column* by 25 comrades waiting downstairs in the Hotel Florida in act 2, scene 3.

commissioner's house   On BIMINI in *Islands in the Stream*. In celebration of Queen Mary's birthday, the drunken Frank HART wants to burn down the commissioner's house by shooting flares at it.

communists   Members of the Communist Party, whether Spaniards or Russians, who fought on the side of the REPUBLICANS in the SPANISH CIVIL WAR. They are called "peasants and workers" in *For Whom the Bell Tolls*.

Como, Lake   In the Lombardy region of northern Italy, in the foothills of the Alps, shaped like an upside-down Y; referred to in *A Farewell to Arms*.

compatriot   American tourist at the GRITTI PALACE HOTEL restaurant, made fun of by Richard CANTWELL and the GRAN MAESTRO, in *Across the River and Into the Trees*, because he does all of his traveling according to Baedeker guides, and "he has no taste in either food or wine."

Compiègne   Town on the Oise River, 42 miles northeast of Paris, with a "flat" racecourse that Hemingway went to occasionally while in Paris during the 1920s.

Compton   In "The Snows of Kilimanjaro," he is the pilot of a plane that HARRY dreams about, which will arrive at the safari campsite to take him to a hospital in Nairobi, Kenya.

Comrade, First   In *The Fifth Column* he falls asleep while guarding a prisoner and is sent to police headquarters by Philip RAWLINGS for questioning and possible torture. He is a member of the Lincoln INTERNATIONAL BRIGADE. The escaped prisoner later returns to shoot Comrade WILKINSON in the back of the head, thinking it is Rawlings.

Comrade, Second   In *The Fifth Column* he is involved with the First Comrade in carelessly allowing a prisoner to escape, and, although he goes to police headquarters with the First Comrade, who is apparently tortured, the Second Comrade is not mentioned again.

"Concert a Success"   Article for Oak Park and River Forest High School newspaper, *The Trapeze* (January 20, 1916), reprinted in *Hemingway at Oak Park High: The High School Writings of Ernest Hemingway, 1916–1917* (1993).

conchs   Some of the "have nots" who live in KEY WEST in *To Have and Have Not*. "Conch" is slang for people who hunt conch shells for a living, hence any working-class native of the area. Harry MORGAN, the novel's main character, is called a "conch" by the lawyer, "BEE-LIPS," but Harry denies being one.

Conch town   Section of KEY WEST, Florida, described by Richard GORDON in *To Have and Have Not* as having, among other things, "lighted Cuban bolito houses," a "Red House, Chicha's," a "pressed stone church," a "filling station and a sandwich place," "three drug stores, the music store, the five Jew stores, three poolrooms, two barbershops, five beer joints, three ice cream parlors, the five poor and the one good restaurant, two magazine and paper places, four second-hand joints. . . ." See CONCHS.

concierge (1)   At the hotel in LAUSANNE, Switzerland, where Frederic HENRY and Catherine BARKLEY, in *A Farewell to Arms*, stay while waiting for her baby to be born.

concierge (2)   At the GRITTI PALACE HOTEL in Venice, the assistant manager, who greets Richard CANTWELL, in *Across the River and Into the Trees*, when he arrives at the hotel.

Concordia   Shop where PEDUZZI (1) buys MARSALA wine for his illegal trout fishing trip with the YOUNG GENTLEMAN in "Out of Season."

concussions   Richard CANTWELL informs his doctor at the beginning of *Across the River and Into the Trees* that he has had 10 concussions, "Counting polo. Give or take three." The concussions and the three heart attacks he has already had let Cantwell know that his death is imminent.

"Condensing the Classics"   Article, published in *The Toronto Star Weekly* (August 20, 1921), reprinted in *Ernest Hemingway: Dateline Toronto* (1985). A tongue-in-cheek response to a five-year effort by "a little group of earnest [literature] condensers, said to be endowed by Andrew Carnegie. . . . *Les Misérables* has been cut to ten pages. *Don Quixote* is said to run to about a column and a half." Hemingway then suggests condensing other classics: Blake's "Tiger, tiger, burning bright," Coleridge's "Ancient Mariner," the opera *Pagliacci*, Shakespeare's *Othello*, etc.

condottieri   Italian for "soldiers of fortune," against whom the Gran Maestro says he wishes he could have fought under Colonel Richard CANTWELL, his friend in *Across the River and Into the Trees*. "[A]ll you had to do," the Gran Maestro says, "was out-think them" and they would give up the fight.

Connolly, Cyril (1903–1974)   British critic and publisher and author of *The Unquiet Grave* (1944; rev. ed. 1945), from which Hemingway takes a two-paragraph quotation for use as a headnote for his article "A Situation Report," written for *Look* magazine (September 4, 1956). The quotation is about the importance of a writer striving always to write the best that he can.

"Conrad, Optimist and Moralist"   Article, an untitled contribution to a special issue on Joseph Conrad for the TRANSATLANTIC REVIEW (October 1924), reprinted in *By-Line: Ernest Hemingway* (1967). Conrad died on August 3, 1924, and Ford Madox FORD, the editor of *transatlantic review,* asked a number of writers to contribute to the commemorative issue. In his article, Hemingway writes: "If I knew that by grinding Mr. [T. S.] ELIOT into a fine dry powder and sprinkling that powder over Mr. Conrad's grave Mr. Conrad would shortly appear . . . and commence writing I would leave for London early tomorrow morning with a sausage grinder."

Constante   Bartender at the FLORIDITA bar in Havana, who, according to Thomas HUDSON in *Islands in the Stream,* makes "great" double frozen daiquiris. His photograph is on the bar's promotional material.

"Constantinople, Dirty White, Not Glistening and Sinister"   Article, published in *The Toronto Daily Star* (October 18, 1922), reprinted in *Ernest Hemingway: Dateline Toronto* (1985). Datelined "Constantinople," the article describes "Stamboul" as Hemingway enters the main part of the city from the train station and arrives at Hôtel de Londres. He reports that "The Golden Horn" looks like the Chicago River.

Constitution   Ship on which Hemingway traveled to Spain in 1959 at the beginning of the bullfight season; the trip is described briefly in *The Dangerous Summer.*

"Convicts Set Fire to Stable at 'Pen' and Made Escape" Article, published in *The Toronto Star* (September 11, 1923), "discovered" by William Burrill at the John F.

Kennedy Library in Boston but not reprinted in his book, *Hemingway: The Toronto Years* (1994), where 25 other recently found articles are reprinted.

cook (1)   Unnamed Negro, a minor character in *The Torrents of Spring;* he works at BROWN'S BEANERY.

cook (2)   At the train station in "The Light of the World." He is homosexual and made fun of by one of the customers.

cook (3)   Minor character on the hunting safari in "The Short Happy Life of Francis Macomber." He helps carry MACOMBER back to camp "in triumph" after he has "killed" the lion.

cook (4)   In "The Killers"; see SAM.

Coolidge, Calvin (1872–1933)   Thirtieth U.S. president (1923–29). In "Banal Story" he is mentioned because his name appears in a booklet advertising *The Forum* magazine, criticized by the story's narrator for its banal treatment of the arts.

He is also alluded to by Robert JORDAN in *For Whom the Bell Tools.* And in *The Garden of Eden* David BOURNE calls him "that thin-lipped bastard Coolidge fishing for trout in a high stiff collar in a fish hatchery in the Black Hills we stole from the SIOUX and CHEYENNE."

Cooper, Gary (1901–1961)   Hollywood film actor and a friend of Hemingway, who joined him for several hunting and fishing trips in Idaho, including one filmed by the gossip columnist Hedda Hopper for a documentary.

Cooper starred in two film adaptations of Hemingway works. He played Frederic HENRY in the 1932 version of *A Farewell to Arms;* and he was nominated for an Academy Award for his role as Robert JORDAN in the 1943 film version of *For Whom the Bell Tolls* with Academy Award nominee Ingrid BERGMAN, for roles they repeated in the first radio adaptation of the novel.

Côpic, Vladimir   Commander of the 15th International Brigade in the Spanish civil war, which included American and British battalions; mentioned in NANA Dispatch No. 20.

copita   Spanish term for a small cup or glass. In "A Clean, Well-Lighted Place," the older waiter closes up his café and goes to a bar, where he orders a small cup of coffee.

Corbett, James J.   U.S. boxer and heavyweight champion (1892–97); he defeated John L. Sullivan for the title in 1892; mentioned in "Fifty Grand."

Córdoba   Capital of Córdoba Province in southern Spain, in Andalusia, at the foot of the Sierra de

Córdoba. It is one of the towns on the Spanish bullfight circuit covered by Hemingway in 1959 in preparation for writing *The Dangerous Summer.*

Córdoban front   Battle site near Córdoba between the Loyalists and the Rebels during the Spanish civil war. In *For Whom the Bell Tolls,* Robert JORDAN was at the Córdoban front at the beginning of the war (1936) before going to Madrid.

Cornet, The   In *Green Hills of Africa* Hemingway tells Kandisky that it is the only book of poems by RILKE that he has read. Kandisky's opinion is that it is full of "snobbery."

Corniche   French for "coastal road," this one between Nice and Villefranche on the French Riviera, driven by Catherine BOURNE in *The Garden of Eden.*

corrida de toros   Or just *corrida.* "Bullfight" is the closest English translation of this Spanish term, a faulty but apparently workable translation. "There is no Spanish word for bullfight," according to Jake BARNES in *The Sun Also Rises.* See BULLFIGHT.

Corriere della Sera   Milan, Italy, newspaper, read by Frederic HENRY in *A Farewell to Arms,* both in Milan and later in MONTREUX, Switzerland, while he is waiting for Catherine BARKLEY to have her hair done.

Corrochano, Gregorio   Bullfight critic for *A.B.C.,* a Madrid newspaper with monarchist political views. The critic is mentioned in *Death in the Afternoon.*

Corsican wine   Otherwise unidentified wine from the French island of Corsica, mentioned in *A Moveable Feast.* Corsican wines, red, white, and rose, are known for being full-bodied, most either *vin ordinaire* (common or ordinary) or *vin de pays* (local wines).

Cortez, Pizarro, Menéndez de Avila, Enrique Lister   A long line of Spanish "sons of bitches" that Robert JORDAN thinks about in *For Whom the Bell Tolls.* "There is no finer and no worse people in the world," he says of the Spanish people. "No kinder people and no crueler." He later also thinks about Pablo Iglesias, "one good man . . . in two thousand years" of Spanish history. All but Lister are 17th-century conquerors, known for their cruelty to indigenous populations and to European enemies. Lister was a contemporary Spanish general.

Cortina d'Ampezzo   Ski resort in the Italian Dolomites, mentioned by Frederic HENRY in *A Farewell to Arms* as a place where he had skiied before World War I.

Hemingway says in *A Moveable Feast* that it was one of the places where he and Hadley enjoyed skiing during the 1920s and that he wrote "Out of Season," a short story set in Cortina, there in April 1923.

Cortina d'Ampezzo is also remembered several times by Richard CANTWELL in *Across the River and Into the Trees.*

Corton   French red wine from the Côte de Beaune, the southern part of Burgundy's Côte d'Or region. The wine is mentioned in *Death in the Afternoon* in a comparison Hemingway makes between acquiring a taste for good wine and acquiring a taste for the bullfight.

corto y derecho   Spanish bullfight term, meaning "short and straight." In "The Undefeated," Manuel GARCIA concentrates on *corto y derecho* when he goes in over the bull's horns for the kill. He is unsuccessful, however, and it takes him six attempts before making the kill.

Cosmopolitan   American magazine for which Dorothy Bridges, in *The Fifth Column,* is writing an article, "just as soon as [she understands] things [about the fighting in Madrid] the *least* bit better."

"Cossacks, The"   Short novel by Leo Tolstoi, published in 1863. Hemingway is reading it on the safari described in *Green Hills of Africa.* He says in it "were the summer heat, the mosquitoes, the feel of the forest in the different seasons, and that river that the Tartars crossed, raiding, and I was living in that Russia again." He also mentions having lived "through Turgenieff" and "in the family Buddenbrooks" and in Stendhal's *Le Rouge et le Noir,* seeing "Salcède torn apart by the horses at the Place de Grèves" in Paris.

cot, double size   Robert WILSON, the white hunting guide in "The Short Happy Life of Francis Macomber," always carries one with him on safari "to accommodate any windfalls he might receive," meaning the wives of hunters.

Côte d'Or   Department in eastern France, with the capital at Dijon, a beautiful region through which Hemingway and Fitzgerald drive on their way back to Paris from Lyon, described in *A Moveable Feast.*

côtes   French for "hills," "shore," or "seacoast." When Catherine BOURNE mentions it after bicycling, in *The Garden of Eden,* she is probably referring to hills: "It [the bicycle trip] was nothing but I'd forgotten about the *côtes.*"

"Count Apponyi and the Loan"   Article, unsigned, published in *The Toronto Daily Star* (October 15, 1923), reprinted in *Ernest Hemingway: Dateline Toronto* (1985).

The headline in the *Daily Star* was "Hungarian Stateman Delighted With Loan." The 77-year-old Apponyi has been for "fifty years one of Hungary's greatest statesmen." Hemingway describes Apponyi's meeting with David LLOYD GEORGE, former British prime minister, at a luncheon in the LaSalle Hotel in Chicago. He also describes Apponyi's response to the news that the League of Nations had voted to provide Hungary with £24-million loan to help reorganize its finances in the aftermath of World War I. This article was Hemingway's last for the *Star.*

country, the other   In *The Garden of Eden* the setting for David BOURNE's AFRICAN STORY, set in East Africa and referred to as "the other country" because David gradually preferred it to the chaotic world he lived in with his wife, Catherine, and MARITA in southern France.

"Country Poem with Little Country"   Poem written in 1949 and first published in *88 Poems* (1979).

course 225°   In *To Have and Have Not,* it is the identified navigational course Harry MORGAN takes when he leaves KEY WEST on his charter fishing boat hired by four Cubans (see CUBANS, FOUR). After hiring him, they rob a Key West bank and then order Morgan to take them to Havana.

cove, the   At LA NAPOULE, France, where, in *The Garden of Eden,* David and Catherine BOURNE and MARITA swim, usually nude.

Cowley, Malcolm (1898–1989)   U.S. literary critic and social historian, best known for his works about the writers of the Lost Generation of the 1920s and their successors. He was literary editor of *The New Republic* (1929–44) and carried a generally leftist position on literary and political matters during the Depression of the 1930s. He also helped to edit and publish two little magazines in Paris, *Secession* and *Broom*. His books include: *Exile's Return: a Narrative of Ideas* (1934; rev. ed. *Exile's Return: A Literary Odyssey of the 1920s,* 1951), *After the Genteel Tradition: American Writers Since 1910* (1937), *Books That Changed Our Minds* (1939), *The Literary Situation* (1954), and *And I Worked at the Writer's Trade* (1976). Perhaps Cowley's most significant contribution to American literature, however, was his reviving the reputation of William FAULKNER with his editing of *The Portable Faulkner* (1946) at a time when all of Faulkner's books were out of print.

Coxey's Army   Group of unemployed men who marched on Washington, D.C. in 1894 to petition Congress for help in their joblessness. Yogi JOHNSON in *The Torrents of Spring* thinks about their fruitless walk (they were arrested in Washington for walking on the Capitol lawn) as he, Johnson, walks toward PETOSKEY, Michigan, near the end of the novel.

crabe mexicain   Crabmeat in a wine sauce of tomato, mushroom, and hot pepper. In *A Moveable Feast* Hemingway writes of having this dinner with oysters and a Sancerre wine at PRUNIERS RESTAURANT in Paris with Hadley. The menu, however, would probably have read either "crabe mexicain" or "crabe à la mexicaine."

cramps   In *The Old Man and the Sea* SANTIAGO's left hand cramps during his painful ordeal in catching the marlin. See CHRISTIAN IMAGERY.

Crane, Stephen (1871–1900)   U.S. author, best known for his novel *The Red Badge of Courage* (1895). Hemingway admired Crane, but in *A Moveable Feast* he writes that Tolstoi's writing about war, "the movement of troops, the terrain and the officers and the men and the fighting," made Crane's writing about the American Civil War "seem like the brilliant imagining of a sick boy who had never seen war but had only read the battles and chronicles and seen the Brady photographs. . . ."

In *Green Hills of Africa,* however, Hemingway tells KANDISKY that the "good" American writers are Henry James, Stephen Crane, and Mark Twain.

C rations   U.S. Army canned food, mentioned by Colonel Richard CANTWELL in *Across the River and Into the Trees.* See K RATIONS.

Crawfish Bar   Shallow area near the harbor entrance at KEY WEST, Florida. In *To Have and Have Not* Harry MORGAN considers running his boat onto the bar in order to stop the escape of four Cubans who have robbed a Key West bank and are now forcing him to take them to Cuba.

crew   Thomas HUDSON has a crew of eight men with him in the "At Sea" section of *Islands in the Stream* as they search the islands off the northeast coast of Cuba for the crew of a German submarine in May 1944. The eight men with Hudson are the chief mate, ANTONIO (2); two Basques, ARA and GEORGE (10); the radioman, PETERS; the navigator, JUAN; and crewmen GIL, HENRY (3), and WILLIE.

Crillon bar   At the Hôtel de Crillon, 10, place de la Concorde in Paris. In *A Moveable Feast* Hemingway writes that when, in the early 1920s, he and Hadley "had money," they ate at the Crillon bar, one of the most expensive places to eat in Paris.

The bar is where David and Catherine BOURNE (*The Garden of Eden*) meet for the first time.

Crime and Punishment Novel by DOSTOYEVSKY, published in 1866, one of the first books borrowed by Hemingway from Sylvia BEACH'S SHAKESPEARE AND COMPANY (1) bookshop. The borrowings are discussed in *A Moveable Feast.*

Cripps, Sir Stafford (1889–1952) British statesman and socialist, thrown out of the Labour Party in 1939 for urging a united front with the Communists; but a year later he was appointed ambassador to the Soviet Union by Prime Minister Winston Churchill. In *Across the River and Into the Trees* Richard CANTWELL makes a sarcastic reference to him by thinking to himself that Cripps "will probably ration" the English language, since about all the English have left is a language named after them.

Criterion, The English quarterly review of literature (1922–39), founded and edited by T. S. ELIOT. Eliot's poem *The Waste Land* appeared in its first issue (October 1922), and later issues included works by W. H. Auden, Ezra POUND, and Stephen Spender; it also included the first writings of Marcel Proust and Jean COCTEAU. Hemingway mentions the review in *A Moveable Feast.*

"Critical Intelligence" Poem written in 1927 and first published in *Ernest Hemingway: Complete Poems* (1992), the revised edition of Nicholas Gerogiannis's *88 Poems* (1979).

Crittenden, Colonel William L. (1822–1851) In *Islands in the Stream* Thomas HUDSON refers to Crittenden's failed attempt to lead an expedition of soldiers, mostly from the United States but paid by the government of Venezuela, to free Cuba from Spanish rule. Crittenden, a U.S. officer trained at West Point, and most of his men were captured and executed. Hudson mentions the castle of Atares, where Crittenden was shot on August 16, 1851. This date helps determine the age of Hudson, who states that the incident took place 40 years before he was born, which makes him about 53 years old during the "At Sea" section of the novel (May 1944).

Croatians Mentioned in *A Farewell to Arms* as soldiers fighting on the side of the Austrians in World War I.

Croix de Guerre French military medal awarded for "bravery in action." Mentioned in *A Moveable Feast;* see JEAN (2).

crooked hand Richard CANTWELL's hand was injured during World War I, although it is not made clear how; and he seems to contradict himself by saying that, in spite of all his wounds, no bones were ever broken.

Crosby, Mr. In *Islands in the Stream* a friend of Thomas HUDSON's when he lived in Paris, remembered by young Tom HUDSON. It is probably a reference to Harry Crosby (1898–1929), the writer and editor, whom Hemingway had known in Paris in the 1920s and who committed suicide in New York on December 9, 1929.

"Cross-Country Snow" Nick ADAMS and his friend GEORGE (4) are skiing in Switzerland in this short story, probably just above MONTREUX, since George mentions that he has to catch a train from there that night. They ride up the mountain on a FUNICULAR car that is finally stopped by snow across its track. The narrator then describes skiing down to an inn. They have a bottle of wine and some apple strudel, talk about the German waitress who is unmarried and pregnant, and about George's return to the United States to go back to school.

Nick is married. George asks Nick when HELEN (2)'s baby is due, and he says, "late next summer." The story suggests the biological trap Nick finds himself in, but either it's not much of a trap or Nick is unaware of it. Neither Nick nor Helen wants to go "back to the States," according to Nick. When George then says, "It's hell, isn't it," it isn't clear whether George is talking about not being able to stay in Switzerland or about being trapped by having a baby. In any case, Nick says, "No. Not exactly."

The ambiguity here is an important part of the story's tension. They have enjoyed skiing together in Switzerland, and they agree that the skiing isn't nearly as good in the States. George wishes they could make a promise about skiing together again, but Nick says, "There isn't any good in promising." They leave the inn, strap on their skis, and the story ends with the narrator stating that, at least, "they would have the run home together." Nick is evidently trying to work out his own ambivalent feelings about skiing, going home, and having a baby.

"Cross-Country Snow" was first published in *transatlantic review* (January 1925) and reprinted in *In Our Time* (1925).

"Crossing the Mississippi" Unfinished story about NICK's first trip across the Mississippi River in October 1917, the date made clear from a reference to the Chicago White Sox beating the New York Giants in the sixth (and "final") game of the World Series. Nick also thinks about Mark Twain, Huck Finn, Tom Sawyer, and LaSalle, "as he looked up the flat, brown plain of slow-moving water. Anyhow I've seen the Mississippi, he thought happily to himself." The fragment was published in Philip Young's *The Nick Adams Stories* (1972).

"Crossroads—An Anthology" Unfinished series of early short sketches published as a "short story" by

Peter Griffin in the first volume of his biography, *Along With Youth: Hemingway, The Early Years* (1985). The sketches are titled "Pauline Snow," "Ed Paige," "Bob White," and "Old Man Hurd—and Mrs. Hurd." Hemingway submitted "Crossroads" to the *Saturday Evening Post*, but it was rejected.

Crowley, Aleister (1875–1947) English writer, best known for his books on black magic rites and as the prototype for the main character in Somerset Maugham's novel *The Magician.* In *A Moveable Feast* Hemingway writes about a conversation with Ford Madox Ford in which it becomes clear that Ford had mistaken Hilaire Belloc for Crowley. Hemingway also states that a "great" friend says Crowley is "supposed to be the wickedest man in the world."

Crystal Palace, the Large exhibition hall built originally in London's Hyde Park and opened by Queen Victoria on May 1, 1851. It was torn down three years later and rebuilt at Sydenham, about seven miles from London.

In the "Bimini" section of *Islands in the Stream,* BOBBY tells Thomas HUDSON that some of his paintings are "fit to hang in the Crystal Palace alongside the masterpieces of all time." The reference is useful for setting the time of the section, because the Crystal Palace burned down in 1936.

cuadrilla Each matador in a Spanish bullfight has a *cuadrilla,* or team, of usually five men who assist him in the bull ring—two PICADORS and three BANDERILLEROS, any one of whom may be asked to kill the bull. It is one of the *cuadrilla* of the bullfighter in the "Chapter 11" vignette who finally has to kill the badly wounded bull.

"Cuba" Title of part 2 of three parts in *Islands in the Stream.* The action takes place during February and March 1944 in the years just before Thomas HUDSON's chasing of German submarines during World War II, which takes place in part 3, titled "at sea." Part 1 is titled "BIMINI." See *Islands in the Stream.*

Cuba House, the Owned by Thomas HUDSON in Cuba and offered, in the "Bimini" section of *Islands in the Stream,* as a sort of love nest to his friend Roger DAVIS for his growing relationship with Audrey BRUCE. But Roger and Audrey leave for Montana instead. In the "Cuba" section of the novel, the Cuba House is called "the farm."

Cuba Libre Cocktail made with rum and coke in *To Have and Have Not.* It is the drink FREDDY, the barman, names when Harry MORGAN asks him what Helen GORDON is drinking. It means, literally, a free Cuba.

Cuban Indians HONEST LIL tells Thomas HUDSON, in *Islands in the Stream,* that they're all *mulatos,* but he says, "No, they're not. Some are real Indians . . . from Yucatan."

Cubans, four Revolutionaries who hire Harry MORGAN to take them to Cuba in his charter fishing boat. They pay him $200 each and "a thousand guaranty [that] nothing happens to the boat." They rob the FIRST STATE TRUST AND SAVINGS BANK in KEY WEST in support of the revolution and then force Morgan to take them to Cuba. Three of four Cubans are identified: ROBERTO, EMILIO (2), and "the pleasant speaking one."

Cubans, three Killed in a gunfight outside the CUNARD BAR in Havana at the beginning of *To Have and Have Not.*

Cuban watchman Guard at the NAVY YARD in KEY WEST in *To Have and Have Not.*

"Cucaracha" In "The Gambler, the Nun, and the Radio," the three Mexican musicians who play for Cayetano RUIZ in the hospital where he is recovering from gunshot wounds, ask Mr. FRAZER to suggest a song, and he asks for "the Cucaracha." According to the story's narrator, it "has the sinister lightness and deftness of so many of the tunes men have gone to die to." *La Cucaracha* is a song that illustrates the tendency of Mexican folk dances to imitate animals; a "cucaracha" is a cockroach.

Cunard Bar In *To Have and Have Not* it is located next door to the PEARL OF SAN FRANCISCO CAFÉ on the square near the docks in Havana, Cuba.

Cunarder Reference in *A Moveable Feast* to one of the Cunard line of passenger ships that sailed from New York to Europe during the 1920s.

Cunningham, Mr. The official at the bank in Frederic HENRY's unnamed hometown who will accept the sight draft on Frederic's GRANDFATHER (2)'s account.

"Current, The" Unfinished early story fragment, written between 1919 and 1921, rejected for publication during Hemingway's lifetime but published, with four other previously unpublished fragments, as a completed "short story" by Peter Griffin in the first volume of his biography, *Along With Youth: Hemingway, The Early Years* (1985).

Curtis, Charlie (1891–1959) Charles Pelham Curtis, United States author, mentioned in *Green Hills of Africa* because of his writing about hunting in East Africa. The book referred to is probably *Hunting in Africa, East and West* (1925), written with Richard C. Curtis.

Custer, George Armstrong (1839–1876) U.S. Army officer, a graduate of West Point, who was at the Civil War battle of Bull Run and distinguished himself under General G. B. McClellan in the Peninsular campaign. He was made a brigadier general in 1863, the youngest general in the Union Army. He was present at the surrender at Appomattox Courthouse and was promoted to major general.

After the Civil War, his career in reorganizing the army for Indian affairs was less distinguished. He died at the battle of the Little Bighorn on June 25, 1876, when he led an attack against the Sioux Indians without realizing how outnumbered were his own troops; every soldier was killed.

Richard CANTWELL refers to him as "General (Brevetted)," meaning an officer nominally promoted but without higher pay or greater authority. And later thoughts of Billings, Montana, remind Cantwell of the place "where they killed that fool George Armstrong Custer."

"Custer's Last Fight" Title of a painting by Cassilly Adams (1884) and made into a lithographic print by F. Otto Becker for the Anheuser-Busch Co. of St. Louis. Robert JORDAN, in *For Whom the Bell Tolls*, thinks about a copy of the print hanging on a poolroom wall in Red Lodge, Montana. He remembers a blond Custer surrounded by Sioux Indians.

It is also the picture on the wall in FREDDIE'S BAR in *To Have and Have Not*, identified as "Custer's Last Stand."

C.W. In *Islands in the Stream* it is the only identification for one of the Chinese millionaires Thomas HUDSON had met in Hong Kong and about whom he tells HONEST LIL. The millionaires were known only by their initials, and they procured prostitutes, surprising Hudson once with a "gift" of three beautiful girls.

Cynara In the "Cuba" section of *Islands in the Stream* Thomas HUDSON's first wife (Mrs. Thomas HUDSON [1]), the mother of Tom, makes a surprise visit to Hudson in Havana and says to him, "Thee hasn't been faithful to me, Cynara, in thy fashion."

Cynara is an otherwise unidentified allusion to a poem by Ernest Dowson (1867–1900), a British poet, known for musical lyrics often reflecting sadness. His most famous poem is popularly known as "Cynara," and the line alluded to is the refrain at the close of each of four verses: "I have been faithful to thee, Cynara, in my fashion." Hudson's first wife is kidding him about being "faithful," because they are divorced, and she has had other lovers herself.

D

dadaists Members of the dada movement in art and literature. In their works, the dadaists used ordinary objects as metaphors for something else, requiring the participation of the observer, whose own imagination provided the work's only meaning. The group was founded by Romanian poet Tristan Tzara (1896–1963) in 1915 in reaction to World War I. See "DIVINE GESTURE, A."

Dain Curse, The Title of a detective novel by Dashiell HAMMETT, published in 1929 and referred to by Hemingway in *Death in the Afternoon.*

Damascus City in Syria, that Thomas HUDSON, in *Islands in the Stream,* remembers visiting on a voyage along the Suez Canal and the Mediterranean. See PRINCESS.

Dan Minor character in *Green Hills of Africa,* sent off in the trucks at one point to recruit porters.

Danby-Smith, Valerie Gregory Hemingway's third wife. She was in the party that helped celebrate Hemingway's 60th birthday at LA CONSULA, the home of Bill and Annie Davis, in Spain in the summer of 1959, while Hemingway was covering the bullfight season and preparing to write *The Dangerous Summer.* She also did some secretarial work for him as he tried to keep up with his correspondence that summer.

dancers, three Riau-riau dancers in PAMPLONA, who would not let Jake BARNES buy drinks and who taught Brett ASHLEY how to drink from wineskins in *The Sun Also Rises.* (See RIAU-RIAU MUSIC.)

Dandolo, Contessa In *Across the River and Into the Trees* her house on the Grand Canal in Venice is pointed out by Richard CANTWELL to the boatman. She is evidently a reference to the ancient Venetian Dandolo family, which produced four doges, a number of naval officers, and several other prominent Venetian citizens.

Dangerous Summer, The (1) Nonfiction work about the 1959 bullfight season in Spain, with an emphasis on the afternoons when two of Spain's best matadors of that time, Antonio ORDÓÑEZ and Luis Miguel DOMINGUÍN,

fought bulls either in the same ring, with a third matador on the card, or "mano a mano"—that is, alternating one after the other, three bulls each.

When the article was first published by *Life* magazine in three installments (September 5, 12, and 19, 1960) Hemingway was criticized for seeming to favor Ordóñez over Dominguín. Hemingway traveled from town to town with Ordóñez and spent time at his ranch, which only added to the criticism. That Ordóñez and Dominguín were brothers-in-law and managed by the same two men, both brothers of Dominguín, didn't make Hemingway's task any easier. As Hemingway described the awkward situation, it "looked very hard on family life and very good for bullfighting."

It was also "dangerous" as Hemingway saw it because Dominguín, 33 years old, considered himself a bigger draw and so felt he should get more money, but Ordóñez was younger by six years and probably the better matador. They would take this psychological friction into the bull ring, which added to the danger.

The best writing in the book concerns what Hemingway refers to as "one of the very greatest bullfights I have ever seen," bullfights taking place on August 14 in Málaga (chapter 11). But the writing elsewhere is unclear at times about the dates and/or the location of some of the fights and even vague about the number of fights Ordóñez and Dominguín fought on the same program (the description of their first fight on the same card does not come until more than halfway through the book). It is still more confusing because Hemingway once or twice refers to a particular fight as "mano a mano" but then mentions a third bullfighter on the same card.

It's difficult to know, however, whether this confusion is the result of Hemingway's carelessness or of the editing of a 65,000-word manuscript down to 45,000 words. The original version, as published by *Life* magazine in 1960, was excerpted from a 65,000-word manuscript, which itself had been cut down by A. E. HOTCHNER from Hemingway's first draft of 120,000 words. Scribner's didn't publish the work in book form until 25 years later (1985), when editor Michael PIETSCH cut it to its final length. Hotchner was a friend of Hemingway's during the last 13 years of his life and was with him for part of the 1959 circuit of the Spanish bull rings.

Ernest with chauffeur Adamo Simon near Burgos, Spain, 1953
(Copyright holder unknown; photo courtesy of the John F. Kennedy Library.)

The three parts of the *Life* version are titled "The Dangerous Summer," "The Pride of the Devil," and "An Appointment with Disaster." At Scribner's, however, Pietsch dropped the three headings and divided the book into 13 chapters. He includes at the back a reprinting of the "Glossary" of bullfight terms Hemingway used in *Death in the Afternoon,* plus an index, which includes a listing of towns where the bullfights occurred. And there's an "Introduction" by James Michener that begins with an interpretive statement difficult to argue against: "This is a book about death written by a lusty sixty-year-old man who had reason to fear that his own death was imminent."

The first of the book's chapters are introductory, describing Hemingway's trips to Spain earlier in the 1950s and his arrival there in the summer of 1959 for the bullfights.

Chapter 7 describes the first fight in the rivalry between Ordóñez and Dominguín, which takes place in Zaragoza near the end of June. The bullfights were not particularly impressive, however, so more than half of the chapter is devoted to a description of the countryside he and Bill Davis drove through on their way across the mountains to Alicante on the Mediterranean coast. Chapter 8 describes a "strong fight on a wild day [in Alicante] and both Luis Miguel and Antonio were wonderful." One of the impressions one gets from the book, which Hemingway does not stress, is that the bullfighters do a lot of traveling during a summer season, sometimes driving all night after an evening's fights to fight again the next evening several hundred kilometers away. The best bullfighters often fly from one city to the next, but most drive or are driven cross-country.

Chapter 9 begins, "Pamplona is no place to bring your wife." It's a man's fiesta, according to Hemingway, and women tend to get in the way. He and Antonio Ordóñez, who was there without his wife, Carmen, spend the week together, averaging "something over three hours sleep a night." Antonio was not on the bullfight schedule, but he gets a horn wound anyway, running with the bulls one morning in a tradition often credited to Hemingway for his description of the fiesta's morning ceremony in *The Sun Also Rises* (Hemingway never ran with the bulls, nor did his novel's hero, Jake BARNES).

The fourth day in Valencia (chapter 10) finds the two matadors on the same card for what Hemingway calls the fifth time, but he has mentioned only three others. It was a fight in which Antonio was so superior that he "gravely wounded" Luis Miguel's confidence.

Chapter 11 provides writing that might remind the reader of the best of Hemingway, the Hemingway, for example, of *Death in the Afternoon.* It is barely two weeks after both matadors had been in the Madrid hospital from horn wounds, and the crowd anticipation in Málaga is tremendous. Hemingway describes carefully and in detail the work of each bullfighter on each of the six bulls. Luis Miguel was tossed six feet into the air by his third bull but not wounded. Ordóñez came out for his last bull, knowing that he had to be "perfect." When it came time for the kill, "[h]e and the bull formed one solid mass and when he came out over the horn the bull had the long steel death in him to the hilt and the aorta was severed. Antonio watched him go down in a foot-gripping, staggering, rolling crash and the second mano a mano was over." All six bulls were killed with one sword thrust each, extremely unusual even for the greatest of matadors.

Chapter 12 describes the mano a mano in Bayonne, France, where Antonio, fighting almost as well as in Valencia, "destroyed [Luis Miguel] mercilessly." The chapter ends with a summary of Antonio's attitude: he "wanted to go to Bilbao now, the most difficult public

EH in the mountains near Burgos, Spain, 1953. (Copyright holder unknown; photo courtesy of the John F. Kennedy Library.)

four of the seven times "mano a mano." There are passages in the book that remind the reader of Hemingway as he once was, but there are not many, and certainly the book as a whole presents a picture of a man at the low ebb of his writing career. The long article that appeared in *Life* during three weeks in September 1960 was the last work published in Hemingway's life. In a little more than two months he would make his first visit to the Mayo Clinic in Rochester, Minnesota, and ten months later he would be dead.

"Dangerous Summer, The" (2)   Title of part 1 of the three-part *Life* magazine version of *The Dangerous Summer,* published by *Life* in its September 5, 1960, issue. Part 2, "The Pride of the Devil," was published in the September 12 issue; part 3, "An Appointment with Disaster," was published in the September 19 issue.

"D'Annunzio"   Poem about the Italian poet and soldier, Gabriele D'ANNUNZIO, written about 1920–21 and first published in *88 Poems* (1979).

D'Annunzio, Gabriele (1863–1938)   Italian novelist, poet, dramatist, journalist, military hero, and political leader, probably the most important Italian writer of the late 19th and early 20th centuries. Richard CANTWELL in *Across the River and Into the Trees* remembers that D'Annunzio had lost an eye "in a crash, flying as an observer, over Trieste or Pola, and . . . he had always worn a patch over" the eye.

Cantwell passes the poet's house as he goes along the Grand Canal toward the GRITTI PALACE HOTEL in Venice. He thinks of him as a "Lieutenant Colonel of Infantry without knowing how to command a company [but a] great, lovely writer of *Notturno* whom we respect and jerk."

Dante (1265–1321)   Dante Alighieri, Italian poet, author of the *Divine Comedy* (c. 1308–21), mentioned by or thought of often by Richard CANTWELL in *Across the River and Into the Trees.*

In *Islands in the Stream* Thomas HUDSON thinks that Dante's hell in *The Divine Comedy* is not at all like the hell he feels as he travels to France for the funeral of his sons David and Andrew and their mother, all killed in an automobile accident.

"Dare Devil Joins Tanks"   Article, unsigned, published in *The Kansas City Star* (April 21, 1918), reprinted in *Ernest Hemingway, Cub Reporter* (1970).

Dark Forest, The   Novel by Hugh WALPOLE, published in 1916 and recommended to NICK by BILL (1) in "The Three-Day Blow." The story is based on Walpole's experiences in Russia during World War I. The date of publication helps to set the time of the story in the autumn of 1916 (see also Heinie ZIM and WORLD SERIES [1]).

in Spain where the bulls are the biggest and the public the most severe and exigent so that no one could ever say that there was ever anything doubtful or shady or dubious about this campaign of 1959 when he was fighting as no one had fought real bulls since Joselito and Belmonte."

Hemingway describes in Chapter 13 Luis Miguel's lost confidence and wounding by the second bull in the final fight on the same card with Antonio. While Luis Miguel is being rushed to the hospital, Antonio finishes the work with Luis Miguel's bull and does it *RECIBIENDO,* a way that "is the oldest and the most dangerous and the most beautiful since the matador instead of running in on the bull stands quietly, provokes the bull's charge and then, when the bull comes, guides him past and to the right with the muleta while he puts the sword in high between the bull's shoulders."

The Dangerous Summer describes seven of the fights in the bullfight season of 1959 in which Antonio Ordóñez and Luis Miguel Dominguín fought on the same card,

Dark Laughter Novel by Sherwood Anderson, published in 1925. In *A Moveable Feast* Hemingway writes that it was "so terribly bad, silly and affected" that he had to write a parody of it. The parody is *The Torrents of Spring* (1926).

daughter (1) In *The Sun Also Rises* she is the daughter of the owner of the BAL MUSETTE, where Jake BARNES takes GEORGETTE and some of his friends early in the novel. She accuses Georgette of being a prostitute, thereby creating a "corking row."

daughter (2) Perhaps the most "caged" of all the characters in "A Canary for One," though she doesn't actually appear in the story. Two years ago her mother broke off her relationship with a man from Vevey, Switzerland, with whom she was "madly in love." Her mother, the AMERICAN LADY, tells the story's narrator that she couldn't allow her daughter to marry a foreigner.

daughter (3) RENATA, the leading female character in *Across the River and Into the Trees*. When she says to Richard CANTWELL, "I can be your daughter as well as everything else," he says, "That would be incest."

daughters, three Of Harry MORGAN and MARIE, the main characters in *To Have and Have Not*. The daughters are not named and, although they live with their parents in KEY WEST, they make only two appearances in the novel.

David Bourne See David BOURNE.

Davidson, Jo (1883–1952) U.S. sculptor, best known for his busts of famous people of his time, including presidents Wilson and Roosevelt and General Pershing. He also edited a pamphlet of short essays on heroes of the Spanish civil war that includes Hemingway's essay on Major Milton Wolff of the International Brigades. Bill GORTON refers to him in *The Sun Also Rises,* not as an artist but as one of America's "biggest business men." See *Spanish Portraits*.

Da Vinci, Leonardo (1452–1519) Italian Renaissance painter, sculptor, architect, musician, engineer, and scientist. Thomas HUDSON, in *Islands in the Stream,* wishes he could draw as well as Leonardo but realizes the wish is "silly."

Davis, Annie Wife of Bill DAVIS and hostess at their home near Málaga, Spain, for Ernest and Mary Hemingway and their friends in the summer of 1959, especially for Ernest's 60th birthday party.

Davis, Bill Friend of Hemingway's, whose home, LA CONSULA, "in the hills above Málaga" was used as a stopover several times during the bullfight season of 1959 when Hemingway was traveling the circuit and preparing to write *The Dangerous Summer*. Davis traveled with Hemingway for a good portion of the season, doing most of the driving.

Davis, Roger In *Islands in the Stream* he is Thomas HUDSON's good friend from their years together in Paris; he owns a fishing shack on BIMINI. He's a writer, author of a novel, *The Storm*, and several film scripts. His 11-year-old brother's death in a boating accident when Roger was "about twelve" is one of the stories that he tells the three Hudson sons. The brother's name was Dave, which accounts for Roger favoring David among Hudson's sons and for his help and sympathy during David's struggle with the 1,000-pound broadbill swordfish. Davis does not appear after the "Bimini" section of the novel.

"Day, The" Poem written, according to Peter Griffin, in 1916 and first published in Griffin's biography, *Along With Youth: Hemingway, The Early Years* (1985).

"Day's Wait, A" The main character in this short story is a nine-year-old boy named SCHATZ, whose father narrates the story. Schatz has the flu and a temperature of 102°. The doctor leaves medicine, one for the fever, one as a purgative, and one "to overcome an acid condition." He tells the father that the "germs of influenza can only exist in an acid condition."

The father reads from Howard PYLE's *Book of Pirates,* but the boy is distracted. The father leaves the house for a short hunting trip nearby, and when he returns Schatz is not letting anyone into his room for fear they might catch what he has. Finally, he says to his father, "About what time do you think I'm going to die?"

The father tries to reassure the boy, but Schatz says that at school in France "the boys told me you can't live with forty-four degrees. I've got a hundred and two." The father then has to explain the difference between Fahrenheit and centigrade measurements, that it's "like miles and kilometers. . . . On that thermometer thirty-seven is normal. On this kind it's ninety-eight." At the end of the story the father says that the "hold" Schatz had over himself "relaxed" slowly and that the next day "he cried very easily at little things that were of no importance."

"A Day's Wait" was first published in *Winner Take Nothing* (1933).

Dayton, Ohio In *The Sun Also Rises* seven train-car loads of Catholics from Dayton have been on a "pilgrimage to Rome" and are now on their way to Biarritz and Lourdes and have reserved the train's diner until mid-afternoon, angering Jake BARNES and Bill GORTON, who are on their way from Paris to Pamplona, Spain.

They have to order sandwiches for lunch on their way to the Spanish border.

death In "The Snows of Kilimanjaro," HARRY feels death approaching his cot while he waits, with a gangrenous right leg, to be taken by plane out to Nairobi and a hospital. Near the end, Harry feels that "death had come and rested its head on the foot of the cot and he could smell its breath."

In a twist at the end of the story, Hemingway depicts two deaths: the first is only in Harry's state of delirium as he envisions the plane coming, the pilot taking off but instead of heading for Arusha, where he had said he would refuel, he turns the plane toward the top of Mt. KILIMANJARO. The second death takes place in reality, as the story's point of view shifts to Helen and she hears the hyena "whimpering in the night" and making the "strange" sound, which she hears but does not wake to. It is only when she *does* wake, after some dreaming of her own, that she looks over at Harry's cot and realizes that he is dead. See the following entry for Hemingway's concept of the importance of violent death to writers.

Death in the Afternoon Nonfiction work, published in 1932, considered by most people who know about bullfighting to be the best book on the subject written by a non-Spaniard. It is a clear exposition of a very complex cultural spectacle; extremely readable, even by those not particularly interested in bullfighting; nearly always light and often funny; and with occasional essays on violent death and on writing.

Published when Hemingway was in his early 30s, it represents the author at his best, first as a writer and second as someone who was never satisfied with knowing only a little about his subject but who always dug deeply until he had both the essence and the smallest details. The book "is intended," Hemingway tells us in a note at the end, "as an introduction to the modern [that is, early 1930s] Spanish bullfight [and] attempts to explain that spectacle both emotionally and practically." It was written, Hemingway says, because nothing like it had been done in either Spanish or English.

Chapter 1 attempts to answer the most obvious question, at least for an American: Why should anyone want to go to a bullfight? Hemingway says that "from a modern moral point of view, that is, a Christian point of view, the whole bullfight is indefensible; there is certainly much cruelty, there is always danger, either sought or unlooked for, and there is always death."

And, in the first of several statements about writing, Hemingway provides his definition of the difference between writing fiction and writing journalism. Fiction is writing that makes the reader feel the emotion that the character feels; journalism is merely telling what happened. The best place for a young writer to learn this, he says, is at moments of "violent death," and since the wars were over, the best place to see violent death was in the bull ring, and he had gone to Spain to study it. As for the morality of bullfighting, Hemingway says that "what is moral is what you feel good after and what is immoral is what you feel bad after."

Chapter 2 defines some key bullfight terms, focusing on the idea that the "bullfight is not a sport in the Anglo-Saxon sense of the word." The Americans and English "are not fascinated by death, its nearness and its avoidance. We are fascinated by victory and we replace the avoidance of death by the avoidance of defeat. . . . It is a very nice symbolism but it takes more *cojones* [testicles] to be a sportsman when death is a closer party to the game."

Chapter 3 concentrates on the bullfight itself, six bulls, two killed by each of three bullfighters. A bullfight in Spanish is called a CORRIDA DE TOROS or "running of bulls." The English word "bullfight" is a faulty translation of the Spanish meaning. The very strict rules of the bullfight are discussed, including those that apply to each member of a matador's "cuadrilla," or team, the BANDERILLEROS and the PICADORS. He describes how the bulls are selected and how to tell the difference between "good" and "bad" bulls. And where to sit for your first bullfight.

Chapter 4 covers the bullfight season in Spain, the best places and the best dates. And "girl inspection is a big part of bullfighting for the spectator." And to use "glasses [for the inspection] from a barrera seat is legitimate, and a compliment, and a means of communication and almost an introduction."

Chapter 5 explains Hemingway's love affair with Madrid. "Madrid is a strange place," he says, yet "when you get to know it, it is the most Spanish of all cities, the best to live in, the finest people, month in and month out the finest climate. . . . [And it] is in Madrid only that you get the essence [of Spain]. . . . [And] when you can have the Prado [Madrid's art museum] and the bullfight season at the same time. . . . it makes you feel very badly, all question of immortality aside, to know that you will have to die and never see it again."

Chapter 6 gives a description of the preliminaries to a bullfight, including the fear and sometimes cynicism of the bullfighter as he prepares for a fight.

Chapter 7 introduces the old lady (see LADY, OLD [2]), a fictional character who asks questions of Hemingway following her first bullfight and who enters into dialogue with him during all but one of the next eight chapters. She liked her first bullfight, but there are a number of things she does not understand, and Hemingway proceeds to explain them to her. He explains the decadence of modern bullfighting, how ranch owners have bred down their bulls in size and length of horn and how bullfighters have compensated. He describes for the Old Lady the competition he has been told about between

Juan BELMONTE and JOSELITO before May 16, 1920, when Joselito was killed in the ring.

Chapters 8 and 9 explain further the decay of bullfighting that has taken place in the decade of the 1920s. Near the end of chapter 9, still explaining the details of bullfighting, Hemingway states that it is the "death," in bullfighting, "that makes all the confusion. . . . Bullfighting is the only art," he says, "in which the artist is in danger of death and in which the degree of brilliance in the performance is left to the fighter's honor"—that is, in his willingness to take himself close to the bull without faking it.

Chapter 10 explains the three "acts" of the bullfight: first, the *suerte de varas* (the trial of the lances), in which the picadors on horseback "pic" the bull to slow it down; second, the banderillas (sticks about a yard long with harpoon-shaped steel points one-and-a-half inches long), which are placed in pairs in the humped muscle at the top of the bull's shoulders and meant to further slow the bull; third, the death of the bull.

The next three chapters present, collectively, an essay on the bulls. Chapter 11 begins, "The fighting bull is to the domestic bull as the wolf is to the dog." The bull is so intelligent that his contacts with humans are kept to a minimum during the four to four-and-a-half years of his preparation for the ring, and he has probably not seen a man on foot in all that time. And the bull "learns so rapidly in the ring that if the bullfight drags, is badly done, or is prolonged an extra ten minutes he becomes almost unkillable by the means prescribed in the rules of the spectacle"—the main reason for a 15-minute time limit on each fight. The fighting bull can outrun a horse for 25 yards from a standing start. And at the end of chapter 11, the Old Lady asks Hemingway about a bull's "love life," and so he tells her.

Chapter 12 includes a separate essay, which Hemingway titled "A Natural History of the Dead" (see the main entry for it) meant, ostensibly, to appease the Old Lady who is for the moment tired of hearing about animals.

Chapter 13 returns to the bull, particularly as he performs in the bull ring: "All of bullfighting is founded on the bravery of the bull, his simplicity and his lack of experience."

Chapter 14 begins with a definition of the "ideal bull" from a bullfighter's perspective—that is a "bull that will charge perfectly straight and will turn by himself at the end of each charge and charge again perfectly straight; a bull that charges as straight as though he were on rails." This wished-for bull comes along "only once in thirty or forty."

Chapter 15 deals with the increased importance of the cape in the modern bullfight, made more important by the work of Belmonte, who became an expert with the cape during the years of World War I and the early 1920s.

Chapter 16 is about the picadors and the horses, especially the decadent way of selecting the horses. The money paid to picadors is so little that they are eager for tips (a *propina*) to accept contractors' horses that are too old, or too weak, or that have been injured by bulls in earlier fights and so are sufficiently afraid to be dangerous. In the last, long paragraph of this chapter he also presents further ideas about writing, providing in particular his definitive statement on the THEORY OF OMISSION, the "iceberg principle."

Chapter 17 returns to further explanation about the role of the banderilleros in placing their banderillas, an act which Hemingway believes to be the most appealing aspect of the bullfight to the first-time spectator. Chapter 18 explains the use of the muleta, a scarlet cloth used by the matador, the artistic merit of which determines a bullfighter's ranking. "It is with the muleta that a reputation is made and it is by the extent of this ability to give a complete, imaginative, artistic and emotional performance with the muleta, granted that he has a good bull, that a bullfighter is paid much or little."

Chapter 19 explains the ways of killing bulls, and Hemingway presents more criticism of the American attitude about death. "Once you accept the rule of death," Hemingway says, "thou shalt not kill is an easily and a naturally obeyed commandment. But when a man is still in rebellion against death he has pleasure in taking to himself one of the Godlike attributes; that of giving it."

Chapter 20 is an apology to the reader for what is lacking in *Death in the Afternoon*. A good book should have "everything in it." By everything, Hemingway means the whole of Spain, because the book presents in detail not just an exposition on the art of bullfighting but an explanation of Hemingway's great love affair with Spain and the Spanish people.

At the end of the book's main text there are 81 black-and-white photographs, mostly superb action shots of bullfighters at work; "An Explanatory Glossary" of bullfight terms; selected reactions to bullfights by unidentified individuals; an essay on the American bullfighter Sidney Franklin; and "Dates on Which Bullfights will Ordinarily be Held in Spain, France, Mexico, and Central and South America."

Death in the Afternoon was published by Charles Scribner's Sons on September 23, 1932. The first edition consisted of 10,300 copies at $3.50 each. "A Natural History of the Dead" (taken from chapter 12) was reprinted as a "short story" in *Winner Take Nothing* (1933), and "A Short Estimate of the American, Sidney Franklin, as a Matador" was reprinted in *Bullfighter from Brooklyn* by Sidney Franklin (1952).

"Dedicated to F.W." Poem to Oak Park High School classmate Fred Wilcoxen. First publication was in the

Oak Park and River Forest High School newspaper, *Trapeze* (November 24, 1916).

Dedos, Cuatro In PILAR'S STORY to Robert JORDAN in *For Whom the Bell Tolls* Dedos helps PABLO push the last FASCISTS out of the *Ayuntamiento* (town hall) in Pilar's village toward their deaths, through a line of Loyalists and over a cliff.

"Defense of Dirty Words: A Cuban Letter" Article, published in *Esquire* (September 1934).

"Defense of Luxembourg" Antiwar poem written in 1945 and first published in *88 Poems* (1979).

Degas, Edgar (1834–1917) One of several impressionist painters whom Richard CANTWELL thinks about in *Across the River and Into the Trees*. Degas was born in Paris.

DelCredo, Enrico See Ralph SIMMONS.

Delys, Gaby (1884–1920) Gaby Deslys was a feather dancer in the music halls of Paris and London during World War I. She and Harry PILCER became a famous dance team. Hemingway misspells her name as "Delys" when he mentions her in "A Way You'll Never Be."

demijohns Large bottle with a narrow neck in a wicker casing, used in *To Have and Have Not* for carrying gasoline on Harry MORGAN's boat.

De Mille, Cecil B. (1881–1959) American movie director and producer, mentioned in *Islands in the Stream* by Roger DAVIS, a former Hollywood scriptwriter. De Mille is best known for Hollywood "spectaculars," particularly *The Greatest Show on Earth* (1953), for which he won an Academy Award, and *The Ten Commandments* (1956).

Dempsey, Jack (1895–1983) U.S. boxer from Manassa, Colorado, and known as "the Manassa Mauler." He was world heavyweight champion (1919–26), knocking out Jess Willard to win the title in Toledo and losing the title to Gene Tunney in Philadelphia. He fought Tunney again in 1927 and lost a 10-round decision in a fight that involved the famous "long count" in the seventh round, with Tunney down for longer than the normal 10-second count. Dempsey's real name was William Harrison.

In the "Cuba" section of *Islands in the Stream* Thomas HUDSON argues that weight is not the primary factor in a good boxer and uses, for example, the Dempsey-Willard championship fight when Willard was much heavier than Dempsey. Hudson argues that weight is unimportant in boxing matches or cat fights.

Dent de Jaman Mountain peak (6,140 feet) northeast of MONTREUX, Switzerland; seen in *A Farewell to Arms* by Frederic HENRY and Catherine BARKLEY.

Dent du Midi Mountain range in southwest Switzerland (10,683 feet), seen from Montreux across the east end of Lake Geneva by Ernest and Hadley Hemingway and their friend Chink DORMAN-SMITH on a trip Hemingway describes in *A Moveable Feast*.

In *A Farewell to Arms* Frederic HENRY and Catherine BARKLEY can see the Dent du Midi across the eastern end of Lake Geneva from their hilltop house above Montreux.

Dent editions J. M. Dent (1849–1926) was an English bookbinder first and then a publisher, beginning with the Temple Library series and then the Everyman's Library series. In *The Garden of Eden* David BOURNE's copy of W. H. Hudson's *Far Away and Long Ago* is one of the Dent editions.

"Denunciation, The" This short story takes place in CHICOTE'S RESTAURANT in Madrid during the Spanish civil war. It is November 1937, and the main character is the narrator, Enrique EMMUNDS, who tells the story of his denunciation of Luis Delgado, a friend who has turned fascist.

Delgado is in Chicote's bar—where only LOYALISTS dared to make an appearance—wearing a Loyalist uniform. Emmunds knows him as a brave man but calls him a "fool" and gives a waiter, who also recognizes him, the telephone number of the counterespionage bureau. Emmunds leaves before the police arrive and later that night feels guilty that he had let the waiter take the responsibility for the denunciation.

He calls a friend at the bureau and asks him to tell Delgado that he, Emmunds, had denounced him to the security police. He realizes it is a small thing, because Delgado will soon be shot, but he is pleased with himself, nevertheless, calling his confession a small act of kindness, because "Delgado was an old client of Chicote's and I did not wish him to be disillusioned or bitter about the waiters there before he died."

The story appeared first in *Esquire* (November 1938) and then as the first of the "stories" in *The Fifth Column and Four Stories of the Spanish Civil War* (1969).

Denver Post In "The Gambler, the Nun, and the Radio," Mr. FRAZER can get a "picture" of Denver from the *Denver Post* newspaper that "corrects" the one he gets from *The Rocky Mountain News*.

De Quincey, Thomas (1785–1859) English essayist, referred to as "Mr. DeQuincey" in *Islands in the Stream*. Roger DAVIS explains to "young Tom" that he had not become involved in the drug trade when he lived in

Paris because De Quincey and Cocteau had "done so well in it."

Derain, André (1880–1954)   French postimpressionist painter and illustrator, associated with the Fauve movement, characterized by the use of violent color. In *The Garden of Eden* Catherine BOURNE suggests to David a list of illustrators for the book he is writing about their marriage and ménage à trois with Marita. Derain is one of the artists she names.

Der Querschnitt   German literary journal, founded in 1920 by Alfred Flechtheim, an art dealer in Frankfurt-am-Main. Flechtheim's Paris representative and later the journal's editor, Count Alfred von Wedderkop, bought five of Hemingway's poems for publication in 1924, and his short story "The Undefeated" was bought for publication in 1925. The magazine's name means "The Cross Section."

Kandisky in *Green Hills of Africa* asks Hemingway if he is *the* Hemingway whose "rather obscene" poems he had recently read in *Querschnitt*.

Desdemona   Character in Shakespeare's *Othello*. In *Across the River and Into the Trees* Richard CANTWELL lies in bed with his 18-year-old lover, RENATA, glad that they are not Othello and Desdemona, although, as he thinks, it's the same town, Venice, and the girl, Renata, is "better looking" than the Shakespearean character.

desert   In East Africa, "broken" and "volcanic," part of the setting for the AFRICAN STORY that David BOURNE writes in *The Garden of Eden*.

detective sergeant   In "The Gambler, the Nun, and the Radio," he interrogates the Russian and Mexican beet workers who are wounded by gunshots in an all-night restaurant in Hailey, Montana.

Detroit News, The   Available for reading at BROWN'S BEANERY in *The Torrents of Spring*.

Deux-Magots, Les   A café located at 170, boulevard Saint-Germain in Paris, at the corner of boulevard Saint-Germain and rue Bonaparte, across from the church of Saint-Germain-des-Prés. It was one of Hemingway's favorite cafés while he lived in Paris during the 1920s.

devil (1)   Name that Thomas HUDSON, in *Islands in the Stream,* sometimes thinks of when he remembers his first wife.

devil (2)   Name David BOURNE gives to his wife, Catherine, as a result of her androgynous, bisexual drive in *The Garden of Eden.*

Dial, The   Quarterly literary journal, founded in Chicago by Francis F. Browne and published from 1880–1929, moving to New York City in 1918. It was the most distinguished literary monthly of its time. Its editors included Conrad Aiken, Van Wyck Brooks, Scofield Thayer, and Marianne Moore; and it published works by T. S. ELIOT, Thomas Mann, D. H. Lawrence, E. E. Cummings, and Sherwood ANDERSON, plus drawings by Henri de Toulouse-Lautrec, Pablo PICASSO, and Marc Chagall. Thayer was the editor from 1919 to 1926, covering Hemingway's first years in Paris.

In *A Moveable Feast* Hemingway refers to the magazine's annual prize of "$1,000" for the best writing done by a contributor, but from 1921–28 the prize was actually $2,000 a year, a lot of money for a young writer, considering the annual per capita income in the United States then was about $750. The prize would have been worth about $40,000 in the 1990s. During those eight years, they went to Sherwood Anderson, T. S. Eliot, Van Wyck Brooks, Marianne Moore, E. E. Cummings, William Carlos Williams, Ezra POUND, and Kenneth Burke.

David BOURNE in *The Garden of Eden* is angered by his publisher's notion that his second novel "validates" his first, and so he questions to whom he promised validation—certainly not to the journals that had reviewed his book, one of which was *The Dial.*

Diana   See Diana SCRIPPS.

"Did Poincaré Laugh in Verdun Cemetery?"   Article, published in *The Toronto Daily Star* (August 12, 1922), reprinted in *Ernest Hemingway: Dateline Toronto* (1985). Dateline "Paris." During U.S. government ceremonies honoring the town of Verdun for its efforts in World War I, a French Communist Party photographer took pictures of French premier Poincaré and U.S. ambassador Herrick laughing in the cemetery. Both gentlemen denied that they had laughed, but there was a debate over the issue and much embarrassment in the Chamber of Deputies, nevertheless.

Dijon   Town in France 195 miles southeast of Paris, where, in "Mr. and Mrs. Elliot," the Elliots go for a summer school and to see friends they had met on the boat to France. The term is also mentioned in *A Moveable Feast.*

DiMaggio, Joe (1914–1999)   Major league baseball player with the New York Yankees (1936–51), with a lifetime batting average of .325. In *The Old Man and the Sea* SANTIAGO remembers him often during his ordeal with the marlin, especially his ability to play baseball in spite of a "bone spur," which the old man wonders about in comparison to his own "cramped" left hand. He also thinks about him because DiMaggio's father was a fisherman.

Dinesen, Isak (1885–1962) Pseudonym of Karen Christence Dinesen, Baroness Blixen-Finecke, Danish novelist and short story writer, best known for her non-fiction book *Out of Africa* (1937) and for her collection of short stories, *Seven Gothic Tales* (1934). She is mentioned in connection with a story about her husband, Baron von Blixen, told by Hemingway in *A Moveable Feast.*

Dingo bar In Paris at 10, rue Delambre, now named l'Auberge du Centre. In *The Sun Also Rises,* Brett ASHLEY and Mike CAMPBELL meet Jake BARNES at the Dingo on June 21, before leaving Paris for Spain on the 26th. Jake describes it as one of the new, popular bars. It is also the setting for "The Sea Change."

And it is, according to Hemingway in *A Moveable Feast,* the place where he and F. Scott FITZGERALD met for the first time in late April 1925. Section 17 of the book is titled "Scott Fitzgerald" and describes the meeting of the two men, one a 25-year-old at the beginning of his writing career, the other a 29-year-old almost at the peak of his, already well known for *The Beautiful and Damned* (1922). *The Great Gatsby* was published in New York on April 10, 1925, just a few days before the two men met at the Dingo bar.

Distinguished Service Cross (D.S.C.) U.S. Army bronze medal, awarded for extraordinary heroism in military action against an armed enemy. Colonel Richard CANTWELL in *Across the River and Into the Trees* received this medal in World War I.

"Divine Gesture, A" Allegory with an obscure meaning. The "Great Lord God" (who looks like Tolstoi) is in a Roman garden on a Sunday, conversing with talking broken flowerpots and bathtubs. There are blackbirds, animated boot jacks, and an absent Adam and Eve. A disgusted and busy God "makes a divine gesture to the angel Gabriel who [follows] him quietly out of the garden," after which they argue about English verb usage.

Dennis Ryan, writing in *The Hemingway Review,* argues that "A Divine Gesture" is an experimental piece in which Hemingway, trying to develop a personal style, "parodies automatic writing" and "burlesques" the Dada movement in art, popular in 1921 when Hemingway wrote the fable.

The DADAISTS created works in which an object was intended as something other than itself and so required the participation of the viewer, whose own imagination provided the meaning. Ryan says that, in this fable, Hemingway used objects like flowerpots and bathtubs and "subjected them to radical recontextualizations to elicit subjective reactions in his readers." But he does it in such a way, Ryan suggests, that it parodies contemporary writers who were participants in the Dada movement. See Ryan's article, "'A Divine

Gesture': Hemingway's Complex Parody of the Modern" in *The Hemingway Review* (Fall 1996).

"A Divine Gesture" was first published in *Double Dealer* magazine (May 1922) and reprinted in a separate, limited edition by Aloe Press in 1974.

Doc NICK's father, the doctor in "The Doctor and the Doctor's Wife." He hires three Indians to cut up logs that have drifted ashore from one of the LOG BOOMS being pulled down the lake to the mill. He sees the logs as driftwood, but Dick BOULTON, one of the Indians, calls taking the logs stealing. The doctor feels "uncomfortable," especially with Nick there. He challenges Boulton to stop calling him "Doc," but the Indian continues, and the doctor walks off, refusing, perhaps afraid, to fight.

The doctor goes back to his cottage, where his wife asks what the trouble was about. She is a Christian Scientist. The tension between them created by his chosen profession and her antithetical spiritual beliefs is evident when he first apologizes to her for the disturbance, then after she asks him to send Nick in to her the doctor allows Nick to follow him into the woods to hunt for black squirrels instead.

doctor (1) NICK's father in "Indian Camp." He performs a CAESARIAN SECTION on an Indian woman with a jackknife and no anesthetic, and then sews the incision with gut leaders from fishing line. It is a successful operation, and the doctor is exhilarated by the event and excited to share it with his young son, a boy of about eight or nine years. But the excitement is checked when they turn to the woman's husband in the bunk above. He had cut his leg badly with an ax three days before and so is there to hear everything. And he slits his throat, apparently because he cannot stand the screaming. The doctor is apologetic to Nick and tries to answer his questions about death and dying as calmly as possible, but it's Nick's story and it ends with Nick feeling sure that "he would never die."

doctor (2) In the "Chapter 14" vignette of *In Our Time* (1925), he has been "sewing up picador horses" when he is called in to sew up the matador MAERA, who has been gored badly but dies before the doctor can operate.

doctor (3) Major in the Italian army, who treats the narrator of "In Another Country" for his knee wound.

doctor (4) Recipient of a letter written by the main character in "One Reader Writes." She got his name from a photograph caption in a Roanoke, Virginia, newspaper.

doctor (5) In "A Day's Wait." He takes SCHATZ's temperature and leaves medicine for his flu condition, one for the fever, one as a purgative, and one "to overcome an acid condition." He tells the father that the "germs of influenza can only exist in an acid condition."

doctor (6)   The last two-plus pages of "A Natural History of the Dead" are devoted to the narrator's story of an Italian captain-doctor who refuses to kill a badly wounded soldier. He gets in an argument with a lieutenant who calls the doctor inhumane for not ending the man's life. After being cursed by the lieutenant, the doctor throws a container of iodine in his face, temporarily blinding him. All of this for "nothing," the doctor says, after the wounded soldier dies without anyone's help.

doctor (7)   In *To Have and Have Not* he helps carry Harry MORGAN off his boat at the KEY WEST docks and to the hospital, where Harry dies. The doctor informs Marie of Harry's death when she arrives at the hospital.

doctor (8)   Richard CANTWELL's doctor, Wes, in *Across the River and Into the Trees*, is a surgeon. He gives Cantwell his physical examination at the beginning of the novel and tells him that his cardiograph is "O.K.," but that they "ought to make you drag a chain like a high-octane truck." The doctor knows that Cantwell has taken NITROGLYCERIN to make the cardiograph look good and to pass the exam so he can go on the duck hunting trip.

"Doctor and the Doctor's Wife, The"   This short story brings together NICK's parents, an uneasy marriage of a Christian Scientist mother, who believes that prayer is preferable to medicine, and a doctor father. The doctor, "Henry" to his wife but "Doc" to the Indians who work for him, hires three Indians to cut up logs that have come loose from one of the large log booms pulled down the lake but considered driftwood by Nick's father.

Dick BOULTON suggests to the doctor that he is stealing the logs from the log companies, since the logs are marked with the company name. The doctor feels "uncomfortable," but walks off, refusing to fight with Boulton.

He goes back to his cottage, where his wife lies on her bed "with the blinds drawn." She hopes he hasn't lost his temper and wants to know what the trouble was about. He apologizes for the disturbance, and she says, "It's all right, dear." The doctor explains that Boulton owes him money and, by getting in a "row," thinks that he won't have to work to pay the debt. She asks him to send Nick in to her, and the doctor gives Nick the message but then allows him to go along with him to hunt black squirrels instead of responding to his mother's request.

"The Doctor and the Doctor's Wife" was first published in *transatlantic review* (December 1924) and reprinted in *In Our Time* (1925).

doctors, Catherine's   In *A Farewell to Arms* the pregnant Catherine BARKLEY has three doctors: in MONTREUX, Switzerland, where she goes for checkups; at the hospital in LAUSANNE, where she goes to have her baby; and, also in Lausanne, a doctor called in to assist with the CAESAREAN SECTION.

doctors, Frederic's   An unspecified number of doctors are at the post hospital where Frederic HENRY is carried after his wounding near the end of book 1 in *A Farewell to Arms*. And, initially, there are three doctors who inspect his wounds at the AMERICAN HOSPITAL (1) in Milan. One is "tall" and "gaunt," another is "bearded," and the third is "the house doctor." Apparently incompetent, these three tell Frederic he must wait six months to allow the metal shell fragments in his legs to "encyst and [for] the synovial fluid" to reform before he has an operation. But then the hospital's regular doctor returns from holiday and, after a quick examination, suggests an operation the next day.

dogfish   Small sharks. In *A Farewell to Arms* Frederic HENRY uses it as a metaphor for people during the war (World War I) who steal food and sell it on the black market. Gino is complaining about the lack of food on the Bainsizza, his home region in Italy, and Frederic tells him the "dogfish are selling it somewhere else."

Dog's Head   Brand of ale, offered to Thomas HUDSON by MR. BOBBY in the "BIMINI" section of *Islands in the Stream*.

Dog's Head ale is the drink of choice for everyone at the INDIAN CLUB in PETROSKEY in *The Torrents of Spring*.

dolphin   A toothed whale in the same family with killer whales, white whales, narwhals, and porpoises. But it is the bottle-nosed dolphin that is most common along the Atlantic coast and the one most likely to be caught by SANTIAGO in the Gulf Stream of *The Old Man and the Sea*.

Dolphin is one of the lesser fish fished for in *The Old Man and the Sea*. Santiago, who refers to dolphin as *dorado*, catches a dolphin on one of his smaller lines and brings him into the skiff while his lines are hooked to the great MARLIN. Inside the dolphin are "two flying fish," which the old man saves for later eating.

Domínguin, Domingo   Brother of Luis Miguel Domínguin and manager, with another brother, Pepé, for both Domínguin and Antonio Ordóñez, the two major bullfighters in *The Dangerous Summer*.

Domínguin, Luis Miguel (1925–1996)   One of the two matadors Hemingway wrote about in *The Dangerous Summer*. He was 33 years old in 1959, the year of his "mano a mano" in Spain's bull rings with

EH with Ava Gardner and Spanish matador Luis Miguel Dominguín (Copyright holder unknown; photo courtesy of the John F. Kennedy Library)

Antonio ORDÓÑEZ. In spite of Hemingway's seeming bias toward Ordóñez, both during the summer of the bullfights and in the *Life* magazine version of *The Dangerous Summer*, Dominguín remained a good friend of the Hemingways. Two of his brothers, Domingo and Pepé, were managers for both bullfighters, which complicated Hemingway's task of covering the bullfight circuit.

Dominguín, Pepé   Brother of Luis Miguel Dominguín and manager, with their brother, Domingo, for both Dominguín and Antonio ORDÓÑEZ, the two major bullfighters described in *The Dangerous Summer*.

Donne, John   (1572–1631)   Seventeenth-century English poet who provides Hemingway with the epigraph of *For Whom the Bell Tolls*, quoted here as it appears opposite page 1 of the Charles Scribner's Sons edition: "No man is an *Iland*, intire of it selfe; every man/is a peece of the *Continent*, a part of the *maine*; if a/*Clod* bee washed away by the *Sea*, *Europe* is the lesse,/as well as if a *Promontorie* were, as well as if a *Mannor*/of the *friends* or of *thine owne* were; any mans/*death* diminishes *me*, because I am in-/volved in *Mankinde*; And therefore/never send to know for/whom the *bell* tolls; It/tolls for *thee*.

In *A Moveable Feast* Hemingway describes a strange conversation he had with Ford Madox Ford that included a discussion of the men they considered to be "gentlemen." When Ford suggests Donne, Hemingway's only comment is, "He was a parson."

Donovan's   Bar in Havana where Harry MORGAN gets a beer in part 1 of *To Have and Have Not*.

Dorman-Smith, Eric Edward "Chink"   (1895–1969)   An Irish captain in His Majesty's Fifth Fusiliers when he and Hemingway first met in Milan in 1918. Hemingway was recovering from wounds suffered while driving an ambulance for the Italian army. The two became good friends immediately, a friendship that lasted until Hemingway's death more than 40 years later. Chink was godfather for Hemingway's oldest son, Jack, baptized in Paris March 16, 1924.

Dorman-Smith was a Lieutenant General and chief of staff under General Claude Auchinleck in WORLD WAR II in the British African campaign. He told Hemingway how he and Auchinleck had lost their command. Prime Minister Winston CHURCHILL visited the troops in North Africa, shortly after General Auchinleck had just won the first battle of Alamein, a turning point in the war against the German Afrika Korps. Dorman-Smith had already designed the plans for the second attack, but Churchill wanted the British to attack immediately, and when Auchinleck declined, Churchill replaced him with General Bernard Montgomery. This incident probably provided the model for a bitter experience remembered by Colonel Richard CANTWELL in *Across the River and Into the Trees* in which he is unjustly demoted.

In *Green Hills of Africa* Hemingway mentions his army friend "Chink" and refers to him as "Captain Eric Edward Dorman-Smith, M.C. of His Majesty's Fifth Fusiliers."

In *A Moveable Feast* Hemingway, writing about his and Hadley's relationship with Chink, states that he was "our best friend." The three of them traveled across northern Italy together and fished for trout near Aigle, Switzerland. He is also mentioned in *Green Hills of Africa*.

Dorothy Bridges   See Dorothy BRIDGES.

Dos Passos, John   (1896–1970)   American writer, one of the LOST GENERATION novelists, best known for *Three Soldiers* (1921) and his trilogy *U.S.A.* (*The 42nd Parallel* [1930], *1919* [1932], and *The Big Money* [1936]). These works are portrayals of the artist trying to cope with the shock of the post–World War I era in the United States.

Dos Passos, like Hemingway, was born in the Chicago area, and, like Hemingway, served in WORLD WAR I with an army ambulance corps. They met for the first time in 1918 in northern Italy during the war, just before Dos Passos was to leave for Paris to join the U.S. Army Ambulance Corps and just before Hemingway was wounded (July 8) while serving as an ambulance driver with the Italian army.

After the war the two writers were friends in France during the 1920s, and in 1929 Dos Passos married Katy SMITH, one of Hemingway's friends from his northern Michigan years. Dos Passos helped write the screenplay of *The Spanish Earth,* produced in 1937, which Hemingway narrated.

Dostoyevsky, Fyodor Mikhaylovich (1821–1881) Russian novelist and short story writer, best known for *Crime and Punishment* (1866) and *The Brothers Karamazov* (1879–80).

In discussing writing in *Green Hills of Africa* Hemingway says that "Dostoevsky was made by being sent to Siberia. Writers are forged in injustice as a sword is forged."

In *A Moveable Feast* Hemingway writes that when Sylvia Beach encouraged him to borrow more than just the one book he had picked out (Turgenev's *A Sportsman's Sketches*) on his first visit to Shakespeare and Company, he chose the Constance Garnett translation of *War and Peace* and Dostoyevsky's *The Gambler and Other Stories*. He says of Dostoyevsky that there were some things "so true" in his writing that "they changed you as you read them; frailty and madness, wickedness and saintliness, and the insanity of gambling. . . ." The Russian author's name is often translated into English as *Dostoevsky*.

double Canfield Solitary card game, mentioned in *Across the River and Into the Trees.* Richard CANTWELL thinks of it in connection with a game he plays while walking the streets of VENICE, a "*solitaire ambulante,*" alone, in which he observes the Venetian landmarks while he walks, without counting streets and yet getting where he wants to go—a difficult task in Venice. The "game was to leave from the Gritti [Hotel] and make the Rialto [bridge] by the *Fondamente Nuove* without a mistake."

Double Dealer Literary journal founded in New Orleans by Julius Weis Friend and published from January 1921 until May 1926. It was the first professional magazine to publish Hemingway's fiction, "A Divine Gesture" (May 1922).

The magazine was supported by Sherwood ANDERSON and H. L. MENCKEN and helped launch the careers of several writers, including Hart Crane and Thornton Wilder.

double frozen daiquiris In the "Cuba" section of *Islands in the Stream* Thomas HUDSON spends a morning drinking daiquiris at the FLORIDITA BAR in Havana. He is drinking to forget the killing of his oldest son, young Tom, in France during the war, but everyone at the bar keeps sympathizing with him and making it impossible for him to forget.

Hudson drinks at least seven double frozen daiquiris "without sugar," and since the barkeep leaves "at least another full daiquiri in the bottom" of the mixer, which he puts in front of Hudson each time he serves him a

drink, the reader is led to believe the real total is 14. Then his first wife shows up, prepared to spend the afternoon with him—most of it in bed—before she, an entertainer with the USO, flies on to a military base she does not identify.

Doyle, Jerry Narrator of the short story "Fifty Grand." He is the trainer for Jack BRENNAN, a boxer who is the story's main character. Doyle realizes that Brennan has agreed to throw a big fight scheduled for New York's Madison Square Garden, but he doesn't do anything about it. Perhaps he feels he's not in a position to do anything; perhaps he realizes that Brennan will probably lose the fight anyway; or perhaps, because he's telling the story, he prefers to seem objective.

Drake, Charles In "My Old Man," he is the owner of the stable where JOE's "old man" keeps his horse, GILFORD.

Drevitts Police officer in the "Chapter 8" vignette of *In Our Time* who is frightened by the cold-blooded shooting by his partner, Jimmy BOYLE, of two Hungarian robbers of a cigar store. Boyle shot the two men because he thought they were "wops" (Italians).

Droopy One of the trackers, "about thirty-five," in part 2 of *Green Hills of Africa*. Hemingway, who likes him perhaps better than any of the other natives, is impressed by Droopy's "trick" of slitting open the stomach of a waterbuck, turning it inside out, and using it as a carrying sack.

drummer Unnamed salesman ("drummer") in *The Torrents of Spring*, a customer at BROWN'S BEANERY, who, midway through the novel, says he wants to tell the waitress and Scripps O'NEIL "about a pretty beautiful thing that happened" to him "once in Bay City." But when they turn to listen, he says: "Tell you about it some other time, brother." In this novel, each of the characters is similarly impotent in his or her inability to think clearly or to even remember events of facts clearly. See also Oscar GARDNER.

D.S.O. Distinguished Service Order, awarded to U.S. military personnel for valor in war. In *The Torrents of Spring* the two Indians brag about winning the D.S.O., probably an exaggeration of their wartime experiences. See INDIANS, TWO.

D.T.'s Slang for delirium tremens, brought on by excessive drinking of alcoholic beverages. In "A Pursuit Race," Mr. TURNER thinks William CAMPBELL has the D.T.'s, but Campbell's delirium turns out to be drug-induced.

Dufy, Raoul (1877–1953) French painter, best known as a member of the fauve movement. In *The Garden of*

Eden Catherine BOURNE suggests to David a list of illustrators for the book he is writing about their marriage and ménage à trois with Marita. Dufy is one of the artists she names.

Dunning, Ralph Cheever (1878–1930) American poet whose first book of poems, *Rococo,* was published by the Black Manikin Press in Paris in 1926. He had won a *Poetry* magazine contest the year before, and both the prize and the book created critical controversy among writers in Paris.

He was supported by Ezra POUND, who was instrumental in getting some of his poetry published. Dunning lived in Paris in a top-floor flat at 70, rue Notre-Dame-des-Champs, a "neighbor" of the Hemingways after they moved to No. 113 in 1924.

Dunning was addicted to opium, and, in *A Moveable Feast,* Hemingway writes that when Pound left Paris in 1924 he made Hemingway promise to take a jar of opium to Dunning in any "emergency" and that when the emergency arrived Hemingway delivered the drug to the dying Dunning, only to have the poet kick him out of his apartment with an epithet and "flying milk bottles."

duomo Cathedral (the word means "cathedral" or "dome" in Italian) in Padua, mentioned in "A Very Short Story." The story's main character, HE, and LUZ go to the cathedral to pray and to get married, but there isn't enough time for the banns, nor do they have birth certificates.

Also the great Duomo in Milan, Italy, is mentioned in *Green Hills of Africa.*

Durán, Gustavo (1906–1969) Spanish composer and pianist and known, in *For Whom the Bell Tolls,* as a "lad about town before the movement." He was commander of the XI International Brigade and later of the XX Army Corps during the SPANISH CIVIL WAR.

Durocher, Leo (1905–1991) Major League baseball player (1925–45), mostly with the St. Louis Cardinals and the Brooklyn Dodgers, but better known as manager of the Dodgers (1939–48) and of the New York Giants (1948–55). In *The Old Man and the Sea* SANTIAGO remembers that Durocher fished once while staying in Santiago's small Cuban village.

Duval In *For Whom the Bell Tolls,* one of three officers to whom Robert JORDAN sends ANDRÉS with a message that a Rebel counterattack is going to take place and that the LOYALIST attack should be called off. Duval makes the emergency call to General GOLZ, only to hear at the other end of the telephone line the beginning of the Loyalist attack.

Duzinell, Madame Concierge at Jake BARNES's flat in Paris, in *The Sun Also Rises.* At first angry at Brett ASHLEY for disturbing her late at night when Brett and Count MIPPIPOPOLOUS want to go up to Jake's flat, she is much friendlier after Brett gives her a big tip.

"Dying, Well or Badly" Article, published in *Ken* (April 21, 1938). Hemingway writes about the accompanying photographs of dead soldiers from the Spanish civil war, including some photographs that Hemingway took.

Eakins, Thomas (1844–1916) American painter, best known perhaps for "The Chess Players," "The Concert Singer," and "The Swimming Hole." While Thomas HUDSON is watching his crew bathe off the stern of his boat in the "At Sea" section of *Islands in the Stream,* he thinks he would like to have Cézanne paint the picture but then decides he would prefer to have it painted by Eakins.

"Earnest Liberal's Lament, The" Poem written in 1922 and first published in the German publication *Der Querschnitt* (Autumn 1924).

earth moves, the The idea is part of Robert JORDAN's INTERIOR MONOLOGUE at the end of a love-making scene with MARÍA in *For Whom the Bell Tolls.* "And he felt the earth move out and away from under them." The two lovers later discuss having felt "the earth move."

Easter Sunday "Old Man at the Bridge," a story out of the Spanish civil war, takes place on Easter Sunday, probably in 1938 (which would make the date April 17).

Ebro River Forming in a lake near Reinosa in northern Spain, about 24 miles from the Bay of Biscay, the Ebro River flows southeast from northern Spain about 450 miles, through Logrone and Zaragoza, emptying into the Mediterranean just southeast of Tortosa, near Amposta. The bridge in "Old Man at the Bridge" crosses the river near Tortosa.

A train station in the valley of the Ebro, probably near Zaragoza, is the setting for "Hills Like White Elephants."

Éclaireur de Nice Supplement to the weekly newspaper *L'Eclaireur du dimanches et la Vie pratique* published in Nice, France (1920–37), and read by David BOURNE in *The Garden of Eden.*

École Alsacienne In Paris, mentioned in *Islands in the Stream* as the school attended by young Tom HUDSON.

Eddie Owner of the *IRYDIA IV* luxury boat and one of the "haves" in *To Have and Have Not.* He is "a professional son-in-law of the very rich." On his boat, he is drunk and asleep next to Dorothy HOLLIS, his mistress.

Eddy (1) One of the Indians, the son of Dick BOULTON, in "The Doctor and the Doctor's Wife."

Eddy (2) Harry MORGAN's rummy friend, Eddy Marshall, and the first mate on board Morgan's fishing boat in part 1 of *To Have and Have Not.* Harry says he "was a good man on a boat once," before he became an alcoholic. Later Harry says of him, "He walked with his joints all slung wrong." After Harry kills Mr. SING, who has arranged for Harry to transport 12 Chinese men out of Havana, Harry realizes that Eddy will talk and plans to kill him before they get back to KEY WEST. But then he discovers that Eddy had arranged to put his name on the crew list and changes his mind, telling him, "God looks after rummies." Harry would have to explain the absence of anyone on the crew list. Eddy's name is sometimes spelled "Eddie."

Eddy (3) A "rummy" in *Islands in the Stream,* Thomas HUDSON's cook, good fishing companion, and friend to Hudson's three sons. It is Eddy who shoots with a sub-

EH on the Ebro River in Spain, April 1938 (Copyright holder unknown; photo courtesy of the John F. Kennedy Library)

machine gun the hammerhead shark that threatens David while the boys are swimming off their father's boat in the novel's "Bimini" section. He also encourages David during his struggle to bring in a 1,000-pound broadbill swordfish and, when David's line breaks, dives overboard in an attempt to grab it.

Editor and Publisher   Magazine for journalists, founded in 1884 for editors, publishers, and reporters, and now of interest to all media people. In *The Sun Also Rises* ambiguity occurs in the sentence in which the name is used: "He [Robert COHN] sat in the outer room and read the papers, and the Editor and Publisher and I [Jake BARNES] worked hard for two hours." It's unlikely that Hemingway would capitalize the two words if he means the editor and publisher of the newspaper for which he works (and would it be one person or two?), but the lack of punctuation makes that meaning possible. Hemingway tended to put quotation marks around the titles of literary works and magazines, though he does not here. Even so, it is probably a reference to the magazine.

Edna   Bill GORTON's "friend from Biarritz," who joins Jake BARNES's crowd of friends in PAMPLONA during the Fiesta SAN FERMÍN in *The Sun Also Rises*.

Edwards, Mr.   Minor character in *Islands in the Stream*, who, according to the narrator, was a "worthless man who turned out to be a fairy."

Eglise de la Madeleine   Church in Paris at place de la Madeleine, just up the rue Royale from the place de la Concorde. Construction of the church was begun by King Louis XV in 1764 with a design by Constant d'Ivry but halted when it was decided the design was too much like the Church of the Invalides, just across the river. Building resumed under the direction of the designer Couture in 1777 but was again interrupted during the French Revolution. The church was finally completed in 1806 by Vignon under Napoleon.

In *The Sun Also Rises* Jake BARNES gets off the S Bus at "the Madeleine" and walks to his office, near the Opéra.

Eglise du Val de Grâce   Paris church that Jake BARNES passes on the rue Saint-Jacques in chapter 8 of *The Sun Also Rises*. The church had been a hospital for wounded soldiers since 1793.

Eglise Saint-Etienne du Mont   Rebuilt on the site of an earlier church in 1491, this Paris edifice underwent further construction in 1537, 1541, 1580, 1610, and 1624, resulting in its wide variety of architectural styles, including late Gothic and Renaissance. It was much admired by Hemingway. He describes in *A Moveable Feast* walking from his apartment at 74, rue

Cardinal Lemoine toward place Saint-Michel by way of Saint-Etienne du Mont and the Panthéon, to the boulevard Saint-Michel, past the Cluny Museum and the boulevard Saint-Germain to a café on the place Saint-Michel.

It is one of several places the taxi passes by as Jake BARNES and Brett ASHLEY ride on their way to the CAFÉ SELECT at the beginning of chapter 4 of *The Sun Also Rises*. Other places mentioned on the taxi ride are the trees and a standing bus at the place de la Contrescarpe, the cobbles of the rue Mouffetard, with "lighted bars" and late open shops on each side of the street, and work being done on the avenue des Gobelins. The details that Jake provides in this scene show his attempt to concentrate on these details in order to avoid thinking about his love for Brett and the fact that he cannot consummate that love.

88's   German artillery guns used against U.S. Army troops at the battle of HÜRTGEN FOREST in WORLD WAR II, described by Richard CANTWELL in *Across the River and Into the Trees* and referred to in the article "War in the Siegfried Line."

eighty-four days   In *The Old Man and the Sea* the length of time SANTIAGO has gone without catching a fish.

Eisenhower, Dwight David (1890–1969)   U.S. military general during WORLD WAR II and president (1953–61). The general is "[s]trictly the Epworth League," indicating high class, according to Richard CANTWELL in *Across the River and Into the Trees*. Other World War II generals mentioned are "[Omar] Bradley, the schoolmaster"; "Lightning Joe [Collins] . . . a good one. . . . Commanded the Seventh Corps when I [Cantwell] was there"; and [General George] Patton.

Eladio   One of the partizans in PABLO's BAND of Spanish guerrilla fighters, helping Robert JORDAN in *For Whom the Bell Tolls*. Eladio, who is André's older brother, is killed after the bridge is blown.

eland   Largest of the African antelopes; the bull can reach six feet in height at the shoulders and weigh more than 1,200 pounds. Its spiral horns extend straight upward. It is the main luncheon course for Francis and Margot MACOMBER after his failure at lion hunting in "The Short Happy Life of Francis Macomber." Margot describes the eland as the "big cowy things that jump like hares." Her husband reminds her that it's "very good meat."

It is also one of the animals hunted on the safari described in *Green Hills of Africa*.

El Crisol   Havana daily newspaper, read by Thomas HUDSON in *Islands in the Stream*. He reads the current news about the Allied forces movement through Italy in February 1944. It helps set the time of the "Cuba" section of the novel.

elephant In *The Garden of Eden* David BOURNE's AFRICAN STORY is about the killing by his father of an old elephant that David had come to admire and that symbolized for him the faithfulness and friendship he did not see in his father. David remembers that as a boy of about eight he told his father where the elephant was located, and, after his father had killed it, David felt guilty for having betrayed the beautiful animal.

El Escorial The palace and monastery complex of Escorial, about 27 miles northwest of Madrid, features in *For Whom the Bell Tolls* as a planning headquarters for General GOLZ's attack following the destruction of the BRIDGE by Robert JORDAN and his Republican friends. David BOURNE also refers to El Escorial in *The Garden of Eden.*

El Escorial was built (1563–84) by King Philip II as a retreat for San Lorenzo del Escorial. The complex includes a monastery, palace, church, college, library, and mausoleum of the kings of Spain. Its art gallery includes works by El GRECO, TINTORETTO, and VELÁZQUEZ.

Elias Leader, with Alejandro, of a band of Spanish guerrilla fighters, five men whom PABLO recruits to help Robert JORDAN blow up the BRIDGE in *For Whom the Bell Tolls;* two of the others are Pepe and Elicio. It is probable that Pablo kills them all after the bridge is blown up in order to have enough horses for Jordan and his own band of guerrillas.

Eliot, T. S. (1888–1965) Thomas Stearns Eliot, American poet, playwright, and literary critic, winner of the Nobel Prize for literature in 1948. He is best known for his poems *The Waste Land* (1922) and *The Four Quartets* (1936–43), for his play *Murder in the Cathedral* (1935), and as founder/editor of the quarterly review *The Criterion* from 1922–39.

The Waste Land is alluded to by Richard CANTWELL in *Across the River and Into the Trees* when he refers to his dead wife as "[d]eader than Phoebus the Phoenician."

Eliot is mentioned in *A Moveable Feast* mostly because of BEL ESPRIT, a plan devised by Ezra POUND to collect money from other writers and artists to give to Eliot so he could quit his bank job in London and devote his time to the writing of poetry.

Elliot, Cornelia The "Mrs." in "Mr. and Mrs. Elliot." She is 40 years old and working in a Boston tea shop when she meets Hubert, who is 25 and in law school at Harvard. She is "very Southern" and is impressed that Hubert is still "clean" and saving himself for marriage.

She is "pure" too when they marry. "Kiss me again like that," she tells him.

They "try to have a baby" in Boston the night of their marriage, and they try again in France on their honeymoon. They try on the boat to Europe too, but she, being "very Southern," is seasick most of the time. Sex is a disappointment to her (to Hubert, too) and she cries a lot. In France she types Hubert's long poems for him, but when she makes a mistake he makes her type over the entire page.

She talks him into sending for her "girl friend," HONEY, who worked with her in a Boston tea shop, and, when she arrives in France, the "girl friend" takes over the responsibility of typing Hubert's manuscripts. After they move to a château in Touraine, Hubert takes a room of his own, and the two women "sleep together" in another room. All three seem to enjoy one another's company, and in the evenings they "make conversation" in the "garden under a plane tree" while Hubert drinks white wine. The three of them "were quite happy."

Elliot, Hubert The "Mr." in "Mr. and Mrs. Elliot." "Hubie" is 25 years old and taking postgraduate law courses at Harvard when he marries Cornelia, a 40-year-old "very Southern" woman who works in a tea shop in Boston.

He has never been to bed with a woman, and, although "nearly all the ['girl friends'] lost interest in him" when he told them how "clean" he was, the same declaration impresses Cornelia. They "try to have a baby" in Boston the night of their marriage, then again on the boat to Europe (although Cornelia is seasick most of the time), and they try several times in France.

He writes poetry and has an income of nearly $10,000 a year—but not from the poetry. He writes "very long poems" and, in France, decides he has enough for a book, arranges a contract with a publisher, and sends a check to help pay for the costs. He agrees to send for Cornelia's "girl friend," and the three of them travel together, along with some other friends. He rents a château in Touraine for the summer and begins drinking white wine. He has a room of his own for writing more poems, and the two women sleep together in a second bedroom. He drinks his white wine in the evenings, and the two women talk. And, as the narrator states in the story's final line, "They were all quite happy."

El Sordo "Santiago," the 52-year-old leader of a band of eight Spanish PARTIZANS, in *For Whom the Bell Tolls,* the last four of whom, including El Sordo, die on a hilltop from a FASCIST airplane attack.

emeralds The young Italian contessa RENATA makes a gift of the precious green gemstones to Richard

CANTWELL in *Across the River and Into the Trees*. He likes to feel them in his pocket during his last weekend and arranges to have them returned to Renata upon his death.

Emerson, Ralph Waldo (1803–1882) American poet and essayist, leader of the American Transcendentalist movement. In *Green Hills of Africa* Hemingway, in explaining American literature to KANDISKY, tells him there were American writers in the 19th century "who wrote like exiled English colonials from an England of which they were never a part to a newer England that they were making." They were good men of letters, "Quakers with a sense of humor." He then names "Emerson, Hawthorne, Whittier, and Company."

Emilio (1) Barman at the "little hotel" in STRESA, who, in *A Farewell to Arms,* lends Frederic HENRY and Catherine BARKLEY a rowboat so they can escape up Lake MAGGIORE to Switzerland.

Emilio (2) "The boy," one of the four Cuban bank robbers in *To Have and Have Not.*

Emily Wife of ANDREA in *Across the River and Into the Trees.*

Emmanuele III, Vittorio Victor Emmanuele III, king of Italy (1900–46), mentioned by Frederic HENRY in *A Farewell To Arms* as "the tiny man with the long thin neck and the goat beard." He lives in UDINE and visits the military units each day "to see how things were going."

Emmunds, Enrique Main character and narrator of "The Denunciation." He is on the LOYALIST side in the SPANISH CIVIL WAR and "denounces" a friend of his who has become a FASCIST.

Employer's Liability Act Renamed "workmen's compensation" late in the 20th century, it provides protection to workers while on the job. In *The Torrents of Spring,* which takes place during the early 1920s, Yogi JOHNSON understands that when the PUMP-FACTORY managers send workers out of the building when the CHINOOK WINDS blow, the factory owners do not want to "get caught under the Employer's Liability Act." They don't want to have to pay their employees extra while they're laid off because of a wind.

encierro Spanish for "the running of the bulls," the driving of the bulls, led by steers, from a temporary corral to the corral of the bull ring. It is described in *The Sun Also Rises,* and every year many Americans go to Pamplona for the Fiesta SAN FERMÍN to run with the bulls. This phenomenon is ironic, however, because neither Hemingway nor his main character in *The Sun Also Rises,* Jake BARNES, ever ran with the bulls.

"End of Something, The" This short story is full of the tension that NICK, a teenager, feels, knowing that he's going to break up with his girlfriend, MARJORIE. But he can't quite bring himself to say the words. The two teenagers beach the rowboat they've been fishing from and build a fire. They sit on a blanket Marjorie has spread for them, but there is a heavy atmosphere for both of them, Marjorie sensing that something is wrong. Nick finally works up the nerve to tell her, "It isn't fun any more." She says, "Isn't love any fun?" and he answers "No."

Without a "scene," she takes the boat and rows away on the lake. Nick's friend BILL (1) walks onto the beach and, clearly in on Nick's intensions, says to him, "Did she go all right?" Nick, still upset at the breakup, tells him to go away. "The End of Something" was first published in *In Our Time* (1925).

Enghien race course French town of Enghien is about nine miles north of Paris. There was a steeplechase racetrack there in the 1920s, where, in "My Old Man," JOE's "old man" was a jockey for several races.

In *A Moveable Feast* Hemingway writes about going to the steeplechase races in Enghien, but he says he stopped going because "it took too much time" and because he suspected some of the races were fixed.

Enormous Room, The Novel by e. e. cummings, published in 1922 and mentioned by the narrator of *The Torrents of Spring* as part of Diana SCRIPPS's thinking about how "strange" the French people are.

The "enormous room" was a concentration camp at La Ferté Macé, about 100 miles west of Paris. Cummings, a driver for the American ambulance corps in France during WORLD WAR I, was mistakenly imprisoned there (August 1917–January 1918), for suspected "treasonable correspondence." The novel is about the author's experiences in prison, enhanced by the idiosyncratic nature of his fellow prisoners, each of whom was imprisoned for irrational "French" reasons.

Enrique (1) In "The Capital of the World," he washes dishes in the PENSION LUARCA, where the main character, PACO (2), is a waiter. He is three years older than Paco and is "very cynical and bitter." When Paco takes a napkin and pretends to be a matador in the kitchen of the pension, Enrique plays the role of the bull, with two meat knives for horns, tied to the legs of a chair. The "play" turns serious, however, as one of the knives accidentally enters Paco's body, and, as Enrique runs for a doctor, Paco dies.

Enrique (2) Twenty-eight-year-old communist revolutionary in "Nobody Ever Dies." He is home in Cuba after 15 months of fighting in the SPANISH CIVIL WAR, and he is doing espionage work for the outlawed

Communist Party of Cuba. He is killed by the Havana police as he tries to escape from a house where the Communists have stored weapons. His lover, MARIA, escapes, but is later captured.

"L'Envoi" Vignette (149 words). The word "envoy" in English means postscript or summary, and Hemingway places it at the end of *In Our Time*. In French "l'envoi" means something sent or goods delivered. The king of Greece, son of King Constantine (George II, though he is not named in the vignette), is being held prisoner in the palace grounds by Colonel Nicholas PLASTIRAS, leader of the revolutionary committee (which overthrew Constantine's government on September 27, 1922). The king and the story's narrator drink a whiskey and soda "at a table under a big tree" and talk about the revolution, the king saying at one point that Plastiras "did right . . . shooting those chaps," a reference to the execution of six of Constantine's ministers and advisers (November 28, 1922), probably the six "cabinet ministers" Hemingway describes being shot in the CHAPTER 5 vignette.

In "L'Envoi" the king also tells the narrator that if KERENSKY had "shot a few men things might have been altogether different," a reference to Aleksandr Kerensky, who became provisional premier of Russia in 1917 but was too weak a leader to withstand the Bolsheviks. "Of course," the king tells the narrator, "the great thing in this sort of an affair is not to be shot oneself!"

"L'Envoi" was first published as "chapter 18" of *in our time* (1924) and reprinted in *In Our Time* (1925) under its present title. It is the last item in the book, following "Big Two-Hearted River, Part II."

Ernest Hemingway: Complete Poems Revised edition of *88 Poems* (1979), edited by Nicholas Gerogiannis and published by the University of Nebraska Press in 1992. It includes a new essay on the collected poems and one additional poem, "Critical Intelligence." Gerogiannis included a footnote stating that there were nine unauthorized, "pirated," editions of Hemingway's poems, published without a publisher's name or date of publication. They contained the poems written by Hemingway in Paris during the 1920s. See also *The Collected Poems of Ernest Hemingway*.

Ernest Hemingway: Cub Reporter Anthology of 11 unsigned articles Hemingway wrote for *The Kansas City Star* during his seven months as a cub reporter between October 1917 and April 1918, when he resigned in order to join the American Red Cross and drive ambulances for the Italian army in WORLD WAR I. *Cub Reporter* was published by University of Pittsburgh Press in 1970 and is edited by Matthew J. Bruccoli.

Ernest Hemingway: Dateline Toronto Anthology of 172 articles Hemingway wrote for *The Toronto Daily Star* between 1920 and 1924, edited by William White and published by Charles Scribner's Sons in 1985; subtitled "The Complete *Toronto Star* Dispatches, 1920–1924." The articles are in chronological order and include 30 articles in part 1 ("Reporting, 1920–1924") from *By-Line: Ernest Hemingway*, also compiled by White. In the four years between February 14, 1920, and January 19, 1924, Hemingway averaged an article a week for the *Star* and often wrote more than one an issue—seven for *The Toronto Star Weekly* of November 24, 1923. Thirty additional articles by Hemingway have been found since the publication of *Dateline Toronto*. See HEMINGWAY: THE TORONTO YEARS.

Ernest Hemingway: Grace Under Pressure **(documentary film)** Produced in 1986 by The Center for Humanities, Inc. in Mount Kisco, New York, this 55-minute film was advertised as "the first major film biography of the man who single-handedly forged the modern novel." It is written and narrated by Anthony Burgess.

"Ernest Hemingway's 'Young Man'" **(film script)** Adaptation, derived from the Nick ADAMS stories, completed in September 1955 by A. E. HOTCHNER and produced by Jerry Wald Productions in August 1962 as "Ernest Hemingway's Adventures of a Young Man."

"Escaped Kingston Convicts Still at Large" Article, unsigned, published in *The Toronto Star* (September 11, 1923), reprinted in William Burrill's *Hemingway: The Toronto Years* (1994). Dateline "Kingston Mills, Sept. 11." This was the first of several stories Hemingway wrote about the escape from prison of the gangster Red Ryan and three other convicts. A fifth convict was captured after being shot in the hand by one of the guards searching for the escapees. He described the plans for the getaway, and Hemingway uses the man's description of what happened to write the details of the escape, including a wild chase by prison guards and their eventual loss of four of the five escapees.

Escorial See EL ESCORIAL.

espadrilles Casual shoes with a canvas upper and a sole of twisted rope, worn by Catherine BOURNE in *The Garden of Eden*.

Esquire Illustrated literary monthly for men, begun and edited by Arnold GINGRICH in 1933. Gingrich published six of Hemingway's short stories, including "The Snows of Kilimanjaro," and 26 articles, all in the 1930s.

The magazine's first issue (Autumn 1933), the only issue not planned as a monthly, carried Hemingway's article "Marlin Off the Morro: A Cuban Letter."

The first issue proclaimed that "Esquire aims to be, among other things, a fashion guide for men." In 1944 the magazine's postal permit was withdrawn because of Postmaster General Walker's disapproval of its contents. The ruling was reversed by the U.S. Supreme Court in 1945.

Estérel   Region of southern France that includes the coastal towns of SAINT-RAPHAËL, CANNES, ANTIBES, and LA NAPOULE, all mentioned in *The Garden of Eden*.

Ethel   One of the five whores in "The Light of the World." She and Hazel are "big," nearly as big as Alice, who weighs, the narrator guesses, 350 pounds. Ethel and Hazel are described as not "very bright."

Eton   Prestigious English "public," that is private, school for boys, established in 1440. Eton's dress code includes hairstyle, and in *The Garden of Eden* Catherine BOURNE wants her hair cut short like the boys at Eton.

Ettore   Waiter at HARRY'S BAR in *Across the River and Into the Trees*.

"European Nightlife: A Disease"   Article, published in *The Toronto Star Weekly* (December 15, 1923), reprinted in *The Wild Years* (1962), reprinted in *Ernest Hemingway: Dateline Toronto* (1985). The headline in the *Star Weekly* was "Night Life in Europe a Disease: Constantinople's Most Hectic." Hemingway says that "Paris nightlife is the most highly civilized and amusing. Berlin is the most sordid, desperate and vicious. Madrid is the dullest, and Constantinople is, or was, the most exciting."

expatriates   People who have withdrawn from residence in or allegiance to their native land. After WORLD WAR I "expatriate" often referred to those American writers, artists, and musicians who moved to France, especially Paris. An important cause of their self-imposed exile was their alienation from the apa-thetic American people, who seemed indifferent to the devastating results of the war. Many Americans felt the war should be forgotten so that things could get back to normal.

Hemingway's *The Sun Also Rises* (1926) is one of the leading novels to explain what it was like to live in Paris after the war, especially for the expatriates. The novel's protagonist, Jake BARNES, is wounded by the war, both physically and psychologically and trying to cope in a seemingly meaningless world. Other American expatriate writers included John DOS PASSOS, Ezra POUND, F. Scott FITZGERALD, Hart Crane, e. e. cummings, and Archibald MACLEISH. See also LOST GENERATION.

Exterminator   American racehorse, mentioned in *Death in the Afternoon*. Exterminator won the 1918 Kentucky Derby and during his nine-year career won 50 of the 100 races in which he ran.

Extremadura   Region in west-central Spain and location of the small village hometown of PACO (2), the main character in "The Capital of the World." It is also where, in *For Whom the Bell Tolls*, Robert JORDAN carries out his first assignment to blow up trains.

Extremaduran   In "Under the Ridge," a character from the Extremadura region of Spain. He is described as hating all foreigners and as having no fear, of bullets or of anything. His great-grandmother was killed by the English, "under Wellington," and his father was killed by North Americans in Cuba. And the Spanish civil war in which he is now fighting further convinces him of the brutality of foreigners.

Extremadura road   In *The Fifth Column*, it is the location of the house that Philip Rawlings and Max attack, capturing a civilian member of the Fifth Column. The road leads west out of Madrid.

F.A.I. Federación Anarchista Iberica, a more radical anarchist organization than the C.N.T. (Confederación Nacional de Trabajo), both referred to in *For Whom the Bell Tolls.*

"Faithful Bull, The" A fable, published along with "The Good Lion" in *Holiday* magazine (March 1951). The faithful bull loves to fight so much that he fights other bulls and reduces their value to the owner, who finally decides that rather than send the bull to the bull ring to be killed, he would put him in with the cows in the pasture and produce more bulls with the good fighting blood. But the bull falls in love with one cow only and refuses to mate with any of the others. So the owner decides that he must, after all, send the "faithful bull" into the bull ring to be killed. The matador is impressed by how well the bull fights, and his sword handler says, "Yes, his owner had to get rid of him because he was so faithful." And the matador says, "Perhaps we should all be faithful."

Falange Name adopted by the mainstream FASCIST party in post-Republican Spain, founded in 1933 during the regime of dictator General Miguel PRIMO DE RIVERA, who had seized power with a fascist dictatorship in 1923. The Falange became the only official political party in Spain under General Francisco FRANCO following the SPANISH CIVIL WAR. See PILAR'S STORY.

"False News to the President" Article, published in *Ken* (September 8, 1938). Hemingway doubts the accuracy of reports President Roosevelt receives from the U.S. State Department about the Spanish civil war.

Far Away and Long Ago Novel (1918) by W. H. HUDSON, a "lovely book," read by David BOURNE in *The Garden of Eden* on the terrace of the hotel in LA NAPOULE, France, where he and his wife, Catherine, are staying. It is a story about a man roaming the Argentina Pampas, studying both natural life and human beings on what at the time was a lawless frontier. David probably thinks of it as "lovely" because the natural beauty of the Pampas reminds him of the East Africa he is writing about in his own AFRICAN STORY.

Farewell to Arms, A Hemingway's third novel, published in 1929, begins in the late summer of 1915, as WORLD WAR I heats up on the northeastern Italian front, and ends in March 1918 with the death in childbirth of the novel's heroine, Catherine BARKLEY.

The protagonist and narrator is Frederic HENRY, an American in his early 20s, who volunteered for the Italian ambulance corps and is a lieutenant. Frederic's military unit is based near a small town south of GORIZIA on the Italian border with Slovenia (which became part of Yugoslavia following the war), where some of the major battles of Italy's war with Austria-Hungary are expected to take place. Catherine, an Englishwoman, is a volunteer assistant nurse assigned to a British medical unit assisting the Italian army, first near Gorizia, and, when the fighting becomes heavier the next year, at the AMERICAN HOSPITAL (1) in Milan.

The novel is divided into five "books." The first three chapters in book 1 introduce the relatively peaceful setting of northeast Italy where Frederic's ambulance corps and the British hospital are located. The novel begins: "In the late summer of that year we lived in a house in a village that looked across the river and the plain to the mountains. In the bed of the river there were pebbles and boulders, dry and white in the sun, and the water was clear and swiftly moving and blue in the channels." The chapter concludes, however, with Frederic's remark that with the winter "came the permanent rain and with the rain came the cholera. But it was checked and in the end only seven thousand died of it in the army." The sarcastic tone of this comment suggests changes in Frederic's view of the war as a result of the experiences he is about to describe.

Chapter 2 moves into the next year (1916), when "there were many victories" for the Italians; but the war's fiercest fighting is taking place in France. Frederic meets Catherine the next spring (chapter 4) in the gardens of the villa that houses the hospital. When he tries to kiss her, she slaps him for his impudence but then gives him a kiss, foreshadowing what she sees as a "strange life" ahead of them. Catherine tells him about her fiancé, who was killed on the SOMME front in France; the reader becomes aware that she has already suffered great loss in the war and that Frederic does not yet fully understand the human devastation that war brings. Frederic apparently does not even know when the Battle of the Somme was fought (it began July 1, 1916), and so is insensitive to Catherine's recent loss.

Ernest in Italian uniform, 1918 (Copyright holder unknown; photo courtesy of the John F. Kennedy Library)

The major events of the novel begin in chapter 9. Frederic is seriously wounded while at the battle front "above PLAVA" with three other ambulance drivers: "I ate the end of my piece of cheese and took a swallow of wine. Through the other noise I heard a cough, then came the chuh-chuh-chuh-chuh—then there was a flash, as when a blast-furnace door is swung open and a roar that started white and went red and on and on in a rushing wind. I tried to breathe but my breath would not come and I felt myself rush bodily out of myself and out and out and out and all the time bodily in the wind. . . ."

The explosion is from a "big trench mortar shell" just in front of Frederic that leaves shrapnel fragments in his legs. Another driver, Passini, is more seriously wounded and, suffering from the pain, begs "some-

one" to shoot him. Frederic tries to help him but can't because of his own wounds. He realizes Passini is dead only when the screaming stops. Frederic is taken to a "dressing station," where he gets special treatment from an Englishman, then to the field hospital, where he is visited by his good friends RINALDI (2) and the unit's PRIEST (2). The priest hates the war and tries to convince Frederic that, in spite of his wounding, he (Frederic) doesn't "see" the hatred of war yet. A day or two later he is transferred to the American Hospital in Milan.

Frederic arrives at the hospital at the beginning of book 2. An operation is performed to remove most of the shrapnel from his legs, but the recovery is slow, allowing him four or five months in Milan with Catherine, who arranges her schedule so she can be with him. After he is sufficiently recovered so that he can get around, first in a wheelchair and then on crutches, he manages various activities for himself while Catherine is working, including mostly ineffective rehabilitation at the OSPEDALE MAGGIORE. When Catherine is off duty, they spend time at their favorite restaurants and at the Siro steeplechase racetrack, just outside of Milan, betting on the mostly crooked races. She becomes pregnant.

They plan a convalescent leave to Lake MAGGIORE before Frederic goes back to the front, but he is sick for two weeks with jaundice. The head nurse, Miss VAN CAMPEN, catches him with a locker full of brandy bottles and accuses him of deliberately getting sick in order to delay his return to the war. She cancels his leave. After a last evening with Catherine in a sleazy hotel across from the train station, Frederic catches the train back to the battlefront.

Book 3 is devoted to Frederic's return to the war, his continuing awareness of the chaos that war brings, and his final escape from it—his "separate peace." He returns to his unit in time for major fighting between the Italians and the Austrian forces in the mountains of northeast Italy. He and the ambulance drivers under his command are involved in the retreat of the Italian army from Caporetto in late October (1917), one of the many battles along the ISONZO River (actually the 12th and last battle, although Frederic doesn't know it; see CAPORETTO, BATTLE OF).

The retreat begins to break down near UDINE, and Frederic leads his drivers and their three cars onto a series of side roads, eventually getting stuck in the mud. After losing two of his drivers, one shot and the other disappearing under suspicious circumstances, Frederic arrives at the TAGLIAMENTO River, where the BATTLE POLICE of the Italian army are pulling officers out of the retreat and shooting them for desertion. When Frederic is pulled out of the line for questioning and realizes that he, too, will be shot, he dives into the Tagliamento and escapes down river. He comes out at a place where he "thinks" he can see the town of San Vito (two and a half miles to the west). He then walks another 12 and a half miles to LATISANA, and hops a westward-moving freight train on the Trieste-Milan line, arriving in Milan early the next morning.

It is during this retreat that Frederic confirms his antiwar feelings. His dive into the waters of the Tagliamento River was both a physical escape from the war and a symbolic escape from any guilt he might otherwise feel over deserting the Italian cause. It is here that he learns the meaning of the words he had merely thought about before the retreat: "I was always embarrassed by the words sacred, glorious, and sacrifice and the expression in vain. . . . I had seen nothing sacred, and the things that were glorious had no glory and the sacrifices were like the stockyards at Chicago if nothing was done with the meat except to bury it. . . . Abstract words such as glory, honor, courage, or hallow were obscene beside the concrete names of villages, the numbers of roads, the names of rivers, the numbers of regiments and the dates." This is the lesson he takes back to Milan.

At the beginning of book 4, Frederic goes to the American Hospital in Milan, only to be told that Catherine and her friend Helen FERGUSON are in STRESA on leave. He finds them there in a small hotel near the railway station, and he and Catherine plan an escape to Switzerland. The hotel's barman, EMILIO, wakes them late one night to warn them that Italian police plan to arrest Frederic in the morning. Emilio lends them a rowboat, and they row the 21 miles from Stresa north on Lake Maggiore to safety in Switzerland, landing at BRISSAGO the next morning. The Swiss confiscate the boat but allow them to stay in the country. They go first to MONTREUX at the eastern end of Lake Geneva, where they rent the second floor of a house in the mountains above the town.

During the final four chapters (book 5) Frederic and Catherine spend the winter skiing and hiking or taking the train through the snow down into Montreux from their idyllic mountain retreat to the town's restaurants and to get Catherine's hair done. Frederic grows a beard, to give him "something to do." In March they move to LAUSANNE, a larger city 18 miles farther west along the lake, where there is a large hospital. Catherine checks in three weeks later, and after a prolonged labor with much hemorrhaging, and finally a CAESARIAN SECTION, the baby is stillborn and Catherine dies. At the end of the novel, Frederic goes into Catherine's room but says it was "like saying good-by to a statue," and, after a while, he leaves "the hospital and walk[s] back to the hotel in the rain," desolated.

What is so final in Frederic's disillusionment is his awareness at the end of the novel that the death of anyone, in war or out, is without meaning. "That was what you did," he had said earlier, thinking about Catherine's impending death. "You died. You did not know what [life] was about. You never had time to learn. They threw you in and told you the rules and the first time they caught you off base they killed you. Or they killed you gratuitously like Aymo. Or gave you the syphilis like Rinaldi. But they killed you in the end. You could count on that. Stay around and they would kill you." In both love and war, the ending is the same.

A Farewell to Arms was published by Charles Scribner's Sons on September 27, 1929, in a first edition of 31,050 copies. SCRIBNER'S MAGAZINE serialized the novel in six parts, May–October, 1929.

Farewell to Arms, A (film 1) Paramount picture (78 minutes), released in December 1932; produced and directed by Frank Borzage, screenplay by Benjamin Glazer and Oliver H. P. Garrett, photography by Charles Lang. Winner of an Academy Award for cinematography; nominated for best picture and production design.

Cast: Helen Hayes (Catherine Barkley), Gary Cooper (Frederic Henry), Adolphe Menjou (Major Rinaldi), Mary Philips (Helen Ferguson), Jack LaRue (priest), Blanche Friderici (head nurse), Henry Armetta (Bonello), George Humbert (Piani), Fred Malatesta (Manera), Mary Forbes (Miss Van Campen), Tom Ricketts (Count Greffi), Robert Cauterio (Gordoni), and Gilbert Emery (British major).

There are two endings to this film. The one that was shown in most theaters and which is seen in the current videotape versions has Catherine dying in the final scene, as she does in the novel, but with doves flying out the window from under her hospital bed, symbolizing her soul's release and the end of the war (church bells are ringing in the distance). In the alternative ending Catherine is still alive and in Frederic's arms.

Farewell to Arms, A (film 2) Selznick Studio/Twentieth Century-Fox picture, released in January 1958 (150 minutes); produced by David O. Selznick, directed by Charles Vidor, screenplay by Ben Hecht, photography by Piero Portalupi and Oswald Morris, music by Mario Nascimbene (conducted by Franco Ferrara), art direction by Mario Garbuglia, set decoration by Veniero Colasanti and John Moore, special effects by Costel Grozea and Willis Cook. The credits also state "Ernest Hemingway's 'A Farewell to Arms.'" Nominated for an Academy Award for best supporting actor (Vittorio De Sica).

Cast: Rock Hudson (Frederic Henry), Jennifer Jones (Catherine Barkley), Vittorio De Sica (Alessandro Rinaldi), Alberto Sordi (Father Galli), Kurt Kasznar (Bonello), Mercedes McCambridge (Miss Van Campen), Oscar Homolka (Doctor Emerich), Elaine Stritch (Helen Ferguson), Leopoldo Trieste (Passini), Franco Interlenghi (Aymo), Jose Nieto (Major Stampi),

Georges Brehat (Captain Bassi), Umberto Sacripanti (ambulance driver), Victor Francen (Colonel Valentini), Joan Shawlee (red-headed nurse), Enzo Fiermonte (officer of the Carabinieri), Alberto D'Amario (arrested officer), Giacomo Rossi Stuart (first Carabiniere), Carlos Pedersoli (second Carabiniere), Alex Revides (officer of the Carabinieri), Peter Meersman (major, the accuser), Stephen Garret (captain, the defendant), Franco Mancinelli (Captain at outpost), Patrick Crean (medical lieutenant), Ina Centrone (Esmeralda), Guidarino Guidi (civilian doctor), Diana King (hospital receptionist), Clelia Metania (hairdresser), Eduard Linkers (Lieutenant Zimmerman), Angiolo Galassi (firing squad commander), Eva Kotthaus (delivery room nurse), Michela Ciustiniani and Margherita Horowitz (nurses in operating room gallery), Gisella Mathews (nurse in Catherine's room).

Farewell to Arms, A (play)   Three-act adaptation of the novel, produced by William Brady and Al Woods, directed by Rouben Mamoulian, script by Laurence Stallings. The cast included Glenn Anders as Frederic Henry, Elissa Landi as Catherine Barkley, and Crane Wilbur as Rinaldi. It had a pre-Broadway run at the Shubert Theatre in Philadelphia beginning September 15, 1930, and opened September 22, 1930, at the National Theatre in New York. According to newspaper reports the audiences were enthusiastic, but the reviews were generally bad, and the play lasted just three weeks, closing October 7, 1930.

According to Frank Laurence in *Hemingway and the Movies* (1981) rights to the Stallings play were bought by Paramount when it purchased the rights for the movie. "Never published, it seems to be a lost play," Laurence says, and "it is impossible to determine whether or not it was actually used in the writing of the screenplay." Stallings's name is in the film credits, however, for both the 1932 and 1957 movies.

Farewell to Arms, A (radio production 1)   CBS production for "The Campbell Playhouse" (December 1938) with Orson Welles producing and reading the role of Frederic Henry. Katharine Hepburn read Catherine Barkley.

Farewell to Arms, A (radio production 2)   NBC (c. World War II) production for "Star Theatre" with Frederic March and Florence Eldridge reading the parts of Frederic Henry and Catherine Barkley.

Farewell to Arms, A (radio production 3)   NBC production for "NBC University Theatre" (August 1948) with John Lund as Frederic Henry and Lurene Tuttle as Catherine Barkley.

Farewell to Arms, A (radio production 4)   CBS production for the "Ford Theatre" (June 1949) with Fletcher Markle and Helen Hayes as Frederic Henry and Catherine Barkley.

Farewell to Arms, A (radio production 5)   Produced for the NBC "Theatre Guild on the Air" (October 22, 1950), adapted for radio by Robert Anderson. Humphrey Bogart and Joan Fontaine read the leads. The production was aired over 167 NBC stations.

Farewell to Arms, A (television play)   A CBS "Chrysler Climax Theater" production (May 1955), starring Guy Madison and Diana Lynn; script by Gore Vidal.

farm   Thomas HUDSON's Cuban house, outside of Havana, referred to once in *Islands in the Stream* as "the Finca" (Spanish for estate or property) and the setting for the "Cuba" section of the novel. It is the same as the CUBA HOUSE mentioned in the earlier "Bimini" section.

The Finca Vigía is the name Hemingway gave to his own house just outside of Havana, which is now the Museo de Hemingway, owned by the Cuban government.

"Farm, The"   Article, published in *Cahiers d'Art* (1934); about Hemingway's purchase of Joan Miró's painting, "The Farm" in 1925.

"Fascism Is a Lie"   Article, published in *New Masses* (June 22, 1937), originally a speech Hemingway delivered before the Second Writers' Congress at Carnegie Hall in New York on June 4, 1937.

fascist (1)   Young man, who asks for a ride to Spezia from the two main characters in "Che Ti Dice La Patria?" He is arrogant in his fascist beliefs, insisting that riding on the running-board of the two-seat Ford coupé is no "discomfort," because he was used to it and to traveling. When he leaves them he uses the word "thanks," which is, for an Italian, the lowest form of gratitude.

fascist (2)   In "Che Ti Dice La Patria?," a bicyclist, with a "heavy revolver in a holster on his back," stops the story's narrator and his traveling friend, Guy, for having a dirty license plate on their car. He charges a 25-lira "fine," which he changes to 50 lire when the narrator tells him that the Italian roads are dirty. This is one of the experiences the narrator describes in his story of the decadence of Mussolini's Fascist Italy in the mid-1920s.

fascist café   Where, in "Out of Season," Arturo, a bank clerk, stares at PEDUZZI (1) when Peduzzi tips his hat to him.

fascist horseman   Man killed by Robert JORDAN, in *For Whom the Bell Tolls,* who discovers by reading some papers from the dead man's pockets that the man is 21 years old and from Tafalla in Navarra, son of a blacksmith, a CARLIST and thus *not* a "fascist."

fascisti   In the article "Genoa Conference," Hemingway writes that "fascisti are a brood of dragons' teeth that were sown in 1920 when it looked as though Italy might go bolshevik." The name *fascisti* means 'organization,' and a unit of *fascisti* is a *fascio.* They are young ex-veterans formed to protect the existing government of Italy against any sort of Bolshevik plot or aggression. They are counterrevolutionaries, and in 1920 they crushed the communist uprising with bombs, machine guns, knives, and kerosene cans to set the Red meeting places afire.

"Fascisti Party Half-Million"   Article, published in *The Toronto Daily Star* (June 24, 1922), reprinted in *The Wild Years* (1962), reprinted in *Ernest Hemingway: Dateline Toronto* (1985). The headline in the Daily Star was "Fascisti Party Now Half-Million Strong."

Datelined "Milan," this is an interview with Benito Mussolini, head of the Fascisti movement in Italy. "We are not out to oppose any Italian government," he tells Hemingway. "We are not against the law. . . . But . . . we have force enough to overthrow any government that might try to oppose or destroy us." At the end of the article, Hemingway states the question on everyone's mind at the time: "[w]hat does Mussolini . . . intend to do with his 'political party organized as a military force'?" The answer came in October of that year when King Victor Emmanuele III asked him to become Italian premier and form a cabinet. He then gradually turned the government into a dictatorship.

fascist(s)   Follower(s) of fascism, a modern revolutionary political ideology with roots in the theories of 19th-century French, Italian, and German intellectuals such as George Sorel and Friederich Nietzsche. Fascists reject the political and economic values of liberal democracy, such as materialism, rationalism, and humanism, in favor of aggressive nationalism, racism, and militarism. The term is related to the Latin word *fasces,* a bundle of rods with an ax, which was a Roman symbol of authority.

In 1919, military dictator Benito MUSSOLINI introduced fascism as a political movement in Italy. He supported a rigid one-party dictatorship, private economic enterprise under centralized government control, and forcible suppression of any opposition. Mussolini's political success influenced rising leaders in other European countries—notably Adolf Hitler in Germany and General Francisco FRANCO in Spain—who combined radical nationalism with anti-Marxist socialism and other ideologies.

Hemingway addresses fascism mainly in his work about the SPANISH CIVIL WAR (1936–38), in which Franco's fascist rebels, with military support from Germany and Italy, fought to overthrow the Spanish Republican government. Many Americans went to Spain to fight for the Republican, or LOYALIST, cause. Hemingway made three trips to Spain in 1937–38 and wrote 30 dispatches about the war for the North American News Alliance (NANA).

Hemingway's novel *For Whom the Bell Tolls* takes place during three days of the war in May 1937. Robert JORDAN, an American, has volunteered his services to the LOYALIST cause, fighting against Franco's REBEL army. Jordan is assigned by General GOLZ, a Russian Communist fighting on the side of the Loyalists, to blow up a bridge across a gorge in the Guadarrama Mountains in order to stall the fascists after a planned REPUBLICAN attack. Jordan is helped by Spanish guerrilla fighters, who have located in the mountains in order to make strikes against the rebels.

In "Old Man at the Bridge," fascists are the enemy from whom the old man is trying to escape. See also FALANGE.

"Fashion Graveyards"   Article, published in *The Toronto Star Weekly* (April 24, 1920), reprinted in *The Wild Years* (1962), reprinted in *Ernest Hemingway: Dateline Toronto* (1985). The headline in the *Star Weekly* was "Stores in the Wild Graveyards of Style." About changing styles in clothing. "[A]ll good styles when they die go to the country"—from Toronto department stores to smaller towns, like Sudbury.

father (1)   In "Ten Indians," NICK's father tells Nick that he had seen Prudence MITCHELL during the afternoon "in the woods with Frank Washburn. . . . threshing around." And in answer to the suddenly unhappy Nick's further questioning, he says that he guesses they were "happy." Nick's father knows that Prudie is Nick's "girl," but it isn't clear whether he is deliberately trying to break up the relationship or merely making fun of his son. Immediately after he tells Nick what he saw in the woods, the narrator informs us that the father "was not looking at" Nick, suggesting, perhaps, that he had a larger purpose. Nick's father gets him his dinner and a "big" piece of huckleberry pie and sends him up to bed. Nick's mother is not mentioned in the story.

father (2)   Of Harold KREBS in "Soldier's Home." He's in the real estate business and only in the story as an influence, mostly as Harold's mother passes on decisions to Harold—including one in which they allow him to use the car "in the evenings." Harold's father is described best when his mother tells Harold not to "muss up the paper. Your father can't read his *Star* if it's been mussed."

father (3)   Of the unnamed main character/narrator in "Now I Lay Me." The narrator remembers that once, when his father was away on a hunting trip, his mother burned all of his Indian relics.

father (4)   Of E. D. HARRIS, the main character of part 3 in "Homage to Switzerland." Harris says that his father had committed suicide the year before.

father (5)   Of Nick ADAMS in "Fathers and Sons." See the entry of the story.

father (6)   Thomas HUDSON's father in *Islands in the Stream*. During the search for a German submarine crew in the "At Sea" section of the novel, Hudson remembers fondly a time when he and his father were in a duck-hunting blind.

father (7)   In *The Garden of Eden* David BOURNE's father is the elephant hunter in David's AFRICAN STORY. David regrets having told his father about having seen the old elephant, because his father then tracks the elephant down and kills it.

father (8)   Catherine BOURNE's father in *The Garden of Eden* was killed in an automobile accident. Her husband, David, is told that it was a strange accident, also killing Catherine's mother and suggesting that it might not have been an accident.

father, mother, daughter   Family of "haves" sleeping on their yacht, *ALZIRA III*, near the end of *To Have and Have Not*. They sleep well even though they are "haves," because they think their money is made honestly. The daughter, Frances, dreams of her fiancé, Harold Tompkins.

"Fathers and Sons"   This short story, the final one in *Winner Take Nothing* (1933), takes place in Nick ADAMS' automobile as the 38-year-old Nick drives with his unnamed son, probably nine or 10 years old, toward an unnamed destination, after "the day's run" (of hunting or fishing, or of some business transaction).

The story is about Nick's memory of his own FATHER (5) and about the questions his own son asks about his grandfather. The boy is asleep on the front seat of the car, and Nick, perhaps because it is the "middle of fall" and he is "hunting the country in his mind as he [goes] by," is reminiscing about his father, who had taught him to hunt and fish. When "he first thought about [his father] it was always the eyes." He could see farther and "quicker" than most men that Nick had known. But Nick remembers that his father was also "very nervous" and "sentimental," and that "like most sentimental people, he was both cruel and abused." And he had "died in a trap that he had

helped only a little to set, and they had all betrayed him in their various ways before he died." His father had committed suicide, but the "they" who had betrayed him are not identified.

Nick, a writer, had loved his father "very much," and he hopes he can write about him some day. He remembers that his father "was as sound [on hunting and fishing] as he was unsound on sex . . . and Nick was glad that it had been that way." Nick's father had offered a warped attitude toward sex. He had defined the word "bugger," for example, as a "man who has intercourse with animals" and "mashing" as "one of the most heinous of crimes," and he had told Nick that "masturbation produced blindness, insanity, and death, while a man who went with prostitutes would contract hideous venereal diseases and that the thing to do was to keep your hands off of people."

Nick remembers his sexual experiences with TRUDY when they were young. Trudy was a member of the OJIBWAY Indian tribe, and, in Nick's remembering, he and she went with her brother BILLY into the Hemlock woods behind the Indian camp where Nick and Trudy have sex twice, once while Billy watches and once while he wanders through the woods hunting for a black squirrel with Nick's gun. While Nick and Trudy are still lying together under the trees, she says to him, "You think we make baby?" Nick is disturbed by the thought and says, "I don't think so."

Nick is in for another shock when Billy returns and informs Nick that his and Trudy's older half-brother, Eddie GILBY, wants to "come some night sleep in bed with you sister Dorothy." Nick tells them that he will kill Eddie if he "ever . . . even speaks to Dorothy."

When Nick's son finally wakes, shaking his father out of the reminiscing, he asks his father to tell him what it was like " when you were a little boy and used to hunt with the Indians?" Nick tells him about the Indians, but not about Trudy. He thinks to himself, instead: "Could you say she did first what no one has ever done better." But he does tell him about his father, the boy's grandfather, that he was a better hunter and fisherman than he, Nick, is and that "he had wonderful eyes." The boy wants to know why they don't "go to pray at the tomb" of his grandfather. Nick tries to explain that they live in a different part of the country, and when his son says that it doesn't feel right "never to have even visited the tomb of [his] grandfather," Nick agrees that they will have to go.

As with Hemingway's title for his first novel, *Torrents of Spring*, the title "Fathers and Sons" is probably taken also from a novel by the 19th-century Russian novelist and short story writer Ivan TURGENEV. Hemingway's story was first published in *Winner Take Nothing* (1933).

fat man   In "Fifty Grand," he is assigned to check the weight of Jack Brennan and Jimmy Walcott before their prizefight at Madison Square Garden.

Fats One of Thomas HUDSON's 11 cats in the "Cuba" section of *Islands in the Stream*. He is referred to once, after a fight with "Boise" that went on for a mile down the road, as "El Gordo," which in Spanish means "fat."

fat woman She runs the inn at the hotel in BURGUETE where, in *The Sun Also Rises*, Jake BARNES and Bill GORTON stay while on their fishing trip to the IRATI RIVER.

fat wop Unnamed gambler, who, with HOLBROOK, tries to get the "old man," in "My Old Man," to throw a race. "Wop" is offensive slang for "Italian."

Faulkner, William (1897–1962) U.S. novelist and short-story writer, winner of the Nobel Prize for literature in 1949. Faulkner is best known for his novels set in the fictional Yoknapatawpha County, Mississippi, particularly *The Sound and the Fury* (1929), *Light in August* (1932), and *Absalom, Absalom!* (1936).

Hemingway tells the old lady in *Death in the Afternoon* that his "operatives tell [him] that through the fine work of Mr. William Faulkner publishers now will publish anything rather than to try to get you to delete the better portions of your works." Hemingway and Faulkner exchanged several letters but never met. Faulkner helped write the screenplay for *To Have and Have Not*, arguably the best of the film adaptations of Hemingway works.

Faulkner's works were effectively out of print in 1945, but *The Portable Faulkner* (1946), with an "Introduction" by Malcolm COWLEY that presented the Yoknapatawpha County legend as a unified whole, brought out reprints and a new Faulkner novel, *Intruder in the Dust* (1948). Besides the Nobel Prize, he won the National Book Award in 1950.

Other works in the Faulkner canon include "The Bear," one of seven short stories in *Go Down, Moses* (1942), *As I Lay Dying* (1930), *Sanctuary* (1931), and the Snopes trilogy, *The Hamlet* (1940), *The Town* (1957), and *The Mansion* (1959).

FBI file During the last 20 years of his life, Hemingway told friends that he was being monitored by the U.S. government. From 1959 to 1961, years during which he suffered many physical and mental ailments, when he mentioned the surveillance, people thought he was paranoid.

Herbert Mitgang, cultural correspondent for *The New York Times*, discovered in FBI dossiers, provided under the Freedom of Information Act, that the CIA, FBI, and other intelligence agencies had waged at 50-year campaign of espionage against not only Hemingway but other writers as well, including William FAULKNER, John Steinbeck, Carl Sandburg, Pearl Buck, Sinclair LEWIS, and John DOS PASSOS.

Mitgang states in his book *Dangerous Dossiers* (1988), that the FBI has a "122-page, heavily censored file" on Hemingway, a file started in Havana in October, 1942, when Hemingway began using his boat, the *Pilar*, with the sanction of the U.S. Navy, to search for German submarines in the Cuban coastal waters. Mitgang reports that FBI director J. Edgar HOOVER was "near-obsessed" by Hemingway and his activities, largely because of Loyalist sympathies during the Spanish civil war.

Mitgang writes that although the government claimed that Hemingway "had not been investigated, his dossier includes a detailed fourteen-page, single-spaced memorandum, complete with table of contents. . . . This *confidential* memorandum, dated April 27, 1943, is still heavily censored, with entire paragraphs blacked out, more than four decades after it was written and long after Hemingway's death."

Felsch, Happy (1891–1964) Major League baseball player with the Chicago White Sox (1915–20), mentioned in "Crossing the Mississippi."

FERA Federal Emergency Relief Administration, part of President Roosevelt's economic recovery plan during the 1930s. It and the Works Progress Administration (WPA) were established to decrease unemployment. In *To Have and Have Not* Freddy, the owner of Freddie's place, thinks about one of the women at the bar, that she is so unattractive that you would have to be a "writer or a F.E.R.A. man to have a wife like that."

Ferguson, Helen Catherine BARKLEY's friend, whom she calls "Fergy," a nurse attached to the British Hospital in GORIZIA at the beginning of *A Farewell to Arms* and later at the AMERICAN HOSPITAL (1) in Milan. She is Scottish, and, as Catherine suggests to Frederic, she "loves Scotland better than England." Frederic tells the reader that he doesn't know much about her, except that she has a brother in the 52nd Division of the British army and another brother in Mesopotamia and that "she was very good to Catherine Barkley."

Feria de Abril Fiesta of Seville, a religious festival, with bullfights, that runs each year from April 18–25. In *The Garden of Eden* David BOURNE tells Catherine that the festivals in Madrid (May 15–22) and Seville are finished, so there is no point in going to Seville.

Fernando One of PABLO's band of guerrilla fighters in *For Whom the Bell Tolls*. He is "about thirty-five" years old. He returns from La Granja with news of a rumor that the LOYALISTS are preparing an offensive "in these parts," a shock to Robert JORDAN who thought the offensive was being kept secret. Fernando is killed during the blowing up of the BRIDGE.

fiacre See HORSE-CAB.

fiamme nere Italian for military facings on the collar of a uniform, referred to by Richard CANTWELL in *Across the River and Into the Trees.*

Fiat The name is an acronym for Fabbrica Italiana Automobili Torino, an international holding company and major Italian manufacturer of cars and trucks, with its headquarters in Turin, Italy.

Fiat is one of the makes of cars used by Frederic HENRY in his work with the Italian ambulance corps in *A Farewell to Arms.*

Fiat garage In VENICE where Colonel Richard CANTWELL and his driver, JACKSON, leave Cantwell's car for the weekend in *Across the River and Into the Trees.*

Fiats Pursuit planes made by the Italian company F.I.A.T. (Fabbrica Italiana Automobili Torino). The planes were used to protect HEINKEL ONE-ELEVEN BOMBERS in the Spanish civil war, seen flying over the mountains in *For Whom the Bell Tolls.*

field hospital After Frederic HENRY is wounded in book 1 of *A Farewell to Arms,* he is taken first to a post hospital, a "dressing station," for a survey of his wounds and then to a field hospital for treatment.

Fielding, Henry (1707–1754) English novelist and playwright, best known for his novel *Tom Jones* (1749). Hemingway quotes Fielding in his epigraphs for each of the four parts of *The Torrents of Spring.* The epigraph for part 1 sets the tone of parody for the novel: "The only source of the true Ridiculous . . . is affectation."

In *A Moveable Feast* Hemingway describes a conversation he had with Ford Madox Ford that included a discussion of men they considered to be "gentlemen." Hemingway thought Fielding might "technically" be considered a gentleman, even though he had been a judge.

Fiesta British title for *The Sun Also Rises.*

fifth column The term was first used in 1936 at the beginning of the SPANISH CIVIL WAR. Lieutenant General Queipo de Llano, a Falangist propagandist in General Francisco FRANCO's rebel army, broadcast the following in an attempt to demoralize the LOYALIST forces in Madrid: "We have four columns on the battlefield against you and a fifth column inside your ranks." The "fifth column" was made up of rebel sympathizers in the city, working "underground" to help prepare the way for Franco's takeover of the country.

Another who is sometimes given credit for coining the term is Falangist commander General Emilio Mola, who oversaw an attack on Madrid from four different directions and spoke of four columns with a fifth inside the city, working secretly for Franco's rebels.

A direct translation of the Spanish *quinta columba,* "fifth column," in contemporary usage, refers to any group who, in war, acts traitorously and subversively out of a secret sympathy for an enemy of their country. See also FALANGE.

Fifth Column, The This three-act play, the only full-length play Hemingway wrote, takes place during the SPANISH CIVIL WAR. The term *fifth column* refers to people who in war act traitorously and subversively out of a secret sympathy for the enemy of their country.

The play is the story of two Loyalists, counterespionage men, one American, one German, who capture a member of the fifth column whose confession under torture leads to the capture of 300 others. MAX (2), the German, is the "scout officer" and in charge of the capture. Philip RAWLINGS, the American and the play's protagonist, assists. Rawlings is bitterly disillusioned about the war, partly because of the betrayal of the government by many Spanish civilians who joined the fifth column in support of General Franco's fascist army, and partly because the war is run so badly by Loyalist leaders. Two other significant characters, Robert PRESTON and Dorothy BRIDGES, both Americans, are writers, living together (but in adjoining rooms) in the HOTEL FLORIDA in Madrid, which is often under attack from the fascist guns.

In act 1, Rawlings orders two guards to be sent to SEGURIDAD (police) headquarters for questioning when he discovers that, through their carelessness, they have allowed a prisoner to escape from another room at the hotel where they were guarding him. Later the prisoner returns to the hotel intending to kill Rawlings, but kills a man named Wilkinson, whom he mistakes for Rawlings. Rawlings moves in with Dorothy Bridges, after her former lover, Preston, gets in a fight with Rawlings; and Philip and Dorothy make romantic plans for traveling after the war, plans which Rawlings knows will never be carried out, plans in which he is not even interested.

Act 2, scene 1 takes place at Seguridad headquarters where Rawlings and ANTONIO (1), the *Comisario de Vigilancia* (literally the commissioner of vigilance) at Seguridad, question the first of the two careless guards. Rawlings convinces Antonio to let the guard go, and he does, but after Rawlings leaves Antonio's office, the Comisario brings the guard back for further questioning, and the audience infers, as the curtain falls, that the guard will be tortured during the follow-up session.

Act 2, scene 2 takes place at "a corner table" in CHICOTE'S RESTAURANT, where Rawlings drinks Booth's gin with Anita, a "Moorish tart," while waiting for Max to show up.

The first part of act 2, scene 3 takes place back at the Hotel Florida (Rooms 109 and 110) and involves a discussion of the war between Dorothy and Petra, the hotel maid. Petra reports that a man has been shot in the street during the night, the shot coming from a window. She tells Dorothy, "they always shoot from windows at night during a bombardment. The fifth column people. . . . If I was killed they would be happy. They would think it was one working person less." Rawlings comes back to his room for the second half of the scene, entering with Max and two unnamed INTERNATIONAL BRIGADE comrades. Rawlings assigns the two "I.B." soldiers to guard the room while he and Max talk about the expected bombardment and the job they must do in disrupting it. While Philip and Max plan their strategy, the 25 Republican comrades waiting downstairs are singing songs of the revolution, including the "Internationale."

In scene 4 Max and Philip return to the room after a failed attempt at an otherwise unexplained bit of espionage. Max says, "I am very sad to fail. I was certain they were coming. But they did not come." And Rawlings tells him that "it's not your fault if they call off the shoot."

Act 3 begins five days later. Scene 1 involves conversations, first between Dorothy and Philip, and second, between Philip and Max about the war. Philip, who is particularly depressed because he blames himself for Wilkinson's death, says to Max, "I've been doing this so long I'm bloody well fed up with it." Max answers with a statement that summarizes the Republican cause against the fascists: "You do it so *every one* will have a good breakfast. . . . You do it so *no one* will ever be hungry. You do it so men will not have to fear ill health or old age; so they can live and work in dignity and not as slaves."

Scene 2 shifts to the climactic action of the play, the preparation by the fascists at their artillery observation post for a midnight bombardment of Madrid. Max and Rawlings, who have sneaked up on the house, knock out the two guards and enter the tower on top of the house, where they tie up the post's commander and a "thin officer," and take as prisoners a civilian member of the fifth column and a "large officer."

Max and Rawlings are back in the Seguridad headquarters in scene 3, having killed the officer en route, because he "was too heavy and he would not walk." They brought the civilian in for questioning by Antonio, but ask to leave before the "questioning" begins, knowing that Antonio will get information from the prisoner by torturing him.

In scene 4, the play's final scene, the two men are back at the Hotel Florida the next afternoon. It turns out that Philip returned, after all, to watch the questioning of the civilian, and he reports on it to Max. Philip goes to Dorothy's room, when she returns from some shopping, and they once again talk about where they might go after the war. The play ends, however, with Philip showing his bitterness about the war and about his love affair with Dorothy.

The Fifth Column was first published by Charles Scribner's Sons in *The Fifth Column and the First Forty-nine Stories* (October 14, 1938). Its first separate publication was by Scribner's (June 3, 1940). And it was published in *The Fifth Column and Four Stories of the Spanish Civil War* in 1969.

Fifth Column, The (stage performance 1) The first stage performance of this play was an adaptation by Benjamin Glazer and produced by the Theatre Guild of New York, directed by Lee Strasberg and starring Lee J. Cobb and Franchot Tone. It opened March 6, 1940, at New York's Alvin Theatre and, although reviews were generally good, it closed on May 18 after 87 performances.

Fifth Column, The (stage performance 2) Adaptation of the play, written in December 1959 by A. E. HOTCHNER and first performed on October 19, 1990, by the Performing Arts Department of Washington University in St. Louis.

Fifth Column, The (television play) Adaptation of the play, written by A. E. HOTCHNER and produced for CBS's "Buick Electra Playhouse" in the fall of 1959 and spring of 1960.

Fifth Column and Four Stories of the Spanish Civil War, The This book was published by Charles Scribner's Sons August 13, 1969, and includes the play *The Fifth Column*, and the short stories: "The Denunciation," "The Butterfly and the Tank," "Night Before Battle," and "Old Man at the Bridge." It was the first time the four stories appeared together and the first time in book form for "The Denunciation" and "Night Before Battle."

Fifth Column and the First Forty-nine Stories, The This book was published by Charles Scribner's Sons October 14, 1938, and includes the following: the short stories of *In Our Time* (1925), *Men Without Women* (1927), and *Winner Take Nothing* (1933); the first printing of Hemingway's Spanish civil war play, *The Fifth Column;* the first appearance in book form of "The Short Happy Life of Francis Macomber," "The Capital of the World," and "Old Man at the Bridge"; and "The Snows of Kilimanjaro." "Snows" appeared in Edward J. O'Brien's *The Best Short Stories of 1937* but was revised for this book.

"Fifth Generation of Family Lives On Old Canadian Manor" Article, unsigned, published in *The Toronto*

Daily Star (October 20, 1923), reprinted in William Burrill's *Hemingway: The Toronto Years* (1994). It was "discovered" by Burrill in the Hemingway Collection at the John F. Kennedy Library in Boston. Dateline "Newmarket, Oct. 20." Hemingway writes, "This is the story of the old Dawson Manor. . . . mixed up with Indians . . . stage coaches and a dark eyed high school girl that lives alone with her grandmother in one of the most beautiful old houses in Canada."

"Fifty Grand"   A boxing short story with a twist at the end. The story is told by Jerry DOYLE, Jack BRENNAN's trainer and friend. Brennan is training for a big fight in New York's Madison Square Garden, and, although he's in good shape and good enough to win against his opponent, Jimmy WALCOTT, Brennan can't get up mentally for the fight.

The training camp is at Danny Hogan's Health Farm across the river in New Jersey, and Brennan misses his wife and two daughters at their home in the city. He's also thinking about giving up the fight game in order to be able to do other things but especially so he can spend more time with his family. So when his corrupt manager, John COLLINS, and two even more corrupt "friends," Happy Steinfelt and Lew Morgan, show up at the camp to talk him into throwing the fight, Brennan accepts their offer. The narrator is not in the room when the offer is made, but Brennan makes it clear to him that fixing the fight was the gist of his conversation with the three men. He tells Doyle that he's going to bet $50,000 on his opponent, and he encourages Doyle to do the same.

Brennan fights well for 10 rounds but tells Collins before the 11th round that he "can't stay" because his "legs are going bad." And, according to the narrator, "He was sick as hell." Brennan knew he was losing, but it was all right. "He didn't want to be knocked out." But in the 11th round, Walcott hits Brennan below the belt, so hard that Doyle says, "I thought the eyes would come out of Jack's head." Brennan knows, however, that if the referee calls the foul, the 50 grand he bet on Walcott would be lost, because Brennan would be declared the winner by default. So when the referee grabs Walcott, Brennan tells him the blow "wasn't low. . . . It was a accident." The referee looks at Brennan's manager, thinking Collins might throw in the towel he's already holding, but, of course, Collins is in on the fix and so doesn't stop the fight.

Meanwhile, Doyle states that Brennan's "face was the worst thing I ever saw—the look on it! He was holding himself and all his body together and it all showed on his face. All the time he was thinking and holding his body in where it was busted."

But then comes the plot twist. Brennan starts to box again, and he lands both gloves solidly at Walcott's groin, sending him down to grab himself in pain. The referee stops the fight and declares Walcott the winner "on a foul." It was a "popular win" for Walcott, because most of the crowd's money was on him. Back in the dressing room, Collins says, "They certainly tried a nice double-cross," suggesting that Morgan and Steinfelt, and probably others in on the double-cross, had bet on Brennan to win the fight, and that's why Walcott fouled him. With most of the money having been bet on Walcott, that would have provided larger winnings for anyone betting on Brennan. At the end of the story, Brennan says, "It's funny how fast you can think when it means that much money."

"Fifty Grand" was first published in *Atlantic* (July 1927) and reprinted in *Men Without Women* (1927).

***Fifty Grand* (television play 1)**   CBS "Schlitz Playhouse of Stars" production, adapted from the short story (July 1952).

***Fifty Grand* (television play 2)**   Adaptation of the short story, written by A. E. HOTCHNER and produced on NBC's "Kraft Television Theatre" (April 1958).

Finca Vigía, La   A "farm," outside of Havana, which Hemingway's third wife, Martha Gellhorn, rented in April 1939. After some alterations, they moved in. After Hemingway's death in 1961 the house became the Museo de Hemingway, owned by the Cuban government. The house still contains nearly 8,000 volumes of books that Hemingway had owned.

fine à l'eau   Brandy and water, often selected by David BOURNE in *The Garden of Eden*. And when he and his wife, Catherine, see MARITA and her friend, NINA, for the first time, it is significant to David that Marita, the "handsome one," orders a *fine à l'eau*.

Firbank, Ronald (1886–1926)   English novelist, a literary innovator and eccentric, whose style of humor influenced Evelyn Waugh and Ivy Compton-Burnett. In *Death in the Afternoon* Hemingway refers to Firbank as a writing "specialist." Born Arthur Annesley Ronald Firbank, in 1914 he expressed a preference to be called Ronald.

In *A Moveable Feast* Hemingway writes that Firbank and F. Scott Fitzgerald were the only writers who had not spoken well of Gertrude Stein.

First Infantry Division   Mentioned by Richard CANTWELL in connection with the U.S. Army division fighting at HÜRTGEN FOREST in World War II. See General Walter Bedell SMITH.

EH at the Finca Vigía in 1939 (Courtesy of the John F. Kennedy Library)

Ernest at the Finca Vigía near Havana. (Courtesy of the John F. Kennedy Library)

"The White Tower" behind the Finca Vigía, built by Mary Hemingway with a writing room for EH on the top floor. It also has a view of Havana eight miles away and the Gulf Stream beyond. (Photo by Robert E. Gajdusek and used with his permission)

"First Poem to Mary in London"   Antiwar prose poem written in 1944 and first published in *Atlantic* (August 1965).

First State Trust and Savings Bank   Key West, Florida, bank in *To Have and Have Not,* robbed by four Cubans before they force Harry MORGAN to take them to Cuba in his charter fishing boat.

Fischer, Doc   In "God Rest You Merry, Gentlemen," Doc tells the narrator most of the story of a 16-year-old boy who, wanting to be castrated but not understanding what the word means, amputates his penis.

HORACE, the story's narrator, always calls Fischer "Doc" and describes him as "thin, sand-blond, with a thin mouth, amused eyes and gambler's hands," and he is Jewish. He also "affected a certain extravagance of speech" that seemed "of the utmost elegance" to Horace. And, according to Horace, Doc Fischer has a "lack of respect for Federal statutes," which has produced "his trouble." The trouble is not identified.

In spite of this background, he is evidently a good doctor, and if he had been on duty when the boy came in at one o'clock in the morning (Christmas day), having cut off his penis, Doc Fischer might have saved the boy's life. At the end of the story he and the incompetent Doctor WILCOX discuss the significance of the boy's mutilation occurring on Christmas day. It is ironic that Fischer, a Jew, sees more significance in the boy's act occurring on Christmas day than does Wilcox.

"Fishing in Baden Perfect"   Article, published in *The Toronto Daily Star* (September 2, 1922), reprinted in *The Wild Years* (1962), reprinted in *Ernest Hemingway: Dateline Toronto* (1985). The headline in the *Daily Star* was "Once Over Permit Obstacle, Fishing in Baden Perfect." Datelined "Triberg-in-Baden, Germany," about the "legal labyrinths" involved in getting permission to fish in Baden but the perfection of the fishing once permission is granted.

"Fishing the Rhône Canal"   Article, published in *The Toronto Daily Star* (June 10, 1922), reprinted in *The Wild Years* (1962), and in *By-Line: Ernest Hemingway* (1967). Datelined "Geneva, Switzerland," the article is about catching a beautiful trout in the canal that connects the west-flowing Rhône River to Lake Geneva and wondering, as the author walks the "straight white road" back to the town of Aigle at the east end of the lake, whether one of Napoleon's soldiers or maybe one of the Romans or Huns who had traveled the same road had not also stopped to fish for trout in that stream. The *TDS* headline read "There Are Great Fist in the Rhône Canal."

Fitzgerald, F. Scott (1896–1940)   Francis Scott Key Fitzgerald, American novelist and short story writer, best known for *The GREAT GATSBY* (1925) and *Tender Is the Night* (1934), was a friend of Hemingway and a literary influence. Three of the last four "sketches" in Hemingway's *A Moveable Feast* (1964) are about Fitzgerald and their friendship in Paris during the 1920s. The sketches include Hemingway's attitude toward Fitzgerald's heavy drinking, his life with his wife, Zelda (whom Hemingway calls a "hawk"), and Fitzgerald's writing.

Fitzgerald attended Princeton but dropped out in 1917 and joined the army. The next year he met Zelda Sayre, the daughter of an Alabama Supreme Court judge, and, after publication of *This Side of Paradise* in 1920, which convinced Zelda that he could support her through his writing, they married.

Fitzgerald and Hemingway were two of the leading members of the "LOST GENERATION" of American writers after World War I, whose fictional characters searched for ways out of the provincial and morally barren attitude of people in the United States following the war. Fitzgerald's early works virtually defined the "Jazz Age" of the 1920s—a period of unconventionality and gaiety: *This Side of Paradise* (1920), *Flappers and Philosophers* (1920), *The Beautiful and Damned* (1922), *Tales of the Jazz Age* (1922)—one of the first times the term was used—*The Vegetable* (1923), *All the Sad Young Men* (1926), and especially *The Great Gatsby* (1925), the most popular of his works, and *Tender Is the Night* (1934).

The Great Gatsby is a powerful and antagonistic portrayal of the wealthy American society of the 1920s, with its attraction for false glamour, immorality, and cultural barrenness.

All of Fitzgerald's major works were published by Charles Scribner's Sons. Fitzgerald wrote to his editor, Maxwell PERKINS, a complimentary letter about Hemingway six months before the two writers met in April 1925: "This is to tell you about a young man named Ernest Hemmingway, who lives in Paris, (an American) writes for the transatlantic Review + has a brilliant future. Ezra Pount published a a collection of his short pieces in Paris, at some place like the Egotist Press, I havn't it hear now but its remarkable + I'd look him up right away. He's the real thing."

By the time Perkins wrote to him, however, Hemingway had already signed a contract with BONI & LIVERIGHT to publish *In Our Time* and his next book. When Horace Liveright refused to publish *The Torrents of Spring* the next year, however, thereby breaking the contract, Hemingway was able to sell the novel to Scribner's, along with *The Sun Also Rises,* both of which were published in 1926. *The Torrents of Spring* is a parody of Sherwood ANDERSON, among other writers, & Liveright refused publication because Anderson was one of Boni & Liveright's principal authors.

Section 17 of *A Moveable Feast* is titled "Scott Fitzgerald" and has the book's only epigraph, a one-paragraph tribute to Fitzgerald that is probably the best example of Hemingway's ambivalent attitude toward his friend. "His talent was as natural as the pattern that was made by the dust on a butterfly's wings. At one time he understood it no more than the butterfly did and he did not know when it was brushed or marred. Later he became conscious of his damaged wings and of their construction and he learned to think and could not fly any more because the love of flight was gone and he could only remember when it had been effortless."

Hemingway describes the first meeting of the two writers and a strange and awkward trip to recover the Fitzgeralds' abandoned automobile in Lyon, France. The first meeting took place at the DINGO BAR in Paris sometime between April 10 and May 1, 1925. Scott wrote a letter to Perkins on April 10 from Capri and then left with Zelda for Paris (April 10 is also the publication date of *The Great Gatsby*). Hemingway describes the meeting as one of many "strange things" that happened with Fitzgerald, "but this one I was never able to forget." Scott came into the bar with a friend of his from Princeton, Duncan Chaplin (although Chaplin later denied to Fitzgerald biographer Matthew J. Bruccoli that he had been there), and Hemingway writes that "Scott was a man then who looked like a boy with a face between handsome and pretty." Fitzgerald got drunk on champagne, and Hemingway writes that "the skin seemed to tighten over [Scott's] face until all the puffiness was gone and then it drew tighter until the face was like a death's head." Hemingway wanted to take Scott to the hospital, but "Chaplin" said that Scott was "all right. . . . That's the way it takes him."

The "strange" trip that Hemingway then describes is a comedy of errors, mostly caused by Fitzgerald's ineptitude. It began by Scott missing the train and Hemingway having to wire his hotel location from Lyon. Scott didn't get the telegram, and Hemingway writes that when they finally got together he could not get Fitzgerald to understand that he hadn't followed his own travel arrangements. The car, a Renault, did not have a top, and when, on their way back to Paris, it started to rain, they had to stop overnight. Hemingway summed up the trip by saying that "[y]ou could not be angry with Scott any more than you could be angry with someone who was crazy."

Hemingway wrote most of the first draft of *The Sun Also Rises* in Spain during the summer of 1925, and in Paris that fall Fitzgerald was upset because he wasn't allowed to see the rough draft. Not long after this incident, however, Hemingway asked Fitzgerald to read the finished novel, and he suggested major cuts at the beginning that Hemingway accepted and that improved considerably the published version.

Hemingway also writes in *A Moveable Feast* that Fitzgerald and Ronald FIRBANK were the only writers who had not spoken well of Gertrude STEIN. There is also an "AUTHOR'S NOTE" in *The Torrents of Spring* in which Hemingway makes fun of one of Fitzgerald's drunken sprees. "It was at this point in [writing] the story, reader, that Mr. F. Scott Fitzgerald came to our home one afternoon, and after remaining for quite a while suddenly sat down in the fireplace and would not (or was it could not, reader?) get up and let the fire burn something else so as to keep the room warm." And in "Homage to Switzerland" (Part II) Mr. JOHNSON asks the waitress if, while she was a student learning English at the Berlitz School, there were "many smoothies? Did you ever run into Scott Fitzgerald?"

The best-known passage in Hemingway, however, that comments negatively on Fitzgerald is in "The Snows of Kilimanjaro," published in *Esquire* (August 1936). The short story's main character, Harry, is thinking about the rich, and he remembers "poor Scott and his romantic awe of [the rich] and how he had started a story once that began, 'The very rich are different from you and me.' And how someone had said to Scott, Yes, they have more money. But that was not humorous to Scott. He thought they were a special glamourous race and when he found they weren't it wrecked him just as much as any other thing that wrecked him." Fitzgerald was stung by this comment and wrote to Hemingway: "Please lay off me in print." Hemingway changed the name "Scott" to "Julian" for reprints of the story.

Hemingway took the Fitzgerald line out of context and gave it a meaning it doesn't have in Scott's original story, "The Rich Boy." The story's narrator says, "Let me tell you about the very rich. They are different from you and me. They possess and enjoy early, and it does something to them, makes them soft where we are hard, and cynical where we are trustful, in a way that, unless you were born rich, it is very difficult to understand. They think, deep in their hearts, that they are better than we are because we had to discover the compensations and refuges of life for ourselves."

Fitzgerald kept notes on his meetings with Hemingway, and, according to Fitzgerald, they met only four times in the 11 years between 1929 and 1940. He notes, "Not really friends since '26." In 1929, after Hemingway and his wife, Pauline, moved back to Paris to an apartment at 6, rue Férou, the Fitzgeralds lived just around the corner, but Fitzgerald notes that there were only "three or four meetings in Autumn 1929."

Hemingway sent Fitzgerald a copy of *For Whom the Bell Tolls* when it was published on October 21, 1940, and Fitzgerald wrote a letter, dated November 8, 1940, thanking Hemingway for the book and congratulating him, saying, "I envy you like hell." Fitzgerald died six weeks later.

Hemingway was ambivalent all his life about his friendship with Fitzgerald and never publicly admitted the help Fitzgerald had provided, not only for suggesting the cuts in *The Sun Also Rises*, but for other critical comments as well. Hemingway wrote to Fitzgerald biographer Arthur Mizener in 1950 that Fitzgerald "was romantic, ambitious, and Christ, Jesus, God knows how talented. He was also generous without being kind. . . . He was a charming cheerful companion when he was sober although a little embarrassing from his tendency always to hero-worship." But seven years later Hemingway started writing *A Moveable Feast*, in which he turns his back on Fitzgerald again, as he does on most of the friends of his years in Paris during the 1920s.

Fitzgerald, Scottie (1921–1986)   Daughter of F. Scott and Zelda Fitzgerald, referred to in *A Moveable Feast*.

Fitzgerald, Zelda Sayre (1900–1948) Wife of F. Scott Fitzgerald and also a writer best known for *Save Me the Waltz* (1932). The novel was reprinted in 1967, and 10 of her short stories were published in *Bits of Paradise* (1974). *Zelda Fitzgerald: The Collected Writings* (1991) includes the novel, her play, *Scandalabra*, 11 short stories, 13 articles, and several letters to Scott.

Zelda also painted, working in watercolors, gouache, and oils. She had two small exhibitions in New York, one at the Cary Ross gallery in 1934, the other at the Algonquin Hotel. She gave away a number of her paintings to servicemen in 1942 so they could reuse the canvases, but about 100 works survive, many reproduced in two books: *The Romantic Egoists* and *Zelda, An Illustrated Life: The Private World of Zelda Fitzgerald*.

Zelda married Scott Fitzgerald in April 1920, shortly after publication of Scott's first novel, *This Side of Paradise*, which reassured Zelda that he could support her. Their only child, Scottie, was born in October 1921.

By 1930 Zelda's behavior had become occasionally erratic, out of control at times, and it was necessary for her husband to hospitalize her first at the Malmaison Clinic near Paris and then at the Val-Mont and Prangins institutes in Switzerland. She was diagnosed as schizophrenic. After her release in September 1931 she suffered a relapse in February 1932 and was taken to the Phipps Clinic at Baltimore's John Hopkins University. She wrote *Save Me the Waltz* during her four-month stay at Phipps. She was in and out of clinics for the rest of her life.

In *A Moveable Feast*, written in the late 1950s, Hemingway describes his feeling that Zelda had interfered with Scott's work in the 1920s, when he knew them in Paris, because she was jealous of Scott's ability as a writer. Hemingway also describes her gradual slide into insanity. At the end of the section on Zelda, "Hawks Do Not Share," Hemingway describes arriving at the Fitzgeralds' villa in Juan-les-Pins, France, with Hadley. The MacLeishes and the Murphys were also there, and no one was drunk. He thought it a good place to write, and Zelda's "[h]awk's eyes were clear and calm. I knew everything was all right and was going to turn out well in the end when she leaned forward and said to me, telling me her great secret, 'Ernest, don't you think Al Jolson is greater than Jesus?'"

Fitzgerald-Hemingway Annual A bound volume of scholarly criticism, biography, and bibliography. It was edited by Matthew J. Bruccoli, 1969 and 1976; Bruccoli and C. E. Frazer Clark, 1970–75; Margaret M. Duggan and Richard Layman, 1977; and Bruccoli and Layman, 1978–79. The *Annual* was published by NCR Microcard (Washington, D.C.), 1969–73; Information Handling Services (Englewood, Co.), 1974–76; and Gale Research (Detroit), 1977–79.

flamboyán tree Better known as royal poinciana or peacock tree, it is a beautiful scarlet and orange flowering tree of the pea family, known for the shade it provides. It is native to Madagascar but widely planted elsewhere in frost-free regions. It grows from 20 to 40 feet tall.

There is a flamboyán tree outside the bedroom window at the farm near Havana where Thomas HUDSON lives alone, mentioned in the "Cuba" section of *Islands in the Stream*. He sees the shadow of the tree's branches on the walls of his room when he can't sleep.

Flanner, Janet (1892–1978) American writer best known as the Paris correspondent for *The New Yorker* magazine, for which she wrote a periodic "Letter from Paris," under the pseudonym Genêt from 1925 to 1975 (except during the war years 1939–44). Her articles covered politics, art, theater, and other aspects of French life and culture.

Flanner and Hemingway were good friends from their first meeting until his death. In *Charmed Circle: Gertrude Stein & Company* (1974) James Mellow suggests that although Flanner made friends rather easily in Paris, her "great friendship was with Ernest Hemingway." She was seven years older than he and liked to mother him, and he recognized in her a woman of strong character and independence who probably understood his fascination with bullfighting better than any other person he ever met. He took her to a boxing match in Paris and she realized he was "a natural quick linguist who learned a language first through his ears because of his constant necessity for understanding people and for communicating." He was quick to pick up the jargon of the French boxers.

In her introduction to *Paris Was Yesterday: 1925–1939* (1972) Flanner writes: "After the publication of Ernest Hemingway's *The Sun Also Rises*, he became that first and foremost famous expatriate American writer. When I look back on the stir created by his individual style of writing, what stands out in my memory is the fact that his heroes, like Ernest himself, were of outsized masculinity even in small matters. In his writing, his descriptions of the color of deep sea water beside his boat or of the trout's fins in the pool where he angled were like reports from the pupil of his eyes transferred by his pen onto his paper."

flashback Stylistic device by which a writer presents events that occurred prior to the opening of a work of fiction. Hemingway's short story "The Snows of Kilimanjaro" includes five flashbacks, all events in the life of the main character, Harry, who thinks about all the stories he had meant to write but hasn't.

Across the River and Into the Trees takes place mostly in flashback as the main character, Richard CANTWELL, remembers events that occurred before the novel begins. Chapters 2 through 39 of the 45-chapter novel are in flashback.

flask   Contains GORDON'S GIN for Richard CANTWELL during the Sunday morning duck shoot in *Across the River and Into the Trees*. The flask is "flat and of silver with a leather cover" and is engraved, "to Richard From Renata With Love."

"Flat Roofs"   Poem about the roofs of a city, written in 1921 and first published in *88 Poems* (1979).

Flaubert, Gustave (1821–1880)   French writer; one of the most significant novelists of the 19th century. Best known for *Madame Bovary* (1857), Flaubert's writing is characterized by meticulous prose, realistic detail, and unusual psychological insight into his characters. Hemingway mentions the "discipline" that Flaubert had as one of the ingredients necessary for achieving the FOURTH AND FIFTH DIMENSION in writing. He had told *New Yorker* reviewer Lillian Ross that Flaubert was one of his "heroes."

Ezra POUND, one of a very few friends left unscathed in *A Moveable Feast*, recommended soon after Hemingway arrived in Paris that he read "Flaubert and Stendhal: *The Red and the Black*, the first half of *The Charter House of Parma, Madame Bovary, Sentimental Education, Three Stories*, and *Bouvard and Pecuchet*." The first two titles on the list are by Stendhal, the others are by Flaubert. According to biographer Michael Reynolds, Hemingway learned from Flaubert "to be detached, ironic, precise. From Stendhal he learned how to deal with panoramic movement."

Fleurie wine   From the town of Fleurie, in the center of France's Beaujolais region, drunk, according to Hemingway in *A Moveable Feast*, by Hemingway and F. Scott Fitzgerald at dinner in Châlon-sur-Saône, on their way back to Paris from Lyon.

flit gun   Used to spray an insecticide. There is "flit gun man" in the short story "The Butterfly and the Tank," who shoots his flit gun full of perfume at an older waiter who doesn't like it. The people in the over-crowded bar laugh at the waiter's anger, however, so the "flit gun man" continues to shoot at the waiter. Later the "flit gun man" overdoes it, and he is killed.

A flit gun is also carried by Thomas HUDSON on his boat as he and his crew search for a German submarine crew in the "At Sea" section of *Islands in the Stream*. This one is probably used against mosquitoes.

Florian   In *Across the River and Into the Trees* restaurant on St. Mark's Square in VENICE, where Richard CANTWELL remembers that he and RENATA met for breakfast on Saturday morning; but they decide break-

fast "is worthless here" and so go to the GRITTI PALACE HOTEL.

Florida Hotel   In Madrid in *For Whom the Bell Tolls*, where Robert JORDAN had stayed before the war begins. He remembers Luis, a porter at the hotel.

Floridita   Havana bar where Thomas HUDSON gets drunk at the beginning of the "Cuba" section of *Islands in the Stream*. He drank "double frozen daiquiris," first with "Cuban politicians," then with "sugar planters and rice planters," with "Cuban government functionaries," with "second and third secretaries of Embassy," with "the inescapable FBI men," with "Navy that he knew," with the "then-called Hooligan Navy or Coast Guard," and, finally, with "old respectable whores." Hudson drinks to try to forget the deaths of his sons David and Andrew and to get over the loneliness that permeates his character during both this section of the novel and the third section, titled "At Sea." See DOUBLE FROZEN DAIQUIRIS.

Flowers, Tiger (1895–1927)   U.S. boxer, who became world middleweight champion on February 28, 1926, by defeating Harry Greb. He lost the title later in the same year to Mickey Walker. In *The Sun Also Rises* Bill GORTON sees a fighter who he says looks like Tiger Flowers.

flying fish   Seen off the Havana, Cuba, harbor by Harry MORGAN in *To Have and Have Not*, in this case "those big ones with the black wings that look like the picture of Lindbergh crossing the Atlantic when they sail off."

SANTIAGO in *The Old Man and the Sea* sees flying fish on the Gulf Stream. They were a sign to the old man that dolphin were close. He "was very fond of the flying fish as they were his principal friends on the ocean."

"Flying Inn, The"   Poem by G. K. CHESTERTON, one verse of which is quoted by NICK to BILL (1) in "The Three-Day Blow." See G. K. CHESTERTON.

Fontan, André   Fourteen-year-old son of Marie and Sam Fontan in "Wine of Wyoming." The narrator picks up a book he is reading, *Frank on a Gunboat*.

Fontan, Marie   She and her husband, Sam, both French, sell illegal homemade wine and beer out of their home on the outskirts of an unnamed Wyoming town in "Wine of Wyoming." She is described as a "plump old woman" but "very clean." Her husband makes the wine and beer (during Prohibition), and she sells it, the wine for a dollar a bottle and the beer for 10 cents. When the story's narrator and the narrator's wife fail to show up at the Fontans for a special good-bye dinner in their honor, Marie has "tears in her eyes" for the sake of her husband, who wanted to share his new vintage of wine with their American friends.

Fontan, Sam   In "Wine of Wyoming," Sam and his wife, Marie, both French, live on the outskirts of a town in Wyoming. He is described as an old man with a "small mine-tired body." He knows English slang words and the popular songs of his period of military service at the end of the 19th century. He makes wine and beer during Prohibition, the story taking place in the fall of 1928, and has been caught and put in jail once, paying a fine of $755.

He and his wife do not understand many of the cultural ways of Americans and so Sam is "crushed" and "disgraced" when the American narrator and his wife fail to show up for a good-bye dinner in their honor. Monsieur Fontan has his new wine ready and is eager to share it with his American friends. But the Americans are insensitive to Sam's feelings.

footman   In RENATA's villa in *Across the River and Into the Trees*. In discussing American slang with Richard CANTWELL, Renata tells him that "Sometimes when we have the British Ambassador and his dull wife for dinner I will teach the footman, who will announce dinner, to say, 'Come and get it, you son of bitches, or we will throw it away.'"

Ford, Ford Madox (1873–1939)   English novelist, editor, and critic, best known for his novels *The Good Soldier* (1915) and a tetralogy consisting of *Some Do Not* (1924), *No More Parades* (1925), *A Man Could Stand Up* (1926), and *Last Post* (1928), the four novels published as *Parades' End* in 1950. Ford was also the editor of the short-lived TRANSATLANTIC REVIEW (January 1924–January 1925). His given name was Ford Hermann Hueffer, but he changed it after World War I.

Ford is mentioned in one of the "AUTHOR'S NOTES" in *The Torrents of Spring*. Hemingway tells his readers that he got the "best of [his] anecdotes from Mr. Ford Madox Ford," an indication that the author is ridiculing Ford in *Torrents*, as well as Sherwood ANDERSON and others.

Ford is referred to in *Death in the Afternoon* in a negative comparison with Waldo Frank, who is not named but only identified as the author of *Virgin Spain* (1926).

In *A Moveable Feast* Hemingway describes how difficult it was to look at Ford's face and that he felt the need to hold his breath when he was with Ford in a closed room. The ninth section of the nonfiction book is titled "Ford Madox Ford and the Devil's Disciple," about a rather drunken conversation Hemingway had with Ford at the café Closerie des Lilas. It begins with

Ford explaining how he had just "cut" Hilaire Belloc, the French writer, but the victim, as it turned out, had not been Belloc but Aleister Crowley, "the diabolist." Hemingway writes that he talked Ford into publishing serially in his review Gertrude Stein's long novel, *The Making of Americans*.

Ford coupé   Automobile driven around northern Italy by the two main characters in "Che Ti Dice La Patria?"

Ford taxi   Used by the four Cuban bank robbers in *To Have and Have Not* to get from the FIRST STATE TRUST AND SAVINGS BANK of Key West, Florida, to Harry MORGAN's boat, docked a block away. See CUBANS, FOUR.

"Foreheads Villainous Low"   Essay by Aldous Huxley that Hemingway quotes in *Death in the Afternoon*.

Forest Lovers   Historical novel by Maurice Hewlitt, published in 1898. It is the story of a rich man who marries a poor girl out of pity, a plot similar to that in Hemingway's "The Three-Day Blow," in which the main character, NICK, has broken up with Marjorie because she is of a lower class. His friend Bill has recommended *Forest Lovers* to him.

Fornaci   Town in northern Italy, from which Nick Adams rides his bicycle to an unnamed town and back in "A Way You'll Never Be."

In *Across the River and Into the Trees* Richard CANTWELL remembers the town (spelled Fornace), because he had fought there with the Italians in WORLD WAR I.

Fort, Paul (1872–1960)   French poet associated with the French Symbolist movement. In *A Moveable Feast* Hemingway writes that Fort was one of the poets who met regularly with other writers at the Closerie des Lilas. Hemingway also says that he had never read any of his poetry.

"[FOR THE HARLOT HAS A HARDLOT . . .]"   First line of a poem written (entirely in capital letters) in 1922, first published in *88 Poems* (1979).

Fortitude   Novel by Hugh WALPOLE, published in 1913. In "The Three-Day Blow" Bill and NICK discuss the book, Nick saying that "[i]t's a real book." According to Nick, it's about a boy whose "old man is after him all the time."

Forum, The   Magazine of opinion, begun in 1886. It is harshly criticized by the narrator of "Banal Story," set in 1925, for its banal stories and articles. The magazine merged with *Century*, and then they both disappeared into the journal, *Current History*.

For Whom the Bell Tolls Hemingway's fourth novel details three days in the life of its main character, Robert JORDAN, an American college teacher from Montana who has volunteered his services to the LOYALIST cause in the SPANISH CIVIL WAR (1936–39). The Loyalists are fighting against the REBEL army of General Francisco FRANCO.

Jordan is assigned by General GOLZ, a Russian communist fighting on the side of the Loyalists, to blow up a bridge in order to stall the FASCISTS after a planned Loyalist attack. Jordan joins a small band of guerrilla fighters living temporarily in a cave in the Guadarrama Mountains just to the southeast of SEGOVIA. The story takes place during "the moon of May" in 1937. The band of guerrillas, led by PABLO and "his woman," PILAR, has already blown up a train and escaped into the mountains where they have been hiding for three months when Jordan joins them.

Jordan meets MARÍA, who is recovering with Pilar's help from psychological wounds she received when the Falangists (a political wing of the fascists) entered her home town, killed her mother and father, the town mayor, and then gang-raped her and several of her friends. She is rescued when the train on which she is being evacuated is blown up by PABLO's band of PARTIZANS. They take her into the mountains, and, three months later, when Jordan joins the group, she becomes his lover. Pilar believes that being with Jordan will help María overcome her mental wounds.

Jordan joins PABLO'S BAND of seven other men and the two women and manages to blow up the bridge at the proper time, but he is wounded during the escape and left to die while covering the retreat of his comrades. He keeps a machine-gun so he can stall the fascists and give his friends time to get away.

Hemingway divided the novel into 43 chapters, without the sort of larger breaks ("books" or "parts") he used in his first three novels. But the novel can be broken down into four main sections, each describing the action of a separate day, from the late afternoon Jordan arrives in the mountains to the morning of the fourth day, a total of about 72 hours.

The first seven chapters cover the first day. Jordan is lying on the "brown, pine-needled floor of the forest" with ANSELMO next to him, the "old man" of Pablo's band, and looking down on a road that leads to the gorge where the bridge is located, Jordan studying the geography and making preliminary notes. There is also a flashback to Jordan's earlier conversation with General Golz about his instructions to blow up the bridge. After meeting the other guerrilla fighters at their cave in chapter 2 and depositing his two heavy bags of explosives, Jordan and Anselmo go back to the area of the bridge for a closer inspection. They return to the cave for the evening meal and for Pilar's reading of death in Jordan's hand. She denies that she sees death, but Jordan understands that she has, and it influences his feeling about the importance of concentrating on the things that are happening to him "now." That night, María joins Jordan in his sleeping bag (chapter 7).

Chapters 8 through 20 cover Jordan's first full day with the partizans. They make plans to meet EL SORDO and his guerrilla band, and Pilar tells Jordan about the beginning of the REPUBLICAN movement when she witnessed the "ugly" killing of 20 fascists in their hometown (see PILAR'S STORY). Pilar leads Jordan, with María, to El Sordo's camp to make plans for the help he will provide at the bridge, and on the way back to their own cave, Pilar leaves Jordan and María to give them the freedom for the second love-making scene, in which "the earth moves." Pilar baits Pablo (chapter 16), calling him a coward for not wanting to help blow up the bridge; he leaves the cave but comes back a little later, saying that he has changed his mind. There is a flashback (chapter 18) in which Jordan remembers his long conversation with KARKOV at GAYLORD's in Madrid about the Russian communist participation on the Republican side (a chapter that was cut from the Russian translation of the novel in 1968). There is an essay on death and its "smell" in chapter 19, followed by the third love-making scene that night of the second day.

The third day (chapters 21 through 37) begins with Jordan killing a fascist horseman who rides into the camp early in the morning. Four other horsemen are later seen following the first rider's tracks in the snow, but that confrontation is avoided. At three o'clock that afternoon, El Sordo is trapped on the top of a hill and he and his five men are killed by planes bombing the location; Jordan and PRIMITIVO see the planes from a distance and hear the bombs exploding. (Hemingway later reprinted this section in a book he edited, titled *Men at War* [1942]).

Chapter 27 presents a vivid description of the tension in El Sordo's last-ditch stand. Anselmo meets Jordan back at the cave and reports on the fascist troop and vehicle movements near the bridge. Jordan realizes from Anselmo's report that Franco's soldiers are preparing for a counterattack and so sends ANDRÉS with a message to General Golz in Navacerrada to warn him of the fascist preparations.

That night (chapter 31), María joins Jordan again in his sleeping bag, but the narrator shifts to other events of the same night: Karkov at Gaylord's discussing with other Russians the next morning's Loyalist attack, and, at two o'clock in the morning, beginning his drive up to the front to meet General Golz (Chapter 31); also at two in the morning, Pilar wakes Jordan to tell him that Pablo has run off with Jordan's detonators (chapter 33); the reader gets Andrés's thoughts as he makes his way to Golz's headquarters (chapter 34); and Jordan returns to his sleeping bag and rages at himself for not following his instincts about the danger that Pablo presented (chapter 35); there is more of Andrés's progress (chapter 36); followed by the final bedroll scene with Jordan and María (chapter 37).

Pablo returns to the cave in the still dark morning of the third full day—the beginning of the novel's fourth part (chapter 38–43)—and has six additional men with him. The guerrilla band moves down the mountain toward the bridge (chapter 39); meanwhile, Andrés proceeds with Jordan's message for General Golz (chapter 40); Jordan and his friends wait for the first light of day so they can attack the bridge, allowing Jordan to set the explosives (chapter 41); Andrés finally gets through to General Golz, but he is too late to stop the attack (chapter 42).

In the final chapter (43), Jordan secures the explosives under the bridge, using hand grenades to detonate the TNT because Pablo has stolen his exploding devices. Despite precautions, a piece of steel from the blown bridge kills Anselmo. Pablo, who with his "extra" men had held off counterattacking fascists, rejoins Jordan with extra horses (implying that he had killed some of his own men in order to enhance the chances for escape). Jordan and the others have to cross a road that is guarded by a fascist tank, and Jordan's horse is shot out from under him, smashing Jordan's leg in the fall. After convincing María that she must leave with the others, he is left alone, waiting for the fascists to come up the road, and hearing "his heart beating against the pine needle floor of the forest."

When *For Whom the Bell Tolls* won The Limited Editions Club's Gold Medal Award in 1941, Sinclair LEWIS, who was one of the three judges, summarized the panel's decision. He wrote that the judges believed the novel was the "American book published during the three years past which was most likely to survive, to be known fifty years from now, or possibly a hundred." Lewis also noted that each judge (the other two were Sterling North and Clifton Fadiman) had argued the novel's merits for entirely different reasons. "To one," Lewis wrote, *For Whom the Bell Tolls* was . . . a great 'love story.' Another judge asserted that it was essentially a galloping chronicle in the tradition of *A Tale of Two Cities* or *Ivanhoe*." And Lewis himself argued that the novel "might just possibly be a masterpiece, a classic, because here was a crystallization of the world revolution that began long ago—perhaps in 1776, perhaps in 1848—and that will not cease till the human world has either been civilized or destroyed—perhaps in 1976, perhaps in 2848."

Lewis closes his essay this way: "Not by pulpiteering shall the people be stirred to resolution and combative common sense. But when the reader, identifying himself with Robert Jordan, actually smells the fighting, then freedom may become an activity to live for, to die for, and brotherhood may become inevitable.

"That is what Ernest Hemingway has done here."

The novel was published by Charles Scribner's Sons October 21, 1940, in an edition of 75,000 copies at $2.75 each.

For Whom the Bell Tolls (film) Paramount picture (170 minutes), released in July 1943; produced by B. G. DeSylva and Sam Wood, screenplay by Dudley Nichols, photography by Ray Rennahan, music score by Victor Young, technicolor color direction by Natalie Kalmus, special effects by Gordon Jennings, set direction by Bert Granger. Winner of an Academy Award for best supporting actress (Katina Paxinou); nominated for best picture, best actress, best actor, best supporting actor (Akim Tamiroff), cinematography, production design, editing, and art direction.

Cast: Gary Cooper (Robert Jordan), Ingrid Bergman (Maria), Akim Tamiroff (Pablo), Arturo De Cordova (Agustin), Joseph Calleia (El Sordo), Katina Paxinou (Pilar), Vladimir Sokoloff (Anselmo), Mikhail Rasumny (Rafael), Fortunio Bonanova (Fernando), Eric Feldary (Andres), Victor Varconi (Primitivo), Lilo Yarson (Joaquin), Alexander Granach (Paco), Adia Kusnetzoff (Gustavo), Leonid Snegoff (Ignacio), Leo Bulgakov (General Golz), Duncan Renaldo (Lieutenant Berrendo), George Coulouris (Andre Massart), Frank Puglia (Captain Gomez), Pedro Cordoba (Colonel Miranda), Michael Visaroff (staff officer), Konstantin Shayne (Karkov), Martin Garralaga (Captain Mora), Jean Del Val (sniper), Jack Mylong (Colonel Duval), and Feodor Chaliapin (Kashkin).

For Whom the Bell Tolls (radio production 1) "Lux Radio Theater" productions (February 1945) did an adaptation of the novel with Gary Cooper and Ingrid Bergman recreating their film rolls as Robert Jordan and María.

For Whom the Bell Tolls (radio production 2) NBC production for "NBC Theater" in November 1949.

For Whom the Bell Tolls (television play) Adaptation from the novel, written by A. E. HOTCHNER and produced in two parts for CBS (March 1959), starring Jason Robards and Maria Schell. It was produced by Fred Coe and directed by John Frankenheimer.

Fossalta Italian town along the PIAVE RIVER northeast of VENICE near where Richard CANTWELL was wounded during WORLD WAR I. Cantwell returns to the place of his wounding as a 50-year-old colonel, "along the sunken road . . . out on the river bank. It was easy to find because of the bend of the river, and where the heavy machine gun post had been, the crater was smoothly grassed."

Cantwell "relieved himself in the exact place where he had determined, by triangulation, that he had been badly wounded thirty years before." It was the "big fifteenth of June offensive in eighteen," which sets the date for *Across the River and Into the Trees* at 1948. Cantwell remembers that the grass there now grows green with the "iron" he has deposited, plus "Gino's leg, both of Randolfo's legs, and my right kneecap."

Fossalta is also the site of the shelling in the "Chapter 7" vignette in which the frightened main character prays to Jesus for delivery from danger.

Fountain of the Medicis   In *A Moveable Feast* Hemingway writes about walking through the Luxembourg Gardens and viewing the Fontaine de Médicis, which is in the northeast corner of the Gardens, near the rue de Médicis. The fountain represents Leda sitting on the banks of the Eurotas, near Jupiter changed into a swan. The fountain was constructed in 1620 and moved to the Gardens in 1860, when the rue de Médicis was completed.

four-gallon jug   In "Up in Michigan," Jim GILMORE gets drunk after getting back to Hortons Bay from a deer hunting trip with D. J. Smith and Charley Wyman. They drink from a four-gallon jug of whiskey, after which Jim seduces Liz COATES.

four-leaf clover   Colonel Richard CANTWELL's divisional insignia. He was the division's commander in World War II but lost his command in the fighting at HÜRTGEN FOREST in *Across the River and Into the Trees*.

fourth and fifth dimension   In *Green Hills of Africa* Hemingway, in talking to KANDISKY about how far good prose writing can be carried if the writer is "serious" and "has luck," says, "There is a fourth and fifth dimension that can be gotten." In discussing it further, he says that first there must be as much "talent" as Kipling had. "Then there must be discipline. The discipline of Flaubert." Hemingway never clearly defined the concept but it may refer to the idea that a talented, disciplined writer can, through implied layers of meaning, intensify a reader's experience of prose beyond what is written on the page.

Fourth C.M.R.   WORLD WAR I military unit to which the two Indians in *The Torrents of Spring* say they belonged. See INDIANS, TWO.

Foxa, Agustín de   Spanish poet, serving as a secretary at the Spanish embassy in Havana in 1954, mentioned by Hemingway in *The Dangerous Summer* as a nightclub-hopping companion of Luis Miguel DOMINGUÍN while the bullfighter visited Hemingway at the Finca Vigía.

"Fox Farming"   Article, published in *The Toronto Daily Star Weekly* (May 29, 1920), reprinted in *Ernest Hemingway: Dateline Toronto* (1985). The headline in the *Star Weekly* was "Canadian Fox-ranching Pays Since the Wild-cats Let the Foxes Alone." It's about Canadian silver fox ranching catching on in the United States and Japan. Silver fox have become less valuable as breeders—once, according to Hemingway, worth about $18,000 for a pair of breeding foxes, now about $1,500—so ranchers are no longer as likely to kill them for the furs.

Foyot's   Paris hotel and restaurant, at 33, rue de Tournon, at the corner of the rue de Vaugirard. In *The Sun Also Rises* it was too expensive for the newspaperman Jake BARNES.

F. Puss (1)   One of Hemingway's first and favorite cats, who lived in Paris with Ernest, Hadley, and their son, Jack ("Bumby"); discussed in *A Moveable Feast.*

F. Puss (2)   Big cat belonging to Thomas HUDSON when he lived in Paris with his first wife and their son, Tom. He is mentioned in *Islands in the Stream,* but he is not one of the 11 cats now owned by Hudson and described in the "Cuba" section of the novel.

Frances (1)   Daughter of one of the "haves" in *To Have and Have Not.* See FATHER, MOTHER, DAUGHTER.

Frances (2)   See Frances CLYNE.

Francesca, Piero della (c. 1420–1492)   Important Italian Renaissance painter; mentioned in "The Revolutionist."

Francis, Ad   Ex-prizefighter in "The Battler," who has only one ear, the other one a mere "stump." He is a little "crazy" as Nick ADAMS learns when he meets Ad. He seems gentle enough at first, until Ad's friend BUGS prevents Nick from lending Ad a knife. Then he sulks silently until he threatens Nick, and Bugs is forced to knock Ad out with a blackjack in order to "change him." While Ad is unconscious, Bugs explains to Nick that Ad is the way he is, not just because of all the boxing matches he had fought.

Ad's fight manager had been a woman who Ad at first claimed was his sister, and the newspapers had written about the brother-sister fight team, but "then they got married in New York and that made a lot of unpleasantness." Bugs explains that they had not actually been brother and sister but that "there was a lot of people didn't like it either way."

Franco, Doña Carmen Polo de Wife of General Francisco FRANCO, Spanish regent of the kingdom of Spain when Hemingway was there in 1959 following the bullfight circuit in preparation for writing *The Dangerous Summer*. According to Hemingway, Doña Carmen was in the presidential box in Bilbao for the final "mano a mano" between Antonio ORDÓÑEZ and Luis Miguel DOMINGUÍN.

Franco, Generalissimo Francisco (1892–1975) Leader of the Spanish REBELS in the SPANISH CIVIL WAR and ruler of Spain as dictator until his death (1939–75). He stayed out of the many military conspiracies in the early 1930s in Spain, gaining the respect of the right-wing conservatives and making enemies of the left-wing Loyalists. In 1935 he was appointed head of the military's general staff. On July 18, 1935, when the Nationalist rebellion began, Franco went to Morocco to command the Spanish garrison there.

His forces invaded southern Spain in the late summer and fall and marched toward Madrid. Franco's rebel forces gradually took over the rest of the country during the next two and a half years, the war ending on April 1, 1939. One of Franco's first actions as dictator was to execute or imprison hundreds of thousands of Loyalists. In *For Whom the Bell Tolls* KARKOV, the communist whom Robert JORDAN meets in Madrid's Gaylord's Hotel, calls Franco a "poor Spanish fascist."

And Richard CANTWELL in *Across the River and Into the Trees* thinks of him as "General Fat Ass Franco."

"Franco-German Situation, The" Article, published in *The Toronto Daily Star* (April 14, 1923), reprinted in *The Wild Years* (1962), reprinted in *Ernest Hemingway: Dateline Toronto* (1985). The headline in the *Daily Star* was "A Victory Without Peace Forced the French to Undertake the Occupation of the Ruhr." This was the first of 10 articles Hemingway wrote for the *Daily Star* on the French-German situation in 1923, five years after the end of World War I. Dateline: "Paris." "To write about Germany," Hemingway begins, "you must begin by writing about France." He discusses the current French political system, its parties and their idiosyncrasies and then explains "causes that forced France into the Ruhr [Valley]."

Francolin See SPUR FOWL.

Frank (1) Bartender at "The Pilot" saloon in "A Man of the World."

Frank (2) Bartender at the Ritz Hotel in Paris when Hemingway was there in the mid-1920s; mentioned in *A Moveable Feast*.

Frank, Waldo (1889–1967) American writer, not named in *Death in the Afternoon*, but identified by a reference Hemingway makes to Frank's book *Virgin Spain* (1926) and an article he wrote for *s4N* magazine explaining his writing habits.

Frankfurter Zeitung Berlin newspaper, one of the publications that bought some of Hemingway's early poems; mentioned in *A Moveable Feast*.

Frankie Sent by Harry MORGAN to find JOHNSON, the tourist who owes Morgan $600 for 18 days of fishing in *To Have and Have Not*. Frankie also helps Harry to get the charter to take 12 Chinese men to Florida.

Franklin, Sidney (1903–1976) U.S. bullfighter, born Sidney Frumpkin. A friend of Hemingway, whom Franklin met in 1929, not realizing he was a writer. They became friends, and Hemingway writes in *Death in the Afternoon* that Franklin was a better bullfighter than all but a handful of Spanish bullfighters. There is also an essay on Franklin at the back of the book. Franklin was with Hemingway in Madrid during one of the writer's trips to Spain to cover the Spanish civil war for the North American Newspaper Alliance. See NANA Dispatch #1.

Franz See SEXTON.

Frazer, Mr. Main character in "The Gambler, the Nun, and the Radio." A writer, he is in the hospital in Hailey, Montana, after falling from a horse and breaking his leg. He has been laid up for at least three months and doesn't seem to be getting any better. He is pessimistic about things in general, although some of the pessimism may be caused by his long stay in the hospital and by the alcohol he consumes.

At the story's beginning, he acts as an interpreter for Cayetano RUIZ, a Mexican beet worker in the hospital with a gunshot wound who is being interrogated by a detective sergeant trying to get as much information from him as possible before he dies. Ruiz is an optimist despite his dire circumstance. At the end of the story Mr. Frazer thinks of all the things that are "opium for the people": religion, music, economics, patriotism (in Italy and Germany—it's 1930), alcohol, sexual intercourse (for some people), the radio, gambling, ambition, new forms of government, and, finally, the one, great opium of the people, that he could not at first think of, *bread*—an opium, like most of the others, never explained but used probably because it is considered essential to life.

Fred Or "Freddy," a character in *Islands in the Stream*, "one of the island boys" hired by the captain of Johnny GOODNER's boat.

Freda Wife of the owner of "this place" in *To Have and Have Not*, where Harry MORGAN, the lawyer, and Albert TRACY meet to plan the illegal transporting of four Cubans from KEY WEST to Cuba. See CUBANS, FOUR.

Freddie's place Bar in KEY WEST, Florida, where much of the drinking in *To Have and Have Not* takes place. Harry MORGAN tells the lawyer, BEE-LIPS, that Freddy is "the only son-of-a-bitch in this town I [would] trust."

Frederichs, Herman In *To Have and Have Not*. He informs BEE-LIPS, the lawyer, that Harry MORGAN's boat has been found by customs officials.

Frederick the Great (1744–1797) Frederick William II, king of Prussia (1786–97). Named, with Maurice de Saxe and Mr. T'sun Su, by Richard CANTWELL in *Across the River and Into the Trees*, as soldiers who were also writers.

Freedman, Solly Jimmy WALCOTT's manager in "Fifty Grand." When Jack BRENNAN, who is getting ready to fight Walcott, asks Freedman for Walcott's nationality, the manager says he's "some sort of Dane."

"Free Shave, A" Article, published in *The Toronto Star Weekly* (March 6, 1920), reprinted in *The Wild Years* (1962), and in *By-Line: Ernest Hemingway* (1967). The article calls Toronto the "true home of the free and brave": free haircuts at the local barber college and free dental service at the local dental college, both available to people "brave" enough to go there; and free medical service at the local hospital for the "needy" poor. And if you want free room, board, and medical attention you can "[w]alk up to the biggest policeman you can find and hit him in the face. . . . [The] amount of your free medical attention will depend on the size of the policeman." The *TSW* headline read "Taking a Chance for a Free Shave."

"Freiburg Fedora, The" Article, published in *The Toronto Star Weekly* (January 19, 1924), reprinted in *Ernest Hemingway: Dateline Toronto* (1985). The headline in the *Star Weekly* was "Must Wear Hats Like Other Folks If You Live in Toronto." About the conforming nature of Toronto's dress code. The byline is "John Hadley," in honor of Hemingway's son, John Hadley Nicanor Hemingway, born October 10, 1923. The article is one of three printed after Hemingway had gone off the *Star*'s payroll on December 31, 1923.

Frenchman In "Under the Ridge," he is a member of an INTERNATIONAL BRIGADE fighting for the Republic in the Spanish civil war. Having had enough of the war, the Frenchman walks away from it. The story's narrator had been through the same battle, and he understands "how a man might suddenly, seeing clearly the stupidity of dying in an unsuccessful attack . . . seeing its hopelessness, seeing its idiocy, seeing how it really was, simply . . . walk away from it as the Frenchman had done." But the battle police (soldiers paid to kill deserters) had "hunted him down, and the death he had walked away from had found him when he was just over the ridge, clear of the bullets and the shelling, and walking toward the river."

"French Royalist Party" Article, published in *The Toronto Daily Star* (April 18, 1923), reprinted in *The Wild Years* (1962), reprinted in *Ernest Hemingway: Dateline Toronto* (1985). The headline in the *Daily Star* was "French Royalist Party Most Solidly Organized." This was the second of 10 articles Hemingway wrote for the *Daily Star* on the French-German situation in 1923, five years after the end of World War I. Datelined "Paris," it is about the impact of the Royalist Party, led by Léon Daudet, son of the novelist Alphonse Daudet. They want France to establish a king as head of the country once again and have chosen Philippe, the duke of Orleans, as their candidate.

"French Speed With Movies on the Job" Article, published in *The Toronto Daily Star* (May 16, 1923), reprinted in *Ernest Hemingway: Dateline Toronto* (1985). The headline in the *Daily Star* was "French Register Speed When Movies Are on Job." This was the 10th and last article that Hemingway wrote for the *Star* on the French-German situation in 1923, five years after the end of World War I. Under the dateline "Düsseldorf," Hemingway delivers sarcastic comments on "personally conducted tours" of economic development in the Ruhr Valley, for example by two Americans who are impressed by what the French have done with German industry and who plan to report about it to their churches back home. And by a "fat [French] movie operator" taking pictures to show how fast the French workers are; when the movie man leaves, the workers sit down again for another smoke and wait for the next tour group.

"Fresh Air on an Inside Story" Article, published in *Ken* (September 22, 1938), reprinted in *By-Line: Ernest Hemingway* (1967). Hemingway explains his method of stopping another, unnamed journalist from sending a false report of the fighting in Madrid during the Spanish civil war.

Friendless The "early name" for Big Goats, or just GOATS, one of Thomas HUDSON's cats in *Islands in the Stream*. He and FRIENDLESS'S BROTHER (really his sister) were the only cats that would sleep with Hudson when he was drunk.

Friendless's Brother   One of Thomas HUDSON's cats in *Islands in the Stream*. But it's really Friendless's sister.

"Friend of Spain: A Spanish Letter, The"   Article, published in *Esquire* (January 1934), reprinted in *By-Line: Ernest Hemingway* (1967). The article is about Hemingway's return to Spain during the late summer of 1933 (on his way to Africa), following the publication the year before of *Death in the Afternoon*, and the subtle difference in the attitude toward him of his Madrid friends.

Fronton, the   Whorehouse in Havana, mentioned in the "Cuba" section of *Islands in the Stream*.

Fuentes   One of the banderilleros in "The Undefeated," a gypsy, who gets the applause of the crowd for his work in the ring.

Fuentes, Gregorio   First mate on Hemingway's fishing boat, *Pilar,* from 1938 to Hemingway's death in 1961. Hemingway writes about him in the article "The Great Blue River."

Fulton, John (1932–1998)   U.S. bullfighter and artist, born in Philadelphia, who, after 40 years of bullfighting, became the first American to be elevated and confirmed as a Spanish matador. Hemingway once helped him through hard times in Spain with a gift of $100.

Fundador bottle   In *The Sun Also Rises* it contains a "smooth amontillado brandy," shared by Jake BARNES and Brett ASHLEY at the Fiesta SAN FERMÍN.

funicular   Steep, usually short, railway having two parallel sets of tracks, upon each of which runs a car raised and lowered by means of a cable that simultaneously lowers or raises the other car so that the two are counterbalanced. In "Cross-Country Snow," Nick ADAMS and GEORGE (4) take a funicular car near Montreux, Switzerland, as high as it can go before being blocked by packed snow.

Furhouse   One of Thomas HUDSON's 11 cats at his home outside of Havana in *Islands in the Stream*.

G('s) U.S. military abbreviation for General(s). Richard CANTWELL uses it in talking with Renata in *Across the River and Into the Trees.*

gaff Pole with a strong hook for bringing in fish that SANTIAGO uses, in *The Old Man and the Sea,* to fight off the sharks. It is used to stick into a tired fish and lift it into the boat or to hold onto a large fish while rigging a hoist to haul it aboard.

Gage, Miss First nurse to take care of Frederic HENRY at the AMERICAN HOSPITAL (1) in Milan after his wounding at the war front in *A Farewell to Arms.*

Galignani's Paris bookstore that, in *The Garden of Eden,* Catherine BOURNE contacts to get books for her husband, David, including W. H. HUDSON's *FAR AWAY AND LONG AGO.* Galignani's was established in 1804 as a publishing house, bookstore, and reading room, and published an English language guide to Paris beginning in 1814 and each year from 1824 to 1894. In 1886 the firm moved to its present location at 224, rue de Rivoli and became a reading room and bookstore. It still claims to be the first English-language bookstore in Europe.

Gall, General Hungarian officer, an unpopular commander in the International Brigades, fighting for the REPUBLIC in *For Whom the Bell Tolls.*

Galleria In Milan, Italy, an indoor shopping and eating area between the cathedral and La Scala theater. It is where gamblers meet with the "old man" in "My Old Man" to try to get him to throw a race.

It is also the location of the Cova Restaurant, where Frederic HENRY eats while convalescing from his war wounds, in *A Farewell to Arms.* He also fantasizes about eating at the Cova during the worst of the fighting back at the warfront.

Gallo Bullfighter in *The Sun Also Rises* without "aficion"; that is, without passion. See AFICIONADO.

"Galloping Dominoes" Article, published in *The Toronto Star Weekly* (May 22, 1920), reprinted in *Ernest Hemingway: Dateline Toronto* (1985). The headline in the *Star Weekly* was "Galloping Dominoes, alias African Golf, Taken Up by Toronto's Smart Set." It's about the "realm of sport of Toronto's smart set." The new game is "Galloping Dominoes" and, "[i]n short, Toronto society is shooting craps."

Galtür Town in southwest Austria, in the Paznauntal Valley about 24 miles southwest of Landeck. It is the setting for "An Alpine Idyll."

Gamble, Jim Hemingway met him in 1918 during the war in northern Italy and writes in *A Moveable Feast* that his wife Hadley remembers an otherwise unidentified story he told Ernest and her about a wisteria vine.

"Gambler, the Nun, and the Radio, The" This short story takes place in a hospital in Hailey, Montana. The main character is Mr. FRAZER, who is in the hospital with a broken leg that never seems to heal; by the end of the story he's been in the hospital for at least three months and seems no better than when he had entered. He listens to a rented radio late at night (because the reception is poor during the day), and he reacts to the "philosophy" of the gambler Cayetano RUIZ, a patient with peritonitis from a gunshot wound, and of the nun, Sister CECILIA, who works at the hospital.

Ruiz, a cardplayer, calls himself a "poor idealist, . . . the victim of illusions." He considers himself "unlucky," since he sometimes wins money at cards only to lose it again in the next game. But when Frazer asks him why he continues to play, Ruiz says, "If I live long enough the luck will change. I have had bad luck now for fifteen years. If I ever get any good luck I will be rich." And the nun, too, is idealistic. She wants to become a saint. "Ever since I was a little girl," she tells Frazer, "I've wanted to be a saint." And she thinks that if she could become a saint, she would be "perfectly happy." Frazer, on the other hand, is a cynic, and when he gets a bit drunk, he lists the various opiums of the people that he has encountered: religion, music, economics, patriotism (in Italy and Germany in 1930), alcohol, sexual intercourse (for some people), the radio, gambling, ambition, new forms of government, and, finaly, the one, great opium of the people, that he could not at first think of, *bread.*

Mr. Frazer is sympathetic, however, to Ruiz's gambling optimism, though he reminds him that he is in the hospital because he was shot by another Mexican while drinking coffee in a local restaurant. And he tries to encourage Sister Cecilia into thinking that she will make it to sainthood, though he doesn't believe in either her prayers or the possibilities of sainthood.

Three Mexicans—friends not of Ruiz but of the man who shot him—come to visit Ruiz, and they return with musical instruments, also entertaining Mr. Frazer in his room down the hall and asking him for requests. He asks them to play "the Cucaracha," which, according to the narrator, "has the sinister lightness and deafness of so many of the tunes men have gone to die to." One of the Mexicans tells Mr. Frazer that "It is the tune of the real revolution," implying the communist revolution. And Mr. Frazer thinks, "Revolution . . . is no opium. Revolution is a catharsis; an ecstasy which can only be prolonged by tyranny." He is glad when they all leave, because then he can have a "little spot of the giant killer and play the radio."

Frazer's cynicism seems mostly alcohol-induced, helping to make this one of Hemingway's funnier stories. But there is humor also in Sister Cecilia's prayers for "Our Lady" (i.e., the Notre Dame football team) and for her own sainthood; and in the police insisting that other Mexicans visit their countryman Ruiz in the hospital, even though the three Mexicans they pick are friends not of Ruiz but of the man who shot him; and even in the idea that the Mexicans are migrant beet workers but living in Montana in the winter.

The story takes place in December 1930 (probably), although the time of the story is confused. The Notre Dame football game was played "on the coast," according to Mr. Frazer, and, although it is not otherwise identified, it is probably the game against the University of Southern California, won in Los Angeles on December 6, 1930, by Notre Dame, 27–0. At one point in the story, Sister Cecilia asks what "fourteen to nothing means." But Mr. Frazer also mentions *Liberty* magazine as "a MacFadden publication," and it was not bought by MacFadden until 1931, which makes the 1930 date suspect. And the World Series between the Philadelphia Athletics and the St. Louis Cardinals, which is also a strain on Sister Cecilia's prayers, is not much of a factor in attempting to date the story since the two teams met in the World Series in both 1930 and 1931.

"The Gambler, the Nun, and the Radio" was first published in *Scribner's Magazine* (May 1933) and reprinted in *Men Without Women* (1933).

Gambler, the Nun and the Radio, The (television play) Adaptation from the short story, written by A. E. Hotchner and produced for CBS "Buick Electra Playhouse" in the fall of 1959 and spring of 1960.

Gambler and Other Stories, The Fyodor Dostoyevsky's book of short stories, published in 1866. In *A Moveable Feast* Hemingway writes that when Sylvia Beach encouraged him to borrow more than just the one book he had picked out (Turgenev's *A Sportsman's Sketches*) on his first visit to Shakespeare and Company, he chose the Constance Garnett translation of *War and Peace* and Dostoyevsky's *The Gambler and Other Stories.*

"Game-Shooting in Europe" Article, published in *The Toronto Star Weekly* (November 3, 1923), reprinted in *The Wild Years* (1962), reprinted in *Ernest Hemingway: Dateline Toronto* (1985). The headline in the *Daily Star* was "More Game to Shoot in Crowded Europe Than in Ontario: Forests and Animals Are Really Protected Over There."

Hunting, Hemingway writes in the article, is the national sport in France, Belgium, Italy, Germany, Czechoslovakia, "and points east." Paris trains are crowded every weekend with hunters heading for the country and probably "more game within twenty miles of Paris, France, than within twenty miles of Toronto, Ontario." The most dangerous game is the wild boar, which manages to kill several hunters every year in France. But licenses are harder to get in Europe. In Italy "you must have a certificate that you have never been in jail signed by the chief of police and the mayor of your hometown." And game is plentiful because it is protected by "rigidly enforced closed seasons" and the fact that governments own the forests.

gamin French word meaning "boy" or "tomboy." MARITA in *The Garden of Eden* says, "Perhaps I am a gamin," suggesting that maybe she is not so different from the androgynous (bisexual) Catherine BOURNE after all.

Ganay, Gustave (d. 1926) "Great" bicycle racer whom Hemingway describes falling at the championships of France at the Parc du Prince, just west of Paris; mentioned in *A Moveable Feast.* Hemingway says he "heard his skull crumple under the crash helmet as you crack a hard-boiled egg against a stone to peel it on a picnic."

Gangeswisch, Mrs. Owner of a chalet above Montreux, Switzerland, where Ernest, his wife Hadley, and their friend Chink Dorman-Smith stayed on a trip Hemingway writes about in *A Moveable Feast.*

Garabitas Hill Outside Madrid, mentioned in *The Fifth Column* as one of the places from which the fascist guns are firing into the city.

Garbo, Greta (1905–1990) Movie actress, born in Sweden and perhaps best known for her role in *Anna Christie.* In "The Capital of the World" PACO (2)'s sisters are returning from a Garbo movie as Paco lies dying on the floor of the hotel kitchen where he works.

Garbo and Jean Harlow are the subjects of Robert JORDAN's occasional dreams in *For Whom the Bell Tolls.* She is also mentioned in *Green Hills of Africa* in a discussion of "beautiful" women.

Garcia, Antonio Brother of the main character in "The Undefeated," Manuel GARCIA. Antonio had been killed nine years before by a bull named Mariposa, whose head was stuffed and now hangs over the desk of the Madrid bullfight promoter Don Miguel RETANA.

Garcia, Don Benito See PILAR'S STORY.

Garcia, Manuel Bullfighter and main character in "The Undefeated." He is just out of the hospital after being gored and wants to fight again, but he's considered too old or not good enough for a regular bullfight in Madrid, so the best he can contract for is a "nocturnal," a nighttime bullfight, more dangerous than regular bullfights because the bulls are either over- or underweight and, usually, have something else wrong with them.

The promoter, Don Miguel RETANA, agrees to let him fight but only offers him 250 pesetas, an insult to a good matador, and finally agrees to pay 300, still an insult. And Garcia has to pay his handlers out of his share. He asks ZURITO (1) to act as a picador for him, and Zurito agrees to do it for no pay, since he knows Garcia can't pay him a proper amount anyway, but he tells the bullfighter that if he turns in a bad performance, he will cut off his COLETA (pigtail), indicating an end to his career.

Garcia works well in the early stages with his first bull, but when he gets to the final stage, where he has to kill, he can't get the sword into the proper spot. Six times he goes in for the kill, each time a failure. The first two times he feels the "shock" of being hit by the bull, but he is not badly hurt. After the fourth time, the crowd throws cushions, and during his fifth attempt he trips on a cushion as he jumps backward, this time the bull's horn going into his side. His handlers try to get him to stop, but he refuses, going in for a sixth try. This time the sword goes all the way in, "[four] fingers and a thumb into the bull."

They rush Garcia to the infirmary, where he is prepared for an operation. Zurito holds up scissors as if to cut off his pigtail, but then, when Garcia pleads with him, relents and says he was only "joking." Just before Garcia goes under the anesthetic, he says to Zurito, "Wasn't I going good, Manos?" And Zurito says, "Sure . . . You were going great."

Garden, Madison Square Major sporting venue in New York City. In "Fifty Grand," it is the site of the boxing match between the story's main character, Jack BRENNAN, and Jimmy Walcott.

garden, the In the "L'Envoi" vignette of *In Our Time,* the KING of Greece is "working in the garden" of his own palace, since he is forbidden by the revolutionary committee, led by Colonel Nicholas PLASTIRAS, to leave the grounds.

Garden of Eden, The This ninth and last published novel (1986)—the second published after Hemingway's death—is one of his most interesting because of the controversy that surrounds it. Hemingway's manuscript was edited to one-third of its original size, from 200,000 words and 48 chapters to 70,000 words and 30 chapters.

A "Publisher's Note" states that "some cuts in the manuscript and some routine copy editing corrections" were made, but some people who have read the original manuscript at the John F. Kennedy Library believe that the cuts were heavy-handed and spoiled the novel. Some go so far as to say that it's not Hemingway's novel at all but the novel of its editor, Tom Jenks, at Scribner's. Others say, however, that *The Garden of Eden* is one of Hemingway's best novels—as published—one that is refreshingly different from all the others. Hemingway wrote the novel over a 15-year period beginning in 1946.

Catherine BOURNE is bisexual (see ANDROGYNOUS) and with symptoms of what might be considered at the end of the 20th century a multiple-personality disorder. The novel's protagonist is David BOURNE, in his mid-20s, a writer with a successful first novel and a second one recently published. The story begins three weeks after their marriage in Paris, and they are on their honeymoon in the south of France, at the small, idyllic town of GRAU DU ROI on the Mediterranean coast, where they eat and drink, make love, swim in the nude, eat and drink, and make love.

The time span of the novel is from March until sometime in late September of the same year, probably 1923. (At one point they buy a copy of the French edition of *Vogue* magazine, which began publication in 1920; and at another time they buy a copy of the Paris edition of *The New York Herald,* which merged with the *Tribune* to form *The New York Herald Tribune* in 1924.)

The first sign of a dark shadow in this otherwise idyllic Garden of Eden comes when Catherine decides to get her hair cut short like a boy's. The story's omniscient narrator states that no "decent girls had ever had their hair cut short like that in this part of the country and even in Paris it was rare and strange and could be beautiful or could be very bad." And she wants to play the part of the "boy" in their love-making and wants to change his name to "Catherine" and hers to "Peter." This initial sexual experimentation frightens David, and he is aware that it foreshadows disaster, but he is unwilling or unable to do anything about it. At one point the reader is told that David wants to avoid the chaos that he sees coming and simply "lie still and quiet and hold [Catherine] and not think at all," but, as the narrator says, "his heart said goodbye" to Catherine, implying David's awareness of what he has gotten himself into.

They drive to Spain in their black BUGATTI, where Catherine begins to lose control over her ability to change from "girl" to "boy" and back again. Her new "classical" boy's haircut, a "surprise" for David, done in BIARRITZ on their way to Madrid, seems to set off the more permanent change. "When you start to live outside yourself," Catherine tells him, "it's all dangerous." And she tries not to change, but David begins to realize that she has no choice.

But the complexity of Catherine's personality is just beginning. They return to the south of France, this time to LA NAPOULE, near CANNES, again on the Mediterranean coast. They meet MARITA, who is attracted to Catherine, first because of her fresh, boy's haircut and her dark-tanned skin color and then by her nonconformity in dressing in a fisherman's shirt and shorts and espadrilles. But after Marita leaves her friend NINA, with whom she has been traveling in a lesbian relationship, and joins David and Catherine, she becomes also attracted to David, because she realizes he is caught in the trap of Catherine's bisexuality. As Marita tells David, she loves them both, and she goes to bed with them both, Catherine presenting Marita to David the first time as a "present."

David is writing a story about his marriage with Catherine, which she refers to as the "narrative." But the more he lives the "narrative," especially after the addition of Marita complicates things, the harder it is for him to write about it, so, as a means of escape, he begins another story, untitled but referred to by them as the AFRICAN STORY. And the more he remembers about his experience of hunting an elephant with his father in East Africa when he was a boy, the more he is able to write about it and escape the complexities of his present life with Catherine and Marita. But the writing of this story adds to the complexity, because Catherine becomes jealous of the African story since it is not about the three of them. She also realizes that David and Marita have become closer, mostly, she knows, because of her own complex nature, and although she loves them both and wants them to love each other, she still realizes that she has become the odd person in the threesome.

At the climax of the novel, she burns the stories David has been working on, and, knowing that she has hurt him badly, she takes the train away from the idyllic life, the Garden of Eden, and into whatever life she has left for herself. At the end of the novel, David tries—

successfully the reader is led to believe—to remember and write again the African story.

The novel's 30 chapters are divided into four "books." Book 1 contains three chapters that set the idyllic nature of the "garden" in which the newly married couple live but with the dark shadows already beginning to appear. Catherine makes her initial change into a boy, and David feels "empty" for the first time. Later he wakes during the night and feels her hands touching him, "and she had made the dark magic of the change again." The "clippings" he has received from his New York publisher frighten her, because she thinks they could "destroy" him if he believes in the reviews of his novel, most of which praise the book. To Catherine the reviews are like death; she tells him they're "like bringing along somebody's ashes in a jar."

Book 2 (chapters 4 through 8) is the Spanish section. They have their first quarrel on their way from France to Madrid. In a drunken state, Catherine argues again about the clippings, showing some of the jealousy that later leads to her burning the reviews and stories. She also begins to show signs of not being able to control her multiple-personality disorder. He realizes that "it had gone further now and he could tell and feel the desperateness." A little later she says to him that she is "always Catherine when [he] need[s] her," but he is beginning to doubt. He realizes, at the end of chapter 7 that there would be no end to the sexual changes. While she is at the PRADO (1) museum in Madrid and seeing the paintings "as a boy" would see them, David meets a friend of his, Colonel John BOYLE, who tells him about Catherine's parents. Both had died in a strange automobile accident. Boyle says that the father killed himself in the accident and implies that it might have been a double suicide. Book 2 ends with Catherine telling David, again after several drinks, how bored she is being a girl and that he should make up his mind about what he wants from her. She becomes "his girl" again and asks him if he had seen her change. "Do you want me to wrench myself around and tear myself in two," she says to him, "because you can't make up your mind? Because you won't stay with anything?"

More than half of the novel is in book 3 (chapters 9 through 24). Back on the French Mediterranean coast, Catherine gets her hair cut short again and convinces David to have his cut by the same coiffeur and lightened like hers. They meet Marita (chapter 10), and although David recognizes her relationship with her friend, NINA, as lesbian, he is attracted to her almost as quickly as is Catherine. And the sexual triangle begins. David uses his African story more and more to escape from the chaos, but he cannot escape except in the vivid memory he has of the elephant hunt with his father. David realizes that Catherine is right when she says that the two of them are "damned" and that the happiness of the Garden is gone.

At the beginning of book 4 (chapters 25 through 30), David and Marita learn that Catherine has burned the clippings and all of David's short stories, except the "narrative." She tries to explain to him why she burned them, but the explanation only makes David aware of just how "crazy" she has become. He tells her that the only reason he doesn't kill her is because she is crazy. She wants to "go away" in the Bugatti, suggesting the possibility of her thoughts of suicide, but David insists that she go by train. She leaves him a letter apologizing for burning the stories and saying that she would be back to "settle things the best we can." At the end of the novel, David gets up from his bed, shared with Marita, and sits down to begin again his African story, which, the narrator states, is "returning to him intact." With Catherine's departure, David has regained his potency as a writer and readers may infer that he regains his potency as a man.

The Garden of Eden was published by Charles Scribner's Sons in May 1986, in a first edition of 100,000 copies. The African story was published separately in *Sports Illustrated* (May 5, 1986), titled "An African Betrayal."

gardener   At Thomas HUDSON's farm near Havana, in the "Cuba" section of *Islands in the Stream*. He advises Mario to feed the cat Goats lightly until he gets over his wounds from his fights with Fats.

Gardner, Ava (1922–1990)   Hollywood film actress, who played roles in three movie adaptations of Hemingway works. She was Lady Brett Ashley in Darryl Zanuck's 1956 production of *The Sun Also Rises;* she was Kitty Collins in the 1946 film version of *The Killers* and sang the Academy Award–nominated song "The More I Know of Love"; and she was Cynthia in the 1952 production of *The Snows of Kilimanjaro*.

Gardner is not mentioned in Hemingway's *The Dangerous Summer*, but she is in one of the photographs with the bullfighter Luis Miguel DOMINGUÍN.

Gardner, George   Jockey riding KZAR in a steeplechase race at St. Cloud in "My Old Man." He tells JOE's "old man" not to bet on Kzar, because KIRCUBBIN would win the race. The "old man" knows the race is fixed, and when Kzar comes in second, he says to Joe, "It sure took a great jock to keep that Kzar horse from winning." Gardner also tries to comfort Joe after his dad is killed in a race at Auteuil near the end of the story.

Gardner, Oscar   In *The Torrents of Spring*, Gardner works at the PUMP-FACTORY in PETOSKEY with Yogi JOHNSON and Scripps O'NEIL, the two main characters. Yogi remembers that "a strange and beautiful thing had

once happened" to Gardner, but Gardner fails to tell anyone what it is. See also DRUMMER.

Gare de Lyon   Train station in Paris on the Right Bank, just southeast of the place de la Bastille, where the rue de Lyon runs into boulevard Diderot. It is where the trains from the south generally arrive and depart. At the end of "A Canary for One," the narrator, his wife, and the AMERICAN LADY say good-bye at the Gare de Lyon.

Gare du Nord   Train station in Paris at 18, rue de Dunkerque, just off the boulevard de Magenta. Trains depart for destinations in northern France, northern Germany, Belgium, the Netherlands, and Great Britain. In *A Moveable Feast* Hemingway writes of taking the train with Hadley from the Gare du Nord to the Auteuil steeplechase track. It's an unlikely starting place for the Auteuil track, located in the Bois de Boulogne on the near west side of Paris.

Gare d'Orsay   Train station in Paris, on the quai Anatole France, from which passengers in the 1920s caught trains to southwestern France. It is now an art museum. In *The Sun Also Rises* Jake BARNES and Bill GORTON leave from the Gare d'Orsay on their way to PAMPLONA, Spain.

Gare Saint-Lazare   Train station in Paris, at rue Saint-Lazare, just north of the Opera, serving passengers going to the northwest; mentioned in *The Sun Also Rises*.

It is also where, in "My Old Man," Joe and his dad, the "old man," caught the train out to Mrs. Meyers' boardinghouse in Maisons-Lafitte.

"Gargoyles as Symbol"   Article, unsigned, published in *The Toronto Star Weekly* (November 17, 1923), reprinted in *Ernest Hemingway: Dateline Toronto* (1985), from which this title is taken. It is a four-paragraph story about the gargoyles of Notre Dame Cathedral in Paris and their possible symbolism. The headline in *TDS* read, "Is France's Present Attitude Toward Germany Symbolized in the Gargoyles of Notre Dame?"

Garner, Carl   One of Joe and Mrs. GARNER's two sons in "Ten Indians." He kids NICK about having an Indian girlfriend and shows his prejudice against Indians by telling Nick that Indians and skunks "smell about the same." His mother tells him that he shouldn't "talk that way," but his father laughs about it, probably leaving the lesson unnoticed.

Garner, Frank   Character in "Ten Indians." When his father, Joe, is back up on the family's horse-drawn wagon after moving a ninth drunken Indian off to the side of the road, Frank says he thought the Indian "was killing a snake."

Garner, Joe In "Ten Indians," he drives the horse-drawn "big wagon" home with his family and their guest, NICK, from the July 4 baseball game in town. He counts nine drunken Indians along the road. His sons kid Nick about having an Indian for a "girl," and when one of them says that "Pa wouldn't ever have had a squaw for a girl," his wife whispers in Joe's ear something with an apparent sexual connotation, because he laughs and then tells his sons that Nick can have Prudie for a girl, because he has his own girl.

Garner, Mrs. At the beginning of "Ten Indians," when she and her family are on their way home in a horse-drawn wagon from a July 4 baseball game and Joe counts nine drunken Indians along the way, Mrs. Garner says, twice, "Them Indians." But later on the same trip, she tries to stop her son Carl from making prejudiced remarks about Indians. When Carl tells NICK that he ought to know skunks because he has "an Indian girl" and they "smell about the same," Mrs. Garner tells him he shouldn't talk that way. But her husband, Joe, laughs too, and so she says to him, "You stop laughing, Joe . . . I won't have Carl talk that way." She's aware of the racial prejudice her son and husband show and tries to guide at least her son away from it.

Garnett, Constance (1861–1946) English translator of late 19th-century Russian novels. She was the first to translate Dostoyevsky and Chekhov into English, and she translated the complete works of Turgenev and Gogol and the major works of Tolstoi. Her nearly 70 translations of the classical works of Russian literature have been a significant influence on English-language readers.

In *A Moveable Feast* Hemingway writes that one of the first books he borrowed in Paris at Sylvia Beach's American bookshop, SHAKESPEARE AND COMPANY (1), was Garnett's translation of *War and Peace*. He later states that he borrowed all of her translations of Tolstoi.

Garrick, David Hemingway's name for the "uneducated" native tracker in *Green Hills of Africa*, named, because of his theatrical expressions, for the famous 18th-century English Shakespearean actor. Garrick, the tracker, is apparently incompetent but difficult to get rid of.

Garrison Bight Near KEY WEST where Harry MORGAN hides his boat after being wounded while bootlegging liquor in part 2 of *To Have and Have Not*. Later, in part 3, Garrison Bight is where Harry thinks one of the

speedboats is "laid up" that might be fast enough to catch the boat he has borrowed to carry four Cuban bank robbers to Cuba. Morgan is worried that the police may find a boat fast enough to catch his.

Gastonia The subject, according to Richard GORDON in *To Have and Have Not*, of a new book he is writing and about which he tells the SHERIFF as the two men go to see Harry MORGAN's boat being towed in near the end of his boat the novel.

Gattorno, Antonio Cuban painter. He and his wife, Lillian, made several fishing trips with Hemingway aboard the latter's boat the *Pilar*.

"Gattorno: Program Note" Article, first published in the art exhibition catalog *Gattorno* (Havana 1935) and reprinted with photographs of several of Gattorno's paintings in *Esquire* (May 1936). Hemingway and the Cuban artist became friends in 1934, and Gattorno joined the Hemingways for several fishing trips on the *PILAR*. In the article, Hemingway writes that Gattorno has a strong color sense and a strong sense of mystery.

Gaudier-Brzeska, Henri (1891–1915) French sculptor and exponent of vorticism, a short-lived abstract art movement (1912–15) which embraced cubist and futurist ideals. He is perhaps best known for his abstract figures "The Dancer" and "The Embracers" and in literary circles for his head of Ezra POUND, which Hemingway saw at Pound's apartment in Paris when they were friends during the early 1920s and which he mentions in *A Moveable Feast*. "Brzeska" is the artist's wife's surname. He was killed during World War I at age 24.

Gavuzzi One of the four ambulance drivers under Frederic HENRY's command during the drive to the war-front in book 1 of *A Farewell to Arms*. He and MANERA carry Frederic to an ambulance after his wounding.

Gaylord's Hotel in Madrid that "the Russians had taken over," important to Robert JORDAN in *For Whom the Bell Tolls* because he met KARKOV there, "the most intelligent man he [Jordan] had ever met," and learned from him about the COMMUNISTS and why they were fighting for the Spanish Republic.

Gaylord's is a luxury hotel, "the place where you met famous peasant and worker Spanish commanders who had sprung to arms from the people at the start of the war without any previous military training and [you] found that many of them spoke Russian." Karkov explained that in preparation for the Spanish civil war many of these "peasants and workers" had gone to the Lenin Institute that the Comintern maintained in Moscow. Karkov also told Jordan about a number of interesting people involved in the war: Valentín

Gonzales, called El Campesino or The Peasant, who had never been a peasant but was an ex-sergeant in the Spanish Foreign Legion; about Enrique Lister, a "simple stonemason" from Galicia, who now commanded a division; and about Juan Modesto from Andalusia, a cabinetmaker, who now commanded an Army corps.

Later in the novel (chapter 32), the scene shifts back to Gaylord's where Karkov is meeting with other communist officers, discussing the LOYALIST attack that is to take place the next morning. And Karkov learns that even his mistress has heard about the "secret" battle plan.

Gazette de Lausanne, La   Swiss newspaper which, in *A Moveable Feast*, Hemingway writes about reading when he and Hadley, and their friend Chink Dorman-Smith, were in Aigle, Switzerland.

Gazzettino   VENICE   newspaper,   which   Richard CANTWELL reads, in *Across the River and Into the Trees,* while at the GRITTI PALACE HOTEL. RENATA tells Cantwell he can publish the statement that she loves him in the *Gazzettino.*

Gellhorn, Martha   Hemingway's   third   wife.   See Martha Ellis Gellhorn HEMINGWAY.

General   In *The Fifth Column* he is in command of the artillery observation post on the Extremadura Road near Madrid. He is apparently German and explains to a Spanish civilian at the post that some of the shells the fascists are firing into Madrid will land in the Salamanca quarter of the city where other "civilians" live, because "Spanish batteries are not as good as ours." He is tied up and gagged by Philip RAWLINGS and MAX (2) when they attack the post.

Génération Perdue, Une   See LOST GENERATION, THE.

Geneva Convention   International agreement on the rules of war, established in 1864 and later revised to cover the care and treatment of the sick, wounded, and dead. In *Across the River and Into the Trees* Colonel Richard CANTWELL indicates, without details, that he "had not fulfilled the complete spirit" of the convention during his fighting in World War II.

"Genio after Josie: A Havana Letter"   Article, published in *Esquire* (October 1934). It is about Hemingway's own fishing for game off the Cuban coast and that it is important to know the age and sexual habits of marlin if one wants to catch them.

Genoa   Conference   International   Economic Conference, held April 10–May 19, 1922, in Genoa, Italy, and attended by representatives of 34 nations to attempt   the   post–World   War I   reconstruction   of European finance and commerce. TCHITCHERIN (also spelled Chicherin) headed the U.S.S.R. delegation, the first time since the Russian Revolution that the Soviets attended a European meeting. When the U.S.S.R. and Germany signed the "Treaty of Rapallo," adding to the mistrust already established between the Allies and Germany, agreement on reconstruction became impossible and the Genoa conference adjourned on May 19. Hemingway covered the conference for *The Toronto Star.*

"Genoa Conference"   Article,   published   in   *The Toronto Daily Star* (April 13, 1922), reprinted in *The Wild Years* (1962), and in *By-Line: Ernest Hemingway* (1967). Datelined "Genoa, Italy," the article is about the clash in northern Italy between the communists of both the U.S.S.R. and Italy, and the FASCISTI, "young ex-veterans [of the Italian army] formed to protect the existing government of Italy against any sort of bolshevik plot or aggression." The clash had been going on for more than a year, but it became centered in the Genoa Economic Conference that opened on April 10, 1922, and which Hemingway covered for *The Toronto Daily Star.* Hemingway writes about the demonstrations and the casualties. The *TDS* headline read "Picked Sharpshooters Patrol Genoa Streets."

"Genoa Scrubs Up for Peace Parley"   Article, published in *The Toronto Star* (April 15, 1922), reprinted in William Burrill's *Hemingway: The Toronto Years* (1994). It was "discovered" by Burrill in the Hemingway Collection at the John F. Kennedy Library in Boston. Datelined "Genoa, April 15," it is about the preparations the Italians have made in Genoa for the International Economic Conference, including interference with the Italian custom of hanging the wash out of windows, avoiding competition with the Union Jack of Great Britain or the Tricolor of France.

gentleman, old   Man in PAMPLONA who subscribes each year for Jake BARNES's bullfight tickets in *The Sun Also Rises*. He is also the town's archivist.

George (1)   NICK's uncle in "Indian Camp." He goes with Nick and Nick's father to assist in the birth of an Indian baby but is apparently traumatized by the Caesarian section Nick's father performs by jackknife, without anesthetic, followed by the suicide of the woman's husband. He disappears, after the operation, probably to get drunk.

George (2)   Husband of the main character in "Cat in the Rain." He is not sympathetic to his wife's desire for a cat, nor does he see the loneliness that prompts her to want all the other things. He tells her to "shut up."

He continues to lie in bed, reading his book and mostly oblivious to his wife's feelings.

George (3)   Barman at the HÔTEL DE CRILLON in *The Sun Also Rises*.

George (4)   Nick ADAM's skiing friend in "Cross-Country Snow." George is returning to the States to go back to school after the day's skiing, and, while they drink a bottle of wine at an inn on their way down the mountain, they discuss the skiing and Nick's future. When Nick says that neither he nor HELEN (2), who is expecting a baby in the late summer, want to leave Switzerland, George says, "It's hell, isn't it." It isn't clear whether George is talking about not being able to stay in Switzerland or about Nick and Helen having the baby. In any case, Nick answers, "No. Not exactly." The ambiguity here is an important part of the story's tension.

George (5)   Apparent owner of HENRY'S LUNCHROOM, the setting for most of "The Killers." George waits on the two "killers," AL and MAX (1), when they enter the lunchroom and discourages other customers from ordering meals while the killers remain there, waiting for Ole ANDRESON to come in for dinner. George is sarcastic in answering the sarcastic questions of the killers and seems unafraid of them, even when they insist on tying up and gagging his cook, SAM, and his only customer, Nick ADAMS. When the killers leave the lunchroom, George tells Nick to go warn Andreson at Hirsch's rooming house. When Nick returns to the lunchroom, George responds to Nick's feeling that what is going to happen to Andreson is "awful" by telling him "you better not think about it."

George (6)   Hebrew wine seller in *Today is Friday*. In a "drinking-place" late at night, he serves wine to three Roman soldiers who assisted at Christ's crucifixion that day. Although Jewish, he tells the soldiers, "It's a thing I haven't taken any interest in." Of the play's four characters, George, because of his indifference to the crucifixion—probably because he's afraid of the Roman authorities—may, nevertheless, be the most dangerous.

George (7)   Headwaiter at the GRAN ITALIA restaurant in the GALLERIA in Milan, the favorite of Frederic HENRY and Catherine BARKLEY during Frederic's convalescence in *A Farewell to Arms*. George also lends him money.

George (8)   In *Across the River and Into the Trees* Colonel Richard CANTWELL's "best friend" during their division's march across France toward Germany during World War II.

George (9)   Probably George Antheil, French concert pianist and composer, whom Hemingway knew in Paris in the 1920s. He is mentioned in *A Moveable Feast* in connection with his having been in Sylvia Beach's bookshop Shakespeare and Company with Count Alfred von Wedderkop, the Paris representative of *Der Querschnitt*.

George (10)   One of the crew members on Thomas HUDSON's boat in *Islands in the Stream*, searching for the crew of a German submarine. The novel's narrator refers to George as "a good athlete and fine seaman, but not nearly as strong as ARA in many ways." His name is Eugenio, but PETERS has difficulty pronouncing it, so they call him George.

Georges   Bartender at the Ritz Hotel in Paris and a friend of Hemingway. In *A Moveable Feast* Hemingway writes, in one of the stories that belittles F. Scott Fitzgerald, that "many years" after the Hemingways and the Fitzgeralds had lived in Paris during the 1920s, Georges once asked him at the Ritz, "Papa, who was this Monsieur Fitzgerald that everyone asks me about?" According to Hemingway, Georges, who claimed to have known everyone back in the 1920s, didn't remember Fitzgerald. Georges was, however, just a "*chasseur*" at that time, a hotel page-boy, and might not have met many of the artists who visited the Ritz.

Georgette   Paris prostitute whom Jake BARNES picks up at the beginning of *The Sun Also Rises*, because he thought it would be fun to have dinner with someone. Jake says, "She grinned and I saw why she made a point of not laughing." He introduces her to some of his friends at the NÈGRE DE TOULOUSE RESTAURANT as "Mademoiselle Georgette Leblanc," but Georgette misses the joke and so immediately corrects him, telling everyone that her name is Georgette Hobin. Georgette Leblanc (c. 1867–1941) was a well-known French actress and singer.

Georgetti   In *A Farewell to Arms*, when Frederic HENRY is being transferred by train from a northern Italian field hospital to the American Hospital in Milan, he meets Georgetti, an Italian soldier also wounded in the war. The two men get drunk together.

gerenuk   Reddish brown antelope of East Africa, "that long-necked antelope that resembles a praying mantis," hunted by Hemingway on the safari described in *Green Hills of Africa*.

"German Blow—Disloyal?"   Article, unsigned, published in *The Toronto Daily Star* (April 18, 1922), reprinted in *Ernest Hemingway: Dateline Toronto* (1985). The headline in the *Daily Star* was "Is Germany's Most Sinister Blow at the Allies, Most Striking Disloyal Act Ever Accomplished?" Under the dateline "Genoa,"

Hemingway quotes the Italian newspaper *Corriere Mercantile* as stating that the Russo-German treaty "is the most sinister blow Germany was able to deliver at the Allies." Other delegations agree.

"German Delegation at Genoa" Article, published in *The Toronto Daily Star* (April 28, 1922), reprinted in *Ernest Hemingway: Dateline Toronto* (1985). The headline in the *Daily Star* was "German Delegation at Genoa Keeps Stinnes in Background." Datelined "Genoa," this is a report of the difficulties the German delegation is having at the Genoa Economic Conference because from the beginning they felt they had "nothing to gain" at the conference "and everything to lose." Hugo Stinnes was "the sinister peacetime kaiser of Republican Germany . . . the industrial dictator," and the German delegation, knowing of his unpopularity outside Germany, felt that it was better if Stinnes was not allowed to speak at the conference.

"German Export Tax Hits Profiteers" Article, published in *The Toronto Star Weekly* (February 25, 1922), reprinted in *Ernest Hemingway: Dateline Toronto* (1985). The headline in the *Star Weekly* was "Exchange Pirates Hit by German Export Tax." Datelined "Basel, Switzerland," this article explains that Germany has a new law taxing exports to prevent foreigners from buying German products cheaply, because of the low value of the German mark, and selling them elsewhere for a 400 to 500 percent profit.

German girl Friend of the Hemingways when they were in Schruns, Austria, during the winter 1925–26. In *A Moveable Feast* Hemingway writes that "[s]he was a great mountain skier, small and beautifully built, who could carry as heavy a rucksack as I could and carry it longer." But no name is given.

"German Inflation" Article, published in *The Toronto Daily Star* (September 19, 1922), reprinted in *The Wild Years* (1962), and in *By-Line: Ernest Hemingway* (1967). Datelined "Kehl, Germany," the article is about Ernest and his wife Hadley walking across the bridge over the Rhine River into Kehl and feeling the impact of German inflation. A dollar was worth 800 marks. They priced coffee at 34 marks per pound; a scythe blade cost 150 marks; beer was 10 marks a stein; Kehl's best hotel served a five-course dinner for 120 marks (15 cents). The *TDS* headline read "Crossing to Germany Is Way to Make Money."

"German Inn-Keepers" Article, published in *The Toronto Daily Star* (September 5, 1922), reprinted in *The Wild Years* (1962), and in *By-Line: Ernest Hemingway* (1967). Datelined "Oberprechtal-in-the-Black-Forest," the article is about Ernest and Hadley Hemingway hiking in the Black Forest with their friends the Bill Birds

and finding the reluctance of German innkeepers or inn customers to be friendly. The inns are "white plastered and clean looking outside and uniformly neat and dirty inside." The Americans find that some Germans still recovering from the war have a hatred of "Auslanders" (foreigners). The *TDS* headline read "German Inn-Keepers Rough Dealing with 'Auslanders.'"

"German Journalists a Strange Collection" Article, published in *The Toronto Daily Star* (May 8, 1922), reprinted in *Ernest Hemingway: Dateline Toronto* (1985). Under the dateline "Genoa," Hemingway writes that if it's "true that the funnier-looking a newspaperman is the better work he does, there were some world-beaters at the Genoa Conference." Especially the Germans.

"German Machiavellianism" Article, published in *The Toronto Daily Star* (April 18, 1922), reprinted in *Ernest Hemingway: Dateline Toronto* (1985). The headline in the *Daily Star* was "Regarded by Allies as German Cunning." Datelined "Genoa," this is a two-sentence report that the Genoa Economic Conference is "like a ship in a hurricane" because of the Russo-German treaty, which Hemingway says is "a return to German Machiavellianism."

German prisoner In *Islands in the Stream* two of Thomas HUDSON's crew members, Willie and Ara, find a wounded German sailor, a member of a submarine crew that Hudson and his crew are hunting in the islands off the northeast coast of Cuba in the "At Sea" section of the novel. The German dies of his wounds before Hudson can get any information from him, and they bury him on CAYO CRUZ.

"German Riots" Article, published in *The Toronto Star Weekly* (September 30, 1922), reprinted in *The Wild Years* (1962), reprinted in *Ernest Hemingway: Dateline Toronto* (1985). The headline in the *Star Weekly* was "Riots are Frequent Throughout Germany." Datelined "Cologne," it is about the conflict between German police and German mobs: riots against the high cost of living, for example, and riots in favor of a return to monarchy.

"Germans Desperate Over the Mark" Article, published in *The Toronto Daily Star* (September 1, 1922), reprinted in *The Wild Years* (1962), reprinted in *Ernest Hemingway: Dateline Toronto* (1985). The headline in the *Daily Star* was "Germans Are Doggedly Sullen Or Desperate Over the Mark." Datelined "Freiberg, Germany," it is about "the plunge to worthlessness" of German money and the reaction of "dogged sullenness or hysterical desperation" by the German people.

German soldier In the "Chapter 3" vignette of *In Our Time*, he gets caught climbing over a garden wall at Mons and is "potted" (shot) by unidentified soldiers.

"Get a Seeing-Eyed Dog"   This short story and "A Man of the World" are the last short stories published in Hemingway's lifetime. They were placed together under the heading "Two Tales of Darkness" in *Atlantic* for November 1957. The "darkness" in the overall title refers to the blindness of the main character in each story. In "Get a Seeing-Eyed Dog," PHILIP is a writer who has recently gone blind. He and his unnamed wife are in Venice in the late winter, and he tries to get her to take a trip in order to better "pace themselves" in getting used to his blindness. She refuses to go, preferring his company and hoping to encourage his memory of things they have done together so he can write about them. In his attempt to get her to go away for awhile, he tells her that he doesn't want her to become "just a seeing-eyed dog." She insists that she's not and corrects him, saying that it's "seeing-eye not seeing-eyed dog." At the end of the story she refuses to go away, and Philip is left thinking of ways to get her to leave without hurting her, because, he says, "I am not doing too well at this" (his blindness).

"Getting into Germany"   Article, published in *The Toronto Daily Star* (May 2, 1923), reprinted in *The Wild Years* (1962), and in *By-Line: Ernest Hemingway* (1967). This was the sixth of 10 articles Hemingway wrote for the *Daily Star* on the French-German situation in 1923, five years after the end of World War I (there is a prefatory note stating that this article was intended to be published before the one of April 25). Datelined "Offenburg, Baden," the article is about the difficulty of getting a visa to visit Germany and of the increased cost of everything since Hemingway last visited Germany less than a year before. Beer is now 350 marks a glass, wine is 500 marks a glass. The *TDS* headline read "Getting into Germany Quite a Job, Nowadays." See also "German Inflation."

Gettysburg, Battle of   Richard CANTWELL describes the American Civil War battle to RENATA in *Across the River and Into the Trees*. He tells her it was "the big kill day of all kill days," comparing it to the World War II battle for HÜRTGEN FOREST.

"G.I. and the General, The"   Article, published in *Collier's* (November 4, 1944), reprinted in *By-Line: Ernest Hemingway* (1967). This article is the fifth of six dispatches from the European sector of World War II, all published in *Collier's*. No date or place is identified in this article, but Hemingway calls it a "clear summer afternoon," which would identify the action as probably before the taking of Paris, which occurred on August 25, 1944. The division he is with is tired. "No one remembered separate days any more, and history, being made each day, was never noticed but only merged into a great blur of tiredness and dust, of the smell of dead cattle, the smell of earth new-broken by TNT, the grinding sound of tanks and bulldozers, the sound of automatic-rifle and machine-gun fire, the interceptive, dry tattle of German machine-pistol fire, dry as a rattler rattling; and the quick, spurting tap of the German light machine guns—and always waiting for others to come up." The general of the article title is not named, but one of the American soldiers argues that he is "sixty miles back if he is an inch" and that he "does not know that men are human." Hemingway knows the general and that the general knows how important it would be for the troops to get some rest. The article describes soldiers who are tired, angry, discouraged, and scared.

Gibbs, .505   In "The Short Happy Life of Francis Macomber," it is the gun Francis MACOMBER carries with him the morning he, his wife, Margot, and the white hunting guide, Wilson, hunt for lions.

Gide, André (1869–1951)   French novelist, essayist, poet, and critic, winner of the Nobel Prize for literature in 1947. He is best known, perhaps, for *L'Immoraliste* (1902; *The Immoralist*).

In *Death in the Afternoon* Hemingway says of Gide that he had a "withered old maid moral arrogance." Gide, however, was rebellious against conventional morality and expressed this sentiment in much of his work.

In *Islands in the Stream* Thomas HUDSON's oldest son, young Tom, had shown as a young boy his understanding of homosexuality by naming a book he had read by Gide, *Si le grain ne meurt* (1924; *If It Die . . .*), an autobiographical work about Gide's life from birth to his marriage with his cousin Madeleine Rondeaux and the discovery of his homosexuality, a book considered one of the great works of confessional literature.

Gil   Member of Thomas HUDSON's crew in the "At Sea" section of *Islands in the Stream*.

Gilby, Eddie   Seventeen-year-old Ojibway Indian and half-brother of Billy and Trudy in "Fathers and Sons." Billy informs Nick ADAMS that Eddie has said he wants to "sleep in bed with you sister Dorothy," and Nick tells him that he will kill Eddie before he lets that happen.

Gilford   In "My Old Man," it is the name of the steeplechase racehorse that JOE's "old man" buys. According to Joe, Gilford is "Irish bred and a nice, sweet jumper." The old man thought that training him and riding him both would be a "good investment." But the horse needs to be put down when he falls at one of the jumps, killing Joe's dad.

Gilmore, Jim   Main male character in "Up in Michigan." He had bought the blacksmith shop when he moved to Hortons Bay from Canada. He is "short and dark with big mustaches and big hands." He eats most of his meals at D. J. Smith's, where Liz COATES works; he "liked her face because it was so jolly," but the narrator informs us that he never thought about her. He talks with D. J. Smith about their work and about the Republican Party, but he doesn't pay much attention to Liz.

When he returns to Hortons Bay from a deer-hunting trip, he gets drunk and makes sexual advances toward Liz. She is frightened but wants Jim's attention, and because she doesn't know what else to do, she lets him take her to the dock, where she tries to stop him from sexual intercourse but can not.

gimlet   Cocktail, ordinarily made with gin or vodka, sweetened lime juice, and sometimes with soda water. It's the drink Robert WILSON chooses, and which Francis and Margot MACOMBER agree to, at the beginning of "The Short Happy Life of Francis Macomber." Mr. Wilson "needs" the drink, following Macomber's cowardice in running from the lion he was hunting the morning the story opens. The gimlet in this case is made of lime juice, gin, sugar, and soda.

It is also a drink that P.O.M. (Poor Old Mama) chooses in *Green Hills of Africa*.

gin and tonic   Drink of choice for Thomas HUDSON in the "Bimini" section of *Islands in the Stream*. At BOBBY's cafe and bar on Bimini, the drink is "Booth's yellow gin" and "Schweppes's Indian Tonic Water." He likes a "piece of lime peel" with the drink, "and a few drops of ANGOSTURA," and the bitter drink brought pleasant memories of his voyages along the coast of East Africa. In the novel's third section, "At Sea," his drink is iced tea.

Gingrich, Arnold (1903–1972)   First editor of both *Coronet* and *Esquire* magazines. Partly as a favor to Gingrich to help get *Esquire* started, Hemingway contributed "Marlin off the Morro: A Cuban Letter" for its first issue, "Autumn 1933" (the only quarterly issue of the magazine). He contributed a total of 26 articles and six short stories to *Esquire*, including "The Snows of Kilimanjaro" (August 1936).

Gingrich, who was both editor and publisher at *Esquire* for a period of time, wrote the autobiographical *Nothing but People* (1971). Gingrich was the fourth husband of Jane MASON, one of Hemingway's Key West and Havana friends in the early 1930s.

Gin Lane   William Hogarth's woodblock print (c. 1751), remembered by Thomas HUDSON in *Islands in the Stream*, because it pictures the human degradation from drinking gin.

Giorgio   Barman at the GRITTI PALACE HOTEL in Venice, mentioned in *Across the River and Into the Trees*.

He is greeted as "Privy Counsellor" by Richard CANTWELL upon his arrival at the hotel. Giorgio is an "anarchist" from Piemonte, an Italian border province.

Giotto (c. 1266–c. 1337)   Giotto di Bondone, a Florentine painter and architect, one of several Italian painters whom Richard CANTWELL thinks about in *Across the River and Into the Trees*. He is also mentioned in "The Revolutionist."

Giovanni, Edouardo   See Edgar SAUNDERS.

girl (1)   Clerk in the Concordia shop, in "Out of Season," who is amused by the idea that one of the three Marsala wines the "Young Gentleman" and his wife order is for a *vecchio*, an old man. PEDUZZI (1) identifies the clerk as his daughter.

girl (2)   In *A Farewell to Arms* a waitress at the restaurant in STRESA where Frederic HENRY finds Catherine BARKLEY and Helen FERGUSON after his escape from the war. The girl is upset because Ferguson is crying due to the sudden appearance of Frederic, whom Ferguson blames for getting Catherine pregnant.

girl (3)   In "A Clean, Well-Lighted Place," probably a prostitute, she has been picked up by a soldier and both are noticed by the two waiters as they walk past their café.

girl (4)   Unnamed character in "The Sea Change," she has just informed her lover, PHIL, that she is leaving him for a woman. The narrator notes that she is wearing a tweed suit; "her skin was a smooth golden brown, her blonde hair was cut short and grew beautifully away from her forehead."

She tries to smooth over Phil's hurt feelings and to argue against both drastic action on his part and calling "it" names (the term lesbianism is not used in the story). When he says, "I'll kill her," she says, "It won't make you happy." And when he calls what she is doing "perversion," she reminds him that "[w]e're made up of all sorts of things. You've known that. You've used it well enough." He says, "You don't have to say that again," implying that they have discussed the idea of "perversion" before, probably as it concerns their own relationship.

She is like JIG, the girl in "Hills Like White Elephants," who discusses with her boyfriend whether she should get an abortion. Just as lesbianism is not mentioned in "The Sea Change," neither is abortion mentioned in "Hills Like White Elephants." And in both stories, the young women are stronger characters than are the young men.

girl (5)   In *The Fifth Column*, she asks the International Brigade soldier she's with in the Hotel

Florida to translate a sign that's on the door of Room 109. It is the room of Dorothy Bridges and Robert Preston, and the sign reads, "Working, Do Not Disturb."

girl (6) In *A Moveable Feast* Hemingway describes seeing a pretty girl in a place Saint-Michel café who "disturbed" him as he tried to write a story. "She was very pretty with a face fresh as a newly minted coin . . ., and her hair was black as a crow's wing and cut sharply and diagonally across her cheek." She "excited" him and he wanted to put her in the story, and he looked at her now and then while he continued to write, but when he looked up after finishing the story she was gone.

girl (7) In *The Garden of Eden* she brings beer in GOURD CUPS to David BOURNE's father and the hunter-tracker JUMA after they kill the old elephant. David remembers the incident from his childhood experience hunting with his father in East Africa and is writing about it in his AFRICAN STORY. The young girl is helped by her "younger brother."

girl assistant In *The Sun Also Rises;* assistant to the MAN WITH JUMPING FROGS.

girls, Cova The narrator of "In Another Country" describes the girls seated at tables in the CAFÉ COVA in Milan as "very patriotic," suggesting that they are either prostitutes or merely waiting for dates with soldiers who drop into the café.

girls, seven From the soldiers' whorehouse in Gorizia in part 1 of *A Farewell to Arms*. They are evacuated at the start of the retreat from Caporetto.

girls, three Waitresses in a restaurant in Spezia, Italy, in "Che Ti Dice La Patria?" They double as prostitutes during the time of the story (April 1927) when Mussolini has closed the brothels, forcing prostitutes to find fronts in other businesses. One of the "waitresses" tries to force herself on Guy, the traveling friend of the story's narrator, and Guy has to beg the narrator to get them out of there.

girls, two (1) On a walk back to the AMERICAN HOSPITAL (1) in Milan after one of his treatments at the Ospedale Maggiore, Frederic HENRY, in *A Farewell To Arms*, sees two "nice-looking girls" posing for a silhouettes artist.

girls, two (2) In *A Farewell To Arms* Italian sisters who ride with AYMO and Frederic HENRY in their retreat from GORIZIA toward Pardonne. They "look" to be about 15 and 16 years old.

girls, two (3) Richard CANTWELL, in *Across the River and Into the Trees*, sees "two lovely looking girls" as he walks toward HARRY'S BAR in Venice, but he realizes, as he feels the "twinges" of a possible heart attack coming, that he needs to "quit window gazing" and get to the bar.

Girones, Vincente In *The Sun Also Rises;* he is from Tafalla, Spain, and is killed during the running of the bulls in PAMPLONA at the Fiesta SAN FERMÍN, attended by Jake BARNES and his friends. Girones is "twenty-eight years old, and had a farm, a wife, and two children. . . . The bull who killed [him] was named Bocanegra, was Number 118 of the bull-breeding establishment of Sanchez Taberno, and was killed by Pedro ROMERO as the third bull of that same afternoon."

The incident, including Girones's wife arriving in Pamplona to take the body home, acts as contrast with the carefree attitude toward everything else involved in the festival.

glasses, twelve-power Binoculars that Thomas HUDSON carries on board his boat, in *Islands in the Stream*, in search of a German submarine crew.

Globe Toronto newspaper for which Hemingway wrote one article, "Moscow Theatre Company Will Not Come to Toronto" (November 27, 1923), while he was still under contract with *The Toronto Star*.

glühwein In *A Farewell to Arms*, "[h]ot red wine" drunk by Frederic HENRY and Catherine BARKELY in Bains de l'Alliaz on one of their winter hikes from Montreux.

G.M. Richard CANTWELL's abbreviated name for the GRAN MAESTRO in *Across the River and Into the Trees*.

G.N.'s Spanish Guardia Nacionals, those "[w]hatyoumacallits nationals," according to Catherine BOURNE to her husband, David, in *The Garden of Eden*. She probably means the Guardia Civil (Civil Guard), describing them in their khaki uniforms, on bicycles and with "black leather pistol holsters." She's in a Madrid café drinking ABSINTHE and nervous about the "G.N.'s" because, although absinthe is not illegal in Spain (as it is in France), waiters serve it discreetly, and Catherine feels she has to "engulp the evidence" quickly.

Goats One of Thomas HUDSON's 11 cats in *Islands in the Stream*. Goats is one of BOISE's sons and officially named "Big Goats." He used to be called FRIENDLESS and has a sister named FRIENDLESS'S BROTHER.

goats, two In "Old Man at the Bridge," the old man takes care of two goats, a cat, and four pairs of pigeons.

"[God is away for the summer . . .]"   First line of a poem about a Chicago Presbyterian minister taking a summer vacation, written about 1920–21 and first published in *88 Poems* (1979).

"God Rest You Merry, Gentlemen"   This short story takes place in a Kansas City hospital on Christmas Day afternoon. HORACE, the narrator, apparently a journalist, visits the city hospital where he visits Doc FISCHER and Doctor WILCOX, who tell him a fascinating story. A boy, "about sixteen," had been to the hospital the day before, pleading with the two doctors to castrate him, because he can't stop sinning. "I've prayed," the boy had told them, "and I've done everything and nothing helps."

Doc Fischer had tried to convince him that nothing is wrong with him, that he is very normal. But the boy didn't listen; he still insisted that he is sinning "against purity," and he begged them to castrate him. The doctors finally got him out of the hospital, but at one o'clock the next morning (Christmas Day) he was back, having mutilated himself with a razor. The boy thinks he has castrated himself, but, not knowing what the word means, he had amputated his penis and was bleeding badly.

The story is really about the doctors, one a Jew, and their seeming incompetence to deal with the boy's problem. Doc Fischer has "gambler's hands," not necessarily a detriment for a good doctor. But it is "Doctor" Wilcox who gets the narrator's satirical focus. Wilcox carries with him a pocket-sized copy of *The Young Doctor's Friend and Guide,* a book which provides symptoms and treatment and cross-references. He had been told by a medical school professor, "Wilcox, you have no business being a physician and I have done everything in my power to prevent you from being certified as one," but he advised him "in the name of humanity," to buy the little book and "learn to use it." So Doctor Wilcox carries the booklet with him at all times. But, as Doc Fischer relates to Horace, Doctor Wilcox was on call when the boy came in self-mutilated, but "he was unable to find this emergency listed in his book."

Left there, this would be a funny story, a slap at Doctor Wilcox and his little book of medical instructions if not at the entire medical profession. But the story's last page is devoted to a dialogue between the two doctors about the significance of the self-mutilation occurring on Christmas Day, which provides an ambiguous twist to the ending and an ironic meaning to the story's title. Doc Fischer is Jewish but reminds Doctor Wilcox that it is the day of "our Saviour's birth." Wilcox reminds him that since he is Jewish, it is not *his* Savior's birthday. Doc Fischer then says that the "significance of the particular day is not important." But the significance of the day is at least accentuated by the boy carrying his religious fundamentalism to an extreme and by the two doctors discussing it, while waiting to see if the boy would live or die.

"God Rest You Merry, Gentlemen" was first published by House of Books in April 1933 and reprinted, with several revisions, in *Winner Take Nothing* (1933).

Gogol, Nikolay (1809–1852)   Russian novelist and playwright, best known for his short story "The Overcoat" (1842) and for his novel *Dead Souls* (1842). In *A Moveable Feast* Hemingway writes that as soon as he discovered Sylvia Beach's American bookshop Shakespeare and Company he began to read the complete works of Turgenev and everything of Gogol's that had been translated.

"Goiter and Iodine"   Article, published in *The Toronto Star Weekly* (December 15, 1923), reprinted in *Ernest Hemingway: Dateline Toronto* (1985). The headline in the *Star Weekly* was "Dose Whole City's Water Supply to Cure Goitre by Mass Medication." It is about an attempt in Rochester, New York, to cure the goiter by introducing iodine into the city's water supply. The opening sentence reads, "Should a whole city be dosed for the ills of a few of its inhabitants?" The byline is "John Hadley," in honor of Hemingway's son, John Hadley Nicanor Hemingway, born October 10, 1923.

Golden Horn   Gulf off the Bosporus at Constantinople (now Istanbul) and close to the eastern wall of the old city; it is about 5 miles long and shaped like a stag's horn. It got the name "Golden" when the richness of the region's products was discovered. In the article "Constantinople, Dirty White, Not Glistening and Sinister," Hemingway writes that the Golden Horn looks like the Chicago River.

Golz, General   Soviet-trained officer ("Général Sovietique"), in *For Whom the Bell Tolls,* the communist commander of the 14th and 35th International Brigades of the REPUBLICAN army; he gives Robert JORDAN the orders for blowing up the BRIDGE. In response to a comment by Jordan that he has enough to think about without thinking about girls, Golz says, "I never think at all. Why should I? I am *Général Sovietique.* I never think. Do not try to trap me into thinking." Later, Jordan sends a message to Golz, warning him that the fascists in the mountains are preparing for a counterattack, but the message reaches the general too late.

Gómez, Rafael (1882–1960)   "El Gallo," Spanish bullfighter mentioned in *Death in the Afternoon,* also known as Rafael El Gallo. He was the younger brother of a more famous bullfighter, JOSELITO.

Gomez, Rogelio   Captain of the 65th Brigade, who takes Andrés LOPEZ by motorcycle to General GOLZ with Robert JORDAN's message in *For Whom the Bell Tolls*.

gonorrhea   Sexually transmitted disease, characterized by inflammation of the urethra or of the vagina. It is what the main character, HE (2), in "A Very Short Story," catches from a salesgirl while riding in a taxi through Chicago's Lincoln Park.

gonorrheal pus   Mentioned in conversation in *Across the River and Into the Trees* between Richard CANTWELL and the GRAN MAESTRO as a device soldiers used, usually contained in a matchbox, for producing an infection that would keep "poor boys who did not want to die" out of the next battle. Jaundice could be produced also, according to Cantwell, by placing big ten-centime pieces under the armpits.

González, Don Federico   See PILAR'S STORY.

Gonzalez, Mike (1890–1997)   Major League baseball player (1912–32) with five different teams but mostly with the St. Louis Cardinals and the Chicago Cubs; he also managed the Cardinals in 1938 and 1940. He was born in Cuba and so was of special interest to SANTIAGO in *The Old Man and the Sea*. He was born Miguel Angel Gonzalez y Cordero.

"Good Generals Hug the Line"   Article, published in *Ken* (August 25, 1938). One of the Spanish civil war pieces not sent to the North American Newspaper Alliance (NANA). Hemingway reports that the generals on both sides in the war "hug the line"; that is, they stay so far behind their front lines that they are often out of touch with events and so lose battles.

"Good Lion, The"   Fable, published along with "The Faithful Bull" in *Holiday* magazine (March 1951), illustrated by Adriana IVANCICH. The lion is "good" because in Africa it won't eat other animals and people as "bad" lions do, and the good lion has wings, so all the other lions make fun of it. It is finally forced to fly away to Venice where its father and mother live and where it can go to Harry's Bar and have a "very dry martini."

Goodner, Johnny   Character in *Islands in the Stream*. He owns a cruiser, the *Narwhal*, tied up at BIMINI and in which he can usually be found with a Tom Collins in one hand and a "long, green Mexican chile pepper" in the other. "He was," according to Thomas HUDSON, the size and build of a middleweight gone a little heavy."

Gordini, Franco   One of the four ambulance drivers under Frederic HENRY's command as the ambulances drive toward the warfront in book 1 of *A Farewell to Arms*. Frederic thinks of him as the "quietest one of the

four." He is wounded by the same "big trench mortar shell" explosion that wounds Frederic.

Gordo, El   One of Thomas HUDSON's 11 cats in *Islands in the Stream*. See FATS. The Spanish word "gordo" means "fat."

Gordon, Helen   "The prettiest stranger in KEY WEST that winter," according to FREDDY in *To Have and Have Not*, with "a lovely Irish face." She is the wife of Richard GORDON but is in an unhappy marriage. When she discovers that Richard has gone to bed with Helène BRADLEY, she leaves him, failing to mention that she has also committed adultery with Prof. MACWALSEY. Once the breakup takes place (chapter 21), Richard goes off to get drunk with MacWalsey, and Helen is not mentioned in the novel again.

The Gordon marriage is meant as a contrast to the happier marriage of Harry and Marie MORGAN. The Gordons represent the "haves" and the Morgans the "have nots." Helen Gordon tells Richard that "[l]ove always hangs up behind the bathroom door. It smells like lysol." She also defines love as "ergoapiol pills" (uterine stimulant), "catheters," and "whirling douches." Helen is expressing here her hatred of the paraphernalia of sex.

Gordon, Richard   He and his wife, Helen GORDON, in *To Have and Have Not*, are used by Hemingway as foils for Harry MORGAN and his wife, Marie MORGAN. The Gordon marriage is a failure, while the Morgan marriage works. Richard is a writer. He has an unsuccessful sexual fling with Helène BRADLEY during the afternoon before the evening that his wife tells him their marriage is over. Richard becomes suddenly impotent that afternoon when Tommy BRADLEY, Helène's husband, appears at the door of her bedroom to watch them making love.

Gordon's gin   Richard CANTWELL's drink on his Sunday morning duck shoot in *Across the River and Into the Trees*. He uses it to wash down the two pills he takes to slow down the heart attacks. When the BOATMAN asks what it is, Cantwell tells him it's "English grappa"—that is, aqua vitae, the water of life.

It is also drunk by David BOURNE near the end of *The Garden of Eden*.

Gorizia   Small town in northeast Italy on the east side of the ISONZO River, just west of the border between Italy and Slovenia. Before WORLD WAR I the national border was the river, and the town belonged to Austria-Hungary. At the beginning of *A Farewell to Arms*, Frederic HENRY is stationed with the Italian ambulance corps in an unnamed village down river from Gorizia.

Several battles were fought at or near Gorizia in the spring and summer of 1916. Referred to as the battles of the Isonzo, it took six separate assaults before the Italians could take Gorizia in August. The Italians had 147,000 casualties and the Austrians 81,000 in the six engagements. There were six additional Isonzo battles later in the war.

Gorizia, also called Görz, was crucial in Italy's declaration of war against Austria-Hungary on May 23, 1915. Although the town was the capital of the Austrian-Hungarian province of Görz before the war, it had a large Italian population, and Italy always considered it part of Italy—Italia Irredenta" (unredeemed territory). After the outbreak of the war in western Europe, the Italian government asked the Austrio-Hungarian government to accept a new Italian frontier, which would include Gorizia, in exchange for Italy's neutrality in the war. When it refused, Italy declared war. It took 15 months of fighting to take the town (August 6, 1916), and a year later it was retaken by the Austrians (October 28, 1917). With the Allied victory in the war, Gorizia was ceded to Italy under the Treaty of Saint-Germain in 1919.

Gorton, Bill   Jake BARNES's friend from Chicago in *The Sun Also Rises*. He arrives in Paris and leaves immediately for Vienna and Budapest, where he gets in trouble with the law for helping an American Negro boxer, who "looked like Tiger Flowers." They have to leave town after the American boxer knocks down Vienna's local favorite.

Gorton spends most of his time drunk, not only on the Vienna-Budapest trip but also in Paris and later in PAMPLONA during the Fiesta SAN FERMÍN. In one memorable scene, Bill, "pie-eyed," wants to buy Jake a stuffed dog; Jake rejects the idea. Bill says, "All right. Have it your own way. Road to hell paved with unbought stuffed dogs." At the end of the novel Jake drops Bill off in Bayonne, where he catches the train back to Paris on his way home to Chicago.

goujon   A "dace-like" fish that Hemingway mentions in *A Moveable Feast* that Paris fishermen caught under the PONT NEUF and which he and Hadley later have for dinner.

gourd cups   David BOURNE's father and the hunter-tracker JUMA drink beer from gourd cups after killing the old elephant, both as David remembers from his childhood experience and as he is writing about it in his AFRICAN STORY in *The Garden of Eden*.

Gourmont, Rémy de (1858–1915)   French novelist, poet, and critic, especially of the French Symbolist movement. Hemingway remembers him in *A Moveable Feast* as a friend of Natalie BARNEY's.

"Government Pays for News"   Article, published in *The Toronto Daily Star* (April 21, 1923), reprinted in *The Wild Years* (1962), reprinted in *Ernest Hemingway: Dateline Toronto* (1985). The headline in the *Daily Star* was "Government Pays For News in French Papers." This was the third of 10 articles Hemingway wrote for the *Daily Star* on the French-German situation in 1923, five years after the end of World War I. Datelined "Paris," Hemingway writes that if the French people are interested in the Ruhr "and the whole German question" they "will not find out by reading the French press."

The French government has bought the news columns and so controls what the French people read. France needs the coal it is getting out of Germany's rich Ruhr Valley, but it takes four or five tanks and a battalion of infantry to protect the 50 French workmen from the German citizens, and the French have also not been told that although their government has been paying reparations to the Germans for the coal, the return on the money has been steadily dwindling.

Goya y Lucientes, Francisco José de (1746–1828)   Leading Spanish painter and etcher of his time. Born in Saragossa of poor parents, he studied art there and in Madrid and Rome before returning to Madrid (c. 1775) to do a series of tapestry designs, which won him the attention of the Spanish royal family. His series of etchings LOS DESASTRES DE LA GUERRA (Disasters of War) is recalled by the narrator in "A Natural History of the Dead" (in *Death in the Afternoon*) on observing dead soldiers and animals.

Goya is also mentioned several times in *Death in the Afternoon*, usually as a way of describing a scene connected with the subject of bullfighting.

Grace Cottage   On Walloon Lake, across from the Hemingway family cottage, Windemere. Grace Hemingway had the cottage built as a studio for herself in May 1919. On the south side of the lake, it was a three-mile walk west to Horton Bay on Lake Charlevoix.

"grace under pressure"   Term used by Hemingway in a statement to Gerald MURPHY but which Murphy apparently misunderstood. When Murphy admitted to being scared during a ski run in Gaschurn, Austria (March 1926), Hemingway told him that courage was "grace under pressure." In a letter to F. Scott FITZGERALD a month later (April 20, 1926), Hemingway writes that he hadn't meant "guts" in his statement to Murphy but "[g]race under pressure," that guts were useful only to "violin string manufacturers." Murphy's comment to Fitzgerald is not recorded, but apparently, in quoting Hemingway, Murphy used the word "guts" instead of "courage." The Hemingway-Fitzgerald letter is the first published use of the term "grace under pressure."

Gracía, Concepción MARÍA's best friend, in *For Whom the Bell Tolls,* who did not recognize her after the GUARDIA CIVILES cut her hair and were dragging her out of the barbershop in preparation for cutting Concepción's hair too. It is implied that she was also raped by the FALANGISTS. See MARÍA'S STORY.

Graflex In *Green Hills of Africa* Hemingway has two cameras with him, a Graflex and a "cinema camera."

grain broker One of the "haves" mentioned near the end of *To Have and Have Not.* He is 60 years old, lying "awake worrying about the report he had received from his office about the activities of the investigators from the Internal Revenue Bureau. [His wife] had divorced him ten years before after twenty years of keeping up appearances."

Granada Town in Spain, home of Federico García Lorca; mentioned in *The Dangerous Summer* because of its famous poet.

Grand Canal Waterway in VENICE, over which Richard CANTWELL in *Across the River and Into the Trees* has a view from his room at the GRITTI PALACE HOTEL, "which was now [Friday evening] becoming as grey as though Degas had painted it on one of his greyest days."

grandfather (1) The earliest memory of the unnamed main character/narrator in "Now I Lay Me" is that he and his parents moved after the death of his grandfather and, in cleaning out the attic before moving, found jars of snakes preserved in alcohol.

grandfather (2) Frederic HENRY, in *A Farewell to Arms,* draws a sight draft money order on his grandfather's bank account in order to have money while he is recuperating from his wounds in Milan. He later receives a letter from him that includes a draft for 200 dollars. A sight draft money order is a check drawn by one bank on another bank.

grandfather (3) Of Nick ADAMS's son in "Fathers and Sons."

grandfather (4) In *For Whom the Bell Tolls* Robert JORDAN, fighting for the Loyalists in the Spanish civil war, remembers that his grandfather fought in the AMERICAN CIVIL WAR. Jordan wishes that the officers he has seen in Spain were as talented as some his grandfather fought with.

Grand Hotel (1) In PAMPLONA, where, in *The Sun Also Rises,* the bullfighters without *aficion* stay; that is, those bullfighters without passion for the bullfights.

Grand Hotel (2) In Zaragoza, Spain, where Hemingway stayed while in town for the bullfights in 1959 in preparation for writing *The Dangerous Summer.*

Grand Hotel (3) One of the hotels open during the off season in STRESA when Frederic HENRY arrives there looking for Catherine BARKLEY in November after his escape from the war in *A Farewell to Arms.* He finds her instead at a "little hotel" near the train station.

G.R. & I. station Grand Rapids and Indiana Railroad. The station in Mancelona, Michigan, is the site of the beginning of *The Torrents of Spring.* The train station in Petoskey is also on the G.R. & I. line, now called the Penn Plaza, located across the street from the upstairs lobby of the Perry Hotel.

Grand Rapids furniture Scripps O'NEIL thinks he might get a job in Grand Rapids, Michigan, working for a furniture company, one of several jobs he thinks about as he walks along the railroad tracks between MANCELONA and PETOSKEY at the beginning of *The Torrents of Spring.*

Granero, Manolo (1902–1922) Spanish bullfighter from Valencia, mentioned in *Death in the Afternoon* as "the one bullfighter the aficion [those with a passion for bullfighting] had great faith in."

He is also a bullfighter PILAR remembers and describes to Robert JORDAN in *For Whom the Bell Tolls.* He was "destroyed," she says, by the bull Pocapena of the ranch of Veragua. Other "real" bullfighters she remembers and mentions to Jordan are "Marcial," "Chicuelo," "Joselito," "Fornos," "Ignacio," "Sanchez," "Mejias Ricardo," and "Felipe Gonzales."

Gran Italia Restaurant in the GALLERIA in Milan, the favorite of Frederic HENRY and Catherine BARKLEY during his convalescence in the summer after his wounding in *A Farewell to Arms.*

Gran Ligas Spanish for "big leagues," the American major leagues of professional baseball, thought of often by SANTIAGO in *The Old Man and the Sea.*

Gran Maestro Richard CANTWELL's name for the maitre d'hotel at Venice's GRITTI PALACE HOTEL, in *Across the River and Into the Trees.* The Gran Maestro is a good friend of both Cantwell and RENATA.

Grant's gazelle Large gazelle, with distinctive, long curved horns, native to the East African plains and one of the animals hunted by Hemingway in *Green Hills of Africa,* referred to most often as a "grant."

Gran Vía   Major thoroughfare in Madrid, where Jake BARNES and Brett ASHLEY ride in a taxi after he goes to "rescue" her near the end of *The Sun Also Rises*.

The Gran Vía is remembered by Robert JORDAN as he tries not to think about the war in *For Whom the Bell Tolls*. The Hotel Florida, setting for *The Fifth Column*, is located just off the Gran Vía. And the famous street is also mentioned in "The Mother of a Queen."

grappa   Unaged brandy, distilled from the pomace of a wine press, drunk by RINALDI (2) and Frederic HENRY in *A Farewell to Arms*. Considered to be aqua vitae to Italians, the water of life.

And it is offered by Captain PARAVICINI to Nicholas ADAMS in "A Way You'll Never Be."

grasshoppers   In "Big Two-Hearted River," NICK uses grasshoppers as bait on his fishing trip. The grasshoppers are all black when he first arrives, because the country has been burned over, but he then climbs into the hills to the north, out of the burned country. Grasshoppers have chromatophores, special cells containing pigment granules that allow color changes, as in the chameleon.

"[Grass smooth on the prairies . . .]"   First line of a poem written about 1922 and first published in *88 Poems* (1979).

Grau du Roi   Small French village on the Mediterranean Sea, about 18 miles east-southeast of Montpellier, near the mouth of the Rhône River. Grau du Roi is the setting for the opening scene of *The Garden of Eden*. "It was a cheerful and friendly town."

Graves, Robert (1895–1985)   English poet, novelist, critic, and scholar, best known for his historical novel *I, Claudius* (1934). In *Green Hills of Africa* Hemingway remembers his friend Chink DORMAN-SMITH quoting Graves.

"Great 'Apéritif' Scandal, The"   Article, published in *The Toronto Star Weekly* (August 12, 1922), reprinted in *The Wild Years* (1962), reprinted in *Ernest Hemingway: Dateline Toronto* (1985). The headline in the *Daily Star* was "Latest Drink Scandal Now Agitates Paris." The 14th of July (Bastille Day) celebration in Paris in 1922 lasted four consecutive nights, somewhat unusual in itself. But the "scandal" occurred because, while the French government "spent some millions of francs on the party," the apéritif industry received "about a million dollars worth of publicity."

The streets where the parties were held—every two blocks, according to Hemingway—were hung with "enormous banners advertising the different brands of apéritifs": "Drink Amourette," for example, or "Vive Anis Delloso—the Finest Apéritif in the World."

"Great Blue River, The"   Article, published in *Holiday* (July 1949), reprinted in *True* (April 1955), reprinted in *By-Line: Ernest Hemingway* (1967). Begins with an explanation of what attracts him to Havana, the "biggest reason" of which "is the great, deep blue river, three quarters of a mile to a mile deep and sixty to eighty miles across, that you can reach in thirty minutes from the door of your farmhouse, riding through beautiful country to get to it, that has, when the river is right, the finest fishing I have ever known." Hemingway describes fishing for marlin off his boat, *Pilar*, with his mate, Gregorio Fuentes, who had been mate since 1938 and is 50 years old at the time of the article (1949). At the end of the article is a list of "Ernest Hemingway's Tackle Specifications."

"Greatest Boy Actor Is a Toronto Lad"   Article, published in the Toronto *Mail and Empire* (January 1924), reprinted in William Burrill's *Hemingway: The Toronto Years* (1994). It was "discovered" by Burrill in the Hemingway Collection at the John F. Kennedy Library in Boston. After Hemingway resigned as a reporter for *The Toronto Daily Star* on January 1, 1924, he wrote two stories for the rival *Mail and Empire*. This one is about a child actor who had been "judged the best child actor on the continent, in competition with 10,000 stage children from all the dramatic schools of the world."

Great Gatsby, The   F. Scott FITZGERALD's best-known novel, published April 10, 1925. The two writers met for the first time about two weeks after the novel's publication, and in *A Moveable Feast*, Hemingway writes of Fitzgerald's "non-conceited" discussion about the book, encouraging Hemingway to want to read it.

The novel is a powerful and antagonistic portrayal of wealthy American society of the 1920s and its embrace of the false glamour, immoral values, and barrenness of "Jazz Age" culture.

Great Isaacs light   About 25 miles due north of North BIMINI island, mentioned in *Islands in the Stream*. It is near here that David HUDSON catches his big fish in the novel's first section, "Bimini."

"Great News from the Mainland"   Unfinished story about a son of the main character, whose "great news from the mainland" is that he's not really insane as everyone thinks but is doing fine, "just fine." The story was first published in *The Complete Short Stories of Ernest Hemingway* (1987).

great well   The name Cuban fishermen give, in *The Old Man and the Sea*, to the "sudden deep of seven hundred fathoms where all sorts of fish congregated because of the swirl the current made against the steep walls of the floor of the ocean. Here there were concentrations of shrimp and bait fish and sometimes schools of squid in the deepest holes. . . ." SANTIAGO crosses the great well early on his way to the Gulf Stream.

grebes Water birds unrelated to loons but having a similar rudimentary tail and lobed toes, making them strong swimmers and divers. At the end of *Green Hills of Africa* Hemingway, sunning himself along the Sea of Galilee and watching the grebes on the water, wonders why they are never mentioned in the Bible.

Greco, El (c. 1541–1614) Spanish painter, born in Candia, Greece. His real name was Doménikos Theotokópoulos. Hemingway says, in *Death in the Afternoon,* that "Greco liked to paint religious pictures because he was very evidently religious and because his incomparable art" was not limited to painting the faces of noblemen. He "could go as far into his other world as he wanted . . . [and] paint saints, apostles, Christs and Virgins with the androgynous faces and forms that filled his imagination."

Catherine BOURNE, in *The Garden of Eden,* also refers to El Greco whose paintings she sees at the Prado Museum in Madrid, most memorably "Toledo."

Greco-Turkish War Fought in 1922 over the boundaries established by the Allies for Greece and Turkey after WORLD WAR I. At the Peace Conference following the war, Greece had received the Bulgarian coast on the Aegean Sea, and the remnants of European Turkey, except the Zone of the Straits (the Dardanelles). The Greeks were encouraged by the Allies to seek even more territory and so invaded Asia Minor in 1921. They were defeated by the Turkish forces of Mustafa KEMAL the next year, which included the burning of Smyrna September 9–14, 1922. The Treaty of Lausanne (1923) restored the Maritsa River as the Greco-Turkish border in Europe. Hemingway covered the evacuation of Greek citizens from Constantinople in 1922, writing several articles for *The Toronto Star.*

Gredos Mountains West of Madrid, an area to which EL SORDO, in *For Whom the Bell Tolls,* suggests Robert JORDAN and his PARTIZAN friends escape after blowing up the BRIDGE.

Greek cavalry In the "Chapter 2" vignette of *In Our Time,* the cavalry "herded along" the refugees as the Greek army evacuated ADRIANOPLE.

Greek princess Customer at HARRY'S BAR in Venice, in *Across the River and Into the Trees,* when ARNALDO calls on behalf of Richard CANTWELL to find out who is there.

"Greek Revolt, The" Article, published in *The Toronto Daily Star* (November 3, 1922), reprinted in *The Wild Years* (1962), reprinted in *Ernest Hemingway: Dateline Toronto* (1985). The headline in the *Daily Star* was "Betrayal Preceded Defeat, Then Came Greek Revolt." Datelined "Muradli, Eastern Thrace," it is about the defeated Greek army evacuating Eastern Thrace after their own government, led by King Constantine, betrayed them by signing the peace treaty with Turkey, which forced Greece out of the territory. "They are the last of the glory that was Greece. This is the end of their second siege of Troy."

Greeks In "After the Storm," the narrator, who wasn't able himself to dive down and enter an ocean liner that had sunk, explains that after his attempts, "Greeks had blown her open and cleaned her out." The Greeks are probably Greek sponge fishermen who lived in the Florida Keys during the 1920s, the time of the story. The Greeks were hated by the natives of the Florida Keys, because the "foreigners" had better diving equipment.

Green, Simon One of the "successful" Indians that NICK mentions in "The Indians Moved Away."

Green Hills of Africa Hemingway says in the "Foreword" to this "nonfiction" work (published in 1937) that "[u]nlike many novels, none of the character or incidents in this book is imaginary. . . . The writer has attempted to write an absolutely true book to see whether the shape of a country and the pattern of a month's action can, if truly presented, compete with a work of the imagination." Nevertheless, none of the major participants is identified in the book, not even Hemingway.

The country is Tanzania in East Africa, and the month's action is big-game hunting, primarily of the male KUDU, a large, beautiful antelope with corkscrew-like horns. *Green Hills* is divided into four parts: "Pursuit and Conversation," "Pursuit Remembered," "Pursuit and Failure," and "Pursuit as Happiness."

Part 1 (chapters 1 and 2) begins the story of the hunt for kudu but is devoted mostly to a conversation between the narrator (Hemingway) and an Austrian named KANDISKY, who is in Tanzania for obscure reasons and who bumps into Hemingway on safari, discovers that he is *the* Hemingway whose poetry he has recently read in the German journal *DER QUERSCHNITT,* and who asks him questions about literature, particularly American.

Kandisky impresses Hemingway with his literary knowledge, and the two strangers enjoy one another's company and liquor. Kandisky asks about American writers. In his answer Hemingway says of Twain: "All modern American literature comes from one book by Mark Twain called *Huckleberry Finn.* . . . There was

Part 2 (chapters 3 through 9) begins with the statement that "It [friction between the hunters and trackers] dated back to the time of DROOPY, after I had come back from being ill in Nairobi and we had gone on a foot safari to hunt rhino in the forest." This opening sentence begins a flashback ("Pursuit Remembered") to the early days of the monthlong safari when they were hunting rhino near Lake MANYARA in northern Tanzania. The description of the country of the RIFT VALLEY is important here—as the lay of the land is important throughout *Green Hills*. The beauty of the land merges often with the purpose of the hunt: "it was a pleasure to walk in the easy rolling country, simply to walk, and to be able to hunt, not knowing what we might see and free to shoot for the meat we needed."

Chapter 3 introduces Droopy, clearly Hemingway's favorite tracker, although he disappears after part 2. Droopy shows Hemingway how to slit open the stomach of a REEDBUCK (another African antelope), turn it inside out, and use it as a bag for carrying other "delicacies." Hemingway is as fastidious in hunting as he is in fishing (see "Big Two-Hearted River"). He carries four

EH reading at safari camp in East Africa (Courtesy of the John F. Kennedy Library)

nothing before," Hemingway says, and "[t]here has been nothing as good since." Hemingway writes about but does not define the "FOURTH AND FIFTH DIMENSIONS" that a good writer can achieve. But this writing takes "talent" and "discipline," the talent of a Kipling and the discipline of a Flaubert.

The relations between the white hunters and the native trackers and gun bearers is introduced in chapter 2, as well as the tension that exists between Hemingway and another white hunter, KARL. Hemingway believes that he is the better hunter, but Karl, who is on the safari but hunts by himself, usually comes back to camp with the bigger, better kills. This "subplot" runs like a thread throughout *Green Hills*, Hemingway in a rather constant state of jealousy over Karl's hunting skills—or "luck" as Pop calls it. And the lion kill of P.O.M. (Poor Old Mama), the first by anyone on the safari, is also described in this chapter. (Neither Pop nor P.O.M. is identified in the book, but the former is Hemingway's white hunter guide, Philip PERCIVAL, and P.O.M. is Hemingway's wife, Pauline.)

EH at safari camp in East Africa (Courtesy of the John F. Kennedy Library)

Ernest at safari camp in East Africa (Courtesy of the John F. Kennedy Library)

handkerchiefs on this safari, for example, in order to wipe the sweat off his eyeglasses, moving them from his left to his right pocket as they become wet.

Chapter 4 provides the recalled description of the hunt, Hemingway getting his rhino but Karl getting a bigger one. Five people are in the main hunting party: the trackers, Droopy and M'Cola; the guide, Pop; and the hunters, P.O.M., and Hemingway. He describes rest periods in the shade, reading Tolstoi's *Sevastopol* and using it to argue "what a great advantage an experience of war was to a writer." And he discusses Stendhal and Dostoyevsky and says, thinking of them, that "[w]riters are forged in injustice as a sword is forged," and he wonders if sending Thomas Wolfe to Siberia (as Dostoyevsky was) might "make a writer of him." He discusses love of country as a value to a writer: "I had loved country all my life; the country was always better than the poeple. I could only care about people a very few at a time." Hemingway shoots his rhino at 300 yards, "a hell of a shot," with his Springfield rifle, enhancing his reputation within the party and to himself. Hemingway knows he's a braggart and confesses it regularly in the narration. But he is brought down considerably when they return to camp, because Karl's rhino is "twice the size of the one I had killed."

Chapter 5 describes the continued hunt for rhino but the killing of a buffalo instead. "Then I saw the black back, the wide-swept, point-lifted horns and then the quick-moving, climbing rush of a buffalo up the other bank." In chapter 6 they move into the Rift Valley, near Lake Manyara, "rose-colored at one end

with a half million tiny dots that were flamingoes." They hunt ducks, the first they've had since an earlier hunt on the Serengeti Plain. Chapter 7 describes the first five to seven days of their hunt for kudu and their move toward the town of BABATI and then south along the "Cape to Cairo road" to new territory and the 10 days remaining on this safari. Chapter 8 describes the new country, "so much like Aragon that I could not believe that we were not in Spain." And there is a lot of optimism in camp for getting kudu. Karl gets his first of two kudus, but Hemingway gets nothing and feels time running out, as he has since the beginning of the book. In chapter 9, the end of the flashback, they make another attempt at the salt licks, where the kudu feed, but again without luck.

Part 3 (chapters 10 and 11), "Pursuit and Failure," brings the reader back to time present and the last two days of the monthlong safari. Chapter 10 begins, "That all seemed a year ago." They fail to see the bull kudu they're looking for, even though the rain makes for good tracking. Hemingway discusses again the value of "country" for the writer, stating that he would "like to try to write something about the country and the animals and what it's like to some one who knows nothing about it." And he and Pop drink and talk about the books they've read.

In chapter 11 two natives come with news of kudu and SABLE a day's walk from the camp—three or four hours, Pop figures, by car. And at the end of the chapter Hemingway leaves camp with M'Cola, the driver, and four other natives for the new country.

Part 4 (chapters 12 and 13) narrates Hemingway's "Pursuit and Happiness," the successful hunt for kudu in country "the loveliest that I had seen in Africa. The grass was green and smooth, short as a meadow that has been mown and is newly grown, and the trees were big, high-trunked, and old with no undergrowth but only the smooth green of the turf." He gets his "huge, beautiful kudu bull, . . . long-legged, a smooth gray with the white stripes and the great, curling, sweeping horns, brown as walnut meats, and ivory pointed." He gets another bull kudu and, resting comfortably, finally, under a tree, reflects, "looking in the fire, not thinking, in complete happiness, feeling the whiskey warm me and smooth me as you straighten the wrinkled sheet in a bed." Although one has the feeling that Hemingway had a number of happy moments during his lifetime, this is the only place anywhere in his works where he actually admits to it.

In chapter 13 he gets his sable, "dead black [identifying it as a bull] and shiny as he hit the sun, and his horns swept up high, then back, huge and dark, in two great curves nearly touching the middle of his back." He writes again about "country," grateful that he can make a living "with two pencils and a few hundred sheets of the cheapest paper." At the end of the book he's bitter, however, not because of the country but because Karl has a kudu with the "biggest, widest, darkest, longest-curling, heaviest, most unbelievable pair of kudu horns in the world." Most of the bitterness is gone by the next morning, but not without an awareness on Hemingway's part that it's "impossible not to be competitive." But he's all right again, and a month later he and P.O.M. and Karl and Karl's wife meet in Haifa, Israel, and are sitting against a stone wall by the Sea of Galilee eating lunch, drinking a bottle of wine, and watching the GREBES on the water, Hemingway wondering why grebes are never mentioned in the Bible.

Green Hills of Africa was serialized in *Scribner's Magazine* (May–November 1935) and published in book form by Charles Scribner's Sons on October 25, 1935, the first printing consisting of 10,500 copies at a price of $2.75 each.

Green Isaac's Special   It is, according to Thomas HUDSON in *Islands in the Stream,* a "tall cold drink made of gin, lime juice, green coconut water, and chipped ice . . . with just enough ANGOSTURA bitters to give it a rusty, rose color."

Green Key   Otherwise unnamed island (*cayo*) in *Islands in the Stream,* near where Thomas HUDSON and his crew finally chase down a German submarine crew in the "At Sea" section of the novel.

Greenwich Meridian   See MONT SAINT-MICHEL.

Greffi, Count   The 94-year-old friend of Frederic HENRY, "with white hair and mustache and beautiful manners," who plays billiards with Frederic in the LITTLE HOTEL in STRESA, where he and Catherine BARKLEY are staying before they escape north across Lake MAGGIORE to Switzerland in *A Farewell to Arms*. In a discussion about the soul, the count asks Frederic if he is *croyant*—meaning, in this context, a believer. Frederic answers that he is *croyant* "at night."

Gris, Juan (1887–1927)   Spanish painter, mentioned in *Islands in the Stream,* especially in connection with his painting "Guitar Player," owned by the novel's main character, Thomas HUDSON. Gris is also mentioned in *A Moveable Feast.*

Gritti Palace Hotel   In Venice, on the Grand Canal, near the Santa Maria del Giglio and the Teatro la Fenice. The hotel is where Richard CANTWELL stays on Friday and Saturday night of his duck-hunting trip in *Across the River and Into the Trees*. He thinks of it as a "three story, rose colored, small, pleasant palace" on the Grand Canal. He thought of it as "probably the best hotel if you did not wish to be fawned on, or fussed over, or over-flunkied, in a city of great hotels," and he

"loved it." He refers to it sometimes as the "Hotel Gritti" or just the "Gritti." It is still one of the most expensive hotels in Venice.

The palace was built during the reign of the 77th doge of Venice, Andrea Gritti, in 1523.

Grosshau   German town east of HÜRTGEN FOREST, one of the objectives in *Across the River and Into the Trees* of Richard CANTWELL's division in its fighting in WORLD WAR II.

grunt fishing boat   In *To Have and Have Not,* Harry MORGAN sees a boat with a "Negro fisherman sitting in the stern holding the tiller." A "grunt" is any of various related saltwater fishes that grunt when they are removed from the water.

Guadalajara   Spanish town, along with the towns of Soria, Siguenza, Cádiz, and Arganda, thought about by Robert JORDAN in *For Whom the Bell Tolls,* pleasant thoughts meant to keep his mind off the present dangers involved in blowing up a bridge. He remembers, particularly, driving past Guadalajara in a staff car on his way to join the PARTIZANS.

guajiro   Spanish for "countryman" or "peasants," the term used by EMILIO (2), one of the four Cuban bank robbers in *To Have and Have Not,* in telling Harry MORGAN that the Cuban revolution is being fought for the peasants.

Thomas HUDSON in *Islands in the Stream* also uses the term to distinguish the country people from the fishermen of COJIMAR, described near the beginning of the "Cuba" section of the novel. Countrymen wear, according to Hudson, "formalized pleated shirts, wide hats, tight trousers, and riding boots," while the fishermen wear the "remnants of any old clothes" they have and are "cheerful, self-confident men."

Guanabacoa   Cuban town near Havana where, SANTIAGO tells MANOLIN at the end of *The Old Man and the Sea,* they can grind the "spring leaf from an old Ford" to make a "good killing lance" for the "next" fishing trip, one which the old man and the boy plan to make together.

Guantánamo   U.S. military base at the eastern end of Cuba, which Thomas HUDSON is trying to reach by ship-to-shore radio in order to report on his search for the crew of a German submarine in the "At Sea" section of *Islands in the Stream.*

Guaranty Trust   Where Hemingway kept his Paris financial accounts, when he lived in Paris in the 1920s. It is at 1, boulevard des Italiens. His friend Mike Ward worked at the travel desk; in *A Moveable Feast*

Hemingway describes meeting Ward and being introduced by him to bicycle racing.

guard   At the railroad bridge at LATISANA, Italy, in *A Farewell to Arms*. He is suspicious of Frederic HENRY, who wants to hop a freight train. The guard walks only partway toward Frederic as he lays along the tracks waiting for a train.

guardia civiles   Spanish civil guards. Most of its members joined the military Rebels of Francisco FRANCO during the Spanish civil war. In *For Whom the Bell Tolls* María tells Robert JORDAN that the *guardia civiles* cut off her hair and then wrote in iodine on her forehead "UHP" (*Unión de Hermanos Proletarios*—Union of Proletarian Brothers). See MARÍA'S STORY.

guardia di finanza   Italian police along Lake MAGGIORE, whom Frederic HENRY thinks "could have seen our boat black on the water if they had been watching" as he and Catherine BARKLEY row toward Switzerland and freedom from the war in *A Farewell to Arms*.

"Guards Were Hoaxed by Call For Help"   Article, published in *The Toronto Star* (September 13, 1923), "discovered" by William Burrill at the John F. Kennedy Library in Boston but not reprinted in his book, *Hemingway: The Toronto Years* (1994), where 25 other recently found articles are reprinted.

guide   Cuban fisherman, captured and killed by German submarine crew members in the "At Sea" section of *Islands in the Stream*.

"Guitar Player"   Painting by Juan Gris, owned by Thomas HUDSON at the "farm" outside of Havana in *Islands in the Stream*. Hudson remembers buying it at the Flechtheim's Gallery in Berlin during the years when he and his first wife had been happy together.

Gulf Stream   Best known of all the ocean currents, "discovered" in 1513 by Ponce de León. It originates in the Gulf of Mexico, moves through the Straits of Florida with a breadth at that point of 50 miles, and then flows northeast, parallel to the United States coast and separated from it by a narrow strip of cold water. It spreads out as it moves north, and at 40° north latitude, 60° west longitude it is no longer distinguishable from the rest of the North Atlantic Drift, and does not, as is often thought, warm up western Europe. The Gulf Stream's average speed is four miles an hour; its temperature in its southern regions is usually 80 degrees Fahrenheit, less as it moves north along the U.S. coast.

The Straits of Florida is the setting for much of the action in *To Have and Have Not*. The Gulf Stream north and east of Havana is where SANTIAGO fishes during the three days of his fishing ordeal in *The Old Man and the Sea*. And it is the "stream" of *Islands in the Stream*. Thomas HUDSON lives in a house on Bimini in the first of the novel's three sections, and at the beginning of the novel the narrator states that the "water of the Stream was usually a dark blue when you looked out at it when there was no wind. But when you walked out into it there was just the green light of the water over that floury white sand and you could see the shadow of any big fish a long time before he could ever come in close to the beach."

gun-bearer, second   Unnamed assistant tracker and one of the two gun bearers in "The Short Happy Life of Francis Macomber." The first gun bearer is named Kongoni.

gun-bearers, two   The narrator of "The Short Happy Life of Francis Macomber" uses the term "native boys" to refer to the African natives responsible for the guns when they are not being used by the story's three main characters. The gun bearers are embarrassed, as is nearly everyone else in the hunting party, when Macomber runs from the lion at the beginning of the story. When the cook, the skinner, and the porters carry Macomber back to camp "in triumph," the gun bearers are described as having "taken no part in the demonstration." They had been forced to go into the bush with Wilson and Macomber when the two hunters searched for the wounded lion, and so the gun bearers had seen up close Macomber's cowardice.

gunner's mate   In "On the Quai at Smyrna," he is accused wrongly of "insulting" a Turkish officer.

Gun Runners, The (film)   Seven Arts/United Artists picture, released in September 1958 (83 minutes), based on Hemingway's *To Have and Have Not*. Produced by Clarence Greene, directed by Don Siegel, art direction by Howard Richmond, screenplay by Daniel Mainwaring and Paul Monash, music by Leith Stevens, songs by Joe Lubin.

Cast: Audie Murphy (Sam Martin), Eddie Albert (Hanagan), Patricia Owens (Lucy Martin), Everett Sloane (Harvey), Gita Hall (Eva), Richard Jaeckel (Buzurki), Paul Birch (Sy Phillips), and Jack Elam (Arnold).

Gutierrez, Carlos   First mate on Hemingway's fishing boat, *Pilar*, from 1935 until 1938 when, as Hemingway writes in his article "The Great Blue River," someone "hired him away" when he (Hemingway) was off covering the Spanish civil war. In his article "Marlin off the Morro: A Cuban Letter," Hemingway calls Gutierrez the "best marlin and swordfisherman around Cuba."

Guttingen, Mr. and Mrs. Owners of the "brown wooden house in the pine trees" on the side of the mountain above MONTREUX, where, in *A Farewell to Arms,* Frederic HENRY and Catherine BARKLEY spend the winter (1917–18) waiting for Catherine's baby to be born. The Guttingens "lived downstairs and we would hear them talking sometimes in the evening and they were very happy together too."

Guy Only named character in "Che Ti Dice La Patria?" He travels with the narrator around fascist northern Italy in the mid-1920s, trying to discover "how things were with the country or the people." He is 38 years old, and the narrator tells a waitress/prostitute in Spezia that he is "South German," although it isn't clear that he's telling her the truth. The narrator says that Guy "takes some pride in the fact that he is taken for a traveling salesman in France." There is some good-natured kidding in this scene about Guy's good looks, but it still isn't clear what he does for a living.

guys, two At the end of "My Old Man," after the "old man" is killed in a steeplechase race, one of the two "guys" says to the other, "Well, Butler [the 'old man'] got his, all right." The other says, "I don't give a good goddam if he did, the crook. He had it coming to him on the stuff he's pulled." JOE, Butler's son, overhears the conversation but isn't old enough to realize that his dad, a jockey, had been involved in fixing some races.

gymnasium In LAUSANNE, Switzerland, where Frederic HENRY goes to box while Catherine BARKLEY stays late in bed during the final weeks of her pregnancy in *A Farewell to Arms.*

H

Haifa City in northwest Israel, on the Mediterranean Sea. At the end of *Green Hills of Africa* Hemingway and his wife (called P.O.M., "Poor Old Mama") meet Karl and Karl's wife in Haifa on their way to the Sea of Galilee for some sun.

Thomas HUDSON, in *Islands in the Stream,* remembers visiting the city on a voyage along the Suez Canal and the Mediterranean.

Hailey, Montana Setting for "The Gambler, the Nun, and the Radio."

Hal One of SEVEN TOURISTS in the "BIMINI" section of *Islands in the Stream.* He is the butt of a joke played by Thomas HUDSON's sons, who, all underage, pretend to be drunk at the Ponce de León bar. Hal wants to buy one of Hudson's paintings.

Hall, Caroline Hancock (1843–1895) Ernest Hemingway's maternal grandmother: born in Bristol, England, September 18, 1843; she died in Oak Park, Illinois, September 10, 1895. She was the daughter of Alexander and Caroline Sydes Hancock. When her mother died in January 1853, her father, a sea captain, took his three children around Cape Horn in the bark *Elizabeth,* intending to homestead some property in Australia. They left Sydney for the United States, however, and he bought a farm in Dyersville, Iowa, in 1854. Caroline married Ernest Hall (see below) November 6, 1865, in Dyersville, and they had three children: Ernest, born and died in 1867; Grace (Ernest Hemingway's mother), born June 15, 1872; and Leicester Campbell, born in 1874.

Hall, Ernest (1840–1905) Ernest's maternal grandfather: born in Sheffield, England, February 21, 1840; died in Oak Park, Illinois, May 10, 1905. He was the son of a silversmith and was educated at St. Saviour's Grammar School in London; he left for the United States in 1855 with his parents, Charles and Mary Miller Hall, where they bought a farm in Dyersville, Iowa. He was a member of the First Iowa Volunteer Calvary, Company L, during the U.S. Civil War and, after the war, a member of the Randall, Hall and Co. Wholesale Cutlery in Iowa.

He married Caroline Hancock HALL November 6, 1865, in Dyersville. They had three children: Ernest,

born and died 1867; Grace (Ernest Hemingway's mother), born June 15, 1872; and Leicester Campbell, born 1874.

Ernest and Caroline Hall lived at 439 North Oak Park Avenue, across from Anson and Adelaide Hemingway at 444, and when Grace Hall and Clarence Hemingway married in 1896 they moved in with her father, a widower of one year.

Hall, Grace See Grace Hall HEMINGWAY.

Halle aux Vins In *A Moveable Feast* Hemingway describes this wine warehouse at the eastern end of boulevard Saint-Germain, where wine was kept until the people or businesses who owned it paid their taxes on it. He writes that it was as "cheerless from the outside as a military depot or as prison camp."

"Hamid Bey" Article, published in *The Toronto Daily Star* (October 9, 1922), reprinted in *The Wild Years* (1962), and in *By-Line: Ernest Hewingway* (1967). Datelined "Constantinople," the article quotes Bismarck as saying that "all men in the Balkans who tuck their shirts into their trousers are crooks." It then proceeds to describe Hamid Bey, one of the "most powerful men in the Angora government," who tucks his shirt in. He denies to Hemingway that a "massacre" will occur when Kemal Atatürk and his men enter Constantinople. Kemal was a Turkish general in 1922 when Hemingway wrote the article and president of Turkey from 1923–38. The *TDS* headline read "Hamid Bey Wears Shirt Tucked In When Seen By *Star.*"

"Hamilton Gag, The" Article, published in *The Toronto Star Weekly* (June 12, 1920), reprinted in *Ernest Hemingway: Dateline Toronto* (1985). The headline in the *Star Weekly* was "It's Time to Bury the Hamilton Gag, Comedians Have Worked It to Death." The Hamilton gag goes like this on the stages of Toronto musical theaters: The first comedian says, "Do you live in the city?" The second comedian says, "No, I live in Hamilton." Hamilton is a large city just south of Toronto.

Hammett, Dashiell (1894–1961) American writer of detective stories, best known for *The Maltese Falcon*

(1930); mentioned in *Death in the Afternoon* as the author of *The Dain Curse* (1929).

ham sandwich Important in "The Battler," because Nick ADAMS walks all the way back to the railroad tracks at the end of the story before he notices that he has a ham sandwich in his hand, emphasizing for the reader the traumatic impact his experience with the boxer Ad FRANCIS and his "caretaker" have had on Nick.

Hamsun, Knut (1859–1952) Norwegian novelist, winner of the Nobel Prize for literature in 1920. One of the "literary" stories that MANDY tells Scripps O'NEIL in *The Torrents of Spring* to seduce him away from his wife, Diana, is about the time when Knut Hamsun was "a streetcar conductor in Chicago," part of the novel's exaggeration and parody.

Handeni Town in Tanzania. In *Green Hills of Africa* Hemingway is concerned about the expected rains and is trying to decide whether to wait out the rains where the safari is located or move to Handeni, about 180 miles to the east.

Handley Pages The Handley Page 0/400 was one of the largest airplanes used in World War I and flew passengers from London to Kenya before World War II. Handley Page (1885–1962) was a British aircraft designer. In *Islands in the Stream* Thomas HUDSON recalls that the prince and princess he met aboard a luxury liner on its way to London preferred the boat to the Handley Page plane they had flown in to Kenya.

Hanley's Restaurant New York City restaurant where, at the beginning of "Fifty Grand," the story's narrator, plus his fighter, Jack Brennan, and Soldier Bartlett discuss Brennan's next fight.

"Hanna Club Members Hear Practical Talk" Article for Oak Park and River Forest High School newspaper, *The Trapeze* (February 3, 1916), reprinted in *Hemingway at Oak Park High: The High School Writings of Ernest Hemingway, 1916–1917* (1993).

"Hanna Club Tomorrow Night" Article for Oak Park and River Forest High School newspaper, *The Trapeze* (January 27, 1916), reprinted in *Hemingway at Oak Park High: The High School Writings of Ernest Hemingway, 1916–1917* (1993).

Harbour Springs See PETOSKEY.

Hardy reel British fishing reel used by Harry MORGAN's customers fishing out of the Havana harbor in part 1 of *To Have and Have Not*. They use the reel "with

six hundred yards of thirty-six thread." The Hardy Brothers fishing tackle company was formed by William and J. J. Hardy in Alnwick, Northumberland, in 1872.

"Harington Won't Demand Evacuation" Article, unsigned, published in *The Toronto Daily Star* (October 2, 1922), reprinted in *Ernest Hemingway: Dateline Toronto* (1985). Datelined "Constantinople," it's a two-paragraph story about a denial by British officials in Constantinople that General Harington, the British commander, had demanded that Turkish troops evacuate the Dardanelles.

Harlow, Jean (1911–1937) U.S. movie star, born in England. She and Greta Garbo are subjects in Robert JORDAN's occasional dreams in *For Whom the Bell Tolls*.

harpoon With its shaft, used by SANTIAGO, in *The Old Man and the Sea,* to bring in large fish, but the old man also uses it to fight off sharks.

Harris Character in *The Sun Also Rises*. See WILSON-HARRIS.

Harris, E. D. Main character in part 3 of "Homage to Switzerland." He is American, probably in his 30s, waiting for a late train in Territet, Switzerland. Unlike the main characters in each of the other two parts, he does not ask his waitress at the station café for sex. Instead, he finds himself forced into a conversation with Dr. Sigismund WYER, a proud member of the National Geographic Society. They discuss various memorable issues of *National Geographic* magazine.

Harris apparently feels it necessary to lie about knowing the names of other Society members that Wyer drops into the conversation, and Harris is also probably lying about his father's membership in the Society. It is likely true, however, that his father committed suicide. When Wyer says that he's sure it was a "blow to science as well as to his family," Harris says, "Science took it awfully well." At the end of the story, the two men exchange calling cards, Wyer's stating his membership in the National Geographic Society.

Harrison, Frederick Washington bureaucrat, one "of the three most important men in the United States today," according to his own secretary aboard CAPTAIN WILLIE's boat in *To Have and Have Not*. Harrison insists that Capt. Willie arrest Harry MORGAN for bootlegging when they see him wounded on his charter boat drifting off KEY WEST, Florida. Capt. Willie, a friend of Morgan's, deliberately refuses Harrison's order and takes him and his other government "customers" farther out into the gulf, but Harrison issues an affidavit, and Morgan's boat is seized by customs, anyway.

Harry   Main character in "The Snows of Kilimanjaro," a writer. He and his wife, HELEN (3), are on a safari in East Africa, a trip that has turned bad because Harry develops gangrene after failing to treat a scratch on his right leg. He spends his time lying on the cot Helen has set up for him outside their tent and either abusing her verbally or wandering off into memory FLASHBACKS about stories he had saved to write about.

Harry Morgan   Main character in *To Have and Have Not*. See Harry MORGAN.

Harry's Bar   Located at 1323 San Marco, Calle Vallaresso in Venice, Italy. It was founded in 1931 by Giuseppe CIPRIANI, who named it after Harry Pickering, a friend who helped him start the bartending business. The bar was passed on to Giuseppe's son, Harry (Arrigo) Cipriani, who is also the proprietor of two New York restaurants, Bellini By Cipriani and Harry Cipriani's.

Harry's in Venice was one of Hemingway's favorite bars and is mentioned several times in *Across the River and Into the Trees*.

Harry's boat   Harry MORGAN's boat in part 1 of *To Have and Have Not:* It is 38 feet long with a 100-horsepower Kermath engine. "It can carry two hundred and sixty-five cases [of liquor] without being loaded" or a dozen men, if they don't carry any baggage. Harry loses his boat to the authorities at the end of part 2.

Harry's New York Bar   At 5, rue Daunou in Paris, famous as an expatriate hangout in the 1920s and birthplace of the Bloody Mary. Hemingway frequented the bar and mentions it in *The Sun Also Rises*.

Hart, Frank   A "worthless sporting character" who plays the banjo in the "Bimini" section of *Islands in the Stream*. During one of his drunken sprees, in celebration of Queen Mary's birthday, he wants to burn down the commissioner's house on Bimini by shooting flares at it. He also shoots flares onto a boat docked nearby. He is called Captain Frank or Mr. Frank.

"Hate in the Ruhr is Real"   Article, published in *The Toronto Daily Star* (May 12, 1923), reprinted in *The Wild Years* (1962), reprinted in *Ernest Hemingway: Dateline Toronto* (1985). The headline in the *Daily Star* was "Hate in Occupied Zone A Real, Concrete Thing." This was the ninth of 10 articles Hemingway wrote for the *Daily Star* on the French-German situation in 1923, five years after the end of World War I. Datelined "Düsseldorf," the article reports that most of the workers of the Ruhr district of Germany are communists, so it is easy for them to hate the French workers and soldiers who are in the district taking their German coal back to France.

The resistance is mostly passive, but there was an incident the Saturday before Easter in which 13 French workmen were killed.

Hatuey beer   Brand of 10-cent beer in Havana during the 1930s, mentioned in *To Have and Have Not*. Made by the Bacardí rum company in Cuba, the beer is named after an Indian chief from the Arawak tribe in Haiti, who migrated to Cuba.

In *The Old Man and the Sea* SANTIAGO drinks Hatuey beer during "supper" with MANOLIN the night before Santiago's three-day fishing ordeal begins.

Haut Brion   French wine from the Bordeaux region. It is referred to in *Death in the Afternoon* in a comparison Hemingway makes between acquiring a taste for good wine and acquiring a taste for the bullfight.

Havana   The setting for part 1 of *To Have and Have Not*. Harry MORGAN, the novel's protagonist and narrator of part 1, thinks, "Looking back, I could see Havana looking fine in the sun and a ship just coming out of the harbor past the MORRO."

It is the largest nearby city from SANTIAGO's north coast village in *The Old Man and the Sea*, which is not named but is probably COJÍMAR.

Havana Coal Company   In *The Old Man and the Sea*, where some of the men worked who watched the hand-wrestling match that SANTIAGO remembers winning when he was a youth.

hawk channel   At KEY WEST in *To Have and Have Not*, through which Harry MORGAN's boat is towed near the end of the novel.

Hawthorne, Nathaniel (1804–1864)   American novelist and short story writer, best known for *The Scarlet Letter* (1950). See Ralph Waldo EMERSON.

haya   Word that David BOURNE in *The Garden of Eden* uses to describe MARITA, who asks what it means. He says, "The one who blushes. The modest one." It's a Swahili word that means "bashful" or "humble."

Hayzooz   A "goofy Cuban" taxi driver in *To Have and Have Not*. The name is a mispronunciation of *Jesús*.

Hazel   One of the five whores in "The Light of the World." She and Ethel are "big," nearly as big as Alice, who weighs, the narrator guesses, 350 pounds. Hazel and Ethel are described as not "very bright."

He (1)   Unnamed character in "On the Quai at Smyrna." He was "senior officer" of a detachment of navy personnel, probably British, trying to maintain order under chaotic conditions during the Greek evacuation from Smyrna. He tells the story's narrator about a Turkish officer who identifies the wrong soldier, a gunner's mate, who had insulted him; and he tells about the women with dead babies, holding on to them until some of his men had to drag the babies out of their arms; and he tells about the Greek soldiers who, when they evacuated Smyrna, broke the forelegs of the baggage animals they couldn't take with them and pushed them off the docks into the water.

He (2)   Main character in "A Very Short Story," an American, fighting with the Italians in northern Italy in WORLD WAR I. He is recuperating from wounds and falls in love with his nurse, LUZ, in the Padua Hospital where they've taken him. They plan to get married but can't because neither has a birth certificate. He wants her to go home to the States with him, but she wants to wait until he has a job to join him.

Home in Chicago, he gets a letter from her telling him she has fallen in love with an Italian major and plans to get married in the spring. He doesn't answer the letter or another one telling him that the marriage is off. At the end of the story, he gets gonorrhea from a Chicago shop girl while riding in the back of a taxi in Lincoln Park.

He (3)   Main character in the "Chapter 7" vignette of *In our Time*. Frightened, he prays to Jesus to be saved from death in the shelling he finds himself in the middle of at Fossalta, Italy. He tells Jesus he will do anything He asks of him, if He allows him to survive the shelling; but the next night he goes with a prostitute, and, as the narrator says, he doesn't tell the prostitute about Jesus, nor does he tell anyone.

He (4)   Main character in "The Revolutionist." He is a "very shy and quite young" communist and the victim of suffering under the "Whites in Budapest" in 1919, particularly Horthy's Men, who "had done some bad things to him." He travels around Italy seeing many paintings in art museums, particularly the paintings of Giotto, Masaccio, and Piero della Francesca; but he makes it clear that he does not like the artist Mantegna.

Although unstated in the story, it may be that the revolutionist knows—as Giorgio Vasari describes Mantegna in his *Lives of the Artists* (1568; translation 1965)—that Mantegna was born of "very humble stock . . . working in the fields as a boy and yet . . . rising to the rank of a knight through his own efforts and good fortune," the sort of individualism that might not be appreciated by a revolutionist with such strict communist ideals.

"He" is helped by the story's unnamed narrator, who talks to him about the "movement" in Italy and puts him on a train to Milan, where he will then go to Aosta and walk across the pass into Switzerland. The last the narrator hears about him is that he was picked up by the police in Switzerland and is in a jail "near Sion."

He (5)   Character in "Banal Story." He eats an orange while reading a "booklet" advertising *The Forum,* a magazine of the arts and culture. He is described by the narrator as making fun of the magazine because of its appeal to readers satisfied with the "banal," the dull or insipid.

health farm, Danny Hogan's   Training site for boxers in "Fifty Grand." The story's main character, Jack BRENNAN, trains there, but he doesn't like it because it takes him away from his wife and kids and because he gets tired of Soldier Bartlett kidding him all the time for training at a health farm.

"Hearst Not Paying Lloyd George"   Article, published in *The Toronto Star Weekly* (October 6, 1923), reprinted in *Ernest Hemingway: Dateline Toronto* (1985). The headline in the *TSW* was "Cope Denies Hearst Paying Lloyd George." Dateline "Aboard Lloyd George's Special," about the former British prime minister's train trip from New York toward Montreal and the public response he gets in upstate New York. Cope, a Lloyd George spokesman, tells Hemingway that, in contrast to what had been printed the day before in the London *Post* and *The New York Times,* neither the Hearst newspaper chain nor the United Press organization was paying Lloyd George's expenses for his tour of the United States and Canada.

"Heat and the Cold, The"   Article, published in *Verve* (Spring 1938), about the filming of *The Spanish Earth.*

Hedda Hopper's Hollywood No. 3 **(film documentary)**   Includes an account of a hunting party in Idaho with Hemingway hosting Gary Cooper, poet Christopher LaFarge, and others. Produced about 1958.

Heineken beer   Drunk with breakfast by Thomas HUDSON, in *Islands in the Stream,* to go with corned beef hash and eggs, coffee with milk, and grapefruit juice.

Heinkel one-eleven bombers   Twin-motor bombers, German built, capable of flying 250 mph, used by the REBELS during the Spanish civil war. Seen and feared by Robert JORDAN and his LOYALIST friends in *For Whom the Bell Tolls.* The Heinkels drop bombs on EL SORDO and his men on top of a hill, killing them all.

The bombers are also referred to in Hemingway's NANA DISPATCH number 24.

Heiress In *The Garden of Eden* it is the name David BOURNE gives to MARITA after the "perversion" (the MÉNAGE Á TROIS) begins.

Held, Anna (1873?–1918) American musical comedy actress, famous for her beauty and her tempestuous off-stage life. In "Fathers and Sons," she is remembered by the 38-year-old Nick ADAMS as the woman pictured on the inside of cigar boxes.

Helen (1) One of Harold KREBS's two sisters, in "Soldier's Home." She plays INDOOR BASEBALL and invites Harold to watch her play. She's the only member of his family with any sympathy for him as he tries to get rid of the traumatizing effects of his WORLD WAR I experiences.

Helen (2) Nick ADAMS's wife in "Cross-Country Snow." She does not appear in the story, but GEORGE (4) asks Nick if she is going to have a baby. Nick says, "Yes. . . . Late next summer."

Helen (3) HARRY's wealthy wife in "The Snows of Kilimanjaro." She tries to comfort Harry as well as she can, but he's dying from gangrene in his right leg, received from a scratch he didn't take care of properly. They are waiting for a plane that will take him to a hospital in Kenya, but Harry knows he is dying and takes his anger out on Helen by abusing her verbally. She is sensitive to his condition but unhappy with Harry's constant anger, seeming to blame her for his impending death.

Helena, Arkansas Town where the husband of the narrator in "One Reader Writes" goes for "a course of injections" for "sifilus." It's his mother's home.

Hem, Old Only once in *Green Hills of Africa* does Hemingway refer to himself in any way other than "I," and that is when POP refers to him as "Old Hem."

His second wife, Pauline, who was with him on the actual safari, is not named either, always referred to as P.O.M. ("Poor Old Mama"). In what is probably another slip, he mentions "Bumby" once, the nickname Hemingway and his first wife, Hadley, gave to their son, Jack. In what is clearly not a mere slip-up, however, he also mentions "Chink," that is, "Captain Eric Edward Dorman-Smith, M.C. of His Majesty's Fifth Fusiliers." Chink was Hemingway's Irish friend from their soldiering days in World War I.

***Hemingway* (television documentary)** Produced in 1987 by the BBC in conjunction with the Arts & Entertainment Network in the United States. There are four one-hour parts, titled: "A Remembered Springtime," "One True Sentence," "On the Ropes," and "The Last Round."

***Hemingway* (television film)** Six-hour biography, coproduced by Daniel Wilson Productions and Alcor Film; starring Stacy Keach as Hemingway, Joséphine Chaplin as "First Wife," Marisa Berenson as Pauline ("Second Wife"), Lisa Banes as "Martha Gellhorn," and Pamela Reed as "Fourth Wife." The film, a German-American cooperative effort, was directed by Bernhard Sinkel.

Hemingway, Adelaide Edmonds (1841–1923) Ernest's paternal grandmother: born near Rock River, Illinois, August 17, 1841; died February 6, 1923, in Oak Park, Illinois. She met Anson Tyler HEMINGWAY as a student at Wheaton College and married him August 27, 1867, after graduation. They moved to Oak Park in 1868 where they were active members of the First Congregational Church. She had a degree in botany from Wheaton and passed on her love of nature to her children.

She and Anson had six children, all of whom attended Oberlin College: Anginette Blanche ("Nettie"), born July 23, 1869; Clarence (Ernest's father), born September 4, 1871; Willoughby Anson, born April 1, 1874; George Roy, born March 10, 1876; Alfred Tyler, born December 4, 1877; and Grace Adelaide, born February 13, 1881.

Hemingway, Anson Tyler (1844–1926) Ernest's paternal grandfather: born in Plymouth, Connecticut, August 26, 1844; died in Oak Park, Illinois, October 7, 1926. He was the son of Allen and Harriet Loisa Tyler Hemingway. His family moved from Connecticut to Norwood Park, near Chicago, when he was 10.

During the Civil War Anson joined Company D of the 72nd Illinois Infantry on July 28, 1862, and fought in June 1863 under General Grant at the battle of Vicksburg, Mississippi. He also fought with Company B of the 70th U.S. Infantry at the battle of Natchez and retired as a first lieutenant.

After the war he attended Wheaton College in Illinois, where he became a friend of evangelist Dwight Moody, and, after graduation, he married a Wheaton student, Adelaide Edmonds, August 27, 1867, in Nashua Township, Illinois; they moved to Oak Park in 1868 and lived at the corner of Oak Park Avenue and Superior Street.

He sold real estate, and he and his wife were active in the First Congregational Church of Oak Park, he as a Sunday School teacher and deacon. They had six children: Anginette Blanche ("Nettie"), born July 23, 1869; Clarence (Ernest's father), born September 4, 1871; Willoughby Anson, born April 1, 1874; George Roy, born March 10, 1876; Alfred Tyler, born December 4, 1877; and Grace Adelaide, born February 13, 1881. All six children attended Oberlin College.

Hemingway, Carol (1911–)   Ernest's sister and the fifth of six children born to Clarence and Grace Hemingway: born July 19, 1911, in Resort Township, Michigan. She married John Fentress Gardner June 25, 1933, in New York City, and they have three children: Elizabeth Linda (b. December 8, 1937), Hilary Paul (b. November 12, 1939), and Mark Andrew (b. November 14, 1948).

Hemingway, Clarence Edmonds (1871–1928)   Ernest's father, known to his friends as Ed: born in Oak Park, Illinois, September 4, 1871; died in Oak Park, December 6, 1928—of self-inflicted pistol wounds. He was the oldest son of Anson Tyler HEMINGWAY and Adelaide HEMINGWAY.

Clarence graduated from Oak Park High School in 1890, and from Oberlin College in 1893; he received his M.D. from Rush Medical College in Chicago and became a general practitioner. He married Grace Hall on October 1, 1896, in Oak Park. They had six children: Marcelline, Ernest Miller, Ursula, Madelaine, Carol, and Leicester Clarence.

Dr. Clarence Hemingway is described as six feet tall, a strong, powerfully built man, with a black beard. He became one of Oak Park's most prominent citizens, both as a physician and surgeon and as a member of Oak Park's First Congregational Church. He was a member of the staff of the Oak Park Hospital from its beginning and held memberships in the Chicago and Illinois State Medical Societies. He studied at the New York Laying-In Hospital in Obstetrics in 1908 and invented the Spinal Forceps.

Clarence shot himself in 1928 with his father's Smith and Wesson .32 revolver. He had been suffering from some financial setbacks but mostly from physical problems, mainly, Ernest believed, from loss of sleep caused by diabetic disorders and angina pectoris. He was 57 years old at the time of his death.

Hadley (Copyright holder unknown; photo courtesy of the John F. Kennedy Library)

Clarence and Grace Hemingway in 1897 (Courtesy of the John F. Kennedy Library)

Hemingway, Elizabeth Hadley Richardson (1891–1979)   Ernest's first wife, born November 9, 1891, in St. Louis; died January 23, 1979, in Lakeland, Florida. She was injured as a child in a fall from a second-story window, a back injury that required months of bed rest.

She graduated from Mary Institute in St. Louis and attended Bryn Mawr College for one year. Her mother, who tended to dominate her childhood, felt that Hadley was too delicate, both physically and emotionally, and so she quit college. Shortly after this, her older sister, Dorothea, died giving birth to a stillborn baby.

Hadley met Ernest in Chicago at a party held by a mutual friend from Horton Bay, Michigan, Katy SMITH, who had invited her for a visit just after Hadley's mother died in the late summer of 1920. She was nearly eight years older than Ernest, but she had spent an unhappy and protected childhood and so was not as mature as most 29-year-old women when she married him on September 3, 1921, in Horton Bay. They had one child, John Hadley Nicanor (b. October 10, 1923), nicknamed "Bumby" as a child but called "Jack" in adulthood. Hadley and Ernest were divorced in 1926 so he could marry Pauline PFEIFFER. The divorce settlement included all of the royalties on his first major novel, *The Sun Also Rises,* published in 1926. Hadley married Paul Scott Mowrer July 3, 1933.

She is described by Ernest in the first chapter of *A Moveable Feast* (1964) as having a "gently modeled face and her eyes and her smile lighted up at decisions as though they were rich presents."

Hemingway, Ernest (1899–1961)   Born July 21, 1899, in Oak Park, Illinois; died July 2, 1961, in Ketchum, Idaho—of self-inflicted shotgun wounds. From maturity until his death, Hemingway lived a life of almost constant excitement.

He saw five wars, was wounded badly as an 18-year-old volunteer ambulance driver for the Italian army in WORLD WAR I, and was among the first Americans to enter Paris after the Allied invasion of Normandy in WORLD WAR II. Between those wars he covered the Greek army's retreat from Constantinople in 1922 for *The Toronto Daily Star,* the Spanish civil war in 1937 and 1938, for the North American Newspaper Alliance (NANA),

and the Sino-Japanese war in 1941 for the *PM* newspaper, seeing frontline action in all five of these wars.

He survived four automobile accidents and two airplane crashes (on consecutive days in 1954), the airplane accidents in East Africa producing obituaries in newspapers all over the world.

During the approximately 43 years of his maturity Hemingway wrote nine novels (a 10th is scheduled for publication in 1999), four books of nonfiction, more than 100 short stories, nearly 400 articles, a play, and 90 poems. He won the 1954 Nobel Prize for literature and a Pulitzer Prize. He was married four times and had three sons. For a period of about 20 years during the 1930s and 1940s he was in the news media almost daily, his experiences covered by reporters and photographers as if he were a Hollywood movie star. He was handsome, active, intelligent, and charismatic. In a Canadian Broadcasting Company interview, Archibald MacLeish said that "the only [other] person I have ever known who could exhaust the oxygen in a room the way Ernest could just by coming into it was Franklin Delano Roosevelt."

Hemingway created a style of writing admired by nearly every writer of fiction and nonfiction and left that style as perhaps his most important legacy. It has been said that half of all 20th-century writers have tried

The Hemingway family: in back left to right, Clarence, Grace, Madelaine ("Sunny"), Ursula, Marcelline, and Ernest; in front, Leicester and Carol (Copyright holder unknown; photo courtesy of the John F. Kennedy Library)

A young Ernest in northern Michigan (Courtesy of the John F. Kennedy Library)

to imitate Hemingway's style and the other half have tried not to.

One problem for the reader of Hemingway's works is that it is sometimes difficult to tell the difference between nonfiction and fiction. Many incidents in his fiction are lifted directly from actual experiences, and many actual experiences are fictionalized—or at least exaggerated—in his nonfiction. Frederic Henry's wounding in *A Farewell to Arms* is a vivid rendering of Hemingway's own wounding along the Piave River near Fossalta on July 8, 1918. And *Green Hills of Africa,* clearly a report of a two-month safari in East Africa with his wife, Pauline, during January and February 1934, begins with an epigraph that states: "Unlike many novels, none of the characters or incidents in this book is imaginary."

This sometimes too-thin line between fiction and nonfiction is perhaps best exemplified and complicated by some biographers who insist on "proving" events in Hemingway's life by quoting from the fiction. One biographer "discovered" the author's first sexual experience and then cites the short story "Up in Michigan" as his source of information. Another identifies real people as characters in the fiction, without qualification. Another biographer assumes that statements in Hemingway's letters and media articles are biographical facts, failing to acknowledge that the author may have lied or exaggerated in the nonfiction as well as in the fiction. In a 1981 review of Carlos Baker's *Ernest Hemingway: Selected Letters, 1917–1961* Morley CALLAGHAN wrote that "[s]ince he had a searing power to make everything he wrote seem real, the letters are captivating because we can never be sure whether he is telling the truth, or whether he is being

seduced by his imagination into believing the legends he created for himself."

All of these factors make it difficult to get biographies right. Hemingway was rejected for the army in 1917 because of a vision problem, so he lied about his age in early 1918 in order to get into the Red Cross to drive ambulances for the Italian army. He gave his birth year as 1898. Since then a number of biographical studies have had his birth date wrong. Even *Life* magazine, in a special issue honoring "The 100 Most Important Americans of the 20th Century," has Hemingway's birth year as "1898."

All of this biographical confusion, more of it perhaps with Hemingway than with any other 20th-century American author, has helped to generate a mythology that grows larger every year. And people have bought into the myth. Hemingway's oldest son, Jack, says that he has yet to recognize his father in any of the biographies. "He may have been an SOB to some people," Jack says, "but he was not an SOB to me." This failure of recognition is probably not unusual in family members, but all three of the Hemingway sons talk about how much fun they had growing up with their father. And they say he was "funny" as well, a characteristic rarely mentioned in the biographies.

EH about 1918 (Copyright holder unknown; photo courtesy of the John F. Kennedy Library)

EH on a freight train headed north (Courtesy of the John F. Kennedy Library)

There are dozens of stories told by well-meaning people of meetings with Hemingway, of seeing him in various places, of things he did, stories told as true but which are not true—often because Hemingway was already dead at the time the event was supposed to have taken place. At least two Hemingway impersonators, one in the United States and one in Europe, have for several years been getting free drinks and dinners at the expense of gullible admirers.

There are enough stories of his prowess as a hunter or boxer or wrestler or drinker or brawler, to justify a biographer's time chasing them down. But it also requires an extra amount of drive to get facts right that most biographers seem unwilling to exhibit. The first editor of *The Hemingway Review* received perhaps a dozen letters either describing incidents that occurred in this or that bar in Albuquerque or Des Moines or Tallahassee, or asking if Hemingway could have been at a certain place at a certain time in order for the letter-writer "to prove correct" whatever story he had recently heard from this or that bartender, most of the writers

seeming to assume that if Hemingway *had* been there, then the story of a "brawl" *must* be true.

And in spite of assumptions to the contrary, Hemingway never ran with the bulls in Pamplona, Spain. The leg wounds he had received in World War I prohibited running at any time, let alone on the mostly cobblestone streets of Pamplona with bulls chasing him. Nor did Jake BARNES, the central character in *The Sun Also Rises,* run with the bulls. Yet the legend is advanced every year in Pamplona where dozens of people, including many Americans, run with the bulls in what they think is an imitation of a Hemingway act of bravery.

Another aspect of the mythology is in the deluge of allusions to Hemingway in the media. There are songs, like "Grace Under Pressure" and "Islands in the Stream"; there is a Doonesbury book of cartoons titled "A Farewell to Alms"; and a Hemingway "Adventure Map." There is a seemingly endless number of advertisements and newspaper headlines derived from Hemingway's works: a *New York Times* sports headline "Sub Also Rises"; a *Punch* magazine food article titled "The Soufflé Also Rises"; a *Time* magazine story headlined "The Bell Tolls for Falwell." And there are at least 10 "Hemingway Restaurants" in the United States, plus one in New Zealand and another in Abu Dhabi, the capitol of the United Arab Emirates, at the southern end of the Persian Gulf. There are numerous Harry's Bars, named after the one in Venice that appears in the novel *Across the River and Into the Trees.* There was a Calvin Klein "Obsession Fragrance" ad that used a "scene" from *The Sun Also Rises;* and there's a catering service in Warrenton, Virginia, named "A Moveable Feast," spelled correctly, with an *e.*

Another of the legends attached to Hemingway has him so drawn to death that he became *its* subject and so foreshadowed his suicide. But it was the *subject* of violent death that attracted him, because the subject allowed him to push life into a corner for examination. Hemingway says at the beginning of *Death in the Afternoon* (1932), a book generally acclaimed as the best book on bullfighting written in English, that "[t]he only place where you could see life and death, *i.e.,* violent death now that the wars were over, was in the bull ring and I wanted very much to go to Spain where I could study it."

Much of Hemingway's seemingly macho stance, his own or that of his fictional characters—courage in the face of death, whether in war, in bullfights, or in hunting big game—was the author's attempt to examine life more closely so that he could write better about it, even as a scientist examines with a microscope so that he can get closer to truth. Hemingway's vision of the human condition as reflected in his fiction is usually that of the individual alone with some loss, attempting to cope with that loss in order to come out the other side of

Ernest at safari camp in East Africa (Courtesy of the John F. Kennedy Library)

more than 60 conferences devoted entirely or in part to Hemingway, including international conferences every two years since 1984; more than 100 books and 1,500 articles about Hemingway or his works; festivals each year in Oak Park and in Key West, Florida; a $7,500 Hemingway Foundation/PEN Award, given each year for the best first book of fiction; all of this plus a line of clothes, a line of hunting gear and fishing tackle, a house design, and even Hemingway wallpaper. A whole industry has developed, all in the name of Ernest Hemingway.

Hemingway won the Nobel Prize for literature in 1954, largely on the basis of a story about an old Cuban fisherman, down on his luck, who catches a marlin two feet longer than his 16-foot boat but who loses it to sharks before he can get it back to shore. The old man learns that "man can be destroyed but not defeated" if he tries to do well what his life has led him to. This experience with a semblance of understanding of himself and of his place in the larger scheme of things.

Meanwhile, Hemingway was having difficulty coping with his own life. He was haunted constantly by physical and mental ailments: blinding headaches, insomnia, high blood pressure, eye and ear problems, diabetes, depression, and paranoia—all problems that his father had had and that were causal factors in *his* suicide in 1928. Other family suicides included Ernest's sister Ursula in 1966 and his brother, Leicester, in 1982; and Leicester suspected suicide when their oldest sister, Marcelline, died in 1963, although the doctors reported natural causes. Four suicides, maybe five, in a family of eight.

During the last years of his life, Ernest told his wife, Mary, and his friends in Idaho that he was being followed by the FBI, a story which everyone thought to be the result of the paranoia and which nearly all the early biographical studies retold. But in a rather interesting twist, it has been discovered that the FBI has large files of information on Hemingway's activities from World War II until his death, including information that could have been gathered only from following him during the last months of his life.

All these legends have not been unproductive. The century's last 20 years have produced a HEMINGWAY SOCIETY (begun in 1980) with a scholarly journal and newsletter with worldwide circulations, plus Hemingway societies in Oak Park, Illinois, in northern Michigan, in Japan, and in Korea. There have been

Ernest at the Finca Vigía near Havana (Courtesy of the John F. Kennedy Library)

affirmation in *The Old Man and the Sea* is, to a large extent, an affirmation readers may see in nearly all of Hemingway's fictional works. But if Hemingway wrote of such affirmation, how then does one account for the final act in the author's own life? His suicide in 1961 shocked readers and writers alike.

Writers as diverse as Ray Bradbury and Norman Mailer have even attempted to rewrite the death as a way of explaining it, first to themselves, as if suicide for a man who had studied death all of his life was not a satisfactory explanation either for them or for the rest of us. And in the process of analysis they have added to the mythology.

Bradbury wrote a science fiction short story for *Life* magazine, titled "The Kilimanjaro Machine" (January 22, 1965), in which the author changes the circumstances of Hemingway's death. Bradbury has his narrator stop for Hemingway along an Idaho dirt road and transport him in his flying pickup truck to the top of Mt. Kilimanjaro, where the main character in one of Hemingway's best short stories, "The Snows of Kilimanjaro," dreams of going at the moment of his own death, the top of the mountain representing for the narrator and for Bradbury a sort of heaven for writers, the place where Bradbury believes Hemingway deserved to be.

Mailer suggested in an address at a Boston conference in 1990 that perhaps it wasn't a suicide at all. "All writers are doctors," Mailer said. "The shotgun was medicine for the dread" that Hemingway lived with during his last years, the dread of the life he faced each day but especially the dread of losing his ability to continue writing. "Perhaps he wasn't a suicide," Mailer said, "in the sense that he took the medicine each evening, testing the trigger tension of the gun," the tension acting as medicine for the dread. On the morning of July 2, 1961, Mailer suggested, the tension went beyond the gun's limits. Gregory Hemingway says of the suicide, in his biography, *Papa: A Personal Memoir* (1976), that his father "showed courage in accepting the only option left."

Late in his life Hemingway's creative powers seemed to be gone, at least in part as a result of electric shock treatments he received at the Mayo Clinic in Rochester, Minnesota, twice a week during December and January, 1960–61. He had led a life full of the kinds of excitement difficult to keep up in a 60-year-old man. Gregory sums it up in his biography by saying that Hemingway had "everything." He was "[h]andsome as a movie star in his youth, with an attraction for women you wouldn't believe unless you saw it; extremely sensitive, blessed with a constitution, energy, and resiliency that allowed him to abuse his body and recover from trauma, both physical and emotional," that might well destroy "lesser men; supremely imaginative and yet possessed of tremendous common sense, perhaps the rarest combi-

nation of qualities; and luck, almost always good, the genetic good luck to have all of the above, and the luck to survive a major war wound with the knowledge of what the edge of nothingness is like."

In spite of all the persistent myth-making, which is only a biographer's way—or anyone's—of trying to explain his or her subject, Hemingway wrote the most popular and some of the best prose of any 20th-century writer in English and created a style of writing which moved Norman Mailer to refer to him as the "literary father" of all current novelists, a writer who made the short, declarative sentence an ideal for nearly every writer who followed.

For year-by-year details of Hemingway's life, see Appendix III, "Chronology and Dateline." For genealogy, see Appendix II, "Hemingway's Family."

Hemingway, Grace Hall (1872–1951) Ernest's mother: born June 15, 1872 in Chicago; died June 29, 1951, in Memphis, Tennessee. She was the daughter of Ernest Hall and Caroline Hancock; she had two brothers, Ernest (b. 1867; d. next day) and Leicester Campbell (b. 1874).

She graduated from Oak Park High School in 1891 and went to New York, where she took voice lessons from opera singer Louisa Cappianni in 1895–96. In order to pay her $1,000 teacher's fee, Grace gave a concert at the Madison Square Garden Theater with the Apollo Club of New York City. Madame Cappianni had been one of Amelita Galli-Curci's teachers and believed that Grace, too, had the potential for a career at the Metropolitan Opera. Grace came from a family of singers: her father was a baritone, and her mother sang soprano and was the owner as a child of the first organ in Dyersville, Iowa, where her family lived, and which she took to Chicago with her. Grace's mother did not teach her to cook, because she wanted her to spend her time practicing voice and piano.

But she gave up a potential operatic career to marry Dr. Clarence Edmonds HEMINGWAY October 1, 1896, in Oak Park. She directed a children's church choir and orchestra at the First Congregational Church. She also had a reputation as an artist and held several exhibitions. She lectured on women's suffrage and was a member of the Suburban Civics Club, a drama group, a Fine Arts Society, and a Hospital Auxiliary. She and Clarence had six children: Marcelline, Ernest Miller, Ursula, Madelaine, Carol, and Leicester Clarence. Grace's eyesight was defective as the result of childhood scarlet fever (when she was blind for several months), and the result in adulthood was almost constant severe headaches.

Hemingway, Gregory Hancock (1931–) Ernest's third son, the second with his second wife, Pauline, born November 12, 1931, in Kansas City, Missouri. A physician, Gregory practiced in New York and Montana, before moving to Miami, Florida. He wrote a biography of his father titled *Papa: A Personal Memoir* (1976). He has been married three times. He and his first wife, Shirley Jane Rhodes, had one child, Lorian (b. December 15, 1951); he and his second wife, Alice Thomas, had three children, John Patrick (b. August 19, 1960), Maria Ann (b. November 28, 1961), and Patrick Edward (b. March 31, 1966); and he and his third wife, Valerie DANBY-SMITH, had three children, Sean (b. April 12, 1967), Edward Brian (b. September 16, 1968), and Vanessa (b. July 16, 1970). Danby-Smith also had a child, Brenden (b. February 12, 1962) by a previous marriage.

Hemingway, John Hadley Nicanor (1923–   )   Ernest's son with his first wife, Hadley, born October 10, 1923, in Toronto, Canada. He was called "Bumby" in childhood and "Jack" as an adult. He was a lieutenant with the OSS in World War II and parachuted into France,

was wounded, captured by the Germans and imprisoned in the Moseburg Prison Camp until his release on April 30, 1945.

An expert fly fisherman, he published a book titled *Misadventures of a Fly Fisherman: My Life With and Without Papa* (1986), which is partly a biography of his father and partly a memoir of his experiences while fly fishing in some of the world's greatest trout streams. He is a retired Colorado Fish and Game Commissioner.

He married Byra Whittlesey (Puck) Whitlock June 25, 1949, in Paris, with former OSS comrade in arms Julia Child as matron of honor and Alice B. Toklas in the audience. Jack and Puck had three children, Joan Whittlesey (b. May 5, 1950), Margot, "Margaux" (b. February 16, 1955; d. July 1, 1996), and Hadley, "Mariel," (b. November 22, 1961).

Jack Hemingway has stated on several occasions that he spent the first half of his life as the son of a famous father and the second half as the father of three famous daughters. Joan is a writer, Margot was a top

Ernest and son Jack ("Bumby") on the Pilar (Courtesy of the John F. Kennedy Library)

fashion model before her suicide in 1996, and Mariel is an actress.

Hemingway, Leicester Clarence (1915–1982)   Ernest's brother and the sixth of six children born to Clarence and Grace Hemingway: born April 1, 1915, in Oak Park, Illinois; died September 13, 1982, in Miami Beach, Florida—by suicide.

He graduated from Oak Park High School in 1933 and worked for various newspapers, including the *Chicago Daily News* (1935–1937), *The Philadelphia Inquirer* (1938), and *PM* newspaper (1940). He also wrote articles for *Everybody's Digest* and *Look* magazine. He wrote two books, *Sound of the Trumpet* and *My Brother, Ernest Hemingway* (1962). He served in World War II with a documentary film unit in Europe and was later a director of Cayman Boats, Ltd., in the Cayman Islands (1945–46). He was an assistant information officer for the State Department, stationed in Bogotá, Colombia (1949–51).

He married Patricia Shedd Hemingway (foster daughter of Ernest's uncle, Alfred Tyler) on June 13, 1936, in Kansas City, Missouri, and they had two children, Jacob Edmonds (b. June 23, 1937) and Peter (b. June 29, 1940). After a divorce, Leicester married Doris Dunning March 24, 1956, and they had two children: Anne Elizabeth Jane (b. November 15, 1957) and Hilary Hancock (b. June 16, 1961).

Hemingway, Madelaine "Sunny" (1904–1995)   Ernest's sister and the fourth of six children born to Clarence and Grace Hemingway: born November 28, 1904 in Oak Park, Illinois; died January 14, 1995.

She married Kenneth Sinclair Mainland January 29, 1938, in River Forest, Illinois and they had one child, Ernest Hemingway (b. December 2, 1938). Madelaine worked as a nurse's aide and as a dental technician. She was also an accomplished musician, playing the harp in the Memphis Symphony Orchestra.

She published a biography of her brother, titled *Ernie: Hemingway's Sister "Sunny" Remembers* (1975) and provided an annual scholarship in creative writing in his name at Indiana University. She also gave a stained glass window to the Emmanuel Episcopal Church of Petoskey, Michigan, in the name of Ernest Miller Hemingway.

Hemingway, Marcelline (1898–1963)   Ernest's older sister and the first of six children born to Clarence and Grace Hemingway: born January 15, 1898, in Oak Park, Illinois; died December 9, 1963, in Grosse Pointe, Michigan.

She was held back from entering grade school so she and Ernest could be together in the same grade, and they graduated from Oak Park and River Forest High School in 1917. She attended Oberlin College, Northwestern University, and the University of Chicago. She married Sterling Sanford January 2, 1923, in Oak Park, and they had three children: Carol Hemingway (b. September 19, 1924), James Sterling (b. May 27, 1929), and John Edmonds (b. December 27, 1930).

Marcelline wrote about her Hemingway roots in *At the Hemingways: A Family Portrait* (1962). She also lectured on theater topics and wrote a column titled "Theater Briefs" for a magazine of the Woman's City Club of Detroit.

Hemingway, Martha Ellis Gellhorn (1908–1998)   Ernest's third wife, "Marty," born in St. Louis. She was the daughter of Dr. George and Edna Gellhorn, Dr. Gellhorn a well-known gynecologist in St. Louis.

Martha graduated from John Burroughs School in St. Louis and attended Bryn Mawr for three years. A journalist, she held jobs with the *New Republic* and the Albany, New York, *Hearst Times Union,* and then went to Paris where she worked for *Vogue* magazine, and United Press, and freelanced for the *St. Louis Post-Dispatch.* One obituary calls her "one of the great war correspondents of the century."

Martha in Idaho, November 1940 (Copyright holder unknown; photo courtesy of the John F. Kennedy Library)

In her book *Travels With Myself and Another* (1978), the "another" is Ernest Hemingway, referred to only as "U.C." (Unwilling Companion). "I was a writer before I met him," she said at another time, "and I have been a writer for 45 years since."

She met Ernest at Sloppy Joe's Bar in Key West in late December 1936. Ernest and Martha married November 21, 1940, in Cheyenne, Wyoming, and divorced December 21, 1945. It was the unhappiest of the four marriages for Ernest, most likely because he and Martha competed as writers and journalists. They both covered the Spanish civil war (1937–38), and when she was assigned by *Collier's* to go to China in 1941 to cover China's war with Japan, Ernest followed along and took away some of her spotlight. Then in early 1944, after *Collier's* had assigned Martha to cover the war in Europe, the editors asked Ernest to be their correspondent.

She sneaked onto a hospital ship going to Omaha Beach on D-Day, June 6, 1944, and went ashore on June 7. She was caught, however, by Allied officers and sent back to England. She later went illegally to the Italian front. She covered the Nuremberg trials and the trial of Adolf Eichmann. She went to Vietnam in 1966–67 and

Mary and Ernest at the Finca Vigía (Courtesy of the John F. Kennedy Library)

Ernest with Martha in Idaho, 1940 (Copyright holder unknown; photo courtesy of the John F. Kennedy Library)

to Panama in 1989. In 1953 she married *Time* magazine editor Tom Matthews; they were divorced in the early 1960s.

When Ernest first met her in Key West, he had heard of her because of her first novel, *What Mad Pursuit* (1934). She wrote 13 novels. Her books include *The Trouble I've Seen* (1936), *A Stricken Field* (1940), *The Heart of Another* (1941), *Two by Two* (1958), *The Face of War* (1959), and *Point of No Return* (1995).

Hemingway, Mary Welsh Monks (1908–1986)   Ernest's fourth wife, born April 5, 1908 in Walker, Minnesota; died November 26, 1986, in New York City. Her father, Tom Welsh, was a Minnesota logger who also ran a riverboat, taking customers up and down the Mississippi River on day trips. Mary's mother, Adeline, was a Christian Scientist.

Mary, an only child, worked her way through three years as a journalism major at Northwestern University

Mary standing in an elephant footprint (Courtesy of the John F. Kennedy Library)

but dropped out to marry, a marriage that broke up after two years. In an interesting bit of irony, Mary got a job with *The Chicago Daily News* under Paul Mowrer as managing editor, Paul the husband since 1933 of Hadley Hemingway, Ernest's first wife. In 1937 she accepted a position with Lord Beaverbrook's London *Daily Mail*, married one of its reporters in 1938, Noel Monks, and in 1940 was hired by *Time* magazine to be its London correspondent. Her circle of London friends during the war included Robert Capa, the *Life* photographer, and writers Irwin Shaw and William Saroyan.

Her marriage with Monks was over when she met Hemingway at a restaurant in London in 1944, introduced by their mutual friend, Shaw. Mary and Ernest were married March 14, 1946, in Havana, Cuba.

For the next fifteen years she was a manager of Ernest's financial affairs and tried to keep under control his bouts with drinking and depression. She took care of him in the late 1950s, during the last years, when his mind began to deteriorate and he twice

attempted suicide before finally managing it successfully on July 2, 1961. Her biography of Ernest, *How It Was,* was published in 1986.

Hemingway, Patrick (1928–) Ernest's second son, the first with his second wife, Pauline, born June 28, 1928, in Kansas City, Missouri. He was for a number of years a teacher at Wildlife Management College in Tanzania, Africa, before retiring and moving to Montana.

He married Henrietta F. Broyles June 17, 1950, and they adopted a child, Edwina, "Mina," (b. July 31, 1960). Henrietta died in October 1963 and Patrick remarried in 1982.

Hemingway, Pauline Pfeiffer (1895–1951) Ernest's second wife, born in 1895 in Parkersburg, Iowa; died October 1, 1951. They met at the Paris home of a mutual friend, Kitty Cannell, who had invited Pauline and her sister, Virginia (Jinny), for drinks. Ernest and Hadley were invited because he and Kitty's friend Harold LOEB were both about to be published by BONI & LIVERIGHT, and she was hosting the celebration. Pauline was working for the Paris edition of *Vogue* magazine.

Pauline had attended the Visitation Convent in St. Louis and had recently graduated from the University of Missouri. She and Jinny were the daughters of wealthy parents living in Piggott, Arkansas.

She joined Ernest and his first wife, Hadley, in Schruns, Austria, Christmas Day, 1925, ostensibly because Ernest had promised to teach her how to ski, and they became attracted to each other during that winter. In March, Ernest stopped in Paris on his way back to Schruns from New York and spent two days with Pauline. Following Hadley's divorce from Ernest, he and Pauline were married May 10, 1927, in Paris.

Ernest and Pauline (Copyright holder unknown; photo courtesy of the John F. Kennedy Library)

EH skiing near Gstaad, Switzerland, February 1927 (Copyright holder unknown; photo courtesy of the John F. Kennedy Library)

Pauline on the **Pilar** (Copyright holder unknown; photo courtesy of the John F. Kennedy Library)

Hemingway, Ursula (1902–1966) Ernest's sister and the third of six children born to Clarence and Grace Hemingway: born April 29, 1902, in Oak Park; died October 30, 1966, in Honolulu, Hawaii—by suicide. She married J. "Jep" Jasper in 1923 in Hawaii, and they had one child, Gayle Hemingway (b. 1924). Ursula was well known in Honolulu for her artwork, and she established the Ernest Hemingway Memorial Award for creative writing at the University of Hawaii.

Hemingway: The Toronto Years Biography of Hemingway's years working for *The Toronto Daily Star,* 1920–24, written by William Burrill and published in 1994 by Doubleday Canada Limited. It includes 25 "lost" articles published by *Toronto Star* newspapers and identified as Hemingway items by Burrill or by a colleague, William McGeary, former librarian at the *Star.* Burrill also identifies five other published articles but chose not to reprint them. The 30 articles supplement the 172 articles published in *Ernest Hemingway: Dateline Toronto* (1985).

Hemingway: The Wild Years Anthology of seventy-three articles, edited by Gene Z. Hanrahan and published by Dell Publishing Co. (as a paperback) in 1962. This was the first collection of Hemingway's nonfiction writing, all articles about the 1920s. The book is divided into 12 parts: "Manners and Morals" (nine articles); "Gangsters and Prohibition" (seven); "An American in Paris" (eight); "In Defeated Germany" (10); "The Troubled Ruhr" (four); "European Miscellany" (seven); "Tragedy at Genoa" (three); "Italy Turns Right" (three); "Politics and War in the Orient" (eight); "Men of Lausanne" (two); "Bullfighting" (two); and "Outdoors—at Home and Abroad" (10).

Hemingway airplane crash injuries Mary HEMINGWAY sustained two broken ribs in the first crash on January 23, 1954; Ernest sustained a concussion in the second crash (January 24, 1954) from knocking the plane's window out with his head. Other injuries to Ernest included a ruptured liver, spleen, and kidney, temporary loss of vision in his left eye, some loss of hearing in his left ear, a crushed vertebra, a sprained right arm and shoulder, a sprained left leg, paralysis of the sphincter, and first-degree burns on his face, arms, and head.

Ernest and Mary got back to a hospital in Nairobi in time to read their own obituaries in several U.S. and world newspapers.

Hemingway in the Autumn (film) Centennial Entertainment/KTVB documentary, released in 1996 (51 minutes); produced and directed by David Butterfield, narrated by Carolyn Holly; interviews with Hemingway's oldest son, Jack Hemingway; Idaho friends Clara

Spiegel, Don Anderson, Bud Purdy, Tillie Arnold, Dr. John Moritz, Clayton Stewart, Ruth Purdy, and Dr. George Saviers; and Hemingway scholars Michael Reynolds and Susan Beegel.

Hemingway Collection, The   At the John F. Kennedy Library in Boston, dedicated July 19, 1980, in conjunction with a Hemingway Conference on Thompson Island, Dorchester Bay. The room is an integral part of the overall design of the JFK presidential library, which is administered by the National Archives. The library offers grants for people interested in doing research in the Hemingway Collection.

The collection contains more than 2,500 original Hemingway letters and manuscript materials for use by researchers. The collection also includes more than 10,000 photographs, as well as newspaper clippings and miscellaneous materials.

Hemingway Hero, The (stage play)   An adaptation, written by A. E. Hotchner in January 1967 but not produced. Following the title in the script, Hotchner adds: "Based on the writings of Ernest Hemingway." The script, which is in the Olin Library at Washington University in St. Louis, is also stamped with the address of "Touring Theatre, Inc.," a New York drama troupe.

Hemingway Newsletter, The   Eight-page newsletter, published in January and June each year, which includes news and trivia of interest to readers of Hemingway's works. The *Newsletter* began in January 1981 and continues. It is sponsored by The Ernest HEMINGWAY SOCIETY.

Hemingway Review, The   Scholarly journal with essays of criticism on the works of Hemingway, reviews of books, and bibliography. The journal began as *Hemingway notes* in the spring 1971, and 14 issues were published during the next 10 years (1971–74 and 1979–80). The name was changed to *The Hemingway Review* with the fall 1981 issue and has continued publication twice each academic year since then. The *Review* is sponsored by The Ernest HEMINGWAY SOCIETY.

"Hemingway on the Town"   Article, published in the London *Daily Express* (September 11, 1956), describing a night at the Floridita Bar in Havana.

Hemingway's Adventures of a Young Man (film) Twentieth Century-Fox picture, released in July 1962 (145 minutes), based on Hemingway's Nick Adams short stories. Produced by Jerry Wald, directed by Martin Ritt, screenplay by A. E. Hotchner, music by Franz Waxman, photography by Lee Garmes, art direction by Jack Martin Smith and Paul Groesse, set decorations by Walter M. Scott and Robert Priestly,

special effects by L. B. Abbott and Emil Kosa. Hotchner's original title was "Ernest Hemingway's 'Young Man.'"

Cast: Richard Beymer (Nick Adams), Diane Baker (Carolyn), Corinne Calvet (Contessa), Fred Clark (Mr. Turner), Dan Dailey (Billy Campbell), James Dunn (telegrapher), Juano Hernandez (Bugs), Arthur Kennedy (Dr. Adams), Ricardo Montalban (Major Padula), Susan Strasberg (Rosana), Jessica Tandy (Mrs. Adams), Eli Wallach (John), Edward Binns (brakeman), Whit Bissell (Ludstrum), Philip Bourneuf (Montecito), Tullio Carminati (Signore Griffi), Marc Cavell (Eddy Bolton), Charles Fredericks (mayor), Simon Oakland (Joe Boulton), Michael Pollard (George), and Paul Newman (the battler).

Hemingway Society, The Ernest   Formed on December 28, 1980; Professor Paul Smith of Trinity College (Connecticut) elected as the first president. The stated purpose of The Ernest Hemingway Society is to "assist and coordinate Hemingway studies." There were 119 individuals and two libraries as charter members in 1980. By 1998 there were more than 500 members in 21 countries. The society became a foundation in 1987.

The society sponsors international conferences every two years, plus sessions on Hemingway at several U.S. meetings each year. International conferences have been held in Madrid (1984); Lignano, Italy (1986); Schruns, Austria (1988); Boston (1990); Pamplona (1992); Paris (1994); Ketchum/Sun Valley, Idaho (1996); Les Saintes-Maries-de-la-Mer, France (1998); and Bimini Island (scheduled for 2000). And the society has supported conferences on Hemingway in Guilin, China, and several in Havana, Cuba, the latter meetings organized by the Curator of the Hemingway Museum at the former Hemingway home outside of Havana.

The society also sponsors two publications, *The Hemingway Review,* a journal of scholarly essays and reviews, and *The Hemingway Newsletter,* providing information about conferences, special events, and the author in the popular culture.

Hemingway's short stories   It is difficult to determine the exact number of "short stories" Hemingway wrote. Some checklists include as short stories the 18 vignettes that Hemingway wrote for *in our time* (1924); some include "fables" as short stories; some include the stories he wrote for his high school literary magazine; some include fragments cut from longer works.

Since Hemingway's death in 1961, several items—mostly fragments cut from longer stories or novels and pieces probably not intended by Hemingway for publication (but not destroyed)—have been published as "short stories." *Hemingway A to Z* has entries for every work published as a "short story"—a total of 104 items—the fragments, juvenilia, and fables identified as such.

In *Green Hills of Africa* Hemingway writes that magazine editors in rejecting his first short stories "would never call them stories, but always anecdotes, sketches, contes, etc."

Hendaye   Small French village on the Atlantic Ocean at the border with Spain. In *The Garden of Eden* David and Catherine BOURNE spend a few days there on their way to MADRID. There's a "big hotel and a casino" in Hendaye facing the ocean, with mimosas and Basque white-washed villas across the road. In spite of this much admired scenery, they argue about the clippings of reviews of David's second novel, which they have just received. Catherine is angry at David for reading them and wanting to keep them. After a morning of writing, David finds her at a small café, where they eat most of their meals, and she is drinking ABSINTHE and is "very far ahead of him."

Henri Quatre statue   Mentioned in *A Moveable Feast*. See PONT NEUF.

Henry (1)   Name of Nick's father in "The Doctor and the Doctor's Wife." He's called "DOC" by the Indians who work for him.

Henry (2)   Count MIPPIPOPOLOUS's chauffeur in *The Sun Also Rises*.

Henry (3)   One of Thomas HUDSON's crew members in the "At Sea" section of *Islands in the Stream*. Henry does not get along with WILLIE, another crew member, but learns to respect him for his bravery.

Henry, Catherine   Name used by Catherine BARKLEY, in *A Farewell to Arms*, when she registers at the hospital in LAUSANNE.

Henry, Edwin   Narrator of "Night Before Battle." He is called "Hank" by one of his American friends. He is with a film crew in Madrid during the SPANISH CIVIL WAR, filming the fighting. He tries to get Al Wagner, a tankman for the Republic and a friend, to forget a premonition Al has had that he is going to die in the next day's battle.

Henry, Frederic   Protagonist and narrator of *A Farewell to Arms*, an American in his early 20s who wants to be an architect. He goes to war instead, and gradually becomes disillusioned by what he sees.

At the beginning of WORLD WAR I, Frederic has volunteered to drive ambulances with Italy's Second Army and is given the rank of lieutenant. He joins the army in northern Italy in the "fall of that year" (1915), after

the Italian campaign against Austria-Hungary had begun in the spring. In August of the next year, following a serious wounding and recuperation, Frederic returns to his unit, which moves to GORIZIA (which was won by Italy, after 15 months of fighting and 147,000 casualties, on August 6, 1916), and it doesn't take long for him to understand the horror that war brings. It is his responsibility, along with other ambulance personnel, to pick up the bodies of the dead and wounded.

In one of several statements that indicate his growing hatred of the war, Frederic says, sarcastically, that with the winter rain there was cholera, "But it was checked and in the end only seven thousand died of it in the army." Frederic declares, egotistically, that "I knew I would not be killed. Not in this war. It did not have anything to do with me. . . . I wished to God it was over though." He thinks he is safe driving ambulances behind the lines.

He is badly wounded, however, by a mortar shell on the "Isonze [ISONZO River] north of Plava" in the spring of the following year (1917). The medical captain at the post hospital dictates to a sergeant-adjutant what Frederic's wounds are: "Multiple superficial wounds of the left and right thigh and left and right knee and right foot. Profound wounds of right knee and foot. Lacerations of the scalp [he probed—Does that hurt?—Christ, yes!] with possible fracture of the skull. Incurred in the line of duty."

Frederic is taken to a field hospital for treatment and then to the AMERICAN HOSPITAL (1) in Milan for an operation to remove some of the shell fragments from his leg. During his recovery in Milan, he and Catherine BARKLEY, an English V.A.D. (assistant nurse) whom he had met earlier that spring in Gorizia, have a summer love affair, and Catherine becomes pregnant. Catherine's fiancé had been "blown up" in the battle of the SOMME in northern France the year before, and when she and Frederic first met, she was "nearly crazy" over the loss and just beginning to put it behind her.

Frederic is a student of the strategy of war. At one point during his Milan convalescence, while worrying about his friends back at the war front, he thinks that the Italians are wrong for fighting the Austrians in the mountains. He thinks that Napoleon would never have fought the Austrians in the mountains but would have beaten them on the plains. "He would have let them come down," Frederic believes, "and whipped them around Verona."

Frederic returns to the front in the late summer and takes part in the retreat from CAPORETTO (which began October 24, 1917). He leads the ambulance drivers under his command away from the stalled trucks and men of the general retreat, but then the three cars they are driving get stuck in the mud of the sideroads, and they have to continue toward the west on foot.

One of the drivers (Bartolomeo AYMO) is killed and one (Aldo BONELLO) disappears mysteriously before Frederic and the fourth driver, Luigi PIANI, finally make it to a bridge over the TAGLIAMENTO RIVER, where there is a general congestion of retreating vehicles and troops. The Italian BATTLE POLICE, made up of CARABINIERI, armed policemen, are pulling officers out of the line for questioning and then shooting them as deserters. Frederic is pulled from the line to be questioned, but when the carabiniere turns to look at the next officer in line, Frederic dives into the river and escapes.

Just before the retreat from Caporetto, Frederic had presented an argument against abstractions: "I was always embarrassed by the words sacred, glorious, and sacrifice and the expression in vain. . . . I had seen nothing sacred, and the things that were glorious had no glory and the sacrifices were like the stockyards at Chicago if nothing was done with the meat except to bury it."

By the time he escapes execution by the battle police at the Tagliamento bridge, he has been changed by both the war and by his love for Catherine. Whatever his reasons for volunteering to join the Italian ambulance corps in the first place, it does not take him long to realize the "hell" that war brings. He watches as his friend RINALDI (2), a doctor, becomes so damaged psychologically by seeing men torn apart by enemy weapons that the doctor becomes morally corrupt, drinking heavily and attending the officers' whorehouses frequently. And even though the unit's PRIEST, another close friend, tries to stay optimistic in his conversations with other officers, Frederic realizes that the war has taken its toll even on him.

By the end of the novel, as Frederic realizes Catherine is going to die, he has become a fatalist. He says: "That was what you did. You died. You did not know what it [life] was about. You never had time to learn. They threw you in and told you the rules and the first time they caught you off base they killed you. Or they killed you gratuitously like Aymo. Or gave you the syphilis like Rinaldi. But they killed you in the end. You could count on that. Stay around and they would kill you."

As he leaves the hospital at the end, after Catherine's death, and walks back to his hotel "in the rain," in his desolation he perceives that her death and the suffering and deaths of others in the war are meaningless.

Henry's lunch-room   Setting in Summit, Illinois, for the beginning and ending of "The Killers." It has been "made over from a saloon into a lunch-counter." GEORGE (5) seems to be the owner now, and Henry, apparently the original owner, is never mentioned.

Henry's Sin House   Whorehouse in Havana, mentioned in the "Cuba" section of *Islands in the Stream*.

Heraldo de Madrid, El   Madrid newspaper, for which the "substitute bull-fight critic" is taking notes during Manuel GARCIA's fight in "The Undefeated."

In *Death in the Afternoon* Hemingway implies that a bullfight reporter for the newspaper exaggerated the ability of the bullfighter, Domingo López Ortega.

Hernandez   Second bullfighter in the "nocturnals" with Manuel GARCIA, the main character in "The Undefeated." The younger Hernandez tries to encourage Garcia and is sympathetic when the crowd turns against him.

Herrick, Myron T. (1854–1929)   American diplomat, governor of Ohio (1903–05); named ambassador to France in 1912 by President Taft. He became something of a hero to the French, because when the French government moved to Bordeaux in 1914 to avoid the German military advance at the beginning of World War I, Herrick was the only foreign diplomat to remain in Paris. He was reappointed as French ambassador in 1921 by President Harding, and he bought the embassy building for the United States out of his own funds. In *A Moveable Feast* Hemingway describes a conversation he had with Ford Madox FORD that included a discussion of men they considered "gentlemen." Herrick was named as one of the possibilities.

"He Who Gets Slap Happy: A Bimini Letter"   Article, published in *Esquire* (August 1935). Hemingway answers his critics who say he should stop writing articles for *Esquire* and write fiction instead.

high country, the   In East Africa, part of the setting for David BOURNE's AFRICAN STORY in *The Garden of Eden*.

"High Lights and Low Lights"   Article for Oak Park and River Forest High School newspaper, *The Trapeze* (May 25, 1917), reprinted in *Hemingway at Oak Park High: The High School Writings of Ernest Hemingway, 1916–1917* (1993).

Hill, Catherine   Catherine BOURNE's maiden name in *The Garden of Eden*.

"Hills Like White Elephants"   In this short story, a young, unmarried couple wait outside the platform café in a train station along the "valley of the Ebro" River in Spain. The station is not identified, but it is probably at the rail junction about 9 miles northwest of Zaragoza, where the main line between Barcelona and Madrid meets the line that runs on to the northwest. The train stops, the narrator tells us, for two minutes.

The story is nearly all dialogue, two young people drinking beer in the hot sun and waiting for a train. The man is identified only as "American," the girl as

"Jig." In spite of what seems to the reader only small talk, it is clear that underneath their conversation is a tension that permeates their relationship. The girl is pregnant, and she is trying to decide whether to have an abortion, but none of this is stated, only hinted to the reader by the man saying to her, "It's really an awfully simple operation, Jig. . . . It's not really an operation at all. . . . I know you wouldn't mind it, Jig. It's really not anything. It's just to let the air in."

Meanwhile, the girl "looked at the ground" or "did not say anything," clearly embarrassed by the predicament and getting angrier at the man for being so insensitive to her dilemma. Hemingway depends almost entirely on what the young people *do not* say to one another for the story's emotional impact (see THEORY OF OMISSION). The situation, including the failure of either individual to say exactly what he or she feels, has a timeless quality about it that helps place it among the most popular of Hemingway's short stories.

The title's significance is ambiguous. The girl looks at the "line of hills" that are "white in the sun" and the country that is "brown and dry" and says to her companion, "They look like white elephants." Later she says the hills "don't really look like white elephants . . . just . . . the coloring of their skin through the trees." But the girl is merely trying to make conversation.

The story is full of tension, created almost entirely by the failure of communication, and a seeming inability of the young man to stop talking. Jig says to him, finally, "Would you please please please please please please please stop talking." A waitress informs them that the train will arrive in five minutes, and the young man carries their bags to the other side of the platform, probably to take a break from the situation. He has a drink at the bar and notices that all the other people are "waiting reasonably for the train." He returns to Jig and asks her if she feels better. She says: "I feel fine. . . . There's nothing wrong with me. I feel fine."

But the reader knows she doesn't feel fine, that they have resolved nothing, and that Jig is still miserable—as much about her lover's insensitivity concerning the decision she has to make as about the decision itself.

"Hills Like White Elephants" was first published in *transition* magazine (August 1927) and reprinted in *Men Without Women* (October 1927).

Hills Like White Elephants (stage play) Adaptation from the short story, written by A. E. HOTCHNER in January 1962 but not produced. Beneath the title in the script, Hotchner adds: "Drawn freely from the writings of Ernest Hemingway" and "copyright H&H, Ltd., 1962." The script is in the Olin Library at Washington University in St. Louis.

Hills Like White Elephants (television production) A David Brown Production in association with HBO Showcase and Granada Television, first shown in the United States in January 1998. Cast: Melanie Griffith (Hadley) and James Wood (Robert). Directed by Tony Richardson.

Hirsch's rooming-house In Summit, Illinois, where, in "The Killers," Ole ANDRESON has a room. Nick ADAMS goes there to warn Andreson about the two men in Henry's lunch-room who say they're going to kill him.

Hitler, Adolf (1889–1945) German dictator, Nazi (National Socialist German Workers Party) leader, master propagandist, and rabid anti-Semite. An ambitious but low-ranking corporal in the German army during WORLD WAR I (1914–18), Hitler believed that Germany's political leaders had dishonored the country by signing the Treaty of Versailles in which they agreed to relinquish German territories. He helped found the Nazi party in 1920, and began his upward drive to political leadership, then dictatorial power over the German people, which he gained in 1933. During the SPANISH CIVIL WAR he sent troops to Spain to support fascist Francisco FRANCO's rebel army. Hitler's rearmament of Germany and expansionist military aggression precipitated WORLD WAR II, and his domestic policies decimated Germany's, and later all of Europe's, Jewish population, through systematic and brutal persecution known as the Holocaust.

Hitler's book *Mein Kampf* ("My Struggle"), published in 1924, was filled with anti-Semitic tirades, worship of power, disdain for morality, and a strategy for world domination.

Hemingway was astonished by Hitler's bold attempt to overthrow the German government in November 1923, when he and other Socialists attempted the "beer-hall putsch," intended as a coup to bring Germany under National Socialist control with support from the army. The coup failed, and Hitler spent nine months in jail, but it gave him the time to write *Mein Kampf*, and it brought him national popularity. Hemingway told Gertrude STEIN in Paris that the newspapers were full of the beer-hall "fiasco." In "Notes on the Next War: A Serious Topical Letter" (*Esquire*, September 1935), Hemingway wrote about the inevitability of war in Europe because of the bullying tactics of Hitler and Mussolini.

"H.M.'s Loyal State Department" Article, published in *Ken* (June 16, 1938). Accuses the "fascists" in the U.S. State Department of "doing the dirty work of a very temporary British policy."

Hobin, Georgette In *The Sun Also Rises.* See GEORGETTE.

Hoffenheimer In *The Sun Also Rises* Jake BARNES asks Harvey STONE what H. L. MENCKEN is like, and, by way of showing that Mencken says "some pretty funny things," Stone quotes Mencken as saying that Hoffenheimer is "a garter snapper." Hoffenheimer is a fictionalized version of, apparently, Joseph Hergesheimer (1880–1954), a U.S. writer who wrote about the decadence of wealthy Americans. The name "Hergesheimer" was used in the novel's original manuscript.

Hogan, Danny   In "Fifty Grand," the owner of a "health farm" in New Jersey, where boxers train. He's a friend of the story's narrator, Jerry DOYLE.

Hogarth, William   (1697–1764)   English painter and engraver, mentioned in *Islands in the Stream* for his woodblock print "Gin Lane" (c. 1751), a caricature of vice in "men of the lowest rank."

hogshead   Large barrel (or cask) holding up to 140 gallons of any liquid, used by Richard CANTWELL for a duck blind on his Sunday duck shoot at the mouth of the Tagliamento River in *Across the River and Into the Trees*.

Holbrook   One of the gamblers who has an argument with the "old man" in "My Old Man." The old man, a jockey named BUTLER, either threw a race at the San Siro steeplechase course in Milan or didn't do what he was paid to do.

Hole in the Wall bar   In *A Moveable Feast* Hemingway writes that he thought Ezra Pound must have gotten the opium he saved for Ralph Cheever DUNNING at the Hole in the Wall bar on the rue des Italiens in Paris.

According to Hemingway the bar was a "hangout for deserters and for dope peddlers during and after the first war." The bar was narrow with a red facade and, so the story was told, had a basement opening into the sewers of Paris.

The bar Hemingway refers to is "Le Trou dans le Mur" (The Hole in the Wall), located not on rue des Italiens as Hemingway has it in *A Moveable Feast* but at 23, boulevard des Capucines, on the south side of the boulevard, across the street from the Grand Hôtel, which housed the Café de la Paix. The facade is still there, about 40 inches wide and about 10 yards deep; the name, "Le Trou dans le Mur/Raouche" is above the door. The mistake in address is probably deliberate since Hemingway's bank and mailing address, the Guaranty Trust Company, was located on the short (half-mile long) rue des Italiens, a street Hemingway knew too well, therefore, to have confused with the boulevard des Capucines.

Hollins, Mr.   Marine warrant officer at the U.S. embassy in Havana, in *Islands in the Stream*, where Thomas HUDSON goes to report to the ONI (Office of Naval Intelligence) about his work searching for German submarines. There is hostility between the two men, probably because Hollins is a lieutenant and Hudson is a civilian.

Hollis, Dorothy   Mistress of EDDIE, on board *IRYDIA IV* in *To Have and Have Not*. She masturbates in order to get to sleep while the drunken Eddie sleeps next to her.

Hollis, John   Unseen husband of Dorothy HOLLIS, mentioned in *To Have and Have Not*. He has a liver condition and is apparently unaware of his wife's affair with EDDIE.

Hollywood fund-raising speech   Speech delivered to an audience of filmmakers and stars in July 1937. The film of "The Spanish Earth," directed by Joris IVENS, had just been shown to President Roosevelt at the White House, and Ivens, Hemingway, and Pauline Hemingway were in Hollywood to provide publicity for the film and to raise money for the Loyalist cause in the Spanish civil war.

"Homage to Ezra"   Article, published in *This Quarter* (Spring [May]1925). This first issue of the magazine was dedicated to Ezra POUND.

"Homage to Switzerland"   There are three separate but parallel stories within this short story. In each story (or "part" as Hemingway designates them), there is an American man waiting for the Simplon-Orient Express in a train station café near the east end of Lake Geneva, the first man in MONTREUX, the second in VEVEY, and the third in TERRITET.

Each man is informed by a waitress that the train is an hour late, held up in Saint Maurice by the snow, and the purpose of each story is to describe the way in which each man spends the hour. They are all headed for Paris.

Each story begins with a description of the station café, each one very much like the others: each "warm and light," with the Territet station "a little too warm"; each with wood tables and chairs that "shone" from wiping; and each with a waitress who speaks "German and French and the dialects," and who is not allowed to eat or drink with the customers, nor does she accept the offer of a cigar, the second and third waitresses laughing at the idea. (It is interesting to note, although probably not significant, that the three stations are not dealt with in the order at which the train heading west will finally arrive: the order of arrival would be Territet, Montreux, and Vevey.

In part 1, titled "Portrait of Mr. Wheeler in Montreux," WHEELER offers his waitress first 100 francs Swiss to "go upstairs" with him, then 200, and finally 300. She turns him down and tries to get him to stop saying "such things," calling him "hateful." Her reaction when alone, however, is to think, "Three hundred francs for a thing that is nothing to do. How many times have I done that for nothing. And no place to go here. . . . Three hundred francs to do that. What people those Americans." And Mr. Wheeler reacts differently too, when alone. "He was very careful about money and did not care for women. He had been in that station before and he knew there was no upstairs to go to. Mr. Wheeler never took chances."

Part 2 is titled "Mr. Johnson Talks About It At Vevey." The "it" is a divorce his wife is seeking. JOHNSON asks his waitress if she wouldn't like to "play" with him, but, after she turns him down, Johnson strikes up a conversation with three old porters and buys two bottles of the station's best champagne. When asked by one of the porters if it is his birthday, Johnson, who is 35 and a writer, tells them that his wife is divorcing him. They discuss how Americans divorce more than the French or Germans, and then Johnson leaves to walk along the station platform, leaving a full bottle of champagne but noticing through the window that the three porters have turned it in for cash.

Part 3, the funniest of the three stories, is titled "The Son of a Fellow Member at Territet." Mr. HARRIS does not ask his waitress for sex but has, instead, a conversation with an "old gentleman," Dr. Sigismund WYER (only identified by the card he hands to Harris at the end of the story), a proud member of the National Geographic Society. Wyer drops several Society names on Harris who then tells Wyer about his father's Society membership. His father "shot himself, oddly enough," Harris tells him, and Wyer says he is "sure his loss was a blow to science as well as to his family." Harris tells him that "Science took it awfully well," leaving the reader to wonder how much of the rest of Harris's story is true. Harris accepts Wyer's National Geographic Society calling card and promises, in the story's last line, to keep Dr. Wyer's card "very carefully."

This is the story of three American men, all about the same age, waiting at three separate train stations for the same, hour-late train, and "this" is what they do. One, who does not like women, spends his hour deliberately embarrassing his waitress, knowing all along how "safe" from her he is. The second man is getting a divorce and discusses it with three station porters, who then take him for a bottle of champagne. And the third gets caught up in the lies he thinks he has to tell in a conversation with a European member of the National Geographic Society, who is so proud of his membership that he carries his certificate of membership in his billfold.

"Homage to Switzerland" was first published in *Scribner's Magazine* (April 1933) and reprinted in *Winner Take Nothing* (1933).

Homer (8th century B.C.) Greek poet and author of the *Iliad* (c. 750 B.C.) and *The Odyssey* (c. 725 B.C.). In *Green Hills of Africa* POP thinks that when Hemingway mentions *Ulysses* he means the hero of the *Odyssey*, but he means the novel by James JOYCE.

"Homes on the Seine" Article, published in *The Toronto Daily Star* (August 26, 1922), reprinted in *Ernest Hemingway: Dateline Toronto* (1985). The headline in the *Daily Star* was "Takes to the Water, Solves Flat Problem." Datelined "Paris," it is about the apartment shortage in Paris, which is driving people to rent "flats" on river barges.

"Home Sweet Home" Poem/song by John Howard Payne (1792–1852). It was first sung in Payne's opera, *Clari, the Maid of Milan*, produced in London in 1823, music by Henry R. Bishop. The song is used as part of the parody in *The Torrents of Spring*. Scripps O'NEIL, one of the novel's main characters, says that his friend Harry Parker knew a "poet chap" who wrote the line, "Through pleasures and palaces though I may roam . . ."—a line from the song. But the story, like so much of what Scripps says, is made up, or at least fantasized. *The Torrents of Spring* takes place in the 1920s, so Parker could not have known Payne.

homosexuality In *Islands in the Stream*, there is a short discussion of homosexuality, involving Thomas HUDSON's sons, particularly David, Hudson's friend Roger DAVIS, and Audrey BRUCE. They mention "Damon and Pythias" and "David and Jonathan," and a book by GIDE "with Oscar Wilde in it." When a homosexual approaches young Tom, the latter tells him he has read the Gide book but that he has only an "academic interest" in the subject.

Honest Lil One of the Havana whores whom Thomas HUDSON knows. "She looked her best when sitting at the far end of the bar when you saw only her lovely dark face and the grossness that had come over her body was hidden by the polished wood of the bar." She and Hudson drink together at the FLORIDITA bar in Havana at the beginning of the "Cuba" section of *Islands in the Stream*. She is drinking with him in sympathy over the death of his son Tom.

Honey Girlfriend of Cornelia ELLIOT in "Mr. and Mrs. Elliot." She and Cornelia work together in a Boston tea shop until Cornelia marries Mr. Elliot. After the Elliots are in France for a while, they send for Honey, who takes over the typing of Hubert's poetry. When Hubert takes a room of his own at the château in Touraine, Honey and Cornelia sleep together in another bedroom.

Hong Kong   In *Islands in the Stream* HONEST LIL asks Thomas HUDSON to tell her a "happy" story, and he tells her about a love affair he had in Kowloon, Hong Kong. He tells her about the Chinese "millionaires" he knew, all by their initials only: H. M., M. Y., T. V., H. J., and C. W., who sent him three "absolutely beautiful Chinese girls." Hudson tells Lil that he had more "close and intimate friends" in Hong Kong than he had had before or since.

Honorable Pacciardi   Italy's minister of defense in 1948, during the time of *Across the River and Into the Trees.* He is the source of a joke between Richard CANTWELL and the bartender at the GRITTI PALACE HOTEL in Venice. A joke because the Italians had no "defense" during the years just after WORLD WAR II.

hook book   A booklike holder for fishing lures. In "Big Two-Hearted River" NICK takes a small hook, "very thin and springy," from his hook book to begin fishing for trout the morning of the story's second day.

Hoover, J. Edgar (1895–1972)   Controversial director of the FBI (1924–72), mentioned in *To Have and Have Not.* One of the drunken veterans at FREDDIE'S PLACE accuses Hoover of running the vets "out of Anticosti flats" and Roosevelt of sending the "scum" among the vets to the camp at BOCA CHICA "to get rid of us."

Hopkins   In "Big Two-Hearted River," NICK remembers an argument he had once with his friend Hopkins over how to make coffee over a campfire. Hopkins had argued for putting the coffee into the water and boiling it, rather than putting the coffee into the already boiling water. "Hop" had gone to Texas and made "millions of dollars" from oil.

Horace   Narrator of "God Rest You Merry, Gentlemen." He relates a story, as it was told to him by two doctors, of a 16-year-old boy who goes to the hospital and asks to be castrated. Horace is sarcastic in his description of Doctor Wilcox, especially about the little book he carries with him, titled *The Young Doctor's Friend and Guide.* But after the first four narrative paragraphs, none of which mentions the incident of the boy, nearly all of the rest of the story is told through quotations from the two doctors as they tell Horace what happened to the boy.

"Horns of the Bull, The"   The original title for "The Capital of the World." The short story was published under the former title in *Esquire* (June 1936) and reprinted under the latter title in *The Fifth Column and First Forty-Nine Stories* (1938). See "Capital of the World, The."

horse-cab   In *The Sun Also Rises,* Jake BARNES takes a ride in one, called a *fiacre,* with the prostitute GEORGETTE.

horsemen, four   FASCIST cavalry in *For Whom the Bell Tolls,* who trail through the snow looking for their comrade, whom Robert JORDAN has killed.

Horthy, Miklós von Nagybánya (1863–1957)   Admiral in the Hungarian navy during World War I and later a statesman. He was a counterrevolutionary, named regent and head of state in 1920, after the Romanian communists had been chased from Budapest in November 1919. In "The Revolutionist," the main character ("He"), a communist, is tortured by "Horthy's Men" in Budapest, before he is able to escape to Italy.

Horton Bay   Small town in northern Michigan, located just off the north shore of Lake Charlevoix, about 12 miles east of Charlevoix on the road to Boyne City. It is the setting for "Up in Michigan." In the story, the town has five houses, a general store, and a post office. There's the Smith house, the Stroud house, the Dillworth house, the Horton house and the Van Hoosen house. The Methodist church is out of town one way on the only road, and the township school is out of town the other way. The blacksmith shop that Jim GILMORE owns is across from the school. Lumbering is the region's primary business, although Liz COATES can see the ore barges out on Lake Michigan headed toward Boyne City.

Horton Bay is named after Sam Horton, its first resident, who moved to the north shore of Lake Charlevoix just before the Civil War. The community was first known as Hortons Bay, the spelling Hemingway uses in his short story. But the town's name was changed to Horton Bay in 1894 by the U.S. Postal Service.

Horton Creek   Trout stream in northern Michigan, mentioned in "The End of Something." The creek flows into Lake Charlevoix (formerly called Pine Lake) at Horton Bay, about 10 miles east of Charlevoix. It is spelled Hortons Creek in Hemingway's story.

hospital (1)   In Milan, the setting for "In Another Country."

hospital (2)   In LAUSANNE, Switzerland, where Catherine BARKLEY goes to have her baby in *A Farewell to Arms.*

hospital, Milan   Setting for "Now I Lay Me."

hospital, post   In *A Farewell to Arms,* a "dressing station" where a survey of Frederic HENRY's wounds is done; he is then taken to a FIELD HOSPITAL for treatment.

hospital wall   The only physical setting mentioned in the "Chapter 5" vignette of *In Our Time*, against which six cabinet ministers are shot.

"Hot Bath an Adventure in Genoa, A"   Article, published in *The Toronto Daily Star* (May 2, 1922), reprinted in *Ernest Hemingway: Dateline Toronto* (1985). The headline in the *Daily Star* was "Getting a Hot Bath an Adventure in Genoa." Under the "Genoa" dateline Hemingway writes of his experience luxuriating in one of the deep Italian bathtubs at his hotel in Genoa during the economic conference he is covering when the gas heater exploded, throwing him out of the tub, "through—or over—an enameled foot tub and a chair. The proof," he says, "was furnished by an eight-inch gash in my right shin and a long, rapidly greening bruise on my left hip. . . . The bottom of the copper heater had blown out."

Hotchner, A. E. (1920–)   Aaron Edward Hotchner was a magazine writer, novelist, playwright, friend, and business partner of Hemingway during the last 13 years of Ernest's life. Hotchner adapted more than a dozen of Hemingway's works for the stage or film and wrote *Papa Hemingway: A Personal Memoir* (1966).

Following service in World War II, Hotchner tried to get a job at *Cosmopolitan* magazine, but instead of writing assignments he was given the task of trying to persuade Edna Ferber, Dorothy Parker, Somerset Maugham, William Faulkner, and Hemingway to write stories for *Cosmopolitan*. Hotchner went to Havana in September 1949 to talk Hemingway into submitting an article to *Cosmo*, which Hemingway refused to do. But because he and Hotchner developed an immediate liking for one another, Hemingway later agreed to serialize *Across the River and Into the Trees* in *Cosmopolitan*'s February to June issues (1950), before Scribner's published the novel in book form on September 7.

Hotchner was also a traveling companion during most of the summer of 1959, when Hemingway was in Spain following the bullfight circuit and preparing to write an article for *Life* magazine, which would become *The Dangerous Summer*. Hemingway invited Hotchner to Cuba that fall to help edit the manuscript. He worked closely with Hemingway, especially by urging him to cut or reword some anti-Semitic and sexually explicit language. Hotchner managed to help cut the "article" from its original 120,000 words to about 65,000, which he then carried to the *Life* editors in New York on behalf of Hemingway. Hotchner and the Scribner's editors managed to cut another 20,000 words for the three-installment publication of 45,000 words (September 5, 12, and 19, 1960).

Controversy developed over Hotchner's description of his relationship with the writer in *Papa Hemingway*. Mary Hemingway was angry, believing that Hotchner

Ernest with A. E. Hotchner in Idaho, 1958 (Copyright holder unknown; photo courtesy of the John F. Kennedy Library)

made himself out to be a closer friend than he was, and she was especially angry at Hotchner's rather vivid description of Hemingway's decline during his last six months and the suicide.

According to Albert J. DeFazio III, however, in his unpublished Ph.D. dissertation, *The HemHotch Letters: The Correspondence and Relationship of Ernest Hemingway and A.E. Hotchner*, the letters between the two men "[corroborate] many of the details of *Papa Hemingway*, substantiating Hotchner's claim that he and his subject were intimate friends." The correspondence also "authenticates Hotchner's narrative," DeFazio argues, "revealing that the men engaged in several professional endeavors: most of them involved Hotchner's acting as agent or adaptor [of Hemingway's works into films and plays] but occasionally the two edited manuscripts together."

hotel (1)   In SAN SEBASTIÁN, where, in *The Sun Also Rises*, Jake BARNES stays while trying to relax after the Fiesta SAN FERMÍN, and to which Brett ASHLEY sends a telegram asking him to rescue her in Madrid.

hotel (2)   A "nice hotel," this one in BAYONNE, France, where, in *The Sun Also Rises*, Robert COHN has gotten rooms for Jake BARNES and Bill GORTON as they travel from Paris to PAMPLONA for the fiesta. They "each had a good small room."

hotel (3) In Milan, where Frederic HENRY and Catherine BARKLEY stay for three or four hours the evening Frederic catches the midnight train back to the war front in *A Farewell to Arms*. The room they rent is "furnished in red plush" and "many mirrors," which makes Catherine feel "like a whore."

hotel (4) In LAUSANNE, Switzerland, where Frederic HENRY and Catherine BARKLEY in *A Farewell to Arms* stay for three weeks while waiting for her baby to be born. At the end of the novel, after Catherine's death, Frederic walks "back to the hotel in the rain."

hotel (5) Where David and Catherine BOURNE stay in GRAU DU ROI on their honeymoon at the beginning of *The Garden of Eden*. It has four rooms upstairs, a restaurant, and billiard tables downstairs with windows onto the canal and the lighthouse.

hotel, little Where Catherine BARKLEY and Helen FERGUSON are staying in STRESA at the beginning of book 4 of *A Farewell to Arms* and where Frederic HENRY finds them before he and Catherine take a rowboat north across Lake MAGGIORE into Switzerland.

Hotel Alfonso XIII In Sevilla, Spain, where Hemingway stayed for the bullfights during the 1959 season in preparation for writing *The Dangerous Summer*.

Hôtel Beau-Rivage In Lausanne, Switzerland, where, during the Lausanne Conference that Hemingway covered for Toronto newspapers in 1922–23, the British and Italian delegations stayed. It is mentioned in the article "The Malady of Power: A Second Serious Letter."

Hotel Carlton In Bilbao, Spain, where Hemingway stayed while covering the bullfight circuit and particularly the final "mano a mano" fight between Antonio Ordóñez and Luis Miguel Dominguín. The author was gathering material for writing *The Dangerous Summer*.

Hôtel de Crillon In Paris, at 10, place de la Concorde, originally a mansion built for aristocrats, turned into a luxury hotel in 1907. It is where, in *The Sun Also Rises*, Jake BARNES was to meet Brett ASHLEY "at five o'clock," but she forgets the appointment. She and Count MIPPIPOPOLOUS join him later at his flat. George is the barman.

The hotel is also where HARRY, in "The Snows of Kilimanjaro," remembers staying with his wife, HELEN (3). See also CAFÉ CRILLON.

Hôtel de Londres In Constantinople, where Hemingway stayed while covering the Greek retreat from the city in 1922. He reports from there to *The Toronto Daily Star*. See, for example, the article "Constantinople, Dirty White, Not Glistening and Sinister."

Hôtel du Grand Veneur Headquarters for the Allied forces in Rambouillet, France, as they move toward Paris in August 1944. See "Battle for Paris."

Hotel Florida In Madrid, it is the setting for the play, *The Fifth Column*. It is used by the main characters as headquarters for their work with the Loyalists during the Spanish civil war.

hotel garden In "Out of Season," PEDUZZI (1) works in the town hotel's garden when he isn't conning tourists into fishing for trout illegally.

Hotel Imperator In *The Garden of Eden* where David and Catherine BOURNE stay in Nîmes, France, while bicycling from Avignon to Grau du Roi.

Hôtel Jacob In Paris, on the north side of rue Jacob, between rue Saint-Benôit and rue des Saints-Pères and across from the Charity Hospital when Hemingway was there in the 1920s. Hemingway and his wife, Hadley, stayed at the Hôtel Jacob when they first arrived in Paris on December 20, 1921. It is now named Hôtel d'Angleterre.

Hotel Löwen In "An Alpine Idyll," the peasant, OLZ, who has amused the sexton but disgusted the old innkeeper in Galtur, Austria, leaves the inn after one drink and goes down the road to the Hotel Löwen.

Hotel Metropole Hotel in LOCARNO where Frederic HENRY and Catherine BARKLEY spend their first night in Switzerland in *A Farewell to Arms* after rowing from STRESA north across Lake MAGGIORE to their freedom.

Hotel Montana In Madrid, where Jake BARNES finds Brett ASHLEY in *The Sun Also Rises* after she sends a telegram to him asking him to rescue her there, because she's "rather in trouble"—meaning she has no money.

Hotel Montoya In Pamplona, Spain, where, in *The Sun Also Rises*, the novel's main characters stay during the week of the Fiesta SAN FERMÍN. According to Jake BARNES, all "the good bullfighters stayed at Montoya's hotel; that is, those with afición [passion for bullfighting] stayed there."

hotel owner The "*padrone*" at the unnamed Italian hotel where the American husband and wife are staying, in "Cat in the Rain." The wife likes the owner because of the "deadly serious way he received any complaints. . . . his dignity. . . . the way he wanted to serve her. . . . [and for] his old, heavy face and big hands." At the end of the story, after the American wife fails to find the cat out in the rain, he shows his kindness to her by sending the maid with another cat, a "big tortoise-shell cat."

Hotel Palace   In Madrid where, in *The Garden of Eden,* David and Catherine BOURNE stay and where Catherine tells him for the first time that she *has* to change, that she has to become a "boy."

Hotel Panier Fleuri   In BAYONNE, France, where, in *The Sun Also Rises,* Jake BARNES stays a night before going on to SAN SEBASTIÁN, Spain, after dropping off Bill GORTON and Mike CAMPBELL, following the Fiesta SAN FERMÍN in PAMPLONA.

Hotel Ritz   Deluxe Paris hotel at 15, place Vendôme. According to the 1924 Baedeker's guide, it had at that time 242 beds and 180 bathrooms at "from 50" francs per night. The Ritz was built by Jules Hardouin-Mansard in 1705 as a private mansion and opened as a hotel by César Ritz in 1898.

The hotel was where Hemingway went first on August 25, 1944, when he entered Paris with Allied troops during World War II. He is said to have ordered 73 dry martinis for himself and the several friends who were with him. The hotel's rue Cambon bar is now named the Hemingway Bar.

In November 1956, according to legend, the hotel's owner Charles Ritz found two trunks belonging to Hemingway in the hotel's basement. The trunks were left there in March 1928, when Hemingway and his second wife, Pauline, left Paris for Key West, Florida. The trunks contained notebooks he had kept during his early Paris years and some newspaper clippings, both of which he apparently used to remind himself of the events and people of those years as he began to write his memoir of Paris, *A Moveable Feast.*

Hotel Sanatoria Ruber   Where Hemingway stayed, along with the bullfighters, Antonio Ordóñez and Luis Miguel Dominguín, during the 1959 Spanish bullfight season. Hemingway was following the circuit in preparation for writing *The Dangerous Summer.*

Hotel Shelby   In "Fifty Grand," it's the hotel in New York, "just around the corner from the Garden" (Madison Square Garden), where the story's main character, Jack Brennan, stays the night of his fight with Jimmy Walcott.

"Hotels in Switzerland, The"   Article, published in *The Toronto Star Weekly* (March 4, 1922), reprinted in *The Wild Years* (1962), in *By-Line: Ernest Hemingway* reprinted (1967). Datelined "Les Avants, Switzerland," this article is about the fashionable hotels of Switzerland that are "scattered over the country, like bill-boards along the right of way of a railroad" and about the usually rich Americans or Canadians who frequent them. You can usually find "charming young men, with rolling white sweaters and smoothly brushed hair, who make a good living playing bridge" with rich, usually older women who deal the cards "with a flashing of platinum rings on plump fingers." The *TSW* headline read "Queer Mixture of Aristocrats, Profiteers, Sheep and Wolves in the Hotels in Switzerland."

Hotel Suecia   In Madrid, where Hemingway, his wife, Mary, and their friends stayed during the San Isidro *feria* (festival) in May 1959, when Ernest was there for the first bullfight on the summer circuit in preparation for writing *The Dangerous Summer.*

Hotel Taube   In *A Moveable Feast* Hemingway writes about staying at the Hotel Taube in SCHRUNS, Austria, during the winters of 1924–25 and 1925–26. "The rooms at the Taube were large and comfortable with big stoves, big windows and big beds with good blankets and feather coverlets. The meals were simple and excellent and the dining room and the wood-planked public bar were well heated and friendly. . . . The pension was about two dollars a day for the three of us" (Ernest, Hadley, and their son, "Bumby").

Hôtel Trois Couronnes   In "A Canary for One," it is in Vevey, Switzerland, where the story's narrator and his wife had stayed on their honeymoon.

Hôtel Voltaire   See QUAI VOLTAIRE.

Hotspur, Lord Harry   Main character in Anthony Trollope's novel *Sir Harry Hotspur of Humblethwaite* (1871). In *A Moveable Feast* Hemingway writes of a conversation he had with Ford Madox FORD that included a discussion of men they considered "gentlemen." Trollope's fictional character Hotspur was named as one of the possibilities.

house, long yellow   A "long, yellow house" is the primary symbol in the dreams of Nick ADAMS in "A Way You'll Never Be." Nick returns to the place where he was badly wounded near FOSSALTA in northern Italy, to look for the house he sees in his dreams of the trauma, but he cannot find the actual house.

house, the   Thomas HUDSON's house on Bimini in *Islands in the Stream,* built "on the highest part of the narrow tongue of land between the harbor [on North

Bimini] and the open sea. It had lasted through three hurricanes and it was built solid as a ship. . . . [O]n the ocean side you could walk out of the door and down the bluff across the white sand and into the Gulf Stream. . . . The house . . . was built into the island as though it were a part of it. . . . It was the highest thing on the island except for the long planting of tall casuarina trees that were the first thing you saw as you raised the island out of the sea."

"How Ballad Writing Affects Our Seniors"   Poem written as a senior English class assignment at Oak Park and River Forest High School. First publication was in the school's literary magazine, *Tabula* (November 1916).

"How We Came to Paris"   Article, published in *Collier's* (October 7, 1944), reprinted in *By-Line: Ernest Hemingway* (1967). This article is the fourth of six dispatches from the European sector of WORLD WAR II, all published in *Collier's,* about the movement of the French partisans, always a little ahead of the Allied armies, toward Paris. Hemingway and his jeep driver, Archie Pelkey, were with some of the French partisans, all of whom were hoping for a chance to kill Germans. Hemingway was just eager to get into Paris.

General Leclerc, commander of the Second French Armored Division, greeted some American officers at Rambouillet with "unprintable" words, which Hemingway writes "will live in my ears forever. . . . 'Buzz off, you unspeakables,' the gallant general said, in effect. . . . In war, my experience has been that a rude general is a nervous general." It was raining on the day they "advanced on Paris," and Hemingway describes his own emotions at the end of the article: "I had a funny choke in my throat and I had to clean my glasses because there now, below us, gray and always beautiful, was spread the city I love best in all the world."

"Hubby Dines First, Wifie Gets Crumbs!"   Article, published in *The Toronto Daily Star* (September 30, 1922), reprinted in *The Wild Years* (1962), reprinted in *Ernest Hemingway: Dateline Toronto* (1985). Dateline "Cologne." The "Hubby" in question are German "gentlemen"; the "wifie" are their wives. And on the crowded trains of postwar Germany it is the men who find their way to the dining car, returning later with scraps for the women.

Hubert   Young son of a Montana couple in *The Sun Also Rises* that Jake BARNES and Bill GORTON meet on the train from Paris to BAYONNE.

Hudson, Andrew   Third of Thomas HUDSON's three sons in *Islands in the Stream*. Both Andy and the second

son, David, are by Hudson's second wife. At the end of the "BIMINI" section, Hudson gets a telegram informing him that David, Andrew, and their mother have been killed in an automobile accident near Biarritz, France. Andrew "was built like a pocket battleship," like his father, only smaller. Hudson thinks of him as "bad" and refers to him as "Devil."

Hudson, David   The second of Thomas HUDSON's three sons in *Islands in the Stream*. Both David and the third son, Andrew, are by Thomas Hudson's second wife. Both boys and their mother are killed in an automobile accident near Biarritz, France. David reminds Hudson of an "otter" because of his "lovely small-animal quality." David's age is difficult to determine. He seems to be a young teenager by the way his father and his brothers treat him, but Roger DAVIS and Hudson wonder if he was driving the car when the accident occurred, and the age limit for getting a driver's license in France during the 1930s was 18, a law Hudson would have known about, having lived in Paris earlier. Why Hudson and Davis wondered if David was driving is not explained in the narration. Andrew is a year or two younger than David, and Hudson thinks Andy's mother "might let him" drive, indicating that he is underage.

Hudson, Thomas   Main character in *Islands in the Stream,* an American. He is a "well established" artist and is "respected both in Europe and in his own country" for his paintings. He works at his profession at his house on BIMINI in the novel's opening section, "Bimini," but his painting plays only a minor role in either of the other two sections, "Cuba" and "At Sea." In the opening section, however, the narrator says, "What he cared about was painting and his children and he was still in love with the first woman he had been in love with."

Half the income from the ranch in Montana that he had inherited from his grandfather provides him with enough security to be able to paint at leisure and so that he can live where he wants. According to the novel's narrator, Hudson weighs 192 pounds, is well tanned, and his "hair [is] faded and streaked from the sun." He is called "Mr. Tom" by the natives on the island but is referred to as "Thomas Hudson" by the narrator.

Hudson was divorced by his second wife, mother of David and Andrew, his youngest sons, in 1933. Near the end of the novel, Hudson is mortally wounded by one of the German submarine crew members he and his own crew have been looking for, and the narrator states that "for the first time he [Hudson] had time to realize that he was probably going to die." At the end of the novel, the reader is told that Hudson "looked across the great lagoon [to CAYO CONTRABANDO] that he was quite sure, now, he would never paint."

Hudson, Mrs. Thomas (1)   Thomas HUDSON's otherwise unnamed first wife in *Islands in the Stream*. She is the mother of "young Tom," the oldest of Hudson's three sons. She is sometimes thought of by Hudson as "Devil," but it is clear throughout the novel that he still loves her. She appears only near the end of part 2, the "Cuba" section, when she, "an actress," makes a stopover in Havana while serving with the Army USO.

Apparently she has done several films, because while she is at the FLORIDITA bar with Hudson, a Cuban customer, Mr. Rodríguez, asks for her autograph, telling her that he has seen all of her "pictures." When she meets Hudson at the bar, she doesn't know that their son has been killed in the war, and it has been three weeks since Hudson received the telegram from the war department. He tells her about young Tom's death that afternoon—after sex. He also tells her that the numbness she feels "will get number."

Hudson, Mrs. Thomas (2)   The otherwise unnamed second wife of Thomas HUDSON, the main character in *Islands in the Stream*. They were divorced in 1933. She is the mother of David and Andrew and is killed with them in an automobile accident in France. Hudson doesn't like her because she tends to make plans for their sons without consulting him, forcing him to accommodate her schedule. When he discusses the auto accident with his friend Roger Davis at the end of the "Bimini" section, Hudson wonders if David, the older of the two boys, had been driving the car or whether their mother might even have let Andrew drive.

Hudson, Tom   In *Islands in the Stream* Thomas HUDSON's oldest son by his first wife. He is referred to by the narrator and in the thinking of his father as "young Tom," and he is perhaps 16 or 17 years old in the "Bimini" section, which takes place in 1934 or 1935 (see the novel's main entry).

He becomes a flight lieutenant during World War II and is killed while parachuting into Germany, although Hudson lies to Tom's mother, an actress, when he tells her about their son's death, telling her that he was "shot down by a flak ship in a routine sweep off Abbeville" and that he had not bailed out. He is described as tall and dark and a "happy boy although in repose his face looked almost tragic." His father sometimes calls him "Schatz."

Hudson, W. H. (1841–1922)   British writer and naturalist. Several of Hemingway's fictional characters read Hudson's work. William Henry Hudson was born in Buenos Aires to American parents who had a sheep farm in Argentina. *FAR AWAY AND LONG AGO* (1918) recalls his childhood experiences roaming the pampas and studying plant and animal life there. After his parents died, he settled in England in 1869 and became a citizen in 1900. His early novels are set in the South America of his childhood and romanticize his experiences. His best-known novels are *THE PURPLE LAND* (1885) and *Green Mansions* (1904), a love story about a mysterious character named Rima, who is half human and half bird, and whose jungle upbringing has made her a part of nature itself. But Hudson is probably better known, at least in England, for his books on the English countryside: *NATURE IN DOWNLAND* (1900), *Afoot in England* (1909), *A Shepherd's Life* (1910), *Dead Man's Plack* (1920), *A Traveller in Little Things* (1921), and *A Hind in Richmond Park* (1922).

In *The Sun Also Rises* Robert COHN has read *The Purple Land* and tries to talk Jake BARNES into going to South America. Jake thinks that Cohn "took every word of 'The Purple Land' as literally as though it had been an R.G. Dun report." In a bit of sarcasm, Jake suggests they might go to British East Africa instead.

In "A Natural History of the Dead" (in *Death in the Afternoon*), Hemingway discusses Hudson's interest in natural history, especially in the "flora and fauna of Patagonia."

David BOURNE in *The Garden of Eden* reads *Far Away and Long Ago* ("Dent edition") and "saves" Hudson's *Nature in Downland* to read during the worst of times with his wife, Catherine.

Hugo's English grammar   RINALDI (2) in *A Farewell to Arms* is studying a copy of this book in order to improve his English.

"Humanity Will Not Forgive This!"   Article, published in *Pravda* (August 1, 1938). Hemingway was asked to write an article about the fascist involvement in the SPANISH CIVIL WAR for the Moscow newspaper in late July 1938. He liked the idea because he was impressed by the work of the Soviet communist officers and soldiers that he had met in the war, all fighting against the fascists of General Francisco Franco's rebel forces.

Hemingway was also angry at the American government's noninterference policy in the war and so saw an opportunity to provide the Soviets with details he felt prevented from stating in U.S. publications.

In the article Hemingway makes a passionate distinction between war and murder. War is "fought to defend your country against an invader and for your right to live and work as a free man." Murder is the indiscriminate killing of women and children, which is the strategy of the German fascists fighting for Franco. They murder, Hemingway writes, in order to "destroy the morale of the Spanish people" and to experiment with "various bombs in preparation for the war that Italy and Germany expect to make"—one of several statements in which Hemingway predicted WORLD WAR II, this one coming just 11 months before Germany invaded Poland to start the war (September 1, 1939).

The *Pravda* article was not published in English until the typescript was discovered in 1982 in the Hemingway collection at the John F. Kennedy Library in Boston. *The Toronto Daily Star* published it November 27, 1982, followed by its publication in other newspapers. It was reprinted in *The Hemingway Review* (Spring 1988), along with all 30 of Hemingway's Spanish civil war dispatches to the North American Newspaper Alliance (NANA).

Hungarians, two   Two cigar store robbers in the "Chapter 8" vignette of *In Our Time,* shot by one of the two police officers called to the scene because he thinks the robbers are Italian ("wops").

Hürtgen Forest   The WORLD WAR II battle of Hürtgen Forest along the Siegfried Line is important in *Across the River and Into the Trees,* because that's where Colonel Richard CANTWELL, the novel's main character, lost his division of troops and subsequently his rank of Brigadier General. Cantwell recalls the battle during his weekend in Venice with RENATA and on his Sunday duck-shoot.

husband   An Indian, who, in "Indian Camp," lies in the bunk above his wife, who is having a CAESARIAN SECTION without anesthetic, performed by NICK's doctor father with a jackknife. He is trapped in the room because he had cut his foot with an ax three days earlier and can't get out of bed. He slits his own throat, apparently because he can't stand to hear his wife's screams.

hut, the   Military headquarters and the setting for "A Simple Enquiry." There are at least two rooms, the main office where the "paper work" is done and the room where the major's bed is located.

Hutchinson, A. S. M. (1879–   )   Popular English novelist of the early 20th century, referred to at the beginning of *The Torrents of Spring* as a "writing fellow" and cited incorrectly by the narrator (part of Hemingway's parody in *Torrents*) as the source for the quotation, "If winter comes can spring be far behind." Hutchinson wrote a novel titled *If Winter Comes* (1921), but the quotation is from Shelley's "Ode to the West Wind." Hutchinson's full name is Arthur Stuart Menteth Hutchinson. His other books include *The Uncertain*

Trumpet (1929), *He Looked for a City* (1940), and *Bring Back the Days* (1958).

Huxley, Aldous (1894–1963)   English novelist, essayist, literary and social critic, best known for *Brave New World* (1932). In *Death in the Afternoon* Hemingway writes about Huxley's essay "Foreheads Villainous Low."

In *A Moveable Feast* Hemingway writes that Huxley was one of the novelists he read during his first years in Paris, borrowing the books from Sylvia Beach's "library" at SHAKESPEARE AND COMPANY (1).

hydro-electric projects   Along the PIAVE RIVER, seen by Richard CANTWELL as he drives toward VENICE at the beginning of *Across the River and Into the Trees.* They were not there, he remembers, during World War I when he was wounded.

hyena, the   Nocturnal, doglike mammal, with front legs shorter than its hind ones, with a coarse coat, a sloping back, and large teeth. It feeds on carrion and can crush bones with its teeth and jaws. Hyenas range over most of Africa, Asia Minor, and India. The African hyenas, the ones in Hemingway's works, are spotted and about two and one-half feet high at the shoulders; they are the largest and boldest of the species.

The hyena is one of the animals shot by Hemingway in part 2 of *Green Hills of Africa:* "Highly humorous was the hyena obscenely loping, full belly dragging, at daylight on the plain, who, shot from the stern, skittered on into speed to tumble end over end."

In "The Snows of Kilimanjaro," the hyena is the animal that HARRY hears, and it represents death for him. When he feels death approaching, he tells his wife, HELEN (2), "Never believe any of that about a scythe and a skull. . . . It can be two bicycle policemen as easily, or be a bird. Or it can have a wide snout like a hyena." As it gets closer to the camp, where Harry lies on his cot with a gangrenous right leg and waiting for a plane to arrive to take him out to Nairobi and a hospital, he hears the hyena more and more, until it "stopped whimpering in the night and started to make a strange, human, almost crying sound."

Harry's wife, Helen, hears it, but "[s]he did not wake." And in the story's last paragraph the hyena makes the "same strange noise that had [finally] awakened her." She looks over at Harry on his cot and realizes that he is dead.

I (1) Unnamed narrator of "The Revolutionist." A communist himself, he helps the "very shy and quite young" communist revolutionist of the story's title when he meets him in Bologna, Italy. He listens to the revolutionist's story of suffering at the hands of "the Whites in Budapest" and of his travels around Italy, viewing the paintings of, particularly, Giotto, Masaccio, and Piero della Francesca.

The narrator tells the reader twice that the revolutionist does not like the paintings of MANTEGNA. He puts him on a train to Milan, where he will then go to Aosta and walk across the pass to Switzerland. The narrator later hears that he had been picked up by the Swiss police and is in a jail near Sion.

I (2) Unnamed soldier/narrator of the "Chapter 3" vignette of *In Our Time*. He and "young Buckley" shoot Germans as they try to climb over a garden wall.

I (3) Unnamed narrator of the "Chapter 11" vignette of *In Our Time* (1925). He sees a defeated bullfighter at a café after the bullfighter has been disgraced in the ring. The bullfighter says, "I am not really a good bull fighter."

I (4) Unnamed narrator of the "Chapter 13" vignette of *In Our Time* (1925). He tries to stop the bullfighter LUIS from drinking and dancing with the riau-riau dancers so he can prepare for the bullfights that afternoon. The third bullfighter on the card, MAERA, complains to the narrator that they will have to kill Luis's bulls "after he gets a COGIDA," that is, after he is gored by one of his bulls.

I (5) Unnamed narrator of "A Canary for One." He describes the caged nature of the life of the AMERICAN LADY, who happens to be in the same compartment with him and his wife for their train trip through Marseilles and Avignon to Paris. Because he uses the term "American Lady" 23 times in the fairly short story, the reader may infer the narrator's sarcastic attitude toward such women. But he too is trapped, as readers learn only in the story's last line when he says that he and his wife "were returning to Paris to set up separate residences."

I (6) Unnamed narrator of "An Alpine Idyll." He and his skiing friend, John, have just come down out of the mountains in southwest Austria from a month of spring skiing. It is now May. They stop at an inn in Galtur and are entertained by an "Alpine idyll," a story about a peasant, OLZ, who has just that day buried his wife; she had been dead since December.

He couldn't bring her down to the parish church for burial because he lives too high in the mountains and so had to wait until the snow melted. He put her in the wood shed, but when she stiffened he stood her against the wall and, when he entered the shed at night to get wood, he hung his lantern from her mouth. By the time he got her down from the mountain for burial, her face was so disfigured the priest didn't want to bury her. The sexton who tells the story is "amused," while the innkeeper is "disgusted." The narrator's reaction to the story is unclear, except that at the end of the telling both he and his friend go back to their dinner.

I (7) Unnamed narrator of "In Another Country." He is an American who joined the Italian army during WORLD WAR I and is badly wounded. He is skeptical of the treatment offered to him in a Milan hospital by the army doctor and says of his wound that his knee won't bend and that "the leg [drops] straight from the knee to the ankle without a calf."

The doctor has him on a machine that moves his legs awkwardly, "as in riding a tricycle," but the doctor promises him that he will play football again. An Italian major, a champion fencer also wounded in the war who has "a little hand like a baby's," is also being treated on one of the doctor's machines. The doctor shows him before-and-after photographs of other withered hands, but the major is not encouraged. Later, after he learns about the sudden death of his young wife, he becomes depressed and the doctor's photographs mean even less to him.

The narrator realizes that he, himself, is a foreigner, struggling with the language and that he is something of an intruder "in another country." He has the same medals as other wounded soldiers, but his wound is not as serious as most of the others. Although others were "polite" about his medals, they had read the papers explaining them, and they knew that what the "beautiful language" really said was that he has been given the medals because he is an American.

I (8)   Unnamed narrator and one of the two main characters in "Che Ti Dice La Patria?" He and his traveling companion, GUY, spend 10 days in April 1927 driving around northern Italy in a Ford coupé, trying to discover "how things [are] with the country or the people." What they discover is that fascism under MUSSOLINI is full of confidence, even arrogance, but dirt poor.

The narrator's age is not given, but he says that Guy is 38, so it's fair to assume that the narrator is about the same age. He tells the waitress/prostitute at the restaurant in Spezia that they are South Germans, but it isn't clear that he's telling her the truth. When she says she speaks German, the conversation is apparently still carried on in broken Italian.

I (9)   Unnamed narrator of "Wine of Wyoming." He is an American writer, who, with his wife, is staying in a hotel in a small Wyoming town to do some hunting in the fall of 1928. They are friends with Sam and Marie FONTAN, a French couple who make their own wine and beer, in spite of Prohibition.

The narrator isn't as aware as the story's readers of just how much cultural difference there is between the two Americans and their French friends, especially when the Americans fail to show up for a dinner in their honor that Sam and Marie have planned.

I (10)   Unnamed narrator of "After the Storm." He describes his attempts to dive for an unidentified treasure on an ocean liner that had sunk during a hurricane. The liner was on its side only about 12 feet under the surface, between the Rebecca Light and the Dry Tortugas islands, about 65 miles west of Key West, Florida.

He is the first person to find the liner, but he can't break through the glass of the nearest porthole in order to get inside. He sees a woman "with her hair floating all out" and "rings on one of her hands," but he is frustrated in his attempts to break into the ship. The police place him under a $500 bond for a fight he had had earlier, just after the storm, and by the time he settles the problem with the police and gets back to the sunken liner, the "Greeks had blown her open and cleaned her out." He says, at the end of the story: "First there was the birds, then me, then the Greeks, and even the birds got more out of her [the ship] than I did."

I (11)   In "A Natural History of the Dead," the "I" is either Hemingway himself if the work is read as a separately titled part of chapter 12 in *Death in the Afternoon,* or as an unnamed narrator character if it is read as a

short story in *Winner Take Nothing.* See "Natural History of the Dead, A."

I (12)   Seventeen-year-old narrator of "The Light of the World." He is unnamed, but it is generally assumed that this is a Nick ADAMS story.

He and his 19-year-old friend TOM (1) are wandering through northern Michigan and enter an unidentified town—the setting for the story—entering "at one end and . . . out the other." They get thrown out of a bar, because Tom insults the bartender, and then, at the railway station they meet "five whores waiting for the train to come in, and six white men and four Indians." Three of the whores are "big," Alice weighing, the narrator guesses, 350 pounds.

He listens to the argument between Alice and Peroxide, one of the other whores, over which one had loved Steve Ketchel better. The narrator is enamored of Alice, and at the end of the story, he notices her smile and states that "she had about the prettiest face I ever saw. . . . But my God she was big." Tom, who has seen him looking at Alice, suggests it's time to go.

I (13)   Unnamed narrator of "A Day's Wait." He tells about his son's confusion over the difference between Celsius and Fahrenheit thermometers, the son thinking that because he has a temperature of 102° he is going to die.

I (14)   Unnamed narrator of *Green Hills of Africa.* Although it is clearly Hemingway himself narrating the events of the safari that he and his second wife, Pauline, took to East Africa in late 1933 and 1934, neither he nor Pauline is named in the book. She is referred to only as P.O.M., "Poor Old Mama."

I (15)   Unnamed narrator of "Old Man at the Bridge." He is a soldier on the Republican side in the Spanish civil war, and it is his assignment to cross a pontoon bridge over the EBRO RIVER, near TORTOSA, in northeast Spain and explore the bridgehead in order to find out how far the FASCISTS have advanced.

He returns from his reconnaissance mission to find an OLD MAN (7) still at the bridge, confused by the chaos of the civilian retreat, and worried about the animals in his care—two goats, a cat, and four pairs of pigeons. The narrator tells of trying to get the old man to cross the bridge and catch a ride toward Tortosa and Barcelona, but the old man has walked more than seven miles already and doesn't think he can go any farther.

At the end of the story the narrator realizes there's nothing he can do about the old man and that the overcast sky, which may keep the enemy planes from bombing the bridge, and the "fact that cats know how to look after themselves" was the only luck left for the old man.

I.B.   See INTERNATIONAL BRIGADES.

Ibarruri, Dolores   See La PASIONARIA.

iceberg principle   See THEORY OF OMISSION.

iced tea   Although the drink Thomas HUDSON most often chooses in the "Bimini" section of *Islands in the Stream* is GIN AND TONIC, in the "At Sea" section he drinks nothing stronger than iced tea until, during the most intense moments of his search for a German submarine crew, he has some rum.

Ida   BILL (1)'s girlfriend, mentioned by him in "The Three-Day Blow." She is beneath Bill's social class, as is Nick's girlfriend MARGE, whom Nick has just dumped. Bill tells Nick that he's better off without her, because she needs to "marry somebody of her own sort."

"[If my Valentine you won't be . . .]"   First line of a two-line poem written in 1956 and first published in Mary Hemingway's *How It Was* (1976).

Ignacio (1)   One of EL SORDO's men, killed, along with El Sordo, Joaquin, and another unnamed guerrilla fighter in *For Whom the Bell Tolls*. HEINKEL ONE-ELEVEN BOMBERS attack them after they are surrounded on top of a hill.

Ignacio (2)   One of three waiters, the "tall" one, at the PENSION LUARCA where PACO (2) works, in "The Capital of the World." Ignacio attends a meeting of the revolutionary anarcho-syndicalists on the night that Paco is killed practicing to be a matador.

"I Guess Everything Reminds You of Something"   Unfinished story about a father's attempt to teach his son how to write and discovering that his son had won a prize for a story he had plagiarized. "I Guess Everything Reminds You of Something" was first published in *The Complete Short Stories of Ernest Hemingway* (1987).

Ile de la Cité   In *A Moveable Feast* Hemingway writes that from the east end of the boulevard Saint-Germain in Paris you could go over to the Ile Saint-Louis and enjoy walking its narrow streets or you could walk west along the Left Bank quais and enjoy looking across at the island and then at Notre-Dame and the Ile de la Cité.

Ile de France   Luxury French liner, which made her maiden voyage in 1927 and on which Ernest and Pauline Hemingway sailed back to the United States after their African safari in 1934. Ernest and his fourth wife, Mary, also sailed to Europe on the *Ile de France* in 1949, returning on the same ship in 1950.

In *Islands in the Stream* it is the ship on which Thomas HUDSON travels to France for the funeral of his sons David and Andrew and their mother.

Ile Saint-Louis   Island in the Seine River, the ancient heart of Paris. In *The Sun Also Rises* Jake BARNES and Bill GORTON eat on the island at Madame LECOMTE's RESTAURANT, Au Rendez-vous des Mariniers, 33, quai d'Anjou. After dinner they stop on a bridge and admire the view of the Cathedral of Notre-Dame.

"I Like Americans"   A short piece published in *The Toronto Star Weekly* (December 15, 1923), reprinted in *Ernest Hemingway: Dateline Toronto* (1985) and in *88 Poems* (1979). Thirty-two one-sentence reasons for liking Americans ("They do not brag about how they take baths"). It is signed "A Foreigner."

"I Like Canadians"   A short piece published in *The Toronto Star Weekly* (December 15, 1923), reprinted in *Ernest Hemingway: Dateline Toronto* (1985) and in *88 Poems* (1979). Thirty-nine one-sentence reasons for liking Canadians ("They are so unlike Americans"). It is signed "A Foreigner."

illustrators   In *The Garden of Eden* Catherine BOURNE is thinking about illustrators for the story David is writing about their marriage and their MÉNAGE-A-TROIS with MARITA. Catherine suggests for illustrators Marie LAURENCIN, Jules PASCIN, Amdré DERAIN, Raoul DUFY, and Pablo PICASSO.

imbarcadero   The place in Venice from which people catch water buses and other public transportation to other points in the city, mentioned in *Across the River and Into the Trees*.

"I'm off'n wild wimmen . . ."   First line of a poem written around 1922 and first published in *88 Poems* (1979).

Imola   Town in north-central Italy, one of the places to which the two main characters travel in "Che Ti Dice La Patria?" (What do you hear from home?).

impala   An African antelope, the male of which has ringed, lyre-shaped horns and which is known for its leaping ability. It is small, about two and one-half feet high at the shoulder and about five and one-half feet long, half the size of another antelope, the ELAND.

In "The Short Happy Life of Francis Macomber," MACOMBER kills an old ram impala "with a very creditable shot" the afternoon of the morning he runs like a coward from an attacking lion.

The impala is among animals hunted in *Green Hills of Africa*. Hemingway sometimes spelled it "impalla."

impotence A man's inability to have sexual intercourse because of an inability to have or sustain an erection. It can be caused by several factors, including anemia or other debilitating diseases, or chronic poisoning, as in alcoholism and drug addiction. There are four principal types of impotence: organic, endocrine, neurologic, and psychic. Organic impotence is most often due to anatomical defects, but can be caused by injury. Endocrine is most often caused by diseases of the endocrine system, but it too can be caused by injury. Neurologic impotence results from organic disease of the nervous system. Psychic impotence is due solely to psychological problems—fear or hostility, for example.

In *The Sun Also Rises* Jake BARNES's denial of impotence to his friend Bill GORTON makes unclear the exact nature of the wound that Jake received in WORLD WAR I that keeps him from consummating his love for Brett ASHLEY. But since the wound occurred at least seven years before the events of the novel, the psychic factors cannot be dismissed.

There is some evidence that Jake gets physical satisfaction from Brett but the satisfaction could be sexual manipulation of some kind or merely a backrub.

Jake's attempt to cope with the war wound that has caused his impotence is thematic in *The Sun Also Rises* and parallels the general impotence of the LOST GENERATION expatriate Americans estranged from their country because of its indifference to the wounding effects of the war. Jake's efforts to transcend his loss of potency provides readers with one of the best examples of a Hemingway character attempting to cope with life the best way he can. Jake says, "I did not care what it [the world] was all about. All I wanted to know was how to live in it."

inaccrochable A French word Gertrude STEIN used to describe why Hemingway could not publish his short story "Up in Michigan." He writes at some length of the incident in *A Moveable Feast* and defines the term by saying that "it is like a picture that a painter paints and then . . . cannot hang . . . when he has a show and nobody will buy it because they cannot hang it either." *Accrocher* means "to hang upon a hook."

"Up in Michigan" involves the drunken seduction/date rape of the main character, and it is that aspect, apparently (no details are given), that Stein thought could not be published. She tells him he should not write stories that are *inaccrochable*.

"[In a magazine . . .]" First line of a poem out of Hemingway's WORLD WAR I experiences, written about 1920 and first published in *88 Poems* (1979).

"In Another Country" The title of this short story is taken from Marlowe's *The Jew of Malta* quoted by T. S.

Eliot as an epigraph to "Portrait of a Lady:" "Thou hast committed—/Fornication: but that was in another country,/ And besides, the wench is dead."

Much scholarly speculation has focused on the "wench," some suggesting a thematic relationship to other Hemingway stories or to *A Farewell to Arms*. But with the possible exception of the Cova Girls, who are declared by the narrator to be "very patriotic," there are no "wenches" in "In Another Country." (See GIRLS, COVA.)

The title suggests, on the other hand, several ideas that work well within this story. The narrator, identified only as "I," is an American fighting with the Italian army during World War I. He has a severe knee wound and is in a Milan hospital getting treatment on a machine that bends the knee "as in riding a tricycle." He is under the supervision of an army doctor who seems to be the only one who believes in the machines. The narrator is skeptical, and so is a "friend" of his, an Italian major, a champion fencer, whose hand is crippled and who goes each day to put his hand in a machine that moves it back and forth and which, the doctor believes, will return the hand to normal use.

At the end of the story, the major gets angry at the narrator for saying that he hopes to get married after the war, the major arguing that a soldier "should not place himself in a position to lose [a wife]." He later apologizes and explains that his own wife has just died. The doctor tells the narrator that she was young and that the death was unexpected. The doctor continues to encourage the major about the healing of his hand, but the photographs of hands supposedly healed by the machines "did not make much difference to the major because he only looked out of the window."

The narrator has also established a kind of camaraderie with four other "boys," all about the narrator's age and all wounded and using the machines. They walk together from the hospital to the CAFÉ COVA through the communist quarter, where some of the "toughs" of Milan live and catcall to them as they pass. All have medals of various sorts for their valor, but they are wounded psychologically as well as physically. They "were all a little detached, and there was nothing that held us together except that we met every afternoon at the hospital"—as well as the idea, which also afforded them some immunity from intimidation by the toughs, that something had happened to them that others did not understand.

Although the focus of the story seems to be on the major, with his wounded hand and his skepticism about the machines, it is the narrator who is most affected by the major's depression. The narrator is a foreigner "in another country," struggling with the language and with his sense of being an intruder. He has the same medals as the other wounded soldiers, but his wound is not as serious as that of the major or of one of the four "boys"—who has no nose and so hides his face behind a black silk handkerchief. Although the boys were "polite" about his medals, they had read the papers explaining them, and they knew that all that the "beautiful language" really said was that he had been given the medals because he was an American.

"In Another Country" was first published in *Scribner's Magazine* (April 1927) and reprinted in *Men Without Women* (1927).

Index, The   In "A Man of the World," a saloon in a small western U.S. town named Jessup. It is also the name of a mountain, visible from Lawrence Nordquist's L-Bar-T Ranch in Wyoming, near Cooke City, Montana, where Hemingway spent several summers during the 1930s hunting, fishing, and writing.

"Indian Camp"   In this short story the main character is NICK, whose father, a doctor, has been sent for by Indians from a camp across the lake to help an Indian woman have a baby. The doctor takes along Nick, a boy of perhaps eight or nine, and Nick's Uncle GEORGE (1).

The young woman has been in labor for two days, and the doctor tries to explain to Nick what is happening. He is going to have to perform a CAESARIAN SECTION without an anesthetic. He tells Nick that her screaming is "unimportant." Nick's father washes his hands, and three Indians and Uncle George hold the woman still. She lies in a lower bunk, while her husband, who had cut his foot badly three days before, is in the upper bunk. When the operation begins he rolls "over against the wall."

It's a breech birth, the operation is performed with a "jack-knife," the baby boy is born, and the doctor is elated by the success of the operation. He sews the incision with gut leaders from his fishing line. Nick watches some of the operation but not the sewing of the incision. The narrator says that by then Nick's "curiosity had been gone for a long time."

When Nick and the doctor check to see about the father in the upper bunk, they discover that the Indian husband has cut his own throat "from ear to ear." Nick sees the blood and realizes what has happened. On the way back to the rowboat, his father apologizes: "'I'm terribly sorry I brought you along, Nickie,' . . . all his post-operative exhilaration gone." Nick, however, is full of questions: about the difficulty of women having babies, about why the father killed himself, about where Uncle George disappeared to (he has evidently gone off to get drunk), and, most important, about whether dying is easy. Nick's father tells him that he thinks dying is "pretty easy. . . . It all depends." And the story ends with Nick feeling "quite sure that he would never die."

"Indian Camp" was first published in *transatlantic review* (April 1924) and reprinted in *In Our Time* (1925).

Indian Club   In *The Torrents of Spring*, two Indians take Yogi JOHNSON to a stable in PETOSKEY, where a ladder leads to the club "upstairs." In the club's "committee room" there are framed autographed photographs of Chief Bender, Francis Parkman, D. H. Lawrence, Chief Meyers, Stewart Edward White, Mary Austin, Jim Thorpe, General Custer, Glenn Warner, Mabel Dodge, and a "full-length oil painting of Henry Wadsworth Longfellow." The significance of the photographs is obscure but probably tied to the overall parody of the novel.

Indians (1)   Hemingway refers to the Indians in *The Torrents of Spring* as the "only real Americans."

Indians (2)   Carl Garner shows prejudice in "Ten Indians" when he tells NICK that he ought to know skunks because he has "an Indian girl" and they "smell about the same." Mrs. Garner tries to squash the remark by telling him to "[s]top talking that way," but her husband, Joe, laughs too.

Indians, four   Characters at the train station in "The Light of the World." The "four" Indians become inexplicably "three" late in the story, and it turns out that Scribner's editors overlooked Hemingway's handwritten correction in the typescript that changes four to three, and the numbers remain "four" and "three" even in the most recent publication of the story in *The Complete Short Stories of Ernest Hemingway* (1987).

Indians, two (1)   In *The Torrents of Spring*, the two otherwise unnamed Indians, one "little" one "big," are friends of Yogi JOHNSON, one of the main characters. Both Indians say they fought in World War I and claim to have won medals: the "little" Indian received the V.C. and the other won the D.S.O. and the M.C. "with bar"; he was a major in the Fourth C.M.R.'s. Both Indians also claim to have attended Carlisle College.

They exaggerate everything they say about themselves, just as Johnson exaggerates his own war record. The "big" Indian and spokesman for the two tells Johnson that the "little" Indian had both arms and both legs shot off "at YPRES." At the pool hall, Johnson notices the "little" Indian's two artificial arms, and later, as they climb the ladder to the INDIAN CLUB, he notices the squeaking of the artificial legs.

Johnson is treated well at the club, but the two Indians are thrown out, through the trapdoor onto the straw on the stable floor below. They are thrown out because they are "woods Indians," whereas the other Indians in the bar are "town Indians." The "little Indian" cries because he has lost one of his artificial arms. The Indians tell Johnson earlier in the novel that they are going to PETOSKEY to join the SALVATION ARMY. At the end of the novel, as Yogi walks up the railroad tracks with a naked "squaw," the wife of the "little" Indian, the two Indians are seen following not far behind.

Indians, two (2)   In "Indian Camp," one of the two Indians takes NICK and his doctor father in one rowboat, and the other takes Nick's Uncle George in a second boat across the lake to their camp, where a woman is going through a difficult labor.

"Indians Moved Away, The"   Unfinished story about NICK's memory of the Indians who lived near his Grandpa Bacon's farm on the road to PETOSKEY (Michigan). It was published in Philip Young's *The Nick Adams Stories* (1972).

Indian woman, young   A woman experiencing difficult labor, in "Indian Camp." NICK's doctor father performs a CAESARIAN SECTION on her, using a jack-knife and no anesthetic. Her baby boy is born without other complications, but the woman's husband, who can't stand her screaming, slits his own throat in the bunk above.

indoor baseball   Softball played indoors, a game popular in the United States at the end of the 19th century. In "Soldier's Home," it is the game Harold KREBS's sister HELEN (1) plays and invites Harold to watch.

"Indoor Fishing"   Article, published in *The Toronto Star Weekly* (November 20, 1920), reprinted in *The Wild Years* (1962), reprinted in *Ernest Hemingway: Dateline Toronto* (1985). The headline in the *Star Weekly* was "A Fight With a 20-Pound Trout." Indoor fishing clubs are popular in Toronto, according to Hemingway; the indoor fishermen have an easier time catching big fish than outdoor fishermen. "It is cheaper and the fish run bigger." The difference is that the fishermen can't then brag about it to their friends, because they have to throw the fish back into the water.

"Inexpressible, The"   Poem in imitation of James Whitcomb Riley, first published in the Oak Park and River Forest High School literary magazine, *Tabula* (March 1917).

"Inflation and the German Mark"   Article, with the byline "John Hadley," a pseudonym in honor of Hemingway's son, who was born in Toronto in October 1923. The article was published in *The Toronto Star Weekly* (December 8, 1923), reprinted in *The Wild Years* (1962), and in *By-Line: Ernest Hemingway* (1967).

The article is about "the Russian ruble, the Austrian kronen and German mark, not worth the paper they are printed on, making a last stand as serious money in Toronto's Ward." A "barker" on a Toronto street corner is trying to convince people that money in those coun-

tries is "bound to come back," and he's offering to sell what he has of it cheap. The *TSW* headline read "German Marks Make Last Stand As Real Money in Toronto's 'Ward.'"

Ingersoll, Ralph   Editor of the newspaper *PM*, which published seven dispatches by Hemingway in 1941 on the Sino-Japanese war. Ingersoll wrote an introductory article for the series of dispatches titled "Hemingway Interviewed by Ralph Ingersoll" (June 9, 1941). A headnote over the reprinted dispatch in *By-Line: Ernest Hemingway*, states that the interview was held in a New York hotel just after Hemingway had returned from an assignment given to him by Ingersoll to "go to the Far East to see for himself whether or not war with Japan was inevitable." Hemingway edited the interview himself.

"In Love and War" (film)   New Line Cinema production, released in the spring of 1997; produced by Richard Attenborough and Dimitri Villard; directed by Attenborough; screenplay by Allan Scott, Clancy Sigal, and Anna Hamilton Phelan, based on the book *Hemingway in Love and War* by Henry S. Villard and James Nagel; music composed by George Fenton, costumes by Penny Rose.

Cast: Chris O'Donnell (Ernest Hemingway), Sandra Bullock (Agnes Von Kurowsky), MacKenzie Astin (Henry Villard), Margot Steinberg (Mabel "Rosie" Rose), Ingrid Lacey (Elsie "Mac" MacDonald), Tara Hugo (Katherine "Gumshoe" De Long), Ian Kelly (Jimmy McBride), Colin Stinton (Tom Burnside), Vincenzo Nicoli (Enrico Biscaglia), Rocco Quarzell (Roberto Zardini), and Emilio Bonucci (Domenico Caracciolo).

inn, an (1)   In "Cross-Country Snow," Nick ADAMS and GEORGE (4) ski down to a "long, low-eaved, weather-beaten building," an inn, where they have a bottle of Sion wine and apple strudel.

inn, an (2)   In the trees at the BAINS DE L'ALLIAZ where Frederic HENRY and Catherine BARKLEY stop for *GLÜHWEIN* on their winter walk from MONTREUX in *A Farewell to Arms*.

innkeeper   Character in "An Alpine Idyll." He's "a tall man and old," and he's "disgusted" by a story the sexton tells about a peasant who, during the past winter, hung a lantern from his dead wife's mouth every night when he went to the shed for wood. He was waiting for the snow to melt so he could bring her down to town for burial. Twice the innkeeper says, in disgust, these "peasants are beasts."

in our time   Volume of 18 short, untitled but numbered "chapters" or vignettes, published in the spring of 1924.

Two of the vignettes appeared as short stories in *In Our Time* (1925): "chapter 11" became "The Revolutionist" and "chapter 10" became "A Very Short Story." The other sixteen "chapters" of *in our time* were used as interchapters in the 1925 book, each but the last one, titled "L'Envoi," appearing between two short stories.

in our time was published in Paris by William Bird at Three Mountains Press in a first edition of 170 copies.

In Our Time Volume of 16 short stories alternating with 16 of the short "chapters" (vignettes) from *in our time* (1924), and ending with "L'Envoi."

In Our Time was published in New York by Boni & Liveright on October 5, 1925, in a first edition of 1,335 copies at $2 each.

"Interclass Meet Saturday" Article for Oak Park and River Forest High School newspaper, *The Trapeze* (February 2, 1917), reprinted in *Hemingway at Oak Park High: The High School Writings of Ernest Hemingway, 1916–1917* (1993).

interior monologue A technique writers sometimes use when they want the reader to know the unspoken thoughts of a character. There are two forms of interior monologue: direct, in which a stream of thought and/or feeling is expressed directly from a character to the reader; and indirect, in which the narrator presents to the reader the thoughts and/or feelings of a character.

Hemingway uses interior monologue in several works of fiction. It is used in "The Snows of Kilimanjaro," for example, to allow the reader into the consciousness of HARRY, the story's main character. He remembers all the experiences he has stored up to write about, but he will not get a chance to write them now, because he is dying. See the story's five memory flashbacks in "The Snows of Kilimanjaro" entry.

International Brigades Non-Spanish volunteers fighting on the side of the Republic in the Spanish civil war (July 1936–March 1939). More than 35,000 men and a few women from 50 countries participated as soldiers, including 10,000 French, 5,000 Germans and Austrians, 5,000 Poles, 3,400 Italians, 3,000 Americans, 2,000 British, and 1,200 Canadians.

About 3,000 foreigners arrived in Spain during August and September 1936, but by autumn an underground railway, provided mostly by communist parties, began carrying foreign fighters into Spain. Most of the volunteers were not communists but wanted to stop the spread of right-wing parties everywhere, and they hoped that by stopping General Francisco FRANCO and his revolutionary rebel following in Spain they would be able to stop similar movements in their own countries.

In the spring of 1937 the International Brigades began organizing on the basis of native languages. The 11th Brigade was made up of Northern Europeans (Germans, Austrians, Scandinavians, and Dutch); the 12th IB was Italian; the 13th Slavic; the 14th, French and Belgian; and the 15th, English. The IB headquarters were at Albacete, a town in southeast Spain, about 120 miles from Madrid. Overseeing the activities of the brigades was André MARTY, a French military hero, Longo ("Gallo"), and Giuseppe ("Nicoletti") di Vittorio of Italy. Each brigade had four battalions of about 700 men each. When the losses became significant, replacements tended to be Spanish.

There were two brigades of Americans—the Abraham Lincoln and George Washington, both training at Villanueva de la Jara, near Albacete. There was a Mackenzie-Papineau Battalion of Canadians within the 15th Brigade, half of whom were killed by the end of the war. The two U.S. brigades lost 50 percent of their troops at the Battle of Brunete in July 1937, after which both units combined into the Abraham Lincoln Brigade. See also SPANISH CIVIL WAR.

"Internationale" A revolutionary anthem, written by Pierre Degeyter and first sung during the French Revolutionary War, urging workers to fight. Hemingway heard it sung in Madrid during the Spanish civil war (1936–39). In his play, *The Fifth Column,* it is sung by 25 Loyalist comrades waiting downstairs in the Hotel Florida in act 2, scene 3.

"L'Internationale" was sung in Lawrence, Massachusetts, during a strike by workers at the Everett Cotton Mill on January 11, 1912. It was sung in 11 different languages by immigrants working for $2 a day, according to Pete Seeger and Bob Reiser in their book, *Carry On!: A History in Song and Picture of the Working Men and Women of America* (1985). Although Seeger says that it still sounds best in French, the first four lines in English read: "Arise, you prisoners of starvation!/ Arise, you wretched of the earth!/ For justice thunders condemnation./ A better world's in birth."

"Interpreters Make or Mar Speeches at Genoa Parley" Article, published in *The Toronto Star* (April 15, 1922), reprinted in William Burrill's *Hemingway: The Toronto Years* (1994). The article was "discovered" by Burrill in the Hemingway Collection at the John F. Kennedy Library in Boston. Dateline "Genoa." It is about the importance of the role the translators play at the International Economic Conference. Hemingway also mentions the hissed s's of TCHITCHERIN, head of the Russian delegation. "His voice is the most peculiar I have ever heard . . . queer, metallic, like sandpaper, running through all the diction."

Intrepid Voyagers Some of the "haves" in the novel *To Have and Have Not.* These characters are Esthonian tourists sailing around the world in various boats "between 28 and 36 feet long and sending back articles to Esthonian newspapers" under the heading "Sagas of Our Intrepid Voyagers." They are mentioned with sarcasm in the novel, as are most of the "haves."

Irati River   A trout stream in northern Spain in which, in *The Sun Also Rises,* Jake BARNES and Bill GORTON fish at least twice during their five-day stay in BURGUETE before they return to Pamplona for the Fiesta SAN FERMÍN. Their English friend Wilson-Harris fishes with them.

There is a bit of ambiguity concerning the Irati, because Jake tells Bill that the Irati is "too far to go and fish and come back the same day, comfortably." The first fishing, then, identified takes place at the Rio de la Fabrica, a stream much closer to Burguete than is the Irati. At the end of the chapter (12), however, Jake says that they went "twice to the Irati River." Unless Hemingway meant to indicate that they spent the night, he probably had the Fabrica River in mind as the location for all of their fishing.

Ireland, Archbishop (1838–1918)   American Roman Catholic prelate, first archbishop of St. Paul's Cathedral in New York, he is mentioned in *A Farewell to Arms* in which Frederic HENRY talks about him with the PRIEST (2).

Irish setter   Dog owned by the unnamed narrator of "A Day's Wait." The narrator hunts quail with the setter while waiting for his son's temperature to drop.

Irish whisky   In "The Three-Day Blow," the liquor that NICK and BILL (1) drink while discussing baseball, literature, and getting drunk.

It is used to make whisky sours in *Islands in the Stream.*

irony and pity   Words to a song Bill GORTON makes up and sings to Jake BARNES in their hotel room in BURGUETE in *The Sun Also Rises.* They are sung, according to Jake, to the tune of "THE BELLS ARE RINGING FOR ME AND MY GAL." In this context "irony and pity" connect to the novel's theme of impotence. Gorton claims Barnes is an "expatriate" and tells him that one group of women "claims [he's] impotent." Jake answers, "No, . . . I just had an accident." See IMPOTENCE.

Irun   An "ancient Spanish town." It is just across the border from HENDAYE, France, on the Bay of Biscay, from which David and Catherine BOURNE in *The Garden of Eden* can see the "green hills [of Irun] across the bay and . . . the lighthouse."

Irydia IV   Boat owned by EDDIE, "a professional son-in-law of the very rich," one of the "haves" in *To Have and Have Not.* Eddie is on board with his mistress, Dorothy

HOLLIS, the wife "of that highly paid Hollywood director, John Hollis."

Isaacs Light   Fishing area to which Thomas HUDSON takes his sons on the day that David catches a thousand-pound broadbill in *Islands in the Stream.* The Great Isaac reef is located about 30 miles north of Alice Town, North Bimini Island.

Islands in the Stream   Eighth and longest of the nine published novels Hemingway wrote. It was the first of two published after his death. The novel has a headnote written by Mary Hemingway, Ernest's fourth wife, who, with Charles Scribner Jr., did the "preparing" for publication of *Islands in the Stream.* In the headnote she says that in spite of "some cuts," the book is "all Ernest's. We have added nothing to it."

Islands received little critical acclaim, but it was on *The New York Times* best-seller list for 24 weeks. Apparently, Hemingway's original plan was to include most or all of the novel in a three-volume novel of the sea, the air, and the land. *The Old Man and the Sea* was to be the first of a three-part novel of the sea, and manuscripts for which he used "Sea Novel" as a working title were to be included in parts two and three; those manuscripts were put together as *Islands in the Stream.* The "air" and "land" novels were never written.

Islands is, therefore, somewhat fragmented, divided as it is into three unequal parts, each having little to do with the others. Thomas HUDSON is introduced as the main character in each part as if it were a separate story. Characters named in part 1 ("Bimini")—particularly Hudson's three sons—are mentioned in part 2 ("Cuba") and part 3 ("At Sea") but only as sad memories, since two of the sons are killed in a car accident at the end of part 1 and the oldest son is dead at the beginning of part 2 when it is reported that his plane was shot down in World War II. Rogert DAVIS, one of Hudson's good friends in part 1, is not mentioned again, nor are EDDY (3) and JOSEPH, both of whom play roles in the "Bimini" section significant enough to be remembered even nine or 10 years later in parts 2 and 3 ("Cuba" and "At Sea").

There is a 25-page essay on cats at the beginning of the "Cuba" section, about the 11 cats that Hudson has acquired, which live with him on his "farm" outside of Havana. Each cat is described, personalized, and clearly loved by Hudson, but the cats have little relevance to the rest of the story—with perhaps one, important, exception. Because of the death of his sons, Hudson is a lonely man, drinking too much and working too hard, both the drinking and the working an attempt to forget the pain of his loss. The cats keep him from being alone. He can talk to them about his sons without receiving pity or sentimentality in return, as he does from his friends.

The Finca Vigía, Hemingway's home outside of Havana (Courtesy of the John F. Kennedy Library)

Part 1, "Bimini" has 15 chapters in approximately 200 pages and covers from six to seven weeks in the early summer of 1934 or 1935. The dating is determined by the narrator's statement that Hudson has been divorced from his second wife since 1933 and from the mention of the CRYSTAL PALACE, an exhibition hall outside of London that was destroyed by fire in 1936. Mr. BOBBY, the owner of Hudson's favorite Bimini bar and a friend, tells Hudson he should send some of his paintings to the Palace for exhibition.

Hudson is a successful painter of Bimini scenes and seascapes and sends the finished paintings to a New York art dealer for display and sale. He is rich enough from sales of the paintings and from oil leases on land in Montana inherited from his grandfather to pay alimony to his two ex-wives and to afford the house on

EH and Mary in Torcello, Italy, November 1948 (Copyright holder unknown; photo courtesy of the John F. Kennedy Library)

they are ready to bring him onto the boat. When David's fish jumped, the ocean broke "open and the great fish rose out of it, rising, shining dark blue and silver, seeming to come endlessly out of the water, unbelievable as his length and bulk rose out of the sea into the air and seemed to hang there until he fell with a splash that drove the water up high and white." Eddy, who sees that the fish is only hooked "by a thread," goes overboard with the gaff, trying to hook onto the fish in the last second, just as it breaks free from the hook. He's too late and the fish is lost.

Eddy gets beat up at Bobby's bar that night, telling about David's fish that nobody else at the bar believes. Eddy tells Hudson the next day, "I kept waiting for truth and right to win and then somebody new would knock truth and right right on its ass." The boys leave the island (chapter 13), David and Andy to join their mother in France. Hudson then gets a radio message (chapter 14), sent to him by the Paris branch of his

Bimini, plus the upkeep on a ranch in Montana and a house outside of Havana.

His three sons arrive (chapter 5) on the day after the British protectorate's celebration of Queen Mary's birthday (May 23), the five-week stay organized by the mother of the two youngest sons, David and Andrew HUDSON. The oldest son, "young Tom," is about 15 and responsible for his younger brothers on their trip together to the island.

There are two particularly memorable scenes in the "Bimini" section. The first one is of David being attacked by a shark (chapter 7) while the three boys and Roger Davis are goggle-fishing (a goggle is a type of fish with bulging eyes). Eddy, the cook on board, comes up for some lunch instructions and sees a hammerhead shark heading for David, who has caught a yellowtail on his spear. While Hudson tries to shoot the shark with his .256 rifle, Eddy grabs the boat's submachine gun and manages to kill the shark about 30 yards from the boy. They guess the shark weighs "eleven hundred pounds."

The second memorable scene occurs when David catches a "one thousand pound" broadbill swordfish in an all-day outing near ISAACS LIGHT but loses him just as

EH in his Finca Vigía library, late 1950s (Courtesy of the John F. Kennedy Library)

New York bank, informing him that the three of them have been killed in a "motor accident near Biarritz." Hudson wonders if David had been driving; he even thinks it possible that their mother might have let Andy drive. Since driver's licenses were not issued in France in the 1930s until the 18th birthday, the ages of the two younger boys are particularly difficult to determine.

At the end of the "Bimini" section (chapter 15), Hudson is on the *Ile de France,* sailing for France and trying to avoid thinking about the death of the two boys.

Part 2, "Cuba," has 125 pages all in one chapter and takes place over a period of two or three days in Havana in February 1944. Hudson awaits further orders from the U.S. embassy in Havana, orders related to his duties chasing German submarines. The time can be established from Hudson's knowledge of where the U.S. Fifth Army is located during the Italian campaign in WORLD WAR II (the Fifth Army invaded the Italian mainland on September 3, 1943, took Naples on October 1, and was threatening Rome in late February, which fell to the Allies on June 4, 1944). So the events in part 2 take place nine or 10 years after the events on "Bimini."

Hudson is now using his fishing boat to chase German submarines in the waters off Cuba's northeast shores. He has a crew of eight men, and, at the beginning of the "Cuba" section, they have just returned from a surveillance trip, the last 19 hours of which Hudson spent on the flying bridge of his boat. The *brisa,* or northeast trade wind, is blowing, so he expects to be on shore for four days. His crew has just left, and he's glad to be home alone with his cats.

The next morning (February 20) he goes to the U.S. embassy in Havana to report on his recent, unidentified work at sea, but the colonel he reports to has gone to Guantánamo. So Hudson spends the rest of the morning at the FLORIDITA bar, where he downs at least seven DOUBLE FROZEN DAIQUIRIS "without sugar" (this counts only the ones he orders; the barkeep always leaves "at least another full daiquiri in the bottom" of the mixer, which he leaves in front of Hudson—so the actual count could be 14).

Hudson is drinking to forget the killing of young Tom in France, but everyone he runs into asks him about Tom and tells him what a nice boy he was. His first wife then arrives at the bar. She is a Hollywood screen actress in the uniform of the USO, and she and her secretary have flown into Cuba to see Hudson on their way to entertain servicemen at a military base she does not identify. She tells Hudson that a boy at the airport told her she might find him at the Floridita. She has to catch a six o'clock plane out of Cuba's Camagüey airfield that evening, but they spend the afternoon together in his bedroom, and he informs her—after sex—that their son, Tom, is dead. He later tells her that

EH on the Pilar *in Havana harbor* (Courtesy of the John F. Kennedy Library)

the numbness she feels will get even "number." At the end of the "Cuba" section, Hudson gets a message from the embassy to report for more duty.

Part 3, "At Sea," is 135 pages, divided into 22 chapters, and takes place over a period of two or three days in May 1944. The wind has been blowing steadily for 50 days, indicating the lapse of time between the end of part 2 and the beginning of part 3. "At Sea" provides in detail the events of the search Hudson makes with his eight-man crew for the German submarine crew among the islands of the Camagüey archipelago (hundreds of islands off Cuba's northeast coast). See Appendix I for a map of the islands mentioned in the chase.

Hudson learns that the sub was sunk "by aviation" off CAYO (key, or island) GUINCHOS 10 days ago. Hudson's crew finds burned houses, the bodies of nine Cuban islanders killed by the Germans on an unidentified key, and a dead German sailor on a second key, executed, so Hudson thinks, by one of the sailor's own men (chapter 1). There is constant trouble with the boat's radio and so Hudson is also worried about reporting his findings and getting help from headquarters in Guantánamo. He steers through the night toward CAYO CONFITES, guessing most of the time about where the Germans might be heading.

CAYO ROMANO is about 50 miles long, and Hudson decides the Germans must be in among the smaller keys along its northeastern coastline (chapter 5). They have to keep off the islands, however, traveling mostly in the Old Bahama Channel, several hundred yards off shore, because the depth of the water around the islands, according to the charts, is as shallow as six and a half feet. At a radio shack on Confites, a lieutenant confirms the earlier reports that there were two German submarines, one sunk by airplanes two weeks ago off Cayo Guinchos and the other still maneuvering, having shot down a blimp off CAYO SAL, a cape off Cuba's southeast coast, the "day before yesterday." The lieutenant also tells Hudson that the Germans from the first sub have taken two Bahaman turtle boats and are running "before the wind" (in this case, toward the west) for CAYO CRUZ.

Cuban turtle boats are sailing vessels, and the two in the novel are apparently without motors (at one point Hudson realizes the turtle boats "have to tack"). Hudson cruises into the area between CAYO CRUZ and CAYO MÉGANO (Grande), anchoring in the lee (with an east wind, this places them on the west side) of CAYO CRUZ, that is, between it and Mégano, where they put ashore.

On Cayo Cruz they find a badly wounded German sailor, but he refuses to talk and dies before they can get any information from him. Hudson takes his boat on a southwesterly heading toward CAYO ANTÓN, where they discover that the Germans had been on Antón and had picked up a Cuban fisherman as a guide. Part of Hudson's guesswork involves the mystery of the second submarine: Why, he wonders, haven't the Germans from the first submarine tried to take over a radio station in order to get help from the second sub? The mystery is never solved.

Hudson goes to the western end of Cayo Romano, along the long northeast-facing wing of CAYO PAREDÓN GRANDE. Still trying to decide what he would do if he were the German captain, Hudson determines that the Germans would continue in the relatively open waters around the north side of Cayo Coco, rather than try to go "inside" just yet; that is, to the south or southwest of the archipelago. After searching along a bay on Coco ("Puerto Coco"), they continue west toward Cayo Guillermo.

Two women on a small island referred to only as "half-moon key" tell Hudson they had seen a turtle boat go into an "inside" channel, and Hudson figures that he is now not more than an hour and a half behind.

The narrow channel runs between the western end of Cayo Coco and Cayo Contrabando (see map) and dozens of smaller keys, including "no-name key," where they find a turtle boat with a wounded German on it. The German sailor manages to kill one of Hudson's crew members, PETERS, before Hudson can kill the German.

After running aground trying to get through the channel, and while waiting for the tide to lift the boat, Hudson has his first drink of alcohol since leaving Havana, and the rum "unlocks" his memory of the times when he and young Tom fished together. Hudson's boat floats free with the tide, and they move slowly in toward "no-name key," an island otherwise unidentified and not on the charts.

It is here that they finally find the Germans, who open fire. Hudson, because he is most vulnerable on the flying bridge, is hit by the first burst of bullets. But the return of fire by Hudson's crew, plus hand grenades, prevent others of his crew from being hit. Hudson is badly wounded with three bullets in his left leg. At the end of chapter 20, Hudson feels "that he [is] probably going to die." They are in open water again, having killed all the Germans and, finished with their work, head toward Caibarién, the closest town on the Cuban coast, in channels that are "clear and well marked."

At the end of the novel Hudson's boat is in the open waters of Bahía Buenavista, southwest of Romano. Hudson is lying wounded on the deck and can "see the blue hills of the Turiguaño." He looks "across the great lagoon that he was quite sure, now, he would never paint."

There are several thematic elements in *For Whom the Bell Tolls* and the other major novels, but *Islands in the Stream* does not open itself to much interpretation. The editing together of three apparently incomplete parts does not make for unity of the whole. Thomas Hudson is an accomplished artist and a good father and friend on Bimini island (part 1), but then his art and friends disappear from the novel, and the memory of his now dead sons haunts him in part 2 ("Cuba"). He becomes a lonely man in parts 2 and 3, content with his cats and chasing German submarines. He certainly performs heroic acts in part 3 ("At Sea"), even "GRACE UNDER PRESSURE," but because of the novel's fragmentation, the acts do not provide the depth of character of Hemingway's major heroes.

Islands in the Stream was published by Charles Scribner's Sons on October 6, 1970, in a first edition of 75,000 copies at $10 each. A 34,000-word excerpt from the "Bimini" section was published in *Esquire* (October 1970, before book publication); a long excerpt from the "Cuba" section was published in *Cosmopolitan* (March 1971).

Islands in the Stream **(film)** Paramount picture, released in March 1977 (105 minutes); produced by Peter Bart and Max Palevsky, directed by Franklin J. Schaffner, screenplay by Denne Bart Petitclerc, photography by Fred J. Koenekamp, music by Jerry Goldsmith, set decoration by Raphael Bretton, special effects by Alex Weldon, orchestrations by Arthur Morton. Nominated for Academy Award for "Cinematography."

Cast: George C. Scott (Thomas Hudson), David Hemmings (Eddy), Gilbert Roland (Captain Ralph), Susan Tyrrell (Lil), Richard Evans (Willy), Claire Bloom (Audrey), Julius Harris (Joseph), Hart Bochner (Tom), Brad Savage (Andrew), Michael-James Wixted (David), Hildy Brooks (Helga Ziegner), Jessica Rains (Andrea), Walter Friedel (Herr Ziegner), and Charles Lampkin (Constable).

Isleño Spanish for islander, a character mentioned in *To Have and Have Not* as having provided a great public "sight" when he had been lynched "years before" and then "hung up to swing from a telephone pole in the lights of all the cars that had come out to see it."

"Isle of Capri" A popular song played on the jukebox at FREDDIE'S PLACE in *To Have and Have Not* and heard by Richard GORDON as he and the SHERIFF stop there on their way to see Harry MORGAN's boat being towed into KEY WEST near the end of the novel.

Ismailia Ismâ'ilîya, a town on the west side of the Suez Canal, about 75 miles south of Port Said. The town is remembered by Thomas HUDSON in *Islands in the Stream.* See PRINCESS.

Isola Bella Island on Lake MAGGIORE in northern Italy, to which Frederic HENRY rows with the hotel barman, EMILIO (1), in *A Farewell To Arms,* while fishing out of STRESA. Emilio also directs Frederic toward the island as a first landmark on his rowboat escape up the lake with Catherine BARKLEY.

Isola Madre Island on Lake MAGGIORE in northern Italy, from which EMILIO tells Frederic HENRY and Catherine BARKLEY, in *A Farewell To Arms,* that they can "go with the wind" up the lake to Switzerland.

Isonzo River in northeastern Italy that forms part of the border with Slovenia (which became part of Yugoslavia in 1929 and is now an independent republic) and along which several battles were fought in WORLD WAR I between the German-Austrian armies and the Italians. One of the most famous of the Isonzo battles (the 12th) was fought near CAPORETTO (now Kobarid) on October 24, 1917. In book 1 of *A Farewell to Arms,* Frederic HENRY is badly wounded on the Isonzo River, "north of Plava," and in book 3 he and his ambulance corps drivers retreat from Caporetto with the Italian army.

In *Across the River and Into the Trees,* the canal BOATMAN's brothers were both killed in the Isonzo fighting.

Isotta Fraschini Car owned by MARITA, in *The Garden of Eden.* It is an old convertible with Swiss plates, bad brakes, and an ignition that needs to be overhauled.

"Italian Premier" Article, unsigned, published in *The Toronto Daily Star* (April 10, 1922), reprinted in *Ernest Hemingway: Dateline Toronto* (1985). The headline in the *Daily Star* was "Italian Premier Strikes Keynote." Datelined "Genoa," it is a one-paragraph quotation about the importance of peace taken from a speech made by the Italian premier Facta at the Genoa Economic Conference.

"Italy—1927" Article, published in *New Republic* (May 18, 1927). See "Che Ti Dice la Patria?"

"Italy's Blackshirts" Article, published in *The Toronto Star Weekly* (June 24, 1922), reprinted in *The Wild Years* (1962), reprinted in *Ernest Hemingway: Dateline Toronto* (1985). The headline in the *Star Weekly* was "'Pot-Shot Patriots' Unpopular in Italy." Dateline "Milan." Hemingway writes that Fascisti, "or extreme Nationalists, which means black-shirted, knife-carrying, club-swinging, quick-stepping, nineteen-year-old pot-shot patriots, have worn out their welcome in Italy." He refers to them as "a sort of Ku Klux Klan." He says a "hitch" came in their work to clear the country of communists when they became overzealous: "They had a taste of killing under police protection and they liked it." See FASCISTS.

"[I think that I have never trod . . .]" First line of a poem written in 1926 and first published in *The New York Times Magazine* (October 16, 1977). It's a parody of Joyce Kilmer's "Trees."

"It's Easy to Spend a Million Marks" Article, published in *The Toronto Daily Star* (May 5, 1923), reprinted in *The Wild Years* (1962) and in *Ernest Hemingway: Dateline Toronto* (1985). The headline in the *Daily Star* was "Quite Easy To Spend A Million, If In Marks." This was the seventh of 10 articles Hemingway wrote for the *Daily Star* on the French-German situation in 1923, five years after the end of World War I. Datelined "Mainz-Kastel," it is about the fluctuating exchange rate of German marks to dollars as you travel in Germany. "A full meal in the country," for example, "costs 2,000 marks. On the train a ham sandwich costs 3,000 marks."

Adriana Ivancich in Venice (Copyright holder unknown; photo courtesy of the John F. Kennedy Library)

Ivancich, Adriana (1930–1983)   Young Italian friend of Hemingway's, whom he met in 1948 while on a hunting trip in northern Italy. She was 18 at the time; he was 49. The Ivancich family had established itself in Venice in 1800 in a palazzo just east of the Piazza San Marco, and Adriana's family still owned the palazzo when Hemingway knew her. She remained a friend of both Ernest and Mary for the rest of his life.

Adriana did the cover illustrations for the first editions of both *Across the River and Into the Trees* and *The Old Man and the Sea*. She also did the illustrations for Hemingway's two fables, "The Good Lion" and "The Faithful Bull" (*Holiday* magazine, March 1951). She was probably the prototype for RENATA, the young Italian countess and love interest for the novel's main character, Richard CANTWELL.

Adriana wrote a book of memoirs, *La Torre Bianca* (1980). She committed suicide at age 53 on her farm in Capalbio, Italy, hanging herself from the limb of a tree. One obituary called her an "aristocratic Venetian socialite."

Ivancich, Gianfranco   Friend of Hemingway's who joined the Hemingway entourage for part of the bullfight circuit in Spain during the summer of 1959 when Hemingway was preparing to write *The Dangerous Summer*. He is the brother of Adriana IVANCICH.

Ivens, Joris (1898–1989)   Dutch filmmaker and important leader in the world documentary film industry during the 1920s and 1930s. He is best known in Hemingway circles for THE SPANISH EARTH (1937), a film about the Spanish civil war, narrated by Hemingway.

Other Ivens films include *The Bridge* (1927) about a Rotterdam bridge; *Rain* (1929), a tone poem about a rainstorm in the city; *Borinage* (1933) about the misery of miners in Holland; *New Earth* (1934) about the dyking of the Zuider Zee; and *The 400 Million* (1938) about China, then being attacked by the Japanese.

jackal Nocturnal wild dog of Asia and Africa, usually seen running in packs. Hemingway sees one alone, "like a gray fox," and mentions it near the end of *Green Hills of Africa*.

Jacks, Nelson A "tall Communist" war veteran at FREDDIE'S PLACE whom Richard GORDON and the SHERIFF meet on their way to see Harry MORGAN's boat being towed in, near the end of *To Have and Have Not*.

Jackson Colonel Richard CANTWELL's driver in *Across the River and Into the Trees*. He has a T5 rank in the 36th Division of the U.S. Army, and is stationed in TRIESTE during 1948, the time of the novel. He has a "combat infantryman badge" and the Purple Heart for fighting in World War II. Before the war he had been partners with his brother in a garage in Rawlings, Wyoming; his brother was killed in the Pacific. Jackson's name is Ronald, but it is used only once in the novel.

Jackson, Baldy American pilot flying planes for the Republic in the Spanish civil war in "Night Before Battle." Under the influence of a lot of champagne, he describes being shot down but parachuting to safety.

Jackson, Peter Pen name used by Hemingway twice on stories he wrote for *The Toronto Star Weekly:* "Wild Gastronomic Adventures of a Gourmet" and "Cars Slaying Toronto's Splendid Oak Trees."

Jackson, Thomas J. (1824–1863) "Stonewall" Jackson, the American Confederate general, is quoted by Colonel Richard CANTWELL in *Across the River and Into the Trees*. Cantwell tells his driver, JACKSON, as they head back to TRIESTE near the end of the novel that "Thomas J. Jackson said on one occasion . . . let us cross over the river and rest under the shade of the trees."

According to Bartlett's *Familiar Quotations*, these were Stonewall Jackson's last words, said May 10, 1863, at the battle of Chancellorsville, where he was killed. Immediately after Cantwell quotes the words, he is "hit" by a final series of heart attacks that kills him.

Jacobson, Jon Master of *ALZIRA III,* a boat owned by "Father," one of the "haves" in *To Have and Have Not*.

James Bartender at the Paris café in "The Sea Change." He doesn't hear the conversation between the GIRL (4) and her lover, PHIL, but James can tell they are breaking up: "He knew these two and thought them a handsome young couple. He had seen many handsome young couples break up and new couples form that were never so handsome long." But he's more interested, at the moment, in finding out how well a horse on which he has bet money had run. James has the story's last line. When Phil tells him several times how different he feels, having just lost a woman to another woman, James says to Phil, "You look very well, sir. . . . You must have had a very good summer."

James, Henry (1843–1916) American novelist, short story writer, and literary critic, perhaps best known for *The Turn of the Screw* (1898) and *The Ambassadors* (1903). According to MANDY in *The Torrents of Spring*, James was awarded the ORDER OF MERIT on his deathbed by the king of England. This is one of Mandy's many literary anecdotes, which, by the end of the novel, help to seduce Scripps O'NEIL away from his wife, Diana. Mandy also tells Scripps that James's last words were "Nurse, put out the candle, nurse, and spare my blushes." As part of Hemingway's parody of other writers in *Torrents*, however, none of the characters can be believed.

In *Green Hills of Africa* Hemingway tells Kandisky that the "good" American writers are Henry James, Stephen Crane, and Mark Twain.

In *A Moveable Feast* Hemingway writes that when he first told his wife, Hadley, about Sylvia BEACH and her American bookshop and lending library, SHAKESPEARE AND COMPANY (1), Hadley was pleased to discover that Sylvia had books by Henry James.

jamón serrano A "smoky, hard cured ham" from pigs that feed on acorns. In *The Garden of Eden* it is eaten for lunch with anchovies and garlic olives and MANZANILLA by David and Catherine BOURNE in Madrid.

Japalac Racehorse, in *A Farewell to Arms,* that won a crooked race at the SAN SIRO track outside of Milan. Frederic HENRY and Catherine BARKLEY, with Helen FERGUSON, pooled their money and bet 100 lire on him.

He started the race at odds of 31 to 1 and won, but people who bet on him to win still lost their money.

"Japanese Earthquake"   Article, unsigned, published in *The Toronto Daily Star* (September 25, 1923), reprinted in *Journalism Quarterly* (Autumn 1966), and in *By-Line: Ernest Hemingway* (1962). The article is from an interview Hemingway and another reporter had with two unnamed survivors of an earthquake in Yokohama, Japan. The *TDS* headline read "Tossed About on Land Like Ships in a Storm."

"Japan Must Conquer China"   Article, published in *PM* (June 13, 1941), reprinted in *By-Line: Ernest Hemingway* (1967). Datelined "Rangoon," the article states that Japan must move into China if it wants essential military supplies, particularly oil, and that the United States and Britain must decide when it is in their best interests to stop the Japanese. This was the third of seven dispatches Hemingway wrote for *PM*. The headline read "Ernest Hemingway Says Japan Must Conquer China Or Satisfy USSR Before Moving South."

"Japan's Position in China"   Article, published in *PM* (June 16, 1941), reprinted in *By-Line: Ernest Hemingway* (1967). Datelined "Rangoon," the article explains the present stalemate between Japan and China, and argues that "Japan can never conquer China" and that she has also lost an opportunity for making peace with China. This was the fifth of seven dispatches Hemingway wrote for *PM*. The headline read "After Four Years of War in China Japs Have Conquered Only Flat Lands."

Jardín Botánico   Botanical gardens next to the Prado Museum in Madrid, which in *For Whom the Bell Tolls* Robert JORDAN remembers visiting.

jaundice   Abnormal yellowing of the eyeballs, the skin, and the urine, caused by bile pigments in the blood. Frederic HENRY is sick for two weeks with it in *A Farewell to Arms.* Nurse VAN CAMPEN causes Frederic to lose the rest of his leave because she accuses him of drinking brandy to deliberately get the jaundice and so delay his return to the front.

The appearance of jaundice was produced by soldiers, according to Richard CANTWELL in *Across the River and Into the Trees,* by placing 10-centime pieces in the armpits.

Javanese   People of Java, an island that is the cultural and political center of Indonesia. Near the end of *The Garden of Eden,* David BOURNE thinks of MARITA: "She was lovely and her coloring and the unbelievable smoothness of her skin were almost Javanese."

Jean (1)   See COIFFEUR (2).

Jean (2)   Waiter at the café Closerie des Lilas, mentioned in *A Moveable Feast.* He had won both the Croix de Guerre and the Médaille Militaire during World War I. Hemingway writes that Jean "loved" Evan Shipman, because the American poet "often" visited Jean at his home in Montrouge to help him with the gardening.

Jeffries, James J. (1875–1953)   U.S. boxer and world heavyweight champion (1899–1905). In *Green Hills of Africa* Hemingway describes his native tracker M'Cola as having "that aged look" one sees in photographs of ex-prizefighters like Jeffries and Sharkey posing thirty years after their last fight, with "ugly, old-man biceps and the fallen pectoral muscles."

Jenks, Tom   Editor at Charles Scribner's Sons, responsible for preparing *The Garden of Eden* for publication in 1986.

Jessup   Otherwise unidentified western U.S. town, the setting for "A Man of the World."

Jeu de Paume   Paris art museum mentioned in *A Moveable Feast.* It is near the MUSÉE DU LOUVRE at the northwest corner of the Tuileries gardens. It exhibited, until 1986, the impressionist paintings transferred to the Louvre from other museums, particularly the MUSÉE DU LUXEMBOURG. In 1986 the paintings were moved to the former Gare d'Orsay railway station, now called MUSÉE D'ORSAY. Only temporary exhibitions are now displayed at the Jeu de Paume. The name Jeu de Paume is from a handball-like game that used to be played in that corner of the Tuileries gardens.

jewfish   Any of several large fishes but especially of two species, the giant sea bass and the groupers, both found in the Atlantic Ocean. In "After the Storm," the narrator, who has attempted unsuccessfully to dive for treasure on an ocean liner that sank during the storm, says that the jewfish now live inside the ship, the implication being that they are eating whatever is left of the people who had been onboard the ship when it went down.

Jig   One of the two main characters in "Hills Like White Elephants." She and her boyfriend, identified only as "American," are waiting at a train station near Zaragosa, Spain, for the train to Madrid. Jig is pregnant, and there is much tension between them, because the young man wants her to abort the baby, even though he says that he will support whatever she does. She is extremely irritated by his insensitivity. She tries to get him to stop talking, but he can't. At the end of the story, she tells him that she feels "fine. . . . There's nothing wrong with me. I feel fine." But the reader knows that she doesn't feel fine, that the tension between them is worse than ever.

Jiménez, Manuel (1902–1967) Spanish bullfighter, known as "Chicuelo"; mentioned in *Death in the Afternoon*.

Jimmy Hanley's place New York City restaurant in "Fifty Grand," where the boxer Jack BRENNAN and Jerry DOYLE, his trainer and the story's narrator, have lunch the day of Brennan's fight.

Joaquín (1) One of EL SORDO's men, killed, along with El Sordo, Ignacio, and an unnamed guerrilla fighter in *For Whom the Bell Tolls* when Heinkel one-eleven planes drop bombs on them. Joaquín is a teenager from Valladolid. See HEINKEL ONE-ELEVEN BOMBERS.

Joaquín (2) Young LOYALIST in PILAR'S STORY, told to Robert JORDAN in *For Whom the Bell Tolls*. Joaquín "cries" from fear during the killing of the FASCISTS in Pilar's village at the beginning of the SPANISH CIVIL WAR.

Joe Narrator and son of the jockey, BUTLER, in "My Old Man." Joe is 13 or 14 years old and does not know that his father is "crooked," that he is involved in fixing races. Because he repeats parts of conversations he overhears, first at the GALLERIA in Milan, Italy, and then in Paris, the reader is able to infer that something is wrong with the way the races are run. But Joe is too young and having too much fun with a father whom he loves and who loves him to pay much attention to the meaning of what he overhears.

Even at the end of the story, when his father is killed in a steeplechase race, Joe doesn't fully understand the meaning of a conversation he overhears between two gamblers who think that Butler got what was coming to him. But he's beginning to understand. When another jockey and a friend of his father's, George GARDNER, tells Joe that his dad was "one swell guy," Joe says, to the reader: "But I don't know. Seems like when they get started they don't leave a guy nothing." Whether he comprehends any of the dealings in which his father had been involved, Joe knows that Gardner is right. His father was a "a swell guy"—at least to him.

Joffre, General Joseph (1852–1931) Popular French general during World War I—known as Jacques Césaire. He was given command of all the French and British forces on the western front and was the "Hero of the battle of the Marne." He is mentioned in *The Torrents of Spring* as part of a story that the "elderly waitress" tells to Scripps O'NEIL, another of the novel's "stories" that is part of Hemingway's PARODY of early 20th-century writers.

John (1) Skiing friend of the narrator of "An Alpine Idyll." He listens with the narrator to a story, an "Alpine idyll" told to them by a sexton.

John (2) Italian orderly for the unnamed main character/narrator of "Now I Lay Me." John had been assigned to the American lieutenant, fighting with the Italian army in World War I, because he had lived in Chicago for 10 years and spoke English. He recommends that the American find a wife as a means of overcoming his sleeplessness.

John (3) Greek comrade of Enrique EMMUNDS, the main character and narrator of "The Denunciation." John had been bombed a month before by the fascists in the trenches at Fuentes del Ebro and still hears a buzzing in his head.

Johnson Hires Harry MORGAN to take him fishing out of HAVANA in part 1 of *To Have and Have Not* and then cheats him of the money he owes—$35 a day for three weeks, plus fishing gear.

Johnson, Jack (1878–1946) A prizefighter mentioned in "The Light of the World" who fought against Stanley KETCHEL in 1909. Johnson won the world heavyweight championship in 1908 by beating Tommy Burns in Sydney, Australia. He lost the title to Jess Willard in Havana in 1915.

Johnson, Mr. Main character in part 2 of "Homage to Switzerland." He is a 35-year-old American writer waiting in the train station café in Vevey, Switzerland, for the Simplon-Orient Express to Paris, which is an hour late because of snow. As in each of the stories in parts 1 and 3 of "Homage," the reader learns how an American man spends an hour waiting for a train that's late.

He asks his waitress if she "wouldn't like to play" with him, and when she turns him down he joins three old porters at another table and orders two bottles of champagne. One of the porters asks him if it is his birthday, but he tells them that his wife has just asked him for a divorce. They discuss the difference in attitude about divorce between Americans and the French and Germans, and then he leaves to walk along the station platform, noticing through the window that the porters turn in the second bottle of champagne for cash.

Johnson, Roger Character in *To Have and Have Not*. See SHERIFF.

Johnson, Yogi One of the two leading characters in *The Torrents of Spring*, Hemingway's parody of contemporary writers, particularly Sherwood Anderson. Yogi works in the PUMP-FACTORY in Petoskey, Michigan, and is saved from thoughts of suicide by the sight of an Indian squaw entering BROWN'S BEANERY "clad only in a pair of worn moccasins." She is the wife of the "little" Indian of Yogi's two Indian friends. Yogi tells some customers about a time in Paris during the war (World War I) when he was taken to bed by a "beautiful" woman with whom he fell instantly in love but whom he later saw taking to bed another man, "a British officer." Yogi had "suffered" ever since, but, now, having seen the naked Indian woman, he is "cured." See INDIANS, TWO.

His best memories are of the war, in which he fought and in which his arm was crippled. Now he is full of war stories, told mainly to his two Indian friends, one of whom has two artificial arms. He befriends the Indians because he finds "true communion" with them and thinks of them as "the only real Americans." The novel's narrator states that "Yogi was not haunted by men he had killed" in the war and that he knew he had killed five. "Probably he had killed more."

The two Indians take Yogi to an Indian club, hidden away in an obscure attic of a barn, where he is treated well by the other Indians and a Negro bartender named BRUCE but where his two Indian friends are thrown out, through the trapdoor onto the straw in the floor of the barn, because they are "woods" Indians and the rest of the bar-goers are "towns" Indians.

At the end of the novel, Yogi is described walking up the railroad tracks with the squaw. He is "silently" stripping off his clothes, until he is down to his "pump-maker" shoes, "Yogi Johnson, naked in the moonlight, walking north beside the squaw." The reader assumes the squaw is still clad only in her moccasins. The two Indian friends follow them up the tracks, picking up Yogi's clothes as they go.

Johnston, Wallace "Wally," a rich co-owner, with Henry Carpenter, of the yacht *New Exuma II* in *To Have and Have Not*. They are two of the "Haves" who pay no attention to the excitement at the Coast Guard pier near the end of the novel as Harry MORGAN's boat is brought in. Johnson is 36 years old and an "M.A. Harvard"; Carpenter is 38, also "M.A. Harvard."

Jolson, Al (1886–1950) American jazz singer and entertainer, born in Russia. In *A Moveable Feast* Hemingway, describing Zelda Fitzgerald's "sickness," writes that she once said to him, "Ernest, don't you think Al Jolson is greater than Jesus?"

Jones, Bobby (1902–1971) Robert Tyre Jones Jr., American golfer from Atlanta, Georgia, the first player to win the U.S. Open and the British Open in the same year (1926)—at age 24, during his second year on the professional tour. Hemingway suggests in *Death in the Afternoon* that for a Spanish bullfighter to take the first name of a famous "old-time stylist" bullfighter (for

example "Cayetano" for Cayetano Sanz) would be like a young Atlanta golfer taking the name Bobby Jones.

Jordan, Robert Main character in *For Whom the Bell Tolls*. He's an American college teacher of Spanish, on leave from the University of Montana and fighting on the side of the REPUBLIC in the SPANISH CIVIL WAR. He's not a communist, but he is antifascist. Jordan has published a book on Spain, which "had not been a success."

He has been assigned by one of the LOYALISTS' commanding officers, General GOLZ, to help in a Loyalist attack on some of Franco's REBELS. He is to contact a band of guerrilla fighters and then, with their help, blow up a BRIDGE in the Guadarrama mountains southeast of SEGOVIA, which will halt an expected counterattack by the FASCISTS. In the three-day time frame of the novel, Jordan arranges to blow up the bridge, but he also falls in love with MARÍA, a young woman rescued by the guerrillas from a train they had blown up three months earlier.

The bridge is blown up, but in attempting to escape in the chaos that follows, Jordan sustains a smashed left leg when his horse falls on him after being hit by a tank's cannon fire. Knowing that he cannot get away without endangering the escape of the guerrilla fighters who have helped him, including María, he asks to be left alone, where he hopes to "hold on to himself" long enough to slow the fascist soldiers trailing him and his friends.

Like Frederic HENRY in *A Farewell to Arms,* Jordan hates war. He says, for example, "Did big words make it [war] more defensible? Did they make killing any more palatable?" But he also knows he is something of an intruder in Spain's civil war, and, although the Loyalists are glad to have any help they can get, the guerrilla fighters with Jordan are never quite sure why an American would come to fight in Spain's war. One of the reasons PABLO, the leader of the guerrilla band, is against Jordan's orders to blow up the bridge is that the bridge is too close to the cave where Pablo and his band are hiding out. He tells Jordan, "You must live in one place and operate in another. . . . I live here and I operate beyond Segovia. . . . It is only by doing nothing here that we are able to live in these mountains."

Jordan understands this, but, as with everything in war, he is merely following the orders of someone above him. He also understands that the chain of command is obscure in a guerrilla band fighting in the hills, especially when there is intrusion by not just an outsider but a foreigner. General Golz had talked to Jordan about the importance of not thinking during a war, and Jordan later realizes the value of this advice. He is a bridge-blower, not a thinker. He is not able to take the advice, however, because several times during the three days of the novel, he thinks about the importance of living life to the fullest. He realizes, in fact, that if he lives these three days well, it can feel like a lifetime. Seventy-two hours can be equated with 72 years. His falling in love with María almost at first sight is merely an element of this rush Jordan feels to make the most of his last three days.

In an article about *For Whom the Bell Tolls* Sinclair Lewis suggests that Robert Jordan exemplifies the true American hero. For politicians, Lewis says, democracy, justice, and freedom are just "words . . . dry and dead. . . . But when the reader, identifying himself with Robert Jordan, actually smells the fighting, then freedom may become an activity to live for, to die for, and brotherhood may become inevitable."

Joselito (1895–1920)   One of the leading Spanish bull-fighters mentioned in *Death in the Afternoon*. His full name was José Miguel Isidro del Sagrado Corazón de Jesús Gómez y Ortega, known in Spain as Joselito el Gallo ("Gallito"), or, as Barnaby Conrad states in *Gates of Fear* (1957), "simply—The Best."

Joselito is also mentioned in both "The Undefeated" and "Banal Story."

Joseph   Thomas HUDSON's houseboy on BIMINI in *Islands in the Stream*. Joe "was tall with a very long, very black face and big hands and big feet." He was usually dressed in a white jacket and trousers and went bare-footed.

Josey   Minor character in *Islands in the Stream*. She is a friend of LOUIS, a native of Bimini.

Josie   Otherwise unidentified woman in *Green Hills of Africa,* mentioned in a discussion of "beautiful" women.

jota   One of the Spanish dance tunes performed during the Fiesta SAN FERMÍN in *The Sun Also Rises*.

Journal of the American Medical Association   In *A Moveable Feast* Hemingway writes about F. Scott Fitzgerald's concern about having "congestion of the lungs" and that he tried to convince Scott it was the same as pneumonia, citing an article he had read recently in the *Journal of the American Medical Association*.

Joyce, James (1882–1941)   Irish novelist and short story writer, best known for a book of short stories, *Dubliners* (1914), and for his novels *A Portrait of the Artist as a Young Man* (1916), *Ulysses* (1922), and *Finnegans Wake* (1939).

At age 18 Joyce was encouraged by the acceptance and publication of his essay on Henrik Ibsen by the London *Fortnightly Review*. Its remarkable success convinced him to make a career of writing. After formal education at University College, Dublin, where he was active in the college's Literary and Historical Society,

Joyce began a lifelong attempt to master the art of writing, constantly experimenting with language. He wrote short prose pieces, which he called "epiphanies"— moments when truth is revealed.

Sylvia Beach, proprietor of SHAKESPEARE AND COMPANY (1) bookshop in Paris published *Ulysses* in 1922, in spite of its difficulty in getting past the censors. But the book, already notorious because of the previous publication of some of its parts in THE LITTLE REVIEW (1918–20), became immediately famous. It was banned from the United States, however, until 1933. During the 1930s Joyce published several extracts titled "Work in Progress," all of which would become parts of *Finnegans Wake,* his last novel, published in 1939. In *Finnegans Wake* Joyce pushed to the limits his language experiments.

Joyce is mentioned in the booklet advertising *The Forum* magazine in "Banal Story." Kandisky, in *Green Hills of Africa,* says that he doesn't have the money to buy a copy of *Ulysses*.

Young Tom Hudson, in *Islands in the Stream,* refers to him as "Mr. Joyce," a friend of his father's in Paris. Tom says that Mr. Joyce "was tall and thin and he had a moustache and a small beard that grew straight up and down on his chin and he wore thick, thick glasses." Young Tom also refers to "Mr. Ford" (probably Ford Madox Ford, 1873–1939), whom Mr. Joyce "couldn't stand," and "Mr. Pound" (Ezra Pound, 1885–1972), who had "gotten on his nerves, too." Tom remembers that Mr. Joyce had said, "Ezra's mad, Hudson."

In *A Moveable Feast* Hemingway remembers eating at Michaud's Restaurant one evening and seeing the Joyces at another table: James Joyce "peering at the menu through his thick glasses"; Nora with him; Giorgio "thin, foppish, sleek-headed from the back"; and Lucia "with heavy curly hair, a girl not quite yet grown; all of them talking Italian." Hemingway also writes that if anyone mentioned Joyce's name "twice" to Gertrude STEIN, that person would not be invited back to Stein's apartment.

Juan   Navigator on Thomas HUDSON's boat, searching for the crew of a German submarine in the "At Sea" section of *Islands in the Stream*.

Juan-les-Pins   Small town on the French Riviera just east of CANNES, where Ernest and Hadley Hemingway joined the Scott Fitzgeralds at their suggestion, renting a villa for a month in late May 1926.

David and Catherine BOURNE, in *The Garden of Eden,* also travel to Juan-les-Pins.

"Judgment of Manitou"   One of three short stories Hemingway published in his high school literary magazine, *Tabula* (February 1916). The other two are "A Matter of Color" and "Sepi Jingan."

"Judgment of Manitou" (Manitou means "Great Spirit" in the Ojibway language, is about two friends, Dick Haywood and Pierre, who are hunting in Manitou, Canada. A trick that Pierre plays on Dick causes him to be killed by wolves, and when Pierre tries to rescue his friend he gets caught in a wolf trap that the two friends had laid earlier. He realizes that his only recourse is to kill himself before the wolves get to him.

Julián Best friend of fascist Lieutenant Paco BERRENDO in *For Whom the Bell Tolls*, killed by EL SORDO before the fascist soldiers discover that El Sordo and his men are not dead but only faking.

Julian In "The Snows of Kilimanjaro," HARRY remembers "poor Julian and his romantic awe" of rich people. Julian once wrote a story that began, "The very rich are different from you and me. And how some one had said to Julian, Yes, they have more money. But that was not humorous to Julian." This is a not very veiled allusion to F. Scott Fitzgerald's short story, "The Rich Boy," published in 1926. And the name was not "Julian" but "Scott" in the first version of "Snows," published in *Esquire* (August 1936).

Juma In *The Garden of Eden* an African tracker and "professional hunter" with "filed teeth," who helped David BOURNE's father track and kill an elephant in East Africa when David was eight years old. David is writing about the incident in his AFRICAN STORY. "Juma" is a Swahili name that is as common in East Africa as the name "Paco" is in Spain.

"Junior Debates" Article for Oak Park and River Forest High School newspaper, *The Trapeze* (May 4, 1916), reprinted in *Hemingway at Oak Park High: The High School Writings of Ernest Hemingway, 1916–1917* (1993).

Kalkaska Town in northern Michigan, 13 miles south of MANCELONA. Nick ADAMS knows that the freight train, from which he has been thrown by the brakeman, had passed through Kalkaska just before dark and that he must, therefore, be fairly close to Mancelona.

Kamau One of the truck drivers in *Green Hills of Africa*. He is one of the KIKUYU tribe of East Africa, "a quiet man of about thirty-five," who in spite of ragged clothes, "managed always to give an impression of great elegance."

Kamba Servant In *The Garden of Eden,* a minor character in David BOURNE's AFRICAN STORY.

Kandisky Austrian war veteran, a "short, bandy-legged man with a Tyroler hat, leather shorts, and an open shirt," who meets Hemingway early in *Green Hills of Africa*. He had read his poetry in *Der Querschnitt,* a German literary journal. He is as opinionated as Hemingway about literature and literary people, but asks the American about several writers. He says that he fought with the famous German General Paul von Lettöw in his East African campaign.

Kansas City Two adjacent cities at the junction of the Missouri and Kansas rivers. The larger of the two cities is in Missouri, and it is assumed that it is Kansas City, Missouri, where Harold KREBS in "Soldier's Home" wants to go to find a job.

An unnamed hotel in Kansas City is the setting for "A Pursuit Race."

Kansas City, Missouri, is where, in *Across the River and Into the Trees,* Richard CANTWELL remembers playing polo at the country club. Cantwell also remembers the Muehlebach hotel in Kansas City, "which has the biggest beds in the world."

Kansas City Star, The Founded September 18, 1880, as *The Kansas City Evening Star* ("Evening" was dropped after a few years) by William Rockhill Nelson and Samuel Morss, and edited by Nelson until his death in 1915.

Hemingway was a cub reporter for *The Star* from October 1917 until April 1918, less than seven months, writing only 12 stories, none of which had a byline. He credited the newspaper and its editors for providing him with important lessons about writing. Rule No. 1 of *The Kansas City Star* stylebook, for example, was and still is: "Use short sentences. Use short first paragraphs. Use vigorous English. Be positive, not negative." Rule No. 21 was and still is: "Avoid the use of adjectives, especially such extravagant ones as splendid, gorgeous, grand, magnificent, etc."

In Hemingway's short story "Soldier's Home," *The Kansas City Star* is the newspaper subscribed to by Harold KREBS's parents. His mother asks him to not "muss up the paper. Your father can't read his *Star* if it's been mussed."

Karagatch road Thoroughfare heading west out of ADRIANOPLE for Karagatch in northwest Turkey. It is a road crowded with Greeks, escaping from the Turkish army in 1922 in THRACE, a region mentioned in the "Chapter 2" vignette of *In Our Time.*

Karkov Russian journalist in *For Whom the Bell Tolls,* a communist, with important political connections, rumored in the novel to reach as high as the Soviet dictator, Josef Stalin. Karkov became Robert JORDAN's political mentor.

Karkov's mistress In *For Whom the Bell Tolls* she tells Karkov at Gaylord's in Madrid that "Every one knows about it," meaning the battle that is to take place the next day, which is supposed to be secret. When Karkov asks her how she knows about the battle, she says that "Richard" had informed her about it.

Karkov's wife In *For Whom the Bell Tolls* she puts up with Karkov's mistress.

Karl One of the white hunters in *Green Hills of Africa*. Hemingway, the book's narrator, and Karl are in constant competition, mostly of a selfish, macho nature (at least on Hemingway's part), for the better, bigger animal kill. Hemingway seems embarrassed from time to time about his own attitude but nevertheless curses the "luck" that POP insists is how Karl gets consistently bigger game. At the end of the hunt for kudu in part 4 of the book, Hemingway returns to camp extremely happy with a 52-inch kudu horn only to discover that Karl had returned earlier with one of 57 inches. The natives call Karl B'wana Kabor.

Kashkeen, Ivan A. (1899–1963) Soviet literary critic and translator, the first to translate any of Hemingway's works into Russian. *Smert' Posle Poludnya* (1934) includes selections from *Death in the Afternoon* and three other books. Kashkeen also edited *Izbrannye proizvedenija* (1959), a two-volume set that includes translations by other Soviet scholars of *The Sun Also Rises, A Farewell to Arms, To Have and Have Not, The Old Man and the Sea, The Fifth Column, The Spanish Earth,* the first 49 short stories, excerpts from *Death in the Afternoon* and *Green Hills of Africa,* and a selection of Hemingway articles.

Kashkin Soviet soldier in *For Whom the Bell Tolls,* a communist, who fought on the side of the LOYALISTS and asked Robert JORDAN to shoot him after he was wounded, rather than allow himself to be captured, in April 1937, shortly before Jordan joins Pablo's partizan band. Kashkin taught Jordan how to blow up bridges.

Kati One of the native helpers in *Green Hills of Africa.*

Kayti Minor character, referred to as a "boy," in *Green Hills of Africa.* He prepares the baths.

Keeley cure In "A Pursuit Race," there is a reference to "the Keeley" cure, suggested by Mr. TURNER for William CAMPBELL, who is "hopped to the eyes" on drugs. Leslie E. Keeley (1842–1900) was an American physician who opened a sanitarium for the cure of alcoholics and drug addicts. He developed a system based on a compound that contained bicholoride of gold and so was also called the "gold" cure. Dr. Keeley graduated from Chicago's Rush Medical College in 1863 and opened the sanitarium in Dwight, Illinois, in 1880. Hemingway's father was a doctor who had also graduated from Rush Medical College (1895).

kek In "Wine of Wyoming" the word is the French pronunciation for "cake," which is offered by Sam and Marie FONTAN to the story's narrator.

Kelly, Spider John H. Kelly, U.S. boxer, undefeated for 13 years (1887–1900) and flyweight and bantamweight champion during part of that time. He retired from the ring and became the boxing coach at Princeton University. In *The Sun Also Rises* Robert COHN was on the Princeton boxing team, and Jake BARNES remembers that Cohn was Spider Kelly's "star pupil."

Kemal, Mustafa (1881–1938) Turkish general, founder of modern Turkey, and its first president (1923–38). He was first known as Mustafa Kemal, but was given the name Kemal Atatürk in 1934. Kemal defeated the Greek army in 1922, ending the GRECO-TURKISH WAR. He is mentioned by Hemingway in several articles, especially in "Hamid Bey" and "Mussolini: Biggest Bluff in Europe." In the latter article Heming-way writes that Kemal "looks more like an Armenian lace seller than a Turkish general. There is something mouselike about him."

Kemal is also a minor character in Hemingway's short story "On the Quai at Smyrna."

"Kemal's One Submarine" Article, published in *The Toronto Daily Star* (November 10, 1922), reprinted in *Ernest Hemingway: Dateline Toronto* (1985). The headline in the *Daily Star* was "Destroyers Were on Lookout For Kemal's One Submarine." Datelined "Constantinople," the article is about the futile attempt by two British destroyers to chase down and stop a Turkish submarine moving around in the Black Sea.

Ken A leftist magazine begun in 1937 by David Smart, publisher at the time of *Esquire* magazine. Hemingway published a short story, "Old Man at the Bridge" and 12 articles in *Ken* during 1937 and 1938.

Kennedy, John F. (1917–1963) The 35th president of the United States (1961–63). President Kennedy invited Hemingway to read at the presidential inauguration in January 1961, but Hemingway had to decline because of poor health. Kennedy admired Hemingway's work, and in a statement released by the White House when Hemingway died, Kennedy stated: "Few Americans have had a greater impact on the emotions and attitudes of the American people than Ernest Hemingway. . . . He almost single-handedly transformed the literature and the ways of thought of men and women in every country in the world." And at the president's dinner for Nobel Prize winners in April 1992, Frederic March read an excerpt from the opening pages of Hemingway's then-unpublished *Islands in the Stream.*

Kennedy also assisted Mary Hemingway in getting into Cuba in 1962 in order to bring out a number of items, including manuscripts, photographs, and rare paintings at the Hemingways' home outside of Havana. After President Kennedy died, Mary arranged to have the manuscripts, photographs, and paintings in her possession sent to Harvard until the presidential library opened in Boston in 1979. See HEMINGWAY COLLECTION.

Kentucky Brew An unlabeled beverage drunk by the main characters in "The Mercenaries," a short story set in the Cafe Cambrinus on Wabash Avenue in Chicago.

Kenya, Mount It is 17,058 feet high, about 90 miles north of Nairobi in Kenya, East Africa. In *Green Hills of Africa* Hemingway says that to find "big rhino you want to go up on Mount Kenya," meaning the foothills, especially on the southwest side.

Kerensky, Aleksandr (1881–1970) Russian revolutionary leader and provisional premier in 1917 mentioned in the "L'Envoi" vignette at the end of *In Our Time* (1925). His insistence on Russia's continued involvement in World War I, his failure to deal with urgent economic problems, and his politics of moderation enabled the Bolsheviks to overthrow his government in 1917.

In "L'Envoi," the Greek king says that if "Kerensky had shot a few men [the way Colonel Nichola PLASTIRAS did as leader of the revolutionary committee in Greece] things might have been altogether different [in Russia]."

"Kerensky, the Fighting Flea" Article, unsigned, published in *The Kansas City Star* (December 16, 1917), reprinted in *Ernest Hemingway, Cub Reporter* (1970). It is about an office boy at *The Star* who looks like Aleksandr Kerensky, the Russian revolutionary.

Kerr, Dick (1893–1963) Major League baseball pitcher for the Chicago White Sox (1919–21 and 1925). In *Islands in the Stream* Andrew HUDSON is kidded about being too short for a pitcher, but he argues that he will be as "big" as Dick Rudolph and Dick Kerr. Rudolph was five feet, nine and one-half inches, and 160 pounds; Kerr was five feet, seven inches and 155. Andy's brother David tells him he'll be as big as Earl SANDE, a famous jockey, who at five feet, six inches was big for a jockey; so it's a backhanded compliment.

Ketchel, Stanley (1886–1910) U.S. prizefighter, famous as the "White Hope" in a fight against the heavyweight champion Jack Johnson in 1909. Ketchel was World Middleweight Champion (1908–10), with the title in dispute 1911–12. He is the source of the argument in "The Light of the World," between two whores, ALICE and PEROXIDE, about which one of them knows him better. But the lover they both argue about is named Steve Ketchel. Because of the confusion over the names Steve and Stanley, it is never clear which if either of the two women ever knew Stanley Ketchel the prizefighter.

In "Crossroads—An Anthology" Ketchel offers $100 to anyone who can stay with him six rounds. One of Boyne City's lumbermen, Ed Paige, stays the six rounds but "hasn't done anything much since," indicating he had been badly beaten.

Ketchel, Steve In "The Light of the World," he may or may not be the same as Stanley KETCHEL, the prizefighter who fought Jack Johnson in 1909. But both Alice and Peroxide, two of the five whores whom the narrator meets in a railway station bar, argue about "Steve," both saying they were once his lover.

Ketchum, Idaho Hemingway first arrived in Ketchum/Sun Valley, Idaho, in the fall 1939 as a guest of the Sun Valley Lodge, a resort built by Averell Harriman and the Union Pacific Railroad and in need

EH with his Polish translator, Bronislaw Zielinski, in November 1958 in Ketchum, Idaho (Copyright holder unknown; photo courtesy of the Special Collections Department, University of Virginia Library)

Bust of EH in Ketchum, Idaho. The inscription reads: "Best of all he loved the fall/ The leaves yellow on the cottonwoods/ Leaves floating on the trout streams/ And above the hills/ The high blue windless skies/ Now he will be a part of them forever." (Photo by Charles M. Oliver)

of guests. Hemingway was invited in order to provide the resort with some publicity.

He returned to Ketchum several times during the next 22 years, finally buying a home there in March 1959. The house is located high enough on the north side of the Ketchum to have a view of the town and the surrounding mountains. Hemingway committed suicide at the house on July 2, 1961, and is buried in the Ketchum Cemetery.

Two miles north of Ketchum, just off Sun Valley Road, is a memorial bronze bust of Hemingway, mounted on a stone pedestal, located in a grove of aspen and willow trees overlooking Trail Creek. Inscribed on a plaque are words Hemingway had written for the funeral of a hunting friend, Gene Van Guilder, in 1939: "Best of all he loved the fall/ The leaves yellow on the cottonwoods/ Leaves floating on the trout streams/ And above the hills/ The high blue windless skies/ Now he will be a part of them forever."

The Hemingway house in Ketchum is now owned and maintained by the Idaho Nature Conservancy.

key Reef or low island. In Spanish the term is *cayo*, or cay.

key points, three Richard CANTWELL remembers the importance in his fighting in northern Italy during World War II of "three key points": the "massif of Grappa," Assalone, and Pertica, all three places where decisive battles were fought.

Key West, Located at the southwestern end of the Florida Keys, 90 miles from Havana and 154 miles from Miami, Key West was originally called Cayo Hueso ("Bone Island") because settlers found human bones among the mangrove clumps. The town was incorporated in 1828.

Descendants of the original settlers and people born in Key West are called "conchs." Hemingway first went to Key West in 1928 and called the island his home for the next 12 years. After renting rooms on Simonton Street and later on South Street, he and his second wife, Pauline Pfeiffer, bought a house in 1931 at 907 Whitehead Street, paid for with money given them by Pauline's father. It was four blocks from the Navy Yards and eight blocks to SLOPPY JOE'S BAR. The Whitehead Street house is now a Hemingway Museum.

Professor MACWALSEY in *To Have and Have Not* informs Richard GORDON that "they call [Key West] the Gibraltar of America and it's 375 miles south of Cairo, Egypt." Harry MORGAN, the novel's main character, has a home and family in Key West.

Kibo (1) The higher of the two peaks of Mount Kilimanjaro in Tanzania in East Africa. Kibo is at 19,341 feet; Mawenzi, the lower of the two peaks, is at 16,896 feet. Mount Kilimanjaro is the highest mountain in Africa. See also KILIMANJARO, MOUNT.

Kibo (2) David BOURNE's dog in *The Garden of Eden*, both the real one he had as a child when he hunted elephants with his father in East Africa and the fictional one that he writes about in his AFRICAN STORY. The dog is named after the higher of the two peaks of Mount Kilamanjaro.

Kid, the The third matador in the "Chapter 9" vignette in *In Our Time* (1925). The other two matadors are gored, so the Kid has to kill bulls "because you can't have more than three matadors." He is so tired by the last bull that he can't get the sword in, and after at least five tries he finally kills the bull and then sits on the sand and vomits. While his handlers hold a cape over him, the "crowd hollered and threw things down into the bull ring."

Kiki's Memoirs Hemingway wrote the "introduction" to this book, published in June 1930, his first of several introductions and prefaces. Kiki, who wrote the text and included 20 of her own paintings, was a celebrated model and the "Queen" of Montparnasse. Hemingway's essay had been published separately on January 22, 1930, in an eight-page pamphlet titled *Kiki of Montparnasse*. Hemingway wrote that Kiki "never had a Room of Her Own" (a slap at Virginia Woolf) and that Kiki was "a woman who was never a lady at any time." Her real name was Alice Prin.

Kikuyu One of the largest East African tribes. Their home is in the foothills of Mount Kenya, north of Nairobi. With Kenya's independence from the British, many Kikuyu became political leaders, including the country's first chief of state, Jomo Kenyatta. One of Hemingway's drivers, KAMAU, in *Green Hills of Africa*, is identified as a Kikuyu.

Kilimanjaro, Mount Volcanic mountain in northern Tanzania, on the border with Kenya, the highest mountain in Africa. Sources disagree in stating the height of Mount Kilimanjaro's two peaks. The most reliable current source is probably the National Geographic Society, which, in its *National Geographic Atlas of the World*, lists Kibo at 19,341 feet and MAWENZI, the second Kilimanjaro peak, at 16,896 feet. The *Guide to Mount Kenya and Kilimanjaro*, published by the Mountain Club of Kenya in 1981, also lists Kibo at 19,341 feet. Other sources, however, list the Kibo height at from 19,321 feet (*Random House Unabridged Dictionary*) to 19,565 feet (*The Columbia Encyclopedia*).

Hemingway, who was usually accurate about such details, has the mountain at 19,710 feet in the epigraph to "The Snows of Kilimanjaro." He wrote the story, however, in 1935, before satellites provided scientists with precise triangulation methods used for measuring mountains at the end of the 20th century. The height of Kilimanjaro is not as important, however, as the mountain's significance. The epigraph reads, in part: "Its western summit is called the Masai 'Ngàje Ngài,' the House of God. Close to the western summit there is the dried and frozen carcass of a leopard. No one has explained what the leopard was seeking at that altitude."

"Kilimanjaro Machine, The" See Ray BRADBURY.

"Killed Piave—July 8—1918" Poem out of Hemingway's war experiences, written in 1921 and first published in *88 Poems* (1979). Hemingway was wounded near the Piave River on July 8, 1918.

"Killers, The" One of Hemingway's best known short stories, "The Killers" is set in Summit, Illinois, a small town 11 miles southwest of Chicago during the early 1920s. AL and MAX (1) have been hired to kill a Swedish heavyweight prizefighter named Ole ANDRESON. The reason the "killers" have been hired is not given, and the killers themselves may not know. It is probably because Andreson failed to throw a fight. But it doesn't matter, because the impact of the story falls not on the killers or on Andreson but on Nick ADAMS, the story's main character.

Al and Max enter Henry's lunchroom and bully the three people there: the owner, GEORGE (5); his Negro cook, SAM; and Nick Adams, the only customer, apparently a local resident since he knows both George and Sam and is familiar enough with the town to know where Hirsch's roominghouse is located when George tells him that Andreson lives there.

The killers know something about Andreson's habits, because they tell George and Nick that they know that the Swede usually comes in for dinner about six o'clock. They tie up and gag Nick and Sam in the kitchen and tell George to discourage other customers from ordering dinner. They wait until a little after seven o'clock and then leave, a shotgun bulging under Al's overcoat. "In their tight overcoats and derby hats they looked like a vaudeville team."

George unties Nick and Sam and suggests to Nick that he go to warn Andreson. He agrees, but when he finds the ex-boxer, Andreson is lying in bed, apparently too depressed to get up even to eat, and he is unwilling to avoid the killers. "There isn't anything I can do about it," he tells Nick. He tells Nick not to go to the police, because "That wouldn't do any good." Nick leaves and, back at the lunchroom, he says to George, "It's an awful thing. . . . I'm going to get out of this town. . . . I can't stand to think about him waiting in the room and knowing he's going to get it. It's too

damned awful." George says, in the story's last line, "you better not think about it."

The story is an example of Hemingway's use of the THEORY OF OMISSION. So much is understated in the story, or not stated at all (for example, how or why Andreson got in trouble), that it is understandable why some readers have difficulty deciding whose story it is. But it is Nick who leaves town. He seems to be the one for whom the violence has the deepest impact. "He had never had a towel in his mouth before." Nick thinks the whole incident is an "awful thing . . . too damned awful." George's advice to Nick to "not think about it" is probably good advice but not possible for someone as young and impressionable as Nick.

"The Killers" was first published in *Scribner's Magazine* (March 1927) and reprinted in *Men Without Women* (1927).

***Killers, The* (film 1)** Universal picture, released in August 1946 (105 minutes); produced by Mark Hellinger, directed by Robert Siodmak, screenplay by Anthony Veiller, photography by Woody Bredell, art direction by Jack Otterson and Martin Obzina, set decorations by Russell A. Gausman and E. R. Robinson, music by Miklos Rozsa (including the song "The More I Know of Love" sung by Ava Gardner), lyrics by Jack Brooks. Nominated for Academy Awards for best director, writer (Anthony Veiller), music, and editing.

Cast: Burt Lancaster (the Swede), Ava Gardner (Kitty Collins), Edmond O'Brien (Riordan), Albert Dekker (Colfax), Sam Levene (Lubinsky), Charles D. Brown (Packy), Donald McBride (Kenyon), Phil Brown (Nick), John Miljan (Jake), Queenie Smith (Queenie), Garry Owen (Joe), Harry Hayden (George), Bill Walker (Sam), Vince Barnett (Charleston), Jack Lambert (Dum Dum), Jeff Corey (Blinky), Wally Scott (Charlie), Virginia Christine (Lilly), Gabrielle Windsor (Ginny), Rex Dale (man), Charles McGraw (Al), and William Conrad (Max).

***Killers, The* (film 2)** Universal picture, released in July 1964 (95 minutes); produced and directed by Donald Siegel, screenplay by Gene L. Coon, photography by Richard L. Rawlings, art direction by Frank Arrigo and George Chan, set decorations by John McCarthy and James S. Redd, music by Johnny Williams, music (including "Too Little Time") by Henry Mancini, lyrics by Don Raye (sung by Nancy Wilson).

Cast: Lee Marvin (Charlie), Angie Dickinson (Shelia Farr), John Cassavetes (Johnny North), Clu Gulager (Lee), Claude Akins (Earl Sylvester), Norman Fell (Mickey), Ronald Reagan (Browning), Virginia Christine (Miss Watson), Don Haggerty (mail truck driver), Robert Phillips (George), Kathleen O'Malley (receptionist), Ted Jacques (gym assistant), Irvin Mosley (mail truck guard), Jimmy Joyce (salesman),

Davis Roberts (maitre d'), Hall Brock (race marshall), Burt Mustin (elderly man), Peter Hobbs (instructor), John Copage (porter), Tyler McVey (steward), Seymour Cassel (postal clerk), and Scott Hale (hotel clerk).

"Killers, The" (television play)   Adaptation from the short story, written by A. E. Hotchner in September 1959 and produced on the CBS "Buick Electra Playhouse" in the fall 1959 and spring 1960.

Killers and Other Stories, The   Published by V. Verlag Ferdinand in Germany (1966), in English. This book contains Hemingway's "The Killers" and Samuel Beckett's "Waiting for Godot," among other stories.

king, the   Of Greece (George II, though he is not named), one of the characters in the "L'Envoi" vignette of *In Our Time* (1925). He is the son of King Constantine who abdicated on September 27, 1922, six days after Colonel Nicholas PLASTIRAS and Colonel Stylianos Gonatas led a revolution against the government. This occurred following Turkey's defeat of the Greek army that included the burning of Smyrna September 9–14, 1922. Plastiras ordered the execution of six of Constantine's ministers and advisers on November 28.

In Hemingway's vignette "L'Envoi," the king tells the narrator that the "revolutionary committee" does not "allow him to go outside the palace grounds." The executions are mentioned when the king says that "Plastiras is a very good man . . . but frightfully difficult. I think he did right though shooting those chaps." The narrator says, at the end, that "[like] all Greeks [the king] wanted to go to America."

"King Business in Europe"   Article, published in *The Toronto Star Weekly* (September 15, 1923), reprinted in *The Wild Years* (1962), and in *By-Line: Ernest Hemingway* (1967). Written in Toronto, the article is about King George II of Greece, the "newest king in Europe," King Ferdinand of Romania, where "the king business isn't flourishing so well either," King Boris of Bulgaria, Alexander of "Yugo-Slavia," Victor Emmanuel of Italy, and King Alfonso of Spain. All of these kings have thrones which "[rest] on volcanoes." On the other hand, there are, according to Hemingway, the "respectable kings": Haakon of Norway, Gustaf of Sweden, Christian of Denmark, Albert of Belgium, John II of Liechtenstein, who had ruled since 1858. The *Star Weekly* headline read "King Business in Europe Isn't What It Used to Be."

King George (1895–1952)   George VI, king of England (1936–52), mentioned in *Islands in the Stream*. Roger DAVIS asks Thomas HUDSON, the novel's main character, to paint a character from one of his (Davis's)

novels large enough so that King George "can read it without his spectacles."

King George II   See "King Business in Europe."

King Lear   Richard CANTWELL, in *Across the River and Into the Trees*, thinks of Shakespeare's play and that "Mister Gene Tunney," the champion boxer, once read it.

King's Highway   Location of Thomas HUDSON's favorite bar, the PONCE DE LEÓN, on Bimini, in *Islands in the Stream*.

"Kipling"   Poem written circa 1922 and first published in *88 Poems* (1979). It is in the style of Rudyard Kipling.

Kipling, Rudyard (1865–1936)   English novelist, short story writer, and poet, best known in the United States for *Barrack-Room Ballads* (1892), *The Jungle Book* (1894), and *Just So Stories* (1902). He won the Nobel Prize for literature in 1907. His full name was Joseph Rudyard Kipling.

Hemingway mentions in *A Moveable Feast* that the "talent" Kipling had is one of the ingredients necessary for the FOURTH AND FIFTH DIMENSION in writing.

Kirby, Mr. and Mrs. Aloysius   In *The Sun Also Rises* Jake BARNES gets a wedding invitation from them for the wedding of their daughter Katherine, but Jake doesn't know any of the three.

Kircubbin   Winning horse in a fixed race at St. Cloud, near Paris, in "My Old Man." JOE's "old man" bets "five thousand" francs on him because he knows the race is fixed, and he wins at "67.50 for 10."

kirsch   Brandy, distilled from a fermented mash of cherries, produced in Germany, Switzerland, eastern France, and western Austria. In *A Moveable Feast* Hemingway writes that he drank the kirsch made in the Voralberg valley of western Austria.

kitchen corporal   Narrator of the "Chapter 1" vignette of *In Our Time*.

Klee, Paul (1879–1940)   Swiss painter and etcher, a member of the Bauhaus group of painters. Hemingway bought one of Klee's paintings while he lived in Paris in the early 1920s, "Monument in Arbeit." In *Islands in the Stream*, the main character, Thomas HUDSON, owns the painting, having bought it in Berlin.

Komm' Süsser Tod   "Come, Sweet Death," the title of a Bach Cantata (No. 161), referred to by Richard CANTWELL and furthering the theme of death in *Across the River and Into the Trees*.

Kongoni   Name of one of the two gun bearers in "The Short Happy Life of Francis Macomber." He is picked by the guide Wilson to help find wounded buffalo near the end of the story.

kongoni   East African animal hunted in *Green Hills of Africa*. It is also one of the animals David BOURNE had shot as a child and about which he is writing in his AFRICAN STORY in *The Garden of Eden*.

K rations   Army emergency field rations for U.S. armed forces when other food was unavailable. K rations (named after physiologist Ancel Keys) usually contained three packaged meals of concentrated and dehydrated food. It wasn't "bad," according to Colonel Richard CANTWELL in *Across the River and Into the Trees*. "C Rations were bad. Ten in ones were good." Cantwell asks his driver, JACKSON, if he has brought any K rations along for their weekend in Venice. "Ten in ones" were a British innovation and "vastly preferable" to K rations, according to one World War II veteran of the front lines. The name means "ten meals for one or one meal for ten, and it came in a large cube-like cardboard box" and included a chocolate bar and cigarettes.

Krebs, Harold   U.S. marine and main character in "Soldier's Home," Krebs is back in his Oklahoma home from WORLD WAR I, where he fought with the U.S. Marines in enough serious battles to leave him depressed over the attitude of hometown folks, especially his parents about the war.

He had fought at BELLEAU WOOD, SOISSONS, the CHAMPAGNE, SAINT-MIHIEL, and in the ARGONNE FOREST, all important battles in the war, involving serious American losses. Fighting in any one of those battles would be enough to traumatize a young U.S. marine, but he had fought in all five. He joined the marines in 1917 and returns home in the summer of 1919, after most of the other American soldiers are already home, and people are trying to get things back to normal as quickly as possible.

His parents are religious fundamentalists, treating him on his return from France and Germany as they had when he was a young teenager before the war. And they have no concept of what their son has been through. They think it's a big favor when they inform him that he can drive the car "in the evenings." He upsets his mother by telling her that "No," he doesn't love her and by refusing to pray for himself when she asks him to kneel with her. His inability to put the war behind him or to satisfy his parents by getting a job, frustrates him and causes him at the end to decide to go to Kansas City to look for work. His young sister HELEN (1) is the only one who seems to sympathize and let him be himself. She invites him to watch her play INDOOR BASEBALL, and, at the end of the story, after he's decided to go to Kansas City, he goes to watch her pitch.

Krum   U.S. correspondent for an unidentified news service in Paris in *The Sun Also Rises*. He, his colleague Woolsey, and Jake BARNES share a taxi ride. See QUAI D'ORSAY.

kudu   Large African antelope, the male of which has large corkscrewlike horns. At the beginning of *Green Hills of Africa*, a book devoted to describing a month-long safari primarily for kudu, Hemingway resists shooting a "lesser kudu bull" because he's afraid the sound of the shot might frighten off the greater kudu he hopes to find later. In part 4 of the book, on the last day of the safari, he gets two large kudus and a sable.

Kurdistan   A region of Southwest Asia, mentioned in *The Garden of Eden*. David BOURNE tells MARITA that the cool breeze they feel at their table outside the hotel in LA NAPOULE, France, on the Mediterranean, "comes all the way from Kurdistan."

Kurowsky, Agnes von (1892–1984)   U.S. Red Cross nurse in northern Italy during World War I when Hemingway was there as a volunteer ambulance driver. She became his nurse in Milan while he recuperated

Agnes von Kurowsky, 1918 (Copyright holder unknown; photo courtesy of the John F. Kennedy Library)

during the summer of 1918 from wounds suffered on the Piave River front, and he fell in love with her. According to Bernice Kert in her book *The Hemingway Women,* the love affair was not consumated.

After less than five months together (they saw each other for the last time on December 9), he left for home (January 4, 1919) and received a letter from her in March breaking off the relationship. She remained devoted to the Red Cross after the war, serving in Romania and later in Haiti during the 1920s. During World War II she worked for the Red Cross in New York City.

Kzar A "great big yellow horse" in "My Old Man," which made JOE feel "all hollow inside he was so beautiful." In a fixed race at Saint-Cloud, Kzar was favored to win but ran second to KIRCUBBIN. Kzar's name is spelled Kazar once in the story.

Hemingway describes in *Death in the Afternoon* having seen the real Kzar run in a steeplechase race in Europe.

"Lack of Passion, A" Unfinished story, published in *The Hemingway Review* (Spring 1990). According to Baker's biography, Hemingway had intended to include this story in *Men Without Women* (1927), but he wrote to the Scribner's editor, Maxwell Perkins, that the story "had grown to about the size of a novel and would not 'come right,'" and so it was dropped.

La Consula Name of the villa owned by Bill and Annie Davis, located "in the hills above Málaga," Spain, and used by Hemingway as a stopover on several occasions during the summer of 1959 when he followed the bullfight season in preparation for writing *The Dangerous Summer*.

Ernest's 60th birthday party (and Annie Davis's 30th) was held there on July 21, hosted by the Davises and including among the guests, David and Evangeline Bruce, Miguel PRIMO DE RIVERA (Spanish ambassador in London), Charles T. LANHAM, Dr. and Mrs. George Saviers, Gianfranco and Cristina Ivancich, Carmen and Antonio Ordóñez. Peter and Mrs. Buckley, Valerie DANBY-SMITH, A. E. HOTCHNER, and two "pretty" American women taken "prisoners" in Pamplona, Mary Schoonmaker and Teddy Jo Paulson.

Ladies' Home Journal One of the magazines "received regularly at the Officer's Club in Trieste," mentioned by Richard CANTWELL in *Across the River and Into the Trees*.

lady, old (1) One of the incidents told about in "On the Quai at Smyrna" is about an "old lady," lying among dead Turkish people on the quai, who, just as the HE (1) of the story takes a look at her, dies and "went absolutely stiff," just as if she had been "dead over night."

Lady, Old (2) Fictional character in *Death in the Afternoon*, inserted by Hemingway to ask questions and comment on his explanation of the details of bullfighting. The questions she asks are ones the reader would probably like to ask.

She appears first in chapter 7 and then in the latter parts of all but one of the next eight chapters. Near the end of chapter 16, Hemingway writes, "What about the Old Lady? She's gone. We threw her out of the book, finally." When, in chapter 12, she tells him she wants "no more about animals today," he then offers her "one of those homilies on life and death that delight an author so to write."

The homily is "A Natural History of the Dead." At the end of it the Old Lady tells Hemingway, "You know I like you less and less the more I know you." And Hemingway tells her, "Madame, it is always a mistake to know an author."

"Lady Poet With Footnotes, The" Poem about six contemporary women poets, written about 1924 and first published in the German magazine, *Der Querschnitt* (November 1924).

La Fe In westernmost Cuba, one of the towns in the "At Sea" section of *Islands in the Stream* where "dispositions" are provided concerning the hunt for German submarines by Thomas HUDSON and his crew.

La Granja Spanish royal summer residence built by Philip V (1721–23) in Limitation of Versailles. La Granja is near the town of San Ildefonso in Segovia province and is described in *The Dangerous Summer*.

"Lakes Aren't Going Dry, The" Article, published in *The Toronto Star Weekly* (November 17, 1923), reprinted in *Ernest Hemingway: Dateline Toronto* (1985). The headline in the *Star Weekly* was "Cheer Up! The Lakes Aren't Going Dry: High Up and Low Down Is Just Their Habit."

Hemingway reassures readers that although the water level in the Great Lakes has fallen during the past two years, it has fallen before only to rise again. "From previous indications there may be a spell of several years of low water before a climb again. But the water level is tricky and knows no regular rules, and there is nothing in the past performances of the harbor to prevent another flood next spring."

This was the first time Hemingway used "John Hadley" as a byline for an article. His and Hadley's son, John Hadley Nicanor Hemingway, had been born a month before (October 10, 1923).

Lalanda, Marcial (1903–1990) Spanish bullfighter, mentioned in *Death in the Afternoon*.

He, as a fictional character, is also one of the bull-fighters performing during the Fiesta SAN FERMÍN in *The Sun Also Rises.*

La Mancha   Plateau region south of Madrid in central Spain, famous as the birthplace of Don Quixote and described in *The Dangerous Summer.*

la mar   In *The Old Man and the Sea* SANTIAGO "always thought of the sea as *la mar* which is what people call her in Spanish when they love her . . . [and] as feminine . . . something that gave or withheld great favours."

La Napoule   Town on the French Riviera, two-and-a-half miles southwest of CANNES. In *The Garden of Eden* David and Catherine BOURNE return to La Napoule after their trip to Spain to see if they can start their marriage over. But book 3 of *The Garden of Eden* begins, "The new plan lasted a little more than a month," at which time they meet MARITA. They stay in a Provençal house "on the Estérel side of La Napoule," where they can see across the bay to Cannes.

Lancia   Italian automobile used by Hemingway during most of his travels in Spain while preparing to write *The Dangerous Summer.* Nicknamed "La Barata," meaning "the cheap one."

"Landscape with Figures"   Short story Hemingway had intended to include in a book of Spanish civil war stories but which Scribner's editors excluded when they published *The Fifth Column and Four Stories of the Spanish Civil War* (1969). The story is about a film crew making a documentary film about the war. The story was first published in *The Complete Short Stories of Ernest Hemingway* (1987).

Lanham, Charles T. (1902–1978)   "Buck" Lanham was a West Point graduate and career officer when Hemingway met him during the Normandy campaign of World War II. They liked each other immediately, and Hemingway followed the U.S. 22nd Regiment under Lanham's command through its bloody engagements in the fall and winter of 1944–45 at Schnee Eifel and Hürtgenwald in western Belgium, where thousands of Americans were killed or wounded.

After the war Lanham worked for General Omar Bradley at the Pentagon and was a frequent visitor and fishing friend of Hemingway's, both at the Finca Vigía outside of Havana and in Ketchum, Idaho. He joined the Hemingway entourage on Spain's bullfight circuit in the summer of 1959, and attended Ernest's 60th birthday party, described in *The Dangerous Summer.*

Lanson   A brut champagne from Lanson Père & Fils, an important champagne house with cellars at Reims,

France. Catherine BOURNE tells her husband, David, that she would like either it or the PERRIER-JOUET for breakfast in HENDAYE. The hotel is out of the latter champagne, so the waiter brings the Lanson.

Lantorna   Name of a steeplechase horse ridden by the "old man" in "My Old Man." He wins the Premio Commercio race at the San Siro track in Milan.

La Pêche Miraculeuse restaurant   Open-air restaurant in Paris built out over the Seine River at Bas Meudon, where Ernest and Hadley could find a good dinner of *goujon,* a dacelike fish, when, as he writes in *A Moveable Feast,* they had money for a trip away from the Latin Quarter, where they lived at the time. With the dinner they had a "good" Muscadet wine.

Larbaud, Valery (1881–1957)   French novelist, critic, and translator into French of works by Walt Whitman and James Joyce. Hemingway refers to him in *A Moveable Feast.*

Lardner, Ring (1885–1933)   American writer, satirist, and storyteller, best known for his collection of baseball stories, *You Know Me Al* (1916). Hemingway admired Lardner's writings and imitated his style in five articles written for his Oak Park and River Forest High School newspaper, *The Trapeze.*

Hemingway also refers to him in "Fifty Grand" as one of the reporters who picked "Willard" to win a fight in Toledo but which Willard lost. According to Danny Hogan, owner of the New Jersey "health farm" where the story's main character, Jack Brennan, is training for his next fight, Lardner "only writes the big fights."

large forwarding envelope   In *The Garden of Eden* it contains three envelopes from David BOURNE's publishers and readdressed from his Paris bank. They contain reviews of his second novel, clippings that his wife, Catherine, later burns out of jealousy of the stories he is writing. The large envelope is also "heavy with enclosed letters from her bank in Paris."

Larry   Otherwise unidentified "friend" of the narrator in "Wine of Wyoming."

Larson, Nils   Captain of the NEW EXUMA II, owned by Wallace Johnson and Henry Carpenter, two of the "Haves" in *To Have and Have Not.*

La Scala   Opera house in Milan, Italy, where, in *A Farewell to Arms,* two American acquaintances of Frederic HENRY's are singing: Enrico DelCredo (Ralph Simmons) and Edoardo Giovanni (Edgar Saunders).

"Last Good Country, The"   Long fragment of a novel (110 manuscript pages), published nevertheless as a "short story," with heavy editing, in Philip Young's *Ernest Hemingway: The Nick Adams Stories* (1972) and reprinted in *The Complete Short Stories of Ernest Hemingway* (1987).

Latin Quarter   In Paris the Latin Quarter (Quartier Latin) is a section on the Left Bank (south side) of the Seine River. It was originally enclosed by walls built under the reign of King Philip Augustus (1180–1223), who is also credited with enlarging Paris and building the original palace where the Louvre now stands.

The Latin Quarter is now bordered on the north by the river, on the south by the boulevard de Port-Royal, on the east by the boulevards Saint-Marcel and de l'Hôpital, and on the west by, vaguely, an area just west of the boulevard Saint-Michel that includes the Luxembourg Palace and gardens.

Generally speaking, the Latin Quarter is the area on both sides of boulevard Saint-Michel around the buildings of the Sorbonne, the original college of the University of Paris. The Latin Quarter got its name when, in the late Middle Ages, the Schools of Latin and Theology moved across the river from the Cité, the island on which Notre-Dame now stands. It became known as the Latin Quarter because Latin was the language used in all classes at the school.

Next to the Cité, the Latin Quarter is the oldest part of Paris. During Philip Augustus's time there were four "*quartiers*"; now there are 80, but, according to a dictionary of Paris streets, none was ever called "Quartier Latin." In *A Moveable Feast* Hemingway, who lived there, refers to it simply as the "quarter."

Latisana   Town in northern Italy, about 13 miles north of where the TAGLIAMENTO RIVER runs into the Adriatic Sea. It is on the main railway line between Trieste and Venice. In *A Farewell to Arms* Frederic HENRY is about nine miles north of Latisana when he dives into the Tagliamento River in order to escape the battle police. He knows that the next railroad bridge across the river to the south is at Latisana. He hops a train there going west toward Milan.

Richard CANTWELL and the Barone Alvarito, in *Across the River and Into the Trees*, do their Sunday morning duck hunting at the mouth of the Tagliamento, and Alvarito asks to be dropped off in Latisana after the shoot. "I can get transportation from there [back to Venice]," he tells Cantwell, who, with his driver, will head east from there, back to Trieste.

La Torre   Bullfighter mentioned by Don Miguel RETANA in "The Undefeated" as one who would draw a crowd, compared to the story's main character, Manuel GARCIA who, Retana argues, would not.

Laughton, James   Unsuccessful writer in *To Have and Have Not*, "very tall, thin, wide-shouldered . . . wearing thick-lensed spectacles" and a regular at FREDDIE'S PLACE on Bimini.

Laughton's wife   Unattractive wife of James Laughton in *To Have and Have Not*. She has "[b]londe curly hair cut short like a man's, a bad complexion, and the face and build of a lady wrestler." When Harry MORGAN enters FREDDIE'S PLACE, she likes his looks and says to her husband, "Buy me that, Papa."

"Laundry Car Over Cliff"   Article, unsigned, published in *The Kansas City Star* (March 6, 1918), reprinted in *Ernest Hemingway, Cub Reporter* (1970).

Laurencin, Marie (1885–1956)   French painter, mostly of sophisticated women. In *The Garden of Eden* Catherine BOURNE suggests to David a list of illustrators for the book he is writing about their marriage and ménage à trois with Marita. She names Laurencin, Jules PASCIN, André Derain, Raoul DUFY, and Pablo PICASSO. She thinks that Laurencin could do an illustration of her and Marita in their car on the way to Nice, when they had their first sexual encounter—a scene David tells her he hasn't written yet.

Lausanne   Swiss city on the north shore of Lake Geneva, where, in *A Farewell to Arms*, Frederic HENRY and Catherine BARKLEY go in March (1918), three weeks before her baby is due.

Lausanne Conference   World War I peace conference where the agreement called the Treaty of Sèvres (1920) was made that virtually destroyed Turkey as a nation state. But following Turkey's defeat of the Greeks in 1922, the country was in a better position to argue for a new peace treaty. And after lengthy negotiations in Lausanne, Switzerland, the treaty was signed in 1923.

Turkey got, among other concessions, Eastern Thrace, several Aegean islands, and an international zone in the Straits of the Dardanelles. It agreed to an exchange with Greece of various minority groups. The treaty also established the Maritsa River as the border in Europe between Greece and Turkey.

Hemingway was in Constantinople from September 26 to October 18, 1922, and wrote 20 articles for the *Toronto Star*, covering the Greco-Turkish War and the retreat of the Greek army and civilians from the city. He then went to Lausanne in November 1922 and wrote two stories about the ongoing negotiations. See also MUDANIA CONFERENCE.

Lavigne, M. and Mme.   Proprietors of the NÈGRE DE TOULOUSE RESTAURANT in Paris and friends of Ernest and Hadley Hemingway when they lived above a sawmill at 113, rue de Notre-Dame-des-Champs in the mid-1920s.

Lavigne's Restaurant The NÈGRE DE TOULOUSE RESTAURANT in Paris at 159, boulevard du Montparnasse, owned by Madame and Monsieur Lavigne and referred to as Lavigne's Restaurant by Jake BARNES in *The Sun Also Rises*. It's where Jake takes the prostitute GEOR-GETTE for dinner.

Lawrence, D. H. (1885–1930) David Herbert Lawrence, English novelist and essayist, best known in the United States for the novels *Sons and Lovers* (1913) and *Lady Chatterley's Lover* (1928), and for a book of liter-ary criticism, *Studies in Classic American Literature* (1923).

In *A Moveable Feast* Hemingway writes that Lawrence was one of the novelists he read during his five years in Paris, borrowing the books from Sylvia Beach's "library" at Shakespeare and Company. He names the novels *Sons and Lovers*, *The White Peacock*, and *Women in Love*, and the short story "The Prussian Officer."

Lawrence, T. E. (1888–1935) "Lawrence of Arabia," an English adventurer, soldier, and writer, author of *The Seven Pillars of Wisdom* (1926). An obscure reference is made to him by E. D. HARRIS, the main character of part 3 in "Homage to Switzerland."

Lawson, Henry (1867–1922) Australian writer, best known for his realistic portrayals of bush life in short stories and ballads. In *Islands in the Stream* Roger DAVIS tells Thomas HUDSON that he likes Lawson's stories.

LCV (P) Landing Craft, Vehicle, Personnel. The boat from which Hemingway observed the landing on Omaha Beach, June 6, 1944. See "Voyage to Victory."

leather briefcases, two Used by four Cubans to carry money they steal from the FIRST STATE TRUST AND SAV-INGS BANK in *To Have and Have Not*. The money is recov-ered by the SHERIFF when Harry MORGAN's boat is brought in by the COAST GUARD at the end of the novel. See CUBANS, FOUR.

Leblanc, Georgette (c. 1867–1941) French actress and singer, who performed in a number of plays by French author Maurice Maeterlinck and who wrote about her association with him in *My Life with Maeterlinck* (1932). Jake BARNES introduces GEORGETTE Hobin, the prostitute he has picked up, as "Georgette Leblanc," but she misses the joke.

Lech Town in western Austria, in the Arlberg, where in the winter 1925–26, according to a story Hemingway describes in *A Moveable Feast*, a number of people were killed in an avalanche.

Leclerc, Jacques Philippe (1902–1947) French com-mander of the Second French Armored Division in World War II, which was given the honor of retaking Paris in August 1944. He is referred to by Hemingway in the *Collier's* articles "Battle for Paris" and "How We Came to Paris." In the latter article, Hemingway writes about meeting Leclerc in Rambouillet, a town about 21 miles southwest of Paris, where the general greeted the U.S. commanding officers with "unprintable" words, which Hemingway writes "will live in my ears forever. . . . 'Buzz off, you unspeakables,' the gallant general said, in effect. . . . In war, my experience has been that a rude general is a nervous general."

Richard CANTWELL says of Leclerc, in *Across the River and Into the Trees*, that he was "a high-born jerk. . . . Very brave, very arrogant, and extremely ambitious."

Lecomte's Restaurant In Paris at 33, quai d'Anjou on the Ile Saint-Louis. In *The Sun Also Rises* the Restaurant Au Rendezvous des Mariniers, owned by Madame Lecomte, is called "Lecomte's Restaurant" by the novel's narrator, Jake BARNES. Jake and Bill GORTON have to wait 45 minutes for dinner, because the guide-books have referred to the restaurant as "quaint," increasing the tourist trade. After dinner, Jake and Bill walk around the island, and, from a bridge over the Seine, they admire the view of the Cathedral of Notre-Dame, on the adjacent Ile de la Cité.

"Leda and the Swan" Marble statue in Madrid's PRADO museum, seen by David and Catherine BOURNE in *The Garden of Eden*.

Ledoux–Kid Francis fight In *The Sun Also Rises* the fight takes place in Paris "the night of the 20th of June," attended by Jake BARNES and Bill GORTON.

légitime According to Hemingway in *A Moveable Feast*, this was a word used to refer to one's wife in the early 1920s ("my *légitime*"), but in the 1950s, when he was writing the book, the word used was *régulière* ("my *régulière*").

Lenglen, Suzanne (1899–1938) French tennis player, winner of several European championships and the women's singles champion at Wimbledon for five straight years (1919–23). In *The Sun Also Rises* Jake BARNES thinks that his tennis partner and friend Robert COHN is as competitive as Lenglen on the courts but with a milder temper.

Lenin Institute in Moscow In *For Whom the Bell Tolls* an institute maintained by the Comintern. The Russian KARKOV recommends that after the Spanish civil war, Robert JORDAN go there to study.

Lent, Herr Walther In *A Moveable Feast* Hemingway writes about learning to alpine ski at Herr Lent's ski school in SCHRUNS, Austria, during the winter 1925–26.

leopard Spotted carnivore, of the cat family, usually tawny with black markings, about two and one-half feet high at the shoulders, now an endangered species. One of the animals hunted in *Green Hills of Africa.*

leopard, the (1) There's a mystery concerning a leopard in the epigraph to "The Snows of Kilimanjaro." Hemingway writes that close to the western summit of Mountain Kilimanjaro, called the "House of God" in the Masai language, "there is the dried and frozen carcass of a leopard. No one has explained what the leopard was seeking at that altitude."

leopard, the (2) In his AFRICAN STORY, David BOURNE, in *The Garden of Eden,* writes about hearing as a child "the leopard cough" at night.

Lerroux Spanish Republican politician, named, along with Indalecio Prieto, as "enemies of the people," by Robert JORDAN in *For Whom the Bell Tolls.*

Les Avants Small town in the mountains above Montreux, Switzerland, near the east end of Lake Geneva. One of the Swiss officials who registers Frederic HENRY and Catherine BARKLEY when they arrive in Brissago from their rowboat trip from Stresa, Italy, recommends the winter sports at Les Avants.

Ernest and Hadley Hemingway went to Les Avants to ski in January 1922 and December 1922–January 1923, and he writes about the skiing in *A Moveable Feast.*

lesbianism One of the significant cultural differences Hemingway found as soon as he arrived in Paris with his wife Hadley in 1923 was the openness of lesbian relationships. He tried to avoid male homosexuals but had a number of friends among the lesbian crowd. He seemed to have a much greater understanding of the possibility of love between two women.

Among his Paris lesbian friends were Gertrude STEIN and Alice B. TOKLAS, Sylvia BEACH and Adrienne Monnier, Djuna BARNES and Thelma Wood, Natalie BARNEY and Romaine Brooks, Janet FLANNER and Solita Solano, and Margaret Anderson and Jane Heap (publishers of *THE LITTLE REVIEW*).

Hemingway wrote about lesbians in "The Sea Change" and *The Garden of Eden.*

Le Toril One of the bullfight papers Jake BARNES reads the night in Paris after his sexually heated but unfulfilling encounter with Brett ASHLEY in the backseat of a taxi in *The Sun Also Rises.*

Lett In *The Sun Also Rises* the "tall dark one" of the homosexuals, who enters the BAL MUSETTE with Brett ASHLEY, while Jake BARNES and GEORGETTE, and several of Jake's friends, are having drinks at the bar.

Lettöw, Paul von (1870–1964) German general who conducted a brilliant defense of German East Africa against superior Allied power during World War I and led a guerrilla campaign against the British, finally surrendering on November 23, 1918, two weeks after the armistice in Europe.

In *Green Hills of Africa* the Austrian KANDISKY says that he fought with von Lettöw. The general's full name is Paul von Lettöw-Vorbeck.

Lewis, Sinclair (1885–1951) American novelist and social critic, the first American winner of the Nobel Prize for literature (1930). He is perhaps best known for *Main Street* (1920) and *Babbitt* (1922). In *Green Hills of Africa* KANDISKY tells Hemingway that Lewis "is nothing."

Lewis was one of the three judges awarding The Limited Editions Club's Gold Medal to Hemingway in 1941 for *For Whom the Bell Tolls* (1940). Lewis commented that the novel "might be a masterpiece, a classic, because here was a crystallization of the world revolution that began long ago. . . . Not by pulpiteering [by politicians] shall the people be stirred to resolution and combative common sense. But when the reader, identifying himself with Robert Jordan, actually smells the fighting, then freedom may become an activity to live for, to die for, and brotherhood may become inevitable."

Lewis, Ted (Kid) Prizefighter whom Jack BRENNAN has "handled" (that is, already beaten in a fight) in "Fifty Grand." He is the source of a restaurant argument at the beginning of the story, because Brennan refers to him as a "kike," and a couple of "broads," who have been drinking, overhear the slur and so call Brennan a "big Irish bum."

Lewis, Wyndham (1884–1957) English novelist and painter, one of the founders of Vorticism, an abstract movement in both painting and literature that sought to tie art into the industrial process.

In *A Moveable Feast* Hemingway writes that he disliked a painting of Lewis's that he saw in Ezra Pound's Paris apartment, but the painting is not identified.

Lewis gun Called a *máquina* (literally "machine") by the Spanish guerrilla fighters working with Robert JORDAN, in *For Whom the Bell Tolls.* It is an automatic rifle that continues "to fire as long as you exert pressure on the trigger."

Libertad One of the Madrid newspapers read by Philip Rawlings in *The Fifth Column.*

Liberty American magazine, founded in 1924 by the McCormick-Patterson newspaper organization and sold to Bernarr Macfadden in 1931. It competed with the *Saturday Evening Post* and *Collier's* as a five-cent weekly "miscellany" publication.

The magazine has a minor but interesting mention in "The Gambler, the Nun, and the Radio," interesting because it confuses the dating of the story. Mr. FRAZER, the main character, mentions *Liberty* as a "Macfadden publication," setting the date of the story not earlier than 1931. But he listens to a Notre Dame football game "out on the coast," meaning, at that time, a game with the University of Southern California. Notre Dame defeated Southern Cal, 27-0, in Los Angeles, on December 6, 1930.

Lido A narrow, sandy island about 3 miles long, separating the Venice lagoon from the Adriatic Sea, mentioned in *Across the River and Into the Trees*, because the island is where the rich go to gamble.

lieutenant (1) In the "Chapter 1" vignette of *In Our Time*, a lieutenant who is drunk, as are all of the men in his army unit, keeps saying, "I'm drunk. . . . Oh, I am so soused."

lieutenant (2) In *A Farewell to Arms* he is a "very thin and military" Swiss officer who questions Frederic HENRY and Catherine BARKLEY following their arrival in BRISSAGO, after their escape from Italy and the war.

lieutenant (3) In "A Natural History of the Dead," this unnamed Italian officer wants a captain-doctor to end the life of a badly wounded soldier who can't seem to die on his own. The lieutenant is so angered by the doctor's attitude that he curses him, saying "F— yourself. . . . F— your mother. F— your sister." The doctor then throws a container of iodine in the officer's face, temporarily blinding him. At the end of the story, the lieutenant is still in pain, screaming at the doctor.

lieutenant (4) Character at the radio station on CAYO CONFITES, from whom Thomas HUDSON gets supplies for the continuing search of the German submarine crew in the "At Sea" section of *Islands in the Stream*.

lieutenant (5) On CAYO FRANCÉS in *Islands in the Stream*. Thomas HUDSON doesn't think the lieutenant will give him "any trouble" when Hudson and his crew drop off the body of Peters, who had been killed by a German submarine crew member.

lieutenant, second In "A Way You'll Never Be," a character who stops Nicholas ADAMS to ask for his military identification and then takes him to Captain PARAVICINI, the battalion commander. The unnamed second lieutenant, who is probably shell-shocked, as is Nick, makes Nick "very nervous."

lieutenant-colonel Character at the WOODEN BRIDGE across the TAGLIAMENTO RIVER, where Frederic HENRY is retreating with Italian soldiers, after the battle of CAPORETTO. This otherwise unidentified Italian officer is pulled out of line by Italian officers and BATTLE POLICE and shot as a "traitor."

"Lieutenants' Mustaches" Article, published in *The Toronto Star Weekly* (April 10, 1920), reprinted in *Ernest Hemingway: Dateline Toronto* (1985). The headline in the *Star Weekly* was "Lieutenants' Mustaches the Only Permanent Thing We Got Out of War." It is about two Canadian veterans of World War I who find themselves without civilian skills. One says to the other, "We didn't get nothing permanent good out of the war except the lieutenant's mustaches. Plenty of them about."

Life **magazine** Begun in 1883 as a weekly, switched to a monthly in 1932; in 1936 it was bought by *Time* magazine and turned into a glossy weekly with photographs and feature stories. It serialized both *The Old Man and the Sea* (1954) and *The Dangerous Summer* (1960).

"Light for Me" A racehorse that Frederic HENRY and Catherine BARKLEY bet on at the SAN SIRO steeplechase track near Milan. The horse finished fourth in a field of five.

lighthouse At GRAU DU ROI, France. The unnamed hotel where David and Catherine BOURNE stay at the beginning of *The Garden of Eden* faces the Rhone canal and the lighthouse.

lighthouse dock On KEY WEST in *To Have and Have Not*.

"Light of the World, The" This short story begins as the unnamed narrator, aged 17, and his friend TOM (1), 19, enter a bar in an unnamed northern Michigan town, and the bartender immediately covers the two free-lunch bowls of pig's feet. He also refuses to serve the teenagers beer until he sees their money. Tom is irritated by this and spits a mouthful of pig's feet onto the barroom floor out of spite, telling the bartender that his "pig's feet stink." The two boys are then kicked out of the bar.

They had "come in that town at one end and . . . were going out the other" anyway, so they move on to the town railway station where at the café-bar they encounter five whores, three of whom look as if they weigh "three hundred and fifty pounds." There are also "six white men and four Indians" in the bar, but only four of the whores and Tom are identified by name. It is generally assumed by Hemingway scholars that the narrator is Nick ADAMS, but he is not named. (The "four" Indians, who never speak, become "three" later in the story but only because Scribner's failed to notice Hemingway's correction in the typescript.)

After the two teenagers arrive at the railway station bar, the story focuses on an argument between two of the "big" whores. Each insists that she knew (and loved) Steve KETCHEL better than the other. They both remember and loved "Steve" Ketchel, but the man they seem to be describing and whom the narrator and other male customers think they are describing is "Stanley" KETCHEL, a former prizefighter, most famous as the "White Hope" for his fight against the black, heavyweight champion, Jack Johnson, in 1909.

The restaurant cook, a homosexual who takes abuse from other customers, says to PEROXIDE, one of the whores who begins talking about Steve Ketchel, "Wasn't his name Stanley Ketchel?" She says, "[h]e was no Stanley. Steve Ketchel was the finest and most beautiful man that ever lived." After this exchange, the name "Stanley" is not mentioned again, but all the references to Steve Ketchel apply to the prizefighter. The cook says, for example, "Didn't Jack Johnson knock him out though?" and Peroxide says, "It was a trick. . . . That big dinge took him by surprise." She claims that after Johnson was knocked down by Ketchel (Johnson was, in fact, knocked down by Ketchel in the 12th round of their 1909 fight), he looked over at her and smiled and "that black son of a bitch from hell jumped up and hit him by surprise." She goes on to say that "They can take my body. My soul belongs to Steve Ketchel. By God, he was a man."

Alice, whom the narrator meanwhile has noticed crying silently next to him during Peroxide's talking, calls her a "dirty liar. . . . You never layed Steve Ketchel in your life and you know it," Alice says. When Peroxide asks Alice what Steve Ketchel had said to her, Alice says he told her, "You're a lovely piece, Alice." Peroxide calls that a lie, because it "wasn't the way he talked." After a few more insults, Peroxide asks to be left with her memories: "With my true, wonderful memories."

Both women may be confusing the Steve Ketchel of their remembering with the prizefighter Stanley Ketchel. The narrator, who has been somewhat enamored of Alice all along, sees that she is smiling and that "she had about the prettiest face I ever saw. . . . and a nice smooth skin and a lovely voice and she was nice all right and really friendly. But my God she was big." Tom notices his friend looking at her and decides it's time to go.

"The Light of the World" was first published in *Winner Take Nothing* (1933).

Lilac Time bar   CONCH TOWN bar in KEY WEST where Richard GORDON goes to get drunk with Prof. John

MACWALSEY after Richard's wife, Helen GORDON, tells him their marriage is finished.

Lincoln Park   On Chicago's North Side, where, in "A Very Short Story," the main character gets gonorrhea from a salesclerk while riding in a taxi through the park.

Lindbergh, Charles (1902–1974)   Pioneer in U.S. aviation, the first person to fly solo nonstop from New York to Paris (1927 in *The Spirit of St. Louis*. In *To Have and Have Not* Harry MORGAN sees flying fish in the Gulf Stream and is reminded of a picture he had seen of Lindbergh crossing the Atlantic.

liner, a   Luxury boat in "After the Storm," sunk during a hurricane between the Rebecca Light and the Dry Tortugas, about 60 miles west of Key West, Florida. The narrator of the short story describes seeing the ship only 12 feet below the surface and trying to break through one of its portholes in order to get out whatever treasure he might find.

"Lines to a Girl 5 Days After Her 21st Birthday"   Poem written to Adriana IVANCICH in 1950 and first published in *88 Poems* (1979).

"Lines to a Young Lady on Her Having Very Nearly Won a Vögel"   Poem written in 1921 and first published in *88 Poems* (1979).

"Lines to Be Read at the Casting of Scott Fitzgerald's Balls into the Sea from Eden Roc (Antibes, Alpes Maritimes)"   Poem written in 1935 and first published in *88 Poems* (1979).

lion (1)   Francis MACOMBER "kills" a lion at the beginning of "The Short Happy Life of Francis Macomber." His license allows one lion, and so this one is his, even though he only wounds him, and the white hunting guide, Robert WILSON, has to go into the bush after the lion to finish him off.

The omniscient narrator allows the reader a one-paragraph description of how the lion feels, lying wounded as he is, just before he rushes against his human enemies. "All of him, pain, sickness, hatred and all of his remaining strength, was tightening into an absolute concentration for a rush."

lion (2)   One of the animals hunted in *Green Hills of Africa*. According to POP, the Memsahib (P.O.M., "Poor Old Mama") got the "best lion."

lion (3)   In *The Garden of Eden* the word "lion" is used in three different ways. Catherine BOURNE refers to it as a color ("tawny") that she wants to be; her husband,

David, refers to his sexual powers, which are "like a lion"; and the café where they eat in Grau du Roi overlooks the "Gulf of Lions."

lions   In *The Old Man and the Sea* SANTIAGO remembers seeing "lions on the beaches in the evening" in Africa when he was the age that MANOLIN is now, when Santiago was "before the mast on square rigged ship that ran to Africa." He often dreams of the lions on the African coast: "he began to dream of the long yellow beach and he saw the first of the lions come down onto it in the early dark and then the other lions came. . . ." And the last sentence of the novel returns to the same childhood memory: "The old man was dreaming about the lions."

Lipp's Brasserie   Restaurant in Paris at 151, boulevard Saint-Germain, near the rue de l'Odéon; mentioned in *Islands in the Stream* and *Green Hills of Africa*. In *A Moveable Feast* Hemingway remembers the good beer there at midnight after boxing matches.

Litri   Bullfighter mentioned by RETANA in "The Undefeated" as one who would draw a crowd, compared to the story's main character, Manuel GARCIA, who, Retana argues, would not.

Little Big Horn   In *Across the River and Into the Trees* Richard CANTWELL thinks about the Little Big Horn and about General George Armstrong CUSTER, "with the ponies making the circle around them in all the dust. . . ." See *CUSTER'S LAST FIGHT*.

"[Little drops of grain alcohol . . .]"   First line of a poem written in 1926 and first published in *88 Poems* (1979).

"[Little Mr. Wilson . . .]"   First line of a poem written in 1930 and first published in *The New York Times Magazine* (October 16, 1977). It is a criticism of novelist and literary critic Edmund Wilson.

Little Review, The   Avant-garde literary magazine published in Chicago (1914–17) and New York's Greenwich Village (1917–29) by editor Margaret Anderson and her artist companion Jane Heap. Despite constant financial difficulty, the magazine became one of the most influential arts magazines of its time. It published works by, among others, Hemingway, Gertrude STEIN, Vachel Lindsay, William Carlos Williams, Ezra POUND, T. S. ELIOT, Wyndham Lewis, and Wallace Stevens.

It also published James JOYCE's *Ulysses* in serial form, which helped give the novel some notoriety before Sylvia BEACH published it in book form in 1922. The serialization began in March 1918, and during the next three years the U.S. Post Office burned entire press runs of four of the issues in which *Ulysses* appeared for alleged obscenity—adding to the financial worries of its editors.

Hemingway published two short stories in *The Little Review*, "Banal Story" and "Mr. and Mrs. Elliot," plus six vignettes that would become interchapters for *In Our Time* (1925) and two poems.

Littless   One of Thomas HUDSON's 11 cats in *Islands in the Stream*.

"Little Welshman Lands, The"   Article, published in *The Toronto Daily Star* (October 6, 1923), reprinted in *Ernest Hemingway: Dateline Toronto* (1985). The headline in the *Daily Star* was "Little Welshman Lands/ Anxious to Play Golf." Datelined "New York," the article is an interview by several newspaper reporters with David LLOYD GEORGE, former British prime minister, his wife, and daughter aboard the *Mauretania*, as it lays at anchor in New York harbor.

"Little White Lies"   A popular song of the 1930s, which is considered by Mr. FRAZER in "The Gambler, the Nun, and the Radio" to be one of the "best tunes they had that winter," meaning the winter of 1940 or 1941, the time of the story.

Liveright, Horace Brisbane (1886–1933)   Owner and editor at BONI & LIVERIGHT Publishers in New York, publishers of Hemingway's *In Our Time* (1925). Hemingway's contract with Liveright included an option on a second book, but when Hemingway submitted *The Torrents of Spring* Liveright rejected it because of its satirical criticism of Sherwood Anderson, one of Liveright's other authors. The rejection broke the contract, and Hemingway immediately took the novel to Charles Scribner's Sons, who published *The Torrents of Spring* and *The Sun Also Rises* in 1926 and all the rest of Hemingway's major works.

Liveright and Albert Boni started the company in 1917 but philosophical differences split up the partnership in 1918 and Liveright won the firm on a toss of a coin. He published works by T. S. ELIOT, Djuna BARNES, Upton SINCLAIR, and Ezra POUND; and, in 1925, besides publishing *In Our Time*, he also published Anderson's *Dark Laughter*, Theodore Dreiser's *An American Tragedy*, and Eugene O'Neill's *Desire Under the Elms*. Liveright changed the company's name to Horace Liveright in 1928, and, when he died in 1933, the firm was purchased for $18,000 and its name changed to Liveright Publishing Corporation.

"Living on $1,000 a Year in Paris"   Article, published in *The Toronto Star Weekly* (February 4, 1922), reprinted in *The Wild Years* (1962), and reprinted in *Ernest*

Hemingway: Dateline Toronto (1985). The headline in the *Star Weekly* was "A Canadian With One Thousand a Year Can Live Very Comfortably and Enjoyably in Paris." Under the dateline "Paris," Hemingway reports on his and his wife's experience of living in "a comfortable hotel in the Rue Jacob." He says that if you pick the right restaurants you can also eat well in Paris.

Lloyd George, David (1863–1945) British statesman, elected to Parliament by the Welsh constituency for 54 years, who was prime minister from 1916 to 1922. He is mentioned in several of Hemingway's articles to Toronto newspapers from the Genoa Economic Conference in 1922 and from interviews with him when he visited Canada in 1923.

"Lloyd George the Great Survivor" Article, first published in William Burrill's *Hemingway: The Toronto Years* (1994). It was "discovered" by Burrill in the Hemingway Collection at the John F. Kennedy Library in Boston. In October 1923 Hemingway was assigned by *The Toronto Star* to cover the visit to the United States and Canada of the former British prime minister, David LLOYD GEORGE. Hemingway wrote 10 articles during the first two days of his assignment.

This article and "On the Golf Course With Lloyd George" were not published by the *Star,* perhaps because he was turning in more stories than the editors wanted. Hemingway writes that of the four world leaders who "sat around a table at Versailles to remake the world" at the Paris Peace Conference in 1919, the former British prime minister, David Lloyd George, is the only one who has "survived." The other three are the U.S. president, Woodrow Wilson, "a broken man, his aims unaccomplished and his accomplishments repudiated"; the French premier, Georges Clemenceau, "a bitter and disillusioned old man"; and the Italian premier, Vittorio Emanuele Orlando, "a voiceless politician in a country that has abandoned parliamentary government."

"Lloyd George's Magic" Article, published in *The Toronto Daily Star* (May 13, 1922), reprinted in *Ernest Hemingway: Dateline Toronto* (1985). The headline in the *Daily Star* was "Lloyd George Gives Magic to the Parley." In the article datelined "Genoa," Hemingway clearly admires the conciliatory role the British prime minister has taken at the conference.

"Lloyd George's Wonderful Voice" Article, published in *The Toronto Daily Star* (October 6, 1923), reprinted in *Ernest Hemingway: Dateline Toronto* (1985). The headline in the *Daily Star* was "Wonderful Voice Is Chief Charm of Lloyd George." Datelined "New York," the article is about a speech the former British prime minister made at the Biltmore Hotel, during a luncheon in his honor given by the United Press news bureau.

"Lloyd George Willing to Address 10,000" Article, published in *The Toronto Daily Star* (October 5, 1923), reprinted in *Ernest Hemingway: Dateline Toronto* (1985). The headline in the *Daily Star* was "Lord George Willing To Address 10,000 Here." Datelined "New York," this is a one-paragraph story about an address the former British prime minister plans to give in Toronto.

Locarno Small Swiss town at the northern end of Lake MAGGIORE, where, in *A Farewell to Arms*, Frederic HENRY and Catherine BARKLEY are taken by a Swiss soldier after their arrival in BRISSAGO.

Lodger, The Novel (1913) by Marie Belloc LOWNDES, mentioned in *A Moveable Feast*. Hemingway says it's about Jack the Ripper, but it is actually the story of a serial murderer, Mr. Sleuth, who escapes from a French prison, eludes a French inspector at Madame Toussaud's in London, and proceeds to commit another seven murders.

Loeb, Harold (1891–1974) Editor and founder of *Broom*, a little magazine published in Paris from 1921 to 1924. Loeb, who had disliked living in Greenwich Village and in Paris's Latin Quarter, edited the magazine from Rome. He dropped the magazine in 1924 in order to write novels.

Hemingway first met Loeb at one of Ford Madox FORD's Thursday literary teas, and Loeb became one of Ernest's poker- and tennis-playing friends. Hemingway biographer Carlos Heard BAKER describes Loeb as "a well-dressed, dark-haired young man with broad shoulders, a firm chin, and the profile of a classical Greek wrestler."

Loeb, whose first novel, *Doodab,* had been accepted for publication by BONI & LIVERIGHT in 1924, introduced Hemingway to Leon Fleischman, the publisher's European agent. The meeting did not go well because Hemingway thought Fleischman was patronizing him, but Hemingway sent his manuscript of *In Our Time* to Boni & Liveright nevertheless, and it was accepted. Several weeks later, at a party in Loeb's apartment to celebrate his new contract, Hemingway met for the first time Pauline Pfeiffer, who was to become his second wife.

Loeb also was part of the Hemingway excursion to Pamplona for the fiesta in July 1925, which also included Hadley Hemingway, Duff Twysden and Pat Guthrie, Bill Smith, and Donald Stewart. Loeb was out of place on this outing—he was a nondrinker in a drinking crowd and he was infatuated with Twysden, who had rejected him. Twysden informed Hemingway that she and Loeb had been to Saint-Jean-de-Luz together, which was why he kept following her around. Further, Loeb announced before the first bullfights that he hated bullfighting—the primary reason for the trip. The "friends" drank heavily to combat the tension, fist-fights occurred, and everyone had a generally miserable time. Hemingway used the trip, however, as his background experience for writing the Pamplona section of *The Sun Also Rises*.

log booms   Large groups of floating logs, tied together and pulled by boats to logging mills. In "The Doctor and the Doctor's Wife," Nick's father hires three Indians to cut up logs that have broken loose from the booms and drifted onto his lake shoreline.

Loggerhead Key   Location of the TORTUGAS lighthouse, about 75 miles west of KEY WEST; mentioned in *To Have and Have Not*.

"London Fights the Robots"   Article, published in *Collier's* (August 19, 1944), reprinted in *Masterpieces of War Reporting* (1962), reprinted in *By-Line: Ernest Hemingway* (1967). This article is the second of six dispatches from the European sector of WORLD WAR II, all published in *Collier's*. This article is about the London Blitz during the summer of 1944.

Hemingway refers to himself as "your pilotless aircraft correspondent" as he describes the incoming robot bombs ("doodlebugs" or "buzz bombs") from Germany toward London and the attempt by RAF Tempest pilots to shoot them down. He also describes his first flight in a Mitchell bomber to bomb an unidentified target and how difficult he found it to understand the English language when spoken by British pilots over a plane's intercom system.

long, low stone house   It is near the landing where Richard CANTWELL meets Barone ALVARITO after the Sunday morning duck shoot in *Across the River and Into the Trees*. The 42 ducks the barone has killed are "laid out on the ground in rows."

Longchamps (1)   Famous Paris steeplechase racecourse, in the Bois de Boulogne, mentioned in *Islands in the Stream* and *The Garden of Eden*, as well as in several of Hemingway's short stories. The track was built about 1850 on the site of a 13th-century abbey.

Longchamps (2)   A Madison Avenue restaurant in New York City, where the military "surgeon" in Trieste, who gives Richard CANTWELL a physical exam at the beginning of *Across the River and Into the Trees*, orders his ducks. Cantwell wants to hunt for the ducks; the doctor prefers to get his already cooked.

Longhena   Architect mentioned in *Across the River and Into the Trees* as the builder of a "ruined country house," destroyed by "mediums" (Austrian cannon shells) and located near a blown bridge over the TAGLIAMENTO RIVER.

Looie   One of the waiters at the café in Madrid where, in "The Undefeated," Manuel GARCIA waits for ZURITO.

Lopez, Andrés   "The bulldog of Villaconejos," one of the guerrilla fighters helping Robert JORDAN in *For Whom the Bell Tolls*. He makes the three-hour trip from the guerrillas' cave in the Guadarrama Mountains to NAVACERRADA with a message from Jordan to General GOLZ in an attempt to stop the LOYALIST attack. But the message gets to Golz too late.

"Lord and Lady Cranworth"   Article, written in September 1923 and first published in William Burrill's *Hemingway: The Toronto Years* (1994). This is a short interview story about a couple, "arrivals from the Old Land, of British aristocracy," in Toronto on vacation. It was "discovered" by Burrill in the Hemingway Collection at the John F. Kennedy Library in Boston.

"Lord Birkenhead"   Article, unsigned, published in *The Toronto Daily Star* (October 4, 1923), reprinted in *Ernest Hemingway: Dateline Toronto* (1985). The headline in the *Daily Star* was "He's a Personality, No Doubt, But a Much Maligned One." It is an interview with Frederick Edwin Smith Birkenhead (1872–1930), First Earl of Birkenhead, British statesman and jurist.

Lorimer, George Horace (1867–1937)   Editor of *The Saturday Evening Post* from 1899–1936 and the person most responsible for the magazine's growth and success. Scripps O'NEIL in *The Torrents of Spring* says he has sold a story to Lorimer and that he has $450 in his pocket to prove it. Scripps seems to have the money, but readers may doubt that he got it from selling a story to Lorimer.

Lorimer is mentioned in *A Moveable Feast* because he had rejected some of Hemingway's early stories.

"Los Desastres de la Guerra"   Series of etchings by Goya, completed between 1810 and 1820, depicting the atrocities committed by French troops during the suppression of a popular uprising against Napoleonic rule in Spain. The etchings remain among the most powerful and disturbing images of war and reflect Goya's despair at the human potential for madness and cruelty. His original title for the series was "Fatal consequences of the bloody war against Napoleon in Spain, and other emphatic caprices," but it was mistitled "Disasters of War" when first published in 1863. See Francisco José de GOYA Y LUCIENTES.

Hemingway refers to the etchings in *Death in the Afternoon*, especially in "A Natural History of the Dead," where the narrator says that Goya might well have painted some of the scenes of dead soldiers and animals that he, the narrator, had observed in war.

lost generation, the   Term Gertrude Stein applied to Hemingway and other American writers who had been in World War I and were living in Paris in the early 1920s. According to a story Hemingway tells in *A Moveable Feast*, Stein got the term from the proprietor of a Paris garage where she had gone to have work done on her Model T Ford. The young man who worked on her car had done a poor job and had been reprimanded by the garage's proprietor, who said to him, "You are all *une génération perdue*." Stein then said to Hemingway: "That's what you are. That's what you all are. . . . All of you young people who served in the war. You are a lost generation. . . . You have no respect for anything. You drink yourselves to death." Later, over a beer, Hemingway thought that "all generations were lost by something." He had used the term as the first epigraph to *The Sun Also Rises*.

Most of the writers Stein referred to had been in the war and had received at least psychic wounds, if not also physical wounds, and so could not understand America's seemingly hurried need to forget the war and, by implication, the soldiers who fought in it. These writers were also "lost" in the sense that they felt a spiritual alienation from an America that seemed hopelessly provincial and emotionally barren. Artists were often inhibited in their work by censorship, the best example of which was the prohibition against James JOYCE's novel, *Ulysses*, published in Paris in 1922, copies of which were burned by the U.S. Post Office authorities in New York and which was not officially allowed into the country until 1933.

The third section of *A Moveable Feast* is titled "Une Génération Perdue." The term has since been made a part of English language vocabulary, defined in dictionaries as the generation of men and women who came of age during World War I and who, because of the war and the social upheaval that followed it, became disillusioned and cynical.

Other writers who are generally considered to be part of this group include Hart Crane, e. e. cummings, F. Scott Fitzgerald, John Dos Passos, and Archibald MacLeish. Malcolm Cowley dealt with the subject in his book, *The Lost Generation* (1933).

Lost Generation, The **(play)**   Written by Hilary Hemingway (a niece) and Jeffry Freundlich, based on Hemingway's life in Paris during the 1920s. The first performance was during the Hemingway Days Festival in Key West in July 1987.

Louis   "Negro boy" in the "Bimini" section of *Islands in the Stream*.

Lowndes, Marie Belloc (1868–1947)   English novelist and playwright, best known for her murder mysteries. Her pseudonym was Mrs. Belloc Lowndes. In *A Moveable Feast* Hemingway writes that he had not heard of Lowndes until Sylvia BEACH recommended her to him at her bookshop, Shakespeare and Company. "If you don't want to read what is bad," she told him, "and want to read something that will hold your interest and is marvelous in its own way, you should read Marie Belloc Lowndes." Beach lent to Hemingway Lowndes's *The Lodger* (1913).

Loyalists   Spaniards loyal to the REPUBLIC and against Generalissimo Francisco FRANCO and the REBELS during the SPANISH CIVIL WAR (1936–39).

Lucius   One of the run-boat's crew in the "Bimini" section of *Islands in the Stream*. The run-boats carry supplies to Bimini from Miami.

luck   Often a factor in Hemingway's thinking and in the thinking of his fictional characters. His definitive statement about luck may be found in *The Old Man and the Sea*. The old fisherman, SANTIAGO, has been 84 days without catching a fish and so feels down on his luck. But he is a skilled fisherman, who knows at exactly what depth to place his baits, and so he thinks: "Maybe today. Every day is a new day. It is better to be lucky. But I would rather be exact. Then when luck comes you are ready."

luge   See "Swiss Luge, The."

Luger   German automatic pistol, used by PANCHO to kill one of the gunmen attacking three Cubans outside of Havana's PEARL OF SAN FRANCISCO CAFÉ at the beginning of *To Have and Have Not*.

Luger, 9mm   Pistol used by the Germans to kill nine Cuban islanders and one of their own crew members in the "At Sea" section of *Islands in the Stream*. The semiautomatic weapon was invented by George Luger (1849–1923) in 1898 while working for the German factory Deutschen Waffen und Munitions werke (DWM). Thomas HUDSON and one of his crew members, ARA, dig the 9mm Luger bullets out of the dead Cuban islanders, but the Luger pistol also shoots SCHMEISSER BULLETS, which they find later.

Lugo   City in northwestern Spain and hometown of one of the Fascist guards at the BRIDGE in *For Whom the Bell Tolls*.

Luis (1)   Bullfighter in the "Chapter 13" vignette of *In Our Time* (1925). He is drunk and dancing with the riau-riau dancers, and the narrator tries to get him back to the hotel so he can rest for the afternoon's bullfights. The narrator is also a matador, and he and the third matador for that afternoon's bullfights know that if Luis doesn't stop drinking they will have to kill his bulls for him. See RIAU-RIAU MUSIC.

Luis (2)   Porter in Madrid's Florida Hotel in *For Whom the Bell Tolls*.

Luque, Adolfo "Dolf" (1890–1957)   Major League baseball pitcher (1914–35) with four different teams but mostly with the Cincinnati Reds and the New York Giants. He was nicknamed "The Pride of Havana." In *The Old Man and the Sea* Manolin asks SANTIAGO, "Who is the greatest manager, really, Luque or Mike GONZALEZ?" Luque never managed a Major League team, but he managed in Cuba in the winter leagues. Due to racial issues Cuban baseball players were unusual in the U.S. major leagues in the late 1940s and early 1950s and the Cubans who were allowed to play were light-skinned.

Luxembourg Gardens   In Paris, on the Left Bank, the only remaining Renaissance gardens in the city. With marble fountains, double staircases, stone balustrades, fountains, paths, trees, and benches, the gardens are a playground for children and a park for strolling adults.

In *A Moveable Feast* Hemingway writes about walking through the gardens on his way from his apartment at 74, rue Cardinal Lemoine to the Luxembourg Art Museum or to Gertrude Stein's apartment at 27, rue de Fleurus. He mentions the Fontaine de Médicis, which is in the northeast corner of the Luxembourg Gardens, near the rue de Médicis. The fountain was constructed in 1620 and moved to the gardens in 1860, when the rue de Médicis was completed. The Luxembourg Gardens are mentioned in several other Hemingway works as well.

Luz   Lover of the main character, HE (2), in "A Very Short Story." She's a nurse in a Padua, Italy, hospital during World War I and falls in love with him while he's there recuperating from wounds he's received fighting for the Italians. She wants to marry him, but she insists that he go home and find a job before she rejoins him. She moves to Pordenone, Italy, to open a hospital and, while there, makes love to an Italian major. She writes to her American lover to tell him she plans to get married in the spring, but she doesn't get a response; nor does she get an answer to her letter a little later, informing him that the marriage is off.

Lyon   Town in France about 285 miles southeast of Paris. In *A Moveable Feast* Hemingway describes, in a section titled "Scott Fitzgerald," the trip he and Fitzgerald took to Lyon, where they picked up Fitzgerald's abandoned car. Fitzgerald missed the train from Paris, and Hemingway had to send him directions in a telegram from Lyon; Scott also missed the telegram.

M

Mac In *Across the River and Into the Trees,* name RENATA has learned from American books and films that refers to the man at the "comfort station" to whom she can say, "fill her up and check the oil, Mac." She also tries to imitate American movie actress Ida Lupino's voice when she says to the GRAN MAESTRO, "Listen, Mac. You hired out to be tough, didn't you?"

Macedonias A brand of cigarettes that Frederic HENRY passes out to his ambulance drivers on their way to the war front in *A Farewell to Arms.*

Machado y Morales, Gerardo (1871–1939) Dictatorial president of Cuba (1925–33); it was his corrupt administration that led to the revolution that put Fulgencio BATISTA Y ZALDÍVAR into power in 1933. In *To Have and Have Not* four Cubans rob a bank in Key West and hire Harry MORGAN to take them to Cuba. The money is to help finance Batista's revolution. The incident helps set the time of the novel at 1934–35.

mackerel boats Seen on the Mediterranean Sea from GRAU DU ROI, France, described by the narrator in *The Garden of Eden.* The boats catch the mood of David BOURNE, who at the time is happy in his marriage to Catherine. "The mackerel fishing boats were coming in now and the women were unloading the shining blue and green and silver mackerel. . . . It was a very good catch and the town was busy and happy."

MacLeish, Archibald (1892–1982) American poet and playwright, best known for his often anthologized poem "Ars Poetica" (1926) and for his verse play *J.B.* (1958). The MacLeishes were good friends of Ernest and Hadley Hemingway in France during the 1920s, and in *A Moveable Feast* Hemingway writes about meeting them, the Gerald Murphys, and the Scott Fitzgeralds at Juan-les-Pins on the Riviera for most of June 1926. The MacLeishes arrived in Paris in 1923, renting an apartment at 23, rue Las-Cases.

MacLeish wrote the *Life* magazine obituary on Hemingway (July 14, 1961) and once said that "the only [other] person I have ever known who could exhaust the oxygen in a room the way Ernest could just by coming into it was Franklin Delano Roosevelt."

Macomber, Francis Main character in "The Short Happy Life of Francis Macomber." He is 35 years old, "very tall, very well built if you did not mind that length of bone, dark, his hair cropped like an oarsman, rather thin-lipped, and was considered handsome." He is wearing the same clothes as the guide, Robert WILSON, except that Macomber's clothes are brand new. And near the beginning of the story he is also described as having "just shown himself, very publicly, to be a coward."

The fear of hunting had begun the night before when he had lain awake listening to a lion roaring, the fear growing steadily inside him, and he remembers a Somali proverb that says, "a brave man is always frightened three times by a lion; when he first sees his track, when he first hears him roar and when he first confronts him." They hear a lion roar the next morning at breakfast, and Macomber begins to ask so many questions about lions attacking that even Wilson begins to wonder about him.

Macomber thinks about the lion so much, that by the time he confronts his first one that day, his fear dominates him and he runs away, "like a coward." But when, the next day he is charged by a wounded buffalo, he has not had time to think about being afraid. This time Macomber stands his ground and is thrilled by the hunt. His "short happy life" ends abruptly, however, when his wife, Margot, shoots him in the back of the head. When she sees the buffalo rushing at her husband, the narrator states that she "shot at the buffalo with the 6.5 Mannlicher as it seemed about to gore Macomber and had hit her husband about two inches up and a little to one side of the base of his skull."

Macomber, Margot Wife of the main character in "The Short Happy Life of Francis Macomber." "She was an extremely handsome and well-kept woman of the beauty and social position which had, five years before, commanded 5,000 dollars as the price of endorsing, with photographs, a beauty product which she had never used." She and Francis have been married 11 years.

They are on a hunting safari in East Africa, and she is embarrassed and ashamed at the beginning of the story, just back from the morning's lion hunt, because her husband had run from a charging lion. She becomes sarcastic, refusing to stay in camp the next morning during Macomber's hunt for buffalo, perhaps anticipating more of her husband's cowardice, and saying, "I wouldn't miss something like today for anything." And when Wilson, the guide, is rather insistent that she not go, she says to him, "I want *so* to see you perform again. You were lovely this morning [during the lion hunt]. That is if blowing things' heads off is lovely."

She goes to bed with Wilson late that night in spite of her attitude about his killing animals, apparently because getting even with her husband for his cowardice is more important to her. She feels trapped in the marriage, because, although she would like to leave Macomber, she is afraid she would not be able to attach herself to anyone else.

In the story's ambiguous ending, Margot shoots her husband as he is about to kill or be killed by a charging buffalo—having regained his courage—but the narrator's wording leaves the reader in some doubt about her intentions: "Mrs. Macomber . . . had shot at the buffalo . . . as it seemed about to gore Macomber and had hit her husband about two inches up and a little to one side of the base of his skull."

She will not be found guilty of murder, partly because Wilson will testify on her behalf. The narrator states that she shot "at the buffalo," but the reader understands her character well enough, as well as her potential motivation for murder, to be at least ambivalent about her guilt.

Macomber Affair, The (film)   United Artists picture, released in April 1947 (89 minutes), based on Hemingway's short story "The Short Happy Life of Francis Macomber." Produced by Benedict Bogeaus and Casey Robinson, directed by Zoltan Korda, screenplay by Casey Robinson and Seymour Bennett, music by Miklos Rozsa, photography by Karl Struss, art direction by Erno Metzner. The credits also state "Ernest Hemingway's 'The Macomber Affair.'"

Cast: Gregory Peck (Robert Wilson), Joan Bennett (Margaret Macomber), Robert Preston (Francis Macomber), Reginald Denny (Captain Smollet), and Jean Gillie (Aimee).

MacWalsey, Prof. John   Character in *To Have and Have Not.* He has a "rather swollen reddish face, a rusty-colored mustache, a white cloth hat with a green celluloid visor, and a trick of talking with a rather extraordinary movement of his lips as though he were eating something too hot for comfort." He goes to bed with Helen GORDON, which contributes to the breakup of an already bad marriage, then tries to help her husband, the drunken Richard GORDON, to get home near the end of the novel. MacWalsey's wife had died during the influenza epidemic in 1918. His name is spelled "McWalsey" once.

Madlener-Haus   One of the Alpine Club huts in the mountains above the southern end of the Montafon Valley, south-southeast of SCHRUNS, Austria; mentioned in *A Moveable Feast.* Skiiers had to haul their skis and equipment up to the hut from the valley. Hemingway writes that it got easier the more you did it.

Madrid   In *Death in the Afternoon* Hemingway says that, although Madrid is a "strange place . . . it is the most Spanish of all cities, the best to live in, the finest people, month in and month out the finest climate and while the other big cities are all very representative of the province they are in, they are either Andalucían, Catalan, Basque, Aragonese, or otherwise provincial. It is in Madrid only that you get the essence."

The Plaza de Toros in Madrid was the first bull ring in Spain (built in 1617) and still is the most important bull ring in the world.

Madrid is the setting for "The Capital of the World" and for *The Fifth Column.*

Maera (1)   Bullfighter in the "Chapter 13" vignette of *In Our Time* (1925). He wants the narrator, also a bullfighter, to stop the third bullfighter on the afternoon's card, LUIS (1), from drinking and dancing with the riau-riau dancers. Maera is angry because he knows that he and the narrator will have to kill Luis's bulls "after he gets a COGIDA," that is after he is tossed by one of his bulls.

Maera (2)   Bullfighter who dies in the "Chapter 14" vignette of *In Our Time.*

Maera, Manuel García (1896–1924)   Spanish bullfighter, one of the three matadors Hemingway saw at his first bullfights in Pamplona, Spain, in July 1923. Hemingway says of him in *Death in the Afternoon* that "he was always one of the finest, most emotional and finished banderilleros that ever nailed a pair; and he became one of the best and most satisfying matadors I have ever watched." The other bullfighters on the Pamplona card that day were Rosario OLMOS and ALGABEÑO.

Maera is also mentioned in the booklet advertising *The Forum* magazine in "Banal Story."

Maggiore, Lake   Northern Italian lake, 40 miles long but only about two and a half miles wide, the northernmost part of which is in Switzerland. In *A Farewell To Arms* Frederic HENRY and Catherine BARKLEY row a boat from Stresa, Italy, up the lake into Swiss territory (about 21 miles) and to freedom from possible arrest by Italian police.

Magic   Name of a steamboat in "The Doctor and the Doctor's Wife" that pulls the LOG BOOMS down (probably) Walloon Lake to logging mills in northern Michigan.

Magnum, .357   A weapon carried by Thomas HUDSON on his boat during the "At Sea" section of *Islands in the Stream.* He and his crew are searching for a German submarine crew.

Magyars   Members of the Finno-Ugric ethnic group that forms the predominant element of the population of Hungary. The terms Magyar and Hungarian are synonymous, but Magyar is used to distinguish the Hungarian-speaking population from the German-, Slavic-, and Romanian-speaking minorities. Hemingway makes this distinction by referring to the "Magyars" who fought against Italy in World War I. They are mentioned briefly in *A Farewell to Arms.*

maid (1)   At the hotel in "Cat in the Rain" where the American wife and her husband are staying. The maid carries the umbrella to protect the wife from the rain when she goes out to look for a cat, and, at the end of the story, the maid carries to the wife the "big tortoise-shell cat" that the hotel owner sent up to her room.

maid (2)   In RENATA's villa in *Across the River and Into the Trees.*

maid (3)   Looks after the hotel rooms in LA NAPOULE, France, for David and Catherine BOURNE in *The Garden of Eden.*

maidservant   At Gertrude STEIN's apartment in Paris at 27, rue de Fleurus. In *A Moveable Feast* Hemingway writes that, when Stein was not at home, the maidservant would offer him a drink and look after him.

Mail and Empire   Toronto newspaper for which Hemingway wrote two articles ("Greatest Boy Actor Is a Toronto Lad" and "Marks Not Caused by Ill-Treatment"), following his resignation from *The Toronto Star* on January 1, 1924. The newspaper later merged with the *Globe* and became known as the *Globe and Mail.*

Main Street   In PETOSKEY, Michigan, mentioned in *The Torrents of Spring.* "It was a handsome, broad street, lined on either side with brick and pressed-stone buildings."

Maisons-Lafitte   Town about 9 miles west of Paris on the left bank of the Seine, near the forest of Saint Germain, where, in "My Old Man," JOE and his "old man" lived at Mrs. Meyer's boardinghouse during the racing season. The "old man" is a jockey, and there was a steeplechase racing season at Maisons-Lafitte during the 1920s when the story takes place.

maitre d'hotel   At the Hotel Montoya in Pamplona, a German who, according to Jake BARNES in *The Sun Also Rises,* tended to eavesdrop on patrons.

Maji-Maji rebellion   East African civil war (1905–07), mentioned by David BOURNE in *The Garden of Eden* as the time of his childhood experience with his father hunting an old elephant in East Africa and about which David is writing in his AFRICAN STORY. The rebellion was by the Maji-Maji people against German rule in East Africa. David was "about eight" at the time of the uprising, which helps determine his age in the novel. The novel takes place in about 1923, which places him in his mid-20s.

major (1)   Italian military officer, in "A Very Short Story," who makes love to LUZ in Pordenone, where, as a nurse, she has helped to open a hospital. They plan to get married "in the spring," but the marriage is called off.

major (2)   Character in the Italian army during World War I and the narrator's friend in "In Another Country." The major is a champion fencer, but he has been wounded in the war and has a hand which is now "little . . . like a baby's," and the army doctor has him on a machine that manipulates the hand and is supposed to return it to normal. The major is skeptical of the treatment, and, when his young wife dies suddenly of pneumonia, he becomes depressed and can only stare out the window when the doctor tries to encourage him with before-and-after photographs of other withered hands, which the doctor insists are now healed.

major (3)   Character in "A Simple Enquiry." He is a homosexual army major, and he attempts to seduce his orderly, PININ, who insists that he is in love with a girl. The major asks Pinin if he is "corrupt," implying homosexuality, but when Pinin says he doesn't understand the question, the major tells him not to be "afraid. . . . I won't touch you." He also says, "you better stay on as my servant. You've less chance of being killed." But he is "really relieved" at his unsuccessful seduction, thinking, "life in the army was too complicated."

This also suggests that the "enquiry" of the title is not so "simple" after all. And at the end of the story, the major thinks, "I wonder if he lied to me," and if Pinin did lie about his love for a girl and about his not understanding the word "corrupt," then the story, too, is not simple.

major (4)   Italian officer in charge of the ward in the FIELD HOSPITAL where, in *A Farewell to Arms,* Frederic

HENRY is taken after his wounding and before he is transferred to Milan.

Making of Americans, The Experimental novel by Gertrude STEIN, completed in 1911 but not published until 1925 because of its length and its lack of plot, dialogue, and action. Stein thought that by generalizing events in her own family history she could create a book that would be about all American families.

In *A Moveable Feast* Hemingway writes that the book is "unbelievably long" and that although there are "great stretches of great brilliance," it then goes on "endlessly in repetitions that a more conscientious and less lazy writer would have put in the waste basket." Nevertheless, he managed to talk Ford Madox FORD into publishing it serially in *transatlantic review,* knowing, as Hemingway says, "that it would outrun the life of the review." Only part 1 was published in the *review.* The book was published by Robert McAlmon at Contact Editions (1925).

"Malady of Power: A Second Serious Letter, The" Article, published in *Esquire* (November 1935), reprinted in *American Points of View: 1936* (1937), and in *By-Line: Ernest Hemingway* (1967). It includes anecdotes from Hemingway's early days in Paris as a reporter for *The Toronto Star,* ending with a three-paragraph editorial on the next war in Europe and America's chances of staying out of it. "War is coming to Europe as surely as winter follows fall. If we [Americans] want to stay out now is the time to decide to stay out. . . . [S]he [the U.S.] will again have a chance to save civilization; she will have a chance to fight another war to end war." Hemingway wrote this in the fall of 1935 six years before WORLD WAR II.

Málaga Town in southern Spain on the Mediterranean coast where Bill and Annie Davis, friends of Ernest and Mary Hemingway, built a villa, LA CONSULA. Hemingway visited them in the summer of 1959 during the bullfight season which he followed in preparation for writing *The Dangerous Summer.* Málaga was also the site of one of the "mano a mano" bullfights between Antonio ORDÓÑEZ and Luis Miguel DOMINGUÍN, which was, Hemingway says, "one of the very greatest bullfights I have ever seen."

Malecon, the Road in Cuba on which, according to Thomas HUDSON in *Islands in the Stream,* General BENÍTEZ practices "learning to ride a motorcycle" in preparation for serving with a motorized division in World War II.

Mama Jini's Lion (play) Written by Patrick and Carol HEMINGWAY, based on a 1960s safari they took in Tanzania with flashbacks to earlier times in Patrick's

father's life. The play had its first public reading March 26, 1988, at a writers' conference at the University of North Dakota.

man (1) Character in a "rubber cape" who, in "Cat in the Rain," crosses the "empty square to the café" as the American wife looks for the cat she had seen from her second-floor hotel window.

man (2) Character at the Fiesta SAN FERMÍN who would not let Jake BARNES pay for drinks at the wine shop in *The Sun Also Rises.*

man (3) Character who orders a rye in "The Light of the World," as the narrator and his friend Tom enter a bar at the beginning of the story.

man (4) One of the drunken brawlers in a fight with Joey that the SHERIFF breaks up at FREDDIE'S PLACE in *To Have and Have Not.* He and Richard GORDON are on their way to watch Harry MORGAN's boat being towed in near the end of the novel. The man tells the sheriff to "mind [his] own business."

man (5) Owner of a cruiser docked at BIMINI, whose boat is shot at with flares by the drunken Frank HART in *Islands in the Stream.* The man gets in a fight with Roger DAVIS about the incident.

"Man, What a Sport" Article, published in *Rotarian* (May 1940), giving advice to Rotary conferees on how to fish the Gulf Stream.

manager (1) Of the hotel in Milan, across from the train station, where, in *A Farewell To Arms,* Frederic HENRY and Catherine BARKLEY stay until midnight the night he returns to the front.

manager (2) Lover of PACO (1), a homosexual bullfighter and the main character in "The Mother of a Queen." The manager has Paco's mother buried, not in perpetuity as he had earlier the father, but for five years, because when the mother died, the manager wasn't sure his relationship with Paco would last much longer.

manager (3) Of the Hotel Florida in Madrid, setting for *The Fifth Column.* He's very nervous about everything going on in his hotel, especially the counterespionage activities of the play's main characters.

Mancelona Town in northern Michigan northeast of Traverse City and about 40 miles south of PETOSKEY. Scripps O'NEIL, one of the main characters in *The Torrents of Spring,* has two wives, one of whom lives with their daughter in Mancelona.

"The Battler" is set in a beechwood forest about two miles south of Mancelona and just off the railroad line that runs from Chicago to Petoskey.

In "The Light of the World," the whore ALICE is from Mancelona and claims to have known Steve KETCHEL there.

Manchester Guardian, The Manchester, England daily newspaper, read, the reader is led to believe, in PETOSKEY, Michigan, by Diana SCRIPPS in *The Torrents of Spring*.

Mandy The "relief" waitress at Brown's Beanery in *The Torrents of Spring* and the woman Scripps O'NEIL takes up with after dumping the "elderly waitress," Diana. Mandy is referred to as the "buxom waitress." She is able to seduce Scripps away from Diana because she is full of literary anecdotes, which entertain Scripps, a would-be short story writer.

Manera One of the four ambulance drivers under Frederic HENRY's command as they drive to the warfront in book 1 of *A Farewell to Arms*. He and GAVUZZI carry Frederic to an ambulance after he is wounded.

Mann, Heinrich (1871–1950) German novelist and essayist, the elder brother of Thomas MANN. Heinrich is best known for his portrayal of the decadence of high society, especially in Germany before World War I. In the United States his best-known work is *The Blue Angel* (1928). In *Green Hills of Africa* when Kandisky asks Hemingway what he thinks of Mann, Hemingway says, "He is no good."

Mann, Thomas (1875–1955) German novelist and essayist, best known for *Buddenbrooks* (1901), *Death in Venice* (1912), and *The Magic Mountain* (1924). He won the Nobel Prize for literature in 1929. In *Green Hills of Africa* Kandisky asks Hemingway about American literature and says, "Who is your Thomas Mann? Who is your Valery?" In other words, who is your best novelist, your best poet.

Manners, Lady Diana (1892–1986) Actress and youngest daughter of the eighth duke of Rutland. She had a short career in silent films and then went on stage in Max Reinhardt's *The Miracle*, a play that opened in New York in January 1924 and then toured across both the United States and Europe. During World War I she was a V.A.D. (Volunteer Aid Detachment) for the British Army, not a trained nurse—the same seminursing position held by Brett ASHLEY in *The Sun Also Rises* and Catherine BARKLEY in *A Farewell to Arms*.

In *A Moveable Feast* Hemingway writes that Scott Fitzgerald told him that his daughter, Scotty, had a cockney accent because he and his wife, Zelda, had hired an English nanny so Scotty would speak like Lady Diana Manners when she got older. Her full name was Diana Olivia Winifred Maud Manners.

Manning, Bishop Probably William Thomas Manning (1866–1949), Episcopal bishop of New York (1921–46). In *The Sun Also Rises* Jake BARNES and Bill GORTON have lunch, including wine, after trout fishing along the Fabrica River in northern Spain; they make joking remarks about Manning, William Jennings BRYAN, and Wayne B. WHEELER.

mannitol hexanitrate Colorless, crystalline, water-insoluble, explosive solid, used as a fulminating agent in percussion caps and in the treatment by doctors of hypertension and coronary insufficiency. In *Across the River and Into the Trees* Richard CANTWELL takes two of these tablets each time he feels a heart twinge during his duck hunting trip to VENICE. He has had four heart attacks when the novel begins.

Mannlicher, 6.5 Rifle used by Margot MACOMBER in "The Short Happy Life of Francis Macomber." This rifle, also developed by Ferdinand Mannlicher (see entry below), is a "straight-pull" bolt-action weapon, first used by Austrian soldiers in 1885.

The narrator of "The Short Happy Life" states that Margot "shot at the buffalo . . . as it seemed about to gore Macomber and . . . hit her husband about two inches up and a little to one side of the base of is skull."

Mannlicher Shoenauer, .256 Named after Count Ferdinand Mannlicher, an Austrian gun designer who worked for the Austrian Arms Company, which produced more than 150 new or improved weapons during the last 40 years of the 19th century. The .256 Mannlicher Shoenauer, invented in 1885, is a carbine rifle with a rotary magazine for rapid fire; it was produced initially as a weapon for sportsmen. Mannlicher designed the rifle's action, and Otto Schoenauer, director of the Company's Steyr, Austria, factory, designed the rotary magazine.

Thomas HUDSON owns one of the rifles and carries it on his boat in the BIMINI section of *Islands in the Stream*, keeping it clean and well oiled. He fires it at a hammerhead shark that is headed for his young son David but misses, and Eddy has to kill the shark with a submachine gun.

A Mannlicher is also one of the rifles used by Hemingway on the one-month safari he describes in *Green Hills of Africa*.

mano a mano Term meaning, literally, "hand to hand" used by Hemingway exclusively in reference to bullfighting. It is a duel between two bullfighters without the usual third matador in the ring, and each of the two bullfighters kills three bulls instead of the usual two.

In *The Dangerous Summer* the term is sometimes confusing, because it is used even though a third matador is on the card with the book's two primary bullfighters, Antonio ORDÓÑEZ and Luis Miguel DOMINGUÍN.

The first clearly defined mano a mano mentioned in the book (and confirmed by the index) was in Valencia, where Dominguín was wounded by his third bull. The second mano a mano was in Málaga on August 14, which, according to Hemingway, "was one of the very greatest bullfights I have ever seen" (chapter 11). The third mano a mano was in Bayonne, France, and the fourth was in Ciudad Real, Spain, on August 17.

"Man of the People, A"   Article, unsigned, published in *The Toronto Daily Star* (October 8, 1923), reprinted in *Ernest Hemingway: Dateline Toronto* (1985). The headline in the *Daily Star* was "'A Man of the People, Will Fight for People.'" Datelined "Montreal," it is about Lloyd George, the former British prime minister, making a statement in one of his speeches that he is "a man of the people."

"Man of the World, A"   This short story and "Get a Seeing-Eyed Dog" were the last stories published in Hemingway's lifetime, placed together under the heading "Two Tales of Darkness" in *Atlantic* magazine for November 1957. The "darkness" in the overall title refers to the blindness of the main character in each story.

"Blindy," the blind man in "A Man of the World" lost his sight in a vicious fight with Willie Sawyer in a western U.S. town called Jessup. Blindy wanders the road between "The Flats" and Jessup and its two saloons, "The Pilot" and "The Index." In the evening of the story, he is picked up by Sawyer who comes along in his car but dropped off suddenly when Blindy reaches over to feel Sawyer's face. In the earlier fight with Sawyer, Blindy had managed to gouge out some of Sawyer's face, and in the car he had reached over to feel the results. "That's why he put me out of the car," Blindy says. "He ain't got no sense of humor at all. . . . You know that Willie Sawyer he'll never be a man of the world."

man-of-war bird   Seen by SANTIAGO on the GULF STREAM in *The Old Man and the Sea*. Also known as a frigate bird, it is the most aerial of the water birds of the Tropics, and has a wingspan of seven feet or more, the widest of any bird in proportion to its body weight (three to four pounds).

Manolete (1917–1947)   Manuel Rodríguez, known as Manolete, one of the great matadors of the "classical period" of Spanish bullfighting, mentioned several times in *The Dangerous Summer*, usually in comparison to Antonio ORDÓÑEZ and Luis Miguel DOMINGUÍN, the bullfighters Hemingway saw in the summer of 1959.

Manolin   Young boy who looks after SANTIAGO in *The Old Man and the Sea*. Because Santiago has been 84 days without a fish, Manolin's parents consider the old man "*salao*, which is the worst form of unlucky," and they have forbidden Manolin to fish with Santiago any longer. But he loves the old man and provides him with food and supplies, including two fresh sardines as bait for his next day's fishing.

Manolin is an important character in the novel, not only because of his role as a caretaker for Santiago, but because the love and friendship he shows the old man is necessary sustenance for a man whose "hope and . . . confidence had never gone" and who the narrator later tells us can be "destroyed but not defeated." The boy asks Santiago where he is going to fish, and, when the old man says "far out to come in when the wind shifts," Manolin tells him that he will ask the fisherman he is working with the next day to go "far out" too so that if Santiago catches something really big they can help him.

And he talks to the old man about "the baseball." Both of them like the Yankees, especially the great Joe DIMAGGIO, whose father was a fisherman, but Manolin fears "the Indians of Cleveland" and they both fear "the Tigers of Detroit." It is September and the American League pennant race is close. The boy asks the old man who he thinks is the greatest manager, Dolf LUQUE or Mike GONZALEZ. Both are Cubans, but Luque only managed in the Cuban winter leagues.

Santiago wakes Manolin the next morning, and the boy carries the rolls of line in a basket and the harpoon and gaff to the old man's boat. They have a coffee together before Santiago sets out.

At the end of the novel, the boy sees the 18-foot-long skeleton of the marlin and cries for the old man's bad luck. He carries a can of coffee to Santiago's hut and waits for him to wake up. He tells Santiago that they will fish together again no matter what his parents say, and when the old man tells him that "I am not lucky anymore," the boy says, "The hell with luck. . . . I'll bring the luck with me." And they make plans for their next fishing trip together.

Manolin's age is difficult to determine, but he is probably about 10 years old. The only internal evidence is in a single, but grammatically ambiguous, comment made by the boy to Santiago about the baseball players George SISLER and Dick SISLER. Manolin says to Santiago that "[t]he great Sisler's father was never poor and he, the father, was playing in the Big Leagues when he was my age." If Manolin's statement is taken literally, the second "he" still refers to the father, and Manolin must be at least 22 years old, since George Sisler's first year in the majors was as a 22-year-old in 1915. The old man might still refer to Manolin as a "boy," but it doesn't seem likely that Manolin is 22.

C. Harold Hurley argues convincingly, on the other hand, that Manolin is 10. The second "he" in the sentence refers to Dick Sisler, not to George, Hurley argues, and Dick Sisler was 10 in his father's final year in the major leagues in 1930 (see "Just 'a boy' or 'already a man'?": Manolin's Age in *The Old Man and the Sea*": *The Hemingway Review,* Spring 1991: 71–72).

The novel's next sentence adds to the age ambiguity, however, when Santiago responds by saying, "When I was your age I was before the mast on a square rigged ship that ran to Africa. . . ." Ten seems young to be "before the mast" on a serious sailing ship (Melville was 20 on his first voyage—as a cabin boy) but not impossible, especially, perhaps, for Santiago, the extremely knowledgeable old man of the sea.

Manolo   See Manuel GARCIA.

Mansfield, Katherine (1888–1923)   New Zealand short story writer, Katherine Mansfield Murry (née Beauchamp), the wife of the English writer John Middleton Murry, is best known for her book *The Garden Party and Other Stories* (1922). In *A Moveable Feast* Hemingway writes that he had been told that she was a good, even "great," short story writer, but he says that reading her after Chekov (a doctor as well as a writer) "was like hearing the carefully artificial tales of a young old-maid compared to those of an articulate and knowing physician who was a good and simple writer. Mansfield was like near-beer. It was better to drink water."

Mansion House   Hotel in Seney, Michigan, in "Big Two-Hearted River." When NICK, the only character, gets there on his fishing trip, it has burned, the hotel sticking "up above the ground. The stone was chipped and split by the fire. It was all that was left of the town of Seney."

Mantegna, Andrea (c. 1431–1506)   Italian painter and engraver and one of the best-known and most celebrated of all the painters in northern Italy. He is mentioned in "The Revolutionist" as the one painter the Revolutionist does not like in his travels around the art museums of Italy.

Although unstated in the story, it may be that the Revolutionist, who is a communist, knows—as Giorgio Vasari describes Mantegna in his *Lives of the Artists* (1568; translation 1965)—that Mantegna was born of "very humble stock . . . , working in the fields as a boy and yet . . . rising to the rank of a knight through his own efforts and good fortune," the sort of individual-

ism that might not be appreciated by a revolutionist with such strong communist ideals.

Mantegna is also mentioned, along with other Renaissance painters, including Michelangelo and Piero della Francesca, by Richard Cantwell in *Across the River and Into the Trees.*

Mantequerías Leonesas   A store in Madrid that Robert JORDAN remembers in *For Whom the Bell Tolls.* He had sent LUIS (2) to the store for a bottle of absinthe.

man with Goebbels' face   A customer in HARRY'S BAR, observed by Richard CANTWELL in *Across the River and Into the Trees.* Goebbels was the German propaganda director for the Nazis during World War II.

man with jumping frogs   In *The Sun Also Rises* Jake BARNES walks along the sidewalk past a man with toy jumping frogs on Jake's way to his office near the Paris Opéra. The man is assisted by a girl who manipulates mechanical men who simulate boxing.

Manyara, Lake   In northern Tanzania southwest of Mount Kilimanjaro and near Babati, just south of which is the setting for much of *Green Hills of Africa.*

Manzanilla   In *The Garden of Eden* David and Catherine BOURNE drink this "light and nutty tasting" sherry in MADRID after spending the morning at the PRADO (1) museum. Manzanilla is a special type of sherry, from, according to the novel's narrator, "the lowland near CADIZ called the Marismas." Some wine connoisseurs believe that Manzanilla's special tang comes from the sea wind off the Atlantic, but it is more likely caused by the humidity of the Sanlucar de Barrameda region.

Maquereau Vin Blanc Capitaine Cook   Name of the tin of marinated mackerel, spiced with wine, mentioned in *The Garden of Eden.* David BOURNE "opened [the tin] and took it, perilous with edge-level juice, with a cold bottle of the Tuborg beer out to the bar." The word mackerel in French means both the fish and pimp or panderer, and both times the tin of Maquereau is mentioned in the novel, David is alone and may be thinking of the pandering he has been involved in with Catherine and MARITA.

máquina   An informal Spanish word for "machine gun," the word used by the guerrilla fighters in *For Whom the Bell Tolls* for the Lewis Gun, an automatic rifle.

Maran, René   (1887–1960)   French novelist from Martinique who won a controversial Goncourt Academy Prize in 1921 for his novel *Batouala.* The novel was critical of French imperialism. The controversy is the subject of Hemingway's article "Black Novel a Storm Center."

Marceliano's   Restaurant in Pamplona, Spain, where Hemingway and Antonio Ordóñez went for breakfast during the Fiesta San Fermín while Hemingway followed the bullfight circuit in 1959 in preparation for writing *The Dangerous Summer*.

March, Juan   Spanish millionaire and enemy of the Spanish Republic during the Spanish civil war; he was jailed in 1931 for corruption. Pilar refers to him as a "criminal" in *For Whom the Bell Tolls*.

Marcial   In *The Sun Also Rises* he is the third bullfighter, with Pedro ROMERO and BELMONTE, to fight on the last day of the Fiesta SAN FERMÍN in Pamplona.

Marconi, Comrade   In *The Fifth Column* it is the ironic name given by Philip RAWLINGS to the drunken electrician at the Hotel Florida, the name an allusion to Guglielmo Marconi (1874–1937), the Italian physicist who invented wireless telegraphy (radio).

Margaret   A singer of "The Star Spangled Banner" "on the radio," whom Richard CANTWELL hears in *Across the River and Into the Trees* (1950). It may be a reference to Margaret Truman, daughter of President Harry S. Truman, who began her singing career in 1947.

Margaux   Wine of choice for Frederic HENRY and Catherine BARKLEY at the GRAN ITALIA restaurant in Milan.

Margot   Unidentified woman in *Green Hills of Africa*, mentioned in a discussion of "beautiful" women.

Margot Macomber   In "The Short Happy Life of Francis Macomber." See Margot MACOMBER.

Maria   In "Nobody Ever Dies," she is a member of the outlawed Communist Party of Cuba in 1939 and doing espionage work in Havana. She brings food to her lover, ENRIQUE (2), who is hiding in a house where the communists have stored weapons. She escapes with him when the police raid the house, and, when Enrique is killed by machine-gun fire, she decides to walk into the police spotlight and gunfire, thinking it is the best way to die.

Instead of shooting her, however, the police capture her, because they believe she can provide them with information. She prays for help, not to the God she could have prayed to in earlier years, but to the dead Enrique and to her brother and friends who were killed in the recent Spanish civil war.

The police think she is crazy for calling to the dead, and, at the end of the story, the Negro "stool pigeon" who had turned Maria and Enrique in to the police, becomes afraid of these calls to the dead and so fingers his blue voodoo beads, because he thinks "he [is] up against an older magic now."

María   One of the major characters in *For Whom the Bell Tolls*. Early in the SPANISH CIVIL WAR—three months before the novel begins—María had been raped by the Falangists in VALLADOLID after her mother and father, the town's mayor, had been shot. She was rescued by PABLO and his band of Spanish LOYALISTS when they blew up the train on which she was being evacuated to the south. They took her into the Guadarrama Mountains, and, when the American, Robert JORDAN, joins the group on his assignment to blow up the BRIDGE, María becomes his lover.

She tells Jordan about the killing of her mother and father by the GUARDIA CIVILES of her own village and about her rape. They cut her hair and then wrote in iodine on her forehead "UHP" (Unión de Hermanos Proletarios—Union of Proletarian Brothers). She tells Jordan that her best friend, Concepción Gracía, did not recognize her as the Falangists dragged Concepción past María into the barbershop to have her hair cut also.

She also tells Jordan that PILAR, Pablo's wife, had told her that "nothing is done to oneself that one does not accept and [Pilar said] that if I loved some one it would take it all away. I wished to die, you see." She is attracted to Jordan in part because he is sensitive toward both Pilar and her, but she is also attracted to him because she believes what Pilar had told her, that if she loves him then what happened to her before would be more easily forgotten. When Jordan is wounded and left to die, following the blowing up of the bridge, María has to be dragged away by other members of the guerrilla band, who are escaping farther into the mountains.

In spite of the early popularity of *For Whom the Bell Tolls*, criticism of the novel tended to focus for nearly 40 years on Hemingway's creation of María as a "mere sex object." Recent criticism, however, has viewed María more as a victim of the social disorder in Spain at the time of the SPANISH CIVIL WAR (1936–39). She is trying, with the help of Pilar, a mother figure for María, to get her life back together; and her love affair with Jordan is an attempt to regain her self.

Marie   *Femme de ménage* (charwoman) in the Paris apartment at 113, rue Notre-Dame-des-Champs where the Hemingways lived in the mid-1920s; mentioned in *A Moveable Feast*.

Marie Antoinette (1755–1793)   In *Across the River and Into the Trees*, Richard CANTWELL tells RENATA that she looks "like Marie Antoinette in the tumbril"—that is, the cart in which they took her to the guillotine. She was wife of Louis XVI and daughter of Maria Theresa and Francis I of Austria.

Mariel   Cuban port town, about 25 miles west of Havana, where Harry MORGAN and his Negro mate, WESLEY, are badly wounded while loading bootleg liquor in part 2 of *To Have and Have Not*.

Marie Morgan   See Marie MORGAN.

Marine Hardware   KEY WEST store in *To Have and Have Not*.

Marine Hospital   In KEY WEST, where the dying Harry MORGAN is taken at the end of *To Have and Have Not*.

Mario   Thomas HUDSON's houseboy at his farm outside of Havana in *Islands in the Stream*. Mario takes care of the cats, goes for the mail, mixes drinks, etc. Hudson likes his efficiency.

Mariposa   Name of the bull that had killed Manuel GARCIA's brother "nine years" before the time of "The Undefeated." The bull's head had been stuffed and now hangs over the desk of the Madrid bullfight promoter Don Miguel RETANA.

marismeño   A Spanish wine, ordered by David BOURNE in Madrid, in *The Garden of Eden*, and enjoyed with Colonel John BOYLE, who tells him about Catherine BOURNE's parents.

Marita   Major character in *The Garden of Eden*, a young, "handsome," woman, who has a "breathless way of speaking" and who becomes sexually involved with both David BOURNE and Catherine BOURNE.

Marita and her friend NINA first meet the Bournes in a café in LA NAPOULE on the Mediterranean Sea near the beginning of book 3. Their nationality is never made clear, but they are probably Swiss, since their car has Swiss plates. David and Catherine consider them "spooky" at first, because of their lesbian relationship, but they are both charmed by Marita and soon accept her into their world.

Marita is attracted to Catherine because of her non-conformity, especially the way she has her hair cut like a boy's, and then, soon after, she is attracted to David too because she realizes he is caught in the trap of Catherine's bisexuality (see ANDROGYNY). Marita blushes in her initial meetings with David and Catherine but loses the embarrassed feeling, as she later tells David, the first time the three swim naked together.

Near the beginning of the MÉNAGE À TROIS, Marita tells David, "Your wife is wonderful and I'm in love with her. . . . I'm in love with you also." After her friend Nina leaves, Marita moves into the hotel at La Napoule, "next door" to David's work room. Marita and Catherine have their first sexual encounter in the car on their way to Nice. Marita and Catherine then sleep together at the hotel, and Catherine then "gives" Marita to David as a "gift." Marita says, "Perhaps I am a gamin," meaning, for her, that maybe she is not so different from Catherine after all—that is, that she is a boy, or at least a tomboy, but bisexual. *Gamin* is a word that David uses to describe Marita, and when she asks, he says it means "The one who blushes. The modest one."

At the end of the novel Catherine leaves, realizing that she has spoiled both her marriage and her relations with Marita. Marita remains with David as he attempts to get his life back together.

Maritza River   Flows for 300 miles from southern Bulgaria along the border between Greece and European Turkey into the Aegean Sea. At the Lausanne Conference (1923) the Maritza became the border between Turkey and Greece. The river is referred to in the "Chapter 2" vignette of *In Our Time* and in articles that Hemingway wrote for *The Toronto Star* when he was in Constantinople in 1922 covering the evacuation of the Greeks.

Marjorie   NICK's girlfriend in "The End of Something." She doesn't realize that the reason Nick is so quiet while they fish the edges of the lake and then build a fire on the shore is because he is about to break off their relationship. When he tells her that "It isn't fun any more," she says, "Isn't love any fun?" When he says "No," she accepts the breakup with less apparent emotion than he and, taking the boat, rows away onto the lake.

In "The Three-Day Blow," a story that follows the action of "The End of Something," Nick's friend BILL (1) makes an issue of Marjorie's lower-class status. In trying to convince Nick that he's better off without her, Bill says, "Now she can marry somebody of her own sort and settle down and be happy. You can't mix oil and water. . . ."

According to Bill in "The Three-Day Blow," Marjorie's mother was "sore as hell" when Nick broke with her daughter. "She told a lot of people you were engaged." The "Marge business" is apparently over, but Nick is still unsure that he had done the right thing.

market   In *Across the River and Into the Trees* Richard CANTWELL "loved the [Venice] market. . . . A market is the closest thing to a good museum like the Prado or as the Accademia is now." The market contains "gray-green lobsters," "small soles," "albacore and bonito," "boat-tailed bullets," "eels," "prawns," and "shrimp," "small crustaceans," "the razor-edge clams you only should eat raw if you had your typhoid shots up to date," and "small delectables." Cantwell buys a quarter kilo of sausage for his Sunday lunch on the duck hunt, thinking that he will give a slice to BOBBY, the retriever.

"Marks Not Caused by Ill-Treatment" Article, published in the Toronto *Mail and Empire* (January 8, 1924), reprinted in William Burrill's *Hemingway: The Toronto Years* (1994). The article was "discovered" by Burrill in the Hemingway Collection at the John F. Kennedy Library in Boston. This was the second of two articles Hemingway wrote for the *Mail and Empire*, following his resignation from *The Toronto Daily Star* on January 1, 1924. Datelined, "Goderich, Ont., Jan. 8," the article is about an inquest into the death of a 16-

year-old boy, found hanging in a barn on a farm a few miles from Goderich, Ontario.

marlin (1) Large fish hooked by JOHNSON, the tourist fisherman on Harry MORGAN's charter fishing boat in part 1 of *To Have and Have Not*. Harry says it is "the biggest black marlin I ever saw in my life." But the careless Johnson loses both the marlin and 650 dollars' worth of Morgan's fishing tackle overboard.

marlin (2) The fish that SANTIAGO catches in *The Old Man and the Sea*, a 1,500-pound Atlantic blue marlin. Here is the reader's introduction to the great fish: "One hundred fathoms down [600 feet] a marlin was eating the sardines that covered the point and the shank of the hook where the hand-forged hook projected from the head of the small tuna."

Lillian Gattner with Hemingway and his 125-pound striped marlin (Courtesy of the John F. Kennedy Library)

When the old man finally lashes him to the boat, he is 18 feet long (two feet longer than the boat) and "over fifteen hundred pounds the way he is. . . . Maybe much more." Santiago figures that, dressed out, even at two-thirds of the 1,500 pounds, at thirty cents a pound, the fish is worth $300. Later, one of the fishermen at the dock measures the skeleton at "eighteen feet from nose to tail." The marlin's significance is practical, but Santiago also knows, when he loses the fish to sharks, that his ambition to go out far enough to catch a great fish is the cause of his losing it.

The world record weight for the Atlantic blue marlin is 1,402 pounds, caught off the coast of Brazil in 1992. But when Hemingway wrote *The Old Man and the Sea* (writing it from late 1950 to March 1952), the world record Atlantic blue, according to the 1952 *World Almanac and Book of Facts* was 742 pounds (12 feet 10 ½ inches long, with a 68-inch girth), caught off Bimini on June 19, 1949. So the fish that Hemingway imagined for Santiago was twice the weight and a third longer than any Atlantic blue marlin ever caught.

Some critics have questioned the type of marlin Hemingway had in mind. Captain Steve Coulter, a sportfisherman out of Hatteras, North Carolina, says he has no problem accepting Hemingway's story. He says that Santiago's marlin is the dream of every deep-sea fisherman. Several 1,500-pound Atlantic blues have probably been caught, Coulter says; they just haven't been recognized, for one reason or another, as official world records. As for the possibility that Hemingway meant for Santiago's marlin to be the black marlin, which tends to be larger than the Atlantic blue but is a Pacific Ocean fish, Coulter says it would be a greater oddity to catch a black marlin off the Cuban coast than a 1,500-pound Atlantic blue.

"Marlin off the Morro: A Cuban Letter" Article, published in *Esquire* (Autumn 1933 [Vol. I, No. 1]), reprinted in *By-Line: Ernest Hemingway* (1967). The article presents the details of fishing for marlin off the Cuban coast. Hemingway fished from the *Anita*, a 34-foot boat, "owned and skippered" by Captain Joe Russell of Key West. They were joined by Carlos Gutiérrez of Havana, 54 years old and "the best marlin and swordfisherman around Cuba."

Marlowe, Christopher (1564–1593) English poet and playwright, best known as Shakespeare's contemporary and for his play *The Jew of Malta* (1633). In *A Moveable Feast* Hemingway describes a conversation he had with Ford Madox FORD that included a discussion of men they considered to be "gentlemen." When Ford suggests Marlowe, Hemingway says "of course not," without further explanation.

Marquez One of the bullfighters who fights in Pamplona during the weeklong Fiesta SAN FERMÍN in *The Sun Also Rises.*

Marsala A sweet, dark, fortified, Italian wine from the vineyards near Marsala, a seaport town in western Sicily. It is the wine that PEDUZZI (1) buys in "Out of Season."

In *Across the River and Into the Trees* Marsala is the wine chosen to go with a dinner of scaloppine, by Richard CANTWELL to share with Renata on Friday evening at the GRITTI PALACE HOTEL in Venice. The wine is also mentioned in *A Moveable Feast.*

Marseilles Major Mediterranean seaport city in France. The characters in "A Canary for One" see the smoking chimneys of Marseilles as they enter the city by train.

Marseilles is also where, in *Islands in the Stream,* Thomas HUDSON remembers leaving the luxury cruise ship, on which he has just finished a love affair with a "plain girl." See PRINCESS.

Marshall, Eddy See EDDY (2).

marsh-birds Thought about by Richard CANTWELL, in *Across the River and Into the Trees,* in connection with the two young men who are threatening him on his early Saturday morning walk in VENICE. When he stops to fight they were "off like marsh-birds."

Martin Owner of the TERRACE café, who provides MANOLIN with food and drink for SANTIAGO in *The Old Man and the Sea.*

Martin, Don Guillermo See PILAR'S STORY.

Martinique rum See RUM ST. JAMES.

Marty, André (1886–1955) French communist commissar and head of the INTERNATIONAL BRIGADES during the Spanish civil war. In *For Whom the Bell Tolls* he is "Comrade Marty," the "insane" officer in General Golz's headquarters who refuses to see the value of Robert JORDAN's message and so delays sending Andrés forward to Golz in time to delay the Loyalist attack.

Marvell, Andrew (1621–1678) British poet, mentioned by Frederic HENRY in *A Farewell to Arms.* He quotes two lines of "To His Coy Mistress" to Catherine BARKLEY in the hotel room in Milan the evening Frederic goes back to the warfront: "But at my back I always hear/Time's wingèd chariot hurrying near."

Masaccio (1401–1428?) Italian painter, one of the early, important painters of the Italian Renaissance and one of the key figures in Florentine art. His real name was Tommaso Guidi. See "The Revolutionist."

Masai   Members of an East African tribe inhabiting the highlands of Kenya and Tanzania and having a largely pastoral economy and a society based on the patrilineal clan. It is their language that Hemingway uses in the epigraph to "The Snows of Kilimanjaro" to describe the western summit of Mount Kilimanjaro as the Masai *Ngàje Ngài*, the House of God.

In *Green Hills of Africa* on the hunt for kudu in part 4 Hemingway and the five natives with him drive through a Masai village, and he notes that they are not "contemptuous like the northern Masai," and that they "[are] the tallest, best-built, handsomest people I had ever seen and the first truly light-hearted happy people I had seen in Africa."

mashing   A slang term meaning the act by a man of making amorous advances toward a woman he does not know. In "Fathers and Sons," Nick ADAMS remembers that as a child he once read that Enrico CARUSO had been arrested for "mashing" and that when Nick asked his father what that meant, his father defined it as "one of the most heinous of crimes," and that he, Nick, imagined Caruso doing "something strange, bizarre, and heinous with a potato masher to a beautiful lady who looked like the pictures of Anna HELD on the inside of cigar boxes." Nick also remembers vowing that when old enough he "would try mashing at least once."

Mason, A. E. W. (1865–1948)   English romantic novelist. In *The Sun Also Rises* Jake BARNES reads one of Mason's stories while resting under a tree on his fishing trip to the Fabrica River near BURGUETE with Bill GORTON. The Mason story concerns a "man who had been frozen in the Alps and then fallen into a glacier and disappeared, and his bride was going to wait twenty-four years exactly for his body to come out on the moraine, while her true love waited too." Mason's initials stand for Alfred Edward Woodley.

Mason, Jane (1909–1981)   Woman whom Hemingway met in 1931 when on board the *Ile de France* returning to the United States. She was 22 years old, beautiful, and immediately attracted to Hemingway. She was the wife of G. Grant Mason, head of Pan American Airways in Cuba, who owned an estate, "Jaimanitas," west of Havana.

Jane Mason visited Ernest and Pauline Hemingway often, usually at their Key West home, and biographers have speculated that there may have been an adulterous affair. In May 1933, in an apparent state of depression, she either jumped or fell from a second-floor window at Hemingway's Key West house and broke her back.

This incident, which put her in a New York hospital for five months and a back brace for a year, followed by a few days an automobile accident in which the car she was driving rolled down a 40-foot embankment. Her passengers were Hemingway's sons Jack and Patrick and her own adopted son. The on-again, off-again relationship between Jane and Ernest had its final, bitter, break in April 1936. Jane Mason had four husbands, including Arnold GINGRICH, editor of *Esquire* magazine.

Masson, André (1896–1987)   French surrealist painter and graphic artist whose paintings Thomas HUDSON, in *Islands in the Stream*, admires. Hudson owns at least one of Masson's paintings and has it on the wall of his bedroom at his house in Cuba.

mast   For SANTIAGO'S SKIFF (1) in *The Old Man and the Sea*. At the end of the novel, when Santiago returns from having won, then lost, the great Marlin, it seems to take on the image of the cross: "He picked the mast up and put it on his shoulder and started up the road. He had to sit down five times before he reached his shack." See CHRISTIAN IMAGERY.

Matacumbe   An island in the GULF STREAM off which, in *To Have and Have Not*, the captain of a tanker sees Harry MORGAN's boat adrift and notifies the COAST GUARD.

matador   Term for a bullfighter who is the formal killer of a bull. See the glossary in *Death in the Afternoon*.

matador, first   In the "Chapter 9" vignette of *In Our Time*, he gets a "horn through his sword hand and the crowd hooted him." The second matador slips on the bullring sand and gets badly gored, fainting as his handlers carry him out of the ring.

Mathaiga Club   In Nairobi, Kenya, where the hunters and their rich colleagues meet socially. It is mentioned in "The Short Happy Life of Francis Macomber" when the white hunting guide, Robert WILSON, becomes angry because of Francis MACOMBER's cowardice but assures the hunter that the story of his running from a wounded lion will not get back to the Mathaiga Club.

The club is also where, in *Islands in the Stream*, Thomas HUDSON remembers meeting a "plain girl" princess and her husband and later having an affair with the princess on their luxury cruise up the Suez Canal. They had all been hunting in East Africa, and they had taken the same cruise ship when it docked at Mombasa.

"Matter of Color, A"   This short story is one of three Hemingway published in his high school literary magazine, *Tabula* (April 1916). The other two are "Judgment of Manitou" and "Sepi Jingan."

"A Matter of Color" is about a crooked boxing match in which the manager for a white fighter, Dan Morgan, arranges to have a Swede stand behind the curtain along the ropes at ringside and hit the black fighter, Joe Gans, over the head with a baseball bat when he is backed against the curtain by Dan. Joe Gans is backed against the curtain and nothing happens, but when he then backs Dan Morgan against the ropes, the Swede clubs him. When the angry manager confronts the Swede about his mistake, the Swede says, "I bane color blind."

"Matter of Wind, A" Article, published in *Sports Illustrated* (August 17, 1959), about the MANO A MANO (man against man, literally "hand to hand") between Spanish bullfighters Antonio ORDÓÑEZ and Luis Miguel DOMINGUÍN during July 1959. See also *The Dangerous Summer*.

Matthews, Herbert (1906–1977) U.S. correspondent for *The New York Times* who covered the SPANISH CIVIL WAR with Hemingway; mentioned in several of Hemingway's dispatches from the war. Matthews wrote a short essay on "Colonel Juan Modesto," commander of the Army of the Ebro, for Jo Davidson's *Spanish Portraits* (no date). His books include *Two Wars and More to Come* (1938), *The Yoke and the Arrows* (1942; revised 1961), *The Education of a Correspondent* (1946), and *Half of Spain Died: a Reappraisal of the Spanish Civil War* (1973).

Mauser guns A single shot, 11 mm bolt-action rifle, designed in 1884 by brothers Wilhelm and Paul Mauser, German weapons manufacturers who opened the Mauser Brothers & Co. factory in 1874. Besides the rifle, they also developed a rear-loading pistol, a revolver, and a repeating rifle, all called Mausers. In *For Whom the Bell Tolls* Pablo takes a Mauser pistol from a dead *guardia civile* and then, after ordering one of the other four to explain how the gun works, shot each of the four with it. Agustín, another character in the story, also carries a Mauser pistol.

In *The Fifth Column* a Mauser pistol is used to kill Comrade Wilkinson by a man "wearing a beret and a trench coat" when he mistakes Wilkinson for the play's main character, Philip Rawlings.

Mawenzi The lower of the two peaks of Mt. Kilimanjaro; it is 16,896 feet (5,149 meters). KIBO, the higher peak, is 19,341 feet (5,895 meters), making Kilimanjaro the highest mountain in Africa.

Max (1) The second of two hitmen in "The Killers." He talks too much about their plans to kill Ole ANDRESON; or at least his partner, AL, thinks so. He tells Max four times that he talks too much. "We're going to kill a Swede," Max tells the lunchroom owner, GEORGE. "We're killing him for a friend. Just to oblige a friend." When the two killers leave the lunchroom, they are described as looking "like a vaudeville team" in "their tight overcoats and derby hats."

Max (2) Character in *The Fifth Column* and Philip RAWLINGS's colleague in counterespionage work for the LOYALISTS in the Spanish civil war. He is supposed to meet Rawlings at Chicote's bar in Madrid but is a day late. He has been "circulating . . . behind fascist lines" and has located an observation post, which he and Rawlings, at the climax of the play, successfully attack, taking an important civilian prisoner, a member of the FIFTH COLUMN, who leads the Loyalists to 300 other Fifth Columnists. Max is described as having a broken face "with his teeth gone in front. With sort of black gums where they [the fascists] burnt them with a red-hot iron."

Mayo Clinic Private medical center in Rochester, Minnesota, where Hemingway was taken in December 1960 and early 1961 to undergo electroshock therapy for hypertension, paranoia, and depression. The clinic was cofounded about 1905 by two brothers, William James Mayo (1861–1939) and Charles Horace Mayo (1865–1939). Their father, William Worrall Mayo (1819–1911), was head of the medical staff of St. Mary's Hospital, from which the Mayo Clinic developed.

"Mayor Tommy Church" Article, written in January 1920 for *The Toronto Star Weekly,* but rejected by editors because of its harsh treatment of Toronto's mayor, Tommy Church. It was identified later as a Hemingway story by *Star* librarian William McGeary, and published for the first time in William Burrill's book, *Hemingway: The Toronto Years* (1994).

Mays, Carl (1891–1971) Major League baseball pitcher from 1915–29 with the Boston Red Sox, New York Yankees, Cincinnati Reds, and New York Giants. In *Islands in the Stream* PETERS, one of Thomas HUDSON's crew members, throws a hand grenade onto the turtle boat at the end of the search for the German submarine crew, and Hudson thinks that it is tossed the way Carl Mays pitched, with an underhand motion.

M.C. British Military Cross. In *The Torrents of Spring,* one of the two Indians brags of having received an "M.C. with bar," along with a V.C. (VICTORIA CROSS) and D.S.O. But the Indians have probably exaggerated, or lied about, their medals, just as Yogi JOHNSON, one of the novel's main characters, has probably exaggerated, or lied about, his own war stories.

McAdams   "Mac," an otherwise unidentified "vice-consul" in Milan, in *A Farewell to Arms*. Frederic HENRY and Catherine BARKLEY meet him while Frederic is convalescing during the summer after his wounding on the northern Italian front in World War I.

McCarthy's barber shop   Scripps O'NEIL, in *The Torrents of Spring*, sees two Indians enter McCarthy's shop in PETOSKEY, Michigan. Scripps walks past the shop and thinks of it as "inviting," but he does not enter.

"McConkey's 1914 Orgy"   Article, published in *The Toronto Star Weekly* (December 29, 1923), reprinted in *Ernest Hemingway: Dateline Toronto* (1985). The headline in the *Star Weekly* was "Wild New Year's Eve Gone Forever: Only Ghost of 1914 Party Remains." New Year's Eve is dead in Toronto, according to Hemingway, thanks to Colonel George Taylor Denison. Denison, so the story goes, sued in court over a drunken "orgy" he witnessed at McConkey's Tavern in February 1914, and Toronto's celebration of the New Year has never been the same since. The byline is "John Hadley," in honor of Hemingway's son, John Hadley Nicanor Hemingway, born October 10, 1923.

McGintys   A type of artificial fishing fly carried by Jake BARNES on his fishing trip to the IRATI RIVER with Bill GORTON, in *The Sun Also Rises*.

McGraw, John J. (1873–1934)   Manager of the New York Giants Major League baseball team (1902–32). In *The Old Man and the Sea* SANTIAGO tells MANOLIN, "He [McGraw] used to come to the TERRACE sometimes . . . in the old days." McGraw is also referred to by Bill and Nick in "The Three-Day Blow."

M'Cola   Hemingway's native tracker, gun bearer, and companion in *Green Hills of Africa*. M'Cola speaks Swahili and wears an "old U.S. Army khaki tunic, complete with buttons," which POP had originally intended as a gift for DROOPY, another tracker, remembered in part 2. M'Cola's tunic, "a pair of shorts, his fuzzy wool curler's cap, and a knitted army sweater he wore when washing the tunic, were the only garments" Hemingway ever saw "the old man" wear. He wore shoes cut from automobile tires. He is as efficient as Hemingway needs on safari, and so the two get along well. There is a bit of friction, however, when M'Cola fails to understand why Hemingway gives his wife, "P.O.M.," credit for shooting the first lion, when, apparently, it was Hemingway's shot that killed it.

"M. Deibler, A Much-Feared Man"   Article, published in *The Toronto Daily Star* (April 1, 1922), reprinted in *Ernest Hemingway: Dateline Toronto* (1985). The headline

in the *Daily Star* was "Much-Feared Man Is Monsieur Deibler." Datelined "Paris," the article concerns the most feared man in Paris who is the public executioner of France and has two guillotines, one for his work in Paris, the other for travel. His neighbors in Paris's avenue de Versailles think he's a jolly man and wonder what he does for a living.

"Mecca of Fakers, The"   Article, published in *The Toronto Daily Star* (March 25, 1922), reprinted in *Ernest Hemingway: Dateline Toronto* (1985). The headline in the *Daily Star* was "The Mecca of Fakers in French Capital." Datelined "Paris," the article states that you can "find more famous American dancers who have never been heard of in America; more renowned Russian dancers who are disclaimed by the Russians; and more champion prizefighters who were preliminary boys before they crossed the ocean, per square yard in Paris than anywhere else in the world."

medaglia d'argento   "Silver medal" awarded by the Italian government to certain wounded soldiers during World War I. In *A Farewell to Arms*, RINALDI (2) tells Frederic HENRY that he will get the *medaglia d'argento* for his wounds and heroism.

In *Across the River and Into the Trees* Colonel Richard CANTWELL also received this medal for his military courage in World War I.

Médaille Militaire   French medal awarded for valor during war, mentioned in *A Moveable Feast*. See JEAN (2).

media-verónica   Half pass with the cape that a bullfighter makes after the bull has charged several times, and the bullfighter finally "[cuts] the bull's charge brusquely" and "[fixes] him to the spot." Described in *Death in the Afternoon*. Also mentioned in "The Short Happy Life of Francis Macomber."

medical captain   At the post hospital in book 1 of *A Farewell to Arms*; he dictates to an adjutant who records the wounds Frederic HENRY has received.

medical kit   Carried by David BOURNE's father on the elephant safari that David remembers from his childhood and which he writes about in his AFRICAN STORY in *The Garden of Eden*.

medical sergeant   Character who bandages both of Frederic HENRY's legs at the post hospital after his wounding in book 1 of *A Farewell to Arms*.

Mediterranean Sea   David and Catherine BOURNE spent most of the seven months of their marriage in *The Garden of Eden* along the Mediterranean coast of France.

The narrator of "Che Ti Dice La Patria?" describes driving along the Italian shoreline of the Mediterranean Sea near Genoa.

"Melanctha"   One of Gertrude STEIN's short stories, referred to in *A Moveable Feast*.

Melville, Herman (1819–1891)   American novelist, best known for *Moby-Dick* (1851). In *Green Hills of Africa* Hemingway tells Kandisky that Melville wrote without much rhetoric but that his writing was nevertheless praised for its rhetoric. "They [the critics] put a mystery in which is not there."

men, five   Sentenced to be hung "at six o'clock in the morning in the corridor of the county jail" in the "Chapter 15" vignette of *In Our Time*. "Three of the men to be hanged were negroes." But the focus is on Sam CARDINELLA, who is so afraid of what's taking place that the guards have to carry him to the gallows.

men, six white   At the train station in "The Light of the World." Two are lumberjacks, two are Swedes, one is a cook, and one "Talks."

men, two   In the "Chapter 11" vignette of *In Our Time* (1925), two men hold down the bullfighter, who has performed badly, while another cuts off his pigtail, indicating that he is no longer a bullfighter.

ménage à trois   Means, literally, triangle. The term is not used in *The Garden of Eden,* but that is what the sexual relationship becomes among David BOURNE, Catherine BOURNE, and MARITA. There is no indication that all three are ever in bed together, but the sexual encounters form a complete triangle.

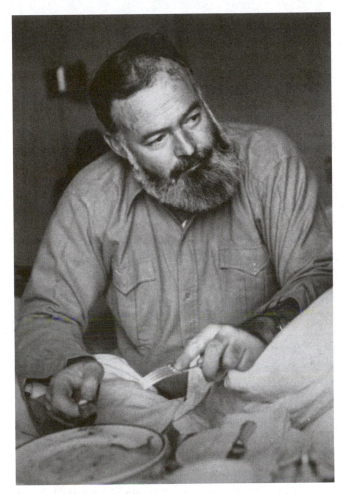

EH during World War II (Copyright holder unknown; photo courtesy of the John F. Kennedy Library)

Men at War: The Best War Stories of All Time   Book of war articles and short stories, edited by Hemingway and published by Crown Publishers in 1942.

In his introduction Hemingway writes: "The editor of this anthology, who took part and was wounded in the last war to end war [World War I], hates war and hates all the politicians whose mismanagement, gullibility, cupidity, selfishness and ambition brought on this present war [World War II] and made it inevitable. But once we have a war there is only one thing to do. It must be won. For defeat brings worse things than any that can ever happen in a war." There are 82 stories in the book divided among eight parts.

Part 1, "War is Part of the Intercourse of the Human Race," includes "The Invasion of Britain" by Julius Caesar and "The Death of Montezuma" by William Hickling Prescott.

Part 2, "War is the Province of Danger, and Therefore Courage Above all Things is the First Quality of a Warrior," includes *The Red Badge of Courage* by Stephen Crane and "The Pass of Thermopylae" by Charlotte Yonge.

Part 3, "War is the Province of Physical Exertion and Suffering," includes "Torture" by T. E. Lawrence and "The March to the Sea" by Xenophon.

Part 4, "War is the Province of Uncertainty," includes "An Egg for the Major" by C. S. Forester and "Manila Bay" by Admiral George Dewey.

Part 5, "War is the Province of Chance," includes "Turn About" by William Faulkner and "The People's War" by Leo Tolstoi.

Part 6, "War is the Province of Friction," includes "Waterloo" by Victor Hugo and "The Victory of Americans at Saratoga by Sir Edward S. Creasy."

Part 7, "War Demands Resolution, Firmness, and Staunchness," includes "After the Final Victory" by Agnes Smedley and "Trafalgar" by Robert Southey.

Part 8, "War is Fought by Human Beings," includes "An Occurrence at Owl Creek Bridge" by Ambrose Bierce and "Soldiers of the Republic" by Dorothy Parker.

Mencken, H[enry] L[ewis] (1880–1956)   American journalist, editor, author, and literary critic, he worked for *The Baltimore Sun* for 50 years (1906–56), was co-editor with George Jean Nathan of *Smart Set* (1914–23), and was founder/editor of the *American Mercury* (1924–33). He published *The American Language* (1919) in order to organize examples of Americanisms and followed the first volume with two supplements in 1945 and 1948. His essays fill six volumes, titled *Prejudices* (1919–27), and, in spite of what Hemingway thought of him, he was probably the most influential American literary critic of the 1920s.

There was little good that either Mencken or Hemingway had to say about the other. In 1925, Hemingway blamed Mencken for the delay in getting editors to read his short stories of *In Our Time*, but the insult for which Hemingway never forgave Mencken came in a review of *in our time* (1924): "The sort of brave, bold stuff that all atheistic young newspaper reporters write. Jesus Christ in lower case. A hanging, a carnal love, and two disembowelings. Here it is set forth solemnly on Rives handmade paper, in an edition limited to 170 copies, and with the imprimatur of Ezra Pound."

Mencken is parodied by Hemingway in *The Torrents of Spring* as someone interested in buying a story by Scripps O'NEIL, a writer of little talent. Scripps's wife, "the elderly waitress," in a desperate effort to impress her husband, who has fallen in love with a younger waitress, tells him that she has just read an article in *American Mercury* on chiropractors by H. L. Mencken. Chiropractors, no doubt, was meant as an insultingly lightweight subject for such an important writer.

Mentone   Small French town on the Mediterranean Sea just west of the border with Italy (the correct French spelling is "Menton"). It is where the narrator and his traveling friend, Guy, spend the night at the end of their 10-day travels around northern Italy in "Che Ti Dice La Patria?" After their experiences in fascist Italy, Mentone "seemed very cheerful and clean and sane and lovely," a comment on how bad things were in Italy.

Men Without Women   Hemingway's second book of short stories, after *Three Stories & Ten Poems* (1923), includes the following: "The Undefeated," "In Another Country," "Hills Like White Elephants," "The Killers," "Che Ti Dice La Patria?" "Fifty Grand," "A Simple Enquiry," "Ten Indians," "A Canary for One," "An Alpine Idyll," "A Pursuit Race," "To-Day is Friday," "Banal Story," and "Now I Lay Me."

The book was published by Charles Scribner's Sons on October 14, 1927, in a first printing of 7,650 copies at $2 each.

"Mercenaries, The"   Short story, written in 1919 but not published until 1985 when Peter Griffin included it and four other previously unpublished stories in the first volume of his biography, *Along With Youth: Hemingway, The Early Years*. Hemingway submitted the story to *Redbook* and to *The Saturday Evening Post*, getting rejection slips from both magazines before giving up on it.

In the story three men discuss their war experiences. The narrator is Rinaldi RENALDO, an American who had spent three years in Italy during World War I. The other two characters are Denis Ricaud and Perry Graves, who are on their way to New York to join the Peruvian army as mercenaries in a war against Chile.

Merito, Peps   The Marquis del Merito, who owned a home near Córdoba, Spain, where Hemingway stayed during the summer of 1959 while he was traveling the bullfight circuit in preparation for writing *The Dangerous Summer.*

mess boy   Minor character in "The Short Happy Life of Francis Macomber." He makes the GIMLETS for Francis and Margot Macomber and for Mr. WILSON.

Messerschmitt pursuit planes   Mentioned in Hemingway's Spanish civil war NANA Dispatch No. 24.

Mestre   Small Italian town just across the canal to the north of Venice, mentioned as the location of the VILLA ROSSA whorehouse in the "Chapter 7" vignette of *In Our Time*.

Frederic HENRY goes through Mestre on his way to Milan after his wounding. The train is sidetracked near Mestre, delaying Frederic's arrival at the hospital. The town is also mentioned in *Across the River and Into the Trees*.

Methodist college   In "Soldier's Home," Harold KREBS attended an otherwise unidentified Methodist college in Kansas before he enlisted in the marines.

Mexicans, three   In "The Gambler, the Nun, and the Radio," three Mexicans visit the badly wounded Cayetano RUIZ in the hospital. Afterward, they visit Mr. FRAZER in his room, for drinks. They are not friends of Ruiz but of "he who wounded him." Two of the three had lost money to Ruiz in card games, and the Mexican who shot Ruiz had lost $38 to him.

They return to the hospital later to sing to Ruiz, who tells Mr. Frazer that "As musicians they are fatal." Mr. Frazer can hear the three Mexicans playing their instruments down the hospital corridor, entertaining Ruiz and other hospital patients: a rodeo rider with a broken back, a carpenter with broken ankles and wrists, and a boy about 16 with a broken leg that was badly set and had to be rebroken. When the Mexicans ask Mr. Frazer what he would like to hear played, he asks for "the Cucaracha."

Meyers   In *A Farewell to Arms* "Old Meyers and his wife" are friends of Frederic HENRY in Milan during his convalescence there. Meyers "was short and old, with a white mustache and walked flat-footed with a cane." He and his wife go to the races, which he thinks are crooked, and he spends the afternoons in the GALLERIA at a table where he tells Frederic he [Meyers] can always be found.

Meyers, Benny   U.S. military administrator, involved in a scandal in the mid-1940s, court-martialed in 1947, and found guilty of procurement violations for negotiating a billion dollar contract for war materials for Howard Hughes's airline company. Meyers was stripped of his World War II medals and half of his pension.

In *Across the River and Into the Trees* Richard CANTWELL uses the Benny Meyers name as a metaphor for corruption in the procurement of Burberry raincoats for military personnel.

Meyers, Mrs. (1)   Owner of the boardinghouse in "My Old Man," where JOE and his "old man" live during the racing season in MAISONS-LAFITTE, west of Paris.

Meyers, Mrs. (2)   Wife of "old Meyers" in *A Farewell to Arms*, both friends of Frederic HENRY during his convalescence in Milan after his wounding. "She was a big-busted woman." She offers some "Marsala and cakes" for her "boys" at the AMERICAN HOSPITAL (1) where Frederic is staying.

Miaja, José (1878–1958)   General in the Spanish army; during Spain's civil war (1936–39) he successfully organized the defense of Madrid for the Republicans. According to Robert JORDAN in *For Whom the Bell Tolls*, he is an "[o]ld bald, spectacled, conceited, stupid-as-an-owl, unintelligent-in-conversation, brave-and-as-dumb-as-a-bull, propaganda-built-up defender of Madrid."

Miami   Named, with New Orleans, in *To Have and Have Not*, as places Harry and Marie MORGAN plan to vacation after his "last" illegal trip from KEY WEST to Cuba to make some extra money. But Harry is killed on his last trip.

Michaud's   Restaurant in Paris when Hemingway was there in the 1920s, at 29, rue des Saints Pères, at the corner of rue Jacob. In *A Moveable Feast* Hemingway remembers a dinner he and Hadley had there when James Joyce and his family, were seated at another table. He says later in the book that he once met F. Scott Fitzgerald there for lunch.

Michelangelo Buonarroti (1475–1564)   Italian painter, sculptor, architect, and poet, referred to by Richard Cantwell in *Across the River and Into the Trees*, along with other Renaissance painters.

Michelangelo is also mentioned in *Islands in the Stream*. Novelist Roger DAVIS asks Thomas HUDSON to paint one of the characters in a novel he's working on, and suggests that he paint upside down "like Michelangelo," a reference to the painter's ability to paint church ceilings while lying on his back.

Michelin map   Map used by David BOURNE in his travels in southern France and Spain with his wife, Catherine. The Michelin Guides and maps cover all European countries. The first Michelin "Red Guide" appeared in 1900, but the guides were limited to France until 1957. The Michelin Company, begun in 1888 by brothers Edouard and André Michelin, was primarily a maker of automobile and bicycle tires.

Michener, James A. (1907–1997)   American novelist and short story writer, winner of the Pulitzer Prize (1948) for *Tales of the South Pacific*. He wrote the introduction to the first book publication of Hemingway's *The Dangerous Summer* (1985). The first sentence reads: "This is a book about death written by a lusty sixty-year-old man who had reason to fear that his own death was imminent." Michener also relates a dramatic story of reading, at the request of *Life* magazine editors, a set of galley proofs for *The Old Man and the Sea*. He read it in "a poorly lighted corner of a Marine hut in a remote corner of the South Korea mountains," where he was stationed during the Korean War in 1954. "From Hemingway's opening words," Michener writes, "through the quiet climaxes to the organlike coda I was enthralled." His "Introduction" to *The Dangerous Summer* also includes bullfight terms and a summary of the parts of the bullfight itself.

Middle Key   One of the islands in the Dry Tortugas, west of Key West; referred to in *Islands in the Stream*.

Midi, the   The south of France. In *The Garden of Eden* Madame AUROL, wife of the proprietor of the hotel in LA NAPOULE where David and Catherine BOURNE stay, kids the flirting David that "he would have to show more evidence he was a man before he roused a woman of the Midi."

"Midwayites Downed by Oak Park Team"   Article for Oak Park and River Forest High School newspaper, *The Trapeze* (November 24, 1916), reprinted in *Hemingway at Oak Park High: The High School Writings of Ernest Hemingway, 1916–1917* (1993).

Miguelillo   Sword handler for Antonio Ordóñez, one of the two major matadors discussed by Hemingway in *The Dangerous Summer*.

Mike   GEORGE (4)'s name for Nick ADAMS in "Cross-Country Snow."

Milan   The largest city in northern Italy, and capitol of Lombardy. In "My Old Man" the San Siro steeplechase racetrack is located in Milan. And the city is also mentioned in "The Revolutionist."

Frederic HENRY and Catherine BARKLEY have their love affair in the AMERICAN HOSPITAL (1) in Milan after his wounding. She is assigned there as a V.A.D. (nurse's assistant).

"Million Dollar Fright: A New York Letter"   Article, published in *Esquire* (December 1935). Report on the Joe Louis–Max Baer prizefight of September 24, 1935, at Madison Square Garden in New York.

minarets   Lofty, usually slender towers or turrets attached to a mosque, the tower surrounded by one or more balconies, from which the muezzin calls the Muslim worshippers to prayer. The "Chapter 2" vignette from *In Our Time* begins, "Minarets stuck up in the rain out of Adrianople across the mud flats."

Minerva   A coral reef just off CAYO ROMANO, near Cuba. In *Islands in the Stream* Thomas HUDSON tells ARA, his helmsman, to "watch for that no-good Minerva. Keep well inside of that and outside the sandspits." Hudson and his crew are searching for a German submarine crew.

Mippipopolous, Count   A rich Greek character in *The Sun Also Rises*, who picks up Brett ASHLEY and Jake BARNES as friends. Brett lets Jake know that the count is "one of us." He likes the best champagne and has his chauffeur carry a bushel basket of MUMMS to Jake's flat one evening after he and Brett had been café-hopping. As a 21-year-old he had fought in the war at ABYSSINIA, where he received two arrow wounds, which he shows to Brett and Jake.

According to the concierge at Jake's flat, he "was very large. Very, very large." Jake, Brett, and the count eat dinner at a restaurant in "Le BOIS" (de Boulogne) the night the count brings the case of champagne to Jake's flat, and at dinner the count orders an 1811 bottle of brandy, explaining his seemingly "ostentatious"

order by telling them, "I get more value for my money in old brandy than in any other antiquities." He owns a "chain of sweetshops" in the United States.

Mirafiore   Steeplechase track in Torino, Italy, mentioned in "My Old Man."

Miranda   Loyalist lieutenant-colonel who recognizes the value of Andrés's message from Robert JORDAN to General Golz in *For Whom the Bell Tolls*. The message tells Golz that the Rebels have prepared a larger counterattack than Golz had expected.

Miró, Joan (1893–1983)   Spanish painter, a member of the dada movement in Europe in the 1920s. Hemingway owned Miró's "The Farm" (1922). Thomas HUDSON, in *Islands in the Stream*, reminds his son "young Tom" that they had known Miró in Paris.

Miroir des Sports   An illustrated sports magazine that David BOURNE buys in CANNES in *The Garden of Eden*. It was published in Paris from 1912 to 1939, initially under the name *Miroir Clé*.

mirror   Placed behind the bar in the hotel in LA NAPOULE where David and Catherine BOURNE and MARITA stay during their MÉNAGE À TROIS in *The Garden of Eden*. The mirror becomes a metaphor for the reflection each of the three casts on the others. After Catherine burns David's stories, the two girls are at the hotel bar when David walks in. Marita looks at him and sees how "things" are with him; Catherine, on the other hand, only looks at his reflection in the mirror.

"Miss Megan George a Hit"   Article, published in *The Toronto Daily Star* (October 6, 1923), reprinted in *Ernest Hemingway: Dateline Toronto* (1985). The headline in the *Daily Star* was "Miss Megan George Makes Hit: 'A Wonder' Reporters Call Her." Datelined "New York," this four-paragraph story is about David LLOYD GEORGE's daughter, a hit with all the reporters covering the former British prime minister's visit to the United States. According to Hemingway biographer Carlos Baker, this article was written for Hemingway at his request by Isabel Simmons of Oak Park, Illinois, then a student in New York.

mistral   Literally a "master" wind, a cold, dry north wind that blows over the Mediterranean coast of southern France. In *The Garden of Eden*, after getting off the Paris-Avignon train, David and Catherine BOURNE "rode [on their bicycles] with the mistral down to Nîmes . . . and then . . . down to AIGUES MORTES still with the heavy wind behind them and then on to le GRAU DU ROI." The mistral is still blowing at LA NAPOULE as MARITA enters the MÉNAGE À TROIS with the Bournes.

Mitchell, Prudence "Prudie" is NICK's "girl" in "Ten Indians." Carl GARNER kids Nick about having an Indian girlfriend, and, although Nick denies it, he "felt hollow and happy inside . . . to be teased" about her. Nick's father tells him, however, that he had seen Prudie that afternoon "in the woods with Frank Washburn . . . threshing around." Nick thinks he has a broken heart, but he is awake the next morning "a long time before he remembered that his heart was broken."

"Mitraigliatrice" Poem using war, particularly a *mitrailleuse* (machine gun), as a metaphor for tapping out stories on a typewriter, written in 1921 and first published in *Poetry* magazine (January 1923). The title was misspelled as "Mitrailliatrice." The poem was published, with the title spelled correctly, in Hemingway's first book, *Three Stories & Ten Poems* (1923).

Miuras Bulls brought in for the bullfights in PAMPLONA the week that Jake BARNES and his friends, in *The Sun Also Rises,* are there for the Fiesta SAN FERMÍN. The bulls are from a ranch near Seville owned by Juan Miura.

"Mix War, Art and Dancing" Article, unsigned, published in *The Kansas City Star* (April 21, 1918), reprinted in *Ernest Hemingway, Cub Reporter* (1970).

M'Kumba, B'wana The Swahili name for Hemingway in *Green Hills of Africa.*

M.O.B. The Montreux Oberland Bernois railway, an electric train that runs from MONTREUX, Switzerland, up the mountain toward Interlocken. In *A Farewell to Arms* Frederic HENRY and Catherine BARKLEY ride the train from Montreux to their rented house near LES AVANTS.

"Modern Version of Polonius' Advice, A" Poem written about 1920 and first published in *88 Poems* (1979).

Mohammedan In *The Garden of Eden* Catherine BOURNE suggests that her husband, David, could marry MARITA too, and David responds that he could if he were Mohammedan, because the men are "allowed three wives."

Molo (1) One of the African native "boys," in "The Snows of Kilimanjaro," working for HARRY and HELEN (2) on their hunting trip in Tanzania. Molo changes the dressings on Harry's leg and brings him whiskey-sodas.

Molo (2) One of the native helpers in *Green Hills of Africa.*

Molo (3) In *The Garden of Eden* Molo is one of the porters in David BOURNE's AFRICAN STORY.

Monastier Town in northern Italy which, in *Across the River and Into the Trees,* Richard CANTWELL remembers in connection with one of the battles he helped fight during WORLD WAR I.

Mondeño Bullfighter, who fought on the same card with Antonio Ordóñez and Luis Miguel Dominguín in Puerto de Santa Maria in 1959 when Hemingway covered the bullfight circuit in preparation for writing *The Dangerous Summer.*

Monet, Claude (1840–1926) French impressionist landscape painter. Hemingway writes in *A Moveable Feast* about seeing the Monet paintings at the Luxembourg Palace when he and Hadley lived in Paris during the early 1920s.

Monfalcone to Latisana The old road between these two Italian towns is the one that Richard CANTWELL takes in *Across the River and Into the Trees* to get from Trieste to Venice. He remembers riding in a CAMION along the same route during WORLD WAR I.

Monfried, Henri de (1879–1974) French writer and friend of Roger DAVIS and Thomas HUDSON in *Islands in the Stream.* He was known in Paris, according to a story Davis had told young Tom HUDSON, for guiding taxi drivers around the city while steering by the stars. Hemingway misspells his name as "Montfried."

Monnier, Adrienne Owner of the French bookshop in Paris at 7, rue de l'Odéon, across the street from Sylvia BEACH's American bookshop SHAKESPEARE AND COMPANY (1) at No. 12.

Monnier's bookshop, La Maison des Amis des Livres (The House of the Friends of Books), was, during the 1920s and 1930s, a place where a number of mostly French writers gathered to read their own works aloud. Readings were given by André Gide, Jules Romains, Paul Valéry, André Breton, Valéry Larbaud, among others, and included what may have been the first public reading by James Joyce of his *Ulysses,* a "work-in-progress."

Monnier later published the French translation of *Ulysses* (1929). Occasionally there would be a program of music at her shop, with Erik Satie or Francis Poulenc. Monnier translated Hemingway's short story "The Undefeated" into French and published it in *Le Navire d'Argent*—his first French translation.

Monnier and Beach shared an apartment at No. 18, rue de l'Odéon from 1921 to 1937. Both bookshop owners are mentioned in *A Moveable Feast,* where Hemingway refers to Monnier simply as "Adrienne."

"Monologue to the Maestro: A High Seas Letter" Article, published in *Esquire* (October 1935), reprinted in *By-Line: Ernest Hemingway* (1967). The "Maestro" is

Arnold Samuelson, a young man who hitchhiked to Key West in 1934 in order to ask Hemingway questions about writing. The article is in the form of a dialogue between "Y.C." (your correspondent) and "Mice."

monos   Short for the Spanish word *monosabios,* the red-shirted assistants to picadors in a bullfight. The short form is used in the "Chapter 10" vignette of *In Our Time* (1925). The term originated when the picador assistants were put into red blouses at a time (1847) when performing monkeys in red jackets were introduced as entertainment in Madrid.

Monroe, Harriet (1860–1936)   Founder in 1912 and longtime editor of *POETRY, A MAGAZINE OF VERSE,* one of the most influential American literary publications during the early part of the 20th century. She and her magazine are referred to in *A Moveable Feast.*

Monroe's poem "Columbian Ode" was read at the dedication of Chicago's World's Columbian Exposition (1892). Her autobiography is titled *A Poet's Life: Seventy Years in a Changing World* (1938).

Mons, garden at   Setting for the "Chapter 3" vignette of *In Our Time.* Mons is the capital of Hainaut province in southwest Belgium, about 30 miles southwest of Brussels. It was the site in August 1914 of the first battle of World War I between the British and the Germans.

Montafon dialect   The only language of the porters, "squat sullen peasants," who, according to Hemingway in *A Moveable Feast,* carried the heaviest loads when skiers climbed to one of the Alpine Club huts in the mountains of the Montafon Valley in western Austria.

Montagne Sainte-Geneviève   In *A Moveable Feast* Hemingway describes walking in the rain back to his apartment at 74, rue Cardinal Lemoine, up the hill (montagne) of the rue Sainte-Geneviève, a short street running from boulevard Saint-Germain to rue des Ecoles. It is also remembered by Thomas HUDSON in *Islands in the Stream.*

Montagny   A village in the Côte Chalonnaise, in Burgundy, and the source of a wine of the same name. In *A Moveable Feast* this was the wine drunk by Hemingway and F. Scott Fitzgerald at dinner in Châlon-sur-Saône, on their way back to Paris from Lyon.

Montalvo, Don Ricardo   See PILAR'S STORY.

Montana family   In *The Sun Also Rises* a man with his wife and their young son, Hubert, who are in the train compartment with Jake BARNES and Bill GORTON as they travel from Paris to Spain for the PAMPLONA fiesta.

Montana National Guard   Richard CANTWELL, in *Across the River and Into the Trees,* served with this unit when he was 16 years old.

Montgomerys   A "very dry Martini" Richard CANTWELL has invented that is "fifteen to one" (15 parts gin or vodka to one part dry vermouth). It is named after British Field Marshal Bernard Montgomery (1887–1976). "Monty" was "a character," according to Cantwell, who "needed fifteen to one [advantage] to move [his troops], and then moved tardily." A super Montgomery is a "fifteen to one" Martini with garlic olives, "not the big ones," still a slap at the famous British officer.

Montmartre   In Paris, a Right-Bank center of nightlife, where, in *The Sun Also Rises,* Jake BARNES, Brett ASHLEY, and Count MIPPIPOPOLOUS go for drinks and dancing at ZELLI's, and where Brett tells Jake that she and her homosexual friends have a "date" at the BAL MUSETTE, across the river.

Montoya, Juanito   In *The Sun Also Rises* the owner of the HOTEL MONTOYA, a friend of Jake BARNES, and a bullfight "aficion." At the end of the Fiesta SAN FERMÍN, he is angry enough at Jake to avoid speaking to him in passing on the hotel stairs, because Jake has allowed Brett ASHLEY to run off with the bullfighter Pedro ROMERO, thereby compromising Romero's art as a bull-fighter. See Juanito QUINTANA.

Montparnasse   Left-Bank quarter of Paris, full of restaurants and cafés, referred to often in *The Sun Also Rises* because the cafés are the center of much of the action in book 1, especially along the boulevard du Montparnasse.

"Montparnasse"   Poem about Bohemians in Paris after World War I, written in 1922 and first published in *Three Stories & Ten Poems* (1923).

Montreux   Town in Switzerland on the north shore and near the east end of Lake Geneva. Hemingway mentions the town in a number of his works.

GEORGE (4), in "Cross-Country Snow," tells Nick ADAMS, at the end of their skiing holiday together, that he has to catch a train from Montreux that night to go back to the States.

The railway station café in Montreux is the setting for part 1 of "Homage to Switzerland."

And Frederic HENRY and Catherine BARKLEY live in the mountains above Montreux (in Les Avants) during the winter of 1917–18, following their escape from Italy and the war.

Montrouge, France   Southern suburb of Paris. It is the location of the STADE BUFFALO where, according to Hemingway in *A Moveable Feast,* he saw bicycle races.

Mont-Saint-Michel   A rocky island in the English Channel about one mile off the Norman coast of France, near Avranches. On the island is a Benedictine abbey, founded in 708.

In *Across the River and Into the Trees*, Colonel Richard CANTWELL talks to RENATA about HARRY'S BAR in Venice, saying that it sometimes filled with people "with the same rushing regularity as the tide coming in at Mont St. Michel." Except, he tells her, that the tide changes every day, whereas the hours at the bar were as steady as the hours at the Greenwich meridian, the standard for time around the world.

Monument in Arbeit   Painting by Paul KLEE, owned by Thomas HUDSON and mentioned in the "Cuba" section of *Islands in the Stream*.

Moorish cavalry   Richard CANTWELL thinks of this military unit in connection with Generalissimo Francisco FRANCO and the Spanish civil war. Franco began the Spanish civil war from towns in North Africa and gathered rebel support as he moved north in Spain toward Madrid.

Moorish tart   In *The Fifth Column*, her name is Anita, but she is described as a "Moorish tart from Cueta" and her lines in the play are identified not by the name "Anita" but by the term "Moorish Tart." She's "very dark, but well built, kinky-haired and tough looking, and not at all shy."

Philip RAWLINGS describes her to Dorothy BRIDGES as the "comrade that bit Vernon Rodgers that time. Laid him up for three weeks. Hell of a bite." Later at CHICOTE's bar, Anita tells Rawlings that Rodgers tried to take 300 pesetas out of her stocking. "What I should do? Say 'Yes, go ahead. All right. Help yourself?' No, I bite." She's not a key character in the play, but she is on stage at the end, after Rawlings has broken off his love affair with Dorothy.

Mora   The Carlist captain in *For Whom the Bell Tolls* who is convinced that El Sordo and his men are dead and so walks up the hill toward the silent El Sordo and is killed.

Moretti, Ettore   In *A Farewell to Arms* he's a 23-year-old Italian from San Francisco, California, enlisted in the Italian army. Frederic HENRY meets him at the CAFÉ COVA in Milan, along with two opera singers. Moretti has been a lieutenant for two years and expects to be made a captain.

Morgan, Harry   Main character in *To Have and Have Not*. He is one of the "Have Nots" in a novel that shows the contrast between socialism and individualism or, at least, the downfall of the individual. Near the end of the novel, while he is lying wounded on the deck of the boat he used to transport four Cuban bank robbers to Havana, Harry is finally able to state a philosophy that has "taken all of his life to learn . . . a man alone ain't got no bloody fucking chance."

He is "alone" in the sense that he is responsible for his own destiny, but he is not alone in the sense that he has a good relationship with his wife, Marie. It is clearly a marriage that works well, in spite of the lack of money. Harry had worked on the Miami police force before moving to Cuba, where the novel begins.

In Havana he has a 38-foot fishing boat that he uses as a charter for wealthy but mostly incompetent fishermen, and he is trying to avoid the temptation to run illegal goods between Havana and Florida. When the wealthy Mr. JOHNSON loses overboard $650 worth of Harry's fishing gear and then cheats him out of another $825 for the 18 days he has chartered the boat, Harry is forced into transporting illegal goods.

He agrees to a deal with Mr. SING to take 12 illegal Chinese aliens to Florida. He is so skeptical of Mr. Sing's honesty and so nervous about the exchange of the money when the men board his boat that when Mr. Sing reaches into his breast pocket, Harry thinks he might be reaching for a gun and so kills him. Harry and his first mate, the rummy EDDY (2), then drop the 12 aliens onto a nearby beach and make their way across to KEY WEST with the money.

In a second illegal act (part 2 of the novel) Harry loses his right arm after being shot by double-crossing Cuban government officials (who until this trip had been looking the other way) while trying to load bootleg liquor in MARIEL, Cuba, for illegal transport to KEY WEST. He and WESLEY are both wounded so badly that they can barely manage to get the 40-pound bags of liquor overboard, trying to avoid being caught by U.S. government officers near Key West. They get caught anyway, and Harry's boat is confiscated.

In spite of losing both his arm and his boat, Harry agrees (part 3) to carry four Cubans to Havana. In desperation, he first steals his own boat from the Navy Yard on Key West, where the Coast Guard has it tied up, and then, when government officials find it again, he rents a boat for $1,200. He doesn't realize that the four Cubans who hire him plan to rob a bank first (to get money for a Cuban revolution).

Harry and his new first mate, Albert TRACY, meet the four Cubans as planned, and, after Albert is killed for hesitating to start the boat's engine, Morgan realizes what the Cubans have done and puts the boat out to sea, hoping to gain an advantage before they get to Havana. There is a gunfight, Harry managing to kill all four of the Cubans but not before he is badly wounded. A Coast Guard cutter finds the drifting boat and tows it back to Key West, where Harry dies in the hospital.

Marie knows that Harry has suffered over the details of this last crossing. Earlier, when he leaves to meet the four Cubans, she "watched him go out of the house, tall, wide-shouldered, flat-backed, his hips narrow, moving, still, she thought, like some kind of animal, easy and swift and not old yet . . . and getting in the car he grinned at her and she began to cry. 'His goddamn face,' she thought. 'Everytime I see his goddamn face it make me want to cry.'" And at the end of the novel, when she sees him at the hospital and the doctor tells her "He didn't suffer at all, Mrs. Morgan," she notices his face: "'Oh, Christ,' she said, and began to cry again. 'Look at his goddamned face.'"

Morgan, Lew   Character in "Fifty Grand," a "bookie," and a prizefighter, managed by John COLLINS, who is also the manager for the story's main character, Jack BRENNAN. Morgan is with Collins and another "friend," Happy STEINFELT, when they talk Brennan into throwing his fight with Jimmy WALCOTT. Morgan and Steinfelt own a poolroom—probably a place where bets are placed—and the two are considered to be "sharpshooters" by Danny HOGAN, the owner of the New Jersey camp where Brennan is training.

Morgan, Marie   The wife of the main character, Harry MORGAN, in *To Have and Have Not*. She is a "big woman, long legged, big handed, big hipped, still handsome, a hat pulled down over her bleached blond hair."

To Harry she is beautiful, and they are happily married. Marie and Harry represent the "Have Nots" in the novel and are contrasted with two of the "Haves," Richard and Helen GORDON, who have an unhappy marriage. Both Helen and Richard commit adultery and eventually split up.

Marie doesn't seem to mind when Harry shifts from legal jobs to illegal ones, but it takes her awhile to get over the loss of his arm during a shootout in MARIEL, Cuba, while he is loading sacks of bootleg liquor. And Hemingway gives Marie the novel's last chapter, "direct" INTERIOR MONOLOGUE as she attempts to come to grips with the death of her husband. "The bastards that shot him. Oh, the dirty bastards. That's the only feeling I got. Hate and a hollow feeling. I'm empty like a empty house."

Morro   Spanish for "moraine." In Havana, Cuba, it is a promontory jutting into the Gulf Stream out of the harbor and the location of the Morro Castle, a historic castle at the entrance to the harbor.

In *Islands in the Stream* Thomas HUDSON, who is constantly aware of the changing moods of the sea, sees at one point that "the sea was very wild and confused and clear green water was breaking over the rock at the base of the Morro, the tops of the seas blowing white in the sun."

The Morro is also referred to in *To Have and Have Not*. See also "Marlin off the Morro: A Cuban Letter."

Moscas   Spanish nickname for Russian-made monoplanes used by the Loyalists in the Spanish civil war; referred to in *For Whom the Bell Tolls*.

"Moscow Theatre Company Will Not Come to Toronto"   Article, unsigned, published in the Toronto *Globe* (November 27, 1923), reprinted in William Burrill's *Hemingway: The Toronto Years* (1994). The article concerns the manager of Toronto's Royal Alexandra Theatre, Lawrence Solman, who canceled the engagement of the Moscow Art Theatre Company, for what seem to be political reasons. Although Hemingway was under contract to *The Toronto Star*, he made some extra money by writing this story for one of the *Star*'s Toronto competitors.

Mosquito Coast   The swampy east coast of Nicaragua and Honduras, where, in *The Old Man and the Sea*, SANTIAGO had gone "turtle-ing" during his youth.

mother (1)   Of Nick in "The Doctor and the Doctor's Wife." She is a Christian Scientist, who prefers the darkness of her bedroom to the light of day and henpecks her husband, the doctor of the story's title. She's lying in her room "with the blinds drawn," her Bible and a copy of *Science and Health* and her *Quarterly* by her bed.

She hopes her husband hasn't lost his temper in the "row" she has overheard between her husband and Dick BOULTON in front of the cottage, and she wants to know what the trouble was about. She accepts her husband's explanation but finds it difficult to believe that Boulton would deliberately start a fight, thinking he could get out of paying a debt he owes her husband. She asks her husband to send NICK in to her, perhaps to make sure he hasn't been upset by the event, and her husband gives Nick the message but then allows him to go along on his hunt for black squirrels.

mother (2)   Of Harold KREBS in "Soldier's Home." She and Harold's father are religious fundamentalists, who fail to understand their son's lethargy after he returns home from World War I. Nor does she understand the trauma he has been through in the war. And she and her husband treat him as if he were still the teenager they knew before he went to war. They think it is a privilege when they offer to let him drive the car "in the evenings."

She asks Harold if he loves her, and she cries when he says "No." When she asks him to kneel in prayer with her and he can't pray for himself, she prays for him.

mother (3)   Of the unnamed main character/narrator of "Now I Lay Me." He remembers that once, while his father was away on a hunting trip, his mother cleaned out the basement of their house and burned all of his father's collection of Indian relics.

"Mother of a Queen, The" PACO (1) is a homosexual Spanish bullfighter, and the "queen" of the short story's title. The story's narrator, ROGER, ties Paco's tightness with money to his homosexuality. Roger is Paco's current manager, responsible for the money he earns in the bull ring.

The setting is Mexico, where Paco has a contract for six fights. There are two incidents that the narrator uses to illustrate Paco's cheapness. The first involves the burial of his mother, not in "perpetuity," which would cost him $20, but for five years, after which he would have to make additional arrangements for the gravesite. The five years are up, and after four warnings from the authorities and constant reminders from Roger, who offers each time to "take care of it" but is turned down, Paco's mother's grave is opened and her bones thrown on the "public boneheap."

Roger is incredulous, but Paco argues that it is *his* mother and that "[n]ow she is so much dearer to me. Now I don't have to think of her buried in one place and be sad. Now she is all about me in the air, like the birds and the flowers. Now she will always be with me." And Roger answers, "Jesus Christ . . . what kind of blood have you anyway?"

The second incident involves a debt of 600 pesos that Paco owes Roger, who knows the money is available in the cashbox. But Paco insists that he needs that money for "something" and so promises to pay the debt but keeps putting it off. The final straw comes when Paco asks Roger to give 50 pesos to a "*paesano*" (sic), a peasant (correctly spelled *paisano*) from Paco's hometown, whom he has picked up off the street. "He is a fellow townsman," Paco says, "and he is in distress." Roger calls Paco a "bitch" and then a "motherless bitch," but gives him the key to the cashbox, and tells him to get the money himself.

At the end of the story and after some time has passed, Roger describes meeting Paco on the GRAN VIA in Madrid. Paco is friendly but asks him about the "unjust" things Roger has been saying about him. In front of three of Paco's friends, Roger says that he had merely been telling people that "you never had a mother," the worst insult of one Spanish man to another. Paco then lies, for the sake of the three friends, saying that it was true. "My poor mother died when I was so young it seems as though I never had a mother." And Roger concludes, "There's a queen for you. You can't touch them. . . . They spend money on themselves or for vanity, but they never pay. . . . What kind of blood is it that makes a man like that?"

"The Mother of a Queen" was first published in *Winner Take Nothing* (1933).

Mother Superior Name the Italian soldiers give to the matron of the soldiers' bordello in *A Farewell to Arms*. "Everybody in the Second Army knows that matron."

motor car, the The otherwise undescribed vehicle in "The Short Happy Life of Francis Macomber," in which Francis and Margot MACOMBER and the white hunting guide, Robert WILSON, hunt big game in Kenya.

mounted policeman On the GRAN VIA in Madrid, noticed by Jake BARNES as he rides in a taxi with Brett ASHLEY at the end of *The Sun Also Rises*.

Moveable Feast, A This nonfiction work is a series of 20 sketches of Paris in the 1920s. Hemingway began writing the book in the fall of 1957 and completed it in spring 1960, a little more than a year before he died.

The memoir began, so the yet unproved story goes, as the result of the discovery of two trunks belonging to Hemingway, found by Charles Ritz in the basement of the HOTEL RITZ in Paris in November 1956. The trunks were left there in March 1928, when Hemingway and his second wife, Pauline, left Paris for Key West, Florida. The trunks contained notebooks he had kept during his early Paris years and some newspaper clippings, both of which he apparently used in writing the memoir only as reminders of some of the events and people of those years.

Ernest and his first wife, Hadley, arrived in Paris in December 1921, and the next few years were clearly happy ones for both of them, until the late spring of 1926 when the marriage began to end. He mentions several times in *A Moveable Feast* how poor they were in those early years. But they were not poor. Hadley had interest income of at least $3,000 a year from an inheritance received from a trust fund set up by her grandfather Richardson and from her mother's estate, plus $10,000 that she received shortly after her wedding in 1921 from an uncle's recent death, which gave them what they thought they needed to go to Paris. And Ernest also had income from articles he was writing for the Toronto newspapers—nearly 200 articles in the four years between 1920 and 1924—and some from poems he sold to two German periodicals.

A. E. HOTCHNER, a friend of Hemingway's, provided the book's title when he told Ernest's fourth wife, Mary, who, with Hotchner, edited the manuscript, that Ernest had once told him that Paris was a "movable feast." Mary then suggested an epigraph for the book: "If you are lucky enough to have lived/ in Paris as a young man, then wherever you/ go for the rest of your life, it stays with/ you, for Paris is a moveable feast." It is signed "Ernest Hemingway/ *to a friend, 1950*"; the friend is Hotchner.

The spelling of "movable" caused a problem at Scribner's, but Mary argued that Ernest often added an extra "e" in words and that "moveable" would, therefore, be her preference (the spelling is an acceptable, alternate spelling in most dictionaries). There is a "Note" written by Mary that provides the dates and places for the writing of the book and states that it is about the years between 1921 and 1926.

There is also a "Preface" by Hemingway that lists some of the people, places, and events left out of the book and with the statement that the reader can, if he or she wants, regard the book as "fiction." The "fiction" might, Hemingway suggests "throw some light on what has been written as fact." This statement is important for readers, because the book often reads like fiction, and one may well consider some of the stories the author tells to be exaggerated if not made up.

Whether the stories are made up or not, they show a Hemingway who has turned his back, sometimes with a great deal of animosity, on a number of former friends, many of whom had helped him during his early years in Paris. This animosity shows particularly in his writing about Ford Madox FORD, Gertrude STEIN, Alice B. TOKLAS, Zelda FITZGERALD, and even Scott FITZGERALD, who was one of his closest friends in those early years. The only Paris friend not turned on to one degree or another in *A Moveable Feast* is Ezra POUND.

The 20 sketches are each titled but not numbered, and they rarely provide dates, so the reader may not feel much continuity from beginning to end. But the whole painting Hemingway provides of Paris and of how it was to live there during the 1920s is as vivid, as emotionally powerful, as readers of Hemingway expect in the best of his writing. It is especially true in the parts where he writes about Paris itself or his struggles with writing, rather than about the people he knew there.

The first sketch is titled "A Good Café on the Place St.-Michel" and is about one of Hemingway's early walks in Paris to a café on place Saint-Michel, a "pleasant café, warm and clean and friendly," where he orders a *café au lait,* followed later by a rum St. James, and where he sits writing a short story. A girl arrives at the café and sits by herself, "pretty with . . . rain-freshened skin, and her hair [as] black as a crow's wing and cut sharply and diagonally across her cheek." He continues his writing, but he looks up at the girl periodically because he is clearly struck by her good looks. He gets deeper and deeper into the story he's writing, however, forgetting about time and place. He finishes the story, and when he looks up again, the girl is gone. He's saddened by the loss, but he orders a dozen oysters and a half-carafe of dry white wine and thinks about plans for a trip to Switzerland with his wife, Hadley.

In the second sketch, "Miss Stein Instructs," Hemingway describes his return to Paris in early 1922 after a short skiing vacation in Switzerland. He and Hadley live in a fourth-floor Left-Bank apartment at 74, rue du Cardinal Lemoine, but he does his writing in a room on the top floor of a hotel where he can look out over the roofs of the Latin Quarter. He writes that he always quit for the day when he knew where the story was going next, so he could begin easily the next morning. Some days he would walk through the Luxembourg Gardens to Gertrude STEIN's studio apartment at 27, rue de Fleurus. He describes the two women who live there, both of whom he likes, but he never mentions Stein's lesbian friend Alice B. TOKLAS by name, referring to her only as "friend" or "companion."

In the next sketch, "*Une Génération Perdue,*" Hemingway continues with his memory of meetings with Stein at her apartment and of her once telling him that he was a member of the *génération perdue,* the "LOST GENERATION" of youths who served in the war. "You have no respect for anything. You drink yourselves to death." He argues with her about the term *lost generation,* especially as she applies it to him, but he uses it, nevertheless, as one of the epigraphs for his first major novel, *The Sun Also Rises,* and attributes it to Stein, "in conversation."

The fourth sketch is titled "Shakespeare and Company" and describes Hemingway's meeting with Sylvia BEACH at her American bookshop at 12, rue de l'Odéon. He says that he and Hadley were too poor to join even the rental library at SHAKESPEARE AND COMPANY (1) but that Sylvia was willing to wait for the deposit.

Sketch five, "People of the Seine," is about the several ways Hemingway had of getting to the river from his apartment on Cardinal Lemoine, of the Left Bank bookstalls along the river where sometimes he found English-language books, and of meeting fishermen under the Pont Neuf who caught *goujon,* a "dace-like" fish that were "delicious fried whole."

In the sixth sketch, "A False Spring," Hemingway writes of the happiness he and Hadley felt in the early morning of a Paris spring. He worked early on the short stories, and he remembers days when they went to the horseraces and at least once when, after they had won some money at the races, they went to PRUNIERS RESTAURANT for a dinner of *crabe mexicaine* and SANCERRE WINE. But it was a "false spring," and from his perspective of the late 1950s Hemingway remembers that the happiness he felt in those early Paris spring days would not last.

Sketch seven, "The End of an Avocation," recalls the giving up of horseracing for bicycle racing at the VÉLODROME D'HIVER or at the STADE BUFFALO, events one of his friends told him he didn't have to bet on. He enjoyed bicycle racing all of his life after that, and he states that he had started a number of stories about bicycle racing, but he could never write a story that was as good as the races.

In "Hunger Was Good Discipline" Hemingway explains the directions he took on his walks in order to avoid passing the good eating places—they would make him hungry. And he writes about the time (in December 1922) when Hadley's suitcase was stolen at the Gare de Lyon when she was on her way to join

Ernest at the Lausanne Peace Conference, which he was covering for the *The Toronto Daily Star*. Her suitcase contained copies (original manuscripts, typescripts, and carbons) of all but two of the short stories Ernest had written. She had intended to surprise him with the stories, so he could revise them while he covered the conference.

Sketch nine is titled "Ford Madox Ford and the Devil's Disciple" and is about a conversation Hemingway had with Ford Madox FORD, over several drinks, at the CLOSERIE DES LILAS. It begins with Ford explaining how he had just "cut" Hilaire BELLOC, the French writer, but who, as it turned out had not been Belloc at all but Aleister CROWLEY, "the diabolist." And the strange conversation ends with Ford and Hemingway discussing the men they thought might be considered "gentlemen": Trollope's Lord Harry HOTSPUR? Trollope himself? Henry FIELDING? Marlowe? Or maybe John DONNE? They couldn't agree on which if any of these men were gentlemen.

In the 10th sketch, "Birth of a New School," Hemingway states that all he needed for writing in the 1920s was the blue-backed school notebooks he used, two pencils and a sharpener, a café where he could write, and luck. But "luck" included uninterrupted writing at a café, and on the occasion described in this sketch an unnamed writer he knew said "Hi, Hem," and that was the end of that day's work for Hemingway. In the ensuing dialogue the reader gets a feeling for the anger and meanness Hemingway was capable of with people he knew.

In sketch 11, "With Pascin at the Dôme," Hemingway describes a conversation at the CAFÉ DU DÔME with the French painter Jules PASCIN and two of his women models. Pascin is nasty toward the two models, who are also his lovers, but at the end of the sketch, Hemingway writes that, after the painter had killed himself (1930), Hemingway liked to remember him the way he was that evening at the Dôme. And he then makes an observation about suicide: "They say the seeds of what we will do are in all of us, but it always seemed to me that in those who make jokes in life the seeds are covered with better soil and with a higher grade of manure."

Sketch 12 is titled "Ezra Pound and His Bel Esprit" and describes how good a friend Pound was and that he was always doing nice things for other people. "Bel Esprit" was a plan to help T. S. ELIOT. Pound suggested that all the writers and painters they knew donate a certain percentage of money earned from their work to a fund that would allow Eliot to quit his job as clerk in a London bank and devote his time to writing poetry. The plan was barely under way when Eliot began to earn money from the publication of *The Waste Land* (1922) and from backing he received for a literary review he wanted to start—*The Criterion*.

Sketch 13, "A Strange Enough Ending," is about Hemingway's perception of the ending of his friendship with Gertrude Stein. It had to do with Hemingway failing to go by Stein's apartment in time to say good-bye to her and Alice B. Toklas before they left on a trip to the south of France. Part of his "failure" was the result, however, of overhearing that morning Toklas making nasty remarks to Stein in their upstairs bedroom and Stein begging her to stop. The language and the pleading that Hemingway overhears apparently add to his disgust with their lesbian relationship. He left the apartment and could not quite get himself to return, even to say good-bye.

Sketch 14 is titled "The Man Who Was Marked for Death," a reference to Ernest WALSH, who died of tuberculosis in 1926 at age 31. The two men met at Ezra Pound's studio apartment, where Walsh had taken two American girls he had recently met on the boat; he had promised them he would introduce them to Pound. Hemingway writes that Walsh was "marked for death as a character is marked for death in a motion picture."

The 15th sketch is titled "Evan Shipman at the Lilas." It begins with Hemingway's comments on the reading he had been doing, especially of Ivan TURGENEV, Nikolay GOGOL, Leo TOLSTOI, and Anton CHEKOV. Someone had earlier recommended Katherine MANSFIELD's short stories, but he says that "trying to read her after Chekov was like hearing the carefully artificial tales of a young old-maid compared to those of an articulate and knowing physician who was a good and simple writer."

Sketch 16, "An Agent of Evil," concerns another good deed of Ezra Pound's that turned out to be a difficult moment for Hemingway. The poet Ralph Cheever DUNNING was a friend of Pound's and addicted to opium. Pound was leaving for Italy and asked Hemingway to keep a jar of opium in case of an "emergency." When the emergency arrived, Hemingway rushed to Dunning's apartment to give him the opium, only to have the jar thrown back at him, along with Dunning's curses at Hemingway's thoughtlessness.

The next three sketches are devoted to F. Scott FITZGERALD. "Scott Fitzgerald" defines Hemingway's ambivalent attitude toward Fitzgerald, who had just published *THE GREAT GATSBY* (April 10, 1925). The sketch begins with their first meeting, an embarrassing encounter at the DINGO BAR, Fitzgerald loudly praising in public Hemingway's work and then suddenly going blank from too much champagne, his face looking like "a death's head. . . . the color of used candle wax." Hemingway then describes a strange trip he took with Scott to recover the Fitzgeralds' car, which he and Zelda had left in Lyon, France, for some repairs. The trip is "strange" because Fitzgerald missed the train and then missed a telegram Hemingway sent to him letting him know where he was staying in Lyon. When they finally got together Fitzgerald had difficulty understanding that it was he who had fouled up his own arrangements.

Sketch 18 is titled "Hawks Do Not Share," the hawk a reference to Zelda Fitzgerald, who, according to Hemingway, "had hawk's eyes and a thin mouth and deep-south manners and accent." Both Scott and Zelda drank heavily, Zelda often passing out to Scott's embarrassment, and Scott drinking to avoid people and places. At the end of the sketch Hemingway quotes Zelda as asking him if he didn't think Al Jolson was "greater than Jesus." That was before, Hemingway suggests, everyone knew she was insane.

In "A Matter of Measurements" (sketch 19), Hemingway describes Fitzgerald's concern—from a statement Zelda had made to him—that he was not "built" in a way to make women happy, that it was a "matter of measurements." Hemingway takes him into a men's room for a look and then assures him that there is nothing wrong with his measurements. Hemingway thinks that Zelda is out to "destroy" Scott out of jealousy for the writing he has done.

Sketch 20 is titled "There Is Never Any End to Paris" but is devoted primarily to a mostly peaceful picture of Schruns, Austria, where he, Hadley, and their two-year-old son, Bumby, enjoy the winter of 1925–26. At the end, however, he writes about "pilot fish," people who find artists or places and then tell the rich about them, creating a rush of the rich and their money, which can spoil artists and places quickly. "All things truly wicked," Hemingway says, "start from an innocence," a reference to the spoiling of good things in general but particularly the spoiling of his marriage to Hadley, which began to fail in the late spring and summer of that year (1926). But he writes in the book's last sentence: "But this is how Paris was in the early days when we were very poor and very happy."

A Moveable Feast was published by Charles Scribner's Sons on May 5, 1964, in a first edition of 85,000 copies at $4.95 each.

M.P.'s   Military Police, probably British, remembered by HARRY in "The Snows of Kilimanjaro." He remembers a fight he had had with a British gunner subaltern and that the M.P.'s had broken it up.

"Mr. and Mrs. Elliot"   This short story begins, "Mr. and Mrs. Elliot tried very hard to have a baby." They try in Boston on their honeymoon; they try on the boat to Europe, but she is seasick most of the time, only "as Southern women are sick"; and they try in Paris, Dijon, Touraine, and Trouville.

Hubert, who is in law school at Harvard, is 25 and proud that he has led a "clean life." Most of his previous "girl friends" lost interest as soon as he told them how clean he was. But Cornelia, who is 40 and a very Southern woman, is clean (pure) too and so impressed by Hubert's purity that, before their marriage, every time he kisses her, she asks him to tell her again how pure he is. "The declaration always set her off again."

The narrator says that Hubert spent several weeks "making love to her" before he kissed her, using an expression (making love) that has changed in meaning since Hemingway wrote the story in 1924; it does not mean that they had sexual intercourse. After the marriage and their attempt to have a baby, both of them become disenchanted with sex, and Cornelia "cries a lot."

In France Cornelia prevails upon Hubert to send for her "girl friend," HONEY, who is still in the Boston tea shop where they had worked together, and the two reunited women have "many good cries together." Honey is a few years older than Cornelia and also "very Southern."

Hubert writes "very long poems very rapidly," and when he thinks he has enough for a book he sends a check with his poems for a publishing contract. Cornelia types his poems, but he's particular and makes her retype an entire page if she makes an error. When the "girl friend" arrives, she takes over the typing responsibility. Hubert rents a château in Touraine for the summer, and he takes "to drinking white wine" and living in a room of his own, in order to write his poetry, while the two women sleep together in another room.

In the evenings the three of them sit under a plane tree while Hubert drinks white wine and the two women talk together, and, as the story's last line says, "they were all quite happy."

"Mr. and Mrs. Elliot" was first published in *The Little Review* (Autumn-Winter 1924–25) and reprinted in *In Our Time* (1925).

"Mr. Quayle Rouses Hanna Club"   Article for the Oak Park and River Forest High School newspaper, *The Trapeze* (February 17, 1916), reprinted in *Hemingway at Oak Park High: The High School Writings of Ernest Hemingway, 1916–1917* (1993).

Mudania Conference   Mudania is a small town on the Bosporus, about 42 miles from Constantinople. A peace conference was held there in 1922 in a mostly unsuccessful attempt to settle the war between Turkey and Greece.

mud flats   A mud-covered, gently sloping tract of land, mentioned in the "Chapter 2" vignette of *In Our Time.* The evacuation of Greeks from Adrianople during the Greco-Turkish War is slowed by carts stuck trying to get across the mud flats along the road to Karagatch.

muleta   In bullfighting the *muleta* is a heart-shaped, scarlet cloth used, as Hemingway says in *Death in the Afternoon,* to "defend the man; to tire the bull and regulate the position of his head and feet; to perform a series of passes of more or less aesthetic value with the bull; and to aid the man in the killing." Hemingway uses the term often in his descriptions of bullfights, both in fiction and nonfiction.

Mumms   Famous champagne of G.H. Mumm and Company, a dry, "light-bodied" champagne from near Epernay, France, and one of the better champagnes. In *The Sun Also Rises* Count MIPPIPOPOLOUS brings a case of it to Jake BARNES's flat when the count and Brett ASHLEY are making the rounds of Paris cafés.

Mundo Obrero, El   Spanish Communist Party newspaper, referred to in *For Whom the Bell Tolls*.

Munich Beer, dark   In *A Farewell to Arms* it is drunk by Frederic HENRY in MONTREUX while he waits for Catherine BARKLEY to have her hair done.

Murano   Island just east of VENICE famous for its glass-blowing plants, pointed out, in *Across the River and Into the Trees,* by Colonel Richard CANTWELL to his driver, JACKSON, as they drive toward Venice.

Murphy, Gerald (1888–1964)   Gerald and Sara Murphy were friends of a number of artists in Paris during the 1920s, including Scott and Zelda Fitzgerald, Ernest and Hadley (and later Pauline) Hemingway, Ada and Archibald MACLEISH, John and Katy DOS PASSOS, and Dorothy Parker. Fitzgerald's novel *Tender Is the Night* is dedicated to Gerald and Sara Murphy.

Gerald, a professional architect, made a number of paintings while in Paris, and he helped the Ballets Russes company restore scenery that had been lost in a fire. While at the scenery shops he met Diaghilev, the company's director, and the French painters Braque, Picasso, and Derain, who were also helping the Russian ballet company recover scenery, especially for its performances of *Scheherazade* and *Pulcinella*.

The Murphys were famous for their parties at their French Riviera summer home, "Villa America," near Cap d'Antibes. They also had an apartment in Paris, at 1, rue Gît-le-Coeur, one floor for themselves and one floor for their three children. And Gerald had a studio apartment at 69, rue Froidevaux, behind the Montparnasse Cemetery, which he lent to Hemingway for the late fall of 1926 and spring of 1927 following his divorce from Hadley and before his marriage to Pauline Pfeiffer.

In *A Moveable Feast* Hemingway writes about meeting the Murphys at Juan-les-Pins on the Riviera during June 1926. Hemingway corrected the page proofs of *The Sun Also Rises* during August 1926, while staying at the Murphys' Paris apartment, across from the Montparnasse Cemetery.

Left to right, Gerald Murphy, Hemingway, and John Dos Passos, in Schruns, Austria, 1926 (Courtesy of the John F. Kennedy Library)

Murphy, Sara (1883–1975)   Sara Sherman Murphy, original surname Wiborg. See Gerard MURPHY.

Muscadet wine   A light, dry wine from the vineyards of the lower Loire Valley near Nantes, France; mentioned in *A Moveable Feast*.

"Muscle Shoals: Cheap Nitrates"   Article, published in *The Toronto Star Weekly* (November 12, 1921), reprinted in *Ernest Hemingway: Dateline Toronto* (1985). The headline in the *Star Weekly* was "Cheap Nitrates Will Mean Cheaper Bread." It is about converting the Muscle Shoals, Alabama, plant that had manufactured ammonium nitrate during World War I, "the base of high explosives," into a peacetime plant and producer of commercial nitrogen for the growing of crops.

Musée d'Orsay   A former Paris railway station, the Gare d'Orsay was renovated and became an art museum in

1986. The museum is devoted to the period 1848 to 1916 and includes nearly all of the impressionist paintings previously on display at the Musée du Luxembourg, when Hemingway was in Paris during the 1920s. The paintings were later moved to the Musée du Louvre or to the Jeu de Paume.

Musée du Louvre Formerly a royal palace, transformed into one of the world's great art museums in 1793. Hemingway refers to it in *A Moveable Feast*. See MUSÉE DU LUXEMBOURG.

Musée du Luxembourg On the north side of the Luxembourg Gardens in Paris, mentioned in *A Moveable Feast*. It was founded in 1750, primarily as a museum for art that belonged to the state. Hemingway writes of seeing paintings at the Luxembourg and that it was always better to look at paintings when you are hungry.

He writes that the great paintings once in the Musée du Luxembourg have been moved to the Louvre or to the JEU DE PAUME. The French impressionists whom he mentions (Manet, Monet, and Cézanne, in particular) were in Room 11, Cabinet D, in the mid-1920s, and the museum's policy was to transfer artworks to the Louvre or provincial galleries 10 years after the death of the artists.

The impressionist paintings transferred to the Louvre were placed in the Jeu de Paume until 1986, when they were transferred to the Musée d'Orsay, the recently renovated railway station, Gare d'Orsay.

musette French word for haversack, which, in "Out of Season," the YOUNG GENTLEMAN carries over his shoulder as he and PEDUZZI (1) start down the road toward the river to fish for trout.

It is called a "musette bag" in *The Garden of Eden* and is carried by David and Catherine BOURNE, along with a "rucksack," to the south of France on their honeymoon.

Mussolini, Benito (1883–1945) Italian dictator and founder of fascism. In 1921 he was elected to parliament, and the National Fascist Party was organized. In October 1922 he sent the Fascists on a march to Rome, where King Victor Emmanuel III permitted them to enter the city, and the king later called on Mussolini to become premier of Italy and to form a cabinet. He chose to join forces with Germany in WORLD WAR II and, when the Allies invaded Italy, Hitler installed Mussolini as head of a puppet state in German-controlled northern Italy. He had to escape the advancing Allied forces, however, and was eventually recognized by Italian PARTIZANS and killed.

Hemingway mentions Mussolini in several articles written for Toronto newspapers in 1922; see especially "Fascisti Party Half-Million," the story written after an interview with Mussolini.

And in "Che Ti Dice La Patria?" the short story's narrator describes experiences that he and his friend, Guy, have as they travel around northern Italy in 1927, discovering how decadent the country has become.

"Mussolini: Biggest Bluff in Europe" Article, published in *The Toronto Daily Star* (January 27, 1923), reprinted in *The Wild Years* (1962), and in *By-Line: Ernest Hemingway* (1967). The dateline is "Lausanne, Switzerland," where Hemingway was covering the LAUSANNE CONFERENCE. In the article Hemingway sums up the character and attitude of each of the major participants: the Soviet leader, TCHITCHERIN; KEMAL Pasha of Turkey; and especially Mussolini, "the biggest bluff in Europe." The *TDS* headline read "Mussolini, Europe's Prize Bluffer, More Like Bottomley Than Napoleon."

M'uto-Umbu camp Name of Hemingway's first camp in Africa, used on the 1933–34 safari that he describes in *Green Hills of Africa*.

"My First Sea Vouge [sic]" This four-paragraph short story, dated "Mon April 17, 1911" was the first Hemingway wrote; he was in the sixth grade at the Holmes Grammar School in Oak Park, Illinois. The story's narrator tells about sailing around the "Horn" to Australia as a four-year-old with his father, the "catain [sic] of the three masted schooner 'Elizabeth.'" It was published in Carlos Baker's *Ernest Hemingway: A Life Story* (1969).

"My Life and the Woman I Love" Article, published in the London *Daily Express* (September 10, 1956). In three parts: "A Situation Report"; "Miss Mary, My Wife"; and "This Fishing is Punishing Work."

"My Old Man" JOE, the narrator of this short story, is the main character, even though the story is about his father, a steeplechase jockey named BUTLER from Kentucky, who turns crooked in European racing.

Joe's language in the narration is that of a young, perhaps 12-year-old, uneducated boy, and it is clear that he does not fully understand why, at the end of the story, two men speak of his dad as if he deserved to be killed: "Well, Butler got his, all right." And the second man says, "I don't give a good goddam if he did, the crook. He had it coming to him on the stuff he's pulled." And the first man tears a "bunch of tickets in two."

Another jockey, a friend of Butler's but who has thrown at least one major race himself, tries to stop Joe's crying and tells him not to listen "to what those bums" say. "Your old man was one swell guy." And the story ends with Joe saying to the reader: "But I don't know. Seems like when they get started they don't leave a guy nothing."

Butler was killed on a horse named GILFORD as it stumbled and fell going over a water-jump at the AUTEUIL steeplechase course in Paris. The horse, recently purchased by Butler, broke its leg and had to be shot. So Joe is left with "nothing," except, perhaps, the memories of how much he loved his father, the fun of traveling with him to the various steeplechase courses, and the idea of his dad having enough money to finally buy his own horse.

Apparently everyone in the steeplechase industry knows about Butler's crookedness. But Joe doesn't, and since Joe is telling the story, it is only by quoting the comments of the two men at the end of the story that the reader is able to infer, finally, the truth about Joe's "old man." There are other hints at his crookedness—he has to leave Italy in a hurry, for example, and he has difficulty getting his license transfered to France—but since the hints come to the reader only through Joe's point of view, they are not clear enough to enable the reader to draw fully developed conclusions.

"My Old Man" was first published in *Three Stories & Ten Poems* (1923).

My Old Man **(television play)** CBS production (December 7, 1979), script by Jerome Kass, directed by John Erman, starring Warren Oates and Kristy McNichol. McNichol plays the original "Joe" but as "Jo" since it was felt at the time that teenage girls would be more interested than boys in a horse story.

"'My Own Life'" Article, published in *The New Yorker* (February 12, 1927). A parody of Frank Harris's "My Life."

"My Pal the Gorilla Gargantua" Article, published in *Ken* (July 28, 1938). It is a report on the Joe Louis–Max Schmeling boxing match, held in New York on June 22, 1938.

N.6 Road to CANNES from LA NAPOULE along the Mediterranean coast that the narrator of *The Garden of Eden* says David BOURNE takes with MARITA in testing the BUGATTI's brakes. Contemporary maps show the shore road as N98 and the main route as N7.

Nairobi Capital of Kenya in East Africa, where Hemingway remembers recovering from an illness at the beginning of part 2 of *Green Hills of Africa*. The city is mentioned elsewhere as well, in fiction and nonfiction.

naked squaw In *The Torrents of Spring*, Yogi JOHNSON and the two Indians are in BROWN'S BEANERY when an Indian squaw comes into the room "clad only in a pair of worn moccasins." She has a papoose on her back and a "husky dog" walking beside her. The "little" Indian says, "Her my squaw," and explains that "Her no like clothes," because "Her woods Indian." She makes such an impression on Yogi that he overcomes his temptation to commit suicide, and at the end of the novel he is walking up the railroad tracks with her, stripping off his own clothing. See INDIANS, TWO.

NANA Acronym for North American Newspaper Alliance, a wire service that distributed for publication in its 60-plus member newspapers 28 of Hemingway's dispatches from the Spanish civil war (1937–38). Hemingway wrote three other dispatches from the war: One was not sent by him and apparently destroyed, and two were submitted to NANA in New York but not distributed (see NANA DISPATCHES No. 11 and No. 28).

Most of the dispatches went from Hemingway to the London office of the wire service, managed by its European editor, H. J. J. Sargint, who then cabled the stories to New York. John N. WHEELER was the general manager of NANA in New York.

Some of the dispatches were reprinted in *The New Republic* and *Time* magazine in the United States and in *Fact* in England. Nine were reprinted in *By-Line: Ernest Hemingway* (1967). All 30 of the extant dispatches were reprinted together for the first time in *The Hemingway Review* (Spring 1988).

In editing the dispatches for publication in *The Hemingway Review* William Braasch Watson used a variety of sources: Hemingway's own, usually penciled arti-
cles or parts of articles or typescripts (those still available); the still extant edited telegrams usually sent from NANA's London office; the wire-service submissions out of New York to its 60 newspaper subscribers; and the published articles in several newspapers, no two of which were the same. Watson says, "Many hands—none of them Hemingway's—intervened in the process of converting his cables to newspaper columns. Cable and telegraph operators introduced errors and changes, and the rewrite editors at NANA refashioned Hemingway's prose to suit the tastes and needs of their newspaper readers."

Individual newspaper editors also cut and edited to suit their own purposes. And Hemingway was in a constant battle of his own with NANA editors, especially Wheeler, who sent him cable messages complaining about the way Hemingway was reporting the war. Wheeler insisted on particular kinds of reporting, later limiting Hemingway to one story a week and then adding that they wanted one story a week only if he had "worthwhile material." Once when Hemingway failed to produce a weekly piece, he got a wire asking him to "file story soon as events warrant." During the early fighting around Madrid, he offered three stories, but Wheeler cabled back that he only wanted two. Later, Wheeler noted to Hemingway that he was sending to NANA the same reports that Herbert MATTHEWS was submitting to his newspaper, *The New York Times*. Wheeler suggested that the two friends split up. And later yet the editors asked for more "color" and less "straight reporting."

The main problem was undoubtedly money. While the usual pay for NANA reporters was $25 an article or less, Hemingway was being paid $500 for each dispatch, and Wheeler was having a hard time justifying the money to NANA's management.

Hemingway signed a contract on January 13, 1937, to write dispatches from Spain for NANA's syndicated newspapers. He was in Spain three times during the war: from March 14–May 9, 1937; from September 6–December 28, 1937; and from March 31–May 3, 1938. On June 4, 1937, he was in New York to deliver an address to the American Writer's Congress. Titled "Fascism Is a Lie," the speech was reprinted in *New Masses* (June 22, 1937).

The titles for the dispatches summarized below are taken from the collection edited by Watson for *The Hemingway Review*.

NANA Dispatch No. 1: "Passport for Franklin" Article, datelined "Paris, March 12" (1937), Hemingway's first as a reporter for the North American Newspaper Alliance wire service. In the article, he argues, not entirely tongue-in-cheek, for using the American bullfighter Sidney Franklin as an "assistant war correspondent" in his work as a reporter for the wire service, offering to pay the wages himself.

NANA Dispatch No. 2: "Italian and German Intervention" Article, datelined "Toulouse" (France, March 15, 1937). The numbers of non-Spanish soldiers going to Spain to fight for the rebel forces of General Francisco Franco are impressive, according to information Hemingway has gathered. Eighty-eight thousand Italians and between 16,000 and 20,000 Germans, and a "small number of Senegalese troops" are now in Spain.

Posters offering 1,000 German marks for "Volunteers for Spain" were seen by Hemingway colleagues at the Reichswehr barracks in Munich. Although Hemingway doesn't state it in the article, these statistics counter the arguments of U.S., French, and British diplomats that there is no non-Spanish intervention in the war. And this intervention also makes ineffective the nonaggression pact signed by both Italy and Germany.

NANA Dispatch No. 3: "Journey to the War" Article, datelined "Valencia, March 17" (1937). An account of a trimotor plane ride Hemingway took down the Mediterranean coast of Spain from Barcelona to Alicante, all still Republican territory in early 1937. He found a few wounded soldiers along the streets, which made the war seem "real," but mostly he saw "celebrating crowds that reminded [him] of the old days of ferias and fiestas more than of war."

NANA Dispatch No. 4: "Loyalist Victory at Guadalajara" Article, datelined "On the Guadalajara front, via Madrid, March 22" (1937). Provides details of the Loyalist victory over the Italians at Guadalajara on March 18. He predicts in the last paragraph (incorrectly, as it turned out) that the victory would be a turning point in the war.

NANA Dispatch No. 5: "Analysis of the Battle of Brihuega" Article, datelined "Madrid, March" (26, 1937). Details of one of the battles for Guadalajara (see Dispatch No. 4), which Hemingway called a "complicatedly planned and perfectly organized military operation only comparable to the finest in the Great War." He writes that the Government Loyalists "could go on the offensive now," and he wonders how Mussolini will accept the Italian defeat.

NANA Dispatch No. 6: "First Combat Experience" Article, datelined "Madrid, April 9" (1937). Reports firsthand on this early battle for Madrid, Hemingway seeing and feeling the Spanish civil war close for the first time. He and Joris IVENS, who is filming the war for what would become *The Spanish Earth,* a film narrated by Hemingway, are on the streets of Madrid where the battle is taking place.

NANA Dispatch No. 7: "Battle in the Casa de Campo" Article, datelined "Madrid, April 11" (1937). Details about the fighting for Madrid, especially indiscriminate bombing and artillery fire that kills civilians.

NANA Dispatch No. 8: "A Wounded American Volunteer" Article, datelined "Madrid, April" (probably 18 or 19). Focuses on a single American volunteer, [Robert J.] Raven, a social worker from Pittsburgh, fighting for the Republican cause, badly wounded and asking Hemingway about the war and the chances of a Government victory.

In war, Hemingway writes, you're always glad it's not you wounded or dead on the street, your body parts blown against a wall; but in the Spanish civil war when you see someone from your own country badly wounded, it "still isn't you . . . but it is your countryman now. Your countryman from Pennsylvania where once we fought at Gettysburg." This article was distributed by NANA after Dispatch No. 9, because it was sent by standard mail whereas Dispatch No. 9 was cabled.

NANA Dispatch No. 9: "Bombardment of Madrid" Article, datelined "Madrid, April 20" (1937). Written on the "tenth day of heavy indiscriminate bombardment [by Franco's fascist forces] of the nonmilitary objective of the central districts of Madrid." But, "[i]n the meantime the military situation remains deadlocked, with the Government still possessing an offensive position."

NANA Dispatch No. 10: "Survey of Madrid's Defenses" Article, datelined "Madrid, April 30" (1937). After 18 days of fighting in Madrid, there is a break, and Hemingway describes the Republican defenses set up for future attacks. "Madrid is the key position on a front 800-miles long."

NANA Dispatch No. 11: "Strategic Situation in Spain Today" Article, datelined "Paris, May" (9, 1937), but not distributed by NANA. Hemingway sums up the current status of the Spanish civil war from the distance of Paris, but the NANA editors are unhappy with his reporting, first because he is sending too many cables, then because he is sending too few, and now because he sent one from Paris, a long way from the action about which the editors expected him to write.

NANA Dispatch No. 12: "The Chauffeurs of Madrid" Article, datelined "Paris, May" (probably 9–13). This was the final article from Hemingway's first trip to the Spanish civil war, a piece that reads more like one of his short stories and which was reprinted in his collection of war articles and stories, titled *Men at War* (1942). The dispatch is in honor of the heroic escapades of the various chauffeurs who drove for Hemingway while he is covering the war in Madrid.

NANA Dispatch No. 13: "Battles of Quinto and Belchite" Article, datelined "Valencia, September 13" (1937). Hemingway did not return to Spain in time for the fighting at Quinto and Belchite, two of the most violent battles of the war, but he interviewed several American volunteers who had fought there, and they are the primary source for this dispatch.

The battles were part of the Government's Aragon offensive of August–October 1937. Government troops, including 500 American volunteers, "captured an area of over 700 square kilometers [273 square miles]." Officials claim to have buried more than 1,200 Fascist dead, having lost 2,000 Government soldiers in the two battles, including 23 Americans dead and 60 wounded. Hemingway also sums up the war to that point, predicting what General Franco must do if he is to make a counteroffensive in the Aragon region.

NANA Dispatch No. 14: "Inspection of Aragon Front Near Teruel" Article, datelined "On the Teruel front, via Madrid, September 23" (1937). From an observation tower near Teruel, Hemingway observes through field glasses the situation in the town. He writes that "I wanted to see the entire front in order to decide on the possibility of Franco making a major offensive toward the coast through Teruel in an effort to cut between Valencia and Barcelona." By mid-November he says, snow will close the mountain passes, making an attack by Rebel forces nearly impossible until April.

NANA Dispatch No. 15: "Madrid Front is Quiet" Article, datelined "Madrid, September 30" (1937). With a lull in the fighting in Madrid, Hemingway provides a description of the life in the city in the midst of war. "Some days there is no shelling and the weather is beautiful and the streets crowded. The shops are full of clothing, and the jewelry stores, camera shops, picture dealers and antiquarians are all open and cafés and bars are crowded."

NANA Dispatch No. 16: "Central Front Around Brunete" Article, datelined "Madrid, October 6," (1937). More reflection on the lull in the fighting for Madrid, a description of the frontline near the town of Brunete, and an attempt to determine what General Franco will do next and the wish that, whatever it is, he

would do it soon. In a draft lead to the story, which Hemingway himself apparently later cut, he describes Belchite after Government troops had taken the town and predicts that Franco needs the German and Italian troops that Hitler and Mussolini are thinking about sending in order to defeat the Republican forces.

NANA Dispatch No. 17: "Attack on Teruel" Article, datelined "Army Headquarters, Teruel front, by car to Madrid, December 19" (1937). Government troops fight for three days, as much against the zero-degree weather as against the Nationalist forces of General Franco. It is a surprise attack by the Loyalists, as much a surprise, Hemingway writes, as the Max Schmeling knockout of Joe Louis.

The Government offers safe conduct to Teruel citizens who leave town by early morning of the day Hemingway sends his dispatch. Hemingway wrote another dispatch about this attack, but because Herbert MATTHEWS was writing similar reports for *The New York Times*, NANA editors wired Hemingway not to send his third dispatch, and no text of the article survives.

NANA Dispatch No. 18: "Fall of Teruel" Article, datelined "Army Headquarters, Teruel front, by courier to Madrid, December 21" (1937). Details of the three days of fighting for Teruel, Hemingway very much in the midst of the fighting as he moves toward the town with the Republican troops. He describes "kids" carrying "bomb pouches" into the town "800 yards from us," and following them into town, which now belongs to Government troops, and where he and two other reporters are treated like heroes.

NANA Dispatch No. 19: "Flight of Refugees" Article, datelined "Barcelona, April 3" (1938). This is the first article from Hemingway's third trip to Spain to cover the Spanish civil war. He arrived in Barcelona on March 31, 1938, and left with Herbert MATTHEWS, reporter for *The New York Times*, on a two-day trip to the front, now extended by General Franco's attack to the East, across Aragon and into Catalunya and to the Mediterranean coast. What Hemingway sees then are the retreating Republican troops and refugees, several of whom he talks to about the retreat.

NANA Dispatch No. 20: "American Volunteers Retreat from Gandesa" Article, datelined "Barcelona, April 4" (1938). Details of the retreating Republican forces, particularly the Lincoln-Washington Battalion of American volunteers retreating from Gandesa.

NANA Dispatch No. 21: "Defense of Tortosa" Article, datelined "Tortosa, April 5" (1938). Tortosa is located on the Ebro River about 18 miles from the

Mediterranean Sea, and false reports have said the town was taken by General Franco's Rebel forces. But Hemingway drives about 9 miles up the left bank of the river to Cherta in order to find where the battle lines are drawn. When he gets back to Tortosa, he reports that he now knows three things: "that the road to Tortosa was being defended stubbornly . . . ; that Franco's forces trying to march down the Ebro to the sea had advanced only five kilometers [3 miles] in the last three days; [and] that the morale of the Government troops defending Tortosa and the Valencia-Barcelona road was excellent. . . ."

NANA Dispatch No. 22: "Survey of the Catalan Front" Article, datelined "Tortosa, April 10" (1938). Hemingway spends five days traveling from the Pyrenees Mountains south to Tortosa and the Ebro delta, making notes of the gradual movement of Franco's forces eastward toward the sea. He sums up Franco's position by stating that he "is trying two main drives to the sea. One is absolutely checked and has been for five days above Tortosa. The other is down from Morella to San Mateo and Vinaroz. The latter has been progressing spottily for several days, but the Government forces still have not fallen back on the best positions."

NANA Dispatch No. 23: "Quiet Day Along the Ebro" Article, datelined "Tarragona, April 13" (1938). Hemingway reports on Franco's tactics along the Ebro River of finding the "soft points" in the Republican defenses and exploiting them, concentrating artillery and planes on the ground forces and then attacking with tanks, armored cars, and infantry. Hemingway sees a few enemy on the other (east) side of the river, but he sees little fighting and so calls it a "quiet day."

NANA Dispatch No. 24: "Bombing of Tortosa" Article, datelined "Tortosa, April 15" (1938). Hemingway describes the bombing raids made by German Heinkel light bombers and Messerschmitt pursuit planes on a Government infantry company trying to defend the Barcelona-Valencia road leading into Tortosa.

NANA Dispatch No. 25: "Awaiting Combat in the Ebro Delta" Article, datelined "Ebro Delta, April 18" (1938). This story is about the beginning of the ground battle for Tortosa, which eventually would be won by Franco's Rebels.

NANA Dispatch No. 26: "James Lardner, Loyalist Volunteer" Article, datelined "Barcelona, April 25" (1938). James Lardner, 24 years old, a Harvard graduate, and Ring LARDNER's son, is interviewed by Hemingway about his enlistment in the Lincoln-

Washington International Brigade and the brigade's recent fighting along the Ebro River. Lardner believes his mathematical skills will help in the fighting of the Loyalist artillery. He was killed five months later (September 22, 1938).

NANA Dispatch No. 27: "Loyalist Defenses on Lérida Front" Article, datelined "Lérida, April 29" (1938). Lérida is about 96 miles west of Barcelona, and Hemingway goes there after the Ebro front at Tortosa had stabilized. The Government forces still hold about a third of the town, Hemingway reports, but there is concern about the weather. The Loyalists are hoping that the usual Spanish spring rains will come, keeping the Segre River high enough so the Rebel troops won't be able to wade across.

NANA Dispatch No. 28: "Front and Rear in Spanish Civil War" Article, datelined [Barcelona, ca. May 1]. Not distributed by NANA and probably not even sent by Hemingway, but both the holograph copy and the typescript are at the John F. Kennedy Library in Boston. It's a propaganda piece, written for publication on May Day, the holiday for the Labor movement and the Communist Party.

The article is a not very subtle plea, particularly to the United States, for planes and guns to help defend the Republican cause in Spain. Hemingway had apparently told Jack WHEELER, NANA's general manager in New York, that he wanted to "sum up" the war, but later he wrote that he had changed his mind. This article may be the summing-up piece.

NANA Dispatch No. 29: "Visit to Castellón Defenses" Article, datelined "Castellón, via courier to Madrid, May 8" (1938). The first of what Hemingway thought would be three articles filed from the central warfront but which, because of a misunderstanding with NANA, turned out to be two.

By now the Loyalists held only a small section of northeastern Spain around Barcelona and a somewhat larger section that included Madrid and the southeast. Hemingway flies to Alicante and reports on the wartime lives of the citizens of Valencia and of the provinces of Murcia, Alicante, and Castellón. "The inhabitants of Castellón do not evacuate the town, but sit outside their houses, the women knitting and the men in cafés, but when the siren sounds everyone dives into holes like a colony of prairie dogs."

NANA Dispatch No. 30: "Madrid Fighting Its Own War" Article, datelined "Madrid, May 10" (1938). Report on the most recent fighting in Madrid and its pride in holding against the Fascists. Hemingway explains the regional pride in Spain that allows the people of isolated provinces to fight harder for their own region than for Spain as a whole: "Madrid now has a war of its own and seems happy with it. . . . Extremadura and Andalucía have their war and don't have to worry about Cataluña. They are relieved. Cataluña is fighting on her own now and considers she has something worth fighting for."

narrative　In *The Garden of Eden* the term is used by Catherine BOURNE for the story her husband, David, is writing, about their seven-month marriage, including the MÉNAGE À TROIS with MARITA.

narrator　Character in "Banal Story." He relates the sarcastic reaction of "He," a man reading in 1925 a "booklet" advertising *The Forum*, a magazine of the arts and culture. His description makes the sarcasm seem deserved, but in the story's last paragraph the narrator gives a serious description of the death of the bullfighter, Manuel García Maera, in Triana, Spain.

National Geographic Society　A nonprofit scientific and educational organization, based in Washington, D.C., chartered in 1890. Dr. Sigismund WYER, a character in "Homage to Switzerland," is very proud to be a card-carrying member.

Nationalists　Self-styled name for military rebels and their anti-Republican allies—fascists, monarchists, Carlists, and right-wing Catholics, all under General FRANCO during the SPANISH CIVIL WAR. They fought against the Republican government and its LOYALIST followers. In *For Whom the Bell Tolls* Robert JORDAN, the novel's main character, is fighting on the side of the Loyalists. The "Nationalists" are referred to as "Rebels" throughout *Hemingway A to Z*.

natural　Left-handed pass with the MULETA that the bullfighter makes in front of the bull. In *Death in the Afternoon* Hemingway calls it the "greatest pass" and the "most dangerous to make and the most beautiful to see."

"Natural History of the Dead, A"　This work was published as part of chapter 12 in *Death in the Afternoon* (1932) and then included as the 11th of 14 short stories in *Winner Take Nothing* (1933). The differences between the two versions are slight, mainly the exclusion in the "short story" version of a dialogue between an "Old Lady" and the "Author," the former asking questions and the author answering them.

In *Death in the Afternoon*, it is clear that it is Hemingway who describes, first, the need for a natural history of the dead and, second, not so much a history as Hemingway's account of his own experiences in WORLD WAR I and at SMYRNA, during the Greek-Turkish War (1922). It is journalism written by a man who was

fascinated by death: "The heat, the flies, the indicative positions of the bodies in the grass [because their pockets had been searched], and the amount of paper scattered are the impressions one retains."

But if readers are to accept the same work as a short story, then the narrator is an unnamed character who describes the dead soldiers he has seen on various battlefields and a scene in the mountains involving a violent argument between a wounded artillery officer and a doctor. The artillery officer, a lieutenant, wants the doctor to give an overdose of morphine to a badly wounded man who cannot seem to die.

The man's "head was broken as a flower-pot may be broken. . . ." The lieutenant accuses the doctor of inhumanity for not killing the wounded man and curses him. The doctor tosses a container full of iodine in the lieutenant's face, and the lieutenant threatens to kill him, as soon as he can see. As the doctor tells a sergeant to wipe out the lieutenant's eyes with "alcohol and water," a stretcher-bearer comes into the cave to inform the doctor that the badly wounded man has finally died. The doctor says to the lieutenant: "It is nothing. . . . Your eyes will be all right. It is nothing. A dispute about nothing."

Nature in Downland　Title of a book (1900) by W. H. HUDSON that David BOURNE, in *The Garden of Eden*, has saved to read during the worst of times with his wife, Catherine. Hudson was a naturalist, and this book is about the flora and fauna of the English downs.

Navacerrada　Spanish town at the foot of the Sierra de Guadarrama, about 30 miles northwest of Madrid and 12 miles north of El Escorial, where, in *For Whom the Bell Tolls*, Robert JORDAN gets his instructions from General Golz at the beginning of the novel. Navacerrada is "three-hours away" by foot from the bridge that Jordan is to blow up. Jordan sends Andrés with a message to General Golz in Navacerrada, warning him that the Rebels are moving troops in preparation for the attack that both Jordan and General Golz had thought was secret.

Naval Attaché　Office in Havana to which Thomas HUDSON reports his observations while hunting German submarines in the "Cuba" section of *Islands in the Stream*.

"Navy Desk Jobs to Go"　Article, unsigned, published in *The Kansas City Star* (April 18, 1918), reprinted in *Ernest Hemingway, Cub Reporter* (1970).

Navy Yard　On the west side of KEY WEST where Hemingway kept his boat, *Pilar*, during the years he lived on the island; the docks were only a few blocks from his home on Whitehead Street. In *To Have and*

Have Not the Navy Yard is where the U.S. COAST GUARD officials keep Harry MORGAN's confiscated boat. The docks are used by the Coast Guard to patrol the area around the southern end of the Florida keys. At the end of the novel, Harry Morgan's boat is towed in to the docks by one of the Coast Guard cutters.

"Near East Censor Too 'Thorough'" Article, published in *The Toronto Daily Star* (October 25, 1922), reprinted in *Ernest Hemingway: Dateline Toronto* (1985). The headline in the *Daily Star* was "Censor Too 'Thorough' in Near East Crisis." Datelined "Constantinople," it is about the difficulties of getting newspaper reports out about the peace process between Turkey and Greece when there is only one telegraph station in Constantinople and one censor on duty at a time.

Nègre de Toulouse restaurant In Paris at 159, boulevard du Montparnasse, where, in *The Sun Also Rises,* Jake BARNES takes GEORGETTE for dinner, and where, in *A Moveable Feast,* Hemingway says that his and Hadley's red and white checkered napkins were always in their napkin rings and waiting to be picked up for dinner. See LAVIGNE'S RESTAURANT.

Negrita One of Thomas HUDSON's dogs, mentioned in the "Cuba" section of *Islands in the Stream.* She is "with puppies again." The other dogs on the farm are not named, as are, in contrast, all 11 of Hudson's cats. Besides Negrita, there is a "pointer" and "other mongrel dogs."

Negro, ebony In *Across the River and Into the Trees* it is a gift from Richard CANTWELL to RENATA, which she picks out in the window of a VENICE shop. The face is made of ebony with a "turban made of chip diamonds with [a] small ruby on the crown of the turban." The pin is "about" three inches long. In looking at it they discuss Shakespeare's *Othello,* a play with a Moor as the main character and set in Venice.

negronis A cocktail of Campari, gin, and sweet vermouth. But in *Across the River and Into the Trees,* the narrator, Richard CANTWELL, refers to people at Harry's Bar in Venice who are drinking "*negronis,* a combination of two sweet vermouths and seltzer water."

Nels, Herr Owner of the Hotel Taube in SCHRUNS, Austria, and a friend of the Hemingways when they stayed at his hotel in the winter of 1925–26; mentioned in *A Moveable Feast.*

"Neothomist Poem" A two-line parody of the opening to the 23rd Psalm, Hemingway's poem was written in 1926 and first published in Ezra Pound's magazine,

The Exile (No. 1, Spring 1927), and misspelled there as "Nothoemist."

nephew Of the MAID (3) at the hotel in LA NAPOULE, France, where in *The Garden of Eden,* David and Catherine BOURNE stay. He is an "apprentice waiter."

Nervesa Small town on the PIAVE RIVER in Italy where Richard CANTWELL in *Across the River and Into the Trees* remembers that the bodies of soldiers that had been floating in the river were finally buried, "in that big *OSSARIO* [charnel house] up by Nervesa."

"New Betting Game: Tennis Tamburello" Article, published in *The Toronto Daily Star* (May 9, 1922), reprinted in *Ernest Hemingway: Dateline Toronto* (1985). The headline in the *Daily Star* was "All Genoa Goes Crazy Over New Betting Game." Datelined "Genoa," this article is about a game in which people bet on which square block painted on a curtain a "tennis player" wielding a tambourine will hit a ball against. Hemingway writes that "the worst of the shady racetracks of the American continent are paradises of justice and honor besides the Tennis Tamburello dives."

"New Ether to Credit of Toronto Surgeon" Article, unsigned, published in *The Toronto Star* (January 27, 1920), reprinted in William Burrill's *Hemingway: The Toronto Years* (1994). This was Hemingway's first accepted story for the *Star,* identified later as a Hemingway item by *Star* librarian William McGeary. The "new ether" was discovered by a Toronto doctor, James H. Cotton, and is, Hemingway writes, "one of the most important discoveries in medical science for many years." The first use of the new ether had been demonstrated at Royal Victoria Hospital in Montreal in June 1917.

New Exuma II The yacht owned by Harry CARPENTER and Wallace JOHNSTON, two of the "Haves" in *To Have and Have Not.* The boat carries a crew of 12 and is tied up in Key West near the Coast Guard dock where Harry MORGAN's boat is being brought in at the end of the novel.

New Orleans In *To Have and Have Not* New Orleans is named, with Miami, as a place where Harry and Marie MORGAN plan to vacation after his "last" illegal trip from KEY WEST to Cuba to make some extra money. He is killed, however, on his last trip.

New Republic, The American magazine of opinion, founded in 1914 by Willard D. Straight. David BOURNE in *The Garden of Eden* is angered by his publisher's notion that his second novel "validates" his first, and so he questions to whom he promised validation—certainly not to the journals that had reviewed his book, one of which was *The New Republic*.

"New Trier Tankers Win From Locals" Article for Oak Park and River Forest High School newspaper, *The Trapeze* (March 2, 1917), reprinted in *Hemingway at Oak Park High: The High School Writings of Ernest Hemingway, 1916–1917* (1993).

New Yorker, The Popular weekly magazine, founded in 1925 by Harold Ross to publish fiction, nonfiction, and cartoons. It is best known in Hemingway circles for Lillian Ross's "Profile" of Hemingway, "How Do You Like It Now, Gentlemen?" (May 13, 1950). In *Islands in the Stream* Thomas HUDSON remembers a "Profile" of Queen Mary.

New York Giants Major League baseball team, mentioned in *A Farewell to Arms* as winning the National League pennant. Frederic HENRY reads about it in the Italian newspapers. This helps set the time of the escape of Frederic with Catherine BARKLEY to Switzerland in the fall of 1917, because that is the only season between 1913 and 1921 in which the Giants won the pennant.

New York Herald Tribune English language Paris newspaper, founded after the merger of the *New York Herald* and the *New York Tribune* in 1924. The *Herald Tribune* became the *International Herald Tribune* in 1967 and continues to publish. According to Jake Barnes in *The Sun Also Rises* (1926), the window of the *Herald Tribune* office on the avenue de l'Opéra is "full of clocks." It is probably the newspaper Jake works for.

In *Across the River and Into the Trees* Richard CANTWELL reads the *Herald Tribune* in his room at the GRITTI PALACE HOTEL in VENICE.

The purchase of an issue of the *New York Herald* by David and Catherine BOURNE, helps set the time of *The Garden of Eden* in 1923, since the merger of the two newspapers took place the next year.

News of the World, The London newspaper, which in *A Farewell to Arms* is brought to Frederic HENRY by the PRIEST (2) when he visits Frederic at the field hospital after Frederic's wounding. See FIELD HOSPITAL.

"Newspapermen's Pockets" Article, published in *The Toronto Star Weekly* (November 6, 1920), reprinted in *Ernest Hemingway: Dateline Toronto* (1985). The headline in the *Star Weekly* was "No Danger of Commercial Tie-Up Because Men Carry Too Much Money." An unidentified editor is worried because a recent survey of manufacturers' employees indicates that each carries an average of 20 dollars in his pocket, a total of 200 million dollars in currency taken out of circulation. Hemingway suggests that the editor not worry about it, and lists the contents of an average newspaperman's pockets: about 20 items, including "$2.85 in cash."

Newsweek U.S. weekly newsmagazine, founded in 1933. In *Islands in the Stream* Thomas HUDSON reads in it about the automobile accident that killed his sons and their mother. He is traveling to France on the *Ile de France* for the funeral. He also has for distraction, besides drinking "OLD PARR," copies of *Time* magazine, where he also reads the obituaries of his sons.

"Next Outbreak of Peace, The" Article, published in *Ken* (January 12, 1939). It's about British prime minister Neville CHAMBERLAIN's policy of appeasement with the Germans.

Ney, Marshal (1769–1815) French general under Napoleon I. Ney's statue is at the corner of the boulevard MONTPARNASSE and the boulevard SAINT-MICHEL in Paris, visible from the outdoor tables of the CLOSERIE DES LILAS and mentioned by Jake BARNES as he walks past the café in *The Sun Also Rises*. "He looked very fine, Marshal Ney in his top-boots, gesturing with his sword among the green new horse-chestnut leaves."

In *Across the River and Into the Trees* RENATA reminds Richard CANTWELL that Napoleon called Ney the "gravest of the brave," to which Cantwell responds, "You can't eat on that."

And in *A Moveable Feast* Hemingway remembers thinking about the "fiasco" Ney made of the Battle of Waterloo.

Ngàje Ngài Masai language for "House of God," used in the epigraph to "The Snows of Kilimanjaro."

Ngoma Swahili word for the Bantu tribal dance that David BOURNE remembers, in *The Garden of Eden*, from his days as a boy in East Africa.

Nick Referred to variously as Nick, Nicholas, or Nick Adams, he is the named protagonist in 12 Hemingway short stories and generally considered to be the protagonist in three other stories in which he is not named. See Nick ADAMS.

Nick Adams See Nick ADAMS.

nickel machine Machine that provides change at FREDDIE'S PLACE, a Key West bar in *To Have and Have Not*. After Harry MORGAN has been told that his fishing boat has been confiscated by customs officials, he stares at the nickel machine, along with "two dime machines, and the quarter machine . . . as though he'd never seen them." He is stunned by the loss of his boat, because it means his attempt to take four Cubans illegally to Havana has been delayed.

nicknames   Hemingway did not seem to like the name "Ernest" and so was constantly encouraging friends and family members to use nicknames. They included the following: "Hemingstein" in high school; "Kid" by Agnes von KUROWSKY; "Ernie," "Oinbones," "Nesto," "Hemmy," "Stein," and "Wemedge" by Michigan boyhood friends; "Nesto," "Ernestoic," "Poo," "Tatie," and "Wax Puppy" by his first wife, Hadley; the "Black Christ" or "the Black Kirsch-drinking Christ" by Montafoners in SCHRUNS, Austria; and, finally, "Papa" by his sons and several friends.

niece   Of Count Greff in *A Farewell to Arms,* a woman who, according to Frederic HENRY, "looked like my grandmother."

"nigger" boxer   Unidentified U.S. boxer in *The Sun Also Rises,* who looks "like Tiger FLOWERS," helped by Bill GORTON when the boxer wins a fight in Vienna and the crowd attacks him for knocking down a "local boy." He leaves town without the money the promoters had promised him and without even his street clothes. Bill tells Jake BARNES that the boxer lives in Cologne, is married with a family, and has promised that he will return the money Bill lent him. Bill says he hopes he "gave him the right address."

"nigger" drummer   At ZELLI's bar in MONTMARTRE in *The Sun Also Rises,* a "great friend" of Brett ASHLEY's.

"Night Before Battle"   The narrator of this story, whose name is Edwin HENRY but who is called "Hank" by at least one friend, is helping to make a film about the Spanish civil war. He and his crew have been filming from a "shell-smashed house" in Madrid, but they are too far away from the action and know they must get closer the next day.

At CHICOTE'S RESTAURANT that April evening (probably 1938) Henry realizes that when "things are really bad and you are all right, a drink just makes it clearer." He knows the people's army is on the offensive but that it's "attacking in a way that could . . . only . . . destroy itself." It is a sort of unstated principle at the core of the drinking in the crowded Chicote's bar.

Henry meets Al WAGNER, a tankman for the Republic and a friend. Al is convinced he is going to die in the next day's battle, and Henry tries to get him to think about other things. They go back to Henry's apartment, where a party is going on, including a crap game, and where they hear Baldy JACKSON, an American Flyer, tell a story about being shot down that afternoon but parachuting to safety.

When the party finally breaks up, Al tells Henry that he will see him the next night at Chicote's, but he doesn't want to "go into the time" of the meeting, and the reader is left, at the end of the story, with the feeling that Al's premonition about death will come true.

The story appeared first in *Esquire* (February 1939) and then as the third of the "stories" in *The Fifth Column and Four Stories of the Spanish Civil War* (1969).

"Night Before Landing"   Story fragment from an unfinished World War I novel, *Along with Youth: A Novel,* but published as a "short story" in Philip Young's *Ernest Hemingway: The Nick Adams Stories* (1972). The main character, NICK, is on board a ship with some Polish officers, the ship zigzagging through the Bay of Biscay but safe from torpedoes they believe, because it carries German mails.

"[Night comes with soft and drowsy plumes . . .]"   First line of a poem about a city at night, written in 1920–21 and first published in *88 Poems* (1979).

night watchman   At the NAVY YARD in Key West, where COAST GUARD officials are keeping Harry MORGAN's confiscated boat in *To Have and Have Not.*

Nimes   Town about 27 miles north of GRAU DU ROI in southern France, referred to in *The Garden of Eden.*

It is also the town where Hemingway saw bullfights in the summer of 1959 when he was preparing to write *The Dangerous Summer.* The two main bullfighters in the book, Luis Miguel Dominguín and Antonio Ordóñez fought there on successive days.

Nina   MARITA's friend in *The Garden of Eden* when the "two girls" introduce themselves to David and Catherine BOURNE. They are lesbians, who have a verbal fight over whether to intrude on the Bournes in order for Marita to ask about Catherine's boyish haircut. Later, when David asks about Nina, Marita says merely that "[s]he's gone away." Catherine refers to her as a "bitch" but quickly admits that she thinks most women are bitches.

"95,000 Wear the Legion of Honor"   Article, published in *The Toronto Daily Star* (April 1, 1922), reprinted in *Ernest Hemingway: Dateline Toronto* (1985). The headline in the *Daily Star* was "95,000 Now Wearing the Legion of Honour." Datelined "Paris," Hemingway reports in this four-paragraph story that "[y]ou cannot walk twenty yards on the Grands Boulevards without seeing the familiar red ribbon of the Legion in someone's buttonhole."

Ninth Division   U.S. military unit that fought at HÜRTGEN FOREST in World War II. See Genwel Walter Bedell SMITH.

nitroglycerin Medicine that Richard CANTWELL has taken in *Across the River and Into the Trees* in order to make his cardiograph look good so the surgeon will okay his weekend duck hunting expedition. Cantwell has taken so many of the little pills that the doctor suggests he drag a chain behind him like a gasoline truck.

Nobel Prize Named after Alfred Bernhard Nobel (1833–96), a Swedish chemist and inventor. He helped develop torpedoes, landmines, gunpowder, and nitroglycerin; but he later had misgivings about these war devices, and eventually became a pacifist. Upon his death he left to the Swedish Academy his great wealth, the income from which would establish monetary awards for work in physics, chemistry, physiology and medicine, literature, and toward the promotion of international peace.

The awards are made each year on December 10, the anniversary of Nobel's death. They were begun in 1901.

Hemingway won the Nobel Prize for literature in 1954. For the other literature awards given between 1901 and Hemingway's death in 1961, see Appendix III: Chronology and Dateline.

"Nobel Prize Speech, The" Speech, written by Hemingway for delivery by the American ambassador to Sweden, John Moors Cabot, at the Nobel Prize ceremonies in Stockholm on December 10, 1954.

The Swedish minister to Cuba presents Hemingway with Nobel Prize medal at the Finca Vigía, in December 1954 (Copyright holder unknown; photo courtesy of the John F. Kennedy Library)

Hemingway disliked making speeches and so used ill health as the reason for not attending the ceremonies.

He won the $35,000 award for *The Old Man and the Sea* (1952). The Swedish Academy citation praises Hemingway's "powerful, style-making mastery of the art of modern narration." It mentions the "brutal, cynical, and callous" writing of his earlier works and the "heroic pathos" that forms "the basic element of his awareness of life" and his "manly love of danger and adventure . . . [his] natural admiration for every individual who fights the good fight in a world of reality overshadowed by violence and death."

Hemingway's message to the Swedish audience is that "Writing, at its best, is a lonely life. . . . For [the writer] does his work alone and if he is a good enough writer he must face eternity, or the lack of it, each day." Hemingway talks about the importance to writers of going out too far: "For a true writer, each book should be a new beginning where he tries again for something that is beyond attainment. . . . It is because we have had such great writers in the past that a writer is driven far out past where he can go, out to where no one can help him."

The speech was first published in English in *Les Prix Nobel en 1954,* printed in Stockholm by Imprimerie Royale P.A. Norstedt & Söner (1955). It was reprinted in the *Mark Twain Journal* (Summer 1962).

"'Nobleman' Yeats" Article, unsigned, published in *The Toronto Star Weekly* (November 24, 1923), reprinted in *Ernest Hemingway: Dateline Toronto* (1985). The headline in the *Star Weekly* was "Learns to Commune With the Fairies, Now Wins the $40,000 Nobel Prize." It presents a cynical view of the procedures for selecting the Nobel Prize for literature and particularly that year's winner (1923), William Butler Yeats. That the Swedish committee has passed up Thomas Hardy and Joseph Conrad is indicative of its inability to read English, according to Hemingway. Yeats may have been selected, Hemingway suggests, because he had just been elected to the Senate of the Irish Free State.

"Nobody Ever Dies" Short story set in Cuba in the aftermath of the Spanish civil war (1939). The main characters, ENRIQUE (2) and MARIA (1) Irtube, are members of the Communist Party in Cuba before the revolution that put Batista into power in 1940.

Enrique, 28 years old, fought with other Cubans in the Spanish civil war and, after 15 months, is back in Havana, trying to hide from the Batista police. At the beginning of the story, he is holed up in a house being watched by "a Negro" stool pigeon, who wears a string of blue voodoo beads around his neck. The police pay him $50 for everyone he turns in. The house has some rifles and boxes of ammunition, which the police apparently already know about.

Maria, Enrique's lover, sneaks food in to him after dark, and, when the police raid begins a little later, they escape separately into the weeds at the back of the house, weeds high enough to hide them. A searchlight catches Enrique, however, as he tries to run across the street, apparently to a better escape route, and the police kill him with a Thompson machine gun. Maria, meanwhile, tries to stay hidden in the weeds, and she prays, not to the god whom she could have prayed to at one time, but to her brother and all their other friends who were killed in the Spanish civil war, a war of failure, according to Maria.

She realizes that Enrique is dead, and she decides to simply walk into the machine gun fire herself, "the best way to do it," she thinks. But there is no shooting. They take her alive instead, because, as someone says, she is Vincent Irtube's sister and so "should be useful." She yells for help to Enrique and to her brother and to the others who have been killed, and when the police tell her that they can't help her because they're all dead, she tells them, "It is the dead that will help me. . . . Can't you see everyone is helping me now. . . . No one dies for nothing. . . . Everyone is helping me now."

And the narrator describes her "strange confidence" as she holds "herself very still against the back of the seat" of the police car. The girl's confidence is so strong and her prayers to the dead friends so powerful, that the Negro who has turned her in is "frightened" and fingers his beads even more tightly. "But they could not help his fear because he was up against an older magic now."

The story was first published in *Cosmopolitan* magazine (March 1939) and then in *The Complete Short Stories of Ernest Hemingway* (1987).

Noghera A town along the Dese River north of Venice where, in *Across the River and Into the Trees,* Richard CANTWELL remembers fighting during World War I. "It is my city," he says, "because I fought for it when I was a boy."

No-name Key In *Islands in the Stream* it is one of the dozens of islands between CAYO GUILLERMO and the west end of CAYO COCO, off the northeast coast of Cuba. At the end of the novel Thomas HUDSON and his crew find on "No-name Key" a German submarine crew they've been looking for, but the Germans wound Hudson before his crew kills the Germans.

Hemingway probably made up the island's name. There is no "No-name Key" listed in *Gazetteer No. 30: Cuba* (January 1957), published by the U.S. Board on Geographic Names. There is, however, a seldom identified island named "No-Name Key" in the Florida Keys, between Johnsons Key and Big Pine Key, about 10 miles south of Marathon, and Hemingway may have used its name for the most important island in Hudson's search for the Germans.

There is also "Anonimo Key" (sometimes called "No-Name" or "Noname Key"), a mangrove island 800 yards northeast of Boca Chica Key (at 24° 35′N; 81° 41′W). It is too far from the search area, however, to be the key Hemingway had in mind at the end of the novel, but the name may have appealed to him.

Normandy In *Across the River and Into the Trees* Richard CANTWELL compares the flatness of the country along the PIAVE RIVER in northern Italy, where he fought and was wounded during WORLD WAR I, to "Normandy only flatter. . . . like fighting in Holland."

"No Room in Canada for European Reds, Preacher Maintains" Article, published in *The Toronto Star* (fall 1923), reprinted in William Burrill's *Hemingway: The Toronto Years* (1994). The article was "discovered" by Burrill in the Hemingway Collection at the John F. Kennedy Library in Boston. The "preacher" is Rev. W. R. Mackay of Toronto's Bond Street Congregational Church, and in an interview with Hemingway, he says: "Not Socialism, in any form, but the Golden Rule, . . . was the logical cure for the ills of the world."

North American Newspaper Alliance (N.A.N.A.) See NANA.

"Notes on Dangerous Game: The Third Tanganyika Letter" Article, published in *Esquire* (July 1934), reprinted in *By-Line: Ernest Hemingway* (1967). It is about two white hunters on East Africa's Serengeti Plain and why they are able to keep their clients and themselves from getting mauled. The hunters are Philip PERCIVAL and Baron Bror von BLIXEN-FINECKE.

"Notes on Life and Letters: Or a manuscript found in a bottle" Article, published in *Esquire* (January 1935). Hemingway thinks that telling stories about writers is a vice, but he tells one, nevertheless, on Alexander Woollcott. And he warns William Saroyan against writing about himself and to write "for" himself instead.

"Notes on the Next War: A Serious Topical Letter" Article, published in *Esquire* (September 1935), reprinted in *The Third New Year: An Etude in the Key of Frankness* (1935), edited by Arnold Gingrich, and reprinted in *By-Line: Ernest Hemingway* (1967).

"Not this August, nor this September," Hemingway writes, but "[i]f there is a general European war we will be brought in if propaganda (think of how the radio will be used for this), greed, and the desire to increase the impaired health of the state can swing us in." Further, "The only way to combat the murder that is war is to show the dirty combinations that make it and the criminals and swine that hope for it and the idiotic way they run it when they get it so that an honest man will distrust it as he would a racket and refuse to be enslaved into it. . . . We were fools to be sucked in once on a European war and we should never be sucked in again."

Notre Dame cathedral Notre-Dame de Paris (Our Lady of Paris), a cathedral of early Gothic architecture on the Ile de la Cité on the Seine River, where originally stood pagan altars. Christian churches were built on the island during the sixth century, but they were in ruins when the architect Maurice de Sully began to build Notre Dame. The cornerstone was laid in 1163 by Pope Alexander III, and the cathedral was finished at the beginning of the 14th century.

In *The Sun Also Rises* Jake BARNES and Bill GORTON stop to admire the cathedral on their walk after dinner on the Ile Saint-Louis. "It's pretty grand," Bill says.

Hemingway, who spells the cathedral name the French way, with a hyphen, in *A Moveable Feast* writes that from the east end of the boulevard Saint-Germain you could go over to the Ile Saint-Louis and enjoy walking its narrow streets or you could walk west along the Left Bank quais and enjoy looking across at the island and then at the Ile de la Cité and to Notre-Dame.

Notre-Dame-des-Champs, 113 Cold-water flat where the Hemingways lived after returning to Paris from Canada in late January 1924. They signed the lease on February 8.

Notre Dame football In "The Gambler, the Nun, and the Radio," Mr. FRAZER asks Sister CECILIA if she wants to listen to the Notre Dame football game that afternoon. She declines on the grounds that she could not take the excitement. She tells him that the World Series nearly finished her off. "No," she says, "I'll be in the chapel. For Our Lady. They're playing for Our Lady." Although not otherwise identified in the story, the game is probably the game with Southern California on December 6, 1930, won by Notre Dame, 27-0.

novillo A bull used in the *novilladas*, bullfights in which the bulls are either too young or too old for the regular bullfights or the bullfighters are either over-the-hill or mere beginners. Either way, they are the most dangerous bullfights, and more bullfighters are killed in the *novilladas* than in the regular fights.

"Now I Lay Me" This short story focuses on the main character's fear of the dark and on his attempt to concentrate on various details in order to get through the night without sleep. The problem is almost universal among Hemingway's fictional characters, especially Jake Barnes in *The Sun Also Rises*, Frederic Henry in *A Farewell to Arms,* and the Nick ADAMS character in several of the short stories, all of whom have been wounded either physically or psychologically and who tend to concentrate on details when the need arises in order not to think about their wounds.

The protagonist in "Now I Lay Me" is from Chicago, an American with the rank of lieutenant, connected with the Italian army in World War I. He and his orderly are in a room in makeshift barracks, about four miles behind the frontlines. It's not that he can't sleep. It's that he does not want to sleep: "I had been living for a long time with the knowledge that if I ever shut my eyes in the dark and let myself go, my soul would go out of my body."

Nick had "different ways of occupying" himself while avoiding sleep. He describes thinking about the trout streams he had fished as a boy, including the "deep holes" and the stream banks and of running out of worms, and he could "fish the whole length" of the stream in his mind. And when he ran out of the real trout streams, he made up other trout streams that he thought would be fun to fish, and he fished them in his mind.

Sometimes he could not fish, so he laid "cold-awake" and prayed for all the people he had ever known back to the house where he had been born, and he remembered details of his childhood, including things that occurred to his grandfather and to his father. Or he would name all of the animals he could think of or birds, fishes, countries, cities, foods, or the names of Chicago streets.

When JOHN, the narrator's Italian orderly, asks him about the sleepless nights, Nick says, "I got in pretty bad shape along early last spring and at night it bothers me." The orderly, who was assigned to the narrator because he spent 10 years in Chicago and speaks English, insists that marriage would help the sleepless nights, and Nick agrees.

In the story's last paragraph, he is listening to his orderly's snores and to the silkworms eating, and he tries to think of all the girls he has known and "what kind of wives they would make." For a while it "kills off trout-fishing," but then he goes back to picturing the trout streams, because he could remember them clearly, whereas the girls became "blurred" after a while. And at the end of the story, as he recalls this army experience sometime later, he's still not married and, apparently, still cannot sleep in the dark.

The story's title comes from a 12th-century prayer, the most common form of which was published in *The New England Primer* (1784): "Now I lay me down to sleep,/ I pray the Lord my soul to keep;/ If I should die before I wake,/ I pray the Lord my soul to take."

"Now I Lay Me" was first published in *Men Without Women* (1927).

nurse (1) At the hospital in LAUSANNE who assists Catherine BARKLEY's doctor in *A Farewell to Arms.*

nurse (2) At the LAUSANNE hospital in *A Farewell to Arms,* who informs Frederic HENRY that Catherine BARKLEY's baby is dead.

nurse, night   Asked by Mr. FRAZER at the beginning of "The Gambler, the Nun, and the Radio" where Cayetano RUIZ has been shot.

nurses, two (1)   At the LAUSANNE hospital in *A Farewell to Arms,* who assist in the CAESAREAN SECTION on Catherine BARKLEY.

nurses, two (2)   In *A Farewell to Arms* they hurry toward the operating room in the Lausanne hospital where Catherine BARKLEY is about to undergo a CAESAREAN SECTION, and they are excited about seeing the operation. "It's a Caesarean. . . . They're going to do a Caesarean."

Oak Park, Illinois Hemingway's birthplace and home-town for his first 18 years. Oak Park is a town of about 55,000 people, located in Cook County, nine miles west of downtown Chicago. It was settled in 1833, incorporated in 1901, and named for the oak forest it displaced.

Ernest's mother and father, Clarence and Grace Hemingway, owned three homes in Oak Park. Ernest's maternal grandparents, Caroline and Ernest HALL, built a house at 439 N. Oak Park Avenue (now 339), and Ernest's parents moved in with Grace's father when they married in 1896; Ernest was born there on July 21, 1899. The Ernest Hemingway Foundation of Oak Park now owns the house, and it is open to the public. While waiting for a new house to be built, the family lived at 161 N. Grove Avenue from September 1905 until October 1906, now owned by the adjacent Oak Park Public Library.

The new house, which was designed by Grace Hemingway, is at 600 N. Kenilworth Avenue and was owned by the Hemingways until Grace's death in 1951. Included in Grace's house plans was a 30-foot by 30-foot music room, where she could teach her piano and singing students. The house is now privately owned.

Besides the three Hemingway homes, Oak Park is also known for its 24 buildings designed by Frank Lloyd

Oak Park home of the Hemingways at 600 N. Kenilworth Avenue (Photo by Robert E. Gajdusek and used with his permission)

Wright, including the one he lived in at the corner of Chicago and Forest Avenues, designed in 1889 with a studio added in 1898.

"Oak Park Athletes Win Beloit Meet" Article for Oak Park and River Forest High School newspaper, *The Trapeze* (May 11, 1917), reprinted in *Hemingway at Oak Park High: The High School Writings of Ernest Hemingway, 1916–1917* (1993).

Oak Park Foundation Officially named "The Ernest Hemingway Foundation of Oak Park," established as a not-for-profit membership organization in 1983 to "foster appreciation for the literary skill and achievements of the author and to explore the influences of his early years in Oak Park." The Foundation owns and is restoring Hemingway's birthplace home at 339 N. Oak Park Avenue (439 when the Hemingways lived there); it sponsors a Hemingway Museum at 200 N. Oak Park Avenue, and offers tours, lectures, and conferences.

"Oak Park Second in Northwestern U" Article for Oak Park and River Forest High School newspaper, *The Trapeze* (April 20, 1917), reprinted in *Hemingway at Oak Park High: The High School Writings of Ernest Hemingway, 1916–1917* (1993).

Ernest's birthplace home at 439 N. Oak Park Avenue (now 339), Oak Park, Illinois (Photo courtesy of The Ernest Hemingway Foundation of Oak Park)

"Oak Park Team Wins From Maine High"   Article for Oak Park and River Forest High School newspaper, *The Trapeze* (March 9, 1917), reprinted in *Hemingway at Oak Park High: The High School Writings of Ernest Hemingway, 1916–1917* (1993).

"Oak Park Victors Over Waite High"   Article for Oak Park and River Forest High School newspaper, *The Trapeze* (November 17, 1916), reprinted in *Hemingway at Oak Park High: The High School Writings of Ernest Hemingway, 1916–1917* (1993).

"Objections to Allied Plan"   Article, unsigned, published in *The Toronto Daily Star* (April 13, 1922), reprinted in *Ernest Hemingway: Dateline Toronto* (1985). The headline in the *Daily Star* was "Russia and Germany Object to Allied Plan." Datelined "Genoa," the article reports that the Allied plan for Russia at the Genoa Economic Conference included: "Russian recognition of czarist and provisional government debts and guarantees for non-aggression and for safety of foreigners in Russia." George TCHITCHERIN, the leader of the Russian delegation objected and "asked for twenty-four hours in which to prepare a formal negative reply."

O'Brien   In "The Gambler, the Nun, and the Radio," Sister CECILIA goes to police headquarters and sends "that O'Brien boy," apparently an officer, to find some Mexicans to visit Cayetano RUIZ in the hospital.

O'Brien, Edward (1890–1941)   Editor of the annual *The BEST SHORT STORIES* (1914–40) and of *Best British Short Stories* (1921–40). Hemingway met O'Brien in 1923 and, when asked for a story, gave him the manuscript of "My Old Man." Even though O'Brien only accepted stories that had been previously published in magazines, he made an exception (the only exception to the rule he ever made; "My Old Man" had been published in the book *Three Stories & Ten Poems* the year before in Paris) and published Hemingway's story in *The Best Short Stories of 1923* (1924), the young author's first hardback publication in the United States.

"Offer Sir Donald Soviet Railroads"   Article, unsigned, published in *The Toronto Star* (September 10, 1923), reprinted in William Burrill's *Hemingway: The Toronto Years* (1994). This is an interview with Canadian Railroad "builder," Sir Donald Mann, who has just returned to Toronto from a 2,500-mile railroad trip across the Soviet Union. Russia is doing well, Mann tells Hemingway, and "[t]here is nothing for the [Western] powers to do except recognize Russia."

officer, large   In *The Fifth Column* he is one of the fascist officers in charge of the artillery observation post on the Extremadura Road near Madrid. He is cap-

tured, along with a civilian, by Philip RAWLINGS and MAX (2) when they attack the outpost, but they are forced to kill him ("lose him") before they get back to Seguridad (police) headquarters. He is too big, and Rawlings and Max can't make him move.

officer, thin   In *The Fifth Column* he is one of the fascist officers in charge of the artillery observation post on the Extremadura Road near Madrid.

officers   Unidentified enemy officers in the "Chapter 4" vignette of *In Our Time*. After their men tried to get over the barricade but were "potted" (shot) by the narrator's side, the officers tried to remove the barricade but could not.

Officer's Club   At the U.S. Army base in TRIESTE, where, in *Across the River and Into the Trees*, Colonel Richard CANTWELL is a member.

official   In LOCARNO, Switzerland, where, in *A Farewell to Arms*, Frederic HENRY and Catherine BARKLEY are taken by Swiss authorities after their escape from Italy. The official encourages them to go to MONTREUX during their internment (until the end of the war). A second official encourages them to stay in Locarno.

"Of Love and Death" (dramatic reading)   Written by A. E. HOTCHNER in 1960 but never performed; the script is at the Olin Library, Washington University.

"Oily Weather"   Poem written about 1922, first published in *Poetry* magazine (January issue, 1923) and in Hemingway's first book, *Three Stories & Ten Poems* (1923).

ojen   Spanish ABSINTHE. In *To Have and Have Not* it is the drink Richard GORDON has at the LILAC TIME BAR in KEY WEST, Florida, after his wife, Helen GORDON, breaks off their marriage. He has three of the "specials," but "the opaque, sweetish, cold, licorice-tasting drink" did not make him feel any better.

Ojibway Indians   Large tribe of North American Indians, located principally around Lakes Huron and Superior but extending as far west as North Dakota and Saskatchewan. The Michigan Indians in Hemingway's short stories are Ojibway. It is the tribe of TRUDY and her brother BILLY in "Fathers and Sons." And it is the tribe of Indians in "The Doctor and the Doctor's Wife." The tribal name is spelled "Ojibwa."

"Oklahoma"   Poem about Indians, written about 1920 and first published in Hemingway's first book, *Three Stories & Ten Poems* (1923).

"Old 'Constan'" Article, published in *The Toronto Daily Star* (October 28, 1922), reprinted in *The Wild Years* (1962), and in *By-Line: Ernest Hemingway* (1967). Datelined "Constantinople," the article reports on life in "Constan," the name used by "old timers," while negotiations are going on to stop the war between Turkey and Greece. Fridays are Muslim holidays, Saturdays are Jewish holidays, Sundays are Christian holidays. And there are weekday holidays for Catholics, Muslims, and Greeks—a total of "one hundred sixty-eight legal holidays in Constan." The *TDS* headline read "Old 'Constan' in True Light Is Tough Town."

older fishermen The narrator of *The Old Man and the Sea* says the older fishermen are "sad" when they look at SANTIAGO, because he has gone 84 days without catching a fish.

oldest girl, the One of the three daughters of Harry Marie MORGAN and in *To Have and Have Not*. None of the girls is named, and they appear only twice in the novel.

old man (1) In *The Sun Also Rises* he is described by Jake BARNES as having "long, sunburned hair and beard, and clothes that looked as though they were made of gunny-sacking." He is turned back by carabinieri at the Spanish border because he has no passport, but it is expected that he will "just wade across the stream."

old man (2) One of the Basques in *The Sun Also Rises*, riding on the top of the bus from PAMPLONA to BURGUETE with Jake BARNES and Bill GORTON.

old man (3) Silhouette-cutter in Milan near OSPEDALE MAGGIORE, in *A Farewell to Arms*, whom Frederic HENRY watches cut a silhouette of two girls posing for him.

old man (4) In *A Farewell to Arms*, a waiter in the café near the hospital in LAUSANNE where Frederic HENRY goes to eat while waiting for Catherine BARKLEY to have her baby.

old man (5) Last customer of the day at the café in "A Clean, Well-Lighted Place." He is deaf, and the waiters think he may be 80 -years old. The old man wants to stay late, because it is a nice café and he has nowhere else to go.

The younger waiter, who has a wife waiting for him at home, wants to close up and so is impatient with the old man. He calls the old man "a nasty thing," but the older waiter says that he is clean and that "[h]e drinks without spilling." The younger waiter, who has been serving him several glasses of brandy, finally refuses the old man "another" drink. The old man counts the saucers, pays for the drinks and leaves the café, "walking unsteadily but with dignity."

old man (6) Proprietor of Havana's DONOVAN's bar in *To Have and Have Not*.

old man (7) Main character in "Old Man at the Bridge." The 76-year-old man has been taking care of animals in San Carlos, a Spanish town on the Mediterranean coast, and when, during the Spanish civil war, the fascist artillery forces him to leave his home and responsibility, he is alone, retreating with the Loyalist forces, worried more about the animals than about his own safety.

He had been taking care of two goats, a cat, and four pairs of pigeons. He realizes that the cat can take care of itself and that, because he left the cage open, the birds will fly, but he does not want to think about the goats in an artillery bombardment.

old man (8) In *The Old Man and the Sea*. See SANTIAGO.

Old Man and the Sea, The This short novel (about 27,000 words) is the one novel specifically mentioned by the Swedish Academy in its citation awarding Hemingway the 1954 Nobel Prize for literature. The committee cited his "powerful, style-making mastery of the art of modern narration."

The Old Man and the Sea is the story of SANTIAGO, an old Cuban fisherman who has gone 84 days without catching a fish. He is an expert fisherman, but he stretches his ability by going "out too far" in order to catch a great fish, and, in spite of all that he knows, sharks destroy the 1,500-pound marlin he catches before he can get it back to his village. His understanding and love of the sea and all of its creatures, and his exhausting but hopeless struggle to keep the sharks away from his great fish, places Santiago among the great heroes of American literature.

The boy, MANOLIN, who is about 10 years old, helps the old man with his fishing gear and reminds Santiago that the two of them had gone 87 days without a fish once before, and then they "caught big ones every day for three weeks." And it no longer bothers the old man that the other fishermen in the village where he lives make fun of him. He thinks he is still strong enough for a big fish, and, as he tells Manolin, "there are many tricks."

Except for the boy, Santiago is a lonely old man. Out at sea, he thinks, "No one should be alone in their old age. . . . But it is unavoidable." His wife had died several years ago, and he has to make up stories for the boy about food that he has not eaten. What Santiago has in abundance, however, is the love of the boy and fishing and baseball and his dreams at night of the lions on the beaches of Africa, which he remembers from when he was before the mast on a square-rigged ship along the African coast.

The novel takes place in September, probably in 1950. The best argument for this dating is offered by C. Harold Hurley in "The World of Spirit or the World of Sport?: Figuring the Numbers in *The Old Man and the Sea*" (see Hemingway's Debt to Baseball in *The Old Man and the Sea*). Hurley argues that the story begins on Tuesday, September 12, 1950, and ends on Saturday morning, September 16.

On Tuesday evening, Santiago's 84th day without a fish, he reads Monday's paper and discovers in Sunday's baseball reports that the Yankees beat the Washington Senators, 8-1, New York's 84th win of the season. And, although the old man doesn't have the scores for the Yankees' double-header on Monday, he knows that if they won one of the two games—their 85th win—it would bring them into a tie for first place with the Detroit Tigers, who were idle that day.

No wonder then that Santiago feels that he will be lucky on his 85th day. He leaves his village (Wednesday morning), intending to go "far out" in search of a big fish. He catches a marlin, at noon on the first day, that turns out to be two feet longer than his 16-foot SKIFF and that weighs, he later believes, over 1,500 pounds (twice the weight and one-third again the length of the world record at that time—see MARLIN [2]).

The marlin pulls the skiff off to the northwest, out of the sight of land (which means at least 12 miles), and then to the northeast to go with the Gulf Stream current. The old man suffers with cramps in his left hand and with the pain of the fishing cord constantly pulling on his shoulder. He doesn't see the fish until mid-morning of the second day (Thursday): "The line rose slowly and steadily and then the surface of the ocean bulged ahead of the boat and the fish came out. He came out unendingly and water poured from his sides."

Santiago is finally able to kill the fish and lash it to the boat, but he wonders whether the marlin is tied to the boat or the boat to the fish. He turns his boat for home, but an hour later the first shark strikes, a "very big Mako shark built to swim as fast as the fastest fish in the sea and everything about him was beautiful except his jaws." Santiago fights back, first with the harpoon and then with the tiller, and then with the splintered tiller. Although he is able to kill or wound two or three of the sharks, they get so much of the marlin that the old man can no longer stand to look at his great fish. And during the second night (still Thursday) the sharks get what is left, in spite of Santiago's still persistent efforts to keep them off.

The old man arrives back at his village late Friday night, leaving his skiff with its 18-foot skeleton still tied to it against a dock in front of the Terrace café, where, in the morning (Saturday), when one of the waiters tries to explain to tourists how the sharks had attacked the marlin, the tourists misunderstand, thinking the skeleton is that of a shark.

Santiago had told Manolin about the confidence he felt and about the "tricks" he could use. He knows the sea and its fish, and he knows how to place the baits at proper distances to catch the marlin, but whatever tricks he has do not work against the sharks, which are quick to attack. He also knows that he went "out too far" and that fishermen should not go out on the sea alone. But when he sees wild ducks "etching themselves against the sky over the water," he knows "no man was ever alone on the sea." He is also too humble to think that there are always sharks out to destroy the great efforts of men. In the novel's last line, the old fisherman is dreaming again about the lions.

Santiago's humility is part of the novel's Christian imagery. Santiago is Spanish for St. James, Spain's patron saint, who was a fisherman before he became Christ's disciple, a "fisher of men." The old man's "left" hand cramps, but it "had always been a traitor and would not do what he called on it to do"; in pain, he says aloud, "Ay," which is, as the narrator says, "just a noise such as a man might make, involuntarily, feeling the nail go through his hands and into the wood." In another image of crucifixion, he "slept face down on the newspapers with his arms out straight and the palms of his hands up." (See CHRISTIAN IMAGERY.)

The Old Man and the Sea also carries one of Hemingway's most important themes. During the most exhausting moments of his struggle to fight off the sharks, Santiago says, "But man is not made for defeat. . . . A man can be destroyed but not defeated." Nearly all of Hemingway's major characters attempt to live by this credo. Jake BARNES in *The Sun Also Rises*, says, "I did not care what it [the world] was all about. All I wanted to know was how to live in it." Robert JORDAN in *For Whom the Bell Tolls*, knows that if he lives his life to the fullest during his last 72 hours, it could be the same as 72 years. Richard CANTWELL in *Across the River and Into the Trees*, struggles to maintain dignity in the face of impending death. They are all "destroyed but not defeated."

Life magazine first published the novel in its September 1, 1952, issue, and it was first published in book form by Charles Scribner's Sons on September 8, 1952, in a first edition of 50,000 copies at $3 each.

Old Man and the Sea, The (1)   (film) Warner Brothers picture, released in October 1958 (89 minutes); produced by Leland Hayward, directed by John Sturges, screenplay by Peter Viertel, photography by James Wong Howe, underwater photography by Lamar

Ernest with Spencer Tracy during filming of The Old Man and the Sea *(Courtesy of John F. Kennedy Library)*

Boren, art direction by Art Loel and Edward Carrere, set decoration by Ralph Hurst, special effects by Arthur S. Rhoads. The credits also state "Spencer Tracy in Ernest Hemingway's Pulitzer and Nobel Prize-winning story 'The Old Man and the Sea.'" Winner of Academy Award for music (Dmitri Tiomkin); nominated for best actor (Spencer Tracy).

Cast: Spencer Tracy (the old man), Felipe Pazos (the boy), and Harry Bellaver (Martin).

Old Man and the Sea, The (2) (film) Produced by Robert E. Fuisz, directed by Jud Taylor, cinematography by Tony Imi, music by Bruce Broughton, adaptation by Roger O. Hirson. Shown first on NBC Television March 25, 1990 (100 minutes), this version adds several characters to the original plot.

Anthony Quinn plays Santiago; other actors include Gary Cole, Patricia Clarkson, Valentina Quinn, Francesco Quinn, Alexis Cruz, Paul Calderon, Joe Santos, and Jaime Tirelli.

"Old Man at the Bridge" This two-and-one-half-page short story is about the impact of war on civilians. The story's narrator is a soldier in the Spanish civil war on a reconnaissance mission to determine how far the fascists have advanced toward the EBRO RIVER. It is Easter Sunday, probably in 1938 (which would make the date April 17).

The narrator sees a tired old man sitting by the side of the road near a pontoon bridge that crosses the river and on which other civilian refugees are crossing to the north. The old man has walked 7.5 miles from his home already and doesn't think he can go any farther. He was a caretaker of animals in SAN CARLOS, and he is more concerned about the animals than he is about his own safety. He knows that the cat can take care of itself and that the birds will fly away (he left their cage open), but he doesn't want to think about the goats if the fascists start bombing the town.

The narrator, who has completed his mission and is now anxious to get back to safety before the fascists bomb the bridge, tries to talk the old man into going up the road a little farther where he can get a ride toward TORTOSA and then to Barcelona. But the old man is too tired to go any farther, and the story ends with the narrator observing that there's nothing he can do about the old man and that the overcast sky, which may keep the enemy planes from bombing the bridge, and the "fact that cats know how to look after themselves" was the only luck the old man had left.

"Old Man at the Bridge" was first published (under the title "The Old Man at the Bridge") in *Ken* magazine (May 19, 1938) and reprinted (under its present title) in *The Fifth Column and the First Forty-nine Stories* (1938).

"Old Newsman Writes: A Letter from Cuba" Article, published in *Esquire* (December 1934), reprinted in *By-Line: Ernest Hemingway* (1967). Hemingway remembers his days as a newspaper reporter and wartime ambulance driver.

"Old Order Changeth in Alsace-Lorraine" Article, published in *The Toronto Daily Star* (August 26, 1922), reprinted in *Ernest Hemingway: Dateline Toronto* (1985). Datelined "Strasbourg, France," the article is about the language barrier in Alsace-Lorraine, the easternmost region of France, which is as German as it is French.

Old Paint An "old broken-down quarter horse" in *Islands in the Stream,* belonging to David HUDSON on the family's Montana farm.

Old Parr A Scotch whisky produced by United Distillers since 1871. It is named for Thomas Parr, who lived near Shrewsbury, England, and became a celebrity in 1635 when it was discovered that he was 152 years old (though, apparently, there's no confirmed birth year). He has been known since as "Old Parr," a man who lived through the reigns of ten English monarchs, was taken to London to meet Charles I, and died the next day of the excitement. United Distillers advertises the whisky as representing "timeless quality in an ever changing world."

Thomas HUDSON has a bottle of Old Parr and PERRIER WATER in his bag on the *Ile de France* at the end of the "Bimini" section (part 1) of *Islands in the Stream*. He is traveling to France for the funeral of his sons David and Andrew and their mother. In his stateroom, late the night the ship leaves New York, he has a tray of sandwiches and fruit, the bottle of Perrier water in a bucket of ice, and a "fifth of good Scotch." At the end of the chapter he notes: "The Old Parr was about gone but he had another bottle. . . ."

old rale, the   A "disease," discussed by Prof. MACWALSEY and Richard GORDON in *To Have and Have Not*. In medical terms, it is a bronchial disease, a chronic viral pneumonia, that produces an abnormal sound, usually a rattling or bubbling noise. The term is from the French word *râler,* to make a rattling sound. Hemingway uses the term in the novel with some ambiguity, the characters discussing it as if it were a disease transmitted sexually.

No one at FREDDIE'S PLACE, however, can tell Prof. MacWalsey, when he asks, just what the term means. They discuss it as a disease transmitted from one boxer to another, one of the boxers rubbing against the "puss" on the "shoulders and back" of the other. They may be thinking of syphilis when they use the term "old rale," but, if they are, they are using it incorrectly.

olives, garlic-flavored   Richard CANTWELL has invented what he calls a "fifteen to one" martini, named after British General Montgomery, "need[ed] fifteen to one to move [his troops], and then moved tardily." The martini contains 15 parts gin or vodka to one part dry vermouth. A "super Montgomery" is a "fifteen to one" martini with garlic olives, "not the big ones."

Garlic olives are also the ones that David BOURNE chooses most often at meals in *The Garden of Eden*.

Olmos, Rosario   One of the three bullfighters whom Hemingway saw at his first bullfights in Pamplona, Spain, in July 1923. The others were MAERA (Manuel García) and ALGABEÑO. In the article "Pamplona in July" (see *By-Line Ernest Hemingway*), Olmos is described as "a chubby faced, jolly looking man. . . ."

Olz   Austrian peasant in "An Alpine Idyll." He has just buried his wife in the town churchyard, though she had been dead for six months. He lives in the mountains above the town and, because of the snow, couldn't get his wife's body down to their parish church for burial.

When she died he put her in the woodshed, and after she became stiff he stood her against the wall and then, each night when he went to the shed for wood, hung his lantern from her mouth. Her face became so distorted that the priest didn't want to bury her. Olz told the priest that, yes, he loved his wife, he "loved her fine."

"On Being Shot Again: A Gulf Stream Letter"   Article, published in *Esquire* (June 1935), reprinted in *By-Line: Ernest Hemingway* (1967). Hemingway writes about shooting himself in "the calves of both legs. . . . with a single bullet . . . while gaffing a shark."

O'Neil, General   Scripps O'NEIL's father in *The Torrents of Spring*. According to Scripps, his father fought in the Civil War. Scripps was a boy then, and he remembers that the general was away from home when General SHERMAN burned the O'Neil house on his "march to the sea." *The Torrents of Spring* takes place after World War I, so Scripps would have to be in his 60s during the time of the novel, making his story improbable and part of the novel's parody.

O'Neil, Lousy   Daughter of Lucy and Scripps O'NEIL in *The Torrents of Spring*. "Lousy" is a nickname for Lucy, and she, like her mother, is referred to but does not appear in the novel.

O'Neil, Lucy   One of Scripps O'NEIL's two wives in *The Torrents of Spring;* she is referred to but does not appear in the novel.

O'Neil, Mrs.   Scripps O'NEIL's mother in *The Torrents of Spring*. Scripps says that she told General SHERMAN that "If General O'Neil were here, you dastard! . . . you'd never have touched a match to that house."

O'Neil, Scripps   One of the two main characters in *The Torrents of Spring*. He, like Yogi JOHNSON, is a parody of main characters in many early 20th-century novels, particularly the Sherwood ANDERSON character John Stockton/Bruce Dudley in *DARK LAUGHTER*.

Scripps has two wives. After either losing or misplacing his first wife in MANCELONA, Michigan, Scripps walks the railroad tracks north to PETOSKEY where he gets a job in the PUMP-FACTORY and meets Yogi Johnson and marries Diana, an "elderly waitress" at BROWN'S BEANERY. Scripps thinks of himself as a writer, because he has sold three short stories, but he is ignorant of literature, quoting often from well-known sayings but confusing his sources. He may have sold a short story to *The Saturday Evening Post* and "two to *The Dial*." Readers can't be sure of his reliability on such matters, but he has $450 in his pocket, which he says comes from the sale of the stories.

He also tells Diana that Scofield THAYER was the "best man" at his first wedding, that he, Scripps, is "a

Harvard man," and that Henry MENCKEN, the famous editor, is "trying to get ahold of [him]," ostensibly to buy one of his stories. He marries Diana, an Englishwoman who remembers attending the Paris Exposition in 1889 as a child. But Diana's story is as unreliable as O'Neil's, so the reader is constantly trying to separate incidents that occur to characters from incidents that the characters either make up or fantasize.

Scripps O'Neil finds a "dead" bird along the tracks on his way from Mancelona to Petoskey and keeps it warm under his coat with its head sticking out now and then. But he doesn't know whether the bird is a hawk, a falcon, a robin, or a parrot, male or female, and neither do the people he meets, indicating their ignorance as much as his. He works "almost a year at the pump-factory," where he is put to work "collaring pistons in the piston-collaring room." The reader is told that in some ways it was the "happiest year of his life." But it may also have been a nightmare. "In the end he grew to like it. In other ways he hated it."

In an improbable biographical note, the narrator says that Scripps's father, General O'NEIL, fought on the side of the South in the Civil War, and that the family home was burned by General SHERMAN, in person, on his "march to the sea." This is just one more questionable item in *Torrents,* since if true it would put Scripps in his 60s, at least, during the time of the novel.

At the end of the novel, Scripps leaves Diana for MANDY, the younger waitress at "The Beanery," because Mandy knows the literary anecdotes with which to seduce Scripps away from the less literate Diana.

"One Reader Writes"   Barely one page long, this story is about a young, "ignorant" woman who writes a letter to a doctor, whose name SHE got from a local newspaper in Roanoke, Virginia. She wants to know if it would be all right for her to safely rejoin her husband who has been discharged from the army after three years in China and who is at his mother's home in Helena, Arkansas, "taking a course of injections" for something that sounds "like . . . sifilus."

She wants to know if it will "ever be safe for me to live with him again." Her father had once told her, she writes, that anyone who had that "malady" might "wish themselves dead"; but she wants to believe her husband who told her that he will be "O K" after the doctor who is treating him finishes the treatments. The narrator then describes the woman's thoughts as she reflects on the letter she has written. "I don't care what he did to get it. But I wish to Christ he hadn't ever got it. . . . I don't know why he had to get a malady."

"One Reader Writes" was first published in *Winner Take Nothing* (1933).

"One Trip Across"   Published as a short story in *Cosmopolitan* (April 1934), it then became part 1 (with some revisions) of *To Have and Have Not* (1937). It was published separately again in *The Complete Short Stories of Ernest Hemingway* (1987).

ONI   Office of Naval Intelligence, where Thomas HUDSON, in *Islands in the Stream,* makes his reports concerning his crew's search for the crew of a German submarine crew.

"On the American Dead in Spain"   Article about American volunteer soldiers killed during the Spanish civil war, published in *New Masses* (February 14, 1939).

"On the Blue Water: A Gulf Stream Letter"   Article, published in *Esquire* (April 1936), reprinted in *Blow the Man Down* (1937), reprinted in *By-Line: Ernest Hemingway* (1967). In writing about the Gulf Stream, Hemingway provides anecdotes, including one that became the nucleus for *The Old Man and the Sea* (1952): "an old man fishing alone in a skiff out of Cabañas hooked a great marlin that, on the heavy sashcord handline, pulled the skiff far out to sea."

"On the Golf Course with Lloyd George"   Article, first published in William Burrill's *Hemingway: The Toronto Years* (1994). It was "discovered" by Burrill in the Hemingway Collection at the John F. Kennedy Library in Boston. In October 1923 Hemingway was assigned by *The Toronto Star* to cover the visit to the United States and Canada of the former British prime minister, David LLOYD GEORGE. Hemingway followed Lloyd George everywhere, even onto a golf course, and wrote 10 articles during the first two days of his assignment.

This article and "Lloyd George the Great Survivor" were not published by the *Star,* perhaps because he was turning in more stories than the editors wanted. This piece is about a golf match at the Royal Montreal Club, where Lloyd George and J. W. McConnell defeated General Sir Arthur Currie and J. J. McGill.

"On the Quai at Smyrna"   More a vignette than a short story, this short piece is about a navy detachment of, probably British, troops assigned to clean up the docks in Smyrna after the Greco-Turkish war in 1922.

The narrator is being told by the detachment's "senior officer" about several unusual events that took place while the detachment was assigned to Smyrna. The officer is referred to in the first sentence as "he" but not named. He tells about several incidents, each of which presents a touch of culture shock to the British navy personnel. The worst incident, he says, concerned trying to take dead babies away from their mothers, who refused to give them up, until finally the men had "to take them away."

The narrator tells about KEMAL Atatürk, the Turkish general and later president, coming down to the docks to dismiss the Turkish commander for exceeding his authority by trying to stop the British from removing the dead from the dock area. And he discusses the Greeks, who "were nice chaps too." When they evacuated the town, they broke the forelegs of any baggage animals they no longer needed and dumped them off the docks into the water to drown. The "he" of the story finishes by telling the narrator, "It was all a pleasant business. My word yes a most pleasant business." See GRECO-TURKISH WAR.

"On the Quai at Smyrna" was first published under the heading "Introduction by the Author" in the Scribner's reissue of *In Our Time* (1930) and reprinted in *The Fifth Column and the First Forty-nine Stories* (1938).

"On Weddynge Gyftes" Article, published in *The Toronto Star Weekly* (December 17, 1921), reprinted in *The Wild Years* (1962), reprinted in *Ernest Hemingway: Dateline Toronto* (1985). The article is about the gifts Ernest and Hadley received at their wedding, September 3, 1921. "Now one traveling clock is a delight," he suggests; "two traveling clocks are a pleasure; three traveling clocks are unnecessary, and four traveling clocks are ridiculous."

"[On Weddynge Gyftes]" Poem written in 1921 as a prologue for an article on weddings for *The Toronto Star Weekly* (December 17, 1921).

"On Writing" Story fragment cut from "Big Two-Hearted River" but published as a separate "short story" in Philip Young's *Ernest Hemingway: The Nick Adams Stories* (1972).

NICK is the main character, fishing for trout and remembering other fishing trips and bullfights and bullfighters. But then Nick thinks about writing and becomes Hemingway himself, describing the help he had received as a young writer from other writers, particularly James JOYCE, Ezra POUND, Theodore Dreiser, Sherwood ANDERSON, and the impressionist artist Paul CÉZANNE.

It's a curious piece, because the narrator says, at one point, after criticizing Joyce for making Daedalus in *Ulysses* autobiographical, that "Nick in the stories was never himself. He made him up." The "himself" and "he" here is Hemingway.

"Open Boat, The" Short story by Stephen CRANE, published in 1898. In *Green Hills of Africa* Hemingway tells Kandisky that Crane wrote "two fine stories" and names "The Open Boat" and "The Blue Hotel," the latter one the better of the two.

"Opening Game, The" Poem about the Chicago Cubs, probably Hemingway's first poem, written when he was 12 years old. Its first publication was in *88 Poems* (1979).

operation, simple The only suggestion in "Hills Like White Elephants" that the short story is about the tension that develops between two young lovers over whether the girl should have an abortion is when the young man tells her that it's "really an awfully simple operation. . . . not really an operation at all. . . . It's just to let the air in." The word abortion is not used.

opium In *A Moveable Feast* Hemingway describes taking a cold-cream-like jar full of what looked like raw opium to the American poet Ralph Cheever DUNNING, who was addicted to the drug. Ezra POUND had asked Hemingway to deliver the drug to the poet in the event of an emergency, but when Ernest received word that Dunning was dying he took the jar to him, only to have the poet send him away from the apartment with an epithet and "flying milk bottles."

Hemingway says that Pound bought the jar from "an Indian chief" on the avenue de l'Opéra near the boulevard des Italiens, "and it had been very expensive." Hemingway thinks he probably bought it at the HOLE IN THE WALL BAR.

"O.P. Places Second in Suburban Classic" Article for Oak Park and River Forest High School newspaper, *The Trapeze* (March 16, 1917), reprinted in *Hemingway at Oak Park High: The High School Writings of Ernest Hemingway, 1916–1917* (1993).

Order, the In *Across the River and Into the Trees* a "purely fictitious organization" imagined by Richard CANTWELL and his friend the GRAN MAESTRO in their playful friendship at the GRITTI PALACE HOTEL in Venice, formed by the two men because they had both fought in northern Italy during WORLD WAR I and remember the various battles. The formal name of the "club" is "El Ordine Militar, Nobile y Espirituoso de los Caballeros de Brusadelli." The motto is "Love is love and fun is fun. But it is always so quiet when the gold fish die."

Order of Merit The "O.M." is a medal that was, according to the waitress MANDY in *The Torrents of Spring*, given to Henry James on his deathbed by the King of England.

Ordóñez, Antonio (1932–1998) One of the two Spanish matadors Hemingway wrote about in *The Dangerous Summer*. Ordóñez was 27 years old in 1959, the year of his "mano a mano" fights in Spain's bull rings with his brother-in-law, Luis Miguel DOMINGUÍN.

Hemingway saw Ordóñez first in Pamplona in 1953, and he says, "I could tell he was great from the first

Spanish matador Antonio Ordóñez, followed by EH, 1959
(Copyright holder unknown; photo courtesy of the John F. Kennedy Library)

long slow pass he made with the cape." Following the *Life* magazine publication of *The Dangerous Summer* in 1960, Hemingway was criticized for showing favoritism in the book toward Ordóñez over Domínguín. Hemingway traveled with Antonio, and he and Mary stayed in his home near Cádiz on several occasions. The author later apologized for the unbalanced treatment he gave in the article.

Antonio was the son of another bullfighter, Cayetano Ordóñez, known as "Niño de la Palma," whom Hemingway had known in the 1920s and who was probably the prototype for Pedro Romero in *The Sun Also Rises.*

Ordóñez, Carmen Wife of Spanish bullfighter Antonio ORDÓÑEZ. Her friendship with Ernest and Mary Hemingway and her hospitality while they were in Spain for the bullfight season of 1959 is described in *The Dangerous Summer.* She was also the younger sister of Luis Miguel DOMINGUÍN, the second of the two major bullfighters discussed in the book. Carmen "was very dark and beautiful with a lovely face and she was beautifully built."

Ordóñez, Cayetano (1) (1904–1961) Father of the bullfighter Antonio Ordóñez. Hemingway had known

Cayetano, called "Niño de la Palma," in the 1920s and had used him in part as the prototype for Pedro Romero in *The Sun Also Rises.* Hemingway says in *The Dangerous Summer* that he had written a "portrait" of Cayetano in *The Sun Also Rises* that was accurate for his work in the bull ring, but outside the ring everything is "imagined." Hemingway says of him in *Death in the Afternoon* that in his first year "he looked like the messiah who had come to save bullfighting if ever any one did."

Ordóñez, Cayetano (2) (1928–   ) Son of "Niño de la Palma" and brother of the bullfighter Antonio Ordóñez, one of the two major bullfighters at the center of *The Dangerous Summer.*

Original Romeike's, the Newspaper clippings service in the 1920s, with a branch in New York, from which writers received reviews of their works. Henry Romeike began the service in 1855 in Paris, moved it to London in 1881, and started the New York branch in 1884. Hemingway used Romeike's clippings service while in Paris in the 1920s.

In *The Garden of Eden* Catherine BOURNE, who is jealous of her husband's writing and has burned the reviews of his first novel, tells MARITA that she wishes her marriage with David "hadn't ended in complete disillusion too but what are you to do if you discover the man is illiterate and practices solitary vice in a wastebasket full of clippings from something called The Original Romeike's, whoever they are."

Orlando, Vittorio Emanuele (1860–1952) Italian statesman and jurist, and Italy's premier from 1917–19.

Left to right, Cayetano Ordóñez, Hemingway, and Antonio Ordóñez, in Ronda, Spain, September 10, 1959 (Photo by Miguel Martin; used by permission of Alex Cardoni)

He was one of the "Big Four" statesmen at the Paris Peace Conference in 1919, along with U.S. president Woodrow WILSON, British prime minister David LLOYD GEORGE, and French premier Georges CLEMENCEAU.

In an article for *The Toronto Star* (written in October 1923), Hemingway writes that Orlando is "a voiceless politician in a country that has abandoned parliamentary government." See "Lloyd George the Great Survivor."

Orquito, Don Manuel   The "fireworks king." In *The Sun Also Rises* he tries unsuccessfully to get his fireworks to go off properly in spite of the rain during the Fiesta SAN FERMÍN in PAMPLONA.

Ortega, Domingo López (1906–1988)   In *Death in the Afternoon* Hemingway implies that the unnamed bullfight reporter for the newspaper *Heraldo de Madrid* exaggerated the ability of Ortega in the ring.

oryx   Large African antelope, gray with black markings and with long, nearly straight horns, now an endangered species. In *Green Hills of Africa* they are hunted "in the dried-up dustiness of the Rift Valley."

Ospedale Maggiore   Hospital in Milan, Italy, located southeast of the Piazza Diaz, built in 1456 by Antonio Filarete. After World War II the area around the piazza changed, and as of this writing, the building is being used by the state university.

The hospital is where Jake BARNES, in *The Sun Also Rises,* was taken after being wounded in the genitals on the Italian "joke front" during World War I. The Padiglione Ponte is the building of the Ospedale Maggiore where Jake recuperated from his war wound, and the Padiglione Zonda, also mentioned in *The Sun Also Rises,* was next to the hospital.

It is also the hospital where Frederic HENRY has X rays taken after his wounding in book 1 of *A Farewell to Arms.* After an operation he also goes there afternoons for treatments: "bending the knees, mechanical treatments, baking in a box of mirrors with violet rays, massage, and baths."

Ostos, Jaime (1933–   )   One of the bullfighters whom Hemingway saw fight during the summer of 1959 as he traveled the Spanish bullfight circuit in preparation for writing *The Dangerous Summer.* Hemingway considered him "almost insanely brave." He fought and killed six bulls in Bordeaux, France, on October 4, 1959, and is considered one of the great bullfighters of the last half of the century.

Otero   Spanish town about 31 miles northwest of Toledo, where, in *For Whom the Bell Tolls,* one of the

Loyalist raids had taken place that Anselmo remembers and about which he tells Robert JORDAN.

Othello   Shakespeare's famous Venetian general, a Moor. In *Across the River and Into the Trees* Richard Cantwell lies in bed with Renata, glad that they are not Othello and Desdemona, although, as he thinks, it's the same town, Venice, and the girl, Renata, is "better looking" than the Shakespearean character. He also thinks that the Moors made excellent soldiers.

Ouchy   Small Swiss town below LAUSANNE, on Lake Geneva, to which Frederic HENRY and Catherine BARKLEY take the cogwheel railway in order to walk by the lake during the last few weeks of Catherine's pregnancy in *A Farewell to Arms.*

Ouida (1839–1908)   Pseudonym of Maria Louise Ramé, or de la Ramée, an English novelist best known for her extravagant melodramatic romance novels. In *A Moveable Feast* Hemingway writes that he could not read her, even when, once on a skiing trip to Switzerland, he ran out of reading material, except for one of her books.

"Our Confidential Vacation Guide"   Article, published in *The Toronto Star Weekly* (May 21, 1921), reprinted in *The Wild Years* (1962), reprinted in *Ernest Hemingway: Dateline Toronto* (1985). The article is about vacation places to avoid—all imagined but recognizable places from the clichéd descriptions.

"Our Modern Amateur Impostors"   Article, published in *The Toronto Star Weekly* (December 29, 1923), reprinted in *The Wild Years* (1962), and reprinted in *Ernest Hemingway: Dateline Toronto* (1985). The headline in the *Star Weekly* was "Weird, Wild Adventures of Some of Our Modern Amateur Impostors." Hemingway wonders about the people who want to pass themselves off as someone else, usually someone famous.

"Our 'Ring Lardner' Jr. Breaks Into Print With All-Cook County Eleven"   Article for Oak Park and River Forest High School newspaper, *The Trapeze* (December 8, 1916), reprinted in *Hemingway at Oak Park High: The High School Writings of Ernest Hemingway, 1916–17* (1993). The article is written in the style of Ring Lardner.

"Out in the Stream: A Cuban Letter"   Article, published in *Esquire* (August 1934), reprinted in *By-Line: Ernest Hemingway* (1967). In the article Hemingway describes the marlin's habitat and habits: "under water, great blue pectorals widespread like the wings of some huge, underwater bird."

Out of Africa   Book by Isak Dinesen, published in 1937. Hemingway mentions it in *A Moveable Feast* as "perhaps the best book about Africa" he had ever read.

"Out of Season"   This short story is ostensibly about fishing "out of season" and the friction between the two main characters, the YOUNG GENTLEMAN and his wife, TINY, because he is fishing illegally. But the "out of season" fishing is merely the surface action that covers the much more subtle friction in the marriage.

The two tourists are led to a trout stream near Cortina, Italy, by a drunken old man, a self-imposed guide, who assures them that he is known in the town and that it will be all right to fish. There is tension from the beginning between the "young gentleman" and Tiny, but the cause of the tension is not made clear. Tiny doesn't want to go fishing, but she follows "rather sullenly," and she "stood sullenly" while waiting for the guide, PEDUZZI (1), to buy some wine. Hints of the tension are provided when, for example, "the young gentleman" apologizes to his wife for whatever they had argued about at lunch. He's sorry she feels "so rotten,"

and he says, "I'm sorry I talked the way I did at lunch. We were both getting at the same thing from different angles." Her reply is ambiguous: "It doesn't make any difference. . . . None of it makes any difference."

A little later, he tells Tiny that he wishes they "weren't in on this damn thing," that is the illegal fishing expedition. She says, "Of course you haven't got the guts to just go back" and tell Peduzzi he doesn't want to fish illegally. These are the only hints the reader has concerning the tension, and they are probably not enough to place the story among the better examples of Hemingway's THEORY OF OMISSION—stories like "Hills Like White Elephants" and "Big Two-Hearted River."

The writing of this story in Cortina d'Ampezzo in April 1923 is described in *A Moveable Feast*. Hemingway explains that he wrote it on a new theory he was working on: "you could omit anything if you knew that you omitted and the omitted part would strengthen the story and make people feel something more than they understood." See THEORY OF OMISSION.

"Out of Season" was first published in *Three Stories & Ten Poems* (1923) and reprinted in *In Our Time* (1925).

Pablo In *For Whom the Bell Tolls,* the coleader, with PILAR, of the PARTIZAN group of LOYALISTS that Robert JORDAN joins in order to blow up a bridge and prevent a fascist counterattack. Pablo has killed a number of FASCISTS, according to ANSELMO, a member of Pablo's band of guerrilla fighters. "He killed more people than the cholera."

Initially Pablo balks at helping Jordan because he does not want to risk losing any of his own band of guerrilla fighters or his power of leadership over them. Another reason Pablo is against Jordan's orders is that the bridge is too close to the cave where Pablo and his guerrilla fighters are hiding out. He tells Jordan, "You must live in one place and operate in another. . . . I live here and I operate beyond Segovia. If you make a disturbance here, we will be hunted out of these mountains." Jordan notes the "sadness" in Pablo and thinks to himself that the sadness is bad. "That's the sadness they get before they quit or before they betray." And, in fact, a little later, Pablo steals the detonating caps and exploder box from Jordan's bags in order to forestall the blowing of the bridge. At nearly the last minute he returns with some additional men he has gathered and helps Jordan complete his work on the bridge.

In the chaos that follows the bridge explosion, Pablo apparently kills four of the men he had recruited, because, as he explains to Jordan, his own friends needed the extra horses for their escape. Pablo has been in the war since midsummer 1936, almost from the beginning. He and his "wife," Pilar, had helped start the Loyalist movement in Pilar's village, where Pablo and other Loyalists had killed the town's priest and other local fascists (see PILAR'S STORY).

Pablo's band Eight men and two women who are Loyalist/guerrilla fighters in the mountains above Segovia where Robert JORDAN is sent to blow up a bridge in *For Whom the Bell Tolls.* The men are Andrés LOPEZ, the "brother with the dark hair"; ELADIO, "the other brother"; PRIMITIVO; FERNANDO; AGUSTÍN; RAFAEL (2), the gypsy; ANSELMO; and PABLO. The women are PILAR and MARÍA.

Pacifico, the Cafe and bar near Havana where, in *Islands in the Stream,* Thomas HUDSON eats and drinks occasionally.

Paco (1) Main character in "The Mother of a Queen." He is a Spanish bullfighter in Mexico, homosexual, and "tight" with money. He and his first manager were lovers, and the manager had Paco's mother buried, not in perpetuity as he had the father, but for five years, because by the time the mother died, the manager wasn't sure his relationship with Paco would last.

When the five years is up, Paco, who now has a new manager—ROGER, the story's narrator—puts off the payment for additional burial time until the authorities finally dig up her body and throw it on the public "boneheap." Roger can't understand why Paco would allow this to happen to his own mother.

The two men meet later in Madrid, and when Paco accuses Roger of saying "unjust" things against him, Roger says, in front of three of Paco's friends, "All I say is you never had a mother," the worst sort of insult from one Spaniard to another. Paco says, "That's true. . . . My poor mother died when I was so young it seems as though I never had a mother." And the narrator has the last word, to the reader: "There's a queen for you. You can't touch them. They spend money on themselves or for vanity, but they never pay. . . . What kind of blood is it that makes a man like that?"

Paco (2) Main character in "The Capital of the World." The narrator describes him as "well built" with "very black, rather curly hair, good teeth and a skin that his sister envied." He loves his sisters; he loves his work as a waiter at the PENSION LUARCA in Madrid; and he loves Madrid.

He is the youngest of three waiters at the pension, and his favorite customers are the bullfighters. He is a romantic young boy and dreams of becoming a bullfighter himself. Paco has no father, but the story's narrator begins with a joke about an ad placed in the personal column of the Madrid newspaper *El Liberal* by a distraught father, which says, "Paco meet me at Hotel Montana noon Tuesday all is forgiven Papa." A squadron of Guardia Civil had to be ordered out to "disperse the eight hundred young men who answered the advertisement."

At the end of the story, Paco, still fantasizing about being a bullfighter, pretends to work a bull by flourishing a napkin in front of another waiter holding a chair with knives attached to two legs. In a *"pase"* Paco is "gored" by one of the knives and dies, "as the Spanish phrase has it, full of illusions."

Paco (3)   A young, frightened boy who deliberately wounds himself in the hand in order to avoid going back into battle in "Under the Ridge," a Spanish civil war story. His hand is amputated at the field hospital and dressed against infection, but then an officer takes him back to the place of his self-wounding and, as an example to the other soldiers, shoots him in the back of the head.

padrone, the   In "Cat in the Rain." See HOTEL OWNER.

Padua   About 21 miles due west of Venice in northern Italy, it is the opening setting for "A Very Short Story."

Pagoda bar   Near the stables at the SAN SIRO racetrack outside of Milan, in *A Farewell to Arms*, where Frederic HENRY and Catherine BARKLEY have a drink after the races.

Palace Hotel (1)   In Lausanne, Switzerland, where, during the Lausanne Conference, which Hemingway covered for Toronto newspapers in 1922–23, the French and Turkish delegations stayed. It is referred to in the article "The Malady of Power: A Second Serious Letter."

Palace Hotel (2)   In Madrid, Spain, where, at the end of *The Sun Also Rises*, Jake BARNES and Brett ASHLEY leave their overnight bags while waiting for the SUD EXPRESS to take them back to Paris.

Palavas   Village in southern France, across the small bay from GRAU DU ROI, mentioned in *The Garden of Eden*.

Palazzo San Giorgio   In Genoa, Italy, site of the 1922 Genoa Conference, which Hemingway attended as a reporter for *The Toronto Daily Star*.

Palermo   Seaport city and capital of the Italian island of Sicily. It is where the AMERICAN LADY in "A Canary for One" bought the canary.

Pallanza   Town on Lake Maggiore in northern Italy. According to Emilio, bartender at the hotel in the town of Stresa, where, in *A Farewell to Arms*, Frederic HENRY and Catherine BARKLEY are staying, the lights of Pallanza will show as Frederic and Catherine row up the lake on their way to Switzerland. But they don't see the lights.

Palma, Nino de la   See Cayetano ORDÓÑEZ.

Palmer engine   A two-cylinder engine on CAPTAIN WILLIE's boat in *To Have and Have Not*. The engine is named for Frank T. Palmer, who founded the Mianus Electric Company in 1888, changed the name to Palmer Engine Works, and moved it to Cos Cob, Connecticut, in 1894, eventually expanding the business to include marine supplies.

Pamplona   City in northern Spain where Jake BARNES, Brett ASHLEY, Robert COHN, Bill GORTON, and Mike CAMPBELL meet for the Fiesta SAN FERMÍN in book 2 of *The Sun Also Rises*. Pamplona is the capital of the Navarra province, about 192 miles northeast of Madrid and about 24 miles south of the mountain border with France.

It is a city made famous, at least for Americans, by Hemingway and by *The Sun Also Rises*. The ritual of running with the bulls, which occurs the morning of the day of the bullfights, attracts Americans every year. It is interesting to note, however, that neither Hemingway nor his novel's main character, Jake Barnes, ever ran with the bulls.

Pamplona is also one of the towns on the bullfight circuit covered by Hemingway in *The Dangerous Summer*. He says of it at the beginning of chapter 9, "Pamplona is no place to bring your wife," implying that the all-night drinking and partying was not as pleasant with wives along. Hemingway and the bullfighter Antonio Ordóñez "do" the fiesta together "for five days and nights," having left their wives elsewhere. Ordóñez is gored one morning during the running of the bulls, and Hemingway says that in his next fight with Luis Miguel Dominguín a few days later it was the only time all summer that Dominguín "outclassed" Ordóñez.

"Pamplona in July"   Article, published in *The Toronto Star Weekly* (October 27, 1923), reprinted in *The Wild Years* (1962), and in *By-Line: Ernest Hemingway* (1967).

The article is about the wild, carnival-like atmosphere that takes over Pamplona, Spain, beginning every July 6, with the Fiesta SAN FERMÍN: beautiful, dark-eyed girls with "black-lace mantillas, Basque riau-riau dancers, military bands, rockets exploding, the running of the bulls (in which Hemingway did *not* participate), and the bullfights. The *TSW* headline read "World's Series of Bull Fighting a Mad, Whirling Carnival." The story was published one week after another article from the author's same trip to Spain, "Bull Fighting a Tragedy."

"Pamplona Letter"   Article, published in *transatlantic review* (October 1924). Hemingway writes about the Fiesta SAN FERMÍN in Pamplona, Spain, as a "quasi-religious festival." He says that "San Fermin is the local deity in the system of local idolatry which the Spaniards substitute for Catholicism." He also states that a writer can destroy the things he loves by "writing about them"

EH at Pamplona bullfights with Pauline (to his right), 1926 (Copyright holder unknown; photo courtesy of the John F. Kennedy Library)

and that "[i]t is only when you can no longer believe in your own exploits that you write your memoirs."

Pancho   The "nasty" one in *To Have and Have Not*, one of three Cubans who try to hire Harry MORGAN to take them from Havana to Florida. Pancho is later killed by machine-gun fire outside the PEARL OF SAN FRANCISCO CAFÉ.

Panthéon   A building in Paris, on the highest point of the Left Bank, place du Panthéon, site of the tomb of Saint Geneviève (420–512), patron saint of Paris. It was converted in 1791 from a church to a "Panthéon," a temple for the burial of famous men.

   In *A Moveable Feast* Hemingway mentions it because it was on his way to most places of interest to him when he and Hadley were home at 74, rue Cardinal Lemoine during 1922–23.

Papa (1)   SHATZ (1)'s father in "A Day's Wait."

papa (2)   MANOLIN's father in *The Old Man and the Sea*. He is only mentioned in the story; he and his wife prohibit Manolin from fishing with SANTIAGO, because they think he is unlucky.

Papa (3)   Nickname for Hemingway, used in his later years both by his sons and by his close friends. See NICK-NAMES.

***Papa* (play)**   Written by John deGroot, based on "the legendary lives of Ernest Hemingway"; directed by Philip M. Church, with William Hindman as Hemingway in the premier performance at the Colony Theatre on Miami Beach, October 1, 1987. Hollywood actor George Peppard purchased the rights to the play and performed the role of Hemingway at Boise State University in 1989.

Papa Dobles   A daiquiri drink, invented, according to legend, by Hemingway at SLOPPY JOE'S BAR in Key West, Florida. Hemingway often refers to the drink in his works, and several cocktail recipe books credit Hemingway's list of ingredients: two ounces of white or light rum, the juice from two limes, the juice from half a grapefruit, Maraschino liqueur floating on the top, served over crushed ice.

"Papal Poll: Behind the Scenes"   Article, published in *The Toronto Star Weekly* (March 4, 1922), reprinted in *Ernest Hemingway: Dateline Toronto* (1985). The headline in the *Star Weekly* was "Behind the Scenes at Papal Election." In the article datelined "Paris," Hemingway writes of the difficulties newspaper reporters are having getting news about the election of a new pope out of the Vatican. "By dint of top hats, bribes, shoving, proxies, and Italians to translate the Italian newspapers, the correspondents got the news."

papaw   Papayalike fruit from a tree of the custard-apple family, having an oblong, yellowish, edible fruit with many seeds; eaten by Thomas HUDSON in *Islands in the Stream*, with "fresh lime squeezed over it."

Paravicini, Captain   In "A Way You'll Never Be," Paravicini is an "acting major," in command of a battalion of Italian soldiers. The story's main character, Nicholas ADAMS, refers to him as "Para" and the commander calls Nicholas "Nicolo."

Paravicini plays an important supporting role in the story, because he helps to explain the kind of wounds Nick has suffered in battle. He knows that besides a wound to the knee, Nick is shell-shocked and that it is the psychological wound that is the more serious. He reminds Nick that he had suggested the wound be trepanned, a medical term usually indicating the boring of a hole in the skull but which is ambiguous in the story, because Nick is wounded in the knee. See TREPAN.

Nick says, "I don't seem crazy to you, do I?" And Paravicini then puns on the "trepanned" idea by saying, "You seem in top-hole shape." The captain sympathizes with Nick, but he also doesn't want him around his military unit, scaring the other soldiers. He tells Nick, "I won't have you circulating around to no purpose."

Parc Montsouris   In the southern part of Paris, where the Cité Universitaire is now located. The university was being built at the time Hemingway lived in Paris in the early 1920s. Jake BARNES refers to the park in *The Sun Also Rises*.

Parc du Prince   Bicycle racing stadium located just south of the Auteuil steeplechase course, west of Paris at the Bois de Boulogne's southeastern corner. In *A Moveable Feast* Hemingway calls this the "wickedest track of all where we saw [the] great rider Ganay fall and heard his skull crumple under the crash helmet as you crack an hard-boiled egg against a stone to peel it on a picnic." It was a cement track, about 733 yards in length.

Paris   Capital city of France, where Hemingway lived for several years during the 1920s, at the beginning of his career. He and Hadley lived in an apartment at 74, RUE CARDINAL LEMOINE and later at 113, RUE NOTRE-DAME-DES-CHAMPS; he lived in Gerald Murphy's studio apartment at 69, RUE FROIDEVAUX while waiting for the divorce from Hadley; and he and Pauline lived at 6, RUE FEROU.

Paris is the setting for the first third of *The Sun Also Rises* and the place where David and Catherine BOURNE are married three weeks before the beginning of *The Garden of Eden*. It is also one of the places where, in "Mr. and Mrs. Elliot," the Elliots "try to have a baby." And it is "remembered" by several characters in other works, novels as well as short stories.

Hemingway's *A Moveable Feast* is a memoir of his first years in Paris, and the book's epigraph states: "If you are lucky enough to have lived/ in Paris as a young man, then wherever you/ go for the rest of your life, it stays with/ you, for Paris is a moveable feast."

Hemingway in Paris (Photo by Helen Breaker; courtesy of the John F. Kennedy Library)

Paris Exposition   Mentioned in *The Torrents of Spring*, probably in reference to the 1889 exposition, which featured the Eiffel Tower. In the novel the "elderly waitress," Diana SCRIPPS, says she was a young girl ("a *jeune fille*") when her mother took her there, and the novel takes place in 1924 or 1925. Of the three possible major expositions held in Paris (1867, 1889, and 1900), all worldwide industrial exhibits attracting millions of visitors, the 1889 date is the most probable one, since Diana would then be about 40 at the time the story takes place.

"Parisian Boorishness"   Article, published in *The Toronto Star Weekly* (April 15, 1922), reprinted in *The Wild Years* (1962), reprinted in *Ernest Hemingway: Dateline Toronto* (1985). The headline in the *Star Weekly* was "French Politeness." The article is datelined "Paris," and in it Hemingway reports that "French politeness has gone the way of absinthe, prewar prices and other legendary things."

"Paris is Full of Russians"   Article, published in *The Toronto Daily Star* (February 25, 1922), reprinted in *Ernest Hemingway: Dateline Toronto* (1985). The headline in the *Daily Star* was "Influx of Russians to All Parts of Paris." Datelined "Paris," the article is about Russian emigrés who have concentrated in Paris, keeping alive, apparently, by selling off the jewels and gold ornaments they brought with them from Russia.

"Paris Letter, A"   Article, published in *Esquire* (February 1934), reprinted in *By-Line: Ernest Hemingway* (1967). The article is about the depression Hemingway feels on visiting Paris for a short time in late 1933, the depression caused by news of old friends who have either committed suicide or lost all their money. Paris "was a fine place to be quite young in. . . . But she is like a mistress who does not grow old and she has other lovers now."

Paris Review, The   English-language literary quarterly published in Paris and founded in 1953 by George Plimpton (editor), Peter Matthiessen, and Harold Humes. The journal is modeled after Paris literary magazines of the 1920s.

It is known for publishing quality fiction and poetry, especially of new or unknown writers; it introduced Philip Roth and Jack Kerouac, among others, and was the first American journal to publish the work of Samuel Beckett. The *Review* is also known for its series of interviews with writers, beginning in 1958, and included one with Hemingway (Spring 1958). See "The Art of Fiction."

Paris-Sport Complet   Sporting newspaper, read for the racing odds and results by JOE's "old man" in "My Old Man." He refers to it as *Paris-Sport*.

In *A Moveable Feast* Hemingway writes of buying the final afternoon edition of this paper in order to get the results from the steeplechase races at Auteuil and the next day's odds at Enghien.

"Paris-to-Strasbourg Flight, A"   Article, published in *The Toronto Daily Star* (September 9, 1922), reprinted in *The Wild Years* (1962), and in *By-Line: Ernest Hemingway* (1967). Datelined "Strasbourg, France," the article is about a flight Ernest and his wife, Hadley, took, somewhat reluctantly, on the "Franco-Rumanian Aero Company" line, leaving Paris at five o'clock one morning and arriving in Strasbourg two and a half hours later. The *TDS* headline read "A Paris-to-Strasbourg Flight Shows Living Cubist Picture."

Paris Times   Newspaper bought by Jake BARNES in *The Sun Also Rises*.

Park, Mungo (1771–1806?)   Scottish explorer. In "A Natural History of the Dead," the narrator relates Park's story of being saved from death in Africa by the inspiration he received in studying the beauty of a "small moss-flower of extraordinary beauty."

Parker, Harry   Referred to once in *The Torrents of Spring* as Scripps O'NEIL's friend who met a "poet chap" in Detroit whom Scripps credits for the quotation, "Through pleasures and palaces though I may roam. . . ." The quotation is incorrectly credited as part of Hemingway's parody in *Torrents*.

The quotation is actually from the poem/song "Home Sweet Home" in the opera *Clari, the Maid of Milan*, by John Howard Payne (1791–1852).

Parma   Town in northern central Italy, mentioned in "Che Ti Dice La Patria?" (What Do You Hear From Home?) to which the two main characters travel.

parody   A literary work that deliberately imitates the characteristic style of another work in an attempt to ridicule. Parodies usually treat serious subjects in nonsensical ways. Hemingway wrote *The Torrents of Spring* in an apparently deliberate attempt to ridicule some novels of the World War I years and particularly Sherwood Anderson's novel *Dark Laughter* (1925). One of the characters in *Torrents* mentions "that fellow Anderson's book," with a "chap" named "Fred Something." See the main entry for *The Torrents of Spring*.

"Partizan, The"   A Spanish civil war song, sung in *The Fifth Column* by 25 "comrades" waiting downstairs in the Hotel Florida in act 2, scene 3.

partizans   Guerrilla fighters in the LOYALIST band led by PABLO and PILAR in *For Whom the Bell Tolls*. They help

Robert JORDAN blow up the bridge. "Partizan" is, according to the novel's narrator, the Russian term for "guerrilla work behind the lines."

Pascin, Jules (1885–1930)   American painter, born in Bulgaria. Pascin went to Paris in 1905, moved to New York in 1914, and became an American citizen, then returned to Paris after the war (1918).

The 11th section of *A Moveable Feast* is titled "With Pascin at the Dôme." In it Hemingway describes a conversation at the café with Pascin and two of his women models. Pascin is nasty toward the two models, who are also his lovers. At the end of the sketch, however, Hemingway writes that, after the painter had killed himself, he liked to remember him the way he was that evening at the Dôme. And he makes an observation about suicide: "They say the seeds of what we will do are in all of us, but it always seemed to me that in those who make jokes in life the seeds are covered with better soil and with a higher grade of manure."

In *The Garden of Eden* Catherine BOURNE suggests to David a list of illustrators for the book he is writing about their marriage and ménage à trois with Marita. Pascin is one of the artists she names. In *Eden* the name is misspelled "Pascen."

Pascin is a "friend" of Roger DAVIS in *Islands in the Stream*. Referred to as Mr. Pascin by young Tom HUDSON, he is one of several painters he and his father, Thomas HUDSON, knew in Paris. Pascin, as Hudson states, committed suicide in 1930.

Pasionaria, La   The Spanish "passion flower" was Dolores Ibarruri (1895–1989), one of the most inspirational leaders for the REPUBLIC during the SPANISH CIVIL WAR. She was a communist and a member of parliament. In *For Whom the Bell Tolls*, while Joaquín and the rest of El Sordo's men wait to die on a hill surrounded by Rebels, Joaquín quotes La Pasionaria's slogan of the resistance: "it is better to die on your feet than to live on your knees."

Passchendaele (Passendale)   A town in western Flanders (Belgium), about 6 miles east-northeast of Ypres, where major fighting took place at the battle of HÜRTGEN FOREST in WORLD WAR II. Richard CANTWELL, in *Across the River and Into the Trees*, talks about "Passchendaele with tree bursts," indicating that the U.S. forces were not prepared for fighting in a forest.

Passini   One of the four ambulance drivers under Frederic HENRY's command as they drive to the warfront in book 1 of *A Farewell to Arms*. Passini is killed by the same "big trench mortar shell" explosion that wounds Frederic.

pasta asciuta   Dry pasta, or any pasta not cooked in soup. Although the waitresses/prostitutes at a Spezia restaurant hassle the two main characters in "Che Ti Dice La Patria?" (What do you hear from home?) the narrator reports that the *pasta asciuta* is good. The wine, however, "tasted of alum," and they had to add water.

pastis   A yellowish liqueur made of aniseed (anise), similar to ABSINTHE but without the wormwood. David BOURNE in *The Garden of Eden* says it is "impossible to drink pastis after absinthe."

patronne   In *The Sun Also Rises*, the proprietor at the BAL MUSETTE in Paris with whom Jake BARNES leaves a 50-franc note. He tells the patronne that if GEORGETTE, the prostitute he has picked up, asks for him after he leaves with Brett ASHLEY then Georgette is to get the money; if she doesn't ask for him then he is to hold it for Jake. The reader is not told the outcome of this event.

Patton, General George S. (1885–1945)   U.S. general in command of the Third Army in its march across France and Germany during World War II. Richard CANTWELL, in *Across the River and Into the Trees*, thinks an extra large lobster served to him looks a "little bit" like Patton.

Paula   A friend of Frances CLYNE, Robert COHN's fiancée, in *The Sun Also Rises*.

Paulson, Teddy Jo   One of the two "pretty" American girls, along with Mary Schoonmaker, taken "prisoner" by Hemingway and his friends in Pamplona in 1959 when Ernest was in Spain for the bullfight season and to write *The Dangerous Summer*. They are not named in the text, but Schoonmaker is identified in one of the book's photographs, and Paulson has been identified by biographers. Both are a part of the Hemingway party not only in Pamplona but "through the feria of Valencia at the end of the month" and at Ernest's 60th birthday party at La Consula on July 21.

Pavillion Henri-Quatre   A hotel in Paris, in Saint Germain, where HARRY, in "The Snows of Kilimanjaro," remembers staying with his wife, HELEN (3).

Paznaun   Valley in southwest Austria where the town of Galtur is located, the setting for "An Alpine Idyll."

Pearl of San Francisco Café   Near the boat docks in Havana, Cuba, in *To Have and Have Not*. Harry MORGAN and EDDY (2) cross the square to the café from their boat at the beginning of the novel to get a cup of coffee. Morgan also refers to it as the "Perla café," where he says he "can get a good meal . . . for twenty-five cents."

pearls In *The Garden of Eden* David BOURNE asks his wife, Catherine, to leave her pearls on while they make love in their hotel room at HENDAYE, France.

pédéraste French for "homosexual." In *Across the River and Into the Trees* RENATA points out to Richard CANTWELL at HARRY'S BAR a boy "with the wave in his hair," the 25-year-old painter of her portrait, which she later gives to Cantwell. Richard refers to him as a *pédéraste*.

Pedrico (1) One of the bartenders at the FLORIDITA in Havana in *Islands in the Stream*. He serves Thomas HUDSON double frozen daiquiris on the morning his first wife flies in to Cuba for the day (February 20, 1944).

Pedrico (2) Owner of the bodega (grocery store) in SANTIAGO's village in *The Old Man and the Sea*. He takes care of the old man's skiff and gear after he returns home from his fishing. Santiago tells MANOLIN to give the skeletal head of the marlin to Pedrico.

Pedro Thomas HUDSON's chauffeur, in the "Cuba" section of *Islands in the Stream*. Hudson doesn't like Pedro, but he can't get rid of him because he knows too much about Hudson's activities chasing German submarines.

Peduzzi (1) Fishing guide in "Out of Season." He's a drunken old man who has imposed himself on two tourists in Cortina, Italy, insisting that it is all right to fish for trout, even if it's illegal, "out of season." He talks "mysteriously" with the YOUNG GENTLEMAN about the fishing and with good humor. But he needs money badly, which is probably why he insists to the gullible "young gentleman" that everything is all right, that they will be safe from the police. Peduzzi, then works the tourists for some lire for wine and supplies.

When the three discover at the river that they have no *piombi* (lead weights) for the fishing lines, the "young gentleman" is relieved that they can't fish; he's afraid of being arrested. But he still accepts Peduzzi's proposal that they leave the hotel the next morning at seven o'clock and try again.

The young gentleman works up the nerve to tell Peduzzi that he "may not be going" with him in the morning, but he gives him four lire anyway for the next day's supplies. At the end of the story, Peduzzi is confident that he will no longer have to work in the hotel's garden because he's earning money as a fishing guide; he believes that his life is "opening out."

Peduzzi (2) Italian ambulance driver in *A Farewell to Arms*. After Frederic HENRY returns to his post at Gorizia, having recovered from his war wound, Peduzzi drives him to Bainsizza, near the front lines.

Peerless Brand of tobacco, the favorite of Billy TABE-SHAW in the juvenilia short story "Sepi Jingan."

It is also the brand which, in *The Torrents of Spring*, Yogi JOHNSON hands to one of his Indian friends.

Peirce, Waldo (1884–1970) American painter, known for his splashy brushwork and color, somewhat in the style of the French impressionists, especially Renoir. Hemingway knew Peirce in Paris in the 1920s, and they went to Spain together for the bullfights, Peirce making sketches for later paintings of bullfight scenes.

In *Islands in the Stream* Peirce is one of several painters Thomas HUDSON and his son, young Tom, remember from their Paris years.

Pension Luarca A boardinghouse in Madrid where PACO (2) lives and works as a waiter, in "The Capital of the World." Second-rate matadors live at the pension, because it has a good address in the Calle San Jeronimo, the food is good, and the rooms are inexpensive. At the time of the story there are three matadors living at the pension, as well as two picadors, and one banderillero.

Pepé Friend of Enrique EMMUNDS, the main character and narrator of "The Denunciation." Pepé works at the counterespionage bureau of the Loyalist forces during the Spanish civil war.

Pera Palace Pera was a section of Constantinople in the 1920s; the palace there is mentioned in "The Snows of Kilimanjaro." The city's name was changed in 1930 to Istanbul, and the Pera section is now called Beyoglu, a commercial and residential area.

Percival, Philip Hope (1885–1966) Hunting guide, whom Hemingway referred to as "the best white hunter in Africa." Percival was an Englishman who had gone to East Africa in 1905 and bought a farm at Machakos, about 20 miles from Nairobi. He had led safaris with Winston CHURCHILL, Teddy Roosevelt, George Eastman, and the Vanderbilts, all before World War I. But it was Hemingway who made the Percival name public by referring to him in his writing. Percival's book, *Hunting, Settling and Remembering*, was completed in 1961 but not published until 1997.

Hemingway thought Percival was the consummate professional. He was the hunting guide when Hemingway and his wife Pauline went to East Africa in 1933–34, and Hemingway hired him again for another safari in 1953–54. Hemingway wrote *Green Hills of Africa* (1935) from his experiences on the first safari. Neither Percival nor Pauline is identified in the book, but Percival is "Pop" and Pauline is P.O.M., "Poor Old Mama."

Percival is one of the two white hunters Hemingway admires and writes about in his article "Notes on Dangerous Game: The Third Tanganyika Letter." The other white hunter is Baron Bror von BLIXEN-FINECKE, the director of guides for Tanganyika and the divorced husband of writer Isak DINESEN.

Père Lachaise   Cemetery in northeast Paris, mentioned in *Across the River and Into the Trees.* The cemetery is named after François d'Aix de La Chaise (1624–1709), a Jesuit priest, confessor of Louis XIV.

Perkins, Maxwell (1884–1947)   Editor at Charles Scribner's Sons, beginning in 1914, later becoming the firm's editorial director and vice president. He is best known as the editor and adviser for Hemingway, F. Scott FITZGERALD, and Thomas WOLFE. Other writers whom Perkins either discovered or assisted during his career at Scribner's were Robert Louis Stevenson, Edmund WILSON, Erskine Caldwell, and John P. Marquand.

In *A Moveable Feast* Hemingway writes that on his first meeting with Fitzgerald in April 1925, Scott told him about Perkins, who was his editor for *The Great Gatsby* which had been published a few days before (April 10). Later, Hemingway writes that he took the manuscript of *The Sun Also Rises* to New York in the late winter of 1925–26 to show to Perkins. He became Hemingway's editor for that novel and for each of the other major works published during Perkins's lifetime.

Pernod   The Frenchman Henry-Louis Pernod produced a brand of green, aromatic anise- and licorice-flavored liqueur in 1797, and it has since become a trade name. See ABSINTHE.

According to Jake BARNES, in *The Sun Also Rises*, adding water makes its greenish color turn milky. "It tastes like licorice and it has a good uplift, but it drops you just as far."

Peroxide   One of the five whores in "The Light of the World." She argues with ALICE about which of them knows Steve/Stanley KETCHEL better. When one of the customers at the railway station bar mentions "Steve Ketchel," Peroxide says, "There aren't any more men like Steve Ketchel."

When the cook says, "Wasn't his name Stanley Ketchel?" she says, "He was no Stanley. Steve Ketchel was the finest and most beautiful man that ever lived." ALICE, one of the other whores, argues that she knew him better and says to Peroxide, "You're a dirty liar. . . . You never layed Steve Ketchel in your life and you know it." And when Alice says that Steve had once told her she was a "lovely piece," Peroxide says, "Steve couldn't have said that. It wasn't the way he talked."

Because of the confusion over the names Steve and Stanley, it is never clear which, if either, of the two women knew Stanley Ketchel the prizefighter.

Perrier-Jouet   Brut (dry) champagne from Epernay, France, now linked with G.H. Mumm and Company and considered "light-bodied," one of the better champagnes. In *The Garden of Eden* Catherine BOURNE tells her husband, David, that she would like either it or the LANSON (another dry champagne) for breakfast in HENDAYE, France.

Perrier-Jouet Brut 1915   In *Islands in the Stream* Thomas HUDSON remembers that he and the PRINCESS drank two bottles of this champagne at the "Ritz bar," located at the stern of the luxury cruise ship they were on going up the Suez Canal.

Perrier-Jouet Brut 1942   The champagne with which, in *Across the River and Into the Trees*, Richard CANTWELL "celebrated" the death of the French general LECLERC.

Perrier water   Sparkling mineral water, first bottled in 1863, though the Perrier source for water was known in Roman times. Produced when fresh rain falls on the hillsides of southern France and seeps into limestone, sand, and gravel deposits. Originally, natural gas formed, and mingled with spring water, rising to the surface at a temperature of 60 degrees Fahrenheit.

Hemingway refers to Perrier water often, in both his fiction and nonfiction, as a mix for alcoholic drinks. In *Islands in the Stream* Thomas Hudson drinks Perrier water and a "fifth of good Scotch," referred to as OLD PARR.

"Personal"   Article for Oak Park and River Forest High School newspaper, *The Trapeze* (January 26, 1917), reprinted in *Hemingway at Oak Park High: The High School Writings of Ernest Hemingway, 1916–1917* (1993).

personal boys   African natives on the hunting safari in "The Short Happy Life of Francis Macomber." They help carry MACOMBER back to camp "in triumph" after he has "killed" the lion. When Macomber's own "personal boy" is told about his master's morning cowardice, he looks "curiously" at him while setting the table for lunch, and the white guide, Wilson, has to threaten to whip him.

pescecani   Italian term for "profiteers," its literal translation is "dogfish." In *Across the River and Into the Trees*, Richard CANTWELL describes his BOATMAN's hopes of profiting from gambling at one of the LIDO Island casinos, near Venice. Cantwell refers to the gamblers as *"pescecani,"* the "post-war rich from Milan."

Peter   The name Catherine BOURNE gives to her husband, David, for the changing sexual role she asks him to play in *The Garden of Eden.*

Peters   One of the crew members on Thomas HUDSON's boat, searching for the crew of a German submarine in *Islands in the Stream*. Peters is the radioman on board but considered incompetent by Hudson and the other crew members, because he cannot get the radio to pick up or deliver reports to Cuban headquarters. He is killed by one of the Germans who fires at him from a turtle boat.

Petoskey Town in northern Michigan on Little Traverse Bay, about 40 miles south of the Straits of Mackinac. The Hemingway family traveled to Petoskey from Oak Park, Illinois, on their way each summer to their cabin on Walloon Lake, a few miles southwest of Petoskey.

In "Ten Indians," NICK can see the lights of Petoskey "and, off across Little Traverse Bay, the lights of Harbour Springs." Petoskey is also the setting for *The Torrents of Spring*.

Petra (1) A "little old woman of about sixty," a maid at Madrid's HOTEL FLORIDA in *The Fifth Column*. She tells Dorothy Bridges that the fascists "always shoot from windows at night during a bombardment. The fifth column people. The people who fight us from inside the city. . . . They are our enemies. Even of me. If I was killed they would be happy. They would think it was one working person less."

Petra (2) The name of one of the maids at the Hotel Florida in *For Whom the Bell Tolls*. See SEGURIDAD.

Pfeiffer, Pauline See Pauline Pfeiffer HEMINGWAY.

Phelps, Miss In *Islands in the Stream* the name given by young Tom HUDSON to a fictitious secretary who supposedly types Roger DAVIS's stories for him. Tom makes up the story for the sake of SEVEN TOURISTS he and his two brothers are trying to trick into thinking the three underage boys are drunk.

Phil Main character in "The Sea Change." He has just been told by his lover, identified only as "GIRL (4)," that she is leaving him for a woman. He argues with her about it, saying, without meaning it, "I'll kill her." He says to the girl, "Couldn't you have gotten into some other jam?"

Phil knows what he would do if it were a man, but this "sea change" clearly frustrates him. He refers to "it" (lesbianism, a word not used in the story) as a "vice," trying to remember lines from a poem he knows. The lines he can't remember are from Alexander Pope's "An Essay on Man": "Vice is a monster of so frightful mien,/ As, to be hated, needs but to be seen;/ Yet seen too oft, familiar with her face,/ We first endure, then pity, then embrace." He remembers properly only the first line, but Pope's idea is that eventually we accept, even "embrace" a vice, which leaves the reader wondering how much of this idea Phil, or even the narrator in telling the story, understands about the "sea change" that has taken place in the girl.

Phil also refers to "it" as "perversion," but the girl reminds him that he, too, has been involved in perversion. She says, "We're made up of all sorts of things. You've known that. You've used it well enough." And he says, "You don't have to say that again," implying that they have discussed the idea of "perversion" before, probably as it concerns their own relationship.

Finally, though, he tells her to leave, even "Right away" and she does, without looking "back at him." He suddenly feels different and goes to the bar to tell James, the bartender, about it. "I'm a different man, James. . . . You see in me quite a different man." And when he looks in the mirror behind the bar he sees "quite a different-looking man."

A "sea change" has taken place in Phil, too, perhaps a change just as significant as the one the girl has gone through.

Philip Main character in "Get a Seeing-Eyed Dog." He is a writer, recently blinded, trying to remember things that he and his wife have done together so he can write about them. He loves his wife but tries to get her to go away for a while so they can "pace themselves" in getting used to his blindness. He feels that he's "not doing too well," and he wants to deal with it alone for awhile.

"[Philip Haines Was a Writer. . .]" Unfinished, untitled story published in *The Hemingway Review* (Spring 1990).

Philippe, Duke of Orleans Candidate of the French Royalist Party in 1923 in its attempt to reestablish a king as the head of France. See "French Royalist Party."

Philip Rawlings *See* Philip RAWLINGS.

Phillip II (1527–1598) King of Spain (1556–98). In describing the beginning of the bullfight in chapter 6 of *Death in the Afternoon*, Hemingway states that the two mounted bailiffs who lead the parade (*paseo*) are dressed in costumes of the time of Philip II.

Phoebus the Phoenician Reference in *Across the River and Into the Trees*, probably taken from T. S. Eliot's *The Waste Land*. Richard CANTWELL tells RENATA about his wife, a journalist, from whom he is now divorced: "I told her about things once, and she wrote about them. But that was in another country and besides the wench is dead. . . . Deader than Phoebus the Phoenician." It is "Phlebas the Phoenician," however, in *The Waste Land*.

"Photo Portraits" Article, published in *The Toronto Star Weekly* (May 29, 1920), reprinted in *Ernest Hemingway: Dateline Toronto* (1985). The headline in the *Star Weekly* was "Prices for 'Likenesses' Run From 25 cents to $500 in Toronto." The article is about having your photograph taken either as you are (the 25-cent version) or as you would like to be (the more expensive one).

Piacenza   Town in northern Italy, one of several mentioned in "Che Ti Dice La Patria?" (What do you hear from home?) to which the two main characters travel.

Piani, Luigi   In *A Farewell to Arms* the last driver to be with Frederic HENRY before Frederic's escape into the TAGLIAMENTO RIVER. Piani may have shot BONELLO, one of the other ambulance drivers, during the chaotic retreat from Caporetto, but the sudden and mysterious disappearance of Bonello is not explained. Piani tells Frederic several times that Bonello "went away," to which Frederic tells the reader, "I did not say anything," implying, perhaps, that he thinks Piani shot him.

Piave   San Dona di Piave, a town near VENICE through which Colonel Richard CANTWELL drives on his way to Venice at the beginning of *Across the River and Into the Trees*.

Piave River   In *Across the River and Into the Trees* it is along the Piave River that Richard CANTWELL was wounded during WORLD WAR I. The river's headwaters are in the Carnic Alps in northeastern Italy near the border with Austria, and it runs almost due south, dumping into the Adriatic a few miles east of Venice.

The Italian army retreated from CAPORETTO (1917) to the Piave River, where they held off the Austrians until October 1918, when the Allied forces joined the Italians to defeat the Austrians.

Piazzale Roma to Ca'Foscari   Section of the Grand Canal in VENICE that is "the dull part," according to Richard CANTWELL in *Across the River and Into the Trees*. Its dullness is not explained, but Cantwell adds, as an afterthought, "though none of it [Venice] is dull."

Piazzetta   Venice plaza near St. Mark's Square, which opens onto the Adriatic Sea, mentioned in *Across the River and Into the Trees*.

Picabia, Francis (1878–1953)   French painter involved in the dadaist movement early in the 20th century. In *A Moveable Feast* Hemingway writes that he "liked" the Picabia painting in Ezra Pound's Paris studio, otherwise unidentified, but thought that it was "worthless."

picador   In bullfights, the picador is the man who, while on horseback, "pics" the bulls for the matador. The picador is a bullfighter under the orders of the matador. The pic is a wooden shaft about two yards long with a steel point at the head of the shaft, and it is placed by the picador into the hump of muscle above the shoulders of the bull in order to slow him down in preparation for the matador's work with the cape.

One of the characters in the "Chapter 10" vignette of *In Our Time* (1925) is a picador.

Picasso, Pablo   (1881–1973)   Spanish painter and sculptor, one of the founders of cubism and surrealism, perhaps best known for his paintings *Guérnica* (1937) and *Les Demoiselles d'Avignon* (1907). Hemingway knew Picasso in Paris during the 1920s. He is mentioned in the booklet advertising *The Forum* magazine in "Banal Story."

In *A Moveable Feast* Hemingway writes of his discussion with Gertrude Stein about sex ("Miss Stein Instructs") and of, at one point during the conversation, looking up at her painting of Picasso's nude of the girl with the basket of flowers.

In *Islands in the Stream* he is one of several painters that Thomas HUDSON and his oldest son, young Tom, knew in Paris when Tom was a boy. Other painters mentioned without further reference are Georges BRAQUE, Joan MIRÓ, André MASSON, Jules PASCIN, and Waldo PEIRCE.

In *The Garden of Eden* Catherine BOURNE suggests to David a list of illustrators for the book he is writing about their marriage and ménage à trois with Marita. Picasso is one of the artists she names.

Pietsch, Michael   An editor at Charles Scribner's Sons, responsible for preparing *The Dangerous Summer* for publication in 1984.

Piga! Piga!   Expression used by hunters in *Green Hills of Africa* to indicate that a hunted animal has been hit or is down.

Pilar   In *For Whom the Bell Tolls*, she is with PABLO, the leader of the guerrilla fighters helping Robert JORDAN. She is 48 years old, "almost as big as Pablo, almost as wide as she was tall, in black peasant skirt and waist, with heavy wool socks on heavy legs, black rope-soled shoes and a brown face like a model for a granite monument. She has big but nice looking hands and her thick curly black hair was twisted into a knot on her neck."

She is Jordan's spiritual support during the three days he is with the LOYALISTS in preparation for fulfilling his assignment of blowing up a bridge. She has "gypsy blood," according to RAFAEL (2), and a "tongue that scalds and that bites like a bull whip." She has been taking care of MARÍA during the three months since they rescued her from the fascist train they blew up. María had been gang-raped by the fascists, and Pilar is providing emotional help in her recovery.

In spite of Rafael's warning to Jordan that Pilar is not letting anyone "come near" María, Pilar does not interfere when María and Jordan begin to fall in love; she encourages the relationship, in fact, because Pilar thinks it would work toward María's emotional recovery.

Pilar dominates Pablo, lashing out at him for seeming to be depressed about the work they have been doing: "What are you doing now, you lazy drunken obscene unsayable son of an unnameable unmarried gypsy obscenity?" But she turns almost immediately to Jordan, whom she has just met and asks him how things are going in the Republic. And the reader is told that she is "looking into his face and smiling and he noticed she had fine gray eyes." She asks to see Jordan's hand and looks at it "carefully," but "then [drops] it" and refuses, when he asks, to tell him what she had seen there. The reader infers that she has seen "death," but she refuses to say more, and Jordan can only think about it later as he, himself, begins to feel the shortness of the time he has left.

In spite of her dominance over Pablo—and the guerrilla band as a whole—she can't keep Pablo from stealing some of Jordan's explosive materials, which puts at risk Jordan's assignment to blow up the bridge.

Pilar, The A diesel-powered, 38-foot fishing boat, with twin engines (a 75hp Chrysler and a 40hp Lycoming—for trolling), double rudders, a galley, and sleeping quarters. Hemingway bought the boat in the spring of 1934 from a catalogue of the Wheeler Shipyard in Brooklyn and had it shipped to Miami, where he picked it up and sailed it to Key West. He paid $7,500 for the boat and named it after the Pilar shrine and *feria* (religious celebration) at Zaragoza, Spain, where he had been for the bullfights in 1926.

While Hemingway was in Key West he docked the *Pilar* at the Navy Yards. During World War II he added electronic gear so he could patrol for German submarines out of Cuba. The boat is now in the yard of the Finca Vigía, Hemingway's home outside Havana, a Hemingway Museum run by the Cuban government.

Pilar's story Chapter 10 of *For Whom the Bell Tolls* is devoted to Pilar's story of the beginning of the LOYALIST movement. She describes the killing by Loyalist townspeople, led by PABLO, of other townspeople, all FASCISTS.

Among those in her emotional story who were forced to run a gauntlet and then thrown over a cliff to their deaths are people she and Pablo knew well: Don Guillermo Martín, a store owner; Don Benito García, the mayor; Don Federico González, owner of a mill and feed store, a "fascist of the first order"; Don Ricardo Montalvo, a landowner; Don Faustino Rivero, oldest son of Don Celestino Rivero, a landowner; Don Anastasio Rivas, "fascist"; and Don José Castro, a dealer

Ernest with Jane Mason on the Pilar, *summer 1934 in Havana* (Courtesy of the John F. Kennedy Library)

in horses. As Pilar tells Jordan, it was an "ugly" beginning to the movement.

Pilcer, Harry Professional dancer who teamed with Gaby DELYS in the music halls of Paris and London during World War I. The two of them are referred to in "A Way You'll Never Be."

Pilot, The Saloon in a small western U.S. town named Jessup, the setting for "A Man of the World." It is also the name of a mountain, visible from Lawrence Nordquist's L-Bar-T Ranch in Wyoming, near Cooke City, Montana, where Hemingway spent several summers during the 1930s hunting, fishing, and writing.

pilot boat In *Islands in the Stream,* the supplies and mail boat that travels to BIMINI from Miami once a week. Also called a "run-boat."

pilot fish A term Hemingway uses at the end of *A Moveable Feast* to refer to a person who finds a potentially good writer or painter, or a good vacation spot, and then tells the rich people he knows, which, after all the rich people arrive, spoils the writer or artist or vacation spot.

Hemingway refers mostly to himself and to the people who told him how great a writer he was; he writes that he "wagged [his] tail," instead of thinking, "[i]f these bastards like it [his writing] what is wrong with it." He says he trusted the pilot fish as he would the tables in *Brown's Nautical Almanac,* an annual publication of the British Admiralty, which is extremely trustworthy.

pinard   French slang term for cheap red wine, wine which, as Richard CANTWELL says in *Across the River and Into the Trees*, "You cannot get . . . at the [Hotel] Ritz," an expensive hotel in Paris.

Pinder, Rupert   A character in the "Bimini" section of *Islands in the Stream*. He is a "very big Negro who was said to have once carried a piano on his back, unaided, from the Government dock all the way up the KING'S HIGHWAY to the old club that the hurricane blew away."

Pinin   Orderly for the MAJOR (3) in "A Simple Enquiry." The major calls him in to make a simple enquiry about his sexual preferences. The major is homosexual and is attracted to the 19-year-old Pinin. He wants to find out whether the young man is in love with a girl or if he might be "corrupt," implying homosexuality. Pinin insists that he loves a girl, and he says he doesn't understand what the major means by "corrupt."

The major does not force the issue and dismisses his orderly but tells him that he "had better stay on" as his "servant. You've less chance of being killed." Pinin is "flushed" when he leaves the room, indicating embarrassment about the questions. He doesn't know about the major's thought at the end of the story: "The little devil. . . . I wonder if he lied to me." But, as Paul Smith has pointed out in *A Reader's Guide to the Short Stories of Ernest Hemingway*, if Pinin lied to the major about being in love with a girl and if he did understand the meaning of "corrupt," then the story is far more complicated than the earliest critics realized.

pin-tails   Ducks. On his Sunday morning duck shoot in *Across the River and Into the Trees*, Richard CANTWELL sees a "pair of pin-tails [that] came, suddenly, from nowhere, slanting down fast in a dive no airplane ever made."

Pisa   Town in northern Italy on the Ligurian coast, about 111 miles southeast of Genoa, mentioned in "Che Ti Dice La Patria?" (What do you hear from home?) to which the two main characters travel.

Pitti   Pitti Palace, an art museum in Florence, Italy, located near the Boboli Gardens. Colonel Richard CANTWELL's driver, JACKSON, tells Cantwell, in *Across the River and Into the Trees*, that he had once visited the Pitti and Uffizi galleries and had looked at paintings of madonnas until they "started to run out of my ears."

place Contrescarpe   In Paris on the Left Bank, located at the top of rue du Cardinal Lemoine and its intersection with rue Rollin, rue l'Acépede, rue Mouffetard, and rue Blanville. Ernest and Hadley Hemingway rented their first apartment at 74, rue Cardinal Lemoine in January 1922. Place Contrescarpe is referred to at the beginning of *A Moveable Feast*.

place de l'Observatoire   In *A Moveable Feast* Hemingway writes that when he was hungry he would look for routes along Paris streets where there were no restaurants. He could walk from the place de l'Observatoire to the rue de Vaugirard on the north side of the Luxembourg Palace and then, after seeing the paintings in the Luxembourg, walk down the rue Férou to the place Saint-Sulpice, all without passing a restaurant.

places   In *The Old Man and the Sea* SANTIAGO "no longer dreamed of storms, nor of women, nor of great occurrences, nor of great fish, nor fights, nor contests of strength, nor of his wife. He only dreamed of places now and of the lions on the beach."

Places are also important to a number of Hemingway protagonists, including Frederic HENRY in *A Farewell to Arms*, Richard CANTWELL in *Across the River and Into the Trees*, Thomas HUDSON in *Islands in the Stream*, and Jake BARNES in *The Sun Also Rises*. See ABSTRACTIONS.

"Plain and Fancy Killings, $400 Up"   Article, published in *The Toronto Star Weekly* (December 11, 1920), reprinted in *The Wild Years* (1962), and in *By-Line: Ernest Hemingway* (1967). Datelined "Chicago," this article is about the exporting of underworld "weasels of death" from the United States to Ireland for "specialized" killings.

A policeman or a member of the Black and Tans is worth $400; a "well-guarded magistrate" is worth $1,000. (Black and Tans were an armed force of about 6,000 soldiers sent by the British government to suppress Irish uprisings in 1920.) And, Hemingway continues, this past summer and fall (1920), rumor has it "that if you throw a stone into a crowd in front of one of the mutual booths at the famous Longchamps race course outside of Paris, you would hit an American gunman, pickpocket or strong-arm artist."

plane   HARRY and HELEN (3), in "The Snows of Kilimanjaro" are waiting for a plane they've called in from Nairobi to take Harry back to a hospital for treatment of gangrene in his right leg. At the end of the short story, Harry dreams that the plane arrives, that "the [native] boys" have lit the fires to guide "old Compton" (the pilot) in to the camp, and that instead of flying toward Nairobi when Compton takes off again, he heads the plane toward the top of Kilimanjaro.

plane, observation   In *Islands in the Stream* an observation plane flies over Thomas HUDSON's boat near CAYO ROMANO as he and his crew look for a German submarine crew.

planes   In *The Garden of Eden* nine planes fly low over the beach at LA NAPOULE where David and Catherine

BOURNE and MARITA are swimming nude. "They passed rapidly, three echelons of three, their big Rhône motors roaring suddenly as they flew over" on their way toward Sainte-Maxime.

Plastiras, Colonel Nicholas Greek revolutionary leader who overthrew his government in September 1922, following Greece's defeat by Turkey and the subsequent burning of Smyrna, which took place from September 9–14, 1922. He is mentioned in "L'Envoi."

Platte River In Nebraska, remembered in *Across the River and Into the Trees* by Colonel Richard CANTWELL's driver, JACKSON, as a place with plenty of good duck shooting.

Plava Town in northeastern Italy on the ISONZO River, just north of which, in *A Farewell to Arms,* Frederic HENRY is wounded.

Plaza Santa Ana In Madrid, where David BOURNE, in *The Garden of Eden,* has breakfast in a café and thinks about Catherine's androgynous (bisexual) mood swings. "We've been married three months and two weeks and I hope I make her happy always but in this [her desire to change into a 'boy'] I do not think anybody can take care of anybody."

pleasant-speaking one, the One of four Cuban bank robbers in *To Have and Have Not,* otherwise not named.

P.L.M. Paris-Lyon-Méditerranée Railway, one of four private companies running lines into Paris during most of the first half of the 20th century. In *The Sun Also Rises,* Jake BARNES compares the "dull riding" along the boulevard Raspail in Paris with a "certain stretch on the P.L.M. between Fontainebleau and Montereau."

PM Square-shaped New York tabloid, short-lived (1940–48), started by Ralph Ingersoll, financed by Marshal Field III, which published seven dispatches by Hemingway between June 10–June 18, 1941 on the Sino-Japanese War. Field sold the publication in April 1948, and the name was changed to *New York Star,* which lasted until January 28, 1949. The letters *"PM"* stand for *Picture Magazine.*

Poe, Edgar Allan (1809–1849) American short story writer and poet, best known for his tales of mystery and the macabre. In *Green Hills of Africa* the Austrian hunter Kandisky asks Hemingway about American writing. After telling Kandisky that "We do not have great writers," Hemingway explains by naming several "skillful" writers, beginning with Poe.

"Poem" Poem against war, written about 1922 and first published in *88 Poems* (1979).

"Poem, 1928" Poem written in 1929 and first published in *88 Poems* (1979).

"Poem Is By Maera, The" Poem about bullfighting in Pamplona, written in 1925 and first published in *88 Poems* (1979).

"Poem to Mary (Second Poem)" Antiwar prose poem written in 1944 and first published in *Atlantic* (August 1965).

"Poem to Miss Mary" Poem Hemingway wrote to his wife, Mary, in 1949 and first published in *88 Poems* (1979).

"Poetry" Poem written in 1944 and first published in Mary Hemingway's *How It Was* (1976).

Poetry, A Magazine of Verse American literary journal, founded and edited by Harriet Monroe from its first issue (October 1912) until her death in 1936. It began during the Chicago Literary Renaissance and published works by such poets as Carl Sandburg, Vachel Lindsay, Sherwood ANDERSON, T. S. ELIOT, and Ezra POUND, who was Monroe's European correspondent.

Six of Hemingway's poems were also published in *Poetry.* In *A Moveable Feast* Hemingway mentions *Poetry* in connection with meeting Ernest Walsh at Pound's apartment in Paris. Walsh had recently had poems published in the magazine. It continues to publish at the end of the century.

"Poincaré's Election Promises" Article, published in *The Toronto Daily Star* (March 11, 1922), reprinted in *Ernest Hemingway: Dateline Toronto* (1985). The headline in the *Daily Star* was "Poincaré Making Good on Election Promises." In the article, datelined "Paris," Hemingway quotes a reporter colleague who says that although "France was quite sick" and had tried several medicines, now she has the ex-president and newly appointed prime minister, Raymond Poincaré, who is just the doctor she needed.

"Poincaré's Folly" Article, published in *The Toronto Daily Star* (February 4, 1922), reprinted in *Ernest Hemingway: Dateline Toronto* (1985). In the article, datelined "Paris," Hemingway reports that whereas France generated much sympathy after World War I, it no longer does because of the present premier, Poincaré, who is one of the blind "reactionaries." But "the French people have been thinking and working while their politicians have been talking . . . (unemployment has almost vanished in France)," and so there is hope. The headline in the *TDS* was "France Now in Hands of Old Professionals."

point, the   Probably Paradise Point on North BIMINI and the place where the character "SUICIDES" washes ashore in the "Bimini" section of *Islands in the Stream*.

Poisoned Buffalo   The name of a friend of the Negro bartender in the INDIAN CLUB in *The Torrents of Spring*.

poler   In *Across the River and Into the Trees*, the person who poles the boats for duck hunters on the Tagliamento River.

polo shirts   Knitted pullover sport shirts, worn by Robert COHN in *The Sun Also Rises*.

P.O.M.   Hemingway's name for his otherwise unnamed wife (Pauline) on safari in *Green Hills of Africa*. The initials are his pet nickname for her, "Poor old Mama." P.O.M. is mentioned often as the story of the safari unfolds but tends to be in the background nonetheless. She and Hemingway—whose name is not used in the narration either—shoot at a lion, and although she is given credit, apparently it is her husband's shot that actually made the kill.

Ponce de León   Thomas HUDSON's favorite café and bar on BIMINI in *Islands in the Stream*. It is more often referred to as "Mr. Bobby's" or "Bobby's place." The owner is Bobby Saunders.

Pont Neuf   Paris bridge that crosses the Seine River at the western point of the Ile de la Cité, mentioned in *A Moveable Feast* because Hemingway enjoyed walking across from the Left Bank to the island to see the statue of Henri Quatre.

Poochy   Character in *To Have and Have Not*. See RED.

Pop   White hunter guide in *Green Hills of Africa*. He is not otherwise identified (nor is Hemingway himself), but he is Philip PERCIVAL, an Englishman who went to Africa in 1905 and became Hemingway's hunting guide on two safaris.

"Popular in Peace—Slacker in War"   Article, published in *The Toronto Star Weekly* (March 13, 1920), reprinted in *The Wild Years* (1962), reprinted in *Ernest Hemingway: Dateline Toronto* (1985). The headline in the *Star Weekly* was "How to be Popular in Peace Though a Slacker in War." The article is about "morally courageous" Canadians who emigrated to the United States during World War I to work in munition plants and who returned to Canada after the war to gain 15 percent on the money they had earned. "Stand in front of your mirror," Hemingway writes in the last paragraph, "and look yourself in the eye and remember that there are fifty-six thousand Canadians dead in France and Flanders. Then turn out the light and go to bed."

Pordenone   Northern Italian town, about 39 miles northeast of Venice, where LUZ, in "A Very Short Story," falls in love with an Italian major.

Pordenone is also the town to which Frederic HENRY, in *A Farewell to Arms*, is ordered to retreat, from GORIZIA, with his four ambulance drivers. It is located about nine and a half miles west of the TAGLIAMENTO RIVER. Frederic says that there "was a note. . . for me to fill the cars with the material piled in the hall [of his billet] and to proceed to Pordenone," where there is a hospital to which they are to report. They leave the next morning in their three ambulance cars.

pork and beans   In "Big Two-Hearted River," NICK makes his first evening's meal of pork and beans and a can of spaghetti, cooked in a frying pan over an open fire.

porpoises   In *The Old Man and the Sea* two come near Santiago's boat after he has hooked the great marlin. He thinks of them, as he does of all fish, as brothers. At one point, he dreams of a "vast school of porpoises that stretched for eight or ten miles. . . ." The porpoise is a sea mammal, related to the whale. It is about four to six feet long, black above and white below, and, unlike the dolphin, its nose is blunt. In the United States, the bottle-nosed dolphin is often called a porpoise.

porter (1)   At the Ayuntamiento (ticket office) in PAMPLONA, Spain, where, in *The Sun Also Rises*, Jake BARNES buys his bullfight tickets.

porter (2)   At the Gare de Lyons in Paris, in "A Canary for One," who takes care of the AMERICAN LADY's bags.

porter (3)   At the American hospital in Milan, where Frederic HENRY is taken at the beginning of book 2 in *A Farewell to Arms*. He helps arrange for a room and bed, because the nurse, Mrs. Walker, is too confused by the early arrival to know what to do.

At the end of his convalescence, Frederic asks the porter and his friend, a "machine-gunner," to go to the railway station at five o'clock in order to save a seat for Frederic on the midnight train back to Udine. The ploy doesn't work, and he has to stand. The porter and his wife greet Frederic warmly, later, when he arrives back in Milan, following his escape from the war.

porter (4)   In *A Farewell to Arms*, the "second porter" at the LITTLE HOTEL in STRESA, where Frederic HENRY and Catherine BARKLEY stay while waiting to escape up Lake

MAGGIORE to Switzerland. He warns them about the rainstorm as they leave the hotel, unaware that they are leaving for good.

porter, hall   Assigned to Richard CANTWELL's floor at the GRITTI PALACE HOTEL in Venice, in *Across the River and Into the Trees;* he slides the *Gazzettino* (Venice newspaper) under the door each day.

"Porter, The"   Fragment from a scene in an unfinished novel, published as a "short story" in *The Complete Short Stories of Ernest Hemingway* (1987).

Porter dock   In *To Have and Have Not* where four Cubans ask Harry MORGAN to meet them to take them, illegally, to Cuba from Key West. The dock is located a block away from the bank they rob, and Morgan is being used by them for their escape.

porters   Minor characters on the hunting safari in "The Short Happy Life of Francis Macomber." They help carry MACOMBER back to camp "in triumph" after he has "killed" a lion.

Portofino Cape   On the Italian Ligurian coast about 15 miles south of Genoa, mentioned in "Che Ti Dice La Patria?" (What do you hear from home?).

Portogruaro   Town in northern Italy on the railway line midway between Venice and Trieste. In *A Farewell to Arms,* after his escape from the Italian battle police, Frederic HENRY knows that he can catch a train in Portogruaro that will take him to Milan and the hospital where his lover, Catherine BARKLEY, is working as a nurse.

"Portrait of the Idealist in Love"   One of the early story fragments, rejected for publication in the early 1920s, but published, with four other fragments, by Peter Griffin in the first volume of his biography, *Along With Youth: Hemingway, The Early Years* (1985).

"Portrait of a Lady"   Prose poem written about 1926 as a parody of Gertrude Stein's writing style, and first published in *88 Poems* (1979).

Portuguese man-of-war   Large, transparent, often colored, swimming or floating jellyfish, with long dangling tentacles that have poison-secreting cells. They are seen on the Gulf Stream by Harry MORGAN in *To Have and Have Not.*

SANTIAGO, in *The Old Man and the Sea,* thinks of them as "whore." He "loved to see the big sea turtles eating them."

post-war rich   The first man Richard CANTWELL sees in the GRITTI PALACE HOTEL bar near the beginning of *Across the River and Into the Trees.* He is from Milan, "fat and hard as only Milanese can be, sitting with his expensive looking and extremely desirable mistress." They are drinking NEGRONIS.

Potsdam   City in northeast Germany, a few miles southwest of Berlin. The narrator's traveling friend, Guy, in "Che Ti Dice La Patria?" (What do you hear from home?) tells the waitress/prostitute in Spezia, Italy, that he is from Potsdam. He's probably lying.

Pouilly-Fuissé wine   A dry white wine made from Chardonnay grapes in four small communes west of the town of Mâcon in southern Burgundy: Solutré, Fuissé, Chaintré, and Vergisson. The wine is usually drunk by Hemingway and by his fictional characters when eating oysters.

poules   French slang word for prostitutes, referred to in *The Sun Also Rises.*

POUM   Partido Obrero Unificado Marxista (the United Marxist Worker's Party) was an anti-Stalinist Communist Party in Spain, located primarily in Catalonia and Aragon during the SPANISH CIVIL WAR; mentioned in *For Whom the Bell Tolls.*

Pound, Dorothy   Painter and wife of Ezra Pound and a friend of Ernest and Hadley Hemingway when they lived in Paris during the early 1920s. In *A Moveable Feast* Hemingway writes that he did not particularly like the Japanese paintings that the Pounds had accumulated in their apartment at 70, rue Notre-Dame-des-Champs. He did like, however, Dorothy's paintings, and he liked the head of Ezra done by Henri GAUDIER-BRZESKA and owned by the Pounds.

Pound, Ezra   (1885–1972)   American poet and literary critic, best known for his profound influence on 20th-century poetry in English. His best-known poems are "Hugh Selwyn Mauberley" (1920) and his volumes of "The Cantos," which he began publishing in the early 1920s and continued writing throughout his lifetime.

He lived in London (1908–20), in Paris (1920–24), and in Italy until he was arrested for his anti-Semitic and pro-Fascist radio broadcasts.

During World War II Pound made several hundred broadcasts (1941–43) from Rome, openly condemning the United States for its war policies. He was arrested by U.S. troops in 1945 and spent six months in a prison camp before being returned to the United States to be tried for treason. He was pronounced "insane and mentally unfit for trial" by a panel of doctors and spent the next 12 years (1946–58) at St. Elizabeth's Hospital for the criminally insane in Washington, D.C.

Hemingway and Pound were good friends, both during their time together in Paris after Hemingway arrived (1922) and after Pound moved to Rapallo, Italy (1924). Hemingway contributed to Pound's defense fund during his insanity trial and later while he was at St. Elizabeth's.

The 12th section of *A Moveable Feast* is titled "Ezra Pound and His Bel Esprit." "Bel Esprit" was a program devised by Pound to get mostly American and English writers and painters to contribute part of their earnings toward a fund to provide T. S. ELIOT with enough money so that he could leave his job in a London bank and devote his time to writing poetry. "Bel Esprit" ended, Hemingway explains, when Eliot began to make money from *The Waste Land*, published in 1922, and from the financial support of a periodical, *The Criterion*, which Eliot edited.

Hemingway also writes of Gertrude Stein's anger at Pound for breaking one of her chairs. But he is the only Hemingway friend mentioned in *A Moveable Feast* toward whom Hemingway shows no animosity.

Pound is mentioned in *Islands in the Stream* as one of several artists and writers whom Thomas HUDSON, young Tom, and their friend Roger DAVIS knew in Paris when they lived there during young Tom's boyhood.

"Practical Education vs. Theoretical"   Article for Oak Park and River Forest High School newspaper, *The Trapeze* (February 10, 1916), reprinted in *Hemingway at Oak Park High: The High School Writings of Ernest Hemingway, 1916–1917* (1993).

Prado   A meadow in Havana that has Spanish laurel trees where, according to Thomas HUDSON in *Islands in the Stream*, blackbirds roost. The word "prado" in Spanish means "meadow."

Prado, the (1)   In Madrid, one of the world's great art museums and probably Hemingway's favorite, if the number of times he mentions it in his works is any indication. It is on the Paseo del Prado in the heart of Madrid. The building was begun by Juan de Villanueva in 1785 for King Charles III and completed under Ferdinand VII, the opening ceremony taking place in 1819.

The museum is mentioned several times in *Death in the Afternoon*, especially in chapter 5 on the city of Madrid itself. Hemingway calls Madrid the "most Spanish of all cities," and he says that "when you can have the Prado and the bullfight season at the same time . . . it makes you feel very badly . . . to know that you will have to die and never see it again."

It is where David and Catherine BOURNE spend a morning. As a reflection of her bisexuality, she wants to view the paintings "as a boy."

Prado, the (2)   Street in Havana, Cuba, remembered with some fondness by Marie MORGAN in *To Have and Have Not*. After her husband, Harry MORGAN, dies in KEY WEST at the end of the novel, Marie tries to think of happier times. In Spanish *prado* means "promenade."

Pravda article   See "Humanity Will Not Forgive This!"

prejudice   There is racial and/or religious prejudicial language in many of Hemingway's works of fiction, the language of several characters who may frequently refer to minority individuals or groups with words like "nigger," "chink," "wop," "mick," "kike," etc. The prejudices of various characters is particularly evident in *To Have and Have Not*.

There is the language of anti-Semitism in *The Sun Also Rises*, most of it focused on Robert COHN, a friend of the main character, Jake BARNES. Jake becomes angry at Cohn for going away for a week with Brett ASHLEY, whom Jake loves. And Jake and his friends know that Cohn is not "one of us," not able to easily mix in with their activities. Cohn doesn't understand the excitement of the Fiesta San Fermín in Pamplona, nor the bullfights. Jake is often sarcastic in his narrative remarks about Cohn, but Brett, her fiancé, Mike CAMPBELL, and Jake's American friend Bill GORTON, all make anti-Semitic remarks in their own anger at Cohn.

Premio Commercio   Special steeplechase race at the San Siro track in Milan, Italy, in "My Old Man."

Prentiss, Robert   A "rising new novelist," one of Jake BARNES's acquaintances in *The Sun Also Rises*.

"President Vanquishes, The: A Bimini Letter"   Article, published in *Esquire* (July 1935). A friend of Hemingway, Henry Strater, is the "president."

Preston, Robert   One of the characters in *The Fifth Column*. He is American, "about thirty-five," wearing, in act 1 of the play, "a leather jacket, corduroy trousers, and very muddy boots." He is a reporter for various unnamed publications, writing about the Spanish civil war and working with others in the International Brigades. His role as Dorothy Bridges's lover is usurped by Philip Rawlings midway through act 1, and he leaves, not to be seen again.

"Pride of the Devil, The"   Title of part 2 of the three-part *Life* magazine version of *The Dangerous Summer*, published by *Life* in its September 12, 1960, issue. Part 1, "The Dangerous Summer," was published on September 5; part 3, "An Appointment with Disaster," was published on September 19. See *The Dangerous Summer* (1).

priest (1) In "An Alpine Idyll" the priest doesn't want to bury a peasant's wife because her face is disfigured. She has been dead for six months, but her husband, who lives in the mountains, couldn't get her down to the town for burial. She is disfigured because after she became frozen stiff he stood her against the wall of his woodshed and hung his lantern from her mouth every evening when he went to the shed for wood.

priest (2) From the ABRUZZI region of east-central Italy, he is assigned to the Italian military unit to which Frederic HENRY is also attached as an ambulance driver in *A Farewell to Arms*. The priest, according to Frederic, is "young and blushed easily and wore a uniform like the rest of us but with a cross in dark red velvet about the left breast pocket of his gray tunic." The priest is made fun of by several of the officers, but he accepts the baiting as part of his assignment to keep up the morale of the soldiers. Frederic and the priest are good friends.

The priest visits Frederic at the FIELD HOSPITAL after his wounding in book 1 and tells him that he should "love God." He says, "What you tell me about in the nights. That is not love. That is only passion and lust. When you love you wish to do things for. You wish to sacrifice for. You wish to serve."

priest (3) In *The Garden of Eden* the priest at GRAU DU ROI who doesn't approve of David and Catherine BOURNE wearing shorts, but he and the other villagers consider it "an eccentricity by foreigners" and so let it go.

priests, two (1) In the "Chapter 15" vignette of *In Our Time*, one of the two priests whispers to Sam CARDINELLA, who is to be hung, "Be a man, my son." The younger priest kneels next to him and "skipped back onto the scaffolding just before the drop fell."

priests, two (2) Minor characters in "The Capital of the World," dining at the PENSION LUARCA, and waiting for an audience with an unidentified authority of the Catholic church in Madrid. They are in Madrid to ask for money for their home province, Galicia. One priest refers to their "abandoned country. When the money runs out we can return [to Madrid to request more]. . . . What does Madrid care about Galicia? We are a poor province."

Prieto, Indalecio (1883–1962) Spanish journalist and politician, a member of the Socialist Party. During the Spanish civil war Prieto was the minister of defense on the side of the Republic until May 1937 when he was ousted because he realized the Republicans were losing the war and said so in public.

In *For Whom the Bell Tolls* Prieto is presented as a leader who has lost his idealism. KARKOV tells Robert JORDAN that the POUM (*Partido Obrero Unificado Marxista*—the United Marxist Worker's Party) had failed in an attempt to assassinate him.

Primitivo One of Pablo's guerrilla fighters who helps Robert JORDAN in *For Whom the Bell Tolls*.

Primo de Rivera (1870–1930) Spanish general, political leader, and dictator (1923–29), mentioned in *Death in the Afternoon*. His full name was Miguel Primo de Rivera y Orbaneja.

Prin, Alice Real name of KIKI of MONTPARNASSE.

prince In *Islands in the Stream*, the husband of the PRINCESS with whom Thomas HUDSON remembers having a love affair on board a luxury cruise ship going up the Suez Canal.

princess Thomas HUDSON remembers, in the "Cuba" section of *Islands in the Stream*, a "plain girl" princess with whom he had a love affair on a luxury cruise ship "going through the [Suez] Canal coming up onto the light of Ismailia." They had all been hunting in East Africa and met at the Muthaiga Club in Nairobi, Kenya, and they had taken the same cruise ship when it docked at Mombasa. It was headed up the canal to the Mediterranean and, eventually, to Southampton, England. Hudson and his friend the BARON left the ship at Marseilles; the princess and her husband went on to Southampton.

Princessa The "grandmother" of all of Thomas HUDSON's cats in *Islands in the Stream*. She would not sleep with Hudson when he was drunk. Her original name was "Baby," but the servants changed it to Princessa. She is a blue Persian, "intelligent, delicate, high-principled, aristocratic, and most loving, but afraid of the catnip."

Princeton University Where Robert COHN, in *The Sun Also Rises*, went to college and was on the boxing team.

Prix du Marat In "My Old Man," it is a 4,500-meter steeplechase race at the AUTEUIL track in Paris, the race in which JOE's "old man" is killed.

"Prizefight Women" Article, published in *The Toronto Star Weekly* (May 15, 1920), reprinted in *Ernest Hemingway: Dateline Toronto* (1985). The headline in the *Star Weekly* was "Toronto Women Who Went to the Prize Fight Applauded the Rough Stuff."

The article begins, "Toronto women were present at prizefights for the first time last Saturday night." Hemingway describes the details of the boxing ring and the events, and quotes some of the women he could hear around him, all of whom enjoyed the fights. Not included was the wife of Georges Carpentier. "Her husband is a fighter and she knows what it means. So she stayed home and waited for Georges."

"Problems of Boyhood Discussed at Hanna Club" Article for Oak Park and River Forest High School newspaper, *The Trapeze* (March 9, 1916), reprinted in *Hemingway at Oak Park High: The High School Writings of Ernest Hemingway, 1916–1917* (1993).

professor, the Of boxing, at the gymnasium in LAUSANNE, Switzerland, in *A Farewell to Arms,* where Frederic HENRY "works out" in the mornings while waiting for Catherine BARKLEY's baby to be born.

"Program for U.S. Realism, A" Article, published in *Ken* (August 11, 1938), reprinted in *By-Line, Ernest Hemingway* (1967). The article is about war: "War is an act of violence intended to compel our opponent to fulfill our will." Hemingway elaborates on this definition and predicts war "in Europe by next summer [1939] at the latest." He quotes Karl von CLAUSEWITZ, a 19-century Prussian general who wrote books on military science.

"[Program Notes]" Article, published in *Esquire* (February 1935). In this untitled essay Hemingway critiques Luis QUINTANILLA's etchings.

proprietor Owner of a wine shop in Milan where in *A Farewell to Arms,* Frederic HENRY drinks a glass of coffee on his arrival in the city after his escape from the war. The proprietor of the shop offers to help Frederic if he's "in trouble."

Provincetown Robert COHN in *The Sun Also Rises* moved the review of the arts he first supported financially, then edited, from Carmel, California, to Provincetown, Massachusetts.

"Provincial Police Are Taking Up Chase" Article, published in *The Toronto Star* (September 12, 1923), "discovered" by William Burrill at the John F. Kennedy Library in Boston but not reprinted in his book, *Hemingway: The Toronto Years* (1994), where 25 other recently found articles are reprinted.

Prudie Nickname for Prudence MITCHELL, a character in "Ten Indians."

Pruniers restaurant At 9, rue Duphot when Hemingway was in Paris in the early 1920s. The Prunier, founded in 1872, was famous for its oysters.

In *A Moveable Feast,* Hemingway describes going there with his wife, Hadley, and having a dinner of oysters with CRABE MEXICAINE and SANCERRE WINE.

"Prussian Officer, The" A. D. H. LAWRENCE short story, published in *The Prussian Officer and Other Stories* (1914), mentioned in *A Moveable Feast* as one of Lawrence's works that Hemingway particularly liked.

Puerta del Sol Area in the center of Madrid, at the intersection of several major streets and near which, in "The Undefeated," Manuel GARCIA waits in a café for the picador ZURITO (1).

Puerto de Santa Maria One of the towns on the bullfight circuit covered by Hemingway in *The Dangerous Summer.* It was the third time that the two main subjects of the book, Antonio ORDÓÑEZ and Luis Miguel DOMINGUÍN, fought on the same card. The third matador was Mondeño.

Pulitzer Prize Annual awards for achievements in U.S. journalism, letters, and music. The prizes were established by newspaper publisher Joseph Pulitzer in 1917 and are presented by the trustees of Columbia University each May. Hemingway won a Pulitzer prize in 1953 for *The Old Man and the Sea.*

pump-factory, the Where Yogi JOHNSON and Scripps O'NEIL meet and work in PETOSKEY, Michigan, at the beginning of *The Torrents of Spring.* The factory is, according to Yogi, famous for its "Peerless Pounder that won the pump race in Italy, where Franky Dawson was killed."

pump-gun A shotgun, one of the weapons carried on Harry MORGAN's charter fishing boat in *To Have and Have Not.* The other guns on board are a THOMPSON SUBMACHINE GUN, a WINCHESTER 30-30, and a SMITH AND WESSON .38 pistol.

"Punt, The" Poem about football, first published as one of three parts under the title "Athletic Verse" in the Oak Park and River Forest High School literary magazine, *Tabula* (March 1917). The other two parts are "The Tackle" and "The Safety Man." All three were reprinted in *88 Poems* (1979) and regarded as separate poems.

puntillo Dagger used in a bullfight to kill the bull or a horse who has been badly wounded. It is used by a member of the bullfighter's CUADRILLA in the "Chapter 11" vignette of *In Our Time.*

Purdey 12 shot-gun One of the James Purdey manufactures, this one with a small (12) gauge, good for shooting birds on the wing. In *Across the River and Into the Trees,* Richard CANTWELL remembers that his grandfather owned a Purdey, and Cantwell wants to buy one for RENATA so she can go duck hunting.

Purple Land, The   Novel by the British author and naturalist W. H. Hudson, published in 1885. The full title, in two volumes, is *The Purple Land that England Lost.* It is set in Argentina and romanticizes the natural quality of the country.

In *The Sun Also Rises* Robert COHN has read the novel and is so caught up in the romance that he urges Jake BARNES to go with him to South America. Jake thinks that Cohn "took every word of 'The Purple Land' as literally as though it had been an R.G. Dun report." In his sarcastic response, Jake suggests they should go to British East Africa instead.

"Pursuit Race, A"   According to the first paragraph of this short story, a "pursuit race" is a bicycle race in which the bicyclists start at "equal intervals," and when one rider passes another that rider is out of the race. If none of the riders is caught, then the winner is the one who has gained the most distance. The pursuit race is meant as a metaphor, because there is no bicycle race in the story.

One of the two characters in the story is William CAMPBELL, an advance man for a burlesque show, whose job is to move from city to city ahead of the show, taking care of logistical matters and the advertising in preparation for the show's arrival. As a sentence in the second paragraph states, "When the burlesque show caught up with [Campbell] he was in bed."

The story's other character, Mr. TURNER, who is one of the show's managers, catches up with Campbell in a Kansas City hotel. Mr. Turner thinks Campbell is drunk, but it turns out that he's "hopped to the eyes" on heroin. "On the forearm, from just above the wrist to the elbow, were small blue circles around tiny dark blue punctures." Mr. Turner likes Campbell and offers to get him help with "the KEELEY cure," but he's also a businessman, and he has to get back to work.

Campbell tells Mr. Turner that he will get up about noon, but when Mr. Turner returns at noon Campbell is still sleeping. At the end of the story the narrator states that "as Mr. Turner was a man who knew what things in life were very valuable he did not wake him."

Campbell has been caught by alcohol and drugs and, since the burlesque show passes him in Kansas City, he is out of the "race." Mr. Turner is still trying, somewhat desperately, to keep ahead of his pursuers—perhaps his own bosses—and so has become a workaholic. He is called "Sliding Billy," suggesting an ability, as Campbell points out, to "slide" through life without an awareness of its possible meanings. Campbell, on the other hand, can't "slide at all. . . . It just catches. Every time I try it, it catches." Mr. Turner knows "what things in life [are] . . . valuable."

But who is the main character? Is it William Campbell, who has been caught by the burlesque show and so is out of the pursuit race? Or is it Mr. Turner, who conforms to society's values, working constantly to stay ahead of his pursuers? And since the story's title is a metaphor, it is not difficult to read the "burlesque show" as a metaphor too, a metaphor for the absurdness of life itself.

"A Pursuit Race" was first published in *Men Without Women* (1927).

Pyle, Howard   (1853–1911)   American illustrator, painter, and author, best known for his book illustrations in early 20th-century Art Nouveau style. He wrote and illustrated several children's books, including *Howard Pyle's Book of Pirates* (1921), the book that the narrator/father in "A Day's Wait" reads to his son, SCHATZ (1), who is ill with the flu.

Q

quai des Grands Augustins In *A Moveable Feast* Hemingway writes that there were no Parisian Left Bank bookstalls that sold English-language books between the TOUR D'ARGENT RESTAURANT at 15, quai de la Tournelle and the quai des Grands Augustins, about a half mile farther west.

quai d'Orléans Embankment along the Seine River on the southwest side of the Ile Saint-Louis, facing the rear of Notre-Dame in Paris, mentioned in *The Sun Also Rises*.

quai d'Orsay Embankment on the Left Bank of the Seine River in Paris, between the Eiffel Tower and the Hotel des Invalides, where, in *The Sun Also Rises*, Jake BARNES meets some other journalists at lunch. Jake shares a taxi back to this office with WOOLSEY and KRUM. The only significance of this scene seems to be that their conversation indicates that Woolsey and Krum hardly ever get to the Left Bank, which is the part of Paris Jake knows best and which any Paris journalist *should* know.

quai Voltaire In *A Moveable Feast* Hemingway writes that there were a lot of Left Bank bookstalls with English-language books between the quai des Grands Augustins and the quai Voltaire, where the proprietors bought books from employees of the Hotel Voltaire; they picked them up from their wealthy clientele.

Hemingway's reference to the hotel may be to the building at No. 27, quai Voltaire, where Voltaire died (May 30, 1778); but it is more likely a reference to the Hôtel du Quai-Voltaire at No. 19, near the Pont du Carrousel.

quarter See LATIN QUARTER.

quartermaster At the wheel of the COAST GUARD cutter bringing in Harry MORGAN's boat at the end of *To Have and Have Not*.

Quatorzième Brigade In *For Whom the Bell Tolls*, the 14th Brigade is one of the two brigades that General GOLZ commands. The other is the 35th Brigade.

queen, the Of Greece, wife of George II, mentioned in the "L'Envoi" vignette of *In Our Time*. She is intro-duced to the narrator, who says she is "clipping a rose bush."

Queen Conch The boat Harry MORGAN borrows from Freddy in order to run the four Cuban bank robbers from KEY WEST to Havana in part 3 of *To Have and Have Not*. It is 34 feet long, with a "V number" engine from Tampa, with the boat's name and home port, "Key West, Florida," painted across her stern.

Queen Mary (1867–1953) Queen consort of George V of England and mother of two kings of England, Edward VIII (1936) and George VI (1936–52). It is her birthday (May 26) that is being celebrated at the opening of *Islands in the Stream*. The year of part 1 ("Bimini") is either 1934 or 1935.

Quesada, Pete Unidentified in *Across the River and Into the Trees*, except as a military officer Richard CANTWELL thought was good with ground support during the Allied advance toward Germany in World War II.

Quevedo y Villegas, Francisco Gómez de (1580–1645) Spanish satirist and novelist whom Robert JORDAN refers to in *For Whom the Bell Tolls*. Quevedo is admired by Jordan for his honesty and realism in writing about 19th-century Spanish society and politics.

Quinet, Edgar (1803–1875) French historian and poet, quoted (incorrectly) by Hemingway in *Green Hills of Africa*. In talking about James Joyce, Hemingway says that one night he kept quoting Quinet: "Fraîche et rose comme au jour de la bataille [fresh and pink as the day of battle]." It's part of a quotation from *Finnegans Wake*, but the word is "riantes" (pleasant), not "rose."

Quintana, Juanito Spanish bullfight aficionado and companion of Hemingway both during the 1920s when they first met in Pamplona at Quintana's hotel and during the 1950s when Hemingway returned for the bullfights and to write *The Dangerous Summer*. Quintana was also the apparent prototype for Montoya, the Pamplona hotel manager in *The Sun Also Rises*.

Quintanilla, Luis (1895–1980) Spanish painter, perhaps best known for his large fresco, "Love Peace and

Hate War," for the Spanish pavilion at the New York World's Fair in 1939. He was sent by the Spanish Republic to help publicize the Spanish civil war and, after the collapse of the Loyalist cause, he was not allowed to return to Spain. He settled in the United States in 1942, and a number of his paintings were widely exhibited. He is also the author of *Latin America Speaks* (1943), *Franco's Black Spain* (1946), and *Pan Americanism and Democracy* (1952).

Hemingway and other writers wrote short essays of appreciation for Quintanilla in 1934 for a catalogue of his sketches, to support his release from a Madrid jail. Hemingway's "note" was also published by *Esquire* (February 1935). Hemingway wrote three prefaces for *All the Brave* (1939), a book of Quintanilla's drawings of Spanish civil war scenes.

quite Spanish bullfight term. According to Hemingway in his glossary for *Death in the Afternoon,* "quite" is "the taking away of the bull from any one who has been placed in immediate danger by him." Pronounced "key-tay."

R

Radiguet, Raymond (1903–1923) French novelist and poet, best known perhaps for *The Devil in the Flesh* (1923). He died at the age of 20 from typhoid fever. Hemingway tells the old lady in *Death in the Afternoon* that Radiguet made his short-lived career with his "pencil" as well as his "pen . . . if you follow me, madame"—a sexual metaphor. Hemingway uses Radiguet—along with the sexual overtones—as an example of why the word "decadence" is so hard to define and why the Spanish bullfight of the 1930s had become decadent.

radio Rented by Mr. FRAZER in "The Gambler, the Nun, and the Radio." He is in the hospital in Hailey, Montana, where he is recovering from a broken leg, and the radio does not work well until dusk. "They said it was because there was so much ore in the ground or something about the mountains." He listens to the popular music of the time of the story (1930) and to at least one Notre Dame football game. He listens during the night to the signing off of the stations, first Denver, then Salt Lake City, then Los Angeles and Seattle.

radio message Telegram in the "Bimini" section of *Islands in the Stream,* notifying Thomas HUDSON that two of his sons and his second wife had been killed in an accident: "Your sons David and Andrew killed with their mother in motor accident near Biarritz attending to everything pending your arrival deepest sympathy." On his way to France for the funeral he thinks, "What the hell do you suppose she was doing at Biarritz? . . . At least she could have gone to St. Jean-de-Luz."

radishes In *The Garden of Eden,* eaten by MARITA with TAVEL wine.

Raeburn, Dick In *Islands in the Stream,* the husband of Audrey BRUCE's mother before he was killed in a bobsled accident.

R.A.F. The British Royal Air Force, mentioned by Richard CANTWELL in *Across the River and Into the Trees,* in connection with the bombing of German General ROMMEL's forces during WORLD WAR II.

In *Islands in the Stream* Thomas HUDSON's son, "young" Tom HUDSON, is killed flying for the R.A.F. during World War II.

Rafael (1) Madrid bullfight critic in *The Sun Also Rises* who is in PAMPLONA for the Fiesta SAN FERMÍN.

Rafael (2) A gypsy, one of PABLO's guerrilla fighters, who helps Robert JORDAN in *For Whom the Bell Tolls.*

"[rail ends do not meet, The . . .]" First line of a poem written about 1927 and first published in *88 Poems* (1979).

railroad station, the Setting for "Hills Like White Elephants." The station is not identified but is probably located at the junction of the mainline route between Barcelona and Madrid and a rail line that continues on to northwestern Spain, about nine miles northwest of Zaragosa.

Ralph, Captain Captain of the "run boat" that carries supplies and mail from Miami to Bimini in *Islands in the Stream.*

Ramadan The ninth month of the Muslim calendar, when Muslims take part in a daylight fast each day. In *Green Hills of Africa* Charo, one of the native gun bearers, observes Ramadan. Hemingway says that "[a]ll Ramadan he never swallowed his saliva until sunset."

ranch, the Thomas HUDSON, in *Islands in the Stream,* owns a ranch in Montana as well as a house in BIMINI and a "farm" near Havana. He inherited the Montana ranch from his grandfather, and Hudson has a "regular income from oil leases" on the land. The land had been sold, but Hudson retained the mineral rights.

Rancho Boyeros A "bar of the crazies" in Havana, mentioned in the "Cuba" section of *Islands in the Stream.*

Rapallo Small Italian port town on the Mediterranean Sea, about 15 miles southeast of Genoa. Ezra Pound moved from Paris to Rapallo in 1924 and lived there for the next 20 years. In *A Moveable Feast,* Hemingway writes about visiting Pound in Rapallo.

Rawlings, Philip The main character in *The Fifth Column.* He is a Loyalist in the Spanish civil war, a counterespionage agent assigned to disrupt the bombardment of Madrid by General Franco's attacking army.

Usually drunk or drinking, he is, nevertheless, instrumental, along with his German friend, MAX, in attacking an artillery outpost and capturing a member of the FIFTH COLUMN, who, under torture, provides enough information for the arrest of 300 other members of the Fifth Column, an organization of Spanish civilians in sympathy with Franco.

Rawlings usurps Robert PRESTON's roll as the lover of Dorothy BRIDGES, the leading female character in the play. Before the war, Rawlings was in Cuba, where he was recruited for the counterespionage work in Spain.

Rawlins, Wyoming JACKSON, Richard CANTWELL's driver in *Across the River and Into the Trees,* lived in Rawlins before the war. There are no wolves there, Jackson tells Cantwell, but plenty of coyotes.

Ray's speedboat One of the four boats Harry MORGAN thinks might be able to catch his boat on the run to Cuba with the four Cuban bank robbers in part 3 of *To Have and Have Not.* He's worried that the Coast Guard might have a boat that is faster than his.

"Real Spaniard, The" Article, published in *Boulevardier* (October 1927). In Louis Henry Cohn's *A Bibliography of the Works of Ernest Hemingway* (1931) Hemingway is quoted as saying that the article "was written partly by me, mostly by my wife, and re-written by . . . [the editor] Arthur Moss," leaving unclear how much and which parts are by Hemingway.

Rebecca Light Lighthouse in the Tortugas Islands, west of Key West, Florida; mentioned in "After the Storm."

Rebel automobiles In *For Whom the Bell Tolls* the FASCIST army general and division staffs drive various kinds of cars: Fords, Fiats, Opels, Renaults, Citroëns, Rolls-Royces, Lancias, Mercedes, and Isottas. The type of car defines the rank of its occupants, but Robert JORDAN's forward observer, ANSELMO, fails to distinguish among them in counting the vehicles he sees along the road toward the BRIDGE, making it difficult for Jordan to determine the numbers of fascist officers, soldiers, and observers.

Rebels In the Spanish civil war (1936–39) the rebels were led by Generalissimo Francisco FRANCO against the government of Spain. See NATIONALISTS and SPANISH CIVIL WAR.

recibiendo Spanish bullfight term meaning, according to Hemingway in *Death in the Afternoon,* that the matador is able to kill the bull without moving his feet once the bull charges.

"Recruits for the Tanks" Article, unsigned, published in *The Kansas City Star* (April 18, 1918), reprinted in *Ernest Hemingway, Cub Reporter* (1970).

Red One of the drunks at FREDDIE'S PLACE when the SHERIFF and Richard GORDON stop at the bar on their way to the KEY WEST docks to watch the COAST GUARD bring in Harry MORGAN's boat near the end of *To Have and Have Not.* Red (also called "Joey") is a "punchie," an ex-boxer, who has the OLD RALE, a disease he and his friends think is sexually transmitted. Others mentioned in this scene are "Poochy" and "Suds" who also have "the old rale." Poochy thinks he got his in Shanghai; Suds got his from a girl in Brest, "coming home" from the war. Red and Poochy fight in front of Gordon and MacWalsey, seated at the bar.

Red Cross International organization, founded at the 1864 Geneva Convention, to provide for the wounded

EH with Red Cross ambulance service in World War I, 1918 (Copyright holder unknown; photo courtesy of the John F. Kennedy Library)

and sick of armies in wartime. Red Cross volunteers from any country were considered neutral and were allowed to retrieve the wounded from battlefields and treat them at field hospitals. Later the Red Cross provided for the promotion of public health at any time.

The U.S. Red Cross was organized in 1881 by Clara Barton and received its first federal charter in 1900. Hemingway enlisted with the U.S. Red Cross in the spring of 1918 to drive ambulances in Italy during World War I. He was badly wounded in northern Italy on July 8, 1918.

The American Frederic HENRY, the main character in *A Farewell to Arms,* drove Red Cross ambulances for an Italian military unit stationed near GORIZIA in northern Italy and was badly wounded.

"Red Flag in Toronto"   Article, unsigned, published in *The Toronto Star Weekly* (February 14, 1920), reprinted in William Burrill's *Hemingway: The Toronto Years* (1994). The article was identified as a Hemingway story by the *Star* librarian, William McGeary. It is about a Communist sympathizer named Sam Stoichi, newly arrived in Toronto, who is arrested for disturbing an auction sale that he thought was a Communist rally because a red flag was flying in front of the building.

Red Lodge (1)   Unidentified drink that Mr. FRAZER offers three Mexicans in "The Gambler, the Nun, and the Radio." Mr. Frazer is from Red Lodge, Montana.

Red Lodge (2)   A town in Montana, named along with Cooke City, as places that Robert JORDAN thinks about in connection with his grandfather and father in *For Whom the Bell Tolls.* In particular, he thinks about an "Anheuser-Busch lithograph" hanging on a poolroom wall in Red Lodge that shows the Sioux Indians closing in on Custer.

Mr. FRAZER, in "The Gambler, the Nun, and the Radio," is from Red Lodge and names an unidentified drink "Red Lodge."

reedbuck   A yellowish African antelope, the male of which has short, forward-curving horns. It is hunted by Hemingway on the safari described in *Green Hills of Africa.*

"Refugees from Thrace"   Article, published in *The Toronto Daily Star* (November 14, 1922), reprinted in *The Wild Years* (1962), and in *By-Line: Ernest Hemingway* (1967). Datelined "Sofia, Bulgaria," this article sums up Hemingway's feelings as he watched the retreat of Greek civilians from Thrace after the Turkish attack. The *TDS* headline read "Refugee Procession is Scene of Horror."

Regla   Cuban town across the harbor from Havana, mentioned in *Islands in the Stream.*

Regoli   Name of a jockey, "a little wop," riding at the San Siro, Italy, steeplechase track in "My Old Man."

régulière   According to Hemingway in *A Moveable Feast,* this was the French word used to refer to one's wife when he wrote the book in the 1950s ("my *régulière*"). But he says that when he lived in Paris during the early 1920s the word was *légitime*" ("my *légitime*").

Reinhardt, Max (1873–1943)   Austrian theatrical producer and director, mentioned in *Across the River and Into the Trees.* There is a woman in mourning at HARRY'S BAR in Venice, a mourning "so theatrical," that it reminds Richard CANTWELL of the actress Lady Diana MANNERS playing the nun in Reinhardt's *The Miracle.*

"Remembering Shooting-Flying: A Key West Letter"   Article, published in *Esquire* (February 1935), reprinted in *By Line: Ernest Hemingway* (1967). It is about hunting in Illinois, in the Vorarlberg of western Austria, in Clark's Fork, Wyoming, and in other places.

Renaldo, Rinaldi   Main character and narrator of the short story "The Mercenaries." He's an American who meets two mercenaries on their way to join the Peruvian army in a war against Chile.

Renata   An Italian contessa, the 18-year-old love of 50-year-old Richard CANTWELL's life in *Across the River and Into the Trees.*

Even though she is the leading female character in the novel, she does not appear directly before the reader, only as Cantwell remembers her during his Sunday morning duck hunt and as he starts back toward his military base in Trieste before his fatal heart attacks near the end of the novel. He remembers that "she came into the room [HARRY'S BAR], shining in her youth and tall striding beauty, and the carelessness the wind had made of her hair. She had pale, almost olive colored skin, a profile that could break your . . . heart, and her dark hair, of an alive texture, hung down over her shoulders."

Later, when Cantwell asked her if she thinks her mother "would mind if we had a baby," Renata answers, "I don't know. . . . But I would have to marry someone, I suppose." Since they both know that Cantwell is going to die soon, the reader may infer that she has in mind the Baron ALVARITO, their mutual good friend.

There are suggestions of sexual intercourse between Renata and Cantwell, and some readers have inferred that she may be pregnant. In his room at the GRITTI PALACE HOTEL, when she says, "I can be your daughter as well as everything else," he says, "That would be incest." And there is a scene in a gondola under an army blanket that also suggests sexual activity.

But Renata is an Italian contessa and must protect her good name, which she suggests is compromised to some extent just by being in his hotel room unescorted. The name Renata means "reborn," and Hemingway once said in another context that she represents the spirit of youth, reborn in the mind of the 50-year-old army colonel.

Renata's father Killed during World War II by German soldiers, he is referred to by Renata in conversation with Richard CANTWELL in *Across the River and Into the Trees.*

Renata's mother Mentioned with fondness by Richard CANTWELL TO RENATA in *Across the River and Into the Trees.*

Renata's painting Richard CANTWELL thinks to himself about the painting of Renata: "It was a beautiful portrait; neither cold, nor snobbish, nor stylised, nor modern. It was the way you would want your girl painted if Tintoretto were still around and, if he were not around, you settled for Velasquez."

Renault Car owned by Scott and Zelda Fitzgerald while they lived in France and which they "abandoned" in Lyon. In *A Moveable Feast* Hemingway writes of agreeing to take the train to Lyon with Fitzgerald in order to help drive the car back to Paris. He is "astonished" to discover that the car has no top.

Renoir, Pierre Auguste (1841–1919) French impressionist and postimpressionist painter and sculptor, known for his paintings of nudes and women with children, especially "Bathers" (c. 1886) and *After the Bath* (1895).

Thomas HUDSON, in *Islands in the Stream,* remembers that Renoir had wondered why Gauguin had gone to Tahiti to paint when "one paints so well here [in Paris] at the Batignolles[.]"

Republicans In *For Whom the Bell Tolls,* Spaniards on the side of the Republic (also called LOYALISTS) in the SPANISH CIVIL WAR. The novel's main character, Robert JORDAN, fights and dies for the Republic.

Retana, Don Miguel In "The Undefeated," the promoter for the Madrid bullfights. Three times on the first page of the story, Retana is described as "a little man." He knows that Manuel GARCIA is desperate for a contract. But he also knows that he is just out of the hospital after being gored by a bull and that he should retire anyway because of his age.

Garcia has been a good bullfighter, but Retana only offers him the "nocturnals," nighttime bullfights that are the most dangerous of all because neither the bull-

fighters nor the bulls are up to Spanish standards. And he adds insult to injury by offering Garcia the least amount of money he thinks he can get by with, 250 pesetas. Retana agrees to pay 300 but still knows that he has gotten away with a cheap arrangement. Later, while Garcia waits in a café for ZURITO (1), waiters argue about Retana's influence in Madrid, one saying that he has done a lot for bullfighters like Villalta, Marcial Lalanda, Nacional, and Nacional II, all "Retana's boys."

Revello, Ignacio Natera One of Thomas HUDSON's drunken acquaintances in *Islands in the Stream.* They meet at the FLORIDITA bar in the "Cuba" section of the novel and roll dice for drinks—Revello usually loses, and Hudson rejects Revello's invitation to lunch.

Revello, Lutecia Wife of Ignacio Natera Revello in *Islands in the Stream.*

Revered One, the In *Across the River and Into the Trees* the "leader" of the ORDER, "our Great Patron, Brusadelli." According to Richard CANTWELL, Brusadelli was "a particularly notorious multi-millionaire non-taxpaying profiteer of Milan, who had, in the course of a dispute over property, accused his young wife, publicly and legally . . . of having deprived him of his judgment through her extraordinary sexual demands."

"Review of Anderson's *A Story-Teller's Story*" Book review by Hemingway, published in *Ex Libris* (March 1925), reprinted in the *Fitzgerald/Hemingway Annual: 1969.*

"Review of Two Christmas Plays" Play review, published in the West Austrian newspaper *Vararlberger Landes-Zeitung* (January 13, 1926), reprinted in *Fitzgerald/Hemingway Annual: 1971.* The plays were *The Hot Iron* by Hans Sachs and *How He Deceived Her Husband* by Bernard Shaw.

revolutionary committee Of Greece in 1922, led by Colonel Nicholas PLASTIRAS and mentioned in the "L'Envoi" vignette of *In Our Time.*

"Revolutionist, The" In this short story, a young, unnamed Communist revolutionist, a MAGYAR, has "suffered" under the "WHITES in Budapest" (1919) and is traveling by train around Italy, visiting art galleries. He likes the painters GIOTTO, MASACCIO, and Piero della FRANCESCA, but not MANTEGNA.

He carries a "square of oilcloth" from party headquarters "written in indelible pencil" urging "comrades" to help him. The revolutionist tells the story's narrator that in spite of what had happened to him in Hungary, where he was tortured by the counterrevolutionaries, he still "believed altogether in the world revolution."

The narrator tells him that the movement in Italy is going "badly," but the revolutionist is optimistic, saying that Italy "will be the starting point of everything." The narrator is skeptical. He puts the revolutionist on a train to Milan, where he will go to Aosta and walk over the pass into Switzerland to escape from the anti-communists. The narrator mentions the Mantegna paintings in Milan and where to eat, and he gives him the addresses of some comrades, but "his [the revolutionist's] mind was already looking forward to walking over the pass." The last word the narrator hears about him is that he had been picked up by the Swiss police.

Although generally considered a short story, "The Revolutionist" is little more than a page in length—barely twice the length of the average Hemingway "vignette" and, as with the 16 "vignettes" (Chapters) of *In Our Time* (1925), this story has little plot, painting instead the picture of a character in a moment of time. It may be argued also, however, that the story is an example of Hemingway's THEORY OF OMISSION, the idea that what is deliberately left out of a story is as important as what goes in.

Because it is mentioned twice that the revolutionist dislikes the painter Mantegna, it may be that the story depends on a bit of unstated information about the painter. The revolutionist may know—as Giorgio Vasari describes Mantegna in his *Lives of the Artists* (1568; translation 1965)—that Mantegna was born of "very humble stock . . . , working in the fields as a boy and yet . . . rising to the rank of a knight through his own efforts and good fortune," the sort of individualism that might not be appreciated by a communist.

"The Revolutionist" was first published as "Chapter 11" of *in our time* (1924) and reprinted in *In Our Time* (1925) under its present title.

rhino   In the part 2 flashback of *Green Hills of Africa* ("Pursuit Remembered") Hemingway describes killing a rhino in the Rift Valley of northern Tanzania. He's proud of the kill until he gets back to camp and finds that KARL has killed a larger rhino.

Rhodesia   Former British colony in South Africa, declared independent in 1965, and called Zimbabwe since 1979. In *Green Hills of Africa* (1935) the Hemingways have only three days left on their safari before the rains are expected from Rhodesia.

Rhône Canal   On the Rhône River near Aigle; Switzerland. In *A Moveable Feast* Hemingway writes about fishing in the canal.

Rhône Valley   The Rhône River has its headwaters in the Rhone glacier in the upper Valais, Switzerland, and it flows west into Lake Geneva near Aigle, then out near Geneva, in a southerly direction, dumping into the Mediterranean west of Marseilles, a total of about 405 miles. For nearly its entire length, the Rhône Valley is covered with vineyards and fruit and vegetable gardens. It is mentioned in book 5 of *A Farewell to Arms* because of the valley's proximity to Montreux and Lausanne, places Frederic HENRY and Catherine BARKLEY stay.

riau-riau music   The music of the streets of PAMPLONA during the Fiesta SAN FERMÍN, heard almost constantly by Jake BARNES and his friends and described in *The Sun Also Rises*. Jake says the music consists of "pipes shrill and . . . drums pounding." And "behind them came the men and boys dancing."

Rice, Alfred (1908–1985)   Hemingway's lawyer from 1948 until Hemingway's death in 1961 and then Mary Hemingway's lawyer until Rice's death.

Richard   Character in *For Whom the Bell Tolls* who tells Karkov's mistress at Gaylord's that "everyone knows" about the battle to take place the next day.

Richard Cantwell   See Richard CANTWELL.

Richard Carvell   Popular historical novel by the American writer Winston Churchill, published in 1899; a Revolutionary War novel in which the hero serves as a naval officer under John Paul Jones. POP is reading it on the safari described in *Green Hills of Africa*.

Richard Feverel   When BILL (1) asks NICK, in "The Three-Day Blow," what he is reading, Nick names this George Meredith novel, published in 1859. The plot of *The Ordeal of Richard Feverel* is related to the plot of Hemingway's story. Both are about young people of different classes, in love but with too much of a cultural divide between them to make the relationship work.

Richard's   Bar in *To Have and Have Not* where BEE-LIPS gets drunk before meeting Harry MORGAN to confirm arrangements for transporting four Cuban men illegally from KEY WEST to Cuba.

Richardson, Hadley   See Elizabeth Hadley Richardson HEMINGWAY.

"Rich Boy, The"   Short story by F. Scott Fitzgerald, published in *All the Sad Young Men* (1926). In Hemingway's "The Snows of Kilimanjaro," HARRY, the main character, makes a not very veiled allusion to "The Rich Boy," as he thinks of "poor Julian and his romantic awe" of rich people. (The name was not "Julian" but "Scott" in the first version of "Snows.") Harry says that Julian once wrote a story that began,

"The very rich are different from you and me. And how some one had said to Julian, Yes, they have more money. But that was not humorous to Julian."

The actual quotation is from the third paragraph of "The Rich Boy" and reads: "Let me tell you about the rich. They are different from you and me. . . . They think . . . they are better than we are because we had to discover the compensations and refuges of life for ourselves."

In *A Moveable Feast* Hemingway writes that in 1925 Fitzgerald had written "one good story, 'The Rich Boy.'"

Richebourg French wine from one of the great red-wine–producing vineyards of Burgundy, situated in the village of Vosne-Romanée. The wine is mentioned in *Death in the Afternoon* in a comparison Hemingway makes between acquiring a taste for good wine and acquiring a taste for the bullfight.

rifle, 22-caliber Owned by Sam FONTAN in "Wine of Wyoming." His son André wants to shoot muskrats with it.

rifles The .303 and .450 rifles, mentioned in *The Garden of Eden*. At the beginning of the narrator's account of David BOURNE's writing his AFRICAN STORY, the reader is told, "He [both David while he is writing the story and the main character of the story he is writing] could feel the weight of the heavy double-barreled rifle carried over his shoulder, his hand on the muzzle." Later, the reader is told that David's father had carried a .450.

Rift, The In *The Garden of Eden* the title of David BOURNE's first novel, about his boyhood experiences in East Africa. His second novel, unnamed, has just been published when *Eden* begins; it is about flying airplanes during World War I. David figures he has earned $500 from the first printing of *The Rift*, but most of the cost of the honeymoon is being financed by his wife, Catherine, which creates tension between them.

Rift Valley In East Africa, a loosely connected series of valleys, often with associated volcanoes, which extend for about 2,400 miles in a north-south direction through East Africa. These valleys are often 30 miles wide. The Kenya rifts extend through Kenya to northern Tanzania. Associated with these rifts are the extinct volcanoes of Mount Kenya and Mount Kilimanjaro. The setting for most of *Green Hills of Africa* is the Rift Valley of northern Tanzania.

Rigel Bright star in the constellation Orion, seen by SANTIAGO, according to the narrator of *The Old Man and the Sea*, though he "did not know the name" of the star. The first-magnitude star would be visible from about midnight to sunrise in mid-September on the Gulf Stream off the north coast of Cuba, where Santiago is fishing.

Rilke, Rainer Maria (1875–1926) Austro-Hungarian (now Czech Republic) poet, best known for his *Duino Elegies* (1923) and his *Sonnets to Orpheus* (1923). When, in *Green Hills of Africa*, Kandisky asks Hemingway about the poet, Hemingway says he has read only *The Cornet*, which he liked.

Rimini Town on the Adriatic Sea in north-central Italy, one of the places mentioned in "Che Ti Dice La Patria?" (What do you hear from home?) to which the two main characters travel.

Rinaldi (1) NICK's friend in the "Chapter 6" vignette of *In Our Time*. Rinaldi lies face down against a wall of a church, not responding to Nick's talk about making a "separate peace," the implication being that Rinaldi is dead.

Rinaldi (2) Nicknamed "Rinin," Lieutenant Rinaldi, in *A Farewell to Arms*, is Frederic HENRY's best friend in the Italian military unit to which they are assigned. Rinaldi is from Amalfi, "good-looking," and about the same age as Frederic (that is, in his early 20s). He is a doctor and tense from seeing too many wounded and dying soldiers. As a result, Rinaldi drinks too much and goes too often to the officers' bordello in Gorizia where the unit is stationed.

After Frederic escapes to Milan and eventually to Switzerland, he worries aloud to Catherine BARKLEY about Rinaldi's health, especially whether he might have contracted syphilis.

Rincon, José "Keeps the bodega" in Aranjuez that ANDRÉS is asked ("tested") about by guards on his way to General GOLZ with Robert JORDAN's message in *For Whom the Bell Tolls*.

Ring, The U.S. boxing magazine, founded in New York in 1922 by Nat Fleischer (1888–1972) and still being published. In *Islands in the Stream* Thomas HUDSON reads a copy on his way to France for the funeral of his sons David and Andrew and their mother, Hudson's second wife.

"'Ring Lardner' on the Bloomington Game, A" Article for Oak Park and River Forest High School newspaper, *The Trapeze* (November 24, 1916), reprinted in *Hemingway at Oak Park High: The High School Writings of Ernest Hemingway, 1916–1917* (1993). An article written in the style of Ring Lardner.

"Ring Lardner, Jr. Discourses on Editorials" Article for Oak Park and River Forest High School newspaper, *The Trapeze* (February 16, 1917), reprinted in *Hemingway at Oak Park High: The High School Writings of Ernest Hemingway, 1916–1917* (1993). An article written in the style of Ring Lardner.

"'Ring Lardner Junior' Writes About Swimming Meet. Oak Park Rivals Riverside" Article for Oak Park and River Forest High School newspaper, *The Trapeze* (February 2, 1917), reprinted in *Hemingway at Oak Park High: The High School Writings of Ernest Hemingway, 1916–1917* (1993). An article written in the style of Ring Lardner. The young Hemingway was learning to write by imitating writers he respected.

"Ring Lardner Returns" Article for Oak Park and River Forest High School newspaper, *The Trapeze* (May 4, 1917), reprinted in *Hemingway at Oak Park High: The High School Writings of Ernest Hemingway, 1916–1917* (1993). An article written in the style of Ring Lardner.

Río de la Fabrica Trout stream near BURGUETE in northern Spain which, in *The Sun Also Rises*, Jake BARNES and Bill GORTON fish during the first full day of their five-day stay in Burguete before they return to Pamplona for the Fiesta San Fermín. See also IRATI RIVER.

rioja alta Wine from the Rioja district of Spain, generally considered to provide the best table wines (especially red) in Spain. It gets its name from the Rio Oja, a small tributary of the Ebro River, which it joins near Pamplona. It is the wine Jake BARNES and Brett ASHLEY choose for the lunch they have together at BOTIN's in Madrid near the end of *The Sun Also Rises*.

"Riparto d'Assalto" Poem out of Hemingway's WORLD WAR I experiences, written in 1922, first published in *Poetry* magazine (January 1923) and again in Hemingway's first book, *Three Stories & Ten Poems* (1923).

Ritz bar (1) In the Hôtel Ritz in Paris, at 15, place Vendôme. The bar, now named "Hemingway's Bar," was originally the smaller "ladies' bar" before women were allowed to drink with the men. Charles Ritz, the hotel's owner after World War II renamed the bar in honor of one of its most famous patrons. See also HOTEL RITZ.

In *The Fifth Column* the hotel is one of the places to which Dorothy BRIDGES "dreams" of going with Philip RAWLINGS.

Hemingway also writes about the bar in *A Moveable Feast*. It is one of the places he "liberated" on August 25, 1944, the day he re-entered Paris during the Allied invasion. He also "liberated" several cafés and Sylvia

BEACH's bookshop, SHAKESPEARE AND COMPANY (1), though it had not been open since the beginning of the war.

Ritz bar (2) Located at the stern of the luxury cruise ship that Thomas HUDSON takes up the Suez Canal in *Islands in the Stream*. He remembers that he and the PRINCESS, with whom he is having an affair, drink two bottles of PERRIER-JOUET BRUT 1915 at the ship's "Ritz bar."

Rivas, Don Anastasio See PILAR'S STORY.

river (1) In the dreams of Nick ADAMS in "A Way You'll Never Be." It is a "river [that] ran so much wider and stiller than it should," and which he cannot locate in the real world, adding to his confusion in his shell-shocked condition.

river (2) In *The Garden of Eden* David BOURNE writes his AFRICAN STORY about a boyhood hunting trip with his father in East Africa and reaching "the river and the great grove of fig trees where they would make their camp." It is a refreshing stop, both for the characters in the story as David remembers the event and for David now, as he writes the story, in part as an escape from the "craziness" of his wife, Catherine, and the chaotic events of the present time.

Rivero, Don Faustino See PILAR'S STORY.

"Road to Avallon, The" Poem written in 1949 and first published in *88 Poems* (1979).

Roanoke City in southwestern Virginia and the return address on a letter that the main character writes in "One Reader Writes."

"Robert Graves" Poem written about 1922 and first published in *88 Poems* (1979).

Robert Jordan See Robert JORDAN.

Roberto One of four Cuban bank robbers, the "big-faced one," in *To Have and Have Not*.

rocks, dark red Overlooking the Côte d'Azur at LA NAPOULE, France, from which David BOURNE dives into the sea near the end of *The Garden of Eden*. After David's wife, Catherine, has left, David and MARITA lie on the sand where David had spread the beach robes and the towels "in the shade of a red rock."

In *The Waste Land* (1922) T. S. Eliot suggests that a way out of the waste land is to "Come in under the shadow of this red rock." Catherine, David's androgynous (bisexual) wife has left the MÉNAGE À TROIS, and

David and Marita are together now, perhaps in the "shade" of a more normal relationship.

Rocky Mountain News, The   In "The Gambler, the Nun, and the Radio," Mr. FRAZER can get a "picture" of Denver from the *Denver Post* that "corrects" the one he gets from *The Rocky Mountain News*.

rod-case, leather   NICK carries one with him on his fishing trip in "Big Two-Hearted River."

Rodgers, Crowell   A young boy in *A Farewell to Arms* who had been "wounded in the eyes" and who was hospitalized with Frederic HENRY at the American hospital in Milan. He attends the races with Frederic, Catherine BARKLEY, and Helen FERGUSON while he and Frederic recover from their respective wounds. Crowell is sent to Rome at the end of the summer (1916) and then back to the United States.

Rodgers, Vernon   Minor character in *The Fifth Column*. He is bitten by the MOORISH TART, which "[l]aid him up for three weeks," according to Philip RAWLINGS, the play's main character.

Rodríguez, Mr.   In *Islands in the Stream* a radio announcer in Havana, and a friend of Thomas HUDSON. He recognizes Hudson's first wife when she walks into the Floridita Bar in Havana in the "Cuba" section of the novel. She is a Hollywood film actress, and Rodríguez tells her he has seen all of her pictures.

Roederer Brut '42   A dry champagne from one of the Louis Roederer vineyards in the Champagne region of France. In *Across the River and Into the Trees* it is served to Richard CANTWELL and RENATA by the Gran Maestro for their dinner at the GRITTI PALACE HOTEL.

Rogelio   An unseen character in *The Old Man and the Sea* who, in the past, has sometimes thrown the fishing net for SANTIAGO.

Roger   Narrator of "The Mother of a Queen." He manages PACO (1), a Spanish bullfighter and a homosexual, who is so "tight" with money that he won't even arrange to save his mother from burial on the "public boneheap." He owes Roger 600 pesos, and, although Paco keeps promising to pay he doesn't, and Roger finally dumps him in disgust, both for the debt and for the way Paco treated his mother. He calls him a "bitch" and later a "motherless bitch."

They meet later in Madrid, and when Paco accuses Roger of saying "unjust" things against him, Roger says, in front of three of Paco's friends, "All I say is you never had a mother," the worst sort of insult in Spanish. Paco says, "That's true. . . . My poor mother died when I

was so young it seems as though I never had a mother." And the narrator has the last word: "There's a queen for you. You can't touch them. They spend money on themselves or for vanity, but they never pay. . . . What kind of blood is it that makes a man like that?"

Roger, Victoriano (1898–1936)   Spanish bullfighter, "Valencia II," mentioned in *Death in the Afternoon*. He was killed in the Spanish civil war.

rognons   French for "kidneys," offered, in *Across the River and Into the Trees,* to Richard CANTWELL and to RENATA by the Gran Maestro for breakfast Saturday morning at the GRITTI PALACE HOTEL in Venice. Also offered are an "omelet with truffles dug by pigs of distinction," and "real Canadian bacon."

Rojo, Vincente   He "manufactures" the Republican offensive in the Spanish civil war, including the plan for blowing up the bridge, which Robert JORDAN takes with him into the Guadarrama Mountains in *For Whom the Bell Tolls*.

Rollers, the   Slang term for a church group on BIMINI island in *Islands in the Stream*.

Romagna   Province in northern Italy. Ravenna is its capital and Bologna a major city, the setting for most of "The Revolutionist."

Roman Soldier, first   In the one-scene play, *Today is Friday,* he keeps repeating to his two soldier colleagues that Christ, whom they had helped crucify earlier "was pretty good in there today." In response to the second Roman soldier's question about why Christ hadn't "come down off the cross," the first soldier says, "That's not his play." And he brags about sticking his spear into Christ's side to hurry his death, even though he knows it could get him in trouble with his officers.

Roman Soldier, second   In *Today is Friday,* he is the skeptic of the three Roman Soldiers. He calls Christ, whom they helped to crucify that day, a "false alarm." He wonders aloud to the two other soldiers why Christ "didn't . . . come down off the cross." He has apparently assisted in other crucifixions, and he says, "Show me a guy that doesn't want to come down off the cross." And to the Hebrew wine-seller, GEORGE (6), who hasn't "taken any interest" in it, he says, "You're a regular Christer, big boy."

Roman Soldier, third   In *Today is Friday,* he has a "gut-ache," caused partly by bad wine but mostly because he and his two drinking colleagues assisted in Christ's crucifixion earlier that day, and it makes him "feel like hell."

Romero, Pedro (1)   Spanish bullfighter and one of Brett ASHLEY's lovers in *The Sun Also Rises*. Jake BARNES says he "stood very straight and unsmiling in his bullfighting clothes. . . . He was the best-looking boy I have ever seen." He is 19 years old and "alone," except for "his sword-handler, and the three hangers-on." Romero was born in Ronda, near Gilbraltar, and started bullfighting in Málaga in the bullfighting school there. He had only been fighting for three years. His older brother is one of his BANDERILLEROS but apparently doesn't have "aficion" (a passion for bullfighting; see AFICIONADO).

Romero fights well the first two days of the PAMPLONA bullfights, does not fight the third day, because it was "Miura bulls, and a very bad bullfight." Jake introduces him to Brett, and, after Romero's last bullfight, he and she leave town together.

Robert COHN beats up Romero in a jealous rage just before the bullfighter's last fight, but Romero is able to "hold on" against the injuries and give his usual, impressive performance, and in front of Brett. She is 15 years older than he and leaves him a few days later in Madrid.

Romero, Pedro (2) (1754–1839)   Spanish bullfighter, who killed 5,600 bulls during a career of 23 years between 1771 and 1794. Hemingway says in *Death in the Afternoon* that Romero killed the bulls *recibiendo;* that is, without moving his feet while awaiting the charging bull. Romero lived long enough to die in his own bed at the age of 95.

Rommel, Erwin (1891–1944)   German field marshal, called "the Desert Fox," commander of the German forces fighting in North Africa in World War II. In *Across the River and Into the Trees* Richard Cantwell tells Renata that he fought against Rommel "halfway" from Cortina to the Grappa in northern Italy.

Roncesvalles   The monastery and commune of Roncesvalles (Roncevaux in French) in the Pyrenees Mountains of Spain, about 30 miles northeast of Pamplona. In *The Sun Also Rises* Jake BARNES calls the monastery to Bill GORTON's attention as they ride by bus from PAMPLONA to BURGUETE.

Roncesvalles, close to the town of Burguete is comprised of a cluster of religious and historical buildings. It is an important way station on the pilgrimage route of Santiago de Compostela, important because of its identification as the place where part of Charlemagne's army was defeated and where Roland died in 778.

On the wall of Jake and Bill's hotel room in Burguete is a "framed steel-engraving of Nuestra Señora de Roncesvalles." And near the end of their stay, they and their English friend, WILSON-HARRIS, walk to Roncesvalles and go through the monastery.

Ronda   One of the Spanish towns on the bullfight circuit covered by Hemingway in *The Dangerous Summer*. It is also the home of Pedro Romero (1754–1839), one of Spain's most famous bullfighters and the name Hemingway chose for his fictional bullfighter in *The Sun Also Rises*.

In *The Dangerous Summer* Hemingway describes a ceremony in Ronda in honor of Antonio ORDÓÑEZ, one of the two major bullfighters Hemingway was covering for the book. Ronda was Ordóñez's hometown.

"Roosevelt"   Poem about Theodore Roosevelt, written in 1922, first published in *Poetry* magazine (January 1923) and again in Hemingway's first book, *Three Stories & Ten Poems* (1923).

Roosevelt, Franklin Delano (1882–1945)   Thirty-second president of the United States (1933–45); he is generally credited with creating plans during the 1930s that got America out of its economic depression. His plans included the "New Deal," the Social Security Act, and the Works Progress Administration (WPA). In *Islands in the Stream* Thomas HUDSON and a drinking friend offer a toast to Roosevelt and to other political leaders of the time (February/March 1944).

One of the drunken veterans at FREDDIE'S PLACE in *To Have and Have Not* accuses President Roosevelt of sending the "scum" among the vets to work on BOCA CHICA in order "to get rid of us." He also accuses [J. Edgar] HOOVER, director of the FBI, of running the vets "out of Anticosti flats."

Rosa, Juan Luis de la (1901–1938)   Spanish bullfighter, mentioned in *Death in the Afternoon*. He was killed in the Spanish civil war.

Rosicrucian pamphlet   Rosicrucians are members of an esoteric society, who claim that the history of their order can be traced to ancient Egypt and has over the course of time included many of the world's sages. Their secret learning deals with occult symbols, particularly the rose and the cross, the swastika, and the pyramid. In *Islands in the Stream* Thomas HUDSON meets a Negro who is reading a Rosicrucian pamphlet.

Ross, Lillian (1927–   )   American writer, best known for her "Profile" column for *The New Yorker,* including her "Portrait of Hemingway" (May 13, 1950). She also wrote a series of articles describing the filming of *The Red Badge of Courage*, which were later published as a book, titled *Picture*. Her preface to the book *Portrait of Hemingway* (1961) was used by the British Broadcasting Corporation as part of a program, "Tribute to Ernest Hemingway," in July 1961 following Hemingway's death.

round dutch collars Worn by girls as part of a new style of dress, "above their sweaters," when Harold KREBS, in "Soldier's Home," returns from World War I.

route of retreat The route Frederic HENRY takes on the retreat from the Battle of CAPORETTO in *A Farewell To Arms:* south along the ISONZO RIVER to GORIZIA, where he picks up his four drivers and three ambulance cars. The next morning they leave on the road to Cormons and toward UDINE, which is crowded with trucks and other equipment already loaded for the retreat. Then they are supposed to head toward the TAGLIAMENTO RIVER and PORDENONE, as per the orders left for Frederic in Gorizia. But because the column of retreating soldiers is stopped by the rain and developing chaos, Frederic and his men try to drive across country on side roads.

After abandoning their cars, which have become stuck in the mud about eight miles southeast of UDINE, they cross a railway bridge at an unnamed river. From this bridge, and after seeing German soldiers crossing the next bridge to the north and also moving toward Udine, Frederic decides to follow railroad tracks that lead toward Pordenone south of Udine. It is about a 10-mile walk to the nearest bridge across the Tagliamento; Frederic and Luigi PIANI arrive there the next morning.

rowboats, two Used by Indians in "Indian Camp" to take NICK, his doctor father, and Nick's Uncle George across the lake to a camp where a woman is going through a difficult labor.

Roy's In *Islands in the Stream,* a shop on BIMINI where conch pearls and other souvenirs may be purchased.

"Rubber Supplies in Dutch East Indies" Article, published in *PM* (June 11, 1941), reprinted in *By-Line: Ernest Hemingway* (1967). Datelined "Rangoon," the article is about the difference between the "pretexts" for the United States going to war with Japan and the "real reasons."

The pretext is that Japan "has attacked the Philippines, or the Dutch East Indies or British Malaya." The real reason is to protect "control of the world supply of rubber," four-fifths of which comes from the area Japan would be attacking. This was the second of seven dispatches Hemingway wrote for *PM.* The headline read "Ernest Hemingway Says We Can't Let Japan Grab Our Rubber Supplies in Dutch East Indies."

Rube Goldberg (1883–1970) Mentioned in *The Garden of Eden.* David BOURNE tells MARITA, sarcastically, that his wife, Catherine, is "going to have her lawyers have them [his stories that she has burned] appraised in some fantastic Rube Goldberg manner and then she's going to

pay me double the appraisal price." Rube Goldberg was a cartoonist of comically involved contrivances, and his name is associated with anything made complex but used for a seemingly simple function.

Rubito Bullfighter mentioned by RETANA in "The Undefeated" as one who would draw a crowd, compared to Manuel GARCIA who, Retana argues, would not.

rucksack Carried by David and Catherine BOURNE to the beaches of the Riviera, in *The Garden of Eden.* It contains their lunches, cold bottles of wine, and a "bottle of oil" in a side pocket.

Rudolph, Dick (1887–1949) Major League baseball pitcher from 1910 to 1927, all but two of those years with the Boston Braves. In *Islands in the Stream* Andrew HUDSON is kidded about being too short for a pitcher, but he argues that he will be as "big" as Rudolph and Dick KERR, another Major League pitcher. Rudolph was five feet, nine and a half inches and 160 pounds; Kerr was five feet, seven inches and 155. Andy's brother David tells him he'll be as big as Earl SANDE, a famous jockey, who at five feet six was big for a jockey.

rue Cardinal Lemoine, 74 Ernest and Hadley Hemingway rented a fourth-floor walkup apartment at this Paris address on January 9, 1922, having arrived in Paris on December 20, 1921. In *A Moveable Feast* Hemingway writes of the odor from the tank wagons that pumped out the cesspools of the apartment houses along the street.

Jake BARNES and Bill GORTON walk up rue Cardinal Lemoine in *The Sun Also Rises* on their way to meet Brett ASHLEY and her fiancé Mike CAMPBELL at the CAFÉ SELECT. Other places mentioned on this walk: Nègre Joyeux, Café aux Amateurs, place Contrescarpe, rue du Pot de Fer, rue Saint-Jacques, Val de Grâce, boulevard du Port Royal, Port Royal, Montparnasse, "the Lilas," Lavigne's, "and all the little cafés, Damoy's, . . . the Rotonde, past its lights and tables to the Select."

rue Delambre Short cross street in Paris, where is located the CAFÉ DU DÔME (at the corner of the BOULEVARD DU MONTPARNASSE); mentioned in *The Sun Also Rises.*

rue Denfert-Rochereau At its juncture with boulevard Saint-Michel in Paris there is a statue, according to Jake BARNES in *The Sun Also Rises,* of the gentleman "who invented pharmacy."

rue Descartes In *A Moveable Feast* Hemingway writes of seeing a herd of goats going down rue Descartes in

Paris, near place Contrescarpe, early one morning when he was out to buy a racing paper.

rue Ferou, 6   Address of the apartment in Paris that Ernest and Pauline Hemingway move into following their marriage in May 1927.

rue de Fleurus, 27   Paris home of Gertrude Stein when Hemingway was in Paris during the 1920s. In *A Moveable Feast* he writes of his many visits with her there and getting to her apartment by walking across the Luxembourg Gardens from his own apartment on Cardinal Lemoine.

rue Froidevaus, 69   Address of Gerald Murphy's studio in Paris, which he lent to Hemingway from late 1926 until May 1927 following his divorce from Hadley and before his marriage to Pauline Pfeiffer.

rue Jacob   In Paris during the 1920s, Michaud's Restaurant was located at the corner of rue Jacob and rue des Saints-Pères; mentioned in *A Moveable Feast*.

rue Mouffetard   In *A Moveable Feast* Hemingway refers to this Paris street as "that wonderful narrow crowded market street which led into the Place Contrescarpe."

rue Notre-Dame-des-Champs, 70   Address of Ezra and Dorothy POUND when they lived in Paris during the early 1920s. In *A Moveable Feast* Hemingway writes of visiting Pound at this flat. Later the Hemingways rented an apartment on the same street at No. 113.

rue Notre-Dame-des-Champs, 113   Location of the second apartment rented in Paris by Ernest and Hadley Hemingway; they signed the lease on February 8, 1924. It was a second-floor, cold-water flat above a sawmill. It is described in *A Moveable Feast*.

rue de l'Odéon, 12   Paris address of Sylvia's BEACH's American bookshop SHAKESPEARE AND COMPANY (1).

rue de Rivoli   One of the major east-west streets on the Right Bank in Paris, mentioned in *The Sun Also Rises*.

rue Soufflot   Jake BARNES walks down "the Boulevard" (BOULEVARD SAINT-MICHEL) to the rue Soufflot for coffee and a brioche at the beginning of chapter 5 of *The Sun Also Rises*. "It was a fine morning. The horse-chestnut trees in the Luxembourg Gardens were in bloom. There was the pleasant early-morning feeling of a hot day."

rue de Tilsit, 14   Location in Paris of the flat that Scott and Zelda Fitzgerald were renting when Hemingway met them in the spring of 1925. In *A Moveable Feast* he writes about being invited to lunch there and that it was a "gloomy" place with little in it other than copies of some of the books Fitzgerald had written.

rue de Vaugirard   Paris street that curves around the north side of the Luxembourg Gardens and in front of the palace. In *A Moveable Feast* Hemingway writes that after his discussion with Gertrude Stein about sex ("Miss Stein Instructs"), he had to walk back to his own apartment by way of the rue de Vaugirard because the park was closed.

"Rug Vendors in Paris"   Article, published in *The Toronto Daily Star* (August 12, 1922), reprinted in *Ernest Hemingway: Dateline Toronto* (1985). The headline in the *Daily Star* was "Rug Vendor Is Fixture in Parisian Life." Datelined "Paris," the article is about fur rug vendors plying their mostly dishonest trade on the streets of Paris.

Ruiz, Cayetano   The gambler in "The Gambler, the Nun, and the Radio." He is a Mexican beet worker (although it's December and in Montana), one of two men wounded and brought to the hospital in Hailey at the beginning of the story. He was shot twice in the abdomen while drinking coffee with a Russian friend in an all-night restaurant.

He tells the detective sergeant that "it was an accident." He develops peritonitis, and they think he will die, but at the end of the story he seems to have recovered but with one leg paralyzed. He has no friends, according to three other Mexicans who are sent by the police to visit him. The three Mexicans are, in fact, friends of the man who shot Ruiz, and he had won money from them in card games.

Ruiz thinks of himself as unlucky at cards but that if he keeps playing long enough his luck will change. "I have bad luck now for fifteen years," he says. If I ever get any good luck I will be rich."

rum   Often the drink of choice in *To Have and Have Not*, especially by EDDY (2), Harry MORGAN's "rummy" sidekick and mate on his charter fishing boat.

"Rum-Running"   Article, published in *The Toronto Star Weekly* (June 5, 1920), reprinted in *The Wild Years* (1962), reprinted in *Ernest Hemingway: Dateline Toronto* (1985). The headline in the *Star Weekly* was "Canuck Whiskey Pouring in U.S." The article is about the organized and disorganized bootlegging of whiskey from Canada to the United States "You hear of cities like Grand Marais in Upper Michigan, which have been dead for twenty years, that are now coming back to a furtive, silent existence since the passage of the Eighteenth Amendment" (passed in 1919, prohibiting the sale of alcoholic beverages, repealed by the 21st Amendment in 1933).

rum St. James In *A Moveable Feast* Hemingway describes making himself thirsty while writing a story in a place Saint-Michel café about characters who are drinking, and so he orders a rum St. James. It is Martinique rum.

run-boat The boat that brings supplies once a week to BIMINI from the mainland in the opening section of *Islands in the Stream*.

Russell, Joe "Josie" Russell owned Sloppy Joe's Bar in Key West, Florida, during the 1930s when Hemingway lived in Key West. They were good friends and fishing companions for nearly 14 years, until Russell's death in 1941. See SLOPPY JOE'S BAR.

Hemingway writes about Russell in his article "Marlin off the Morro: A Cuban Letter" (*Esquire*, Autumn 1933). He was Captain of the *Anita*, a 34-foot fishing boat, and it was "Russell of Key West who brought the first load of liquor that ever came into that place from Cuba and who knows more about swordfish than most Keywesters do about grunts."

Russian A worker in the beet fields of Montana during the early 1930s, one of the two men wounded and brought to the hospital at the beginning of "The Gambler, the Nun, and the Radio." He was wounded when "someone" came into an all-night restaurant where he and a Mexican beet worker friend were having coffee and opened fire at the Mexican. The Russian still has pain from the wound but is released from the hospital after one week.

"Russian Claims" Article, unsigned, published in *The Toronto Daily Star* (April 14, 1922), reprinted in *Ernest Hemingway: Dateline Toronto* (1985). The headline in the *Daily Star* was "Russian Claims to Offset Allies." Datelined "Genoa," it is a one-paragraph story stating that the Russian delegation at the Genoa Economic Conference claims that the Allied claims against Russia would make it a "slave state."

"Russian Girls at Genoa" Article, published in *The Toronto Daily Star* (April 24, 1922), reprinted in *The Wild Years* (1962), and in *By-Line: Ernest Hemingway* (1967).

Datelined "Genoa, Italy," the article is about the Genoa Conference and the various delegations in attendance, the reporters, the movie people taking pictures, and, last to enter the great hall, the Russian delegation, followed by a "mass of secretaries . . . including two girls with fresh faces, hair bobbed in the fashion started by the actress Irene Castle, and modish tailored suits. They are far and away the best looking girls in the conference hall." The *TDS* headline read "Two Russian Girls the Best-Looking at Genoa Parley."

"Russian Toy Soldier, A" Article, published in *The Toronto Daily Star* (February 10, 1923), reprinted in *The Wild Years* (1962), and in *By-Line: Ernest Hemingway* (1967).

Datelined "Lausanne, Switzerland," this article is from an interview Hemingway had with the leader of the Soviet delegation to the Lausanne Conference, Georgi TCHITCHERIN. His major aim at the conference is to get an agreement to block the Straits of the Dardanelles and the Bosporus to warships. The *TDS* headline read "Gaudy Uniform Is Tchitcherin's Weakness: A 'Chocolate Soldier' of the Soviet Army."

"Russians Hold Up Progress" Article, unsigned, published in *The Toronto Daily Star* (April 17, 1922), reprinted in *Ernest Hemingway: Dateline Toronto* (1985). The headline in the *Daily Star* was "Progress Held Up at Genoa Parley by the Russians." Datelined "Genoa," Hemingway writes that the Russian delegation to the Genoa Economic Conference is holding up progress in resolving Europe's economic problems. Hemingway refers to it as the "Russian difficulty."

"Russia Spoiling the French Game" Article, published in *The Toronto Daily Star* (October 23, 1922), reprinted in *The Wild Years* (1962), reprinted in *Ernest Hemingway: Dateline Toronto* (1985). The headline in the *Daily Star* was "Russia to Spoil The French Game With Kemalists." The dateline is "Constantinople."

The French backed the victorious Turks during Turkey's war with Greece, while Britain's prime minister, Lloyd George, backed the Greeks. So now, the French influence is seen in Constantinople. KEMAL, the Turkish leader, is beginning to lean toward Russian influence, however, and Hemingway believes that if the British fail to stop the Soviet drive into the Balkans, they may have to "fight Gallipoli over again." It is Kemal's affiliations with the Russians that will, "next to the conflict between Islam and Christianity," make for "the greatest danger to the peace of the world."

"Russo-Japanese Pact" Article, published in *PM* (June 10, 1941), reprinted in *By-Line: Ernest Hemingway* (1967). The article was the first of seven dispatches which Hemingway wrote on the war in the Far East for *PM*, a New York tabloid newspaper.

Datelined "Hong Kong," the article concerns the assistance the U.S.S.R. was giving China in its war with Japan. The headline in *PM* read "Ernest Hemingway Says Russo-Jap Pact Hasn't Kept Soviet from Sending Aid to China."

Ruth, Babe (1895–1948) Baseball player, first with the Boston Red Sox (1914–19) and then with the New York Yankees (1920–35), probably the best known of all

Major League baseball players. His 714 home runs is the second-highest record in baseball history; his 8.5 home runs per 100 times at bat is first.

He is mentioned in *A Farewell to Arms* as a pitcher with Boston. Ruth had a 24–13 pitching record in 1917, the year to which Frederic HENRY refers.

In *Green Hills of Africa* Hemingway describes his native tracker M'Cola as having "slim, handsome legs with well-turned ankles on the style of Babe Ruth's."

Ryall, Bill (1890–1930) William Bolitho Ryall, European correspondent for the Manchester *Guardian* and friend of Hemingway during his early years in Paris. In an article "The Malady of Power: A Second Serious Letter" Hemingway writes that Ryall taught him about international politics. Ryall later moved to New York and wrote for the New York *World* under the name William Bolitho. He wrote the novels *Murder for Profit* (1926) and *Twelve Against the Gods* (1929).

sable Large African antelope, hunted in *Green Hills of Africa*. It is about five feet high at the shoulders, six and one-half feet long, with two-and-one-half-foot-long slightly backward-curving horns. POP tells Hemingway that the bull is easily identified, because he is black and the female is brown. As the hunters get close, one of the animals "looked up . . . nervously and I [Hemingway] saw the dark, heavy-built antelope with scimitar-like horns swung back staring at us. I had never seen a sable."

It is technically called a "sable antelope," but it is referred to only as "sable" in *Green Hills*. The sable antelope is now on the list of endangered species.

Sachs, Hans In *A Moveable Feast* Hemingway writes that while in Schruns, Austria, during the winter 1925–26, he wrote a review for a local newspaper of a play written by a German named Hans Sachs, apparently a local writer.

sack Covers the bait box on SANTIAGO's skiff in *The Old Man and the Sea*, but he also uses it to protect himself from the fishing lines which cut into his back. The sack may also be seen as part of the novel's CHRISTIAN IMAGERY, as in sackcloth.

Sacré Coeur Basilica in Paris and well-known landmark at the top of Montmartre. It was built (1875–1914) with Catholic church subscriptions as a votive offering after the Franco-Prussian War (1870–71). It was consecrated in 1919 after World War I.

In "A Way You'll Never Be," Nick ADAMS confuses in a dream the dancers Gaby DESLYS (Hemingway spells her name "Delys") and Harry PILCER getting out of a cab on the hill leading up to Sacré Coeur with his own traumatic experience on a hill in the war.

"Sacred Heart of Jesus" Picture "in color" on the wall of SANTIAGO's shack in *The Old Man and the Sea*.

"Safari" Article, published in *Look* (January 26, 1954), describing the two plane crashes (January 23 and 24) that ended the hunting safari of Ernest and Mary Hemingway in East Africa.

Ernest and Mary on African safari, 1954 (Courtesy of the John F. Kennedy Library)

"Safety Man, The" Poem about football, first published as one of three poems under the general title, "Athletic Verse," in the Oak Park and River Forest High School literary magazine, *Tabula* (March 1917). The other two poems are "The Tackle" and "The Punt." All three were reprinted in *88 Poems* (1979) and regarded as separate poems.

sail, furled The narrator of *The Old Man and the Sea* states that the sail on SANTIAGO's boat, "was patched with flour sacks and, furled, it looked like the flag of permanent defeat." But later in the novel the narrator states, in reference to the pain Santiago has gone through trying to catch the great marlin, that "[a] man can be destroyed but not defeated."

"Sailfish Off Mombasa: A Key West Letter" Article, published in *Esquire* (March 1935). Written a year after the event, Hemingway devotes much of the article to a criticism of the "lousy boat called the Xanadu" he and some friends had rented for fishing in the Indian

Ocean. "The boat never ran for more than twenty minutes at a time and never at decent trolling speed and we used to discuss what we would like to do to the man who had chartered her to us. . . ." But he describes catching kingfish, "very big jacks" and "snapper-like fish that looked rather like a hog-fish, two kinds of groupers. . . ." Hemingway's friend Philip PERCIVAL was along, and so was Alfred Vanderbilt, who caught a 97-pound sailfish.

sailing barges, twelve   In *Across the River and Into the Trees* Richard CANTWELL sees them "running with the wind for Venice" as he and his driver, JACKSON, drive toward Venice.

sailors, two   One of Richard CANTWELL's memories while duck hunting, in *Across the River and Into the Trees,* is of a time when he beat up two sailors who were harassing him and RENATA while they were walking at night in Venice.

Saint Anthony medal   Of religious significance to Roman Catholics who believe Saint Anthony (1195–1231) to be a miracle worker, especially in the finding of lost articles. That significance is lost on Frederic HENRY, however, who is presented with the medal by Catherine BARKLEY as he leaves for the battle front and his eventual wounding in book 1 of *A Farewell to Arms.* He loses the medal somewhere in the chaos of his wounding and subsequent transportation to the hospital in Milan.

Saint Bernard Pass   Mountain pass from Switzerland into northwestern Italy. The pass is at 8,230 feet. In *A Moveable Feast* Hemingway remembers that Hadley reminded him of the time when the two of them and their friend Chink DORMAN-SMITH walked through the snow of the Saint Bernard Pass into Italy and "walked down all day in the spring to Aosta." The distance from the top would have been about 21 miles and a drop of about 6,000 feet.

Saint-Cloud   Town on the left bank of the Seine, just across from the Bois de Boulogne in Paris. In "My Old Man," a steeplechase horse race course is mentioned for Saint-Cloud, where JOE's "old man" was a jockey for several races. Thomas HUDSON, in *Islands in the Stream,* also remembers attending races there.

Saint-Emilion wine   Saint-Emilion is a small town located about 21 miles east of Bordeaux. It produces one of the great French red wines, from vineyards dating back to the third century.

In *A Moveable Feast* Hemingway describes drinking a bottle of Saint-Emilion for lunch in Montereau, while en route from Paris to Lyon.

Saint-Estèphe   Northernmost wine-producing township of the Haut-Médoc district of Bordeaux, France. In *A Farewell to Arms* Frederic HENRY and Catherine BARKLEY order one of the Saint-Estèphe red wines, along with a bottle of CAPRI, the evening Frederic catches the midnight train back to the war front.

Saint-Etienne-du-Mont   Built during 1517–1618, this Paris church combines late-Gothic and Renaissance architecture and was much admired by Hemingway. He describes in *A Moveable Feast* walking from his apartment at 74, rue Cardinal Lemoine toward place Saint-Michel by way of Saint-Etienne-du-Mont and the Panthéon, to the boulevard Saint-Michel, past the Cluny Museum and the boulevard Saint-Germain to a café on the place Saint-Michel.

The church is also one of several places the taxi passes by as Jake BARNES and Brett ASHLEY ride on their way to the CAFÉ SELECT at the beginning of chapter 4 of *The Sun Also Rises.*

Saint-Ignace   On the north side of the Straits of Mackinac in Michigan's Upper Peninsula, the last place where NICK had eaten before setting up camp near SENEY in "Big Two-Hearted River."

Saint-Jean-de-Luz   On the southwest coast of France, an ocean resort town near the border with Spain, where, in *The Sun Also Rises,* Mike CAMPBELL goes after the Fiesta SAN FERMÍN.

Saint-Lô   The World War II Allied invasion of this Normandy town is mentioned in *Across the River and Into the Trees.*

Saint-Mihiel   A town in northeast France, on the Meuse River, northwest of Nancy, captured by American forces in World War I (1918) and one of the places mentioned in "Soldier's Home" where Harold KREBS fought with the U.S. Marines.

Sainte-Odile   Celebrated pilgrimage site in the Vosges in eastern France, 25 miles from Strasbourg. In *The Sun Also Rises* Jake BARNES mentions it to Robert COHN as a possible destination for a trip.

Saint-Raphaël   Where, according to Hemingway writing about F. Scott Fitzgerald in *A Moveable Feast,* Scott's wife, Zelda, had fallen in love with a French naval aviator. Apparently, it turned out, not to be serious.

salao   In Spanish it means, according to the narrator in *The Old Man and the Sea,* "the worst form of unlucky." It is the word MANOLIN's parents use to explain to him why they don't want him to go any more in SANTIAGO's boat. He had been 40 days without a fish at the time, and now, at the beginning of the novel, the old man has been 84 days without a fish.

salchichón   Spicy "dark sausage" from VICH, Spain, eaten for lunch in MADRID by David and Catherine BOURNE, in *The Garden of Eden.* They eat the sausage along with anchovies, garlic olives, and MANZANILLA wine.

Salvador   In "The Undefeated," Manuel GARCIA, who has just agreed to fight in the "nocturnals," remembers that fighting in the nocturnals, the most dangerous of the bullfights, was how the bullfighter Salvador got killed.

Salvation Army   International organization, semimilitary and religious, devoted to helping the poor. The two INDIANS in *The Torrents of Spring* say they are going to join up in PETOSKEY.

salvoconducto   Spanish for safe-conduct pass given to Andrés by Robert JORDAN to help him make his way to General Golz with Jordan's urgent message in *For Whom the Bell Tolls.*

Sam   Negro cook at Henry's lunchroom in "The Killers," called "nigger" by the two killers but "Sam" by the owner of the lunchroom and by Nick ADAMS. He is the only character who wants nothing to do with either the killers or with Ole Andreson, the heavyweight boxer whom the killers are after.

Sampson, Benny   An otherwise unidentified boxer who gave "The OLD RALE" to the Red-headed One in *To Have and Have Not.* "Every time they'd go into a clinch he'd [Benny] rub his shoulder under Red's nose or across his puss." See RED.

Samuelson, Arnold   Young man from Minnesota who hitchhiked to Key West in 1934 because he wanted to ask Hemingway some questions about writing. He spent several weeks in Key West, getting answers and fishing with Hemingway and his crew, out of both Key West and Havana. Hemingway mentions him in two *Esquire* articles, "Monologue to the Maestro: A High Seas Letter" and "There She Breaches! or Moby Dick off the Morro." Samuelson also wrote a book about his experiences, *With Hemingway: A Year in Key West and Cuba* (1984).

San Carlos   Hometown in Spain of the OLD MAN (7) in "Old Man at the Bridge." San Carlos de la Rapita is located on the Mediterranean coast, about 6 miles south of Tortosa.

Sancerre wine   French white wine from the region around the Sancerre village in the upper Loire Valley, about 108 miles south of Paris. Hemingway refers to the wine several times in his works, but especially in *A Moveable Feast,* when he describes a dinner of CRABE MEXICAINE with a Sancerre wine.

Sánchez   A soldier Andrés LOPEZ meets on his way to General Golz in *For Whom the Bell Tolls.*

Sánchez, Gregorio (1930–)   The third bullfighter on the card with Antonio ORDÓÑEZ and Luis Miguel DOMINGUÍN in Valencia in the summer of 1959 when Hemingway followed the Spanish bullfight circuit in preparation for writing *The Dangerous Summer.*

Sánchez, Ignacio   The name of one of the ranches in Spain that furnished bulls for the Valencia fights, mentioned in *The Dangerous Summer.* The owner, Ignacio Sánchez, had been killed in the ring in 1935.

Sande, Earl (1898–1968)   American jockey, winner of 967 races and a member of the Racing Hall of Fame. He rode Gallant Fox to the Triple Crown in 1930, winning the Kentucky Derby, the Preakness, and the Belmont Stakes.

Sande is mentioned in "Fifty Grand," when the story's narrator, Jerry Doyle, tells Danny Hogan that, according to the papers, "he [Sande] booted three of them in yesterday."

In *Islands in the Stream* Andrew HUDSON is kidded about being too short for a pitcher, but he argues that he will be as "big" as Major League pitchers Dick Rudolph and Dick Kerr. Rudolph was five feet, nine and a half inches, and 160 pounds; Kerr was five feet, seven inches, and 155. Andy's brother David tells him he'll be as big as Earl Sande, who at five feet six was big for a jockey.

Sandhurst   English military college west of London where the Hemingways' friend Chink DORMAN-SMITH went to school before World War I. The school is mentioned in *A Moveable Feast* in connection with their friendship.

Sand Key   A few miles south of KEY WEST, noticed by Harry MORGAN in *To Have and Have Not* as he heads toward Cuba with the four Cuban bank robbers. Morgan sees the Sand Key Light.

San Fermín, Fiesta   In PAMPLONA, Spain, beginning every July 6. A religious festival and procession from church to church in honor of Saint Fermín, the patron saint of the Navarre Province. But the fiesta also includes eating and drinking, and bullfights in the afternoons.

Fermín was an evangelist and the first Bishop of Pamplona. He was beheaded for his faith, and festival-goers honor his martyrdom by wearing red necker-chiefs. It is to this fiesta that Jake BARNES and his friends go in *The Sun Also Rises*. "It kept up day and night for seven days. The dancing kept up, the drinking kept up, the noise went on," until everything became so unreal that it was as if there were no "consequences."

San Francisco dock   In Havana where Harry MORGAN has his charter boat tied up in *To Have and Have Not*.

San Gabriele   One of the towns north of Gorizia, Italy, that the World War I allies "could not take" during the fall "of that year" (1916) in book 1 of *A Farewell to Arms*.

San Isidro   Patron saint of Madrid. The saint's feast day is May 15 and marks the beginning of a week of fiesta in Madrid, including bullfights.

San Isidro is one of the towns on the bullfight circuit covered by Hemingway in *The Dangerous Summer*. And in *The Garden of Eden* David BOURNE tells Catherine that the festivals in Madrid and Seville (April 18–25) are over.

San Isidro Street   In Havana, mentioned in *Islands in the Stream*. It is "below the main railway station and opposite the entrance to the old P. and O. docks." At one time, according to Thomas HUDSON, the street had been "the great whorehouse street of the waterfront."

San Pedro   Saint Peter, who, SANTIAGO remembers, was a fisherman "as was the father of the great DiMaggio." The reference to San Pedro is part of the CHRISTIAN IMAGERY in *The Old Man and the Sea*.

San Pier d'Arena   An "industrial suburb" of Genoa, where the narrator of "Che Ti Dice La Patria?" (What do you hear from home?) and his traveling friend, Guy, have their car splashed by a "sheet of muddy water" from the arrogant, probably fascist, driver of a "big car" passing them on the main street.

San Rafael   Town near Segovia, northwest of Madrid. In *For Whom the Bell Tolls*, there are rumors in San Rafael of FASCIST troop movements in the Guadarrama Mountains where Robert JORDAN and Pablo's band of guerrilla fighters are preparing to blow up a bridge.

San Relajo   Small town near the mouth of the TAGLIA-MENTO RIVER near where Richard CANTWELL duck hunts in *Across the River and Into the Trees*.

San Sebastián   Town in northwest Spain, on the ocean and about 12 miles south of the French border. In *The Sun Also Rises* it is the town where Jake BARNES goes to relax after the Fiesta SAN FERMÍN in PAMPLONA and where Brett ASHLEY's telegram reaches him, asking him to rescue her from "trouble" in Madrid. It is also the

town where Brett and Robert COHN go to have their weeklong affair earlier in the novel.

San Siro   Steeplechase horse racing track near Milan, Italy, where, in *A Farewell to Arms*, Frederic HENRY and Catherine BARKLEY go while he is recovering from his wound. The two of them and "old Meyers" and his wife drive to San Siro "in an open carriage."

The track is also mentioned in "My Old Man" as the site of fixed races in which the father of JOE, the story's main character, rides.

In *A Moveable Feast*, Hemingway, who is writing about when he and Hadley were in Paris in 1923–24, remembers San Siro "from the good old days," meaning when he was in World War I six or seven years earlier.

Santa Maria del Giglio   Venetian church, around the corner from the GRITTI PALACE HOTEL, mentioned in *Across the River and Into the Trees*.

Santiago   The main character in *The Old Man and the Sea*. He is described as "thin and gaunt with deep wrinkles in the back of his neck." The brown blotches of "skin cancer the sun brings . . . ran well down the sides of his face and his hands had the deep-creased scars from handling heavy fish on the cords. But none of these scars were fresh. They were as old as erosions in a fishless desert."

Santiago has been 84 days without a fish, and the parents of MANOLIN, the boy who had earlier assisted the old man, stopped him from going with the old fisherman after 40 days, because they considered Santiago to be "*salao* . . . the worst form of unlucky." Manolin reminds Santiago that the two of them went 87 days without a fish once before, and then they "caught big ones every day for three weeks." And it no longer bothers the old man that the other fishermen in the village where he lives make fun of him. He thinks he is still strong enough for a big fish, and, as he tells Manolin, "there are many tricks."

Except for the boy, Santiago is a lonely old man. Later, out at sea, he thinks, "No one should be alone in their old age. . . . But it is unavoidable." His wife had died several years earlier. What Santiago does have, however, is the love of the boy and fishing and baseball and his dreams of the lions on the beaches of Africa, which he remembers from when he was before the mast on a square-rigged ship along the African coast.

Santiago is an expert fisherman. He knows to the fathom how far down in the water are his baits: "One was down forty fathoms. The second was at seventy-five and the third and fourth were down in the blue water at one hundred and one hundred and twenty-five fathoms. Each bait hung head down with the shank of the hook inside the bait fish, tied and sewed solid and all the projecting part of the hook, the curve and the point, was covered with fresh sardines." Santiago says, "It is better to be lucky. But I would rather be exact. Then when luck comes you are ready."

Santiago loves the sea, which he thinks of as "*la mar*, which is what people call her in Spanish when they love her." And he knows the birds on the sea. He sees a man-of-war bird flying low over the water, signaling the presence of dolphin. And he feels sorry for a warbler, resting on one of the lines. He feels a kinship with the tiny bird, because he knows that just as he has gone "out too far" in pursuit of the big fish he has hooked, so the warbler has gone out too far. "Take a good rest small bird, [then] go in and take your chance like any man or bird or fish."

The old man had told Manolin that he planned to go far out, but now, having hooked the marlin, which pulls him even farther away from land, he knows that he has gone too far. In the end, what he has accomplished in catching the marlin and fighting off the sharks is misunderstood. Two tourists are looking down at the "long backbone of the great fish that was now just garbage waiting to go out with the tide," and a waiter tries to explain to the tourists how the sharks had attacked the great fish, but the tourists think that the skeleton is that of a shark: "I didn't know," the woman says, "sharks had such handsome, beautifully formed tails." Her male companion says, "I didn't either." The great acts of men often go misunderstood.

San Vito   Town about two and a half miles west of the Tagliamento River in northern Italy. When, in *A Farewell to Arms*, Frederic HENRY dives into the river to avoid being shot by the Italian battle police, he comes out of the river across from a town he can see in the distance and which he thinks is San Vito.

Sarabande   A dance in slow triple time found in 18th-century musical suites. A recording of a Bach "sarabande" is played on board *NEW EXUMA II*, owned by Nils LARSON, in *To Have and Have Not*.

Sargasso Sea   A region of calm water extending from the West Indies to the Azores and from about 20° to 35° N latitude, best known for its floating seaweed. The main stem of the seaweed has flattened; there are leaflike outgrowths and branches with berrylike air sacs.

SANTIAGO in *The Old Man and the Sea* sees "patches of yellow, sun-bleached Sargasso weed and the purple, formalized, iridescent, gelatinous bladder of a Portuguese man-of-war floating close beside [his] boat."

Sargint, H. J. J.   European editor for the North American Newspaper Alliance during the Spanish civil war. See NANA.

Saturday Evening Post, The   American popular magazine, begun on August 18, 1821 and still being published. Since 1897 the cover page has noted that the publication was founded by Benjamin Franklin in 1728, but the only connection to Franklin is that it was originally published from an office once occupied by Franklin's *Pennsylvania Gazette*, one of whose later publishers founded the *Post*.

It was purchased by Cyrus Curtis in 1897 and edited by George Horace LORIMER from 1899–1936. The *Post* was a weekly until 1962 when it became a semimonthly during July and August and from mid-December to mid-January. In *A Moveable Feast* Hemingway writes that F. Scott Fitzgerald explained when they met in Paris in 1925 that he was writing stories for the *Post* in order to make some quick money. Hemingway also states that Gertrude Stein told him, in the mid-1920s, that he was not yet a good enough writer to be published in the *Post*.

Saunders, Edgar   In *A Farewell to Arms* he is an American opera singer singing under the Italian name, Edouardo Giovanni, at La Scala in Milan. Frederic HENRY meets him during his convalescence in Milan during the summer after his wounding.

Saviers, Dr. George   Doctor-friend of Ernest and Mary Hemingway from Sun Valley, Idaho, who cleaned and dressed a wound received by Antonio ORDÓÑEZ in Pamplona during the running of the bulls and described in *The Dangerous Summer*.

sawed-off automatic shotgun   Used to kill the four Cuban bank robbers who hire Harry MORGAN to run them to Cuba in part 3 of *To Have and Have Not*. A sawed-off shotgun is also used to kill the three Cubans outside Havana's PEARL OF SAN FRANCISCO CAFÉ in chapter 1.

S Bus   In *The Sun Also Rises* Jake BARNES takes a Paris "S Bus" to the Madeleine.

Scala, La   See LA SCALA.

Schatz (1)   Main character in "A Day's Wait." He's a nine-year-old boy sick with the flu, and he thinks he's going to die because he has a temperature of 102°. After spending most of the day in bed in something of a stupor, he finally asks his father, the story's narrator, how long he has to live. He says that the boys in his school in France had told him that "you can't live with forty-four degrees. I've got a hundred and two."

Schatz's father then has to explain the difference between the Celsius and Fahrenheit thermometers. "It's like miles and kilometers" he tells him. Schatz then begins to relax "very slowly," his father says, "and the next day . . . he cried very easily at little things that were of no importance."

Schatz (2) In *Islands in the Stream* a nickname Thomas HUDSON sometimes uses for his oldest son, Tom HUDSON.

Schmeisser bullet Used by a German submarine crew in *Islands in the Stream* and found by Thomas HUDSON on a Cuban turtle boat the Germans have stolen in their attempt to escape. The bullet is 9mm, used in a pistol that fires 400 rounds per minute; the bullet can also be fired from a Luger pistol. The bullet was named for its designer, Hugo Schmeisser.

Schmeisser machine pistol There are two on board the turtle boat the Germans have captured in the "At Sea" section of *Islands in the Stream*. Thomas HUDSON also has two Schmeisser pistols on board his boat as he and his crew search for the Germans. The gun uses 9mm standard issue bullets.

Schmidt See Al SMITH.

Schnapps In Europe it's any strong, dry spirit; drunk by the peasant in "An Alpine Idyll." In *A Moveable Feast* Hemingway writes about it as a KIRSCH, "distilled from mountain gentian."

Schnautz Dog owned by Thomas HUDSON and his first wife and son when they lived in Europe, remembered by young Tom in the "Bimini" section of *Islands in the Stream*.

Schnauz Dog belonging at the Hotel Taube in Schruns, Austria, but which, according to Hemingway in *A Moveable Feast,* liked to sleep at the end of his and his wife Hadley's bed and who "loved to go on ski trips."

Schnee-Eifel fight In *Across the River and Into the Trees* Richard CANTWELL mentions having been in Paris during the two days between the World War II battles at Schnee-Eifel ridge and HÜRTGEN FOREST in western Belgium.

Schneider, Hannes In *A Moveable Feast* Hemingway mentions Schneider as "the great Arlberg skier" of the early 1920s and a partner with Herr Walther Lent, the Hemingways' ski instructor.

"Schober Every Inch a Chancellor" Article, published in *The Toronto Daily Star* (April 26, 1922), reprinted in *Ernest Hemingway: Dateline Toronto* (1985). The headline in the *Daily Star* was "Schober of Austria, at Genoa, Looks Every Inch a Chancellor." In the article, date-lined "Genoa," Hemingway writes a biographical sketch of Austria's Chancellor Schober, "the only man at the Genoa [Economic] Conference, with the exception of Lloyd George, that looks the romantic conception of what a chancellor should look."

schooner, three-masted In "After the Storm," the narrator describes a sunken three-masted schooner as too deep to get anything out of her. Then he finds the sunken ocean liner which is the focus of his story.

Schoonmaker, Mary One of two young American women, "captured" by Hemingway and his friends in Pamplona during the Fiesta SAN FERMÍN in 1959 while Hemingway was following the bullfight circuit in preparation for writing *The Dangerous Summer*. She is not named in the text, but she is identified in one of the book's photographs.

The other young woman, according to biographers, was Teddy Jo Paulson. Both are a part of the Hemingway party not only in Pamplona but "through the feria of Valencia at the end of the month" and including Ernest's 60th birthday party on July 21.

Schruns Small town in the Vorarlberg of western Austria, where Ernest and Hadley Hemingway went for skiing in the winters of 1924–25 and 1925–26. He writes about Schruns in *A Moveable Feast*, especially in the final section, "There Is Never Any End to Paris." He finished the rewriting of *The Sun Also Rises* in Schruns. He says that he and Hadley "loved" both the Vorarlberg and Schruns.

Schwarzwald German name for the Black Forest, a large region in southwestern Germany. Ernest and Hadley Hemingway took a hiking tour through the Schwarzwald with friends in August 1922. The forest is mentioned in "Cross-Country Snow."

"Schwarzwald" Poem about Germany's Black Forest, written in 1922 and first published in *88 Poems* (1979).

Science and Health Book by Mary Baker Eddy on the power of the Bible in daily life, published in 1875. It is read by NICK's mother in "The Doctor and the Doctor's Wife."

Scotch NICK and BILL (1) start on a bottle of Scotch after they finish the Irish Whisky in their deliberate attempt to get drunk in "The Three-Day Blow."

Scribner, Charles I (1821–1871) Founder with Isaac D. Baker of a New York publishing house in 1846, which had the Scribner name (except for 1871–78) from 1850, when Baker died, until 1984, when it was bought by Macmillan Publishing Company.

Scribner, Charles II (1854–1930) Son of Charles Scribner I) and head of Charles Scribner's Sons publishing house for 51 years, from 1879 to 1930. He founded *Scribner's Magazine* in 1887 and attracted several leading writers to the firm during the pre– and post–World War I years, including Hemingway, F. Scott Fitzgerald, Robert Louis Stevenson, Henry van Dyke, and Ring Lardner. Charles's older brother, John Blair Scribner, was head of the firm from 1871–79, and Charles's younger brother, Arthur Hawley Scribner, was director from 1930–32.

Hemingway published nearly all of his books under the Charles Scribner's Sons label. Important exceptions are *Three Stories & Ten Poems* (Contact Publishing Co., 1923), *in our time* (Three Mountains Press, 1924), *Today is Friday* (The As Stable Publications, 1926), *God Rest You Merry Gentlemen* (House of Books, Ltd., 1933), and *The Spanish Earth* (J.B. Savage Co., 1938).

Scribner, Charles III (1890–1952)   Son of Charles Scribner (2) and head of Charles Scribner's Sons from 1932–52. Hemingway, who considered "Charlie" Scribner a close friend, dedicated *The Old Man and the Sea* to him and to his editor at Scribner's, Maxwell PERKINS.

Scribner, Charles, IV (1921–1995)   Son of Charles SCRIBNER III and head of Charles Scribner's Sons publishing house from 1952–84, when the firm was purchased by Macmillan Publishing Company.

Scribner's Magazine   Literary and artistic magazine begun in 1886 by Scribner's Publishing House in New York. Hemingway published seven short stories in the magazine between 1927 and 1930, including "The Killers" and "A Clean, Well-Lighted Place."

Scripps, Diana   In *The Torrents of Spring*, she is the "elderly waitress" who works at BROWN'S BEANERY in PETOSKEY, where she meets and marries Scripps O'NEIL the day he arrives in town and eats at her restaurant. The novel's narrator refers to her most often as "Mrs. Scripps" or by her full name, "Diana Scripps," but never as "Diana" or "Mrs. O'Neil."

She is English, having come from the Lake District and looks, according to Scripps, like an actress named Lenore Ulric, whom Scripps remembers seeing in *Peter Pan*. Diana says that her father was a "great admirer of Gladstone" and that the two had attended Eton together. She tells Scripps that she was a young girl when her mother took her to the PARIS EXPOSITION. Of the three possible expositions held in Paris (1867, 1889, and 1900) the 1889 date is the most logical one, since she would then be about 40 at the time the story takes place.

Very little of what the reader is told in the novel, however, even by the narrator, is reliable (see the novel's main entry), so little can be accurately documented. Diana tells Scripps an incredible story about the disappearance of her mother and being told by the police and others that she had not been with her mother at all, but with a "General So-and-so." And she "never saw Mummy again."

She suggests to Scripps that he work at the Petoskey PUMP-FACTORY; even if he is a writer why shouldn't he work with his hands, and she names Rodin, Cézanne, Renoir, Picasso, Gilbert Stuart, Emerson, and James Russell Lowell as other artists who had worked with their hands. She reads a lot of literary magazines—*The Forum, The Mentor, Scribner's, The Literary Digest* "Book Review," *The Bookman, The Saturday Review of Literature, The New York Times* "Literary Section," and *Harper's Magazine*—all in an attempt to hold onto her husband, the "writer." She reads the magazines, because she wants to compete with the younger waitress, MANDY, who is full of literary anecdotes, but all of Diana's reading of literary materials does her no good. At the end of the novel, Scripps leaves Diana for Mandy.

Scuola San Rocco   One of the art museums in Venice, mentioned in *Across the River and Into the Trees* as one of the two places (with the Accademia) where Richard CANTWELL would like to "go every day to see the Tintorettos." The San Rocco is famous for its series of paintings by Tintoretto.

sea bass   David BOURNE catches a 15-pound sea bass on a bamboo pole in front of his hotel in the GRAU DU ROI at the beginning of *The Garden of Eden*.

"Sea Change, The"   The term "sea change" originally meant an irreversible change in form wrought by the sea. The earliest known usage was in Ariel's speech in Shakespeare's *The Tempest* (Act I, scene 2): "Full fathom five thy father lies;/ Of his bones are coral made;/ Those are pearls that were his eyes:/ Nothing of him that doth fade/ But doth suffer a sea-change/ Into something rich and strange."

The meaning has evolved since 1611 and now usually refers to a significant transformation that takes place within a person and is used most often as a metaphor for any change in an individual's personality or character.

The title of Hemingway's short story refers to a change in sexual preference for the "GIRL (4)." As with "Hills Like White Elephants," where the subject of the story, abortion, is not named, so here the subject, lesbianism, is not named. And, as with "Hills," the story is almost entirely in dialogue, the "girl" and Phil seated in a Paris café early on a late-summer morning discussing their breakup, she having just told him about her newly formed lesbian relationship.

He has apparently just asked her to give up her female lover, because he is pushing her for an answer: "All right. . . . What about it?" And she says, "No. . . . I can't." He wonders why she couldn't have gotten into some other kind of "jam," and he pretends to know what he would do if it were a man. She insists that she still loves him, and that she will "come back." He refers to "it" first as a "vice" and remembers a quotation about "vice": "Vice is a monster of such fearful mien." But he can't remember the next lines. The lines he is trying to remember are from Alexander Pope's "An Essay on Man," neither author or title identified: "Vice is a monster of so frightful mien,/ As, to be hated, needs but to be seen;/ Yet seen too oft, familiar with her face,/ We first endure, then pity, then embrace." We accept, even "embrace" vice.

When Phil refers to "it" as "perversion," the "girl" says, "We're made up of all sorts of things. You've known that. You've used it well enough." When he says, "You don't have to say that again," the reader is left with the impression that there may have been some "perversion" in their own relationship that they have talked about before. She is quite relieved when he tells her to go, and she leaves the café and does "not look back at him."

Phil moves to the bar and tells the bartender, James, "vice . . . is a very strange thing." And when he looks in the mirror he thinks he sees "quite a different-looking man," repeating the idea to the barman and to himself. The repetition of the idea that he is "different" suggests that both the "girl" and Phil have gone through a "sea change," Phil's change perhaps the result of the jolt to his own male self-esteem caused by the "girl" leaving him for another woman.

The story is an example of Hemingway's THEORY OF OMISSION. What is *not* said by the girl and Phil to each other and even by the narrator in telling the story is more important than what *is* said. See other examples, particularly "Hills Like White Elephants" and "Big Two-Hearted River."

"The Sea Change" was first published in *This Quarter* (December 1931) and reprinted in *Winner Take Nothing* (1933).

Sea of Galilee   At the end of *Green Hills of Africa* Hemingway and his wife (still P.O.M., "Poor old Mama"), and Karl and Karl's wife, sun themselves "against a stone wall by the Sea of Galilee eating some lunch and drinking a bottle of wine and watching the grebes out on the lake."

"Search for Sudbury Coal"   Article, published in *The Toronto Daily Star* (September 25, 1923), reprinted in *Ernest Hemingway: Dateline Toronto* (1985). The headline in the *Daily Star* was "Search for Sudbury Coal a Gamble, Driller Tells of What He Has Found." The article, datelined "Sudbury, Ontario," is about the continuing search for good coal in the mines of Sudbury, Ontario, where for 30 years mine operators have been searching and have found only mixed seams of good and bad coal.

Seconal   Trademark for a brand of secobarbital, a sedative and some of the medicine that Richard CANTWELL takes, in *Across the River and Into the Trees*, in order to avoid his next heart attack. He also takes NITROGLYCERIN and MANNITOL HEXANITRATE.

In *Islands in the Stream* Thomas HUDSON, after drinking DOUBLE FROZEN DAIQUIRIS, takes the last "big double Seconal capsule" he has in order to sleep and wake in the morning without a hangover.

secretary   In *The Sun Also Rises* Jake BARNES's secretary at his newspaper office in Paris, probably the Paris edition of the *New York Herald Tribune*.

section eight   Dishonorable discharge from the U.S. Army, mentioned in *Across the River and Into the Trees*.

Segovia   Capital of Segovia Province in central Spain, in Old Castile, one of the towns taken by the fascists at the beginning of the SPANISH CIVIL WAR and which the Loyalists hoped to take back. The band of guerrilla fighters, to which Robert JORDAN is attached in *For Whom the Bell Tolls*, is operating in the Guadarrama Mountains just to the southeast of Segovia.

Seguridad   Police headquarters in Madrid, where Robert JORDAN, in *For Whom the Bell Tolls*, tells MARÍA they will go after the war to get marriage papers. He also tells her that the hotel where they will stay is the Hotel Florida on the Plaza del Callao and that the servant girl they will hire is named Petra.

Seguridad headquarters   In *The Fifth Column*, the office of the Madrid security police, where Philip RAWLINGS sends the two comrades who have allowed a prisoner to escape.

Seldes, Gilbert (1893–1970)   Editor of the literary journal *Dial* (1920–23) and author of *The Seven Lively Arts* (1924). In *A Moveable Feast* Hemingway writes that F. Scott Fitzgerald showed him a review of *The Great Gatsby* that Seldes had written, and according to Hemingway, it "could not have been better."

semaphore   A statue of the inventor of the semaphore flag-signaling system "engaged in doing same" is mentioned by Jake BARNES in *The Sun Also Rises*.

Seney   Small town in Michigan's Upper Peninsula, about 85 miles northwest of St. Ignace at the Straits of Mackinac. It is the setting for "Big Two-Hearted River." Seney is actually on the Fox River, and although there is no Big Two-Hearted River in Michigan, there is a Two Hearted River that originates in an area of small lakes and swamps about 20 miles northeast of Seney.

In Hemingway's story, Seney has burned down with very little left to show that there had been a town there. There is "nothing but the rails [for trains] and the burned-over country." There used to be "thirteen saloons that had lined the one street," but they were gone, and the "foundation of the Mansion House hotel stuck up above the ground."

sentry, first   In *The Fifth Column* he is guarding the fascist artillery observation post on the Extremadura Road near Madrid. The sentry is at the foot of the ladder leading to the upstairs tower of a shelled house where the observers are located. The "second sentry" is at the top of the ladder.

sentry box   One at each end of the BRIDGE in *For Whom the Bell Tolls,* the two ends guarded by "seven men and a corporal."

"Sepi Jingan"   This short story is one of three Hemingway published in his high school literary magazine, *Tabula* (November 1916). The other two are "Judgment of Manitou" and "A Matter of Color."

Sepi Jingan is a dog owned by Billy TABESHAW, an Indian friend of the story's narrator, who tells him about being trapped by another Indian, Paul Black Bird, and being saved when the dog attacks and kills him. Everybody had thought that Paul Black Bird had gotten drunk and fallen on the tracks, but Billy Tabeshaw explains the real story, that after Sepi Jingan had killed him, Billy had then placed the dead man on the railroad tracks and that the "Pere Marquette Resort Limited [train] removed all the traces."

"Sequel"   Poem written about 1926 and first published in *88 Poems* (1979).

Serafín   Barman at the Floridita Bar in Havana in the "Cuba" section of *Islands in the Stream.* He offers Thomas HUDSON food to counter the drinking Hudson is doing.

Serengeti plain   Extensive plain, about 5,610 square miles in northwest Tanzania, in which a national wildlife preserve, the Serengeti National Park, is located. Hemingway writes about the Serengeti in *Green Hills of Africa,* where he remembers that they had killed ducks that were "marvellous." Hemingway spells the name "Serengetti."

sergeant   Near the end of "A Natural History of the Dead," a sergeant is asked by a military doctor to wipe out the eyes of a lieutenant, who has been temporarily blinded by a container of iodine thrown in his face by the doctor.

sergeant, white   The narrator of "A Canary for One" notices a group of "negro soldiers" on the station platform in Avignon, France, who are led by a "short white sergeant."

sergeants of engineers, two   In *A Farewell to Arms* they hitch a ride with Aldo BONELLO in his retreat with Frederic HENRY after the Battle of CAPORETTO. They later disobey an order to help push one of the ambulance cars out of the mud and run off down the road. One of them is shot, first by Frederic and then killed by Bonello; the other gets away.

Sermione arch   In *A Moveable Feast* Hemingway and his wife, Hadley, walking back to their Paris apartment one night, see the Arc du Carrousel and the Arc de Triomphe and wonder to one another if it were true, as the story was told, that the two Paris arches are in line with the Sermione arch in Milan, Italy.

There is no arch in Milan named Sermione, but there is the Arco della Pace (the triumphal peace arch, built 1806–38) at the northwest end of Milan's Nuovo Parco and which faces northwest onto the Corso Sempione and is framed by the two gates of the Porta del Sempione (where Hemingway no doubt got the arch's name). It could be argued that the Arco della Pace lines up with the two Paris arches.

Sestri   Italian town, about 21 miles southeast of Genoa, one of the towns mentioned in "Che Ti Dice La Patria?" to which the two main characters travel. Hemingway creates some geographical confusion in the story, however, because the narrator states that the Mediterranean is on their left as they pass "through the suburbs of Genoa," which means they're driving north toward Genoa and, according to their itinerary, back to the starting point of their 10-day trip, Ventimiglia, near the border with France. But they stop for lunch in Sestri, which would be behind them, 21 miles southeast of Genoa.

Sevastopol   Novel of the Crimean War by Tolstoi, published in 1855–56. Mentioned in *Green Hills of Africa.* See Leo Nikolayevich TOLSTOI.

seven tourists   In the "BIMINI" section of *Islands in the Stream,* the crew of five men and two women on a visiting yacht is tricked by Thomas HUDSON's three young sons, who pretend to be drunken, underage drinkers at the PONCE DE LEÓN bar.

seventy-sevens German cannon shells, fired at the Italian army in World War I and seen exploding in the mountains of northern Italy by Frederic HENRY in *A Farewell to Arms*.

sexton Named Franz in "An Alpine Idyll." He's "a little man with a mustache," and he's "amused" by the "idyll" he tells the short story's narrator.

The idyll is about the Austrian peasant, OLZ, whose wife had died six months earlier, in December, but who had just gotten her down to the village for burial because his mountain home had been snowed in all winter. Franz is amused because the priest didn't want to bury her. Her face had become horribly disfigured because Olz had stood her in the woodshed when she became stiff and then hung a lantern from her mouth every evening when he went to the shed to get wood.

S4N Spanish periodical referred to in *Death in the Afternoon* as a "now dead little magazine," one in which Waldo FRANK once published an article on his writing habits.

shack Where SANTIAGO lives in his unnamed village (probably Cojimar) near Havana. According to the narrator of *The Old Man and the Sea*, the "shack was made of the tough budshields of the royal palm [tree] which are called *guano* and in it there was a bed, a table, one chair, and a place on the dirt floor to cook with charcoal."

SHAEF Supreme Headquarters of the Allied Expeditionary Forces, based in Versailles, outside of Paris, during the Allied advance toward Germany in World War II and mentioned by Colonel Richard CANTWELL in *Across the River and Into the Trees*.

Shakespeare Richard CANTWELL, in *Across the River and Into the Trees*, thinks of Shakespeare as the "winner and still the undisputed champion." He also thinks about "King Lear," which "Mister Gene Tunney" read, and later about "Othello and Desdemona," which he and RENATA were not, "thank God."

Shakespeare and Company (1) American bookshop at 12, rue de l'Odéon in Paris, owned by Sylvia BEACH. It was opened on November 19, 1919, and closed in 1941, when the Germans threatened to confiscate the books.

The shop was a haven for Left Bank American and British citizens, particularly writers, during the 1920s and '30s, because it was both a shop for buying books and a lending library. Hemingway and his wife, Hadley, borrowed dozens of books, and although Beach kept careful records, those for the Hemingway borrowings from late December 1921, when he first entered the shop, until 1925 are lost.

In her book *Shakespeare & Company* Beach has a chapter titled "My Best Customer," a reference to Hemingway, who apparently gave the title to himself but which was, according to Beach, "a title that no one disputed with him."

The fourth section of *A Moveable Feast* is titled "Shakespeare and Company." And in section 15 he writes of the great value he received from being allowed to borrow so many books from the bookshop. In referring especially to books by the great Russian writers—Turgenev, Gogol, Tolstoi, Chekov, and Dostoyevsky—Hemingway says: "To have come on all this new world of writing . . . was like having a great treasure given to you."

The name of the shop has been written as Shakespeare & Company (even on the cover of Beach's book) or as Shakespeare & Co. But the name over the door of the shop was Shakespeare and Company.

Shakespeare and Company (2) American bookshop at 37, rue de la Bucherie in Paris, "Kilometer Zero," established in 1964 by George Whitman and named in honor of Sylvia Beach's bookshop at 12, rue de l'Odéon, which closed in 1941. And Whitman named his daughter Sylvia Beach Whitman in honor of the owner of the first Shakespeare and Company.

Sylvia Beach Whitman published a booklet titled *Shakespeare & Company: Biography of a Bookstore in Pictures and Poems*, which was to help pay for damage caused by a fire on July 18, 1990.

The shop has provided American scholars studying in Paris with beds and tea for a number of years and has been the site of readings that have included Allen Ginsberg, Lawrence Ferlinghetti, Langston Hughes, and Brenden Beehan, plus an annual reading of James Joyce's *Ulysses* on Bloomsday, June 16. The shop has an inscription over the door to one of the rooms: "Be not inhospitable to strangers/ lest they be angels in disguise."

shamba An East African (Swahili) term for village huts or a plantation, or any cultivated plot of ground, perhaps a garden, owned by an individual or a family. When, in *Green Hills of Africa*, P.O.M. (Poor Old Mama) asks the Austrian KANDISKY what the word "shamba" means, he tells her it means a "plantation."

The word "shamba" is also used in *The Garden of Eden* as part of David BOURNE's AFRICAN STORY about his father drinking at the "beer shamba."

Shanghai fighting Mentioned by the narrator of "Che Ti Dice La Patria?" (What do you hear from home?). It helps set the time of the story in April 1927. The narrator states that he reads about the "Shanghai fighting" in

Madame Chiang Kai-shek with Ernest and Martha Gellhorn Hemingway in Chungking, China, 1941 (Copyright holder unknown; photo courtesy of the John F. Kennedy Library)

the newspapers during lunch in Sestri, Italy. It's a reference to the "massacre" that took place when Chiang Kai-shek led the Kuomintang against the Communist labor movement in Shanghai in April 1927.

shark factory "On the other side of the cove" from SANTIAGO's unnamed fishing village in *The Old Man and the Sea*.

shark liver oil In *The Old Man and the Sea* SANTIAGO drinks a cup "each day from the big drum in the shack where many of the fishermen kept their gear."

sharks In *The Old Man and the Sea* a 1,500-pound MARLIN (2) that SANTIAGO catches is destroyed by sharks. "The shark was not an accident," the narrator says. "He had come up from deep down in the water as the dark cloud of [marlin] blood had settled and dispersed in the mile deep sea." The first one is a "very big Mako shark built to swim as fast as the fastest fish in the sea and everything about him was beautiful except his jaws. . . . *Dentuso*, [Santiago] thought. Bad luck to your mother."

The mako shark is common in the Atlantic Ocean and can grow to 13 feet and 1,000 pounds. There are also shovel-nosed sharks, *galanos*, identified by their "brown, triangular fin and the sweeping movements of the tail. . . . He could see their wide, flattened, shovel-pointed heads . . . and their white-tipped wide pectoral fins."

Santiago kills the mako and three shovel-nosed sharks, but the damage they do, sometimes pulling off 40 pounds of meat in one bite, and the damage done by the sharks that come after nightfall, strip the marlin of nearly all its meat.

Shaw, George Bernard (1856–1950) Irish dramatist and critic and winner of the Nobel Prize for literature (1925), mentioned in the booklet advertising *The Forum* magazine in "Banal Story."

Shaw, Mr. Yogi JOHNSON tells Scripps O'NEIL in *The Torrents of Spring* that Mr. Shaw is "probably the greatest living pump-maker," referring to the pumps made at the PUMP-FACTORY, where Yogi Johnson works in PETOSKEY.

She   Main character in "One Reader Writes." She writes a letter to a doctor, whose name she gets from under a photograph in a local newspaper, asking him "for some very important advice." The story's narrator presents the letter.

She had married a soldier in 1929, and after three years in China he returned to his mother's home in Arkansas and is "taking a course of injections" for "sifilus." In the letter, she asks the doctor if it will "ever be safe for me to live with him again." Her father had once told her, she writes, that anyone who had that "malady" might "wish themselves dead"; but she wants to believe her husband who told her that he will be "O K after [the doctor who is treating him] finishes with him."

The narrator then describes her thoughts as she reflects on the letter she has written. "I don't care what he did to get it. But I wish to Christ he hadn't ever got it. . . . I don't know why he had to get a malady."

The letter is addressed from Roanoke, Virginia, but one assumes that her husband is still in Helena, Arkansas, with his mother and taking the injections. It is clear that she doesn't understand the impact of syphilis on her marriage.

sheath knife   Carried by SANTIAGO in *The Old Man and the Sea* and, tied to the end of a pole, he uses it in his attempt to keep the sharks off the 1,500-pound MARLIN he has caught.

Sheepshead   Racetrack mentioned in "Fifty Grand," as a place where Danny HOGAN says he remembers seeing Jack BRENNAN making bets. The reference may foreshadow Brennan's willingness to accept his manager's offer to throw his upcoming fight with Jimmy WALCOTT.

Shelley, Percy Bysshe (1792–1822)   British poet. The narrator of "Che Ti Dice La Patria?" (What do you hear from home?) tells his traveling friend, Guy, that "they [indicating the Italians] drowned Shelley somewhere along here," meaning near Sestri, Italy, on the Ligurian Sea, but Guy tells him it was "down by Viareggio," about 48 miles farther south. Shelley actually drowned in an apparent accident while sailing along the coast near Spezia.

Shenton, Edward (1895–1977)   Philadelphia artist, who did the pen-and-ink illustrations for the *Scribner's Magazine* serialization of *Green Hills of Africa*. A specialist in black-and-white illustrations, Shenton also provided drawings for William Faulkner's *The Unvanquished* (1938) and *Big Woods* (1955) and for Marjorie Kinnan Rawlings' novels *The Yearling* (1938) and *Cross Creek* (1942).

sheriff   Invites Richard GORDON to go along to see Harry MORGAN's boat towed into KEY WEST in *To Have and Have Not*. His name is Roger Johnson, used only once near the end of the novel.

Sherman, General William Tecumseh (1820–1891)   Union general in the American Civil War, best known for his burning of Atlanta and his subsequent "march to the sea," destroying much of the territory between Atlanta and Savannah and then northward through South Carolina.

According to Scripps O'NEIL in *The Torrents of Spring*, Sherman burned his father's house during that march.

"She Sacrifices Herself That Children May Live"   Article, published in *The Toronto Star* (before Christmas 1923), reprinted in William Burrill's *Hemingway: The Toronto Years* (1994). Reporters at the *Star* were (and still are) asked to write a story appealing for money for the newspaper's Santa Claus Fund. This is Hemingway's contribution, about a woman raising three children on her own, who had worked until she had become a "shadow."

"Ship, The"   Poem written aboard the troopship *Chicago* on its way to Europe in 1918 where Hemingway was to become an ambulance driver for the Italian army. The full title is "The Ship: Translated Being La Paquebot," with a subtitle on the typescript page, "The Ship Doeth Pitch/Like a Son of a Bitch." First published in the *Fitzgerald/Hemingway Annual 1972*.

Shipman, Evan (1904–1957)   American poet and race-horse fancier, writing for *American Horse Breeder* magazine during the time Hemingway knew him in Paris from 1924 to 1927. Section 15 of *A Moveable Feast* is titled "Evan Shipman at the Lilas," referring to a mostly small-talk conversation the two men had on the terrace at the café CLOSERIE DES LILAS. Hemingway dedicated his book of short stories, *Men Without Women*, to Shipman.

He is described by Carlos Baker in *Ernest Hemingway: A Life Story* as a "seedy young American poet and race-horse fancier." Hemingway mentions him in *Death in the Afternoon*, also in connection with horse racing. His full name is Evan Biddle Shipman.

"Shock Troops"   Poem written about 1922 and first published in *88 Poems* (1979).

shooters   Otherwise unidentified characters in *Across the River and Into the Trees*, one for each of the six boats on Richard CANTWELL's duck hunting expedition.

shooting stool   Used by the duck hunters, including Richard CANTWELL, in the blinds along the TAGLIAMENTO RIVER in *Across the River and Into the Trees*.

"Shootism Versus Sport: The Second Tanganyika Letter" Article, published in *Esquire* (June 1934), reprinted in *By-Line Ernest Hemingway* (1967). The article begins, "There are two ways to murder a lion." It defines the difference between "shootism" and "sport," covering the rules for hunting with a car on East Africa's Serengeti plain.

"Short Happy Life of Francis Macomber, The" When this popular short story begins, Francis MACOMBER, the main character, has already embarrassed himself and his wife, Margot, by proving himself a "coward" during the morning's hunt for a lion.

There is an 11-page flashback to the incident, a sort of INTERIOR MONOLOGUE for Macomber, and it is in the flashback that the reader learns about Macomber's sleepless night when he hears the lion roar in the distance, and where he thinks of the Somali proverb that says a "brave man is always frightened three times by a lion: when he first sees his track, when he first hears him roar and when he first confronts him."

He feels the fear again in the morning at breakfast when they hear the lion's roar and Macomber begins to ask their guide, Robert WILSON, questions about hunting lions: "where should I hit him? . . . What range will it be? . . . At under a hundred yards?" He's working up his fear, so that neither Macomber nor the reader should be surprised that he runs at the first confrontation. Macomber wounds the lion, but then, when Wilson tells him that they have to go into the tall grass to finish him off, Macomber loses his courage. He follows Wilson into the grass, but, when the lion finally lurches at them the narrator states that the "next thing he [Macomber] knew he was running . . . in panic . . . toward the stream."

Wilson kills the wounded lion, and Macomber's reputation as a coward is made—at least for that day. On the way to the location of the lion hunt, Wilson and Margot sat together on the back seat, but on the return to the camp, Macomber and Margot sit together, signifying Wilson's contempt for both of them. Margot reaches forward and puts "her hand on Wilson's shoulder" and kisses him "on the mouth," Margot showing contempt for her own husband, whom she now thinks of as something less than a man.

The narrator states that Macomber's "wife had been through with him before but it never lasted. He was very wealthy, and would be much wealthier, and he knew she would not leave him ever now." And as the narrator further states, the married couple "had a sound basis of union. Margot was too beautiful for Macomber to divorce her and Macomber had too much money for Margot ever to leave him."

He regains his courage the next day. When three old bull buffalo suddenly appear, Macomber has no time to think about fear, so he holds his ground when the buffalo attacks. Wilson thinks that he and Macomber have killed all three of the huge animals, but one is merely wounded and waiting in the bush. Macomber wants to "go in after him now," much to the surprise of Wilson, who knows it's prudent to wait at least a little while to allow the animal to get sick.

Meanwhile, Margot, who has seen the change take place in her husband is described as turning white and looking ill. The climax of the story comes as Macomber, described as feeling "a wild unreasonable happiness," says, "By God, that was a chase. . . . I've never felt any such feeling. Wasn't it marvellous, Margot?" And she says, "I hated it," setting up the ambiguous ending to the story.

When Margot sees the buffalo rushing at her husband, the narrator states that she "shot at the buffalo with the 6.5 Mannlicher as it seemed about to gore Macomber and . . . hit her husband about two inches up and a little to one side of the base of his skull." In spite of this clear narration critics argue over whether Margot deliberately shot Macomber. Others suggest that the shooting may have been precipitated by subconscious wish for his death.

Wilson, who had begun to like Macomber, calls it an accident but can't help getting in one final jab at Margot: "He *would* have left you too." But they are merely even, because Margot reminds Wilson that he had shot from a moving car, which is illegal.

"The Short Happy Life of Francis Macomber" was first published in *Cosmopolitan* (September 1936) and reprinted in *The Fifth Column and First Forty-nine Stories* (1938).

Short Happy Life of Francis Macomber (radio production) "NBC University Theater" produced the radio version of Hemingway's short story on November 21, 1948, and rebroadcast it on June 5, 1949. The radio script is by Ernest Canoy, and Preston Foster reads the role of Francis Macomber.

Short Happy Life, A (stage play) Adaptation from the short story, written in 1962 by A. E. Hotchner and produced in October 1961. Frank Corasra was director and Joe Mielziner the set designer.

"Shot, The" Article, published in *True* (April 1951), reprinted in *By-Line: Ernest Hemingway* (1967). About hunting for pronghorn antelope near Goldburg, Wyoming, with his friend Taylor Williams, a man Hemingway refers to as "the Old-timer," and his youngest son, "Gigi."

At the end of the article he writes of making "a very lucky shot" on an antelope with his .30-06: "I picked the biggest buck when they came streaming over the edge of the hump and swung ahead of him and squeezed gently and the bullet broke his neck."

shotgun Belonging to the father of the unnamed main character/narrator of "Now I Lay Me."

shotgun, 28-gauge In *Green Hills of Africa* it belongs to P.O.M., "Poor old Mama."

shotgun, sawed-off Carried by AL in "The Killers."

Sidney, Sylvia Movie actress, mentioned by Herbert SPELLMAN in *To Have and Have Not* as someone who should play a roll in the movie version of Richard GORDON's novel-in-progress.

Siegfried Line Zone of fortifications in western Germany, built before WORLD WAR II but in preparation for the war. Called the "Westwall," it was located along Germany's border opposite France, Luxembourg, and Belgium from Basel, Switzerland, at the south end to north of Aachen, Germany, a series of fortifications covering more than 240 miles of territory and sometimes as deep into Germany as 18 miles. It consisted of gun emplacements, "bunkers," for infantry machine guns, antitank guns, and artillery guns.

Each bunker was self-sufficient, containing underground headquarters and barracks, hospitals, storage rooms, and tunnels connecting the observation posts and gun emplacements with the main headquarters and barracks. The guns were fired either from heavy steel turrets or from ports in concealed concrete walls with roofs more than five feet thick. Barbed-wire entanglements and antitank obstacles covered the territory between bunkers throughout the length of the fortified zones.

Hemingway mentions the fortifications specifically in his article "War In the Siegfried Line" and by indirection in other works.

Sierra de Gredos Mountains in the same range as but west of the Guadarrama Mountains in Spain and considered a possible escape route after the bridge is blown up in *For Whom the Bell Tolls*.

Sierra de Guadarrama Mountain range north and northwest of Madrid and a few miles southeast of SEGOVIA, the setting in *For Whom the Bell Tolls*.

sifilus Spelling for syphilis, used by the ignorant main character in the letter she writes to a doctor in "One Reader Writes."

"Sights of Whitehead Street, The: A Key West Letter" Article, published in *Esquire* (April 1935), reprinted in *By-Line: Ernest Hemingway* (1967). The article tells what it's like to live in a house that is listed "as number eighteen in a compilation of the forty-eight things for a tourist to see in Key West," Florida. Especially if one is trying to write.

signallers, two In *The Fifth Column,* two men at the fascist observation post, operating telephones, sending signals to the artillery batteries.

Sikorsky amphibian Type of plane, one of the "old coffee mills," that takes Thomas HUDSON's three sons back to the mainland from BIMINI in *Islands in the Stream.*

Sile canal Seen by Richard CANTWELL as he and his driver, Jackson, notice a big red sail on a barge headed for Venice on their drive into Venice at the beginning of *Across the River and Into the Trees.*

"Silent, Ghastly Procession, A" Article, published in *The Toronto Daily Star* (October 20, 1922), reprinted in *The Wild Years* (1962), and in *By-Line: Ernest Hemingway* (1967). Datelined "Adrianople," this article is about the retreat of the Christian population of eastern Thrace toward Macedonia in 1922 during the war between Greece and Turkey. The *TDS* headline read "A Silent, Ghastly Procession Wends Way from Thrace."

silk-worms The main character/narrator of "Now I Lay Me" lies awake at night trying to avoid going to sleep, and he hears silkworms eating.

Silver Star U.S. Army bronze medal with a small silver star at the center, awarded to a soldier for gallantry in action but when the citation does not warrant the award of a Medal of Honor or the Distinguished Service Cross. Colonel Richard CANTWELL in *Across the River and Into the Trees* received this medal in World War I.

Silvretta The Silvretta is an Alpine range on the border between the Vorarlberg and the Tyrol mountain ranges in Austria and the Grisons in Switzerland. The Piz Buin at 11,040 feet is its highest peak on the Austrian side. It is where the narrator of "An Alpine Idyll" and his friend, John, have been spring skiing at the beginning of the short story.

Hemingway also refers to the Silvretta in *A Moveable Feast.*

Sim See Ralph SIMMONS.

S.I.M. *Servicio de Inteligencia Militar,* a military intelligence organization active during the SPANISH CIVIL WAR, looking for traitors and spies inside the military; mentioned in *For Whom the Bell Tolls.*

Simenon, Georges (1903–1989) Pseudonym of Joseph Chrétien, Belgian-French mystery novelist, famous for his detective Inspector Jules Maigret. In *A Moveable Feast* Hemingway writes that he enjoyed reading the

Simenon novels *L'Ecluse Numéro I* and *La Maison du Canal*, both of which had been recommended to him by Janet FLANNER.

Simmons, Charley   In "Soldier's Home," he is used by Harold KREB's mother as an example of someone Harold's age who is also, apparently, back from World War I and who has a job and is on his "way to being really a credit to the community."

Simmons, Mr.   "BEE-LIPS," the lawyer in *To Have and Have Not* who negotiates the terms for Harry MORGAN to illegally transport four Cubans to Cuba. He is later killed when the Cubans rob a KEY WEST bank.

Simmons, Ralph   "Sim," American opera singer in *A Farewell to Arms*, singing under the Italian name, Enrico DelCredo, at La Scala in Milan. When Frederic HENRY first meets him, during his convalescence in the summer after his wounding, the singer has just come from Piacenza, where he sang in *Tosca*. Frederic goes to him for help after his escape to Milan in the fall of the following year (1917) after the retreat from CAPORETTO.

Simmons, Walt   A friend of Scripps O'NEIL in *The Torrents of Spring* who says he once saw a horse "run over by a passing autobus in the place Vendôme in Paris."

"Simple Enquiry, A"   A short story involving homosexuality. The three characters are a major, an adjutant, and the major's orderly. The major turns some paperwork over to Tonani, the adjutant, and goes to his room to lie down for a rest. He tells Tonani that he wants to see PININ, the orderly. He asks the 19-year-old Pinin several questions about his relations with a girlfriend, especially if he loves her. Pinin, who may have lied about the girl, assures the major that he loves her. The major then makes the "simple enquiry": You "are quite sure. . . . that you are not corrupt?" Pinin says he doesn't understand "corrupt." The major goes on: "And you don't really want—. . . . That your great desire isn't really—." He also suggests that Pinin stay on as his adjutant, since he is less likely to get killed.

The major is "relieved" by Pinin's embarrassment, the major thinking, "life in the army was too complicated." The major reassures Pinin by telling him, "Don't be afraid. . . . I won't touch you." Pinin is "flushed" when he walks by the adjutant on his way out of the hut. At the end of the story, the major, still lying on his bunk, thinks, "The little devil . . . I wonder if he lied to me."

The story is an incident of war, perhaps suggesting the corrupting nature of war. But Paul Smith, in *A Reader's Guide to The Short Stories of Ernest Hemingway* (1989), also points out the story's irony. First, the "enquiry" of the story's title is not at all "simple." It is so complex, in fact, that, as Smith points out, the major can't even complete the sentences in his conversation with Pinin and feels "relieved" to be turned down. Second, the major wonders if Pinin invented the girl he tells the major he is in love with: "I wonder if he lied to me." Does Pinin realize how much the major's attraction for him makes him safer than he would be in the frontlines? And, as Smith points out, if Pinin does understand all of this, then which of the two is the more "corrupt"? An important question, because the answer helps determine the story's main character.

"A Simple Enquiry" was first published in *Men Without Women* (1927).

Simplon-Orient Express   Famous Orient Express train, which began operation in 1893, has four routes: the "Orient Express" from Paris to Constantinople via Strasbourg, Munich, and Vienna; the "Arlberg Orient Express" from Paris to Bucharest via Zurich, Salsburg, and Vienna; the "Ostend Orient Express" from Ostend to Linz, Austria, via Brussels and Frankfurt or to Warsaw via Brussels, Nuremberg, and Prague; and the "Simplon Orient Express" from Paris to Bucharest or Constantinople or Athens via Lausanne, Montreux, the Simplon Pass to Italy, Venice, and Trieste.

The "Simplon-Orient" is the train that each of the characters in the three parts of "Homage to Switzerland" is waiting to catch, each at a different station near the east end of Lake Geneva. The train is an hour late because of snow.

Sinclair, Upton (1878–1968)   American novelist and social critic, best known for *The Jungle* (1906). In *Green Hills of Africa* the Austrian hunter Kandisky, who wants to talk to Hemingway about American writers, asks him who he thinks is the "greatest writer in America. . . . Certainly not Upton Sinclair," he says, before Hemingway can answer. "Certainly not Sinclair Lewis."

Sinclair gas station   In *To Have and Have Not* Albert TRACY has been asked to pick up 150 gallons of gasoline for Harry MORGAN's boat at the Sinclair station in Key West.

"Sinclair Lewis's Horsebacking"   Article, published in *The Toronto Star Weekly* (August 5, 1922), reprinted in *Ernest Hemingway: Dateline Toronto* (1985). The headline in the *Star Weekly* was "Expecting Too Much in Old London Town." Datelined "Paris," this is a four-paragraph story "they are telling on Sinclair Lewis" about a recent trip he made to London.

Sing, Mr.   Chinese man in *To Have and Have Not*, "just about the smoothest-looking thing" Harry MORGAN had ever seen, who negotiates with Harry to transport 12 "chinks" illegally from Havana to Florida for "a hundred dollars apiece." Mr. Sing tells Harry that it doesn't matter where he takes them. He says they could be taken to the Tortugas, "where a schooner would pick them up." Harry, afraid of having been set up, kills Mr. Sing during the exchange of money and men and dumps his body overboard.

"Sing Something Simple" One of the "best tunes they had that winter" (early 1930s) that Mr. FRAZER hears on his radio in "The Gambler, the Nun, and the Radio."

"Singsong Girl" Considered by Mr. FRAZER in "The Gambler, the Nun, and the Radio" to be one of the "best tunes they had that winter," that is during one of the winters of the early 1930s.

Sion wine From any of several Rhône Valley vineyards near the Swiss town of Sion, about 24 miles south-southeast of Aigle. Sion is the capital of the Valais canton in southwestern Switzerland. The wines of the Valais include fresh, light dry whites made from the Chasselas grape, known locally as Fendant, and red wine known as Dôle, made from Pinot Noir and Gamay grapes.

It is served to Mr. Wheeler in part 1 of "Homage to Switzerland." It is also drunk by Nick ADAMS and GEORGE (4) in "Cross-Country Snow" and mentioned by Hemingway in *A Moveable Feast.*

Sioux American Indian tribe of the Dakotas, mentioned in *The Garden of Eden:* David BOURNE refers to "that thin-lipped bastard [U.S. President] Coolidge fishing for trout in a high stiff collar in a fish hatchery in the Black Hills we stole from the Sioux and Cheyenne."

Sisler, Dick (1920–1998) Major League baseball player (1946–53), who played all of his eight-year career with either the St. Louis Cardinals or the Philadelphia Phillies; mentioned along with "the great" DIMAGGIO and other players of the late 1930s and 1940s in *The Old Man and the Sea.* Sisler also played winter baseball in Cuba.

SANTIAGO remembers seeing Sisler, who used to come to his village near Havana to fish, and both he and Manolin regret not inviting him to fish with them. They refer to Dick Sisler as the "great" Sisler, although Dick's father, George, had a much more distinguished career, including election to the Baseball Hall of Fame in 1939. The reference to the Sislers helps determine Manolin's age.

Sisler, George (1893–1973) Major League baseball player (1915–30), who played the first 13 years of his 15-year career with the St. Louis Browns/Washington Senators. He also managed the Browns 1924–26. His lifetime batting average was .340, and he is in the Baseball Hall of Fame.

He is mentioned in *The Old Man and the Sea* only as the father of Dick Sisler, another Major League baseball player, not in the Hall of Fame but who gets more respect than his father from the novel's two main characters, SANTIAGO and MANOLIN. But the age of the boy can be determined by a reference he makes to the older Sisler.

sister (1) The second but unnamed sister of Harold KREBS, mentioned but not seen in "Soldier's Home." HELEN is the sister to whom Krebs pays attention.

sister (2) Of Ad FRANCIS, in "The Battler." She was his fight manager, until the newspaper discovered that they were getting married, "which made a lot of unpleasantness."

sisters, two older Of PACO (2) in "The Capital of the World." They are chambermaids at the Pension Luarca, where they and Paco live. They had gotten Paco his job as an apprentice waiter. One of the two sisters has to fight off the advances of one of the matadors staying at the pension. They are on their way home from a Greta GARBO movie as Paco lies dying on the floor of the pension's dining room after playing at bullfighting.

Sitting Bull The name of a friend of the bartender in the INDIAN CLUB in *The Torrents of Spring.*

"Situation Report, A" Article, published in *Look* magazine (September 4, 1956), reprinted in *By-Line: Ernest Hemingway* (1967). The title used in *Look* is "A Visit With Hemingway: A Situation Report." Datelined "Havana," the article is about his life in Cuba. He loves Cuba, but he's disturbed because most of the other places he loves—Wyoming, Montana, and Idaho—are overrun with tourists.

His "situation" seems not particularly happy. He is rereading *The Old Man and the Sea* in order to help with the film version, which he clearly hates; and he is interrupted regularly by autograph seekers and others who want him for nonprofessional reasons.

"Six Men Become Tankers" Article, unsigned, published in *The Kansas City Star* (April 17, 1918), reprinted in *Ernest Hemingway, Cub Reporter* (1970). It is about six men who enlist in the U.S. tank corps.

Sixth Parachute Division Mentioned in *Across the River and Into the Trees* in connection with Richard CANTWELL's memory of Allied attacks on German positions in World War II.

skates Horse track term for the horses in "My Old Man." Horses are also called "skins."

skiff (1)   SANTIAGO's fishing boat in *The Old Man and the Sea*. It is 16 feet long, with rope-lashed oars in thole pins and a mast for sailing that is "nearly as long as the one room of the shack" where he lived. The MARLIN (2) that Santiago catches is two feet longer than the skiff.

skiff (2)   From the turtle boat the Germans have stolen in the "At Sea" section of *Islands in the Stream*. When Thomas HUDSON and his crew find the turtle boat, the skiff is gone, presumably with the Germans on board. One German was left on the turtle boat, however, and he kills PETERS before being killed himself.

skinner   Minor character on the hunting safari in "The Short Happy Life of Francis Macomber." He is one of the natives who helps "skin" the animals the hunters have killed. He helps carry Francis MACOMBER back to camp "in triumph" after he has "killed" the lion.

skins   Horse track term for the horses in "My Old Man." Horses are also called "skates."

Skoda guns   Frederic HENRY identifies these artillery weapons as the ones firing on the Italian soldiers and Frederic's ambulance crew in the fighting of book 1 of *A Farewell to Arms*.

sleek-headed boy   The second waiter at the GRITTI PALACE HOTEL, in *Across the River and Into the Trees*, who brings the dinner to Richard CANTWELL and RENATA.

"Sling and the Pebble, The"   Article, published as the "Foreword" to the *Treasury of the Free World* (February 1946) and reprinted in the monthly journal *Free World* (March 1946). The editor of *Free World* states that the publication "is delighted to bring to its readers this outstanding liberal statement by one of America's most distinguished novelists."

The two-page article argues the value of educating both the winners and losers of WORLD WAR II. "We have come out of the time," Hemingway writes, "when obedience, the acceptance of discipline, intelligent courage and resolution were most important into that more difficult time when it is a man's duty to understand his world rather than simply fight for it."

Hemingway states, further: "We have invented the sling and pebble that will kill all giants; including ourselves. It is simple idiocy to think that the Soviet Union will not possess and perfect the same weapon."

Sloppy Joe's Bar   In Key West, Florida, at 428 Greene Street during most of the time Hemingway lived in Key West during the 1930s. The bar was owned by Joe ("Josie") Russell, one of Hemingway's friends and fish-

ing companions. It is the bar, according to legend, where Hemingway "invented" the rum drink "PAPA DOBLE."

Russell opened the bar at the 428 Greene Street location soon after Prohibition ended in 1933, and then moved it to its present location at the corner of Greene and Duval on May 5, 1937. Russell died in 1941. The bar at the old Greene Street address is now Captain Tony's Bar, still the oldest active bar in Florida. Hemingway met Martha Gellhorn at Sloppy Joe's in December 1936.

smacks   Fishing boats whose owners fish for mutton fish "on the rock bottom by the MORRO" outside of Havana in *To Have and Have Not*.

smistimento   Italian word for a casualty clearing station where wounded soldiers are sorted out before being sent to various hospitals for treatment; used in *A Farewell to Arms*.

Smith, Al (1873–1944)   U.S. politician, defeated by Herbert Hoover in the 1928 presidential election. His political handicap as a Catholic is discussed by Sam and Marie FONTAN and the narrator of "Wine of Wyoming." The Fontans, who are French, call him "Schmidt."

Smith, Bill (1895–1972)   Childhood friend of Hemingway's at Horton Bay, Michigan, who was an occasional visitor during Ernest's Paris years and a fishing companion. He and his sister, Katy, were from a St. Louis family that summered in northern Michigan. Bill accompanied Ernest and Hadley to Pamplona for fishing and the bullfights in 1925.

Smith, D. J.   Owner of the only restaurant in Hortons Bay, setting for "Up in Michigan." He goes on a deer hunting trip with Jim GILMORE and Charley Wyman.

Smith, Katy (1891–1947)   A friend, with her brother, Bill, of the Hemingway family during their summers at Horton Bay, Michigan. She was one of Hadley's attendants at her marriage to Ernest in 1921. She was also a roommate of Pauline Pfeiffer at the University of Missouri and on her side when Ernest divorced her in order to marry Martha Gellhorn. Katy married Hemingway's friend John DOS PASSOS in 1929.

Smith, General Walter Bedell (1895–1961)   U.S. Army general in World War II. According to Richard CANTWELL in *Across the River and Into the Trees*, General Smith had "explained" to Cantwell and other Allied division commanders how "easy" the taking of HÜRTGEN FOREST would be. But, according to Cantwell, the German High Command had "figured, exactly" where the main fighting after Aachen would take place and so were prepared.

In discussing the fighting with RENATA, Cantwell goes into detail about the bad judgment of General Smith in the placement of troops and in the general strategy of the battle. Cantwell later remembers that they lost three battalion commanders in the forest and that "good battalion commanders have never yet grown on trees; not even Christmas trees which was the basic tree of that woods."

Smith, Mrs. Runs D. J. Smith's restaurant in Hortons Bay, setting for "Up in Michigan." She's a "very large clean woman" and liked Liz COATES, who works for her, because she is the "neatest girl she'd ever seen."

Smith, Red (1905–1982) Walter Wellesley Smith, sports columnist for the New York *Herald Tribune*, mentioned in *Across the River and Into the Trees*. Richard CANTWELL reads his columns in the European edition of the *Herald Tribune* and "[likes] him very much."

Smith and Wesson In *For Whom the Bell Tolls* Robert JORDAN remembers that his grandfather owned a Smith & Wesson, a single action "officer's model .32 caliber" without a trigger guard, which he had used during the American Civil War. Jordan's father had committed suicide with the same gun, and, when the the gun was given to Jordan, he eventually threw it into a deep mountain lake on the Montana-Wyoming border.

The weapon is also referred to as a "thirty-eight special" by Harry MORGAN in *To Have and Have Not* and carried on his charter fishing boat. He also carries a Thompson submachine gun, a pump-gun, and a Winchester 30-30. The Smith and Wesson .38 is also mentioned near the end of the novel as one of the methods, along with jumping out the windows of tall buildings, that the "Haves" use to commit suicide in their unhappiness.

Smyrna In "A Natural History of the Dead," the Greek city is one of the places where the narrator observed death, in this case the death of baggage animals whose legs were broken by Greek soldiers, who then pushed them off into the water to drown.

"Snows of Kilimanjaro, The" Main character in this short story is a writer named HARRY, who, with his wife, HELEN (3), is on a hunting safari in East Africa when he fails to disinfect properly a scratch on his leg and dies from the gangrene that sets in.

While they are waiting for a plane from Nairobi, Kenya, that will fly Harry out to a hospital, he spends his time—most of one day and that night—either verbally abusing Helen or thinking about some experiences he has had which he has saved to write about but which he now knows he will never complete. As he says to Helen, "We quarrel and that makes the time pass."

But he's the one doing all the quarreling. Helen tries to make him as comfortable as possible, offering to read to him and supervising the food and drink prepared by the African "boys" on the safari with them.

They had gone to Africa, "where he had been happiest in the good time of his life" in order to "work the fat off his soul." But as he acknowledges, he "had destroyed his talent by not using it . . . by drinking so much that he blunted the edge of his perceptions" and by a "catalogue" of other things that always interfere with a writer's work. The experiences he has saved to write about are presented in the form of five FLASH-BACKS to better times in Harry's life.

The first flashback begins in the railway station in Karagatch in 1922, where he is waiting for the Simplon-Orient Express to take him out of Thrace following the retreat of the Greeks during the Greek-Turkish war. He also remembers times in western Austria, where he and his first wife rented houses during the winter; and he remembers a World War I pilot who had bombed an Austrian officers' leave train and bragged about machine-gunning the officers as they ran from the train. Each of the experiences he remembers are ones he thought would make good stories, but now he knows he will never get the chance to write about them.

The second flashback begins in CONSTANTINOPLE (the name was changed to Istanbul in 1930, which helps to place the time of the story in the mid to late 1920s). He remembers the city well, because he "whored the whole time," trying to forget that his first wife, whom he still loves, had just left him. He also remembers that when he got back to Paris he saw an American poet with a "pile of saucers in front of him . . . talking about the Dada movement with a Roumanian who said his name was Tristan TZARA." And he remembers that a letter had come to his apartment from a woman and that his wife asked, "Who is the letter from, dear?" and, as Harry remembers it, "that was the end of the beginning of that," implying the breakup of his marriage.

The third flashback begins with the log house his grandfather owned, which burned to the ground and destroyed all of his grandfather's guns. And he remembers that after the war (World War I) "we" rented a trout stream in the Black Forest (in southwest Germany) and that the proprietor of the hotel in Triberg, a little town on the Brigach River, had a fine season. And he remembers the place Contrescarpe in Paris and the whores at the BAL MUSETTE, which he and his first wife lived above just after the war. And he remembers Marie, a neighbor, protesting shortening the work day to eight hours, saying, "If a husband works until six he gets only a little drunk on the way home and does not waste too much. If he works only until five he is drunk every night and one has no money. It is the wife of the working man who suffers from this shortening of hours."

The short fourth flashback begins with Harry thinking that he had never written about Paris: "Not the Paris that he cared about."

The fifth flashback begins with a bombing officer named Williamson whom Harry had known in the war. He had been hit by a "stick bomb" as he was coming through some wire and, screaming, he "had begged every one to kill him." Harry remembers that earlier he and Williamson had argued about "our Lord never sending you anything you could not bear and some one's theory had been that . . . at a certain time the pain passed you out automatically." But Harry remembers how much suffering Williamson had been through, without passing out.

This memory corresponds to his statement to Helen in the story's opening sentence: "The marvellous thing is that it's painless" (the gangrene). Throughout "The Snows of Kilimanjaro," impending death is represented for Harry by various things that pass across his mind: a puff of wind, the wheels of a bicycle, birds circling, or a hyena making a noise. He feels death "come by" more and more until, finally, it sits on the edge of his bed and then on his chest. And then the weight lifts from his chest and he dies.

The narrator then describes a dream that Harry had just before he died, a dream in which his pilot friend Compton arrives in the morning, and there is room for only one passenger on the plane. It takes off, but instead of going toward ARUSHA, where Compton had said they would refuel, the plane turns "left" and flies toward the "square top of Kilimanjaro." At the end of the story, Helen is also dreaming—of her house on Long Island in an earlier marriage—but the noise the hyena makes wakes her, and she sees that Harry has died.

Hemingway wrote an epigraph to the story, which explains that the Masai people of the highlands around Kilimanjaro think of the mountain as the "House of God." The epigraph states that "Close to the western summit there is the dried and frozen carcass of a leopard. No one has explained what the leopard was seeking at that altitude." Kilimanjaro represents an ideal for the writer but Harry has wasted his talent and so will never fulfill his "dream."

"The Snows of Kilimanjaro" was first published in *Esquire* (August 1936) and reprinted in *The Fifth Column and the First Forty-nine Stories* (1938).

"Snows of Kilimanjaro, The" (dramatic reading) Adaptation of the short story, written by A. E. HOTCHNER in 1955, but not performed; the script is at the Alderman Library, University of Virginia.

Snows of Kilimanjaro, The **(film)** Twentieth Century-Fox picture, released in September 1952 (117 minutes); produced by Darryl F. Zanuck, directed by Henry King, screenplay by Casey Robinson, music by Bernard Herrmann, art direction by Lyle Wheeler and John De Cuir, set decorations by Thomas Little and Paul S. Fox, special effects by Ray Kellogg. Gregory Peck and Susan Hayward played the leads; Ava Gardner had a minor role. Hemingway was paid $125,000 for the rights to this film, the most ever paid to that time by Hollywood for a novel. The film received a nomination for an Academy Award for production design.

Snows of Kilimanjaro, The **(television play)** Adaptation from the short story, written by A. E. HOTCHNER and produced for the CBS "Buick Electra Playhouse" in the fall 1959 and spring 1960.

sobrepuertos Area of seats "with wooden backs, halfway up the amphitheatre" of a bull ring. Jake BARNES buys three tickets in this section, for the first day of the bullfights in PAMPLONA, in case there are those among his friends who might be concerned about the blood. He also buys three BARRERAS (front row) seats.

Soissons City in northern France, on the Aisne River, which marked the Allied frontlines during much of World War I, one of the places mentioned in "Soldier's Home," where Harold KREBS fought with the U.S. Marines in 1918.

soldier (1) Italian minor character in *A Farewell to Arms* who has deliberately wounded himself in order to get out of the fighting. Frederic HENRY, driving an ambulance down out of the mountains toward GORIZIA in northern Italy, sees him along the road. Frederic has a load of wounded but promises to come back for him; but when he returns, the "hernia man" has been picked up by his own brigade.

soldier (2) In *A Farewell to Arms* a Swiss soldier who stands guard over the boat Frederic HENRY and Catherine BARKLEY have rowed to BRISSAGO.

soldier (3) In "A Clean, Well-Lighted Place," he has picked up a "girl," probably a prostitute, and they are noticed by the waiters as they walk by the café.

soldiers, Negro In "A Canary for One," they are seen by the story's narrator waiting on the station platform in Avignon, France. They are led by a "short white sergeant."

soldiers, two (1) In the "Chapter 5" vignette of *In Our Time*, they carry one of the six cabinet ministers who is sick out of the hospital into the rain for his execution with the other five.

soldiers, two (2) In *A Farewell to Arms* they are drunk in the bar where Frederic HENRY stops for a glass of wine after he gets off the train in Milan, following his escape from the Italian BATTLE POLICE in the retreat from CAPORETTO.

"Soldier's Home" This short story is about Harold KREBS, who returns from WORLD WAR I in the summer of 1919 to an Oklahoma hometown no longer interested in returning servicemen. The people had held parades for the first group of soldiers returning from the war, but Krebs came back with the second division of marines from the Rhine River, and, by that time, the people had lost interest in parades.

Krebs had fought at BELLEAU WOOD, SOISSONS, the CHAMPAGNE, SAINT-MIHIEL, and in the ARGONNE FOREST, all important battles in the war, involving serious American losses. Fighting in any one of those battles would be enough to traumatize a young U.S. Marine, but he had fought in all five. He didn't want to talk about the war at first, and, later, when he wanted to talk about it, nobody wanted to listen. Or he had to lie to get attention, and the lying spoiled the memories.

The impact of the war on Krebs is understated in the story (see THEORY OF OMISSION), but it is clear that his lethargy—perhaps even depression—is the result of his experiences in the war. The story's narrator only names the five battles in which Krebs fought, without stating anything about the importance of each, or how heroic were the U.S. Marines who fought in them, or that Krebs, having survived, is no doubt traumatized by memories of those battles.

He lives with his religious fundamentalist parents, who treat him as they did when he was a young teenager before the war. His mother, for example, tells him that his father has agreed to allow him to use the car "in the evenings." His mother keeps after him to get a job: "Have you decided what you are going to do yet, Harold? . . . There can be no idle hands in His Kingdom." She tells him that his father thinks he has lost his "ambition." He tries to ignore her concerns, and when she says, "Don't you love your mother, dear boy?" he says, "No." When she starts crying, he tells her that he doesn't love anybody. He apologizes for saying he doesn't love her, and she asks him to kneel in prayer with her. After she prays for him, he kisses her and leaves the house. His sister HELEN (1) is the only one who treats him with respect. She wants him to see her pitch INDOOR BASEBALL.

The trauma of what must have been horrifying war experiences, coupled with the treatment he receives upon his return home, particularly from his parents but also from the town's citizens, allows the reader to infer far greater complications than Krebs is aware of. At the end of the story, however, he decides to go to Kansas City to get a job, and, before he leaves, he goes to watch Helen play indoor baseball.

"Soldier's Home" was first published in the *Contact Collection of Contemporary Writers* (1925) and reprinted in *In Our Time* (1925).

Soldier's Home **(television play)** Robert Geller's adaptation of Hemingway's short story was one of the PBS series "The American Short Story" in 1977.

solitaire ambulante See DOUBLE CANFIELD.

Sollinger clasp knife In *Across the River and Into the Trees,* it is the knife Richard CANTWELL uses to complete the "monument" to his wounding. See FOSSALTA.

Sologne Large region south of Paris, where Hemingway hunted in the 1920s and which he recalls in *Green Hills of Africa*. The area is just south of Orleans, bordered on the north by the Loire valley, on the south by the Cher valley, and on the east by the hills of the Sancerrois. A flat region, it is covered with moors, forests, and ponds, perfect for pheasants and rabbits.

Somali proverb Quoted by the narrator of "The Short Happy Life of Francis Macomber." A "brave man is always frightened three times by a lion; when he first sees his track, when he first hears him roar and when he first confronts him."

Sombrero Lighthouse on KEY WEST that shines on the COAST GUARD cutter and Harry MORGAN's boat as they approach the NAVY YARD near the end of *To Have and Have Not*.

"[Some day when you are picked up . . .]" First line of a poem written in 1924 and first published in *88 Poems* (1979).

"Some Space Filled by Ernest MacNamara Hemingway" Article for Oak Park and River Forest High School newspaper, *The Trapeze* (May 11, 1917), reprinted in *Hemingway at Oak Park High: The High School Writings of Ernest Hemingway, 1916–1917* (1993).

Somme, Battle of the The Somme is a river in northern France, mentioned in *A Farewell to Arms* as the site of Catherine BARKLEY's fiancé's death in the war. Historically there were two battles of the Somme, the first fought from June 24 to November 13, 1916, and the second from March 21 to April 5, 1918. Since most of the novel takes place during 1916 and 1917, Catherine's fiancé was no doubt killed in the first battle. The dating is significant because it means that Catherine is just getting over the shock of his death when she meets Frederic HENRY in the late summer or early fall of that year (1916).

son   Unnamed son of Nick ADAMS in "Fathers and Sons." He is nine or 10 years old and asleep for most of the story, riding on the front seat of his father's car while Nick drives toward an unnamed destination. When the boy wakes, however, he asks his father what it was like when he was a little boy and what the Indians were like.

Nick doesn't tell him about making love to Trudy, his Ojibway girlfriend, whom he has just been thinking about, but he does tell him about the boy's grandfather, especially what a good hunter and fisherman he was and that "he had wonderful eyes." The boy wants to pray at the tomb of his grandfather, and, at the end of the story, Nick says to his son, "We'll have to go [to the grave site]. . . . I can see we'll have to go."

Sons and Lovers   D. H. LAWRENCE novel (1913), mentioned in *A Moveable Feast*. Hemingway says that Lawrence is "pathetic and preposterous," but he liked *Sons and Lovers* and *The White Peacock*.

"So This Is Chicago"   Article, published in *The Toronto Star Weekly* (January 19, 1924), reprinted in *Ernest Hemingway: Dateline Toronto* (1985). It includes 11 short paragraphs of minor events in Chicago and is one of three articles printed after Hemingway had gone off the *Star*'s payroll on December 31, 1923.

soto-tenente   Italian term for second-lieutenant (spelled *sottotenente*). It is used in *A Farewell to Arms* as part of a joke against Frederic HENRY, who is being kidded by fellow officers and in front of THE PRIEST about going on leave and finding too many women. The captain holds up his hand and says, starting with the thumb, "soto-tenente (the thumb), tenente (first finger), capitano (next finger), maggiore (next to the little finger). You go away soto-tenente! You come back soto-colonello." He goes on leave fat but comes back thin, wasted.

"Soul of Spain with McAlmon and Bird the Publishers, The"   Poem written in 1923 and first published in *Der Querschnitt* (Autumn 1924).

"Soul of Spain with McAlmon and Bird the Publishers, The" (Part Two)   Poem written in 1923 and first published in *Der Querschnitt* (Autumn 1924).

Southern Cross, The   Popular name of "Crux," a constellation of stars in the Southern Hemisphere consisting of four bright stars that appear to form a Latin cross. In *Green Hills of Africa* Hemingway states that each morning on safari he stood at the latrine, in the dark, and "observed the Southern Cross in solemn ceremony."

South Island   Larger of the two main Bimini islands, located about 80 miles east of Miami. The North Bimini Island is the setting for part 1 of *Islands in the Stream*.

Sovora mustard   In *The Garden of Eden,* eaten by David BOURNE with stuffed eggs and roast chicken and later with *oeufs au plat avec jambon* (ham and eggs).

spaghetti   In "Big Two-Hearted River," NICK makes his first evening's meal of pork and beans and a can of spaghetti, cooked over an open fire in a frying pan.

Spagnolini   Italian soldier, who made Nick ADAMS's World War I military uniform in "A Way You'll Never Be." The uniform is supposed to make Nick look like an American soldier in order to encourage the Italian soldiers he is with to think that the United States is about to enter the war.

Spalding, Albert (1888–1953)   American violinist, born in Chicago, mentioned by Scripps O'NEIL in *The Torrents of Spring*. It's one of the few times in this parody that O'Neil, or any other character, connects correctly a famous name with that person's occupation.

Spanish civil war   The 1936 election victory in Spain of the Popular Front—made up of liberals, socialists, and COMMUNISTS—promised the Spanish people a renewal of leftist reforms. The war began in mid-July 1936, as Generalissimo Francisco FRANCO led a revolt from Morocco against these reforms, and right-wing groups also rebelled in Spain, the officers leading most of the Spanish army into the revolutionary—that is, "NATIONALIST" or REBEL—camp.

By November 1936, four columns of experienced Rebel troops had besieged Madrid. The Rebels claimed that in addition to these four columns a "FIFTH COLUMN" within the city of Madrid was working to hasten the city's fall. While the REPUBLICAN government of Largo Caballero struggled to organize an effective defense of Madrid, the first INTERNATIONAL BRIGADES helped the LOYALISTS to hold the capital city.

Foreign intervention, in fact, played a large part in the war. From the beginning, Italy and Germany aided Franco with airplanes and tanks; Italy also supplied about 50,000 soldiers, Germany 10,000. American and British volunteers, as well as volunteers from many other countries, fought on the side of the Republic. Twenty-seven nations, including Great Britain, France, Italy, Germany, and the USSR, signed a nonintervention pact in August 1936, but the latter three nations failed to comply. The Spanish republic, therefore, became dependent for supplies on the Soviet Union, which used military aid to achieve its own political goals, including the infiltration of Loyalist brigades by communist soldiers, which, because of their incompetence, ultimately led to inefficiency at all levels of command.

Franco had difficulty with some extremists—mainly with the FALANGE, a FASCIST political organization—but was able to control it and even to consolidate his position. Gradually the Rebels wore down Republican strength. Bilbao, the last Republican center in the north, fell in June 1937; Franco cut the country in two during attacks from March to June 1938; Barcelona fell in January 1939. With the loss of the region of Catalonia the Republican cause became hopeless, and on March 27, 1939, Franco led his victorious army into Madrid.

For Italy and Germany the war served as a testing ground for military techniques used in World War II; for European democracies it was another step on the road to appeasement; for politically conscious youth, who joined the International Brigades, it was the idealistic cause of the 1930s, for which many gave their lives.

Hemingway went to Spain as a journalist three times during the war, first in the spring 1937 (March–May), then in the fall of that year (September–December), and again in the spring 1938 (March–May). He wrote 31 dispatches for NANA (North American Newspaper Alliance) during the three trips. He returned briefly in November 1938 to say good-bye to his civil war comrades. See NANA.

Besides reporting on the war for NANA, Hemingway also wrote a novel (*For Whom the Bell Tolls*), a play (*The Fifth Column*), and eight short stories ("The Chauffeurs of Madrid" [see NANA Dispatch number 12], "The Old Man at the Bridge," "The Denunciation," "The Butterfly and the Tank," "Night Before Battle," "Landscape With Figures," "Nobody Ever Dies," and "Under the Ridge"), all drawn from his experiences while in Spain during the Spanish civil war. See NANA DISPATCHES.

Spanish Earth, The This book is the transcript of Hemingway's narration for the soundtrack of the film *The Spanish Earth*. There is an "Introduction" by the publisher, Jasper Wood, and Hemingway dedicated it "To all the friends of Loyalist Spain."

The book was published in Cleveland by The J.B. Savage Company on June 15, 1938, in a limited edition of 1,000 numbered copies at $3.50 each.

Spanish Earth, The (film) Contemporary Historians documentary (54 minutes), released July 5, 1937; produced and directed by Joris Ivens, screenplay by Archibald MacLeish, John Dos Passos, and Lillian Hellman, photography by Joris Ivens and John Ferno, music compiled by Virgil Thompson and Marc Blitzstein, commentary written and spoken by Ernest Hemingway.

Actor Orson Welles was asked to narrate the film but withdrew, and Ivens suggested that Hemingway read his own commentary. It's Hemingway, voice on the film's soundtrack, but the opening credits on some copies of the film still list Orson Welles as the narrator. Jean Renoir did the voice-over for the French version.

Hemingway c. 1937 (Copyright holder unknown; photo courtesy of the John F. Kennedy Library)

Spanish-English Method book Language book, owned by Catherine BOURNE in *The Garden of Eden*.

Spanish Portraits Title of a pamphlet of short essays by various writers on the Spanish civil war, edited by the artist Jo Davidson. It includes Hemingway's three-paragraph tribute to Milton Wolff, commander in the INTERNATIONAL BRIGADES and one of its heroes. There are 10 essays in the pamphlet, including Vincent Sheean's tribute to "PASIONARIA" (Dolores Ibarruri) and a tribute by Dorothy Parker to Jo Davidson, the editor-artist. Davidson sculpted bronze busts of each of the pamphlet's 10 subjects, which are pictured next to the essay.

"Sparrow Hat On Paris Boulevards" Article, published in *The Toronto Star Weekly* (March 18, 1922), reprinted in *The Wild Years* (1962), reprinted in *Ernest Hemingway: Dateline Toronto* (1985). The headline in the *Star Weekly* was "Sparrow Hat Appears On Paris Boulevards." Datelined "Paris," this three-paragraph story is about Parisian milliners, who are selling new hats, a "brown, mushroom-shaped affair with a girdle of stuffed English sparrows."

Specialty of Domestic and Foreign Wines shop   When PEDUZZI (1) wants to buy wine at this shop in "Out of Season," he discovers that it's closed until two o'clock.

Speiser, Maurice   Hemingway's first lawyer and agent, from the late 1920s until Speiser's death in 1948.

Spellman, Herbert   A wealthy "tall, very thin young man," from Brooklyn, referred to as "Harold" by his companion/caretaker in *To Have and Have Not*. Richard GORDON meets Spellman at the LILAC TIME BAR. Spellman says he is an admirer of Gordon's books and tells him they had met once at a party at "Margaret Van Brunt's." The bar's proprietor indicates to Gordon that Spellman is crazy; that's why he needs the caretaker.

Spezia   Town in northern Italy, on the Mediterranean coast about 48 miles southeast of Genoa, where the narrator of "Che Ti Dice la Patria?" (What do you hear from home?) and his traveling friend, Guy, have lunch and are harassed by a waitress/prostitute, who keeps putting her arms around Guy and trying to get him to go with her.

Spitfires   Type of World War II British fighter plane in which young Tom HUDSON is killed over Belgium in *Islands in the Stream*. The plane was considered both fast and maneuverable, a single-seater with eight machine guns.

"Sport of Kings, The"   Article, a vignette, maybe a poem, published in *The Toronto Star Weekly* (November 24, 1923), reprinted in *Ernest Hemingway: Dateline Toronto* (1985), and in *88 Poems* (1979). Bylined "Hem," it is about betting on a sure-thing horse race and losing. It contains 16 lines, each beginning with "The." For example: "The friend who calls up over the telephone./ The horse that has been especially wired from Pimlico."

"Sporting Mayor"   Article, published in *The Toronto Star Weekly* (March 13, 1920), reprinted in *The Wild Years* (1962), reprinted in *Ernest Hemingway: Dateline Toronto* (1985). The headline in the *Star Weekly* was "Sporting Mayor at Boxing Bouts." The article is about attending boxing matches at Massey Hall with a distracted Toronto mayor.

Sportsman   Champagne, ordered by Mr. JOHNSON in part 2 of "Homage to Switzerland."

Sportsman   Name of a horse racing publication, bought by JOE for his "old man" in "My Old Man."

Sportsman's Sketches, A   Collection of short stories by the Russian writer Ivan Turgenev, published in 1852. In *A Moveable Feast* Hemingway writes that *A Sportsman's Sketches* (in two volumes) was the first work he borrowed from Sylvia BEACH at her American bookshop in Paris, SHAKESPEARE AND COMPANY (1), and that he began to read it in Lyon during a bizarre trip with F. Scott Fitzgerald.

Springfield   One of the rifles used by Hemingway on the one-month safari described in *Green Hills of Africa*. Although not otherwise identified, it is probably the bolt-operated, magazine-fed, .30-caliber rifle used by the U.S. Army during World War I. In *Green Hills* Hemingway's Springfield fires a "220-grain solid bullet."

Francis MACOMBER's gunbearer carries Macomber's Springfield as they leave on the lion hunt the morning he runs from a lion in "The Short Happy Life of Francis Macomber."

Spur   Popular magazine of the 1920s, which, in "The Snows of Kilimanjaro," carried advertisements with HELEN's picture in them. See also *TOWN AND COUNTRY*.

spur fowl   African bird, a type of francolin, which is an African or Eurasian partridge with sharply spurred legs. In *The Garden of Eden* David BOURNE refers to spur fowl in the AFRICAN STORY he is writing: "David had killed two spur fowl with his slingshot out of a small flock that had walked across the trail just before the sunset."

Stade Buffalo   Outdoor arena near Paris where Hemingway saw bicycle racing in the Vélodrome Buffalo stadium, housed inside the large arena. Stade Buffalo was located in Montrouge, France, a southern suburb of Paris. In *A Moveable Feast* Hemingway describes the outdoor stadium "where they [the bicylists] raced behind big motorcycles."

Staib, John   Wyoming friend of Hemingway, mentioned in *Green Hills of Africa*. He thinks Staib would be interested in seeing DROOPY's "trick" of slitting open the stomach of a waterbuck, turning it inside out, and using it as a carrying sack. Hemingway thinks Staib would say, "By Godd, Urnust, dot's smardt."

Stalin, Joseph (1879–1953)   Ruthless Soviet dictator. Active in the revolutionary movement in the late 1890s, Stalin sided with the Bolsheviks and in 1912 went to St. Petersburg as a member of the Central Committee. He was made general secretary of the Communist Party's Central Committee in 1922, and by 1927 he was in command of the Communist Party and the government of the Soviet Union. Stalin's collectivization of the country's farms resulted in mass famine, and the purging of all who were suspected of opposing him resulted in a blood bath that took the lives of millions.

The Soviet Union supported the Spanish Loyalists during the SPANISH CIVIL WAR (1936–39), in opposition to Italy and Germany, the two fascist nations that helped Generalissimo Francisco FRANCO establish his government in Spain.

In *To Have and Have Not* EMILIO, one of the four Cuban bank robbers who have forced HARRY to take them from Key West to Cuba, explains the revolution going on in Cuba. "We want to do away with all the old politicians," Emilio tells Harry, "with all the American imperialism that strangles us, with the tyranny of the army. We want to start clean and give every man a chance. . . . We just raise money now for the fight. . . . To do that we have to use means that later we would never use. . . . But the end is worth the means. They had to do the same thing in Russia. Stalin was a sort of brigand for many years before the revolution."

"Stambouliski of Bulgaria"   Article, published in *The Toronto Daily Star* (April 25, 1922), reprinted in *Ernest Hemingway: Dateline Toronto* (1985). The headline in the *Daily Star* was "Strongest Premier at Parley Is Stambouliski of Bulgaria." In the article, datelined "Genoa," Hemingway provides a biographical sketch of Aleksandr Stambouliski, prime minister of Bulgaria and leader of his country's "agrarian, or Farmers', party." He had fought to keep Bulgaria out of the Balkan wars, and Hemingway sees him as the "strongest premier in Europe—bar none."

Standard Oil dock   One of the Havana docks in *To Have and Have Not* where Harry MORGAN fills his charter boat's gas tanks.

Stanley, Arthur Penrhyn (1815–1881)   Bishop of Norwich, England, an ornithologist, mentioned in "A Natural History of the Dead" as someone interested in natural history. The narrator says that "Bishop Stanley has given us a valuable, although popular, *Familiar History of Birds*."

Star gun   There are two types of Star pistols, a "Star Model A" and a "Super Star Model B" (slightly longer), both of which take a 9 mm Largo bullet. In *For Whom the Bell Tolls*, as Andrés tries to get to General Golz with Robert JORDAN's message about the Rebel counteroffensive, one of the guards near Golz's headquarters, Gómez, carries a Star gun and threatens a subordinate with it. Also, El Sordo uses a Star gun when he shoots six times into the air in order to make the Rebels think he has killed his men and himself.

"Starvers Out of Sight"   Article, published in *The Toronto Daily Star* (May 9, 1923), reprinted in *The Wild Years* (1962), reprinted in *Ernest Hemingway: Dateline Toronto* (1985). The headline in the *Daily Star* was "Amateur Starvers Keep Out of View in Germany." Datelined "Cologne," this was the eighth of 10 articles Hemingway wrote for the *Daily Star* about the French-German situation in 1923, five years after the end of World War I.

Hemingway writes that the tourist, with an itinerary by "the Messrs. Cook" (a British travel agent) sees no suffering in Europe. But for "every ten professional beggars in Italy there are a hundred amateur starvers in Germany. An amateur starver does not starve in public." They are usually suffering in bed, and that's why no one ever sees them. And he "appends" five examples of "amateur starvers."

station   In "The Light of the World," the train station where the story's narrator and his friend TOM (1) go for drinks after being thrown out of another bar. They meet the five whores at the station.

Stearns, Harold Edmund (1891–1943)   American journalist, best known for his books *Liberalism in America* (1919) and *America and the Young Intellectual* (1921). After graduating from Harvard in 1913, he wrote book and drama reviews for a number of publications, including the *New York Press*, the *Chicago Sun*, and *The Bookman*.

He spent most of the 1920s in Paris, as a columnist for *Town and Country*, a talent scout for the U.S. publisher Horace Liveright, as a stringer for several American newspapers, and, from 1925–29, as the writer of a horse-racing column for the Paris edition of *The Chicago Tribune*. He became a heavy drinker in Paris and was recognized as a regular part of the Left Bank café scene. Stearns is generally considered to be the prototype of the Harvey Stone character in *The Sun Also Rises*.

In *A Moveable Feast* Hemingway remembers seeing Stearns at the Café Select and trying to avoid him because he wanted to stop betting on horse races at the time, and he knew Stearns would talk about horses.

steeplechase races   Horse race over a turf course with hurdles and other obstacles over which the horses must jump. The name originates from the first recorded race, a four and one-half mile race in Ireland from Buttevant Church to St. Leger Church—from steeple to steeple. The race is often referred to as a point-to-point race.

When Hemingway was in Paris during the 1920s, he could see steeplechase races at AUTEUIL, ENGHIEN, VINCENNES, and MAISONS-LAFFITTE. The "flat race" courses were at LONGCHAMPS (1), CHANTILLY, Maisons-Laffitte, SAINT-CLOUD, TREMBLAY, and COMPIÈGNE.

Steffens, Lincoln (1866–1936)   American journalist, one of several writers Theodore Roosevelt referred to as "muckrakers." In *A Moveable Feast* Hemingway remembers that one of the two stories he had left after the theft of Hadley's SUITCASE (which contained all the other manuscripts) was "My Old Man," which Steffens had sent to *Cosmopolitan* magazine on Hemingway's behalf and, rejected by the editors, was on its way back to Hemingway in Paris.

Stein, Gertrude (1874–1946) American avant-garde writer, whose Paris apartment at 27, rue de Fleurus was a salon for the leading writers and artists of the period between the two world wars. She was a major influence on a number of writers, including Hemingway.

Her published works include: *Three Lives* (1909), *Tender Buttons* (1914), *The Making of Americans* (1925), *The Autobiography of Alice B. Toklas* (1933), *Wars I Have Seen* (1945), and two operas with Virgil Thompson's musical scores, *Four Saints in Three Acts* (1934) and *The Mother of Us All* (1947), an opera about Susan B. Anthony.

Hemingway was a frequent visitor to her apartment during the early 1920s while he lived in Paris, and he quotes her as part of his epigraph for *The Sun also Rises:* "You are all a lost generation." (See LOST GENERATION). She was a legend in Paris during World War II, because she stayed in the city during the German occupation and because she befriended U.S. servicemen who visited her after the Americans took over the French capital.

Hemingway writes about her in *A Moveable Feast,* usually in unflattering terms. His first mention of her, however, in the book's second section, titled "Miss Stein Instructs," is not unflattering: "Miss Stein was very big but not tall and was heavily built like a peasant woman. She had beautiful eyes and a strong German-Jewish face . . . and she reminded me of a northern Italian peasant woman. . . . She talked all the time and at first it was about people and places."

He writes that she informed him that his short story "Up in Michigan" was "*inaccrochable*" (unpublishable). Although they did not discuss the details, she felt he could not publish a story about a drunken seduction/rape of the main character.

In section 13 of *A Moveable Feast,* "A Strange Enough Ending," Hemingway explains how their relationship came to an end. It had to do with Hemingway failing to go by Stein's apartment in time to say good-bye to her and Alice B. TOKLAS before they left on a trip to the south of France. Part of his "failure" was the result, however, of overhearing that morning Toklas making nasty remarks about Stein to her in their upstairs bedroom and Stein begging her to stop. The overheard conversation added to Hemingway's disgust at their lesbian relationship. He left the apartment and could not quite get himself to return, even to say good-bye.

Yogi JOHNSON thinks about Stein near the end of *The Torrents of Spring,* and Hemingway imitates her writing style in describing Johnson's thoughts: "Ah, there was a woman! Where were her experiments in words leading her? What was at the bottom of it? All that in Paris. Ah, Paris. How far it was to Paris now." Etcetera, etcetera—part of Hemingway's parody in *Torrents.*

Hemingway also refers to Stein on the first page of *Death in the Afternoon* as having spoken "of her admiration for Joselito." She had some photographs of him in the ring and of herself and Alice Toklas in the first row at the bull ring in Valencia.

She and Alice B. Toklas were godmothers for Hemingway's oldest son, Jack, baptized in Paris March 16, 1924.

Steinfelt, Happy One of Jack Brennan's "friends" in "Fifty Grand." He is with Brennan's manager, John Collins, when he talks to Brennan about throwing a fight. He and Lew Morgan own a poolroom, and the two are considered to be "sharpshooters" by Danny Hogan.

Stendhal (1783–1842) Pseudonym of Marie-Henri Beyle, French novelist, best known for his novels *Le Rouge et le noir* (*The Red and the Black,* 1830) and *La Chartreuse de Parme* (*The Charterhouse of Parma,* 1839). Hemingway says in *Death in the Afternoon* that Stendhal and Goya were alike in that "the sight of a priest could stimulate either of those good anticlericals into a rage of production."

In discussing writing in *Green Hills of Africa* Hemingway says that "Stendhal had seen a war and Napoleon taught him to write." See also TOLSTOI.

And in *A Moveable Feast* Hemingway writes about his first reading of *Chartreuse de Parme,* that Stendhal's account of the battle of Waterloo was "wonderful . . . an accidental piece in a book that had much dullness."

step-father In *A Farewell to Arms* Catherine BARKLEY asks Frederic HENRY about his father, and he tells her he has a step-father.

"Stevenson" Poem written about 1922 and first published in *88 Poems* (1979). It is in the style of Robert Louis Stevenson.

Stockalper River in Switzerland that empties into Lake Geneva near AIGLE at the lake's eastern end. It is mentioned in both *Green Hills of Africa* and *A Moveable Feast* in connection with the town of Aigle.

"Stoker, The" Poem written, according to Peter Griffin, in 1916, and first published in Griffin's biography, *Along With Youth: Hemingway, The Early Years* (1985).

Stokes mortar   A 76 mm (3″) portable gun, designed by Sir Frederick Wilfrid Scott Stokes (1860–1927), an English engineer and inventor. One of the Rebel officers in *For Whom the Bell Tolls,* Lieutenant BERRENDO, knows that if he had been issued a Stokes gun his brigade would not have suffered so many losses.

Stone, Harvey   One of Jake BARNES's American writer friends in *The Sun Also Rises.* They carry on a conversation at the CAFÉ SELECT, interrupted by Robert COHN, whom Stone thinks is a "moron." When Stone asks Cohn what he would rather be doing, Cohn tells him that he would rather play football again. Stone says, "You're not a moron. You're only a case of arrested development."

"Stop Hellstrom"   Article for Oak Park and River Forest High School newspaper, *The Trapeze* (November 3, 1916), reprinted in *Hemingway at Oak Park High: The High School Writings of Ernest Hemingway, 1916–1917* (1993).

"Store Thieves' Tricks"   Article, published in *The Toronto Star Weekly* (April 3, 1920), reprinted in *The Wild Years* (1962), reprinted in *Ernest Hemingway: Dateline Toronto* (1985). The headline in the *Star Weekly* was "Store Thieves Use Three Tricks." The article is about shoplifters in Toronto department stores who are automatically suspect if they are "carrying a bag of candy, an umbrella or wheeling a baby carriage."

Straits of Florida   A 50-mile area of the GULF STREAM between the Florida Keys and Cuba. In *To Have and Have Not* Harry MORGAN takes his charter fishing boat across the straits in running illegal goods between KEY WEST and HAVANA.

"Strange Country, The"   According to the headnote over the title of this 45-page "short story" in *The Complete Short Stories of Ernest Hemingway* (1987), it "comprises four chapters of an unfinished novel, . . . preliminary material for an early version of *Islands in the Stream,*" a fragment cut by Hemingway during the writing of *Islands,* which was published posthumously in 1970.

Strattons   People unidentified in "The Three-Day Blow," except as owners of a place where BILL (1)'s girlfriend, IDA, works.

street-car motorman   One of the customers turned away by George in "The Killers" while the two "killers" are waiting for Ole Andreson to come into the lunchroom.

Strega   Brand name for a spicy, orange-flavored liqueur made in Italy and drunk by Frederic HENRY in *A Farewell to Arms.*

Stresa   Town near the southern end of Lake MAGGIORE in northern Italy, about 39 miles northwest of Milan. In *A Farewell to Arms,* Catherine BARKLEY and Helen FERGUSON go on leave there from the American hospital in Milan, and Frederic HENRY joins them at the beginning of book 4. It is November 1917, and Frederic, who has deserted from the Italian ambulance corps, is afraid of being picked up by the Italian police, so he and Catherine leave in a small boat to row from Stresa up the lake into Switzerland.

stretcher bearers (1)   The wounded NICK waits for them in the "Chapter 6" vignette of *In Our Time.*

stretcher bearers (2)   An unspecified number of them are seen by Frederic HENRY while he is in the post hospital after his wounding in book 1 of *A Farewell to Arms.*

stretcher bearers (3)   In "A Natural History of the Dead," the stretcher bearers bring wounded soldiers to the doctor in a mountain cave, and one of them reports, near the end of the story, that the badly wounded man whom everyone hoped would die, has died.

striped fishermen's shirts   Worn by both David and Catherine BOURNE along the French Riviera in *The Garden of Eden.*

sub-base   For submarines near the NAVY DOCKS at KEY WEST in *To Have and Have Not.*

submarine (1) German submarine in *Islands in the Stream,* reportedly destroyed by an explosion northeast of Havana. Thomas HUDSON and his eight-man crew search for the sub's crew in the "At Sea" section of the novel.

submarine (2)   In *Islands in the Stream,* a second German sub is reported to have shot down a blimp off CAYO SAL, one of the islands off the northeast coast of Cuba, "day before yesterday" (in May 1944). Thomas HUDSON wonders why the crew of the first submarine, the one he and his crew are searching for, hasn't made radio contact with the second.

sucker fish   They swim around Harry MORGAN's borrowed boat, *Queen Conch,* in *To Have and Have Not,* attracted by the blood dripping over the side from one of the four Cuban bank robbers killed by Harry. See CUBANS, FOUR.

sucking fish In *The Old Man and the Sea* "two gray sucking fish" swim around the 1,500-pound MARLIN that SANTIAGO has just caught. "They were each over three feet long, and when they swam fast they lashed their whole bodies like eels."

Suckow, Ruth (1892–1960) American writer probably best known for her novels *Country People* (1924) and *The Odyssey of a Nice Girl* (1925). Diana SCRIPPS in *The Torrents of Spring* reads one of her stories and tells her husband, Scripps O'NEIL, about it.

Sud Express The Paris-Madrid train that Jake BARNES catches at SAN SEBASTIÁN, in *The Sun Also Rises,* in order to rescue Brett ASHLEY in Madrid after she sends him a telegram telling him she's "rather in trouble." They then buy tickets on the Sud Express for the trip back to Paris.

It is also the train that brings the English and American papers and the bullfight weeklies to Madrid and which, in *The Garden of Eden,* David BOURNE reads.

Suds See RED.

suertes Spanish term which means, in Hemingway terms, "the predetermined maneouvres in a bullfight." The word "suerte" in the singular also means "luck."

suicide Ernest Hemingway committed suicide on July 2, 1961, shooting himself with a double-barreled shotgun he had hunted with most of his life. His son Gregory writes about the suicide in his book, *Papa* (1976), that his father "showed courage in accepting the only option left." Ernest was suffering from depression, paranoia, hypertension, an enlarged liver, and high blood pressure. And in the early months of 1961 he was getting electroshock therapy at the Mayo Clinic in Rochester, Minnesota.

Ernest was not the only Hemingway to commit suicide. Others included his father, Clarence (1928), his sister Ursula (1966), and his brother, Leicester (1982). Leicester also suspected suicide when their oldest sister, Marcelline, died in 1963, although the doctors reported natural causes. And Hemingway's granddaughter, "Margaux," committed suicide on July 1, 1996.

The father of Ernest's first wife, Hadley Richardson, committed suicide (1903), and Ernest's friend Adriana IVANCICH, the probable prototype for Renata in *Across the River and Into the Trees,* hanged herself from a tree on her farm in Capalbio, Italy (in April 1983).

Suicides Name for a character in one of the stories told by BOBBY the bartender in the BIMINI section of *Islands in the Stream.* It is one of several stories Bobby tells about the tourists who visit the island. This one is about the "suicide" who wants to take someone with him when he kills himself. BIG HARRY volunteers, but Suicides decides to do it alone, diving off Johnny BLACK's dock one night "with the tide going out" and washing up on "the POINT" two days later. Big Harry decides that Suicides was "crazy," suffering "from a thing called Mechanic's Depressive."

Suisse Romande French-speaking region of Switzerland, mentioned in "Homage to Switzerland." One of the three porters in Part II tells Mr. JOHNSON that they are speaking French because they are in the Suisse Romande.

suitcase A "Vuitton" suitcase, used by David BOURNE, in *The Garden of Eden,* to hold the story manuscripts he is writing and which his wife, Catherine, unlocks in order to take the stories out for burning.

suitcase, Hadley's In *A Moveable Feast* Hemingway describes the loss of several short story manuscripts when they were apparently stolen in a suitcase belonging to his wife, Hadley (December 2, 1922). She was at the Gare de Lyon waiting for a train when the suitcase was stolen.

According to Hemingway the theft left him with two stories: "My Old Man," which was in the mail, having been rejected by *Cosmopolitan,* and "Up in Michigan," which he says was "in a drawer somewhere."

"Summer People" Written in 1924, this fragment of a longer work was published as a "short story" in Philip Young's *Ernest Hemingway: The Nick Adams Stories* (1972), but it is incomplete and too quickly edited in Young's version. The word "Slut," for example, is a misprint of "Stut," a nickname the main character uses for his girlfriend. And one of the manuscript pages is left out. The story was reprinted, with "Stut" corrected but with the page of manuscript still missing in *The Complete Short Stories of Ernest Hemingway* (1987).

Summit Small town in Illinois about 11 miles southwest of downtown Chicago, the setting for "The Killers." It is now a suburb about three miles due west of Midway Airport.

Sun Also Rises, The Published in 1926, this is probably Hemingway's best-known novel, certainly the one upon which much of his reputation stands. It defines how it was to live in the Paris of the 1920s, especially for EXPATRIATES, those Americans who felt incompatible with the America of the post–World War I years and left home in order to find the greater freedom offered by Europe after the war, particularly in Paris.

Hemingway sets the tone and theme for the novel in two epigraphs. The first is a statement made to him by Gertrude STEIN "in conversation," in which she told him "You are all a lost generation." She was referring mostly to American writers, many of whom had fought in the war, as Hemingway had, and who had become cynical about the American attitude that implied the war should be forgotten as soon as possible so things could get back to normal. Writers felt a spiritual alienation from an America that seemed hopelessly provincial and emotionally barren.

There was also less freedom to be artistic in America than in Europe; artists were often inhibited by censorship. The best example was the prohibition against James Joyce's novel *Ulysses,* published in Paris in 1922; copies were burned by the New York Post Office authorities, and the novel was not officially allowed into the country until 1933.

The main character and narrator in *The Sun Also Rises* is Jake BARNES, an American journalist in his mid-20s and wounded physically and psychologically by the war. He is an expatriate in Paris trying to cope with a world he thinks no longer has meaning. He is in love with Brett ASHLEY, but he has been rendered "IMPOTENT" by war wounds to the genitals and cannot consumate his love for her. He struggles to maintain any sort of "normal" life, in spite of the wounds that still fester seven years after the war.

Jake denies that he's impotent, and it's probable that he receives some form of sexual gratification from Brett in at least two scenes. But the exact nature of Jake's wound and the nature of his "impotence" is never made clear. "The Catholic Church had an awfully good way of handling all that," Jake says. "Good advice, anyway. Not to think about it. Oh, it was swell advice. Try and take it sometime. Try and take it."

Meanwhile, Brett has gone through two marriages since the war and several love affairs. She and Jake find that stoicism and an effort to move through life with a certain amount of what Hemingway called GRACE UNDER PRESSURE are the best antidotes to a world that makes so little sense.

The second epigraph is a quotation from Ecclesiastes I: 4–7: "One generation passeth away, and another generation cometh; but the earth abideth forever . . . The sun also ariseth, and the sun goeth down, and hasteth to the place where he arose . . . The wind goeth toward the south, and turneth about unto the north; it whirleth about continually, and the wind returneth again according to his circuits . . . All the rivers run into the sea; yet the sea is not full; unto the place from whence the rivers come, thither they return again." (The series of dots do not represent ellipses but merely Hemingway's way of showing the ends of the verses in the King James Bible.)

Ecclesiastes is one of the most poetic and mysterious books ever written, but it conveys a pessimistic outlook on life. "Vanity of vanities, saith the Preacher, vanity of vanities; all *is* vanity" (v. 2). The word "vanity" in Ecclesiastes evokes a world in which nothing anyone does matters very much. We are born, we kick at the traces, and then we die. *The Sun Also Rises* attempts to show how one might cope with such a world.

The novel is divided into three "books."

Book 1, set in Paris, opens with Jake making a sarcastic remark about Robert COHN, Jake's tennis-playing friend: "Robert Cohn was once middleweight boxing champion of Princeton. Do not think that I am very much impressed by that as a boxing title, but it meant a lot to Cohn." Although Jake refers to Robert as a "friend," this sarcasm permeates Jake's attitude toward their relationship. And at the novel's climax, which takes place at the Fiesta SAN FERMÍN in PAMPLONA, Spain, Cohn gets into a fight with Jake and Mike CAMPBELL, Brett's fiancé, and becomes an outcast from the rest of the group. Jake is also sarcastic about Cohn's various notions about life, mostly taken from the romance novels he reads. From the beginning, Cohn is the antagonist in a novel about the importance of learning how to deal with a meaningless world.

In chapter 3, Jake picks up a prostitute, GEORGETTE, who sympathizes with his impotence; he leaves her at a BAL MUSETTE (a dancing club) while she is dancing with some homosexuals who had arrived with Brett. Jake and Brett leave together in a taxi, the chapter ending with Brett telling Jake, "Oh, darling, I've been so miserable," suggesting the frustration she feels over Jake's impotence.

Chapter 4 introduces Count MIPPIPOPOLOUS, a rich Greek who received two arrow wounds when he was 22 years old, fighting in the war in ABYSSINIA. Because of his wounds he is able to empathize with Jake and is, as Brett says, "one of us," suggesting that he too is an expatriate, wounded physically and perhaps psychologically. In Chapter 5, Cohn interrupts Jake's attempt to write some stories for the newspaper he works for by asking questions about Brett, with whom he has become infatuated.

Cohn's fiancée, Frances CLYNE, is introduced in chapter 6 by way of a fight she has with Robert. They've been together for three years, but now he wants her to leave, and she tells Jake that she now realizes that Robert only wanted a "mistress," not a wife. The last chapter in book 1 revolves around the Paris cafés where, Jake, Brett, and Count Mippipopolous, now also infatuated with Brett, drink champagne. Brett informs Jake that she is "going away" for a while but does not tell him why or with whom.

In book 2, Jake knows that both Brett and Robert Cohn are out of town, but it is only later that Jake learns they have been together in SAN SEBASTIAN. Two new characters enter the story, and join Jake, Brett, and Cohn for Pamplona in late June: Bill GORTON, Jake's friend from New York who has come to Europe for some fishing, and Mike Campbell, Brett's fiancé from Scotland.

Jake and Bill leave Paris by train for BAYONNE in southwestern France on their way to Pamplona. Jake's jealousy of Cohn becomes more evident, and the reader infers that Jake can't get over the affair Brett had with Cohn in San Sebastian. Cohn meets Jake and Bill for a fishing trip the three had planned to BURGUETE, north of Pamplona, but decides against going with them because he wants to wait for Brett. Jake tells the reader that "Cohn had a wonderful quality of bringing out the worst in anybody." The bus ride to Burguete is full of tension as Jake tries to avoid thinking about his jealousy of Cohn, manifested for the reader (as it was earlier during the Paris taxi ride with Brett in book 1) through Jake's detailed description of the beauty of the northern Spanish countryside.

Jake and Bill spend five days in Burguete, fishing and relaxing in a small hotel there—the calm before the storm of Pamplona. During this time together, Jake denies to Bill that he is impotent. When Bill tells Jake that some people "claim" that Jake is impotent, Jake says, "No . . . I just had an accident." The accident occurred during the war, causing apparent damage to his genitals, but he refuses to talk about it. In this scene, however, he jokes about it with Bill to let him know it's okay that Bill asked him about it.

In Pamplona for the fiesta and the bullfights (beginning in chapter 13), the drinking takes on more serious overtones. Cohn becomes the enemy of the rest of the group and yet cannot break away as long as Brett remains. Jake describes "much wine, an ignored tension, and a feeling of things coming that you could not prevent happening." Jake is not so drunk that he can't think about the great moral question that still bothers him: "I did not care what it [the world] was all about. All I wanted to know was how to live in it. Maybe if you found out how to live in it you learned from that what it was all about." This echoes the novel's epigraph from Ecclesiastes, as Jake struggles to live in a world that is so seemingly empty of purpose.

The fiesta begins in the next chapter (chapter 15), including what is probably the best description by an American of the annual Fiesta San Fermín in Pamplona, a week of constant eating and drinking and running with the bulls (which Jake does not do). As Jake explains, the fiesta "kept up day and night for seven days. The dancing kept up, the drinking kept up, the noise went on. The things that happened could only have happened during a fiesta." After a while everything seemed unreal and "without consequences."

Jake introduces Brett to Pedro ROMERO, a handsome bullfighter, in the next chapter, making Jake feel later, after Brett and Romero had run off together, that it was "not pleasant" being a pimp. Mike Campbell, who is the worst drunk of the group, baits Cohn, creating even greater tension among the friends. The fistfights between Cohn and Jake, Cohn and Mike, and Cohn and Romero occur in chapter 17; Cohn knocks out Jake and knocks down Mike. Cohn also beats up Romero in his hotel room, though Brett tries to stop the fight. Brett and Romero leave Pamplona together, and Cohn disappears (not to be mentioned in the novel again). The fight scene recalls Jake's sarcastic remark with which the novel begins, about Cohn's boxing ability at Princeton.

Jake's description of the bullfights (chapter 18) is just as clear as Hemingway's in *Death in the Afternoon*, one of the best books on bullfighting written by a non-Spaniard. Whatever drinking Jake has been doing at this point in the novel does not interfere with his ability to describe the bullfights, especially the excellence of Pedro Romero. Book 2 ends as the fiesta ends, with Jake's statement: "The three of us [Jake, Bill, and Mike] sat at the table, and it seemed as though about six people were missing."

Book 3 returns the three friends to a sober atmosphere: "In the morning it was all over. The fiesta was finished." They hire a car to take them to Bayonne: Mike stays in Saint-Jean-de-Luz, Bill catches the train for Paris, and Jake returns to San Sebastian for some swimming and the sun. There he receives a telegram from Brett in Madrid asking him to rescue her: "Could you come Hotel Montana Madrid am rather in trouble Brett." He answers the telegram and tells the reader, "That seemed to handle it. . . . Send a girl off with one man. Introduce her to another to go off with him. Now go and bring her back. And sign the wire with love. That was it all right."

He catches the SUD EXPRESS for Madrid, where Brett tells him that she is going back to Mike. She sums up her feelings by telling Jake that she feels "rather good deciding not to be a bitch. . . . It's sort of what we have instead of God." Jake's response is that some people "have God quite a lot," suggesting that her comment offends him. The novel ends with Brett's statement, "Oh, Jake, . . . we could have had such a damned good time together," and Jake's reply, "Yes. . . . Isn't it pretty to think so?"

Although the time of the novel is not specified, it is probably 1925. On their fishing trip to the Irati during the first week of July, Jake tells Bill that William Jennings BRYAN has just died ("I read it in the paper yesterday"). Bryan died on July 26, 1925. Since the Fiesta San Fermín always begins on July 6, it may be assumed, even though Hemingway has the exact date of Bryan's death wrong in the novel, that the story takes place in that year. Also, Brett tells Jake that Pedro Romero was born in 1905; since readers also know he is 19 years old, that sets the time of the novel at either 1924 or 1925.

In *A Moveable Feast* Hemingway writes about the weeks he spent in the late summer of 1925 writing the rough draft of his first "serious" novel and of finishing it in Schruns, Austria, during the winter of 1925–26 on a skiing vacation with Hadley.

The Sun Also Rises was published by Charles Scribner's Sons on October 22, 1926, in a first edition of 5,090 copies at $2 each. At the end of the century, one of those first editions in a dust jacket could sell for as much as $20,000.

Sun Also Rises, The (film)   Twentieth Century-Fox picture, released in August 1957 (129 minutes); produced by Darryl F. Zanuck, directed by Henry King, screenplay by Peter Viertel, music by Hugo Friedhofer (conducted by Lionel Newman), photography by Leo Tover, art direction by Lyle R. Wheeler and Mark-Lee Kirk, set decorations by Walter M. Scott, Paul S. Fox, and Jack Stubbs.

Cast: Tyrone Power (Jakes Barnes), Ava Gardner (Lady Brett Ashley), Mel Ferrer (Robert Cohn), Errol Flynn (Mike Campbell), Eddie Albert (Bill Gorton), Gregory Ratoff (Count Mippipopolous), Juliette Greco (Georgette), Marcel Dalio (Zizi), Henry Daniell (doctor), Bob Cunningham (Harris), Danik Patisson (the girl), Robert Evans (Romero), Eduardo Noriega (Mr. Braddock), Jacqueline Evans (Mrs. Braddock), Carlos Muzquiz (Montoya), Rebecca Iturbi (Frances), and Carlos David Ortigos (Romero's manager).

Sun Also Rises, The (television play)   Two-part NBC/Twentieth Century-Fox adaptation of the Twentieth Century-Fox movie version (December 1984). The TV miniseries (170 minutes, with another 70 minutes of advertisements) starred Hart Bochner as Jake Barnes, Jane Seymour as Brett Ashley, Robert Carradine as Robert Cohn, Zeljko Ivanek as Bill Gorton, Ian Charleson as Mike Campbell, and Leonard Nimoy as Count Mippipopolous. It was produced by John Furia, directed by James Goldstone, with writing credits to Hemingway and Robert L. Joseph.

"Superman Myth, The"   Article, published in *The Toronto Daily Star* (June 25, 1921), reprinted in William Burrill's *Hemingway: The Toronto Years* (1994). It was "discovered" by Burrill in the Hemingway Collection at the John F. Kennedy Library in Boston. In the article Hemingway predicts that Georges CARPENTIER will defeat Jack DEMPSEY in their July 2 (1921) prizefight. The article is also a good review of Dempsey's championship fights since winning the title from Jess Willard in Toledo on July 4, 1919. The Dempsey "myth" sur-

vived the Carpentier fight, in spite of Hemingway's prediction, by a knockout in the fourth round.

"Support the Swimming Team"   Article for Oak Park and River Forest High School newspaper, *The Trapeze* (February 9, 1917), reprinted in *Hemingway at Oak Park High: The High School Writings of Ernest Hemingway, 1916–1917* (1993).

Swahili   Arabic word meaning "coastal people." Swahili is the language of the Bantu tribes of East Africa, the descendants of Bantu Negroes and Arab traders. It is the generic name for the native populations of the coastal regions of Kenya and Tanzania, and of the island of Zanzibar, off the coast of Tanzania. The Swahili language is the lingua franca of much of East Africa.

It is the language of the two gun bearers in "The Short Happy Life of Francis Macomber," of M'COLA in *Green Hills of Africa,* and of the tracker-hunter JUMA in David BOURNE's AFRICAN STORY in *The Garden of Eden.*

swamp (1)   In "The Battler," Nick ADAMS knows that he has three or four miles to walk along the railroad tracks with swamp on either side before he gets to Mancelona.

swamp (2)   In "Now I Lay Me," the main character/narrator remembers fishing in a trout stream and finding insects for bait in a nearby swamp.

swamp (3)   In "Big Two-Hearted River," the swamp is across and slightly downriver from NICK's campsite and represents for Nick whatever traumatic, but unidentified, experience is now behind him and which he is trying not to think about on the fishing trip. At the end of the story's part 2, however, Nick feels as if he may be able one day to fish the swamp.

Swift and Armour   In one of HARRY's self-deprecating and selfish outbursts at HELEN (3) in "The Snows of Kilimanjaro," he plays on the name of the American meatpacking firm by saying to her, "Your damned money was my armour. My Swift and my Armour." "Amour" is the French word for "love" or "passion."

"Swiss Avalanches"   Article, published in *The Toronto Star Weekly* (January 12, 1924), reprinted in *The Wild Years* (1962), and reprinted in *Ernest Hemingway: Dateline Toronto* (1985). The headline in the *Star Weekly* was "Skiers' Only Escape From Alpine Avalanche is to Swim! Snow Slides Off Mountain as Fast as Off Roof of House." In the article Hemingway writes that "[a]valanches are the skeleton in the winter sport's [skiing's] closet." It was one of three articles printed by *Star* newspapers after Hemingway had gone off the *Star*'s payroll on December 31, 1923.

"Swiss Luge, The" Article, published in *The Toronto Star Weekly* (March 18, 1922), reprinted in *The Wild Years* (1962), and in *By-Line: Ernest Hemingway* (1967). Datelined "Chamby sur Montreux, Switzerland," the article is about the Swiss luge (pronounced "looge"), a winter pastime involving "old grandmothers" and "street children, coasting solemnly down the steep mountain roads, sitting on these little elevated pancakes. . . . [steering] with their feet stuck straight out in front and [coming] down a twelve mile run at a speed of from twelve to thirty miles an hour."

On Sunday you can choose among as many as 12 special trains that run from Montreux on Lake Geneva to the top of Col du Sonloup at 4,000 feet. You take a picnic, Hemingway suggests, and "spend the day sliding gloriously down the long, icy mountain road." The *TSW* headline read "Flivver, Canoe, Pram and Taxi Combined in the Luge, Joy of Everybody in Switzerland."

Switzerland Mentioned by Catherine BOURNE in *The Garden of Eden* as a place where she and her husband, David, might go after MARITA leaves. David had suggested that she could see a doctor there, Catherine realizing that she is "crazy." She has what would be called at the end of the 20th century a multiple personality disorder. "It's an easy drive and beautiful," David tells her. But she won't go.

Switzerland is also where Frederic HENRY and Catherine BARKLEY escape to after Frederic's break from the war in *A Farewell to Arms*. They spend the winter in Montreux at the east end of Lake Geneva and then go to Lausanne, where Catherine dies in childbirth.

In *A Moveable Feast* Hemingway writes of the fishing and hiking he, his wife HADLEY, and their friend Chink DORMAN-SMITH did together in Aigle, Switzerland.

swordfish Related to the sailfish, the swordfish is named for its sharp, broad, elongated upper jaw. In *To Have and Have Not,* one is described as a "big brown buggar with a spear on him longer than your arm." He is one of the fish missed by JOHNSON, the tourist fisherman who has hired Harry MORGAN's charter fishing boat.

A 1,000-pound broadbill swordfish is caught and lost by David HUDSON in chapter 9 of the "BIMINI" section of *Islands in the Stream.* "Then, astern of the boat and off to starboard, the calm of the ocean broke open and the great fish rose out of it, rising, shining dark blue and silver, seeming to come endlessly out of the water, unbelievable as his length and bulk rose out of the sea into the air and seemed to hang there until he fell with a splash that drove the water up high and white." After a six-hour fight for the fish, it gets free just as EDDY (3) is reaching for it with a gaff.

T

Tabeshaw, Billy Main character, an OJIBWAY Indian, in "Sepi Jingan," one of Hemingway's juvenilia short stories, published in *Tabula,* his high school literary magazine and reprinted in *Hemingway at Oak Park High: The High School Writings of Ernest Hemingway* (1993).

He is also one of the Indians, who, with Dick BOULTON and his son, Eddy, are hired to cut up logs by NICK's father, the "DOC" in "The Doctor and the Doctor's Wife."

And Tabeshaw is mentioned in "Ten Indians." When Joe GARNER, on his way home with his family from a July 4 picnic, climbs down from his wagon to remove from the road a ninth drunken Indian they have passed since leaving town, his son Carl asks if it is Billy Tabeshaw.

Tabula Literary magazine of Oak Park and River Forest High School while Hemingway was a student and for which he wrote three short stories during his junior year: "Judgment of Manitou," "A Matter of Color," and "Sepi Jingan," all reprinted in *Hemingway at Oak Park High: The High School Writings of Ernest Hemingway, 1916–1917* (1993). Four of Hemingway's poems were also published in *Tabula.*

Tabula was founded in 1896 as a student newspaper and evolved into a literary magazine, published five times a year, the last issue each year titled *Senior Tabula,* for which Hemingway wrote the "Class Prophecy" in 1917. The magazine became the school yearbook in 1950, and another publication, *Crest,* was then created as the literary magazine.

"Tackle, The" Poem about football, first published as one of three poems under the general title, "Athletic Verse," in the Oak Park and River Forest High School literary magazine, *Tabula* (March 1917). The other two are "The Punt" and "The Safety Man." All three were reprinted in *88 Poems* (1979) and counted as separate poems.

Tafalla Spanish town 19 miles south of Pamplona. In *The Sun Also Rises,* the hometown of Vicente GIRONES, a man killed during the running of the bulls in Pamplona.

Tagliamento River In northern Italy with headwaters in the Dolomite Alps, running generally south, emptying into the Adriatic Sea at Lignano, 36 miles east of Venice. It is where, in *Across the River and Into the Trees,* Richard CANTWELL goes duck shooting with the Barone ALVARITO. They hunt "in the marshes at the mouth" of the river.

In *A Farewell to Arms* it is the river the Italian army must cross in its retreat from CAPORETTO and into which Frederic HENRY dives in order to escape execution at the hands of the Italian battle police.

"Talking with the Tiger" Article, published in William Burrill's *Hemingway: The Toronto Years* (1994). It was "discovered" by Burrill in the Hemingway Collection at the John F. Kennedy Library in Boston. The article is datelined "Les Sables-D'Ollone, France."

An interview with the former French premier Georges CLEMENCEAU at his home in the south of France in September 1922, the article was rejected by editors at *The Toronto Star* because of negative comments made about Canada by Clemenceau. The premier told Hemingway he would not visit Canada on his trip to North America, because Canada had "rejected compulsory [military] service and refused to help France" during World War I.

Tamames, Dr. Manolo Spanish friend of Hemingway and private surgeon for Antonio Ordóñez and Luis Miguel Dominguín during the bullfight season of 1959 when Hemingway followed the Spanish bullfight circuit in preparation for writing *The Dangerous Summer.*

"Tancredo Is Dead" Article, published in *The Toronto Star Weekly* (November 24, 1923), reprinted in *Ernest Hemingway: Dateline Toronto* (1985). Tancredo was known for receiving 5,000 dollars each time he stood in the middle of a bull ring and stared down a charging bull for 10 minutes. "Tancredo never moved. To move would have been fatal. He simply fixed his eyes on the bull." The charging bull "always stopped." But then came the imitators, and the government had to stop the act and, with it, the livelihood of Don Tancredo who died penniless "and a failure because he was too perfect." The byline is "E.M. Heminway" [sic].

tank Near the end of *For Whom the Bell Tolls* the fascists bring up a tank to cut off the escape of Robert JORDAN and his Spanish Loyalist friends after the bridge is blown up. It has a "low-bodied, angled snout and squat green, gray and brown-splashed turret with the projecting machine gun." A shell from the tank wounds the horse on which Robert JORDAN is riding, which then falls on Jordan, crushing his leg.

tanker The captain of this boat, in *To Have and Have Not,* heading north off the Florida Keys, sees Harry MORGAN's boat adrift "off Matacumbe" in the GULF STREAM and notifies the COAST GUARD.

tank wagons These "brown and saffron" wagons "worked" the streets of Paris in the 1920s pumping out the apartment house cesspools. In *A Moveable Feast* Hemingway describes the "strong" smell that came from them along rue Cardinal Lemoine, where he and Hadley lived. He says "their wheeled, horse-drawn cylinders looked like Braque paintings."

Taskforce One of Thomas HUDSON's 11 cats at the farm in the "Cuba" section of *Islands in the Stream.*

Tatie Nickname Hadley Hemingway gave to Ernest, used once in quoting her in *A Moveable Feast.*

Tauchnitz editions Book publications begun in 1841 by the German publisher Christian Bernhard Tauchnitz (1816–95) and continued after Christian's death by the family Tauchnitz. These books were a "Collection of British and American Authors" in English-language editions for sale on the Continent and not legally for sale in either Great Britain or the United States. Hemingway refers to these editions in *A Moveable Feast. A Farewell to Arms* is Tauchnitz edition number 4935, published May 3, 1930.

Tavel Pronounced tah-vel, it is the most famous of the French rosé wines. It is a Côtes du Rhône wine from the village vineyards of Tavel just northwest of AVIGNON.

In *Islands in the Stream,* Thomas HUDSON remembers drinking with his friend the BARON at a café in Marseilles. The Tavel "tasted the way Provence looked." In *The Garden of Eden* it is one of the regional wines of choice for David and Catherine BOURNE in their travels along the French Riviera.

Tchitcherin, George Leader of the Soviet delegation to the Lausanne Conference in 1922–23; the subject of several Hemingway articles for *The Toronto Star.*

"Tchitcherin Speaks at Genoa Conference" Article, published in *The Toronto Daily Star* (April 10, 1922), reprinted in *The Wild Years* (1962), reprinted in *Ernest Hemingway: Dateline Toronto* (1985). The headline in the *Daily Star* was "World Economic Conference Opens in Genoa: Tchitcherin Speaks."

Datelined "Genoa," it is about the Russian delegation at the Genoa Economic Conference, led by George Tchitcherin. He tells Hemingway that Soviet social revolutionaries are being persecuted for real offenses, such as blowing up banks, shooting at Lenin, blowing up ammunition dumps, and attempting to dynamite Trotsky's train. "We are changing our penitentiary system to educate and reform criminals."

"Tchitcherin Wants Japan Excluded" Article, published in *The Toronto Daily Star* (April 11, 1922), reprinted in *Ernest Hemingway: Dateline Toronto* (1985). The headline in the *Daily Star* was "Tchitcherin At It Again, Wants Jap Excluded."

Datelined "Genoa," this three-paragraph story is about the second-day scene at the Genoa Economic Conference when Tchitcherin, the leader of the Russian delegation, "protested against the presence of Japan and Rumania." A commission was appointed to consider the question.

T.D. In its context in *Across the River and Into the Trees* the initials stand for "Tank Destroyer." It is used in reference to Colonel Richard CANTWELL's car, which sounds to Cantwell, a military officer, like a "stricken tank or T.D., except the noises were in miniature from the lack of power."

"Ted's Skeeters" Article, published in *The Toronto Star Weekly* (August 7, 1920), reprinted in *The Wild Years* (1962), reprinted in *Ernest Hemingway: Dateline Toronto* (1985). The headline in the *Star Weekly* was "When You Go Camping Take Lots of Skeeter Dope and Don't Ever Lose it." It is about protecting yourself from mosquitoes while camping. "He is one of the few wild animals that are not afraid of man. He scents him afar off and with a zooming cry attacks him and sucks his blood."

telegrapher At the railroad station in PETOSKEY, Michigan, in *The Torrents of Spring* who asks Scripps O'NEIL if he knows a girl in MANCELONA named Ethel Enright.

telemark position Skiing position for turning, in which the skier places the uphill ski forward of the other and gradually angles the tip of the forward ski downward in the direction to be turned. Described in "Cross-Country Snow."

10-fathom bar Sandbar off BIMINI island, mentioned in *Islands in the Stream* because of its good fishing.

"Ten Indians" Nick, the short story's main character, has been to a July 4 baseball game with Joe GARNER's family. He is riding home late in the evening in the "big" Garner wagon with Joe, Mrs. Garner, and their two sons, Carl and Frank. They pass "nine drunken Indians along the road," the ninth one pulled off to the side of the road by Joe. "Them Indians," Mrs. Garner says.

Carl kids Nick about having an Indian girlfriend, Prudence MITCHELL—the 10th Indian. Nick denies that she is his girl but is pleased about the kidding. When he gets home and, at dinner, asks his father what he had been doing that day, his father tells him about seeing Prudie "in the woods" with Frank WASHBURN. And they "were having quite a time." Nick is immediately curious and wants to know what they were doing. "I don't know," his father said, "I just heard them threshing around."

His father goes outside, and when he comes back into the kitchen, Nick had been crying. Nick goes to bed and "lay . . . with his face in the pillow. My heart's broken. . . . If I feel this way my heart must be broken." The story ends, however, with Nick awake in the morning "a long time before he remembered that his heart was broken." Nick, who is in his early teens or younger, learns in this experience how easy it is to move in and out of "love."

When his father first tells Nick about seeing Prudie in the woods with Frank Washburn, the narrator states that Nick's "father was not looking at him," suggesting that his father knows that Prudie is Nick's "girl" and that he is deliberately upsetting Nick in an attempt to cause him to break up with her. Readers may also wonder about the ambiguity in the story's early emphasis on the Indians being drunk on July 4, in apparent celebration of a white man's holiday.

"Ten Indians" was first published in *Men Without Women* (1927).

ten in ones   U.S. Army rations, mentioned in *Across the River and Into the Trees*. See K RATIONS.

Ten Mile point   Although the name of the lake is not given in "The Three-Day Blow," Ten Mile point is on Lake Charlevoix in northern Michigan at the southern-most point of Horton Bay. NICK and BILL (1) can see the wind "blowing straight down the lake," and they can "see the surf along Ten Mile point."

Tenniel, John (1820–1914)   English illustrator, best known in the United States as illustrator of Lewis Carroll's *Alice in Wonderland* (1865). In *Islands in the Stream* Audrey BRUCE remembers that Roger DAVIS had once told her she looked like a Tenniel illustration.

tent   In "Big Two-Hearted River," NICK makes his tent by hanging canvas over a rope tied between two pine trees for a ridge-pole and then "pegging out the sides."

terns, dark   In *The Old Man and the Sea* SANTIAGO feels sorry for the birds at sea, "especially the small delicate dark terns that were always flying and looking and almost never finding."

Terrace   In *The Old Man and the Sea* it's the café/bar in the Cuban village where MANOLIN and SANTIAGO live and where they get their fishing supplies, food, and beer.

Territet   Small Swiss town at the east end of Lake Geneva, half a mile east of Montreux. Its railway station café is the setting for part 3 of "Homage to Switzerland."

tessera   Italian for identification card or pass, used by Nicholas ADAMS in "A Way You'll Never Be." It has a "photograph and identification and the seal of the third army."

Thayer, Scofield (1890–1982)   Co-owner and one of the editors of *DIAL* magazine from 1918, when it moved from Chicago to New York, until its demise in 1929.

In *The Torrents of Spring* SCRIPPS claims that Thayer was the best man at his wedding, but, as with nearly all of Scripps's stories, he has made it up.

Hemingway mentions Thayer in *A Moveable Feast* in connection with a strange conversation Ernest had with Harold STEARNS, who informed him that he, Hemingway, would win the annual *Dial* prize for the best writing of 1924. Stearns had told other writers that *they* would win the prize.

Theatre Gayarre   In *The Sun Also Rises* it is across the plaza from the HOTEL MONTOYA in PAMPLONA.

theory of omission   In a statement that Hemingway makes in *Death in the Afternoon* about writing, he provides readers with his theory of the importance in writing of omission, an idea that has become known as the "iceberg principle."

"If a writer of prose knows enough about what he is writing about he may omit things that he knows and the reader, if the writer is writing truly enough, will have a feeling of those things as strongly as though the writer had stated them. The dignity of movement of an ice-berg is due to only one-eighth of it being above water. A writer who omits things because he does not know them only makes hollow places in his writing."

Hemingway describes the difference between a writer of fiction and a newspaper reporter by using the example of seeing a little girl hit by a train. The reporter doesn't have to see the accident, in fact is better off not seeing it in order to remain objective—the necessary details can be obtained from the police blotter. But the writer of fiction has to know what "you [the writer] really felt, rather than what you were supposed to feel, and had been taught to feel . . . what the actual things were which produced the emotion that you experienced." If the writer doesn't know the felt experience, he or she will not be able to convey it to the reader.

Most of Hemingway's short stories and several scenes in novels employ the theory of omission. One of the best examples is in the short story, "Big Two-Hearted River," where what is clear is that the main character, Nick, is concentrating on the details of camping and fishing to avoid thinking about some unspecified traumatic event in his immediate past. But the story is not a riddle. What is most important is the tension Nick feels in his struggle to hold on to the present moment to help him avoid thinking about past events. That tension is felt by the reader.

"Soldier's Home" presents another example. Hemingway knew well the details of the World War I battles of SOISSONS, CHAMPAGNE, BELLEAU WOOD, SAINT-MIHIEL, and the ARGONNE, five of the bloodiest battles in the war. The main character in the short story, Harold KREBS, had fought with the U.S. Marines in all five. In the story only the names of the battles are given; the details are omitted. Hemingway must have felt that if he wrote the story well enough, the reader would understand that Krebs's terrifying war experiences were the cause of his lethargy and depression after he returns to his Oklahoma hometown.

Thérèse   One of the two salesgirls in a Paris store from whom the AMERICAN LADY, in "A Canary for One," buys all of her dresses.

"There She Breaches! *or* Moby Dick off the Morro"   Article, published in *Esquire* (May 1936), reprinted in *By-Line: Ernest Hemingway* (1967). The article is about Hemingway's running onto a pod of 20 sperm whales while fishing for marlin off the Cuban north coast (October 10, 1934). He and his crew chased them the rest of the day, harpooning one but losing it because, as he found out later, "you do not harpoon sperm whales in the head. . . . There is too much bone."

"[There was Ike and Tony and Jaque and me . . .]"   First line of a poem about a three-day leave in Schio during Hemingway's work with the Italian ambulance corps in World War I. First published in *88 Poems* (1979).

"They All Made Peace—What Is Peace?"   Poem about the dehumanizing contributions of conferees at the Lausanne Peace Conference in 1922, written in 1922 and first published in *The Little Review* (Spring 1923).

Third Army   World War I Italian military unit to which Nick ADAMS is attached in "A Way You'll Never Be." He is badly wounded on the Carso plateau in northern Italy in what was probably the "eleventh" battle of the ISONZO River, where the Third Army was beaten by the Austrians, the battle ending on September 12, 1917.

This Quarter   Literary publication which bought three of Hemingway's early short stories: "Big Two-Hearted River," Parts I and II (Spring 1925), "The Undefeated" (Autumn–Winter 1925–1926), and "The Sea Change" (December 1931). During 1925–27 the magazine's printing offices were at 338, rue Saint-Honoré in Paris and its editors were Ernest Walsh and Ethel Moorhead.

Thomas Hudson   See Thomas HUDSON.

Thompson submachine gun   Called a "tommy," it is a portable, .45 caliber automatic weapon, designed to be fired from the shoulder or hip. The gun is named after J(ohn) T(aliaferro) Thompson (1860–1940), an American Army officer who aided in its invention.

In *To Have and Have Not* Harry MORGAN keeps a tommy gun on his charter fishing boat, along with other weapons, including a Winchester 30-30, a pump-gun, and a Smith and Wesson .38 pistol. Roberto, one of four Cuban bank robbers, uses the Thompson to kill Harry's first mate, Albert TRACY, when they force Harry to take them to Havana.

When Harry helps Roberto dump Albert's body overboard, Harry manages to kick the gun over the side. A Thompson submachine gun is also used to kill the three Cubans outside the PEARL OF SAN FRANCISCO CAFÉ in chapter 1, Cubans who had just failed to talk Harry into taking them from Havana to Florida.

The Spanish word for the Thompson submachine gun, used in *To Have and Have Not*, is *ametralladora*.

Thomas HUDSON carries at least three Thompsons on board his boat as he and his crew search for a German submarine crew in the "At Sea" section of *Islands in the Stream*. The guns are kept well oiled in "full-length sheep-wool cases." They are called *niños* by the Basque crew members on board, meaning "little children."

Thoreau, Henry David (1817–1862)   American essayist and philosopher, best known for *Walden* (1854) and for attempting to live the doctrines of Transcendentalism. In *Green Hills of Africa* Hemingway tells KANDISKY that Thoreau "is supposed to be really good," but "I have not yet been able to read it. But that means nothing because I cannot read other naturalists unless they are being extremely accurate and not literary."

Thrace   Region in the eastern part of the Balkan peninsula, the Aegean Sea along its southern border and the Black Sea at its eastern end; Istanbul on the Bosporus is its major city. Thrace is divided between

Turkey (Eastern Thrace) and Greece (Western Thrace). The region is mentioned in the "Chapter 2" vignette of *In Our Time* and in several of Hemingway's articles written for *The Toronto Star*. In the article "Turk Red Crescent Propaganda Agency," Hemingway calls Thrace "an unproductive barren country."

"Three-Day Blow, The"   This short story takes place in the autumn following the summer breakup of NICK with his girlfriend, MARJORIE (see "The End of Something"), probably in 1916 (see Heinie ZIM, WORLD SERIES, and *The Dark Forest*). Nick goes to the lake cottage of his friend BILL (1), where the two teenagers talk baseball and literature while getting slowly drunk on Irish whisky.

The main conflict in the story isn't mentioned, however, until two-thirds of the way through, when Bill finally says to Nick, "You were very wise. . . . [to] bust off that Marge business." Three times the narrator states that "Nick said nothing." Bill continues to tell Nick how "absolutely bitched" married men are and that if he had married Marjorie he would have married the "whole family." Then he states his main argument: "Now she can marry somebody of her own sort. . . . You can't mix oil and water . . . ," implying that Marjorie is not good enough for Nick.

Meanwhile, the "liquor had all died out of [Nick]," and he remembers how he broke up with Marjorie, that "he had once had [her] and that he had lost her." He says to Bill, "All of a sudden everything was over"—like the three-day blow, coming off Lake Michigan. Nick thinks, however, that he might see her again, and that makes him feel better, even "happy," and he leaves the cottage thinking that the "Marge business was no longer so tragic. . . . The wind blew everything like that away." But still, he thought, "he could always go into town Saturday night. It was a good thing to have in reserve." He is "happy," not because he has decided Bill is right about breaking up with Marge, but because the breakup is no longer so "absolute," because he thinks there may be a chance to start over.

"The Three-Day Blow" was first published in *In Our Time* (1925).

"Three Shots"   Story fragment, cut as the opening to "Indian Camp," but published as a "short story" in Philip Young's *Ernest Hemingway: The Nick Adams Stories* (1972). Young placed the story at the beginning of his book, because he thought it was the earliest of the Nick ADAMS stories. Nick is left alone in a tent while his father and Uncle George are fishing at night. He is frightened by the silence of the woods, but he is also frightened by thoughts of death, and so he fires a rifle three times out the tent's front flap—the signal agreed upon in an emergency—but he is asleep before his father and uncle get back from the lake. He lies about what spooked him and his father says, "You don't want to ever be frightened in the woods, Nick. There is nothing that can hurt you."

Three Stories & Ten Poems   Hemingway's first book, published in 1923 by Robert McAlmon at the Contact Publishing Co., in Paris. It contains the stories "Up in Michigan," "Out of Season," and "My Old Man"; and the poems "Mitraigliatrice," "Oklahoma," "Oily Weather," "Roosevelt," "Captives," "Champs d'Honneur," "Riparto d'Assalto," "Montparnasse," "Along With Youth," and "Chapter Heading." The 64-page book was published in a first edition of 300 copies at $2 each.

"Throng at Smallpox Case"   Article, unsigned, published in *The Kansas City Star* (February 18, 1918), reprinted in *Ernest Hemingway, Cub Reporter* (1970).

Timber Creek   Area of Wyoming, mentioned by Hemingway in *Green Hills of Africa*. He compares the country in Tanzania where he's hunting with the "south slope of Timber Creek." Hemingway fished and hunted in the region of Timber Creek.

Time   Popular U.S. weekly newsmagazine, founded in 1923 and still publishing at the end of the century. In *Islands in the Stream* Thomas HUDSON, while traveling to France on the *Ile de France* for the funeral of his sons David and Andrew, and their mother, reads about their deaths in *Time*'s "Milestones" column. He also reads about the automobile accident that killed the boys and their mother in *Newsweek*.

"Time Now, The Place Spain, The"   Article, published in *Ken* (April 7, 1938). In it Hemingway suggests that a second world war can be avoided if Mussolini and fascism are defeated in Spain. It is the first issue of *Ken* and the first of 13 articles Hemingway wrote for the publication. The editors also published Hemingway's short story "The Old Man at the Bridge."

Tintoretto (1518–1594)   One of several Italian painters whom Richard CANTWELL thinks about in *Across the River and Into the Trees*. Tintoretto was Venetian. Cantwell thinks to himself about the painting of Renata: "It was a beautiful portrait; neither cold, nor snobbish, nor stylised, nor modern. It was the way you would want your girl painted if Tintoretto were still around and, if he were not around, you settled for VELÁSQUEZ."

Tiny   Wife of the YOUNG GENTLEMAN in "Out of Season." She is described as "following rather sullenly" behind her husband and PEDUZZI (1), the drunken, old fishing guide, as they walk through the town toward a trout stream to fish for trout illegally, "out of season." She and her husband have quarreled about something, but it is not clear what the argument is about or how serious.

He apologizes to her for the quarrel and says that they "were both getting at the same thing from different angles." Her reply is ambiguous: "It doesn't make any difference. . . . None of it makes any difference." This can be taken literally, that whatever they argued about doesn't matter, or it can mean that she's given up trying to reason with him. She is certainly upset with him for being so easily taken in by Peduzzi.

Tio Pepe   A drink that MARITA has, in *The Garden of Eden,* at a CANNES café where she and David BOURNE stop after testing the brakes of the BUGATTI that David's wife, Catherine, owns.

"Tip the Postman Every Time?"   Article, published in *The Toronto Star Weekly* (March 11, 1922), reprinted in *The Wild Years* (1962), and reprinted in *Ernest Hemingway: Dateline Toronto* (1985). The headline in the *Star Weekly* was "How'd You Like to Tip Postman Every Time?" In the article, datelined "Paris," it seems that tipping the postman in Spain is the only way to be sure of getting your mail.

Titanic   British luxury passenger liner that hit an iceberg and sank in the North Atlantic in April 1912, with the lost of 1,517 lives. In *Islands in the Stream* the owner of Thomas HUDSON's favorite bar on Bimini, Bobby Saunders, suggests that Hudson might do a painting of the sinking of the *Titanic.*

TNT   Trinitrotoluene, the explosive material Robert JORDAN uses to blow up the bridge in *For Whom the Bell Tolls.*

"To a Tragic Poetess"   Poem of nasty criticism of Dorothy Parker, written in 1926 and first published in *88 Poems* (1979).

"To Chink Whose Trade is Soldiering"   Poem about Hemingway's friend Eric Edward "Chink" DORMAN-SMITH , written in 1924 and first published in *88 Poems* (1979).

"To Crazy Christian"   Poem in honor of one of Hemingway's favorite cats at the Finca Vigía in Cuba, written about 1946 and first published in *88 Poems* (1979).

Today is Friday   This four-page, one-scene play is set in a "drinking-place" at 11 o'clock the night of Christ's crucifixion. Three Roman soldiers, who assisted at the morning's event, are "a little cock-eyed" from the red wine served to them by the Hebrew wine-seller, and they are discussing what they had witnessed that day.

The first ROMAN SOLDIER, in his progressing inebriation, keeps repeating that he thinks Christ "was pretty good in there today," and he brags that he stuck his spear in Christ's side, a merciful act that might get him in trouble. The second soldier is skeptical, arguing that Christ is a "false alarm" and not understanding why he didn't come down off the cross: "When they first start nailing him, there isn't none of them wouldn't stop it if they could." The third Roman soldier feels "like hell," partly from the red wine but mostly from his feelings about what they had done that day.

GEORGE (6), the Hebrew wine-seller, tries to stay out of the discussion: "I'll tell you, gentlemen, I wasn't out there. It's a thing I haven't taken any interest in." He's a Jew but is indifferent to the crucifixion, probably because he wants to stay out of trouble with the Roman officials. At least two of the soldiers may be seen as sympathetic to Christ—although they also show some sympathy to others they have crucified.

Today is Friday was first published as a pamphlet by The As Stable Publications, Englewood, New Jersey, in the summer of 1926 and reprinted in *Men Without Women* (1927).

"To Good Guys Dead"   Poem against war, written in 1922 and first published in *88 Poems* (1979).

To Have and Have Not   Hemingway's third novel (1937) and considered by most critics to be one of his least successful ones. It is, however, a powerful comment on the effects of the Depression on the people of Key West, Florida. The "Haves," rich tourists, including college professors and government officials, winter in Key West, spend their money, and pay little or no attention to the plight of the poor, the "Have Nots," in the town.

The novel was written in 1936 and set in 1934 or 1935; one of the characters mentions that "prohibition's over" (Prohibition ended in 1933).

Harry MORGAN, 43 years old, one of the "Have Nots," is trying to make a living either honestly by chartering his fishing boat or dishonestly by running illegal goods between KEY WEST, Florida, where he and his wife, Marie, 45, lives, and Havana, Cuba. Neither of these occupation is successful, sometimes because of Harry's poor judgment but mostly for reasons beyond his control, and in the end he dies trying to come to terms with a philosophy that has taken "all of his life to learn." He says that "a man alone ain't got no bloody fucking chance." This statement contradicts ideas Harry had held earlier (chapter 10) as he plans the crossing from Key West to Havana with four (illegal) Cubans. He's arguing with himself about whether to take a first mate, and he thinks, "It would be better alone, anything is better alone but I don't think I can handle it alone. It would be much better alone."

There is also irony in his socialism vs. individualism idea, because, although Harry spends a great deal of time alone, it is clear that he and Marie have a good marriage and that they are happy together. The novel's subplot is devoted to the contrast between their marriage and the relationship that Richard and Helen GORDON have, in spite of their wealth, a marriage broken apart finally by adultery on both sides. Richard is a writer with enough money to attract women and other rich people. And throughout the novel the reader is given vivid pictures of other "Haves," most of them as unhappy as the Gordons.

Harry and Marie are happy, in spite of their struggle to make ends meet. At the end of the novel, while Harry is lying badly wounded on the deck of the QUEEN CONCH, being towed into Key West, he tries to tell the captain and mate of the towing Coast Guard cutter what had happened at sea and especially about his new philosophy. But he can only get out a few words, mostly incomprehensible to the two men.

To Have and Have Not is divided into three parts: part 1 is headed "Harry Morgan (Spring)," part 2 is headed "Harry Morgan (Fall)," and part 3 is headed "Harry Morgan (Winter)." In contrast with his first two novels, *The Sun Also Rises* (1926) and *A Farewell to Arms* (1929), each of which is narrated by the main character, Hemingway uses a variety of points of view in *To Have and Have Not*. Part 1 is written in the first person—like the first two novels—with Harry telling his own story. But the short part 2 is written from the point of view of an omniscient narrator, and part 3, almost 60 percent of the novel, is a mix, beginning with two chapters of first-person narration and then switching to an omniscient narrator for the story of four Cubans who hire Harry to take them to Havana. (See FOUR CUBANS.)

Harry Morgan is the main character throughout, but his language usage is different in parts 2 and 3 from the first-person, literate narration of part 1. He is semiliterate at best in parts 2 and 3, saying, for example, "It don't do you any good to talk like that" and "But I can't get no anchor up." Hemingway thought of the novel, however, as the Morgan stories, so to have three somewhat separate stories is, perhaps, not so surprising, even though the main character seems to change.

Part 1 (chapters 1 through 5) begins in the Havana PEARL OF SAN FRANCISCO CAFÉ with three Cubans trying to talk Harry into taking them to Florida; he is trying to stay legal by chartering his boat to fishermen. The Cubans leave the café and are killed on the street by two "fellows," evidently Cubans preparing for revolution and stopping other Cubans from leaving the country.

Also in chapter 1, the first "Have" to appear, Mr. JOHNSON, hires Harry for a fishing trip, but it is a disastrous affair with the incompetent and selfishly exploitative Johnson not only losing overboard $650 worth of Harry's fishing gear—a Hardy reel and 600 yards of No. 36 thread—but also leaving town without paying the $850 for 18 days of charter boat rental fees.

Because of this setback, Harry is forced to make arrangements with a Chinese man, Mr. SING, to carry 12 illegal Chinese aliens from Havana to Florida. Just as he is receiving the final payment from Mr. Sing, Harry, who has been suspicious all along, thinks Mr. Sing is reaching for a gun and so kills him. He and his "rummy" first mate, EDDY, then drop the 12 aliens off on a nearby beach and take the boat on to Key West, where Harry rejoins Marie for a quiet evening at home, while their three daughters have gone to a movie.

In part 2 (chapters 6 through 8), Harry and his Negro mate, WESLEY, are both wounded and trying to get Harry's boat, loaded with illegal liquor, back to Key West. They had picked up the liquor in MARIEL, a Cuban town on the north side of the island about 25 miles southwest of Havana, and, although Mariel had been "wide open" for six months—they've been running liquor all summer—on this trip they are shot at and wounded by Cuban officials, Harry now with an arm no longer of use. They manage to get back to the Florida Keys, but Harry decides to dump the liquor because he and Wesley are too badly wounded to avoid being caught.

As they are dropping the 40-pound sacks overboard, they are seen by men on a fishing charter, including two "government men." Luckily for Harry and Wesley, however, the boat is owned by a friend of Harry's, Captain WILLIE, and he immediately takes his boat farther out to sea, allowing Harry to continue into Key West.

Part 3, the longest of the three parts (chapters 9 through 26), begins with Harry lying to a lawyer about how he lost his arm, a clear transition from part 2. Hemingway informs the reader that it is "Albert Speaking" in chapter 9, that is, Albert TRACY, who narrates the events at FREDDIE'S PLACE in Key West where a lawyer whom Harry calls BEE-LIPS tries to argue Harry into carrying four Cuban illegal aliens to Havana.

Harry is able to rationalize accepting the job because his boat has been confiscated by the government and he has lost his arm. He says, "let me tell you, my kids ain't going to have their bellies hurt and I ain't going to dig sewers for the government. . . ." Albert, who also needs the money, agrees to be first mate. The novel's two plots are then presented in more or less alternating chapters to the end of the book. In chapter 10 the reader gets Harry's INTERIOR MONOLOGUE as he plans the "crossing," including which local boats he thinks are fast enough to catch his boat. Harry steals his boat from the government docks, but customs officers take it away again, forcing Harry to rent Freddie's boat for $1,200 (chapter 13).

Harry is at home with Marie in chapters 12 and 14, telling her about the plans, the scene showing again the pleasant relationship they have together in contrast with that between Richard and Helen Gordon. The falling apart of the Gordon marriage is described in chapters 15, 19, and 21.

Chapter 18 is the climactic chapter of the novel. Unknown to Harry, the four Cubans have set him up for a far worse scenario than he had envisioned. They rob the FIRST STATE TRUST AND SAVINGS BANK in Key West, which is just a block from the dock where Harry's rented boat is tied and waiting. The Cubans climb on board, and, when Albert hesitates in casting off the lines, the "biggest Cuban" kills him with a Thompson submachine gun he used in the bank robbery. The four Cubans have robbed the bank, Harry finds out later, to help finance the revolution against the Cuban government, the "Have Nots" in Cuba fighting against the "Haves" in the present corrupt government. But Harry thinks to himself, "[t]o help the working man he robs a bank and kills a fellow works with him and then kills that poor damned Albert that never did any harm. That's a working man he kills. He never thinks of that. With a family. . . . The hell with their revolutions." Harry, knowing that he will be killed once they get to Havana, manages to kill the four men but is wounded in the process, badly enough that he loses consciousness.

Chapters 22 and 24 again present the contrasting plots, first a drunken fight at Freddie's Place involving Richard Gordon and Professor John MACWALSEY with some other customers, and then a chapter that describes in greater detail than before the "Haves" on their luxury yachts, almost all of them leading miserable lives.

Chapters 23 through 26 complete the Harry Morgan plot, first his attempt to get out his philosophy of life ("a man alone ain't got no bloody fucking chance") to the Coast Guard captain and his mate, followed by Harry's death in the hospital (chapter 25) and Marie's subsequent suffering over his death (chapter 26). This last chapter presents Marie's interior monologue as she thinks about the good times with Harry, the happiness of a good marriage, even if the couple is poor.

To Have and Have Not was published by Charles Scribner's Sons October 15, 1937, in a first edition of 10,130 copies. The price was $2.50. Two of the novel's three parts were published previously as short stories: Part 1 as "One Trip Across" in *Cosmopolitan* (April 1934) and part 2 as "The Tradesman's Return" in *Esquire* (February 1936). Part 1 was slightly revised for the Scribner's novel, but part 2 was considerably changed (see Hanneman's bibliography).

To Have and Have Not (film)   Warner Brothers picture, released in October 1944 (100 minutes); produced by Jack Warner, produced and directed by Howard Hawks, screenplay by Jules Furthman and William Faulkner, photography by Sid Hickox, art direction by Charles Novi, special effects by Roy Davidson, set decoration by Casey Roberts, music (including the song "How Little We Know") by Hoagy Carmichael, lyrics by Johnny Mercer.

Cast: Humphrey Bogart (Harry Morgan), Walter Brennan (Eddie), Lauren Bacall (Marie), Dolores Moran (Helene De Bursac), Hoagy Carmichael (Cricket), Walter Molnar (Paul De Bursca), Sheldon Leonard (Lieutenant Coyo), Marcel Dalio (Gerard), Walter Sande (Johnson), Dan Seymour (Captain Renard), Aldo Nadi (Renard's bodyguard), Paul Marion (Beauclerc), Patricia Shay (Mrs. Beauclerc), Pat West (bartender), Emmet Smith (Emil), and Sir Lancelot (Horatio).

To Have and Have Not (radio production)   The "Lux Radio Theater" production (October 1946) starred Humphrey Bogart and Lauren Bacall in their film roles as Harry Morgan and Marie.

To Have and Have Not (television play)   NBC "Lux Video Theatre" production (January 1957), starring Edmond O'Brien and Beverly Garland.

Toklas, Alice B. (1877–1967)   Secretary and lesbian companion to Gertrude STEIN from 1907 until Stein's death in 1946, most of those years in Paris at 27, rue de Fleurus. Toklas wrote *The Alice B. Toklas Cook Book* (1955) and *What is Remembered* (1963). Gertrude Stein, however, wrote *The Autobiography of Alice B. Toklas* (1933). Toklas and Stein were godmothers for Hemingway's oldest son, Jack, baptized in Paris March 16, 1924. The two women are buried in the Pére Lachaise cemetery in Paris.

In *A Moveable Feast* Hemingway writes little about Toklas. He states that he liked her, but he never uses her name, referring to her only as Stein's "friend" or "companion." He says that she "had a very pleasant voice, was small, very dark, with her hair cut like Joan of Arc in the Boutet de Monvel illustrations and had a very hooked nose."

Toledo Blade, The   This newspaper and the "Grand Rapids paper" are read by Jim GILMORE in "Up in Michigan."

Tolstoi, Leo Nikolayevich (1828–1910)   Russian novelist and short story writer, best known for *War and Peace* (1865–69) and *Anna Karenina* (1875–77). In *Green Hills of Africa* Hemingway reads Tolstoi's *Sevastopol* in his safari camp. "I thought about Tolstoi and about what a great advantage an experience of war was to a writer."

In *A Moveable Feast* Hemingway writes that upon arriving in Paris in late 1921 the Constance GARNETT translations of Tolstoi were some of the first books he borrowed from Sylvia BEACH's American bookshop, SHAKESPEARE AND COMPANY (1). The name is more commonly spelled Tolstoy.

Tom (1)   Nineteen-year-old friend of the narrator in "The Light of the World." He gets angry when the bartender at the first bar they go to is suspicious of the two young men, refusing to serve them until he sees their money, and Tom spits onto the floor a mouthful of the free-lunch pig's feet. The bartender then kicks them out of his bar.

Tom also gets the story's final sentence. The cook at the railway station restaurant, where the boys go next, is homosexual and made fun of by other customers. At the end of the story, as the boys are leaving, the cook asks them which way they are going, and Tom answers, "The other way from you."

Tom (2)   Narrator of "A Man of the World," one of the few narrators in a Hemingway short story who isn't also the main character.

Tom Collins   One of Thomas HUDSON's drinks in *Islands in the Stream,* made, for him, with coconut water and bitters.

It's also a drink that David BOURNE, in *The Garden of Eden,* describes to "the boy" at the hotel in LA NAPOULE, France, so that he can make one.

Tomini   A drink made, according to Thomas HUDSON in *Islands in the Stream,* of gin, coconut water, with ANGOSTURA and lime.

tommy gun   See THOMPSON SUBMACHINE GUN.

Tompkins, Harold   Fiancé of Frances and one of the "Haves" in *To Have and Have Not.*

Tonani   An adjutant in "A Simple Enquiry." He does some of the MAJOR (3)'s paperwork while the major, lying on his bed in the adjacent room, attempts to seduce PININ, the major's 19-year-old orderly. Although Tonani apparently does not hear the conversation in the next room, he notices that Pinin is "flushed and moved differently," when he leaves the hut, and Tonani "smiles," indicating that he knows that the major is homosexual and that he probably attempted to seduce the young orderly.

"Tooth Pulling No Cure-All"   Article, published in *The Toronto Star Weekly* (April 10, 1920), reprinted in *Ernest Hemingway: Dateline Toronto* (1985). The headline in the *Star Weekly* was "Toothpulling Not a Cure-for-All." It is about the shifting fads in medical practice: first appen-

dicitis, then tonsils and adenoids, blood pressure, and now "our teeth."

Torcello   Island town just east of VENICE where Richard CANTWELL in *Across the River and Into the Trees* points out to his driver, Jackson, the tower of the church at Torcello and the *campanile* of Burano beyond it, which Cantwell thinks leans almost as much as the Leaning Tower of Pisa. Cantwell tells Jackson it was a Torcello boy who "located the body of St. Mark . . . and brought the remains . . . to Venice" where they built St. Mark's cathedral. Cantwell also points out that Torcello is where the Venetians escaped to when the Visigoths attacked their city in the fifth century.

torero   Professional bullfighter. Matadors (the actual killer of the bull), BANDERILLEROS, and PICADORS are all *toreros. Torero* means, according to Hemingway in *Death in the Afternoon,* anyone connected with bullfighting. The term "toreador" is obsolete.

Torino   In "My Old Man," the Mirafiore steeplechase racetrack is located in Torino, Italy.

Toronto Daily Star, The   Newspaper founded in 1892, known as *The Toronto Star* from November 6, 1971. While Hemingway worked for *The Star* in the early 1920s, the offices were at 18–20 King Street West. Hemingway's articles appeared in the *Daily Star* beginning on January 27, 1920, with "New Ether to Credit of Toronto Surgeon." Most of the stories he wrote for the *Star* newspapers would be as European correspondent. He wrote 202 articles for the *Daily Star* and the *Star Weekly* in the four years he worked for them. See *Ernest Hemingway: Dateline Toronto,* edited by William White (1985) and *Hemingway: The Toronto Years* (1994), written by William Burrill.

Toronto Star Weekly, The   Newspaper founded in 1910, published on Saturdays as a supplement to *The Toronto Daily Star.* Hemingway's first article for the *Star Weekly* appeared on February 7, 1920, titled "Truth-telling Ether a Secret," a follow-up story to the article published a week earlier in *The Daily Star.* Hemingway's last Toronto article, "The Freiburg Fedora," appeared in *The Star Weekly* on January 19, 1924, although Hemingway's contract with the newspaper officially ended at the end of 1923. Ernest and his wife Hadley left Toronto by train for New York on January 10, 1924, on their way back to Paris, where his career as a novelist and short story writer would begin.

Toros celebres   Title of a book mentioned in *Death in the Afternoon* that lists "alphabetically by the names the breeders gave them, the manner of dying and feats of some three hundred and twenty-two pages of celebrated bulls."

EH passport photo, December 1921 (Courtesy of the John F. Kennedy Library)

Torrents of Spring, The This short novel is a parody—although Hemingway never admitted it in public—of the style of some of his contempory novelists: Gertrude STEIN, H. L. MENCKEN, James JOYCE, D. H. LAWRENCE, John DOS PASSOS, and particularly Sherwood ANDERSON and his novel DARK LAUGHTER (1925).

The Torrents of Spring is, however, a novel humorous on its own. It is subtitled "A Romantic Novel in Honor of the Passing of a Great Race," the "great race" probably indicating the race of writers whom Hemingway refused to imitate (when he was writing serious fiction) and whom he thought of as "passing."

Torrents is set in northern Michigan after World War I, probably 1924 or 1925. There are two "main" characters, Scripps O'NEIL and Yogi JOHNSON, both of whom work in PETOSKEY in a PUMP-FACTORY. Scripps marries Diana, an "elderly waitress" at BROWN'S BEANERY ("The Best by Test"), shortly after he arrives in Petoskey, having lost or misplaced a wife in Mancelona. He soon becomes interested, however, in a younger waitress, MANDY, who regales Scripps with literary anecdotes, thereby winning his affection.

Diana, meanwhile, tries to hold onto him by reading everything she can that she thinks will impress her husband: *The New York Times Book Review, Harper's Magazine,* etc., all of which reading does her no good. At the end of the novel, Scripps tells Mandy that she is "his woman," a line he had given to Diana earlier.

Yogi Johnson is a war veteran whose life was changed "forever" by being taken to bed by a Paris prostitute, whom he later sees take to bed a "British officer," thus sending him into a sort of permanent depression. But an Indian squaw in Michigan, the wife of one of Yogi's two Indian friends, comes into Brown's Beanery "clad only in a pair of worn mocassins," and Yogi falls immediately in love. At the end of the novel, while Scripps is taking up with Mandy, Yogi is seen walking up the railroad tracks with the still naked squaw and stripping off his own clothes one item at a time.

Hemingway uses a flashback and "Author's Notes" in telling the story. Part 1, "Red and Black Laughter," and part 2, "The Struggle for Life," concern, primarily, Scripps O'Neil. Part 3, "Men in War and the Death of Society," and part 4, "The Passing of a Great Race and the Making and Marring of Americans," are, primarily, about Yogi Johnson. The latter title is a parody of Gertrude Stein's *The Making of Americans,* a novel without plot, dialogue, or action. The two "plots" in *Torrents* are separate, O'Neil and Johnson coming together only at the factory and at Brown's Beanery. The "Author's Notes" are letters to the reader from Hemingway as he writes the story. He says he wrote the novel in 10 days at various Paris watering holes, and he wants to explain the novel or add essays about writing. The "notes" are sometimes as long as the chapter upon which Hemingway is elaborating.

Each of the four parts has an epigraph from Henry FIELDING, the 18th-century English writer of *Tom Jones* and other novels. The first epigraph states, "The only source of the true Ridiculous (as it appears to me) is affectation." This idea sets the tone for Hemingway's humor, his own affectation in *Torrents* meant to reflect his attitude toward the style of some of his contemporaries, but also the affectation of the novel's narrator and of the main characters. At one point the narrator describes Scripps O'Neil's thoughts: "Who was that waitress, anyway? What was it had happened to her in Paris? . . . Who was Yogi, anyway? Had he really been in the war? . . . Where was Cadillac, anyway? Time would tell."

The narrator is occasionally confused, at one point saying of Scripps O'Neil, "There was nothing rococo about [Mancelona High School], like the buildings he had seen in Paris. No, he had never been in Paris. That was not he. That was his friend Yogi Johnson." And Scripps remembers being a boy in the South during the Civil War, highly improbable since that would make him too old for the time of the novel—the mid-1920s.

The first "Author's Note" is at the beginning of chapter 10, the final chapter in part 2. Hemingway informs readers that with the narrator's statement that "Spring was coming," we are to note that chapter 10 begins on "the same day on which the story starts." (Readers of *Hemingway A to Z* should keep in mind as they discover individual entries for the novel, that *The Torrents of Spring* is a parody and that each entry should be taken in the spirit in which Hemingway wrote the novel.)

There is speculation among scholars, though no firm evidence, that Hemingway, who was under contract to BONI & LIVERIGHT, publishers of *In Our Time* (1925) and also Sherwood ANDERSON's publishers, sent them *The Torrents of Spring* knowing they would reject it, and so give him the freedom to break his contract with them and publish, instead, with Scribner's.

There is little scholarly criticism of the novel, probably because it is a merely interesting first novel, with little of the seriousness of Hemingway's later work, such as *The Sun Also Rises,* which was published by Scribner's less than five months after *Torrents.*

The Torrents of Spring was published by Charles Scribner's Sons on May 28, 1926, in a first edition of 1,250 copies, at $1.50 each.

Tortosa   Spanish town on the Mediterranean coast, about 96 miles southwest of Barcelona. The bridge in "Old Man at the Bridge" crosses the Ebro River near Tortosa.

Tortugas   The Dry Tortugas, islands about 65 miles west of KEY WEST, Florida. In "After the Storm," the narrator locates a sunken ocean liner between the Dry Tortugas islands and the REBECCA LIGHT.

Touraine   Province in France's Loire Valley where, in "Mr. and Mrs. Elliot," the Elliots rent a château for the summer.

Tour d'Argent restaurant   In Paris at 15, quai de la Tournelle, near the east end of the boulevard Saint-Germain, still frequented by Americans as it was when Hemingway lived in Paris in the early 1920s and ate at least one meal there. It's the oldest restaurant in Paris and still one of the most expensive; it was founded as a hostelry in 1582.

tourists (1)   Two in Paris are being "urged" by the MAN WITH JUMPING FROGS to buy mechanical toys, and three other tourists are looking on as the man and his GIRL ASSISTANT manipulate the toys on the sidewalk near the Paris Opéra, all observed and noted by Jake BARNES in *The Sun Also Rises.*

tourists (2)   At the TERRACE café in *The Old Man and the Sea,* looking down at the 18-foot-long skeleton remains of the marlin caught by SANTIAGO. The skeleton lies "among the beer cans and dead barracudas." The tourists do not understand what they are seeing. The waiter tries to explain by telling them about the sharks that attacked the marlin, but the tourists think the skeleton is that of a shark and so miss the significance of what has happened.

tourists (3)   BOBBY talks about the pictures tourists take, in the "BIMINI" section of *Islands in the Stream.* "People paying money for pictures of UNCLE EDWARD. Pictures of Negroes in the water. Negroes on land. Negroes in boats. Turtle boats. Sponge boats. Squalls making up. Waterspouts. Schooners that got wrecked. Schooners building. Everything they could see free."

"Tourists Scarce at Swiss Resorts"   Article, published in *The Toronto Daily Star* (February 4, 1922), reprinted in *The Wild Years* (1962), and reprinted in *Ernest Hemingway: Dateline Toronto* (1985). The headline in the *Daily Star* was "Tourists Are Scarce at the Swiss Resorts." Datelined "Les Avants. Switzerland," this article reports that the exchange rate of Swiss francs has fallen to five for one dollar and so has chased away American tourists. What Americans don't know, according to Hemingway, is that the exchange rate is no better anywhere else in Europe, so Switzerland is as good a spot for tourists as any other place.

Tour du Pays Basque   Bicycle-race in *The Sun Also Rises* of which Jake BARNES sees part when the riders stop over in SAN SEBASTIÁN while Jake is there relaxing after the Fiesta SAN FERMÍN.

Tovarich   Russian term meaning "friend," "comrade," or "countryman." In *The Fifth Column* it is the name Max uses for Philip RAWLINGS when the two counterespionage agents talk to the fascists at the observation post on the Extremadura Road. Max uses the term because he wants the fascists to think that he and Rawlings are Russians.

"To Will Davies"   Poem about the hanging of two men, written "to" the Welsh-born poet William Henry Davies (1871–1940), who spent several years wandering across America before writing several books of poetry and *The Autobiography of a Super-tramp* (1907). The poem was first published in *88 Poems* (1979).

town   Unnamed in "A Way You'll Never Be," located in northern Italy, close enough to FORNACI that Nick ADAMS, the story's main character, can ride his bicycle between the two towns in a single day.

town beggar   In "Out of Season," he is the only person in Cortina to lift his hat to PEDUZZI (1) and the YOUNG

GENTLEMAN as they pass on their way to fish illegally for trout.

Town and Country   Popular magazine of the 1920s, which, in "The Snows of Kilimanjaro," published advertisements with HELEN (3)'s picture in them. According to the narrator, she also appeared in a magazine called *Spur*. HARRY thinks of her now, as he looks at her, as "only a little the worse for drink, only a little the worse for bed."

Townsend, Geoffrey   See Audrey BRUCE.

"Track Team Loses to Culver"   Article for Oak Park and River Forest High School newspaper, *The Trapeze* (March 30, 1917), reprinted in *Hemingway at Oak Park High: The High School Writings of Ernest Hemingway, 1916–1917* (1993).

Tracy, Albert   Harry MORGAN's first mate for the illegal voyage to Cuba from KEY WEST in part 3 of *To Have and Have Not*. The story is written from his point of view at the beginning of part 3, as they make plans at FREDDIE'S PLACE to take four Cubans to Havana, using Freddie's boat. Once at sea, the "biggest Cuban" kills Albert with a burst of bullets from his THOMPSON SUBMACHINE GUN at point-blank range. "You don't need no mate," he tells Harry. Only once is Albert's last name used.

Tracy, Mrs.   Albert TRACY's wife, who asks about her husband when Harry MORGAN's boat is brought in to the NAVY YARD at KEY WEST near the end of *To Have and Have Not*. Nobody knows that Albert was killed by Roberto, one of the four Cuban bank robbers, and then thrown overboard. Mrs. Tracy accidentally falls in the water and has to be rescued by two coast guardsmen.

"Tradesman's Return, The"   Published as a short story in *Esquire* (February 1936), but it then became part 2 of *To Have and Have Not* (1937). It was published separately again in *The Complete Short Stories of Ernest Hemingway* (1987). See *To Have and Have Not*.

"Trading Celebrities"   Article, published in *The Toronto Star Weekly* (February 19, 1921), reprinted in *Ernest Hemingway: Dateline Toronto* (1985). The headline in the *Star Weekly* was "Why Not Trade Other Public Entertainers Among the Nations as the Big Leagues Do Baseball Players?" In the article Hemingway suggests that if trades were made, then countries could trade politicians, newspapers ("the *Toronto Telegram*" for the "*London Times*"), writers ("Anatole France, Jean Jacques Rousseau and Voltaire" for "Harold Bell Wright, Owen Johnson, Robert W. Chambers and $800,000 in gold"), boxers, and mountains.

"Train Trip, A"   Fragment from an unfinished novel, published as a "short story" in *The Complete Short Stories of Ernest Hemingway* (1987).

transatlantic review   Short-lived magazine (January 1924–January 1925) published in Paris and edited by Ford Madox FORD. Three of Hemingway's short stories were first published in the *transatlantic*: "Indian Camp," titled "Work in Progress" (April 1924 issue); "The Doctor and the Doctor's Wife" (December 1924); and "Cross Country Snow" (January 1925). In *A Moveable Feast* Hemingway writes of talking Ford into serializing Gertrude Stein's long novel *The Making of Americans*, "knowing that it would outrun the life of the review."

When Ford started the magazine, Bill Bird, publisher at Three Mountains Press, suggested on a whim that Ford put the name in lowercase letters. He did, but most references to the journal capitalize the first letters of each word. In *A Moveable Feast* Hemingway refers to it as "*The Transatlantic Review*" in one place and correctly, as "*transatlantic review*" in another.

"Translations from the Esquimaux: There Are Seasons"   Poem written about 1922 and first published in *88 Poems* (1979).

Trapeze, The   Newspaper of Oak Park and River Forest High School while Hemingway was a student and for which he wrote 37 articles during his junior and senior years (1916–17), all reprinted in *Hemingway at Oak Park High: The High School Writings of Ernest Hemingway, 1916–1917* (1993). He was editor in his senior year. The newspaper was founded in 1912 and continues to be published at the end of the century.

"Travel Poem"   Poem written to Mary Hemingway in 1949 and first published in *88 Poems* (1979).

"Treachery in Aragon"   Article, published in *Ken* (June 30, 1938), about German treachery in the Spanish civil war which led to the breakthrough on the Aragon front in March 1938.

Treaty of Sèvres   In 1920 a World War I peace treaty was signed in Sèvres, France, that virtually abolished the nation of Turkey. The treaty was signed by Turkish Sultan Mohammed VI but was rejected by the rival nationalist government of Pasha KEMAL Atatürk. Atatürk signed a separate agreement with the Soviet Union and then led his Turkish army to defeat the Greeks at Constantinople, a battle that Hemingway witnessed and reported for *The Toronto Star*. The Allies were forced to write a new peace agreement in 1923 in Lausanne, Switzerland.

Tremblay   Near Vincennes, just southeast of Paris, where, in the 1920s, there was a racetrack just east of the Bois de Vincennes. In "My Old Man," JOE's "old man" raced there. Hemingway also saw races there.

trench mortars   Frederic HENRY identifies these weapons as the ones firing on the Italian soldiers and his ambulance crew in the fighting in book 1 of *A Farewell to Arms*. Frederic is wounded by trench mortar shells.

trepan   A tool for cutting shallow holes by removing a core. As a surgical term, it means to bore small holes in bone, usually in the skull. In "A Way You'll Never Be" Nick's wound is in the knee, but he is also shell-shocked and making nonsensical statements, and Captain PARAVICINI, who is not a doctor and so may not know the precise definition of the word, says, "it should have been trepanned." The "it" may refer to Nick's knee, where he specifically mentions being wounded, but it may also refer to either a literal or a figurative head wound.

Triana   Small town across the river from Seville in Spain, where the bullfighters, Manuel Garcia MAERA and JOSELITO, are buried. Triana is mentioned in the booklet advertising *The Forum* magazine in "Banal Story."

"Tribute to Mamma from Papa Hemingway, A"   Article, published in *Life* (August 18, 1952), about Marlene Dietrich.

Trieste   Seaport city at the northeast corner of the Adriatic Sea, designated a free territory by the United Nations in 1947. Trieste's "Northern Zone" was turned over to Italy in 1954; the "Southern Zone" was incorporated into Yugoslavia, now part of Slovenia.
   Richard Cantwell is stationed at a U.S. Army base in Trieste during the time of *Across the River and Into the Trees*, the late 1940s. After World War I the city was claimed by Italy, but after World War II it was claimed by Yugoslavia; as a compromise it became U.N. free zone.

Tristan Tzara (1896–1963)   Romanian-born French poet and essayist, founder of the Dada movement, a nihilistic revolution in the arts intended to devalue everything in modern civilization; he is remembered by HARRY in "The Snows of Kilimanjaro."

Trollope, Anthony (1815–1882)   English novelist, best known for his Barsetshire series of novels and his Palliser novels. Lord Harry Hotspur, the main character in *Sir Harry Hotspur of Humblethwaite* (1871), is mentioned in *A Moveable Feast*. Hemingway writes of a strange conversation he had with Ford Madox FORD that included a discussion of men they considered "gentlemen." The fictional character Hotspur was named as one of the possibilities.

Tropical beer ice wagon   In front of the CUNARD BAR in *To Have and Have Not*, used by two gunmen to hide behind while they machine-gun three Cubans. Tropical beer is also the brand drunk by Harry MORGAN in part 1 of *To Have and Have Not*.

"Trout Fishing"   Article, unsigned, published in *The Toronto Star Weekly* (April 10, 1920), and reprinted in *Ernest Hemingway: Dateline Toronto* (1985). The headline in the *Star Weekly* was "Are You All Set for the Trout?" In the article, Hemingway writes that "[s]pring is only spring to the majority of the city dwellers." But to kids and fishermen, it's a special time.

"Trout Fishing in Europe"   Article, published in *The Toronto Star Weekly* (November 17, 1923), reprinted in *Fisherman* (January 1958), in *The Wild Years* (1962), and in *By-Line: Ernest Hemingway* (1967). The article is the result of several trout fishing trips Hemingway took during his early years in Paris. The *TSW* headline read "Trout Fishing All Across Europe: Spain Has the Best, Then Germany."

"Trout-Fishing Hints"   Article, published in *The Toronto Star Weekly* (April 24, 1920), reprinted in *The Wild Years* (1962), and reprinted in *Ernest Hemingway: Dateline Toronto* (1985). The headline in the *Star Weekly* was "Fishing for Trout in a Sporting Way." In the article Hemingway wrote that contrary to what the sporting magazines say in their articles and advertisements about the importance of trout fishing with flies, the "old-timer" knows that "bait fishing for trout with light tackle and a leader is as sportsmanlike as fly fishing. . . . Worms, grubs, beetles, crickets and grasshoppers are some of the best trout baits."

Trouville   Friends of "Mr. and Mrs. Elliot" go to a resort near Trouville in southern France after becoming disenchanted with TOURAINE.

Trudy   Ojibway Indian and childhood girlfriend of Nick ADAMS in "Fathers and Sons." According to the 38-year-old Nick, as he remembers his sexual experiences with her, "she did first what no one has ever done better." He remembers a time when they made love twice in the hemlock woods behind the Indian camp, once while her brother Billy looked on and again a little later while Billy hunted with Nick's shotgun. "You think we make a baby?" Trudy says to him. "We make plenty baby what the hell." She "folded her brown legs together happily and rubbed against him. Something inside Nick had gone a long way away."

True at First Light   Novel, scheduled for publication by Charles Scribner's Sons, an imprint of Macmillan Publishing Company in the summer of 1999. Edited by Hemingway's second son, Patrick, the novel is considered the last of four book-length manuscripts left unpublished at Hemingway's death in 1961. The others are *A Moveable Feast* (published in 1964), *Islands in the Stream* (1970), and *The Garden of Eden* (1986). There is another unfinished manuscript in the Hemingway Collection at the John F. Kennedy Library in Boston, a 20-chapter manuscript, in pencil, with the working title "Jimmy Breen." An alternate title, "A New Slain Knight: A Novel," is crossed out.

True at First Light was written from experiences Hemingway and his wife Mary had on an African safari from the end of 1953 to the beginning of 1954. An excerpt appeared in *Sports Illustrated* (December 20, 1971, January 3, 1972, and January 10, 1972). The title was "African Journal" and included the details of two plane crashes the Hemingways survived.

Trumbo dock   KEY WEST dock in *To Have and Have Not* where the car ferries loaded, before there was a highway to the north.

"Truth-telling Ether a Secret"   Article, unsigned, published in *The Toronto Star* (February 7, 1920), reprinted in William Burrill's *Hemingway: The Toronto Years* (1994). It was identified as a Hemingway story by *Star* librarian William McGeary. The article was a follow-up story to "New Ether to Credit of Toronto Surgeon," about the importance to medical science of the new ether, discovered by Toronto's Dr. James H. Cotton. It also turns out to be, according to Hemingway, a truth serum.

"Try Bobsledding If You Want Thrills"   Article, published in *The Toronto Daily Star* (March 4, 1922), reprinted in *Ernest Hemingway: Dateline Toronto* (1985). The headline in the *Daily Star* was "Try Bob-sledding If You Want Thrills." In the article, datelined "Les Avants, Switzerland," Hemingway provides a how-to-do-it article on the art of bobsledding. "If you want a thrill of the sort that starts at the base of your spine in a shiver and ends with your nearly swallowing your heart, as it leaps with a jump into your mouth, try bobsledding on a mountain road at fifty miles an hour."

Tschagguns   Western Austrian town "across the valley" from Schruns; mentioned in *A Moveable Feast*. It was a lumber village in the 1920s when the Hemingways were there.

"Tuna Fishing in Spain"   Article, published in *The Toronto Star Weekly* (February 18, 1922), reprinted in *The Wild Years* (1962), and in *By-Line: Ernest Hemingway*

(1967). Datelined "Vigo, Spain," this article is about the tuna industry in Vigo, a "pasteboard looking village, cobble streeted, white and orange plastered," on an "almost landlocked harbor . . . large enough to hold the entire British navy."

Hemingway says you can go out with the fisherman for a dollar a day, and if you are lucky enough to catch one of the "green-blue and silver" fish and survive the six-hour fight it will take to haul him in, you will feel afterwards as if you are in "the presence of the very elder gods and they will make you feel welcome." The *TSW* headline read "At Vigo, in Spain, Is Where You Catch the Silver and Blue Tuna, the King of All Fish."

Tunney, Gene (1897–1979)   U.S. boxer, the world heavyweight champion (1926–29). He defeated Jack Dempsey for the title and beat him again in the famous "long-count" fight (1928), and retired undefeated. Tunney's official name was James Joseph Tunney.

He is thought about by Richard CANTWELL in *Across the River and Into the Trees* because Tunney had said once that he had read Shakespeare's *King Lear*.

In *Islands in the Stream*, Tunney is one of several people Thomas HUDSON and his friends drink to at Havana's Floridita Bar.

Turgenev, Ivan (1818–1883)   Russian novelist, poet, and playwright, best known in the United States for *A Sportsman's Sketches* (1852), *Fathers and Sons* (1862), and *A Month in the Country* (1855). Hemingway admired Turgenev and titled his parody of Sherwood Anderson's *Dark Laughter* after the Russian writer's *The Torrents of Spring* (1872), a novel of a quasi-fantastic nature.

Turgenev's *A Sportsman's Sketches* is read by Jake BARNES while in PAMPLONA waiting for the Fiesta SAN FERMÍN to begin.

In *A Moveable Feast* Hemingway writes that as soon as he discovered Sylvia BEACH's American bookshop, SHAKESPEARE AND COMPANY (1), he began to read the entire works of Turgenev, all of Gogol that had been translated into English, the Constance GARNETT translations of Tolstoi, and the translations of Chekhov. Hemingway says of Turgenev that there were things so true in his fiction, like the descriptions of landscape, that they changed you. And he writes that while waiting for F. Scott Fitzgerald to show up in Lyon, where they were to pick up Fitzgerald's car, Hemingway read the first volume of *A Sportsman's Sketches*.

Turiguaño   Near the end of *Islands in the Stream*, as Thomas HUDSON lies dying on his boat, his crew headed for CAIBARIÉN, on Cuba's north coast, where they can get a doctor, Hudson can see across the Bahia Buenavista to the "blue hills of the Turiguaño," an island just off the coast, near the town of Morón.

Turin train   Taken by JOE and his "old man" when they leave Milan for Paris in "My Old Man."

Turkish officer   In "On the Quai at Smyrna," he picks out a gunner's mate as a man who had insulted him, though the British "senior officer" in charge knows that he's picked the wrong man.

"Turk Red Crescent Propaganda Agency"   Article, published in *The Toronto Daily Star* (October 4, 1922), reprinted in *Ernest Hemingway: Dateline Toronto* (1985). In the article, datelined "Constantinople," Hemingway reports that the chances of peace between Greece and Turkey are good now, because British General Harington wants peace and the Franco-Turk accord seems strong enough. But possession of THRACE is the key, because the Greek government considers it essential to Greece's well-being. The "Red Crescent" is the Turkish equivalent of the Red Cross.

"Turks Distrust Kemal Pasha"   Article, published in *The Toronto Daily Star* (October 24, 1922), reprinted in *The Wild Years* (1962), and reprinted in *Ernest Hemingway: Dateline Toronto* (1985). The headline in the *Daily Star* was "Turks Beginning To Show Distrust Of Kemal Pasha." Datelined "Constantinople," the article is about Mustapha KEMAL Pasha, who was the hero of the Muslim world while they thought he was fighting a holy war for Turkey against the Greeks. But now that he has conquered Constantinople, he has turned into something of a businessman, more interested in oil in Mesopotamia than in continuing the holy war with Greece.

"Turks Near Constantinople"   Article, unsigned, published in *The Toronto Daily Star* (October 9, 1922), reprinted in *Ernest Hemingway: Dateline Toronto* (1985). Datelined "Constantinople," Hemingway reports that with a British destroyer anchored on the Black Sea coast, British General Harington, responsible for keeping the peace between Turkey and Greece, has forced a Turkish withdrawal from the Ismed neutral zone. The headline in *TDS* read, "Turk Forces Draw Near to Constantinople."

Turner, Mr.   One of two characters in "A Pursuit Race." He is the manager, or at least an administrator, of a burlesque show. He catches his advance man, William CAMPBELL, in a Kansas City hotel room "hopped to the eyes" on drugs. He is sympathetic and even offers to help him into rehabilitation, but he's also a man pursued by his work and so has to get back to the burlesque show.

The story ends with the narrator stating that "Mr. Turner was a man who knew what things in life were. . . valuable." He's a workaholic and so is pursued by his own demons. And because the story's title is clearly a metaphor (see the main entry), it is not difficult to also see "burlesque show" as a metaphor for life itself.

Turner's stables   At the San Siro steeplechase racetrack in Milan, Italy, where the "old man" in "My Old Man" auctions off "everything we couldn't get into a trunk and a suit case."

turtle-ing   Hunting for turtles, referred to in *The Old Man and the Sea*. The types of turtles mentioned are green turtles, hawksbills, and loggerheads, "yellow in their armour-plating, strange in their love-making, and happily eating the PORTUGUESE MEN-OF-WAR with their eyes shut." SANTIAGO remembers how clearly he could see fish below the surface of the GULF STREAM from "the cross-trees of the mast-head" of the turtle boats on which he used to work.

Twain, Mark   (1835–1910)   American novelist, humorist, and lecturer, best known for *Huck Finn* (1884). In *Green Hills of Africa* Hemingway tells Kandisky that the "good" American writers are Henry James, Stephen Crane, and Mark Twain. Hemingway says that "[a]ll modern American literature comes from one book by Mark Twain called *Huckleberry Finn*. . . . All American writing comes from that. There was nothing before. There has been nothing as good since."

12th Brigade   An INTERNATIONAL BRIGADE that fought against the Italians near Trijueque during the SPANISH CIVIL WAR. Mentioned in *For Whom the Bell Tolls*.

28th Division   The men of this U.S. Army division fought at HÜRTGEN FOREST in World War II, remembered by Richard CANTWELL in *Across the River and Into the Trees*. The "T.S. [tough shit] division," Cantwell called it—because they had a lot of hard luck and yet attracted little sympathy. See General Walter Bedell SMITH.

27th Army Corps   This Italian army corps is broken apart by a brigade of Austrians after a "great battle," according to a rumor in *A Farewell to Arms* that Frederic HENRY hears and that later proves to be true. It is one of the battles that begins the Italian retreat from CAPORETTO: "The next night the retreat started." Historically it is the 12th battle of the Isonzo River along the eastern Italian border with Yugoslavia that generated the Italian army's retreat.

Two Christmas Tales   "A North of Italy Christmas" and "Christmas in Paris" were both first published in *The Toronto Star Weekly* (December 22, 1923) as the second and third stories under the general heading "Christmas on the Roof of the World." They were reprinted by Hart Press in Berkeley, California, in *Two Christmas Tales* as a Christmas gift booklet in 1959 and reprinted in *By-Line: Ernest Hemingway* (1967), under the original *Star Weekly* heading, "Christmas on the Roof of the World."

"Two Revolutions Are Likely If Germany Suffers Collapse" Article, unsigned, published in *The Toronto Daily Star* (March 7, 1923), reprinted in William Burrill's *Hemingway: The Toronto Years* (1994). The arti-cle is about the economic dominance of France during Germany's period of inflation following World War I and the meaning to the West if Germany's economy should collapse.

Two Stories Published, in English, by Grafisk Forlag of Copenhagen (1967), this booklet contains Hemingway's short stories "Fifty Grand" and "The Undefeated."

U

Ubiitsi (film) Soviet Union film version of *The Killers*, produced in 1958; directed by Andrei Tarkovsky.

U-boat German submarine, used in World War II. Thomas HUDSON is searching for a German U-boat crew in the "At Sea" section of *Islands in the Stream*. The German crew has stolen a Cuban turtle boat after their sub is destroyed, and they are trying to hide among the islands of the Archipiélago de Camagüey off the northeastern Cuba coast.

Udet, Ernst (1896–1941) One of the many Germans that Richard CANTWELL tells RENATA he likes "best," in *Across the River and Into the Trees*. Udet flew with the German Richthofen squadron in World War I and is said to have shot down 62 Allied planes. In the 1930s he developed the dive-bombing technique used by the German air force in World War II. Cantwell tells Renata that he would like to "talk over certain things [about war]. . . with [ROMMEL] and with Ernst Udet."

Udine In northern Italy, about 54 miles northeast of Venice. It is the town near where Frederic HENRY is wounded in book 1 of *A Farewell to Arms*.

It is also mentioned in "A Natural History of the Dead" in connection with its place in the Battle of CAPORETTO during World War I.

Uffizi Art museum in Florence, Italy, located along the Arno river near the Ponte Vecchio. In *Across the River and Into the Trees*, Colonel Richard Cantwell's driver, JACKSON, tells Cantwell that he had once visited the Pitti and Uffizi galleries and had looked at paintings of madonnas until they "started to run out of my ears."

UHP *Union de Hermanos Proletarianos* (Union of Proletarian Brothers) a small, radical left-wing party active during the SPANISH CIVIL WAR. In *For Whom the Bell Tolls*, the FALANGISTS, who cut off MARÍA's hair and then rape her, write in iodine on her forehead "UHP."

"Ultimately" Poem written in 1921 and first published in *Double-Dealer* (June issue, 1922). It was reprinted in *Salmagundi* (April 30, 1932), a book of early William FAULKNER items.

Ulysses In *Green Hills of Africa* Pop thinks that when Hemingway mentions *Ulysses* he is referring to Homer, but he means the novel by James JOYCE.

The Joyce novel, published in 1922, is also discussed in *Islands in the Stream* because Thomas HUDSON remembers that his oldest son, "young Tom," was expelled from school in Paris for reading the book to his classmates.

In *A Moveable Feast* Hemingway refers to the novel in connection with its banning by the U.S. Postal Service. In his book *Published in Paris* (1975), Hugh Ford describes Hemingway's plan for getting 40 copies of *Ulysses* into the United States by having a friend of his, the painter Barnet Braverman, carry the book by ferryboat between Windsor, Ontario, and Detroit, Michigan. There was no embargo on the novel in Canada, so copies could be mailed to Windsor for Braverman, who then carried them across the river one copy at a time in his painting equipment. Joyce was so pleased with the transaction, according to Ford, that he sent Braverman a signed copy.

Uncle Edward An "old Negro" character in *Islands in the Stream*, one of several BIMINI natives who gets his picture taken regularly by the TOURISTS (3).

Uncle Woolfie One of Thomas HUDSON's 11 cats in *Islands in the Stream*. He's a gray Persian who would never touch catnip.

"Undefeated, The" This short story is set in Madrid in 1918 and is about an out-of-luck bullfighter, Manuel GARCIA, who is just out of the hospital after a long stay, recovering from being badly gored. He is passionate about bullfighting, but he knows that he will have difficulty getting a contract to fight again.

A promoter in Madrid, whom Garcia goes to, thinks he is dead, or at least says so when Garcia enters his office. The promoter, RETANA, described three times on the story's first page as "a little man," offers Garcia a spot in the "nocturnals," nighttime fights in which neither the bulls nor the bullfighters are up to Spanish standards, making the nocturnals more dangerous. Garcia has no choice but to accept not only the nocturnals but also an insulting amount of money, 300 pesetas. He reminds Retana that VILLALTA gets 7,000 pesetas; but Retana reminds Garcia that he is not Villalta, one of the great Spanish bullfighters.

Garcia needs a good picador, someone who will be accurate with the *pica*, the steel-pointed pole used to weaken the bull enough so that the bullfighter is less likely to be injured or killed. Garcia wants ZURITO (1) to "pic" for him, but Zurito usually gets more for pic-ing than Garcia is getting to kill the bulls. Zurito tries to talk Garcia into retiring, but finally agrees to pic for him if he promises to cut his pigtail (symbolic of quit-ting the ring) if he does not do well.

Garcia is on a card with a younger fighter, HERNAN-DEZ, who is sympathetic toward Garcia and encour-ages him throughout the fight. Garcia does well, in fact, in the early stages of the fight, showing skills appreciated by his own handlers and Hernandez but not especially by the crowd. Crowds at nocturnals pay about half the cost of tickets to the regular bullfights and are less knowledgeable, so good bullfighters are less likely to please them. That's what happens in the early stages of Garcia's working with his first bull. He works well, but his luck runs out when he makes his first attempt at killing.

It takes Garcia six attempts before he can kill the bull. He is thrown on the first two attempts and gets a horn in his side on the fifth. After the fourth attempt the people throw cushions to show their disgust, and Garcia trips over one of them as he makes his fifth and fatal attempt to get his sword into the "little spot about as big as a five-peseta piece straight in back of the neck, between the sharp pitch of the bull's shoulders." He fights off his handlers who want to get him to the infir-mary and then manages, on his sixth attempt, to get the "sword. . . in all the way. . . up to the guard."

In the infirmary, as the doctor places the mask over Garcia's face to apply the anesthetic, he begs Zurito not to cut off his pigtail. "I was going good," he said. "I did-n't have any luck. That was all. . . ." "Sure," Zurito says to him. "You were going great." "The Undefeated" is a story about the consequences of self-delusion and obsession.

The story was first published in *This Quarter* (Autumn–Winter 1925–1926) and reprinted in *Men Without Women* (1927).

"Undefeated, The"   Short story published in English by Higher School Publishing House in Moscow (1968), a separate issue of Hemingway's short story "The Undefeated."

"Undefeated, The" (film)   Adaptation of the short story, written in 1956 by A. E. HOTCHNER but not produced.

***Under My Skin* (film)**   Twentieth Century-Fox picture, released in March 1950 (86 minutes), based on Hemingway's short story "My Old Man." Produced by Casey Robinson, directed by Jean Negulesco, screen-play by Casey Robinson, music by Daniele Amfitheatrof, photography by Joseph La Shelle, sets by Thomas Little and Walter M. Scott, orchestration by Maurice de Packh and Earle Hagen, songs by Alfred Newman, Mack Gordon, and Jacques Surmagne, spe-cial effects by Fred Sersen.

Cast: John Garfield (Dan Butler), Micheline Prelle (Paule Manet), Luther Adler (Louis Bork), Orley Lindgren (Joe), Noel Drayton (George Gardner), A. A. Merola (Maurice), Ott George (Rico), Paul Bryar (Max), Ann Codee (Henriette), Steve Geray (bar-tender), Joseph Warfield (Rigoli), Eugene Borden (doctor), Loulette Sablon (nurse), Alphonse Martell (detective), Ernesto Morelli (hotel clerk), Jean Del Val (express man), Hans Herbert (attendant), Esther Zeitlin (flower woman), Maurice Brierre (doorman), Gordon Clark (barman), Frank Arnold (official), Elizabeth Flournoy (American mother), Mario Siletti (Italian officer), Guy Zanette (porter), Andre Charise (gendarme), and Harry Martin (Drake).

"Under the Ridge"   This is the second of the SPAN-ISH CIVIL WAR short stories in which the narrator is a member of an American film crew filming the war (the first is "Night Before Battle"). The Americans are filming an attack by an International Brigade against the REBELS, and they are back from the day's battle and resting along a "ridge above the river where the Spanish troops lay in reserve." The time is April, prob-ably in 1938.

The narrator describes three men who react to the war in various ways. He talks with an Extremaduran soldier who hates all foreigners and has "no fear of bullets" nor of anything. His great-grandmother was killed by the English, "under Wellington," and his father was killed by North Americans in Cuba. And the war he is now in further convinces him of the bru-tality of foreigners.

There is also a middle-aged Frenchman in an International Brigade uniform who walks down over the edge of the ridge out of sight, followed a little later by two civilians, battle police, in leather coats with Mauser pistols "strapped to their legs," asking about him. The two battle police disappear over the ridge and pistol shots are heard. Later the Frenchman is found dead on the side of the hill. The narrator had been through the battle that day, and he understands "how a man might suddenly, seeing clearly the stupidity of dying in an unsuccessful attack. . . seeing its hopeless-ness, seeing its idiocy, seeing how it really was, simply. . . walk away from it as the Frenchman had done." But the battle police had "hunted him down, and the death he had walked away from had found him when he was just over the ridge, clear of the bullets and the shelling, and walking toward the river."

The third soldier is Paco (3), a young, frightened boy, who shoots himself in the hand in order to get out of the battle. At the field hospital they amputate his hand and dress the wound carefully against infection, but then an officer takes him back to the place where he shot himself and, after a speech to the other soldiers that Paco must be "punished as an example," shoots him in the back of the head.

But the "oddest thing about that day," according to the narrator, "was how marvelously the pictures we took of the tanks came out." To his credit, however, he realizes that the "nearest any man was to victory was probably the Frenchman who came, with his head held high, walking out of the battle." "Under the Ridge" may be regarded as a comment on the distorting effects of war on human perception.

The story appeared first in *Cosmopolitan* (October 1939) and then as the fourth of the "stories" in *The Fifth Column and Four Stories of the Spanish Civil War* (1969).

unfinished jokes   In *A Farewell to Arms,* Frederic HENRY and other army and ambulance corps buddies tell jokes that are only hinted at by Frederic, the novel's narrator. Here are the jokes but with the punchlines assumed by the characters in the novel and so left out by Frederic: there is the English private soldier who was placed under the shower bath; there are the eleven Czechoslovaks and the Hungarian corporal; there is the jockey who found the penny; there is the duchess who could not sleep at night; and (after the priest has left, so that no one will be embarrassed in telling it) there is the traveling salesman who arrived at five o'clock in the morning at Marseilles when the mistral was blowing.

"United We Fall Upon *Ken*"   Article, published in *Ken* (June 2, 1938). The article is about letters Hemingway has received urging him to stop writing for this publication, a socialist magazine.

"Unworldly Russians, The"   Article, published in *The Toronto Daily Star* (April 27, 1922), reprinted in *Ernest Hemingway: Dateline Toronto* (1985). The headline in the *Daily Star* was "Russian Delegates at Genoa Appear Not to Be of This World." The dateline is "Genoa." The Russians at the Genoa Economic Conference are unpopular with the world's newspaper reporters because "of [their] utter lack of judgment and [their] complete lack of any grasp of the situation of their relation with the press."

"Up in Michigan"   Gertrude STEIN told Hemingway he couldn't publish this short story, that it was *inaccrochable*, like a painting that could not be hung. It concerns a seduction/rape, which, at the end of the century, would be called "date-rape."

Liz COATES, a young girl who waits tables for Mrs. Smith at D. J. Smith's restaurant in HORTONS BAY, Michigan, likes Jim GILMORE. He had come from Canada to Hortons Bay and bought the blacksmith shop. He is "short and dark with big mustaches and big hands." Nearly every description of Liz's feelings for Jim is sensual: "Liz liked. . . the way the hair was black on his arms and how white they were above the tanned line when he washed up. . . outside the house." Liking him and thinking about his body "made her feel funny."

Jim, D. J. SMITH, and Charley Wyman go on a deer hunting trip to the "pine plains beyond Vanderbilt." While they are gone, Liz can think of nothing else but how much she likes Jim. She can't sleep for thinking about him. "It was awful while he was gone."

She's excited the day he returns, and when she sees the "wagon coming down the road she felt weak and sick sort of inside." But the three deer hunters get drunk from their leftover whiskey, and Jim, who had never paid much attention to Liz before, enters the kitchen where Liz is seated in a chair, and reaches around from behind to touch her breasts. Liz is frightened, but she thinks, "He's come to me finally. He's really come." They walk down to the dock, and Jim kept feeling for her breasts and trying to get his hands up her dress.

She tries to stop him but can't, and then finds herself on her back on the hard planks of the dock with Jim on top of her. "She was frightened but she wanted it. She had to have it but it frightened her." Again she tries to stop him, telling him that they "mustn't do it," but it's too late.

He falls asleep on her, and she has to struggle out from under him. She cries, partly from fear and partly because she realizes that the reality of sex with Jim is so different from the dreams she had had of it. She tries to wake him but can't and so lays her coat over him and walks back to the house, crying. "There was a mist coming up from the bay. She was cold and miserable and everything felt gone."

"Up in Michigan" was first published in *Three Stories & Ten Poems* (1923). It was reprinted in the *Short Stories of Ernest Hemingway* (1954).

"U.S. Aid to China"   Article published in *PM* (June 15, 1941), reprinted in *By-Line: Ernest Hemingway* (1967). In the article, datelined "Rangoon," Hemingway argues that Japan "has temporarily lost her chance of making a peace with China" and that for 70 to 100 million dollars in aid to China, the United States could keep most of the Japanese army in China for six to 10 months. China would not make peace with Japan, Hemingway argues, as long as China continues to receive aid from America.

Hemingway's idea was that keeping Japanese troops busy in China would allow the United States a longer time to prepare for its own war with Japan. "Insurance against having to fight in the Far East until the U.S.A. has built a two-ocean navy that can destroy any Eastern enemy, and thus probably never have to fight, is cheap at that price."

This was the fourth of seven dispatches Hemingway wrote for *PM*. The headline read "Ernest Hemingway Says Aid to China Gives U.S. Two-Ocean Navy Security for Price of One Battleship."

USO   United Service Organizations, supplier of mostly volunteer social, recreational, welfare, and spiritual facilities and programs for the U.S. military. Organized in 1941, the USO provided entertainment during WORLD WAR II for American troops at their stations around the world. It was discontinued in 1947 but resumed in 1949 at the request of President Truman.

In *Islands in the Stream* Thomas HUDSON's first wife is a member of the USO and, in the "Cuba" section, shows up in Havana for an afternoon of conversation, drinking, and sex with Hudson. She has to leave that evening, however, because she is on her way to an unspecified place to entertain the troops.

U.S.O.D. blanket   United States Olive Drab, military issue. Used by Richard CANTWELL and RENATA to keep them warm in the gondola and to hide their lovemaking from the gondolier.

U.S.S. Nokomis   A 243-foot World War I U.S. steam yacht converted into a survey boat in the 1930s with duty in the Caribbean. It surveyed the islands off the northeast coast of Cuba for the Hydrographic Office, and it is those maps that Thomas HUDSON uses in chasing after a German submarine crew in the "At Sea" section of *Islands in the Stream*.

Hudson finds that "[m]any things have happened since the U.S.S. Nokomis had boats sounding in here," particularly in the channels off CAYO CONTRABANDO, just before Hudson and his crew make contact with the Germans. The charts are unreliable, in part because many of the smaller islands near Contrabando are essentially sandbars that shift with storms, tides, and changing currents.

V

V.A.D.   Volunteer Aid Detachment, a nurse's aide during World War I. In *A Farewell to Arms,* Catherine BARKLEY is with the British nurse corps, and she is, as she says, "something called a V.A.D. We work very hard but no one trusts us. . . . A V.A.D. is a short cut." Brett ASHLEY, in *The Sun Also Rises,* had also been a V.A.D.

Val Carlos dancers   One of the groups of riau-riau dancers seen by Jake BARNES and his friends during the Fiesta SAN FERMÍN in PAMPLONA.

Valdepeñas   A region of Spain south of Madrid and inland from the Alicante coast; also the wine produced there. In "The Capital of the World," Valdepeñas is drunk from customers' glasses by the waiters PACO (2), ENRIQUE (1), and the "middle-aged" waiter at the PENSION LUARCA, after the last customers have left. It is the only wine mentioned by Hemingway in *The Dangerous Summer,* about his travels around Spain during the 1959 bullfight season.

Valdepeñas wine is drunk from a pitcher by David and Catherine BOURNE in *The Garden of Eden.* David tells Catherine that it's "an African wine," explaining further that "Africa begins at the Pyrenees" and mentioning in particular the Spanish regions of Asturias and Galicia.

Valencia   Spanish city on the Mediterranean Sea coast. The bullfights held there each year are mentioned in *Death in the Afternoon.*

In *For Whom the Bell Tolls,* Robert JORDAN suggests to PILAR that Valencia is a place where María can go to "work with children" after the war.

Valencia is one of the towns on the bullfight circuit covered by Hemingway in *The Dangerous Summer.* Luis Miguel DOMINGUÍN, one of the two main bullfighters Hemingway followed, is gored in a bullfight there.

"Valentine"   Poem written in criticism of critics, written about 1927 and first published in the *The Little Review* (May 1929).

Valentini, Dr.   In *A Farewell to Arms* he is an Italian doctor at the AMERICAN HOSPITAL (1) in Milan who is called in for a "second opinion" about Frederic HENRY's wounds. In contrast to the three doctors who have just told Frederic he should wait six months for an opera-

tion, Dr. Valentini wants to operate the next morning. And as Frederic escapes to Milan after the retreat from CAPORETTO, he thinks about the "fine job" the doctor had done on his legs.

Valéry, Paul   (1871–1945)   French poet mentioned in *Green Hills of Africa.* The German, Kandisky, asks Hemingway about American literature: "Who is your Thomas Mann? Who is your Valery?" In other words, who is your best novelist, your best poet?

Valhalla Express   Richard CANTWELL's term for the line of Allied airplanes "going back toward the east further than you could see" over the "Kraut positions," dropping, first, "coloured smoke" and then "everything in the world" in preparation for an attack by the "brave boys from the Sixth Parachute Division."

Vallalta (1897–1980)   Spanish bullfighter, described by Jake BARNES in *The Sun Also Rises.*

Valpolicella   One of northern Italy's most famous red wines, from the region above Verona. In *Across the River and Into the Trees* it is the wine chosen by Richard CANTWELL and RENATA on their Friday evening at the GRITTI PALACE HOTEL in Venice.

Van Campen, Miss   In *A Farewell to Arms* she is the head nurse at the AMERICAN HOSPITAL (1) in Milan, where Frederic HENRY is taken after he is wounded. She "did not like me and I did not like her. She was small and neatly suspicious and too good for her position. She asked many questions and seemed to think it was somewhat disgraceful that I was with the Italians." She accuses him of drinking brandy to get jaundice and so delay his return to the front, and she orders his leave to be revoked.

Vanderbilt   Small town about 25 miles southeast of Horton Bay in northern Michigan. In "Up in Michigan," Jim GILMORE, D. J. Smith, and Charley Wyman go deer hunting in "the pine plains beyond Vanderbilt."

Van Dyke, Dr. Henry (1852–1933)   U.S. clergyman and professor of English at Princeton, best known as the author of *The Other Wise Man* (1896). In "Banal Story" he's mentioned because his name appears in the booklet advertising *The Forum* magazine, criticized by the story's narrator for its banal treatment of the arts.

Vanity Fair   Popular magazine of the early 20th century, mentioned in *The Torrents of Spring* as one of the magazines read by Diana SCRIPPS. (The current-day publication of the same name is a revival.)

Varella, Dr.   The first captain at the AMERICAN HOSPITAL (1) in Milan where Frederic HENRY is being treated for wounds in book 2 of *A Farewell to Arms*.

Varini, Capitano   In *A Farewell to Arms* he is the third of the three doctors who examine Frederic HENRY at the AMERICAN HOSPITAL (1) in Milan and agree that an operation should be put off for six months.

Varloff   Officer in General GOLZ's command in *For Whom the Bell Tolls*.

V.C.   See VICTORIA CROSS.

Vega, Lope de (1562–1635)   Spanish dramatic poet, writer of as many as 1,800 plays, of which more than 400 are extant. His full name was Lope Félix de Vega Carpio, called "The Phoenix of Spain." He is best known for his "cloak-and-sword" plays of the manners and intrigue of his time. In *Death in the Afternoon* Hemingway compares the art of bullfighting to the art of painting or writing. The two Spanish writers mentioned are Lope de Vega and his contemporary CERVANTES. Hemingway spelled it "da Vega."

Velázquez (1599–1660)   Great master of the Spanish baroque, one of several painters whom Richard CANTWELL thinks about in *Across the River and Into the Trees*. He is also remembered by Robert JORDAN in *For Whom the Bell Tolls*.

The painters's full name was Diego Rodríguez de Silva y Velázquez.

Velázquez 63   Madrid palace headquarters of the INTERNATIONAL BRIGADE during the Spanish civil war, mentioned in *For Whom the Bell Tolls*.

Vélodrome d'Hiver   Bicycle racing track at 8, boulevard de Grenelle in Paris, which Hemingway writes about in *A Moveable Feast*. Hemingway says that the races were better than his writing about them but that he was able to render the track itself, "with the smoky light of the afternoon and the high-banked wooden track and the whirring sound the tires made on the wood as the riders passed." The indoor course was built in 1910 and was the site of the six-day bicycle races that were so popular in France in the 1920s. It was torn down in 1959.

vendeuse   French, for "salesgirl," or "saleswoman," particularly one at a couture house who personally takes charge of clients. In "A Canary for One," the AMERICAN LADY has for 20 years been buying dresses in a Paris clothing store from the same salesgirls, Thérèse and Amelie, because they have her proper measurements.

Venetian plain   A region of northeast Italy between the Alps and the Adriatic Sea; Venice and Verona are the principal cities. In *A Farewell to Arms* Frederic HENRY crosses the plain between SAN VITO—a small town he can see to the west when he emerges from the TAGLIAMENTO RIVER after escaping from the Italian battle police—and LATISANA, where he hops a train west to Milan.

Referred to as the Veneto plain by Richard CANTWELL, in *Across the River and Into the Trees*, he remembers that the Austrians "attacked again and again and again late through the winter [of 1918], to try to get onto this fine road that they [Cantwell and his driver, Jackson] were rolling on now which led straight to Venice."

Venice   Setting for the FLASHBACK part of *Across the River and Into the Trees*. The setting for the novel is the mouth of the TAGLIAMENTO RIVER and the road back toward TRIESTE, but Venice plays a key role in Cantwell's memory, because that's where RENATA lives and where their affair had developed.

Cantwell tells his driver on their way into the city that Venice is "a tougher town than Cheyenne [Wyoming] when you really know it, and everybody is very polite. . . a tougher town than Casper, . . . as tough as Cooke City, Montana, on the day they have the Old Timers' Fish Fry."

Venice stores   Noticed by Richard CANTWELL as he walks from the GRITTI PALACE HOTEL to HARRY'S BAR in *Across the River and Into the Trees*: "charcuterie with the Parmesan cheeses and the hams from San Daniele . . . the cutlery store. . . an antique dealer's" and a "second-rate restaurant."

Ventimiglia   Italian town on the Mediterranean coast, about three miles from the French border, the starting point for the 10-day trip of the two main characters in "Che Ti Dice La Patria?" (What do you hear from home?)

Verey pistol   Named after Edward Wilson Very (1847–1910)—Hemingway misspelled the name—a U.S. naval officer and weapons expert. After the

American Civil War, Very invented a signal pistol that shoots flares. In the "Bimini" section of *Islands in the Stream,* the drunken Frank HART shoots off several flares in celebration of Queen Mary's birthday and shoots at the Commissioner's house to see if he can burn it down.

Verlaine, Paul (1844–1896) French poet. Hemingway describes, in *A Moveable Feast,* doing his own writing in a rented room on the top floor of the hotel in Paris where Verlaine died.

vermouth Ordered, with soda, by David BOURNE in *The Garden of Eden,* to celebrate the reviews of his second novel and the news from his publisher that it was going into a second printing.

Vermouth is also the drink of choice, sometimes, for Richard GORDON in *To Have and Have Not.*

verónica Bullfighter's slow pass with the cape in front of the bull. Hemingway says in *Death in the Afternoon* that it is called a "verónica" because "the cape was originally grasped in the two hands in the manner in which Saint Veronica is shown in religious paintings to have held the napkin with which she wiped the face of Christ."

"Very Short Story, A" A one-and-a-half-page story about a World War I love affair that turns sour. The man is an American soldier identified only as "HE (2)," the girl a nurse named LUZ. He is in a Padua hospital recuperating from a wound. Luz stays on night duty for three months so she can be with him. They want to get married, but neither of them has a birth certificate.

She writes him love letters after he's returned to the front, but after the armistice, they decide that he should go home and get a job before Luz joins him in the United States. They quarrel about her unwillingness to go home with him. After he leaves, she finds herself lonely in a small Italian town where she is opening a hospital. An Italian officer makes love to her, and she writes to her American lover to tell him that theirs had been merely a "boy and girl affair" and that she expects to be married in the spring. The Italian doesn't marry her, and, when she writes to Chicago about it, she gets no answer. "A short time after," the reader is told, "He" gets gonorrhea from a "girl" while riding in a taxi in Lincoln Park.

"A Very Short Story" was first published as "Chapter 10" of *in our time* (1924) and reprinted in *In Our Time* (1925) under its present title.

V.E. soldiers In *A Farewell to Arms,* MANERA tells PASSINI that the V.E. soldiers (otherwise unidentified) would go to the war no matter what the CARABINIERI did to them or to their families.

"Veteran Visits the Old Front, A" Article, published in *The Toronto Daily Star* (July 22, 1922), reprinted in *Ernest Hemingway: Dateline Toronto* (1985). The headline in the *Star* was "A Veteran Visits Old Front, Wishes He Had Stayed Away." The story is datelined "Paris." Hemingway himself is the veteran, and he writes of returning to northern Italy, visiting Schio, Porto Grande on the Piave, and to Fossalta to show his wife, Hadley, where he had been during the war. But, he concludes, "Chasing yesterdays is a bum show."

Vevey Small Swiss town four miles west of Montreux near the east end of Lake Geneva, where the narrator of "A Canary for One" and his wife stayed during their honeymoon. The narrator learns that the American woman with whom he is traveling stopped a love affair between her daughter and a man from Vevey, because a friend had told her that foreign men made poor husbands.

The railway station café at Vevey is the setting for part 2 of "Homage to Switzerland."

Via Manzoni Street in Milan, running northeast from the great cathedral, with "lots of shops." In *A Farewell to Arms,* Catherine BARKLEY buys a nightgown the evening that Frederic HENRY returns to the front on a midnight train.

Viareggio Italian town on the Ligurian coast about nine miles north of Pisa, which, according to Guy, one of the two main characters in "Che Ti Dice La Patria?" (What do you hear from home?) is where the Italians "drowned" the English poet Percy Bysshe SHELLEY. Actually, Shelley drowned while sailing off the coast near Spezia.

Vicente Chauffeur, who drives ANDRÉS and Gomez to General GOLZ's headquarters in *For Whom the Bell Tolls.*

Vich Spanish town in Catalunya, about 42 miles north of Barcelona, famous for its *salchichón,* a spicy dark sausage. In *The Garden of Eden* David BOURNE orders the sausage.

Victoria Cross British military medal, awarded to soldiers and sailors for acts of conspicuous bravery in the presence of the enemy. Colonel Richard CANTWELL in *Across the River and Into the Trees* received the V.C. in World War I.

The V.C. was also received by one of the two Indians, according to them, in *The Torrents of Spring.*

Villa 206 House where Frederic HENRY is billeted in Gorizia in book 1 of *A Farewell to Arms.*

Villacastín Spanish town near Segovia, northwest of Madrid. In *For Whom the Bell Tolls,* there are rumors circulating there and in "San Rafael" of FASCIST troop movements in the Guadarrama Mountains. Robert JORDAN is concerned about the troop movements, because they are close to where he and Pablo's band of guerrilla fighters are preparing to blow up a bridge.

village, a   Twelve miles north of Spezia, Italy, otherwise unidentified (could be Berghetto di Vara), where the narrator of "Che Ti Dice La Patria?" (What do you hear from home?) and his friend, Guy, have their first experience with the decadence of fascist Italy under Mussolini in 1927.

Villalta   The name of a matador in the "Chapter 12" vignette of *In Our Time*. The description of his performance shows a bullfighter at his best, both in his work with the cape and with the sword.

Villalta, Nicanor (1899–   )   Spanish bullfighter. Hemingway says of him in *Death in the Afternoon* that if "you saw him in Madrid you could think he was splendid and see something very fine because, in Madrid, he keeps his feet together when he uses the cape and muleta and thus keeps from being grotesque and he always, in Madrid, kills very valiantly. Villalta is a "strange case," according to Hemingway. "He has a neck three times as long as that of the average man. He is six feet tall to start with and those six feet are mostly legs and neck." Ernest and Hadley named their son after Villalta.

In "The Undefeated" the main character, Manuel GARCIA, argues with the Madrid promoter, RETANA, that Villalta gets 7,000 pesetas a fight. Retana offers Garcia 250 pesetas, reminding him that he is not Villalta.

Villar bulls   The first bulls brought in for the bullfights in PAMPLONA, in *The Sun Also Rises*, the week that Jake BARNES and his friends are there for the Fiesta SAN FERMÍN. The bulls are from the ranch of Francisco Villar de Zamora, but MONTOYA, the owner of the hotel where Jake and his friends stay, does not think much of the bulls.

Villa Rossa (1)   In *In Our Time*, the whorehouse where the main character of the "Chapter 7" vignette goes the night after praying to Jesus to save him from being killed in the shelling at Fossalta.

Villa Rossa (2)   In *A Farewell to Arms* the Villa Rossa is the officers' whorehouse in GORIZIA, where the Italian military unit is stationed to which Lieutenant Frederic HENRY is attached.

Ville d'Avray   Forest painted by the French painter André MASSON, the painting owned by Thomas HUDSON at his "farm" outside of Havana.

Vincennes   Town, just east of Paris known best for its castle and its large woods (Bois de Vincennes). Hemingway attended steeplechase races at the Stade Pershing in the woods during his years in Paris in the 1920s. The stadium, which at that time had grandstands for 30,000 spectators, was presented to France by the United States after World War I.

vino secco   Dry white wine from Vesuvius, Italy, which, in *Across the River and Into the Trees*, Richard CANTWELL orders to go with "the small soles" for lunch on Saturday at the GRITTI PALACE HOTEL.

Virgin of Cobre   Our Lady of Charity, La Virgen de la Caridad del Cobre, the patron saint of Cuba. Her shrine is located in the town of El Cobre, just west of Santiago de Cuba. In *The Old Man and the Sea* there is a picture of the Virgin of Cobre on the wall of SANTIAGO's shack. Also, he promises to make a pilgrimage to the Virgin of Cobre if he is allowed to catch the 1,500-pound marlin.

HONEST LIL in *Islands in the Stream,* in an attempt to comfort Thomas HUDSON about the loss of his son in the war, tells him that the virgin is "looking after Tom day and night."

Virgin Spain   Title of a nonfiction book written by Waldo FRANK, published in 1926, and discussed favorably by Hemingway in *Death in the Afternoon*.

"Visit With Hemingway, A: A Situation Report"   Article, published in *Look* (September 4, 1956), regarding life in Cuba for the Hemingways; reprinted in *By-Line: Ernest Hemingway* (1967).

V.M.I.   Virginia Military Institute, where Richard CANTWELL, in *Across the River and Into the Trees*, went to school; at least he has a ring from there, or did have; he has lost it.

Vogue   A "new French" magazine, mentioned in *The Garden of Eden*. It is actually the French edition of the U.S. magazine, founded in 1892 as a society weekly. *Vogue* added a British edition in 1916 and a French edition in 1920. In 1936 it merged with *Vanity Fair*.

Voix   Short for Charlevoix, a town in northern Michigan on a channel between Lake Charlevoix and Lake Michigan, about 15 miles southwest of Petoskey; mentioned in "The Three-Day Blow."

Vorarlberg   Province in western Austria, with the capital at Bregenz. It includes the town of SCHRUNS, where Ernest and Hadley Hemingway spent the winters of 1924–25 and 1925–26 and which he writes about, especially in the last section of *A Moveable Feast,* titled "There is Never Any End to Paris."

"Voyage to Victory"   Article, published in *Collier's* (July 22, 1944), reprinted in *The United States Navy in World War II* (1966), reprinted in *By-Line: Ernest Hemingway* (1967).

This article is the first of six dispatches from the European sector of World War II, all published in *Collier's*. Hemingway was listed on the masthead as a staff correspondent from July 8, 1944, to May 12, 1945. He viewed the Normandy invasion on June 6, 1944, from as close to the French beaches as it was possible for a correspondent to get on the first day. He transferred from the attack transport ship *Dorothea M. Dix* to an "LCV(P)" (Landing Craft Vehicle, Personnel), that looked "like iron bathtubs," and moved in toward the "Fox Green" beach sector of Omaha Beach.

The article begins: "No one remembers the date of the Battle of Shiloh. But the day we took Fox Green beach was the sixth of June, and the wind was blowing hard out of the northwest." Hemingway writes about a dialogue between a "Lieutenant (jg) Robert Anderson of Roanoke, Virginia," and his "coxswain, Frank Currier of Saugus, Massachusetts. . . . [T]he boat crew, who were making their first landing under fire, knew this officer had taken LCV(P)s in to the African landing, Sicily and Salerno, and they had confidence in him."

The battleships *Texas* and *Arkansas* fired their 14-inch guns at the cliffs beyond the beaches: "There would be a flash like a blast furnace. . . . It struck your near ear like a punch with a heavy, dry glove. . . . I found if I kept my mouth open from the time I saw the guns flash until after the concussion, it took the shock away." The only map of the beaches Anderson had was lost overboard in the wind and spray, and a great deal of confusion followed; but Hemingway had memorized the map and so felt confident of where they were. "That's all Fox Green to the right. There is the Colleville church. There's the house on the beach. There's the Ruquet Valley on Easy Red to the right. This is Fox Green absolutely."

He describes the chaos along the Omaha Beach, tanks burning, soldiers dead, "looking like so many heavily laden bundles on the flat pebbly stretch between the sea and the first cover." Anderson ran the boat "in to a good spot we had picked on the beach and put our troops and their TNT and their bazookas and their lieutenant ashore, and that was that."

Hemingway sums up the action: "It had been a frontal assault in broad daylight, against a mined beach defended by all the obstacles military ingenuity could devise. The beach had been defended as stubbornly and as intelligently as any troops could defend it. . . . There is much that I have not written. You could write for a week and not give everyone credit for what he did on a front of 1,135 yards. Real war is never like paper war, nor do accounts of it read much the way it looks. But if you want to know how it was in an LCV(P) on D-Day when we took Fox Green beach and Easy Red beach on the sixth of June, 1944, then this is as near as I can come to it."

Vuitton luggage   In *The Garden of Eden* David and Catherine BOURNE travel with luggage designed by the Louis Vuitton trunks and suitcases manufacturer. David keeps his writing notebooks in a Vuitton suitcase.

Wagner, Al American friend of the narrator in "Night Before Battle," a story of the Spanish civil war. Wagner has a premonition that he is going to die in the next day's battle.

Wahl, le Capitaine Man in Paris whom young Tom HUDSON, in *Islands in the Stream,* remembers from his childhood there, because the "captain" wrestled crocodiles.

waiter (1) At the Café de la Paix in Maisons-Lafitte, France, near Paris, in "My Old Man." It's there that JOE's "old man" has a "big drag" with the waiter, because the "old man drank whisky and it cost five francs, and that meant a good tip when the saucers were counted up."

waiter (2) At the CAFÉ IRUNA in PAMPLONA, in *The Sun Also Rises.* He is the only character mentioned who is against the bullfights. In talking about a man who is gored during the running of the bulls (see Vincent GORONES), he tells Jake BARNES, sarcastically, "Badly cogido (gored). All for sport. All for pleasure."

waiter (3) At the CAFÉ near the hospital in LAUSANNE in *A Farewell to Arms* where Frederic HENRY goes while Catherine BARKLEY is having her baby.

waiter (4) At a "small cafe" in HENDAYE, France, in *The Garden of Eden,* where David and Catherine BOURNE eat most of their meals while on their way to Madrid.

waiter, older At an unnamed café in "A Clean, Well-Lighted Place." He is not in a hurry to get home, even though it's after two o'clock in the morning. He understands why the OLD MAN (5) wants to stay at the café and have another drink. "I am of those who like to stay late at the café," he says to the younger waiter. "With all those who do not want to go to bed. With all those who need a light for the night." When the younger waiter tells him that the old man can "buy a bottle and drink at home," the older waiter tells him, "It's not the same." And he tells him, "Each night I am reluctant to close up because there may be some one who needs the café."

He closes the café and then goes to a bar "with a shining steam pressure coffee machine." He has a "lit-tle" cup of coffee, but he doesn't like bars and bodegas. "A clean, well-lighted café was a very different thing." He goes home, but he knows he will just lie in bed until daylight when he will finally go to sleep. "After all, he said to himself, it is probably only insomnia. Many must have it."

waiter, younger At an unnamed café in "A Clean, Well-Lighted Place." He is in a hurry to get home to his wife and so has little patience with the OLD MAN who wants another drink, even though it's after two o'clock in the morning. He refuses to serve him another drink. When the older WAITER questions him about it, the younger waiter tells him, "I want to go home to bed." He says that the old man can "buy a bottle and drink at home," and he doesn't understand when the older waiter tells him that "[i]t's not the same." The younger waiter agrees ("He did not wish to be unjust"), but he is in a hurry to get home, never-theless.

"Waiting for an Orgy" Article, published in *The Toronto Daily Star* (October 19, 1922), reprinted in *Ernest Hemingway: Dateline Toronto* (1985). The headline in the *Daily Star* was "Constantinople Cut-Throats Await Chance for an Orgy." The article is datelined "Constantinople." In it Hemingway reports that the "cutthroats, robbers, bandits, thugs and Levantine pirates" from Batum to Bagdad and from Singapore to Sicily have gathered in Constantinople waiting for the orgy of looting that will begin when the Turkish troops, led by Mustapha KEMAL Pasha, enter the city. It will be a test for Kemal to see if he can control his troops, which "will be of greater permanent value to Turkey than many victories in Thrace."

waitress (1) At the station café in Montreux, Switzerland, in "Homage to Switzerland." She waits on Mr. WHEELER in part 1 of the short story. His train is an hour late, and she serves him coffee and a bottle of wine, but rejects his offer, first, of a cigar, and then of money to go "upstairs" with him. "Please do not say such things," she tells him. "You are hateful." Later, however, she thinks to herself that "Three hundred francs for a thing that is nothing to do. How many times have I done that for nothing. And no place to go here. . . . Three hundred francs to do that. What people those Americans."

waitress (2)   At the train station café in Vevey, Switzerland, in "Homage to Switzerland" (part 2). She laughs when Mr. JOHNSON offers her a cigar, and she is less emphatic about turning him down when he asks her for sex, than is the waitress in part 1 of the story.

waitress (3)   At the train station café in Territet, Switzerland, in "Homage to Switzerland" (part 3). She laughs when E. D. HARRIS, the story's main character, offers her a cigar.

waitress, elderly   See SCRIPPS, Diana.

Wakamba   East African language, spoken at one point by M'Cola in *Green Hills of Africa,* although the language he normally uses is SWAHILI.

Walcott, Jimmy   Welterweight boxer on whom Jack Brennan and his manager, John Collins, bet heavily in "Fifty Grand." In an O. Henry sort of twist at the end of the story, Walcott fouls Brennan badly, intending to throw the fight to him; but Brennan manages to recover quickly enough to allow the fight to go on. He then fouls Walcott, and the referee stops the fight in Walcott's favor, thus allowing Brennan and Collins to win their bets.

Walker, Mrs.   In *A Farewell to Arms* a "gray-haired" nurse at the American hospital in Milan, who is confused by Frederic HENRY's arrival at the hospital because the hospital is not quite ready to open and she isn't expecting anyone.

Wallace, Freddy   See FREDDIE'S PLACE.

Walloon Lake   A lake in northern Michigan, a few miles southwest of PETOSKEY, where Hemingway's parents, Clarence and Grace, bought property in 1898 and built their cottage, "WINDEMERE," in 1899. The lake is about eight miles long, extending northwest to southeast, and there is a two-mile extension off to the north from the southern end. It was called Bear Lake when the Hemingways bought the cottage, but the name was changed to Walloon Lake in 1901.

The Hemingways named their cottage after Lake Windermere in the English Lake District, although family members spelled it *Windemere.* Grace Hemingway built a studio across the lake from Windemere on Longfield Farm in the Mackinaw State Forest.

It was a three-mile walk from Grace Cottage due west to HORTON BAY on Lake CHARLEVOIX. Walloon Lake was a good fishing lake, with a camp of OJIBWAY INDIANS near the north end of the southeast "extension," near

what is now Indian Garden Road. There was a lumber camp there originally, but when the best lumber was gone and the white men left, the Indians moved in as squatters and proceeded to log the remaining hardwoods and hemlocks.

Walpole, Sir Hugh (1884–1941)   British novelist, mentioned in "The Three-Day Blow" as the author of *The Dark Forest* and *Fortitude,* novels recommended by BILL (1) to the story's main character, NICK. Bill also recommends Maurice Hewlitt's *Forest Lovers* and George Meredith's *Richard Feverel.*

Walsh, Ernest (1895–1926)   Founder, with Ethel Moorhead, of the literary journal THIS QUARTER in Paris in 1925. Section 14 of *A Moveable Feast* is titled "The Man Who Was Marked for Death," a reference to Walsh who died of tuberculosis in 1926 at age 31.

Hemingway and Walsh first met at Ezra Pound's studio apartment, where Walsh had taken two American girls he had recently met on the boat from the United States. He had promised them he would introduce them to Pound. Hemingway writes of Walsh that he was "dark, intense, faultlessly Irish, poetic and clearly marked for death as a character is marked for death in a motion picture." While Walsh talked to Pound, Hemingway talked to the girls, who showed him a copy of *Poetry* magazine with Walsh's poetry in it. Walsh had apparently told them he received $1,200 for each poem, an exaggeration that Hemingway explains to the reader in detail.

Hemingway also writes of having lunch with Walsh at the latter's expense and being told that he, Hemingway, would win a $1,000 prize from the American literary quarterly *Dial,* which Walsh helped edit. Hemingway discovered later that Walsh had told Joyce that he (Joyce) had won the prize and that perhaps he had told others that they too had won.

Three of Hemingway's short stories were published in *This Quarter*—"Big Two-Hearted River" (May 1925), "The Undefeated" (Autumn–Winter 1925–1926), and "The Sea Change" (December 1931).

Walton   In *To Have and Have Not* the owner of a speedboat that Harry MORGAN thinks of hiring so that ALBERT can take four Cubans to Harry's own hidden boat at the beginning of the illegal run from KEY WEST to Cuba.

Walton Junction   Where Nick ADAMS hops the freight train, in "The Battler," on his way from Chicago to northern Michigan. The village of Walton Junction was located in the southeast corner of Grand Traverse County, about four miles southwest of the village of Fife Lake. It became a town in 1873, developed around the junction of the Grand Rapids & Indiana (GR & I) and the Traverse City Railroads.

Wami River in Tanzania, East Africa, running from above Kongwa in central Tanzania eastward to the sea, emptying into the Indian Ocean opposite the island of Zanzibar. Hemingway remembers, in *Green Hills of Africa*, that POP "galloped lion on the plain below Wami."

Wanderobo hunters Members of an East African tribe of people living in the highlands of Kenya and Tanzania. Also called Dorobos. They are mentioned occasionally in *Green Hills of Africa* as trackers and as "frightful shots."

War Aces Pulp fiction monthly magazine, published from April 1930 to July 1932. In *To Have and Have Not* a "veteran" at FREDDIE'S PLACE reads the magazine and asks Richard GORDON, a writer, if any of his stories has been published in it or in WESTERN STORIES. *War Aces* is also mentioned in "Night Before Battle."

warbler In *The Old Man and the Sea* the small bird lands on SANTIAGO's skiff, first on the stern and then on the fishing line on which the great marlin is hooked. Arriving from the north, perhaps from one of the Bahama islands, the bird "[is] very tired." Santiago talks to it, and it disappears suddenly when the marlin jerks the line. Santiago realizes that just as he has gone "out too far" to fish for the great marlin, the bird has "gone out too far," and so is vulnerable to the hawks that come out from the Cuban coast to meet the smaller birds.

Ward, Mike In *A Moveable Feast* Hemingway describes meeting Ward, who ran the travel desk at the Guaranty Trust in Paris, where Ernest had his Paris account, going to lunch with him, and being introduced by him to bicycle racing. Hemingway was interested in bicycle racing because he was tired of losing money on horse races, and Ward told him he wouldn't have to bet on the bicycles.

"War Medals for Sale" Article, published in *The Toronto Star Weekly* (December 8, 1923), reprinted in *The Wild Years* (1962), and in *By-Line: Ernest Hemingway* (1967). The article is about Canadian soldiers trying to sell their World War I medals in Toronto coin or pawn shops and discovering that there is no "market price for valor." The *TSW* headline read "Lots of War Medals for Sale but Nobody Will Buy Them."

War and Peace Leo TOLSTOI's novel, published 1865–69. In *A Moveable Feast* Hemingway writes that when Sylvia BEACH encouraged him to borrow more than just the one book he had picked out (Turgenev's *A Sportsman's Sketches*) on his first visit to SHAKESPEARE AND COMPANY (1), Hemingway then chose the Constance Garnett translation of *War and Peace* and DOSTOYEVSKY's *The Gambler and Other Stories*.

"War in the Siegfried Line" Article, published in *Collier's* (November 18, 1944), reprinted in *By-Line: Ernest Hemingway* (1967). This article is the sixth of six dispatches from the European sector of World War II, all published in *Collier's*.

This account of the American army crossing into German territory is mostly from a "Captain Howard Blazzard of Arizona," whom Hemingway met and interviewed. The article begins: "A lot of people will tell you how it was to be first into Germany and how it was to break the Siegfried Line and a lot of people will be wrong." Wrong, because war on paper is always different from real war, and no account of any battle can come close to what really happened.

This dispatch is an account of the Germans in retreat but trying to hold on as long as possible, of "L Company" and "K Company" of an unidentified U.S. Army division moving across northeastern France into (probably) Luxembourg and finally fording an unnamed river (probably the Saar) into Germany just south of the Schnee Eifel forest.

Captain Blazzard describes how easily shells from the 105-millimeter Wump guns on the U.S. tank destroyers ("T.D.s") were able to penetrate the steel doors of the German bunker emplacements and how much damage six or seven rounds fired point blank could do to the bunkers and to the men inside. After much detailed description of the devastation provided to Hemingway in the interview, he writes: "There is a lot more to the story. Maybe that is as much as you [the *Collier's* readers] can take today."

wart-hog African wild swine, with large tusks and warty protuberances on the face. On the hunt for kudu in *Green Hills of Africa* Hemingway and the five natives with him see a wart-hog, "less than twenty yards" away, that doesn't "bolt off," Hemingway explaining that it's because it's "virgin country, an un-hunted pocket in the million miles of bloody Africa," and the wart-hog had probably never seen a hunter before.

Washburn, Frank Character in "Ten Indians" whom NICK's father says he saw "in the woods. . . . threshing around" with Nick's girlfriend, Prudence MITCHELL.

Wassermann, Jakob (1873–1934) Austrian novelist. The reference in *Across the River and Into the Trees* is not clear, but when Richard CANTWELL says that he has just read his "third Wassermann," he is probably referring to the Austrian writer. Some readers think Cantwell may be referring to his third Wassermann Test for Syphilis. The test is named after August von

Wassermann (1866–1925), a German physician and bacteriologist. It seems unlikely, however, that Cantwell is worried about syphilis. Nearly all of the novel takes place in Cantwell's mind, and he doesn't think of Wassermann again.

wastebasket In criticizing her husband's writing, Catherine BOURNE says, in *The Garden of Eden*, that a wastebasket is "the most important thing for a writer." She later burns his stories and the reviews of his second novel in a wastebasket.

Waste Land, The Poem by T. S. ELIOT, published in 1922, and considered by many readers to be the best poem written in English in the 20th century. In *A Moveable Feast* Hemingway mentions the poem in connection with Ezra Pound's project Bel Esprit, an attempt to collect money from other writers and artists in order to help Eliot quit his banking job in London and devote his time to writing poetry. The plan died when Eliot began to make money from *The Waste Land* and to receive financial backing for a new quarterly review he edited, *The Criterion*.

waterbuck Large African antelope, about four feet high at the shoulder, described by Hemingway in *Green Hills of Africa* as "worthless for meat."

water-jump Steeplechase jump at the AUTEUIL track in Paris, where, in "My Old Man," the "old man" is killed when his horse, GILFORD, stumbles and falls while trying to clear a hedge in front of the water.

Watson, Ginny Secretary for Mrs. Thomas HUDSON (1)'s first wife in *Islands in the Stream*. Both women are with the Army USO during World War II. They find Hudson at the FLORIDITA bar, and Ginny accepts a luncheon invitation from Mr. Rodríguez.

"Way You'll Never Be, A" This short story is set in northern Italy during WORLD WAR I. Nicholas ADAMS, the main character, has been wounded and is shell-shocked and remembers seeing the Austrian soldier who shot him just before he pulled the trigger. At night, when he closes his eyes, he sees "the man with the beard who looked at him over the sights of the rifle, quite calmly before squeezing off, the white flash and clublike impact, on his knees, hot-sweet choking, coughing it onto the rock. . ." And he keeps seeing, also at night, "a long, yellow house with a low stable and the river much wider than it was and stiller."

Captain PARAVICINI, Nick's friend, says that the wound should have been "trepanned"—in this case a surgical term meaning to bore a hole in the bone and which usually refers to the skull. Nick remembers that he was wounded in the "knees," but he immediately

says to Paravicini, "What's the matter? I don't seem crazy to you, do I?," suggesting also a figurative wound to the head. Paravicini may well clinch the head-wound idea when he next says, "You seem in top-hole shape." And Nick says, in return, "It's a hell of a nuisance once they've had you certified as nutty."

Nick, an American, who moves in and out of "craziness," has been assigned to wear an American uniform to encourage Italian soldiers to believe that the United States is about to enter the war. He rides a bicycle from FORNACI to an unnamed town as a way of displaying the uniform. On the way into town he sees the fields of battle where soldiers still lie unburied, bloating in the sun and with their papers, mostly letters, blowing around the fields. "The hot weather had swollen them all alike regardless of nationality." He is stopped by an Italian second lieutenant, who doesn't accept his identification card as proper and so takes him to the battalion commander, Nick's friend Paravicini.

The captain realizes that Nick is having difficulty and so suggests that he lie down. Nick's thinking provides background information about his wounding and the fear he now has that prevents him from sleeping without a light. In his thoughts he is frightened by "that long yellow house and the different width of the river." He is "mixed up" by this waking dream, because he has been back to the town, and there is "no house." Nor is the river the way it was in his dreams. So why, he wonders, is he so afraid of "a house and a long stable and a canal?" After the dream, he talks to two soldiers, who become frightened by Nick's nonsensical conversation and send for Paravicini.

The captain tells Nick that he can't have him "circulating around to no purpose," and, after he feels "it" again (the "craziness"), Nick tells the captain that the Italians should have buried their dead, suggesting that what has "set him off" this time is his remembering the dead soldiers with all the scattered papers around that he had witnessed on his way into town. And he leaves to find his bicycle, thinking to himself, "I don't want to lose the way to Fornaci." Partly through third-person narration and partly through Nick's own INTERIOR MONOLOGUE, Hemingway presents in this story the understated picture of a soldier torn apart by the war but trying to keep himself together.

"A Way You'll Never Be" was first published in *Winner Take Nothing* (1933).

"W.B. Yeats a Night Hawk" Article, unsigned, published in *The Toronto Star Weekly* (December 22, 1923), reprinted in *Ernest Hemingway: Dateline Toronto* (1985). The headline in the *Star Weekly* was "W.B. Yeats A Night Hawk: Kept Toronto Host Up." It is an interview with a man who hosted William Butler Yeats on a visit to Toronto on February 2, 1920. The recent Nobel Prize winner is remembered "not as a nightingale but as a nighthawk and a nightmare."

We (1)   Unnamed narrator of the "Chapter 4" vignette of *In Our Time.* The language he uses indicates that he is probably British: "simply priceless," "absolutely topping," "frightfully put out."

We (2)   Unnamed wife of the narrator of "Wine of Wyoming." She is referred to only as part of the "we" near the end of the story. She realizes, as does her husband, that they should have gone to dinner with Sam and Marie FONTAN, because they have hurt badly the feelings of the French couple.

Wedderkop, Count Alfred von   Paris representative for the German magazine *Der Querschnitt,* who bought four Hemingway poems in 1924. In *A Moveable Feast* he is referred to as "Dear Mr. Awfully Nice." Hemingway thinks "It's damned funny" that Germany is the only place where he can sell his work.

"Wedding Day"   The wedding day in this fragment of a story is NICK's with Helen. They marry among mostly drunken friends and row across a lake to a honeymoon cottage. It was published as a "short story" in Philip Young's *Ernest Hemingway: The Nick Adams Stories* (1972).

"Well-Guarded Russian Delegation"   Article, published in *The Toronto Daily Star* (May 4, 1922), reprinted in *Ernest Hemingway: Dateline Toronto* (1985). The headline in the *Daily Star* was "Russian Delegation Well Guarded at Genoa." In the article, datelined "Genoa," Hemingway writes that "the hardest-working delegation at [the] Genoa [Economic Conference] is the Russian." But they are also difficult to interview because they stay so well guarded. But one of Hemingway's "most prized trophies," is the pass he got that gives him access to the Hotel Imperial at Santa Margherita, outside of Genoa, where the Russians are staying during the conference.

Welsh, Mary   See Mary Welsh Monks HEMINGWAY.

Wemedge   Nickname BILL (1) uses for NICK in "The Three-Day Blow."

Wesley   Negro in *To Have and Have Not,* hired by Harry MORGAN to help bait the hooks of the tourists who hire his fishing boat. Wesley is "smart and gloomy, with blue voodoo beads around his neck under his shirt, and an old straw hat." He is wounded, along with Harry, at the beginning of part 2, following an attempt to run rum from Havana to KEY WEST. Harry refers to him as a "nigger" in part 1, but calls him "Wesley" in part 2 when they are both wounded and trying to get back to Key West.

Western Stories   Pulp magazine, along with WAR ACES, mentioned in *To Have and Have Not.* Richard GORDON, a writer, is asked by a "veteran" at FREDDIE'S PLACE if he has ever written for either magazine.

Westwall   See SIEGFRIED LINE.

Wetzel's   Restaurant in Paris at 1, place de l'Opera, where, in *The Sun Also Rises,* Jake BARNES and Robert COHN eat lunch, because Wetzel's has "good hors d'oeuvres."

"What Professional Boxers Fight For"   Article, published in William Burrill's *Hemingway: The Toronto Years* (1994). What boxers fight for is money. Written in June 1921, the article was rejected by the sports editor of *The Toronto Star,* perhaps because of some of the language or because it reads more like a short story than a piece of journalism. It was "discovered" by Burrill in the Hemingway Collection at the John F. Kennedy Library in Boston.

Wheeler, John N. (Jack)   Managing editor at the North American Newspaper Alliance (NANA) in New York when Hemingway cabled 30 dispatches to NANA from the Spanish civil war (1937–38).

Wheeler, Mr.   Main character in part 1 of "Homage to Switzerland." He is American, probably in his thirties, waiting in the train station café in Montreux, Switzerland, for the SIMPLON-ORIENT EXPRESS to Paris, which is an hour late because of snow. As in each of the stories in parts 2 and 3 of "Homage," the reader learns how an American man spends an hour waiting for a train.

Wheeler orders coffee from the waitress and then offers her a cigar, which she declines. Then he offers her 100 francs to go upstairs with him and makes it 200 and then 300, she refusing each time and getting more and more upset with him, telling him that he should not "say such things" to her and that he is "hateful." At the end, the reader learns that Wheeler is "very careful with money and did not care for women" and that he knows there is no "upstairs" at the station. "Mr. Wheeler never took chances." That he does not care for women suggests he may be homosexual, but it is clear that he is just playing games to embarrass the waitress and to pass the time.

Wheeler, Wayne B. (1869–1927)   American prohibitionist leader, who fought for the adoption of the 18th Amendment. In *The Sun Also Rises* Jake BARNES and Bill GORTON have lunch, with wine, after trout fishing on the Fabrica River in northern Spain. The wine has an impact, both men humorously insisting that they had gone to college with Wheeler, a man at least 30 years older than they. They also make jokes about William Jennings BRYAN and Bishop MANNING.

wheel metaphor   In *For Whom the Bell Tolls* (chapter 18) Robert JORDAN remembers seeing a wheel of fortune on the avenue du Maine in Paris and thinking of it as having meaning for life itself. But the wheel of life, he says, makes "only one turn; one large elliptical, rising and falling turn and you are back where you have started."

The wheel of fortune, on the other hand, makes several turns during a lifetime: "There will be Pablo" (for example, worried whether Pablo will rejoin the guerrilla fighters and help Jordan blow up the bridge) "or there will be no Pablo. I care nothing about it either way. But I am not going to get on that wheel again."

He's afraid if he gets on the wheel of fortune—worrying about things he can't control—he'll not be able to get off again, and he will lose even those things he feels he *can* control. In order to better direct his own destiny, Jordan prefers to fight against the fate that a wheel of fortune represents.

whiskey and Perrier   The "giant killer," according to David BOURNE in *The Garden of Eden*, drunk at LA NAPOULE, France, while "cooling out" after working at writing. See also OLD PARR.

whiskey and soda   In the "L'Envoi" vignette of *In Our Time*, the narrator has a whiskey and soda with "the KING" of Greece.

HARRY, in "The Snows of Kilimanjaro," insists on a whiskey-soda instead of broth, which HELEN (3) tries to get him to take.

White, Rev. Gilbert (1720–1793)   English clergyman, naturalist, and writer. In "A Natural History of the Dead," White is mentioned as someone interested in natural history, writing about "the Hoopoe [a European, fanlike crested bird] on its occasional and not at all common visits to Selborne," a village in Hampshire, England. White, who was born in Selborne, wrote *Natural History and Antiquities of Selborne*.

White, William (1911–1995)   Compiler and editor of *By-Line: Ernest Hemingway: Selected Articles and Dispatches of Four Decades* (1967) and *Ernest Hemingway: Dateline Toronto, The Complete Toronto Star Dispatches, 1920–1924* (1985). He was also bibliographer for *Hemingway notes* (1971–74) and for *The Hemingway Review* from 1981 to 1987.

Whitehead Street, 907   In KEY WEST, Florida, Hemingway's home from December 1931 until he moved to Havana in 1939. It is now a privately run Hemingway Museum. Ernest and his second wife, Pauline Pfeiffer, moved into the house on Whitehead Street in December 1931.

White Peacock, The   D. H. LAWRENCE novel (1911), mentioned in *A Moveable Feast*. Hemingway says that Lawrence is "pathetic and preposterous," but he liked *Sons and Lovers* and *The White Peacock*.

Whites, the   Reference in "The Revolutionist" to the White Russians, or Byelorussians, who fought against the Bolsheviks during the Russian Revolution following World War I. The "He" of the short story, a Communist, is tortured by the "whites" in Budapest before he escapes to Italy.

Whitman, Walt (1819–1892)   U.S. poet, journalist, and essayist, known for his free verse, particularly *Leaves of Grass* (first of nine editions, 1855). Richard Cantwell, who is waiting for his own death in *Across the River and Into the Trees*, thinks about Whitman because of the poet's attitude toward death as one of life's most important experiences.

In *Death in the Afternoon* Hemingway says of Whitman's homosexuality that it is a "nasty, sentimental pawing of humanity."

Whittier, John Greenleaf (1807–1892)   American poet and abolitionist, best known perhaps for his poem "Snow-Bound" (1866). See also Ralph Waldo EMERSON.

"Who Is He?"   Article, published in *The Toronto Star Weekly* (September 11, 1923), "discovered" by William Burrill at the John F. Kennedy Library in Boston but not reprinted in his book, *Hemingway: The Toronto Years* (1994), where 25 other recently found articles are reprinted.

"Who Murdered the Vets"   Article, published in *New Masses* (September 17, 1935). Datelined, "Key West, Florida," the article is about a Florida hurricane that destroyed the C.C.C. work camp and killed 458 war veterans.

"Who's Who in Beau Brummel?"   Article for Oak Park and River Forest High School newspaper, *The Trapeze* (February 23, 1917), reprinted in *Hemingway at Oak Park High: The High School Writings of Ernest Hemingway, 1916–1917* (1993).

wicker fish traps   At the side of the fishing boats, seen by Richard CANTWELL along the canal between Mestre and Venice at the beginning of *Across the River and Into the Trees*.

widgeon   Genus of duck killed by Richard CANTWELL on the Sunday morning duck shoot near VENICE in *Across the River and Into the Trees*. It is probably the European widgeon, the male of which has a cream-colored crown and reddish-brown head and neck.

Wiesbadener-Hütte   One of the Alpine Club huts in the mountains above the southern end of the Montafon Valley, south-southeast of Schruns, Austria, where the Hemingways skied during the winter 1925–26.

It is also where the narrator of "An Alpine Idyll" and his skiing friend, John, stayed during their spring skiing.

wife (1)   Unnamed main character in "Cat in the Rain." She and her husband are the only Americans in a hotel in an unnamed Italian town on the sea, and she is bored with her life. She sees a cat outside, under a table in the rain, but it's gone when she goes out to get it. "She was suddenly disappointed," and, back in the room, she begins to think of all the other things she wants, using the expression "I want" 16 times in complaining to her husband, who continues to read his book and shows little understanding of her loneliness.

wife (2)   Of the narrator of "A Canary for One." It is she to whom the AMERICAN LADY tells her story of breaking off the love relationship between her daughter and a man from Vevey, Switzerland, because she didn't want her marrying a foreigner. In the story's last line the narrator states that he and his wife are "returning to Paris to set up separate residences."

Wilcox, Doctor   In "God Rest You Merry, Gentlemen," he carries around a booklet titled *The Young Doctor's Friend and Guide*, because a medical school professor, who told him he had "no business being a physician," had recommended it and told him to "use it."

He is on call when a 16-year-old boy comes to the hospital, who the day before had asked to be castrated in order to avoid "sinning," and who, not understanding what "castration" means, has amputated his penis with a razor. But Doctor Wilcox "was unable to find this emergency listed in his book" and so botches an attempt to stop the bleeding. And while they wait to see if the boy lives, Wilcox and Doc FISCHER, a Jew, argue about the significance of the incident occurring on Christmas Day.

Wilde, Oscar (1854–1900)   Irish novelist, playwright, and poet, best known for his novel and his plays *The Picture of Dorian Gray* (1891) *Lady Windermere's Fan* (1893) and *The Importance of Being Earnest* (1899).

In *Death in the Afternoon* Hemingway says of Wilde's homosexuality that he "betrayed a generation."

In *Islands in the Stream* young Tom had shown as a young boy his understanding of homosexuality by naming a book he had read by André GIDE, which mentions Wilde. According to Roger Davis, the book was *Si le grain ne meurt* (1924; "If It Die. . ."), a confessional work about his life from birth to his marriage in 1895 to his cousin Madeleine Rondeaux.

wildebeeste   East African oxlike antelope, about four feet high at the shoulder and about seven feet long, better known as a gnu. But not by Hemingway, who mentions hunting "wildebeestes" in *Green Hills of Africa*.

"Wild Gastronomic Adventures of a Gourmet"   Article, published in *The Toronto Star Weekly* (November 24, 1923), reprinted in *Ernest Hemingway: Dateline Toronto* (1985). The headline in the *Star Weekly* was "Wild Gastronomic Adventures of a Gourmet, Eating Sea Slugs, Snails, Octopus, Etc. for Fun." In the article Hemingway writes of his good and bad eating experiences and good and bad cities where he has had them. Of the many and various exotic foods he has eaten over time, the "most toothsome" are bamboo sprouts and beaver tail, the worst is mule meat.

But Hemingway ends the article by stating: "But I have discovered that there is romance in food when romance has disappeared from everywhere else. And as long as my digestion holds out I will follow romance." The byline on this article is "Peter Jackson," a pen name Hemingway used twice on *TSW* articles. The other was for "Cars Slaying Toronto's Splendid Oak Trees."

"Wild Night Music of Paris"   Article, published in *The Toronto Star Weekly* (March 25, 1922), reprinted in *The Wild Years* (1962), reprinted in *Ernest Hemingway: Dateline Toronto* (1985). The headline in the *Star Weekly* was "Wild Night Music of Paris Makes Visitor Feel a Man of the World." Datelined "Paris," it is about the cost, especially for Americans, of a night on the town in Paris. Champagne, for example, is 18 francs a bottle before 10 o'clock and 85 to 150 francs after 10.

"Wild West: Chicago"   Article, published in *The Toronto Star Weekly* (November 6, 1920), reprinted in *Ernest Hemingway: Dateline Toronto* (1985). The headline in the *TSW* was "The Wild West Is Now in Chicago." In it Hemingway writes that there have been 150 killings in Chicago from January to November "during the present year [1920]." And "[t]here have been to date four hundred and twenty people killed this year in Chicago by motor cars."

Wilkinson   Agent for Thomas HUDSON's paintings in *Islands in the Stream*.

Wilkinson, Comrade In *The Fifth Column,* he is a 20-year-old Loyalist sent by an officer of the INTERNATIONAL BRIGADE to Philip RAWLINGS for orders. Rawlings sends him out of the Hotel Florida for a walk, and when he returns a little later he is shot in the back of the head by someone who mistakes him for Rawlings.

Willard, Jess (1883–1968) U.S. boxer, world heavyweight champion (1915–19). Willard, who was six feet, seven inches tall and at times 265 pounds, won the title by beating Jack Johnson and lost it to Jack DEMPSEY. Willard is referred to in "Fifty Grand" as a fighter picked by reporters to win a fight in Toledo, which in fact he lost.

In *Islands in the Stream* Thomas HUDSON argues that weight is not important in a boxer and uses Willard's loss to Dempsey, who was much smaller and lighter, as an example.

Willie "The dark boy," one of the crew on Thomas HUDSON's boat in the "At Sea" section of *Islands in the Stream.* He is something of an explosives expert and the only crew member identified as an American. Before they go to sea, Willie tries to talk Hudson into joining him and Henry Wood in looking for whores.

Willis "Secretary" to Frederick HARRISON, the government authority in *To Have and Have Not.*

Willy One of Thomas HUDSON's 11 cats in *Islands in the Stream.* He will not sleep with Hudson when he is drunk.

"Will You Let These Kiddies Miss Santa Claus?" Article, published in *Co-operative Commonwealth* (December 1920), the only article Hemingway wrote for the Chicago publication, although he helped edit it during the winter of 1920–21. The article offers a picture of the waiting room at the Chicago Court of Domestic Relation, which "four thousand women for whom the Romance of life is a finished story go through. . . every month." A court fund has been set up, according to Hemingway, to help provide Christmas presents for the children of fatherless homes.

Wilson, Edmund (1895–1972) American literary critic and editor. He was managing editor of *Vanity Fair* (1920–21) and associate editor of *The New Republic* (1926–31) before developing a reputation as one of the leading literary critics in the United States.

His first book was *Axel's Castle* (1931), about the symbolist poets, followed by several other books of criticism, including *The Wound and the Bow* (1941) and *The Twenties* (1975), published posthumously.

Wilson devoted a section of *The Wound and the Bow* to Hemingway in the book he agrees with John DOS PASSOS whom he quotes as saying that Hemingway "had one of the shrewdest heads for unmasking political pretensions [he had] ever run into." Wilson says that it was "an error of the politicos. . . to accuse [Hemingway] of an indifference to society. His whole work is a criticism of society: he has responded to every pressure of the moral atmosphere of the time, as it is felt at the roots of human relations, with a sensitiveness almost unrivalled."

Wilson, Frances One of the five whores in "The Light of the World." She is one of two blondes, not nearly as fat as the three "big" women, ALICE, HAZEL, and ETHEL, and the only one of the five given a last name by the narrator.

Wilson, Fred "Freddy," a "worthless sporting character" who plays the guitar in the "Bimini" section of *Islands in the Stream.*

Wilson, Robert White hunting guide in "The Short Happy Life of Francis Macomber." "He was about middle height with sandy hair, a stubby mustache, a very red face and extremely cold blue eyes with faint white wrinkles at the corners that grooved merrily when he smiled." After he is forced by Francis MACOMBER's cowardice to kill the lion on the morning the story opens, Wilson tries to break with both Macomber and his wife, Margot, but he is unable to, in part because Macomber is not easily insulted.

Wilson gives Macomber the hunter's line that "in Africa no woman ever misses her lion and no white man ever bolts." But Macomber is apologetic, quickly admitting that he "bolted like a rabbit," and Wilson realizes that he will not be able to break from this client easily. And when Margot shows up in his tent that night, he accepts her offer of sex, complicating yet further relations with his clients. Wilson gives Macomber another chance at the hunt and is pleased when his client kills a buffalo the next day. He is doubly angry at Margot, therefore, for murdering her husband—even though Wilson believes, as the narrator states, that Margot "shot at the buffalo."

Although his nationality is not specified, Wilson is probably British. He's somewhat prejudiced against Americans, thinking to himself several times that Macomber is American and that one can never figure Americans. He's especially prejudiced against women, thinking American women are the "hardest in the world; the hardest, the cruelest, the most predatory and the most attractive and their men have softened or gone to pieces nervously as they have hardened."

Nevertheless, Wilson carries a double-size cot with him on the safaris he leads, "to accommodate any windfalls he might receive." He insists, at least to himself, that he has moral standards when it comes to shooting big game, but, as Margot reminds him after she has killed her husband, even those standards are questionable, since he had chased buffalo in a car, which is illegal.

Wilson, Sir Henry (1864–1922) British soldier, born in Ireland. During WORLD WAR I, he was a friend of Marshal Foch of the French forces and was a liaison officer between the British and French armies. He is quoted by Nick ADAMS in "A Way You'll Never Be" as saying, "Gentlemen, either you must govern or you must be governed."

Wilson, Woodrow (1856–1924) Twenty-eighth president of the United States and one of the "Big Four" statesmen at the Paris Peace Conference in 1919. In an article for *The Toronto Star* (written in October 1923) Hemingway writes that Wilson is "a broken man, his aims unaccomplished and his accomplishments repudiated." See "Lloyd George the Great Survivor."

Wilson-Harris In *The Sun Also Rises* an Englishman whom Jake BARNES and Bill GORTON befriend and fish with at least twice on their trip to BURGUETE and the FABRICA and IRATI Rivers. He is so pleased with their companionship that he presents Jake with some homemade flies when he and Gorton leave for PAMPLONA.

Winchell, Walter (1897–1972) Newspaper gossip columnist and radio broadcaster, thought about by Dorothy HOLLIS, one of the "Haves" in *To Have and Have Not*. She won't know if she's turned into a "bitch," because Winchell doesn't provide that kind of gossip.

Winchester 30–30 One of the guns carried on the charter fishing boat by Harry MORGAN in *To Have and Have Not*. He carries it above the boat's wheel. The other guns on board are a Thompson submachine gun, a pump-gun, and a Smith and Wesson .38 pistol. The 30–30 was developed by Oliver Fisher Winchester (1810–80), who bought a weapons company in 1857 and renamed it the Winchester Repeating Arms Company.

Windemere Cottage The Hemingway cottage on WALLOON LAKE in northern Michigan, built by Clarence and Grace Hemingway in 1899. It's on the lake's north side, on Lake Grove Drive, a few hundred yards west of the intersection of Lake Grove and Resort Pike Road, about six miles south of PETOSKEY.

Windemere Cottage on Walloon Lake in northern Michigan (Courtesy of the John F. Kennedy Library)

The Hemingways named their cottage after Lake Windermere in the English Lake District, although family members spelled it Windemere. Ernest's sister Marcelline was taken to the property at age seven months in 1898, after the land was purchased but before the cottage was built. Ernest was at the cottage less than two months after his birth in July 1899, and he spent parts of every summer there until he was 18. Grace Hemingway built a studio across the lake from Windemere on Longfield Farm in the Mackinaw State Forest and about three miles east of HORTON BAY.

wine-shop   In Pamplona in *The Sun Also Rises* at the Fiesta SAN FERMÍN, where Jake BARNES fills his wineskins.

wine-skin   Leather wine bottle with a screw-on nozzle, which is filled with wine drunk by holding the wineskin away from the face and squeezing a fine stream of wine into the mouth. According to Jake BARNES, in *The Sun Also Rises,* it takes a lot of practice to do it without spilling any wine.

"Wine of Wyoming"   Cultural differences dominate this short story. The setting is the home of the French-speaking FONTAN family on the outskirts of an unnamed town in Wyoming in the fall of 1928 (the date is not given, but they discuss the coming presidential election involving Al SMITH).

Sam Fontan makes wine and beer, which places him in constant danger of being caught by the police, because the story is set during Prohibition. His wife, MARIE, sells the homemade brews mostly to friends and neighbors, the wine for a dollar a bottle and the beer for 10 cents. They have been caught once, costing them $755 in fines and Sam some time in jail.

The language of the Fontans, as given by the story's narrator, is a mix of French with a few English words, although there is very little that isn't made clear to the reader. The Fontans don't understand why wine is illegal, let alone why they are not allowed to make it for sale to their neighbors and friends. They also don't understand why some of their customers only want the wine in order to get drunk. They once had a dinner for some young people, and even the young women drank too much and threw up all over the dinner table. The Fontans were disgusted by their American guests and wouldn't allow them into their home again.

The narrator and his wife are friends of the Fontans and enjoy having dinner with them or drinking beer during kitchen conversations. Some of the conversation concerns the cultural differences between Americans and Europeans, especially the differences among the Catholics of the two cultures. The narrator and his wife are staying in a hotel in town but are getting ready to leave, and the Fontans invite them for a good-bye dinner, at which time Sam's wine, made that summer, should be ready for consumption.

But the Americans have gone on a "shooting trip" for prairie chickens, and when they get back to the hotel they decide they are too tired to go to the Fontans' house for dinner. They "did not want [to struggle with] a foreign language." They go the next morning, however, just to say good-bye, and they discover how disappointed Sam and Marie are that their friends had not joined them for dinner and the wine-tasting the night before. Sam is proud of the wine he makes and is "crushed" and "disgraced" at being unable to offer the new wine to their American friends. They had three bottles ready for the dinner, and Sam, who is "crazy pour le vin," drank it all. Marie Fontan now has "tears in her eyes," mostly out of feeling sorry for her husband.

As the narrator and his wife drive down the dirt road in their car, the narrator's wife says, "We ought to have gone last night," and he says, "Yes, we ought to have." But it is too late; they have hurt badly the feelings of their French friends, emphasizing the very cultural differences the two couples had been discussing.

"Wine of Wyoming" was first published in *Scribner's Magazine* (August 1930) and reprinted in *Winner Take Nothing* (1933).

"Wings Always Over Africa: An Ornithological Letter" Article, published in *Esquire* (January 1936), reprinted in *By-Line: Ernest Hemingway* (1967). The article is about Mussolini's attack on Ethiopia in late 1935. It's "An Ornithological Letter" because it is also about the birds that attack the wounded and dying, an "aspect of the war in Africa which Il Duce [Mussolini] will do well to keep censored out of his newspapers."

Winner Take Nothing   Hemingway's third book of short stories—after *Three Stories & Ten Poems* (1923) and *Men Without Women* (1927)—includes the following: "After the Storm," "A Clean, Well-Lighted Place," "God Rest You Merry, Gentlemen," "The Sea Change," "A Way You'll Never Be," "The Mother of a Queen," "One Reader Writes," "Homage to Switzerland," "A Day's Wait," "A Natural History of the Dead," "Wine of Wyoming," "The Gambler, the Nun, and the Radio," and "Fathers and Sons."

The book was published by Charles Scribner's Sons on October 27, 1933, in a first printing of 20,300 copies at $2 each.

"Win Two—Lose One"   Article for Oak Park and River Forest High School newspaper, *The Trapeze* (May 4, 1917), reprinted in *Hemingway at Oak Park High: The High School Writings of Ernest Hemingway, 1916–1917* (1993).

"Wives Buy Clothes for French Husbands"   Article, published in *The Toronto Star Weekly* (March 11, 1922), reprinted in *The Wild Years* (1962), reprinted in *Ernest Hemingway: Dateline Toronto* (1985). In the article, datelined "Paris," Hemingway explains why "the balloon-shaped, narrow-at-the-bottom trousers" are so popular among French workmen. Their wives buy them. They also buy shoes, and cut hair, among other things. And "the reign of feminism will probably continue."

Wolfe, General James (1727–1759)   British officer in the French and Indian Wars of the late 1750s, who helped defeat the French on the Plains of Abraham during the siege of Quebec but died during the battle (September 13, 1959). He became one of the characters in Thackeray's *The Virginians* (1857–1859). Hemingway wrote about him for *The Toronto Star Weekly* (see WOLFE'S DIARIES).

Wolfe, Thomas (1900–1938)   American novelist, best known for *Look Homeward, Angel* (1929). In discussing writing in *Green Hills of Africa* Hemingway suggests that Wolfe needed a "necessary shock to cut the over flow of words and give him a sense of proportion," and that both of these things might have been improved if he had been sent to Siberia like Dostoyevsky.

"Wolfe's Diaries"   Article, published in *The Toronto Star Weekly* (November 24, 1923), reprinted in *Ernest Hemingway: Dateline Toronto* (1985). The headline in the *Star Weekly* was "Gen. Wolfe's Diaries Saved for Canada." It is about the "Monckton Papers," which contain the diaries of General James Wolfe, a British officer and hero of the French and Indian Wars, particularly at the siege of Quebec.

woman (1)   In the "Chapter 2" vignette of *In Our Time,* "having a kid" on a mattress in the back of a cart during the Greek evacuation of ADRIANOPLE.

woman (2)   She sells roasted chestnuts on one of three bridges crossed by the narrator of "In Another Country."

woman (3)   Waitress at the train station bar in "Hills Like White Elephants."

woman (4)   In *A Farewell to Arms,* a clerk at a gun store in Milan, Italy, who sells Frederic HENRY the pistol he buys the night he goes back to the war front.

woman (5)   At the hospital in LAUSANNE, Switzerland, in *A Farewell to Arms,* who checks in Catherine BARKLEY, there to have a baby.

woman (6)   Dead, "with her hair floating all out," seen through one of the portholes of the sunken ocean liner by the narrator of "After the Storm."

woman, old Indian   In "Indian Camp," she holds the lantern for Nick's doctor-father when they arrive to help a young Indian woman have a baby.

"Woman Takes Crumbs"   Article, unsigned, published in *The Toronto Daily Star* (April 15, 1922), reprinted in *Ernest Hemingway: Dateline Toronto* (1985). The headline in the *Daily Star* was "Woman, Lovely Woman, Resents Slight, Is Forced to Take Crumbs at Genoa."

In the article, datelined "Genoa," Hemingway reports in a three-paragraph story that women have little to say at the Genoa Economic Conference. "Alexandra Kollantay, leader of the feminist movement in Russia, objected because the secretary of the conference did not include a woman member." Hemingway lists a few women who have roles, particularly with the Italian delegation—for example, the granddaughter of Dante Gabriel Rossetti, one of the conference's chief interpreters.

Women in Love   D. H. LAWRENCE novel (1921), mentioned in *A Moveable Feast.* Hemingway liked Lawrence's *Sons and Lovers* and *The White Peacock,* but he "couldn't read" *Women in Love.*

Wood, Henry   In *Islands in the Stream,* he's the "biggest man" whom Thomas HUDSON knew, and the most cheerful and well mannered. He's "hunting girls" when Hudson meets him at the FLORIDITA bar in the "Cuba" section of the novel. He is also a member of Hudson's boat crew, searching, in the "At Sea" section, for German submarines.

wooden box   In *The Old Man and the Sea* it is in SANTIAGO's skiff, containing, among other items, extra "rolls of line."

wooden bridge   Bridge on which Frederic HENRY, in *A Farewell to Arms,* crosses the TAGLIAMENTO RIVER during the retreat of the Italian soldiers from CAPORETTO. The bridge is "nearly three-quarters of a mile across, and the river," running in narrow channels among the stones "far below the bridge, was close under the wooden planking." Frederic dives into the river from the end of the bridge to avoid being shot by the battle police.

Woolf Brothers' Saloon   Where HORACE, the narrator of "God Rest You Merry, Gentlemen," gets a free Christmas lunch before going to the city hospital, where he hears a story about a 16-year-old boy who asked to be castrated.

Woolsey   In *The Sun Also Rises,* a U.S. correspondent for an unidentified news service in Paris. He, his colleague Krum, and Jake BARNES share a taxi ride. See QUAI D'ORSAY.

"Worker, The"   Poem about a stoker on a Great Lakes steamer. First publication was in the Oak Park and River Forest High School literary magazine, *Tabula* (March 1916).

workmen   In the hotel in LA NAPOULE, France, where, in *The Garden of Eden,* David and Catherine BOURNE stay during the late summer months. The workmen put up a mirror on the wall behind the bar.

Work-in-Progress   James Joyce's novel that would be printed piecemeal between 1928 and 1937 and then published in its entirety as *Finnegans Wake* in 1939. Hemingway refers to Joyce's "work-in-progress" in *A Moveable Feast.*

World of Nick Adams, The **(television play)**   Adaptation from five Nick Adams short stories, written in November 1957 by A. E. HOTCHNER as a stage play but adapted for CBS's "7 Lively Arts [TV] Theatre" and aired October 9, 1957. It was produced by John Houseman and directed by Robert Mulligan and Robert Herridge.

World Series (1)   In "The Three-Day Blow" NICK tells BILL (1) that he would like to see the World Series. Bill says, "Well, they're always in New York or Philadelphia now." Teams from either Philadelphia or New York were in the World Series from 1910–17. The likely date of the story is 1916, since the two characters also discuss the trade of Heinie Zimmerman (see Heinie ZIM) from the Chicago Cubs to the New York Giants, which took place during the 1916 season.

World Series (2)   In "The Gambler, the Nun, and the Radio," Sister CECILIA tells Mr. FRAZER that she cannot listen to the Notre Dame football game on the radio that afternoon because the excitement of the World Series nearly finished her off. Although the year is not clear, it was probably the 1930 World Series between the Philadelphia Athletics and the St. Louis Cardinals, won by the Athletics four games to two—probably 1930 because the reader is told that the Notre Dame game is on the West Coast, probably its game with Southern California on December 6, 1930, won by Notre Dame, 27-0.

World War I (1914–1918)   No historical event had more of an impact on Hemingway's writing career than World War I. Both of the main characters in his novel *A Farewell to Arms* are directly involved in the war. In *The*

Sun Also Rises, which takes place seven years after World War I, the main character is war casualty. Several of Hemingway's short stories also include characters who are directly affected by the war. Beginning in December 1921, as a European correspondent for *The Toronto Daily Star,* Hemingway also wrote more than 100 articles in two years about the continuing consequences of the war.

When the war began in Europe during the summer of 1914, Ernest was about to begin his sophomore year at Oak Park and River Forest High School, west of Chicago. By the time the United States entered the war on April 2, 1917, Hemingway was still two months from graduation, but his career as a journalist would begin that fall.

Hemingway's direct participation in World War I was short but decisive. After high school, he moved to Kansas City to work as a reporter for *The Kansas City Star,* and the next spring (1918) he and his colleague at the *Star* Ted BRUMBACK enlisted in the American Red Cross to drive ambulances for the Italian army. They left New York for France on May 23 with other ambulance drivers, and arrived in Schio, Italy, on June 4. Hemingway volunteered to deliver chocolate and cigarettes to Italian troops near FOSSALTA along the PIAVE River on June 22, and on July 8 he was wounded badly by an Austrian trench mortar shell, removed to the American Red Cross Hospital in Milan and out of the war.

Hemingway's own war experience lasted barely a month, but, as with nearly everything else that was important to him throughout his life, he studied the war so thoroughly that he was able to describe places and events well enough to cause early critics of the novel to think he had been to the places and had seen the events. His description of the retreat from Caporetto is accurate enough to cause even Italian readers years later to think that Hemingway had been there.

Several factors precipitated the "Great European War," the "war to end all wars," but the single most deciding factor was the assassination of Archduke Francis Ferdinand of Austria-Hungary in Sarajevo on June 28, 1914. Economic rivalries, territorial disputes, and nationalism had for several years created animosities in Europe, especially between Germany and France and Great Britain and between Russia and Austria-Hungary, which at that time included all of the territory that is now divided among Slovenia, Croatia, Bosnia-Herzegovina, and Yugoslavia.

Austria-Hungary, supported by Germany, declared war against Serbia—now a constituent republic of Yugoslavia, including the provinces of Kosovo and Vojvodina. Russian mobilization precipitated Germany's declaration of war on Russia (August 1). Germany then declared war on France (August 3), and immediately sent troops through Belgium and

Luxembourg toward France. Germany's violation of Belgium's neutrality gave the British the pretext and popular support necessary for entry into the war. Montenegro and Japan soon joined the "Allies," which consisted of Great Britain, France, Italy, Russia, Serbia, Belgium, and, later, Portugal, Romania, and Greece. The Ottoman Empire (Turkey) joined the "Central Powers," which consisted of Germany and Austria-Hungary.

The United States remained neutral for most of the war, but two incidents precipitated its declaration of war on Germany. A British passenger ship, the *Lusitania*, was sunk off the Irish coast by a German submarine on May 7, 1915, with 1,195 passengers lost, including 128 Americans. The crucial motivation, however, didn't come until nearly two years later, when the Germans announced unrestricted submarine warfare in order to break British naval power. The United States broke off relations with Germany in February 1917, and entered the war on April 6.

The war was the largest conflict among nations the world had ever seen and the most devastating. Airplanes and submarines were used for the first time, as well as armored tanks and poison gas. In one battle at Ypres in western Belgium, the British lost 400,000 men to gain just five miles of territory. At Verdun, France, the longest and bloodiest battle took place, with two million men engaged and one million killed. It is estimated that the total number of casualties in the war was 10 million dead and 20 million wounded. Starvation and flu epidemics raised the total in the years immediately following the war.

Austria-Hungary surrendered November 4, 1918, after an Italian victory at Vittorio Veneto, but Germany capitulated only after German morale collapsed and a revolt against the war began among the German people. The armistice was signed at Compiègne, France, on November 11, 1918—"at the 11th hour of the 11th day of the 11th month."

Five peace treaties were negotiated in France over the next two years: Versailles, Saint-Germain-en-Laye, Trianon, Neuilly, and Sèvres—all of which changed significantly the boundaries of Europe. The Treaty of Versailles was ratified on May 7, 1919, although the United States didn't sign it until July 2, 1921. The League of Nations was formed in 1919 as part of the Treaty of Versailles, but the League was weak against the nationalistic attitudes of its most powerful members. The League survived, however, until 1946, when it gave way to the United Nations.

When the Armistice was signed on November 11, 1918, Hemingway was still in the American Hospital in Milan, in love with his nurse, Agnes von KUROWSKY, seven years his senior. He was back in Oak Park, on crutches, when the Peace Conferences began in Paris on January 18, 1919. Agnes broke off the relationship that March. And when the Treaty of Versailles was signed on May 7, Hemingway was already at WALLOON LAKE for the summer, and writing short stories.

Although most of the events that would be important in Hemingway's *A Farewell to Arms* (published in 1929) had already occurred before Hemingway graduated from high school, his experiences as a war casualty clearly shaped the novel. Catherine BARKLEY's fiancé was killed in the first battle of the Somme in July 1916, and the scene in which Frederic HENRY is seriously wounded takes place in the spring of 1917, just before the United States entered the war.

The novel's theme concerns Frederic's growth into awareness of the disastrous effects of war on individual human lives. He says, "I was always embarrassed by the words sacred, glorious, and sacrifice and the expression in vain. . . . I had seen nothing sacred, and the things that were glorious had no glory and the sacrifices were like the stockyards at Chicago if nothing was done with the meat except to bury it. . . . Abstract words such as glory, honor, courage . . . were obscene beside the concrete names of villages, the numbers of roads, the names of rivers, the numbers of regiments and the dates."

In the story "Soldier's Home," Hemingway mentions the western European battles of SOISSONS, CHAMPAGNE, BELLEAU WOOD, SAINT-MIHIEL, and the ARGONNE forest, five of the bloodiest battles in the war. Harold KREBS, the story's main character, had fought with the U.S. Marines in all five, but the details are left out (see THEORY OF OMISSION). Hemingway felt that if he wrote the story well enough, the reader would understand that Krebs's terrifying, even traumatizing war experiences are the reason he is so lethargic and depressed back in his Oklahoma hometown. When Krebs first returns home from the war he doesn't want to talk about his experiences, and when he finally wants to talk about them, nobody wants to listen. Neither his parents nor his friends care to understand what he has gone though or why he is now despondent.

Gertrude STEIN told Hemingway in Paris that he was part of the "LOST GENERATION" of postwar Americans. "That's what you are," she said. "All of you young people who served in the war. You are a lost generation. . . . You have no respect for anything. You drink yourselves to death." Stein referred to everyone who had fought in the war and afterward felt a spiritual alienation from an America that seemed hopelessly provincial and emotionally barren. "Lost generation" has since been made a part of English language vocabulary, defined as the generation of men and women who came of age during World War I and who, because of the war and the social upheaval that followed it, became disillusioned and cynical. Hemingway used the quotation, "You are all a lost generation," as the first epigraph to *The Sun Also Rises*.

The main character of *The Sun Also Rises* (1926), Jake BARNES, is still trying, seven years after the war, to cope with wounds that have made him impotent. The mental wounds he suffers as a result of the physical wounds make him cynical about the world in which he lives.

Other Hemingway works show his perspectives on the war and why Gertrude STEIN would include him among her lost generation postwar Americans. In "The Snows of Kilimanjaro" the main character, HARRY, has been in the war and remembers, in flashback, two war incidents. One is about a pilot named Barker, who flew bombing missions and told of machine-gunning Austrian soldiers as they ran from a train he had bombed. Harry describes how quiet it got at mealtime when Barker told the story, and that someone finally said to Barker, "You bloody murderous bastard." The second incident is about an officer named Williamson who had been hit by a "stick bomb" coming through a wire fence and begged someone to kill him to end his suffering. Harry remembers that he and Williamson had argued about whether the pain from serious wounds would "pass you out automatically." Williamson had not passed out.

"In Another Country" describes an Italian army officer who was a champion fencer until a war wound left him with a crippled hand. The army doctor has a machine that manipulates the hand, and he insists the hand will be normal again. "Now I Lay Me" concerns the main character's fear of the dark and his greater fear of sleep. "I had been living for a long time," he says, "with the knowledge that if I ever shut my eyes in the dark and let myself go, my soul would go out of my body. I had been that way . . . ever since I had been blown up at night and felt [my body] go out of me and go off and then come back." In "A Way You'll Never Be" Nicholas ADAMS is tortured by the memory of seeing, just before he felt the bullet, the Austrian soldier who shot him. In the "Natural History of the Dead" the main character describes picking up the fragments of bodies on the battlefield and how surprised he is at the amount of paper "scattered about the dead," mostly letters from home and identification papers.

Three years after Hemingway returned from the war, he married Hadley Richardson and returned to Paris as the European correspondent for *The Toronto Daily Star*, covering, especially, the GENOA CONFERENCE (April 1922) and the LAUSANNE CONFERENCE (late 1922–early 1923). He wrote 202 articles for the *Star*, more than half about the conferences or about postwar European politics. He went back to Toronto in September 1923, for some local assignments, but by February 1924, he was back in Paris, this time to develop a career as a writer of fiction.

World War II (1939–1945) Hemingway was 40 years old at the beginning of World War II, and although he

would see more of the fighting in that war than he did as an 18-year-old in WORLD WAR I, he wrote less about the second war than he did about the first. By the time Germany invaded Poland on September 1, 1939, he was the most popular living author, recognized everywhere. He had been to the SPANISH CIVIL WAR in 1937–38 and published *For Whom the Bell Tolls* in 1940, a novel about that "prelude" to World War II.

Hemingway was directly involved in World War II in two ways: first as captain of his fishing boat, *Pilar*, doing amateur, but official, U.S. counterintelligence work hunting German submarines off the Cuban coasts in 1942–43; and second as a writer for *Collier's* magazine, reporting on the Allied invasion of France and the move of Allied forces across France and Belgium into Germany.

Hemingway's best writing about the Second World War came as a feature writer for *Collier's* magazine. In the summer of 1944 he wrote six articles about the Allied invasion of Europe and the march into Germany. Each article focused on a single aspect of the fighting, and all of them represent some of the best journalism to come out of the war. Hemingway had also written seven articles in June 1941 for *PM*, a New York tabloid, about China's war with Japan and its potential consequences.

World War II also provides background for three works of Hemingway's fiction (against a major novel and a dozen short stories that focus on World War I). *Across the River and Into the Trees* (1950) is a novel about a 50-year-old U.S. army colonel who fought in the war and remembers the details but, four years later, is concerned more with his impending death from a series of heart attacks. In the "At Sea" section of *Islands in the Stream*, the main character uses his fishing boat to search for German submarines off the northeast coast of Cuba in 1944. An unfinished World War II short story titled "Black Ass at the Cross Roads" focuses on Allied soldiers guarding a retreat route for Germans trying to get out of France.

Several factors developed during the 1920s and 30s that created an environment for World War II. The peace treaties after World War I failed to solve a number of European border disputes, and the League of Nations, weakened from the beginning by nationalistic policies of the most powerful countries and especially by the defection of the United States, was unable to persuade member nations to disarm. In particular, the League could not stop the Sino-Japanese war when it began in 1931, and which Hemingway would report about 10 years later. A worldwide economic depression in the 1930s contributed to the rise of totalitarian governments in Germany, Italy, and Japan, and each of these nations eventually adopted a form of dictatorship. Adolf HITLER came to power in Germany in 1933 and immediately re-established the German Army and prepared it for war. He also sent German soldiers in support of Generalissimo Francisco FRANCO's rebels in the SPANISH CIVIL WAR (1936–39). Italy's Benito MUSSOLINI went to war against Ethiopia in 1935–36, and he too sent troops to Spain in support of Franco's forces in Spain.

Germany annexed Austria in March 1938, and with the British and French policy of appeasement toward Germany in the "Munich Pact" of September 1938, the Germans were able to occupy Czechoslovakia by March 1939. Italy seized Albania in April. When the Soviet Union signed a nonaggression pact with Germany in August, the Germans were ready to invade Poland on September 1—the official beginning of World War II.

England and France declared war on Germany September 3, 1939. In spite of the Soviet Union's nonaggression agreement with Germany, the Soviets entered the war on September 17 in order to protect eastern Poland. The British and French sent troops to the Maginot Line, fortifications that extended along the eastern frontier of France from the Swiss border to Belgium. The Germans invaded Norway and Denmark (April 9, 1940) and Belgium and the Netherlands (May 10). On May 13, 1940, the Germans outflanked the Maginot Line, and their armored divisions drove on to the English Channel, where the outnumbered and unprepared British and French soldiers barely escaped from Dunkirk across the channel to England (May 26–June 4). France then signed armistices with Germany and Italy, which entered the war on June 10.

The Germans attempted to defeat the British by destroying London with a series of bombing attacks, but England eventually won the "Battle of Britain" under the leadership of Prime Minister Winston CHURCHILL. The Italians broadened the war by attacking the British forces in Africa (August 1940) and by invading Greece in October. Meanwhile, the Germans increased their submarine warfare in the Atlantic Ocean.

The Soviet Union entered the war on England's side when Germany attacked the USSR on June 22, 1941. German mechanized forces destroyed a large part of the Soviet army and managed to overrun much of the territory in western USSR before a counterattack and the Russian winter of 1941–42 stopped them, just short of Moscow.

The Japanese attack on Pearl Harbor, the Philippine Islands, and Malaya on December 7, 1941, brought the United States into the war. The United States had tried to stay neutral, as it had at the beginning of World War I, but it was clear from early that autumn that its "lend-lease" of military equipment to Britain was not sufficient help for its European allies, and that the United States needed to prepare for war.

By mid-1942 the Japanese had reached the Aleutian Islands, their farthest point of attack in the Pacific. The war then began to turn in favor of the Allies. On August 7, 1942, American troops landed on Guadalcanal in the Solomon Islands, and began to move north toward Japan. In Africa, British field marshal Bernard MONTGOMERY's troops defeated German field marshal Erwin ROMMEL's army at Alamein in North Africa (October 1942), and the Americans invaded Algeria on November 8. Africa was cleared of Axis forces by May 12, 1943. The Soviet stand against the Germans at Stalingrad and the subsequent counteroffensive led by Premier Joseph STALIN brought about the surrender of all the German forces remaining in the Soviet Union. The Allies invaded Italy, first Sicily (July–August 1943) and then the mainland, which surrendered on September 8. The German divisions in Italy did not surrender, however, and the Allies could not take Rome until the next summer (June 4, 1944).

Two days later (June 6, 1944) the Allies invaded northern France. Nearly 4,000 transports, 800 warships, innumerable small boats, and 11,000 aircraft supported the D-Day invasion by American, British, and Canadian troops. After nearly a week of fierce fighting on the Normandy beaches, the Allies began their march across France, Belgium, and Luxembourg, pushing most of the German army across the Rhine River by October. Soviet forces pushed into Germany from the east, meeting their western allies on April 25, 1945, in Torgau, Germany. Germany's unconditional surrender was signed at Rheims, France, on May 7 and ratified in Berlin on May 8.

Allied victory in the Pacific came three months later when the United States dropped atomic bombs on the Japanese cities of Hiroshima (August 6) and Nagasaki (August 9). The Japanese government surrendered on August 14, and the surrender papers were signed (September 2, 1945) on the U.S. battleship *Missouri* in Tokyo Bay.

Hemingway's article "Voyage to Victory" (published July 22, 1944) was the first of the six he wrote for *Collier's*. He viewed the Normandy invasion the morning of June 6 from as close to the beaches as correspondents were allowed to get. The article begins: "No one remembers the date of the Battle of Shiloh. But the day we took Fox Green beach was the sixth of June, and the wind was blowing hard out of the northwest." As with his knowledge of the details of "place" that he demonstrated in his best World War I fiction, he knew the territory that he wrote about in the six *Collier's* articles. From his description of the D-Day invasion in June to his account of the crossing of the Rhine River into Germany by Allied armies in November, Hemingway's writing is at its best, and no journalist did it any better.

Hemingway did not write for public consumption about his "liberation" of the bar at the famous Ritz Hotel in Paris on the day of that city's liberation by Allied troops (August 25, 1944). What is known is that as French general Charles de Gaulle was leading the Allied forces under the Arc de Triomphe and along the

Champs Élysées to the cheers of thousands of celebrating French people, Hemingway was setting up drinks for his friends at the RITZ BAR (1). (See HOTEL RITZ.)

"Would 'Treat 'Em Rough'"   Article, unsigned, published in *The Kansas City Star* (April 18, 1918), reprinted in *Ernest Hemingway, Cub Reporter* (1970). The article is about recruits at the army recruiting office in Kansas City and whether they are to be "treated rough" by the recruitment sergeant.

WPA truck   In part 2 of *To Have and Have Not* two customs men spot Harry MORGAN's hidden boat from the top of a WPA (Works Projects Administration) truck; they then confiscate the boat. One of President Roosevelt's ideas for reducing unemployment during the 1930s was the WPA, which provided jobs in several locations, including Key West, Florida, where most of this novel takes place.

***Wrestling Ernest Hemingway* (film)**   Warner Brothers, released in 1993 (123 minutes); produced by Todd Black, directed by Randa Haines, written by Steve Conrad.

Cast: Robert Duvall (Walter), Richard Harris (Frank), Shirley MacLaine (Helen), Sandra Bullock (Elaine), Piper Laurie (Georgia). About two lonely old men, one a retired sea captain, the other a Cuban barber, meeting at a park in Florida and managing an unlikely friendship. One of their similarities is an interest in Hemingway.

"Writer as a Writer, The"   Article, published in *Direction* (May–June 1939), the official program for the Third Writers' Congress.

Wyer, Dr. Sigismund   In "Homage to Switzerland" he is a proud Swiss (or German) member of the National Geographic Society, and carries calling cards with him to prove it. He gives one to E. D. HARRIS.

Wyman, Charley   Minor character in "Up in Michigan." He goes deer hunting with Jim GILMORE and D. J. SMITH.

Wyoming   Setting for "Wine of Wyoming." "It looked like Spain," the narrator says, "but it was Wyoming."

X-ray machine   In the hospital at Hailey, Montana, in "The Gambler, the Nun, and the Radio." The people in Hailey "protested" its use, especially at nine o'clock every morning, because it interfered with radio reception.

Y

yacht, large white   Owned by one of the "Haves" in *To Have and Have Not* and noticed by Marie MORGAN at the end of the novel. Because Marie is one of the "Have Nots" and has just lost her husband, Harry MORGAN, the novel's main character, Marie's noticing the boat is a final comment on the difference between the Haves and Have Nots.

yachtsman, the   A drunken tourist on Bimini in part 1 of *Islands in the Stream*. He insults nearly everyone he meets and starts fights, threatening to shoot Roger DAVIS after Roger beats him up. During the drunken celebration of Queen Mary's birthday, he yells obscenities from his yacht at Thomas HUDSON, Roger Davis, and others who are shooting off flares; he tells them his wife is trying to sleep below deck. Fred Wilson tells him that if he knew how to satisfy his wife, she would be able to sleep.

"You can't two time—"   Otherwise unidentified song sung by the NIGGER [SIC] DRUMMER at ZELLI's bar in *The Sun Also Rises*. Other words to the song are indicated only by dots in Hemingway's text.

Young Catherine   In *A Farewell to Arms,* it's the name Catherine BARKLEY and Frederic HENRY use most often in referring to their unborn child. In Frederic's dream, however, he thinks of the baby as a boy. The child, a male, is stillborn.

"Young Communists"   Article, unsigned, published in *The Toronto Star Weekly* (December 22, 1923), reprinted in *Ernest Hemingway: Dateline Toronto* (1985). The headline in the *Star Weekly* was "Toronto 'Red' Children Don't Know Santa Claus." It's about 300 children of Russian families in Toronto who have become Communists and so do not celebrate Christmas.

Young Doctor's Friend and Guide, The   In "God Rest You Merry, Gentlemen," it is a little leather-bound, pocket-sized book that Doctor WILCOX carries with him in the Kansas City hospital where he practices. It was recommended to him by a medical school professor who told him that he had "no business being a physician" but that at least he should buy the book.

When a 16-year-old boy attempts self-mutilation with a razor, thinking he is castrating himself but not knowing what the word castrate means, Doctor Wilcox is frustrated because he is "unable to find this emergency listed in his book."

young gentleman, the   One of three characters in "Out of Season." He is not named, as are the other two, but each of the 37 times the narrator refers to him in this seven-page story he is called "the young gentleman." The significance of the repetition is not clear, but the young gentleman is so easily taken in by PEDUZZI (1), the old, drunken fishing guide, that the identification the narrator gives him may simply reflect on his gullibility as a tourist, or on the fact, as his wife insists, that he hasn't the "guts" to walk away.

young girl   In the "Chapter 2" vignette of *In Our Time,* a young girl is holding a blanket over a "woman having a kid" and crying, scared "sick looking at it."

young men   "A crowd of young men," homosexuals, who come into the BAL MUSETTE with Brett ASHLEY while Jake BARNES and his friends are there for the dancing, in *The Sun Also Rises*.

young Tom   *See* Tom HUDSON.

Ypres   Town in northwest Belgium where one of the major battles of World War I was fought and where the "little" one of the two Indians in *The Torrents of Spring* says he lost both arms and both legs in the war.

Zaragoza One of the towns on the 1959 bullfight circuit covered by Hemingway in *The Dangerous Summer.* It is where Antonio ORDÓÑEZ and Luis Miguel DOMINGUÍN fought on the same card for the first time.

Zeiss glasses, small German-manufactured field glasses used by Hemingway in *Green Hills of Africa.*

Zelli's Paris bar in Montmartre, at 16 (bis), rue Fontaine, Pigalle. It was known as a loud but friendly place, featuring the best dancers, singers, and comedians of the day. It was also where Joe Zelli, the American owner, arranged "dates" for his special customers with his bar girls.

In *The Sun Also Rises* Jake BARNES, Brett ASHLEY, and Count MIPPIPOPOLOUS go to Zelli's after a dinner that included an 1811 bottle of brandy that the count buys at a restaurant in the BOIS. Zelli's is also where Brett and the count get a dozen bottles of MUMMS champagne to take back to Jake's flat at the end of chapter 4.

Zim, Heinie (1887–1969) Major League baseball player, mostly with the Chicago Cubs, traded to the New York Giants in 1916. This fact helps to set the time of "The Three-Day Blow," since NICK and BILL (1) discuss Heinie Zim's trade and the idea that the manager of the Giants, John J. MCGRAW, makes players "discontented [with the teams they are on] so they have to trade them to him."

Zizi In *The Sun Also Rises* a "little Greek portrait-painter, who called himself a duke." Zizi introduces Brett ASHLEY and Jake BARNES to Count MIPPIPOPOLOUS. Zizi is the son of a "great friend" of the count's father.

Zona di Guerra post-cards World War I war zone post-cards, with messages already printed. In *A Farewell to Arms,* Frederic HENRY sends "a couple" of them home, "crossing out everything except, I am well."

Zurito (1) Bullfight picador in "The Undefeated" who agrees to "pic" for Manuel GARCIA in the "nocturnals." He usually gets paid more for pic-ing than Garcia is getting as a matador, but he accepts only if Garcia agrees to let his pigtail be cut if he does badly (the cutting is symbolic of a bullfighter's retirement from the ring).

Zurito supports Garcia, especially during the early stages with his first bull, but after the matador cannot kill the bull even after six tries and is finally gored and rushed to the infirmary, Zurito wants to cut the pigtail and stops only because Garcia begs him not to. Zurito's nickname is Manosduros, or Manos.

Zurito (2) (1868–1936) Spanish bullfighter whose real name was Manuel de la Haba. He was known as a great picador. His ability in the bull ring is referred to in *Death in the Afternoon.*

APPENDICES

APPENDIX I

Map from "At Sea" Section of *Islands in the Stream*

Opposite: Map for **Islands in the Stream** *Camagüey archipelago off the northeast coast of Cuba, site of Thomas Hudson's May 1944 hunt for a German submarine in the "At Sea" section of* Islands in the Stream. *Hudson and his crew begin their search at Cayo Confites, moving northwestward, staying offshore as much as possible to avoid shallow water but going ashore periodically to get information from islanders. They find the Germans near "No-Name Island," a name Hemingway probably made up and one of hundreds of islands extending south of Cayo Guillermo and west of Coco—islands that constantly move with the winds. After Hudson's wounding, his crew takes the boat through the islands into the open waters of Bahía Buenavista and on toward the town of Caibarién.* (This map is adapted from U.S. Naval Chart 27060, "Cayo Larela to Cayo Verde, including Andros.")

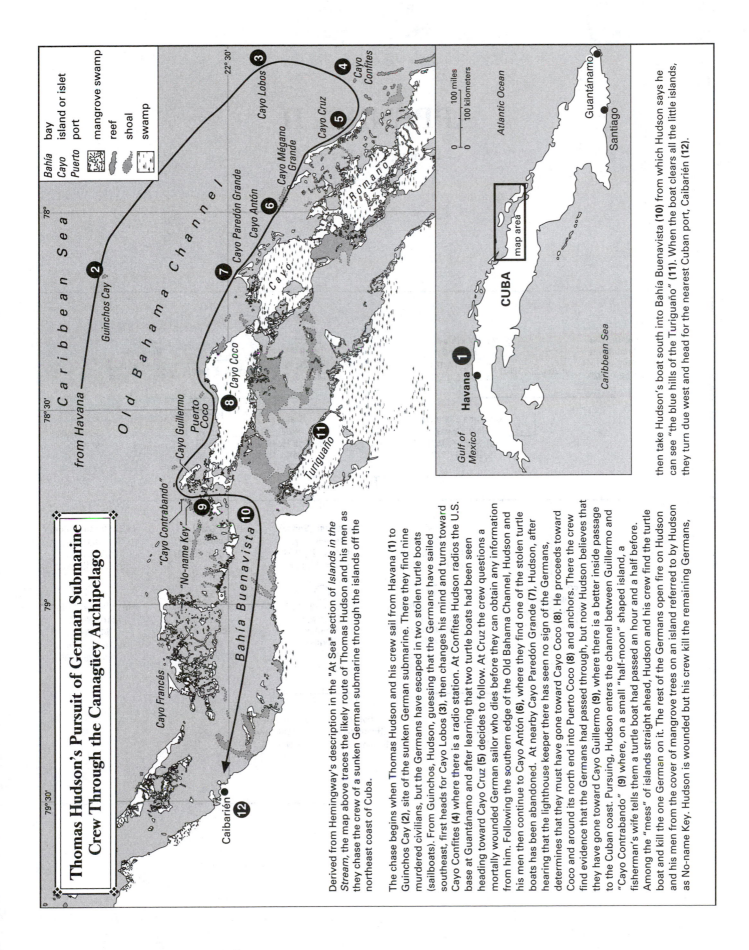

Thomas Hudson's Pursuit of German Submarine Crew Through the Camagüey Archipelago

Bahía	bay
Cayo	island or islet
Puerto	port

mangrove swamp
reef
shoal
swamp

Derived from Hemingway's description in the "At Sea" section of *Islands in the Stream*, the map above traces the likely route of Thomas Hudson and his men as they chase the crew of a sunken German submarine through the islands off the northeast coast of Cuba.

The chase begins when Thomas Hudson and his crew sail from Havana (1) to Guinchos Cay (2), site of the sunken German submarine. There they find nine murdered civilians, but the Germans have escaped in two stolen turtle boats (sailboats). From Guinchos, Hudson, guessing that the Germans have sailed southeast, first heads for Cayo Lobos (3), then changes his mind and turns toward Cayo Confites (4) where there is a radio station. At Confites Hudson radios the U.S. base at Guantánamo and after learning that two turtle boats had been seen heading toward Cayo Cruz (5) decides to follow. At Cruz the crew questions a mortally wounded German sailor who dies before they can obtain any information from him. Following the southern edge of the Old Bahama Channel, Hudson and his men then continue to Cayo Antón (6), where they find one of the stolen turtle boats has been abandoned. At nearby Cayo Paredón Grande (7), Hudson, after hearing that the lighthouse keeper there has seen no sign of the Germans, determines that they must have gone toward Cayo Coco (8). He proceeds toward Coco and around its north end into Puerto Coco (8) and anchors. There the crew find evidence that the Germans had passed through, but now Hudson believes that they have gone toward Cayo Guillermo (9), where there is a better inside passage to the Cuban coast. Pursuing, Hudson enters the channel between Guillermo and "Cayo Contrabando" (9) where, on a small "half-moon" shaped island, a fisherman's wife tells them a turtle boat had passed an hour and a half before. Among the "mess" of islands straight ahead, Hudson and his crew find the turtle boat and kill the one German on it. The rest of the Germans open fire on Hudson and his men from the cover of mangrove trees on an island referred to by Hudson as No-name Key. Hudson is wounded but his crew kill the remaining Germans,

then take Hudson's boat south into Bahía Buenavista (10) from which Hudson says he can see "the blue hills of the Turiguaño" (11). When the boat clears all the little islands, they turn due west and head for the nearest Cuban port, Caibarién (12).

APPENDIX II

Hemingway's Family

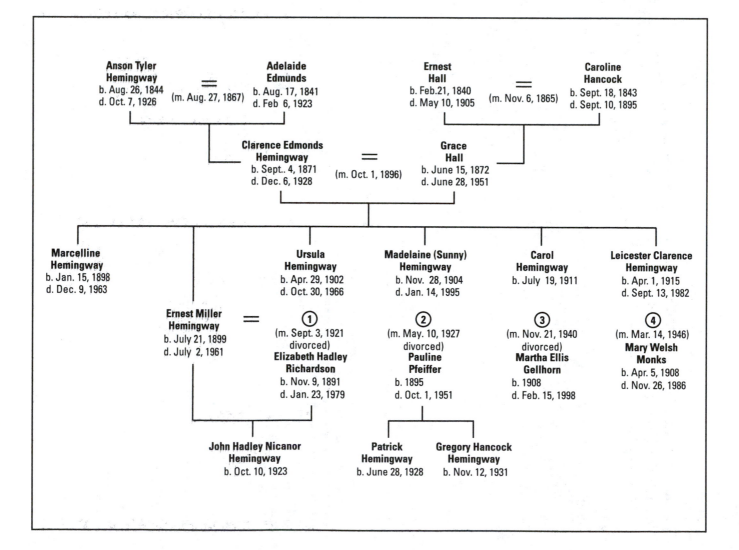

Anson Tyler Hemingway
b. Aug. 26, 1844
d. Oct. 7, 1926

= (m. Aug. 27, 1867)

Adelaide Edmunds
b. Aug. 17, 1841
d. Feb 6, 1923

Ernest Hall
b. Feb.21, 1840
d. May 10, 1905

= (m. Nov. 6, 1865)

Caroline Hancock
b. Sept. 18, 1843
d. Sept. 10, 1895

Clarence Edmonds Hemingway
b. Sept.. 4, 1871
d. Dec. 6, 1928

= (m. Oct. 1, 1896)

Grace Hall
b. June 15, 1872
d. June 28, 1951

Marcelline Hemingway
b. Jan. 15, 1898
d. Dec. 9, 1963

Ursula Hemingway
b. Apr. 29, 1902
d. Oct. 30, 1966

Madelaine (Sunny) Hemingway
b. Nov. 28, 1904
d. Jan. 14, 1995

Carol Hemingway
b. July 19, 1911

Leicester Clarence Hemingway
b. Apr. 1, 1915
d. Sept. 13, 1982

Ernest Miller Hemingway
b. July 21, 1899
d. July 2, 1961

=

① (m. Sept. 3, 1921 divorced)
Elizabeth Hadley Richardson
b. Nov. 9, 1891
d. Jan. 23, 1979

② (m. May. 10, 1927 divorced)
Pauline Pfeiffer
b. 1895
d. Oct. 1, 1951

③ (m. Nov. 21, 1940 divorced)
Martha Ellis Gellhorn
b. 1908
d. Feb. 15, 1998

④ (m. Mar. 14, 1946)
Mary Welsh Monks
b. Apr. 5, 1908
d. Nov. 26, 1986

John Hadley Nicanor Hemingway
b. Oct. 10, 1923

Patrick Hemingway
b. June 28, 1928

Gregory Hancock Hemingway
b. Nov. 12, 1931

APPENDIX III

Hemingway Chronology and Dateline

Date	Personal	Writing and Publishing	Other Literary Events	Nobel Prize (Literature)	Historical Events
1896	Grace Hall and Clarence Hemingway marry October 1 and move in with her father at 439 North Oak Park Ave. in Oak Park, Illinois, a suburb west of Chicago.				
1898	Marcelline Hemingway born January 15.				
1899	Ernest Miller Hemingway born in Oak Park, Illinois (July 21), the second of six Hemingway children. Hemingways leave in September for Walloon Lake in northern Michigan, where they have a summer cottage. EH and his family will go to Windemere Cottage every summer until he joins the American Red Cross for duty in northern Italy in Jan. 1918.		Henry James, *The Awkward Age*; Leo Tolstoi, *Resurrection*; Frank Norris, *McTeague*; b. Hart Crane; b. Federico García Lorca; b. James Weldon Johnson; d. Horatio Alger Jr. (b. 1832).		
1900			Theodore Dreiser, *Sister Carrie*; L. Frank Baum, *The Wonderful Wizard of Oz*; b. Joseph Conrad, *Lord Jim*; b. Thomas Wolfe; b. Antoine St.-Exupéry; b. Margaret Mitchell.		William McKinley defeats William Jennings Bryan for U.S. presidency; Boxer Rebellion begins in Peking; Galveston hurricane (Sept. 8) with 6,000 killed; bacteriologist Walter Reed discovers that mosquitoes carry yellow fever.
1901			Thomas Mann, *Buddenbrooks*; Rudyard Kipling, *Kim*; b. Zora Neale Hurston.	Sully Prudhomme (France)	Orville and Wilbur Wright make powered flight near Kitty Hawk, NC; U.S.-Cuba treaty allows U.S. occupation of Guantánamo.
1902	Ursula Hemingway born April 29.		Joseph Conrad, *Heart of Darkness, Typhoon, and Youth*; d. Bret Harte (b. 1836); d. Émile Zola (b. 1840).	Theodor Mommsen (Germany)	
1903			Henry James, *The Ambassadors*; Jack London, *The Call of the Wild*; W. E. B. DuBois, *The Souls of Black Folk*.	Björnstjerne Björnson (Norway)	

Year	Hemingway	Literature	Nobel Prize	Historical Events
1904	Madelaine (Sunny) Hemingway born Nov. 28.	Knut Hamsun, *Dreamers*; d. Kate Chopin (b. 1851).	Frédéric Mistral (France) and José Echegaray y Eizaguirre (Spain)	Theodore Roosevelt wins U.S. presidency over Alton B. Parker; Russo-Japanese War begins; Panama Canal Zone ceded to United States.
1905	EH begins first grade in Oak Park.	Edith Wharton, *The House of Mirth*; d. Jules Verne (b. 1828).	Henryk Sienkiewicz (Poland)	Albert Einstein presents theory of relativity; Bloody Sunday (Jan. 17) in St. Petersburg as Russian troops kill 100 protesters at Winter Palace; Irish Republican political organization Sinn Fein becomes official party.
1906		John Galsworthy, *Man of Property*; Upton Sinclair, *The Jungle*; d. Paul Laurence Dunbar (b. 1872).	Giosuè Carducci (Italy)	San Francisco earthquake (April 18) destroys most of city, 800 killed; Mahatma Gandhi begins nonviolence civil disobedience campaign in South Africa.
1907		Henry Adams, *The Education of Henry Adams*.	Rudyard Kipling (England)	U.S. financial panic, depression diverted by financiers led by J. Pierpont Morgan; August von Wasserman develops first blood test for syphilis.
1908		E. M. Forster, *A Room With a View*; John Fox, Jr., *Trail of the Lonesome Pine*; d. Joel Chandler Harris (b. 1848).	Rudolf Eucken (Germany)	
1909		Gertrude Stein, *Three Lives*; d. Sarah Orne Jewett (b. 1849).	Selma Lagerlöf (Sweden)	
1910		d. Leo Tolstoi (b. 1828); d. Mark Twain (b. 1835); d. O. Henry (b. 1862).	Paul von Heyse (Germany)	Mexican Revolution begins, eventually killing 1 million (1910–20); Union of South Africa established.
1911	Carol Hemingway born July 19 at summer cottage in Michigan.	Edith Wharton, *Ethan Frome*; Ambrose Bierce, *The Devil's Dictionary*.	Maurice Maeterlinck (Belgium)	Chinese Revolution begins, Sun Yat-sen elected provisional president; Italy declares war on Turkey; Japan annexes Korea.
1912		Thomas Mann, *Death in Venice*; Zane Grey, *The Riders of the Purple Sage*; d. Bram Stoker (b. 1847).	Gerhart Hauptmann (Germany)	

Date	Personal	Writing and Publishing	Other Literary Events	Nobel Prize (Literature)	Historical Events
1913	EH and Marcelline begin freshman year at Oak Park and River Forest High School.		Marcel Proust, *Remembrance of Things Past*; D. H. Lawrence, *Sons and Lovers*; Willa Cather, *O Pioneers!*.	Rabindranath Tagore (India)	Treaty of London ends First Balkan War, creating Albania and giving much of western Turkey to the Balkan League; Second Balkan War begins with Bulgarian attacks on Serbia and Greece.
1914			James Joyce, *Dubliners*; Robert Frost, *North of Boston*; *The Little Review* begins publication (1914-1929); Edgar Rice Burroughs, *Tarzan of the Apes*; d. Ambrose Bierce (b. 1842).	no winner	Bosnian nationalists assassinate Austro-Hungarian Archduke Francis Ferdinand (June 28), starting World War I; First Battle of the Marne (Sept. 5–10); First Battle of Ypres (Oct. 20–Nov. 24); Margaret Sanger coins term "birth control."
1915	Leicester Hemingway born April 1; EH begins writing for high school newspaper, *The Trapeze*; also plays football with reserves.		Franz Kafka, *The Metamorphosis*; Somerset Maugham, *Of Human Bondage*; Edgar Lee Masters, *Spoon River Anthology*; d. Rupert Brooke (b. 1887).	Romain Rolland (France)	British liner *Lusitania* sunk by German submarine off Irish coast, 1,198 people killed, including 128 Americans; Second Battle of Ypres (April 22–May 25), Germans use chlorine gas against British; Italy enters war on Allied side.
1916	EH writes for high school literary magazine, *Tabula*; plays varsity football.	Publishes first article (Jan. 20), "Concert a Success," in high school newspaper, *The Trapeze*; publishes first short story, "Judgment of Manitou," in high school literary magazine, *Tabula* (Feb. issue); he will publish 18 more articles for the newspaper and two more short stories and a poem for the magazine this year.	Carl Sandburg, *Chicago Poems*; Ring Lardner, *You Know Me, Al*; d. Henry James (b. 1843); d. Jack London (b. 1876); d. Sholem Aleichem (b. 1859).	Verner von Heidenstam (Sweden)	Pres. Woodrow Wilson wins second term; First Battle of the Somme (July 1–Nov. 13) with more than 1 million deaths, British introduce tanks; Battle of Verdun (Feb. 21–Dec. 18) with nearly a million casualties, phosgene gas used by Germans; Irish Easter Rising (April 24–29) in Dublin; David Lloyd George becomes British prime minister; first news reports carried by radio.

	EH	Publications	Nobel Prize in Literature	Literature	History
1917	EH in *Beau Brummel*, the high school senior play; he and Marcelline graduate from high school (June); he moves to Kansas City (Oct.) for job as cub reporter with *The Kansas City Star.*	Publishes 18 articles in *The Trapeze* plus three more poems and the "Class Prophecy" in *Tabula*.	Karl A. Gjellerup (Denmark) and Hendrik Pontoppidan (Denmark)	William Butler Yeats, *The Wild Swans at Coole*; Hamlin Garland, *A Son of the Middle Border*; Sara Teasdale, *Love Songs*.	Russian Revolution begins (Jan.). Nicholas II abdicates (March 15); Lenin returns to Russia (April 6); U.S. Congress declares war on Germany (April 2); Leon Trotsky leads forces against St. Petersburg's Winter Palace (Nov. 7), which begins Russian Civil War (1917–1922); Third Battle of Ypres, at Passchendaele (July 31–Nov. 10), a failed British offensive that costs 320,000 lives; Dutch dancer Mata Hari executed by French as German spy (Oct. 15); Battle of Caporetto on northern Italian front (Oct. 24–Nov. 12).
1918	EH and friend Ted Brumback join American Red Cross (May) to drive ambulances in Italy; report for physicals in New York; leave on the *Chicago* for France (May 23); arrive in Italy (June 4) and are stationed at Schio in northern Italy with Ambulance Section 4; EH volunteers (June 22) to take chocolate and cigarettes to frontline Italian troops near FOSSALTA, northeast of Venice on the Piave River; wounded at forward observation post by trench mortar shell (night of July 8)—the first American wounded in World War I; spends rest of year at Red Cross Hospital in Milan; falls in love with his nurse Agnes von Kurowsky; Agnes reassigned to Treviso where EH visits her (Dec. 9), the last time they see each other.		no winner	Willa Cather, *My Antonia*; d. Henry Adams (b. 1838); d. Joyce Kilmer (b. 1886); d. Wilfred Owen (b. 1893).	"Spanish flu," a mainly untreatable pandemic, kills estimated 25–50 million people in Europe, Britain, and U.S. (1918–19); abolition of private property in Russia; first U.S. action in war at Battle of Cantigny (May 28–29); Battle of Belleau Wood (May 30–June 17); Battle of Chateau-Thierry (May 30–June 17); Second Battle of the Marne (July 15–Aug. 5); Battle of Vittorio Veneto (Oct. 24–Nov. 4); Austrian army defeated; German revolution forces abdication of Emperor Wilhelm II (Nov. 9); Armistice (Nov. 11); Woodrow Wilson's "Fourteen Point Plan" includes formation of League of Nations; equal voting rights for British women over 30.

Date	Personal	Writing and Publishing	Other Literary Events	Nobel Prize (Literature)	Historical Events
1919	EH discharged from Red Cross because of wounds (Jan. 4); arrives in New York on *Giuseppe Verdi* (Jan. 21), less than eight months after leaving for Italy; returns to Oak Park; Agnes breaks relationship with EH in a letter (March); he goes to northern Michigan (May); returns to Oak Park in December.	Writes series of short stories at Walloon Lake (summer), none of which is published during his lifetime.	Sherwood Anderson, *Winesburg, Ohio*; H. L. Mencken, *The American Language*; d. L. Frank Baum (b. 1856).	Carl Spitteler (Switzerland)	Paris Peace Conference (Jan. 18–June 28) concludes with Treaty of Versailles; League of Nations established; Red Army defeats White Army in Russian Civil War; German Workers' Party, forerunner of Nazi Party, established; Sinn Fein declares Ireland independent republic (Jan. 21), Eamon de Valera is first president; U.S. passes 18th Amendment, Prohibition; Benito Mussolini establishes first Italian Fascist group.
1920	EH moves to Toronto (Jan. 8) for temporary job as companion to Ralph Connable Jr., 19-year-old partially crippled son of editor of *The Toronto Daily Star*; spends summer at Walloon Lake and Horton Bay; moves to Chicago (Oct.) where he meets Hadley Richardson, a 29-year-old St. Louis woman (b. Nov. 9, 1891) with whom he corresponds during the next year; takes job with *Cooperative Commonwealth*, a journal for midwestern farmers.	Freelances for *The Toronto Star* (Jan.–April); his first published article is "New Ether to Credit of Toronto Surgeon" (Jan. 27); writes and edits for *Cooperative Commonwealth* in Chicago (Dec. 1920–Oct. 1921).	Edith Wharton, *The Age of Innocence*; Sinclair Lewis, *Main Street*; D. H. Lawrence, *Women in Love*; F. Scott Fitzgerald, *This Side of Paradise*; Katherine Mansfield, *Bliss and Other Stories*; d. William Dean Howells (b. 1837).	Knut Hamsun (Norway)	U.S. passes 19th Amendment, women's suffrage; League of Women Voters founded; Warren Harding defeats James M. Cox for U.S. presidency; anti-Jewish pogroms in Ukraine; Turkish forces led by Mustapha Kemal defeat Greek forces in western Turkey; Kemal first president of Turkish Republic; American Civil Liberties Union established.
1921	EH and Hadley marry (Sept. 3) at Horton Bay, Michigan; they live in Chicago in apartment in 1300 block of North Clark St., and EH continues to write for *Cooperative Commonwealth* until its founder is accused of cheating farmers in a cooperative scheme and the journal folds (Oct.); EH gets job with *The Toronto Star* to send feature stories from Europe, and he and Hadley leave for Paris (Dec. 8) aboard *Leopoldina*; arrive in Paris (Dec. 20), where they stay at Hotel Jacob.	Writes short story "Up in Michigan" at Walloon Lake (summer); continues to write feature stories for *Toronto Star*; continues to write and edit for *Cooperative Commonwealth* (until it folds in October).	Marianne Moore, *Poems*; John Burroughs (b. 1837).	Anatole France (France)	Irish Civil War begins; Nicola Sacco and Bartolomeo Vanzetti convicted of murder in Braintree, MA; Margaret Sanger founds American Birth Control League, forerunner of Planned Parenthood.

1922	EH and Hadley rent apartment at 79, rue Cardinal Lemoine (Jan. 9) and leave for Chamby sur Montreux, Switzerland, on a two-week skiing vacation; return to Paris (Feb. 2); visit Gertrude Stein (March 8); EH leaves for Genoa Economic Conference (April 6); returns to Paris (April 27); EH and Hadley return to Chamby sur Montreux, where they and friend Chink Dorman-Smith hike over the St. Bernard Pass into Italy; they see places in northern Italy EH remembers from the war, including Fossalta, near where he was wounded; return to Paris (June 18); EH leaves (Sept. 25) for Constantinople to cover the Greco-Turkish war for *The Toronto Daily Star*; he sees retreat of Greek army (Oct. 14); returns to Paris (Oct. 21); leaves for Lausanne, Switzerland (Nov. 21) to cover the Peace Conference.	Publishes first *Toronto Star* article from Europe (Feb. 4), "Tourists Scarce at Swiss Resorts"; *Star* will publish 86 more of his articles from Europe this year; the *Double Dealer* publishes his allegory "A Divine Gesture"; finishes short story "My Old Man" (Sept. 2); Hadley's suitcase stolen (Dec. 2), containing nearly all of EH's short story manuscripts and the beginning of a novel.	Italy's Fascist Blackshirts march on Rome, Benito Mussolini becomes premier (Oct. 31); U.S. Teapot Dome scandal.
		Jacinto Benavente (Spain)	
		James Joyce, *Ulysses*; T. S. Eliot, *The Waste Land*; Sinclair Lewis, *Babbitt*; Hermann Hesse, *Siddharta*; e. e. cummings, *The Enormous Room*; Willa Cather, *One of Ours*; Katherine Mansfield, *The Garden Party*; d. Marcel Proust (b. 1871).	
1923	EH and Hadley on skiing vacation in Switzerland through January; visit Ezra Pound in Rapallo, Italy (Feb. 7), where they meet Maggie and Henry Strater, who paints EH's portrait, and Edward O'Brien, the editor of an annual anthology of short stories; they vacation in Cortina, Italy; EH goes to Germany's Ruhr Valley (March 30) to cover French and Belgian "occupation," while Hadley stays in Cortina; EH returns to Cortina (April 12); they leave for Paris (May 2) and for Spain (late May), where EH sees his first bullfight (May 30) in Aranjuez; return to Paris in mid-June; leave for Pamplona (July 6) for their first Fiesta San Fermín; leave Europe (Aug. 26) on the *Andania*, landing in Montreal (Sept. 4); EH takes full-time job with *The Toronto Daily Star*; signs lease on apartment on Bathurst Street; EH	Publishes six poems in *Poetry* (Jan. issue); finishes six sketches in Cortina, Italy (March 10), which are published in *The Little Review* (Spring issue) and which will become first six sketches of *in our time* (1924); his first book, *Three Stories & Ten Poems*, is published (no date, but late July/early Aug.) by Robert McAlmon at Contact Publishing Co., Paris; EH checks galley proofs of *in our time* (Dec. 20) while in New York.	Hitler writes *Mein Kampf*, released from prison a national hero; Pres. Warren Harding dies, succeeded by Vice Pres. Calvin Coolidge; French and Belgian army forces occupy Ruhr Valley because Germany refuses to pay reparations established by Treaty of Versailles.
		William Butler Yeats (Ireland)	
		D. H. Lawrence, *Studies in American Literature*; Khalil Gibran, *The Prophet*; Rainer Maria Rilke, *Duino Elegies*; Wallace Stevens, *Harmonium*; d. Katherine Mansfield (b. 1888).	

Date	Personal	Writing and Publishing	Other Literary Events	Nobel Prize (Literature)	Historical Events
	goes to New York to cover arrival of former British prime minister Lloyd George for his visit to Canada; Hadley delivers baby (Oct. 10), John Hadley Nicanor Hemingway; EH resigns position with *Star* (late Dec.) in order to return to Paris and write fiction.				
1924	EH and Hadley leave Toronto (Jan. 10) by train for New York; they sail on the *Antonia* (Jan. 19); arrive Cherbourg (Jan. 30) and sign lease on apartment in Paris at 113, rue Notre-Dame-des-Champs, a Left Bank cold-water flat; their son, nicknamed "Bumby," is baptized (March 16), with friend Chink Dorman-Smith as godfather and Gertrude Stein and Alice B. Toklas as godmothers; EH leaves (April 6) on six-day trip alone through Provence; returns to Paris (May 1); EH and Hadley leave for Pamplona (June 25), where they are joined by Dorman-Smith, John Dos Passos, Donald Ogden Stewart, and George O'Neil; Fiesta San Fermín begins (July 6) and Bill and Sally Bird and Robert McAlmon arrive; EH, Hadley, and friends move to Burguete, Spain (July 13), for fishing in the Irati River; EH and Hadley return to Paris (July 27); they leave for Schruns, Austria (Dec. 20) for winter vacation.	Finishes "Cat in the Rain" and "The End of Something" in Paris (by Feb. 20) and begins "Indian Camp," which is published in *transatlantic review* (April issue); his second book, *in our time*, published by William Bird at Three Mountains Press in Paris (no date, but probably mid March); finishes "The Doctor and the Doctor's Wife," "Soldier's Home," "Mr. and Mrs. Eliot," and "Cross Country Snow" (April 25); edits the August issue of *transatlantic review* for Ford Madox Ford; finishes "Big Two-Hearted River" (mid-Aug.); 14 short stories ready for publication in *In Our Time* (1925)—John Dos Passos takes the typescript to New York to find a publisher; *transatlantic review* publishes EH's "Homage to Conrad" and "Pamplona Letter" (Oct.); *Der Querschnitt* publishes two poems (Oct. 5); *Harper's* magazine rejects "Soldier's Home" (Oct. 27); *transatlantic review* publishes "The Doctor and the Doctor's Wife" (Nov.); *Harper's* rejects "Cross Country Snow" (Nov.) but *Der Querschnitt* publishes it (Dec.).	E. M. Forster, *A Passage to India*; Thomas Mann, *The Magic Mountain*; William Faulkner, *The Marble Faun*; Pablo Neruda, *Twenty Love Songs*; I. A. Richards, *Principles of Literary Criticism*; *Saturday Review* (of Literature) begins publication; d. Joseph Conrad (b. 1857); d. Franz Kafka (b. 1883); d. Anatole France (b. 1844).	Wladislaw S. Reymont (Poland)	Pres. Calvin Coolidge defeats John W. Davis for U.S. presidency; Defense Attorney Clarence Darrow pioneers "insanity plea" and frees murderers Nathan Leopold and Richard Loeb; Bolshevik Party leader Lenin dies; J. Edgar Hoover becomes director of FBI.
1925	EH and Hadley spend week (mid February) skiing from the Madlener Hut in the mountains south of Schruns; return to Paris (March 14); EH meets Pauline and Virginia (Jinny) Pfeiffer through mutual	*In Our Time* rejected by two New York publishers (by Jan. 5); "The Undefeated" rejected by *The Saturday Evening Post* (mid Jan.); "Mr. and Mrs. Eliot" published in *The Little Review* (Autumn–Winter	Theodore Dreiser, *An American Tragedy*; F. Scott Fitzgerald, *The Great Gatsby*; T. S. Eliot, *The Hollow Men*; Virginia Woolf, *Mrs. Dalloway*; Ezra Pound, *The Cantos*; Sherwood Anderson,	George Bernard Shaw (Ireland)	Scopes Trial in Tennessee; Locarno Treaties establish French and German borders; German military hero Paul von Hindenburg becomes president of the Weimar Republic.

friends Harold Loeb and Kitty Cannell; EH meets F. Scott and Zelda Fitzgerald (May) and introduces them to Gertrude Stein (June); EH and Fitzgerald make trip to Lyons (June); EH buys Joan Miró's "The Farm" (June 12) for 3,500 francs; EH and Hadley leave for Pamplona (June 25), where they are joined by Bill Smith, Donald Stewart, Harold Loeb, Lady Duff Twysden, and her fiance, Pat Guthrie; Fiesta San Fermín begins (July 6)—each day begins with the running of the bulls (EH views but does not participate) and afternoon bullfights; EH and Hadley go to Madrid (July 13) for more bullfights and the Prado Museum; Hadley returns to Paris (Aug. 11); he returns (Aug. 18); EH and Hadley leave for Schruns (Dec. 11); mutual friend Pauline Pfeiffer arrives in Schruns (Dec. 25).

issue, 1924–1925); Boni & Liveright Publishers accept *In Our Time* (March 16) but insist on replacement of "Up in Michigan" and editing out offensive parts of "Mr. and Mrs. Elliot"; EH sends signed contract to Boni & Liveright and "The Battler" to replace "Up in Michigan" (March 31); "Big Two-Hearted River" published in *This Quarter* (May issue); *Der Querschnitt* publishes "The Undefeated" in German translation (June); EH begins writing *The Sun Also Rises* (mid July); finishes the first draft (mid Sept.); begins "Fifty Grand" and "Ten Indians" (end Sept.); *This Quarter* publishes "The Undefeated"; EH's third book, *In Our Time*, published by Boni & Liveright in New York (Oct. 5); finishes "Fifty Grand" (Nov. 8); begins *The Torrents of Spring* (late Nov.); Boni & Liveright reject *Torrents* (Dec. 30), allowing EH to break his contract and move to publishers Charles Scribner's Sons.

Dark Laughter; Ole Rolvaag, *Giants in the Earth*; William Carlos Williams, *In the American Grain*; John Dos Passos, *Manhattan Transfer*; Mikhail Sholokov, *The Tales of the Don*; *The New Yorker* magazine founded by Harold Ross; d. Amy Lowell (b. 1874).

British troops break miners' union strike (May 4–12); U.S. physicist and rocket pioneer Robert Hutchings Goddard launches first liquid-propellant rocket (March 16); Hirohito becomes emperor of Japan.

1926

Pauline returns to Paris (mid Jan.); EH arrives in Paris (end Jan.) en route to New York to work out book contract with Horace Liveright; Hadley remains in Schruns; EH departs Cherbourg (Feb. 3) on *Mauretania*; arrives in New York (Feb. 9); Liveright agrees that contract is broken (Feb. 10); EH meets Maxwell Perkins at Scribner's (Feb. 11) to work out contract for both *The Torrents of Spring* and *The Sun Also Rises*; EH signs with Scribner's (Feb. 17); he sails for France on the *Roosevelt* (Feb. 20); he arrives Cherbourg (March 1); stays in Paris with Pauline (March 2–3); returns to Schruns (March 4); EH and Hadley return to Paris (end of March); Hadley, Pauline and Jenny Pfeiffer travel together through the

EH revises *The Sun Also Rises* while wintering in Schruns; receives offer from Jonathan Cape for British rights to *In Our Time* (April 7); mails typescript of *The Sun Also Rises* to Perkins (April 24); mails "An Alpine Idyll" to *Scribner's Magazine* (May 6); finishes "Today is Friday" in Madrid and the second draft of "The Killers" (May 14); EH's fourth book, *The Torrents of Spring*, published by Scribner's (May 28); "A Banal Story" published in *The Little Review* (Spring–Summer issue); his short play, *Today is Friday*, published by The As Stable Publications (summer); at Scott Fitzgerald's suggestion, EH writes Perkins to cut first 16 pages of *The Sun Also Rises* (June 5); "The Killers" accepted by *Scribner's Magazine* (Sept. 8); Scribner's publishes EH's fifth book,

William Faulkner, *Soldier's Pay*; Edna Ferber, *Show Boat*; Henry W. Fowler, *A Dictionary of Modern English Usage*; Book-of-the-Month Club founded; d. Rainer Maria Rilke (b. 1875).

Grazia Deledda (Italy)

377

Date	Personal	Writing and Publishing	Other Literary Events	Nobel Prize (Literature)	Historical Events
	Loire Valley (late May–early April), Hadley learning of Ernest's affair with Pauline; EH goes to Spain alone (May 14); EH and Hadley, with Murphys and Pauline, arrive in Pamplona (July 1) for Fiesta San Fermin; EH and Hadley go to Madrid (July 15) and Valencia (July 24) for more bullfights; they inform the Murphys and Stewarts in Antibes (in August) of their plans to separate; Hadley agrees to divorce (Sept. 24) if EH and Pauline will undergo a 100-day separation period; Pauline leaves for home in Piggott, Arkansas; EH takes care of Bumby while Hadley travels to Chartres with Winifred Mowrer (Nov. 8); Hadley releases EH from separation trial period with Pauline (Nov. 16); Hadley returns to Paris from Chartres (Nov. 17); EH files divorce papers (Dec. 8); he has supper at Sylvia Beach's with James and Nora Joyce, Ada and Archibald MacLeish; Pauline sails from New York (Dec. 30) on the *New Amsterdam*; EH travels to Gstaad, Switzerland (end Dec.), for week's vacation with MacLeishes.	*The Sun Also Rises*, (Oct. 22); *Scribner's Magazine* accepts "A Canary for One" (Nov. 11) and "In Another Country" (Dec. 4).			
1927	EH meets Pauline at Cherbourg (Jan. 8); they arrive Gstaad (Jan. 12); EH meets Sherwood Anderson in Paris (Jan. 20); Hadley gets divorce (Jan. 27), winning cause of desertion and custody of Bumby; EH, Pauline, and Jenny move from Hotel Rossli in Gstaad to Hotel Eiger in Wengen, Switzerland (late Feb.); EH returns to Paris to get Bumby for 10-day visit to Switzerland (Feb. 16–28); EH and Pauline back in Paris with Bumby	*Scribner's Magazine* publishes "The Killers," (March issue), "In Another Country" and "A Canary for One" (April issue); *New Republic* publishes "Italy—1927"; *Atlantic Monthly* publishes "Fifty Grand" (July issue); *transition* publishes "Hills Like White Elephants" (Aug. issue); Scribner's publishes EH's sixth book, *Men Without Women* (Oct. 14).	Sinclair Lewis, *Elmer Gantry*; Virginia Woolf, *To the Lighthouse*; Hermann Hesse, *Steppenwolf*; Thornton Wilder, *The Bridge of San Luis Rey*; Don Marquis, *archy and mehitable*; Willa Cather, *Death Comes for the Archbishop*.	Henri Bergson (France)	Charles A. Lindbergh makes first solo trans-Atlantic flight, New York to Paris in *Spirit of St. Louis* (May 20–21); Sacco and Vanzetti executed (Aug. 23); Chiang Kai-shek breaks with communist allies in Kuomintang (April), beginning with Shanghai Massacre of 5,000–6,000 communists, which sets off Civil War (1927–1949); fossil remains of Peking Man found near Peking, China.

(March 8); Hadley returns to Chartres with Winifred Mowrer (March 11–13); Hadley and Bumby sail for New York (April 16); EH receives dispensation from Archdiocese of Paris permitting him to remarry; EH and Pauline marry (May 10) in Eglise de St-Honore-d'Eylan in Paris; leave Paris (May 11) for honeymoon in Le Grau-du-Roi on the Mediterranean; Hadley takes Bumby to Oak Park (May 25) to visit Grace and Clarence Hemingway, the first time they've seen their grandson; EH and Pauline back in Paris (June 7); they enter Spain (July 1) for Fiesta San Fermín (July 6–12); EH writes to his father about his divorce from Hadley and marriage to Pauline; EH and Pauline return to Paris (Sept. 24) and new apartment at 6, rue Ferou; they visit Berlin (Nov. 3) for six-day bicycle races, meeting Sinclair Lewis there; back in Paris (Nov. 12); then to Gstaad with Bumby and Jinny Pfeiffer (Dec. 13).

1928 Hemingways still in Gstaad (Jan. 15), EH's eye scratched by Bumby badly enough that he can't work or ski; EH back in Paris (Feb. 12); causes apartment skylight to fall on his head, stitches taken (March 6–7); EH and Pauline leave for Key West by way of Havana on *Orita* (March 17); Key West apartment on Simonton Street; EH and Pauline in Piggott, AR (May 31); drive to Kansas City (June 17) for birth of Pauline's first baby, Patrick Hemingway born (June 28); return to Piggott by train (July 29–30); EH to Kansas City (July 25) to meet Chicago friend Bill Horne for train trip to Wyoming; Pauline arrives Sheridan, WY (Aug. 18), back in Piggott (Sept. 26); leave for Chicago

EH begins *A Farewell to Arms* (March); finishes rough draft (Aug. 20–22).

D. H. Lawrence, *Lady Chatterley's Lover*; Stephen Vincent Benét, *John Brown's Body*; A. A. Milne, *The House at Pooh Corner*; final volumes of the *Oxford English Dictionary* published; d. Thomas Hardy (b. 1840).

Sigrid Undset (Norway)

Herbert Hoover defeats Alfred E. Smith for U.S. presidency; Kuomintang army defeats China warlords.

Date	Personal	Writing and Publishing	Other Literary Events	Nobel Prize (Literature)	Historical Events
	and points east (Oct.); to New York (Nov. 8–12) for prizefights and to see Perkins at Scribner's; they see Yale-Princeton football game (Nov. 17) meeting Scott and Zelda Fitzgerald there; visit Fitzgeralds' home, Ellerslie Mansion, near Wilmington, DE; leave by train for Piggott by way of Chicago (Nov. 18); move to Key West, 1100 South Street (late Nov.); EH goes to New York to meet Hadley with Bumby and to return with him to Key West (Dec. 6); EH receives telegram on train in Trenton, NJ, from Oak Park that his father is dead; EH places Bumby and $100 in hands of a porter for continuing trip to Key West and leaves for Chicago; Clarence Hemingway committed suicide (Dec. 6); EH returns to Key West following the funeral (Dec. 7).				
1929	EH asks his mother to put pistol his father used to kill himself in bank vault (March 6); EH borrows $50,000 from Scribner's and Pauline's father for trust fund for Grace Hemingway (March 11); EH, Pauline, Bumby, and Patrick leave Key West for Havana by ferry (March 16); leave for France (April 5); move into Paris flat at 6, rue Ferou (April 21); EH, Pauline, her father, Gus, and Jinny go to Pamplona, Hotel Quintana, for Fiesta San Fermín (July 6–14); EH buys three Goya lithographs as present for Hadley (Sept. 16); he and Pauline invited to party by James and Nora Joyce (Oct. 8); EH and Pauline and several friends, including the Fitzgeralds, go to Montana-Vermala, Switzerland, where Gerald	*A Farewell to Arms* serialized in *Scribner's Magazine* (May, June, July, Aug., Sept., Oct. issues), the May and June issues banned in Boston; *FTA* published in book form, EH's seventh book, by Scribner's (Sept. 27).	Erich Maria Remarque, *All Quiet on the Western Front*; William Faulkner, *The Sound and the Fury*; Thomas Wolfe, *Look Homeward, Angel*; I. A. Richards, *Practical Criticism*.	Thomas Mann (Germany)	U.S. stock market crash (Oct. 29), "Black Tuesday"; Lateran Treaty allows Catholic Church to "recognize" Mussolini; St. Valentine's Day massacre of seven people in Chicago by Al Capone; Geneva Convention establishes fair treatment of war prisoners.

and Sara Murphy's son is in a sanitorium; Hemingways return to Paris (Dec. 31).

	1930	**1931**	**1932**
History		Japan seizes Manchuria; NAACP elects Walter Francis White executive secretary (1931–55).	Soviet Union famine kills estimated 5 million; Franklin Delano Roosevelt defeats Pres. Herbert Hoover for U.S. presidency; Gen. Douglas
Nobel Prize	Sinclair Lewis (U.S.)	Erik Axel Karlfeldt (Sweden)	John Galsworthy (England)
Literature	T. S. Eliot, *Ash Wednesday*; *Poems*; W. H. Auden, *Poems*; Dashiell Hammett, *The Maltese Falcon*; Edna Ferber, *Cimarron*; Katherine Anne Porter, *Flowering Judas*; Hart Crane, *The Bridge*; d. Arthur Conan Doyle (b. 1859); d. D. H. Lawrence (b. 1885).	William Faulkner, *Sanctuary*; Pearl Buck, *The Good Earth*; Edmund Wilson, *Axel's Castle*; d. Arnold Bennett (b. 1867); d. Vachel Lindsay (b. 1879); d. Ole Edvart Rolvaag (b. 1876); d. Khalil Gibran (b. 1883).	Aldous Huxley, *Brave New World*; William Faulkner, *Light in August*; Erskine Caldwell, *Tobacco Road*; James Farrell, *Young Lonigan*; Ellen Glasgow,
Publishing	*Kiki of Montparnasse* published by Black Manikin Press with Hemingway's "Introduction" (Jan. 22); EH begins *Death in the Afternoon* (March); *Scribner's Magazine* publishes "Wine of Wyoming" (Aug. issue); stage adaptation of *A Farewell to Arms* by Lawrence Stallings opens in New York (Sept.) and closes after three weeks; movie rights for *FTA* sold to Paramount Pictures for $80,000 (Nov. 15).	*This Quarter* publishes "The Sea Change" (Dec. issue); EH finishes *Death in the Afternoon* (Dec.); first bibliography of EH's works compiled by Louis Henry Cohn, published by Random House (Aug.).	*Cosmopolitan* publishes "After the Storm" (May issue); EH writes "The Light of the World" (Aug.); his eighth book, *Death in the Afternoon*, published by Scribner's (Sept. 23).
EH Life	EH and Pauline leave for U.S. on *La Bourdonnais* (Jan. 10); arrive Havana (Jan. 22); EH, Maxwell Perkins, and friends stranded (March 16) on Dry Tortugas by storm during fishing trip, "rescued" (March 30); EH, Pauline, and Bumby arrive Nordquist's L-Bar-T ranch near Cooke City, MT (July 13); on hunting trip with Dos Passos (Nov.) EH in automobile accident, breaks his arm, requiring three operations before arm is satisfactorily set; Hemingways leave St. Vincent's Hospital in Billings for Piggott (Dec. 21); arrive (Dec. 24).	EH and Pauline return to Key West and rent house at 907 Whitehead Street (Jan 3); Perkins arrives for fishing trip and the group is stranded again on Dry Tortugas (March 1–13); Pauline, Patrick, and nurse leave for France (early May); EH sails from Havana (May 4) on *Volendam*; spends summer following Spanish bullfights; including Fiesta San Fermín in Pamplona (July 6–14); Pauline ships Paris apartment belongings to Key West house; EH and Pauline buy Juan Gris painting, "The Guitar Player" (Sept. 7); EH, Pauline, and Patrick arrive New York on *Ile de France* (Sept. 29); on board EH meets Grant and Jane Mason; birth of Gregory Hemingway (Nov. 12) in Kansas City by Cesarean section; leave for Piggott (Dec. 12); back to Key West (Dec. 19).	EH on fishing trip to Havana (April 20), where he stays two months at Hotel Ambos Murdos fishing for marlin and meeting Jane Mason; she leaves for New York (May 10)

Date	Personal	Writing and Publishing	Other Literary Events	Nobel Prize (Literature)	Historical Events
	but returns (June 11); Pauline to Havana (June 6); EH and Pauline arrive at Nordquist ranch near Cooke City, MT (July 12); EH returns to Key West (by Oct. 27).		*In This Our Life*; d. Hart Crane (b. 1899).		MacArthur uses tanks and troops to disperse 5,000 World War I veterans in Washington, D.C.; son of Charles Lindbergh kidnapped (March 1) and murdered; Mahatma Gandhi, in prison, begins lifelong campaign on behalf of India's "untouchables"; Eamon De Valera becomes prime minister of Ireland.
1933	EH to New York and then back to Key West (Jan. 20); leaves for Cuba (early April); Jane Mason suffers injuries in car accident with Bumby and Patrick (May 27) and then breaks her back falling or jumping from second floor of Havana hotel, sent to New York for surgery; Hadley marries Paul Scott Mowrer in London (July 3); EH returns to Key West (July 20); EH, Pauline, Patrick, Bumby, and Jinny Pfeiffer leave for Havana during Cuban revolution which overthrows President Machado; Hemingways leave for Spain (Aug. 7); EH in Paris (Oct. 26), invites James and Nora Joyce to dinner (Nov. 20); EH and Pauline leave Paris (Nov. 22) with hunting friend Charles Thompson for African safari, arriving New Stanley Hotel in Nairobi (Dec. 10); leave with Philip Percival as their hunting guide for two-month safari on the Serengeti plain (Dec. 20).	"A Clean Well-Lighted Place" published by *Scribner's Magazine* (March issue); *Scribner's* publishes "Homage to Switzerland" (April issue) and "Give Us a Prescription, Doctor" (May issue); EH agrees to write a series of "Letters" for a new magazine, *Esquire* (April 3); short story "God Rest You Merry, Gentlemen" published by House of Books (mid April); first issue of *Esquire* (Aug.) includes "Marlin Off the Morro" by EH; his ninth book, *Winner Take Nothing*, published by Scribner's (Oct. 27).	James Hilton, *Lost Horizon*; Gertrude Stein, *The Autobiography of Alice B. Toklas*; Erskine Caldwell, *God's Little Acre*; d. John Galsworthy (b. 1863); d. George Moore (b. 1852); d. Ring Lardner (b. 1885); d. Sara Teasdale (b. 1884).	Ivan Bunin (U.S.S.R.)	Adolf Hitler becomes German dictator (Feb. 28); Germans establish Buchenwald Prison; Roosevelt declares "bank holiday" (March 5–13) and establishes Emergency Relief Administration, Civilian Conservation Corps, Federal Deposit Insurance Corp, and Public Works Administration; U.S. passes 21st Amendment, ending Prohibition.
1934	EH has amoebic dysentery, flown out to Nairobi hospital (Jan. 14); rejoins safari (Jan. 22); he and Pauline leave for Paris (Feb. 28) by boat through Suez Canal; they sail	*Cosmopolitan* publishes "One Trip Across" (April issue), which would become part 1 of novel *To Have and Have Not*; EH begins *Green Hills of Africa* (May).	F. Scott Fitzgerald, *Tender is the Night*; James M. Cain, *The Postman Always Rings Twice*; Robert Graves, *I, Claudius*; Agatha Christie, *Murder on the*	Luigi Pirandello (Italy)	FBI agents kill John Dillinger, "Pretty Boy" Floyd, Bonnie Parker and Clyde Barrow.

Year	EH's Life	Works	Literary/Cultural Events	Nobel Prize for Literature	Historical Events
	for New York on the *Ile de France* (March 27); EH orders fishing boat at Wheeler Shipyard in Brooklyn (April 4); back in Key West (mid April); EH picks up his new boat, the *Pilar*, in Miami and sails it to Key West (May 11); he sails to Havana (July 18); returns to Key West (Oct. 26); EH, Pauline, and Patrick in Piggott for Christmas.		*Orient Express*; Malcolm Cowley, *An Exile's Return*.		
1935	EH accidentally shoots himself in both legs with a .22 pistol while shooting at a boated shark en route to Bimini for tuna fishing (April 7); back in Key West (Aug. 15), hurricane hits nearby Matecumbe Key (Sept. 2–3) killing 458 war veterans working in a CCC camp, EH helps in the hurricane cleanup; he covers Joe Louis–Max Baer heavyweight championship fight in New York for *Esquire* (Sept. 24); in Key West with Pauline and sons for Christmas.	*Scribner's Magazine* serializes *Green Hills of Africa* (May, June, July, Aug., Sept., Oct., Nov. issues); *Green Hills* published in book form by Scribner's (Oct. 25), EH's 10th book.	John Steinbeck, *Tortilla Flat*; C. S. Forester, *The African Queen*; Thomas Wolfe, *Of Time and the River*; d. Edwin Arlington Robinson (b. 1869); d. Æ (George William Russell) (b. 1867).	no winner	Italy invades Ethiopia; Pres. Roosevelt's "New Deal" creates millions of jobs; U.S. Social Security System established; John L. Lewis organizes the Congress of Industrial Organizations (C.I.O.); U.S. seismologist Charles Richter develops scale to measure earthquakes.
1936	EH in period of depression, insomnia, and talk of suicide (Jan.); Grant and Jane Mason arrive Key West (early March); EH leaves on *Pilar* (April 24) for month of fishing out of Havana, Pauline takes children to Piggott; EH meets Pauline, they leave for Nordquist Ranch in Wyoming (Aug. 1); back to Key West by way of Piggott to pick up their sons (late Oct.); EH meets journalist Martha Gellhorn in Sloppy Joe's Bar in Key West (end Dec.).	*Esquire* publishes "The Tradesman's Return" (February issue), which will become part 2 of novel *To Have and Have Not*; *Esquire* publishes "On the Blue Water: A Gulf Stream Letter" (April issue), which includes a sketch that EH will use for basic plot of *The Old Man and the Sea*; *Esquire* publishes "The Horns of the Bull" (June issue) and "The Snows of Kilimanjaro" (Aug. issue); *Cosmopolitan* publishes "The Short Happy Life of Francis Macomber" (Sept. issue); EH agrees to write a series of articles on Spanish civil war for North American Newspaper Alliance, NANA (Nov.).	William Faulkner, *Absalom, Absalom!*; Margaret Mitchell, *Gone With the Wind*; John Steinbeck, *In Dubious Battle*; Van Wyck Brooks, *The Flowering of New England*; Anaïs Nin, *The House of Incest*; Dorothy Parker, *Not So Deep a Well*; Ayn Rand, *We, the Living*; *Life* magazine begins publication; d. Rudyard Kipling (b. 1865); d. Federico García Lorca (b. 1899); d. Maxim Gorky (b. 1868); d. A. E. Housman (b. 1859); d. G. K. Chesteron (b. 1874).	Eugene O'Neill (U.S.)	Spanish civil war begins (July 18); U.S. athlete Jesse Owens stars in Berlin Olympics; Britain's Edward VIII abdicates crown to marry Wallis Simpson; Italian forces take Addis Ababa (May) and occupy Ethiopia.
1937	EH signs contract in New York (Jan. 13) to write dispatches from the Spanish civil war for NANA (North America Newspaper Alliance); sails for Spain (Feb. 27); EH at Hotel	NANA publishes first EH dispatch from Spanish civil war, "Passport for Franklin" (March 12); EH works on filming of *The Spanish Earth* (April); gives speech, "Fascism Is a Lie"	John Steinbeck, *Of Mice and Men*; Zora Neale Hurston, *Their Eyes Were Watching God*; Isak Dinesen, *Out of Africa*; J. R. R. Tolkien, *The Hobbit*; J. P.	Roger Martin Du Gard (France)	Sino-Japanese War begins (July 7); International Brigade units see first action at Madrid in Spanish civil war; Amelia Earhart lost in Pacific

Date	Personal	Writing and Publishing	Other Literary Events	Nobel Prize (Literature)	Historical Events
	Florida in Madrid (March 21), under siege; Martha Gellhorn, American bullfighter Sydney Franklin, and Dos Passos also at Hotel Florida (end March); EH returns to Paris (May 9); flies from New York to Hollywood with filmmaker Joris Ivens (July 10) for publicity and fundraising for their war film, *The Spanish Earth*; EH sails for France and Spain (Aug. 17); in Paris, with Martha Gellhorn (end Aug.); EH, Martha, and *New York Times* reporter Herbert Matthews are at Hotel Florida in Madrid (most of fall); EH in Paris with Pauline (end December), he with a liver disorder.	(June 4) to American Writer's Congress in New York; speech is published by *New Masses* (June 22); EH's 11th book, *To Have and Have Not*, published by Scribner's (Oct. 15); begins writing play, *The Fifth Column* (Oct. 15).	Marquand, *The Late George Apley*; Kenneth Roberts, *Northwest Passage*; Kawabata Yasunari, *The Snow Country*; d. Edith Wharton (b. 1862).		during around-the-world flight; German zeppelin *Hindenburg* catches fire and crashes at Lakehurst, NJ (May 6) killing 36.
1938	EH and Pauline sail for New York on *Gripsholm* (Jan. 12); back in Key West (Jan. 29); EH to Havana on *Pilar* (Jan. 29); he sails on *Ile de France* from New York to Spain (March 15) where new offensive has begun; back in New York (May 30), leaves for Key West; in New York for Joe Louis–Max Schmeling fight (June 22); EH and Pauline leave Key West for Nordquist Ranch (Aug. 4); EH and Martha Gellhorn in Paris (early September) together through most of October; EH, Martha, Herbert Matthews and Vincent Sheean leave for Spain (Nov. 3); EH arrives in New York (Nov. 24) to rejoin Pauline; Martha to Czechoslovakia on assignment for *Collier's*; EH and Pauline return to Key West (Dec. 5).	*To Have and Have Not* banned in Detroit (May 14); "The Old Man at the Bridge" published by *Ken* magazine (May 19); transcript of EH's narration of film, *The Spanish Earth*, published by The J.B. Savage Co. in Cleveland (June 15), EH's 12th book; his 13th book, *The Fifth Column and the First Forty-nine Stories*, published by Scribner's (Oct. 14); *Esquire* publishes "The Denunciation" (Nov. issue) and "The Butterfly and the Tank" (Dec. issue).	George Orwell, *Homage to Catalonia*; Richard Wright, *Uncle Tom's Children*; Graham Greene, *Brighton Rock*; Marjorie Kinnan Rawlings, *The Yearling*; Daphne du Maurier, *Rebecca*; d. James Weldon Johnson (b. 1899); d. Thomas Wolfe (b. 1900).	Pearl S. Buck (U.S.)	Germany annexes Austria (March 12); Munich Agreement (Sept. 29–30) allows Germany to take Czechoslovakia, British prime minister Neville Chamberlain says that the agreement brings "peace in our time"; Republican forces in Spain stop Fascist drive toward Barcelona but are defeated when they go on offensive, and next Fascist offensive takes Barcelona and virtually ends the war.
1939	EH takes *Pilar* to Havana (Feb. 14); Martha Gellhorn joins him there (April 10); she rents a farm, the Finca Vigía, near Havana, and EH	*Esquire* publishes "Night Before Battle" (Feb. issue); *New Masses* publishes "On the American Dead in Spain" (Feb.); EH begins writing *For*	James Joyce, *Finnegans Wake*; John Steinbeck, *The Grapes of Wrath*; Raymond Chandler, *The Big Sleep*; William Faulkner, *The*	Frans Emil Sillanpää (Finland)	Barcelona falls to Fascists (Jan.), France and Great Britain recognize Franco's government (Feb.), Madrid

	moves in with her; Pauline drops children at summer camp and leaves with friends for Europe (June 12); EH and Martha drive west, Martha to home in St. Louis, EH to Nordquist Ranch; he meets Hadley and Paul Mowrer near Cody, WY (Aug. 29), joined by three sons at ranch (Aug. 30); EH and Martha at Sun Valley Lodge in Idaho (Sept. 20–Dec.) as nonpaying guests; Martha leaves for *Collier's* assignment to report on war in Finland (Oct.); EH packs Key West belongings and moves to Havana (Dec.), sailing *Pilar* to Cuba (Dec. 24).	*Whom the Bell Tolls* (Feb. 14; *Cosmopolitan* publishes "Nobody Ever Dies" (March issue) and "Under the Ridge" (Oct. issue).	*Wild Palms*; T. S. Eliot, *Old Possum's Book of Practical Cats*; Katherine Anne Porter, *Pale Horse, Pale Rider*; C. S. Forester, *Captain Horatio Hornblower*; Thomas Wolfe, *The Web and the Rock*; d. Ford Madox Ford (b. 1873); d. Zane Grey (b. 1872); d. William Butler Yeats (b. 1865).		and Valencia surrender (March); Hitler occupies Czechoslovakia (March), signs Nazi-Soviet nonaggression pact (Aug. 23–24); Italy invades Albania (April); World War II begins (Sept. 1 with German invasion of Poland; France and Britain declare war (Sept. 3); Soviets invade Finland (Nov. 30); physicists Lise Meitner and Otto Frisch believe uranium can be split into atoms, calling it nuclear fission; floods on China's Yangtse River cause estimated 500,000 deaths.
1940	Martha returns to Havana (mid Jan.); EH's three sons arrive on vacation (March–April); Pauline files for divorce (May), EH to pay $500 a month alimony; EH and Martha leave Cuba for St. Louis and Sun Valley (Sept. 1); Martha accepts *Collier's* assignment to report on war in China (Oct.); Pauline's divorce from EH final (Nov. 4); EH and Martha buy the Finca Vigía for $12,500 (Dec. 28).	Three-act play, *The Fifth Column*, opens in New York (March 7), directed by Lee Strasberg, lasts for 87 performances; play published by Scribner's (June 3), EH's 14th book, *For Whom the Bell Tolls*, published by Scribner's (Oct. 21); Paramount Pictures offers $100,000 for movie rights to *FWBT* (Oct. 25).	Richard Wright, *Native Son*; William Faulkner, *The Hamlet*; Thomas Wolfe, *You Can't Go Home Again*; Arthur Koestler, *Darkness at Noon*; Carson McCullers, *The Heart Is a Lonely Hunter*; Somerset Maugham, *The Razor's Edge*; Graham Greene, *The Power and the Glory*; Walter Van Tilburg Clark, *The Oxbow Incident*; d. Edwin Markham (b. 1852); d. F. Scott Fitzgerald (b. 1896); d. Hamlin Garland (b. 1860); d. Nathanael West (b. 1903).	no winner	Pres. Roosevelt defeats Wendell Willkie for third term; Winston Churchill becomes prime minister of Great Britain (1940–1945); Soviet troops murder estimated 10,000 Polish soldiers at Katyn Forest; Germans take Denmark and Norway (April), invade France (May 13), Holland surrenders (May 14), Belgium (May 28); Germans in Paris (June 14), France surrenders (June 21); British evacuate Dunkirk (June 4), taking out 200,000 soldiers; "Battle of Britain" begins; *Bismarck* sunk by British navy; Italian and German forces take Greece (Oct. 1940–April 1941); Japanese troops take French Indochina (Sept. 22).
1941	EH and Martha sail from San Francisco to Hawaii (Jan. 31) on the *Matsonia*; leave for Hong Kong and Martha's China assignment (mid Feb.), Martha goes alone to the Burma Road; EH and Martha fly to	Limited Editions Club presents gold medal to EH for *For Whom the Bell Tolls* (Nov. 26), main speaker is Sinclair Lewis but EH does not attend.	James Hilton, *Random Harvest*; Thomas Wolfe, *The Hills Beyond*; Budd Schulberg, *What Makes Sammy Run?*; Edna Ferber, *Saratoga Trunk*; Daphne du Maurier, *Frenchman's Creek*;	no winner	German forces take Yugoslavia and Greece (April) and invade Soviet Union (June 22; stopped at Moscow outskirts (Dec.); Japanese bomb Pearl Harbor (Dec. 7),

Date	Personal	Writing and Publishing	Other Literary Events	Nobel Prize (Literature)	Historical Events
	Canton front and Chiang Kai-shek's army and the battlefronts (March 24); they fly back to U.S. separately; in Havana together (most of summer); leave for Sun Valley (Sept. 15) by train, guests of Union Pacific Railroad; return to Cuba (before Christmas).		Virginia Woolf, *Between the Acts*; d. James Joyce (b. 1882); d. Virginia Woolf (b. 1882); d. Isaak Babel (b. 1894); d. Rabindranath Tagore (b. 1861; d. Sherwood Anderson (b. 1876).		take Manila (Dec. 14), invade Malaya, take Hong Kong and several Pacific islands.
1942	EH in Cuba (most of year); American Ambassador and Cuban prime minister agree to EH's suggestion of counterintelligence scheme, EH suggesting that the *Pilar* be turned into a Q-boat to hunt German submarines (mid-May); Patrick and Gregory arrive at Finca and EH begins sub patrols (June 12); Martha reports for *Collier's* on German submarines' impact on Caribbean life (mid-July); Martha back in Havana (late Oct.); EH gives up sub patrol to others and is drinking heavily (Nov.–Dec.); Martha leaves for visit with mother in St. Louis (Dec. 30).	*Men at War*, an anthology subtitled "The Best War Stories of All Time," edited with "Introduction" by EH, is published by Crown Publishers (Oct. 22).	Albert Camus, *The Myth of Sisyphus*; Alfred Kazin, *On Native Grounds*; James Thurber, *My World and Welcome to It*; Mary McCarthy, *The Company She Keeps*; Nelson Algren, *Never Come Morning*.	no winner	Roosevelt and Churchill meet off Newfoundland (Aug. 9–12); Battle of Stalingrad, won by Soviet forces; Battle of the Coral Sea, stopping Japanese invasion of New Guinea; Battle of Midway, allies stopping Japanese invasion in decisive battle for the Pacific; Battle of El Alamein (Oct. 23–Nov. 4), British under Montgomery beating attacking German and Italian troops under Erwin Rommel; allied forces invade North Africa (Nov. 8–11); U.S. places more than 110,000 Japanese-Americans living in California in concentration camps; U.S. Col. James Doolittle leads bombing flights over Tokyo; U.S. "Manhattan Project" begins search for atom bomb.
1943	EH in Cuba (entire year); marriage with Martha deteriorates; EH resumes two-month submarine patrol on the *Pilar* (May 21); Patrick and Gregory arrive for summer (June 7); EH and sons return from sub patrol (July 18); Martha sails from New York to Lisbon to cover war in Europe (Oct. 25); EH jealous of Martha's war assignment, drinking heavily; Patrick and Gregory visit Havana (Christmas holidays).		William Saroyan, *The Human Comedy*; Antoine De St-Exupéry, *The Little Prince*; Ayn Rand, *The Fountainhead*; Betty Smith, *A Tree Grows in Brooklyn*; Jean-Paul Sartre, *Being and Nothingness*; Sholem Asch, *The Apostle*; Wallace Stegner, *The Big Rock Candy Mountain*; d. Beatrix Potter (b. 1866); d. Stephen Vincent Benét (b. 1898).	no winner	German sixth army surrenders at Stalingrad; allied bombing of Europe begins; Warsaw Ghetto uprising (April–May), 60,000 Jews choosing to fight rather than be imprisoned and most killed by Germans; allied troops take Tunis (May 7), 250,000 German soldiers surrender, ending the war in

North Africa; allies invade Sicily (July 23) and Italy (Sept. 3), forcing Italy to sign armistice (Sept. 7); Roosevelt, Churchill, and Stalin meet in Tehran (Nov. 28–Dec. 1) to set timing of allied invasion of Western Europe; U.S. troops win back Guadalcanal Island; J. Robert Oppenheimer's group of scientists begin to build atomic bomb at Los Alamos, NM.

Pres. Roosevelt wins fourth presidential term, defeating Thomas E. Dewey; allied troops move north through Italy, taking Rome (June 4); German rocket-powered V-1 attacks on Britain begin (June), V-2 attacks (Sept.); first jet-powered warplane, Germany's Messerschmidt, flies in combat; Normandy invasion begins (D-Day, June 6), allies take St.-Lô (July), arrive in Paris (late Aug.), move into Germany (Oct.); Battle of the Bulge (Dec. 1944–Jan. 1945); 20 German officers fail to assassinate Hitler (July 20); Bretton Woods, Potsdam, and Dumbarton Oaks conferences begin to set postwar strategies.

Johannes V. Jensen (Denmark)

Howard Fast, *Freedom Road*; d. Anne Frank (b. 1929); d. Antoine De St.-Exupéry (b. 1900); d. Romain Rolland (b. 1866).

Collier's publishes "Voyage to Victory" (July 22), a promotional booklet; reader's poll taken by *Saturday Review of Literature* selects EH as America's leading novelist; *Collier's* publishes "London Fights the Robots" (Aug. 19); *The Viking Portable Library: Hemingway*, edited by Malcolm Cowley, published by Viking Press (Sept. 18); *Collier's* publishes "Battle for Paris" (Sept. 30), "How We Came To Paris" (Oct. 7), "The GI and the General" (Nov. 4), and "War in the Siegfried Line" (Nov. 18).

1944   EH agrees to cover war for *Collier's* (March), upstaging Martha's assignment; she leaves New York by ship (May 13), he flies to London (May 17); he meets journalist Mary Welsh Monks (mid May); EH receives concussion in car accident (May 24); Martha arrives at London hospital (May 28), where he is surrounded by friends and champagne; he leaves hospital (May 29) but headaches persist for two months; EH boards correspondents' transport ship, *Dorothea L. Dix* to view D-Day landing on Normandy beaches (June 6); Martha sneaks onto hospital ship going to Omaha Beach and goes ashore (June 7); she's sent back to England by army officials but leaves soon after on illegal trip to Italian front; EH allowed to fly on RAF bombing mission (June 19–20); visits RAF headquarters at Thorney Island (June 28); flies twice on missions to intercept German rockets (June 29); EH attaches himself to Gen. George Patton's division (July 18–23); "transfers" to 4th Infantry Division (July 24); joins Col. Charles "Buck" Lanham's 22nd Regiment (July 28) and remains on assignment with the 22nd the rest of the year; in jeep accident (Aug. 5) gaining new con-

Date	Personal	Writing and Publishing	Other Literary Events	Nobel Prize (Literature)	Historical Events
	cussion and double vision; spends week (Aug. 18–24) at command post near Rambouillet, helping with interrogation of prisoners; EH enters Paris (Aug. 25), he and some friends "liberate" the Traveler's Club, the Café de la Paix, and the Ritz Hotel bar; Mary Welsh also stays at the Ritz; EH "liberates" (Aug. 26) the Negre de Toulouse, Lipp's Brasserie, and Sylvia Beach's bookshop; he leaves Paris (Sept. 1) to rejoin 22nd Regiment near the Belgium frontier; sees U.S. tanks enter Germany (Sept. 12); ordered to report to 3rd Army for Court of Inquiry (early Oct.) about his bearing arms and combat status at Rambouillet; receives clearance from court (Oct. 8); oldest son, Jack Hemingway, reported missing in action (Oct. 27), later as captured; EH rejoins 22nd Regiment for Hürtgenwald offensive (Nov. 15); Lanham's regiment reaches Luxembourg (Dec. 4); EH goes back to Paris sick with pneumonia (Dec. 7–8); tries to get back for German counteroffensive against 22nd Regiment (c. Dec. 17) but is still sick and misses most of the				
1945	EH in Paris (most of January), learns that oldest son, Jack, is German prisoner; leaves for New York (March 6); stops in London (March 7) to see Martha and start divorce proceedings; arrives in Cuba (mid March) with Patrick and Gregory; Mary arrives in Havana (May 2); Jack arrives (early June) after six months as German POW; EH wrecks car driving Mary to airport (June 20), he breaks four ribs and she has facial cuts; Mary flies to	EH writes preface for *Studio: Europe* by John Groth (Aug.); sells movie rights for "The Killers" to Universal Studio and for "The Short Happy Life of Francis Macomber" to Paramount (Nov.).	George Orwell, *Animal Farm*; Norman Mailer, *The Naked and the Dead*; John Steinbeck, *Cannery Row*; Jessamyn West, *The Friendly Persuasion*; Richard Wright, *Black Boy*; Sinclair Lewis, *Kingsblood Royal* and *Cass Timberlane*; James Thurber, *The Thurber Carnival*; d. Theodore Dreiser (b. 1871); d. Paul Valéry (b. 1871); d. Ellen Glasgow (b. 1874); d. Robert Benchley (b. 1889).	Gabriela Mistral (Chile)	Yalta Conference where Roosevelt, Churchill, and Stalin redraw postwar map of Europe; Pres. Roosevelt dies (April 12); first atom bomb exploded at Alamogordo, NM (July 16); Allies bomb Dresden and Berlin falls to Soviet forces (April 22–May 2); Hitler and Eva Braun commit suicide (April 30); Germany surrenders (May 7); Allies take Okinawa and the

Year	Hemingway's Life	Hemingway's Works	Nobel Prize	Literary Events	World Events
	Chicago (Aug. 31) to complete her own divorce; returns to Havana (October); EH's divorce from Martha final (Dec. 21).				Philippines, begin bombing Japan; U.S. drops atom bombs on Hiroshima (Aug. 6) and Nagasaki (Aug. 9), killing an estimated 150,000 citizens outright and another estimated 200,000 over time; Japan surrenders (Aug. 14); Ho Chi Minh becomes first president of Democratic Republic of Vietnam (1946–69).
1946	EH and Mary marry in Havana (March 14); she becomes pregnant, but complications create emergency in Casper, WY (Aug. 19), and, after the doctor gives her up for dead, EH inserts an IV tube and saves her life; EH and Mary stay in Casper until mid September; they and his three sons move into rented house in Ketchum, ID (Sept. 13); EH back in Havana (mid December).	EH begins writing *The Garden of Eden* (Jan.).	Hermann Hesse (Switzerland)	John Hersey, *Hiroshima*; Robert Penn Warren, *All the King's Men*; William Carlos Williams, *Paterson*; Erich Maria Remarque, *Arch of Triumph*; Carson McCullers, *The Member of the Wedding*; Eudora Welty, *Delta Wedding*; Sholem Asch, *East River*; Denise Levertov, *The Double Image*; d. H. G. Wells (b. 1866); d. Booth Tarkington (b. 1869); d. Countee Cullen (b. 1903); d. Damon Runyon (b. 1884); d. Gertrude Stein (b. 1874).	Nuremberg war-crimes trial (Nov. 1945–Oct. 1946); Indochina War begins, as Vietnamese fight French colonial forces (1946–1954); Winston Churchill delivers "Iron Curtain" speech at Westminster College, Fulton, MO (March 5); Juan Perón elected president of Argentina, becoming dictator (1946–55); Philippines become independent (July 4); Trygve Lie of Norway becomes first secretary-general of United Nations.
1947	Patrick arrives in Havana (January) to study for college entrance exams; becomes seriously ill (April 14), delirious and violent and doesn't fully recover until July; Pauline arrives (April 16) to help; EH awarded Bronze Star (June 13) for services in France during 1944; EH leaves for Idaho by way of northern Michigan (Aug.); Mary, Pauline, and Patrick stay at Finca Vigía.		André Gide (France)		Pres. Truman introduces "Loyalty Oath," allowing witch-hunting period of Sen. Joseph McCarthy; Marshall Plan developed, allowing aid to Europe; India partitioned into India and Pakistan, leading to riots that kill estimated 10–18 million people; U.S. aviator Charles Yeager breaks sound barrier in *Bell X-1*; baseball player Jackie Robinson breaks the color line by playing with Brooklyn Dodgers; Thor Heyerdahl sails across Pacific on balsawood raft, *Kon-Tiki*.

Date	Personal	Writing and Publishing	Other Literary Events	Nobel Prize (Literature)	Historical Events
1948	EH and Mary back in Havana (mid Feb.); leave for Italy aboard the *Jagiello* (Sept. 7); arrive in Genoa (c. Sept. 20), visit northern italy; EH takes Mary to Fossalta, where he was wounded in World War I; EH meets Adriana Ivancich (early December); EH and Mary rent the Villa Aprile (Dec. 15) in Cortina d'Ampezzo for the ski season.	EH begins writing *Islands in the Stream* (spring); refuses membership in American Academy of Arts and Letters (June); sells short story "My Old Man" to Twentieth Century Fox for $45,000 (late Dec.).	William Faulkner, *The Fable*; Alan Paton, *Cry, the Beloved Country*; Truman Capote, *Other Voices, Other Rooms*; Evelyn Waugh, *The Loved One*; Thornton Wilder, *The Ides of March*; B. F. Skinner, *Waldon Two*.	T. S. Eliot (England)	Mahatma" Gandhi assassinated in New Delhi (Jan. 30); Eleanor Roosevelt writes United Nations Declaration of Human Rights; first Arab-Israeli War begins (May 1948–Jan. 1949); Israeli independence proclaimed (May 14); Pres. Truman defeats Dewey for full term as U.S. president; Soviet forces blockade West Berlin (June 22), allies respond with Berlin Airlift (June 26, 1948–Sept. 30, 1949); U.S. diplomat Alger Hiss accused by Whittaker Chambers of being Communist spy; racist National Party comes to power in South Africa, establishing system of apartheid; Korea divided into Northern and Southern republics.
1949	EH and Mary remain in Cortina until mid March; Mary breaks ankle skiing (Jan. 20); EH has eye infection, diagnosed as erysipelas (March) and is hospitalized in Padua; EH and Mary leave Genoa for Havana (April 30); Gen. Buck Lanham arrives in Havana (June) before taking a new command in Europe; Jack Hemingway marries in Paris (June 25); EH and Mary sail for Europe on the *Ile de France* (Nov. 19); arrive Paris (end Nov.); leave with friend A. E. Hotchner for tour of southern France and Italy (Dec. 24).	Malcolm Cowley's essay "A Portrait of Mister Papa" published by *Life* magazine (Jan. 10); EH begins writing *Across the River and Into the Trees* (April); Lillian Ross interviews EH for her "Profile" column in *The New Yorker* (Nov. 17–18).	George Orwell, *1984*; Shirley Jackson, *The Lottery*; Nelson Algren, *The Man with the Golden Arm*; Elizabeth Bowen, *The Heat of the Day*; Eudora Welty, *The Golden Apples*; Tom Lea, *The Brave Bulls*; d. Margaret Mitchell (b. 1900); d. Sigrid Undset (b. 1882).	William Faulkner (U.S.)	Peking falls to Communist forces (Jan. 22) and then the rest of China; Kuomintang government moves to Formosa; Federal Republic of Germany (West Germany) becomes independent state (May), the German Democratic Republic (East Germany) becomes independent (Oct.).
1950	EH and Mary arrive in Cortina (early Feb.) for skiing holiday, Adriana Ivancich visits them there; EH and Mary leave Le Havre for New York on the *Ile de France* (March	*Cosmopolitan* serializes *Across the River and Into the Trees* (Feb., March, April, May, June issues); *ARIT* published by Scribner's (Sept. 7), EH's 15th book; he finishes *Islands in the Stream* (Dec.	Ray Bradbury, *The Martian Chronicles*; Nevil Shute, *A Town Like Alice*; Edna Ferber; *Giant*; Doris Lessing, *The Grass Was Singing*; Lionel Trilling, *The*	Bertrand Russell (England)	Korean War (1950–53) begins (June 25); Owen Lattimore falsely accused of being a Soviet spy by Sen. McCarthy, cleared by Senate

Year	Hemingway's Life	Career	Nobel Prize	Literature	History
	22); arrive in Havana (April 7) for rest of year; EH injures his head in boating accident (July 1), and headaches return, right leg swells and foot numbs when pieces of encysted metal from war wounds come loose during the boating accident; Adriana and her mother arrive at Finca (Oct. 28).	24); begins *The Old Man and the Sea* (early December).		*Liberal Imagination*; National Book Awards established; d. George Orwell (b. 1903); d. Albert Camus (b. 1913); d. Edna St. Vincent Millay (b. 1892); d. Edgar Lee Masters (b. 1868); d. Edgar Rice Burroughs (b. 1875).	committee; McCarthy's anti-Communist McCarran Internal Security Act passes U.S. Senate over Pres. Truman's veto.
1951	Ivancichs leave Cuba for New York (Feb. 6) and return to Italy; Grace Hemingway dies in Memphis (June 28); Pauline dies in Los Angeles (Oct. 1); EH, who has already refused to cooperate with biographers Charles Fenton and Carlos Baker, refuses Philip Young's request for permission to quote from the fiction (Dec. 9).	*Holiday* magazine publishes two fables, "The Good Lion" and "The Faithful Bull" (March issue); *True* magazine publishes "The Shot" (April issue).	Pär Lagerkvist (Sweden)	J. D. Salinger, *The Catcher in the Rye*; Marianne Moore, *Collected Poems*; James Jones, *From Here to Eternity*; Herman Wouk, *The Caine Mutiny*; William Faulkner, *Requiem for a Nun*; William Styron, *Lie Down in Darkness*; d. Sinclair Lewis (b. 1885); d. André Gide (b. 1869); d. Harold Ross (b. 1892).	Chinese forces take Seoul, Korea (Jan. 4); Gen. Douglas MacArthur dismissed by Pres. Truman for demanding that the U.S. bomb China's Manchurian bases; Winston Churchill re-elected prime minister (1951–53); U.S. passes 22nd Amendment, limiting presidents to two terms.
1952	EH and Mary leave (Jan. 10) for month of sailing around Cuba; Charles Scribner dies (Feb. 11); Batista seizes power in Cuba with a military coup (March); EH gives Philip Young permission to quote from fiction (March 6); Mary flies to New York (Sept. 25) for Scribner's celebration of success of *The Old Man and the Sea*, EH does not go; he plans another African safari (Oct.).	*Life* magazine publishes *The Old Man and the Sea* (Sept. 1 issue); Scribner's publishes *OMS* in book form (Sept. 8), EH's 16th book; *Hemingway: The Writer as Artist* by Carlos Baker published by Princeton University Press (Oct.).	François Mauriac (France)	Ralph Ellison, *The Invisible Man*; John Steinbeck, *East of Eden*; Bernard Malamud, *The Natural*; E. B. White, *Charlotte's Web*; Dylan Thomas, *Collected Poems*; Shelby Foote, *Shiloh*; Flannery O'Connor, *Wise Blood*; d. Knut Hamsun (b. 1859).	Dwight D. Eisenhower defeats Adlai Stevenson for U.S. presidency; European Coal and Steel Community established, the model for the European Economic Community (EEC); North Atlantic Treaty Organization (NATO), established; Jonas Salk discovers polio vaccine.
1953	EH receives Pulitzer Prize for *The Old Man and the Sea* (May 4); EH and Mary leave for Europe (June); arrive Pamplona (July 4) for Fiesta San Fermín; leave Marseilles (Aug. 6) for Africa safari (Sept. 1–Jan. 21, 1954).	EH agrees to write series of articles on his hunting safari in Africa (April 4); Scribner's publishes *The Hemingway Reader* (Sept.), edited by Charles Poore.	Sir Winston Churchill (England)	James Baldwin, *Go Tell It on the Mountain*; Ray Bradbury, *Fahrenheit 451*; Saul Bellow, *The Adventures of Augie March*; William Styron, *The Long March*; J. D. Salinger, *Nine Stories*; d. Dylan Thomas (b. 1914); d. Ivan Bunin (b. 1870); d. Marjorie Kinnan Rawlings (b. 1896).	Convicted Soviet spies, Ethel and Julius Rosenberg, executed; Korean War ends (June 27); Edmund Hillary and Tenzing Norgay are first to climb Mt. Everest (May 29).
1954	EH and Mary fly to Belgian Congo; on way to Murchison Falls (Jan. 23) plane hits telegraph wire and crashes, newspapers publish obituaries; party picked up by riverboat (Jan. 24) and taken to Butiaba on	*Look* magazine publishes "Safari" with EH on cover (Jan. 25); *Look* publishes "The Christmas Gift" (April 20); *Time* magazine publishes "An American Storyteller" (Dec. 13), with EH on cover.	Ernest Hemingway (U.S.)	J. R. R. Tolkien, *The Lord of the Rings*; William Golding, *Lord of the Flies*; Louise Bogan, *Collected Poems*; d. James Hilton (b. 1900); d. Colette (b. 1873).	North Vietnamese forces take French stronghold at Dien Bien Phu, ending the Indochina War; French troops withdraw from Vietnam and country divides into North

Date	Personal	Writing and Publishing	Other Literary Events	Nobel Prize (Literature)	Historical Events
	Lake Albert; plane flying them out to Entebbe (still Jan. 24) catches fire, and, to escape, EH breaks cockpit glass with his head, more newspaper obituaries; on fishing trip EH falls into a brush fire he is helping to put out (Feb. 2), sustaining second-degree burns; EH recuperates from his injuries in Venice (April); he and A. E. Hotchner leave Venice (May 6) for Spain, Hotchner driving; Mary joins them in Madrid (May 12); EH and Mary leave Genoa for Havana (June 6) aboard *Francesco Morosini*; back in Havana EH receives news that he has won Nobel Prize (Oct. 28); he writes acceptance speech (Nov. 30) to be delivered in Stockholm by U.S. ambassador to Sweden, John Cabot (Dec. 11).				and South Vietnam, civil war begins; Army-McCarthy hearings (April–May) expose Sen. McCarthy's witchhunt; U.S. Supreme Court case Brown v. Topeka Board of Education makes school segregation illegal.
1955	EH and Mary sail Cuban waters (in April), partly to avoid reporters and partly so EH can regain his health; return to Finca (May 4); receives Cuban Order of San Cristobal (Sept. 17); foot swells up again, along with a kidney infection (Sept. 19), and EH remains at Finca Vigía until second week of January.		Boris Pasternak, *Doctor Zhivago*; Vladimir Nabokov, *Lolita*; McKinley Kantor, *Andersonville*; James Donleavy, *The Ginger Man*; Flannery O'Connor, *A Good Man Is Hard to Find*; Sholem Asch, *The Prophet*; d. James Agee (b. 1909); d. Wallace Stevens (b. 1879).	Halldór Laxness (Iceland)	African-American Rosa Parks arrested in Montgomery, AL, for failing to give up her seat on public bus; 381-day Montgomery bus boycott begins; Nikita Khrushchev wins power struggle in Soviet Union; Warsaw Pact formed among Soviet-bloc countries to parallel NATO; Juan Perón deposed by military coup in Argentina.
1956	EH sends check for $1,000 to Ezra Pound (July), a mental patient at St. Elizabeth's Hospital in New York; EH and Mary sail (Sept. 1) for Europe on the *Ile de France*; arrive at Hotel Ritz in Paris (Sept. 7); leave for Spain (Sept. 17); back in Paris (Nov. 17) for rest of year at Ritz Hotel; EH signs a petition (Dec. 21) urging the release of Pound from St. Elizabeth's.	EH writes "A Room on the Garden Side" and "Get Yourself a Seeing-Eyed Dog" (June); writes text and photo cutlines for *Look* photo article on him at Finca Vigía, published as "A Visit With Hemingway: A Situation Report" (Sept. 4).	Nelson Algren, *A Walk on the Wild Side*; Mark Harris, *Bang the Drum Slowly*; James Baldwin, *Giovanni's Room*; Allen Ginsberg, *Howl and Other Poems*; d. H. L. Mencken (b. 1880); d. A. A. Milne (b. 1881); d. Max Beerbohm (b. 1872); d. Louis Bromfield (b. 1896).	Juan Ramón Jiménez (Puerto Rico)	Pres. Eisenhower wins second term over Adlai Stevenson; second Arab-Israeli War begins; Cuban revolution begins (Dec. 2), led by Fidel Castro.

1957	EH and Mary sail (late Jan.) for New York on the *Ile de France*; EH sends $1,500 (June) to the fund established to get Pound out of St. Elizabeth's Hospital; Mary's mother dies (Dec. 31).	EH writing Paris memoirs (Sept.); *Atlantic* publishes "Two Tales of Darkness" (Nov. issue) — "A Man of the World" and "Get a Seeing-Eyed Dog"; he continues writing *A Moveable Feast* and *The Garden of Eden* (Dec.).	James Agee, *A Death in the Family*; Jack Kerouac, *On the Road*; William Faulkner *The Town*; Ayn Rand, *Atlas Shrugged*; Alain Robbe-Grillet, *Jealousy*; James Gould Cozzens, *By Love Possessed*; d. Joyce Cary (b. 1899); d. Christopher Morley (b. 1890) ; d. Dorothy Sayers (b. 1893); d. Kenneth Roberts (b. 1885); d. Sholem Asch (b. 1887).	Albert Camus (France)	Martin Luther King Jr., and other civil-rights leaders establish Southern Christian Leadership Conference; Harold Macmillan succeeds Anthony Eden as British prime minister; *Sputnik 1* becomes first artificial satellite to orbit earth (Oct. 4).
1958	EH in Cuba until October, during which time Castro revolution begins; EH and Mary leave for Ketchum (early Oct.); A. E. Hotchner and Gary Cooper visit in Ketchum (Nov.).	*Paris Review* publishes George Plimpton's interview "The Art of Fiction XXI: Ernest Hemingway" (spring issue).	Chinua Achebe, *Things Fall Apart*; Truman Capote, *Breakfast at Tiffany's*; Brendan Behan, *Borstal Boy*; Leon Uris, *Exodus*; Shirley Ann Grau, *The Hard Blue Sky*; d. Rose Macaulay (b. 1889); d. Dorothy Canfield (b. 1879); d. James Branch Cabell (b. 1879).	Boris Pasternak (U.S.S.R.; forced to decline)	European Economic Community (EEC) established; Robert Welch establishes John Birch Society.
1959	EH and Mary buy house in Ketchum; return to Cuba (March 29); leave for New York (April 22); sail for Spain on the *Constitution* (April 26); EH spends the summer following the Spanish bullfight circuit; he celebrates 60th birthday (July 21) at La Consula, the Bill Davises' home near Málaga; EH and Mary leave for Paris; Mary flies to Cuba (Oct. 16); EH sails for New York on the *Liberté* (late October); EH and Mary are in their new Ketchum home (end Dec.).	The Hart Press publishes *Two Christmas Tales* (Dec.) — "A North of Italy Christmas" and "Christmas in Paris." EH begins writing *The Dangerous Summer*.	Allen Drury, *Advise and Consent*; Alan Sillitoe, *The Loneliness of the Long Distance Runner*; William Faulkner, *The Mansion*; Langston Hughes, *Selected Poems*; Robert Lowell, *Life Studies*; Philip Roth, *Goodbye, Columbus, and Five Short Stories*; E. B. White, *The Elements of Style*; d. Raymond Chandler (b. 1888).	Salvatore Quasimodo (Italy)	Charles de Gaulle becomes president of France; Castro's guerrilla forces take Havana (Jan. 8); North Vietnamese open Ho Chi Minh Trail military supply route through Laos and Cambodia to South Vietnam; Hawaii wins statehood; Xerox Corp. introduces first copier.
1960	EH suffering from hypertension and insomnia (Jan. 12); EH and Mary leave by train for Cuba (Jan. 16); Hotchner arrives at Finca Vigía to help cut *The Dangerous Summer* for *Life* magazine (June 21), EH in serious depression; he flies to Spain (Aug. 4) by way of Paris; at the Davises' in Málaga he has symptoms of nervous depression and his behavior is erratic; he writes Mary	*Life* serializes *The Dangerous Summer* (Sept. 5 and Sept. 19 issues), but Scribner's will not publish it in book form until 1985; first of nine unauthorized, "pirated," editions of EH's poems published, all without indication of publisher or date of publication.	Harper Lee, *To Kill a Mockingbird*; John Updike, *Rabbit, Run*; John Knowles, *A Separate Peace*; William Styron, *Set This House on Fire*; Flannery O'Connor, *The Violent Bear It Away*; John Barth, *The Sot-Weed Factor*; d. Boris Pasternak (b. 1890); d. Richard Wright (b. 1908); d. Nevil Shute (b. 1899); d. Zora Neale Hurston (b. 1901).	Saint-John Perse (France)	John F. Kennedy defeats Richard Nixon for U.S. presidency; U-2 spy plane pilot Francis Gary Powers shot down over Soviet Union (May 1).

Date	Personal	Writing and Publishing	Other Literary Events	Nobel Prize (Literature)	Historical Events
	(Sept. 3) that he is having a nervous breakdown; becomes paranoid with uncontrollable temper (Oct.); he flies to New York (Oct. 8) and takes train to Ketchum (Oct. 22); enters Mayo Clinic in Rochester, MN, under a false name (Nov. 30), treated for hypertension, enlarged liver, fluctuating blood pressure, paranoia, and depression; electroshock therapy is administered (Dec. and Jan.) for depression.				
1961	EH invited (Jan. 12) to read at inauguration of John F. Kennedy, but declines because of illnesses; leaves Mayo Clinic (Jan. 22) and returns to Ketchum; attempts suicide with gun, but Mary stops him (April 21); tries again with shotgun (April 23), but the gun is taken away before he can pull trigger; EH is flown to Mayo Clinic (April 25) for more electroshock treatment; discharged from clinic (June 26) and arrives by car in Ketchum (June 30); EH kills himself with shotgun (7:30 a.m., July 2).	Scribner's publishes *The Snows of Kilimanjaro and Other Stories* (Jan.).	Muriel Spark, *The Prime of Miss Jean Brodie*; Joseph Heller, *Catch-22*; J. D. Salinger, *Franny and Zooey*; John Steinbeck, *The Winter of Our Discontent*; Günter Grass, *Cat and Mouse*; d. Dashiell Hammett (b. 1894); d. James Thurber (b. 1894); d. Hilda Doolittle (H.D.) (b. 1886); d. Louis-Ferdinand Céline (b. 1894).	Ivo Andrić (Yugoslavia)	U.S. military involvement in Vietnam begins; East Germans build Berlin Wall overnight (Aug. 12); CIA-organized Bay of Pigs invasion of Cuba fails; African-American James Meredith wins right to enter Univ. of Mississippi; Soviet cosmonaut Yuri Gagarin becomes first human in outer space (April 12); Alan Shepard pilots U.S. Mercury spacecraft *Freedom 7* (May 5); U.S. Peace Corps established; Amnesty International established in London; Kuwait becomes independent nation (June 19); South Korean gen. Park Chunghee takes power in military coup.
1962		*The Mark Twain Journal* publishes EH's Nobel Prize Speech, from 1954 award (Summer issue); *The Wild Years*, an anthology of 73 newspaper articles written by EH for *The Toronto Star* newspapers, edited by Gene Z. Hanrahan, published by Dell Publishing Co. (Dec.).			

1964

Passages from *A Moveable Feast* published by *Life* magazine (April 10); Scribner's publishes *A Moveable Feast* (May 5), EH's 17th book.

1967

Scribner's publishes *By-Line: Ernest Hemingway* (March), an anthology of 76 newspaper articles, edited by William White; *Ernest Hemingway: A Comprehensive Bibliography*, compiled by Audre Hanneman, is published by Princeton University Press.

1969

Scribner's publishes *The Fifth Column and Four Stories of the Spanish Civil War* (Aug. 13).

1970

Ernest Hemingway: Cub Reporter, anthology of articles written for *The Kansas City Star*, edited by Matthew J. Bruccoli, published by University of Pittsburgh Press (May 4); Scribner's publishes *Islands in the Stream* (Oct. 6), EH's 18th book; *Esquire* publishes the "Bimini" section (Oct. issue) from *Islands*.

1971

Ernest Hemingway's Apprenticeship, an anthology of writings from EH's years at Oak Park and River Forest High School, edited by Matthew J. Bruccoli, is published by Microcard Editions (July 2); "African Journal," a selection from *The Garden of Eden*, is serialized by *Sports Illustrated* (Dec. 20, Jan. 3, and Jan. 10 issues).

1972

Scribner's publishes *The Nick Adams Stories* (April 17), edited by Philip Young.

Date	Personal	Writing and Publishing	Other Literary Events	Nobel Prize (Literature)	Historical Events
1974		Scribner's publishes *The Enduring Hemingway*, an anthology, edited by Charles Scribner, Jr.			
1975		*Supplement to Ernest Hemingway: A Comprehensive Bibliography*, compiled by Audre Hanneman, published by Princeton University Press.			
1979		*Ernest Hemingway: Complete Poems*, edited by Nicholas Gerogiannis, published by University of Nebraska Press.			
1981		Scribner's publishes *Ernest Hemingway: Selected Letters, 1917–1961*, selected and edited by Carlos Baker.			
1984		Scribner's publishes *Ernest Hemingway on Writing*, selected and edited by Larry W. Phillips.			
1985		Scribner's publishes *The Dangerous Summer* in book form, EH's 19th book. Scribner's publishes *Ernest Hemingway: Dateline Toronto*, an anthology of 172 articles written for *Toronto Star* newspapers, edited by William White.			
1986		Scribner's publishes *The Garden of Eden* (May), EH's 20th book.			

1987   Scribner's publishes *The Complete Short Stories of Ernest Hemingway* (Dec. 2), the Finca Vigía edition.

1993   *Hemingway at Oak Park High: The High School Writings of Ernest Hemingway, 1916–1917* published by Oak Park and River Forest High School, edited by Cynthia Maziarka and Donald Vogel, Jr.

1999   Scribner's scheduled to publish EH novel *True at First Light*, edited by Patrick Hemingway and commemorating the 100th anniversary of EH's birth (July).

APPENDIX IV

Film, Stage, Television, and Radio Adaptations of Hemingway's Works
(and Works about Hemingway)

Note that for each entry below there is a more complete discussion in the text of *Hemingway A to Z,* including, for most productions, members of the cast.

Battler, The   Film, produced in 1962.

Battler, The   Television play, produced in 1955.

Breaking Point, The   Film, produced in 1950.

"Capital of the World"   Ballet, performed in 1953.

"Ernest Hemingway's 'Young Man'"   Film script, written in 1955 and produced in 1962 as *Ernest Hemingway's Adventures of a Young Man.*

Ernest Hemingway: Grace Under Pressure   Documentary film, produced in 1986.

Farewell to Arms, A   Film 1, produced in 1932.

Farewell to Arms, A   Film 2, produced in 1958.

Farewell to Arms, A   Radio production 1, produced in 1938.

Farewell to Arms, A   Radio production 2, produced about 1942.

Farewell to Arms, A   Radio production 3, produced in 1948.

Farewell to Arms, A   Radio production 4, produced in 1949.

Farewell to Arms, A   Radio production 5, produced in 1950.

Farewell to Arms, A   Stage play, produced in 1930.

Farewell to Arms, A   Television play, produced in 1955.

Fifth Column, The   Stage play, performed in 1940.

Fifth Column, The   Stage play, performed in 1990.

Fifth Column, The   Television play, performed in 1959.

Fifty Grand   Television play, produced in 1952.

Fifty Grand   Television play, produced in 1958.

For Whom the Bell Tolls   Film, produced in 1943.

For Whom the Bell Tolls   Radio production 1, produced in 1945.

For Whom the Bell Tolls   Radio production 2, produced in 1949.

For Whom the Bell Tolls   Television play, produced in 1959.

Gambler, the Nun and the Radio, The   Television play, produced in 1959.

Gun Runners, The   Film, produced in 1958.

Hedda Hopper's Hollywood No. 3   Documentary film, produced about 1958.

Hemingway in the Autumn   Documentary film, produced in 1996.

Hemingway   Television documentary, produced in 1987.

Hemingway   Television film, produced about 1994.

Hemingway's Adventures of a Young Man   Film, produced in 1962.

Hills Like White Elephants   Television production, January 1998.

In Love and War   Film, produced in 1997.

Islands in the Stream   Film, produced in 1977.

Killers, The   Film 1, produced in 1946.

Killers, The   Film 2, produced in 1964.

Killers, The   Television play, produced in 1959.

Lost Generation, The   Stage play, produced in 1987.

Macomber Affair, The   Film, produced in 1947.

Mama Jini's Lion   Stage play, produced in 1988.

My Old Man   Television play, produced in 1979.

Old Man and the Sea, The   Film 1, produced in 1958.

Old Man and the Sea, The   Film 2, produced in 1990.

Papa   Stage play, produced in 1987.

Short Happy Life of Francis Macomber   Radio play, produced in 1948.

Short Happy Life, A   Stage play, produced in 1961.

Snows of Kilimanjaro, The   Film, produced in 1952.

Snows of Kilimanjaro, The   Television play, produced in 1959.

Soldier's Home   Television play, produced in 1977.

Spanish Earth, The   Documentary film, produced in 1937.

Sun Also Rises, The   Film, produced in 1957.

Sun Also Rises, The   Television play, produced in 1984.

To Have and Have Not   Film, produced in 1944.

To Have and Have Not   Radio play, produced in 1946.

To Have and Have Not   Television play, produced in 1957.

Ubiitsi (The Killers)   Soviet film, produced in 1958.

Under My Skin   Film, produced in 1950.

World of Nick Adams, The   Television play, produced in 1957.

Wrestling Ernest Hemingway   Film, produced in 1993.

APPENDIX V
Bibliography

1. Comprehensive list of Hemingway's work

Novels
Torrents of Spring, The (Scribner's, 1926)
Sun Also Rises, The (Scribner's, 1926)
Farewell to Arms, A (Scribner's, 1929)
To Have and Have Not (Scribner's, 1937)
For Whom the Bell Tolls (Scribner's, 1940)
Across the River and Into the Trees (Scribner's, 1950)
Old Man and the Sea, The (Scribner's, 1952)
Islands in the Stream (Scribner's, 1970)
Garden of Eden, The (Scribner's, 1986)
True at First Light (Scheduled by Scribner's for 1999)

Nonfiction books
Death in the Afternoon (Scribner's, 1932)
Green Hills of Africa (Scribner's, 1935)
Moveable Feast, A (Scribner's, 1964)
Dangerous Summer, The (Scribner's, 1985)

Collections of short stories
Three Stories & Ten Poems (Contact Publishing Co., 1923)
in our time (Three Mountains Press, 1924)
In Our Time (Boni & Liveright, 1925)
Men Without Women (Scribner's, 1927)
Winner Take Nothing (Scribner's, 1933)
Fifth Column and the First Forty-nine Stories, The (Scribner's, 1938)
Fifth Column and Four Stories of the Spanish Civil War, The (Scribner's, 1969)
Complete Short Stories of Ernest Hemingway, The Finca Vigía Edition (Scribner's/Macmillan, 1987)

Short stories
The first entry in parentheses is the source and date of first publication; following the semicolon are the anthologies in which the story is reprinted.
Abbreviations used:

3STP	*Three Stories & Ten Poems* (1923)
iot	*in our time* (1924)
IOT	*In Our Time* (1925)
MWW	*Men Without Women* (1927)

WTN	*Winner Take Nothing* (1933)
SS	*The Fifth Column and the First Forty-nine Stories* (1938) and *The Short Stories of Ernest Hemingway* (1954)
5thC&4	*The Fifth Column and Four Unpublished Stories of the Spanish Civil War* (1969)
NA	*Ernest Hemingway: The Nick Adams Stories* (1972)
CS	*The Complete Short Stories of Ernest Hemingway* (1987)
HR	*The Hemingway Review* (Spring 1990)
Tab	*Tabula* (1916–17) [Oak Park and River Forest High School Literary Magazine]; stories reprinted in *Ernest Hemingway's Apprenticeship: Oak Park, 1916–1917* (1971) and in *Hemingway at Oak Park High* (1993)

"After the Storm" (*Cosmopolitan*, May 1932; WTN, SS, CS)

"African Betrayal, An" (*Sports Illustrated*, May 5, 1986; CS as "An African Story")

"Alpine Idyll, An" (*American Caravan*, September 1927; MWW, SS, NA, CS)

"Ash Heel's Tendon—A Story, The" [fragment] (Griffin, *Along With Youth: Hemingway, The Early Years*, 1985)

"Banal Story" (*The Little Review*, Spring/Summer 1926; MWW, SS, CS)

"Battler, The" (IOT; SS, NA, CS)

"Big Two-Hearted River" (*This Quarter*, Spring 1925; IOT, SS, NA, CS)

"Black Ass at the Cross Roads" [fragment] (CS)

"Butterfly and the Tank, The" (*Esquire*, December 1938; 5thC&4, CS)

"Canary for One, A" (*Scribner's Magazine*, April 1927; MWW, SS, CS)

"Capital of the World, The" (*Esquire*, June 1936 as "The Horns of the Bull"; SS, CS)

"Cat in the Rain" (IOT; NA, CS)

"Chapter 1" [vignette: "Everybody was drunk"] (*The Little Review*, Spring 1923; iot as "chapter 1," IOT, SS, CS)

"Chapter 2" [vignette: "Minarets stuck up in the rain"] (*The Little Review*, Spring 1923; iot as "chapter 3"; IOT, SS, CS as "Chapter II")

"Chapter 3" [vignette: "We Were in a Garden at Mons"] (*The Little Review,* Spring 1923; iot as "chapter 4"; IOT, SS, CS as "Chapter III")

"Chapter 4" [vignette: "It was a frightfully hot day"] (*The Little Review,* Spring 1923; iot as "chapter 5"; IOT, SS, CS as "Chapter IV")

"Chapter 5" [vignette: "They shot the six cabinet ministers"] (*The Little Review,* Spring 1923; iot as "chapter 6"; IOT, SS, CS as "Chapter V")

"Chapter 6" [vignette: "Nick sat against the wall"] (iot as "chapter 7"; IOT, SS, CS as "Chapter VI")

"Chapter 7" [vignette: "While the bombardment"] (iot as "chapter 8"; IOT, SS, CS as "Chapter VII")

"Chapter 8" [vignette: "At two o'clock in the morning"] (iot as "chapter 9"; IOT, SS, CS as "Chapter VIII")

"Chapter 9" [vignette: "The first matador got the horn"] (*The Little Review,* Spring 1923; iot as "chapter 2"; IOT, SS, CS as "Chapter IX")

"Chapter 10" [vignette: "They whack-whacked the white horse"] (iot as "chapter 12"; IOT, SS, CS as "Chapter X")

"Chapter 11" [vignette: "The crowd shouted all the time"] (iot as "chapter 13"; IOT, SS, CS as "Chapter XI")

"Chapter 12" [vignette: "If it happened right down close in front of you"] (iot as "chapter 14"; IOT, SS, CS as "Chapter XII")

"Chapter 13" [vignette: "I heard the drums coming down the street"] (iot as "chapter 15"; IOT, SS, CS as "Chapter XIII")

"Chapter 14" [vignette: "Maera lay still, his head on his arms"] (iot as "chapter 16"; IOT, SS, CS as "Chapter XIV")

"Chapter 15" [vignette: "They hanged Sam Cardinella"] (iot as "chapter 17"; IOT, SS, CS as "Chapter XV")

"Che Ti Dice La Patria?" (*New Republic,* May 18, 1927, as "Italy—1927"; MWW, SS, CS)

"Christmas in Paris" [article published later as a short story] (*Toronto Star Weekly,* December 22, 1923; *Two Christmas Tales,* 1959)

"Clean, Well-Lighted Place, A" (*Scribner's Magazine,* March 1933; WTN, SS, CS)

"Cross-Country Snow" (*transatlantic review,* January 1925; IOT, SS, NA, CS)

"Crossing the Mississippi" [fragment: "The Kansas City train"] (NA)

"Crossroads—An Anthology" [unfinished sketches] (Griffin's *Along With Youth: Hemingway, The Early Years,* 1985)

"Current—A Story, The" [fragment] (Griffin's *Along With Youth: Hemingway, The Early Years,* 1985)

"Day's Wait, A" (WTN; SS, CS)

"Denunciation, The" (*Esquire,* November 1938; 5thC&4, CS)

"Divine Gesture, A" [allegory] (*Double Dealer,* May 1922; *A Divine Gesture,* 1974)

"Doctor and the Doctor's Wife, The" (*transatlantic review,* December 1924; IOT, SS, NA, CS)

"End of Something, The" (IOT; SS, NA, CS)

"Faithful Bull, The" [a fable] (*Holiday,* March 1951; CS)

"Fathers and Sons" (WTN; SS, NA, CS)

"Fifty Grand" (*Atlantic,* July 1927; MWW, SS, CS)

"Gambler, the Nun, and the Radio, The" (*Scribner's Magazine,* April 1933 as "Give Us a Prescription, Doctor"; WTN, SS, CS as "The Gambler . . .")

"Get a Seeing-Eyed Dog" (*Atlantic,* November 1957; CS)

"God Rest You Merry, Gentlemen" (*God Rest You Merry, Gentlemen,* 1933; WTN, SS, CS)

"Good Lion, The" [a fable] (*Holiday,* March 1951; CS)

"Great News from the Mainland" [fragment] (CS)

"Hills Like White Elephants" (*transition,* August 1927; MWW, SS, CS)

"Homage to Switzerland" (*Scribner's Magazine,* April 1933; WTN, SS, CS)

"I Guess Everything Reminds You of Something" [fragment] (CS)

"In Another Country" (*Scribner's Magazine,* April 1927; SS, NA, CS)

"Indian Camp" (*transatlantic review,* April 1924; SS, NA, CS)

"Indians Moved Away, The" [fragment] (NA)

"Judgment of Manitou, The" [juvenilia] (Tab)

"Killers, The" (*Scribner's Magazine,* March 1927; MWW, SS, NA, CS)

"L'Envoi" [vignette: "The King was working in the garden"] (iot as "chapter 18"; IOT as "L'Envoi")

"Lack of Passion, A" [fragment] (HR)

"Landscape with Figures" [fragment] (CS)

"Last Good Country, The" [fragment of unfinished novel] (NA)

"Light of the World, The" (WTN; SS, NA, CS)

"Man of the World, A" (*Atlantic,* November 1957; CS)

"Matter of Color, A" [juvenilia] (Tab)

"Mercenaries—A Story, The" [fragment] (Griffin, *Along With Youth: Hemingway, The Early Years,* 1985)

"Mother of a Queen, The" (WTN; SS, CS)

"Mr. and Mrs. Elliot" (*The Little Review,* Autumn/Winter 1924; SS, CS)

"My Old Man" (3STP; IOT, SS, CS)

"Natural History of the Dead, A" (part of chapter 12 of *Death in the Afternoon;* revised for WTN, SS, CS)

"Night Before Battle" [fragment of unfinished novel] (*Esquire,* February 1939; 5thC&4, CS)

"Nobody Ever Dies" (*Cosmopolitan,* March 1939; CS)

"North of Italy Christmas, A" [article published later as a short story] (*Toronto Star Weekly,* December 22, 1923; *Two Christmas Tales,* 1959)

"Now I Lay Me" (MWW; SS, NA, CS)

"Old Man at the Bridge" (*Ken,* May 19, 1938; SS, CS)

"One Reader Writes" (WTN; SS, CS)

"One Trip Across" (*Cosmopolitan*, April 1934; part 1 of *To Have and Have Not*, CS)

"On the Quai at Smyrna" [vignette] (IOT; SS, CS)

"On Writing" [fragment] (NA)

"Out of Season" (3STP; IOT, SS, CS)

"Paris, 1922" [sketches] (Baker, *Ernest Hemingway: A Life Story*, 1969)

"[Philip Haines Was a Writer . . .]" [fragment] (HR)

"Porter, The" [fragment of unfinished novel] (CS)

"Portrait of the Idealist in Love—A Story" [fragment] (Griffin, *Along With Youth: Hemingway, The Early Years*, 1985)

"Pursuit Race, A" (MWW; SS, CS)

"Revolutionist, The" [vignette: "In 1919 he was traveling on the railroads in Italy"] ("chapter 11" of iot; IOT, SS, CS as "The Revolutionist")

"Sea Change, The" (*This Quarter*, December 1931; WTN, SS, CS)

"Sepi Jingan" [juvenilia] (Tab)

"Short Happy Life of Francis Macomber, The" (*Cosmopolitan*, September 1936; SS, CS)

"Simple Enquiry, A" (MWW; SS, CS)

"Snows of Kilimanjaro, The" (*Esquire*, August 1936; SS, CS)

"Soldier's Home" (*Contact Collection of Contemporary Writers*, 1925; IOT, SS, CS)

"Strange Country, The" [fragment of unfinished novel] (CS)

"Summer People" [fragment] (NA)

"Ten Indians" (MWW; SS, NA, CS)

"Three-Day Blow, The" (IOT; SS, NA, CS)

"Three Shots" [fragment] (NA)

"Today is Friday" [one-scene play] (*Today is Friday*, 1926; MWW, SS, CS)

"Tradesman's Return, The" (*Esquire*, February 1936; part 2 of *To Have and Have Not*, CS)

"Train Trip, A" [fragment of unfinished novel] (CS)

"Undefeated, The" (*Der Querschnitt*, Summer 1925; MWW, SS, CS)

"Under the Ridge" (*Cosmopolitan*, October 1939; 5thC&4, CS)

"Up in Michigan" (3STP; SS, CS)

"Very Short Story, A" [vignette: "One hot evening in Milan"] ("chapter 10" of iot; "One hot evening in Padua" in IOT, SS, CS)

"Way You'll Never Be, A" (WTN; SS, NA, CS)

"Wedding Day, A" [fragment] (NA)

"Wine of Wyoming" (*Scribner's Magazine*, August 1930; SS, CS)

Plays

Fifth Column, The (*The Fifth Column and the First Forty-nine Stories*, 1938; *The Fifth Column*, Scribner's, June 3, 1940; *The Fifth Column and Four Stories of the Spanish Civil War*, 1969)

Collections of articles

Hanrahan, Gene Z., ed. *Hemingway: The Wild Years*. Dell, 1962.

White, William, ed. *By-Line: Ernest Hemingway*. Scribner's, 1967.

Bruccoli, Matthew J., ed. *Ernest Hemingway: Cub Reporter*. Univ. of Pittsburgh Press, 1970.

White, William, ed. *Ernest Hemingway: Dateline Toronto*. Scribner's, 1985.

Maziarka, Cynthia and Donald Vogel, Jr., eds. *Hemingway at Oak Park High*. Oak Park and River Forest High School, 1993.

Burrill, William, ed. *Hemingway: The Toronto Years*. Doubleday Canada, 1994.

Articles

The first entry in parentheses is the source and date of first publication; following the semicolon are the most accessible books in which the item is reprinted. Some articles have not been reprinted.

Abbreviations used:

TDS	*The Toronto Daily Star*
TSW	*The Toronto Star Weekly*
KC	*The Kansas City Star*
Wild	*Hemingway: The Wild Years* (1962)
By-Line	*By-Line: Ernest Hemingway* (1967)
Cub	*Ernest Hemingway, Cub Reporter* (1970)
Dateline	*Ernest Hemingway: Dateline Toronto* (1985)
OP	*Hemingway at Oak Park High* (1993)
TY	*Hemingway: The Toronto Years* (1994)
HR	*The Hemingway Review*

"A.D. in Africa: A Tanganyika Letter" (*Esquire*, April 1934; By-Line)

"a.d. Southern Style: A Key West Letter" (*Esquire*, May 1935)

"Absolute Lie, Says Dr. Banting, of Serum Report, An" (TDS, Oct. 11, 1923; TY)

"Across from the Post Office" (TY)

"Active French Anti-Alcohol League" (TDS, April 8, 1922; Dateline)

"Afghans: Trouble for Britain" (TDS, Oct. 31, 1922; Wild, Dateline)

"African Journal" (*Sports Illustrated*, Dec. 20, 1971, Jan. 3 and 10, 1972)

"Air Line' Contribution" (*Trapeze*, Nov. 10, 1916; OP)

"Air Line' Contributions" (*Trapeze*, Nov. 24, 1916; OP)

"American Bohemians in Paris" (TSW, March 25, 1922; Wild, By-Line)

"And Out of "America" (*transatlantic review*, August 1924)

"Arrival of Lloyd George, The" (TDS, Oct. 5, 1923; Dateline)

"Art of the Short Story, The" (Benson, *New Critical Approaches to the Short Stories of Ernest Hemingway*)

"At the End of the Ambulance Run" (KC, Jan. 20, 1918; Cub)

"At the Theater with Lloyd George" (TSW, Oct. 6, 1923; Dateline)

"Athletic Association to Organize Next Week" (*Trapeze*, Nov. 3, 1916; OP)

"Athletic Notes" 1 (*Trapeze*, Nov. 24, 1916; OP)

"Athletic Notes" 2 (*Trapeze*, Dec. 22, 1916; OP)

"Athletic Notes" 3 (*Trapeze*, Feb. 2, 1917; OP)

"Athletic Notes" 4 (*Trapeze*, Feb. 9, 1917; OP)

"Balkans: A Picture of Peace, Not War" (TDS, Oct. 16, 1922; Dateline)

"Ballot Bullets" (TSW, May 28, 1921; Wild, Dateline)

"Bank Vaults vs. Cracksmen" (TSW, Dec. 1, 1923; Wild, Dateline)

"Barthou Crosses Hissing Tchitcherin" (TDS, April 24, 1922; Wild, Dateline)

"Barthou Refuses Conference" (TDS, April 18, 1922; Dateline)

"Basketball Seasons Opens; Poor Lightweight Prospects" (*Trapeze*, Dec. 8, 1916; OP)

"Battle for Paris" (*Collier's*, Sept. 30, 1944; By-Line)

"Battle of Raid Squads" (KC, Jan. 6, 1918; Cub)

"Battle' of Offenburg, The" (TDS, April 25, 1923; Wild, Dateline)

"Before You Go on a Canoe Trip, Learn Canoeing" (TDS, June 3, 1922; TY)

"Belgian Lady and the German Hater, The" (TDS, April 28, 1923; Wild, Dateline)

"Best Rainbow Trout Fishing, The" (TSW, Aug. 28, 1920; Wild, By-Line)

"Betting in Toronto" (TSW, Dec. 29, 1923; Wild, Dateline)

"Big Dance on the Hill, The" (TSW, Nov. 24, 1923; Dateline)

"Big Day for Navy Drive" (KC, April 17, 1918; Cub)

"Big Hanna Club Meeting Hears Rousing Talk" (*Trapeze*, March 23, 1916; OP)

"Black Novel a Storm Center" (TSW, March 25, 1922: Dateline)

"Blind Man's Christmas Eve, The" (TSW, Dec. 22, 1923; Dateline)

"British Can Save Constantinople" (TDS, Sept. 30, 1922; Wild, Dateline)

"British Order Kemal to Quit Chanak" (TDS, Sept. 30, 1922; Dateline)

"British Planes" (TDS, Sept. 30, 1922; Dateline)

"Bull Fighting a Tragedy" (TSW, Oct. 20, 1923; Wild, By-Line)

"Bullfighting, Sport and Industry" (*Fortune*, March 1930)

"Buying Commission Would Cut Out Waste" (TSW, April 26, 1920; Dateline)

"Call for Greatness" (*Ken*, July 14, 1938)

"Camping Out" (TSW, June 26, 1920; Wild, Dateline)

"Canada's Recognition of Russia" (TDS, April 10, 1922; Dateline)

"Canadians: Wild/Tame" (TSW, Oct. 9, 1920; Dateline)

"Car Prestige" (TSW, May 1, 1920; Dateline)

"Cardinal Picks a Winner, The" (*Ken*, May 5, 1938)

"Carpentier vs. Dempsey" (TSW, Oct. 30, 1920; Dateline)

"Cars Slaying Toronto's Splendid Oak Trees" (TSW, fall 1923; TY)

"Changed Beliefs" (TSW, Nov. 24, 1923; Dateline)

"Chicago Never Wetter Than Today" (TSW, July 2, 1921; Wild, Dateline)

"China's Air Needs" (*PM*, June 17, 1941; By-Line)

"Chinese Build Air Field" (*PM*, June 18, 1941; By-Line)

"Christians Leave Thrace to Turks" (TDS, Oct. 16, 1922; Dateline)

"Christmas Gift, The" (*Look*, April 20/May 4, 1954; By-Line)

"Christmas on the Roof of the World" (TSW, Dec. 22, 1923; By-Line)

"Circulating Pictures" (TSW, Feb. 14, 1920; Wild, By-Line, Dateline)

"Circus, The" (*Ringling Bros. and Barnum & Bailey Circus Magazine & Program* 1953)

"Clark's Fork Valley, Wyoming, The" (*Vogue*, February 1939; By-Line)

"Class Prophecy" (*Tabula*, 1917; OP)

"Clemenceau Politically Dead" (TDS, Feb. 18, 1922; Dateline)

"Concert a Success" (*Trapeze*, Jan. 20, 1916; OP)

"Condensing the Classics" (TSW, Aug. 20, 1921; Dateline)

"Conrad, Optimist and Moralist" (*transatlantic review*, October 1924; By-Line)

"Constantinople, Dirty White, Not Glistening and Sinister" (TDS, Oct. 18, 1922; Dateline)

"Convicts Set Fire to Stable at 'Pen' and Made Escape" (TDS, Sept. 11, 1923; TY)

"Count Apponyi and the Loan" (TDS, Oct. 15, 1923; Dateline)

"Dare Devil Joins Tanks" (KC, April 21, 1918; Cub)

"Defense of Dirty Words: A Cuban Letter" (*Esquire*, September 1934)

"Did Poincaré Laugh in Verdun Cemetery?" (TDS, Aug. 12, 1922; Dateline)

"Dying, Well or Badly" (*Ken*, April 21, 1938)

"Escaped Kingston Convicts Still at Large" (TDS, Sept. 11, 1923; TY)

"European Nightlife: A Disease" (TSW, Dec. 15, 1923; Wild, Dateline)

"False News to the President" (*Ken*, Sept. 8, 1938)

"Farm, The" (*Cahiers d'Art,* 1934)

"Fascism Is a Lie" (*New Masses,* June 22, 1937)

"Fascisti Party Half-Million" (TDS, June 24, 1922; Wild, Dateline)

"Fashion Graveyards" (TSW, April 24, 1920; Wild, Dateline)

"Fifth Generation of Family Lives On Old Canadian Manor" (TDS, Oct. 21, 1923; TY)

"Fishing in Baden Perfect" (TDS, Sept. 2, 1922; Wild, Dateline)

"Fishing the Rhone Canal" (TDS, June 10, 1922; Wild, By-Line)

"Fox Farming" (TSW, May 29, 1920; Dateline)

"Franco-German Situation, The" (TDS, April 14, 1923; Wild, Dateline)

"Free Shave, A" (TSW, March 6, 1920; Wild, By-Line, Dateline)

"Freiburg Fedora, The" (TSW, Jan. 19, 1923; Dateline)

"French Royalist Party" (TDS, April 18, 1923; Wild, Dateline)

"French Speed With Movies on the Job" (TDS, May 16, 1923; Dateline)

"Fresh Air on an Inside Story" (*Ken,* Sept. 22, 1938; By-Line)

"Friend of Spain, The" (*Esquire,* January 1934; By-Line)

"G.I. and the General, The" (*Collier's,* Nov. 4, 1944; By-Line)

"Galloping Dominoes" (TSW, May 22, 1920; Dateline)

"Game-Shooting in Europe" (TSW, Nov. 3, 1923; Wild, Dateline)

"Gargoyles as Symbol" (TSW, Nov. 17, 1923; Dateline)

"Genio after Josie: A Havana Letter" (*Esquire,* October 1934)

"Genoa Conference" (TDS, April 13, 1922; Wild, By-Line)

"Genoa Scrubs Up for Peace Parley" (TDS, April 15, 1922; TY)

"German Blow—Disloyal?" (TDS, April 18, 1922; Dateline)

"German Delegation at Genoa" (TDS, April 28, 1922; Dateline)

"German Export Tax Hits Profiteers" (TSW, Feb. 25, 1922; Dateline)

"German Inflation" (TDS, Sept. 19, 1922; Wild, By-Line)

"German Inn-Keepers" (TDS, Sept. 5, 1922; Wild, By-Line)

"German Journalists a Strange Collection" (TDS, May 8, 1922; Dateline)

"German Machiavellianism" (TDS, April 18, 1922; Dateline)

"German Riots" (TSW, Sept. 30, 1922; Wild, Dateline)

"Germans Desperate Over the Mark" (TDS, Sept. 1, 1922; Wild, Dateline)

"Getting into Germany" (TDS, May 2, 1923; Wild, By-Line)

"Goiter and Iodine" (TSW, Dec. 15, 1923; Dateline)

"Good Generals Hug the Line" (*Ken,* Aug. 25, 1938)

"Government Pays for News" (TDS, April 21, 1923; Wild, Dateline)

"Great 'Apéritif' Scandal, The" (TSW, Aug. 12, 1922; Wild, Dateline)

"Great Blue River, The" (*Holiday,* July 1949; By-Line)

"Greatest Boy Actor Is a Toronto Lad" (Toronto *Mail and Empire,* n.d.; TY)

"Greek Revolt, The" (TDS, Nov. 3, 1922; Wild, Dateline)

"Guards Were Hoaxed by Call for Help" (TDS, Sept. 13, 1923; TY)

"H. M.'s Loyal State Department" (*Ken,* June 16, 1938)

"Hamid Bey" (TDS, Oct. 9, 1922; Wild, By-Line)

"Hamilton Gag, The" (TSW, June 12, 1920; Dateline)

"Hanna Club Tomorrow Night" (*Trapeze,* Jan. 27, 1916; OP)

"Harington Won't Demand Evacuation" (TDS, Oct. 2, 1922; Dateline)

"Hate in the Ruhr is Real" (TDS, May 12, 1923; Wild, Dateline)

"He Who Gets Slap Happy: A Bimini Letter" (*Esquire,* August 1935)

"Hearst Not Paying Lloyd George" (TSW, Oct. 6, 1923; Dateline)

"Heat and the Cold, The" (*Verve,* Spring 1938)

"Hemingway on the Town" (London *Daily Express,* Sept. 11, 1956)

"High Lights and Low Lights" (*Trapeze,* May 25, 1917; OP)

"Homage to Ezra" (*This Quarter,* Spring 1925)

"Homes on the Seine" (TDS, Aug. 26, 1922; Dateline)

"Hot Bath an Adventure in Genoa, A" (TDS, May 2, 1922; Dateline)

"Hotels in Switzerland, The" (TSW, March 4, 1922; Wild, By-Line)

"How We Came to Paris" (*Collier's,* Oct. 7, 1944; By-Line)

"Hubby Dines First, Wifie Gets Crumbs" (TDS, Sept. 30, 1922; Wild, Dateline)

"Humanity Will Not Forgive This" (*Pravda,* Aug. 1, 1938; TDS, Nov. 27, 1982, HR, Spring 1988)

"I Like Americans" (TSW, Dec. 15, 1923; Dateline)

"I Like Canadians" (TSW, Dec. 15, 1923; Dateline)

"Indoor Fishing" (TSW, Nov. 20, 1920; Wild, Dateline)

"Inflation and the German Mark" (Dateline, Dec. 8, 1923; Wild, By-Line)

"Interclass Meet Saturday" (*Trapeze,* Feb. 2, 1917; OP)

"Interpreters Make or Mar Speeches at Genoa Parley" (TDS, April 15, 1922; TY)

"It's Easy to Spend a Million Marks" (TDS, May 5, 1923; Wild, Dateline)

"Italian Premier" (TDS, April 10, 1922; Dateline)

"Italy's Blackshirts" (TSW, June 24, 1922; Wild, Dateline)

"Italy—1927" (*New Republic,* May 18, 1927; later became short story, "Che Ti Dice La Patria?")

"Japan Must Conquer China" (*PM,* June 13, 1941; By-Line)

"Japan's Position in China" (*PM,* June 16, 1941; By-Line)

"Japanese Earthquake" (TDS, Sept. 25, 1923; *Journalism Quarterly,* Autumn 1966, By-Line)

"Junior Debates" (*Trapeze,* May 4, 1916; OP)

"Kemal's One Submarine" (TDS, Nov. 10, 1922; Dateline)

"Kerensky, the Fighting Flea" (KC, Dec. 16, 1917; Cub)

"King Business in Europe" (TSW, Sept. 15, 1923; Wild, By-Line)

"Lakes Aren't Going Dry, The" (TSW, Nov. 17, 1923; Dateline)

"Laundry Car Over Cliff" (KC, March 6, 1918; Cub)

"Lieutenants' Mustaches" (TSW, April 10, 1920; Dateline)

"Little Welshman Lands, The" (TDS, Oct. 6, 1923; Dateline)

"Living on $1,000 a Year in Paris" (TDS, Feb. 4, 1922; Dateline)

"Lloyd George the Great Survivor" (TY)

"Lloyd George Willing to Address 10,000" (TDS, Oct. 5, 1923; Dateline)

"Lloyd George's Magic" (TDS, May 13, 1922; Dateline)

"Lloyd George's Wonderful Voice" (TDS, Oct. 6, 1923; Dateline)

"London Fights the Robots" (*Collier's,* Aug. 19, 1944; By-Line)

"Lord and Lady Cranworth" (TY)

"Lord Birkenhead" (TDS, Oct. 4, 1923; Dateline)

"M. Deibler, A Much-Feared Man" (TDS, April 1, 1922; Dateline)

"Malady of Power, The: A Second Serious Letter" (*Esquire,* November 1935; By-Line)

"Man of the People, A" (TDS, Oct. 8, 1923; Dateline)

"Man, What a Sport" (*Rotarian,* May 1940)

"Marks Not Caused by Ill-Treatment" (Toronto *Mail and Empire,* Jan. 8, 1924; TY)

"Marlin off the Morro: A Cuban Letter" (*Esquire,* Autumn 1933; By-Line)

"Matter of Wind, A" (*Sports Illustrated,* Aug. 17, 1959)

"Mayor Tommy Church" (TY)

"McConkey's 1914 Orgy" (TSW, Dec. 29, 1923; Dateline)

"Mecca of Fakers, The" (TDS, March 25, 1922; Dateline)

"Midwayites Downed by Oak Park Team" (*Trapeze,* Nov. 24, 1916; OP)

"Million Dollar Fright: A New York Letter" (*Esquire,* December 1935)

"Miss Megan George a Hit" (TDS, Oct. 6, 1923; Dateline)

"Mix War, Art And Dancing" (KC, April 21, 1918; Cub)

"Monologue to the Maestro: A High Seas Letter" (*Esquire,* October 1935; By-Line)

"Moscow Theatre Company Will Not Come to Toronto" (*Toronto Globe,* Nov. 27, 1923; TY)

"Mr. Quayle Rouses Hanna Club" (*Trapeze,* Feb. 17, 1916; OP)

"Muscle Shoals: Cheap Nitrates" (TSW, Nov. 12, 1921; Dateline)

"Mussolini: Biggest Bluff in Europe" (TDS, Jan. 27, 1923; Wild, By-Line)

"My Own Life" (*New Yorker,* Feb. 12, 1927)

"My Pal the Gorilla Gargantua" (*Ken,* July 28, 1938)

"NANA Dispatch No. 1: Passport for Franklin" (March 12, 1937; HR)

"NANA Dispatch No. 2: Italian and German Intervention" (March 15, 1937; HR)

"NANA Dispatch No. 3: Journey to the War" (March 17, 1937; By-Line, HR)

"NANA Dispatch No. 4: Loyalist Victory at Guadalajara" (March 22, 1937; HR)

"NANA Dispatch No. 5: Analysis of the Battle of Brihuega" (March 26, 1937; HR)

"NANA Dispatch No. 6: First Combat Experience" (April 9, 1937; HR)

"NANA Dispatch No. 7: Battle in the Casa de Campo" (April 11, 1937; By-Line, HR)

"NANA Dispatch No. 8: A Wounded American Volunteer" (c. April 18, 1937; By-Line, HR)

"NANA Dispatch No. 9: Bombardment of Madrid" (April 20, 1937; HR)

"NANA Dispatch No. 10: Survey of Madrid's Defenses" (April 30, 1937; HR)

"NANA Dispatch No. 11: Strategic Situation in Spain Today" (May 9, 1937; HR)

"NANA Dispatch No. 12: The Chauffeurs of Madrid" (c. May 9, 1937; By-Line, HR)

"NANA Dispatch No. 13: Battles of Quinto and Belchite" (Sept. 13, 1937; HR)

"NANA Dispatch No. 14: Inspection of Aragon Front Near Teruel" (Sept. 23, 1937; HR)

"NANA Dispatch No. 15: Madrid Front is Quiet" (Sept. 30, 1937; By-Line, HR)

"NANA Dispatch No. 16: Central Front Around Brunete" (Oct. 6, 1937; HR)

"NANA Dispatch No. 17: Attack on Teruel" (Dec. 19, 1937; HR)

"NANA Dispatch No. 18: Fall of Teruel" (Dec. 21, 1937; By-Line, HR)

"NANA Dispatch No. 19: Flight of Refugees" (April 3, 1918; By-Line, HR)

"NANA Dispatch No. 20: American Volunteers Retreat from Gandesa" (April 4, 1918; HR)

"NANA Dispatch No. 21: Defense of Tortosa" (April 5, 1918; HR)

"NANA Dispatch No. 22: Survey of the Catalan Front" (April 10, 1928; HR)

"NANA Dispatch No. 23: Quiet Day Along the Ebro" (April 13, 1918; HR)

"NANA Dispatch No. 24: Bombing of Tortosa" (April 15, 1918; By-Line, HR)

"NANA Dispatch No. 25: Awaiting Combat in the Ebro Delta" (April 18, 1918; By-Line, HR)

"NANA Dispatch No. 26: James Lardner, Loyalist Volunteer" (April 25, 1918; HR)

"NANA Dispatch No. 27: Loyalist Defenses on Lérida Front" (April 29, 1918; HR)

"NANA Dispatch No. 28: Front and Rear in Spanish Civil War" (c. May 1, 1918: HR)

"NANA Dispatch No. 29: Visit to Castellón Defenses" (May 8, 1918; HR)

"NANA Dispatch No. 30: Madrid Fighting Its Own War" (May 10, 1918; HR)

"Navy Desk Jobs to Go" (KC, April 18, 1918; Cub)

"Near East Censor Too 'Thorough'" (TDS, Oct. 25, 1922; Dateline)

"New Betting Game: Tennis Tamburello" (TDS, May 9, 1922; Dateline)

"New Ether to Credit of Toronto Surgeon" (TDS, Jan. 27, 1920; TY)

"New Trier Tankers Win From Locals" (*Trapeze*, March 2, 1917; OP)

"Newspapermen's Pockets" (TSW, Nov. 6, 1920; Dateline)

"Next Outbreak of Peace, The" (*Ken,* Jan. 12, 1939)

"95,000 Wear the Legion of Honor" (TDS, April 1, 1922; Dateline)

"No Room in Canada for European Reds, Preacher Maintains" (TDS, fall 1923; TY)

"Nobel Prize Speech, The" (*Mark Twain Journal,* Summer 1962)

"'Nobleman' Yeats" (TSW, Nov. 24, 1923; Dateline)

"Notes on Dangerous Game: The Third Tanganyika Letter" (*Esquire,* July 1934; By-Line)

"Notes on Life and Letters: Or a manuscript found in a bottle" (*Esquire,* January 1935)

"Notes on the Next War: A Serious Topical Letter" (*Esquire,* September 1935; By-Line)

"O.P. Places Second in Suburban Classic" (*Trapeze,* March 16, 1917; OP)

"Oak Park Athletes Win Beloit Meet" (*Trapeze,* May 11, 1917; OP)

"Oak Park Second in Northwestern U" (*Trapeze,* April 20, 1917; OP)

"Oak Park Team Wins From Maine High" (*Trapeze,* March 9, 1917; OP)

"Oak Park Victors Over Waite High" (*Trapeze,* Nov. 17, 1916; OP)

"Objections to Allied Plan" (TDS, April 13, 1922; Dateline)

"Offer Sir Donald Soviet Railroads" (TDS, Sept. 10, 1923; TY)

"Old Constan'" (TDS, Oct. 28, 1922; Wild, By-Line)

"Old Newsman Writes: A Letter from Cuba" (*Esquire,* December 1934; By-Line)

"Old Order Changeth in Alsace-Lorraine" (TDS, Aug. 26, 1922; Dateline)

"On Being Shot Again: A Gulf Stream Letter" (*Esquire,* June 1935; By-Line)

"On the American Dead in Spain" (*New Masses,* Feb. 14, 1939)

"On the Blue Water: A Gulf Stream Letter" (*Esquire,* April 1936; By-Line)

"On the Golf Course with Lloyd George" (TY)

"On Weddynge Gyftes" (TSW, Dec. 17, 1921; Wild, Dateline)

"Our 'Ring Lardner' Jr. Breaks Into Print With All-Cook County Eleven" (*Trapeze,* Dec. 8, 1916; OP)

"Our Confidential Vacation Guide" (TSW, May 21, 1921; Wild, Dateline)

"Our Modern Amateur Impostors" (TSW, Dec. 29, 1923; Wild, Dateline)

"Out in the Stream: A Cuban Letter" (*Esquire,* August 1934; By-Line)

"Pamplona in July" (TSW, Oct. 27, 1923; Wild, By-Line)

"Pamplona Letter" (*transatlantic review,* October 1924)

"Papal Poll: Behind the Scenes" (TSW, March 4, 1922; Dateline)

"Paris is Full of Russians" (TDS, Feb. 25, 1922; Dateline)

"Paris Letter, A" (*Esquire,* February 1934; By-Line)

"Paris-to-Strasbourg Flight, A" (TDS, Sept. 9, 1922; Wild, By-Line)

"Parisian Boorishness" (TSW, April 15, 1922; Wild, Dateline)

"Personal" (*Trapeze,* Jan. 22, 1917; OP)

"Photo Portraits" (TSW, May 29, 1920; Dateline)

"Plain and Fancy Killings, $400 Up" (TSW, Dec. 11, 1920; Wild, By-Line)

"Poincaré's Election Promises" (TDS, March 11, 1922; Dateline)

"Poincaré's Folly" (TDS, Feb. 4, 1922; Dateline)

"Popular in Peace—Slacker in War" (TSW, March 13, 1920; Wild, Dateline)

"Practical Education vs. Theoretical" (*Trapeze,* Feb. 10, 1916; OP)

"President Vanquishes, The: A Bimini Letter" (*Esquire,* July 1935)

"Prizefight Women" (TSW, May 15, 1920; Dateline)

"Problems of Boyhood Discussed at Hanna Club" (*Trapeze,* March 9, 1916; OP)

"Program for U.S. Realism, A" (*Ken,* August 11, 1938; By-Line)

"[Program Notes]" (*Esquire,* February 1935)

"Provincial Police Are Taking Up Chase" (TDS, Sept. 12, 1923; TY)

"Recruits for the Tanks" (KC, April 18, 1918; Cub)

"Red Flag in Toronto" (TSW, Feb. 14, 1920; TY)

"Refugees from Thrace" (TDS, Nov. 14, 1922; Wild, By-Line)

"Remembering Shooting-Flying: A Key West Letter" (*Esquire*, February 1935; By-Line)

"Review of Anderson's *A Story-Teller's Story*" (*Ex Libris*, March 1925; *Fitzgerald/Hemingway Annual, 1969*)

"Review of Two Christmas Plays" (*Vararlberger Landes-Zeitung*, Jan. 13, 1926; *Fitzgerald/Hemingway Annual 1971*)

"'Ring Lardner Junior' Writes About Swimming Meet. Oak Park Rivals Riverside" (*Trapeze*, Feb. 2, 1917; OP)

"Ring Lardner Returns" (*Trapeze*, May 4, 1917; OP)

"'Ring Lardner' on the Bloomington Game, A" (*Trapeze*, Nov. 24, 1916; OP)

"Ring Lardner, Jr. Discourses on Editorials" (*Trapeze*, Feb. 16, 1917; OP)

"Rubber Supplies in Dutch East Indies" (*PM*, June 11, 1941; By-Line)

"Rug Vendors in Paris" (TDS, Aug. 12, 1922; Dateline)

"Rum-Running" (TSW, June 5, 1920; Wild, Dateline)

"Russia Spoiling the French Game" (TDS, Oct. 23, 1922; Wild, Dateline)

"Russian Claims" (TDS, April 14, 1922; Dateline)

"Russian Girls at Genoa" (TDS, April 24, 1922; Wild, By-Line)

"Russian Toy Soldier, A" (TDS, Feb. 10, 1923; Wild, By-Line)

"Russians Hold Up Progress" (TDS, April 17, 1922; Dateline)

"Russo-Japanese Pact" (*PM*, June 10, 1941; By-Line)

"Safari" (*Look*, Jan. 26, 1954)

"Sailfish Off Mombasa: A Key West Letter" (*Esquire*, March 1935)

"Schober Every Inch a Chancellor" (TDS, April 26, 1922; Dateline)

"Search for Sudbury Coal" (TDS, Sept. 25, 1923; Dateline)

"She Sacrifices Herself That Children May Live" (TDS, c. Christmas 1923; TY)

"Shootism Versus Sport: The Second Tanganyika Letter" (*Esquire*, June 1934; By-Line)

"Shot, The" (*True*, April 1951; By-Line)

"Sights of Whitehead Street, The: A Key West Letter" (*Esquire*, April 1935; By-Line)

"Silent, Ghastly Procession, A" (TDS, Oct. 20, 1922; Wild, By-Line)

"Sinclair Lewis's Horsebacking" (TSW, Aug. 5, 1922; Dateline)

"Situation Report, A" (*Look*, Sept. 4, 1956; By-Line)

"Six Men Become Tankers" (KC, April 17, 1918; Cub)

"Sling and the Pebble, The" (*Free World*, March 1946)

"So This is Chicago" (TSW, Jan. 19, 1923; Dateline)

"Some Space Filled by Ernest MacNamara Hemingway" (*Trapeze*, May 11, 1917; OP)

"Sparrow Hat on Paris Boulevards" (TSW, March 18, 1922; Wild, Dateline)

"Sport of Kings, The" (TSW, Nov. 24, 1923; Dateline)

"Sporting Mayor" (TSW, March 13, 1920; Wild, Dateline)

"Stambouliski of Bulgaria" (TDS, April 25, 1922; Dateline)

"Starvers Out of Sight" (TDS, May 9, 1923; Wild, Dateline)

"Stop Hellstrom" (*Trapeze*, Nov. 3, 1916; OP)

"Store Thieves' Tricks" (TSW, April 3, 1920; Wild, Dateline)

"Superman Myth, The" (TDS, June 25, 1921; TY)

"Support the Swimming Team" (*Trapeze*, Feb. 9, 1917; OP)

"Swiss Avalanches" (TSW, Jan. 12, 1924; Wild, Dateline)

"Swiss Luge, The" (TSW, March 18, 1922; Wild, By-Line)

"Talking with the Tiger" (TY)

"Tancredo is Dead" (TSW, Nov. 24, 1923; Dateline)

"Tchitcherin Speaks at Genoa Conference" (TDS, April 10, 1922; Wild, Dateline)

"Tchitcherin Wants Japan Excluded" (TDS, April 11, 1922; Dateline)

"Ted's Skeeters" (TSW, Aug. 7, 1920; Wild, Dateline)

"There She Breaches! or Moby Dick off the Morro" (*Esquire*, May 1936; By-Line)

"Throng at Smallpox Case" (KC, Feb. 18, 1918; Cub)

"Time Now, The Place Spain, The" (*Ken*, April 7, 1938)

"Tip the Postman Every Time?" (TSW, March 11, 1922; Wild, Dateline)

"Tooth Pulling No Cure-All" (TSW, April 10, 1920; Dateline)

"Tourists Scarce at Swiss Resorts" (TDS, Feb. 4, 1922; Wild, Dateline)

"Track Team Loses to Culver" (*Trapeze*, March 30, 1917; OP)

"Trading Celebrities" (TSW, Feb. 19, 1921; Dateline)

"Treachery in Aragon" (*Ken*, June 30, 1938)

"Tribute to Mamma from Papa Hemingway, A" (*Life*, Aug. 18, 1952)

"Trout Fishing" (TSW, April 10, 1920; Dateline)

"Trout Fishing in Europe" (TSW, Nov. 17, 1923; Wild, By-Line)

"Trout-Fishing Hints" (TSW, April 24, 1920; Wild, Dateline)

"Truth-telling Ether a Secret" (TDS, Feb. 7, 1920; TY)

"Try Bobsledding If You Want Thrills" (TDS, March 4, 1922; Dateline)

"Tuna Fishing in Spain" (TSW, Feb. 18, 1922; Wild, By-Line)

"Turk Red Crescent Propaganda Agency" (TDS, Oct. 4, 1922; Dateline)

"Turks Distrust Kemal Pasha" (TDS, Oct. 24, 1922; Wild, Dateline)

"Turks Near Constantinople" (TDS, Oct. 9, 1922; Dateline)

"Two Revolutions Are Likely If Germany Suffers Collapse" (TDS, March 7, 1923; TY)

"U.S. Aid to China" (*PM,* June 15, 1941; By-Line)

"United We Fall Upon *Ken*" (*Ken,* June 2, 1938)

"Unworldly Russians, The" (TDS, April 27, 1922; Dateline)

"Veteran Visits the Old Front, A" (TDS, July 22, 1922; Dateline)

"Visit With Hemingway, A: A Situation Report" (*Look,* Sept. 4, 1956)

"Voyage to Victory" (*Collier's,* July 22, 1944; By-Line)

"W.B. Yeats a Night Hawk" (TSW, Dec. 22, 1923; Dateline)

"Waiting for an Orgy" (TDS, Oct. 19, 1922; Dateline)

"War in the Siegfried Line" (*Collier's,* Nov. 18, 1944; By-Line)

"War Medals for Sale" (TSW, Dec. 8, 1923; Wild, By-Line)

"Well-Guarded Russian Delegation" (TDS, May 4, 1922; Dateline)

"What Professional Boxers Fight For" (TY)

"Who Is He?" (TDS, Sept. 11, 1923; TY)

"Who Murdered the Vets" (*New Masses,* Sept. 17, 1935)

"Who's Who in Beau Brummel?" (*Trapeze,* Feb. 23, 1917; OP)

"Wild Gastronomic Adventures of a Gourmet" (TSW, Nov. 24, 1923; Dateline)

"Wild Night Music of Paris" (TSW, March 25, 1922; Wild, Dateline)

"Wild West: Chicago" (TSW, Nov. 6, 1920; Dateline)

"Will You Let These Kiddies Miss Santa Claus?" (*Co-operative Commonwealth,* December 1920; *Fitzgerald/Hemingway Annual 1970*)

"Win Two—Lose One" (*Trapeze,* May 4, 1917; OP)

"Wings Always Over Africa: An Ornithological Letter" (*Esquire,* January 1936; By-Line)

"Wives Buy Clothes for French Husbands" (TSW, March 11, 1922; Wild, Dateline)

"Wolfe's Diaries" (TSW, Nov. 24, 1923; Dateline)

"Woman Takes Crumbs" (TDS, April 15, 1922; Dateline)

"Would 'Treat 'Em Rough,'" (KC, April 18, 1918; Cub)

"Writer as a Writer, The" (*Directions,* May-June 1939)

"Young Communists" (TSW, Dec. 22, 1923; Dateline)

Collections of poems

Hemingway, Ernest. *Three Stories & Ten Poems* (Contact Publishing Co., 1923). [Abbreviated 3STP below]

Gerogiannis, Nicholas, ed. *Ernest Hemingway: 88 Poems* (Harcourt Brace Jovanovich, Inc., 1979). [Abbreviated *88 Poems* below]

———, ed. *Ernest Hemingway: Complete Poems* (Univ. of Nebraska Press, 1992). [Abbreviated *Complete Poems* below]

Poems

The first entry in parentheses is the source and date of first publication; following the semicolon are the two accessible collections listed above in which the poem is reprinted. Several of these poems were published in pirated editions, not mentioned below; for information about these editions see *The Collected Poems of Ernest Hemingway* in the *Hemingway A to Z* text.

"Across the Board" (*88 Poems;* Complete *Poems*)

"Advice to a Son" (*Omnibus: Almanach auf das Jahr 1932; 88 Poems, Complete Poems*)

"Age Demanded, The" (*Der Querschnitt* February 1925; *88 Poems, Complete Poems*)

"[All armies are the same . . .]" (*88 Poems, Complete Poems*)

"Along With Youth" (3STP; *88 Poems, Complete Poems*)

"[And everything the author knows . . .]" (*88 Poems, Complete Poems*)

"[Arsiero, Asiago . . .]" (*88 Poems, Complete Poems*)

"[At night I lay with you . . .]" (*88 Poems, Complete Poems*)

"Athletic Verse: The Tackle, The Punt, The Safety Man" (*Tabula,* March 1917; *88 Poems, Complete Poems*)

"Battle of Copenhagen, The" (*88 Poems, Complete Poems*)

"Big Dance on the Hill, The" (TSW, Nov. 24, 1923; *88 Poems, Complete Poems*)

"Bird of Night" (*88 Poems, Complete Poems*)

"Black-Ass Poem After Talking to Pamela Churchill" (*88 Poems, Complete Poems*)

"[Blank Verse]" (*Trapeze; 88 Poems, Complete Poems*)

"['Blood is thicker than water . . .']" (Baker, *Ernest Hemingway: A Life Story* 1969; *88 Poems, Complete Poems*)

"Captives" (3STP; *88 Poems, Complete Poems*)

"Champs d'Honneur" (*Poetry,* January 1923; 3STP, *88 Poems, Complete Poems*)

"Chapter Heading" (*Poetry,* January 1923; 3STP, *88 Poems, Complete Poems*)

"Country Poem with Little Country" (*88 Poems, Complete Poems*)

"Critical Intelligence" (*Complete Poems* 1992)

"D'Annunzio" (*88 Poems, Complete Poems*)

"Day, The" (Griffin, *Along With Youth: Hemingway, The Early Years,* 1985)

"Dedicated to F.W." (*Trapeze,* Nov. 24, 1916; *88 Poems, Complete Poems*)

"Defense of Luxembourg" (*88 Poems, Complete Poems*)

"Earnest Liberal's Lament, The" (*Der Querschnitt* Autumn 1924; *88 Poems, Complete Poems*)

"First Poem to Mary in London" (*Atlantic,* August 1965; *88 Poems, Complete Poems*)

"Flat Roofs" (*88 Poems, Complete Poems*)

"[FOR THE HARLOT HAS A HARDLOT . . .]" (*88 Poems, Complete Poems*)

"[God is away for the summer . . .]" (*88 Poems, Complete Poems*)

"[Grass smooth on the prairies . . .]" (*88 Poems, Complete Poems*)

"How Ballad Writing Affects Our Seniors" (*Tabula,* November 1916; *88 Poems, Complete Poems*)

"I Like Americans" (TSW, Dec. 15, 1923; *88 Poems, Complete Poems*)

"I Like Canadians" (TSW, Dec. 15, 1923; *88 Poems, Complete Poems*)

"[I think that I have never trod . . .]" (*New York Times Magazine*, Oct. 16, 1977; *88 Poems, Complete Poems*)

"[I'm off'n wild wimmen . . .]" (*88 Poems, Complete Poems*)

"[If my Valentine you won't be . . .]" (Mary Hemingway, *How It Was*, 1976; *88 Poems, Complete Poems*)

"[In a magazine . . .]" (*88 Poems, Complete Poems*)

"Inexpressible, The" (*Tabula*, March 1917; *88 Poems, Complete Poems*)

"Killed Piave—July 8—1918" (*88 Poems, Complete Poems*)

"Kipling" (*88 Poems, Complete Poems*)

"Lady Poets With Foot Notes, The" (*Der Querschnitt*, November 1924; *88 Poems, Complete Poems*)

"Lines to a Girl 5 Days After Her 21st Birthday" (*88 Poems, Complete Poems*)

"Lines to a Young Lady on Her Having Very Nearly Won a Vögel" (*88 Poems, Complete Poems*)

"Lines to Be Read at the Casting of Scott Fitzgerald's Balls into the Sea from Eden Roc (Antibes, Alpes Maritimes)" (*88 Poems, Complete Poems*)

"[Little drops of grain alcohol . . .]" (*88 Poems, Complete Poems*)

"[Little Mr. Wilson . . .]" (*New York Times Magazine*, Oct. 16, 1977)

"Mitrailliatrice" (*Poetry*, January 1923; *3STP, 88 Poems, Complete Poems*)

"Modern Version of Polonius' Advice, A" (*88 Poems, Complete Poems*)

"Montparnasse" (*3STP, 88 Poems, Complete Poems*)

"Neothomist Poem" (*Exile*, Spring 1927; *88 Poems, Complete Poems*)

"[Night comes with soft and drowsy plumes . . .]" (*88 Poems, Complete Poems*)

"Oily Weather" (*Poetry* January 1923; *3STP, 88 Poems, Complete Poems*)

"Oklahoma" (*3STP, 88 Poems, Complete Poems*)

"[On Weddynge Gyftes]" (TSW, Dec. 17, 1921; *88 Poems, Complete Poems*)

"Opening Game, The" (*88 Poems, Complete Poems*)

"Part Two of The Soul of Spain with McAlmon and Bird the Publishers" (*Der Querschnitt*, Autumn 1924; *88 Poems, Complete Poems*)

"Poem is By Maera, The" (*88 Poems, Complete Poems*)

"Poem to Miss Mary" (*88 Poems, Complete Poems*)

"Poem to Mary (Second Poem)" (*Atlantic*, August 1965; *88 Poems, Complete Poems*)

"Poem" (*88 Poems, Complete Poems*)

"Poem, 1928" (*88 Poems, Complete Poems*)

"Poetry" (Mary Hemingway, *How It Was*, 1976; *88 Poems, Complete Poems*)

"Portrait of a Lady" (*88 Poems, Complete Poems*)

"[rail ends do not meet, The . . .]" (*88 Poems, Complete Poems*)

"Riparto d'Assalto" (*Poetry*, January 1923; *3STP, 88 Poems, Complete Poems*)

"Road to Avallon, The" (*88 Poems, Complete Poems*)

"Robert Graves" (*88 Poems, Complete Poems*)

"Roosevelt" (*Poetry*, January 1923; *3STP, 88 Poems, Complete Poems*)

"Schwarzwald" (*88 Poems, Complete Poems*)

"Sequel" (*88 Poems, Complete Poems*)

"Ship, The" (*Fitzgerald/Hemingway Annual 1972; 88 Poems, Complete Poems*)

"Shock Troops" (*88 Poems, Complete Poems*)

"[Some day when you are picked up . . .]" (*88 Poems, Complete Poems*)

"Soul of Spain with McAlmon and Bird the Publishers, The" (*Der Querschnitt*, Autumn 1924; *88 Poems, Complete Poems*)

"Sport of Kings, The" (TSW, Nov. 24, 1923; *88 Poems, Complete Poems*)

"Stevenson" (*88 Poems, Complete Poems*)

"[There was Ike and Tony and Jaque and me . . .]" (*88 Poems, Complete Poems*)

"They All Made Peace—What Is Peace?" (*The Little Review*, Spring 1923; *88 Poems, Complete Poems*)

"To a Tragic Poetess" (*88 Poems, Complete Poems*)

"To Chink Whose Trade is Soldiering" (*88 Poems, Complete Poems*)

"To Crazy Christian" (*88 Poems, Complete Poems*)

"To Good Guys Dead" (*88 Poems, Complete Poems*)

"To Will Davies" (*88 Poems, Complete Poems*)

"Translations from the Esquimaux" (*88 Poems, Complete Poems*)

"Travel Poem" (*88 Poems, Complete Poems*)

"Ultimately" (*Double-Dealer*, June 1922; *88 Poems, Complete Poems*)

"Valentine" (*The Little Review* May 1929; *88 Poems, Complete Poems*)

"Worker, The" (*Tabula* March 1917; *88 Poems, Complete Poems*)

Letters

Baker, Carlos. *Ernest Hemingway: Selected Letters, 1917–1961*. New York: Charles Scribner's Sons, 1981.

2. Recommended reading

See first part of this bibliography for a comprehensive list of Hemingway's work.

There have been more than 40 biographical studies of Hemingway published during the last 20 years and more than 100 books of criticism, plus hundreds of articles in scholarly and popular magazines. This listing of the most useful and most accessible sources is not meant to be exhaustive.

Biographical studies of Hemingway

Baker, Carlos. *Ernest Hemingway: A Life Story*. New York: Charles Scribner's Sons, 1969.

Beegel, Susan. "Hemingway and Hemochromatosis." *The Hemingway Review* (Vol. X, No. 1: 57–66).

Burrill, William. *Hemingway: The Toronto Years*. Toronto: Doubleday Canada, 1994. [See also under 1. "Articles"]

DeFazio, Albert J. III. *The HemHotch Letters: The Correspondence and Relationship of Ernest Hemingway and A.E. Hotchner.* Unpublished dissertation, University of Virginia (1992).

Diliberto, Gioia. *Hadley*. New York: Ticknor & Fields, 1992.

Donaldson, Scott. *By Force of Will: The Life and Art of Ernest Hemingway*. New York: The Viking Press, 1977.

Fuentes, Norberto. *Hemingway in Cuba*. Secaucus, N.Y.: Lyle Stuart Inc., 1984.

Griffin, Peter. *Along With Youth: Hemingway, the Early Years*. Oxford: Oxford University Press, 1985.

———. *Less Than a Treason: Hemingway in Paris.* Oxford: Oxford University Press, 1990.

Hemingway, Patricia S. *The Hemingways: Past & Present and Allied Families.* Genealogy, revised edition. Baltimore: Gateway Press, 1988.

Hotchner, A. E. *Papa Hemingway*. New York: Random House, 1966.

Kert, Bernice. *The Hemingway Women: Those Who Loved Him—the Wives and Others.* New York: W.W. Norton & Company, 1983. Rpt. Norton, 1998.

Lynn, Kenneth S. *Hemingway*. New York: Simon and Schuster, 1987.

Mellow, James R. *Hemingway: A Life Without Consequences.* New York: Houghton Mifflin Company, 1992.

Meyers, Jeffrey. *Hemingway: A Biography*. New York: Harper & Row, 1985.

Montgomery, Constance Cappel. *Hemingway in Michigan.* New York: Fleet Publishing Corporation, 1966.

Reynolds, Michael. *The Young Hemingway*. Oxford: Basil Blackwell, 1986.

———. *Hemingway: The Paris Years.* Oxford: Basil Blackwell, 1989.

———. *Hemingway: The American Homecoming.* Oxford: Blackwell, 1992.

———. *Hemingway: The 1930s.* New York: W.W. Norton, 1997.

———. *Hemingway: The Final Years.* New York: Norton, (July) 1999.

Sanford, Marcelline Hemingway. *At The Hemingways: A Family Portrait.* Boston: Little, Brown and Company, 1962. Rpt. University of Idaho Press, 1999.

Sokoloff, Alice Hunt. *Hadley: The First Mrs. Hemingway.* New York: Dodd, Mead & Company, 1973.

Personal memoirs

Castillo-Puche, José Luis. *Hemingway in Spain: A Personal Reminiscence of Hemingway's Years in Spain by His Friend.* Garden City: Doubleday & Company, Inc., 1974.

Hemingway, Gregory H. *Papa: A Personal Memoir.* Boston: Houghton Mifflin Company, 1976.

Hemingway, Jack. *Misadventures of a Fly Fisherman: My Life With and Without Papa.* Dallas: Taylor Publishing Company, 1986.

Hemingway, Leicester. *My Brother, Ernest Hemingway.* Cleveland: The World Publishing Company, 1962.

Hemingway, Mary Welsh. *How It Was.* New York: Alfred A. Knopf, 1976.

Miller, Madelaine Hemingway. *Ernie: Hemingway's Sister "Sunny" Remembers.* New York: Crown Publishers, Inc., 1975.

Samuelson, Arnold. *With Hemingway: A Year in Key West and Cuba.* New York: Random House, 1984.

Critical studies

Baker, Carlos. *Hemingway: The Writer as Artist.* Princeton, N.J.: Princeton University Press, 1973.

Beegel, Susan F. *Hemingway's Craft of Omission: Four Manuscript Examples.* Ann Arbor, Mich.: UMI Research Press, 1988.

Benson, Jackson J. *New Critical Approaches to the Short Stories of Ernest Hemingway.* Durham, N.C.: Duke University Press, 1990.

Brenner, Gerry. *Concealments in Hemingway's Works.* Columbus: Ohio State University Press, 1983.

Flora, Joseph M. *Ernest Hemingway: A Study of the Short Fiction.* Boston: Twain Publishers, 1989.

Hinkle, James. "What's Funny in *The Sun Also Rises*." *The Hemingway Review* (Vol. IV, No. 2: 31–41).

Hurley, C. Harold. *Hemingway's Debt to Baseball in* The Old Man and the Sea: *A Collection of Critical Readings.* Lewiston, N.Y.: The Edwin Mellen Press, 1992.

Joost, Nicholas. *Ernest Hemingway and the Little Magazines: The Paris Years.* Barre, Mass.: Barre Publishers, 1968.

Laurence, Frank M. *Hemingway and the Movies.* Jackson: University Press of Mississippi, 1981.

Lewis, Robert W. *Hemingway on Love.* Austin: University of Texas Press, 1965.

Oliver, Charles M., ed. *A Moving Picture Feast: The Filmgoer's Hemingway.* New York: Praeger, 1989.

Phillips, Gene D. *Hemingway and Film.* New York: Frederick Ungar Publishing Co., 1980.

Plimpton, George. "Ernest Hemingway: The Art of Fiction XXI." *The Paris Review* (Spring 1958: 60–89).

Reynolds, Michael S. *Hemingway's First War: The Making of* A Farewell to Arms. Princeton, N.J.: Princeton University Press, 1976.

Ross, Lillian. *Portrait of Hemingway: The Celebrated Profile.* New York: Simon and Schuster, 1961.

Smith, Paul. *A Reader's Guide to the Short Stories of Ernest Hemingway.* Boston: G.K. Hall, 1989.

Spilka, Mark. *Hemingway's Quarrel With Androgyny.* Lincoln: University of Nebraska Press, 1990.

Stephens, Robert O. *Hemingway's Nonfiction: The Public Voice.* Chapel Hill: The University of North Carolina Press, 1968.

Stoneback, H. R. "From the rue Saint-Jacques to the Pass of Roland to the 'Unfinished Church on the Edge of the Cliff.'" *The Hemingway Review* (Vol. VI, No. 1: 2–29).

Tavernier-Courbin, Jacqueline. *Ernest Hemingway's A Moveable Feast: The Making of a Myth.* Boston: Northeastern University Press, 1991.

Watson, William Braasch. "Hemingway's Spanish Civil War Dispatches." *The Hemingway Review* (Vol. VII, No. 2: 2–113).

Williams, Wirt. *The Tragic Art of Ernest Hemingway.* Baton Rouge: Louisiana State University Press, 1981.

Young, Philip. *Ernest Hemingway: A Reconsideration.* University Park: The Penn State University Press, 1966.

Bibliographies and chronologies

Cohn, Louis Henry. *A Bibliography of the Works of Ernest Hemingway.* New York: Random House, 1931.

Hanneman, Audre. *Ernest Hemingway: A Comprehensive Bibliography.* Princeton, N.J.: Princeton University Press, 1967.

———. *Supplement to Ernest Hemingway: A Comprehensive Bibliography.* Princeton, N.J.: Princeton University Press, 1975.

Larson, Kelli A. *Ernest Hemingway: A Reference Guide, 1974–1989.* Boston: G.K. Hall, 1991.

Reynolds, Michael S. *Hemingway: An Annotated Chronology.* Detroit: Omnigraphics, Inc., 1991.

Other works of interest

Arnold, Lloyd R. *High on the Wild With Hemingway.* Caldwell, Idaho: The Caxton Printers, Ltd., 1968.

Beach, Sylvia. *Shakespeare and Company.* New York: Harcourt, Brace and Company, 1959.

Bellavance-Johnson, Marsha. *Hemingway in Key West: A Guide.* Ketchum, Idaho: The Computer Lab, 1987.

———. *Ernest Hemingway in Idaho.* Ketchum, Idaho: The Computer Lab, 1989.

Boreth, Craig. *The Hemingway Cookbook.* Chicago: Chicago Review Press, 1998.

Brasch, James D. and Joseph Sigman. *Hemingway's Library: A Composite Record.* New York: Garland Publishing, Inc., 1981.

Burgess, Anthony. *Ernest Hemingway and His World.* London: Thames and Hudson, 1978.

Conrad, Barnaby. *Gates of Fear: Great Exploits of the World's Bullrings.* New York: Thomas Y. Crowell, 1957.

———. *Barnaby Conrad's Encyclopedia of Bullfighting.* Cambridge, Mass.: The Riverside Press, 1961.

Cortada, James W., ed. *Historical Dictionary of the Spanish Civil War, 1936–1939.* Westport, Conn.: Greenwood Press, 1982.

Fall, Cyril. *The Battle of Caporetto.* New York: J.B. Lippincott, 1965.

Fitch, Noel Riley. *Sylvia Beach and the Lost Generation: A History of Literary Paris in the Twenties & Thirties.* New York: W.W. Norton, 1983.

———. *Literary Cafés of Paris.* Philadelphia: Starrhill Press, 1989.

———. *Walks in Hemingway's Paris: A Guide to Paris for the Literary Traveler.* New York: St. Martin's Press, 1990.

Flanner, Janet. *An American in Paris: Profile of an Interlude Between Two Wars.* New York: Simon and Schuster, 1940.

Ford, Hugh. *Published in Paris: American and British Writers, Printers, and Publishers in Paris, 1920–1939.* New York: Macmillan Publishing Co., 1975.

Gajdusek, Robert E. *Hemingway's Paris.* New York: Charles Scribner's Sons, 1978.

Hansen, Arlen J. *Expatriate Paris: A Cultural and Literary Guide to Paris of the 1920s.* New York: Arcade Publishing, 1990.

Huddleston, Sisley. *Paris Salons, Cafés, Studios.* Philadelphia: J.B. Lippincott, 1928.

Mandel, Miriam B. *Reading Hemingway: The Facts in the Fictions.* Metuchen, N.J.: The Scarecrow Press, 1995.

Mellow, James R. *Charmed Circle: Gertrude Stein & Company.* New York: Praeger, 1974.

Mitgang, Herbert. *Dangerous Dossiers: Exposing the Secret War Against America's Greatest Authors.* New York: Donald I. Fine, Inc., 1988.

Ohle, William H. *How It Was in Horton Bay.* Horton Bay, Boyne City, Mich.: Ohle Publications, 1989.

Phillips, Larry W., ed. *Ernest Hemingway On Writing.* New York: Charles Scribner's Sons, 1984.

Reynolds, Michael S. *Hemingway's Reading, 1910–1940: An Inventory.* Princeton, N.J.: Princeton University Press, 1981.

Wagner, Linda W., ed. *Ernest Hemingway: Six Decades of Criticism.* Lansing: Michigan State University Press, 1987.

Wilson, Edmund. *The Twenties: From Notebooks and Diaries of the Period.* New York: Farrar, Straus and Giroux, 1975.

Young, Philip, and Charles W. Mann. *The Hemingway Manuscripts: An Inventory.* University Park: Penn State University Press, 1969.

INDEX

"How to be Popular in Peace Though a Slacker in War" (article) 268
"How We Came to Paris" (article) **160,** 194
"Hubby Dines First, Wifie Gets Crumbs!" (article) **160**
Hubert
    in "Mr. and Mrs. Elliot" 85, 228
    in *The Sun Also Rises* **160**
Hudson, Andrew **160,** 172, 185
Hudson, David **160,** 172, 185
Hudson, Mrs. Thomas **161**
Hudson, Thomas **160,** 170–174
    age of 67
Hudson, Tom 2, **161,** 172, 173, 263
Hudson, W. H. 76, 89, **161,** 236, 273
Hugo's English grammar **161**
"Humanity Will Not Forgive This!" (article) **161–162**
Humes, Harold 259
Hungarians, in *In Our Time* **162**
"Hungarian Statesman Delighted With Loan" (article) 66
Hungary 36, 66, 205
hunting *See also* animals, hunted
    articles about 59, 112, 241, 278, 301
    in *Green Hills of Africa* 128–131
    in "The Short Happy Life of Francis Macomber" 203–204
    short story about 181–182
Hurley, C. Harold 209, 247
Hürtgen Forest **162**
husband, in *Indian Camp* **162,** 167
hut(s)
    Alpine Club 204, 351
    in "A Simple Enquiry" **162**
Hutchinson, A. S. M. **162**

Huxley, Aldous 104, **162**
hydro-electric projects **162**
hyena **162**

I

I
    in "After the Storm" **164**
    in "An Alpine Idyll" **163**
    in "A Canary for One" **163**
    in "Chapter 3" vignette **163**
    in "Chapter 11" vignette **163**
    in "Chapter 13" vignette **163**
    in "Che Ti Dice La Patria?" **164**
    in "A Day's Wait" **164**
    in *Green Hills of Africa* **164**
    in "In Another Country" 3, **163–164,** 166–167
    in "The Light of the World" **164**
    in "A Natural History of the Dead" **164**
    in "Old Man at the Bridge" **164,** 248
    in "The Revolutionist" **163**
    in "Wine of Wyoming" **164**
I.B. (International Brigades) 1, **169,** 213, 235, 309, 310, 334, 341
Ibarruri, Dolores 260
iceberg principle *See* theory of omission
iced tea **165**
Ida **165**
"[If my Valentine you won't be . . .]" (poem) **165**
Iglesias, Pablo 65
Ignacio
    in "The Capital of the World" 45, **165**
    in *For Whom the Bell Tolls* **165**
"I Guess Everything Reminds You of Something" (unfinished story) **165**

Ile de la Cité **165**
Ile de France (liner) **165,** 173, 214, 238
Ile Saint-Louis **165**
"I Like Americans" (article) **165**
"I Like Canadians" (article) **165**
illustrator(s) **165,** 193, 260, 264, 273, 300, 322
imbarcadero **165**
"I'm off'n wild wimmen . . ." (poem) **165**
Imola **165**
impala **165**
impotence 19, **166**
    in *The Sun Also Rises* 23, 166, 170, 316, 317
    in *To Have and Have Not* 33, 124
inaccrochable **166**
"[In a magazine . . .]" (poem) **166**
"In Another Country" (short story) **166–167,** 358
    boys in 33
    characters in 205, 355
    narrator of 3, 163–164
Index, The **167**
"Indian Camp" (short story) 41, **167**
    characters in 78, 117, 128, 162, 168, 355
    protagonist in 4
Indian Club 79, **167,** 180
Indians
    Cuban, in *Islands in the Stream* 68
    in "The Doctor and the Doctor's Wife" 78, 79, 320
    in "Fathers and Sons" 94
    in "Indian Camp" **168,** 180
    in "The Light of the World" **167,** 196
    Ojibway **245,** 346
    in "Ten Indians" **167,** 322
    in *The Torrents of Spring* 81, 107, **167–168,** 215
    tribes 55, 304
"Indians Moved Away, The" (unfinished story) **168**

Indian woman
    old, in "Indian Camp" **355**
    in *The Torrents of Spring* 180, 232, 329
    young, in "Indian Camp" **168**
individualism, in *To Have and Have Not* 223, 325
indoor baseball **168,** 189
"Indoor Fishing" (article) **168**
"Inexpressible, The" (poem) **168**
inflation, German, articles on 119, 168
"Inflation and the German Mark" (article) **168**
"Influx of Russians to All Parts of Paris" (article) 259
Ingersoll, Ralph **168**
"In Love and War" (film) **168**
inn
    in "Cross-Country Snow" **168**
    in *A Farewell to Arms* **168**
innkeeper, in *An Alpine Idyll* **168**
In Our Time **169**
    "Chapter 1" vignette **52,** 188, 196
    "Chapter 2" vignette 48, **52,** 128, 183, 220, 228
        characters in 355, 362
    "Chapter 3" vignette **52,** 163, 222
    "Chapter 4" vignette **52,** 245, 349
    "Chapter 5" vignette 40, **52,** 307
    "Chapter 6" vignette **52–53,** 281
    "Chapter 7" vignette **53,** 58, 137, 218
    "Chapter 8" vignette 32, **53,** 81
    "Chapter 9" vignette **53,** 186, 214
    "Chapter 10" vignette **53**
    "Chapter 11" vignette 37, **53,** 68, 163, 217